AUG 2 0 1999

D1466932

Congressional Roll Call 1998

Congressional Roll Call 1998

A Chronology and Analysis of Votes in the House and Senate
105th Congress, Second Session

CONGRESSIONAL QUARTERLY INC.
1414 22ND STREET, N.W.
WASHINGTON, D.C. 20037

991082

Congressional Quarterly Inc.

Congressional Quarterly Inc., an editorial research service and publishing company, serves clients in the fields of news, education, business, and government. It combines the specific coverage of Congress, government, and politics contained in the CQ *Weekly* with the more general subject range of an affiliated service, the CQ *Researcher*.

Under the CQ Press imprint Congressional Quarterly also publishes college political science textbooks, public affairs paperbacks on developing issues and events, information directories, and reference books on the federal government, national elections, and politics, including the *Guide to the Presidency*, the *Guide to Congress*, the *Guide to the U.S. Supreme Court*, the *Guide to U.S. Elections*, and *Politics in America*. CQ's A–Z collection is a four-volume reference series providing essential information about American government and the electoral process. The CQ *Almanac*, a compendium of legislation for one session of Congress, is published each year. *Congress and the Nation*, a record of government for a presidential term, is published every four years.

CQ publishes the *Daily Monitor*, a report on current and future activities of congressional committees. An electronic online information system, cq.com, provides immediate access to CQ's databases of legislative action, votes, schedules, profiles, and analyses.

CQ Press
A Division of Congressional Quarterly Inc.
1414 22nd St. N.W.
Washington, D.C. 20037

(202) 822-1475; (800) 638-1710

http://books.cq.com

Copyright © 1999 Congressional Quarterly Inc.

All rights reserved. No part of this publication may be reproduced or transmitted in any form or by any means, electronic or mechanical, including photocopy, recording, or any information storage and retrieval system, without permission in writing from the publisher.

Printed in the United States of America

Library of Congress catalogued the first volume of this title as follows:

Congressional Quarterly Inc.
    Congressional Roll Call (91st Congress—)
    1. United States. Congress — Periodicals. 2. Legislation — United States.
Periodicals. 1. Title.
JK1.C6635   328.73.'07,'75'2   72-77849

ISBN 1-56802-469-X
ISSN 0191-1473

Table of Contents

Editor's Note. *Congressional Roll Call 1998* provides a member-by-member survey and analysis of votes in the House and Senate during the second session of the 105th Congress.

Following the introductory legislative summary, the book is divided into two sections. The first section contains Congressional Quarterly's special voting studies. These studies examine congressional support of the president's position on specific votes, the percentage of all recorded votes on which members voted or took stands, votes on which a majority of Democrats opposed a majority of Republicans, and votes on which an alliance of Republicans and Southern Democrats opposed a majority of Northern Democrats. Summaries and charts of the key votes are also included.

The second section of the book contains a compilation of roll call votes in the Senate and House in 1998 followed by indexes of the roll call votes and bills on which roll call votes were taken.

Congressional Roll Call 1998

Members Made the Deals, But Scandal Made the News

Sidetracked by Clinton impeachment, Congress compiled a modest record

The House took 547 roll call votes in 1998 and the Senate took 314, but history is likely to take note of just two: the House votes Dec. 19 to impeach President Clinton.

SUMMARY

Those votes closed out a year in which the president's affair with former White House intern Monica Lewinsky and his denial under oath of a sexual relationship cast a long shadow over Washington. From the time the titillating details of the relationship began to emerge in January, the scandal was never far in the background for the administration or for Congress.

Sometimes it took center stage, such as when Clinton went to Capitol Hill on Jan. 27 to deliver his State of the Union address, six days after the first reports of the Lewinsky affair. Though many pundits and members of Congress predicted that Clinton had finally used up his nine political lives, the president ignored the embarrassing reports and steadily delivered his legislative agenda.

Other times, the scandal seemed to take a back seat to initiatives facing floor votes or other pivotal decisions. But even then, Republicans and Democrats, the powerful and the obscure, found themselves asked time and again for their opinion on the president's conduct and possible punishments, not about legislative details.

Congress had a hand in creating much of the quagmire that ensued, especially when the House voted Sept. 11 to release the salacious details of Independent Counsel Kenneth W. Starr's report on Clinton's behavior and Starr's conclusion that 11 counts of impeachable offenses could be upheld. That action, which came before anyone in Congress had read the report, significantly added to the frenzy that consumed much of Congress' energy.

Splits Slow GOP Agenda

Many Republican leaders believed that voter support for Clinton would eventually wane as it became clear that he had at least misled the public and at worst had lied to a grand jury, and they thought Republicans would reap the benefits at election time.

As a result, they did not push a legislative agenda as strongly as they had in previous years. In any case, recurrent divisions within the party would have made it difficult to push a coherent agenda, even if leaders had tried.

The GOP split its votes on issues that ranged from transportation funding, to a ban on cloning, to military training for men and women in the same units. Democrats also faced some divisive votes, splitting on an education savings account plan in the Senate and on the resolution to release the Starr report in the House.

The distractions and fractures, particularly among House Republicans, created a political vacuum that allowed the president and a few congressional lone wolves, such as House Transportation Committee Chairman Bud Shuster, R-Pa., and Rep. Nita M. Lowey, D-N.Y., a family planning and abortion rights proponent, to step in and win passage of legislation that would have likely met with defeat in the earlier, headier days of the Republican revolution.

The second session of the 105th Congress also was notable for what it did not do, including the failure to pass a budget resolution or a major tax cut bill.

As 1998 began, perhaps the most important domestic issue on Congress' plate was the groundbreaking $368.5 billion agreement between tobacco companies and state attorneys general to combat teenage smoking.

The failure of legislation to implement the tobacco settlement — which expanded well beyond the parameters of the original deal — served as an apt metaphor for the entire year. That bill died in the Senate when GOP conservatives objected to its sharply higher cigarette taxes and new bureaucracies. In other words, it was simply too big.

Congress did clear consequential measures on foreign policy, immigration, housing and other matters. In April, the Senate voted overwhelmingly to expand NATO's borders to include three former Warsaw Pact nations. With concerns over the budget deficit quickly fading, Congress passed a $217.9 billion transportation bill that boosts spending on highways and mass transit by 40 percent.

Yet those achievements were largely predictable and had all the political difficulty of a three-foot putt. None of Congress' accomplishments approached the magnitude of last year's budget agreement, which helped wipe away the deficit and provided the first tax cut since Ronald Reagan's first term as president.

Busting the Budget

This year, just completing the routine business of governing proved to be a formidable challenge. For the first time since the modern budget process was established in 1974, Congress did not produce a fiscal budget resolution. House and Senate Republicans were simply unable to agree on a spending plan.

That slowed the appropriations process to a crawl, eventually forcing GOP leaders to cobble together a $500 billion, budget-busting omnibus spending bill that wrapped in eight individual appropriations measures and served as the vehicle for much of this year's limited legislative output.

The huge catchall bill, defended as a practical necessity by departing House Speaker Newt Gingrich, R-Ga., was roundly denounced by GOP

'Cloture' Was the Senate's Byword

In the second session of the 105th Congress, the Senate voted 11 times in 29 attempts to invoke cloture, thereby limiting debate and providing for an up-or-down vote on a particular piece of legislation. Cloture requires a 60-vote majority to succeed.

The result was a 38 percent success rate for Majority Leader Trent Lott, R-Miss. In the first session, cloture was invoked seven times in 24 attempts, a 29 percent rate.

As the chart below shows, when the Senate invoked cloture this year, it always did so by a wide margin. The closest successful cloture vote was 71-24, 11 more votes than necessary.

On successful cloture motions, the majority averaged 88 votes. In most instances, Lott sought cloture votes in order to restrict the use of a piece of legislation as a vehicle for extraneous amendments.

But two other times, Lott came within just one vote of winning cloture on one of his top priorities for the year. On May 13 and Sept. 9, 59-41 tallies kept the Senate from taking up legislation (S 1873) to make it U.S. policy to deploy an anti-missile defense system.

Those were not the only "do overs" on this year's cloture list. Sometimes a series of votes were held — even when failure was a certainty — so that sponsors could drive home their view that an obstinate minority was holding up action. It took four votes against invoking cloture on the sweeping tobacco legislation (S 1415) before the measure was shelved. And the Senate voted three times against invoking cloture on similar forms of campaign finance legislation.

Technically, invoking cloture allows the leaders to break off filibusters. But true filibusters — in which opponents hold the floor for hours on end to stymie supporters of a bill — have become rare. Now, simply the threat of a filibuster prompts leaders to file a cloture motion to gauge support for a measure.

The number of cloture votes also speaks to the continued level of partisanship in the Senate. Democrats spent all year assailing Republicans for minimal accomplishments, and Republicans spent the year declaring that was because the Democrats were thwarting the popular will. "How can the president accuse us of doing little when his own party is blocking bill after bill," Lott said toward the end of the session.

"The minority has rights in the Senate, and we intend to exercise them," replied Minority Leader Tom Daschle, D-S.D., who often pressed his troops to vote against cloture in an effort to make bills available as vehicles for top Democratic priorities — proposals that he knew would never be brought to the floor for debate any other way.

DATE	BILL	VOTE	DESCRIPTION	VOTE
Feb. 10		**8**	**To confirm David Satcher to be surgeon general**	**75-23**
Feb. 11	S 1601	10	To ban human cloning research	42-54
Feb. 26	S 1663	16	To add campaign finance bill (S 25) to bill to restrict political use of union dues	51-48
Feb. 26	S 1663	17	To restrict political use of union dues	45-54
March 11	**S 1173**	**28**	**To reauthorize highway and mass transit programs**	**96-3**
March 17	**HR 2646**	**34**	**Motion to proceed to bill to expand benefits of education savings accounts**	**74-24**
March 19	HR 2646	38	To expand benefits of education savings accounts	55-44
March 26	HR 2646	46	To expand benefits of education savings accounts	58-42
May 13	S 1873	131	Motion to procede to a bill to make it U.S. policy to deploy an anti-missile defense	59-41
June 2	HR 1270	148	To create interim facility near Yucca Mountain, Nev., to store nuclear waste	56-39
June 9	S 1415	150	To set an array of federal policies to curb smoking	42-56
June 10	S 1415	153	To set an array of federal policies to curb smoking	43-55
June 11	S 1415	156	To set an array of federal policies to curb smoking	43-56
June 17	S 1415	161	To set an array of federal policies to curb smoking	57-42
July 7	**S 648**	**184**	**Motion to proceed to bill to limit punitive damages in product liability suits**	**71-24**
July 9	S 648	188	To limit punitive damages in product liability lawsuits	51-47
July 13	S 2271	197	Motion to proceed to bill to allow federal court challenges of local zoning decisions	52-42
July 21	**HR 4112**	**213**	**To make fiscal 1999 legislative branch appropriations**	**83-16**
Sept. 9	S 1873	262	Motion to procede to a bill to make it U.S. policy to deploy an anti-missile defense	59-41
Sept. 9	**S 1301**	**263**	**Motion to proceed to a bill to overhaul consumer bankruptcy laws**	**99-1**
Sept. 10	S 2237	264	To add campaign finance bill (S 25) to fiscal 1999 Interior appropriations bill	52-48
Sept. 11	**S 1645**	**265**	**Motion to proceed to bill to punish evasion of abortion parental consent laws**	**97-0**
Sept. 14	S 1981	266	Motion to proceed to a bill to place curbs on union organizing	52-42
Sept. 22	S 1645	282	To punish evasion of abortion parental consent laws	54-45
Sept. 24	**S 2176**	**285**	**Motion to proceed to bill to limit presidential appointment powers**	**96-1**
Sept. 28	S 2176	289	To limit presidential appointment powers	53-38
Sept. 29	**S 442**	**292**	**Motion to proceed to bill to ban taxes on sales over the Internet for two years**	**89-6**
Oct. 5	**HR 10**	**297**	**To overhaul laws separating banking, brokerage and insurance**	**93-0**
Oct. 7	**S 442**	**302**	**To ban taxes on sales over the Internet for two years**	**94-4**

Note: Instances when cloture was invoked are in bold.

conservatives and moderates alike as a cave-in to Clinton. Just as galling to Republican activists was watching their hopes for a sizable tax cut go up in smoke without even a Senate vote.

Despite Republicans' early hopes for a tax cut of about $100 billion over five years, their leadership gave up because party members in the House and Senate could not reach agreement on the numbers. In addition, Clinton scared many Republicans by calling on Congress to "save Social Security first" and not to use any budget surplus for major tax breaks.

Clinton took advantage of the protracted budget negotiations to shift the focus, at least temporarily, from his own troubles to the Democrats' agenda of 100,000 new teachers and tighter curbs on managed care.

While Democrats were surprisingly effective in communicating their election-year message, they were frustrated in the legislative arena. The demise of the tobacco bill was especially disappointing to them, because Clinton and the Democrats were counting on money from new cigarette taxes to expand aid for child care and other programs.

Democrats managed to pick up a modest amount of GOP backing for initiatives to impose new restrictions on managed care health plans and tough rules on political fundraising. But while the House shocked nearly everyone by approving a campaign finance bill, that measure met a predictable demise in the Senate.

The House also approved a GOP-backed bill on managed care. But the Senate never addressed the issue as Republicans and Democrats squabbled over parameters of the debate.

Democrats did score some important victories in the budget deal, including a $1.1 billion down payment on Clinton's new teacher program. In a bitter defeat for social conservatives, the final version of that bill included a provision requiring federal employee health plans to cover contraceptives if they cover other prescription drugs.

Achievements Subdued

While the two parties spent most of the year locked in conflict, they came together on some important issues. With little fanfare, Congress enacted a major reauthorization of the Head Start program. Lawmakers also agreed on a badly needed overhaul of federal public housing programs.

The high-tech community had considerable success, reflecting its growing political muscle. Congress passed measures to impose a three-year moratorium on taxes on Internet commerce and to expand copyright protection for digitally produced works.

And after a bitter battle, lawmakers provided $17.9 billion in new credits for the International Monetary Fund (IMF), in return for modest reforms by the global lender.

But even when Democrats and Republicans could agree, it was seldom a cause for celebration. Clinton never had a public signing ceremony for the Head Start bill — an extraordinary act by a Democratic president — because he did not want to hand Republicans a victory on education.

The omnibus budget bill included generous funding for a host of GOP priorities, including $1 billion for an anti-missile defense program. But Gingrich's attempt to highlight those provisions was drowned by a cacophony of conservative criticism of the bill.

The outgoing Speaker accurately summarized the session in his last regular speech on the House floor, when he defended the budget agreement. In a divided government, he said, some compromises are necessary: "If we don't work together on the big issues, nothing gets done." Certainly, that was true in 1998.

Clinton's 1998 Vetoes

President Clinton vetoed five bills in 1998, bringing the total for the 105th Congress to eight. Lawmakers did not attempt to override any of the 1998 vetoes. The five bills would have:

● Expanded the tax benefits of education savings accounts (HR 2646). Vetoed July 21.

● Created school vouchers in the District of Columbia (S 1502). Vetoed May 20.

● Punished countries, especially Russia, that offered technical assistance to Iran's missile program (HR 2709). Vetoed June 23.

● Appropriated less for agriculture and nutrition programs than the president wanted (HR 4101). Vetoed Oct. 7.

● Reauthorized and reorganized the State Department (HR 1757). Vetoed Oct. 21.

However, lawmakers did succeed in overriding one of the three 1997 vetoes, salvaging a bill (HR 2631) that restored $287 million in military construction spending. Clinton had tried to block the spending with his short-lived line-item veto. The measure became law without the president's signature (PL 105-159) on Feb. 25.

An attempt to override a second 1997 veto — of a bill (HR 1122) to ban what sponsors describe as "partial birth" abortions — failed in the Senate Sept. 18.

Following is a summary of what Congress did and did not accomplish this year. ◆

Session's Highlights

Congress did:

● Bust its own balanced-budget caps, set in 1997, to reach compromises on spending for fiscal 1999.

● Pass a six-year, $217.9 billion authorization bill for highway and mass transit projects.

● Overhaul federal public housing policy.

● Impose a three-year moratorium on state taxes on Internet commerce.

● Overhaul the Internal Revenue Service to make it more "customer friendly."

● Expand Head Start, move to increase aid for hiring new teachers and reauthorize college student loans.

● Make it a crime to transport a minor across state lines to get an abortion, thereby circumventing her home state's parental-consent law.

● Block U.S. implementation of the Kyoto treaty on global warming.

● Partially reorganize the foreign affairs bureaucracy to consolidate functions in the State Department.

● Increase funding for the International Monetary Fund by $18 billion.

● Launch an impeachment inquiry based on allegations that President Clinton lied about an illicit affair.

● Rename Washington National Airport in honor of former President Ronald Reagan.

Congress did not:

● Act to restrict advertising of cigarettes or sales of tobacco products to minors.

● Revise campaign finance laws despite spotlighting bipartisan abuses in the 1996 election cycle.

● Address rising rates of juvenile crime.

● Increase protections for patients in managed care health plans.

● Override Clinton's veto of a bill that would have banned an abortion procedure that opponents call "partial birth" abortion.

● Update Depression-era banking laws to meet the needs of today's financial-services industry, or update personal bankruptcy rules.

● Increase the minimum wage.

● Complete work on an overhaul of the superfund hazardous waste cleanup program.

● Deregulate the electric power industry.

● Pass a significant tax cut despite an unexpected budget surplus.

● Extend "fast track" trade negotiating authority for the president.

● Resolve a partisan dispute over the way the 2000 census will be conducted.

● Pass a constitutional amendment to ban desecration of the American flag.

SECOND SESSION BY THE NUMBERS

The second session of the 105th Congress closed at 2:36 p.m. on Dec. 19, 1998, when the House adjourned *sine die*. The Senate had adjourned sine die at 2:33 p.m. on Oct. 21. Both chambers started the year Jan. 27.

Here is a statistical portrait of the session compared with the past 10 years:

		1998	1997	1996	1995	1994	1993	1992	1991	1990	1989
Days in Session	Senate	143	153	132	211	138	153	129	158	138	136
	House	119	132	122	168	123	142	123	154	134	147
Time in Session	Senate	1,095	1,093	1,037	1,839	1,244	1,270	1,091	1,201	1,250	1,003
(hours)	House	999	1,004	919	1,525	905	982	857	939	939	749
Avg. Length Daily	Senate	7.7	7.1	7.9	8.7	9.0	8.3	8.5	7.6	9.1	7.4
Session (hours)	House	8.4	7.6	7.5	9.1	7.4	6.9	7.0	6.1	7.0	5.1
Public Laws Enacted		241	153	245	88	255	210	347	243	410	240
Bills/Resolutions	Senate	1,321	1,839	860	1,801	999	2,178	1,544	2,701	1,636	2,548
Introduced	House	2,253	3,662	1,899	3,430	2,104	4,543	2,714	5,057	2,769	4,842
	Total	3,574	5,501	2,759	5,231	3,103	6,721	4,258	7,758	4,405	7,390
Recorded Votes	Senate	314	298	306	613	329	395	270	280	326	312
	House[1]	547	640	455	885	507	615	488	444	536	379
	Total	861	938	761	1,498	836	1,010	758	724	862	691
Vetoes		5	3[2]	6	11	0	0	21[3]	4[3]	11[3]	10[3]

[1] Includes quorum calls; [2] does not include line-item vetoes, [3] includes pocket vetoes

VOTE STUDIES

President's Success Score Droops As White House Priorities Make Scant Headway

President Clinton's historic defeat on two articles of impeachment in the House on Dec. 19 dwarfs all other votes when it comes to assessing his success in the 1998 session of Congress.

In fact, even without the votes that made him the first elected president in U.S. history to be impeached, Clinton's legislative year has to be scored as a failure — if the goal was to advance a policy agenda. Virtually all of his major proposals died.

But if — as cynics would have it — the main thing in politics is to triumph over one's political adversaries, then Clinton performed rather well. He effectively shut down the Republican agenda, including tax cuts and reduced regulations, helped deliver unexpected Democratic victories at the polls in November and, indirectly, contributed to the stunning downfall of then-House Speaker Newt Gingrich, R-Ga.

On paper, Clinton ended the year with a 51 percent success score, according to Congressional Quarterly's annual study of voting patterns. This means he prevailed on 51 percent of the 154 House and Senate floor votes on which he took a position.

That is, on the surface, a fairly low score. It is lower than the scores of Presidents Dwight D. Eisenhower (76 percent) and Ronald Reagan (56.1 percent) in their sixth years in office. It is lower, even, than President Richard M. Nixon's (59.6 percent) in his sixth year — the year he resigned rather than face impeachment.

In fact, Clinton's score was the sixth lowest of any president since Congressional Quarterly began keeping track of such things at the beginning of the Eisenhower administration 46 years ago.

Almost none of the priorities that Clinton set at the beginning of the year became law, and few of them even got a floor vote. Tobacco legislation, campaign finance overhaul, "fast

CQ Vote Studies

track" trade legislation and a "bill of rights" for patients in managed health care all fell far short of enactment.

But Clinton seems to resist being judged by ordinary standards.

Like a clutch quarterback in the final seconds of play, he came through when he had to. After losing a series of House appropriations floor votes, he managed to recover most of his losses when eight of the measures were folded into a massive end-of-session omnibus bill.

The resulting package (PL 105-277) funded several Democratic priorities, including increased spending for teachers, while excluding most of the conservative policy "riders" added in the House.

And with the Republicans in post-election disarray, it was Clinton — despite his lame-duck status — who set much of the legislative tone for this year. His call to save Social Security first, for example, continues to undercut Republican efforts to cut taxes.

In that sense, Clinton fared better than Eisenhower and Reagan, both of whom suffered big congressional setbacks at the polls at this point in their presidencies and saw their power wane.

"Given the partisan tensions that culminated in the impeachment vote, it's quite surprising that Clinton did as well as he did in Congress," said Norman J. Ornstein, a congressional scholar at the American Enterprise Institute, a Washington think tank.

Personal Scandal

For Clinton to merely survive the year in office, let alone win enactment of any major initiatives, was a kind of victory. He was haunted by charges of lying under oath about a sexual liaison with a White House intern, leading members of both parties to support an impeachment inquiry.

Although Clinton took no formal position on early House votes related to the scandal, such as a Sept. 11 vote to publicly release a sexually explicit report by Independent Counsel Kenneth W. Starr, the issue dominated the landscape, giving Clinton scarce chance to pursue his vigorous agenda.

On the other hand, it meant he had nothing to lose by battling GOP initiatives, thereby turning the subject away from scandal. By threatening vetoes on a battery of issues from tax cuts to restrictions on overseas family planning funds, the president stymied congressional conservatives just when it seemed that they should be piling up political points.

When threats were not enough, Clinton wielded his veto pen to stop five bills.

The measures would have expanded the tax benefits of education savings accounts (HR 2646); created school vouchers in the District of Columbia (S 1502); punished countries that offered technical assistance to Iran's missile program (HR 2709); appropriated less money than Clinton wanted for agriculture programs in fiscal 1999 (HR 4101); and tied reauthorization of State Department programs to anti-abortion restrictions in international family planning (HR 1757).

In a year marked by sharply drawn

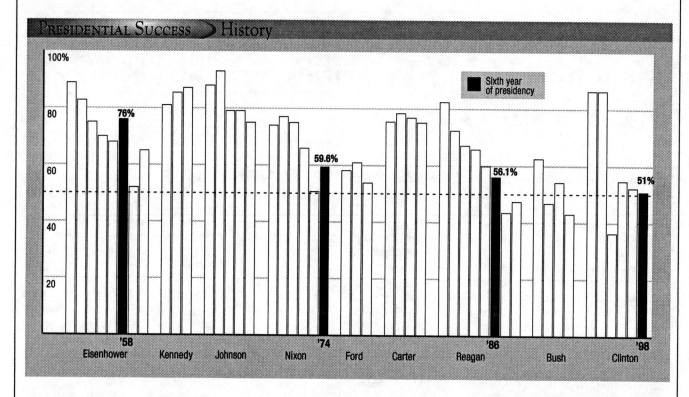

PRESIDENTIAL SUCCESS ❯ History

Sixth year of presidency

76% (Eisenhower '58)

59.6% ('74 Nixon)

56.1% ('86 Reagan)

51% ('98 Clinton)

Eisenhower · Kennedy · Johnson · Nixon · Ford · Carter · Reagan · Bush · Clinton

partisan lines, House Democrats supported Clinton 74 percent of the time; Senate Democrats averaged 82 percent support. Regionally, Clinton fared best with Eastern Senate Democrats (84 percent support) and worst with Southern House Republicans (22 percent support).

His most reliable Republican supporters in the Senate were John H. Chafee of Rhode Island (77 percent) and James M. Jeffords of Vermont (69 percent). In the House, the most GOP support came from Constance A. Morella of Maryland (71 percent) and Sherwood Boehlert of New York (60 percent).

Domestic Setbacks

In his 1998 State of the Union address, Clinton laid out an ambitious domestic agenda. He called for a health care bill of rights to protect consumers; comprehensive regulation of tobacco; tightened campaign finance laws; expanded Medicare benefits; an increased minimum wage; expanded child care programs; and the hiring of 100,000 new teachers.

He got virtually nothing.

Most of his proposals, such as permitting uninsured people as young as 55 to enroll in Medicare, never made it out of the gate. Other plans, including tobacco and campaign finance legislation, were extensively debated in Congress before falling to Senate procedural motions.

Clinton also failed on environmental issues. Proposals to create tax credits to promote energy efficiency and launch clean water initiatives received scant attention on the Hill, and the administration was unable to generate enthusiasm for ratifying a global warming treaty.

The president did somewhat better on his proposal for $7.4 billion over five years to hire 100,000 new teachers. After an extensive appropriations battle, he won the $1.2 billion needed for the first year — but no authorizing language that would give momentum for additional funding.

"Clinton had a big agenda, and it just didn't happen," said George C. Edwards III, director of the Center for Presidential Studies at Texas A&M University. "It's very difficult to point to a very important piece of legislation that has Bill Clinton's stamp on it."

Overall, on domestic issues, Clinton lost on 43 of 69 House votes, and 19 of 36 Senate votes, not counting nominations. Many of his defeats came on conservative-backed policy riders to appropriations bills, such as proposals to limit access to abortion or create vouchers for private schools.

In the end, however, most of those

Definition

How often the president won his way on roll call votes on which he took a clear position.

1998 Data

Senate	48 victories
	24 defeats
House	30 victories
	52 defeats

Total Clinton success rate: 51%

For More Information

riders fell by the wayside. Demonstrating that even an embattled White House wields considerable clout, Clinton carried the day on much of the end-of-session negotiating on fiscal 1999 spending.

The omnibus appropriations bill opened the gates for a flood of new spending, giving the president victories for such items as funding for the Bosnia peacekeeping mission, Year 2000 computer fixes, anti-terrorism efforts and farm relief.

Although Republicans also scored a

Leading Scorers: Presidential Support

Support indicates those who in 1998 voted most often for President Clinton's position; **opposition** shows those who voted most often against the president's position.

Scores are based on actual votes cast; members are listed alphabetically when their scores are tied. Members who missed half or more of the votes are not listed.

Support				Opposition			
SENATE							
Republicans		**Democrats**		**Republicans**		**Democrats**	
Chafee, R.I.	77%	Glenn, Ohio	96%	Inhofe, Okla.	86%	Byrd, W.Va.	26%
Jeffords, Vt.	69	Kennedy, Mass.	96	Smith, N.H.	81	Hollings, S.C.	26
Roth, Del.	64	Kerry, Mass.	94	Nickles, Okla.	77	Conrad, N.D.	25
Collins, Maine	63	Rockefeller, W.Va.	94	Ashcroft, Mo.	76	Dorgan, N.D.	24
D'Amato, N.Y.	60	Dodd, Conn.	93	Hutchinson, Ark.	74	Ford, Ky.	23
Specter, Pa.	60	Levin, Mich.	93	Allard, Colo.	72	Moynihan, N.Y.	22
Domenici, N.M.	57	Sarbanes, Md.	92	Sessions, Ala.	72	Torricelli, N.J.	22
Smith, Ore.	55	Akaka, Hawaii	91	Craig, Idaho	71	Breaux, La.	21
Snowe, Maine	55	Biden, Del.	91	Faircloth, N.C.	71	Reid, Nev.	21
Lugar, Ind.	54	Mikulski, Md.	91	Enzi, Wyo.	69	Baucus, Mont.	19
Stevens, Alaska	54			Helms, N.C.	68	Murray, Wash.	18
Bennett, Utah	53			Gramm, Texas	67	Feingold, Wis.	17
Cochran, Miss.	53			Kyl, Ariz.	67	Graham, Fla.	17
DeWine, Ohio	51			Kempthorne, Idaho	66	Leahy, Vt.	17
Mack, Fla.	50			Shelby, Ala.	66	Lieberman, Conn.	17
HOUSE							
Republicans		**Democrats**		**Republicans**		**Democrats**	
Morella, Md.	71%	McDermott, Wash.	95%	Collins, Ga.	88%	Goode, Va.	74%
Boehlert, N.Y.	60	Skaggs, Colo.	93	Coble, N.C.	84	Hall, Texas	70
Johnson, Conn.	57	Watt, N.C.	91	Coburn, Okla.	84	Taylor, Miss.	67
Shays, Conn.	57	Conyers, Mich.	90	Deal, Ga.	84	Danner, Mo.	54
Leach, Iowa	53	Eshoo, Calif.	90	Schaefer, Colo.	84	Traficant, Ohio	53
Campbell, Calif.	52	Hastings, Fla.	90	Weldon, Fla.	84	Stenholm, Texas	51
Castle, Del.	51	Meeks, N.Y.	90	Blunt, Mo.	83	John, La.	50
Houghton, N.Y.	49	Wexler, Fla.	90	Christensen, Neb.	83	Lipinski, Ill.	50
Gilman, N.Y.	46	Barrett, Wis.	89	Doolittle, Calif.	83	Condit, Calif.	49
Ramstad, Minn.	43	Carson, Ind.	89	Istook, Okla.	83	McIntyre, N.C.	48
Forbes, N.Y.	41	Obey, Wis.	89	Solomon, N.Y.	83	Turner, Texas	47
Kelly, N.Y.	41	Payne, N.J.	89			Cramer, Ala.	46
Porter, Ill.	41	Sabo, Minn.	89			Peterson, Minn.	45
Kolbe, Ariz.	40	Scott, Va.	89				
		Yates, Ill.	89				

few victories, they never recovered from the eleventh-hour negotiations, which took place just weeks before their Nov. 3 electoral setbacks. "We have failed in this process," said a disheartened Rep. Jon Christensen, R-Neb.

Foreign Policy

Presidents traditionally do best in the foreign policy and defense arena, and Clinton has been no exception.

In 1998, he prevailed in the Senate on 15 of 20 foreign policy and defense votes. In the House, however, which proved more difficult terrain for the president across the board, Clinton won on just four of 13 votes.

One of Clinton's biggest victories came when the Senate voted to open the doors of the North Atlantic Treaty Organization, allowing Hungary, Poland and the Czech Republic

to join the strategic alliance (Treaty Doc 105-36).

Clinton also won on repeated votes to fund the U.S. mission in Bosnia. And after a yearlong battle, he prevailed upon lawmakers to appropriate $18 billion for the International Monetary Fund, which he considered an essential step in staving off a global economic downturn.

Yet the president failed to win rati-

fication of a comprehensive nuclear test ban treaty. Lawmakers also refused his repeated requests to pay off debts to the United Nations.

The House twice voted to restrict technology transfers to China, despite administration opposition. It also rebuffed Clinton by passing a bill (HR 2709) that would have punished overseas research laboratories and companies that provided missile technology to Iran. Clinton vetoed the measure.

Taxes and Trade

Clinton may have scored his most resounding victories on an issue that Republicans had hoped to convert into Election Day gains: tax cuts.

By urging Congress to set aside the budget surplus for the Social Security trust fund, rather than use it for tax reduction, he divided conservatives and ultimately paralyzed GOP efforts to cut taxes by $100 billion or more.

To some GOP leaders, it was Clinton's use of the Social Security debate, as much as any issue, that fueled Democratic gains at the polls. "We should have been more aggressive," Gingrich said after the elections.

But for Clinton, the tax issue proved a rather hollow victory. He failed to stir much debate about ways to ensure the future solvency of Social Security, meaning that both he and Congress will have to wrestle with the "third rail" of politics this year.

The president could also point to victories on other tax-related issues. The House failed to pass a constitutional amendment, opposed by the White House, that would have made it more difficult for Congress to impose new taxes. And the Senate turned back a plan that would have terminated the internal revenue code.

In addition, Clinton claimed victory when Congress cleared a measure

(PL 105-206) to overhaul the IRS. However, GOP lawmakers also took credit for the bill, which was one of the few concrete achievements that elected officials of either party could point to in 1998.

Clinton's biggest economic setback may have come Sept. 25, when the House voted overwhelmingly against giving him fast-track trade negotiating authority. The White House took no formal position on that vote because of unusual political currents, but urged GOP leaders to hold off until early 1999 before bringing the top administration priority to the floor.

With many House lawmakers going on record to oppose the plan, GOP leaders are skeptical about reviving the issue before 2001. That would leave Clinton with greatly reduced leverage when he tries to negotiate overseas trade agreements in his final two years in office. ◆

Partisan Voting on the Rise: Ideology Impedes Bills; Some Welcome the Contrast

The end-of-session decision in the House to impeach the president on a pair of party-line votes brought an emotionally draining end to a year marked throughout by a rise in partisan voting.

An analysis of 1998 roll call votes compiled by Congressional Quarterly found that 56 percent of the votes in each chamber (55.7 percent in the Senate; 55.5 percent in the House) pitted a majority of one party against a majority of the other. That is an increase of about 5 percentage points over 1997 party-unity vote ratios, reversing a two-year decline in the proportion of such votes.

Roger Davidson, a congressional scholar at the University of Maryland, says even those figures did not fully reflect the depth of differences between the two parties, because Congress passed relatively few major bills.

"It was a low workload year. You could argue that both parties were distracted by impeachment in 1998," he

said. Yet the parties continued to have passionate differences on emotional issues such as abortion, school vouchers, gay rights, affirmative action and the minimum wage.

In fact, Davidson argues, Congress is in the midst of the most partisan era since Reconstruction at the end of the Civil War. "There is a very deep chasm between the parties," he said.

Whether the emotions unleashed in the impeachment fight will spill over into other issues in 1999 is unclear. While members of both parties decried the acrid tone of the impeachment debate, there were differing views on whether the rising tide of party-unity votes in 1998 was a troubling development or a welcome one.

For moderates such as Rep. David E. Price, D-N.C., the increase in partisanship was worrisome because it could hinder agreement in 1999 on key issues including education funding and a Social Security overhaul.

"Partisan feelings have been rubbed

Definition

The percentage of recorded floor votes in each chamber on which a majority of one party voted against a majority of the other party.

1998 Data

	Partisan Votes	Total Votes	Percent
Senate	175	314	55.7%
House	296	533	55.5%

For More Information

raw. We're just going to have to see what will happen in 1999," Price said in an interview. "Voters want issues resolved. There is not a lot of sympathy for excessive partisanship."

But for some lawmakers who had partisan political objectives, and less compromising legislative goals, 1998 was, if anything, not partisan enough.

"We failed to put bills on the floor with more of a partisan pattern to define differences," said Rep. Tom

Coburn, R-Okla.

Coburn said it was important for parties to stake out positions in 1999 on abortion, proposals to cut government and other issues.

Reversing a Trend

Partisan voting spiked in 1995, when more than two of every three votes were party-unity votes, but it declined over the next two years. In 1997, party-unity votes accounted for 50 percent of votes in either chamber, the lowest level since 1990 in the House and 1991 in the Senate.

The balanced-budget agreement of 1997, in which Democrats and Republicans agreed on a plan to eliminate the deficit in five years, was emblematic of the spirit of bipartisanship that marked the first year of the 105th Congress. But that tone changed quickly in 1998.

Joseph Cooper, a Johns Hopkins University political scientist, says Independent Counsel Kenneth W. Starr's investigation of Clinton's sexual relationship with a White House intern prodded both parties to form battle lines in 1998. "Republicans thought the Monica Lewinsky case would be a silver bullet," he said. "They became rigid in their policy goals."

In one of the first floor votes of the year, Republicans on Feb. 5 backed legislation to rename Washington National Airport after a GOP hero, former President Ronald Reagan. Democrats were strongly opposed to the measure in the House, and evenly split in the Senate. Supporters said the legislation would honor Reagan, but opponents said it was a blatant political act.

Similar skirmishing continued to erupt periodically through the rest of 1998.

Bitter disputes over policy "riders" contributed to long delays in the pas sage of major appropriations bills, culminating in the late-October rush to wrap eight unfinished spending bills into a huge omnibus measure (PL 105-277).

Battle Over Riders

Typical of the partisan trench warfare on spending bill riders was the dispute over the Census Bureau proposal, supported by Democrats, to use statistical sampling in the 2000 census in

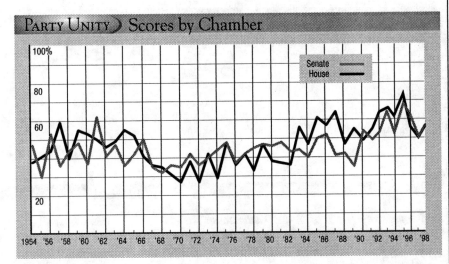

PARTY UNITY Scores by Chamber

order to improve the accuracy of the count and include citizens who might otherwise be missed because of poor English, the lack of a permanent residence or other reasons. Results of the census will determine House district boundaries for the 2002 election.

In a party-line floor vote Aug. 5, Republicans defeated a Democratic amendment to permit sampling. The omnibus spending bill ultimately provided funding for the departments of Commerce, Justice and State only through June 15, 1999, in order to provide more time to work out the sampling dispute.

Social issues, such as abortion, provided fertile ground for other disputes in 1998. The House voted to override Clinton's veto of a bill (HR 1122) to ban "partial birth" abortion, but the Senate failed by three votes to follow suit.

Republicans elected to cut short some other abortion battles to clear the way for the omnibus spending bill. For example, they agreed to strip from the agricultural appropriations bill a House floor amendment approved along party lines that would have barred the Food and Drug Administration from using funds to test or approve the French abortion pill, RU-486.

Despite the increase in partisan voting in 1998, Congress reached bipartisan agreement on significant legislation, including the $217.9 billion surface transportation reauthorization law (PL 105-178), an overhaul of housing programs (PL 105-276), Internal Revenue Service reforms (PL 105-206), and reauthorization of Head Start (PL 105-285).

Some of the biggest partisan battles were fought over bills that were designed to delineate clear political differences. For example, Republicans forced a showdown on education policy and won passage of a bill (HR 2646) to create tax-preferred savings accounts for elementary and secondary school expenses, including private school tuition — a bill that Clinton vetoed.

Democrats also sought confrontation. For example, Sen. Richard J. Durbin of Illinois said Democrats wanted Republicans to take a stand on managed care. While a House-passed GOP bill (HR 4250) encouraged increased patient protections, it stopped short of a Democratic proposal to allow patients to sue health plans in state courts. The House bill was tabled, or killed, in the Senate. "We wanted there to be a clear message showing what the parties were for in the election," Durbin said.

A $368.5 billion settlement reached by state attorneys general with cigarette makers to resolve tobacco-related lawsuits fell apart in the Senate, after the two parties staked out divergent positions. A number of Democrats joined John McCain, R-Ariz., to support a broad bill (S 1415) to raise the price of a pack of cigarettes by $1.10 and require "lookback" penalties if cigarette companies failed to meet youth smoking reduction targets. GOP leaders backed a narrower approach for reducing teen smoking. The Senate fell three votes short of invoking cloture on the McCain bill.

Campaign finance was another

Leading Scorers: Party Unity

Support indicates those who in 1998 voted most consistently with their party's majority against the other party; **opposition** shows how often members voted against their party's majority. Scores are based on votes cast; members are listed alphabetically when their scores are tied. Members who missed half or more of the votes are not listed.

Support		Opposition	

SENATE

Republicans		Democrats		Republicans		Democrats	
Craig, Idaho	99%	Kennedy, Mass.	100%	Jeffords, Vt.	51%	Byrd, W.Va.	28%
Smith, N.H.	99	Glenn, Ohio	99	Specter, Pa.	51	Breaux, La.	27
Ashcroft, Mo.	98	Sarbanes, Md.	99	Chafee, R.I.	43	Lieberman, Conn.	20
Hutchinson, Ark.	98	Wellstone, Minn.	99	D'Amato, N.Y.	38	Hollings, S.C.	19
Nickles, Okla.	98	Harkin, Iowa	98	Snowe, Maine	35	Reid, Nev.	19
Sessions, Ala.	98	Levin, Mich.	98	Collins, Maine	33	Ford, Ky.	17
Allard, Colo.	97	Reed, R.I.	98	Roth, Del.	21	Robb, Va.	17
Gramm, Texas	97	Lautenberg, N.J.	97	Campbell, Colo.	18	Baucus, Mont.	16
Grams, Minn.	97	Mikulski, Md.	97	DeWine, Ohio	18	Graham, Fla.	15
Helms, N.C.	97	Akaka, Hawaii	96	Stevens, Alaska	18	Torricelli, N.J.	15
Inhofe, Okla.	97						

HOUSE

Republicans		Democrats		Republicans		Democrats	
Paxon, N.Y.	98%	Becerra, Calif.	99%	Morella, Md.	60%	Hall, Texas	77%
Archer, Texas	97	Lee, Calif.	99	Shays, Conn.	42	Goode, Va.	72
Armey, Texas	97	Lewis, Ga.	99	Boehlert, N.Y.	41	Traficant, Ohio	67
Hastings, Wash.	97	Olver, Mass.	99	Gilman, N.Y.	38	Taylor, Miss.	59
Sessions, Texas	97	Roybal-Allard, Calif.	99	Johnson, Conn.	38	Stenholm, Texas	50
Shadegg, Ariz.	97	Clay, Mo.	98	Castle, Del.	37	Peterson, Minn.	46
Snowbarger, Kan.	97	Furse, Ore.	98	Leach, Iowa	37	John, La.	44
		Stark, Calif.	98	Campbell, Calif.	36	Lipinski, Ill.	42
		Tierney, Mass.	98	Forbes, N.Y.	35	Turner, Texas	42
				Houghton, N.Y.	34	Danner, Tenn.	41
				Kelly, N.Y.	34		

battleground. Reps. Christopher Shays, R-Conn., and Martin T. Meehan, D-Mass., overcame obstacles erected by the leadership to win House passage of legislation (an amended version of HR 2183) to ban "soft money" contributions in federal elections and expand regulation of advertising. But the drive foundered Sept. 10 when the Senate came eight votes short of ending debate on a proposal to attach a bill (S 25) sponsored by McCain and Russell D. Feingold, D-Wis., to the Interior appropriations bill (S 2237).

The lack of a broad consensus on partisan issues such as campaign fi-

nance changes gave a minority of members a powerful tool to block legislation in the Senate. Of 29 cloture motions considered — including the failed attempt to end debate on McCain's campaign finance bill — only 11 were approved. On the 18 defeated cloture motions, Democrats cast 755 votes in line with their own caucus, and 30 votes in agreement with Republicans.

While Democrats were often a frustrated minority in Congress, they won enough Republican support to win 61 of 175 party-unity votes in the Senate, and 80 of 296 such votes in the House. Many of the votes

amounted to Pyrrhic victories, however. For example, while Democrats were able to marshall enough GOP support to defeat two the four articles of impeachment against Clinton Dec. 19, they could not attract enough Republicans to defeat the other two.

In recent years, both parties have shown a high degree of loyalty on votes when the parties disagree, and that pattern continued in 1998 as Republicans succeeded in keeping an average of 86 percent of their conference in line on party-unity votes in both the House and Senate. Democrats kept an average of 87

percent of caucus members unified on these votes in the Senate, and 82 percent in the House.

Crossing Party Lines

Lawmakers who voted most often against their caucus tended to be Republican moderates, mainly from the Northeast, and conservative Democrats, typically from that party's former stronghold in the South.

In the Senate, no Republican voted with Democrats more often than

any Democrat. And no Democrat voted against his party more often than any Republican did.

Republicans who voted in agreement most often with the other party were James M. Jeffords of Vermont and Arlen Specter of Pennsylvania in the Senate, and Constance A. Morella of Maryland and Christopher Shays of Connecticut in the House.

Democrats who voted most often with Republicans were Robert C. Byrd of West Virginia and John B. Breaux of

Louisiana in the Senate, and Ralph M. Hall of Texas and Virgil H. Goode Jr. of Virginia in the House.

While the ongoing impeachment proceeding may spawn further division in the Senate this year, in the House, some members said emotions may cool.

"We are at the point where we hit rock bottom, and I now hope we are coming back," Appropriations Committee Chairman C.W. "Bill" Young, R-Fla., said Dec. 19. ◆

Influential Since the 1940s, The Conservative Coalition Limps Into History in 1998

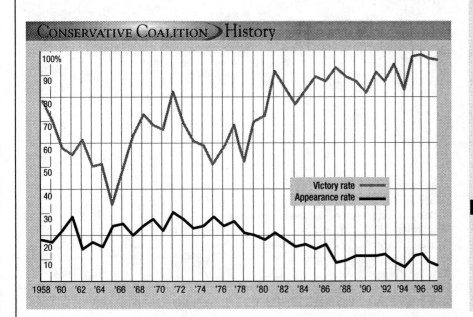

CONSERVATIVE COALITION ▶ History

Victory rate
Appearance rate

1958 '60 '62 '64 '66 '68 '70 '72 '74 '76 '78 '80 '82 '84 '86 '88 '90 '92 '94 '96 '98

Definition

A voting bloc in the House and Senate consisting of a majority of Republicans and majority of Southern Democrats, combined against a majority of Northern Democrats.

Appearance indicates how often the coalition voted as a group. Victory indicates how often the coalition prevailed on these votes.

1998 Data

Senate	8 victories
	0 defeats
	8 appearances in 314 votes

House	40 victories
	2 defeats
	42 appearances in 533 votes

Total Congress appearance rate: 6%
Total Congress victory rate: 96%

For More Information

Eclipsed by rigid partisanship and the shift of the South toward the Republican Party, the conservative coalition — a tool of political analysis for much of the century — became moribund in 1998.

The voting alliance of Republicans and Southern Democrats, which once determined the outcome of major civil rights, labor and economic legislation, finally ran out of steam. Specifically:

● In the Senate, Southern Democrats left their party on only eight votes, too few to be statistically significant.

● No significant bill was enacted because of the votes of the coalition.

● The House showed that it could take the most momentous step possible, impeachment of the president, with the votes of only four Southern Democrats.

Accordingly, Congressional Quarterly, which has maintained the conservative coalition vote study since 1957, is downgrading it. In future years, CQ will collect and publish members' scores for purposes of continuity and research, but will not write

about them — unless the North-South axis reasserts itself as a significant factor on more than regional issues. In a chamber as closely divided as the current House, any bloc of votes that develops cohesion could become significant.

The coalition has been on life support since the mid-1980s. In 1995, it became largely irrelevant as a political force because Republicans no longer needed the votes of Southern Democrats to pass their legislation.

Coalition scores retained some use-

Leading Scorers: Conservative Coalition

Support indicates those who in 1998 voted most often with the conservative coalition. **Opposition** indicates those who voted most often against the coalition. Scores are based on votes cast, and members are listed alphabetically when scores are tied. Members who missed half the votes are not listed.

Support						Opposition					

HOUSE *

Republican		Southern Democrat		Northern Democrat		Republican		Southern Democrat		Northern Democrat	
Baker, La.	100%	John, La.	100%	Traficant, Ohio	95%	Morella, Md.	61%	Lewis, Ga.	93%	Jackson, Ill.	100%
Boehner, Ohio	100	Cramer, Ala.	98	Boswell, Iowa	93	Shays, Conn.	50	McKinney, Ga.	90	Gutierrez, Ill.	98
Brady, Texas	100	Stenholm, Texas	98	Skelton, Mo.	93	Paul, Texas	44	Watt, N.C.	81	Tierney, Mass.	98
Calvert, Calif.	100	Hall, Texas	95	Danner, Mo.	88	Boehlert, N.Y.	36	Hastings, Fla.	80	Lee, Calif.	97
Cannon, Utah	100	Turner, Texas	95	Condit, Calif.	80	Campbell, Calif.	36	Hilliard, Ala.	78	Payne, N.J.	97
Chambliss, Ga.	100	McIntyre, N.C.	93	Pomeroy, N.D.	79	Johnson, Conn.	33	Doggett, Texas	76	Davis, Ill.	95
DeLay, Texas	100	Goode, Va.	90			Sensenbrenner, Wis.	31	Brown, Fla.	71	Owens, N.Y.	95
Granger, Texas	100	Pickett, Va.	90					Meek, Fla.	71	Roybal-Allard, Calif.	95
Hastings, Wash.	100	Tanner, Tenn.	90							Rush, Ill.	95
Lewis, Ky.	100	Sandlin, Texas	88							Stark, Calif.	95
McCrery, La.	100	Sisisky, Va.	88							Meeks, N.Y.	94
Oxley, Ohio	100										
Packard, Calif.	100										
Pickering, Miss.	100										
Redmond, N.M.	100										
Rogers, Ky.	100										
Sessions, Texas	100										
Smith, Ore.	100										
Smith, Texas	100										
Tauzin, La.	100										
Taylor, N.C.	100										
Wicker, Miss.	100										
Wilson, N.M.	100										
Young, Fla.	100										

*Note: CQ's statistical methodology did not yield enough Senate votes in 1998 to serve as a reliable way to align members on a liberal-conservative spectrum.

fulness to political scientists because they constituted a statistically derived scale of political ideology. But in 1998, they became too rare in the Senate, and the votes were often on issues without clear ideological coloration.

A Powerful Force

The occasional alliance of Southern Democrats with conservative Republicans first became a force in President Franklin D. Roosevelt's second term, when it stopped his plan to "pack" the Supreme Court. In the 1940s and '50s, it blocked Democratic initiatives on civil rights, education and labor bills. In 1981, it passed President Ronald Reagan's budget. As recently as 1993, it formed to win approval of the North American Free Trade Agreement.

As a concept, the term also referred to the clout of Southern committee chairmen, who used the one-party dominance of their region to amass seniority. This reached its zenith in the 1950s, as Virginia Democrat Howard W. Smith (1931-67) refused to convene the House Rules Committee, which he chaired, to consider legislation he did not like.

But Smith lost his autonomy in 1961, and three years later, Arizona Sen. Barry Goldwater's presidential campaign gave Republicans a foothold in the South. Thirty years later, Republicans took a majority of Southern seats for the first time since Reconstruction on their way to control of Congress.

Not only are there fewer Democrats from the South, there is also greater diversity among them. Many House districts have been drawn to elect black (or, in Texas, Hispanic) members who are less conservative, and the urbanization of Southern cities has added a few white liberals. Southern is no longer a synonym for conservative.

CQ's statistical methodology did not yield enough Senate votes in 1998 to serve as a reliable way to align members on a liberal-conservative spectrum. While proud liberals Edward M. Kennedy, D-Mass., and Paul Wellstone, D-Minn., scored 0 percent support, those scoring 100 percent included several Republicans (such as William V. Roth Jr. of Delaware and Slade Gorton of Washington) who scored in the 60 percent to 70 percent range on the more subjective ratings of the American Conservative Union (ACU).

And none of the eight Senate votes on which the coalition formed are included in the votes chosen for ratings by the ACU or the liberal Americans for Democratic Action. None are CQ key votes.

In the House, the only CQ conservative coalition vote that was chosen by the ideological groups was a July 23

vote on overriding President Clinton's veto of an abortion-procedure bill. Without the formation of the coalition, the vote probably would not have hit the two-thirds majority needed for overrides. The bill died in the Senate in September on a key vote when the coalition did not form to pass it.

The 42 votes in the House database (7.9 percent of all House roll call votes) are more in line with prior years, and they yield results that seem to track with other ideological measuring sticks.

Three of the four Southern Democrats who voted for impeachment (Ralph M. Hall and Charles W. Stenholm of Texas and Virgil H. Goode Jr. of Virginia) rank among those voting with the coalition 90 percent of the time.

Those voting in opposition to the coalition rank high in other indices, and GOP opponents such as Constance A. Morella of Maryland and Christopher Shays of Connecticut voted against impeachment.

The one anomaly is Ron Paul of Texas, who ranked third in opposition and yet is considered one of the most conservative members. But the former Libertarian Party candidate for president is a maverick who led his party in opposition to the coalition in 1997. ◆

Lawmakers Sustain Historically High Voting Participation Rate

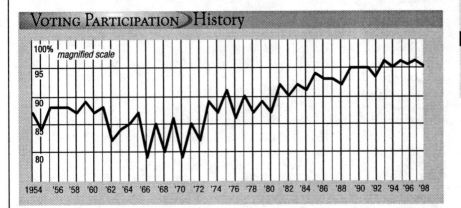

VOTING PARTICIPATION History

Members of Congress continued to rack up strong voting records in 1998 with a 95.7 percent overall participation rate. That was only slightly lower than the previous election-year record of 95.8 percent set two years earlier.

In a repeat of the pattern set in 1995-96, however, 1998 saw a drop from the preceding year, due in significant part to campaign demands and retirements. The overall participation rate in 1997, as in 1995, was 96.5.

Voting participation — measured by how often members vote yea or nay on roll call votes — has climbed during the past decade, reaching at least 95 percent in every year but one. Members' voting diligence stems in part from a desire to avoid the kind of ugly campaign brawls seen most recently in last fall's race between Sen. Alfonse M. D'Amato, R-N.Y., and his challenger, Rep. Charles E. Schumer, D-N.Y.

D'Amato targeted Schumer's voting record, accusing him of failing to represent his constituents by missing more than 100 floor votes and posting a 79 percent voting participation rate in 1998 — in contrast to D'Amato's 97 percent score. Schumer argued that his 1998 record was out of line with his usual voting diligence and that his previous participation scores had regularly been over 90 percent.

D'Amato's strategy backfired, however, when his own voting record as a member of supervisory boards for Nassau County and the Town of Hempstead was examined. It was reported that in 1980, while D'Amato was running for the U.S. Senate, he missed more than 900 votes before the two boards. He went on to win his race for

Definition

How often a member voted yea or nay on roll call votes on the floor of the House or Senate.

1998 Data

	Recorded Votes	Percent
Senate	314	97.4%
House	533	95.5%
Total Congress	847	95.7%

For More Information

Senators' scores B-29
House members' scores B-30

the Senate that year.

In the end, voters were not as impressed with D'Amato's Senate attendance record as he would have liked, and he lost his re-election bid to Schumer. While the race may not have hinged on the attendance issue, the negative campaign is a continuing reminder of the potential cost of missing a large number of roll call votes.

Sixteen senators maintained 100 percent voting scores in 1998. Nine had perfect scores for both sessions of the 105th Congress, including Charles E. Grassley, R-Iowa, who currently has the longest streak of perfect attendance of any member in Congress. Grassley has not missed a vote since July 1993.

Few members had an absence excuse as airtight as that of Sen. John Glenn, D-Ohio, whose participation rate of 76.4 percent was the lowest in the Senate. After casting his last vote Sept. 29, he began preparations with NASA to serve as a payload specialist aboard the space shuttle Discovery. Only four other senators had scores lower than 90 percent: Ernest F. Hollings, D-S.C., Arlen Specter, R-Pa., Daniel K. Inouye, D-Hawaii, and

Jesse Helms, R-N.C. Helms and Specter underwent surgery in 1998.

Overall, the average Senate participation rate was 97.4 percent, lower than last year's rate of 98.7 percent, which was the highest recorded for either chamber in the 46 years that Congressional Quarterly has been tracking participation levels.

The average in the House was 95.5 percent, also lower than last year's 96.3 percent rate. Nine members had perfect attendance, including three freshmen.

Only three House members had a 100 percent attendance rate for the entire 105th Congress: Jim Ramstad, R-Minn., Michael Pappas, R-N.J., and Jesse L. Jackson Jr., D-Ill. Pappas, however, will not be able to add to his streak; he lost his bid for re-election to Democratic challenger Rush D. Holt.

Thirty-four House members fell below 90 percent, compared with 19 members in 1997. Of the 10 members below 80 percent, five were running for higher offices: Jane Harman, D-Calif., Frank Riggs, R-Calif., Glenn Poshard, D-Ill., Barbara B. Kennelly, D-Conn., and Schumer. All five had participated in more than 90 percent of the roll call votes in 1997. Of the five, only Schumer was successful in his race.

Jackson, with a three-year streak that began Jan. 3, 1996, has the longest perfect attendance record of any House member. But he has more than three decades to go before he nears the record of former Rep. William Natcher, D-Ky. (1953-94), who did not miss a roll call vote in 40 years. ◆

Guide to CQ's Voting Analyses

Since 1945, Congressional Quarterly has analyzed the voting behavior of members of Congress. These studies have become references for academics, journalists, politicians and students who want information on how Congress behaves as an institution and how individual members vote.

What votes are used: CQ bases its vote studies on all roll call votes in which members were asked to vote "yea" or "nay." In 1998 there were 533 such votes in the House and 314 in the Senate.

Those totals include votes in the House to approve the Journal (11 in 1998) and in the Senate to instruct the sergeant at arms to request members' presence in the chamber (three in 1998). They do not include quorum calls, which require only that members vote "present." The House held 14 such votes in 1998.

The separate studies on presidential support, party unity and the conservative coalition cover specific votes selected from the total according to the criteria described on pp. B-4, B-6 and B-9.

Individual scores: In most of the charts that follow, a member's scores are calculated two ways: the first based on all votes, regardless of whether the member voted; the second based only on the votes the individual member actually cast.

The lists of leading scorers on pp. B-5, B-8 and B-10 are based on votes cast, not counting absences.

Overall scores: For consistency with previous years, graphs and breakdowns of chambers, parties and regions are based on the first set of scores.

Rounding: Scores are rounded to the nearest percentage point, except that rounding is not used to bring any score up to 100 percent.

Regions: Congressional Quarterly defines regions of the United States as follows: **East:** Conn., Del., Maine, Md., Mass., N.H., N.J., N.Y., Pa., R.I., Vt., W.Va. **West:** Alaska, Ariz., Calif., Colo., Hawaii, Idaho, Mont., Nev., N.M., Ore., Utah, Wash., Wyo. **South:** Ala., Ark., Fla., Ga., Ky., La., Miss., N.C., Okla., S.C., Tenn., Texas, Va. **Midwest:** Ill., Ind., Iowa, Kan., Mich., Minn., Mo., Neb., N.D., Ohio, S.D., Wis.

References to Northern Democrats and Northern Republicans include all members who do not represent the 13 Southern states, as defined by CQ.

Presidential Support Background

Congressional Quarterly determines presidential positions on congressional votes by examining the statements made by President Clinton or his authorized spokesmen.

Support measures the percentage of the time members voted in accord with the position of the president.

Opposition measures the percentage of the time members voted against the president's position. **Success** measures the percentage of the contested votes on which the president prevailed. Absences lowered parties' scores. Scores for 1997 are given for comparison.

National Security vs. Domestic Issues

Following are presidential success scores broken down into domestic and national security issues, with national security comprising votes on issues of foreign policy and defense.

	National Security		Domestic		Average	
	1998	1997	1998	1997	1998	1997
Senate	75%	58%	63%	75%	67%	71%
House	31	18	38	47	37	39
Average	**58**	**32**	**49**	**61**	**51**	**54**

Average Scores

	Support					Opposition			
	Republicans		Democrats			Republicans		Democrats	
	1998	1997	1998	1997		1998	1997	1998	1997
Senate	41%	60%	82%	85%	Senate	56%	39%	13%	13%
House	26	30	74	71	House	71	68	21	26

Regional Averages

	Support								Opposition							
	East		West		South		Midwest			East		West		South		Midwest	
	1998	1997	1998	1997	1998	1997	1998	1997		1998	1997	1998	1997	1998	1997	1998	1997
Republicans									**Republicans**								
Senate	53%	66%	41%	60%	35%	56%	40%	58%	Senate	43%	31%	55%	39%	61%	42%	59%	41%
House	34	39	24	28	22	27	26	31	House	64	60	72	68	74	71	72	68
Democrats									**Democrats**								
Senate	84	84	81	87	81	83	83	86	Senate	12	12	14	12	17	17	13	13
House	77	73	79	77	68	66	73	69	House	19	24	16	20	27	31	23	28

Success Rate History

Average score for both chambers of Congress:

Eisenhower

1953	89.0%
1954	82.8
1955	75.0
1956	70.0
1957	68.0
1958	76.0
1959	52.0
1960	65.0

Kennedy

1961	81.0%
1962	85.4
1963	87.1

Johnson

1964	88.0%
1965	93.0
1966	79.0
1967	79.0
1968	75.0

Nixon

1969	74.0%
1970	77.0
1971	75.0
1972	66.0
1973	50.6
1974	59.6

Ford

1974	58.2%
1975	61.0
1976	53.8

Carter

1977	75.4%
1978	78.3
1979	76.8
1980	75.1

Reagan

1981	82.4%
1982	72.4
1983	67.1
1984	65.8
1985	59.9
1986	56.1
1987	43.5
1988	47.4

Bush

1989	62.6%
1990	46.8
1991	54.2
1992	43.0

Clinton

1993	86.4%
1994	86.4
1995	36.2
1996	55.1
1997	53.6
1998	50.6

1998 House Presidential Position Votes

The following is a list of House votes in 1998 on which there was a clear presidential position. Votes are categorized by topic and listed by roll call number with a brief description.

Domestic Policy

21 Victories

Vote Number	Description
17	Voter identification
25	Telecommunications
37	Puerto Rico
38	Telecommunications
39	Child support
80	Environment
100	Law enforcement
101	Federal courts
133	Affirmative action
139	Child support
140	Law enforcement
197	Vocational aid
201	Religious freedom amendment
204	Legal immigrants
297	Nutrition
312	NEA
398	Executive orders
426	Head Start
489	National parks
544	Impeachment
546	Impeachment

38 Defeats

Vote Number	Description
9	Education
24	Federal agencies
50	Federal agencies
51	Property rights
52	Property rights
74	Small business
78	Union organizing
96	Transportation
114	Needle exchange
119	Education
151	Financial services
160	Federal mandates
163	Federal courts
171	Abortion
225	Bankruptcy law
228	Minimum wage
243	Education
280	Abortion
282	Environment
296	Housing
325	Abortion (veto override)
327	Environment
336	Health care
339	Health care
349	Domestic partners
388	Census sampling
411	Education
412	Needle exchange
414	Adoption
416	D.C. appropriations
424	Education
451	Education
452	Education
479	Agriculture appropriations
506	Bankruptcy law
542	Censure
543	Impeachment
545	Impeachment

Defense and Foreign Policy

4 Victories

Vote Number	Description
58	Bosnia policy
71	Visas
317	China MFN
356	Vietnam policy

9 Defeats

Vote Number	Description
155	Religious persecution
168	China policy
169	China policy
170	China policy
181	Nuclear exports
211	Iran sanctions
377	Iran sanctions
442	Drug interdiction
449	Foreign aid

Economic Affairs and Trade

5 Victories

Vote Number	Description
47	Trade
63	International environment
102	Tax limit amendment
274	IRS overhaul
538	Omnibus appropriations

5 Defeats

Vote Number	Description
10	Line item veto (veto override)
88	Supplemental appropriations
239	Tax code
464	Budget
469	Tax code

House Success Score

Victories	30
Defeats	52
Total	**82**
Success rate	36.6%

1998 Senate Presidential Position Votes

The following is a list of Senate votes in 1998 on which there was a clear presidential position. Votes are categorized by topic and listed by roll call number with a brief description.

Domestic Policy

14 Victories

Vote Number	Description
20	Transportation
23	Affirmative action
119	Job training
128	Legal immigrants
129	Legal immigrants
130	Telecommunications
137	Digital copyright
148	Nuclear waste (cloture)
197	Property rights (cloture)
238	Banking
239	Credit unions
266	Union organizing (cloture)
277	Abortion (veto override)
290	Education

18 Defeats

Vote Number	Description
86	Education
90	Education
91	Education
94	Education
102	Education
138	Immigration
139	Immigration
141	Immigration
145	Tobacco policy
161	Tobacco policy (cloture)
162	Tobacco policy
169	Education
176	Abortion
192	Education
194	Education
268	Mining
294	Environment
298	Agriculture appropriations

Defense and Foreign Policy

15 Victories

Vote Number	Description
47	Mexico drug policy
106	NATO expansion
109	NATO expansion
110	Bosnia policy
111	NATO expansion
112	NATO expansion
117	NATO expansion
131	Anti-missile defense (cloture)
171	Bosnia policy
172	Women in the military
180	Women in the military
249	Bosnia policy
254	Nuclear test ban
256	International Monetary Fund
262	Anti-missile defense (cloture)

5 Defeats

Vote Number	Description
24	Intelligence policy
105	Family planning
146	Iran sanctions
174	Base closures
257	North Korea policy

Economic Affairs and Trade

3 Victories

Vote Number	Description
189	IRS overhaul
241	Tax code
314	Omnibus appropriations

1 Defeat

Vote Number	Description
13	Line-Item veto (veto override)

Nominations

16 Victories

Vote Number	Description
1	Ann L. Aiken
2	Carlos R. Moreno
3	Christine O.C. Miller
9	Dr. David Satcher
11	Margaret M. Morrow
18	Richard L. Young
33	Jeremy D. Fogel
35	Susan Graber
48	M. Margaret McKeown
61	G. Patrick Murphy
104	Scott Snyder Fleming
166	Susan Oki Mollway
182	A. Howard Matz
183	Victoria A. Roberts
295	Sonia Sotomayor
309	William A. Fletcher

Senate Success Score

Victories	48
Defeats	24
Total	**72**
Success rate	67%

Presidential Support and Opposition: House

1. Clinton Support Score. Percentage of 82 recorded votes in 1998 on which President Clinton took a position and on which a representative voted "yea" or "nay" in agreement with the president's position. Failures to vote lowered both support and opposition scores.

2. Clinton Opposition Score. Percentage of 82 recorded votes in 1998 on which President Clinton took a position and on which a representative voted "yea" or "nay" in disagreement with the president's position. Failures to vote lowered both support and opposition scores.

3. Clinton Support Score (adjusted for absences). Percentage of 82 recorded votes in 1998 on which President Clinton took a position and on which a representative was present and voted "yea" or "nay" in agreement with the president's position. In this version of the study, absences were not counted; therefore, failures to vote did not lower support or opposition scores. Opposition scores, not listed here, are the inverse of the support score; i.e., the opposition score is equal to 100 percent minus the individual's support score.

[1] *Barbara Lee, D-Calif., was sworn in April 21, replacing Ronald V. Dellums, D-Calif., who resigned Feb. 6. Lee was eligible for 62 presidential support votes in 1998. Dellums was eligible for two presidential support votes in 1998 but did not vote on either of them.*

[2] *Lois Capps, D-Calif., was sworn in March 17, replacing Walter Capps, D-Calif., who died Oct. 28, 1997. Lois Capps was eligible for 70 presidential support votes in 1998.*

[3] *Mary Bono, R-Calif., was sworn in April 21, replacing Sonny Bono, R-Calif., who died Jan. 5. Mary Bono was eligible for 62 presidential support votes in 1998. Sonny Bono was eligible for no presidential support votes in 1998.*

[4] *Newt Gingrich, R-Ga., as Speaker of the House, voted at his discretion on 30 presidential support votes in 1998.*

[5] *Heather Wilson, R-N.M., was sworn in June 25, replacing Stephen H. Schiff, R-N.M., who died March 25. Wilson was eligible for 37 presidential support votes in 1998. Schiff was eligible for 14 presidential support votes in 1998 but did not vote on any of them.*

[6] *Gregory W. Meeks, D-N.Y., was sworn in Feb. 5, replacing Floyd H. Flake, D-N.Y., who resigned on Nov. 15, 1997. Meeks was eligible for 80 presidential support votes in 1998.*

[7] *Robert A. Brady, D-Pa., was sworn in May 21, replacing Thomas M. Foglietta, D-Pa., who resigned Nov. 11, 1997. Brady was eligible for 46 presidential support votes in 1998.*

Democrats   Republicans   Independent

		1	2	3
ALABAMA				
1	*Callahan*	23	72	24
2	*Everett*	20	79	20
3	*Riley*	18	82	18
4	*Aderholt*	21	79	21
5	*Cramer*	52	44	54
6	*Bachus*	20	79	20
7	Hilliard	84	13	86
ALASKA				
AL	*Young*	27	70	28
ARIZONA				
1	*Salmon*	26	73	26
2	Pastor	82	18	82
3	*Stump*	20	80	20
4	*Shadegg*	22	77	22
5	*Kolbe*	40	60	40
6	*Hayworth*	23	77	23
ARKANSAS				
1	Berry	61	35	63
2	Snyder	80	18	81
3	*Hutchinson*	26	72	26
4	*Dickey*	24	74	25
CALIFORNIA				
1	*Riggs*	20	66	23
2	*Herger*	22	76	23
3	Fazio	77	18	81
4	*Doolittle*	16	79	17
5	Matsui	82	18	82
6	Woolsey	84	15	85
7	Miller	74	15	84
8	Pelosi	80	16	84
9	Lee[1]	85	11	85
10	Tauscher	77	23	77
11	*Pombo*	23	77	23
12	Lantos	80	18	81
13	Stark	82	12	87
14	Eshoo	87	10	90
15	*Campbell*	51	48	52
16	Lofgren	84	11	88
17	Farr	84	12	87
18	Condit	50	49	51
19	*Radanovich*	20	79	20
20	Dooley	80	20	80
21	*Thomas*	28	71	28
22	Capps[2]	73	23	73
23	*Gallegly*	21	78	21
24	Sherman	72	28	72
25	*McKeon*	23	74	24
26	Berman	76	13	85
27	*Rogan*	27	73	27
28	*Dreier*	26	73	26
29	Waxman	84	15	85
30	Becerra	82	11	88
31	Martinez	77	16	83
32	Dixon	76	13	85
33	Roybal-Allard	80	13	86
34	Torres	77	11	88
35	Waters	76	13	85
36	Harman	52	15	78
37	Millender-McD.	78	15	84
38	Horn	34	63	35
39	*Royce*	20	73	21
40	*Lewis*	32	65	33
41	*Kim*	28	72	28
42	Brown	77	13	85
43	*Calvert*	24	76	24
44	*Bono*[3]	23	59	23
45	*Rohrabacher*	26	74	26
46	Sanchez	71	20	78
47	*Cox*	26	70	27
48	*Packard*	20	74	21
49	*Bilbray*	34	65	35
50	Filner	84	15	85
51	*Cunningham*	22	67	25
52	*Hunter*	20	78	20
COLORADO				
1	DeGette	85	13	86
2	Skaggs	83	6	93
3	*McInnis*	26	72	26
4	*Schaffer*	18	82	18
5	*Hefley*	21	78	21
6	*Schaefer*	16	80	16
CONNECTICUT				
1	Kennelly	70	17	80
2	Gejdenson	83	17	83
3	DeLauro	82	18	82
4	*Shays*	57	43	57
5	Maloney	66	32	68
6	*Johnson*	57	43	57
DELAWARE				
AL	*Castle*	51	49	51
FLORIDA				
1	*Scarborough*	24	71	26
2	Boyd	61	38	62
3	Brown	77	15	84
4	*Fowler*	26	71	27
5	Thurman	77	23	77
6	*Stearns*	18	82	18
7	*Mica*	22	73	23
8	*McCollum*	26	73	26
9	*Bilirakis*	20	78	20
10	*Young*	20	61	24
11	Davis	73	26	74
12	*Canady*	22	78	22
13	*Miller*	30	66	32
14	Goss	28	59	32
15	*Weldon*	16	80	16
16	Foley	38	61	38
17	Meek	80	12	87
18	*Ros-Lehtinen*	27	65	29
19	Wexler	88	10	90
20	Deutsch	79	17	82
21	*Diaz-Balart*	32	66	33
22	*Shaw*	34	66	34
23	Hastings	84	10	90
GEORGIA				
1	*Kingston*	20	80	20
2	Bishop	57	41	58
3	*Collins*	12	87	12
4	McKinney	87	13	87
5	Lewis	74	11	87
6	*Gingrich*[4]	5	32	13
7	Barr	20	77	20
8	*Chambliss*	22	78	22
9	*Deal*	16	84	16
10	Norwood	17	78	18
11	Linder	20	76	21
HAWAII				
1	Abercrombie	82	18	82
2	Mink	83	15	85
IDAHO				
1	*Chenoweth*	29	71	29
2	*Crapo*	29	67	30
ILLINOIS				
1	Rush	79	15	84
2	Jackson	83	17	83
3	Lipinski	48	48	50
4	Gutierrez	80	17	83
5	Blagojevich	74	22	77
6	*Hyde*	20	79	20
7	Davis	84	15	85
8	*Crane*	23	74	24
9	Yates	68	9	89
10	*Porter*	39	57	41
11	*Weller*	26	72	26
12	Costello	67	32	68
13	*Fawell*	35	56	39

ND Northern Democrats   SD Southern Democrats

	1	2	3
14 Hastert	21	78	21
15 Ewing	27	66	29
16 Manzullo	21	78	21
17 Evans	82	17	83
18 LaHood	28	71	28
19 Poshard	52	20	73
20 *Shimkus*	24	72	25

INDIANA

	1	2	3
1 Visclosky	79	21	79
2 *McIntosh*	23	73	24
3 Roemer	61	39	61
4 *Souder*	24	73	25
5 *Buyer*	23	73	24
6 *Burton*	20	72	21
7 *Pease*	23	74	24
8 *Hostettler*	24	76	24
9 Hamilton	77	22	78
10 Carson	83	10	89

IOWA

	1	2	3
1 *Leach*	51	46	53
2 *Nussle*	27	72	27
3 Boswell	65	35	65
4 *Ganske*	33	63	34
5 *Latham*	24	76	24

KANSAS

	1	2	3
1 *Moran*	29	71	29
2 *Ryun*	21	77	21
3 *Snowbarger*	22	77	22
4 *Tiahrt*	20	79	20

KENTUCKY

	1	2	3
1 *Whitfield*	23	74	24
2 *Lewis*	20	80	20
3 *Northup*	24	74	25
4 *Bunning*	20	77	20
5 *Rogers*	22	76	23
6 Baesler	60	38	61

LOUISIANA

	1	2	3
1 *Livingston*	23	74	24
2 Jefferson	73	15	83
3 *Tauzin*	22	73	23
4 *McCrery*	24	71	26
5 *Cooksey*	23	71	25
6 *Baker*	20	79	20
7 John	43	43	50

MAINE

	1	2	3
1 Allen	82	16	84
2 Baldacci	79	20	80

MARYLAND

	1	2	3
1 *Gilchrest*	37	61	38
2 *Ehrlich*	24	73	25
3 Cardin	74	21	78
4 Wynn	82	17	83
5 Hoyer	80	18	81
6 *Bartlett*	18	80	19
7 Cummings	82	17	83
8 *Morella*	71	29	71

MASSACHUSETTS

	1	2	3
1 Olver	85	12	88
2 Neal	77	20	80
3 McGovern	78	20	80
4 Frank	80	18	81
5 Meehan	82	11	88
6 Tierney	80	17	83
7 Markey	76	17	82
8 Kennedy	78	17	82
9 Moakley	67	18	79
10 Delahunt	83	17	83

MICHIGAN

	1	2	3
1 Stupak	73	24	75
2 *Hoekstra*	24	76	24
3 *Ehlers*	33	67	33
4 *Camp*	27	73	27
5 Barcia	60	39	60
6 *Upton*	33	67	33
7 *Smith*	26	73	26
8 Stabenow	73	21	78
9 Kildee	74	26	74
10 Bonior	80	16	84
11 *Knollenberg*	24	76	24
12 Levin	83	17	83
13 Rivers	76	24	76
14 Conyers	79	9	90
15 Kilpatrick	77	11	88
16 Dingell	77	17	82

MINNESOTA

	1	2	3
1 *Gutknecht*	24	76	24
2 Minge	71	28	72
3 *Ramstad*	43	57	43
4 Vento	85	15	85
5 Sabo	88	11	89
6 Luther	71	23	75
7 Peterson	55	45	55
8 Oberstar	83	15	85

MISSISSIPPI

	1	2	3
1 *Wicker*	23	74	24
2 Thompson	77	17	82
3 *Pickering*	20	77	20
4 *Parker*	24	65	27
5 Taylor	33	66	33

MISSOURI

	1	2	3
1 Clay	73	10	88
2 *Talent*	20	79	20
3 Gephardt	73	16	82
4 Skelton	57	41	58
5 McCarthy	80	18	81
6 Danner	45	52	46
7 *Blunt*	17	83	17
8 *Emerson*	22	78	22
9 *Hulshof*	24	74	25

MONTANA

	1	2	3
AL *Hill*	27	68	28

NEBRASKA

	1	2	3
1 *Bereuter*	28	72	28
2 *Christensen*	16	76	17
3 *Barrett*	27	73	27

NEVADA

	1	2	3
1 *Ensign*	27	73	27
2 *Gibbons*	22	78	22

NEW HAMPSHIRE

	1	2	3
1 *Sununu*	24	74	25
2 *Bass*	33	66	33

NEW JERSEY

	1	2	3
1 Andrews	77	23	77
2 *LoBiondo*	35	65	35
3 *Saxton*	30	66	32
4 *Smith*	27	72	27
5 *Roukema*	34	66	34
6 Pallone	78	22	78
7 *Franks*	38	62	38
8 Pascrell	70	29	70
9 Rothman	80	17	83
10 Payne	82	10	89
11 *Frelinghuysen*	37	63	37
12 *Pappas*	23	77	23
13 Menendez	74	21	78

NEW MEXICO

	1	2	3
1 *Wilson* [5]	22	35	22
2 *Skeen*	27	73	27
3 *Redmond*	24	68	26

NEW YORK

	1	2	3
1 *Forbes*	41	59	41
2 *Lazio*	37	63	37
3 *King*	30	67	31
4 McCarthy	68	32	68
5 Ackerman	82	13	86
6 Meeks [6]	79	9	90
7 Manton	71	20	78
8 Nadler	76	20	79
9 Schumer	67	12	85
10 Towns	76	13	85
11 Owens	83	11	88
12 Velázquez	79	18	81
13 *Fossella*	23	77	23
14 Maloney	79	17	82
15 Rangel	77	11	88
16 Serrano	80	15	85
17 Engel	79	17	82
18 Lowey	82	17	83
19 *Kelly*	41	59	41
20 Gilman	45	54	46
21 McNulty	65	21	76
22 *Solomon*	17	82	17
23 *Boehlert*	60	40	60
24 *McHugh*	34	65	35
25 *Walsh*	35	63	36
26 Hinchey	82	17	83
27 *Paxon*	17	76	18
28 Slaughter	82	18	82
29 LaFalce	82	17	83

	1	2	3
30 Quinn	30	65	32
31 Houghton	44	46	49

NORTH CAROLINA

	1	2	3
1 Clayton	80	17	83
2 Etheridge	71	27	73
3 *Jones*	21	79	21
4 Price	77	23	77
5 *Burr*	23	73	24
6 *Coble*	16	83	16
7 McIntyre	51	48	52
8 Hefner	70	18	79
9 *Myrick*	18	77	19
10 *Ballenger*	22	77	22
11 *Taylor*	17	80	18
12 Watt	89	9	91

NORTH DAKOTA

	1	2	3
AL Pomeroy	72	24	75

OHIO

	1	2	3
1 *Chabot*	27	73	27
2 *Portman*	29	71	29
3 Hall	65	33	66
4 *Oxley*	24	72	25
5 *Gillmor*	28	70	29
6 Strickland	66	34	66
7 *Hobson*	28	71	28
8 *Boehner*	24	74	25
9 Kaptur	67	28	71
10 Kucinich	78	22	78
11 Stokes	82	12	87
12 *Kasich*	24	73	25
13 Brown	82	17	83
14 Sawyer	88	12	88
15 *Pryce*	26	59	30
16 *Regula*	28	72	28
17 Traficant	46	52	47
18 *Ney*	27	73	27
19 *LaTourette*	38	61	38

OKLAHOMA

	1	2	3
1 *Largent*	26	71	27
2 *Coburn*	16	80	16
3 *Watkins*	23	73	24
4 *Watts*	21	79	21
5 *Istook*	16	77	17
6 *Lucas*	22	78	22

OREGON

	1	2	3
1 Furse	74	11	87
2 *Smith*	17	72	19
3 Blumenauer	83	15	85
4 DeFazio	77	20	80
5 Hooley	77	22	78

PENNSYLVANIA

	1	2	3
1 Brady [7]	83	6	88
2 Fattah	80	11	88
3 Borski	78	21	79
4 Klink	70	23	75
5 Peterson	24	76	24
6 Holden	61	39	61
7 *Weldon*	28	71	28
8 *Greenwood*	35	57	38
9 *Shuster*	24	71	26
10 *McDade*	18	55	25
11 Kanjorski	82	18	82
12 Murtha	72	27	73
13 *Fox*	34	66	34
14 Coyne	82	17	83
15 McHale	73	27	73
16 *Pitts*	21	78	21
17 *Gekas*	21	77	21
18 Doyle	66	30	68
19 *Goodling*	18	77	19
20 Mascara	73	27	73
21 *English*	35	63	36

RHODE ISLAND

	1	2	3
1 Kennedy	79	21	79
2 Weygand	73	27	73

SOUTH CAROLINA

	1	2	3
1 *Sanford*	33	67	33
2 *Spence*	18	82	18
3 *Graham*	22	78	22
4 *Inglis*	18	78	19
5 Spratt	71	27	73
6 Clyburn	83	17	83

SOUTH DAKOTA

	1	2	3
AL *Thune*	23	77	23

TENNESSEE

	1	2	3
1 *Jenkins*	20	80	20
2 *Duncan*	22	78	22
3 *Wamp*	18	82	18
4 *Hilleary*	20	79	20
5 Clement	65	34	65
6 Gordon	61	38	62
7 *Bryant*	20	79	20
8 Tanner	55	39	58
9 Ford	61	21	75

TEXAS

	1	2	3
1 Sandlin	61	37	63
2 Turner	52	46	53
3 *Johnson*	20	78	20
4 Hall	29	70	30
5 *Sessions*	20	78	20
6 *Barton*	20	78	20
7 *Archer*	21	77	21
8 *Brady*	20	77	20
9 Lampson	80	18	81
10 Doggett	80	18	81
11 Edwards	80	18	81
12 *Granger*	28	72	28
13 *Thornberry*	23	77	23
14 Paul	30	67	31
15 Hinojosa	76	20	79
16 Reyes	73	21	78
17 Stenholm	49	51	49
18 Jackson-Lee	78	16	83
19 *Combest*	22	78	22
20 Gonzalez	12	1	91
21 *Smith*	22	74	23
22 *DeLay*	20	78	20
23 *Bonilla*	29	67	30
24 Frost	71	26	73
25 Bentsen	78	22	78
26 *Armey*	22	77	22
27 Ortiz	66	30	68
28 Rodriguez	78	18	81
29 Green	68	28	71
30 Johnson	79	13	86

UTAH

	1	2	3
1 *Hansen*	18	72	20
2 *Cook*	18	78	19
3 *Cannon*	17	72	19

VERMONT

	1	2	3
AL **Sanders**	83	15	85

VIRGINIA

	1	2	3
1 *Bateman*	21	57	27
2 *Pickett*	60	39	60
3 Scott	89	11	89
4 Sisisky	63	37	63
5 Goode	26	74	26
6 *Goodlatte*	23	77	23
7 *Bliley*	23	77	23
8 Moran	80	18	81
9 Boucher	77	21	79
10 *Wolf*	24	76	24
11 *Davis*	33	65	34

WASHINGTON

	1	2	3
1 *White*	29	70	30
2 *Metcalf*	21	79	21
3 *Smith*	20	77	20
4 *Hastings*	22	76	23
5 *Nethercutt*	27	73	27
6 Dicks	84	15	85
7 McDermott	89	5	95
8 *Dunn*	23	76	23
9 Smith	79	20	80

WEST VIRGINIA

	1	2	3
1 Mollohan	63	28	69
2 Wise	74	21	78
3 Rahall	74	22	77

WISCONSIN

	1	2	3
1 *Neumann*	22	77	22
2 *Klug*	33	62	35
3 Kind	77	23	77
4 Kleczka	74	24	75
5 Barrett	88	11	89
6 *Petri*	30	68	31
7 Obey	88	11	89
8 Johnson	72	27	73
9 *Sensenbrenner*	22	78	22

WYOMING

	1	2	3
AL *Cubin*	21	79	21

Southern states - Ala., Ark., Fla., Ga., Ky., La., Miss., N.C., Okla., S.C., Tenn., Texas, Va.

Democrats   *Republicans*

State / Senator	1	2	3
ALABAMA			
Shelby	33	65	34
Sessions	28	71	28
ALASKA			
Stevens	53	44	54
Murkowski	38	51	42
ARIZONA			
McCain	46	47	49
Kyl	31	61	33
ARKANSAS			
Hutchinson	24	68	26
Bumpers	85	13	87
CALIFORNIA			
Feinstein	88	13	88
Boxer	85	10	90
COLORADO			
Campbell	47	53	47
Allard	28	72	28
CONNECTICUT			
Dodd	93	7	93
Lieberman	83	17	83
DELAWARE			
Roth	58	33	64
Biden	83	8	91
FLORIDA			
Mack	50	50	50
Graham	83	17	83
GEORGIA			
Coverdell	39	58	40
Cleland	86	13	87
HAWAII			
Inouye	75	11	87
Akaka	81	8	91
IDAHO			
Craig	29	71	29
Kempthorne	33	65	34
ILLINOIS			
Moseley-Braun	75	13	86
Durbin	86	10	90
INDIANA			
Lugar	54	46	54
Coats	39	56	41
IOWA			
Grassley	39	61	39
Harkin	81	11	88
KANSAS			
Brownback	36	63	37
Roberts	35	64	35
KENTUCKY			
McConnell	39	61	39
Ford	75	22	77
LOUISIANA			
Breaux	78	21	79
Landrieu	85	14	86
MAINE			
Snowe	54	44	55
Collins	63	38	63
MARYLAND			
Sarbanes	92	8	92
Mikulski	86	8	91
MASSACHUSETTS			
Kennedy	92	4	96
Kerry	90	6	94
MICHIGAN			
Abraham	46	54	46
Levin	88	7	93
MINNESOTA			
Grams	39	61	39
Wellstone	85	13	87
MISSISSIPPI			
Cochran	53	47	53
Lott	39	60	39
MISSOURI			
Bond	38	61	38
Ashcroft	24	76	24
MONTANA			
Burns	38	63	38
Baucus	71	17	81
NEBRASKA			
Hagel	42	57	42
Kerrey	89	10	90
NEVADA			
Reid	76	21	79
Bryan	88	13	88
NEW HAMPSHIRE			
Smith	19	81	19
Gregg	42	54	43
NEW JERSEY			
Lautenberg	90	10	90
Torricelli	75	21	78
NEW MEXICO			
Domenici	53	40	57
Bingaman	81	13	87
NEW YORK			
D'Amato	56	38	60
Moynihan	71	19	78
NORTH CAROLINA			
Helms	25	53	32
Faircloth	25	63	29
NORTH DAKOTA			
Conrad	75	25	75
Dorgan	75	24	76
OHIO			
DeWine	51	49	51
Glenn	72	3	96
OKLAHOMA			
Nickles	22	76	23
Inhofe	13	76	14
OREGON			
Smith	54	44	55
Wyden	79	14	85
PENNSYLVANIA			
Specter	49	32	60
Santorum	40	60	40
RHODE ISLAND			
Chafee	76	22	77
Reed	90	10	90
SOUTH CAROLINA			
Thurmond	44	56	44
Hollings	67	24	74
SOUTH DAKOTA			
Daschle	90	10	90
Johnson	89	11	89
TENNESSEE			
Thompson	42	58	42
Frist	44	54	45
TEXAS			
Gramm	32	64	33
Hutchison	35	60	37
UTAH			
Hatch	47	51	48
Bennett	47	42	53
VERMONT			
Jeffords	68	31	69
Leahy	81	17	83
VIRGINIA			
Warner	38	58	39
Robb	90	10	90
WASHINGTON			
Gorton	49	51	49
Murray	82	18	82
WEST VIRGINIA			
Byrd	74	26	74
Rockefeller	82	6	94
WISCONSIN			
Kohl	85	14	86
Feingold	83	17	83
WYOMING			
Thomas	39	60	39
Enzi	31	68	31

ND Northern Democrats   SD Southern Democrats

Southern states - Ala., Ark., Fla., Ga., Ky., La., Miss., N.C., Okla., S.C., Tenn., Texas, Va.

Presidential Support and Opposition: Senate

1. Clinton Support Score. Percentage of 72 recorded votes in 1998 on which President Clinton took a position and on which a senator voted "yea" or "nay" in agreement with the president's position. Failures to vote lowered both support and opposition scores.

2. Clinton Opposition Score. Percentage of 72 recorded votes in 1998 on which President Clinton took a position and on which a senator voted "yea" or "nay" in disagreement with the president's position. Failures to vote lowered both support and opposition scores.

3. Clinton Support Score (adjusted for absences). Percentage of 72 recorded votes in 1998 on which President Clinton took a position and on which a senator was present and voted "yea" or "nay" in agreement with the president's position. In this version of the study, absences were not counted; therefore, failures to vote did not lower support or opposition scores. Opposition scores, not listed here, are the inverse of the support score; i.e., the opposition score is equal to 100 percent minus the individual's support score.

Party Unity Background

Party unity votes. Recorded votes that split the parties, with a majority of voting Democrats opposing a majority of voting Republicans. Members who switched parties are accounted for.

Party unity support. Percentage of party unity votes on which members voted "yea" or "nay" *in agreement* with a majority of their party. Failures to vote lowered scores for chambers and parties.

Opposition to party. Percentage of party unity votes on which members voted "yea" or "nay" *in disagreement* with a majority of their party. Failures to vote lowered scores for chambers and parties.

Average Scores by Chamber

	Republicans		Democrats			Republicans		Democrats	
	1998	**1997**	**1998**	**1997**		**1998**	**1997**	**1998**	**1997**
Party Unity	**86%**	**88%**	**83%**	**82%**	**Opposition**	**12%**	**9%**	**13%**	**15%**
Senate	86	87	87	85	Senate	12	12	10	14
House	86	88	82	82	House	11	9	13	15

Sectional Support, Opposition

Senate	Support	Opposition	House	Support	Opposition
Northern Republicans	84	15	Northern Republicans	84	13
Southern Republicans	91	7	Southern Republicans	88	8
Northern Democrats	88	9	Northern Democrats	85	11
Southern Democrats	83	15	Southern Democrats	74	20

1998 Victories, Defeats

	Senate	House	Total
Republicans won, Democrats lost	114	216	330
Democrats won, Republicans lost	61	80	141

Unanimous Voting by Parties

The number of times each party voted unanimously on party unity votes:

	Senate		House		Total	
	1998	**1997**	**1998**	**1997**	**1998**	**1997**
Republicans voted unanimously	33	38	42	63	75	101
Democrats voted unanimously	46	35	8	11	54	46

Party Unity Average Scores

Average score for each party in both chambers of Congress:

Year	Republicans	Democrats	Year	Republicans	Democrats
1963	72%	71%	1981	76%	69%
1964	69	67	1982	71	72
1965	70	69	1983	74	76
1966	67	61	1984	72	74
1967	71	66	1985	75	79
1968	63	57	1986	71	78
1969	62	62	1987	74	81
1970	59	57	1988	73	79
1971	66	62	1989	73	81
1972	64	57	1990	74	81
1973	68	68	1991	78	81
1974	62	63	1992	79	79
1975	70	69	1993	84	85
1976	66	65	1994	83	83
1977	70	67	1995	91	80
1978	67	64	1996	87	80
1979	72	69	1997	88	82
1980	70	68	1998	86	83

1998 Party Unity Votes

Following are the votes, by roll call number, on which a majority of Democrats voted against a majority of Republicans.

House

(296 of 533 "yea/nay" votes)

2	37	85	120	160	216	244	280	311	347	384	406	447	481	514
3	43	86	121	165	217	246	281	312	349	385	407	448	484	520
4	45	87	123	166	218	247	282	313	351	386	408	449	485	522
5	46	88	124	171	219	248	283	315	352	387	409	450	488	523
6	47	91	130	173	220	249	284	320	356	388	411	451	489	530
7	50	93	132	176	221	259	285	321	357	389	412	452	490	534
8	51	94	133	179	222	260	286	325	358	390	413	459	493	535
9	52	102	134	180	223	263	287	327	359	391	414	461	494	537
12	58	103	136	182	224	265	288	328	360	392	415	462	497	540
15	68	104	137	186	225	267	290	329	362	393	416	463	498	541
17	69	106	145	188	227	269	291	330	365	394	421	464	500	542
19	72	107	146	191	228	270	292	331	366	395	422	465	501	543
20	73	108	147	196	234	271	293	332	367	396	423	466	502	544
22	74	109	150	200	235	272	295	334	368	398	424	468	503	545
23	75	113	151	201	236	273	296	335	370	400	433	469	504	546
24	76	114	153	202	238	275	302	336	375	401	436	470	505	547
29	78	115	156	205	239	276	306	337	376	402	439	473	506	
30	79	117	157	208	241	277	307	338	379	403	440	476	508	
34	80	118	158	209	242	278	308	339	381	404	443	478	512	
36	83	119	159	210	243	279	310	343	382	405	446	480	513	

Senate

(175 of 314 "yea/nay" votes)

1	19	52	68	82	96	125	153	169	194	216	230	249	277	296
4	21	53	69	83	97	131	154	171	197	217	231	254	278	298
5	22	54	70	84	98	133	155	172	198	218	233	258	279	300
6	23	55	71	86	99	134	156	174	200	219	236	262	280	305
9	34	56	73	87	100	138	157	175	201	220	237	264	281	309
10	36	57	74	88	102	139	158	176	204	221	238	266	282	311
11	38	58	76	89	105	142	159	177	205	222	240	267	283	312
12	42	60	77	90	109	144	160	180	207	223	241	268	286	
14	45	62	78	91	120	148	161	187	208	224	242	272	287	
15	46	64	79	93	122	150	162	188	210	225	243	273	289	
16	47	65	80	94	123	151	164	191	212	226	244	274	294	
17	50	67	81	95	124	152	166	192	215	227	246	275	295	

Proportion of Partisan Roll Calls

How often a majority of Democrats voted against a majority of Republicans:

Year	House	Senate	Year	House	Senate	Year	House	Senate	Year	House	Senate
1955	41%	30%	1966	41%	50%	1977	42%	42%	1988	47%	42%
1956	44	53	1967	36	35	1978	33	45	1989	55	35
1957	59	36	1968	35	32	1979	47	47	1990	49	54
1958	40	44	1969	31	36	1980	38	46	1991	55	49
1959	55	48	1970	27	35	1981	37	48	1992	64	53
1960	53	37	1971	38	42	1982	36	43	1993	65	67
1961	50	62	1972	27	36	1983	56	44	1994	62	52
1962	46	41	1973	42	40	1984	47	40	1995	73	69
1963	49	47	1974	29	44	1985	61	50	1996	56	62
1964	55	36	1975	48	48	1986	57	52	1997	50	50
1965	52	42	1976	36	37	1987	64	41	1998	56	56

	1	2	3
ALABAMA			
Shelby	91	9	91
Sessions	98	2	98
ALASKA			
Stevens	82	18	82
Murkowski	91	7	93
ARIZONA			
McCain	81	15	84
Kyl	93	4	96
ARKANSAS			
Hutchinson	94	2	98
Bumpers	95	5	95
CALIFORNIA			
Feinstein	87	13	87
Boxer	88	10	90
COLORADO			
Campbell	82	18	82
Allard	96	3	97
CONNECTICUT			
Dodd	90	9	91
Lieberman	80	20	80
DELAWARE			
Roth	75	21	79
Biden	85	13	87
FLORIDA			
Mack	86	13	87
Graham	85	15	85
GEORGIA			
Coverdell	90	8	92
Cleland	87	13	87
HAWAII			
Inouye	79	6	93
Akaka	89	4	96
IDAHO			
Craig	99	1	99
Kempthorne	96	4	96
ILLINOIS			
Moseley-Braun	85	8	91
Durbin	94	5	95
INDIANA			
Lugar	84	16	84
Coats	87	10	89

	1	2	3
IOWA			
Grassley	86	14	86
Harkin	92	2	98
KANSAS			
Brownback	96	4	96
Roberts	94	5	95
KENTUCKY			
McConnell	95	5	95
Ford	82	17	83
LOUISIANA			
Breaux	73	27	73
Landrieu	88	11	89
MAINE			
Snowe	65	35	65
Collins	67	33	67
MARYLAND			
Sarbanes	99	1	99
Mikulski	94	3	97
MASSACHUSETTS			
Kennedy	98	0	100
Kerry	95	5	95
MICHIGAN			
Abraham	91	9	91
Levin	95	2	98
MINNESOTA			
Grams	97	3	97
Wellstone	98	1	99
MISSISSIPPI			
Cochran	86	14	86
Lott	94	4	96
MISSOURI			
Bond	86	12	88
Ashcroft	98	2	98
MONTANA			
Burns	94	6	94
Baucus	80	15	84
NEBRASKA			
Hagel	89	11	89
Kerrey	88	11	89
NEVADA			
Reid	78	19	81
Bryan	90	10	90

	1	2	3
NEW HAMPSHIRE			
Smith	98	1	99
Gregg	90	9	91
NEW JERSEY			
Lautenberg	97	3	97
Torricelli	83	14	85
NEW MEXICO			
Domenici	81	16	83
Bingaman	83	13	87
NEW YORK			
D'Amato	60	37	62
Moynihan	83	10	89
NORTH CAROLINA			
Helms	75	2	97
Faircloth	89	9	91
NORTH DAKOTA			
Conrad	87	13	87
Dorgan	87	13	87
OHIO			
DeWine	82	18	82
Glenn	77	1	99
OKLAHOMA			
Nickles	98	2	98
Inhofe	95	3	97
OREGON			
Smith	85	15	85
Wyden	86	12	88
PENNSYLVANIA			
Specter	41	43	49
Santorum	91	9	91
RHODE ISLAND			
Chafee	57	42	57
Reed	98	2	98
SOUTH CAROLINA			
Thurmond	91	9	91
Hollings	74	17	81
SOUTH DAKOTA			
Daschle	90	10	90
Johnson	93	7	93
TENNESSEE			
Thompson	87	13	87
Frist	94	6	94

Democrats **Republicans**

	1	2	3
TEXAS			
Gramm	97	3	97
Hutchison	89	8	92
UTAH			
Hatch	87	13	87
Bennett	81	15	84
VERMONT			
Jeffords	49	50	49
Leahy	86	13	87
VIRGINIA			
Warner	83	14	85
Robb	83	17	83
WASHINGTON			
Gorton	83	17	83
Murray	91	9	91
WEST VIRGINIA			
Byrd	72	28	72
Rockefeller	88	7	93
WISCONSIN			
Kohl	87	13	87
Feingold	86	14	86
WYOMING			
Thomas	94	5	95
Enzi	96	4	96

ND Northern Democrats   SD Southern Democrats

Southern states - Ala., Ark., Fla., Ga., Ky., La., Miss., N.C., Okla., S.C., Tenn., Texas, Va.

Party Unity and Party Opposition: Senate

1. Party Unity. Percentage of 175 party unity recorded votes in 1998 on which a senator voted "yea" or "nay" in agreement with a majority of his or her party. (Party unity roll calls are those on which a majority of voting Democrats opposed a majority of voting Republicans.) Failures to vote lowered both party unity and party opposition scores.

2. Party Opposition. Percentage of 175 party unity recorded votes in 1998 on which a senator voted "yea" or "nay" in disagreement with a majority of his or her party. Failures to vote lowered both party unity and party opposition scores.

3. Party Unity (adjusted for absences). Percentage of 175 party unity recorded votes in 1998 on which a senator was present and voted "yea" or "nay" in agreement with a majority of his or her party. In this version of the study, absences were not counted; therefore, failures to vote did not lower unity or opposition scores. Opposition scores, not listed here, are the inverse of the unity score; i.e., the opposition score is equal to 100 percent minus the individual's unity score.

Party Unity and Party Opposition: House

1. Party Unity. Percentage of 296 party unity recorded votes in 1998 on which a representative voted "yea" or "nay" in agreement with a majority of his or her party. (Party unity roll calls are those on which a majority of voting Democrats opposed a majority of voting Republicans.) Failures to vote lowered both party unity and party opposition scores.

2. Party Opposition. Percentage of 296 party unity recorded votes in 1998 on which a representative voted "yea" or "nay" in disagreement with a majority of his or her party. Failures to vote lowered both party unity and party opposition scores.

3. Party Unity (adjusted for absences). Percentage of 296 party unity recorded votes in 1998 on which a representative was present and voted "yea" or "nay" in agreement with a majority of his or her party. In this version of the study, absences were not counted; therefore, failures to vote did not lower unity or opposition scores. Opposition scores, not listed here, are the inverse of the unity score; i.e., the opposition score is equal to 100 percent minus the individual's unity score.

[1] Barbara Lee, D-Calif., was sworn in April 21, replacing Ronald V. Dellums, D-Calif., who resigned Feb. 6. Lee was eligible for 249 party unity votes in 1998. Dellums was eligible for eight party unity votes in 1998. His support score was 75 percent; opposition score, zero; support score adjusted for absences 100 percent.

[2] Lois Capps, D-Calif., was sworn in March 17, replacing Walter Capps, D-Calif., who died Oct. 28, 1997. Lois Capps was eligible for 268 party unity votes in 1998.

[3] Mary Bono, R-Calif., was sworn in April 21, replacing Sonny Bono, R-Calif., who died Jan. 5. Mary Bono was eligible for 249 party unity votes in 1998. Sonny Bono was eligible for no party unity votes in 1998.

[4] Newt Gingrich, R-Ga., as Speaker of the House, voted at his discretion on 61 party unity votes in 1998.

[5] Heather Wilson, R-N.M., was sworn in June 25, replacing Stephen H. Schiff, R-N.M., who died March 25. Wilson was eligible for 162 party unity votes in 1998. Schiff was eligible for 29 party unity votes in 1998 but did not vote on any of them.

[6] Gregory W. Meeks, D-N.Y., was sworn in Feb. 5, replacing Floyd H. Flake, D-N.Y., who resigned on Nov. 15, 1997. Meeks was eligible for 288 party unity votes in 1998.

[7] Robert A. Brady, D-Pa., was sworn in May 21, replacing Thomas M. Foglietta, D-Pa., who resigned Nov. 11, 1997. Brady was eligible for 211 party unity votes in 1998.

Democrats **Republicans**
Independent

	1	2	3
ALABAMA			
1 *Callahan*	89	6	93
2 *Everett*	94	6	94
3 *Riley*	93	6	94
4 *Aderholt*	90	9	91
5 Cramer	58	39	60
6 *Bachus*	89	10	89
7 Hilliard	90	5	94
ALASKA			
AL *Young*	84	11	89
ARIZONA			
1 *Salmon*	93	6	94
2 Pastor	91	9	91
3 *Stump*	93	7	93
4 *Shadegg*	97	3	97
5 *Kolbe*	80	19	81
6 *Hayworth*	94	6	94
ARKANSAS			
1 Berry	68	29	70
2 Snyder	79	20	80
3 *Hutchinson*	85	10	90
4 *Dickey*	91	7	93
CALIFORNIA			
1 *Riggs*	74	6	92
2 *Herger*	93	4	96
3 Fazio	88	10	90
4 *Doolittle*	91	6	94
5 Matsui	92	7	92
6 Woolsey	95	5	95
7 Miller	90	2	97
8 Pelosi	94	3	97
9 Lee[1]	98	1	99
10 Tauscher	79	19	81
11 *Pombo*	92	7	93
12 Lantos	92	5	95
13 Stark	92	2	98
14 Eshoo	92	5	95
15 *Campbell*	64	36	64
16 Lofgren	90	8	92
17 Farr	90	5	95
18 Condit	62	37	63
19 *Radanovich*	90	4	96
20 Dooley	79	19	80
21 *Thomas*	89	10	89
22 Capps[2]	90	8	91
23 *Gallegly*	90	10	90
24 Sherman	82	17	83
25 *McKeon*	94	5	95
26 Berman	83	4	95
27 *Rogan*	88	8	92
28 *Dreier*	90	9	91
29 Waxman	94	3	97
30 Becerra	90	1	99
31 Martinez	77	15	84
32 Dixon	85	5	95
33 Roybal-Allard	91	1	99
34 Torres	81	4	95
35 Waters	85	5	94
36 Harman	63	13	83
37 Millender-McD.	89	4	96
38 *Horn*	73	27	73

	1	2	3
39 *Royce*	83	9	90
40 *Lewis*	86	12	88
41 *Kim*	84	15	85
42 Brown	90	6	94
43 *Calvert*	93	6	94
44 *Bono*[3]	92	7	92
45 *Rohrabacher*	90	10	90
46 Sanchez	86	9	90
47 *Cox*	89	7	92
48 *Packard*	91	6	94
49 *Bilbray*	73	26	74
50 Filner	94	3	97
51 *Cunningham*	82	6	93
52 *Hunter*	91	7	93
COLORADO			
1 DeGette	96	3	97
2 Skaggs	84	5	94
3 *McInnis*	89	8	92
4 *Schaffer*	89	11	89
5 *Hefley*	91	8	92
6 *Schaefer*	90	4	96
CONNECTICUT			
1 Kennelly	68	8	90
2 Gejdenson	93	5	94
3 DeLauro	96	3	97
4 *Shays*	58	42	58
5 Maloney	79	21	79
6 *Johnson*	62	38	62
DELAWARE			
AL *Castle*	63	36	63
FLORIDA			
1 *Scarborough*	85	8	91
2 Boyd	68	31	69
3 Brown	89	4	95
4 *Fowler*	87	9	91
5 Thurman	86	13	87
6 *Stearns*	91	8	92
7 *Mica*	89	8	92
8 *McCollum*	90	7	92
9 *Bilirakis*	89	9	91
10 *Young*	77	9	92
11 Davis	80	19	81
12 *Canady*	93	6	94
13 *Miller*	87	9	90
14 *Goss*	84	6	93
15 *Weldon*	91	6	94
16 *Foley*	82	16	84
17 Meek	86	6	93
18 *Ros-Lehtinen*	76	18	81
19 Wexler	90	8	92
20 Deutsch	84	11	88
21 *Diaz-Balart*	79	20	80
22 *Shaw*	86	12	88
23 Hastings	85	5	95
GEORGIA			
1 *Kingston*	94	6	94
2 Bishop	70	29	71
3 *Collins*	93	5	95
4 McKinney	92	8	92
5 Lewis	82	1	99
6 *Gingrich*[4]	21	0	100
7 *Barr*	90	7	93
8 *Chambliss*	94	5	95
9 *Deal*	93	5	94
10 *Norwood*	91	3	96
11 *Linder*	92	4	96
HAWAII			
1 Abercrombie	91	8	92
2 Mink	93	5	95
IDAHO			
1 *Chenoweth*	88	11	89
2 *Crapo*	86	10	89
ILLINOIS			
1 Rush	93	4	95
2 Jackson	96	4	96
3 Lipinski	55	40	58
4 Gutierrez	92	6	93
5 Blagojevich	85	11	88
6 *Hyde*	91	7	92
7 Davis	93	4	95
8 *Crane*	93	4	96
9 Yates	72	4	95
10 *Porter*	69	30	69
11 *Weller*	86	12	88
12 Costello	75	24	76
13 *Fawell*	75	19	80

ND Northern Democrats   SD Southern Democrats

	1	2	3
14 Hastert	95	4	96
15 Ewing	86	10	90
16 Manzullo	95	5	95
17 Evans	91	8	92
18 LaHood	83	17	83
19 Poshard	63	13	83
20 Shimkus	91	7	93
INDIANA			
1 Visclosky	82	17	83
2 McIntosh	91	6	94
3 Roemer	66	33	66
4 Souder	89	9	90
5 Buyer	85	8	91
6 Burton	86	6	93
7 Pease	91	8	91
8 Hostettler	91	9	91
9 Hamilton	70	27	72
10 Carson	92	4	96
IOWA			
1 Leach	62	36	63
2 Nussle	89	11	89
3 Boswell	65	35	65
4 Ganske	75	23	76
5 Latham	94	6	94
KANSAS			
1 Moran	90	10	90
2 Ryun	94	4	96
3 Snowbarger	96	3	97
4 Tiahrt	96	4	96
KENTUCKY			
1 Whitfield	88	10	90
2 Lewis	93	6	94
3 Northup	91	8	91
4 Bunning	90	8	92
5 Rogers	90	8	92
6 Baesler	65	32	67
LOUISIANA			
1 Livingston	92	5	95
2 Jefferson	82	8	91
3 Tauzin	87	7	92
4 McCrery	90	5	94
5 Cooksey	88	5	95
6 Baker	92	5	94
7 John	48	39	56
MAINE			
1 Allen	91	7	93
2 Baldacci	91	8	92
MARYLAND			
1 Gilchrest	71	29	71
2 Ehrlich	85	12	87
3 Cardin	86	9	91
4 Wynn	91	6	93
5 Hoyer	88	11	89
6 Bartlett	94	5	95
7 Cummings	95	5	95
8 Morella	39	60	40
MASSACHUSETTS			
1 Olver	96	1	99
2 Neal	91	5	95
3 McGovern	93	3	97
4 Frank	90	6	94
5 Meehan	93	3	97
6 Tierney	96	2	98
7 Markey	85	4	95
8 Kennedy	90	6	93
9 Moakley	73	5	94
10 Delahunt	95	3	97
MICHIGAN			
1 Stupak	80	17	83
2 Hoekstra	93	7	93
3 Ehlers	77	21	78
4 Camp	91	8	92
5 Barcia	66	32	67
6 Upton	79	21	79
7 Smith	87	11	88
8 Stabenow	85	13	87
9 Kildee	84	16	84
10 Bonior	94	5	95
11 Knollenberg	94	6	94
12 Levin	93	7	93
13 Rivers	89	10	90
14 Conyers	84	5	95
15 Kilpatrick	90	3	96
16 Dingell	82	10	89

	1	2	3
MINNESOTA			
1 Gutknecht	91	8	92
2 Minge	80	19	81
3 Ramstad	68	32	68
4 Vento	97	3	97
5 Sabo	89	10	90
6 Luther	85	10	89
7 Peterson	53	46	54
8 Oberstar	89	10	90
MISSISSIPPI			
1 Wicker	91	6	94
2 Thompson	89	5	95
3 Pickering	90	4	95
4 Parker	76	9	89
5 Taylor	41	58	41
MISSOURI			
1 Clay	83	2	98
2 Talent	93	7	93
3 Gephardt	85	6	93
4 Skelton	63	36	64
5 McCarthy	88	8	92
6 Danner	58	40	59
7 Blunt	93	4	95
8 Emerson	91	8	92
9 Hulshof	87	11	89
MONTANA			
AL Hill	87	8	92
NEBRASKA			
1 Bereuter	83	16	84
2 Christensen	88	5	95
3 Barrett	87	13	87
NEVADA			
1 Ensign	81	18	82
2 Gibbons	93	7	93
NEW HAMPSHIRE			
1 Sununu	89	9	91
2 Bass	78	22	78
NEW JERSEY			
1 Andrews	84	14	86
2 LoBiondo	75	25	75
3 Saxton	79	20	80
4 Smith	78	21	79
5 Roukema	74	26	74
6 Pallone	92	7	92
7 Franks	72	27	73
8 Pascrell	85	14	86
9 Rothman	84	13	87
10 Payne	88	2	97
11 Frelinghuysen	76	23	77
12 Pappas	85	15	85
13 Menendez	90	10	90
NEW MEXICO			
1 Wilson [5]	86	13	87
2 Skeen	89	11	89
3 Redmond	87	10	90
NEW YORK			
1 Forbes	63	34	65
2 Lazio	72	27	73
3 King	80	17	82
4 McCarthy	82	18	82
5 Ackerman	94	3	97
6 Meeks [6]	86	3	97
7 Manton	81	11	88
8 Nadler	94	4	96
9 Schumer	79	5	94
10 Towns	82	6	93
11 Owens	95	3	97
12 Velázquez	93	3	96
13 Fossella	90	9	91
14 Maloney	91	7	93
15 Rangel	85	5	95
16 Serrano	91	4	95
17 Engel	93	3	97
18 Lowey	93	6	94
19 Kelly	66	34	66
20 Gilman	61	38	62
21 McNulty	72	8	89
22 Solomon	93	4	96
23 Boehlert	58	41	59
24 McHugh	78	20	80
25 Walsh	73	27	73
26 Hinchey	94	4	96
27 Paxon	90	2	98
28 Slaughter	92	4	96
29 LaFalce	88	10	90

	1	2	3
30 Quinn	74	23	76
31 Houghton	63	32	66
NORTH CAROLINA			
1 Clayton	90	5	95
2 Etheridge	79	18	81
3 Jones	92	8	92
4 Price	86	13	87
5 Burr	89	8	92
6 Coble	91	6	93
7 McIntyre	60	39	61
8 Hefner	80	8	91
9 Myrick	92	5	94
10 Ballenger	92	6	94
11 Taylor	93	4	95
12 Watt	95	4	96
NORTH DAKOTA			
AL Pomeroy	78	20	80
OHIO			
1 Chabot	91	9	91
2 Portman	91	9	91
3 Hall	74	24	76
4 Oxley	89	8	91
5 Gillmor	85	13	87
6 Strickland	84	15	85
7 Hobson	90	9	91
8 Boehner	95	4	96
9 Kaptur	80	15	85
10 Kucinich	83	16	84
11 Stokes	91	3	97
12 Kasich	92	6	93
13 Brown	94	3	97
14 Sawyer	93	6	94
15 Pryce	70	10	88
16 Regula	86	13	87
17 Traficant	32	66	33
18 Ney	82	15	85
19 LaTourette	78	22	78
OKLAHOMA			
1 Largent	87	8	91
2 Coburn	91	6	94
3 Watkins	93	6	94
4 Watts	91	8	92
5 Istook	89	4	96
6 Lucas	95	5	95
OREGON			
1 Furse	86	2	98
2 Smith	82	7	92
3 Blumenauer	91	8	92
4 DeFazio	89	7	93
5 Hooley	88	12	88
PENNSYLVANIA			
1 Brady [7]	92	2	97
2 Fattah	91	3	96
3 Borski	89	9	91
4 Klink	80	17	82
5 Peterson	93	5	95
6 Holden	73	27	73
7 Weldon	77	18	81
8 Greenwood	64	31	68
9 Shuster	90	4	95
10 McDade	58	11	84
11 Kanjorski	86	14	86
12 Murtha	71	26	73
13 Fox	71	27	72
14 Coyne	95	5	95
15 McHale	83	16	84
16 Pitts	96	4	96
17 Gekas	90	7	93
18 Doyle	76	21	79
19 Goodling	90	6	94
20 Mascara	80	20	80
21 English	81	19	81
RHODE ISLAND			
1 Kennedy	90	9	91
2 Weygand	87	13	87
SOUTH CAROLINA			
1 Sanford	76	23	76
2 Spence	95	5	95
3 Graham	89	8	92
4 Inglis	89	6	93
5 Spratt	77	18	81
6 Clyburn	93	5	95
SOUTH DAKOTA			
AL Thune	95	5	95

	1	2	3
TENNESSEE			
1 Jenkins	94	5	95
2 Duncan	88	13	88
3 Wamp	89	10	89
4 Hilleary	91	7	93
5 Clement	74	24	76
6 Gordon	72	25	74
7 Bryant	95	4	96
8 Tanner	65	29	69
9 Ford	76	7	91
TEXAS			
1 Sandlin	70	27	72
2 Turner	56	41	58
3 Johnson	91	4	96
4 Hall	23	75	23
5 Sessions	97	3	97
6 Barton	92	6	94
7 Archer	95	3	97
8 Brady	90	5	94
9 Lampson	84	14	86
10 Doggett	91	8	92
11 Edwards	83	16	84
12 Granger	90	9	91
13 Thornberry	92	8	92
14 Paul	74	23	76
15 Hinojosa	85	9	91
16 Reyes	81	12	87
17 Stenholm	49	50	50
18 Jackson-Lee	90	6	94
19 Combest	95	5	95
20 Gonzalez	16	0	98
21 Smith	93	5	95
22 DeLay	93	4	95
23 Bonilla	83	15	85
24 Frost	80	15	84
25 Bentsen	85	15	85
26 Armey	94	3	97
27 Ortiz	72	23	76
28 Rodriguez	88	8	92
29 Green	81	14	86
30 Johnson	87	6	93
UTAH			
1 Hansen	92	4	96
2 Cook	87	10	90
3 Cannon	87	5	94
VERMONT			
AL **Sanders**	94	5	95
VIRGINIA			
1 Bateman	77	6	92
2 Pickett	59	40	60
3 Scott	91	9	91
4 Sisisky	64	35	65
5 Goode	27	71	28
6 Goodlatte	92	8	92
7 Bliley	93	6	94
8 Moran	78	20	79
9 Boucher	78	18	81
10 Wolf	88	11	88
11 Davis	80	19	81
WASHINGTON			
1 White	87	13	87
2 Metcalf	85	14	86
3 Smith	83	14	86
4 Hastings	97	3	97
5 Nethercutt	93	5	95
6 Dicks	84	15	85
7 McDermott	92	4	96
8 Dunn	93	5	94
9 Smith	83	17	83
WEST VIRGINIA			
1 Mollohan	70	25	74
2 Wise	81	14	85
3 Rahall	76	21	78
WISCONSIN			
1 Neumann	83	14	86
2 Klug	76	19	80
3 Kind	84	14	86
4 Kleczka	84	15	85
5 Barrett	93	7	93
6 Petri	85	14	86
7 Obey	91	8	92
8 Johnson	83	15	85
9 Sensenbrenner	84	14	86
WYOMING			
AL *Cubin*	95	4	96

Southern states - Ala., Ark., Fla., Ga., Ky., La., Miss., N.C., Okla., S.C., Tenn., Texas, Va.

Conservative Coalition Background

Conservative coalition. As used in this study, "conservative coalition" means a voting alliance of Republicans and Southern Democrats against the Northern Democrats in Congress. This meaning, rather than any philosophic definition of the "conservative coalition" position, is the basis for CQ's selection of coalition votes.

Conservative coalition vote. Any vote in the Senate or the House on which a majority of voting Southern Democrats and a majority of voting Republicans opposed a majority of voting Northern Democrats. Votes on which there was an even division within the ranks of voting Northern Demo-

crats, Southern Democrats or Republicans are not included.

Conservative coalition support score. Percentage of conservative coalition votes on which a member voted "yea" or "nay" *in agreement* with the position of the conservative coalition. Failures to vote, even if a member announced a stand, lower the score.

Conservative coalition opposition score. Percentage of conservative coalition votes on which a member voted "yea" or "nay" *in disagreement* with the position of the conservative coalition. Failures to vote, even if a member announced a stand, lower the score.

Average Scores

In percentages

| | Support | | | | | | | Opposition | | | | | |
| | Southern Democrats | | Republicans | | Northern Democrats | | | Southern Democrats | | Republicans | | Northern Democrats | |
	1998	1997	1998	1997	1998	1997		1998	1997	1998	1997	1998	1997
Senate	74	73	85	87	34	32	Senate	24	27	13	12	61	67
House	59	63	88	86	31	33	House	35	34	10	10	65	64

Regional Averages

In percentages

| | Support | | | | | | | | Opposition | | | | | | | |
| | East | | West | | South | | Midwest | | East | | West | | South | | Midwest | |
	1998	1997	1998	1997	1998	1997	1998	1997	1998	1997	1998	1997	1998	1997	1998	1997
Republicans									**Republicans**							
Senate	68	70	91	91	91	95	81	94	24	30	10	9	6	5	20	15
House	78	82	89	86	91	89	88	86	19	16	9	9	6	7	10	12
Democrats									**Democrats**							
Senate	32	27	47	37	74	73	28	34	67	72	45	65	24	27	67	62
House	27	31	26	27	59	63	40	40	68	66	70	69	35	34	58	57

Conservative Coalition History

Following is the percentage of the recorded votes on which the coalition appeared and its percentage of victories on those votes.

Year	Appearance	Victories	Year	Appearance	Victories
1971	30%	83%	1985	14%	89%
1972	27	69	1986	16	87
1973	23	61	1987	8	93
1974	24	59	1988	9	89
1975	28	50	1989	11	87
1976	24	58	1990	11	82
1977	26	68	1991	11	91
1978	21	52	1992	12	87
1979	20	70	1993	9	94
1980	18	72	1994	8	82
1981	21	92	1995	11	98
1982	18	85	1996	12	99
1983	15	77	1997	9	98
1984	16	83	1998	6	96

1998 Conservative Coalition Votes

The following is a list of votes cast in 1998 on which a majority of Southern Democrats and a majority of Republicans voted against a majority of all other Democrats.

House Victories & Defeats

40 Victories

Vote Number	Description
20	Law enforcement
68	Copyright
69	Copyright
74	Small business
113	Needle exchange
114	Needle exchange
137	Intelligence authorization
144	Financial services
160	Federal mandates
166	Defense policy
180	Border control
219	Bankruptcy law
221	Bankruptcy law
222	Bankruptcy law
223	Bankruptcy law
225	Bankruptcy law
252	Nuclear energy
258	Price supports
263	Agriculture appropriations
273	IRS overhaul
286	Gun control
308	Campaign finance
321	Abortion
325	Abortion
328	Environment
343	Radioactive waste
344	Environment
346	Veterans' funding
351	Consumer protection
352	VA/HUD appropriations
389	Environment
401	Federal powers
415	Tobacco policy
420	Hunting
435	Drug policy
436	Law enforcement
440	Border control
460	Immigration
494	Treasury/Postal appropriations
520	Consumer protection

2 Defeats

Vote Number	Description
259	Agriculture appropriations
447	Foreign aid

Senate Victories & Defeats

8 Victories

Vote Number	Description
144	Tobacco policy
174	Base closures
178	Defense policy
185	Space station
204	Foreign aid
233	Immigration
275	Bankruptcy law
287	Transportation

0 Defeats

House Victory Score

Victories	40
Defeats	2
Total	**42**
Success rate	95%

Senate Victory Score

Victories	8
Defeats	0
Total	**8**
Success rate	100%

Conservative Coalition Support and Opposition: House

1. Conservative Coalition Support. Percentage of 42 recorded votes in 1998 on which the conservative coalition appeared and on which a representative voted "yea" or "nay" in agreement with the position of the conservative coalition. Failures to vote lowered both support and opposition scores.

2. Conservative Coalition Opposition. Percentage of 42 recorded votes in 1998 on which the conservative coalition appeared and on which a representative voted "yea" or "nay" in disagreement with the position of the conservative coalition. Failures to vote lowered both support and opposition scores.

3. Conservative Coalition Support (adjusted for absences). Percentage of 42 recorded votes in 1998 on which the conservative coalition appeared and on which a representative was present and voted "yea" or "nay" in agreement with the position of the conservative coalition. In this version of the study, absences were not counted; therefore, failures to vote did not lower support or opposition scores. Opposition scores, not listed here, are the inverse of the support score; i.e., the opposition score is equal to 100 percent minus the individual's support score.

[1] Barbara Lee, D-Calif., was sworn in April 21, replacing Ronald V. Dellums, D-Calif., who resigned Feb. 6. Lee was eligible for 38 conservative coalition votes in 1998. Dellums was eligible for no conservative coalition votes in 1998.

[2] Lois Capps, D-Calif., was sworn in March 17, replacing Walter Capps, D-Calif., who died Oct. 28, 1997. Lois Capps was eligible for 41 conservative coalition votes in 1998.

[3] Mary Bono, R-Calif., was sworn in April 21, replacing Sonny Bono, R-Calif., who died Jan. 5. Mary Bono was eligible for 38 conservative coalition votes in 1998. Sonny Bono was eligible for no conservative coalition votes in 1998.

[4] Newt Gingrich, R-Ga., as Speaker of the House, voted at his discretion on five conservative coalition votes in 1998.

[5] Heather Wilson, R-N.M., was sworn in June 25, replacing Stephen H. Schiff, R-N.M., who died March 25. Wilson was eligible for 22 conservative coalition votes in 1998. Schiff was eligible for one conservative coalition vote in 1998 but did not vote.

[6] Gregory W. Meeks, D-N.Y., was sworn in Feb. 5, replacing Floyd H. Flake, D-N.Y., who resigned on Nov. 15, 1997. Meeks was eligible for 42 conservative coalition votes in 1998.

[7] Robert A. Brady, D-Pa., was sworn in May 21, replacing Thomas M. Foglietta, D-Pa., who resigned Nov. 11, 1997. Brady was eligible for 32 conservative coalition votes in 1998.

Democrats *Republicans* **Independent**

	1	2	3
ALABAMA			
1 *Callahan*	98	2	98
2 *Everett*	98	2	98
3 *Riley*	93	5	95
4 *Aderholt*	95	5	95
5 *Cramer*	95	2	98
6 *Bachus*	88	12	88
7 Hilliard	19	69	22
ALASKA			
AL *Young*	90	7	93
ARIZONA			
1 *Salmon*	93	7	93
2 Pastor	45	55	45
3 *Stump*	93	7	93
4 *Shadegg*	90	7	93
5 *Kolbe*	83	17	83
6 *Hayworth*	88	12	88
ARKANSAS			
1 Berry	79	17	83
2 Snyder	57	43	57
3 *Hutchinson*	81	12	87
4 *Dickey*	93	2	98
CALIFORNIA			
1 *Riggs*	74	7	91
2 *Herger*	98	2	98
3 Fazio	45	52	46
4 *Doolittle*	90	10	90
5 Matsui	31	69	31
6 Woolsey	17	83	17
7 Miller	10	86	10
8 Pelosi	12	83	13
9 Lee[1]	3	97	3
10 Tauscher	62	36	63
11 *Pombo*	88	12	88
12 Lantos	24	76	24
13 Stark	5	88	5
14 Eshoo	21	79	21
15 *Campbell*	64	36	64
16 Lofgren	24	76	24
17 Farr	19	69	22
18 Condit	79	19	80
19 *Radanovich*	83	12	88
20 Dooley	62	38	62
21 *Thomas*	93	5	95
22 Capps[2]	29	71	29
23 *Gallegly*	90	10	90
24 Sherman	38	62	38
25 *McKeon*	98	2	98
26 Berman	10	74	11
27 *Rogan*	83	17	83
28 *Dreier*	88	12	88
29 Waxman	14	86	14
30 Becerra	7	88	8
31 Martinez	45	50	48
32 Dixon	17	71	19
33 Roybal-Allard	5	90	5
34 Torres	12	74	14
35 Waters	12	79	13
36 Harman	40	31	57
37 Millender-McD.	14	74	16
38 *Horn*	83	17	83

	1	2	3
39 *Royce*	64	24	73
40 *Lewis*	95	2	98
41 *Kim*	95	5	95
42 Brown	21	79	21
43 *Calvert*	100	0	100
44 *Bono*[3]	95	5	95
45 *Rohrabacher*	79	21	79
46 Sanchez	43	52	45
47 *Cox*	81	14	85
48 *Packard*	95	0	100
49 *Bilbray*	83	17	83
50 Filner	7	93	7
51 *Cunningham*	90	2	97
52 *Hunter*	88	10	90
COLORADO			
1 DeGette	14	86	14
2 Skaggs	21	71	23
3 *McInnis*	88	7	93
4 *Schaffer*	88	12	88
5 *Hefley*	88	12	88
6 *Schaefer*	90	2	97
CONNECTICUT			
1 Kennelly	26	55	32
2 Gejdenson	19	79	20
3 DeLauro	10	88	10
4 *Shays*	50	50	50
5 Maloney	55	45	55
6 *Johnson*	67	33	67
DELAWARE			
AL *Castle*	76	24	76
FLORIDA			
1 *Scarborough*	83	17	83
2 Boyd	86	14	86
3 Brown	26	64	29
4 *Fowler*	95	5	95
5 Thurman	57	43	57
6 *Stearns*	90	7	93
7 *Mica*	88	10	90
8 *McCollum*	86	12	88
9 *Bilirakis*	90	7	93
10 *Young*	76	0	100
11 Davis	69	31	69
12 *Canady*	95	5	95
13 *Miller*	88	12	88
14 *Goss*	81	7	92
15 *Weldon*	95	2	98
16 *Foley*	88	10	90
17 Meek	29	69	29
18 *Ros-Lehtinen*	76	24	76
19 Wexler	31	69	31
20 Deutsch	52	48	52
21 *Diaz-Balart*	83	17	83
22 *Shaw*	90	10	90
23 Hastings	19	79	20
GEORGIA			
1 *Kingston*	86	14	86
2 Bishop	83	17	83
3 *Collins*	90	7	93
4 McKinney	10	90	10
5 Lewis	5	67	7
6 *Gingrich*[4]	100	0	100
7 *Barr*	86	10	90
8 *Chambliss*	95	0	100
9 *Deal*	90	7	93
10 *Norwood*	90	5	95
11 *Linder*	95	5	95
HAWAII			
1 Abercrombie	24	76	24
2 Mink	14	86	14
IDAHO			
1 *Chenoweth*	86	14	86
2 *Crapo*	90	7	93
ILLINOIS			
1 Rush	5	88	5
2 Jackson	0	100	0
3 Lipinski	57	40	59
4 Gutierrez	2	95	2
5 Blagojevich	36	60	38
6 *Hyde*	83	12	88
7 Davis	5	95	5
8 *Crane*	86	10	90
9 Yates	10	74	11
10 *Porter*	79	21	79
11 *Weller*	86	14	86
12 Costello	57	43	57
13 *Fawell*	81	14	85

	1	2	3
14 *Hastert*	98	2	98
15 *Ewing*	90	5	95
16 *Manzullo*	93	7	93
17 Evans	19	81	19
18 *LaHood*	86	14	86
19 Poshard	29	45	39
20 *Shimkus*	98	2	98

INDIANA

	1	2	3
1 Visclosky	48	52	48
2 *McIntosh*	81	17	83
3 Roemer	71	29	71
4 *Souder*	83	14	85
5 *Buyer*	88	10	90
6 *Burton*	93	5	95
7 *Pease*	90	10	90
8 *Hostettler*	88	12	88
9 Hamilton	64	31	68
10 Carson	17	79	18

IOWA

	1	2	3
1 *Leach*	90	10	90
2 *Nussle*	98	2	98
3 Boswell	93	7	93
4 *Ganske*	86	12	88
5 *Latham*	98	2	98

KANSAS

	1	2	3
1 *Moran*	98	2	98
2 *Ryun*	90	7	93
3 *Snowbarger*	95	5	95
4 *Tiahrt*	98	2	98

KENTUCKY

	1	2	3
1 *Whitfield*	86	12	88
2 *Lewis*	100	0	100
3 *Northup*	93	7	93
4 *Bunning*	98	2	98
5 *Rogers*	100	0	100
6 Baesler	76	21	78

LOUISIANA

	1	2	3
1 *Livingston*	93	2	98
2 Jefferson	45	45	50
3 *Tauzin*	90	0	100
4 *McCrery*	95	0	100
5 *Cooksey*	98	2	98
6 *Baker*	95	0	100
7 John	98	0	100

MAINE

	1	2	3
1 Allen	19	81	19
2 Baldacci	33	67	33

MARYLAND

	1	2	3
1 *Gilchrest*	79	19	80
2 *Ehrlich*	79	14	85
3 Cardin	33	60	36
4 Wynn	38	57	40
5 Hoyer	50	50	50
6 *Bartlett*	93	5	95
7 Cummings	26	74	26
8 *Morella*	38	60	39

MASSACHUSETTS

	1	2	3
1 Olver	7	93	7
2 Neal	19	74	21
3 McGovern	7	93	7
4 Frank	19	76	20
5 Meehan	10	83	10
6 Tierney	2	98	2
7 Markey	10	74	11
8 Kennedy	10	86	10
9 Moakley	14	64	18
10 Delahunt	7	93	7

MICHIGAN

	1	2	3
1 Stupak	40	57	41
2 *Hoekstra*	83	17	83
3 *Ehlers*	74	26	74
4 *Camp*	93	7	93
5 Barcia	69	29	71
6 *Upton*	79	21	79
7 *Smith*	88	12	88
8 Stabenow	48	50	49
9 Kildee	40	60	40
10 Bonior	7	93	7
11 *Knollenberg*	95	5	95
12 Levin	31	69	31
13 Rivers	19	81	19
14 Conyers	7	86	8
15 Kilpatrick	12	86	12
16 Dingell	40	52	44

MINNESOTA

	1	2	3
1 *Gutknecht*	90	10	90
2 Minge	69	31	69
3 *Ramstad*	79	21	79
4 Vento	14	86	14
5 Sabo	36	64	36
6 Luther	40	57	41
7 Peterson	76	24	76
8 Oberstar	26	74	26

MISSISSIPPI

	1	2	3
1 *Wicker*	98	0	100
2 Thompson	31	60	34
3 *Pickering*	95	0	100
4 *Parker*	90	2	97
5 Taylor	86	14	86

MISSOURI

	1	2	3
1 Clay	10	76	11
2 *Talent*	93	5	95
3 Gephardt	38	57	40
4 Skelton	90	7	93
5 McCarthy	36	64	36
6 Danner	86	12	88
7 *Blunt*	95	2	98
8 *Emerson*	93	7	93
9 Hulshof	86	12	88

MONTANA

	1	2	3
AL *Hill*	95	2	98

NEBRASKA

	1	2	3
1 *Bereuter*	93	7	93
2 *Christensen*	88	7	93
3 *Barrett*	95	2	98

NEVADA

	1	2	3
1 *Ensign*	76	21	78
2 *Gibbons*	86	14	86

NEW HAMPSHIRE

	1	2	3
1 *Sununu*	81	19	81
2 *Bass*	81	19	81

NEW JERSEY

	1	2	3
1 Andrews	40	57	41
2 *LoBiondo*	71	29	71
3 *Saxton*	81	17	83
4 *Smith*	69	29	71
5 *Roukema*	79	21	79
6 Pallone	31	69	31
7 *Franks*	71	29	71
8 Pascrell	45	52	46
9 Rothman	29	64	31
10 Payne	2	83	3
11 *Frelinghuysen*	83	17	83
12 *Pappas*	76	24	76
13 Menendez	29	71	29

NEW MEXICO

	1	2	3
1 *Wilson* [5]	100	0	100
2 *Skeen*	93	7	93
3 *Redmond*	98	0	100

NEW YORK

	1	2	3
1 *Forbes*	71	26	73
2 *Lazio*	83	17	83
3 *King*	88	10	90
4 McCarthy	36	64	36
5 Ackerman	14	81	15
6 Meeks [6]	5	79	6
7 Manton	33	55	38
8 Nadler	10	83	10
9 Schumer	14	57	20
10 Towns	17	67	20
11 Owens	5	88	5
12 Velázquez	7	83	8
13 *Fossella*	86	14	86
14 Maloney	21	74	23
15 Rangel	14	74	16
16 Serrano	12	79	13
17 Engel	10	81	11
18 Lowey	29	71	29
19 Kelly	74	26	74
20 Gilman	74	26	74
21 McNulty	29	62	32
22 *Solomon*	90	5	95
23 *Boehlert*	64	36	64
24 *McHugh*	83	12	88
25 *Walsh*	86	12	88
26 Hinchey	7	90	7
27 *Paxon*	86	5	95
28 Slaughter	21	71	23
29 LaFalce	36	62	37
30 Quinn	86	10	90
31 Houghton	79	14	85

NORTH CAROLINA

	1	2	3
1 Clayton	33	55	38
2 Etheridge	76	19	80
3 *Jones*	88	12	88
4 Price	64	31	68
5 *Burr*	93	5	95
6 *Coble*	86	12	88
7 McIntyre	88	7	93
8 Hefner	43	38	53
9 *Myrick*	95	2	98
10 *Ballenger*	93	2	98
11 *Taylor*	95	0	100
12 Watt	19	81	19

NORTH DAKOTA

	1	2	3
AL Pomeroy	79	21	79

OHIO

	1	2	3
1 *Chabot*	81	19	81
2 *Portman*	95	2	98
3 Hall	60	40	60
4 *Oxley*	98	0	100
5 *Gillmor*	93	5	95
6 Strickland	50	50	50
7 *Hobson*	90	7	93
8 *Boehner*	100	0	100
9 Kaptur	48	50	49
10 Kucinich	29	71	29
11 Stokes	17	79	18
12 *Kasich*	88	10	90
13 Brown	12	88	12
14 Sawyer	33	67	33
15 *Pryce*	76	5	94
16 *Regula*	95	5	95
17 Traficant	93	5	95
18 *Ney*	88	12	88
19 *LaTourette*	81	19	81

OKLAHOMA

	1	2	3
1 *Largent*	93	5	95
2 *Coburn*	95	2	98
3 *Watkins*	95	2	98
4 *Watts*	95	5	95
5 *Istook*	95	5	95
6 *Lucas*	98	2	98

OREGON

	1	2	3
1 Furse	10	88	10
2 *Smith*	88	0	100
3 Blumenauer	24	74	24
4 DeFazio	14	86	14
5 Hooley	36	64	36

PENNSYLVANIA

	1	2	3
1 Brady [7]	9	84	10
2 Fattah	7	90	7
3 Borski	29	71	29
4 Klink	48	50	49
5 Peterson	95	5	95
6 Holden	67	33	67
7 Weldon	76	19	80
8 Greenwood	76	21	78
9 Shuster	90	2	97
10 McDade	64	10	87
11 Kanjorski	36	64	36
12 Murtha	67	29	70
13 Fox	79	21	79
14 Coyne	21	79	21
15 McHale	45	52	46
16 Pitts	90	10	90
17 Gekas	95	5	95
18 Doyle	57	38	60
19 Goodling	81	14	85
20 Mascara	62	38	62
21 English	81	19	81

RHODE ISLAND

	1	2	3
1 Kennedy	26	71	27
2 Weygand	45	55	45

SOUTH CAROLINA

	1	2	3
1 *Sanford*	74	26	74
2 *Spence*	95	5	95
3 *Graham*	95	5	95
4 *Inglis*	86	12	88
5 Spratt	83	17	83
6 Clyburn	33	62	35

SOUTH DAKOTA

	1	2	3
AL *Thune*	98	2	98

TENNESSEE

	1	2	3
1 *Jenkins*	93	5	95
2 *Duncan*	76	24	76
3 *Wamp*	86	14	86
4 *Hilleary*	90	10	90
5 Clement	86	14	86
6 Gordon	71	24	75
7 *Bryant*	98	2	98
8 Tanner	90	10	90
9 Ford	36	40	47

TEXAS

	1	2	3
1 *Sandlin*	83	12	88
2 Turner	93	5	95
3 *Johnson*	90	2	97
4 Hall	95	5	95
5 *Sessions*	100	0	100
6 *Barton*	95	5	95
7 *Archer*	93	5	95
8 *Brady*	93	0	100
9 Lampson	62	36	63
10 *Doggett*	24	76	24
11 *Edwards*	69	31	69
12 *Granger*	98	0	100
13 *Thornberry*	98	2	98
14 *Paul*	55	43	56
15 *Hinojosa*	55	38	59
16 Reyes	64	33	66
17 Stenholm	98	2	98
18 Jackson-Lee	29	62	32
19 *Combest*	98	2	98
20 Gonzalez	0	7	0
21 *Smith*	98	0	100
22 *DeLay*	100	0	100
23 *Bonilla*	86	12	88
24 Frost	79	19	80
25 Bentsen	67	33	67
26 *Armey*	93	2	98
27 Ortiz	64	33	66
28 Rodriguez	50	48	51
29 Green	62	36	63
30 Johnson	38	52	42

UTAH

	1	2	3
1 *Hansen*	95	2	98
2 *Cook*	93	5	95
3 *Cannon*	83	0	100

VERMONT

	1	2	3
AL **Sanders**	17	83	17

VIRGINIA

	1	2	3
1 *Bateman*	81	2	97
2 *Pickett*	90	10	90
3 Scott	43	57	43
4 Sisisky	88	12	88
5 Goode	90	10	90
6 *Goodlatte*	93	7	93
7 *Bliley*	93	7	93
8 Moran	67	33	67
9 Boucher	67	29	70
10 *Wolf*	86	14	86
11 *Davis*	90	10	90

WASHINGTON

	1	2	3
1 *White*	95	5	95
2 *Metcalf*	81	19	81
3 *Smith*	83	10	90
4 *Hastings*	100	0	100
5 *Nethercutt*	90	5	95
6 Dicks	60	40	60
7 McDermott	14	79	15
8 *Dunn*	93	5	95
9 Smith	55	45	55

WEST VIRGINIA

	1	2	3
1 Mollohan	67	33	67
2 Wise	52	48	52
3 Rahall	52	48	52

WISCONSIN

	1	2	3
1 *Neumann*	74	24	76
2 *Klug*	86	12	88
3 Kind	57	43	57
4 Kleczka	48	48	50
5 Barrett	26	74	26
6 *Petri*	71	29	71
7 Obey	31	69	31
8 Johnson	55	45	55
9 *Sensenbrenner*	69	31	69

WYOMING

	1	2	3
AL *Cubin*	95	2	98

Southern states - Ala., Ark., Fla., Ga., Ky., La., Miss., N.C., Okla., S.C., Tenn., Texas, Va.

Column 1	1	2	3
ALABAMA			
Shelby	100	0	100
Sessions	100	0	100
ALASKA			
Stevens	88	13	88
Murkowski	88	13	88
ARIZONA			
McCain	75	25	75
Kyl	88	13	88
ARKANSAS			
Hutchinson	63	13	83
Bumpers	25	75	25
CALIFORNIA			
Feinstein	50	50	50
Boxer	38	63	38
COLORADO			
Campbell	100	0	100
Allard	100	0	100
CONNECTICUT			
Dodd	38	63	38
Lieberman	38	63	38
DELAWARE			
Roth	75	0	100
Biden	50	50	50
FLORIDA			
Mack	100	0	100
Graham	88	13	88
GEORGIA			
Coverdell	88	0	100
Cleland	88	13	88
HAWAII			
Inouye	50	38	57
Akaka	38	38	50
IDAHO			
Craig	100	0	100
Kempthorne	100	0	100
ILLINOIS			
Moseley-Braun	25	63	29
Durbin	13	88	13
INDIANA			
Lugar	50	50	50
Coats	75	25	75

Column 2	1	2	3
IOWA			
Grassley	75	25	75
Harkin	13	88	13
KANSAS			
Brownback	88	13	88
Roberts	88	13	88
KENTUCKY			
McConnell	100	0	100
Ford	88	13	88
LOUISIANA			
Breaux	100	0	100
Landrieu	75	25	75
MAINE			
Snowe	75	25	75
Collins	88	13	88
MARYLAND			
Sarbanes	25	75	25
Mikulski	38	63	38
MASSACHUSETTS			
Kennedy	0	100	0
Kerry	38	63	38
MICHIGAN			
Abraham	88	13	88
Levin	13	88	13
MINNESOTA			
Grams	75	25	75
Wellstone	0	88	0
MISSISSIPPI			
Cochran	88	13	88
Lott	88	0	100
MISSOURI			
Bond	100	0	100
Ashcroft	75	25	75
MONTANA			
Burns	100	0	100
Baucus	38	38	50
NEBRASKA			
Hagel	88	13	88
Kerrey	75	25	75
NEVADA			
Reid	63	38	63
Bryan	38	63	38

Column 3	1	2	3
NEW HAMPSHIRE			
Smith	88	0	100
Gregg	88	13	88
NEW JERSEY			
Lautenberg	25	75	25
Torricelli	63	38	63
NEW MEXICO			
Domenici	88	13	88
Bingaman	50	38	57
NEW YORK			
D'Amato	63	38	63
Moynihan	25	75	25
NORTH CAROLINA			
Helms	100	0	100
Faircloth	100	0	100
NORTH DAKOTA			
Conrad	50	50	50
Dorgan	50	50	50
OHIO			
DeWine	88	13	88
Glenn	13	38	25
OKLAHOMA			
Nickles	100	0	100
Inhofe	100	0	100
OREGON			
Smith	75	25	75
Wyden	50	38	57
PENNSYLVANIA			
Specter	25	38	40
Santorum	88	13	88
RHODE ISLAND			
Chafee	50	50	50
Reed	25	75	25
SOUTH CAROLINA			
Thurmond	88	13	88
Hollings	50	25	67
SOUTH DAKOTA			
Daschle	38	63	38
Johnson	13	88	13
TENNESSEE			
Thompson	88	13	88
Frist	100	0	100

Democrats *Republicans*

Column 4	1	2	3
TEXAS			
Gramm	88	13	88
Hutchison	88	13	88
UTAH			
Hatch	100	0	100
Bennett	100	0	100
VERMONT			
Jeffords	38	50	43
Leahy	13	88	13
VIRGINIA			
Warner	63	38	63
Robb	75	25	75
WASHINGTON			
Gorton	100	0	100
Murray	50	50	50
WEST VIRGINIA			
Byrd	25	75	25
Rockefeller	38	38	50
WISCONSIN			
Kohl	25	75	25
Feingold	38	63	38
WYOMING			
Thomas	75	25	75
Enzi	75	25	75

ND Northern Democrats   SD Southern Democrats

Southern states - Ala., Ark., Fla., Ga., Ky., La., Miss., N.C., Okla., S.C., Tenn., Texas, Va.

Conservative Coalition Support and Opposition: Senate

1. Conservative Coalition Support. Percentage of 8 recorded votes in 1998 on which the conservative coalition appeared and on which a senator voted "yea" or "nay" in agreement with the position of the conservative coalition. Failures to vote lowered both support and opposition scores.

2. Conservative Coalition Opposition. Percentage of 8 recorded votes in 1998 on which the conservative coalition appeared and on which a senator voted "yea" or "nay" in disagreement with the position of the conservative coalition. Failures to vote lowered both support and opposition scores.

3. Conservative Coalition Support (adjusted for absences). Percentage of 8 recorded votes in 1998 on which the conservative coalition appeared and on which a senator was present and voted "yea" or "nay" in agreement with the position of the conservative coalition. In this version of the study, absences were not counted; therefore, failures to vote did not lower support or opposition scores. Opposition scores, not listed here, are the inverse of the support score; i.e., the opposition score is equal to 100 percent minus the individual's support score.

	1	2			1	2			1	2
ALABAMA				**IOWA**				**NEW HAMPSHIRE**		
Shelby	98	99		*Grassley*	100	100		*Smith*	99	99
Sessions	97	98		Harkin	96	95		*Gregg*	98	98
ALASKA				**KANSAS**				**NEW JERSEY**		
Stevens	99	99		*Brownback*	99	99		Lautenberg	99	99
Murkowski	96	95		*Roberts*	99	99		Torricelli	98	98
ARIZONA				**KENTUCKY**				**NEW MEXICO**		
McCain	94	96		*McConnell*	99	99		*Domenici*	95	95
Kyl	94	94		Ford	99	99		Bingaman	95	95
ARKANSAS				**LOUISIANA**				**NEW YORK**		
Hutchinson	95	95		Breaux	99	99		*D'Amato*	97	97
Bumpers	98	98		Landrieu	99	99		Moynihan	93	93
CALIFORNIA				**MAINE**				**NORTH CAROLINA**		
Feinstein	99	99		*Snowe*	99	99		*Helms*	78	78
Boxer	97	98		*Collins*	100	100		*Faircloth*	96	96
COLORADO				**MARYLAND**				**NORTH DAKOTA**		
Campbell	99	99		Sarbanes	99	99		Conrad	99	99
Allard	99	99		Mikulski	96	96		Dorgan	99	99
CONNECTICUT				**MASSACHUSETTS**				**OHIO**		
Dodd	99	99		Kennedy	97	96		*DeWine*	100	100
Lieberman	100	100		Kerry	98	98		Glenn	76	76
DELAWARE				**MICHIGAN**				**OKLAHOMA**		
Roth	96	96		*Abraham*	100	100		*Nickles*	99	99
Biden	96	96		Levin	97	97		*Inhofe*	95	95
FLORIDA				**MINNESOTA**				**OREGON**		
Mack	99	99		*Grams*	99	99		*Smith*	99	99
Graham	100	100		Wellstone	97	97		Wyden	96	96
GEORGIA				**MISSISSIPPI**				**PENNSYLVANIA**		
Coverdell	97	97		*Cochran*	100	100		*Specter*	86	86
Cleland	99	99		*Lott*	98	100		*Santorum*	99	99
HAWAII				**MISSOURI**				**RHODE ISLAND**		
Inouye	85	85		*Bond*	98	98		*Chafee*	99	99
Akaka	93	93		*Ashcroft*	99	99		Reed	100	100
IDAHO				**MONTANA**				**SOUTH CAROLINA**		
Craig	100	100		*Burns*	99	99		*Thurmond*	99	99
Kempthorne	99	99		Baucus	95	95		Hollings	89	90
ILLINOIS				**NEBRASKA**				**SOUTH DAKOTA**		
Moseley-Braun	92	92		*Hagel*	99	99		Daschle	100	100
Durbin	98	98		Kerrey	98	98		Johnson	100	100
INDIANA				**NEVADA**				**TENNESSEE**		
Lugar	100	100		Reid	98	98		*Thompson*	100	100
Coats	97	97		Bryan	99	99		*Frist*	99	99

	Democrats	*Republicans*

	1	2
TEXAS		
Gramm	99	99
Hutchison	96	95
UTAH		
Hatch	99	99
Bennett	95	95
VERMONT		
Jeffords	99	99
Leahy	99	99
VIRGINIA		
Warner	97	97
Robb	100	100
WASHINGTON		
Gorton	99	99
Murray	99	99
WEST VIRGINIA		
Byrd	100	100
Rockefeller	93	93
WISCONSIN		
Kohl	99	99
Feingold	100	100
WYOMING		
Thomas	99	99
Enzi	99	99

ND Northern Democrats   SD Southern Democrats

Southern states - Ala., Ark., Fla., Ga., Ky., La., Miss., N.C., Okla., S.C., Tenn., Texas, Va.

Voting Participation: Senate

1. **Voting Participation.** Percentage of 314 recorded votes in 1998 on which a senator voted "yea" or "nay."

2. **Voting Participation (without motions to instruct).** Percentage of 311 recorded votes in 1998 on which a senator voted "yea" or "nay." In this version of the study, three votes to instruct the sergeant at arms to request the attendance of absent senators are not included.

Absences due to illness. *Congressional Quarterly no longer designates members who missed votes due to illness. In the past, notations to that effect were based on official statements published in the Congressional Record, but these were found to be inconsistently used.*

Rounding. *Scores are rounded to nearest percentage, except that no scores are rounded up to 100 percent. Members with a 100 percent score participated in all recorded votes for which they were eligible.*

Voting Participation: House

1. **Voting Participation.** Percentage of 533 recorded votes in 1998 on which a representative voted "yea" or "nay."

2. **Voting Participation (without Journal votes).** Percentage of 522 recorded votes in 1998 on which a representative voted "yea" or "nay." In this version of the study, 11 votes on approval of the House Journal were not included.

Absences due to illness. Congressional Quarterly no longer designates members who missed votes due to illness. In the past, notations to that effect were based on official statements published in the Congressional Record, but these were found to be inconsistently used.

Rounding. Scores are rounded to the nearest percentage, except that no scores are rounded up to 100 percent. Members with a 100 percent score participated in all recorded votes for which they were eligible.

[1] *Barbara Lee, D-Calif., was sworn in April 21, replacing Ronald V. Dellums, D-Calif., who resigned Feb. 6. Lee was eligible for 438 votes in 1998. Dellums was eligible for 10 votes in 1998. His voting participation score was 67 percent, both with and without the inclusion of Journal votes.*

[2] *Lois Capps, D-Calif., was sworn in March 17, replacing Walter Capps, D-Calif., who died Oct. 28, 1997. Lois Capps was eligible for 482 votes in 1998.*

[3] *Mary Bono, R-Calif., was sworn in April 21, replacing Sonny Bono, R-Calif., who died Jan. 5. Mary Bono was eligible for 438 votes in 1998. Sonny Bono was eligible for no votes in 1998.*

[4] *Newt Gingrich, R-Ga., as Speaker of the House, voted at his discretion on 73 votes in 1998.*

[5] *Heather Wilson, R-N.M., was sworn in June 25, replacing Stephen H. Schiff, R-N.M., who died March 25. Wilson was eligible for 267 votes in 1998. Schiff was eligible for 64 votes in 1998 but cast no votes.*

[6] *Gregory W. Meeks, D-N.Y., was sworn in Feb. 5, replacing Floyd H. Flake, D-N.Y., who resigned on Nov. 15, 1997. Meeks was eligible for 523 votes in 1998.*

[7] *Robert A. Brady, D-Pa., was sworn in May 21, replacing Thomas M. Foglietta, D-Pa., who resigned Nov. 11, 1997. Brady was eligible for 362 votes in 1998.*

Democrats **Republicans**
Independent

		1	2
ALABAMA			
1	*Callahan*	95	95
2	*Everett*	99	99
3	*Riley*	99	99
4	*Aderholt*	99	99
5	Cramer	98	98
6	*Bachus*	99	99
7	Hilliard	94	94
ALASKA			
AL	*Young*	94	95
ARIZONA			
1	*Salmon*	97	97
2	Pastor	99	99
3	*Stump*	99	99
4	*Shadegg*	99	99
5	*Kolbe*	98	98
6	*Hayworth*	99	99
ARKANSAS			
1	Berry	98	98
2	Snyder	99	99
3	*Hutchinson*	94	94
4	*Dickey*	97	98
CALIFORNIA			
1	*Riggs*	75	75
2	*Herger*	96	96
3	Fazio	97	97
4	*Doolittle*	95	95
5	Matsui	99	99
6	Woolsey	99	99
7	Miller	92	92
8	Pelosi	94	94
9	Lee[1]	99	99
10	Tauscher	98	98
11	*Pombo*	99	99
12	Lantos	96	96
13	Stark	93	93
14	Eshoo	96	96
15	*Campbell*	99	99
16	Lofgren	95	96
17	Farr	95	95
18	Condit	99	99
19	*Radanovich*	93	93
20	Dooley	99	99
21	*Thomas*	99	99
22	Capps[2]	99	99
23	*Gallegly*	99	99
24	Sherman	99	99
25	*McKeon*	99	99
26	Berman	87	87
27	*Rogan*	96	96
28	*Dreier*	99	99
29	Waxman	94	94
30	Becerra	92	92
31	Martinez	88	89
32	Dixon	89	89
33	Roybal-Allard	93	93
34	Torres	81	81
35	Waters	89	89
36	Harman	68	69
37	Millender-McD.	92	92
38	*Horn*	99	99

		1	2
39	*Royce*	92	92
40	*Lewis*	97	97
41	*Kim*	99	99
42	Brown	96	96
43	*Calvert*	99	99
44	*Bono*[3]	99	99
45	*Rohrabacher*	99	99
46	Sanchez	95	95
47	*Cox*	95	95
48	*Packard*	97	97
49	*Bilbray*	97	98
50	Filner	98	98
51	*Cunningham*	91	91
52	*Hunter*	95	95
COLORADO			
1	DeGette	99	99
2	Skaggs	88	88
3	*McInnis*	96	96
4	*Schaffer*	100	100
5	*Hefley*	98	98
6	*Schaefer*	93	93
CONNECTICUT			
1	Kennelly	77	76
2	Gejdenson	98	98
3	DeLauro	99	99
4	*Shays*	99	99
5	Maloney	97	98
6	*Johnson*	99	99
DELAWARE			
AL	*Castle*	99	99
FLORIDA			
1	*Scarborough*	92	93
2	Boyd	99	99
3	Brown	93	93
4	*Fowler*	95	95
5	Thurman	99	99
6	*Stearns*	98	98
7	*Mica*	97	98
8	*McCollum*	97	97
9	*Bilirakis*	97	97
10	*Young*	83	83
11	Davis	99	99
12	*Canady*	99	99
13	*Miller*	97	97
14	Goss	89	89
15	*Weldon*	95	95
16	*Foley*	96	96
17	Meek	94	94
18	*Ros-Lehtinen*	92	91
19	Wexler	95	95
20	Deutsch	93	93
21	*Diaz-Balart*	96	97
22	*Shaw*	98	98
23	Hastings	91	90
GEORGIA			
1	*Kingston*	99	99
2	Bishop	99	99
3	*Collins*	97	97
4	McKinney	99	99
5	Lewis	81	81
6	*Gingrich*[4]	14	14
7	*Barr*	95	95
8	*Chambliss*	99	99
9	Deal	98	98
10	*Norwood*	93	93
11	*Linder*	96	96
HAWAII			
1	Abercrombie	99	99
2	Mink	98	98
IDAHO			
1	*Chenoweth*	98	98
2	*Crapo*	96	96
ILLINOIS			
1	Rush	93	93
2	Jackson	100	100
3	Lipinski	93	93
4	Gutierrez	96	96
5	Blagojevich	95	95
6	*Hyde*	95	96
7	Davis	96	96
8	*Crane*	94	95
9	Yates	75	75
10	*Porter*	98	98
11	*Weller*	98	98
12	Costello	98	99
13	*Fawell*	92	92

ND Northern Democrats   SD Southern Democrats

	1	2
14 *Hastert*	98	99
15 *Ewing*	95	95
16 *Manzullo*	98	98
17 Evans	99	99
18 *LaHood*	99	99
19 Poshard	65	65
20 *Shimkus*	98	98

INDIANA

	1	2
1 Visclosky	97	98
2 *McIntosh*	96	96
3 Roemer	99	99
4 *Souder*	96	97
5 *Buyer*	92	93
6 *Burton*	92	93
7 *Pease*	99	99
8 *Hostettler*	99	99
9 Hamilton	97	97
10 Carson	93	93

IOWA

	1	2
1 *Leach*	98	98
2 *Nussle*	99	99
3 Boswell	99	99
4 *Ganske*	98	98
5 *Latham*	99	99

KANSAS

	1	2
1 *Moran*	100	100
2 *Ryun*	98	98
3 *Snowbarger*	99	99
4 *Tiahrt*	98	98

KENTUCKY

	1	2
1 *Whitfield*	97	97
2 *Lewis*	99	99
3 *Northup*	99	99
4 *Bunning*	99	99
5 *Rogers*	97	98
6 Baesler	96	96

LOUISIANA

	1	2
1 *Livingston*	96	97
2 Jefferson	88	88
3 *Tauzin*	93	93
4 *McCrery*	92	92
5 *Cooksey*	91	91
6 *Baker*	95	95
7 John	86	86

MAINE

	1	2
1 Allen	98	98
2 Baldacci	99	99

MARYLAND

	1	2
1 *Gilchrest*	97	98
2 *Ehrlich*	95	95
3 Cardin	95	95
4 Wynn	96	96
5 Hoyer	98	99
6 *Bartlett*	99	99
7 Cummings	99	99
8 *Morella*	98	98

MASSACHUSETTS

	1	2
1 Olver	98	98
2 Neal	95	95
3 McGovern	96	96
4 Frank	95	95
5 Meehan	94	94
6 Tierney	98	98
7 Markey	91	91
8 Kennedy	93	93
9 Moakley	79	79
10 Delahunt	99	99

MICHIGAN

	1	2
1 Stupak	97	97
2 *Hoekstra*	99	99
3 *Ehlers*	98	98
4 *Camp*	99	99
5 Barcia	98	98
6 *Upton*	100	100
7 *Smith*	98	98
8 Stabenow	97	97
9 Kildee	99	99
10 Bonior	99	99
11 *Knollenberg*	99	100
12 Levin	99	99
13 Rivers	99	99
14 Conyers	90	90
15 Kilpatrick	90	90
16 Dingell	94	94

MINNESOTA

	1	2
1 Gutknecht	98	98
2 Minge	99	99
3 *Ramstad*	100	100
4 Vento	99	99
5 Sabo	98	98
6 Luther	96	96
7 Peterson	99	99
8 Oberstar	98	98

MISSISSIPPI

	1	2
1 *Wicker*	96	96
2 Thompson	94	94
3 *Pickering*	94	95
4 Parker	84	84
5 Taylor	98	99

MISSOURI

	1	2
1 Clay	87	87
2 *Talent*	99	99
3 Gephardt	90	90
4 Skelton	99	99
5 McCarthy	96	96
6 Danner	97	97
7 *Blunt*	96	96
8 *Emerson*	99	99
9 Hulshof	98	98

MONTANA

	1	2
AL *Hill*	96	96

NEBRASKA

	1	2
1 *Bereuter*	99	99
2 *Christensen*	90	90
3 *Barrett*	99	99

NEVADA

	1	2
1 *Ensign*	97	98
2 *Gibbons*	99	99

NEW HAMPSHIRE

	1	2
1 *Sununu*	98	98
2 *Bass*	99	99

NEW JERSEY

	1	2
1 Andrews	98	98
2 *LoBiondo*	99	99
3 *Saxton*	98	98
4 *Smith*	98	99
5 *Roukema*	98	98
6 Pallone	99	99
7 *Franks*	99	99
8 Pascrell	98	98
9 Rothman	96	96
10 Payne	91	91
11 *Frelinghuysen*	99	99
12 *Pappas*	100	100
13 Menendez	98	98

NEW MEXICO

	1	2
1 *Wilson*[5]	99	98
2 *Skeen*	99	100
3 Redmond	98	98

NEW YORK

	1	2
1 *Forbes*	96	96
2 *Lazio*	99	99
3 *King*	97	97
4 McCarthy	99	99
5 Ackerman	92	92
6 Meeks[6]	86	86
7 Manton	92	92
8 Nadler	94	94
9 Schumer	79	79
10 Towns	82	82
11 Owens	94	94
12 Velázquez	94	94
13 *Fossella*	98	98
14 Maloney	94	94
15 Rangel	86	86
16 Serrano	95	95
17 Engel	93	93
18 Lowey	97	97
19 *Kelly*	99	99
20 *Gilman*	99	99
21 McNulty	83	83
22 *Solomon*	97	97
23 *Boehlert*	99	99
24 *McHugh*	98	98
25 *Walsh*	98	98
26 Hinchey	98	98
27 *Paxon*	92	91
28 Slaughter	96	97
29 LaFalce	98	98

RHODE ISLAND

	1	2
1 Kennedy	99	99
2 Weygand	99	99

SOUTH CAROLINA

	1	2
1 *Sanford*	98	98
2 *Spence*	99	99
3 *Graham*	95	95
4 *Inglis*	89	90
5 Spratt	94	94
6 Clyburn	97	98

SOUTH DAKOTA

	1	2
AL *Thune*	99	99

	1	2
30 Quinn	95	95
31 Houghton	94	94

NORTH CAROLINA

	1	2
1 Clayton	94	94
2 Etheridge	98	98
3 *Jones*	99	99
4 Price	99	99
5 *Burr*	97	97
6 *Coble*	96	96
7 McIntyre	97	97
8 Hefner	81	81
9 *Myrick*	97	97
10 *Ballenger*	97	97
11 *Taylor*	94	94
12 Watt	98	98

NORTH DAKOTA

	1	2
AL Pomeroy	97	98

OHIO

	1	2
1 *Chabot*	99	99
2 *Portman*	98	98
3 Hall	96	97
4 *Oxley*	96	96
5 *Gillmor*	98	98
6 Strickland	99	99
7 *Hobson*	99	99
8 *Boehner*	99	99
9 Kaptur	94	94
10 Kucinich	99	99
11 Stokes	93	93
12 *Kasich*	98	98
13 Brown	97	97
14 Sawyer	98	98
15 *Pryce*	77	77
16 *Regula*	99	99
17 Traficant	97	97
18 *Ney*	97	97
19 *LaTourette*	99	99

OKLAHOMA

	1	2
1 *Largent*	94	94
2 *Coburn*	97	97
3 *Watkins*	98	98
4 *Watts*	99	99
5 *Istook*	93	93
6 *Lucas*	100	100

OREGON

	1	2
1 Furse	86	87
2 *Smith*	89	89
3 Blumenauer	98	98
4 DeFazio	95	96
5 Hooley	97	98

PENNSYLVANIA

	1	2
1 Brady[7]	96	96
2 Fattah	92	93
3 Borski	97	97
4 Klink	97	97
5 *Peterson*	98	98
6 Holden	99	99
7 Weldon	96	96
8 *Greenwood*	94	94
9 *Shuster*	94	94
10 *McDade*	67	68
11 Kanjorski	99	99
12 Murtha	95	96
13 *Fox*	99	99
14 Coyne	99	99
15 McHale	99	99
16 *Pitts*	99	99
17 *Gekas*	97	97
18 Doyle	97	97
19 *Goodling*	95	95
20 Mascara	100	100
21 *English*	98	98

TENNESSEE

	1	2
1 *Jenkins*	98	98
2 *Duncan*	99	99
3 *Wamp*	98	98
4 *Hilleary*	99	99
5 Clement	97	98
6 Gordon	97	97
7 *Bryant*	99	99
8 Tanner	96	96
9 Ford	85	84

TEXAS

	1	2
1 Sandlin	97	97
2 Turner	97	97
3 *Johnson*	92	92
4 Hall	99	99
5 *Sessions*	98	98
6 *Barton*	97	98
7 *Archer*	97	97
8 *Brady*	95	96
9 Lampson	95	96
10 Doggett	99	99
11 Edwards	98	99
12 *Granger*	98	99
13 *Thornberry*	99	99
14 *Paul*	98	98
15 Hinojosa	95	95
16 Reyes	92	93
17 Stenholm	99	99
18 Jackson-Lee	97	97
19 *Combest*	99	99
20 Gonzalez	16	16
21 *Smith*	98	98
22 *DeLay*	96	96
23 *Bonilla*	98	98
24 Frost	94	94
25 Bentsen	99	100
26 *Armey*	97	97
27 Ortiz	94	94
28 Rodriguez	97	97
29 Green	94	93
30 Johnson	94	94

UTAH

	1	2
1 *Hansen*	96	96
2 *Cook*	97	97
3 *Cannon*	89	89

VERMONT

	1	2
AL *Sanders*	98	98

VIRGINIA

	1	2
1 *Bateman*	81	81
2 Pickett	98	98
3 Scott	100	100
4 Sisisky	99	99
5 Goode	98	98
6 *Goodlatte*	99	99
7 *Bliley*	99	99
8 Moran	97	97
9 Boucher	94	94
10 *Wolf*	99	99
11 *Davis*	98	98

WASHINGTON

	1	2
1 *White*	98	98
2 *Metcalf*	99	99
3 *Smith*	94	94
4 *Hastings*	99	99
5 *Nethercutt*	98	98
6 Dicks	99	99
7 McDermott	96	96
8 *Dunn*	98	98
9 Smith	98	99

WEST VIRGINIA

	1	2
1 Mollohan	93	93
2 Wise	96	96
3 Rahall	97	97

WISCONSIN

	1	2
1 *Neumann*	97	97
2 *Klug*	95	95
3 Kind	99	99
4 Kleczka	99	99
5 Barrett	99	99
6 *Petri*	99	99
7 Obey	98	98
8 Johnson	98	98
9 *Sensenbrenner*	99	99

WYOMING

	1	2
AL *Cubin*	98	98

Southern states - Ala., Ark., Fla., Ga., Ky., La., Miss., N.C., Okla., S.C., Tenn., Texas, Va.

KEY VOTES

Distracted by Impeachment, Republicans Hand Clinton A Few Legislative Victories

Since 1945, Congressional Quarterly has selected a series of key votes on major issues of the year. An issue is judged by the extent to which it represents:

● A matter of major controversy.

● A matter of presidential or political power.

● A matter of potentially great impact on the nation and lives of Americans.

For each group of related votes on an issue, one key vote is usually chosen — one that, in the opinion of CQ editors, was most improtant in determining the outcome.

Charts showing how each member of Congress voted on these key issues begin on p. C-16.

KEY SENATE VOTES

10 CLONING BAN

After scientists in Scotland announced in 1997 that they had cloned a sheep named Dolly, legislation to ban human cloning was put on a fast track. For much of 1997 and early 1998, it looked as if a broad cloning ban would pass the Senate. But a Feb. 11 decision to block debate on an anti-cloning bill (S 1601) showed how medical research groups and biotech companies were able to make their case, even amid the clamor over Dolly.

It also showed how the cloning issue would not be fought along the same battle lines as abortion. Anti-abortion forces entered the debate on cloning early, hoping to have some products of genetic manipulation defined as human life even though scientists disagreed. They lost when not only Democrats, but also abortion opponents such as Sens. Connie Mack,

R-Fla., and Strom Thurmond, R-S.C., sided with researchers and cited their own experiences with serious diseases in concluding that there is a huge gray area that could be valuable ground for advances in medical knowledge.

The measure was halted when Dianne Feinstein, D-Calif., objected to bringing it up. Sixty votes are necessary to overcome such an objection; the vote on the motion to proceed failed, 42-54: R 42-12; D 0-42 (ND 0-34; SD 0-8).

There was, and is, consensus in Congress that human cloning is morally repugnant. But medical groups and many senators contended that the measure, sponsored by Republicans Bill Frist of Tennessee and Christopher S. Bond of Missouri, was too broad and could interfere with research. For example, they argued that reproducing masses of human cells for the purposes of replacing badly burned skin could be halted by the legislation. The same could be true of an experimental process of cloning human cells into animals for the purposes of having the animals produce human antibodies.

The measure would have banned a process known as somatic cell nuclear transfer for the purposes of creating a human embryo. The process involves replacing the nucleus of an egg cell with the nucleus of some other cell — an adult cell that would not multiply if left in its original state. Scientists have found that the remaining portion of the cell can somehow "reprogram" the new nucleus into multiplying.

Bond and Frist argued that this new cell could be considered an embryo, and thus worthy of the same protection as an embryo created through sexual intercourse. They were backed by The National Right to Life Committee and other groups opposed to abortion.

But scientific groups said the language was too broad. Feinstein offered an alternative that would have banned

creating a human being through the somatic cell transfer process. It was opposed by anti-abortion groups and by some medical organizations.

16 CAMPAIGN FINANCE

In October 1997, Senate Democrats put heavy pressure on Majority Leader Trent Lott, R-Miss., to schedule a vote on a campaign finance bill that he and most of his GOP colleagues vehemently opposed. Democrats threatened to bring the Senate to a halt in the session's closing days unless they got their way.

Displaying his pragmatic streak, Lott acceded to the Democrats' demands and agreed to permit a debate on the matter in early 1998. But Lott could afford to be magnanimous: He had the votes.

Joined by Mitch McConnell, R-Ky., Lott led a successful filibuster against the campaign finance proposal, which was sponsored by John McCain, R-Ariz., and Russell D. Feingold, D-Wis.

The outcome was scripted in advance. Before the debate, McCain acknowledged that his side would not be able to amass the 60 votes needed to break the filibuster. But campaign finance advocates were hoping to do better than they had in October 1997, when they managed to garner 52.

Instead, they fared exactly the same — or would have, had all members been present. Tom Harkin, D-Iowa, a supporter of the McCain-Feingold proposal, was absent. On the key vote, which occurred Feb. 26, the Senate failed to end the filibuster, 51-48. Forty-four Democrats and seven Republicans supported a motion to limit debate; 48 Republicans opposed it.

The vote came on an amendment to a GOP bill (S 1663) that would have limited the use of union dues for political activity. The amendment,

proposed by McCain and Feingold, was a modified version of their campaign finance bill (S 25).

The decisive factor was the willingness of GOP senators who faced reelection in 1998 — such as Alfonse M. D'Amato of New York, Christopher S. Bond of Missouri and Sam Brownback of Kansas — to stand with Lott and McConnell. McConnell said that the 48 Republicans who opposed the bill the previous autumn remained "rock solid."

The McCain-Feingold bill would have banned "soft money," unregulated donations to political parties by unions, corporations and wealthy individuals. It also would have imposed new restrictions on issue-oriented television ads run by interest groups.

The legislation had picked up momentum in 1997 as Congress probed fundraising excesses in the 1996 presidential campaign. But opponents charged that the measure infringed on constitutionally protected political speech. And many Republicans feared that it would diminish their substantial fundraising advantage over Democrats.

The vote of Feb. 26 took much of the steam out of the Senate's campaign finance debate. McConnell was gleeful in declaring victory. "This undeserving legislation is dead," he said after the vote. But Lott's bill on union dues also was defeated. The Senate failed to end a Democratic filibuster on that bill, 45-54.

There were efforts to revive the McCain-Feingold bill later in 1998, but they also failed. On Sept. 10, Democrats again fell short of closing debate on the proposal by the same 52-48 vote.

44 IMF FUNDING

The Senate's strong early vote — 84-16 on March 26 — to appropriate $17.9 billion for the International Monetary Fund (IMF) set the tone for months of high-stakes maneuvering between pro-trade business interests and an unlikely array of environmentalists, free-trade conservatives and others opposed to the funding.

Early in 1998, President Clinton requested the appropriation as part of an emergency supplemental bill (PL 105-174) to shore up IMF reserves, which had been drawn down by massive loans to economically troubled Asian nations. Clinton and many top lawmakers in both parties said the money was necessary to stabilize economies across much of the world.

But House leaders turned a cool shoulder to the request. Majority Leader Dick Armey, R-Texas, denounced the IMF for interfering with free markets, while critics on the left blamed the organization for contributing to deteriorating labor and environmental conditions overseas.

When the House Appropriations Committee on March 24 split IMF funding off from the main supplemental bill (HR 3579), all eyes turned to the Senate. The upper chamber had historically been a bastion of support for trade and international commerce measures, and if the IMF appropriation was to have any chance of reaching the president's desk, it needed a strong Senate vote.

But Senate appropriators also had given IMF a rough ride. The Senate Appropriations Committee approved the funding, but attached such contentious provisions that it was unclear whether the 182-nation organization would be able to comply. For example, the committee insisted that the IMF make loans only to countries that honored certain trade agreements.

When the supplemental bill (S 1768) went to the floor, Mitch McConnell, R-Ky., proposed an amendment that would ease the IMF conditions. It would require that the United States and its major "G-7" industrial partners agree to push for such IMF measures as requiring borrowing countries to abide by international trade agreements.

McConnell's conditions fell far short of what IMF critics demanded. Conservatives such as Connie Mack, R-Fla., and Spencer Abraham, R-Mich., assailed the IMF for pressuring governments to raise taxes, devalue currencies and delay regulatory changes, and said the organization would have to be completely revamped before getting their support.

On the left, Democrats such as Paul Wellstone, D-Minn., criticized the international organization for promoting austerity policies that reduced the standard of living in recipient countries.

But funding supporters such as Chuck Hagel, R-Neb., and Patrick J. Leahy, D-Vt., carried the day by contending that the funding was needed to restore confidence in the global economy.

The Senate passed the amendment on March 26 by a vote of 84-16: R 41-14, D 43-2 (ND 35-2, SD 8-0). The overwhelming vote gave considerable momentum to the administration's funding request.

Still skeptical, House leaders refused to include the funding in the supplemental bill. Instead, the IMF issue lingered all year, as appropriators wrestled with the issue in the fiscal 1999 foreign operations spending bill (HR 4328 — PL 105-277).

But with the resounding Senate vote echoing throughout the negotiations, Congress finally cleared the IMF funding in the final days of the session.

112 NATO EXPANSION

The Senate strongly endorsed admitting Poland, Hungary and the Czech Republic to NATO on April 30, but only after sending a clear signal that the alliance should not rush to invite any more former Soviet satellites to join.

Expansion of the alliance had a powerful head of steam by the time it reached the Senate floor in the spring. It was strongly backed by President Clinton and most Republican and Democratic congressional leaders. And the Clinton administration orchestrated support from labor, veterans and ethnic groups with ties to the three countries.

Opponents of expansion were a politically diverse lot. Conservative isolationists warned that expanding the alliance would overextend U.S. overseas commitments. Some liberals argued that for Poland, Hungary and the Czech Republic to meld their armed forces into NATO would distract them from needed economic reforms. And several foreign policy experts worried that adding the three countries to NATO would exacerbate relations with Russia.

The critics faced an uphill fight from the beginning. And it was apparent by April 27, when the Senate began its final four days of debate, that they had no momentum. For instance, the argument that expansion would undermine

relations with Russia was blunted by Moscow's public acquiescence.

It was clear that the protocol amending the treaty to add the three new countries (Treaty Doc 105-36) would be supported by considerably more than the required two-thirds majority of the Senate. But the critics by then had shifted their focus to delaying, at least for a few years, any invitations to other countries.

The leading candidates for a second round of expansion were Romania and Slovenia. But nine other countries also had applied for NATO membership, including the three Baltic republics — Estonia, Latvia and Lithuania.

The Baltic states posed a particularly awkward problem for NATO. On the one hand, all three had made progress in establishing democratic institutions and free-market economies, which are among the prerequisites of membership. But all three would be difficult to defend, because they are small and adjacent to Russia. Moreover, the Soviet Union had annexed all three in 1940. Although the United States never recognized the annexation, it was widely believed that Russia would object strenuously to NATO membership for countries it deemed former Soviet republics.

For months, even some staunch supporters of admitting the first three countries made it clear they wanted to see how that phase of expansion panned out before admitting additional countries.

The test came on an amendment to the treaty protocol offered by John W. Warner of Virginia, the second-ranking Republican on the Senate Armed Services Committee. Warner's proposal would have barred any additional invitations for three years after the first group was admitted. The amendment was rejected, 41-59. But it garnered more "yea" votes than the one-third that would be needed to block admission a second group of countries, if they were invited too quickly.

Both parties split on the Warner amendment, Republicans opposing it, 24-31, and Democrats, 17-28 (ND 15-22, SD 2-6).

The Senate also rejected several other amendments that would have made admission of Poland, Hungary and the Czech Republic dependent on various developments. But it adopted,

by voice vote, two amendments by Ted Stevens, R-Alaska, chairman of the Appropriations Committee. One required congressional authorization of any U.S. spending related to NATO enlargement. The other urged the president to propose to other alliance members a gradual reduction in the U.S. share of NATO's budget.

The Senate than approved the treaty amendment, 80-19. The three countries are to formally join NATO April 4 at a 50th anniversary meeting of the alliance in Washington.

141 SKILLED-WORKER VISAS

In 1996, Congress greatly restricted immigration policy, cutting off welfare benefits to legal immigrants and passing tough new provisions against illegal immigration. The Senate's May 18 vote to expand the so-called H-1B visa program was perhaps the best evidence of how much things had changed in two years.

The vote was 78-20: R 51-2; D 27-18 (ND 20-17, SD 7-1).

The H-1B program is for skilled immigrants, most of whom go to work in the computer industry, but many of whom fill medium-skilled jobs as medical technicians, physical therapists, even fashion models.

Unlike lesser-skilled immigrants, H-1B recipients had business lobbies, particularly Silicon Valley, arguing their case. But they are still immigrants, and they touch a nerve among groups that argue the country is already swamped with too many foreigners. Groups such as the Federation for American Immigration Reform argued that the program is a way for companies to import cheap labor instead of hiring equally skilled American workers. Labor unions said the program is a ruse for depressing wages.

The overwhelming vote in the Senate showed the increasingly strong nexus between a pro-business stance and a pro-immigration stance. It also showed that taking an anti-immigration position is increasingly difficult.

The vote created the momentum for an H-1B expansion to be enacted. A similar bill ran into some trouble in the House, but was eventually included in the omnibus spending package (HR 4328 — PL 105-277)

passed at year's end.

The Senate bill, increasing the annual allotment of H-1B visas from 65,000 to 115,000, sailed through both the Judiciary Committee and full Senate. Only two Republicans, and fewer than half the Democrats, voted against it.

In committee, and on the floor, Edward M. Kennedy, D-Mass., tried to amend the measure with labor-backed provisions that would have made it much harder for employers to participate in the program. They would have been required to demonstrate their efforts to attract American workers before being allowed to go into the H-1B program. They would have been barred from it if they had laid off any U.S. workers with skills comparable to those of foreigners they wanted to sponsor.

But even these provisions got little Senate support. Both were voted down with near unanimous Republican opposition and a handful Democratic defections.

Later in the legislative process, Republican immigration hard-liners would emerge in the House. The vote put the Senate clearly on the pro-immigration side.

The vote was a significant victory for a new lobby — high-technology companies. Many of the companies that pushed hard for the H-1B expansion were small businesses just a few years ago. Today, these companies, including Sun Microsystems Inc., Intel Corp. and Microsoft Corp., have grown into corporate giants.

Their lobbying and political contributions had not grown as fast as their profits, however. Many of them had a corporate culture that was somewhat anti-Washington; they saw it necessary to open D.C. offices only in the last few years.

The H-1B debate was their first industry-wide cooperative effort, and it was a resounding success. At the beginning of 1998, few members outside of those who represent high-tech states had given much thought to the issue. But by spring the high-tech lobby had put it squarely on senators' agendas. They aggressively argued that they could not continue to grow as fast as they had if they could not get their hands on the skilled workers they needed. They implicitly threatened to

take jobs overseas if overseas workers could not be brought here.

The lopsided vote showed how effectively the lobby had done its homework. Even some Democratic senators had a hard time fighting them. Many, like Dianne Feinstein of California, chose their business constituents over their labor union backers, after some attempts to mollify both sides.

161 TOBACCO LEGISLATION

By the time the Senate floor debate on tobacco legislation (S 1415) reached its fourth week, the action had come to resemble an old serial drama at the movies, complete with cliffhanger moments of suspense, its audience unsure what would happen from one week to the next.

Finally, on June 17, Majority Leader Trent Lott, R-Miss., had seen enough. He shut down the Senate in the morning to convene in his office a meeting of some three dozen Republicans. The decision was made to hold a cloture vote later in the day and, when that failed, to bring the bill down.

During the meeting, Mitch McConnell of Kentucky, chairman of the National Republican Senatorial Committee, reportedly assured nervous colleagues that the tobacco industry would run ads against the bill for their political protection.

The tobacco industry had spent more than $40 million on issue ads that attacked S 1415, and a like amount on lobbying. S 1415 would have raised fees on cigarettes by $1.10 per pack over five years, given the federal government broad control over the distribution and marketing of tobacco products, and restricted tobacco advertising.

"I've never discounted the effect of a lot of money on ads," bill sponsor John McCain, R-Ariz., told a news conference. "If cloture is not invoked, tobacco companies have made a wise investment, and they have won because they have changed the views of a significant number of Americans."

The creation of a federal tobacco policy had seemed almost a foregone conclusion at earlier stages of the legislative process. But as the bill bogged down in the Senate and both its friends and enemies bloated it with big-dollar amendments, it became clear that there was no longer a clear political consensus to lend the effort momentum.

"What killed this bill was that the public never bought into the logic of it — they never saw this as a tool to fight teen smoking," Phil Gramm, R-Texas, told a gaggle of reporters after Lott's meeting broke up. "This bill has no support in America, and it has lost its support in Congress."

There had been three previous cloture votes on the bill, but those had been filed by Democrats and were seen more as maneuvering over control of the schedule than about the bill. As Lott's strategy became clear, the bill's strongest supporters were angered.

"What they did was spread DDT here — first delay, then destroy, then terminate any action on tobacco," Frank R. Lautenberg, D-N.J., said of S 1415's opponents, several of whom could be seen laughing in response on the Senate floor.

Senators for and against the bill had spent the better part of the day counting noses. Asked by a reporter whether his side didn't enjoy a three-vote cushion, Majority Whip Don Nickles, R-Okla., a leading opponent of the bill, replied, "I wouldn't say that yet."

But that is just how the vote turned out. The motion to invoke cloture fell three votes short of the 60 required, 57-42: R 14-40; D 43-2 (ND 37-0, SD 6-2). S 1415 was then taken down on a budget point of order.

169 EDUCATION SAVINGS ACCOUNTS

Opinion polls show that Americans are worried about school quality. Unfortunately for Republicans, the surveys also show that voters believe Democrats do a better job on education issues.

Trying to assuage public concern on both counts, congressional Republicans pushed legislation (HR 2646) that would have allowed families to contribute up to $2,000 per child per year in special savings accounts for private school tuition, tutoring, computer equipment and other education expenses. The legislation passed the House, 230-198, on Oct. 23, 1997, and was taken up by the Senate this year.

Despite White House veto threats and a determined effort by Minority Leader Tom Daschle, D-S.D., to persuade Democrats not to vote for the legislation, the Senate approved the final conference report on June 24, by a vote of 59-36: R 51-2; D 8-34 (ND 6-28, SD 2-6).

The vote indicated a growing willingness among Democrats to buck the White House and search for new ways to give parents more control over their childrens' education. But it also showed the two parties were still far from consensus, a fact that the White House exploited later in the year, when Clinton browbeat Republicans into adding $1.2 billion to the omnibus spending bill (HR 4328 — PL 105-277) as a down payment on his plan to hire 100,000 new teachers.

The savings account bill, sponsored by Paul Coverdell, R-Ga., was designed to move Republicans beyond their narrow emphasis on federally funded vouchers for private schools. Because parents, rather than the government, could choose how to manage the accounts, Republicans hoped they would appeal to Democrats. Robert G. Torricelli, D-N.J., was a chief cosponsor of the bill.

The middle ground turned out to be elusive. The Clinton administration charged that the legislation would mainly benefit upper-income taxpayers. Democrats used debate on the Coverdell bill to force votes on Clinton's proposals to hire teachers and allow local governments to issue $22 billion in federally backed bonds for school construction. Both those initiatives were defeated.

Senate Republicans offered competing amendments that they said would limit the federal role in education and return more power to the states. In a surprise vote, the Senate by 50-49 adopted an amendment by Slade Gorton, R-Wash., that would turn $10.3 billion in annual elementary and secondary programs into broad block grants.

The Senate also adopted an amendment by John Ashcroft, R-Mo., to bar Clinton from proceeding with his plans for voluntary math and reading tests.

With those provisions attached, several Democrats who had said they might have voted for the underlying Coverdell bill decided to vote "nay."

In the end, five Democrats voted for the measure, which passed the Senate, 56-43, on April 23.

House-Senate conferees dropped the proposals on testing and block grants. The final bill retained some bipartisan sweeteners attached in the Senate, including making prepaid college tuition completely tax free. The conference report passed the House, 225-197, on June 18. Twelve Democrats voted for it, 10 Republicans against. Republicans did not even attempt an override after Clinton, as promised, vetoed the bill July 21. They have promised to revive the legislation next year.

180 SAME-SEX TRAINING

Hoping to capitalize on support from a national commission, social conservatives tried to force the Army, Navy and Air Force to follow the Marine Corps' example and segregate male and female recruits during training. But the effort, which came to a head in amendments to the fiscal 1999 defense authorization bill (HR 3616), was rejected by the Senate.

The underlying issue, a battle more than two decades old, was the proper role of women in the armed forces. Starting in 1975, when an amendment to the fiscal 1976 defense bill (PL 94-106) required the admission of women to the national military academies, Congress and successive administrations had eliminated or scaled back rules intended to keep women out of jobs involving any risk of combat. Women's rights groups and female officers vigorously promoted these changes, contending that excluding women from combat jobs — the most prestigious in the services — effectively barred them from rising to the highest ranks.

Social conservatives, however, argued that allowing women into more jobs had undermined combat readiness by lowering standards for physical strength and creating sexual tensions in small units.

The long-running debate gained new urgency in 1996 following allegations of sexual abuse by drill sergeants at some Army training bases. Although the incidents occurred at advanced training facilities, conserva-

tives seized on them to push for legislation that would require the services to organize new recruits in separate units and to house men and women in separate barracks.

Efforts to pass such a bill yielded nothing in 1997, partly because those who challenged mixed-gender training did not want to appear to be condoning the abusive behavior.

But in December 1997, a special commission created by Defense Secretary William S. Cohen and chaired by former Kansas Republican Sen. Nancy Kassebaum Baker (1978-97), recommended separate housing and training units for male and female recruits. The change, Baker said, would reduce distractions for recruits and drill instructors.

The Army, Navy and Air Force vigorously objected, arguing that training men and women together helped acclimate them to working in mixed-gender teams.

Cohen adopted several other recommendations by the Baker panel aimed at making basic training more rigorous and improving the quality of the sergeants and petty officers who supervise recruits. But he allowed the services to continue mixing men and women in the same small units and allowed them to be housed in the same barracks, with physical barriers and supervision.

The House version of the fiscal 1999 defense authorization bill (H Rept 105-532) included a requirement that men and women recruits be housed in separate buildings and trained in separate small units. The House debated the bill under a rule that prohibited any amendments dealing with the issue.

The version of the bill drafted by the Senate Armed Services Committee (S 2057 — S Rept 105-189) would have required only that current policies remain until a commission mandated by Congress in the fiscal 1998 defense authorization bill (PL 105-85) completed its review in 1999.

The issue arose on the Senate floor in a flurry of votes. But in the most sweeping decision, the Senate on June 25 rejected, 39-53, an amendment by Robert C. Byrd, D-W. Va., that would have barred the services from putting male and female recruits in the same small unit, or housing them in the

same building. Republicans supported the amendment, but not overwhelmingly, 31-21, while Democrats opposed it, 8-32 (ND 5-27, SD 3-5).

The conference report on the bill (H Rept 105-736) required only that sleeping areas for male and female recruits housed in the same building be separated by permanent walls. In an unusual move, the conference report also included a non-binding expression of the sense of the House that men and women should be trained in separate small units.

201 SANCTIONS

For months, Richard G. Lugar of Indiana, a senior Republican on the Senate Foreign Relations Committee, had been waging an often lonely and seemingly hopeless fight to slow down the use of overseas economic sanctions by Congress and the executive branch.

Despite the cost of sanctions to U.S. businesses and the restrictions they impose on the administration's diplomatic flexibility, many lawmakers came to believe sanctions are an effective and relatively painless way of exerting influence over other nations and the conduct of U.S foreign policy.

Lugar and influential Reps. Lee H. Hamilton, D-Ind., and Philip M. Crane, R-Ill., believed otherwise, arguing that while some sanctions might have merit, their cumulative weight had partially crippled American foreign policy, harmed U.S. exporters and had little substantive effect on the behavior of foreign countries. The three were supported by USA Engage, an influential coalition of businesses that had joined together expressly to overturn sanctions that critics contended cost the U.S. economy as much as $20 billion a year.

Lugar introduced a bill (S 1413) that would have slowed down the imposition of new sanctions by instituting a formal process under which lawmakers would have to weigh the costs and benefits of new restrictions on aid and trade. The bill also would have put a two-year limit on any sanctions unless Congress renewed them.

But their arguments made little headway until India and Pakistan tested nuclear weapons in May. The tests triggered automatic sanctions under the Arms Export Control Act, con-

tained in the 1994 State Department authorization bill (PL 103-236).

The Arms Export Control Act, originally sponsored by Sen. John Glenn, D-Ohio, cuts off non-humanitarian aid, bars the export of defense material and certain other technology, and halts U.S. credit and loan guarantees to non-nuclear nations that detonate nuclear weapons. It does not permit a presidential waiver.

The sanctions hit Pakistan, a poorer, smaller country, much harder than they hit India. U.S. farmers also were threatened when the Clinton administration decided that the law's credit ban would prevent the United States from guaranteeing bank loans on exports of wheat and other crops to Pakistan.

With U.S wheat farmers about to be squeezed out of a major wheat auction, the Senate unanimously approved legislation (S 2282) allowing India and Pakistan to continue to use guaranteed loans to import American food, fertilizer and other agricultural commodities.

Congress later allowed Clinton to waive sanctions against the two South Asian countries for a year.

But with farmers up in arms about the sanctions and other restrictions on trade, Lugar saw an opportunity to advance his broader bill. On July 15, he introduced it as an amendment to the agriculture appropriations bill (S 2159).

Lugar tried to use the pressure of the farm lobby to make his case, noting that the measure was backed by the American Farm Bureau Federation. "There is a passionate cry of farmers to take this action — that they are being thought of," Lugar said.

Lugar was opposed by Senate Foreign Relations Committee Chairman Jesse Helms, R-N.C., the co-author of a 1996 law (PL 104-114) that tightened the decades-old U.S. embargo on trade with Cuba, as well as other sanctions laws.

Helms argued that sanctions often were a crucial tool in addressing issues such as terrorism, drugs, and nuclear proliferation. "Obviously, sanctions are not always the answer," Helms said. "But we cannot escape the conclusion that sometimes they are the only answer."

Although a majority of GOP senators voted with him, Lugar's amendment was tabled (killed), 53-46: R 27-28; D 26-18 (ND 22-14, SD 4-4).

277 'PARTIAL BIRTH' ABORTION

Call it the showdown that never happened. For months, opponents of abortion rights had hoped to gain support in their effort to override President Clinton's veto of legislation (HR 1122) to ban a procedure they refer to as "partial birth" abortion.

Despite such efforts, the tally when they finally voted Sept. 18 was the same as in May 1997, when the Senate failed to override Clinton's veto by three votes. The outcome indicated that in a year when both sides had hoped to capitalize on the 25th anniversary of the Supreme Court's affirmation of the right to an abortion, neither side had gained ground, leaving the battle lines fairly static. The vote on passage was 64-36: R 51-4; D 13-32 (ND 9-28, SD 4-4).

Clinton vetoed the bill on Oct. 10, 1997, because he said it did not provide exceptions to permit the procedure when necessary to protect a woman's health. Under the legislation, doctors who performed the abortion procedure could have been sentenced to two years in prison and could have faced fines and lawsuits for civil damages. The measure would have exempted the woman from criminal penalties. The House voted, 296-132, on July 23 to override the veto.

Rick Santorum, R-Pa., the leader of the override effort, called the procedure "infanticide." Bill Frist, R-Tenn., a heart surgeon, said the procedure is dangerous for women and inhumane to the fetus.

Abortion-rights supporters such as Barbara Boxer, D-Calif., said the bill would "force doctors to make decisions that jeopardize women's health" because they could perform the procedure only to save the woman's life, not just to protect her health.

Carol Moseley-Braun, D-Ill., and others urged Congress to allow doctors and their patients — rather than legislators — to make decisions about abortion. Congress "does not have the right to practice medicine," said Moseley-Braun.

As in 1997, a bipartisan group of senators proposed an alternative they hoped would provide a middle ground. The backers said their proposal, which never received a floor vote, would have outlawed the procedure on a viable fetus — one that can live outside the womb — except when necessary to prevent "grievous injury" to the woman's physical health. Minority Leader Tom Daschle, D-S.D., proposed a similar measure in 1997, but it was rejected, 36-64.

Even though abortion opponents lost their battle to override Clinton's veto, John Ashcroft, R-Mo., said the issue will return. "This will not be the end of the debate," he said. "We will come back; we will vote again."

314 OMNIBUS APPROPRIATIONS

Senate leaders had hoped there would not be a recorded vote on the $500 billion-plus omnibus spending bill for fiscal 1999. Most senators had already left for home as congressional leaders and the White House hashed out a deal.

But the end product — which busted the 1997 balanced-budget agreement — doled out hundreds of hometown projects and served as the engine to drive unrelated bills into law. It was thus deemed either too important to pass without putting members on record — or too offensive, which was why several senators demanded a recorded vote.

For many fiscal conservatives, the Senate's final vote of the 105th Congress was a dismaying retreat from fiscal discipline, as President Clinton and congressional Democrats won billions of dollars in late-stage concessions from Republicans eager to go home and campaign.

Democrats were energized by the opportunity to trumpet their education priorities and portray a scandal-plagued Clinton as strong.

The bill (HR 4328 — PL 105-277) combined eight of the 13 annual spending bills. It contained $21 billion in "emergency" spending that was not subject to budget "caps" set in place under the 1997 balanced-budget law (PL 105-33). Some of this emergency spending, such as financing for the Bosnia peacekeeping mission and year 2000 computer fixes, had already been passed by the Senate. Veterans

such as Budget Committee Chairman Pete V. Domenici, R-N.M., and Appropriations Committee Chairman Ted Stevens, R-Alaska, felt the caps were too tight.

Senators generally are more permissive on spending than House members, and getting federal spending for one's state is part of a senator's job description. But the process that produced the bill — with decisions made by a small group of GOP leaders and administration aides — earned withering criticism from many, especially the top Democrat on the Appropriations Committee, Robert C. Byrd of West Virginia. He particularly bristled at the presence of administration aides in negotiating sessions to which he was excluded.

"Now someone said ... that making legislation is like making sausage," Byrd said. "Don't kid yourself. I have made sausage, and I can tell you that what we did this year was significantly more sloppy." After giving a classic stemwinder in which he said he would hold his nose and vote for the bill, Byrd decided that he had given such a good speech that he had changed his own mind. He voted "nay."

The Senate's No. 2 Republican, Don Nickles of Oklahoma, also was dismayed by the spending orgy and boycotted a Republican pep rally for the measure.

When Republicans failed to make gains in the Nov. 3 elections, disappointment among core voters over the omnibus bill was deemed one of the reasons.

GOP leaders had hoped to pass the bill by voice vote, but several dissatisfied senators called for a recorded vote to register their opposition. The bill passed easily, however, on Oct. 21 by a vote of 65-29: R 33-20; D 32-9 (ND 26-9, SD 6-0).

The Senate had been in this position before, most notably in 1996, when Clinton extracted almost $7 billion in late-stage talks over a comparable omnibus bill. Those talks occurred in the Senate Appropriations Committee offices in the Capitol, which prompted Stevens to declare he would never again permit White House aides in his office to help write bills. So the 1998 sessions took place in the suite of House Speaker Newt Gingrich, R-Ga.

The bills had been delayed by troubles in the House as well as by political gamesmanship by Senate Democrats, who on several occasions used the spending bills to force votes on their election year agenda.

The must-pass bill also became loaded with lawmakers' pet initiatives. It contained non-spending items that were of little interest to voters but that represented major accomplishments for lawmakers who had toiled for years on relatively obscure issues. For example, the bill reorganized U.S. foreign policy agencies, increased the number of visas for high-tech workers, curbed minors' access to pornography on the Internet and implemented the recently passed Chemical Weapons Convention. It included an extension of popular corporate tax breaks, such as the research and development tax credit.

Clinton won a $1.2 billion down payment on his initiative to subsidize the hiring of 100,000 new teachers, obtained his full $17.9 billion request for the International Monetary Fund and got many "emergency" spending items, including financing for the Bosnia peacekeeping mission and $5.9 billion in farm disaster aid. ◆

10 LINE-ITEM VETOES

The House set the stage Feb. 5 for the final act in Congress' experiment with the line-item veto as it restored funding for 38 military construction projects that President Clinton had killed in 1997 by exercising his short-lived but historic power.

The 1996 line-item veto law (PL 104-130) set forth a complicated mechanism for permitting the president to eliminate individual projects from spending bills that he otherwise had little choice but to sign. Under the law, which raised questions about the separation of power between the executive and legislative branches of government, the president's line-item vetoes would automatically take effect unless Congress passed a bill to void them.

The president could then veto that "disapproval" bill, which would require a two-thirds vote to overturn.

The fiscal 1998 military construction spending bill (PL 105-45) was the first appropriations bill to be presented to a president wielding the line-item veto. Clinton enraged members on both sides of the aisle by carving $287 million in projects from the low-profile bill. Most of the 38 projects were included in the Pentagon's long-term plans, though none were included in Clinton's fiscal 1998 budget. The White House later admitted that Clinton vetoed some projects based on faulty information about them, which added momentum to the drive to roll back the vetoes.

The House and Senate passed the disapproval bill (HR 2631) in November 1997, and Clinton promptly vetoed it just as the House adjourned. It was one of the few items in line for an early vote in 1998.

The House overrode Clinton's veto 347-69: R 197-23; D 149-46 (ND 100-41, SD 49-5); I 1-0. The Senate cleared the bill Feb. 25 in a 78-20 vote.

By the time Congress was ready to overturn the veto, much of Capitol Hill's trepidation over potential abuse of the new power had faded. When applying the veto to spending bills that came after the military construction bill, Clinton had used a much lighter hand.

The successful override came as a constitutional challenge to the 1996 law was poised to erase Clinton's 1997 vetoes anyway. The Supreme Court struck down the law in a 6-3 ruling in June.

95 TRANSPORTATION PROJECTS

House Transportation and Infrastructure Committee Chairman Bud Shuster, R-Pa., had patiently waited to reverse a bitter 1997 defeat at the hands of "deficit hawks."

On April 1, he got his chance. He cleared the way for passage of the $219 billion House version of the six-year surface transportation reauthorization bill (HR 2400) by defeating a campaign led by Lindsey Graham, R-S.C., to strip members' designated projects, known as

earmarks, from the bill. Graham's amendment would have deleted $9 billion in road projects and erased money for specified transit and bus projects.

For Shuster, it was a sweet victory. In May 1997, the House had scrapped by a two-vote margin his proposal to pare tax cuts and slice discretionary spending across the board in order to raise transportation spending by $12 billion over five years. A stalemate ensued, and Congress passed a temporary extension of funding (PL 105-130).

For Graham and many other members of the GOP Class of 1994, the vote was a clash between old-fashioned "pork barrel" politics and the budget-balancing spirit of the House GOP's "Contract With America."

Shuster turned the tide against less senior rivals with the help of economic projections showing a likely budget surplus. His bill called for a 40 percent increase in spending and required unspecified offsets because it exceeded the budget caps set in the balanced-budget deal by about $20 billion.

Shuster said the payoff would come in new jobs and economic growth. And he offered a tempting sweetener: a project selection process that guaranteed each member a shot at earmarking $15 million in highway funds.

At a GOP Conference meeting before the vote, Shuster was tacitly supported by House leaders, who hoped projects would help win elections. But House Budget Committee Chairman John R. Kasich, R-Ohio, spoke in opposition, arguing that the bill spent too much money. On the floor, Kasich offered an amendment to cut the federal gasoline tax from 18.3 cents to 7.4 cents a gallon over four years; it was defeated.

But the most pitched battle was fought over the project-killing Graham amendment. Shuster said the alternative to projects was to give money to states, and, he argued, "It is not reasonable to believe somehow there is a non-political, pure process back in the statehouses, as compared to the decisions made here." He suggested that Graham's opposition was "mystifying" because Graham had requested project funding in a letter.

Graham replied that he had decided to reject the $15 million for his district. He said the bill made a "sham" of the balanced-budget agreement.

Bob Inglis, R-S.C., summed up the feelings of many: "This is probably the most embarrassing night that I have ever spent in this Congress. We came here to change things, and we are not. We are participating in the big old trough that has characterized this place in the past."

In the end, Shuster won big. The final vote on the Graham amendment was 79-337: R 67-152; D 12-184 (ND 6-137, SD 6-47); I 0-1.

133 AFFIRMATIVE ACTION

The Republican Party has been deeply divided about whether to push for elimination of race- or sex-based preferences in education and hiring. From presidential elections to House campaigns, the GOP has been unable to reconcile its objection to what some term special treatment with a political need to reach out to women and minorities.

The House GOP leadership decided to support an amendment to the Higher Education Act reauthorization (HR 6) by Frank Riggs of California that would have eliminated affirmative action at public colleges and universities.

The Riggs amendment, modeled after California's 1996 Proposition 209, would have ended admissions preferences based on race, sex, ethnicity or national origin. "I believe we must focus on equality of opportunity in this country, not mandate equality of results," Riggs said.

Rather than serving to make affirmative action a defining issue between the Republican and Democratic parties, however, the amendment exposed internal fissures within the GOP. It was rejected by a vote of 171-249: R: 166-55; D: 5-193 (ND 2-143; SD 3-50); I: 0-1.

House Republican leaders voted for the amendment, but in a move that likely ensured its demise, J.C. Watts of Oklahoma, the House's only African-American Republican, joined John Lewis, D-Ga., a noted civil rights leader, in a letter to colleagues urging them to vote against the amendment.

Top Democrats spoke out against the measure. "This amendment would travel us down the retrograde road of racial divisiveness," said Minority Leader Richard A. Gephardt, D-Mo.

The House on April 1 defeated a similar amendment by Marge Roukema, R-N.J., to the surface transportation reauthorization bill (HR 2400) that would have softened requirements that the Transportation Department use female- or minority-owned businesses for 10 percent of construction projects.

151 BANKING

With the securities and insurance industries pressuring Congress to take another run at overhauling Depression-era financial services laws, House Republican leaders launched an all-out effort May 13 to pass a bill that would allow cross-ownership of banks, brokerages and insurance firms.

Speaker Newt Gingrich, R-Ga., and GOP Conference Chairman John A. Boehner of Ohio, the House leaders most active in crafting the bill (HR 10), knew that without their pressure, the measure would never make it past strong opposition from all but the largest banks. That opposition had contributed to a hasty decision to pull the bill from floor consideration in late March, after it became clear that the legislation, then attached to a credit union expansion measure (HR 1151), would not pass.

History was also against them: The House had never passed a bill to tear down the 1933 Glass-Steagall Act and subsequent laws aimed at keeping securities and insurance separate from banking.

Because the House had not considered a measure like HR 10 since 1991 and had never passed one, many members found themselves faced with a complex bill they did not fully understand. In addition, many banks lobbied hard against the measure, and the Clinton administration expressed concern about core provisions.

As the voting began May 13, Republican leaders appeared uncertain what the final outcome would be. With the regular 15-minute voting period coming to a close, a defeat seemed imminent, as "nays" outnumbered "yeas."

But when the deficit reached more than a dozen votes, Gingrich emerged and began methodically working the GOP side of the chamber, persuading members one by one to support the measure. After talking to Gingrich,

several Republicans went to the well to cast an "yea" vote or to change their vote from "nay" to "yea."

Among the last to switch were four Florida Republicans — Michael Bilirakis, Dan Miller, Cliff Stearns and Dave Weldon — leading to speculation that Gingrich had promised benefits for the Sunshine State. But members and lobbyists said the four did not appear to receive any special guarantees. Their conversions brought the "yeas" and "nays" to a tie, until Connecticut Democrat Jim Maloney switched his vote from "yea" to "nay."

Then Gingrich called on Education Committee Chairman Bill Goodling, R-Pa., a moderate facing a tight election, to cast the deciding vote. Goodling had stood near the well for several minutes holding both a red "nay" card and a green "yea" card. He cast the deciding "yea" vote. The vote was 214-213: R 153-73, D 61-139 (ND 47-100, SD 14-39), I 0-1.

Opponents scoffed at the one-vote victory, saying the bill was as good as dead because Senate Banking Committee Chairman Alfonse M. D'Amato, R-N.Y., had pledged to bring it up only if it received broad bipartisan support in the House.

But supporters said the vote was nothing short of historic. Given the House's history of refusing to even bring such bills to the floor, "a one-vote victory looks like a landslide," Boehner said.

Despite skepticism that the vote would spur Senate action on the bill, D'Amato — facing a tough re-election battle he would eventually lose — moved the measure through his committee. It eventually died on the Senate floor, as conservatives Phil Gramm, R-Texas, and Richard C. Shelby, R-Ala., held it up, demanding changes to community investment provisions.

188 FOOD STAMPS FOR LEGAL IMMIGRANTS

Even before he signed a broad welfare overhaul (PL 104-193) in August 1996, President Clinton warned that he would seek to reverse provisions of the measure that eliminated federal benefits to legal immigrants.

In the 1997 budget law (PL 105-33), Congress restored disability aid to legal immigrants. This year, Republicans and the White House sparred over Clinton's request to re-instate food stamps.

The White House insisted that legislation (S 1150) to create new mandatory spending programs for agriculture research also include funding to restore nutrition aid to many of the 935,000 legal immigrants dropped from the food stamp rolls under the welfare law.

The White House and Democrats chose the research bill as their vehicle in part because the agriculture program was to be funded by reducing federal payments to states to administer the food stamp program.

The initial Senate version of the bill focused on agriculture research. After Democrats and the White House weighed in, House and Senate negotiators worked out a conference report (H Rept 105-492) that included $818 million over five years to restore food stamps to elderly and disabled legal immigrants who were in the country when the welfare law was signed, as well as children under age 18.

Overall, the legislation would restore benefits to an estimated 250,000 legal immigrants. The conference report included $600 million for agriculture research programs and $1 billion in mandatory crop insurance funding over five years.

Sen. Phil Gramm, R-Texas, held up the consideration of the measure for weeks. When it finally got to the Senate floor on May 12, the bill passed by a vote of 92-8.

In the House, a determined group of conservatives, led by Majority Leader Dick Armey, R-Texas, opposed restoration of food stamp benefits. Despite a deteriorating farm economy, some lawmakers also opposed the agriculture spending.

When the bill came to the House floor on May 22, Republican leaders brought it up under a rule that would have automatically stripped the food stamp provisions. Nearly 100 Republicans voted against the rule, which was defeated 120-289: R 118-98; D 2-190 (ND 1-140, SD 1-50); I 0-1.

The defeat of the rule marked a turning point. With the House at an impasse, farm-state lawmakers were forced to go home for the Memorial Day recess without the promised agriculture and food stamp legislation.

Under pressure from their rank and file, House GOP leaders were forced to stage a quick political turnabout. The House took up the bill again June 4 under a rule that protected the immigrant provisions. The conference report passed, 364-50, with Armey among those voting yea.

In the weeks that followed, Republicans also backed off their opposition to expanding aid to farmers affected by drought and falling prices. Congress ultimately approved a fiscal 1998 omnibus spending bill (105-277) that included nearly $6 billion in emergency agriculture aid.

290 CONTRACEPTIVE COVERAGE

For years, abortion rights supporters have pushed unsuccessfully to require health plans that cover prescription drugs to also cover contraceptives.

Rep. Nita M. Lowey, D-N.Y., scored a partial victory on that issue as part of the House debate over legislation (HR 4104) to fund the Treasury Department, Postal Service and general government spending for fiscal 1999.

After several attempts, Lowey pushed through an amendment requiring health care plans for federal workers to provide coverage for contraceptives if they also cover other prescription drugs. The vote, which splintered Republicans and Democrats, illustrated that the GOP may have more flexibility than in previous years on family planning issues. It also provided lawmakers with one of the year's few floor votes on the politically sensitive topic.

Before that victory, however, Lowey had to fend off attacks from several abortion rights opponents.

First, Todd Tiahrt, R-Kan., succeeded in striking Lowey's contraceptive language, which had been inserted into the legislation in committee, because it sought to legislate on an appropriations bill. Since the Treasury-Postal measure had been brought to the House floor under a rule that protected only one provision in the bill — language to block an annual cost of living increase for members of Congress — measures such as Lowey's were left vulnerable to deletion.

Tiahrt and Christopher H. Smith, R-N.J., one of Congress' most vocal

abortion opponents, objected to federal funding for contraceptives. Smith contended that some of them can be used to chemically induce abortions.

But Democrats, led by Lowey, outmaneuvered Smith and his allies, scoring a surprising victory when they returned to the floor with a slightly reworded version of the amendment. The new language barred federal funds from being used to renew contracts with health care plans for federal employees that provide coverage for prescription drugs but do not include coverage for contraceptives. That new language made the amendment in line with House rules, which allow for limitations on how money is spent. Lowey also added language to exempt five health care plans with a religious orientation that opposed her amendment.

The vote on passage was 224-198: R 48-177; D 175-21 (ND 130-17, SD 45-4); I 1-0.

Smith then countered with an amendment seeking to bar the use of contraceptives that chemically induce abortions. Lowey charged that Smith was trying to outlaw funding for all contraceptives.

"The gentleman from New Jersey is saying to every woman who may take a birth control pill or use another one of the five accepted methods of contraception that they are abortionists," Lowey said, to applause from many female lawmakers. Smith's amendment was rejected, 198-222.

296 PUBLIC HOUSING OVERHAUL

Twice in two years the House and Senate had passed measures to overhaul the nation's public housing system as part of the GOP's effort to remake government social programs.

So when House Banking and Financial Services Committee Chairman Jim Leach, R-Iowa, and Rick A. Lazio, R-N.Y., chairman of the committee's housing panel, appealed to Republican leaders to attach their bill (HR 2) to the fiscal 1999 spending measure for housing, veterans, and science programs, they were given a chance to make their case on the House floor.

On July 17, Leach and Lazio offered HR 2 as an amendment to the spending bill (HR 4194) and argued that a ride on the appropriations measure of-

fered the best chance for their bill to become law.

Lazio and his Senate counterpart, Housing Subcommittee Chairman Connie Mack, R-Fla., had not been able to agree on the details of a bill, despite consensus on broad concepts, during more than three years of negotiating. Both chambers' bills sought to transfer block grants and most operating decisions to local authorities. Both aimed to allow authorities to break up welfare dependence in housing projects by enticing higher-income tenants. But Lazio and Mack could not agree on the specific number of units to reserve for the very poor, nor on a handful of other issues.

Leach and Lazio believed that attaching the measure to the spending bill would rejuvenate talks and provide an extra incentive for another principal, Housing and Urban Development (HUD) Secretary Andrew M. Cuomo, to negotiate.

But the amendment was not without detractors. Both the chairman and ranking Democrat on the VA-HUD Appropriations Subcommittee vociferously opposed joining the bills, saying that attaching the 400-page bill made a mockery of House rules prohibiting authorization provisions on spending legislation.

Ranking Democrat Louis Stokes of Ohio abandoned his usual reserved manner and complained that the Banking Committee had "not been able to do their job. This year, they seem to be admitting defeat earlier than usual."

Not all Banking panel members wanted to combine the housing measure and spending bill. The panel's ranking Democrat, John J. LaFalce of New York, and top Housing Subcommittee Democrat Joseph P. Kennedy II of Massachusetts argued that Lazio and Leach should consent to convene a separate conference on HR 2 and the Senate housing overhaul measure (S 462).

Kennedy said Republicans were trying to "jam" the bill "down the throat of the administration." Cuomo released a statement calling HR 2 "repugnant."

Nonetheless, the House voted to attach HR 2 to the spending measure. The vote was 230-181: R 215-4; D 15-176 (ND 8-136, SD 7-40); I 0-1.

As Leach and Lazio had predicted, pressure to complete work on the spending bill eventually forced a com-

promise. The final version was more moderate than the House bill, reserving more of public and subsidized housing for those with the lowest incomes, but it contained elements of the House and Senate bills and the administration's proposals.

339 MANAGED CARE REGULATIONS

Trying to wrest momentum away from Democrats on the politically explosive issue of regulating managed health care was no easy task for the GOP, especially for House Republicans eager to gain cover on the issue before the fall elections.

The solution came in the form of a package of changes developed by a House Republican task force after meeting for months behind closed doors. The group produced a bill (HR 4250) that allowed GOP members to say they had supported a managed care overhaul. But it split the House, mostly along party lines, and provided a glimpse of where members stood on one of the most controversial issues of the year. The White House threatened a veto.

The task force, led by Dennis Hastert, R-Ill., included many of the patient protections that both sides of the managed care debate had endorsed, such as giving broader rights to emergency-room care and allowing patients to appeal coverage decisions to an outside panel. The GOP bill would not, however, have allowed consumers in managed care plans that are exempt from state regulation to sue their health plans under state laws, a key element of a competing Democratic bill.

Commerce Committee Chairman Thomas J. Bliley Jr., R-Va., a member of the task force, said the proposal would put "patients back in the driver's seat, where they belong." Minority Leader Richard A. Gephardt, D-Mo., dismissed the bill as "rhetoric but not a remedy."

Gephardt and other Democrats blasted the GOP leadership for not holding committee hearings on the proposal, but instead taking it directly to the House floor for a vote. "This whole thing is designed not to have any discussion," said Jim McDermott, D-Wash.

GOP leaders, citing the fact that many chairman of committees with jurisdiction for health care were on the

task force, said such hearings were unnecessary. They also charged that Democrats would attempt to "demonize" the GOP managed care bill. "We knew early on that moving it through the committee process was not practical," said GOP Conference Chairman John A. Boehner, R-Ohio.

The administration said the legislation was "seriously flawed." A statement from the Office of Management and Budget said the bill would cover too few people, provide too few patient protections and "contains unnecessary and irrelevant provisions that undermine the chances for a bipartisan agreement on a patients' bill of rights."

Despite such objections, the bill passed July 24. The vote was 216-210: R 213-12; D 3-197 (ND 2-147, SD 1-50); I 0-1.

Shortly before that vote, the House turned back a Democratic alternative (HR 3605) on a tally of 212-217. Supporters of Democratic bill, including the American Medical Association and a host of provider and consumer groups, said it would have given patients broader rights than the GOP plan, such as the ability to sue their plans for damages. Republicans criticized the Democratic plan as a costly creation of the trial lawyers' lobby.

Ten Republicans, however, broke with the GOP leadership to endorse the Democrats' measure, including plastic surgeon Greg Ganske, R-Iowa.

405 CAMPAIGN FINANCE OVERHAUL

The House vote on Aug. 6 to overhaul campaign finance laws marked the first time in six years that either chamber had acted to rewrite the laws.

Although the effort died in the Senate, the House's action raised the prospect that Congress was inching closer to its first significant revision of campaign finance laws in nearly 20 years.

House passage of HR 2183 came only after an arduous process. Its advocates endured numerous attempts by GOP leaders to block or delay its passage over several months.

From the outset, the leading vehicle of overhaul advocates was a bipartisan measure (HR 3526), sponsored by Christopher Shays, R-Conn., and Martin T. Meehan, D-Mass. It was based on a similar Senate plan (S 25) by John McCain, R-Ariz., and Russell D. Feingold, D-Wis.

The legislation would ban national parties from receiving or spending "soft money" — unlimited and largely unregulated donations to political parties. It also would set new restrictions on campaign-related expenditures by third-party groups.

GOP leaders initially squelched debate on campaign finance March 30 by prohibiting the Shays-Meehan measure from coming to the House floor. But the ploy only encouraged the bill's supporters to embrace a procedural device that would have let them debate a variety of campaign finance bills on their own terms.

GOP leaders finally relented to an open debate on the issue in May. But they made the bill open to dozens of amendments, then forced it to compete with 10 other substitute amendments to the underlying bill. Whichever of the 11 substitute amendments got the most votes — and at least a majority — would prevail.

A crowning moment for supporters of the Shays-Meehan measure came Aug. 3, when the House voted for their substitute amendment, 237-186. Fifty-one Republicans voted for the measure, outweighing the 11 Democrats who voted against it.

The relatively strong vote prompted the authors of several other substitute amendments to withdraw their measures.

The final hurdle was a substitute amendment by Asa Hutchinson, R-Ark., and Tom Allen, D-Maine, based on the so-called freshman bill.

The freshman bill would have taken a somewhat less aggressive stance against soft money and issue advocacy advertising. Its advocates said that approach gave the legislation a better chance of passing in the Senate and surviving a constitutional challenge.

GOP leaders toyed with embracing the freshman proposal to get the 238 votes needed to top — and topple — the Shays-Meehan bill. That prompted supporters of the proposal to elaborately praise the freshmen for their efforts but urge its defeat. The freshman measure ultimately failed, 147-222, with 61 members voting "present."

That cleared the way for final passage of the bill, amended along the lines of the Shays-Meehan proposal, by a vote of 252-179: R 61-164; D 190-15 (ND 142-9, SD 48-6); I 1-0.

Advocates of a campaign finance overhaul vowed afterward to push the Senate to act after the August recess.

McCain and Feingold tried to revive the issue in the Senate by attaching S 25 to the Interior appropriations bill (S 2237). But they fell eight votes short of cutting off debate on Sept. 10, 52-48. It marked the third time in less than a year that the Senate stymied overhaul advocates.

425 RELEASE OF STARR REPORT

Within the White House, the week of Sept. 7 must have felt like one of the lowest points of Bill Clinton's presidency. On Sept. 9, Independent Counsel Kenneth W. Starr sent a report to the House suggesting that Clinton be impeached. Two days later, the House voted to release the report to the public.

The report gave Starr's version of Clinton's affair with former intern Monica Lewinsky and subsequent events, and Clinton's representatives cautioned that it should be viewed as a one-sided document. But the vote on the resolution to release the report (H Res 525) signaled that Republicans, in their effort to impeach Clinton, were willing to accept Starr's allegations and move forward despite a lack of public support. The resolution was adopted by a vote of 363-63: R 224-0; D 138-63 (ND 102-46, SD 36-17); I 1-0.

However, rather than reading the salacious details of the Starr report as evidence of Clinton's immorality and lack of respect for laws, much of the public was repulsed by the fact that these details were released, polls showed. The vote also represented the last time GOP plans for investigating Clinton were able to pick up Democratic support.

No one in Congress had read the report before it was released, and many felt blindsided when they learned of its explicit descriptions of Clinton's liaisons with Lewinsky. The report was posted on the Internet and became the subject of voluminous media coverage. The report was lampooned as X-rated; numerous observers argued that the vote to release it would have been a vi-

olation of the Congress' own Communications Decency Act — a portion of the 1996 telecommunications overhaul (PL 104-104) bill limiting indecent content on the Internet that was declared unconstitutional by the Supreme Court. Starr and his prosecutors insisted the details were necessary to document Clinton's lies and efforts to get others to lie.

Supporting material, including a videotape of Clinton's Aug. 17 testimony before a grand jury, was released in subsequent weeks, after having been screened — and to some extent, redacted — by committee members.

When the dust cleared, the public was clearly still opposed to impeachment and vehemently objected to being subjected to all of the details of the relationship.

The fact that most Democrats joined in the vote was lost on the public. The most vocal Democrats were those on the Judiciary Committee who voted against the release, on the grounds it violated due process and basic fairness. Those Democrats who voted for the release generally declined to defend their vote, and in some cases expressed remorse.

The vote to release was a turning point in the Republican impeachment effort, one that Democrats say vividly demonstrated how out of step the GOP was with popular sentiment. And within days, bipartisan cooperation on impeachment began eroding. By the time a vote authorizing an impeachment inquiry was taken Oct. 8, the two parties had separated like oil and water.

460 SKILLED-WORKER VISAS

The House in 1998 was a major stumbling block for legislation designed to increase the number of skilled temporary workers allowed to immigrate to the United States.

While a bill (S 1723) increasing the number of so-called H-1B visas sailed through the Senate, an unlikely coalition of labor-backed Democrats and Republican immigration hardliners held up the House bill (HR 3736) for most of the year. But behind-the-scenes negotiating helped get the measure enacted.

The major turning point was House

passage Sept. 24, by a vote of 288-133: R 189-34; D 99-98 (ND 66-76; SD 33-22); I 0-1.

The vote represented a big success for a new lobby — the high-tech industry. It also represented a major departure from the anti-immigration policies pushed by House hard-liners in 1996. Since that year, Congress has voted to restore welfare benefits to legal immigrants, loosen requirements on immigrants waiting for permanent visas, and give partial or complete amnesty to a category of Central American refugees who came to America to escape civil wars in the 1980s.

The vote to expand the number of skilled immigrant visas was more than merely a retreat from previous policies. It was an affirmative decision to expand immigration, at least for skilled workers.

The vote was not the last chapter in the year's debate. With the House acting so late, a handful of senators was able to block action on a conference report. In the end, the measure was added to the omnibus spending package (HR 4328 — PL 105-277) passed at the end of the year. But the House vote was clearly the highest hurdle in a difficult year.

The legislation will increase the number of H-1B visas allotted each year from 65,000 to as many as 115,000. The measure was the principal 1998 legislative goal of a new lobby — high-tech companies.

At the beginning of the year, few lawmakers had given much thought to the issue of these visas. But by spring, companies such as Microsoft Corp., Sun Microsystems Inc. and Intel Corp. made them take notice. They persuasively argued that their phenomenal rates of growth would be stymied if they could not find enough programmers and other skilled workers. They implicitly threatened to take plants overseas if they could not get enough workers from overseas to come here.

But it was a difficult lobbying job. In the House Judiciary Committee's Immigration Subcommittee on April 30, Chairman Lamar Smith, R-Texas, a leader among immigration hawks, added two provisions the high-tech lobby found unacceptable. One would have required companies hoping to sponsor H-1B immigrants to show that they had gone to great lengths to

find American workers first. The second would have barred companies from using the H-1B program if they had laid off any workers with comparable skills.

The industry spent the summer trying to round up support from the GOP leadership and sympathetic senators in an effort to pressure Smith to relent. Shortly before the August recess, he agreed to a compromise that would keep the requirements, but apply them to only a certain percentage of companies.

The measure, however, was left to languish over the August recess after President Clinton objected. By late September, though, a new compromise — similar to Smith's bill — was developed. The revised bill passed with relatively little floor debate.

538 OMNIBUS APPROPRIATIONS

Republican leaders portrayed the massive, year-end omnibus spending bill as a win for their party and an inevitable result of divided government, but many in the rank and file saw it as an embarrassing retreat from GOP principles.

For Democrats, the vote — and behind-the-scenes negotiations that led up to it — provided a rejuvenating breather. They got to change the subject from impeachment to their election year agenda, especially education.

The vote capped a year of gridlock on the budget after President Clinton and congressional Republicans spent months talking past each other and trying to use the budget to score political points, mostly in vain. Action on most of the 13 annual appropriations bills for fiscal 1999 — the approximately one-third of the budget upon which Congress and Clinton must agree each year — slid past deadline, and eight of the measures were lumped together into an everything-but-the-kitchen-sink bill (HR 4328 — PL 105-277) that broke through budget targets set only a year earlier.

The eight bills had been slowed by numerous disagreements among Republicans, and between them and the White House.

Despite the impeachment inquiry hanging over his head, Clinton entered the talks with a strong hand. Ever since

Republicans took the political fallout for the 1995-96 partial government shutdowns and for a vetoed 1997 flood aid bill, Clinton had used veto threats to extract concessions from them on spending bills.

The talks started Oct. 7 but moved slowly as White House Chief of Staff Erskine Bowles, under pressure from Democrats in Congress, played hard ball. As negotiations dragged on, Democrats took delight in having a forum for their agenda for the election year.

Clinton won a $1.2 billion down payment on his initiative to subsidize the hiring of 100,000 new teachers, obtained his full $17.9 billion request for the International Monetary Fund, and got many "emergency" spending items, including financing for the Bosnia peacekeeping mission and $5.9 billion in farm disaster aid.

Such emergency spending did not count against budget "caps" set in place in 1997. By the time such add-ons were totaled — including GOP-sought money for drug interdiction, intelligence and missile defense — the emergency spending took a $21 billion bite from future budget surpluses.

Republican conservatives were appalled. "At a time when we are dealing with a weakened president . . . you would think that our leadership, who professed to be conservatives leading this revolution, could stand tough within that budget cap and stay true to the commitment that we . . . came here for in 1994," said Jon Christensen, R-Neb.

Democrats were generally pleased with the bill's spending provisions, but they railed against the chaotic process that produced the 16-inch thick, 40-pound, nearly 4,000- page measure. It was also filled with many parochial projects of the kind that Republicans had criticized under Democratic-controlled congresses.

House Speaker Newt Gingrich, R-Ga., fired back in an impassioned speech criticizing the "perfectionist caucus" in his own party, saying that concessions were necessary to obtain Clinton's signature. But the bill was far larger than it would have been had the 13 annual spending bills been negotiated individually.

Despite grumbling from junior GOP conservatives, the bill passed Oct. 20 by a vote of 333-95: R 162-64; D 170-31 (ND 120-26, SD 50-5); I 1-0.

After the agreement was sealed, Democrats and Republicans staged competing pep rallies. Clinton and the Democrats seemed happy while Republicans seemed to be putting on a brave face. The GOP chairmen of the Budget and Appropriations committees were notably absent.

543 IMPEACHMENT

By the time the House was ready to vote Dec. 19 to make Bill Clinton only the second president ever to be impeached, the environment had become surreal.

On the eve of the scheduled vote, Clinton had ordered a military strike against Iraq. That postponed debate for a day, enough time for Speaker-designate Robert L. Livingston, R-La., to publicly acknowledge that he, like Clinton, had been unfaithful to his wife.

When debate finally began Dec. 18 on the four articles of impeachment, nerves were raw. The articles, approved Dec. 11 and 12 by the House Judiciary Committee along party lines, accused the president of two counts of perjury, one count of obstruction of justice and one count of abuse of power.

Through it all, Democrats bitterly complained that the votes should be delayed until hostilities with Iraq ended. Their anger was increased by Republicans' move to block consideration of a censure resolution.

"To be spending the time of this House to smear our commander in chief when brave men and women are risking their lives for their country shocks the conscience," John Conyers Jr. of Michigan, the Judiciary Committee's ranking Democrat, said on the floor.

Then came the bombshell from Livingston that he would not serve as Speaker and would leave Congress — setting an example for Clinton to follow, he said.

"Infidelity — adultery — is not a public act, it's a private act, and the government, the Congress, has no business intruding into private acts," Judiciary Chairman Henry J. Hyde, R-Ill., said in closing debate. "But it is our business, it is our duty to observe, to characterize public acts by public officials. . . . And when you have a serial violator of the oath who is the chief law enforcement officer of the country — who appoints the judges and the Supreme Court, the attorney general — we have a problem."

The House adopted the first article, which accuses Clinton of lying to a grand jury about his affair with Monica Lewinsky, by a vote of 228-206: R 223-5; D 5-200 (ND 1-149, SD 4-51); I 0-1. A second count, accusing Clinton of obstructing justice, was also adopted, 221-212.

The two other recommended articles were rejected. ◆

	1	2	3	4	5	6
ALABAMA						
Sessions	Y	N	N	Y	Y	N
Shelby	Y	N	Y	Y	Y	N
ALASKA						
Murkowski	Y	N	Y	N	Y	N
Stevens	Y	N	Y	Y	Y	N
ARIZONA						
Kyl	Y	N	N	N	Y	N
McCain	Y	Y	Y	N	Y	Y
ARKANSAS						
Hutchinson	Y	N	Y	Y	N	N
Bumpers	N	Y	Y	Y	N	Y
CALIFORNIA						
Boxer	N	Y	Y	N	Y	Y
Feinstein	N	Y	Y	Y	Y	Y
COLORADO						
Allard	Y	N	N	N	Y	N
Campbell	N	N	N	Y	Y	N
CONNECTICUT						
Dodd	N	Y	Y	N	Y	Y
Lieberman	N	Y	Y	N	Y	Y
DELAWARE						
Roth	N	N	Y	N	Y	Y
Biden	N	Y	Y	N	N	Y
FLORIDA						
Mack	N	N	N	N	Y	N
Graham	N	Y	Y	N	Y	Y
GEORGIA						
Coverdell	Y	N	N	N	Y	N
Cleland	N	Y	Y	N	Y	Y
HAWAII						
Akaka	N	Y	Y	N	N	Y
Inouye	N	Y	Y	N	Y	Y
IDAHO						
Craig	Y	N	Y	N	Y	N
Kempthorne	Y	N	Y	Y	Y	N
ILLINOIS						
Durbin	N	Y	Y	N	N	Y
Moseley-Braun	N	Y	Y	N	N	Y
INDIANA						
Coats	Y	N	Y	N	Y	N
Lugar	N	N	Y	N	Y	N

	1	2	3	4	5	6
IOWA						
Grassley	Y	N	Y	N	Y	Y
Harkin	N	?	Y	Y	N	Y
KANSAS						
Brownback	Y	N	Y	N	Y	N
Roberts	Y	N	Y	Y	Y	N
KENTUCKY						
McConnell	Y	N	Y	N	Y	N
Ford	N	Y	Y	N	Y	N
LOUISIANA						
Breaux	N	Y	Y	N	Y	Y
Landrieu	N	Y	Y	Y	Y	Y
MAINE						
Collins	N	Y	Y	N	Y	Y
Snowe	N	Y	Y	Y	Y	Y
MARYLAND						
Mikulski	N	Y	Y	N	N	Y
Sarbanes	N	Y	Y	N	N	Y
MASSACHUSETTS						
Kennedy	N	Y	Y	N	N	Y
Kerry	N	Y	Y	N	N	Y
MICHIGAN						
Abraham	Y	N	N	N	Y	Y
Levin	?	Y	Y	N	N	Y
MINNESOTA						
Grams	Y	N	Y	N	Y	N
Wellstone	N	Y	N	Y	N	Y
MISSISSIPPI						
Cochran	Y	N	Y	N	Y	N
Lott	Y	N	Y	N	Y	N
MISSOURI						
Ashcroft	Y	N	Y	N	Y	N
Bond	Y	N	Y	Y	Y	N
MONTANA						
Burns	Y	N	Y	N	Y	N
Baucus	N	Y	Y	N	Y	Y
NEBRASKA						
Hagel	Y	N	Y	N	Y	N
Kerrey	N	Y	Y	N	Y	Y
NEVADA						
Bryan	–	Y	Y	N	Y	Y
Reid	?	Y	Y	Y	Y	Y

	1	2	3	4	5	6
NEW HAMPSHIRE						
Gregg	Y	N	Y	N	Y	Y
Smith	Y	N	N	Y	Y	N
NEW JERSEY						
Lautenberg	N	Y	Y	N	Y	Y
Torricelli	N	Y	Y	Y	N	Y
NEW MEXICO						
Domenici	Y	N	Y	N	Y	N
Bingaman	N	Y	Y	Y	Y	Y
NEW YORK						
D'Amato	Y	N	Y	N	?	Y
Moynihan	N	Y	Y	N	Y	Y
NORTH CAROLINA						
Faircloth	Y	N	N	Y	?	N
Helms	Y	N	N	Y	N	N
NORTH DAKOTA						
Conrad	N	Y	Y	Y	Y	Y
Dorgan	N	Y	Y	Y	Y	Y
OHIO						
DeWine	Y	N	Y	N	Y	Y
Glenn	N	Y	Y	N	N	Y
OKLAHOMA						
Inhofe	Y	N	N	Y	Y	N
Nickles	Y	N	N	Y	Y	N
OREGON						
Smith	N	N	Y	N	Y	Y
Wyden	N	Y	Y	Y	Y	Y
PENNSYLVANIA						
Santorum	Y	N	Y	N	Y	N
Specter	N	Y	Y	Y	Y	?
RHODE ISLAND						
Chafee	N	Y	Y	N	Y	Y
Reed	N	Y	Y	Y	Y	Y
SOUTH CAROLINA						
Thurmond	N	N	Y	N	Y	N
Hollings	N	Y	Y	Y	Y	Y
SOUTH DAKOTA						
Daschle	N	Y	Y	N	Y	Y
Johnson	N	Y	Y	N	Y	Y
TENNESSEE						
Frist	Y	N	Y	N	Y	Y
Thompson	Y	Y	N	N	Y	N

	1	2	3	4	5	6
TEXAS						
Gramm	Y	N	Y	N	Y	N
Hutchison	Y	N	Y	Y	Y	N
UTAH						
Bennett	N	N	N	Y	N	Y
Hatch	Y	N	Y	N	Y	N
VERMONT						
Jeffords	N	Y	Y	Y	Y	Y
Leahy	N	Y	Y	Y	Y	Y
VIRGINIA						
Warner	?	N	Y	Y	Y	N
Robb	N	Y	Y	N	Y	N
WASHINGTON						
Gorton	Y	N	Y	N	Y	N
Murray	N	Y	Y	Y	Y	Y
WEST VIRGINIA						
Byrd	N	Y	Y	Y	N	Y
Rockefeller	N	Y	Y	N	N	Y
WISCONSIN						
Feingold	N	Y	N	N	N	Y
Kohl	N	Y	Y	Y	Y	Y
WYOMING						
Enzi	Y	N	Y	Y	Y	N
Thomas	Y	N	Y	N	N	N

Key

Y	Voted for (yea).
#	Paired for.
+	Announced for.
N	Voted against (nay).
X	Paired against.
–	Announced against.
P	Voted "present."
C	Voted "present" to avoid possible conflict of interest.
?	Did not vote or otherwise make a position known.

Democrats   *Republicans*

ND Northern Democrats   SD Southern Democrats

Southern states - Ala., Ark., Fla., Ga., Ky., La., Miss., N.C., Okla., S.C., Tenn., Texas, Va.

Following are Senate votes from 1998 selected by Congressional Quarterly as key votes. Original vote numbers are in parentheses.

1. S 1601. Human Cloning Ban. Motion to invoke cloture (thus limiting debate) on the motion to proceed to the bill banning creation of a human embryo through cloning. Motion rejected 42-54: R 42-12; D 0-42 (ND 0-34, SD 0-8). Feb. 11, 1998. Three-fifths of the total Senate (60) is required to invoke cloture. (*Senate vote 10*)

2. S 1663. Campaign Finance Overhaul. Motion to invoke cloture (thus limiting debate) on the McCain, R-Ariz., substitute amendment that would revise financing of federal political campaigns. Motion rejected 51-48: R 7-48; D 44-0 (ND 36-0, SD 8-0). Feb. 26, 1998. Three-fifths of the total Senate (60) is required to invoke cloture. (*Senate vote 16*)

3. S 1768. IMF Funding. McConnell, R-Ky., amendment to provide $17.9 billion for the International Monetary Fund, including $3.4 billion for a new program aimed at preventing global financial crises and $14.5 billion for the U.S. "quota" to the international agency. The amendment would prohibit release of the quota funds unless the IMF agrees to certain conditions, including restricting aid to nations that do not conform to trade agreements. Adopted 84-16: R 41-14; D 43-2 (ND 35-2, SD 8-0). March 26, 1998. (*Senate vote 44*)

4. S 1768. NATO Expansion. Warner, R-Va., amendment to add language to the resolution of ratification that would require the president to certify to Congress that the United States will not support any further NATO expansion for three years from the date Poland, Hun-

gary and the Czech Republic join the alliance. Rejected 41-59: R 24-31; D 17-28 (ND 15-22, SD 2-6). April 30, 1998. A "nay" was a vote in support of the president's position. (*Senate vote 112*)

5. S 1723. Skilled-Worker Visas. Passage of the bill to increase the number of so-called H-1B visas, which allow highly skilled immigrants to work in the United States for six years, from the current cap of 65,000 per year to 95,000 for the remainder of fiscal 1998. The measure also would increase the cap on the visas to 105,000 for fiscal 1999 and 115,000 for the following three fiscal years, but would sunset the cap to its original level at the end of fiscal 2002. The bill also would increase the authorization for certain educational grants, authorize funding for an Internet job bank and authorize funding to provide training opportunities in information technology. Passed 78-20: R 51-2; D 27-18 (ND 20-17, SD 7-1). May 18, 1998. A "nay" was a vote in support of the president's position. (*Senate vote 141*)

6. S 1415. Tobacco Restrictions. Motion to invoke cloture (thus limiting debate) on the modified Senate Commerce, Science and Transportation Committee substitute amendment to the bill to increase tobacco restrictions. The substitute would require the tobacco industry to pay $516 billion over 25 years for anti-smoking, education and research programs; raise taxes on cigarettes by $1.10 per pack over five years; and impose penalties on the tobacco industry if youth smoking does not decrease by 60 percent over 10 years. Motion rejected 57-42: R 14-40; D 43-2 (ND 37-0, SD 6-2). June 17, 1998. Three-fifths of the total Senate (60) is required to invoke cloture. A "yea" was a vote in support of the president's position. (*Senate vote 161*)

	7	8	9	10	11
ALABAMA					
Sessions	Y	Y	N	Y	N
Shelby	Y	Y	Y	Y	Y
ALASKA					
Murkowski	Y	Y	N	Y	?
Stevens	Y	Y	Y	Y	Y
ARIZONA					
Kyl	Y	Y	Y	Y	N
McCain	Y	N	Y	Y	N
ARKANSAS					
Hutchinson	Y	?	Y	Y	Y
Bumpers	N	Y	N	N	?
CALIFORNIA					
Boxer	N	N	Y	N	Y
Feinstein	Y	N	N	N	Y
COLORADO					
Allard	Y	N	N	Y	N
Campbell	Y	Y	Y	Y	Y
CONNECTICUT					
Dodd	N	N	N	N	Y
Lieberman	Y	N	Y	N	Y
DELAWARE					
Roth	Y	?	N	Y	Y
Biden	Y	N	N	Y	Y
FLORIDA					
Mack	Y	N	Y	N	Y
Graham	N	N	Y	N	Y
GEORGIA					
Coverdell	Y	Y	Y	Y	Y
Cleland	Y	N	N	N	Y
HAWAII					
Akaka	?	?	Y	N	Y
Inouye	N	Y	Y	N	?
IDAHO					
Craig	Y	Y	N	Y	Y
Kempthorne	Y	N	N	Y	Y
ILLINOIS					
Durbin	N	N	N	N	Y
Moseley-Braun	N	N	N	N	Y
INDIANA					
Coats	Y	Y	N	Y	N
Lugar	Y	N	N	Y	N

	7	8	9	10	11
IOWA					
Grassley	Y	Y	Y	Y	N
Harkin	N	N	Y	N	Y
KANSAS					
Brownback	Y	Y	N	Y	Y
Roberts	Y	Y	N	Y	Y
KENTUCKY					
McConnell	Y	Y	Y	Y	Y
Ford	N	Y	Y	Y	Y
LOUISIANA					
Breaux	Y	N	Y	Y	Y
Landrieu	N	N	N	Y	Y
MAINE					
Collins	Y	N	Y	N	N
Snowe	Y	N	Y	N	N
MARYLAND					
Mikulski	N	N	Y	N	Y
Sarbanes	N	N	Y	N	Y
MASSACHUSETTS					
Kennedy	N	N	Y	N	Y
Kerry	N	N	Y	N	Y
MICHIGAN					
Abraham	Y	Y	Y	Y	Y
Levin	N	N	Y	N	N
MINNESOTA					
Grams	Y	Y	N	Y	N
Wellstone	N	N	Y	N	N
MISSISSIPPI					
Cochran	Y	N	N	Y	Y
Lott	Y	Y	Y	Y	Y
MISSOURI					
Ashcroft	Y	Y	Y	Y	N
Bond	Y	N	N	Y	N
MONTANA					
Burns	Y	Y	N	Y	Y
Baucus	?	?	N	N	N
NEBRASKA					
Hagel	Y	N	N	Y	N
Kerrey	N	N	N	N	N
NEVADA					
Bryan	N	N	Y	N	Y
Reid	N	N	Y	N	Y

	7	8	9	10	11
NEW HAMPSHIRE					
Gregg	Y	Y	N	Y	Y
Smith	Y	Y	Y	Y	N
NEW JERSEY					
Lautenberg	N	N	Y	N	Y
Torricelli	Y	Y	Y	N	Y
NEW MEXICO					
Domenici	+	N	N	Y	Y
Bingaman	N	N	Y	N	Y
NEW YORK					
D'Amato	Y	N	Y	Y	Y
Moynihan	N	Y	N	Y	N
NORTH CAROLINA					
Faircloth	Y	Y	Y	Y	Y
Helms	Y	Y	Y	Y	?
NORTH DAKOTA					
Conrad	N	Y	N	Y	Y
Dorgan	N	N	N	Y	Y
OHIO					
DeWine	Y	Y	Y	Y	Y
Glenn	N	?	?	N	?
OKLAHOMA					
Inhofe	Y	Y	Y	Y	N
Nickles	Y	Y	Y	Y	Y
OREGON					
Smith	Y	N	N	Y	Y
Wyden	N	–	Y	N	Y
PENNSYLVANIA					
Santorum	Y	Y	N	Y	Y
Specter	?	?	Y	Y	N
RHODE ISLAND					
Chafee	N	N	N	N	Y
Reed	N	N	Y	N	Y
SOUTH CAROLINA					
Thurmond	Y	N	Y	Y	Y
Hollings	N	Y	Y	Y	Y
SOUTH DAKOTA					
Daschle	N	N	N	Y	Y
Johnson	N	N	N	Y	Y
TENNESSEE					
Frist	Y	Y	N	Y	Y
Thompson	Y	N	Y	Y	Y

Key

Y	Voted for (yea).
#	Paired for.
+	Announced for.
N	Voted against (nay).
X	Paired against.
–	Announced against.
P	Voted "present."
C	Voted "present" to avoid possible conflict of interest.
?	Did not vote or otherwise make a position known.

Democrats	*Republicans*

	7	8	9	10	11
TEXAS					
Gramm	Y	N	N	Y	N
Hutchison	Y	N	N	Y	Y
UTAH					
Bennett	Y	Y	Y	Y	Y
Hatch	Y	Y	Y	Y	Y
VERMONT					
Jeffords	N	N	N	N	Y
Leahy	N	N	Y	N	Y
VIRGINIA					
Warner	Y	N	N	Y	N
Robb	N	N	N	N	N
WASHINGTON					
Gorton	Y	Y	N	Y	N
Murray	N	N	Y	N	Y
WEST VIRGINIA					
Byrd	Y	Y	N	Y	N
Rockefeller	?	?	N	N	Y
WISCONSIN					
Feingold	N	N	Y	N	N
Kohl	Y	N	Y	N	N
WYOMING					
Enzi	Y	Y	N	Y	N
Thomas	Y	N	N	Y	N

ND Northern Democrats   SD Southern Democrats

Southern states - Ala., Ark., Fla., Ga., Ky., La., Miss., N.C., Okla., S.C., Tenn., Texas, Va.

7. HR 2646. Education Savings Accounts. Adoption of the conference report on the bill to allow individuals to contribute up to $2,000 a year of after-tax funds in tax-sheltered savings accounts that may be used to pay for educational expenses. Adopted (thus cleared for the president) 59-36: R 51-2; D 8-34 (ND 6-28, SD 2-6). June 24, 1998. A "nay" was a vote in support of the president's position. (*Senate vote 169*)

8. S 2057. Same-Sex Military Training. Byrd, D-W.Va., amendment to the Gramm, R-Texas, amendment. The Byrd amendment would prohibit the armed forces from housing male and female recruits in the same barracks and would prohibit them from conducting gender-integrated basic training. The Gramm amendment would remove restrictions on recipients of Naval Reserve Officers' Training Corps scholarships. Rejected 39-53: R 31-21; D 8-32 (ND 5-27, SD 3-5). June 25, 1998. (Subsequently, the Gramm amendment was adopted by voice vote.) A "nay" was a vote in support of the president's position. (*Senate vote 180*)

9. S 2159. Economic Sanctions. Stevens, R-Alaska, motion to table (kill) the Lugar, R-Ind., amendment that would revise the process the president and Congress use to impose unilateral economic sanctions by establishing guidelines for future sanctions and setting up procedures for consideration and implementation of sanctions proposals. The amendment would prohibit the president from implementing any unilateral economic sanction without 45 days' notice, and it would express the sense of Congress that all future unilateral sanctions end within two years of their enactment unless extended by law. Motion agreed to 53-46: R 27-28; D 26-18

(ND 22-14, SD 4-4). July 15, 1998. (*Senate vote 201*)

10. HR 1122. "Partial-Birth" Abortion. Passage, over President Clinton's Oct. 10, 1997, veto, of the bill to ban a certain late-term abortion procedure, in which the physician partially delivers the fetus before completing the abortion. Anyone convicted of performing such an abortion would be subject to a fine and up to two years in prison. Rejected 64-36: R 51-4; D 13-32 (ND 9-28, SD 4-4). Sept. 18, 1998. A two-thirds majority of those present and voting (67 in this case) of both houses is required to override a veto. A "nay" was a vote in support of the president's position. (*Senate vote 277*)

11. HR 4328. Fiscal 1999 Omnibus Appropriations. Adoption of the conference report on the bill to provide almost $500 billion in new budget authority for those Cabinet departments and federal agencies whose fiscal 1999 appropriations bills were never enacted. The measure incorporates eight previously separate appropriations bills: Labor-HHS-Education, Interior, Treasury-Postal, Foreign Operations, Commerce-Justice-State, District of Columbia, Agriculture and Transportation. In addition, the bill provides $20.8 billion in "emergency" supplemental spending, including $6.8 billion for military spending ($1.9 billion of it for Bosnia operations), $5.9 billion for relief to farmers, $2.4 billion for anti-terrorism programs, $3.35 billion to address Year 2000 computer problems and $1.55 billion for disaster relief from Hurricane Georges. The measure also contains language to extend expiring tax provisions (at a cost of $9.7 billion over nine years). Adopted (thus cleared for the president) 65-29: R 33-20; D 32-9 (ND 26-9, SD 6-0). Oct. 21, 1998. A "yea" was a vote in support of the president's position. (*Senate vote 314*)

Following are House votes from 1998 selected by Congressional Quarterly as key votes. Original vote number in parentheses.

1. HR 2631. Line-item vetoes. Passage, over President Clinton's Nov. 13, 1997, veto, of the bill to disapprove Clinton's line-item vetoes of 38 projects, totaling $287 million, in the fiscal 1998 military construction appropriations bill (HR 2016 — PL 105-45). Passed 347-69: R 197-23; D 149-46 (ND 100-41, SD 49-5); I 1-0. Feb. 5, 1998. A two-thirds majority of those present and voting (277 in this case) of both chambers is required to override a veto. A "nay" was a vote in support of the president's position. *(House vote 10)*

2. HR 2400. Special Transportation Projects. Graham, R-S.C., amendment to strike provisions that provide funds for specified projects, including about $9 billion for highway projects, and other funding for specified transit and bus projects. Rejected 79-337: R 67-152; D 12-184 (ND 6-137, SD 6-47); I 0-1. April 1, 1998. *(House vote 95)*

3. HR 6. Affirmative Action. Riggs, R-Calif., amendment to prohibit any public institution of higher education that participates in any Higher Education Act program from discriminating against, or granting preferential treatment to any person or group in admissions based in whole or in part on race, sex, color, ethnicity or national origin. Rejected 171-249: R 166-55; D 5-193 (ND 2-143, SD 3-50); I 0-1. May 6, 1998. A "nay" was a vote in support of the president's position. *(House vote 133)*

4. HR 10. Financial Services Overhaul. Passage of the bill to eliminate current Glass-Steagall Act and Bank Holding Company Act barriers against affiliations between banking, securities, insurance and other firms. Passed 214-213: R 153-73; D 61-139 (ND 47-100, SD 14-39); I 0-1. May 13, 1998. A "nay" was a vote in support of the president's position. *(House vote 151)*

5. S 1150. Food Stamps for Legal Immigrants. Adoption of the rule (H Res 446) to dispose of the conference report on the bill to reauthorize agricultural research and education programs through fiscal 2002. The rule would have allowed a point of order to strike $818 million in funding in the conference report to restore food stamps to 250,000 legal immigrants. Rejected 120-289: R 118-98; D 2-190 (ND 1-140, SD 1-50); I 0-1. May 22, 1998. *(House vote 188)*

[1] Barbara Lee, D-Calif., was sworn in April 21, replacing Ronald V. Dellums, D-Calif., who resigned Feb. 6.

[2] Lois Capps, D-Calif., was sworn in March 17, replacing Walter Capps, D-Calif., who died Oct. 28, 1997.

[3] Mary Bono, R-Calif., was sworn in April 21, replacing Sonny Bono, R-Calif., who died Jan. 5.

[4] Newt Gingrich, R-Ga., as Speaker of the House, voted at his discretion.

[5] Heather Wilson, R-N.M., was sworn in June 25, replacing Stephen H. Schiff, R-N.M., who died March 25.

[6] Gregory W. Meeks, D-N.Y., was sworn in Feb. 5, replacing Floyd H. Flake, D-N.Y., who resigned Nov. 15, 1997.

[7] Robert A. Brady, D-Pa., was sworn in May 21, replacing Thomas M. Foglietta, D-Pa., who resigned Nov. 11, 1997.

Key

Y	Voted for (yea).	
#	Paired for.	
+	Announced for.	
N	Voted against (nay).	
X	Paired against.	
–	Announced against.	
P	Voted "present."	
C	Voted "present" to avoid possible conflict of interest.	
?	Did not vote or otherwise make a position known.	

Democrats **Republicans** *Independent*

	1	2	3	4	5
ALABAMA					
1 *Callahan*	Y	N	Y	N	N
2 *Everett*	Y	N	Y	N	N
3 *Riley*	Y	N	Y	N	N
4 *Aderholt*	Y	N	Y	N	N
5 Cramer	Y	N	N	Y	N
6 *Bachus*	Y	N	Y	N	N
7 Hilliard	Y	N	N	N	N
ALASKA					
AL *Young*	Y	N	N	N	N
ARIZONA					
1 *Salmon*	N	Y	Y	Y	Y
2 Pastor	Y	N	N	N	N
3 *Stump*	Y	Y	Y	Y	N
4 *Shadegg*	Y	Y	Y	Y	Y
5 *Kolbe*	Y	Y	Y	Y	N
6 *Hayworth*	Y	Y	Y	Y	N
ARKANSAS					
1 Berry	Y	N	N	N	N
2 Snyder	Y	N	N	N	N
3 *Hutchinson*	Y	N	Y	N	N
4 Dickey	N	N	N	N	N
CALIFORNIA					
1 *Riggs*	Y	N	Y	Y	?
2 *Herger*	?	N	Y	Y	N
3 Fazio	Y	N	N	Y	N
4 *Doolittle*	Y	N	Y	Y	Y
5 Matsui	Y	N	Y	N	N
6 Woolsey	Y	N	N	N	N
7 Miller	Y	N	N	N	?
8 Pelosi	Y	N	N	N	N
9 Lee[1]			N	N	N
9 Dellums	?				
10 Tauscher	Y	N	N	Y	N
11 *Pombo*	Y	N	Y	N	Y
12 Lantos	Y	N	N	N	N
13 Stark	N	N	N	N	?
14 Eshoo	?	N	N	N	N
15 *Campbell*	Y	Y	Y	N	N
16 Lofgren	N	P	N	N	N
17 Farr	Y	N	N	N	N
18 Condit	Y	Y	N	Y	N
19 *Radanovich*	Y	N	?	Y	Y
20 Dooley	N	N	N	Y	N
21 *Thomas*	Y	Y	Y	Y	Y
22 Capps, L.[2]		N	N	N	N
23 *Gallegly*	Y	N	Y	Y	Y
24 Sherman	N	N	N	N	N
25 *McKeon*	+	N	Y	Y	Y
26 Berman	Y	N	N	N	N
27 *Rogan*	Y	Y	Y	Y	N
28 *Dreier*	Y	N	Y	N	Y
29 Waxman	N	N	N	N	N
30 Becerra	+	N	N	N	N
31 Martinez	N	N	N	N	N
32 Dixon	Y	N	N	N	N
33 Roybal-Allard	Y	N	N	N	N
34 Torres	Y	?	N	N	?
35 Waters	Y	?	N	N	N
36 Harman	N	N	N	?	?
37 Millender-McD.	Y	N	N	N	N

	1	2	3	4	5
38 *Horn*	Y	N	Y	Y	N
39 *Royce*	N	?	Y	Y	Y
40 *Lewis*	Y	N	Y	N	Y
41 *Kim*	Y	N	Y	N	N
42 Brown	Y	N	N	N	N
43 *Calvert*	Y	N	Y	Y	N
44 Bono, M.[3]			Y	Y	Y
45 *Rohrabacher*	N	Y	Y	Y	Y
46 Sanchez	N	N	N	N	N
47 *Cox*	Y	Y	Y	Y	Y
48 *Packard*	Y	N	Y	Y	N
49 *Bilbray*	Y	N	Y	Y	N
50 Filner	N	N	N	N	N
51 *Cunningham*	Y	N	Y	Y	Y
52 *Hunter*	Y	Y	Y	N	Y
COLORADO					
1 DeGette	N	N	N	Y	N
2 Skaggs	N	Y	–	–	–
3 *McInnis*	Y	N	Y	N	Y
4 *Schaffer*	Y	Y	Y	N	Y
5 *Hefley*	Y	N	Y	N	Y
6 *Schaefer*	Y	N	?	Y	Y
CONNECTICUT					
1 Kennelly	Y	N	N	Y	N
2 Gejdenson	Y	N	N	N	N
3 DeLauro	Y	N	N	Y	N
4 *Shays*	N	Y	Y	N	N
5 Maloney	Y	N	N	N	N
6 *Johnson*	Y	N	N	Y	N
DELAWARE					
AL *Castle*	Y	Y	N	Y	N
FLORIDA					
1 *Scarborough*	Y	Y	Y	N	Y
2 Boyd	Y	N	N	Y	N
3 Brown	N	N	N	N	N
4 *Fowler*	Y	N	Y	N	N
5 Thurman	Y	N	N	N	N
6 *Stearns*	Y	N	Y	N	N
7 *Mica*	Y	N	Y	Y	N
8 *McCollum*	Y	Y	Y	Y	N
9 *Bilirakis*	Y	N	Y	Y	N
10 *Young*	Y	Y	Y	Y	Y
11 Davis	N	N	N	N	N
12 *Canady*	N	Y	Y	Y	Y
13 *Miller*	N	Y	Y	Y	N
14 *Goss*	Y	Y	Y	Y	Y
15 *Weldon*	Y	N	Y	Y	N
16 *Foley*	Y	Y	Y	N	?
17 Meek	Y	N	N	N	N
18 *Ros-Lehtinen*	Y	?	N	Y	N
19 Wexler	N	Y	N	Y	?
20 Deutsch	Y	N	Y	N	N
21 *Diaz-Balart*	Y	N	N	Y	N
22 *Shaw*	Y	N	Y	Y	N
23 Hastings	Y	N	?	N	N
GEORGIA					
1 *Kingston*	Y	Y	Y	Y	Y
2 Bishop	Y	N	N	Y	N
3 *Collins*	Y	N	Y	Y	Y
4 McKinney	N	N	N	N	N
5 Lewis	Y	N	N	N	N
6 *Gingrich*[4]				Y	Y
7 *Barr*	Y	Y	Y	Y	Y
8 *Chambliss*	Y	N	Y	N	N
9 *Deal*	Y	Y	Y	Y	Y
10 *Norwood*	Y	N	Y	Y	Y
11 *Linder*	Y	N	Y	Y	Y
HAWAII					
1 Abercrombie	Y	N	N	N	N
2 Mink	Y	N	N	N	N
IDAHO					
1 *Chenoweth*	Y	N	Y	N	N
2 *Crapo*	Y	N	Y	Y	N
ILLINOIS					
1 Rush	Y	N	N	N	N
2 Jackson	Y	N	N	N	N
3 Lipinski	Y	N	Y	N	N
4 Gutierrez	N	N	N	N	N
5 Blagojevich	Y	N	N	Y	N
6 *Hyde*	Y	Y	Y	Y	N
7 Davis	Y	N	N	N	N
8 *Crane*	Y	N	Y	Y	N
9 Yates	N	?	?	N	N
10 *Porter*	+	Y	N	Y	N
11 *Weller*	Y	N	Y	Y	N
12 Costello	Y	N	N	N	N

ND Northern Democrats   SD Southern Democrats

	1	2	3	4	5
13 ***Fawell***	Y	N	Y	Y	Y
14 ***Hastert***	Y	N	Y	Y	Y
15 ***Ewing***	N	N	Y	N	N
16 ***Manzullo***	Y	N	Y	N	Y
17 Evans	Y	N	N	N	N
18 ***LaHood***	Y	N	N	N	N
19 Poshard	Y	N	N	N	N
20 ***Shimkus***	Y	N	Y	Y	N
INDIANA					
1 Visclosky	Y	N	N	N	N
2 ***McIntosh***	Y	?	Y	Y	Y
3 Roemer	Y	N	N	N	N
4 ***Souder***	Y	Y	N	Y	N
5 ***Buyer***	Y	N	N	Y	Y
6 ***Burton***	+	N	Y	Y	N
7 ***Pease***	Y	N	Y	Y	N
8 ***Hostettler***	Y	N	Y	Y	Y
9 Hamilton	Y	N	N	N	N
10 Carson	N	N	–	N	N
IOWA					
1 ***Leach***	N	Y	N	Y	N
2 ***Nussle***	N	N	N	Y	N
3 Boswell	N	N	N	N	N
4 ***Ganske***	N	N	Y	Y	N
5 ***Latham***	Y	N	Y	Y	N
KANSAS					
1 ***Moran***	Y	N	N	N	N
2 ***Ryun***	Y	N	Y	N	N
3 ***Snowbarger***	Y	N	N	N	Y
4 ***Tiahrt***	Y	N	Y	N	Y
KENTUCKY					
1 ***Whitfield***	Y	N	Y	Y	Y
2 ***Lewis***	Y	N	Y	N	Y
3 ***Northup***	Y	N	Y	Y	N
4 ***Bunning***	Y	N	Y	Y	N
5 ***Rogers***	Y	N	Y	N	Y
6 Baesler	Y	N	Y	N	N
LOUISIANA					
1 ***Livingston***	Y	N	Y	Y	N
2 Jefferson	Y	?	N	N	N
3 ***Tauzin***	Y	N	Y	Y	Y
4 ***McCrery***	Y	P	Y	Y	Y
5 ***Cooksey***	Y	N	Y	Y	N
6 ***Baker***	Y	N	Y	Y	N
7 John	Y	N	N	Y	N
MAINE					
1 Allen	Y	N	N	N	N
2 Baldacci	Y	N	N	N	N
MARYLAND					
1 ***Gilchrest***	Y	N	N	Y	N
2 ***Ehrlich***	Y	Y	Y	Y	Y
3 Cardin	Y	N	N	N	N
4 Wynn	?	N	N	N	N
5 Hoyer	Y	N	N	N	N
6 ***Bartlett***	Y	N	Y	Y	Y
7 Cummings	Y	N	N	N	N
8 ***Morella***	Y	Y	N	Y	N
MASSACHUSETTS					
1 Olver	Y	N	N	N	N
2 Neal	Y	N	N	Y	N
3 McGovern	Y	N	N	Y	N
4 Frank	N	N	N	N	N
5 Meehan	N	N	N	N	N
6 Tierney	Y	N	N	N	N
7 Markey	N	N	N	Y	N
8 Kennedy	Y	N	N	N	N
9 Moakley	Y	N	N	N	N
10 Delahunt	Y	N	N	Y	N
MICHIGAN					
1 Stupak	N	N	N	Y	N
2 ***Hoekstra***	Y	Y	Y	Y	Y
3 ***Ehlers***	Y	N	N	Y	N
4 ***Camp***	Y	N	Y	N	Y
5 Barcia	Y	N	N	Y	N
6 ***Upton***	N	N	N	Y	N
7 ***Smith***	N	Y	N	Y	N
8 Stabenow	Y	N	N	Y	N
9 Kildee	Y	N	N	N	N
10 Bonior	Y	N	N	N	N
11 ***Knollenberg***	Y	N	Y	Y	Y
12 Levin	Y	N	N	Y	N
13 Rivers	N	N	N	N	N
14 Conyers	N	N	N	N	?
15 Kilpatrick	Y	N	N	N	N
16 Dingell	Y	N	N	Y	N

	1	2	3	4	5
MINNESOTA					
1 ***Gutknecht***	Y	Y	Y	N	N
2 Minge	N	Y	N	N	N
3 ***Ramstad***	N	N	Y	N	N
4 Vento	N	N	N	N	N
5 Sabo	Y	N	N	N	N
6 Luther	N	N	N	N	N
7 Peterson	Y	N	N	N	N
8 Oberstar	Y	N	N	N	N
MISSISSIPPI					
1 ***Wicker***	Y	N	Y	N	?
2 Thompson	Y	N	N	N	N
3 ***Pickering***	Y	N	Y	N	Y
4 ***Parker***	Y	Y	Y	Y	?
5 Taylor	Y	N	Y	N	N
MISSOURI					
1 Clay	Y	N	N	N	N
2 ***Talent***	Y	N	Y	Y	N
3 Gephardt	Y	N	N	N	N
4 Skelton	Y	N	N	N	N
5 McCarthy	N	N	N	N	N
6 Danner	Y	N	N	N	N
7 ***Blunt***	Y	N	Y	N	Y
8 ***Emerson***	Y	N	Y	Y	Y
9 ***Hulshof***	Y	N	Y	N	Y
MONTANA					
AL ***Hill***	Y	Y	Y	Y	N
NEBRASKA					
1 ***Bereuter***	Y	N	Y	N	N
2 ***Christensen***	Y	Y	?	N	N
3 ***Barrett***	Y	Y	N	N	N
NEVADA					
1 ***Ensign***	N	N	N	Y	Y
2 ***Gibbons***	Y	N	N	Y	Y
NEW HAMPSHIRE					
1 ***Sununu***	Y	N	Y	Y	Y
2 ***Bass***	Y	N	Y	Y	Y
NEW JERSEY					
1 Andrews	N	N	N	Y	N
2 ***LoBiondo***	Y	N	Y	Y	N
3 ***Saxton***	Y	N	N	Y	Y
4 ***Smith***	Y	N	Y	Y	N
5 ***Roukema***	Y	N	Y	Y	Y
6 Pallone	Y	N	N	Y	N
7 ***Franks***	N	N	Y	Y	N
8 Pascrell	Y	N	N	Y	N
9 Rothman	N	N	N	N	N
10 Payne	N	?	N	N	N
11 ***Frelinghuysen***	Y	Y	Y	Y	Y
12 ***Pappas***	Y	Y	Y	Y	N
13 Menendez	Y	N	N	N	N
NEW MEXICO					
1 ***Schiff*** [5]	?				
2 ***Skeen***	Y	N	N	N	N
3 ***Redmond***	Y	N	N	N	N
NEW YORK					
1 ***Forbes***	Y	N	N	Y	N
2 ***Lazio***	Y	N	N	Y	N
3 ***King***	Y	N	N	Y	?
4 McCarthy	Y	N	N	Y	N
5 Ackerman	N	N	N	Y	N
6 Meeks [6]		N	N	Y	?
7 Manton	Y	N	N	Y	N
8 Nadler	Y	N	N	Y	N
9 Schumer	Y	N	N	Y	N
10 Towns	N	N	N	Y	?
11 Owens	N	N	N	N	N
12 Velázquez	Y	N	N	N	N
13 ***Fossella***	Y	N	Y	Y	N
14 Maloney	Y	N	N	Y	N
15 Rangel	N	?	N	Y	N
16 Serrano	Y	N	N	N	N
17 Engel	N	N	N	Y	N
18 Lowey	Y	N	N	Y	N
19 ***Kelly***	Y	N	N	Y	N
20 ***Gilman***	Y	N	N	Y	N
21 McNulty	Y	N	?	Y	N
22 ***Solomon***	Y	N	Y	Y	Y
23 ***Boehlert***	Y	N	N	Y	N
24 ***McHugh***	Y	N	Y	N	N
25 ***Walsh***	Y	N	N	Y	N
26 Hinchey	Y	N	N	N	N
27 ***Paxon***	Y	N	Y	Y	Y
28 Slaughter	Y	N	N	N	N
29 LaFalce	Y	N	N	N	N

	1	2	3	4	5
30 ***Quinn***	Y	N	N	Y	–
31 ***Houghton***	Y	N	N	Y	Y
NORTH CAROLINA					
1 Clayton	Y	N	N	N	N
2 Etheridge	Y	N	N	N	N
3 ***Jones***	Y	Y	Y	N	Y
4 Price	Y	N	N	Y	N
5 ***Burr***	Y	Y	N	N	Y
6 ***Coble***	Y	N	Y	Y	Y
7 McIntyre	Y	N	N	N	N
8 Hefner	Y	N	N	?	N
9 ***Myrick***	Y	Y	N	Y	Y
10 ***Ballenger***	Y	Y	Y	Y	Y
11 ***Taylor***	Y	Y	Y	Y	?
12 Watt	Y	N	N	N	N
NORTH DAKOTA					
AL Pomeroy	Y	Y	N	Y	N
OHIO					
1 ***Chabot***	N	Y	Y	Y	Y
2 ***Portman***	Y	N	Y	Y	Y
3 Hall	+	N	N	Y	N
4 ***Oxley***	Y	N	Y	Y	N
5 ***Gillmor***	Y	N	Y	Y	N
6 Strickland	N	N	N	Y	N
7 ***Hobson***	Y	Y	N	Y	Y
8 ***Boehner***	Y	Y	Y	Y	Y
9 Kaptur	Y	N	N	N	N
10 Kucinich	Y	N	N	N	N
11 Stokes	Y	N	N	N	N
12 ***Kasich***	Y	Y	Y	Y	N
13 Brown	N	N	N	Y	N
14 Sawyer	Y	N	N	Y	N
15 ***Pryce***	Y	N	N	Y	N
16 ***Regula***	Y	N	N	Y	N
17 Traficant	Y	N	N	N	Y
18 ***Ney***	Y	N	N	Y	N
19 ***LaTourette***	Y	N	N	Y	N
OKLAHOMA					
1 ***Largent***	Y	Y	N	N	Y
2 ***Coburn***	Y	Y	Y	N	Y
3 ***Watkins***	Y	N	N	N	N
4 ***Watts***	Y	N	N	N	N
5 ***Istook***	Y	Y	Y	N	Y
6 ***Lucas***	Y	N	Y	N	N
OREGON					
1 Furse	?	N	N	N	?
2 ***Smith***	Y	N	Y	N	P
3 Blumenauer	Y	N	N	N	N
4 DeFazio	N	N	N	N	?
5 Hooley	Y	N	N	N	N
PENNSYLVANIA					
1 Brady [7]					N
2 Fattah	Y	N	N	N	N
3 Borski	Y	N	N	N	N
4 Klink	?	N	N	N	N
5 ***Peterson***	Y	N	Y	N	N
6 Holden	Y	N	N	Y	N
7 ***Weldon***	Y	N	N	Y	N
8 ***Greenwood***	N	N	Y	Y	Y
9 ***Shuster***	Y	N	?	N	Y
10 ***McDade***	Y	N	N	Y	N
11 Kanjorski	N	N	N	N	N
12 Murtha	Y	N	N	Y	N
13 ***Fox***	Y	N	N	Y	N
14 Coyne	Y	N	N	Y	N
15 McHale	Y	N	N	N	N
16 ***Pitts***	Y	N	Y	Y	Y
17 ***Gekas***	Y	N	Y	Y	Y
18 Doyle	Y	N	?	Y	N
19 ***Goodling***	Y	N	Y	Y	Y
20 Mascara	Y	N	N	N	N
21 ***English***	Y	N	N	Y	Y
RHODE ISLAND					
1 Kennedy	Y	N	N	N	N
2 Weygand	Y	N	N	N	N
SOUTH CAROLINA					
1 ***Sanford***	N	Y	N	Y	Y
2 ***Spence***	Y	N	Y	Y	Y
3 ***Graham***	Y	Y	Y	N	Y
4 ***Inglis***	Y	Y	Y	Y	Y
5 Spratt	Y	N	N	Y	N
6 Clyburn	Y	N	N	N	N
SOUTH DAKOTA					
AL ***Thune***	Y	N	Y	N	N

	1	2	3	4	5
TENNESSEE					
1 ***Jenkins***	Y	N	Y	N	Y
2 ***Duncan***	N	N	Y	N	Y
3 ***Wamp***	Y	Y	Y	Y	Y
4 ***Hilleary***	Y	Y	Y	N	Y
5 Clement	Y	N	N	N	N
6 Gordon	Y	N	N	Y	N
7 ***Bryant***	Y	N	Y	Y	N
8 Tanner	Y	N	N	Y	N
9 Ford	Y	N	N	Y	N
TEXAS					
1 Sandlin	Y	N	N	N	N
2 Turner	Y	N	N	N	N
3 ***Johnson, Sam***	Y	Y	Y	N	?
4 Hall	Y	Y	Y	N	N
5 ***Sessions***	Y	Y	Y	N	Y
6 ***Barton***	Y	Y	Y	N	Y
7 ***Archer***	Y	Y	Y	Y	Y
8 ***Brady***	Y	N	Y	N	Y
9 Lampson	Y	N	N	N	N
10 Doggett	N	N	N	N	N
11 Edwards	Y	Y	N	N	N
12 ***Granger***	Y	N	Y	N	N
13 ***Thornberry***	Y	Y	Y	N	N
14 ***Paul***	Y	N	Y	N	Y
15 Hinojosa	Y	N	N	N	N
16 Reyes	Y	N	N	N	?
17 Stenholm	Y	Y	N	N	N
18 Jackson-Lee	Y	N	N	N	N
19 ***Combest***	Y	N	Y	N	N
20 Gonzalez	?	?	?	?	?
21 ***Smith***	Y	N	Y	N	Y
22 ***DeLay***	Y	N	Y	Y	Y
23 ***Bonilla***	Y	Y	N	N	N
24 Frost	Y	N	N	Y	N
25 Bentsen	Y	N	N	N	N
26 ***Armey***	?	N	Y	Y	Y
27 Ortiz	Y	N	N	N	N
28 Rodriguez	Y	N	N	N	N
29 Green	Y	N	N	N	?
30 Johnson, E.B.	Y	N	N	Y	N
UTAH					
1 ***Hansen***	Y	N	Y	Y	N
2 ***Cook***	Y	N	Y	Y	N
3 ***Cannon***	Y	?	Y	N	Y
VERMONT					
AL *Sanders*	Y	N	N	N	N
VIRGINIA					
1 ***Bateman***	Y	N	+	+	–
2 Pickett	Y	N	N	N	N
3 Scott	Y	N	N	N	N
4 Sisisky	Y	N	N	N	N
5 Goode	Y	N	N	N	Y
6 ***Goodlatte***	Y	N	Y	Y	Y
7 ***Bliley***	Y	N	Y	Y	Y
8 Moran	Y	N	N	Y	N
9 Boucher	Y	N	N	N	N
10 ***Wolf***	Y	Y	N	Y	N
11 ***Davis***	Y	N	N	N	N
WASHINGTON					
1 ***White***	Y	Y	N	Y	Y
2 ***Metcalf***	Y	N	Y	Y	Y
3 ***Smith, Linda***	Y	N	Y	Y	N
4 ***Hastings***	Y	N	Y	Y	Y
5 ***Nethercutt***	Y	Y	Y	Y	N
6 Dicks	Y	N	N	Y	N
7 McDermott	N	N	N	N	N
8 ***Dunn***	Y	N	Y	Y	Y
9 Smith, Adam	Y	N	N	Y	N
WEST VIRGINIA					
1 Mollohan	Y	N	N	Y	N
2 Wise	Y	N	N	Y	N
3 Rahall	Y	N	N	Y	N
WISCONSIN					
1 ***Neumann***	N	Y	?	Y	Y
2 ***Klug***	N	?	N	Y	Y
3 Kind	N	Y	N	N	N
4 Kleczka	Y	N	N	N	N
5 Barrett	N	Y	N	N	N
6 ***Petri***	N	N	Y	N	Y
7 Obey	Y	N	N	N	N
8 Johnson	N	N	N	N	N
9 ***Sensenbrenner***	N	Y	Y	Y	Y
WYOMING					
AL ***Cubin***	Y	Y	Y	Y	Y

Southern states - Ala., Ark., Fla., Ga., Ky., La., Miss., N.C., Okla., S.C., Tenn., Texas, Va.

Key

Y	Voted for (yea).
#	Paired for.
+	Announced for.
N	Voted against (nay).
X	Paired against.
−	Announced against.
P	Voted "present."
C	Voted "present" to avoid possible conflict of interest.
?	Did not vote or otherwise make a position known.

Democrats **Republicans**
Independent

6. HR 4104. Contraceptive Coverage. Lowey, D-N.Y., amendment to prohibit the Office of Personnel Management from accepting a contract that provides coverage for prescription drugs unless the plan also provides equivalent coverage for prescription contraception drugs. Adopted 224-198: R 48-177; D 175-21 (ND 130-17, SD 45-4); I 1-0. July 16, 1998. (*House vote 290*)

7. HR 4194. Public Housing Overhaul. Lazio, R-N.Y., amendment to overhaul public housing management and allow increased local control over rents and occupancy standards. Adopted 230-181: R 215-4; D 15-176 (ND 8-136, SD 7-40); I 0-1. July 17, 1998. (*House vote 296*)

8. HR 4250. Managed Care Regulations. Passage of the bill to revise managed care and medical insurance regulations. The bill would provide a range of patient protections, create a two-step appeals process for challenging a health plan administrator's decisions and expand the availability of medical savings accounts. Passed 216-210: R 213-12; D 3-197 (ND 2-147, SD 1-50); I 0-1. July 24, 1998. A "nay" was a vote in support of the president's position. (*House vote 339*)

9. HR 2183. Campaign Finance Overhaul. Passage of the bill to ban soft money contributions for federal elections, expand regulations on advertising that advocates a candidate and tighten the definition of what constitutes coordination with a federal candidate. The text of the bill is the Shays-Meehan substitute adopted by the House on Aug. 3. Passed 252-179: R 61-164; D 190-15 (ND 142-9, SD 48-6); I 1-0. Aug. 6, 1998. (*House vote 405*)

[1] Barbara Lee, D-Calif., was sworn in April 21, replacing Ronald V. Dellums, D-Calif., who resigned Feb. 6.

[2] Lois Capps, D-Calif., was sworn in March 17, replacing Walter Capps, D-Calif., who died Oct. 28, 1997.

[3] Mary Bono, R-Calif., was sworn in April 21, replacing Sonny Bono, R-Calif., who died Jan. 5.

[4] Newt Gingrich, R-Ga., as Speaker of the House, voted at his discretion.

[5] Heather Wilson, R-N.M., was sworn in June 25, replacing Steven H. Schiff, R-N.M., who died March 25.

[6] Gregory W. Meeks, D-N.Y., was sworn in Feb. 5, replacing Floyd H. Flake, D-N.Y., who resigned Nov. 15, 1997.

[7] Robert A. Brady, D-Pa., was sworn in May 21, replacing Thomas M. Foglietta, D-Pa., who resigned Nov. 11, 1997.

	6	7	8	9
ALABAMA				
1 *Callahan*	N	?	Y	N
2 *Everett*	N	Y	Y	N
3 *Riley*	N	Y	Y	N
4 *Aderholt*	N	Y	Y	N
5 Cramer	Y	N	N	Y
6 *Bachus*	N	Y	Y	N
7 Hilliard	Y	N	N	Y
ALASKA				
AL *Young*	N	Y	Y	N
ARIZONA				
1 *Salmon*	N	Y	Y	N
2 Pastor	Y	N	N	Y
3 *Stump*	N	Y	Y	N
4 *Shadegg*	N	Y	Y	N
5 *Kolbe*	Y	Y	Y	N
6 *Hayworth*	N	Y	Y	N
ARKANSAS				
1 Berry	Y	N	N	Y
2 Snyder	Y	?	N	Y
3 *Hutchinson*	N	Y	Y	N
4 *Dickey*	N	Y	Y	N
CALIFORNIA				
1 *Riggs*	Y	Y	Y	Y
2 *Herger*	N	Y	Y	N
3 Fazio	Y	N	N	Y
4 *Doolittle*	N	+	Y	N
5 Matsui	Y	N	N	Y
6 Woolsey	Y	N	N	Y
7 Miller	Y	N	N	Y
8 Pelosi	Y	N	N	Y
9 Lee[1]	Y	N	N	Y
10 Tauscher	Y	N	N	Y
11 *Pombo*	N	Y	Y	N
12 Lantos	Y	N	N	Y
13 Stark	Y	N	N	Y
14 Eshoo	Y	N	N	Y
15 *Campbell*	Y	Y	Y	Y
16 Lofgren	Y	N	N	Y
17 Farr	Y	N	N	Y
18 Condit	Y	N	N	Y
19 *Radanovich*	N	Y	Y	N
20 Dooley	Y	N	N	Y
21 *Thomas*	Y	Y	Y	Y
22 Capps, L.[2]	Y	N	N	Y
23 *Gallegly*	Y	Y	Y	Y
24 Sherman	Y	N	N	Y
25 *McKeon*	N	Y	Y	N
26 Berman	Y	N	N	Y
27 *Rogan*	Y	Y	Y	N
28 *Dreier*	N	Y	Y	N
29 Waxman	Y	N	N	Y
30 Becerra	Y	N	N	Y
31 Martinez	Y	N	N	Y
32 Dixon	Y	N	N	Y
33 Roybal-Allard	+	−	N	Y
34 Torres	Y	N	N	Y
35 Waters	Y	N	N	Y
36 Harman	Y	?	N	Y
37 Millender-McD.	Y	−	N	Y
38 *Horn*	Y	Y	Y	Y

	6	7	8	9
39 *Royce*	N	Y	Y	N
40 *Lewis*	N	Y	Y	N
41 *Kim*	N	Y	Y	Y
42 Brown	Y	N	N	Y
43 *Calvert*	Y	Y	Y	N
44 *Bono, M.*[3]	Y	Y	Y	N
45 *Rohrabacher*	N	Y	Y	N
46 Sanchez	Y	N	N	Y
47 *Cox*	N	Y	Y	N
48 *Packard*	N	Y	Y	N
49 *Bilbray*	Y	Y	Y	Y
50 Filner	#	−	N	Y
51 *Cunningham*	N	Y	Y	?
52 *Hunter*	N	Y	Y	N
COLORADO				
1 DeGette	Y	N	N	Y
2 Skaggs	Y	N	N	Y
3 *McInnis*	N	Y	Y	N
4 *Schaffer*	N	Y	Y	N
5 *Hefley*	N	Y	Y	N
6 *Schaefer*	N	Y	Y	N
CONNECTICUT				
1 Kennelly	?	?	N	Y
2 Gejdenson	Y	N	N	Y
3 DeLauro	Y	N	N	Y
4 *Shays*	Y	Y	Y	Y
5 Maloney	Y	N	N	Y
6 *Johnson*	Y	Y	Y	Y
DELAWARE				
AL *Castle*	Y	Y	Y	Y
FLORIDA				
1 *Scarborough*	N	Y	Y	N
2 Boyd	Y	N	N	Y
3 Brown	Y	N	N	Y
4 *Fowler*	Y	Y	Y	N
5 Thurman	Y	N	N	Y
6 *Stearns*	N	Y	Y	N
7 *Mica*	N	+	Y	N
8 *McCollum*	N	Y	Y	N
9 *Bilirakis*	N	Y	Y	N
10 *Young*	N	Y	?	N
11 Davis	Y	N	N	Y
12 *Canady*	N	Y	Y	N
13 *Miller*	N	Y	Y	N
14 *Goss*	N	Y	Y	N
15 *Weldon*	N	Y	Y	N
16 *Foley*	Y	Y	Y	Y
17 Meek	Y	N	N	Y
18 *Ros-Lehtinen*	Y	Y	Y	N
19 Wexler	Y	N	N	Y
20 Deutsch	Y	N	N	Y
21 *Diaz-Balart*	N	Y	Y	N
22 *Shaw*	Y	Y	Y	N
23 Hastings	Y	N	N	N
GEORGIA				
1 *Kingston*	N	Y	Y	N
2 Bishop	Y	N	N	N
3 *Collins*	N	Y	Y	N
4 McKinney	Y	N	N	Y
5 Lewis	?	?	N	Y
6 *Gingrich*[4]		Y		
7 *Barr*	N	Y	N	N
8 *Chambliss*	N	Y	Y	N
9 *Deal*	N	Y	Y	Y
10 *Norwood*	N	Y	Y	N
11 *Linder*	N	Y	?	N
HAWAII				
1 Abercrombie	Y	N	N	N
2 Mink	Y	N	N	N
IDAHO				
1 *Chenoweth*	N	Y	N	N
2 *Crapo*	N	Y	N	N
ILLINOIS				
1 Rush	Y	N	N	Y
2 Jackson	Y	N	N	Y
3 Lipinski	N	N	N	Y
4 Gutierrez	Y	N	N	Y
5 Blagojevich	Y	N	N	Y
6 *Hyde*	N	Y	Y	N
7 Davis	Y	N	N	Y
8 *Crane*	N	Y	Y	N
9 Yates	Y	N	?	Y
10 *Porter*	Y	Y	Y	Y
11 *Weller*	N	Y	Y	N
12 Costello	N	N	N	Y
13 *Fawell*	Y	Y	Y	Y

	6	7	8	9
14 Hastert	N	Y	Y	N
15 Ewing	N	Y	Y	N
16 Manzullo	N	Y	Y	N
17 Evans	Y	N	N	Y
18 LaHood	N	Y	Y	N
19 Poshard	Y	N	N	Y
20 Shimkus	N	Y	Y	Y

INDIANA

	6	7	8	9
1 Visclosky	Y	N	N	Y
2 McIntosh	N	Y	Y	N
3 Roemer	Y	N	N	Y
4 Souder	N	Y	Y	N
5 Buyer	N	Y	Y	N
6 Burton	N	Y	Y	N
7 Pease	N	Y	Y	N
8 Hostettler	N	Y	Y	N
9 Hamilton	Y	N	N	Y
10 Carson	Y	N	N	Y

IOWA

	6	7	8	9
1 Leach	Y	Y	Y	Y
2 Nussle	N	Y	Y	N
3 Boswell	Y	N	Y	N
4 Ganske	Y	Y	N	Y
5 Latham	N	Y	Y	N

KANSAS

	6	7	8	9
1 Moran	N	Y	Y	N
2 Ryun	N	Y	Y	N
3 Snowbarger	N	Y	Y	N
4 Tiahrt	N	Y	Y	N

KENTUCKY

	6	7	8	9
1 Whitfield	N	Y	Y	N
2 Lewis	N	Y	Y	N
3 Northup	N	Y	Y	N
4 Bunning	N	Y	Y	N
5 Rogers	N	Y	Y	N
6 Baesler	Y	Y	N	Y

LOUISIANA

	6	7	8	9
1 Livingston	N	?	Y	N
2 Jefferson	Y	?	N	Y
3 Tauzin	N	Y	Y	N
4 McCrery	N	Y	Y	N
5 Cooksey	N	Y	Y	N
6 Baker	N	Y	Y	N
7 John	?	?	?	N

MAINE

	6	7	8	9
1 Allen	Y	N	N	Y
2 Baldacci	Y	N	N	Y

MARYLAND

	6	7	8	9
1 Gilchrest	Y	Y	Y	Y
2 Ehrlich	Y	Y	Y	N
3 Cardin	Y	N	N	Y
4 Wynn	Y	N	N	Y
5 Hoyer	Y	N	N	Y
6 Bartlett	N	Y	Y	N
7 Cummings	Y	N	N	Y
8 Morella	Y	Y	N	Y

MASSACHUSETTS

	6	7	8	9
1 Olver	Y	N	N	Y
2 Neal	Y	N	N	Y
3 McGovern	Y	N	N	Y
4 Frank	Y	N	N	Y
5 Meehan	Y	N	N	Y
6 Tierney	Y	N	N	Y
7 Markey	Y	N	?	Y
8 Kennedy	Y	N	N	Y
9 Moakley	Y	?	N	Y
10 Delahunt	Y	N	N	Y

MICHIGAN

	6	7	8	9
1 Stupak	N	N	N	N
2 Hoekstra	N	Y	Y	N
3 Ehlers	N	Y	Y	N
4 Camp	N	Y	Y	N
5 Barcia	N	N	N	N
6 Upton	Y	Y	Y	Y
7 Smith	N	Y	Y	N
8 Stabenow	Y	N	N	Y
9 Kildee	N	N	N	Y
10 Bonior	Y	N	N	Y
11 Knollenberg	N	Y	Y	N
12 Levin	Y	N	N	Y
13 Rivers	Y	N	N	Y
14 Conyers	Y	N	N	Y
15 Kilpatrick	Y	N	N	Y
16 Dingell	Y	N	N	Y

MINNESOTA

	6	7	8	9
1 Gutknecht	N	Y	Y	N
2 Minge	Y	N	N	Y
3 Ramstad	Y	Y	Y	Y
4 Vento	Y	N	N	Y
5 Sabo	Y	N	N	Y
6 Luther	Y	N	N	Y
7 Peterson	N	N	N	Y
8 Oberstar	Y	N	N	Y

MISSISSIPPI

	6	7	8	9
1 Wicker	N	Y	Y	N
2 Thompson	Y	N	N	Y
3 Pickering	N	Y	Y	N
4 Parker	?	?	N	Y
5 Taylor	N	Y	N	Y

MISSOURI

	6	7	8	9
1 Clay	Y	N	N	Y
2 Talent	N	Y	Y	N
3 Gephardt	Y	N	N	Y
4 Skelton	N	Y	Y	N
5 McCarthy	Y	N	N	Y
6 Danner	Y	Y	N	Y
7 Blunt	N	Y	Y	N
8 Emerson	N	Y	Y	N
9 Hulshof	N	Y	Y	Y

MONTANA

	6	7	8	9
AL Hill	?	?	Y	Y

NEBRASKA

	6	7	8	9
1 Bereuter	Y	Y	Y	Y
2 Christensen	N	Y	Y	N
3 Barrett	N	Y	Y	N

NEVADA

	6	7	8	9
1 Ensign	Y	Y	Y	N
2 Gibbons	Y	Y	Y	N

NEW HAMPSHIRE

	6	7	8	9
1 Sununu	N	Y	Y	N
2 Bass	Y	Y	Y	Y

NEW JERSEY

	6	7	8	9
1 Andrews	Y	N	N	Y
2 LoBiondo	N	Y	Y	Y
3 Saxton	N	Y	Y	N
4 Smith	N	Y	Y	N
5 Roukema	Y	Y	N	Y
6 Pallone	Y	N	N	Y
7 Franks	Y	Y	Y	N
8 Pascrell	Y	N	N	Y
9 Rothman	Y	N	N	Y
10 Payne	Y	N	N	Y
11 Frelinghuysen	Y	Y	Y	Y
12 Pappas	N	Y	Y	N
13 Menendez	Y	N	N	Y

NEW MEXICO

	6	7	8	9
1 Wilson [5]	Y	Y	Y	N
2 Skeen	N	Y	Y	N
3 Redmond	N	Y	Y	N

NEW YORK

	6	7	8	9
1 Forbes	N	Y	N	Y
2 Lazio	Y	Y	Y	Y
3 King	N	Y	Y	N
4 McCarthy	Y	N	N	Y
5 Ackerman	Y	N	N	Y
6 Meeks [6]	Y	N	N	Y
7 Manton	Y	N	N	Y
8 Nadler	Y	N	N	Y
9 Schumer	Y	N	N	Y
10 Towns	Y	N	N	Y
11 Owens	Y	N	N	Y
12 Velázquez	Y	N	N	Y
13 Fossella	N	Y	Y	N
14 Maloney	Y	N	N	Y
15 Rangel	Y	N	N	Y
16 Serrano	Y	N	N	Y
17 Engel	Y	N	N	Y
18 Lowey	Y	N	N	Y
19 Kelly	Y	Y	Y	Y
20 Gilman	Y	Y	Y	Y
21 McNulty	?	?	N	Y
22 Solomon	N	Y	Y	N
23 Boehlert	Y	Y	Y	Y
24 McHugh	N	N	Y	Y
25 Walsh	N	N	Y	N
26 Hinchey	Y	N	N	Y
27 Paxon	N	Y	Y	N
28 Slaughter	Y	N	N	Y
29 LaFalce	N	N	N	Y
30 Quinn	N	Y	Y	Y
31 Houghton	Y	Y	Y	Y

NORTH CAROLINA

	6	7	8	9
1 Clayton	?	N	N	Y
2 Etheridge	Y	N	N	Y
3 Jones	N	Y	Y	N
4 Price	Y	N	N	Y
5 Burr	N	Y	Y	N
6 Coble	N	Y	Y	N
7 McIntyre	Y	Y	N	Y
8 Hefner	Y	N	N	Y
9 Myrick	N	Y	Y	N
10 Ballenger	N	Y	Y	N
11 Taylor	N	Y	Y	N
12 Watt	Y	N	N	Y

NORTH DAKOTA

	6	7	8	9
AL Pomeroy	Y	N	N	Y

OHIO

	6	7	8	9
1 Chabot	N	Y	Y	N
2 Portman	N	Y	Y	N
3 Hall	N	N	N	Y
4 Oxley	Y	Y	Y	N
5 Gillmor	N	Y	Y	N
6 Strickland	Y	N	N	Y
7 Hobson	Y	Y	N	Y
8 Boehner	N	Y	Y	N
9 Kaptur	Y	N	N	Y
10 Kucinich	N	N	N	Y
11 Stokes	Y	N	N	Y
12 Kasich	N	Y	Y	N
13 Brown	Y	N	N	Y
14 Sawyer	Y	N	N	Y
15 Pryce	N	Y	Y	N
16 Regula	N	Y	Y	N
17 Traficant	Y	N	N	Y
18 Ney	N	Y	Y	N
19 LaTourette	N	Y	Y	Y

OKLAHOMA

	6	7	8	9
1 Largent	N	Y	Y	N
2 Coburn	N	Y	Y	N
3 Watkins	N	Y	Y	N
4 Watts	N	Y	Y	N
5 Istook	N	Y	Y	N
6 Lucas	N	Y	Y	N

OREGON

	6	7	8	9
1 Furse	Y	N	N	Y
2 Smith	N	Y	Y	N
3 Blumenauer	Y	N	N	Y
4 DeFazio	Y	N	N	Y
5 Hooley	Y	N	N	Y

PENNSYLVANIA

	6	7	8	9
1 Brady [7]	Y	N	N	Y
2 Fattah	Y	N	N	Y
3 Borski	Y	Y	N	Y
4 Klink	N	Y	N	Y
5 Peterson	N	Y	Y	N
6 Holden	N	N	N	Y
7 Weldon	Y	Y	Y	N
8 Greenwood	Y	Y	Y	Y
9 Shuster	N	Y	Y	N
10 McDade	N	Y	Y	Y
11 Kanjorski	Y	N	N	Y
12 Murtha	Y	N	N	N
13 Fox	Y	Y	Y	Y
14 Coyne	Y	N	N	Y
15 McHale	Y	N	N	Y
16 Pitts	N	Y	Y	N
17 Gekas	N	Y	Y	N
18 Doyle	N	N	N	Y
19 Goodling	N	Y	Y	N
20 Mascara	N	N	N	Y
21 English	N	Y	Y	N

RHODE ISLAND

	6	7	8	9
1 Kennedy	Y	N	N	Y
2 Weygand	Y	N	N	Y

SOUTH CAROLINA

	6	7	8	9
1 Sanford	N	Y	N	Y
2 Spence	N	Y	Y	N
3 Graham	N	Y	Y	N
4 Inglis	N	Y	Y	?
5 Spratt	Y	N	N	Y
6 Clyburn	Y	N	N	Y

SOUTH DAKOTA

	6	7	8	9
AL Thune	N	Y	Y	Y

TENNESSEE

	6	7	8	9
1 Jenkins	N	Y	Y	N
2 Duncan	N	Y	Y	Y
3 Wamp	N	Y	Y	Y
4 Hilleary	N	Y	Y	N
5 Clement	Y	N	N	Y
6 Gordon	Y	N	N	Y
7 Bryant	N	Y	Y	N
8 Tanner	Y	?	N	Y
9 Ford ·	+	–	–	Y

TEXAS

	6	7	8	9
1 Sandlin	Y	N	N	Y
2 Turner	Y	N	N	Y
3 Johnson, Sam	N	Y	Y	N
4 Hall	Y	N	Y	N
5 Sessions	N	?	Y	N
6 Barton	N	Y	Y	N
7 Archer	N	Y	Y	N
8 Brady	N	Y	Y	N
9 Lampson	Y	N	N	Y
10 Doggett	Y	Y	N	Y
11 Edwards	Y	N	N	Y
12 Granger	Y	Y	Y	Y
13 Thornberry	N	Y	Y	N
14 Paul	N	N	N	N
15 Hinojosa	Y	N	N	Y
16 Reyes	Y	N	N	Y
17 Stenholm	Y	N	N	Y
18 Jackson-Lee	Y	N	N	Y
19 Combest	N	Y	Y	N
20 Gonzalez	?	?	?	?
21 Smith	N	Y	Y	N
22 DeLay	N	Y	Y	N
23 Bonilla	N	Y	N	N
24 Frost	Y	N	N	Y
25 Bentsen	Y	N	N	Y
26 Armey	N	Y	Y	N
27 Ortiz	X	–	N	Y
28 Rodriguez	Y	N	?	Y
29 Green	Y	N	N	Y
30 Johnson, E.B.	Y	N	N	Y

UTAH

	6	7	8	9
1 Hansen	N	Y	Y	N
2 Cook	Y	Y	Y	Y
3 Cannon	N	Y	Y	N

VERMONT

	6	7	8	9
AL Sanders	Y	N	N	Y

VIRGINIA

	6	7	8	9
1 Bateman	N	Y	Y	N
2 Pickett	Y	N	N	Y
3 Scott	Y	N	N	Y
4 Sisisky	Y	N	N	Y
5 Goode	N	Y	Y	N
6 Goodlatte	N	Y	Y	N
7 Bliley	N	Y	Y	N
8 Moran	Y	N	N	Y
9 Boucher	Y	N	N	Y
10 Wolf	N	Y	Y	N
11 Davis	Y	Y	Y	N

WASHINGTON

	6	7	8	9
1 White	N	Y	Y	Y
2 Metcalf	N	Y	Y	Y
3 Smith, Linda	N	Y	Y	Y
4 Hastings	N	Y	Y	N
5 Nethercutt	Y	N	Y	N
6 Dicks	Y	N	N	Y
7 McDermott	Y	N	N	Y
8 Dunn	Y	?	Y	N
9 Smith, Adam	Y	N	N	Y

WEST VIRGINIA

	6	7	8	9
1 Mollohan	N	N	N	N
2 Wise	Y	N	N	Y
3 Rahall	N	N	N	N

WISCONSIN

	6	7	8	9
1 Neumann	N	Y	Y	N
2 Klug	Y	Y	?	Y
3 Kind	Y	N	N	Y
4 Kleczka	Y	N	N	Y
5 Barrett	Y	N	N	Y
6 Petri	N	Y	Y	N
7 Obey	Y	N	N	Y
8 Johnson	Y	N	N	Y
9 Sensenbrenner	N	Y	Y	N

WYOMING

	6	7	8	9
AL Cubin	N	Y	Y	N

Southern states - Ala., Ark., Fla., Ga., Ky., La., Miss., N.C., Okla., S.C., Tenn., Texas, Va.

10. H Res 525. Release of Starr Report. Adoption of the resolution to provide for the release and distribution of the report from Independent Counsel Kenneth W. Starr regarding allegations of criminal offenses and other misconduct by President Clinton. Under the resolution, the Judiciary Committee will review the materials to determine whether they contain grounds for impeachment. It also requires the committee to immediately release the initial 445-page report, and release other documents to the public on Sept. 28 unless the committee votes not to release certain materials. Adopted 363-63: R 224-0; D 138-63 (ND 102-46, SD 36-17); I 1-0. Sept. 11, 1998. (*House vote 425*)

11. HR 3736. Skilled-Worker Visas. Passage of the bill to increase the number of six-year H-1B skill- and profession-based visas for foreign workers from 65,000 to 115,000 in fiscal 1999 and 2000 and 107,500 in fiscal 2001. The bill also would require some employers using H-1B workers to prove they have tried to recruit qualified U.S. workers and have not laid off U.S. workers. Passed 288-133: R 189-34; D 99-98 (ND 66-76, SD 33-22); I 0-1. Sept. 24, 1998. A "nay" was a vote in support of the president's position. (*House vote 460*)

12. HR 4328. Fiscal 1999 Omnibus Appropriations. Adoption of the conference report on the bill to provide almost $500 billion in new budget authority for those Cabinet departments and federal agencies whose fiscal 1999 appropriations bills were never enacted. The measure incorporates eight previously separate appropriations bills: Labor-HHS-Education, Interior, Treasury-Postal, Foreign Operations, Commerce-Justice-State, District of Columbia, Agriculture and Transportation. In addition, the bill provides $20.8 billion in "emergency" supplemental spending, including $6.8 billion for military spending ($1.9 billion of it for Bosnia operations), $5.9 billion for relief to farmers, $2.4 billion for anti-terrorism programs, $3.35 billion to address Year 2000 computer problems and $1.55 billion for disaster relief from Hurricane Georges. The measure also contains language to extend expiring tax provisions (at a cost of $9.7 billion over nine years), increase the number of H-1B visas for high-tech foreign workers, impose a three-year moratorium on new taxes on Internet access, implement the Chemical Weapons Convention and extend for six months Chapter 12 of the bankruptcy code, which is designed to help struggling farmers. Adopted 333-95: R 162-64; D 170-31 (ND 120-26, SD 50-5); I 1-0. Oct. 20, 1998. (HR 4328 was originally the fiscal 1999 Transportation appropriations bill.) A "yea" was a vote in support of the president's position. (*House vote 538*)

13. H Res 611. Impeachment of President Clinton/Article I — Grand Jury Perjury. Adoption of Article I of the resolution, which would impeach President Clinton for "perjurious, false and misleading testimony" during his Aug. 17, 1998, federal grand jury testimony about his relationship with former White House intern Monica Lewinsky, his prior testimony in the Paula Jones sexual harassment lawsuit and his attempts to influence others' testimony in both. Adopted 228-206: R 223-5; D 5-200 (ND 1-149, SD 4-51); I 0-1. Dec. 19, 1998. A "nay" was a vote in support of the president's position. (*House vote 543*)

[1] *Barbara Lee, D-Calif., was sworn in April 21, replacing Ronald V. Dellums, D-Calif., who resigned Feb. 6.*

[2] *Lois Capps, D-Calif., was sworn in March 17, replacing Walter Capps, D-Calif., who died Oct. 28, 1997.*

[3] *Mary Bono, R-Calif., was sworn in April 21, replacing Sonny Bono, R-Calif., who died Jan. 5.*

[4] *Newt Gingrich, R-Ga., as Speaker of the House, voted at his discretion.*

[5] *Heather Wilson, R-N.M., was sworn in June 25, replacing Stephen H. Schiff, R-N.M., who died March 25.*

[6] *Gregory W. Meeks, D-N.Y., was sworn in Feb. 5, replacing Floyd H. Flake, D-N.Y., who resigned Nov. 15, 1997.*

[7] *Robert A. Brady, D-Pa., wa s sworn in May 21, replacing Thomas M. Foglietta, D-Pa., who resigned Nov. 11, 1997.*

Key

Y	Voted for (yea).
#	Paired for.
+	Announced for.
N	Voted against (nay).
X	Paired against.
−	Announced against.
P	Voted "present."
C	Voted "present" to avoid possible conflict of interest.
?	Did not vote or otherwise make a position known.

Democrats **Republicans**
Independent

	10	11	12	13
ALABAMA				
1 *Callahan*	Y	Y	Y	Y
2 *Everett*	Y	Y	Y	Y
3 *Riley*	Y	Y	Y	Y
4 *Aderholt*	Y	Y	Y	Y
5 Cramer	Y	Y	Y	N
6 *Bachus*	Y	N	N	Y
7 Hilliard	N	N	Y	N
ALASKA				
AL *Young*	?	N	Y	Y
ARIZONA				
1 *Salmon*	Y	Y	N	Y
2 Pastor	Y	Y	Y	N
3 *Stump*	Y	N	N	Y
4 *Shadegg*	Y	Y	Y	Y
5 *Kolbe*	Y	Y	Y	Y
6 *Hayworth*	Y	Y	Y	Y
ARKANSAS				
1 Berry	Y	N	Y	N
2 Snyder	Y	Y	Y	N
3 *Hutchinson*	Y	N	Y	Y
4 *Dickey*	Y	Y	Y	Y
CALIFORNIA				
1 *Riggs*	Y	N	N	Y
2 *Herger*	Y	Y	Y	Y
3 Fazio	Y	Y	?	N
4 *Doolittle*	Y	Y	Y	Y
5 Matsui	Y	Y	Y	N
6 Woolsey	N	Y	Y	N
7 Miller	N	Y	N	?
8 Pelosi	N	Y	Y	N
9 Lee[1]	N	N	N	N
10 Tauscher	Y	Y	Y	N
11 *Pombo*	Y	Y	Y	Y
12 Lantos	Y	Y	Y	N
13 Stark	N	N	?	N
14 Eshoo	Y	Y	Y	N
15 *Campbell*	Y	Y	N	Y
16 Lofgren	Y	Y	Y	N
17 Farr	Y	Y	Y	N
18 Condit	Y	N	N	N
19 *Radanovich*	Y	Y	Y	Y
20 Dooley	Y	Y	Y	N
21 *Thomas*	Y	Y	Y	Y
22 Capps, L.[2]	Y	Y	Y	N
23 *Gallegly*	Y	N	Y	Y
24 Sherman	Y	Y	Y	N
25 *McKeon*	Y	Y	Y	Y
26 Berman	Y	Y	Y	N
27 *Rogan*	Y	Y	Y	Y
28 *Dreier*	Y	Y	Y	Y
29 Waxman	Y	Y	Y	N
30 Becerra	N	Y	Y	N
31 Martinez	N	N	Y	N
32 Dixon	Y	Y	Y	N
33 Roybal-Allard	N	N	Y	N
34 Torres	N	?	Y	N
35 Waters	N	?	Y	N
36 Harman	Y	Y	Y	Y
37 Millender-McD.	Y	N	Y	N
38 *Horn*	Y	N	Y	Y

	10	11	12	13
39 *Royce*	Y	N	N	Y
40 *Lewis*	Y	Y	Y	Y
41 *Kim*	Y	Y	Y	Y
42 Brown	N	N	Y	N
43 *Calvert*	Y	Y	Y	Y
44 *Bono, M.*[3]	Y	Y	Y	Y
45 *Rohrabacher*	Y	N	N	Y
46 Sanchez	Y	+	Y	N
47 *Cox*	Y	Y	Y	Y
48 *Packard*	Y	Y	Y	Y
49 *Bilbray*	Y	Y	Y	Y
50 Filner	N	N	N	N
51 *Cunningham*	Y	Y	Y	Y
52 *Hunter*	Y	N	Y	Y
COLORADO				
1 DeGette	Y	N	N	N
2 Skaggs	N	Y	N	N
3 *McInnis*	Y	Y	Y	Y
4 *Schaffer*	Y	N	N	Y
5 *Hefley*	Y	N	N	Y
6 *Schaefer*	Y	?	Y	Y
CONNECTICUT				
1 Kennelly	Y	?	Y	N
2 Gejdenson	Y	N	Y	N
3 DeLauro	Y	N	Y	N
4 *Shays*	Y	N	N	N
5 Maloney	Y	N	Y	N
6 *Johnson*	Y	Y	Y	Y
DELAWARE				
AL *Castle*	Y	Y	N	Y
FLORIDA				
1 *Scarborough*	?	Y	N	Y
2 Boyd	Y	N	N	N
3 Brown	N	N	Y	N
4 *Fowler*	Y	Y	Y	Y
5 Thurman	Y	N	N	N
6 *Stearns*	Y	Y	N	Y
7 *Mica*	Y	Y	Y	Y
8 *McCollum*	Y	Y	Y	Y
9 *Bilirakis*	Y	Y	Y	Y
10 *Young*	Y	Y	Y	Y
11 Davis	Y	Y	Y	N
12 *Canady*	Y	Y	Y	Y
13 *Miller*	Y	Y	Y	Y
14 *Goss*	Y	+	Y	Y
15 *Weldon*	Y	Y	Y	Y
16 *Foley*	Y	Y	Y	Y
17 Meek	N	N	Y	N
18 *Ros-Lehtinen*	Y	Y	Y	Y
19 Wexler	N	N	Y	N
20 Deutsch	N	N	Y	N
21 *Diaz-Balart*	Y	Y	Y	Y
22 *Shaw*	Y	Y	Y	Y
23 Hastings	N	Y	Y	N
GEORGIA				
1 *Kingston*	Y	N	Y	Y
2 Bishop	Y	Y	Y	N
3 *Collins*	Y	N	N	Y
4 McKinney	Y	N	Y	N
5 Lewis	N	N	Y	N
6 *Gingrich*[4]	Y	Y	Y	Y
7 *Barr*	Y	N	N	Y
8 *Chambliss*	Y	Y	Y	Y
9 *Deal*	Y	N	N	Y
10 *Norwood*	Y	N	Y	Y
11 *Linder*	Y	Y	Y	Y
HAWAII				
1 Abercrombie	Y	N	Y	N
2 Mink	Y	N	Y	N
IDAHO				
1 *Chenoweth*	Y	N	Y	Y
2 *Crapo*	Y	Y	Y	Y
ILLINOIS				
1 Rush	N	N	Y	N
2 Jackson	N	N	Y	N
3 Lipinski	Y	N	Y	N
4 Gutierrez	Y	N	Y	N
5 Blagojevich	Y	N	Y	N
6 *Hyde*	Y	Y	N	Y
7 Davis	N	N	Y	N
8 *Crane*	Y	Y	N	Y
9 Yates	N	?	Y	N
10 *Porter*	Y	Y	Y	Y
11 *Weller*	Y	Y	Y	Y
12 Costello	Y	N	N	N
13 *Fawell*	Y	Y	Y	Y

ND Northern Democrats   SD Southern Democrats

	10	11	12	13
14 Hastert	Y	Y	Y	Y
15 Ewing	Y	Y	Y	Y
16 Manzullo	Y	Y	N	Y
17 Evans	Y	N	Y	N
18 LaHood	Y	Y	N	Y
19 Poshard	?	?	?	N
20 Shimkus	Y	Y	Y	Y

INDIANA

	10	11	12	13
1 Visclosky	Y	N	Y	N
2 McIntosh	Y	Y	N	Y
3 Roemer	Y	Y	Y	N
4 Souder	Y	Y	Y	N
5 Buyer	Y	Y	Y	Y
6 Burton	Y	+	Y	Y
7 Pease	Y	Y	Y	Y
8 Hostettler	Y	N	N	Y
9 Hamilton	Y	Y	Y	N
10 Carson	N	N	Y	N

IOWA

	10	11	12	13
1 Leach	Y	Y	Y	Y
2 Nussle	Y	Y	Y	Y
3 Boswell	Y	Y	Y	N
4 Ganske	Y	Y	Y	Y
5 Latham	Y	Y	Y	Y

KANSAS

	10	11	12	13
1 Moran	Y	Y	Y	Y
2 Ryun	Y	Y	Y	Y
3 Snowbarger	Y	Y	Y	Y
4 Tiahrt	Y	Y	Y	Y

KENTUCKY

	10	11	12	13
1 Whitfield	Y	N	Y	Y
2 Lewis	Y	Y	Y	Y
3 Northup	Y	Y	Y	Y
4 Bunning	Y	Y	Y	Y
5 Rogers	Y	Y	Y	Y
6 Baesler	Y	N	Y	N

LOUISIANA

	10	11	12	13
1 Livingston	Y	Y	Y	Y
2 Jefferson	N	N	Y	N
3 Tauzin	Y	Y	Y	Y
4 McCrery	Y	Y	Y	Y
5 Cooksey	Y	Y	Y	Y
6 Baker	Y	Y	Y	Y
7 John	Y	Y	Y	N

MAINE

	10	11	12	13
1 Allen	Y	Y	Y	N
2 Baldacci	Y	Y	Y	N

MARYLAND

	10	11	12	13
1 Gilchrest	Y	Y	Y	Y
2 Ehrlich	Y	Y	Y	Y
3 Cardin	Y	Y	N	N
4 Wynn	Y	N	Y	N
5 Hoyer	Y	Y	Y	N
6 Bartlett	Y	Y	Y	Y
7 Cummings	N	N	Y	N
8 Morella	Y	Y	Y	N

MASSACHUSETTS

	10	11	12	13
1 Olver	Y	N	Y	N
2 Neal	N	Y	Y	N
3 McGovern	Y	Y	Y	N
4 Frank	N	Y	Y	N
5 Meehan	N	Y	?	N
6 Tierney	N	Y	Y	N
7 Markey	N	Y	Y	N
8 Kennedy	N	Y	Y	N
9 Moakley	Y	N	Y	N
10 Delahunt	N	Y	Y	N

MICHIGAN

	10	11	12	13
1 Stupak	Y	N	N	N
2 Hoekstra	Y	Y	N	Y
3 Ehlers	Y	Y	Y	Y
4 Camp	Y	Y	Y	Y
5 Barcia	?	N	Y	N
6 Upton	Y	Y	N	Y
7 Smith	Y	N	N	Y
8 Stabenow	Y	Y	Y	N
9 Kildee	Y	N	Y	N
10 Bonior	N	Y	Y	N
11 Knollenberg	Y	Y	Y	Y
12 Levin	Y	Y	Y	N
13 Rivers	Y	Y	Y	N
14 Conyers	N	N	Y	N
15 Kilpatrick	N	N	Y	N
16 Dingell	Y	N	Y	N

MINNESOTA

	10	11	12	13
1 Gutknecht	Y	Y	Y	Y
2 Minge	Y	Y	N	N
3 Ramstad	Y	Y	Y	N
4 Vento	Y	Y	Y	N
5 Sabo	N	Y	Y	N
6 Luther	Y	Y	N	N
7 Peterson	Y	N	N	N
8 Oberstar	Y	N	Y	N

MISSISSIPPI

	10	11	12	13
1 Wicker	Y	Y	Y	Y
2 Thompson	N	N	Y	N
3 Pickering	Y	Y	Y	Y
4 Parker	Y	Y	Y	Y
5 Taylor	Y	N	N	Y

MISSOURI

	10	11	12	13
1 Clay	N	N	Y	N
2 Talent	Y	Y	Y	N
3 Gephardt	Y	Y	Y	N
4 Skelton	Y	?	Y	N
5 McCarthy	Y	N	Y	N
6 Danner	Y	N	Y	N
7 Blunt	Y	N	Y	Y
8 Emerson	Y	N	Y	N
9 Hulshof	Y	Y	Y	Y

MONTANA

	10	11	12	13
AL Hill	Y	Y	Y	Y

NEBRASKA

	10	11	12	13
1 Bereuter	Y	Y	Y	Y
2 Christensen	Y	Y	N	Y
3 Barrett	Y	Y	Y	Y

NEVADA

	10	11	12	13
1 Ensign	Y	Y	N	Y
2 Gibbons	Y	Y	Y	Y

NEW HAMPSHIRE

	10	11	12	13
1 Sununu	Y	Y	Y	Y
2 Bass	Y	Y	Y	Y

NEW JERSEY

	10	11	12	13
1 Andrews	Y	N	Y	N
2 LoBiondo	Y	N	Y	Y
3 Saxton	Y	Y	Y	Y
4 Smith	Y	N	N	Y
5 Roukema	Y	Y	N	Y
6 Pallone	Y	N	Y	N
7 Franks	Y	N	Y	N
8 Pascrell	Y	N	Y	N
9 Rothman	Y	N	Y	N
10 Payne	N	N	Y	N
11 Frelinghuysen	Y	Y	Y	Y
12 Pappas	Y	Y	N	Y
13 Menendez	Y	Y	Y	N

NEW MEXICO

	10	11	12	13
1 Wilson[5]	Y	Y	Y	Y
2 Skeen	Y	Y	Y	Y
3 Redmond	Y	Y	Y	Y

NEW YORK

	10	11	12	13
1 Forbes	Y	Y	Y	Y
2 Lazio	Y	Y	Y	Y
3 King	Y	Y	N	N
4 McCarthy	Y	Y	Y	Y
5 Ackerman	N	Y	Y	N
6 Meeks[6]	N	N	Y	N
7 Manton	Y	?	Y	N
8 Nadler	N	Y	Y	N
9 Schumer	Y	Y	Y	N
10 Towns	N	N	Y	N
11 Owens	N	N	Y	N
12 Velázquez	N	N	Y	N
13 Fossella	Y	Y	Y	Y
14 Maloney	Y	N	Y	N
15 Rangel	Y	N	Y	N
16 Serrano	N	N	N	N
17 Engel	N	N	Y	N
18 Lowey	Y	Y	Y	N
19 Kelly	Y	Y	Y	Y
20 Gilman	Y	Y	Y	Y
21 McNulty	Y	N	Y	N
22 Solomon	Y	N	Y	Y
23 Boehlert	Y	Y	Y	Y
24 McHugh	Y	Y	Y	Y
25 Walsh	Y	Y	Y	Y
26 Hinchey	N	N	Y	N
27 Paxon	Y	Y	Y	Y
28 Slaughter	Y	Y	Y	N
29 LaFalce	Y	Y	Y	N

	10	11	12	13
30 Quinn	Y	Y	Y	Y
31 Houghton	Y	Y	Y	N

NORTH CAROLINA

	10	11	12	13
1 Clayton	N	Y	Y	N
2 Etheridge	Y	Y	Y	N
3 Jones	Y	Y	N	Y
4 Price	Y	Y	Y	N
5 Burr	Y	Y	N	Y
6 Coble	Y	Y	N	Y
7 McIntyre	Y	Y	Y	N
8 Hefner	N	Y	Y	N
9 Myrick	Y	Y	Y	Y
10 Ballenger	Y	Y	N	Y
11 Taylor	Y	Y	Y	Y
12 Watt	N	Y	Y	N

NORTH DAKOTA

	10	11	12	13
AL Pomeroy	Y	Y	Y	N

OHIO

	10	11	12	13
1 Chabot	Y	Y	N	Y
2 Portman	Y	Y	Y	Y
3 Hall	Y	Y	Y	Y
4 Oxley	Y	Y	Y	Y
5 Gillmor	Y	Y	Y	Y
6 Strickland	Y	N	Y	N
7 Hobson	Y	Y	Y	Y
8 Boehner	Y	Y	Y	Y
9 Kaptur	Y	N	N	N
10 Kucinich	Y	N	Y	N
11 Stokes	N	N	Y	N
12 Kasich	Y	N	Y	N
13 Brown	Y	N	Y	N
14 Sawyer	Y	Y	Y	N
15 Pryce	+	+	+	Y
16 Regula	Y	Y	Y	Y
17 Traficant	Y	N	Y	N
18 Ney	Y	N	Y	Y
19 LaTourette	Y	Y	Y	Y

OKLAHOMA

	10	11	12	13
1 Largent	Y	Y	N	Y
2 Coburn	Y	Y	N	Y
3 Watkins	Y	Y	Y	Y
4 Watts	Y	N	Y	Y
5 Istook	Y	Y	N	Y
6 Lucas	Y	Y	Y	Y

OREGON

	10	11	12	13
1 Furse	?	Y	Y	N
2 Smith	Y	Y	Y	Y
3 Blumenauer	Y	Y	N	N
4 DeFazio	Y	N	N	N
5 Hooley	Y	Y	Y	N

PENNSYLVANIA

	10	11	12	13
1 Brady[7]	N	N	Y	N
2 Fattah	N	N	Y	N
3 Borski	Y	N	Y	N
4 Klink	Y	N	N	N
5 Peterson	Y	Y	Y	Y
6 Holden	Y	N	N	N
7 Weldon	Y	Y	N	Y
8 Greenwood	Y	Y	Y	Y
9 Shuster	Y	Y	Y	Y
10 McDade	Y	Y	Y	Y
11 Kanjorski	Y	N	N	N
12 Murtha	Y	?	Y	N
13 Fox	Y	Y	Y	Y
14 Coyne	Y	N	Y	N
15 McHale	Y	Y	Y	Y
16 Pitts	Y	Y	Y	Y
17 Gekas	Y	Y	Y	Y
18 Doyle	Y	N	Y	N
19 Goodling	Y	Y	Y	Y
20 Mascara	Y	N	Y	N
21 English	Y	Y	Y	Y

RHODE ISLAND

	10	11	12	13
1 Kennedy	N	Y	Y	N
2 Weygand	Y	Y	Y	N

SOUTH CAROLINA

	10	11	12	13
1 Sanford	Y	Y	N	Y
2 Spence	Y	N	Y	Y
3 Graham	Y	Y	N	Y
4 Inglis	Y	Y	Y	Y
5 Spratt	Y	Y	Y	N
6 Clyburn	N	N	Y	N

SOUTH DAKOTA

	10	11	12	13
AL Thune	Y	Y	Y	Y

TENNESSEE

	10	11	12	13
1 Jenkins	+	Y	Y	Y
2 Duncan	Y	N	N	Y
3 Wamp	Y	N	N	Y
4 Hilleary	Y	N	Y	Y
5 Clement	Y	Y	Y	N
6 Gordon	Y	Y	Y	N
7 Bryant	Y	Y	Y	Y
8 Tanner	Y	Y	Y	N
9 Ford	N	Y	Y	N

TEXAS

	10	11	12	13
1 Sandlin	Y	N	Y	N
2 Turner	Y	N	Y	N
3 Johnson, Sam	Y	N	N	Y
4 Hall	Y	Y	Y	Y
5 Sessions	Y	Y	N	Y
6 Barton	Y	Y	N	Y
7 Archer	Y	Y	Y	Y
8 Brady	Y	+	N	Y
9 Lampson	Y	N	Y	N
10 Doggett	Y	Y	N	N
11 Edwards	Y	Y	Y	N
12 Granger	Y	Y	Y	Y
13 Thornberry	Y	Y	Y	Y
14 Paul	Y	Y	N	Y
15 Hinojosa	Y	Y	Y	N
16 Reyes	Y	Y	Y	N
17 Stenholm	Y	Y	Y	N
18 Jackson-Lee	N	Y	N	Y
19 Combest	Y	N	Y	Y
20 Gonzalez	?	N	Y	N
21 Smith	Y	Y	Y	Y
22 DeLay	Y	Y	Y	Y
23 Bonilla	Y	Y	Y	Y
24 Frost	Y	Y	Y	N
25 Bentsen	Y	Y	Y	N
26 Armey	Y	Y	Y	Y
27 Ortiz	Y	Y	Y	N
28 Rodriguez	Y	N	Y	N
29 Green	Y	Y	Y	N
30 Johnson, E.B.	–	Y	Y	N

UTAH

	10	11	12	13
1 Hansen	Y	Y	?	Y
2 Cook	Y	Y	Y	Y
3 Cannon	Y	Y	Y	Y

VERMONT

	10	11	12	13
AL Sanders	Y	N	Y	N

VIRGINIA

	10	11	12	13
1 Bateman	Y	Y	Y	Y
2 Pickett	Y	Y	Y	N
3 Scott	N	Y	Y	N
4 Sisisky	Y	Y	Y	N
5 Goode	Y	N	N	Y
6 Goodlatte	Y	Y	Y	Y
7 Bliley	Y	Y	Y	Y
8 Moran	N	Y	Y	N
9 Boucher	Y	N	Y	N
10 Wolf	Y	Y	N	Y
11 Davis	Y	Y	Y	Y

WASHINGTON

	10	11	12	13
1 White	Y	Y	N	Y
2 Metcalf	Y	Y	N	Y
3 Smith, Linda	Y	Y	N	Y
4 Hastings	Y	Y	Y	Y
5 Nethercutt	Y	Y	Y	Y
6 Dicks	Y	Y	Y	N
7 McDermott	N	Y	N	N
8 Dunn	Y	Y	Y	Y
9 Smith, Adam	Y	Y	N	N

WEST VIRGINIA

	10	11	12	13
1 Mollohan	N	N	?	N
2 Wise	Y	N	Y	N
3 Rahall	Y	N	Y	N

WISCONSIN

	10	11	12	13
1 Neumann	Y	Y	N	Y
2 Klug	Y	Y	Y	Y
3 Kind	Y	Y	N	N
4 Kleczka	Y	N	N	N
5 Barrett	Y	N	N	N
6 Petri	Y	Y	N	Y
7 Obey	Y	N	Y	N
8 Johnson	Y	N	N	N
9 Sensenbrenner	Y	Y	N	Y

WYOMING

	10	11	12	13
AL Cubin	Y	Y	Y	Y

Southern states - Ala., Ark., Fla., Ga., Ky., La., Miss., N.C., Okla., S.C., Tenn., Texas, Va.

SENATE ROLL CALL VOTES

Senate Roll Call Votes
By Bill Number

Senate Bills	House Bills
S 414, S-16	**HR 6,** S-31, S-45
S 442, S-45, S-46, S-47	**HR 10,** S-46
S 648, S-30	**HR 629,** S-40
S 1092, S-45	**HR 1122,** S-43
S 1173, S-6, S-7, S-8	**HR 1150,** S-22
S 1244, S-22	**HR 1151,** S-37, S-38
S 1260, S-22, S-23	**HR 1270,** S-25
S 1301, S-42, S-43, S-44	**HR 1273,** S-22
S 1415, S-24, S-25, S-26, S-27	**HR 1385,** S-20
S 1575, S-4	**HR 1757,** S-18
S 1618, S-22	**HR 2400,** S-24
S 1645, S-41, S-44	**HR 2431,** S-48
S 1663, S-5, S-6	**HR 2631,** S-5
S 1668, S-7	**HR 2646,** S-8, S-9, S-10, S-16, S-17,
S 1671, S-5	S-18, S-28
S 1723, S-23, S-24	**HR 2676,** S-21
S 1768, S-9, S-10	**HR 2709,** S-24
S 1873, S-22, S-41	**HR 3150,** S-44, S-48
S 1882, S-31	**HR 3579,** S-20
S 1981, S-41	**HR 3616,** S-45
S 2037, S-23	**HR 4057,** S-45
S 2057, S-23, S-27, S-28, S-29	**HR 4059,** S-40
S 2132, S-39	**HR 4101,** S-46
S 2138, S-27	**HR 4103,** S-39, S-45
S 2159, S-32, S-33	**HR 4104,** S-41, S-48
S 2168, S-30, S-33, S-34	**HR 4112,** S-34
S 2176, S-44, S-45	**HR 4194,** S-47
S 2237, S-41, S-42	**HR 4250,** S-48
S 2260, S-34, S-35, S-36, S-37	**HR 4328,** S-48
S 2271, S-32	
S 2279, S-44	
S 2307, S-37	
S 2312, S-38, S-39	
S 2334, S-40	
S 2676, S-30	
S 4101, S-33	
S Con Res 107, S-31	
S Con Res 78, S-8	
S Con Res 86, S-10, S-11, S-12, S-13,	
S-14, S-15	
S J Res 42, S-10	
S Res 187, S-8	

Senate Votes 1, 2, 3, 4, 5, 6, 7

ALABAMA	1	2	3	4	5	6	7
Sessions	Y	Y	Y	N	Y	N	Y
Shelby	Y	Y	Y	N	Y	N	Y
ALASKA							
Murkowski	N	Y	Y	N	Y	N	Y
Stevens	Y	Y	Y	N	Y	N	Y
ARIZONA							
Kyl	N	Y	Y	N	Y	N	Y
McCain	N	Y	Y	N	Y	N	Y
ARKANSAS							
Hutchinson	N	Y	Y	N	Y	N	Y
Bumpers	Y	Y	Y	Y	N	Y	N
CALIFORNIA							
Boxer	Y	Y	Y	N	N	N	Y
Feinstein	Y	Y	Y	N	N	N	Y
COLORADO							
Allard	N	Y	Y	N	Y	N	Y
Campbell	Y	Y	Y	N	Y	N	Y
CONNECTICUT							
Dodd	Y	Y	Y	N	Y	N	Y
Lieberman	Y	Y	Y	N	Y	N	Y
DELAWARE							
Roth	Y	Y	Y	N	Y	N	Y
Biden	Y	?	?	Y	N	N	Y
FLORIDA							
Mack	Y	Y	Y	N	Y	N	Y
Graham	Y	Y	Y	Y	Y	N	Y
GEORGIA							
Coverdell	N	Y	Y	N	Y	N	Y
Cleland	Y	Y	Y	Y	N	Y	N
HAWAII							
Akaka	Y	Y	Y	N	Y	N	N
Inouye	Y	Y	Y	Y	N	Y	N
IDAHO							
Craig	N	Y	Y	N	Y	N	Y
Kempthorne	Y	Y	Y	N	Y	N	Y
ILLINOIS							
Durbin	?	Y	Y	N	N	N	Y
Moseley-Braun	?	Y	Y	N	Y	N	N
INDIANA							
Coats	Y	?	?	?	?	?	?
Lugar	Y	Y	Y	N	Y	N	Y

IOWA	1	2	3	4	5	6	7
Grassley	N	Y	Y	N	Y	N	Y
Harkin	Y	Y	Y	Y	N	Y	N
KANSAS							
Brownback	N	Y	Y	N	Y	N	Y
Roberts	N	Y	Y	N	Y	N	Y
KENTUCKY							
McConnell	N	Y	Y	N	Y	N	Y
Ford	Y	Y	Y	Y	N	Y	N
LOUISIANA							
Breaux	Y	Y	Y	N	Y	Y	Y
Landrieu	Y	Y	Y	Y	N	Y	Y
MAINE							
Collins	Y	Y	Y	N	Y	N	Y
Snowe	N	Y	Y	N	Y	N	Y
MARYLAND							
Mikulski	Y	Y	Y	Y	N	Y	N
Sarbanes	Y	Y	Y	Y	N	Y	N
MASSACHUSETTS							
Kennedy	Y	Y	Y	Y	N	Y	N
Kerry	Y	Y	Y	Y	N	Y	N
MICHIGAN							
Abraham	N	Y	Y	N	Y	N	Y
Levin	Y	Y	Y	Y	N	Y	N
MINNESOTA							
Grams	N	Y	Y	N	Y	N	Y
Wellstone	Y	Y	Y	Y	Y	Y	N
MISSISSIPPI							
Cochran	Y	Y	Y	N	Y	N	Y
Lott	N	Y	Y	N	Y	N	Y
MISSOURI							
Ashcroft	N	Y	Y	N	Y	N	Y
Bond	N	Y	Y	N	Y	N	Y
MONTANA							
Burns	N	Y	Y	N	Y	N	Y
Baucus	Y	Y	Y	Y	Y	Y	N
NEBRASKA							
Hagel	N	Y	Y	N	Y	N	Y
Kerrey	Y	Y	Y	Y	N	Y	Y
NEVADA							
Bryan	Y	Y	Y	Y	N	Y	Y
Reid	Y	Y	Y	Y	N	Y	Y

NEW HAMPSHIRE	1	2	3	4	5	6	7
Gregg	N	Y	Y	N	Y	N	Y
Smith	N	Y	Y	N	Y	N	Y
NEW JERSEY							
Lautenberg	Y	Y	Y	Y	N	Y	N
Torricelli	Y	Y	Y	Y	N	Y	N
NEW MEXICO							
Domenici	Y	Y	Y	N	Y	N	Y
Bingaman	Y	?	?	Y	N	Y	N
NEW YORK							
D'Amato	N	Y	Y	N	Y	N	Y
Moynihan	Y	+	+	?	?	?	?
NORTH CAROLINA							
Faircloth	–	Y	Y	N	Y	N	Y
Helms	N	Y	Y	N	Y	N	Y
NORTH DAKOTA							
Conrad	Y	Y	Y	Y	N	Y	N
Dorgan	Y	Y	Y	Y	N	Y	N
OHIO							
DeWine	Y	Y	Y	N	Y	N	Y
Glenn	Y	Y	Y	Y	N	Y	N
OKLAHOMA							
Inhofe	N	Y	Y	N	Y	N	Y
Nickles	N	Y	Y	N	Y	N	Y
OREGON							
Smith	Y	Y	Y	N	Y	N	Y
Wyden	Y	Y	Y	N	N	N	Y
PENNSYLVANIA							
Santorum	Y	Y	Y	N	Y	N	Y
Specter	Y	Y	Y	N	Y	N	Y
RHODE ISLAND							
Chafee	Y	Y	Y	N	N	N	Y
Reed	Y	Y	Y	Y	N	Y	N
SOUTH CAROLINA							
Thurmond	Y	Y	Y	N	Y	N	Y
Hollings	Y	Y	Y	N	Y	N	N
SOUTH DAKOTA							
Daschle	Y	Y	Y	N	Y	N	Y
Johnson	Y	Y	Y	Y	N	Y	N
TENNESSEE							
Frist	N	Y	Y	N	Y	N	Y
Thompson	Y	Y	Y	N	Y	N	Y

TEXAS	1	2	3	4	5	6	7
Gramm	N	Y	Y	N	Y	N	Y
Hutchison	N	Y	Y	N	Y	N	Y
UTAH							
Bennett	Y	Y	Y	N	Y	N	Y
Hatch	Y	Y	Y	N	Y	N	Y
VERMONT							
Jeffords	Y	Y	Y	N	Y	N	Y
Leahy	Y	Y	Y	Y	N	Y	Y
VIRGINIA							
Warner	N	Y	Y	N	Y	N	Y
Robb	Y	Y	Y	Y	N	Y	N
WASHINGTON							
Gorton	Y	Y	Y	N	N	N	Y
Murray	Y	Y	Y	Y	N	Y	Y
WEST VIRGINIA							
Byrd	Y	Y	Y	N	Y	N	Y
Rockefeller	Y	Y	Y	N	Y	N	Y
WISCONSIN							
Feingold	Y	Y	Y	Y	Y	Y	Y
Kohl	Y	Y	Y	Y	Y	Y	Y
WYOMING							
Enzi	N	Y	Y	N	Y	N	Y
Thomas	Y	Y	Y	N	Y	N	Y

Key

- **Y** Voted for (yea).
- **#** Paired for.
- **+** Announced for.
- **N** Voted against (nay).
- **X** Paired against.
- **–** Announced against.
- **P** Voted "present."
- **C** Voted "present" to avoid possible conflict of interest.
- **?** Did not vote or otherwise make a position known.

Democrats   *Republicans*

ND Northern Democrats   SD Southern Democrats

Southern states - Ala., Ark., Fla., Ga., Ky., La., Miss., N.C., Okla., S.C., Tenn., Texas, Va.

1. Aiken Nomination/Confirmation. Confirmation of President Clinton's nomination of Ann L. Aiken of Oregon to be United States District Judge for the District of Oregon. Confirmed 67-30: R 24-30; D 43-0 (ND 35-0, SD 8-0). Jan. 28, 1998. A "yea" was a vote in support of the president's position.

2. Moreno Nomination/Confirmation. Confirmation of President Clinton's nomination of Carlos R. Moreno of California to be U.S. District Judge for the central district of California. Confirmed 96-0: R 54-0; D 42-0 (ND 34-0, SD 8-0). Feb. 3, 1998. A "yea" was a vote in support of the president's position.

3. Miller Nomination/Confirmation. Confirmation of President Clinton's nomination of Christine O.C. Miller of the District of Columbia to be a judge of the U.S. Court of Federal Claims. Confirmed 96-0: R 54-0; D 42-0 (ND 34-0, SD 8-0). Feb. 3, 1998. A "yea" was a vote in support of the president's position.

4. S 1575. Renaming National Airport/Advisory Group. Robb, D-Va., amendment to establish an advisory group to review all proposals to rename federal facilities, including the proposed renaming of Washington National Airport for former President Ronald Reagan. Rejected 35-63: R 0-54; D 35-9 (ND 28-8, SD 7-1). Feb. 4, 1998.

5. S 1575. Renaming National Airport/FBI Building. Coverdell, R-Ga., motion to table (kill) the Reid, D-Nev., amendment to remove former FBI director J. Edgar Hoover's name from the FBI headquarters building in Washington, DC. Motion agreed to 62-36: R 52-2; D 10-34 (ND 8-28, SD 2-6). Feb. 4, 1998.

6. S 1575. Renaming National Airport/Local Approval. Daschle, D-S.D., amendment to require the approval of the Metropolitan Washington Airports Authority before changing the airport's name. Rejected 35-63: R 1-53; D 34-10 (ND 27-9, SD 7-1). Feb. 4, 1998.

7. S 1575. Renaming National Airport/Passage. Passage of the bill to rename Washington National Airport the "Ronald Reagan Washington National Airport" after former President Ronald Reagan. Passed 76-22: R 54-0; D 22-22 (ND 19-17, SD 3-5). Feb. 4, 1998.

	8	9	10	11	12	13	14
ALABAMA							
Sessions	N	N	Y	N	Y	Y	Y
Shelby	N	N	Y	N	Y	Y	Y
ALASKA							
Murkowski	Y	N	Y	N	Y	Y	Y
Stevens	Y	Y	Y	Y	Y	Y	Y
ARIZONA							
Kyl	N	N	Y	N	Y	N	Y
McCain	Y	Y	Y	Y	N	N	N
ARKANSAS							
Hutchinson	N	N	Y	N	Y	N	Y
Bumpers	Y	Y	N	Y	N	N	N
CALIFORNIA							
Boxer	Y	Y	N	Y	N	Y	N
Feinstein	Y	Y	N	Y	N	Y	?
COLORADO							
Allard	N	N	Y	N	Y	Y	Y
Campbell	N	N	N	Y	N	Y	Y
CONNECTICUT							
Dodd	Y	Y	N	Y	N	N	N
Lieberman	Y	Y	N	Y	N	Y	N
DELAWARE							
Roth	Y	Y	N	Y	N	Y	N
Biden	Y	Y	N	Y	N	Y	N
FLORIDA							
Mack	Y	Y	N	Y	Y	Y	Y
Graham	Y	Y	N	Y	N	Y	N
GEORGIA							
Coverdell	Y	Y	Y	N	Y	Y	Y
Cleland	Y	Y	N	Y	N	Y	N
HAWAII							
Akaka	Y	Y	N	Y	N	Y	N
Inouye	Y	Y	N	Y	N	Y	N
IDAHO							
Craig	Y	N	Y	N	Y	Y	Y
Kempthorne	N	N	Y	N	Y	Y	Y
ILLINOIS							
Durbin	Y	Y	N	Y	N	Y	N
Moseley-Braun	Y	Y	N	Y	N	Y	N
INDIANA							
Coats	N	N	Y	N	Y	N	Y
Lugar	N	N	N	Y	Y	Y	Y

	8	9	10	11	12	13	14
IOWA							
Grassley	N	N	Y	N	Y	N	Y
Harkin	Y	Y	N	Y	?	?	?
KANSAS							
Brownback	N	N	Y	N	Y	Y	Y
Roberts	N	N	Y	N	Y	Y	Y
KENTUCKY							
McConnell	N	N	Y	N	Y	Y	Y
Ford	Y	Y	N	?	N	Y	N
LOUISIANA							
Breaux	Y	Y	N	Y	N	Y	N
Landrieu	Y	Y	N	Y	N	N	N
MAINE							
Collins	Y	Y	N	Y	N	Y	N
Snowe	Y	Y	N	Y	N	Y	N
MARYLAND							
Mikulski	Y	Y	N	Y	N	Y	N
Sarbanes	Y	Y	N	Y	N	Y	N
MASSACHUSETTS							
Kennedy	Y	Y	N	Y	N	+	–
Kerry	Y	Y	N	Y	N	Y	N
MICHIGAN							
Abraham	Y	N	Y	Y	Y	N	Y
Levin	?	?	?	?	N	Y	N
MINNESOTA							
Grams	Y	N	Y	N	Y	Y	Y
Wellstone	Y	Y	N	Y	N	N	N
MISSISSIPPI							
Cochran	Y	Y	Y	Y	Y	Y	Y
Lott	Y	N	Y	N	Y	N	N
MISSOURI							
Ashcroft	N	N	Y	N	Y	N	Y
Bond	Y	Y	Y	N	Y	Y	Y
MONTANA							
Burns	N	N	Y	N	Y	Y	Y
Baucus	Y	Y	N	Y	N	Y	N
NEBRASKA							
Hagel	Y	N	Y	N	Y	Y	Y
Kerrey	Y	Y	N	Y	N	N	N
NEVADA							
Bryan	Y	Y	–	Y	N	Y	N
Reid	Y	Y	?	?	N	Y	N

	8	9	10	11	12	13	14
NEW HAMPSHIRE							
Gregg	Y	N	Y	Y	Y	Y	Y
Smith	N	N	Y	N	Y	Y	Y
NEW JERSEY							
Lautenberg	Y	Y	N	Y	N	Y	N
Torricelli	Y	Y	N	Y	N	Y	N
NEW MEXICO							
Domenici	Y	Y	Y	Y	Y	Y	Y
Bingaman	Y	Y	N	Y	N	Y	N
NEW YORK							
D'Amato	N	N	Y	N	Y	Y	Y
Moynihan	Y	Y	N	Y	N	Y	N
NORTH CAROLINA							
Faircloth	N	N	Y	N	Y	Y	Y
Helms	N	N	Y	N	Y	Y	Y
NORTH DAKOTA							
Conrad	Y	Y	N	Y	N	Y	N
Dorgan	Y	Y	N	Y	N	Y	N
OHIO							
DeWine	Y	N	Y	Y	Y	Y	Y
Glenn	Y	Y	N	Y	N	Y	N
OKLAHOMA							
Inhofe	N	N	Y	N	Y	Y	Y
Nickles	Y	N	Y	N	Y	Y	Y
OREGON							
Smith	Y	N	N	Y	Y	Y	Y
Wyden	Y	Y	N	Y	N	N	N
PENNSYLVANIA							
Santorum	N	N	Y	N	Y	Y	Y
Specter	Y	Y	N	?	N	Y	N
RHODE ISLAND							
Chafee	Y	Y	N	Y	N	Y	N
Reed	Y	Y	N	Y	N	Y	N
SOUTH CAROLINA							
Thurmond	Y	Y	N	Y	N	Y	Y
Hollings	Y	Y	N	Y	N	Y	N
SOUTH DAKOTA							
Daschle	Y	Y	N	Y	N	N	N
Johnson	Y	Y	N	Y	N	N	N
TENNESSEE							
Frist	Y	Y	Y	Y	Y	Y	Y
Thompson	Y	Y	Y	Y	Y	N	Y

	8	9	10	11	12	13	14
TEXAS							
Gramm	N	N	Y	N	Y	N	Y
Hutchison	Y	N	Y	Y	Y	Y	Y
UTAH							
Bennett	Y	Y	N	Y	Y	Y	Y
Hatch	Y	Y	Y	Y	Y	Y	Y
VERMONT							
Jeffords	Y	Y	N	Y	N	Y	N
Leahy	Y	Y	N	Y	N	Y	N
VIRGINIA							
Warner	?	?	?	?	Y	Y	Y
Robb	Y	Y	N	Y	N	N	N
WASHINGTON							
Gorton	Y	Y	Y	Y	Y	Y	Y
Murray	Y	Y	N	Y	N	Y	N
WEST VIRGINIA							
Byrd	Y	Y	N	Y	N	Y	N
Rockefeller	Y	Y	N	Y	N	Y	N
WISCONSIN							
Feingold	Y	Y	N	Y	N	N	N
Kohl	Y	Y	N	Y	N	N	N
WYOMING							
Enzi	N	N	Y	N	Y	Y	Y
Thomas	Y	N	Y	N	Y	Y	Y

Key

Y	Voted for (yea).
#	Paired for.
+	Announced for.
N	Voted against (nay).
X	Paired against.
–	Announced against.
P	Voted "present."
C	Voted "present" to avoid possible conflict of interest.
?	Did not vote or otherwise make a position known.

Democrats   *Republicans*

ND Northern Democrats   SD Southern Democrats

Southern states - Ala., Ark., Fla., Ga., Ky., La., Miss., N.C., Okla., S.C., Tenn., Texas, Va.

8. Satcher Nomination/Cloture. Motion to invoke cloture (thus limiting debate) on the confirmation of President Clinton's nomination of Dr. David Satcher of Tennessee to be U.S. surgeon general and assistant secretary for health in the Department of Health and Human Services. Motion agreed to 75-23: R 31-23; D 44-0 (ND 36-0, SD 8-0). Feb. 10, 1998. Three-fifths of the total Senate (60) is required to invoke cloture.

9. Satcher Nomination/Confirmation. Confirmation of President Clinton's nomination of Dr. David Satcher of Tennessee to be U.S. surgeon general and assistant secretary for health in the Department of Health and Human Services. Confirmed 63-35: R 19-35; D 44-0 (ND 36-0, SD 8-0). Feb. 10, 1998. A "yea" was a vote in support of the president's position.

10. S 1601. Ban Human Cloning/Cloture. Motion to invoke cloture (thus limiting debate) on the motion to proceed to the bill banning creation of a human embryo through cloning. Motion rejected 42-54: R 42-12; D 0-42 (ND 0-34, SD 0-8). Feb. 11, 1998. Three-fifths of the total Senate (60) is required to invoke cloture.

11. Morrow Nomination/Confirmation. Confirmation of President Clinton's nomination of Margaret M. Morrow of California to be U.S. District judge for the central district of California. Confirmed 67-28: R 25-28; D 42-0 (ND 35-0, SD 7-0). Feb. 11, 1998. A "yea" was a vote in support of the president's position.

12. S 1663. Campaign Finance Revisions/Labor Union Dues. McConnell, R-Ky., motion to table (kill) the McCain, R-Ariz., substitute amendment that would revise financing of federal political campaigns. Motion rejected 48-51: R 48-7; D 0-44 (ND 0-36, SD 0-8). Feb. 24, 1998.

13. HR 2631. Military Construction Line-Item Veto Disapproval/Veto Override. Passage, over President Clinton's Nov. 13, 1997, veto, of the bill to disapprove Clinton's line-item vetoes of 38 projects, totaling $287 million, in the fiscal 1998 military construction appropriations bill (HR 2016 - PL 105-45). Passed (thus enacted into law) 78-20: R 46-9; D 32-11 (ND 27-8, SD 5-3). Feb. 25, 1998. A two-thirds majority of those present and voting (66 in this case) of both houses is required to override a veto. A "nay" was a vote in support of the president's position.

14. S 1663. Campaign Finance Revisions/Snowe Amendment. McConnell, R-Ky., motion to table (kill) the Snowe, R-Maine, amendment to the McCain, R-Ariz., substitute amendment that would replace language redefining express advocacy with language to increase certain disclosure requirements and prohibit the use of labor or corporate money to broadcast campaign ads shortly before a primary or general election. Motion rejected 47-50: R 47-8; D 0-42 (ND 0-34, SD 0-8). Feb. 25, 1998. (Subsequently, the Snowe amendment was adopted by voice vote.)

	15	16	17	18	19	20	21
ALABAMA							
Sessions	Y	N	Y	Y	Y	N	N
Shelby	Y	N	Y	?	Y	Y	N
ALASKA							
Murkowski	Y	N	Y	?	Y	Y	Y
Stevens	Y	N	N	Y	Y	Y	Y
ARIZONA							
Kyl	Y	N	Y	Y	Y	N	N
McCain	N	Y	N	Y	Y	C	C
ARKANSAS							
Hutchinson	Y	N	Y	Y	Y	N	N
Bumpers	N	Y	N	Y	N	Y	Y
CALIFORNIA							
Boxer	N	Y	N	?	N	Y	Y
Feinstein	N	Y	N	Y	N	Y	Y
COLORADO							
Allard	Y	N	Y	Y	?	N	N
Campbell	Y	N	N	Y	Y	N	N
CONNECTICUT							
Dodd	N	Y	N	Y	N	Y	Y
Lieberman	N	Y	N	Y	N	Y	Y
DELAWARE							
Roth	Y	N	Y	Y	Y	Y	N
Biden	N	Y	N	?	N	Y	Y
FLORIDA							
Mack	Y	N	Y	Y	Y	N	N
Graham	N	Y	N	Y	N	N	N
GEORGIA							
Coverdell	Y	N	Y	Y	Y	N	N
Cleland	N	Y	N	?	N	Y	Y
HAWAII							
Akaka	N	Y	N	Y	N	Y	Y
Inouye	?	Y	N	Y	?	#	Y
IDAHO							
Craig	Y	N	Y	Y	Y	N	N
Kempthorne	Y	N	Y	Y	Y	N	N
ILLINOIS							
Durbin	N	Y	N	Y	N	Y	Y
Moseley-Braun	N	Y	N	?	N	Y	Y
INDIANA							
Coats	Y	N	Y	Y	Y	N	N
Lugar	Y	N	Y	Y	Y	Y	Y

	15	16	17	18	19	20	21
IOWA							
Grassley	Y	N	Y	Y	Y	N	N
Harkin	?	?	?	Y	N	Y	Y
KANSAS							
Brownback	Y	N	Y	Y	Y	N	N
Roberts	Y	N	Y	Y	Y	?	N
KENTUCKY							
McConnell	Y	N	Y	Y	Y	Y	N
Ford	N	Y	N	Y	N	N	N
LOUISIANA							
Breaux	N	Y	N	Y	N	Y	N
Landrieu	N	Y	N	?	N	N	N
MAINE							
Collins	N	Y	N	Y	N	Y	Y
Snowe	N	Y	N	?	Y	Y	N
MARYLAND							
Mikulski	N	Y	N	?	N	Y	Y
Sarbanes	N	Y	N	Y	N	Y	Y
MASSACHUSETTS							
Kennedy	N	Y	N	Y	N	Y	Y
Kerry	N	Y	N	?	N	Y	Y
MICHIGAN							
Abraham	Y	N	Y	Y	Y	N	N
Levin	N	Y	N	Y	N	Y	Y
MINNESOTA							
Grams	Y	N	Y	Y	Y	N	N
Wellstone	N	Y	N	Y	N	Y	Y
MISSISSIPPI							
Cochran	Y	N	Y	Y	Y	N	N
Lott	Y	N	Y	Y	Y	Y	N
MISSOURI							
Ashcroft	Y	N	Y	Y	Y	N	N
Bond	Y	N	Y	Y	Y	Y	N
MONTANA							
Burns	Y	N	Y	Y	Y	N	N
Baucus	N	Y	N	Y	N	X	N
NEBRASKA							
Hagel	Y	N	Y	Y	Y	N	N
Kerrey	N	Y	N	?	N	Y	Y
NEVADA							
Bryan	N	Y	N	Y	N	N	Y
Reid	N	Y	N	Y	N	N	Y

	15	16	17	18	19	20	21
NEW HAMPSHIRE							
Gregg	Y	N	Y	Y	Y	N	N
Smith	Y	N	Y	Y	Y	N	N
NEW JERSEY							
Lautenberg	N	Y	N	Y	N	Y	Y
Torricelli	N	Y	N	Y	N	Y	Y
NEW MEXICO							
Domenici	Y	N	Y	Y	Y	N	N
Bingaman	N	Y	N	Y	N	Y	Y
NEW YORK							
D'Amato	Y	N	N	?	Y	Y	Y
Moynihan	N	Y	N	Y	N	Y	Y
NORTH CAROLINA							
Faircloth	Y	N	Y	?	Y	Y	N
Helms	Y	N	Y	?	Y	Y	N
NORTH DAKOTA							
Conrad	N	Y	N	Y	N	Y	Y
Dorgan	N	Y	N	?	N	Y	Y
OHIO							
DeWine	Y	N	Y	Y	Y	Y	Y
Glenn	N	Y	N	Y	?	?	Y
OKLAHOMA							
Inhofe	Y	N	Y	?	Y	N	N
Nickles	Y	N	Y	?	Y	N	N
OREGON							
Smith	Y	N	Y	Y	Y	Y	Y
Wyden	N	Y	N	Y	N	Y	Y
PENNSYLVANIA							
Santorum	Y	N	Y	Y	Y	N	N
Specter	N	Y	N	Y	Y	Y	Y
RHODE ISLAND							
Chafee	N	Y	N	Y	Y	Y	Y
Reed	N	Y	N	Y	N	Y	Y
SOUTH CAROLINA							
Thurmond	Y	N	Y	Y	Y	N	N
Hollings	N	Y	N	Y	N	Y	Y
SOUTH DAKOTA							
Daschle	N	Y	N	Y	N	Y	Y
Johnson	N	Y	N	Y	N	Y	Y
TENNESSEE							
Frist	Y	N	Y	Y	Y	N	N
Thompson	N	Y	N	Y	Y	N	N

	15	16	17	18	19	20	21
TEXAS							
Gramm	Y	N	Y	Y	Y	Y	N
Hutchison	Y	N	Y	Y	Y	Y	N
UTAH							
Bennett	Y	N	Y	?	Y	N	N
Hatch	Y	N	Y	Y	Y	Y	Y
VERMONT							
Jeffords	N	Y	N	Y	Y	?	N
Leahy	N	Y	N	Y	N	Y	N
VIRGINIA							
Warner	Y	N	Y	?	Y	Y	Y
Robb	N	Y	N	Y	N	Y	Y
WASHINGTON							
Gorton	Y	N	Y	Y	Y	Y	Y
Murray	N	Y	N	Y	N	Y	Y
WEST VIRGINIA							
Byrd	N	Y	N	Y	N	Y	Y
Rockefeller	N	Y	N	Y	N	Y	Y
WISCONSIN							
Feingold	N	Y	N	Y	N	N	N
Kohl	N	Y	N	Y	Y	Y	Y
WYOMING							
Enzi	Y	N	Y	Y	Y	N	N
Thomas	Y	N	Y	Y	Y	N	N

Key

Y	Voted for (yea).
#	Paired for.
+	Announced for.
N	Voted against (nay).
X	Paired against.
–	Announced against.
P	Voted "present."
C	Voted "present" to avoid possible conflict of interest.
?	Did not vote or otherwise make a position known.

Democrats *Republicans*

ND Northern Democrats   SD Southern Democrats

Southern states - Ala., Ark., Fla., Ga., Ky., La., Miss., N.C., Okla., S.C., Tenn., Texas, Va.

15. S 1663. Campaign Finance Revisions/McCain Substitute. McConnell, R-Ky., motion to table (kill) the McCain, R-Ariz., substitute amendment that would revise financing of federal political campaigns. Motion rejected 48-50: R 48-7; D 0-43 (ND 0-35, SD 0-8). Feb. 25, 1998.

16. S 1663. Campaign Finance Revisions/Cloture. Motion to invoke cloture (thus limiting debate) on the McCain, R-Ariz., substitute amendment that would revise financing of federal political campaigns. Motion rejected 51-48: R 7-48; D 44-0 (ND 36-0, SD 8-0). Feb. 26, 1998. Three-fifths of the total Senate (60) is required to invoke cloture.

17. S 1663. Campaign Finance Revisions/Cloture. Motion to invoke cloture (thus limiting debate) on the bill that would require labor organizations, banks or corporations to secure voluntary authorization from their members before using any membership dues, initiation fees or other payments to fund political activities. Motion rejected 45-54: R 45-10; D 0-44 (ND 0-36, SD 0-8). Feb. 26, 1998. Three-fifths of the total Senate (60) is required to invoke cloture.

18. Young Nomination/Confirmation. Confirmation of President Clinton's nomination of Richard L. Young of Indiana to be U.S. District judge for the Southern District of Indiana. Confirmed 81-0: R 45-0; D 36-0 (ND 30-0, SD 6-0). March 2, 1998. A "yea" was a vote in support of the president's position.

19. S 1173. Highway and Transit Reauthorization/Welfare Report. Chafee, R-R.I., motion to table (kill) the Wellstone, D-Minn., amendment to the Senate Environment and Public Works Committee substitute amendment. The Wellstone amendment would require the Health and Human Services Department to report on former welfare recipients' ability to achieve self-sufficiency. Motion Agreed to 54-43: R 53-1; D 1-42 (ND 1-34, SD 0-8). March 3, 1998.

20. S 1173. Highway and Transit Reauthorization/National Blood Alcohol Level. Lautenberg, D-N.J., amendment to the Senate Environment and Public Works Committee substitute amendment. The Lautenberg amendment would establish a national standard to prohibit driving by individuals with a blood-alcohol content of 0.08 percent or greater. Adopted 62-32: R 26-26; D 36-6 (ND 31-3, SD 5-3). March 4, 1998. A "yea" was a vote in support of the president's position.

21. S 1173. Highway and Transit Reauthorization/Open Container Ban. Dorgan, D-N.D., amendment to the Senate Environment and Public Works Committee substitute amendment that would establish a nationwide ban on having an open container of alcohol in a moving vehicle. Adopted 52-47: R 14-40; D 38-7 (ND 34-3, SD 4-4). March 5, 1998.

	22	23	24	25	26	27	28
ALABAMA							
Sessions	N	N	Y	Y	?	?	Y
Shelby	N	N	Y	Y	?	?	Y
ALASKA							
Murkowski	N	Y	Y	Y	N	Y	Y
Stevens	N	Y	Y	Y	N	Y	Y
ARIZONA							
Kyl	N	N	Y	Y	Y	N	N
McCain	C	Y	Y	Y	Y	N	N
ARKANSAS							
Hutchinson	N	N	Y	Y	Y	N	Y
Bumpers	Y	Y	Y	Y	N	Y	Y
CALIFORNIA							
Boxer	Y	Y	?	Y	N	Y	Y
Feinstein	Y	Y	Y	Y	N	Y	Y
COLORADO							
Allard	N	N	Y	Y	N	Y	Y
Campbell	N	Y	Y	Y	N	Y	Y
CONNECTICUT							
Dodd	Y	Y	Y	Y	N	Y	Y
Lieberman	Y	Y	Y	Y	N	N	Y
DELAWARE							
Roth	N	Y	Y	Y	N	Y	Y
Biden	Y	Y	Y	Y	N	Y	Y
FLORIDA							
Mack	N	N	Y	Y	N	Y	Y
Graham	N	Y	Y	Y	Y	Y	Y
GEORGIA							
Coverdell	N	N	Y	Y	Y	N	Y
Cleland	Y	Y	N	Y	N	Y	Y
HAWAII							
Akaka	Y	Y	Y	Y	N	Y	Y
Inouye	Y	Y	Y	Y	N	Y	Y
IDAHO							
Craig	N	N	Y	Y	N	Y	Y
Kempthorne	N	Y	Y	Y	N	Y	Y
ILLINOIS							
Durbin	Y	Y	?	Y	N	Y	Y
Moseley-Braun	Y	Y	Y	Y	N	Y	Y
INDIANA							
Coats	Y	?	?	Y	Y	Y	Y
Lugar	Y	N	Y	Y	Y	Y	Y

	22	23	24	25	26	27	28
IOWA							
Grassley	N	N	Y	N	Y	Y	Y
Harkin	Y	Y	Y	Y	N	Y	Y
KANSAS							
Brownback	N	N	Y	Y	Y	Y	Y
Roberts	N	N	Y	Y	N	Y	Y
KENTUCKY							
McConnell	N	N	Y	Y	Y	N	Y
Ford	N	Y	Y	Y	N	Y	Y
LOUISIANA							
Breaux	N	Y	Y	Y	N	Y	Y
Landrieu	N	Y	Y	Y	N	Y	Y
MAINE							
Collins	N	Y	Y	Y	N	N	Y
Snowe	N	Y	Y	Y	N	N	Y
MARYLAND							
Mikulski	Y	Y	Y	Y	N	Y	Y
Sarbanes	Y	Y	Y	Y	N	Y	Y
MASSACHUSETTS							
Kennedy	Y	Y	Y	Y	N	?	?
Kerry	Y	Y	Y	Y	N	Y	Y
MICHIGAN							
Abraham	N	N	Y	Y	Y	Y	Y
Levin	Y	Y	Y	Y	Y	Y	Y
MINNESOTA							
Grams	N	N	Y	Y	Y	Y	Y
Wellstone	Y	Y	Y	Y	N	Y	Y
MISSISSIPPI							
Cochran	N	N	Y	Y	Y	Y	Y
Lott	N	N	Y	Y	Y	Y	Y
MISSOURI							
Ashcroft	N	N	Y	Y	Y	Y	Y
Bond	N	Y	Y	Y	N	Y	Y
MONTANA							
Burns	N	N	Y	Y	N	Y	Y
Baucus	N	Y	Y	Y	N	Y	Y
NEBRASKA							
Hagel	N	N	Y	Y	Y	N	Y
Kerrey	Y	Y	Y	Y	N	Y	Y
NEVADA							
Bryan	N	Y	Y	Y	N	Y	Y
Reid	N	Y	Y	Y	N	Y	Y

	22	23	24	25	26	27	28
NEW HAMPSHIRE							
Gregg	N	N	Y	N	N	N	Y
Smith	N	N	Y	N	Y	N	Y
NEW JERSEY							
Lautenberg	Y	Y	Y	Y	N	N	Y
Torricelli	Y	Y	Y	Y	N	Y	Y
NEW MEXICO							
Domenici	Y	Y	Y	Y	N	Y	Y
Bingaman	Y	Y	Y	Y	N	Y	Y
NEW YORK							
D'Amato	Y	Y	Y	Y	N	Y	Y
Moynihan	Y	Y	Y	Y	N	Y	Y
NORTH CAROLINA							
Faircloth	N	N	Y	Y	N	Y	Y
Helms	N	?	Y	N	N	Y	Y
NORTH DAKOTA							
Conrad	Y	Y	Y	Y	N	Y	Y
Dorgan	Y	Y	Y	Y	N	Y	Y
OHIO							
DeWine	Y	N	Y	Y	N	Y	Y
Glenn	Y	?	?	Y	N	Y	Y
OKLAHOMA							
Inhofe	N	N	Y	Y	Y	N	Y
Nickles	N	N	Y	N	Y	N	Y
OREGON							
Smith	Y	N	Y	N	Y	N	Y
Wyden	Y	Y	?	Y	N	N	N
PENNSYLVANIA							
Santorum	N	N	Y	N	Y	N	Y
Specter	Y	Y	Y	Y	N	N	N
RHODE ISLAND							
Chafee	N	Y	Y	Y	N	Y	Y
Reed	N	Y	Y	Y	N	Y	Y
SOUTH CAROLINA							
Thurmond	N	N	Y	Y	Y	Y	Y
Hollings	Y	N	Y	Y	N	Y	Y
SOUTH DAKOTA							
Daschle	Y	Y	Y	Y	N	Y	Y
Johnson	Y	Y	Y	Y	N	Y	Y
TENNESSEE							
Frist	N	N	Y	Y	N	N	Y
Thompson	N	N	Y	Y	Y	N	Y

	22	23	24	25	26	27	28
TEXAS							
Gramm	N	N	Y	Y	N	Y	Y
Hutchison	N	?	Y	Y	Y	N	Y
UTAH							
Bennett	N	?	Y	Y	N	Y	Y
Hatch	Y	N	Y	Y	N	Y	Y
VERMONT							
Jeffords	N	Y	Y	Y	N	Y	Y
Leahy	N	Y	?	Y	N	N	Y
VIRGINIA							
Warner	Y	Y	Y	Y	N	Y	Y
Robb	Y	Y	Y	Y	N	Y	Y
WASHINGTON							
Gorton	N	N	Y	Y	N	Y	Y
Murray	Y	Y	Y	Y	N	Y	Y
WEST VIRGINIA							
Byrd	Y	Y	Y	Y	N	N	Y
Rockefeller	Y	Y	Y	Y	N	N	Y
WISCONSIN							
Feingold	N	Y	Y	Y	N	N	Y
Kohl	N	Y	Y	Y	N	Y	Y
WYOMING							
Enzi	N	N	Y	Y	N	Y	Y
Thomas	N	N	Y	Y	N	Y	Y

Key

Y	Voted for (yea).
#	Paired for.
+	Announced for.
N	Voted against (nay).
X	Paired against.
−	Announced against.
P	Voted "present."
C	Voted "present" to avoid possible conflict of interest.
?	Did not vote or otherwise make a position known.

Democrats   *Republicans*

ND Northern Democrats   SD Southern Democrats

Southern states - Ala., Ark., Fla., Ga., Ky., La., Miss., N.C., Okla., S.C., Tenn., Texas, Va.

22. S 1173. Highway and Transit Reauthorization/Drive-Through Liquor Sales. Bingaman, D-N.M., amendment to the Senate Environment and Public Works Committee substitute amendment that would establish a national ban on drive-through alcohol sales. Rejected 43-56: R 9-45; D 34-11 (ND 30-7, SD 4-4). March 5, 1998.

23. S 1173. Highway and Transit Reauthorization/Minority Construction Set-Asides. Chafee, R-R.I., motion to table (kill) the McConnell, R-Ky., amendment to the Senate Environment and Public Works Committee substitute amendment that would eliminate a program to reserve a portion of construction funds for disadvantaged business enterprises. Motion agreed to 58-37: R 15-36; D 43-1 (ND 36-0, SD 7-1). March 6, 1998. A "yea" was a vote in support of the president's position.

24. S 1668. Whistleblower Protection/Passage. Passage of the bill to allow government employees in the intelligence community to disclose to members of Congress evidence of possible misconduct at federal intelligence agencies. Passed 93-1: R 54-0; D 39-1 (ND 32-0, SD 7-1). March 9, 1998. A "nay" was a vote in support of the president's position.

25. S 1173. Highway and Transit Reauthorization/Mass Transit Funding. D'Amato, R-N.Y., amendment to the Senate Environment and Public Works Committee substitute amendment that would authorize $41.3 billion over fiscal 1998-2003 for mass transit programs. Adopted 96-4: R 51-4; D 45-0 (ND 37-0, SD 8-0). March 10, 1998.

26. S 1173. Highway and Transit Reauthorization/Gas Tax. Mack, R-Fla., motion to waive the Budget Act with respect to the Warner, R-Va., point of order against the Mack amendment to the Roth, R-Del., amendment to the Senate Environment and Public Works Committee substitute amendment. The Mack amendment would eliminate the 4.3-cent tax on transportation fuels. Motion rejected 18-80: R 16-37; D 2-43 (ND 1-36, SD 1-7). March 11, 1998. A three-fifths majority vote (60) of the total Senate is required to waive the Budget Act. (Subsequently, the chair upheld the point of order, and the amendment fell.)

27. S 1173. Highway and Transit Reauthorization/Ethanol Tax Break. Lott, R-Miss., motion to table (kill) the McCain, R-Ariz., amendment to the Roth, R-Del., amendment to the Senate Environment and Public Works Committee substitute amendment. The McCain amendment would remove language in the Roth amendment that would extend an ethanol tax break from 2000 to 2007. Motion agreed to 71-26: R 35-18; D 36-8 (ND 29-7, SD 7-1). March 11, 1998.

28. S 1173. Highway and Transit Reauthorization/Cloture. Motion to invoke cloture (thus limiting debate) on the Senate Environment and Public Works Committee substitute amendment which would authorize $214.3 billion over fiscal years 1998-2003 for transportation funding. Motion agreed to 96-3: R 52-3; D 44-0 (ND 36-0, SD 8-0). March 11, 1998. Three-fifths of the total Senate (60) is required to invoke cloture.

	29	30	31	32	33	34	35
ALABAMA							
Sessions	Y	Y	Y	Y	Y	Y	Y
Shelby	N	Y	Y	Y	Y	Y	Y
ALASKA							
Murkowski	Y	Y	Y	Y	Y	Y	Y
Stevens	Y	Y	N	Y	Y	Y	Y
ARIZONA							
Kyl	Y	Y	Y	?	Y	Y	Y
McCain	Y	Y	Y	?	Y	Y	Y
ARKANSAS							
Hutchinson	Y	Y	Y	Y	Y	Y	Y
Bumpers	Y	Y	Y	Y	Y	Y	Y
CALIFORNIA							
Boxer	N	Y	Y	Y	Y	Y	Y
Feinstein	N	Y	Y	Y	Y	Y	Y
COLORADO							
Allard	Y	Y	Y	Y	Y	Y	Y
Campbell	N	Y	Y	Y	Y	Y	Y
CONNECTICUT							
Dodd	Y	Y	Y	Y	Y	Y	Y
Lieberman	Y	Y	Y	Y	Y	Y	Y
DELAWARE							
Roth	Y	Y	Y	Y	Y	Y	Y
Biden	Y	Y	Y	Y	Y	Y	Y
FLORIDA							
Mack	Y	Y	Y	Y	Y	Y	Y
Graham	Y	Y	Y	Y	Y	Y	Y
GEORGIA							
Coverdell	Y	Y	Y	Y	Y	Y	Y
Cleland	Y	Y	Y	Y	Y	N	Y
HAWAII							
Akaka	Y	Y	Y	Y	Y	N	Y
Inouye	Y	Y	Y	?	?	?	?
IDAHO							
Craig	Y	Y	Y	Y	Y	Y	Y
Kempthorne	Y	Y	Y	Y	Y	Y	Y
ILLINOIS							
Durbin	N	Y	Y	Y	Y	N	Y
Moseley-Braun	Y	Y	Y	?	N	Y	
INDIANA							
Coats	Y	Y	Y	Y	Y	Y	Y
Lugar	Y	Y	Y	Y	Y	Y	Y

	29	30	31	32	33	34	35
IOWA							
Grassley	Y	Y	Y	Y	Y	Y	Y
Harkin	N	Y	Y	Y	Y	N	Y
KANSAS							
Brownback	Y	Y	Y	Y	Y	Y	Y
Roberts	Y	Y	Y	Y	Y	Y	Y
KENTUCKY							
McConnell	Y	Y	Y	Y	Y	Y	Y
Ford	N	Y	Y	Y	Y	N	Y
LOUISIANA							
Breaux	Y	Y	Y	Y	Y	Y	Y
Landrieu	Y	Y	Y	Y	Y	N	Y
MAINE							
Collins	Y	Y	Y	Y	Y	Y	Y
Snowe	Y	Y	Y	Y	Y	Y	Y
MARYLAND							
Mikulski	N	Y	Y	Y	?	N	Y
Sarbanes	N	Y	Y	Y	Y	N	Y
MASSACHUSETTS							
Kennedy	N	Y	Y	Y	Y	N	Y
Kerry	N	Y	Y	Y	?	Y	Y
MICHIGAN							
Abraham	Y	Y	Y	Y	Y	Y	Y
Levin	Y	Y	Y	Y	Y	N	Y
MINNESOTA							
Grams	Y	Y	N	Y	Y	Y	Y
Wellstone	N	Y	Y	Y	Y	N	Y
MISSISSIPPI							
Cochran	Y	Y	Y	Y	Y	Y	Y
Lott	Y	Y	Y	Y	Y	Y	Y
MISSOURI							
Ashcroft	Y	Y	Y	Y	Y	Y	Y
Bond	Y	Y	Y	Y	Y	Y	Y
MONTANA							
Burns	Y	Y	Y	Y	Y	Y	Y
Baucus	Y	Y	Y	Y	Y	N	Y
NEBRASKA							
Hagel	Y	Y	Y	Y	Y	Y	Y
Kerrey	Y	Y	Y	Y	Y	N	Y
NEVADA							
Bryan	N	Y	Y	Y	Y	N	Y
Reid	N	Y	Y	Y	Y	N	Y

	29	30	31	32	33	34	35
NEW HAMPSHIRE							
Gregg	Y	Y	Y	Y	Y	Y	Y
Smith	Y	Y	Y	Y	Y	Y	Y
NEW JERSEY							
Lautenberg	N	Y	Y	Y	Y	N	Y
Torricelli	N	Y	Y	Y	?	Y	Y
NEW MEXICO							
Domenici	Y	Y	Y	Y	Y	Y	Y
Bingaman	Y	Y	Y	Y	Y	N	Y
NEW YORK							
D'Amato	Y	Y	Y	Y	Y	Y	Y
Moynihan	Y	Y	Y	Y	Y	Y	Y
NORTH CAROLINA							
Faircloth	Y	Y	Y	+	?	Y	Y
Helms	Y	Y	Y	Y	Y	Y	Y
NORTH DAKOTA							
Conrad	Y	Y	Y	Y	Y	?	Y
Dorgan	Y	Y	Y	Y	Y	N	Y
OHIO							
DeWine	Y	Y	Y	Y	Y	Y	Y
Glenn	Y	Y	N	Y	Y	N	Y
OKLAHOMA							
Inhofe	Y	Y	Y	?	?	Y	Y
Nickles	Y	Y	Y	Y	Y	Y	Y
OREGON							
Smith	Y	Y	Y	Y	?	Y	Y
Wyden	Y	Y	Y	Y	?	N	Y
PENNSYLVANIA							
Santorum	N	N	Y	Y	Y	Y	Y
Specter	N	N	Y	Y	Y	Y	Y
RHODE ISLAND							
Chafee	Y	Y	N	Y	Y	Y	Y
Reed	Y	Y	Y	Y	Y	N	Y
SOUTH CAROLINA							
Thurmond	Y	Y	N	Y	Y	Y	Y
Hollings	N	Y	Y	Y	Y	N	Y
SOUTH DAKOTA							
Daschle	Y	Y	Y	Y	Y	Y	Y
Johnson	Y	Y	Y	Y	Y	Y	Y
TENNESSEE							
Frist	Y	Y	Y	Y	Y	Y	Y
Thompson	Y	Y	Y	Y	Y	Y	Y

	29	30	31	32	33	34	35
TEXAS							
Gramm	Y	Y	Y	?	Y	Y	Y
Hutchison	Y	Y	Y	Y	Y	Y	Y
UTAH							
Bennett	Y	Y	Y	Y	Y	Y	Y
Hatch	Y	Y	Y	Y	Y	Y	Y
VERMONT							
Jeffords	N	Y	Y	?	Y	Y	Y
Leahy	N	Y	Y	Y	Y	Y	Y
VIRGINIA							
Warner	Y	Y	Y	Y	Y	Y	Y
Robb	Y	Y	Y	Y	Y	Y	Y
WASHINGTON							
Gorton	Y	Y	Y	Y	Y	Y	Y
Murray	Y	Y	Y	Y	Y	N	Y
WEST VIRGINIA							
Byrd	N	Y	Y	Y	Y	N	Y
Rockefeller	Y	Y	Y	Y	Y	Y	+
WISCONSIN							
Feingold	Y	N	Y	Y	Y	N	Y
Kohl	Y	N	Y	Y	Y	N	Y
WYOMING							
Enzi	Y	Y	Y	?	Y	Y	Y
Thomas	Y	Y	Y	Y	Y	Y	Y

Key

Y	Voted for (yea).
#	Paired for.
+	Announced for.
N	Voted against (nay).
X	Paired against.
–	Announced against.
P	Voted "present."
C	Voted "present" to avoid possible conflict of interest.
?	Did not vote or otherwise make a position known.

Democrats *Republicans*

ND Northern Democrats   SD Southern Democrats

Southern states - Ala., Ark., Fla., Ga., Ky., La., Miss., N.C., Okla., S.C., Tenn., Texas, Va.

29. S 1173. Highway and Transit Reauthorization/Demonstration Projects. McCain, R-Ariz., amendment to the Senate Environment and Public Works Committee substitute amendment. The McCain amendment would require that funding for future demonstration projects be taken from a state's annual highway funding allocation, not the highway trust fund. Adopted 78-22: R 50-5; D 28-17 (ND 22-15, SD 6-2). March 12, 1998.

30. S 1173. Highway and Transit Reauthorization/Environment Committee Substitute. Senate Environment and Public Works Committee substitute amendment that would authorize $214.3 billion over fiscal years 1998-2003 for transportation programs. The amendment would authorize $41.3 billion of the six-year total for mass transit programs. Adopted 96-4: R 53-2; D 43-2 (ND 35-2, SD 8-0). March 12, 1998. (Subsequently, the Senate passed the underlying bill by voice vote. But the Senate held the bill at the desk pending receipt of the House version.)

31. S Res 187. China Human Rights/Adoption. Adoption of the resolution to urge President Clinton to push for passage of a measure criticizing China for human rights abuses when the U.N. Commission on Human Rights meets the week of March 16, in Geneva. Adopted 95-5: R 51-4; D 44-1 (ND 36-1, SD 8-0). March 12, 1998.

32. S Con Res 78. Saddam Hussein as War Criminal/Adoption. Adoption of the resolution to express the sense of Congress that the president should call for a U.N. tribunal to try Iraqi President Saddam Hussein as a war criminal. Adopted 93-0: R 49-0; D 44-0 (ND 36-0, SD 8-0). March 13, 1998.

33. Fogel Nomination/Confirmation. Confirmation of President Clinton's nomination of Jeremy D. Fogel of California to be U.S. District judge for the Northern District of California. Confirmed 90-0: R 51-0; D 39-0 (ND 31-0, SD 8-0). March 16, 1998. A "yea" was a vote in support of the president's position.

34. HR 2646. Expanding Education Savings Accounts/Cloture. Motion to invoke cloture (thus limiting debate) on the motion to proceed to the bill to allow parents, relatives or outside corporations to contribute up to a combined total of $2,000 a year of after-tax funds in tax-free savings accounts designated for educational expenses. Motion agreed to 74-24: R 55-0; D 19-24 (ND 15-20, SD 4-4). March 17, 1998. Three-fifths of the total Senate (60) is required to invoke cloture.

35. Graber Nomination/Confirmation. Confirmation of President Clinton's nomination of Susan Graber of Oregon to be judge for the 9th U.S. Circuit Court of Appeals. Confirmed 98-0: R 55-0; D 43-0 (ND 35-0, SD 8-0). March 17, 1998. A "yea" was a vote in support of the president's position.

	36	37	38	39	40	41	42
ALABAMA							
Sessions	Y	Y	Y	Y	N	Y	N
Shelby	Y	Y	Y	Y	Y	Y	Y
ALASKA							
Murkowski	Y	Y	Y	Y	Y	Y	N
Stevens	Y	Y	Y	Y	Y	Y	Y
ARIZONA							
Kyl	Y	Y	Y	N	N	Y	N
McCain	Y	Y	Y	N	N	Y	N
ARKANSAS							
Hutchinson	Y	Y	Y	N	N	Y	N
Bumpers	N	Y	N	Y	Y	Y	Y
CALIFORNIA							
Boxer	N	Y	N	Y	Y	Y	Y
Feinstein	N	Y	N	N	Y	Y	Y
COLORADO							
Allard	Y	Y	Y	N	N	Y	N
Campbell	Y	Y	Y	Y	Y	Y	Y
CONNECTICUT							
Dodd	N	Y	N	Y	Y	Y	Y
Lieberman	N	Y	N	Y	Y	Y	Y
DELAWARE							
Roth	Y	Y	Y	N	Y	Y	?
Biden	N	Y	N	?	Y	Y	Y
FLORIDA							
Mack	Y	+	Y	Y	N	Y	Y
Graham	N	Y	N	N	Y	Y	Y
GEORGIA							
Coverdell	Y	Y	Y	Y	Y	Y	Y
Cleland	N	Y	N	Y	Y	Y	Y
HAWAII							
Akaka	N	Y	N	Y	Y	Y	Y
Inouye	?	?	N	Y	Y	Y	Y
IDAHO							
Craig	Y	Y	Y	Y	Y	Y	N
Kempthorne	Y	Y	Y	N	Y	Y	N
ILLINOIS							
Durbin	N	Y	N	Y	Y	Y	Y
Moseley-Braun	N	Y	–	N	Y	Y	Y
INDIANA							
Coats	Y	Y	Y	N	N	Y	N
Lugar	Y	Y	Y	N	Y	Y	Y

	36	37	38	39	40	41	42
IOWA							
Grassley	Y	Y	Y	Y	Y	N	Y
Harkin	N	Y	N	Y	Y	Y	Y
KANSAS							
Brownback	Y	Y	Y	N	N	N	N
Roberts	Y	Y	Y	Y	Y	Y	Y
KENTUCKY							
McConnell	Y	Y	Y	Y	Y	Y	Y
Ford	N	Y	N	Y	Y	Y	Y
LOUISIANA							
Breaux	N	Y	N	Y	Y	Y	Y
Landrieu	N	Y	N	?	Y	Y	Y
MAINE							
Collins	Y	Y	Y	Y	Y	Y	Y
Snowe	Y	Y	Y	Y	Y	Y	Y
MARYLAND							
Mikulski	N	Y	N	?	Y	Y	Y
Sarbanes	N	Y	N	Y	Y	Y	Y
MASSACHUSETTS							
Kennedy	N	Y	N	Y	Y	Y	Y
Kerry	N	Y	N	N	Y	Y	Y
MICHIGAN							
Abraham	Y	Y	Y	N	N	Y	N
Levin	N	Y	N	N	Y	Y	Y
MINNESOTA							
Grams	Y	Y	Y	N	N	Y	N
Wellstone	N	Y	N	Y	Y	Y	Y
MISSISSIPPI							
Cochran	Y	Y	Y	Y	Y	Y	Y
Lott	Y	Y	Y	Y	Y	Y	Y
MISSOURI							
Ashcroft	Y	Y	Y	N	N	N	N
Bond	Y	Y	Y	?	Y	Y	Y
MONTANA							
Burns	Y	Y	Y	Y	Y	Y	N
Baucus	N	Y	N	Y	Y	Y	Y
NEBRASKA							
Hagel	Y	Y	Y	Y	Y	Y	N
Kerrey	N	Y	N	–	Y	Y	Y
NEVADA							
Bryan	N	Y	N	N	Y	Y	Y
Reid	N	Y	N	Y	Y	Y	Y

	36	37	38	39	40	41	42
NEW HAMPSHIRE							
Gregg	Y	Y	Y	N	Y	N	N
Smith	Y	Y	Y	N	N	Y	N
NEW JERSEY							
Lautenberg	N	Y	N	Y	Y	Y	Y
Torricelli	N	Y	N	Y	Y	Y	Y
NEW MEXICO							
Domenici	Y	Y	Y	Y	Y	Y	Y
Bingaman	N	Y	N	Y	Y	Y	Y
NEW YORK							
D'Amato	Y	Y	Y	?	Y	Y	Y
Moynihan	N	Y	N	Y	Y	Y	Y
NORTH CAROLINA							
Faircloth	Y	Y	Y	N	N	Y	N
Helms	Y	Y	Y	Y	N	Y	N
NORTH DAKOTA							
Conrad	N	Y	N	Y	Y	Y	Y
Dorgan	N	Y	N	Y	Y	Y	Y
OHIO							
DeWine	Y	Y	Y	Y	Y	Y	Y
Glenn	N	Y	N	N	Y	Y	Y
OKLAHOMA							
Inhofe	Y	Y	Y	?	N	Y	N
Nickles	Y	Y	Y	N	N	N	N
OREGON							
Smith	Y	Y	Y	N	N	Y	Y
Wyden	N	Y	N	?	Y	Y	Y
PENNSYLVANIA							
Santorum	Y	Y	Y	N	N	Y	N
Specter	Y	Y	Y	Y	Y	Y	Y
RHODE ISLAND							
Chafee	Y	Y	Y	Y	Y	Y	Y
Reed	N	Y	N	Y	Y	Y	Y
SOUTH CAROLINA							
Thurmond	Y	Y	Y	N	Y	Y	Y
Hollings	N	Y	N	Y	Y	Y	Y
SOUTH DAKOTA							
Daschle	N	Y	N	N	Y	Y	Y
Johnson	N	Y	N	N	Y	N	Y
TENNESSEE							
Frist	Y	Y	Y	N	Y	Y	Y
Thompson	Y	Y	Y	N	Y	Y	N

	36	37	38	39	40	41	42
TEXAS							
Gramm	Y	Y	Y	N	N	N	N
Hutchison	Y	Y	Y	N	Y	N	N
UTAH							
Bennett	Y	Y	Y	Y	Y	Y	Y
Hatch	Y	Y	Y	Y	Y	Y	N
VERMONT							
Jeffords	Y	Y	Y	Y	Y	Y	Y
Leahy	N	Y	N	Y	Y	Y	Y
VIRGINIA							
Warner	Y	Y	Y	Y	Y	Y	Y
Robb	N	Y	N	N	N	N	Y
WASHINGTON							
Gorton	Y	Y	Y	Y	Y	Y	Y
Murray	N	Y	N	Y	Y	Y	Y
WEST VIRGINIA							
Byrd	N	Y	N	Y	Y	Y	Y
Rockefeller	N	Y	N	Y	Y	Y	Y
WISCONSIN							
Feingold	N	Y	N	N	N	N	N
Kohl	N	Y	N	N	N	N	N
WYOMING							
Enzi	Y	Y	Y	N	Y	N	N
Thomas	Y	Y	Y	N	Y	N	N

Key

Y	Voted for (yea).
#	Paired for.
+	Announced for.
N	Voted against (nay).
X	Paired against.
–	Announced against.
P	Voted "present."
C	Voted "present" to avoid possible conflict of interest.
?	Did not vote or otherwise make a position known.

Democrats   *Republicans*

ND Northern Democrats   SD Southern Democrats

Southern states - Ala., Ark., Fla., Ga., Ky., La., Miss., N.C., Okla., S.C., Tenn., Texas, Va.

36. NATO Expansion/Motion to Proceed. Motion to proceed to the protocol (Treaty Doc. 105-36) revising the 1949 North Atlantic Treaty to admit Poland, Hungary and the Czech Republic into the North Atlantic Treaty Organization (NATO). Motion agreed to 55-44: R 55-0; D 0-44 (ND 0-36, SD 0-8). March 18, 1998.

37. Violence in Kosovo/Adoption. Adoption of the concurrent resolution to express the sense of Congress that the United States should condemn the Serbian government for human rights abuses and violence against the Albanian population in Kosovo and that the United States should demand that human rights monitors be allowed to return to Kosovo. Adopted 98-0: R 54-0; D 44-0 (ND 36-0, SD 8-0). March 18, 1998.

38. HR 2646. Expanding Education Savings Accounts/Cloture. Motion to invoke cloture (thus limiting debate) on the bill to allow parents, relatives or outside corporations to contribute up to a combined total of $2,000 a year of after-tax funds in tax-free savings accounts designated for educational expenses. Motion rejected 55-44: R 55-0; D 0-44 (ND 0-36, SD 0-8). March 19, 1998. Three-fifths of the total Senate (60) is required to invoke cloture.

39. S 1768. Fiscal 1998 Supplemental Appropriations/Spending Reductions. Stevens, R-Alaska, motion to table (kill) the McCain, R-Ariz., amendment to cut $78 million in unrequested projects from the overall amount provided by the bill. The amendment would strike $33 million by eliminating funding for levee and waterway repairs in Alabama and Mississippi. Motion agreed to 61-31: R 32-20; D 29-11 (ND 24-9, SD 5-2). March 23, 1998.

40. S 1768. Fiscal 1998 Supplemental Appropriations/Spending Offsets. Stevens, R-Alaska, motion to table (kill) the Gramm, R-Texas, amendment that would require that only that portion of spending in the bill that is obligated in fiscal 1998 be designated as emergency spending exempt from budgetary and spending caps. Motion agreed to 76-24: R 34-21; D 42-3 (ND 35-2, SD 7-1). March 24, 1998.

41. S 1768. Fiscal 1998 Supplemental Appropriations/Bosnia Spending Offsets. Stevens, R-Alaska, motion to table (kill) the Feingold, D-Wis., amendment that would remove the "emergency" designation from the provision providing about $400 million for troop deployments in Bosnia. The effect of the amendment would be to require reductions in other Pentagon programs to comply with discretionary spending caps. Motion agreed to 92-8: R 50-5; D 42-3 (ND 34-3, SD 8-0). March 25, 1998.

42. S 1768. Fiscal 1998 Supplemental Appropriations/FEMA Spending Offsets. Bond, R-Mo., motion to table (kill) the Nickles, R-Okla., amendment to the Bond amendment. The Nickles amendment would remove the "emergency" designation from all funds provided to the Federal Emergency Management Agency under the Bond amendment that are to be spent in future fiscal years. The effect would be to require reductions in other domestic programs to comply with discretionary spending caps. The Bond amendment would allocate $1.6 billion to FEMA for disaster relief programs. Motion agreed to 68-31: R 26-28; D 42-3 (ND 35-2, SD 7-1). March 25, 1998. (Subsequently, the Bond amendment was adopted by voice vote.)

ALABAMA	43	44	45	46	47	48	49
Sessions	Y	N	Y	Y	Y	Y	Y
Shelby	Y	Y	Y	Y	Y	Y	Y
ALASKA							
Murkowski	Y	Y	Y	Y	Y	Y	Y
Stevens	Y	Y	Y	Y	Y	Y	Y
ARIZONA							
Kyl	Y	N	Y	Y	N	N	Y
McCain	Y	Y	Y	Y	N	Y	Y
ARKANSAS							
Hutchinson	Y	Y	Y	Y	Y	?	Y
Bumpers	Y	Y	N	N	N	Y	Y
CALIFORNIA							
Boxer	Y	Y	N	N	Y	Y	Y
Feinstein	N	Y	N	N	Y	Y	Y
COLORADO							
Allard	Y	N	Y	Y	Y	Y	N
Campbell	Y	N	Y	Y	N	Y	Y
CONNECTICUT							
Dodd	N	Y	N	N	N	Y	Y
Lieberman	Y	Y	Y	N	Y	Y	Y
DELAWARE							
Roth	Y	Y	Y	Y	N	Y	Y
Biden	Y	Y	N	N	N	Y	Y
FLORIDA							
Mack	Y	N	Y	Y	Y	N	Y
Graham	Y	Y	Y	N	N	Y	Y
GEORGIA							
Coverdell	Y	N	Y	Y	N	Y	Y
Cleland	Y	Y	N	N	N	Y	Y
HAWAII							
Akaka	Y	Y	N	N	N	Y	Y
Inouye	Y	Y	N	N	N	Y	Y
IDAHO							
Craig	Y	Y	Y	Y	N	Y	Y
Kempthorne	Y	Y	Y	Y	Y	Y	Y
ILLINOIS							
Durbin	Y	Y	N	N	Y	Y	Y
Moseley-Braun	Y	Y	N	Y	Y	Y	Y
INDIANA							
Coats	Y	Y	Y	Y	Y	N	Y
Lugar	Y	Y	Y	Y	N	Y	Y

IOWA	43	44	45	46	47	48	49
Grassley	Y	Y	Y	Y	N	N	Y
Harkin	Y	Y	N	N	Y	Y	Y
KANSAS							
Brownback	Y	Y	Y	Y	Y	N	Y
Roberts	Y	Y	Y	Y	Y	Y	Y
KENTUCKY							
McConnell	Y	Y	Y	Y	Y	N	Y
Ford	Y	Y	N	N	N	N	Y
LOUISIANA							
Breaux	Y	Y	Y	Y	N	Y	Y
Landrieu	Y	Y	N	N	N	Y	Y
MAINE							
Collins	Y	Y	Y	Y	Y	Y	Y
Snowe	Y	Y	Y	Y	Y	Y	Y
MARYLAND							
Mikulski	Y	Y	N	N	N	Y	?
Sarbanes	N	Y	N	N	N	Y	Y
MASSACHUSETTS							
Kennedy	N	Y	N	N	N	Y	Y
Kerry	N	Y	N	N	N	?	Y
MICHIGAN							
Abraham	Y	N	Y	Y	Y	N	Y
Levin	Y	Y	N	N	N	Y	Y
MINNESOTA							
Grams	Y	Y	Y	Y	Y	N	Y
Wellstone	N	N	N	N	N	Y	Y
MISSISSIPPI							
Cochran	Y	Y	Y	Y	N	Y	Y
Lott	Y	Y	Y	Y	N	Y	Y
MISSOURI							
Ashcroft	Y	N	Y	Y	Y	N	Y
Bond	Y	Y	N	Y	Y	Y	Y
MONTANA							
Burns	Y	Y	Y	Y	N	Y	Y
Baucus	Y	Y	N	N	N	Y	Y
NEBRASKA							
Hagel	Y	Y	Y	Y	Y	N	Y
Kerrey	Y	Y	N	N	N	Y	Y
NEVADA							
Bryan	Y	Y	N	N	N	Y	Y
Reid	Y	Y	N	N	N	Y	Y

NEW HAMPSHIRE	43	44	45	46	47	48	49
Gregg	Y	Y	Y	Y	Y	Y	Y
Smith	Y	N	Y	Y	Y	N	Y
NEW JERSEY							
Lautenberg	N	Y	N	N	N	Y	Y
Torricelli	Y	Y	N	Y	N	Y	Y
NEW MEXICO							
Domenici	Y	Y	Y	N	Y	N	Y
Bingaman	N	Y	N	N	N	Y	Y
NEW YORK							
D'Amato	Y	Y	N	Y	Y	N	Y
Moynihan	Y	Y	N	N	N	Y	Y
NORTH CAROLINA							
Faircloth	Y	N	Y	Y	Y	?	Y
Helms	Y	N	Y	Y	Y	?	Y
NORTH DAKOTA							
Conrad	Y	Y	N	Y	N	Y	Y
Dorgan	Y	Y	N	Y	N	Y	Y
OHIO							
DeWine	Y	Y	Y	Y	N	N	Y
Glenn	Y	Y	N	N	N	Y	Y
OKLAHOMA							
Inhofe	Y	N	Y	Y	?	?	?
Nickles	Y	N	Y	Y	Y	N	?
OREGON							
Smith	Y	Y	Y	Y	N	Y	Y
Wyden	Y	Y	N	N	Y	Y	Y
PENNSYLVANIA							
Santorum	Y	Y	Y	Y	Y	N	Y
Specter	Y	Y	Y	Y	N	Y	Y
RHODE ISLAND							
Chafee	Y	Y	N	Y	N	Y	Y
Reed	Y	Y	N	N	N	Y	Y
SOUTH CAROLINA							
Thurmond	Y	Y	Y	Y	N	Y	Y
Hollings	Y	Y	N	N	N	Y	Y
SOUTH DAKOTA							
Daschle	Y	Y	N	N	N	Y	Y
Johnson	Y	Y	N	N	N	Y	Y
TENNESSEE							
Frist	Y	Y	Y	Y	Y	Y	Y
Thompson	Y	N	Y	Y	Y	Y	Y

Key

Y	Voted for (yea).
#	Paired for.
+	Announced for.
N	Voted against (nay).
X	Paired against.
−	Announced against.
P	Voted "present."
C	Voted "present" to avoid possible conflict of interest.
?	Did not vote or otherwise make a position known.

Democrats *Republicans*

TEXAS	43	44	45	46	47	48	49
Gramm	Y	Y	Y	Y	Y	?	Y
Hutchison	Y	Y	Y	Y	N	Y	Y
UTAH							
Bennett	Y	Y	Y	Y	N	?	?
Hatch	Y	Y	Y	Y	N	+	+
VERMONT							
Jeffords	Y	Y	N	Y	N	Y	Y
Leahy	N	Y	N	N	Y	Y	Y
VIRGINIA							
Warner	Y	Y	Y	Y	N	N	Y
Robb	Y	Y	N	N	N	Y	Y
WASHINGTON							
Gorton	Y	Y	Y	Y	N	Y	Y
Murray	Y	Y	N	N	Y	Y	Y
WEST VIRGINIA							
Byrd	Y	Y	N	Y	N	Y	Y
Rockefeller	N	Y	N	N	N	Y	Y
WISCONSIN							
Feingold	Y	N	N	N	N	Y	Y
Kohl	Y	Y	N	Y	N	Y	Y
WYOMING							
Enzi	Y	Y	Y	Y	Y	?	Y
Thomas	Y	N	Y	Y	Y	Y	Y

ND Northern Democrats   SD Southern Democrats

Southern states - Ala., Ark., Fla., Ga., Ky., La., Miss., N.C., Okla., S.C., Tenn., Texas, Va.

43. S 1768. Fiscal 1998 Supplemental Appropriations/U.N. Peacekeeping. Helms, R-N.C., amendment to express the sense of the Senate that the United Nations should immediately reduce the percentage of U.S. dues for U.N. peacekeeping operations from 30.4 percent to 25 percent. The amendment also would urge the president to ask the U.N. Security Council to release to all U.N. members a U.S. Defense Department report on the amount the United States has spent since Jan. 1, 1990, implementing or supporting U.N. Security Council resolutions. Adopted 90-10: R 55-0; D 35-10 (ND 27-10, SD 8-0). March 25, 1998.

44. S 1768. Fiscal 1998 Supplemental Appropriations/IMF Funding. McConnell, R-Ky., amendment to provide $17.9 billion for the International Monetary Fund, including $3.4 billion for a new program aimed at preventing global financial crises and $14.5 billion for the U.S. "quota" to the international agency. The amendment would prohibit release of the quota funds unless the IMF agrees to certain conditions, including restricting aid to nations that do not conform to international trade agreements or that provide subsidies to certain industries such as steel, textile and automobile manufacturers. Adopted 84-16: R 41-14; D 43-2 (ND 35-2, SD 8-0). March 26, 1998.

45. S 1768. Fiscal 1998 Supplemental Appropriations/Health Care Portability. Nickles, R-Okla., motion to table (kill) the Kennedy, D-Mass., amendment that would replace the language proposed to be stricken by the Nickles amendment with $8 million for the Health Care Financing Administration (HCFA) to hire more employees to enforce the 1996 health care portability law (PL 104-191). Motion agreed to 51-49: R 51-4; D 0-45 (ND 0-37, SD 0-8). March 26, 1998. (Subsequently, the Nickles amendment was adopted

by voice vote and a motion to advance to third reading on the bill was agreed to by voice vote.

46. HR 2646. Expanding Education Savings Accounts/Cloture. Motion to invoke cloture (thus limiting debate) on the bill to allow parents, relatives or outside corporations to contribute up to a combined total of $2,000 a year of after-tax funds in tax-free savings accounts designated for educational expenses. Motion rejected 58-42: R 55-0; D 3-42 (ND 2-35, SD 1-7). March 26, 1998. Three-fifths of the total Senate (60) is required to invoke cloture.

47. S J Res 42. Reverse Mexico Anti-Drug Certification/Passage. Passage of the joint resolution to reverse the president's certification of Mexico as an ally in the fight against drugs. Rejected 45-54: R 30-24; D 15-30 (ND 14-23, SD 1-7). March 26, 1998. A "nay" was a vote in support of the president's position.

48. McKeown Nomination/Confirmation. Confirmation of President Clinton's nomination of M. Margaret McKeown of Washington to be a judge for the 9th U.S. Circuit Court of Appeals. Confirmed 80-11: R 36-11; D 44-0 (ND 36-0, SD 8-0). March 27, 1998. A "yea" was a vote in support of the president's position.

49. S Con Res 86. Fiscal 1999 Budget Resolution/At-Home Parents. Sessions, R-Ala., amendment to express the sense of Congress recognizing the importance of parents who forgo a second income to stay at home and raise children, and to call for tax breaks for these families. Adopted 96-0: R 52-0; D 44-0 (ND 36-0, SD 8-0). March 31, 1998.

	50	51	52	53	54	55	56
ALABAMA							
Sessions	N	N	N	Y	N	Y	Y
Shelby	N	Y	N	Y	N	Y	Y
ALASKA							
Murkowski	N	N	Y	N	Y	N	Y
Stevens	N	N	N	Y	N	N	Y
ARIZONA							
Kyl	N	Y	N	Y	N	Y	Y
McCain	N	Y	N	Y	N	Y	Y
ARKANSAS							
Hutchinson	–	?	?	Y	N	Y	Y
Bumpers	Y	Y	Y	N	Y	N	N
CALIFORNIA							
Boxer	Y	Y	Y	N	Y	N	N
Feinstein	Y	Y	Y	N	Y	N	N
COLORADO							
Allard	N	N	Y	N	Y	Y	Y
Campbell	N	N	N	Y	N	Y	Y
CONNECTICUT							
Dodd	Y	Y	Y	N	Y	N	N
Lieberman	Y	Y	Y	N	Y	N	N
DELAWARE							
Roth	N	N	Y	N	Y	Y	Y
Biden	Y	Y	Y	N	Y	N	N
FLORIDA							
Mack	N	Y	N	Y	N	N	Y
Graham	Y	Y	Y	N	Y	N	N
GEORGIA							
Coverdell	N	Y	N	Y	N	Y	Y
Cleland	Y	Y	Y	N	Y	N	N
HAWAII							
Akaka	Y	Y	Y	N	Y	N	N
Inouye	Y	Y	Y	N	Y	N	N
IDAHO							
Craig	N	Y	N	Y	N	Y	Y
Kempthorne	N	Y	N	Y	N	Y	Y
ILLINOIS							
Durbin	Y	Y	Y	N	Y	N	N
Moseley-Braun	Y	Y	Y	N	Y	N	N
INDIANA							
Coats	N	N	N	Y	N	N	N
Lugar	N	Y	N	Y	N	N	Y

	50	51	52	53	54	55	56
IOWA							
Grassley	N	Y	N	Y	N	N	Y
Harkin	Y	Y	Y	N	Y	N	N
KANSAS							
Brownback	N	Y	N	Y	N	Y	Y
Roberts	N	Y	N	Y	N	Y	Y
KENTUCKY							
McConnell	N	N	N	Y	N	Y	Y
Ford	Y	N	Y	N	N	N	N
LOUISIANA							
Breaux	Y	Y	Y	N	Y	N	Y
Landrieu	Y	Y	Y	N	Y	N	N
MAINE							
Collins	N	N	N	N	N	N	N
Snowe	N	Y	N	N	N	N	N
MARYLAND							
Mikulski	?	?	?	N	Y	N	N
Sarbanes	Y	Y	Y	N	Y	N	N
MASSACHUSETTS							
Kennedy	Y	Y	Y	?	Y	N	N
Kerry	Y	Y	Y	?	Y	N	N
MICHIGAN							
Abraham	N	Y	N	Y	N	N	Y
Levin	Y	Y	Y	N	Y	N	N
MINNESOTA							
Grams	N	Y	N	Y	N	Y	Y
Wellstone	Y	Y	Y	N	Y	N	N
MISSISSIPPI							
Cochran	N	N	Y	N	Y	N	Y
Lott	N	N	N	Y	N	Y	Y
MISSOURI							
Ashcroft	N	Y	N	Y	N	Y	Y
Bond	N	Y	N	Y	N	N	N
MONTANA							
Burns	N	N	N	Y	N	Y	Y
Baucus	Y	Y	Y	N	Y	N	N
NEBRASKA							
Hagel	N	N	N	Y	N	N	Y
Kerrey	Y	Y	Y	N	Y	N	N
NEVADA							
Bryan	Y	Y	Y	N	Y	N	N
Reid	Y	Y	Y	N	Y	N	N

	50	51	52	53	54	55	56
NEW HAMPSHIRE							
Gregg	N	Y	N	Y	N	Y	Y
Smith	N	Y	N	Y	N	Y	Y
NEW JERSEY							
Lautenberg	Y	Y	Y	N	Y	N	N
Torricelli	Y	Y	Y	N	Y	N	N
NEW MEXICO							
Domenici	N	Y	N	Y	N	N	Y
Bingaman	Y	Y	Y	N	Y	N	N
NEW YORK							
D'Amato	Y	Y	Y	N	N	N	N
Moynihan	Y	Y	Y	N	Y	N	N
NORTH CAROLINA							
Faircloth	Y	N	Y	Y	Y	Y	Y
Helms	N	N	N	Y	N	Y	Y
NORTH DAKOTA							
Conrad	Y	Y	Y	N	Y	N	N
Dorgan	Y	Y	Y	N	Y	N	N
OHIO							
DeWine	N	Y	N	Y	N	N	Y
Glenn	Y	Y	Y	N	Y	N	N
OKLAHOMA							
Inhofe	N	N	N	Y	N	Y	Y
Nickles	N	Y	N	Y	N	Y	Y
OREGON							
Smith	N	Y	N	Y	N	Y	Y
Wyden	Y	Y	Y	N	Y	N	N
PENNSYLVANIA							
Santorum	N	Y	N	Y	N	Y	Y
Specter	N	Y	N	Y	N	N	Y
RHODE ISLAND							
Chafee	N	Y	N	Y	N	N	Y
Reed	Y	Y	Y	N	Y	N	N
SOUTH CAROLINA							
Thurmond	N	Y	N	Y	N	Y	Y
Hollings	Y	N	Y	N	Y	N	N
SOUTH DAKOTA							
Daschle	Y	Y	Y	N	Y	N	N
Johnson	Y	Y	Y	N	Y	N	N
TENNESSEE							
Frist	N	Y	N	Y	N	Y	Y
Thompson	N	Y	N	Y	N	Y	Y

	50	51	52	53	54	55	56
TEXAS							
Gramm	N	Y	N	Y	N	Y	Y
Hutchison	N	Y	N	Y	N	Y	Y
UTAH							
Bennett	N	N	N	Y	N	Y	Y
Hatch	N	N	N	Y	N	Y	Y
VERMONT							
Jeffords	N	N	Y	Y	Y	N	N
Leahy	Y	Y	Y	N	Y	N	N
VIRGINIA							
Warner	N	Y	N	Y	N	Y	Y
Robb	Y	Y	Y	N	Y	N	Y
WASHINGTON							
Gorton	N	N	N	Y	N	Y	Y
Murray	Y	Y	Y	N	Y	N	N
WEST VIRGINIA							
Byrd	Y	Y	Y	N	Y	N	N
Rockefeller	Y	Y	Y	N	Y	N	N
WISCONSIN							
Feingold	Y	Y	Y	N	Y	N	N
Kohl	Y	Y	Y	N	Y	N	N
WYOMING							
Enzi	N	N	N	Y	N	Y	Y
Thomas	N	Y	N	Y	N	Y	Y

Key

Y	Voted for (yea).
#	Paired for.
+	Announced for.
N	Voted against (nay).
X	Paired against.
–	Announced against.
P	Voted "present."
C	Voted "present" to avoid possible conflict of interest.
?	Did not vote or otherwise make a position known.

Democrats   ***Republicans***

ND Northern Democrats   SD Southern Democrats

Southern states - Ala., Ark., Fla., Ga., Ky., La., Miss., N.C., Okla., S.C., Tenn., Texas, Va.

50. S Con Res 86. Fiscal 1999 Budget Resolution/Additional Teachers. Murray, D-Wash., motion to waive the Budget Act with respect to the Domenici, R-N.M., point of order against the Murray amendment to provide $7.3 billion over five years to hire as many as 100,000 additional school teachers. Motion rejected 46-52: R 2-52; D 44-0 (ND 36-0, SD 8-0). March 31, 1998. A three-fifths majority vote (60) of the total Senate is required to waive the Budget Act. (Subsequently, the chair upheld the point of order and the amendment fell.)

51. S Con Res 86. Fiscal 1999 Budget Resolution/Tobacco Manufacturers Immunity. Gregg, R-N.H., amendment to the Gregg amendment that would extend the list to include class-action suits. The underlying Gregg amendment would express the sense of the Senate that any tobacco settlement legislation not provide tobacco manufacturers with immunity from liability in health-related lawsuits. Adopted 79-19: R 37-17; D 42-2 (ND 36-0, SD 6-2). March 31, 1998. (Subsequently, the underlying Gregg amendment as amended was adopted by voice vote.)

52. S Con Res 86. Fiscal 1999 Budget Resolution/Child Care Funding. Dodd, D-Conn., motion to waive the Budget Act with respect to the Domenici, R-N.M., point of order against the Dodd amendment to establish a reserve fund to provide funding for child care improvements. Motion rejected 50-48: R 6-48; D 44-0 (ND 36-0, SD 8-0). March 31, 1998. A three-fifths majority vote (60) of the total Senate is required to waive the Budget Act. (Subsequently, the chair upheld the point of order and the amendment fell.)

53. S Con Res 86. Fiscal 1999 Budget Resolution/Medicare Physicians. Kyl, R-Ariz., amendment to express the sense of Congress that there should be no constraints on physicians who want to privately contract with Medicare patients for Medicare-covered services. Adopted 51-47: R 50-5; D 1-42 (ND 0-35, SD 1-7). April 1, 1998.

54. S Con Res 86. Fiscal 1999 Budget Resolution/Tobacco Settlement Revenues. Conrad, D-N.D., motion to waive the Budget Act with respect to the Domenici, R-N.M., point of order against the Conrad amendment. The Conrad amendment would permit the federal share of revenue from any tobacco settlement to be used for programs to reduce child smoking, increase health research, to provide transition assistance for tobacco farmers and help Medicare financing. Motion rejected 46-54: R 2-53; D 44-1 (ND 37-0, SD 7-1). April 1, 1998. A three-fifths majority vote (60) of the total Senate is required to waive the Budget Act. (Subsequently, the chair upheld the point of order, and the amendment fell.)

55. S Con Res 86. Fiscal 1999 Budget Resolution/Tax Cuts. McCain, R-Ariz., motion to waive the Budget Act with respect to the Lautenberg, D-N.J., point of order against the Coverdell, R-Ga., amendment. Coverdell's amendment would reduce tax revenues by $195.5 billion over five years by raising the income thresholds for the 15 percent and 28 percent tax brackets. Motion rejected 38-62: R 38-17; D 0-45 (ND 0-37, SD 0-8). April 1, 1998. A three-fifths majority vote (60) of the total Senate is required to waive the Budget Act. (Subsequently, the chair upheld the point of order, and the amendment fell.)

56. S Con Res 86. Fiscal 1999 Budget Resolution/Social Security Personal Retirement Accounts. Roth, R-Del., amendment to express the sense of the Senate that the Senate Finance Committee should in 1998 report legislation that would dedicate the federal budget surplus to the establishment of Social Security "personal retirement accounts." Adopted 51-49: R 49-6; D 2-43 (ND 0-37, SD 2-6). April 1, 1998.

	57	58	59	60	61	62	63
ALABAMA							
Sessions	Y	N	Y	Y	Y	Y	N
Shelby	Y	N	Y	Y	Y	Y	N
ALASKA							
Murkowski	Y	N	Y	Y	Y	Y	N
Stevens	Y	N	Y	Y	Y	Y	N
ARIZONA							
Kyl	Y	N	Y	Y	Y	Y	N
McCain	Y	N	Y	Y	Y	Y	N
ARKANSAS							
Hutchinson	Y	N	Y	Y	Y	Y	N
Bumpers	N	Y	Y	N	Y	N	N
CALIFORNIA							
Boxer	N	Y	Y	N	Y	N	N
Feinstein	N	Y	Y	N	Y	N	N
COLORADO							
Allard	Y	N	Y	Y	Y	Y	N
Campbell	Y	N	Y	Y	Y	Y	N
CONNECTICUT							
Dodd	N	Y	Y	N	Y	N	N
Lieberman	N	Y	Y	N	Y	N	N
DELAWARE							
Roth	Y	N	Y	Y	Y	Y	N
Biden	N	Y	Y	N	Y	N	N
FLORIDA							
Mack	Y	N	Y	Y	Y	Y	N
Graham	N	Y	Y	N	Y	N	N
GEORGIA							
Coverdell	Y	N	Y	Y	Y	Y	N
Cleland	N	Y	Y	N	Y	N	N
HAWAII							
Akaka	N	Y	Y	N	Y	N	N
Inouye	N	Y	Y	N	Y	N	N
IDAHO							
Craig	Y	N	Y	Y	Y	Y	N
Kempthorne	Y	N	Y	Y	Y	Y	N
ILLINOIS							
Durbin	N	Y	Y	N	Y	N	N
Moseley-Braun	N	Y	Y	N	Y	Y	N
INDIANA							
Coats	Y	N	Y	Y	Y	Y	N
Lugar	Y	N	Y	Y	Y	Y	N
IOWA							
Grassley	Y	N	Y	Y	Y	Y	N
Harkin	N	Y	Y	N	Y	N	N
KANSAS							
Brownback	Y	N	Y	Y	Y	Y	N
Roberts	Y	N	Y	Y	Y	Y	N
KENTUCKY							
McConnell	Y	N	Y	Y	Y	Y	N
Ford	N	Y	Y	N	Y	N	N
LOUISIANA							
Breaux	N	Y	Y	N	Y	N	N
Landrieu	N	Y	Y	N	Y	N	N
MAINE							
Collins	Y	N	Y	Y	Y	Y	N
Snowe	Y	N	Y	Y	Y	Y	N
MARYLAND							
Mikulski	N	Y	Y	N	Y	N	N
Sarbanes	N	Y	Y	N	Y	N	N
MASSACHUSETTS							
Kennedy	N	Y	Y	N	Y	N	N
Kerry	N	Y	Y	N	Y	N	N
MICHIGAN							
Abraham	Y	N	Y	Y	Y	Y	N
Levin	N	Y	Y	N	Y	N	N
MINNESOTA							
Grams	Y	N	Y	Y	Y	Y	N
Wellstone	N	Y	Y	N	Y	N	N
MISSISSIPPI							
Cochran	Y	N	Y	Y	Y	Y	N
Lott	Y	N	Y	Y	Y	Y	N
MISSOURI							
Ashcroft	Y	N	Y	Y	Y	Y	N
Bond	Y	N	Y	Y	Y	Y	N
MONTANA							
Burns	Y	N	Y	Y	Y	Y	N
Baucus	N	N	Y	Y	Y	N	N
NEBRASKA							
Hagel	Y	N	Y	Y	Y	Y	N
Kerrey	N	N	Y	Y	Y	N	N
NEVADA							
Bryan	N	Y	Y	N	Y	N	N
Reid	N	Y	Y	N	Y	N	N
NEW HAMPSHIRE							
Gregg	Y	N	Y	Y	Y	Y	N
Smith	Y	N	Y	Y	Y	Y	N
NEW JERSEY							
Lautenberg	N	Y	Y	N	Y	N	N
Torricelli	N	Y	Y	N	Y	N	N
NEW MEXICO							
Domenici	Y	N	Y	Y	Y	Y	N
Bingaman	N	N	Y	N	Y	N	N
NEW YORK							
D'Amato	N	N	Y	Y	Y	N	N
Moynihan	N	Y	Y	N	Y	N	N
NORTH CAROLINA							
Faircloth	Y	Y	Y	Y	N	Y	N
Helms	Y	N	Y	Y	+	+	−
NORTH DAKOTA							
Conrad	N	Y	Y	N	Y	N	N
Dorgan	N	Y	Y	N	Y	N	N
OHIO							
DeWine	Y	N	Y	Y	Y	Y	N
Glenn	N	Y	Y	N	Y	N	N
OKLAHOMA							
Inhofe	Y	N	Y	Y	Y	Y	N
Nickles	Y	N	Y	Y	Y	Y	N
OREGON							
Smith	Y	N	Y	Y	Y	Y	N
Wyden	N	Y	Y	N	Y	Y	N
PENNSYLVANIA							
Santorum	Y	N	Y	Y	Y	Y	N
Specter	N	N	Y	N	Y	N	N
RHODE ISLAND							
Chafee	Y	N	Y	Y	Y	Y	N
Reed	N	Y	Y	N	Y	N	N
SOUTH CAROLINA							
Thurmond	Y	N	Y	Y	Y	Y	N
Hollings	N	Y	Y	N	Y	N	N
SOUTH DAKOTA							
Daschle	N	Y	Y	N	Y	N	N
Johnson	N	Y	Y	N	Y	N	N
TENNESSEE							
Frist	Y	N	Y	Y	Y	Y	N
Thompson	Y	N	Y	Y	Y	Y	Y
TEXAS							
Gramm	Y	N	Y	Y	Y	Y	N
Hutchison	Y	N	Y	Y	Y	Y	N
UTAH							
Bennett	Y	N	Y	Y	Y	Y	N
Hatch	Y	N	Y	Y	Y	Y	N
VERMONT							
Jeffords	Y	N	Y	Y	Y	Y	N
Leahy	N	N	Y	N	Y	N	N
VIRGINIA							
Warner	Y	N	Y	Y	Y	Y	N
Robb	N	Y	Y	N	Y	N	N
WASHINGTON							
Gorton	Y	N	Y	Y	Y	Y	N
Murray	N	Y	Y	N	Y	N	N
WEST VIRGINIA							
Byrd	Y	Y	Y	Y	Y	N	N
Rockefeller	N	Y	?	?	Y	N	N
WISCONSIN							
Feingold	N	Y	Y	N	Y	N	N
Kohl	N	Y	Y	N	Y	N	N
WYOMING							
Enzi	Y	N	Y	Y	Y	Y	N
Thomas	Y	N	Y	Y	Y	Y	N

Key

Y	Voted for (yea).
#	Paired for.
+	Announced for.
N	Voted against (nay).
X	Paired against.
−	Announced against.
P	Voted "present."
C	Voted "present" to avoid possible conflict of interest.
?	Did not vote or otherwise make a position known.

Democrats *Republicans*

ND Northern Democrats   SD Southern Democrats

Southern states - Ala., Ark., Fla., Ga., Ky., La., Miss., N.C., Okla., S.C., Tenn., Texas, Va.

57. S Con Res 86. Fiscal 1999 Budget Resolution/School Modernization Bonds. Domenici, R-N.M., motion to table (kill) the Moseley-Braun, D-Ill., amendment that would express the sense of the Senate that Congress should enact legislation to allow states and school districts to issue $21.8 billion in school modernization bonds, and that the federal government should provide income tax credits to purchasers of the bonds in lieu of interest. Motion agreed to 54-46: R 53-2; D 1-44 (ND 1-36, SD 0-8). April 1, 1998.

58. S Con Res 86. Fiscal 1999 Budget Resolution/Social Security Point of Order. Hollings, D-S.C., motion to waive the Budget Act with respect to the Domenici, R-N.M., point of order against the Hollings amendment. The Hollings amendment would revise Senate rules to require a three-fifths majority vote (60) to consider any provision that would revise budget procedures regarding Social Security. Motion rejected 42-58: R 1-54; D 41-4 (ND 33-4, SD 8-0). April 1, 1998. A three-fifths majority vote (60) of the total Senate is required to waive the Budget Act. (Subsequently, the chair upheld the point of order, and the amendment fell.)

59. S Con Res 86. Fiscal 1999 Budget Resolution/Marriage Penalty. Faircloth, R-N.C., amendment to express the sense of the Senate that Congress should begin to phase out the marriage penalty, under which some married couples pay more in income taxes than they would if filing separately, in 1998. Adopted 99-0: R 55-0; D 44-0 (ND 36-0, SD 8-0). April 1, 1998.

60. S Con Res 86. Fiscal 1999 Budget Resolution/Entitlement Spending Supermajority. Craig, R-Idaho, motion to waive the Budget Act with respect to the Lautenberg, D-N.J., point of order against the Craig amendment. The Craig amendment would revise Senate rules to require a supermajority point of order against provisions that would increase mandatory spending without offsetting the increase with reductions. Motion rejected 54-45: R 51-4; D 3-41 (ND 2-34, SD 1-7). April 1, 1998. A three-fifths majority vote (60) of the total Senate is required to waive the Budget Act. (Subsequently, the chair upheld the point of order, and the amendment fell.)

61. Murphy Nomination/Confirmation. Confirmation of President Clinton's nomination of G. Patrick Murphy of Illinois to be U.S. district judge for the Southern District of Illinois. Confirmed 98-1: R 53-1; D 45-0 (ND 37-0, SD 8-0). April 2, 1998. A "yea" was a vote in support of the president's position.

62. S Con Res 86. Fiscal 1999 Budget Resolution/Tax Code Sunset. Hutchinson, R-Ark., substitute amendment to the Dorgan, D-N.D., amendment. The Hutchinson amendment would express the sense of the Senate that the chamber should pass an IRS restructuring bill that includes taxpayer protections, expanded oversight and IRS employee accountability. It would express the sense of Congress that the federal Tax Code should sunset by the end of 2001. Adopted 59-40: R 54-0; D 5-40 (ND 5-32, SD 0-8). April 2, 1998.

63. S Con Res 86. Fiscal 1999 Budget Resolution/Federal Tax Deductions. Domenici, R-N.M., motion to table (kill) the Dorgan, D-N.D., amendment to the modified Dorgan amendment. The second-degree Dorgan amendment would express the sense of Congress that the current tax deductions for interest on home mortgages and charitable contributions should continue. Motion rejected 1-98: R 1-53; D 0-45 (ND 0-37, SD 0-8). April 2, 1998. (Subsequently, both the Dorgan amendment and the modified Dorgan amendment were adopted by voice vote.)

	64	65	66	67	68	69	70
ALABAMA							
Sessions	Y	N	Y	Y	Y	N	Y
Shelby	Y	N	Y	Y	Y	N	Y
ALASKA							
Murkowski	Y	N	Y	Y	Y	N	Y
Stevens	Y	N	Y	Y	Y	N	Y
ARIZONA							
Kyl	Y	N	Y	Y	Y	N	Y
McCain	Y	N	Y	Y	Y	N	Y
ARKANSAS							
Hutchinson	Y	N	Y	Y	Y	N	Y
Bumpers	N	Y	Y	N	N	Y	N
CALIFORNIA							
Boxer	N	Y	Y	N	N	Y	N
Feinstein	N	Y	Y	N	N	Y	N
COLORADO							
Allard	Y	N	Y	Y	Y	N	Y
Campbell	Y	N	Y	Y	Y	N	Y
CONNECTICUT							
Dodd	N	Y	Y	N	N	Y	Y
Lieberman	Y	Y	Y	N	N	Y	N
DELAWARE							
Roth	Y	N	Y	Y	Y	N	Y
Biden	N	Y	Y	N	N	Y	N
FLORIDA							
Mack	Y	N	Y	Y	Y	N	Y
Graham	N	Y	Y	N	N	Y	Y
GEORGIA							
Coverdell	Y	N	Y	Y	Y	N	Y
Cleland	Y	Y	Y	N	N	Y	N
HAWAII							
Akaka	N	Y	Y	N	N	Y	N
Inouye	N	Y	Y	N	?	?	?
IDAHO							
Craig	Y	N	Y	Y	Y	N	Y
Kempthorne	Y	N	Y	Y	Y	N	Y
ILLINOIS							
Durbin	N	Y	Y	N	N	Y	N
Moseley-Braun	N	Y	Y	N	N	Y	N
INDIANA							
Coats	Y	N	N	N	Y	N	Y
Lugar	Y	N	Y	N	Y	N	Y

	64	65	66	67	68	69	70
IOWA							
Grassley	Y	N	Y	Y	Y	N	N
Harkin	N	Y	Y	N	N	Y	N
KANSAS							
Brownback	Y	N	Y	Y	Y	N	Y
Roberts	Y	N	Y	Y	Y	N	Y
KENTUCKY							
McConnell	Y	N	Y	Y	Y	N	Y
Ford	N	Y	Y	N	N	Y	N
LOUISIANA							
Breaux	N	Y	Y	Y	N	Y	Y
Landrieu	–	Y	Y	N	N	Y	Y
MAINE							
Collins	Y	N	Y	N	Y	N	N
Snowe	Y	N	Y	N	N	N	N
MARYLAND							
Mikulski	N	Y	Y	N	N	Y	N
Sarbanes	N	Y	Y	N	N	Y	N
MASSACHUSETTS							
Kennedy	N	Y	Y	N	N	Y	N
Kerry	N	Y	Y	N	N	Y	N
MICHIGAN							
Abraham	N	N	Y	Y	Y	N	Y
Levin	N	Y	Y	N	N	Y	N
MINNESOTA							
Grams	Y	N	Y	Y	Y	N	Y
Wellstone	N	Y	Y	N	N	Y	N
MISSISSIPPI							
Cochran	Y	N	Y	Y	Y	N	Y
Lott	Y	N	Y	Y	Y	N	Y
MISSOURI							
Ashcroft	Y	N	Y	Y	Y	N	Y
Bond	N	N	Y	Y	Y	N	Y
MONTANA							
Burns	Y	N	Y	Y	Y	N	Y
Baucus	N	Y	Y	N	N	Y	N
NEBRASKA							
Hagel	N	N	Y	Y	Y	N	Y
Kerrey	N	Y	Y	N	N	Y	Y
NEVADA							
Bryan	N	Y	Y	N	N	Y	Y
Reid	N	Y	Y	Y	Y	Y	N

	64	65	66	67	68	69	70
NEW HAMPSHIRE							
Gregg	Y	N	Y	N	N	N	Y
Smith	Y	N	Y	Y	N	Y	N
NEW JERSEY							
Lautenberg	N	Y	Y	N	N	Y	N
Torricelli	N	Y	Y	N	N	Y	N
NEW MEXICO							
Domenici	Y	N	Y	Y	Y	N	Y
Bingaman	N	Y	Y	Y	N	Y	N
NEW YORK							
D'Amato	Y	Y	Y	N	Y	N	N
Moynihan	N	Y	Y	N	N	Y	Y
NORTH CAROLINA							
Faircloth	Y	Y	Y	N	Y	N	Y
Helms	+	–	+	+	+	–	+
NORTH DAKOTA							
Conrad	N	Y	Y	Y	N	Y	Y
Dorgan	N	Y	Y	Y	N	Y	Y
OHIO							
DeWine	Y	N	Y	Y	Y	N	N
Glenn	N	Y	Y	N	N	Y	N
OKLAHOMA							
Inhofe	Y	N	Y	Y	Y	?	Y
Nickles	Y	N	N	Y	Y	Y	Y
OREGON							
Smith	Y	N	Y	Y	Y	N	Y
Wyden	Y	Y	Y	N	Y	Y	N
PENNSYLVANIA							
Santorum	N	N	Y	Y	N	N	Y
Specter	Y	Y	Y	N	N	N	N
RHODE ISLAND							
Chafee	Y	N	Y	N	N	N	Y
Reed	N	Y	Y	N	N	Y	N
SOUTH CAROLINA							
Thurmond	Y	N	Y	Y	Y	N	Y
Hollings	N	Y	Y	N	N	N	N
SOUTH DAKOTA							
Daschle	N	Y	Y	N	N	Y	N
Johnson	N	Y	Y	Y	N	Y	N
TENNESSEE							
Frist	Y	N	Y	N	Y	N	N
Thompson	Y	N	Y	Y	Y	N	Y

ND Northern Democrats   SD Southern Democrats

Southern states - Ala., Ark., Fla., Ga., Ky., La., Miss., N.C., Okla., S.C., Tenn., Texas, Va.

Key

Y	Voted for (yea).
#	Paired for.
+	Announced for.
N	Voted against (nay).
X	Paired against.
–	Announced against.
P	Voted "present."
C	Voted "present" to avoid possible conflict of interest.
?	Did not vote or otherwise make a position known.

Democrats   *Republicans*

	64	65	66	67	68	69	70
TEXAS							
Gramm	Y	N	Y	Y	Y	N	Y
Hutchison	Y	N	Y	Y	Y	N	Y
UTAH							
Bennett	Y	N	Y	Y	Y	N	Y
Hatch	Y	N	Y	Y	Y	N	Y
VERMONT							
Jeffords	Y	N	Y	N	N	N	N
Leahy	N	Y	Y	N	N	Y	N
VIRGINIA							
Warner	Y	N	Y	Y	Y	N	Y
Robb	N	Y	Y	N	N	Y	N
WASHINGTON							
Gorton	Y	N	Y	Y	Y	N	Y
Murray	N	Y	Y	N	N	Y	N
WEST VIRGINIA							
Byrd	N	N	Y	N	Y	N	Y
Rockefeller	N	Y	Y	N	N	Y	N
WISCONSIN							
Feingold	Y	Y	Y	N	N	N	N
Kohl	N	Y	Y	N	N	Y	N
WYOMING							
Enzi	Y	N	Y	Y	Y	N	Y
Thomas	Y	N	Y	Y	Y	N	Y

64. S Con Res 86. Fiscal 1999 Budget Resolution/Federal Debt Repayment. Domenici, R-N.M., motion to waive the Budget Act with respect to the Lautenberg, D-N.J., point of order against the Allard, R-Colo., amendment. The Allard amendment would prohibit the Senate, beginning in fiscal 2000, from considering any budget measure that would create a budget deficit or fail to reduce the federal debt enough to eliminate it by fiscal 2028. Motion rejected 53-45: R 50-4; D 3-41 (ND 3-34, SD 0-7). April 2, 1998. A three-fifths majority vote (60) of the total Senate is required to waive the Budget Act. (Subsequently, the chair upheld the point of order, and the amendment fell.)

65. S Con Res 86. Fiscal 1999 Budget Resolution/Environmental Reserve Fund. Lautenberg, D-N.J., motion to waive the Budget Act with respect to the Domenici, R-N.M., point of order against the Lautenberg amendment. The Lautenberg amendment would establish a deficit-neutral reserve fund to provide funding for the environment and natural resources. Motion rejected 47-52: R 3-51; D 44-1 (ND 36-1, SD 8-0). April 2, 1998. A three-fifths majority vote (60) of the total Senate is required to waive the Budget Act. (Subsequently, the chair upheld the point of order, and the amendment fell.)

66. S Con Res 86. Fiscal 1999 Budget Resolution/Elderly Housing. Bond, R-Mo., amendment to express the sense of the Senate that the Department of Housing and Urban Development's Section 202 Elderly Housing program should receive at least as much funding in each of the next five fiscal years as it received in fiscal 1998. Adopted 97-2: R 52-2; D 45-0 (ND 37-0, SD 8-0). April 2, 1998.

67. S Con Res 86. Fiscal 1999 Budget Resolution/Education for the Disabled. Domenici, R-N.M., motion to table (kill) the Bumpers, D-Ark., amendment to raise the aggregate revenue and spending recommendations by $311 million over five years. The amendment called for raising the revenue an additional $311 million by repealing a tax break for hard-rock mining companies and allocate it for grants to states to fund programs under the Individuals with Disabilities Education Act. Motion agreed to 55-44: R 44-10; D 11-34 (ND 9-28, SD 2-6). April 2, 1998.

68. S Con Res 86. Fiscal 1999 Budget Resolution/Discretionary Spending Cuts. Brownback, R-Kan., amendment to express the sense of the Senate that savings from the elimination of any discretionary spending program should be used for tax cuts or to revise the Social Security program. Adopted 52-46: R 48-6; D 4-40 (ND 4-32, SD 0-8). April 2, 1998.

69. S Con Res 86. Fiscal 1999 Budget Resolution/Democratic Substitute. Lautenberg, D-N.J., motion to waive the Budget Act with respect to the Domenici, R-N.M., point of order against the Lautenberg substitute amendment. The Lautenberg amendment would replace the underlying resolution with a version of President Clinton's fiscal 1999 budget. Motion rejected 42-55: R 0-53; D 42-2 (ND 35-1, SD 7-1). April 2, 1998. A three-fifths majority vote (60) of the total Senate is required to waive the Budget Act. (Subsequently, the chair upheld the point of order, and the amendment fell.)

70. S Con Res 86. Fiscal 1999 Budget Resolution/Health Research. Domenici, R-N.M., motion to table (kill) the Specter, R-Pa., amendment intended to increase fiscal 1999 funding for biomedical research by $2 billion by decreasing all discretionary spending by $2 billion through a four-tenths of 1 percent across-the-board cut. Motion agreed to 57-41: R 45-9; D 12-32 (ND 8-28, SD 4-4). April 2, 1998.

	71	72	73	74	75	76	77
ALABAMA							
Sessions	Y	Y	Y	Y	Y	Y	Y
Shelby	Y	Y	Y	Y	Y	Y	Y
ALASKA							
Murkowski	Y	Y	Y	Y	Y	Y	Y
Stevens	Y	Y	Y	Y	Y	Y	Y
ARIZONA							
Kyl	Y	Y	Y	Y	Y	Y	Y
McCain	Y	Y	Y	Y	Y	Y	Y
ARKANSAS							
Hutchinson	Y	Y	Y	Y	Y	Y	Y
Bumpers	N	Y	N	N	Y	N	N
CALIFORNIA							
Boxer	N	Y	N	N	Y	N	N
Feinstein	N	Y	N	N	Y	N	N
COLORADO							
Allard	Y	Y	Y	Y	Y	Y	Y
Campbell	Y	Y	Y	Y	Y	N	Y
CONNECTICUT							
Dodd	N	Y	N	N	Y	N	N
Lieberman	N	Y	N	Y	Y	N	N
DELAWARE							
Roth	Y	Y	Y	Y	Y	Y	Y
Biden	N	Y	N	N	Y	N	N
FLORIDA							
Mack	Y	Y	Y	Y	Y	Y	Y
Graham	N	Y	N	N	Y	N	N
GEORGIA							
Coverdell	Y	Y	Y	Y	Y	N	Y
Cleland	N	Y	N	N	Y	N	Y
HAWAII							
Akaka	N	Y	N	N	Y	N	N
Inouye	?	?	?	?	?	?	?
IDAHO							
Craig	Y	Y	Y	Y	Y	Y	Y
Kempthorne	Y	Y	Y	Y	Y	Y	Y
ILLINOIS							
Durbin	N	Y	N	N	Y	N	N
Moseley-Braun	N	Y	N	N	Y	N	N
INDIANA							
Coats	Y	Y	Y	Y	Y	Y	Y
Lugar	N	Y	Y	Y	Y	Y	Y
IOWA							
Grassley	Y	Y	Y	Y	Y	Y	Y
Harkin	N	Y	N	N	Y	N	N
KANSAS							
Brownback	Y	Y	Y	Y	Y	Y	Y
Roberts	Y	Y	Y	Y	Y	Y	Y
KENTUCKY							
McConnell	Y	Y	Y	Y	Y	Y	Y
Ford	N	Y	N	N	Y	Y	N
LOUISIANA							
Breaux	N	Y	N	Y	Y	Y	N
Landrieu	N	Y	N	N	Y	Y	N
MAINE							
Collins	Y	Y	Y	Y	Y	N	N
Snowe	Y	Y	Y	N	Y	N	N
MARYLAND							
Mikulski	N	Y	N	N	Y	N	N
Sarbanes	N	Y	N	N	Y	N	N
MASSACHUSETTS							
Kennedy	N	Y	N	N	Y	N	N
Kerry	N	Y	N	N	Y	N	N
MICHIGAN							
Abraham	Y	Y	Y	Y	Y	Y	Y
Levin	N	Y	N	N	Y	N	N
MINNESOTA							
Grams	Y	Y	Y	Y	Y	Y	Y
Wellstone	N	Y	N	N	Y	N	N
MISSISSIPPI							
Cochran	Y	Y	Y	Y	Y	Y	Y
Lott	Y	Y	Y	Y	Y	Y	Y
MISSOURI							
Ashcroft	Y	Y	Y	Y	Y	Y	Y
Bond	Y	Y	Y	Y	Y	Y	N
MONTANA							
Burns	Y	Y	Y	Y	Y	Y	Y
Baucus	N	Y	N	N	Y	Y	N
NEBRASKA							
Hagel	Y	Y	Y	Y	Y	Y	Y
Kerrey	N	Y	N	N	Y	Y	N
NEVADA							
Bryan	N	Y	N	N	Y	N	N
Reid	N	Y	N	N	Y	N	N
NEW HAMPSHIRE							
Gregg	Y	Y	Y	Y	Y	Y	Y
Smith	Y	Y	Y	Y	Y	Y	Y
NEW JERSEY							
Lautenberg	N	Y	N	N	Y	N	N
Torricelli	N	Y	N	N	Y	N	N
NEW MEXICO							
Domenici	Y	Y	Y	Y	Y	Y	Y
Bingaman	N	Y	N	N	Y	N	N
NEW YORK							
D'Amato	Y	Y	N	N	Y	N	Y
Moynihan	N	Y	N	N	Y	N	N
NORTH CAROLINA							
Faircloth	Y	Y	Y	Y	Y	Y	Y
Helms	+	+	+	+	+	+	+
NORTH DAKOTA							
Conrad	N	Y	N	N	Y	N	N
Dorgan	N	Y	N	N	Y	N	N
OHIO							
DeWine	N	Y	Y	Y	Y	N	N
Glenn	N	Y	N	N	Y	N	N
OKLAHOMA							
Inhofe	Y	Y	Y	Y	Y	Y	Y
Nickles	Y	Y	Y	Y	Y	Y	Y
OREGON							
Smith	Y	Y	Y	Y	Y	Y	Y
Wyden	Y	Y	N	Y	Y	N	N
PENNSYLVANIA							
Santorum	Y	Y	Y	Y	Y	Y	Y
Specter	N	Y	N	N	Y	N	Y
RHODE ISLAND							
Chafee	N	Y	N	N	Y	N	N
Reed	N	Y	N	N	Y	N	N
SOUTH CAROLINA							
Thurmond	Y	Y	Y	Y	Y	Y	Y
Hollings	N	Y	N	N	Y	N	N
SOUTH DAKOTA							
Daschle	N	Y	N	N	Y	N	N
Johnson	N	Y	N	N	Y	N	N
TENNESSEE							
Frist	Y	Y	Y	Y	Y	Y	Y
Thompson	Y	Y	Y	Y	Y	Y	Y
TEXAS							
Gramm	Y	Y	Y	Y	Y	Y	Y
Hutchison	Y	Y	Y	Y	Y	Y	Y
UTAH							
Bennett	Y	Y	Y	Y	Y	Y	Y
Hatch	Y	Y	Y	Y	Y	Y	Y
VERMONT							
Jeffords	N	Y	Y	N	Y	N	N
Leahy	N	Y	N	N	Y	N	N
VIRGINIA							
Warner	Y	Y	Y	Y	Y	Y	Y
Robb	N	Y	N	N	Y	N	N
WASHINGTON							
Gorton	Y	Y	Y	Y	Y	Y	Y
Murray	N	Y	N	N	Y	N	N
WEST VIRGINIA							
Byrd	N	Y	N	N	Y	Y	N
Rockefeller	N	Y	N	N	Y	N	N
WISCONSIN							
Feingold	N	Y	N	N	Y	N	N
Kohl	N	Y	N	N	Y	N	N
WYOMING							
Enzi	Y	Y	Y	Y	Y	Y	Y
Thomas	Y	Y	Y	Y	Y	Y	Y

ND Northern Democrats   SD Southern Democrats

Southern states - Ala., Ark., Fla., Ga., Ky., La., Miss., N.C., Okla., S.C., Tenn., Texas, Va.

Key

Y	Voted for (yea).
#	Paired for.
+	Announced for.
N	Voted against (nay).
X	Paired against.
−	Announced against.
P	Voted "present."
C	Voted "present" to avoid possible conflict of interest.
?	Did not vote or otherwise make a position known.

Democrats   *Republicans*

71. S Con Res 86. Fiscal 1999 Budget Resolution/Tax Increase Super-majority. Kyl, R-Ariz., amendment to express the sense of the Senate that the Constitution should be amended to require more than a simple majority in each chamber of Congress in order to approve tax increase. Adopted 50-48: R 49-5; D 1-43 (ND 1-35, SD 0-8). April 2, 1998.

72. S Con Res 86. Fiscal 1999 Budget Resolution/Health Care Costs. Nickles, R-Okla., amendment to express the sense of the Senate that the Senate should not pass any health care legislation that would increase the costs of health care for families or divert resources away from treating patients. Adopted 98-0: R 54-0; D 44-0 (ND 36-0, SD 8-0). April 2, 1998.

73. S Con Res 86. Fiscal 1999 Budget Resolution/Patient's Bill of Rights. Nickles, R-Okla., motion to table (kill) the Kennedy, D-Mass., amendment that would express the sense of the Senate that a "patient's bill of rights" should be established for participants in health plans. The "bill of rights" would guarantee access to coverage, prohibit so-called gag clauses, and establish a procedure to provide for an independent, impartial entity to review appeals when a health plan decides to deny care. Motion agreed to 51-47: R 51-3; D 0-44 (ND 0-36, SD 0-8). April 2, 1998.

74. S Con Res 86. Fiscal 1999 Budget Resolution/Budget Surplus. Hutchison, R-Texas, amendment to express the sense of the Senate that any federal budget surplus should be dedicated to debt reduction or tax cuts.

Adopted 53-45: R 49-5; D 4-40 (ND 2-34, SD 2-6). April 2, 1998.

75. S Con Res 86. Fiscal 1999 Budget Resolution/Veterans' Benefits. Rockefeller, D-W.Va., perfecting amendment to the Rockefeller amendment that would raise allocations for veterans programs by $10.5 billion in order to reinstate a Veterans' Affairs Department policy that grants compensation to veterans for smoking-related illnesses. The amendment would offset the spending by reducing highway spending by $10.5 billion. Adopted 98-0: R 54-0; D 44-0 (ND 36-0, SD 8-0). April 2, 1998.

76. S Con Res 86. Fiscal 1999 Budget Resolution/VA Smoking Benefit Study. Domenici, R-N.M., amendment to the Rockefeller, D-W.Va., amendment. The Domenici amendment would reduce veterans programs by $10.5 billion over five years by granting compensation to veterans only for smoking-related illnesses caused during a veteran's term of service. Adopted 52-46: R 47-7; D 5-39 (ND 3-33, SD 2-6). April 2, 1998. (Subsequently, the Rockefeller amendment as amended was adopted by voice vote.)

77. S Con Res 86. Fiscal 1999 Budget Resolution/Social Security Payroll Tax. Grams, R-Minn., amendment to express the sense of the Senate that any federal budget surplus should be used to reduce the Social Security payroll tax and to establish personal retirement accounts. Adopted 50-48: R 49-5; D 1-43 (ND 0-36, SD 1-7). April 2, 1998.

	78	79	80	81	82	83	84
ALABAMA							
Sessions	Y	Y	Y	Y	N	N	Y
Shelby	Y	Y	Y	Y	N	N	Y
ALASKA							
Murkowski	Y	Y	Y	Y	N	N	Y
Stevens	Y	Y	Y	Y	N	N	Y
ARIZONA							
Kyl	Y	Y	Y	Y	N	N	Y
McCain	Y	Y	Y	Y	N	N	Y
ARKANSAS							
Hutchinson	Y	Y	Y	Y	N	N	Y
Bumpers	N	N	N	N	Y	N	N
CALIFORNIA							
Boxer	N	N	N	N	Y	N	N
Feinstein	N	N	N	N	Y	N	N
COLORADO							
Allard	Y	Y	Y	Y	N	N	Y
Campbell	Y	Y	Y	Y	N	N	Y
CONNECTICUT							
Dodd	N	N	N	N	N	N	N
Lieberman	N	N	Y	N	N	N	N
DELAWARE							
Roth	Y	Y	Y	Y	N	N	Y
Biden	N	N	N	N	Y	N	N
FLORIDA							
Mack	Y	Y	Y	Y	N	N	Y
Graham	Y	N	N	N	Y	Y	N
GEORGIA							
Coverdell	Y	Y	Y	Y	N	Y	Y
Cleland	Y	Y	Y	Y	N	Y	Y
HAWAII							
Akaka	N	N	N	N	Y	Y	N
Inouye	?	?	?	?	?	?	?
IDAHO							
Craig	Y	Y	Y	Y	N	N	Y
Kempthorne	Y	Y	Y	Y	N	N	Y
ILLINOIS							
Durbin	N	N	N	N	Y	N	N
Moseley-Braun	N	N	N	N	Y	N	N
INDIANA							
Coats	Y	Y	Y	Y	N	N	Y
Lugar	Y	Y	Y	Y	N	Y	Y

	78	79	80	81	82	83	84
IOWA							
Grassley	Y	Y	Y	Y	N	N	Y
Harkin	N	N	N	N	Y	Y	N
KANSAS							
Brownback	Y	Y	Y	Y	N	N	Y
Roberts	Y	Y	Y	Y	N	N	Y
KENTUCKY							
McConnell	Y	Y	Y	Y	N	Y	Y
Ford	N	N	N	N	Y	Y	N
LOUISIANA							
Breaux	N	N	Y	N	Y	Y	N
Landrieu	N	N	N	N	Y	Y	N
MAINE							
Collins	Y	Y	Y	Y	N	N	Y
Snowe	Y	Y	Y	Y	N	N	Y
MARYLAND							
Mikulski	N	N	N	N	Y	Y	N
Sarbanes	N	N	N	N	Y	Y	N
MASSACHUSETTS							
Kennedy	N	N	N	N	Y	Y	N
Kerry	N	N	N	N	Y	Y	N
MICHIGAN							
Abraham	Y	Y	Y	Y	N	N	Y
Levin	N	N	N	N	Y	Y	N
MINNESOTA							
Grams	Y	Y	Y	Y	N	N	Y
Wellstone	N	N	N	N	Y	Y	N
MISSISSIPPI							
Cochran	Y	Y	Y	Y	N	N	Y
Lott	Y	Y	Y	Y	N	N	Y
MISSOURI							
Ashcroft	Y	Y	Y	Y	N	N	Y
Bond	Y	Y	Y	Y	N	N	Y
MONTANA							
Burns	Y	Y	Y	Y	N	N	Y
Baucus	N	N	N	N	Y	Y	N
NEBRASKA							
Hagel	Y	Y	Y	Y	N	N	Y
Kerrey	N	N	N	N	Y	Y	N
NEVADA							
Bryan	N	N	N	N	Y	N	N
Reid	N	N	N	N	Y	N	N

	78	79	80	81	82	83	84
NEW HAMPSHIRE							
Gregg	Y	N	Y	Y	N	N	Y
Smith	Y	Y	Y	Y	N	N	Y
NEW JERSEY							
Lautenberg	N	N	N	N	Y	Y	N
Torricelli	N	N	N	N	Y	Y	N
NEW MEXICO							
Domenici	Y	Y	Y	Y	N	N	Y
Bingaman	N	Y	N	N	Y	N	N
NEW YORK							
D'Amato	Y	Y	Y	Y	N	N	Y
Moynihan	N	N	N	N	Y	Y	Y
NORTH CAROLINA							
Faircloth	Y	Y	Y	Y	N	Y	N
Helms	+	+	?	+	−	+	−
NORTH DAKOTA							
Conrad	N	N	N	N	Y	Y	N
Dorgan	N	N	N	N	Y	N	N
OHIO							
DeWine	Y	Y	Y	Y	N	N	Y
Glenn	N	N	N	N	Y	N	N
OKLAHOMA							
Inhofe	Y	Y	Y	Y	N	N	Y
Nickles	Y	Y	Y	Y	N	N	Y
OREGON							
Smith	Y	Y	Y	Y	N	N	Y
Wyden	N	N	N	N	Y	N	N
PENNSYLVANIA							
Santorum	Y	Y	Y	Y	N	N	Y
Specter	N	Y	Y	Y	N	N	Y
RHODE ISLAND							
Chafee	Y	Y	Y	Y	N	N	Y
Reed	N	N	N	N	Y	Y	N
SOUTH CAROLINA							
Thurmond	Y	Y	Y	Y	N	N	Y
Hollings	N	N	N	N	Y	Y	N
SOUTH DAKOTA							
Daschle	N	N	N	N	Y	Y	N
Johnson	N	N	N	N	Y	Y	N
TENNESSEE							
Frist	Y	Y	Y	Y	N	N	Y
Thompson	Y	Y	Y	Y	N	Y	Y

Key

Y	Voted for (yea).
#	Paired for.
+	Announced for.
N	Voted against (nay).
X	Paired against.
−	Announced against.
P	Voted "present."
C	Voted "present" to avoid possible conflict of interest.
?	Did not vote or otherwise make a position known.

Democrats   *Republicans*

	78	79	80	81	82	83	84
TEXAS							
Gramm	Y	Y	Y	Y	N	N	Y
Hutchison	Y	Y	Y	Y	N	N	Y
UTAH							
Bennett	Y	Y	Y	Y	N	N	Y
Hatch	Y	Y	Y	Y	N	N	Y
VERMONT							
Jeffords	N	Y	N	N	Y	N	Y
Leahy	N	N	N	N	Y	N	N
VIRGINIA							
Warner	Y	Y	Y	Y	N	N	Y
Robb	N	N	Y	N	Y	Y	Y
WASHINGTON							
Gorton	Y	Y	Y	Y	N	N	Y
Murray	N	N	N	N	Y	N	N
WEST VIRGINIA							
Byrd	Y	N	Y	Y	N	Y	N
Rockefeller	N	N	N	N	Y	Y	N
WISCONSIN							
Feingold	N	N	N	N	Y	N	N
Kohl	N	N	N	N	Y	N	N
WYOMING							
Enzi	Y	Y	Y	Y	N	N	Y
Thomas	Y	Y	Y	Y	N	N	Y

ND Northern Democrats   SD Southern Democrats

Southern states - Ala., Ark., Fla., Ga., Ky., La., Miss., N.C., Okla., S.C., Tenn., Texas, Va.

78. S Con Res 86. Fiscal 1999 Budget Resolution/Education Spending. Grassley, R-Iowa, motion to table (kill) the Kennedy, D-Mass., amendment to recommend increasing spending on education programs by $1.5 billion over five years, financed by across-the-board cuts in non-defense discretionary spending. Motion agreed to 55-43: R 52-2; D 3-41 (ND 1-35, SD 2-6). April 2, 1998.

79. S Con Res 86. Fiscal 1999 Budget Resolution/Public Land Sales. Kempthorne, R-Idaho, amendment to the Reid, D-Nev., amendment. The Kempthorne amendment would express the sense of the Senate that the landowner incentive program of the Endangered Species Recovery Act may be financed from multiple funding sources, including the sale of public lands. The Reid amendment would urge that no public lands be sold to finance the program. Adopted 55-43: R 53-1; D 2-42 (ND 1-35, SD 1-7). April 2, 1998. (Subsequently, the Reid amendment as amended was adopted by voice vote.)

80. S Con Res 86. Fiscal 1999 Budget Resolution/Non-binding Amendments. Nickles, R-Okla., motion to waive the Budget Act with respect to the Lautenberg, D-N.J., point of order against the Nickles amendment. The Nickles amendment would establish a point of order under the budget act against non-binding amendments, such as those expressing the sense of Congress or the sense of the Senate, to budget resolutions during floor consideration. Motion rejected 59-39: R 54-0; D 5-39 (ND 2-34, SD 3-5). April 2, 1998. A three-fifths majority vote (60) of the total Senate is required to waive the Budget Act. (Subsequently, the chair upheld the point of order, and the amendment fell.)

81. S Con Res 86. Fiscal 1999 Budget Resolution/Education Spending. Domenici, R-N.M., motion to table (kill) the Murray, D-Wash., amendment that would recommend $5.9 billion over four years for increased education spending. Motion agreed to 55-43: R 54-0; D 1-43 (ND 1-35, SD 0-8). April 2, 1998.

82. S Con Res 86. Fiscal 1999 Budget Resolution/Disability Programs. Feingold, D-Wis., motion to waive the Budget Act with respect to the Domenici, R-N.M., point of order against the Feingold amendment. The Feingold amendment would establish a deficit-neutral reserve fund to finance programs to allow disabled individuals to function independently in society. The amendment, which would permit tax increases to finance the programs, calls for $2 billion for the fund. Motion rejected 47-51: R 4-50; D 43-1 (ND 35-1, SD 8-0). April 2, 1998. A three-fifths majority vote (60) of the total Senate is required to waive the Budget Act. (Subsequently, the chair upheld the point of order, and the amendment fell.)

83. S Con Res 86. Fiscal 1999 Budget Resolution/Tobacco Farmers. Robb, D-Va., motion to waive the Budget Act with respect to the Domenici, R-N.M., point of order against the Robb amendment. The Robb amendment would reserve federal revenue from any potential tobacco settlement for transition assistance to tobacco farmers or the Medicare hospital insurance trust fund. Motion rejected 31-67: R 7-47; D 24-20 (ND 17-19, SD 7-1). April 2, 1998. A three-fifths majority vote (60) of the total Senate is required to waive the Budget Act. (Subsequently, the chair upheld the point of order, and the amendment fell.)

84. S Con Res 86. Fiscal 1999 Budget Resolution/Adoption. Adoption of the concurrent resolution to adopt a five-year budget plan that maintains the budget surplus expected in fiscal 1998. The plan calls for any federal revenues generated from a possible tobacco settlement to be used to bolster the solvency of the Medicare program. The resolution does not provide for net tax cuts, but anticipates five-year tax cuts of $30 billion, offset by new tax revenues or reductions in mandatory spending. It also contains non-binding language calling for expiration of the tax code by Dec. 31, 2001. The resolution sets budget levels for the fiscal year ending Sept. 30, 1999: budget authority, $1,730 billion; outlays, $1,730 billion; revenues, $1,738 billion; and surplus, $8.4 billion. Adopted 57-41: R 54-0; D 3-41 (ND 1-35, SD 2-6). April 2, 1998.

	85	86	87	88	89	90	91
ALABAMA							
Sessions	N	Y	Y	Y	Y	Y	Y
Shelby	Y	Y	Y	Y	Y	Y	Y
ALASKA							
Murkowski	N	Y	Y	Y	Y	Y	Y
Stevens	N	Y	Y	Y	Y	Y	Y
ARIZONA							
Kyl	N	Y	Y	Y	Y	Y	Y
McCain	N	Y	Y	Y	Y	Y	Y
ARKANSAS							
Hutchinson	N	Y	Y	Y	Y	Y	Y
Bumpers	Y	N	N	N	N	N	N
CALIFORNIA							
Boxer	Y	N	N	Y	N	N	N
Feinstein	Y	N	Y	Y	Y	N	N
COLORADO							
Allard	N	Y	Y	Y	Y	Y	Y
Campbell	Y	Y	Y	Y	Y	Y	Y
CONNECTICUT							
Dodd	Y	N	N	N	N	N	N
Lieberman	Y	Y	Y	N	N	N	N
DELAWARE							
Roth	Y	Y	Y	Y	Y	Y	Y
Biden	Y	Y	Y	N	N	Y	N
FLORIDA							
Mack	Y	Y	Y	Y	Y	Y	Y
Graham	Y	Y	N	N	Y	N	N
GEORGIA							
Coverdell	Y	Y	Y	Y	Y	Y	Y
Cleland	Y	N	N	N	N	N	N
HAWAII							
Akaka	Y	N	N	N	N	N	N
Inouye	?	?	N	N	N	N	N
IDAHO							
Craig	Y	Y	Y	Y	Y	Y	Y
Kempthorne	Y	Y	Y	Y	Y	Y	Y
ILLINOIS							
Durbin	Y	N	N	N	N	N	N
Moseley-Braun	Y	N	N	N	N	N	N
INDIANA							
Coats	N	Y	Y	Y	Y	Y	Y
Lugar	Y	Y	Y	Y	Y	Y	Y

	85	86	87	88	89	90	91
IOWA							
Grassley	N	Y	Y	Y	Y	Y	Y
Harkin	Y	N	N	N	N	N	N
KANSAS							
Brownback	N	Y	Y	Y	Y	Y	Y
Roberts	N	Y	Y	Y	Y	Y	Y
KENTUCKY							
McConnell	N	Y	Y	Y	Y	Y	Y
Ford	Y	N	N	N	N	N	N
LOUISIANA							
Breaux	Y	Y	Y	Y	Y	N	N
Landrieu	Y	Y	N	Y	N	N	N
MAINE							
Collins	Y	Y	Y	Y	Y	Y	N
Snowe	Y	Y	Y	Y	Y	Y	N
MARYLAND							
Mikulski	Y	N	N	N	N	N	N
Sarbanes	Y	N	N	N	N	N	N
MASSACHUSETTS							
Kennedy	Y	N	N	N	N	N	N
Kerry	Y	N	N	N	N	N	N
MICHIGAN							
Abraham	Y	Y	Y	Y	Y	Y	Y
Levin	Y	N	N	N	N	N	N
MINNESOTA							
Grams	N	Y	Y	Y	Y	Y	Y
Wellstone	Y	N	N	N	N	N	N
MISSISSIPPI							
Cochran	Y	Y	Y	Y	Y	Y	Y
Lott	Y	Y	Y	Y	Y	Y	Y
MISSOURI							
Ashcroft	Y	Y	Y	Y	Y	Y	Y
Bond	Y	Y	Y	Y	Y	Y	Y
MONTANA							
Burns	N	Y	Y	Y	Y	Y	Y
Baucus	Y	N	N	N	N	N	N
NEBRASKA							
Hagel	Y	Y	Y	Y	Y	Y	Y
Kerrey	Y	N	N	N	N	N	N
NEVADA							
Bryan	Y	N	N	N	Y	N	N
Reid	Y	N	N	N	Y	N	N

	85	86	87	88	89	90	91
NEW HAMPSHIRE							
Gregg	Y	Y	Y	Y	Y	Y	Y
Smith	N	Y	Y	Y	Y	Y	Y
NEW JERSEY							
Lautenberg	Y	N	N	N	N	N	N
Torricelli	Y	Y	Y	Y	Y	Y	N
NEW MEXICO							
Domenici	N	Y	Y	Y	Y	Y	Y
Bingaman	Y	N	N	N	Y	N	N
NEW YORK							
D'Amato	Y	N	Y	Y	Y	N	Y
Moynihan	+	–	?	?	?	?	N
NORTH CAROLINA							
Faircloth	Y	Y	Y	Y	Y	Y	Y
Helms	N	Y	Y	Y	Y	Y	?
NORTH DAKOTA							
Conrad	Y	N	N	N	Y	N	N
Dorgan	Y	N	N	N	N	N	N
OHIO							
DeWine	Y	Y	Y	Y	Y	Y	Y
Glenn	Y	N	N	N	N	N	N
OKLAHOMA							
Inhofe	Y	Y	Y	Y	Y	Y	Y
Nickles	N	Y	Y	Y	Y	Y	Y
OREGON							
Smith	Y	Y	Y	Y	Y	Y	Y
Wyden	Y	N	N	N	N	N	N
PENNSYLVANIA							
Santorum	Y	Y	Y	Y	Y	Y	Y
Specter	Y	N	Y	Y	Y	Y	N
RHODE ISLAND							
Chafee	Y	N	Y	Y	Y	Y	N
Reed	Y	N	N	N	N	N	N
SOUTH CAROLINA							
Thurmond	Y	Y	Y	Y	Y	Y	Y
Hollings	Y	N	Y	N	Y	N	N
SOUTH DAKOTA							
Daschle	Y	N	N	N	N	N	N
Johnson	Y	N	N	N	N	N	N
TENNESSEE							
Frist	Y	Y	Y	Y	Y	Y	Y
Thompson	Y	Y	Y	Y	Y	Y	Y

	85	86	87	88	89	90	91
TEXAS							
Gramm	N	Y	Y	Y	Y	Y	Y
Hutchison	Y	Y	Y	Y	Y	Y	Y
UTAH							
Bennett	?	?	?	?	?	?	Y
Hatch	Y	Y	Y	Y	Y	Y	Y
VERMONT							
Jeffords	N	N	N	Y	Y	Y	N
Leahy	Y	N	N	Y	N	N	N
VIRGINIA							
Warner	Y	Y	Y	Y	Y	Y	Y
Robb	Y	N	N	N	Y	N	N
WASHINGTON							
Gorton	N	Y	Y	Y	Y	Y	Y
Murray	Y	N	N	N	Y	N	N
WEST VIRGINIA							
Byrd	N	Y	Y	N	Y	N	N
Rockefeller	Y	N	N	N	Y	N	N
WISCONSIN							
Feingold	Y	N	N	N	N	N	N
Kohl	Y	N	N	N	Y	N	N
WYOMING							
Enzi	N	Y	Y	Y	Y	Y	Y
Thomas	N	Y	Y	Y	Y	Y	Y

Key

Y	Voted for (yea).
#	Paired for.
+	Announced for.
N	Voted against (nay).
X	Paired against.
–	Announced against.
P	Voted "present."
C	Voted "present" to avoid possible conflict of interest.
?	Did not vote or otherwise make a position known.

Democrats   *Republicans*

ND Northern Democrats   SD Southern Democrats

Southern states - Ala., Ark., Fla., Ga., Ky., La., Miss., N.C., Okla., S.C., Tenn., Texas, Va.

85. S 414. Ocean Shipping/Shipping Intermediaries. Hutchison, R-Texas, motion to table (kill) the Gorton, R-Wash., amendment to the Hutchison substitute amendment. The Gorton amendment would allow shipping intermediaries the same proprietary rights to offer service contracts to shippers as other ocean common carriers would have under the substitute amendment. The underlying substitute would eliminate requirements that ocean carriers file tariff rate increases or decreases with the Federal Maritime Commission and instead would require carriers to publish their shipping rates through a World Wide Web page or other non-governmental publication. Motion agreed to 72-25: R 30-24; D 42-1 (ND 34-1, SD 8-0). April 21, 1998. (Subsequently, the underlying substitute was adopted and the bill was passed by voice vote.)

86. HR 2646. Expanding Education Savings Accounts/Teacher Loan Forgiveness. Coverdell, R-Ga., motion to table (kill) the Kennedy, D-Mass., amendment to replace the bill's language expanding the accounts with language authorizing $7.2 million over two years to establish a federal program to forgive as much as $8,000 in unpaid student loans for each college graduate who becomes a full-time public school teacher. Motion agreed to 56-41: R 50-4; D 6-37 (ND 4-31, SD 2-6). April 21, 1998.

87. HR 2646. Expanding Education Savings Accounts/Higher Education. Gramm, R-Texas, motion to table (kill) the Glenn, D-Ohio, amendment to require that the expanded tax-free accounts may only be used for post-secondary education expenses. Motion agreed to 60-38: R 54-0; D 6-38 (ND 5-31, SD 1-7). April 21, 1998.

88. HR 2646. Expanding Education Savings Accounts/Teacher Merit Pay and Testing. Mack, R-Fla., amendment to provide incentives for states and localities to establish merit pay programs for teachers and implement teacher testing programs. Adopted 63-35: R 54-0; D 9-35 (ND 6-30, SD 3-5). April 21, 1998.

89. HR 2646. Expanding Education Savings Accounts/Same Gender Schooling. Hutchison, R-Texas, amendment to add proposals for same gender classrooms and schools to the list of "innovative assistance programs" identified under current law as eligible to receive targeted federal funding, as long as the same gender school and classroom programs offer comparable educational opportunities to students of both sexes. Adopted 69-29: R 54-0; D 15-29 (ND 11-25, SD 4-4). April 21, 1998.

90. HR 2646. Expanding Education Savings Accounts/School Construction Bonds. Coverdell, R-Ga., motion to table (kill) the Moseley-Braun, D-Ill., amendment to provide $10 billion in tax credits over ten years for purchasers of interest-free bonds to fund school construction. Motion agreed to 56-42: R 52-2; D 4-40 (ND 4-32, SD 0-8). April 21, 1998.

91. HR 2646. Expanding Education Savings Accounts/Education Block Grants. Gorton, R-Wash., amendment to require each state to decide within one year how it would like to receive its future federal education funding: administered as it is currently, sent directly to the states or sent directly to the local school districts. Adopted 50-49: R 50-4; D 0-45 (ND 0-37, SD 0-8). April 22, 1998.

	92	93	94	95	96	97	98
ALABAMA							
Sessions	Y	N	Y	Y	Y	N	N
Shelby	Y	N	Y	Y	Y	N	N
ALASKA							
Murkowski	Y	N	Y	N	Y	N	N
Stevens	Y	N	Y	Y	Y	N	N
ARIZONA							
Kyl	Y	N	Y	Y	Y	N	N
McCain	Y	N	Y	Y	Y	N	N
ARKANSAS							
Hutchinson	Y	N	Y	Y	Y	N	N
Bumpers	Y	Y	N	N	N	Y	Y
CALIFORNIA							
Boxer	Y	Y	N	N	N	Y	Y
Feinstein	Y	Y	N	N	N	N	Y
COLORADO							
Allard	Y	N	Y	Y	Y	N	N
Campbell	Y	Y	Y	Y	Y	N	–
CONNECTICUT							
Dodd	Y	Y	N	N	N	Y	Y
Lieberman	Y	Y	N	Y	Y	N	Y
DELAWARE							
Roth	Y	N	Y	Y	Y	N	N
Biden	Y	Y	N	N	N	N	Y
FLORIDA							
Mack	Y	N	Y	Y	Y	N	N
Graham	Y	Y	N	N	N	N	Y
GEORGIA							
Coverdell	Y	N	Y	Y	Y	N	N
Cleland	Y	Y	N	Y	Y	N	N
HAWAII							
Akaka	Y	Y	N	N	N	N	Y
Inouye	Y	Y	N	N	N	N	Y
IDAHO							
Craig	Y	N	Y	Y	Y	N	N
Kempthorne	Y	N	Y	Y	Y	N	N
ILLINOIS							
Durbin	Y	Y	N	N	N	Y	Y
Moseley-Braun	Y	Y	N	N	N	Y	Y
INDIANA							
Coats	Y	N	Y	Y	Y	N	N
Lugar	Y	N	Y	Y	Y	N	N

	92	93	94	95	96	97	98
IOWA							
Grassley	Y	N	Y	N	Y	N	N
Harkin	Y	Y	N	N	N	N	Y
KANSAS							
Brownback	Y	N	Y	Y	Y	N	N
Roberts	Y	N	Y	Y	Y	N	N
KENTUCKY							
McConnell	Y	N	Y	Y	Y	N	N
Ford	Y	Y	N	N	N	N	Y
LOUISIANA							
Breaux	Y	Y	N	N	N	N	Y
Landrieu	Y	Y	N	N	N	Y	Y
MAINE							
Collins	Y	N	Y	Y	Y	N	N
Snowe	Y	N	Y	Y	Y	N	N
MARYLAND							
Mikulski	Y	Y	N	N	N	N	Y
Sarbanes	Y	Y	N	N	N	N	Y
MASSACHUSETTS							
Kennedy	Y	Y	N	N	N	N	Y
Kerry	Y	Y	N	N	N	N	Y
MICHIGAN							
Abraham	Y	N	Y	Y	Y	N	N
Levin	Y	Y	N	N	N	N	Y
MINNESOTA							
Grams	Y	N	Y	Y	Y	N	N
Wellstone	Y	Y	N	N	N	N	Y
MISSISSIPPI							
Cochran	Y	N	Y	Y	Y	N	N
Lott	Y	N	Y	Y	Y	N	N
MISSOURI							
Ashcroft	Y	N	Y	Y	Y	N	N
Bond	Y	N	Y	Y	Y	N	N
MONTANA							
Burns	Y	Y	Y	Y	Y	N	N
Baucus	Y	Y	N	N	N	N	Y
NEBRASKA							
Hagel	Y	N	Y	Y	Y	N	N
Kerrey	Y	Y	N	N	N	Y	Y
NEVADA							
Bryan	Y	Y	N	N	N	N	Y
Reid	Y	Y	N	N	N	N	Y

	92	93	94	95	96	97	98
NEW HAMPSHIRE							
Gregg	Y	N	Y	Y	Y	N	N
Smith	Y	N	Y	Y	Y	N	N
NEW JERSEY							
Lautenberg	Y	Y	N	N	N	Y	Y
Torricelli	Y	Y	N	N	N	N	Y
NEW MEXICO							
Domenici	Y	N	Y	Y	Y	N	N
Bingaman	Y	Y	N	N	N	N	Y
NEW YORK							
D'Amato	Y	N	Y	Y	Y	N	N
Moynihan	Y	Y	N	N	N	N	Y
NORTH CAROLINA							
Faircloth	Y	N	Y	Y	Y	N	N
Helms	?	?	?	Y	Y	N	N
NORTH DAKOTA							
Conrad	Y	Y	N	N	N	N	Y
Dorgan	Y	Y	N	N	N	N	Y
OHIO							
DeWine	Y	N	Y	Y	Y	N	N
Glenn	Y	Y	N	N	N	N	Y
OKLAHOMA							
Inhofe	Y	N	Y	Y	Y	N	N
Nickles	Y	N	Y	Y	Y	N	N
OREGON							
Smith	Y	N	Y	Y	Y	N	N
Wyden	Y	Y	N	N	N	N	Y
PENNSYLVANIA							
Santorum	Y	N	Y	Y	Y	N	N
Specter	Y	Y	N	Y	Y	N	N
RHODE ISLAND							
Chafee	Y	N	Y	Y	Y	N	N
Reed	Y	Y	N	N	N	N	Y
SOUTH CAROLINA							
Thurmond	Y	N	Y	Y	Y	N	N
Hollings	Y	Y	N	N	N	N	Y
SOUTH DAKOTA							
Daschle	Y	Y	N	N	N	N	Y
Johnson	Y	Y	N	N	N	N	Y
TENNESSEE							
Frist	Y	N	Y	Y	Y	N	N
Thompson	Y	N	Y	Y	Y	N	N

	92	93	94	95	96	97	98
TEXAS							
Gramm	Y	N	Y	Y	Y	N	N
Hutchison	Y	N	Y	Y	Y	N	N
UTAH							
Bennett	Y	N	Y	Y	Y	N	N
Hatch	Y	N	Y	Y	Y	N	N
VERMONT							
Jeffords	Y	Y	N	N	N	Y	N
Leahy	Y	Y	N	N	N	N	Y
VIRGINIA							
Warner	Y	N	Y	Y	Y	N	N
Robb	Y	Y	N	N	N	N	Y
WASHINGTON							
Gorton	Y	N	Y	Y	Y	N	N
Murray	Y	Y	N	N	N	N	Y
WEST VIRGINIA							
Byrd	Y	Y	N	N	N	N	N
Rockefeller	Y	Y	N	N	N	N	Y
WISCONSIN							
Feingold	Y	Y	N	N	N	N	Y
Kohl	Y	Y	N	N	N	N	Y
WYOMING							
Enzi	Y	N	Y	Y	Y	N	N
Thomas	Y	N	Y	Y	Y	N	N

Key

Y	Voted for (yea).
#	Paired for.
+	Announced for.
N	Voted against (nay).
X	Paired against.
–	Announced against.
P	Voted "present."
C	Voted "present" to avoid possible conflict of interest.
?	Did not vote or otherwise make a position known.

Democrats   *Republicans*

ND Northern Democrats   SD Southern Democrats

Southern states - Ala., Ark., Fla., Ga., Ky., La., Miss., N.C., Okla., S.C., Tenn., Texas, Va.

92. HR 2646. Expanding Education Savings Accounts/Federal Education Funding. Hutchinson, R-Ark., amendment to express the sense of Congress that 95 percent of all federal education funds should be spent for children "in their classrooms." Adopted 99-0: R 54-0; D 45-0 (ND 37-0, SD 8-0). April 22, 1998.

93. HR 2646. Expanding Education Savings Accounts/National Class Sizes. Murray, D-Wash., amendment to express the sense of Congress that Congress should support hiring 100,000 new teachers to reduce first-through third-grade class sizes to a national average of 18 students. Rejected 49-50: R 4-50; D 45-0 (ND 37-0, SD 8-0). April 22, 1998.

94. HR 2646. Expanding Education Savings Accounts/National Education Testing. Ashcroft, R-Mo., amendment to the Levin, D-Mich., amendment. The Ashcroft amendment would restore the bill's savings account expansion and would prohibit the use of any federal funds for national education testing unless Congress passes explicit authorizing legislation. The Levin amendment would replace the savings account language with a provision to increase the current 20 percent lifetime tax credit on college costs to 50 percent for elementary and secondary school teachers who return to school to receive technology training. Adopted 52-47: R 51-3; D 1-44 (ND 1-36, SD 0-8). April 22, 1998.

95. HR 2646. Expanding Education Savings Accounts/Education Tax Deductions. Coats, R-Ind., amendment to allow taxpayers to deduct from their income tax returns 110 percent of charitable contributions to groups that provide scholarships to pre-college students whose family income is below 185 percent of the poverty line. Rejected 46-54: R 45-10; D 1-44 (ND 1-36, SD 0-8). April 23, 1998.

96. HR 2646. Expanding Education Savings Accounts/High School Performance Awards. Kempthorne, R-Idaho, amendment to the Landrieu, D-La., amendment. The Kempthorne amendment would restore the bill's savings account expansion and allow states to use some of their federal education funds to provide awards to public high schools based on the schools' performance on statewide tests composed entirely by the state. Adopted 58-42: R 55-0; D 3-42 (ND 2-35, SD 1-7). April 23, 1998. (Subsequently, the Senate agreed by voice vote to consider the Kempthorne amendment as an amendment directly to the underlying bill, thus not altering the Landrieu amendment.)

97. HR 2646. Expanding Education Savings Accounts/Blue Ribbon Schools. Landrieu, D-La., amendment to replace the savings account language with language to establish a program to award $100,000 each to nationally recognized public or private "Blue Ribbon" schools. Rejected 34-66: R 0-55; D 34-11 (ND 29-8, SD 5-3). April 23, 1998.

98. HR 2646. Expanding Education Savings Accounts/IDEA Funding. Dodd, D-Conn., motion to waive the Budget Act with respect to the Coverdell, R-Ga., point of order against the Dodd amendment. The Dodd amendment would remove the bill's education savings account language and direct that any revenue generated by other provisions of the bill be used to fund special education programs under the Individuals with Disabilities Education Act. Motion rejected 46-53: R 4-50; D 42-3 (ND 35-2, SD 7-1). April 23, 1998. A three-fifths majority vote (60) of the total Senate is required to waive the Budget Act. (Subsequently, the chair upheld the point of order, and the amendment fell.)

	99	100	101	102	103	104	105
ALABAMA							
Sessions	Y	N	N	Y	Y	Y	Y
Shelby	Y	N	N	Y	Y	Y	Y
ALASKA							
Murkowski	Y	N	Y	Y	Y	?	Y
Stevens	Y	N	Y	Y	Y	Y	Y
ARIZONA							
Kyl	Y	N	Y	Y	Y	Y	Y
McCain	Y	N	Y	?	?	Y	Y
ARKANSAS							
Hutchinson	Y	N	N	Y	Y	Y	Y
Bumpers	N	Y	Y	Y	Y	Y	N
CALIFORNIA							
Boxer	N	Y	Y	N	Y	Y	N
Feinstein	Y	Y	Y	N	Y	Y	N
COLORADO							
Allard	Y	N	N	Y	Y	Y	Y
Campbell	Y	N	Y	Y	Y	Y	Y
CONNECTICUT							
Dodd	N	Y	N	Y	Y	Y	N
Lieberman	Y	Y	Y	Y	Y	Y	N
DELAWARE							
Roth	Y	N	Y	Y	Y	Y	N
Biden	Y	Y	N	Y	Y	Y	N
FLORIDA							
Mack	Y	N	N	Y	Y	Y	Y
Graham	N	Y	Y	Y	Y	Y	N
GEORGIA							
Coverdell	Y	N	Y	Y	Y	Y	Y
Cleland	Y	Y	Y	N	Y	Y	N
HAWAII							
Akaka	N	Y	Y	N	Y	Y	N
Inouye	N	Y	Y	N	Y	?	N
IDAHO							
Craig	Y	N	Y	Y	Y	Y	Y
Kempthorne	Y	N	Y	Y	Y	Y	Y
ILLINOIS							
Durbin	N	Y	Y	N	Y	?	N
Moseley-Braun	N	Y	Y	N	Y	Y	N
INDIANA							
Coats	Y	N	N	Y	Y	Y	Y
Lugar	Y	N	N	Y	Y	Y	Y

	99	100	101	102	103	104	105
IOWA							
Grassley	Y	N	N	Y	Y	Y	Y
Harkin	N	Y	Y	N	Y	Y	N
KANSAS							
Brownback	Y	N	N	Y	?	Y	Y
Roberts	Y	N	N	Y	Y	Y	Y
KENTUCKY							
McConnell	Y	N	Y	Y	Y	Y	Y
Ford	N	Y	Y	N	Y	Y	Y
LOUISIANA							
Breaux	Y	Y	Y	Y	Y	Y	Y
Landrieu	N	Y	Y	N	Y	Y	N
MAINE							
Collins	Y	N	Y	Y	Y	Y	Y
Snowe	Y	Y	Y	Y	Y	Y	Y
MARYLAND							
Mikulski	N	Y	Y	N	Y	Y	N
Sarbanes	N	Y	Y	N	Y	Y	N
MASSACHUSETTS							
Kennedy	N	Y	Y	N	Y	?	N
Kerry	N	Y	Y	N	Y	Y	N
MICHIGAN							
Abraham	Y	N	Y	Y	Y	Y	Y
Levin	N	Y	Y	N	Y	Y	N
MINNESOTA							
Grams	Y	N	N	Y	Y	Y	Y
Wellstone	N	Y	Y	N	Y	Y	N
MISSISSIPPI							
Cochran	Y	N	N	Y	Y	Y	Y
Lott	Y	N	N	Y	Y	Y	Y
MISSOURI							
Ashcroft	Y	N	N	Y	Y	Y	Y
Bond	Y	Y	Y	Y	Y	Y	Y
MONTANA							
Burns	Y	N	Y	Y	Y	Y	Y
Baucus	N	Y	Y	N	Y	Y	N
NEBRASKA							
Hagel	Y	N	N	Y	Y	Y	Y
Kerrey	N	Y	Y	N	Y	Y	N
NEVADA							
Bryan	N	Y	Y	N	Y	Y	N
Reid	N	Y	Y	N	Y	Y	N

	99	100	101	102	103	104	105
NEW HAMPSHIRE							
Gregg	Y	N	N	Y	Y	?	Y
Smith	Y	N	Y	Y	Y	Y	Y
NEW JERSEY							
Lautenberg	N	Y	Y	N	Y	Y	N
Torricelli	Y	Y	Y	N	Y	Y	N
NEW MEXICO							
Domenici	Y	N	Y	Y	Y	Y	Y
Bingaman	N	Y	Y	N	Y	Y	N
NEW YORK							
D'Amato	Y	Y	Y	Y	Y	Y	Y
Moynihan	N	Y	Y	N	Y	Y	N
NORTH CAROLINA							
Faircloth	Y	N	Y	Y	Y	?	Y
Helms	Y	N	N	Y	Y	Y	Y
NORTH DAKOTA							
Conrad	N	Y	Y	N	Y	Y	N
Dorgan	N	Y	Y	N	Y	Y	N
OHIO							
DeWine	Y	N	Y	Y	Y	Y	Y
Glenn	N	Y	Y	N	Y	Y	N
OKLAHOMA							
Inhofe	Y	N	N	Y	Y	?	Y
Nickles	Y	N	N	Y	Y	Y	Y
OREGON							
Smith	Y	N	Y	Y	Y	Y	Y
Wyden	N	Y	Y	N	Y	Y	N
PENNSYLVANIA							
Santorum	Y	N	Y	Y	Y	Y	Y
Specter	Y	Y	Y	Y	Y	Y	N
RHODE ISLAND							
Chafee	Y	N	Y	Y	Y	Y	N
Reed	N	Y	Y	N	Y	Y	N
SOUTH CAROLINA							
Thurmond	Y	N	N	Y	Y	Y	Y
Hollings	N	Y	Y	N	Y	Y	N
SOUTH DAKOTA							
Daschle	N	Y	Y	N	Y	Y	N
Johnson	N	Y	Y	N	Y	Y	N
TENNESSEE							
Frist	Y	N	N	Y	Y	Y	Y
Thompson	Y	N	N	Y	Y	Y	Y

Key

Y	Voted for (yea).
#	Paired for.
+	Announced for.
N	Voted against (nay).
X	Paired against.
−	Announced against.
P	Voted "present."
C	Voted "present" to avoid possible conflict of interest.
?	Did not vote or otherwise make a position known.

Democrats *Republicans*

	99	100	101	102	103	104	105
TEXAS							
Gramm	Y	N	Y	Y	Y	Y	Y
Hutchison	Y	N	Y	Y	Y	Y	Y
UTAH							
Bennett	Y	N	Y	Y	?	Y	Y
Hatch	Y	N	Y	Y	Y	Y	Y
VERMONT							
Jeffords	N	N	Y	N	Y	Y	N
Leahy	N	Y	Y	N	Y	Y	N
VIRGINIA							
Warner	Y	N	Y	Y	Y	Y	Y
Robb	N	Y	Y	N	Y	Y	N
WASHINGTON							
Gorton	Y	N	N	Y	Y	Y	Y
Murray	N	Y	Y	N	Y	Y	N
WEST VIRGINIA							
Byrd	Y	Y	Y	Y	Y	Y	N
Rockefeller	N	Y	Y	N	Y	Y	N
WISCONSIN							
Feingold	N	Y	N	N	Y	Y	N
Kohl	N	Y	Y	N	Y	?	N
WYOMING							
Enzi	Y	N	N	Y	Y	Y	Y
Thomas	Y	N	N	Y	Y	Y	Y

ND Northern Democrats   SD Southern Democrats

Southern states - Ala., Ark., Fla., Ga., Ky., La., Miss., N.C., Okla., S.C., Tenn., Texas, Va.

99. HR 2646. Expanding Education Savings Accounts/Technology Training. Coverdell, R-Ga., motion to table (kill) the Levin, D-Mich., amendment to the modified Levin amendment. The second-degree Levin amendment would require that the expanded savings accounts could only be used for post-secondary education expenses and would increase the current 20 percent lifetime tax credit on college costs to 50 percent for elementary and secondary school teachers who return to school to receive technology training. Motion agreed to 61-39: R 54-1; D 7-38 (ND 5-32, SD 2-6). April 23, 1998. (Subsequently, the underlying Levin amendment as amended was adopted by voice vote.)

100. HR 2646. Expanding Education Savings Accounts/After-School Programs. Boxer, D-Calif., amendment to establish a $50 million annual grant program for five years to develop after-school programs. Rejected 49-51: R 4-51; D 45-0 (ND 37-0, SD 8-0). April 23, 1998.

101. HR 2646. Expanding Education Savings Accounts/School Drop-Out Prevention. Bingaman, D-N.M., amendment to establish a national grant program to help schools create dropout prevention programs. Adopted 74-26: R 30-25; D 44-1 (ND 36-1, SD 8-0). April 23, 1998.

102. HR 2646. Expanding Education Savings Accounts/Passage. Passage of the bill to allow parents, relatives or outside corporations to contribute up to a combined total of $2,000 a year of after-tax funds in tax-free savings accounts designated for educational expenses. Current law allows up to $500 for college expenses, but the bill would raise the limit to $2,000 and allow the accounts to be used for public or private elementary and secondary education expenses. The bill also would prohibit federal funding for national education testing, give states the option of receiving federal education funds through

block grants directly to the state or local level and provide incentives for states and localities to establish merit pay and testing programs for teachers. Passed 56-43: R 51-3; D 5-40 (ND 3-34, SD 2-6). April 23, 1998. A "nay" was a vote in support of the president's position.

103. Northern Ireland Peace Agreement/Adoption. Adoption of the concurrent resolution to express the sense of Congress that all of the participants in the recent negotiations that led to a peace agreement concerning Northern Ireland deserve congratulations for their efforts. The resolution singles out British Prime Minister Tony Blair, Irish Taoiseach Bertie Ahern, President Clinton and former Senate Majority Leader George Mitchell, D-Maine, for particular praise. Adopted 97-0: R 52-0; D 45-0 (ND 37-0, SD 8-0). April 23, 1998.

104. Fleming Nomination/Confirmation. Confirmation of President Clinton's nomination of Scott Snyder Fleming of Virginia to be assistant secretary for legislation and congressional affairs in the Department of Education. Confirmed 92-0: R 51-0; D 41-0 (ND 33-0, SD 8-0). April 27, 1998. A "yea" was a vote in support of the president's position.

105. HR 1757. Fiscal 1998 State Department Authorization/Conference Report. Adoption of the conference report on the bill to authorize $1.75 billion in fiscal 1998 and $1.69 billion in fiscal 1999 for State Department diplomatic and consular functions, authorize $819 million over fiscal years 1998 through 2000 to pay part of the U.S. debt to the United Nations, codify restrictions on U.S. funds for international family planning and consolidate several U.S. foreign policy agencies. Adopted (thus cleared for the president) 51-49: R 49-6; D 2-43 (ND 0-37, SD 2-6). April 28, 1998. A "nay" was a vote in support of the president's position.

	106	107	108	109	110	111	112
ALABAMA							
Sessions	N	Y	Y	Y	Y	N	Y
Shelby	N	Y	Y	Y	N	N	Y
ALASKA							
Murkowski	N	Y	Y	N	Y	N	N
Stevens	N	Y	Y	Y	N	N	Y
ARIZONA							
Kyl	N	Y	Y	Y	N	N	N
McCain	N	Y	Y	N	N	N	N
ARKANSAS							
Hutchinson	Y	Y	Y	Y	Y	N	Y
Bumpers	Y	N	Y	Y	N	Y	Y
CALIFORNIA							
Boxer	N	Y	Y	N	N	N	N
Feinstein	N	Y	Y	N	N	N	Y
COLORADO							
Allard	N	Y	Y	Y	Y	N	N
Campbell	N	Y	Y	Y	N	N	N
CONNECTICUT							
Dodd	N	Y	Y	N	N	N	N
Lieberman	N	Y	Y	N	N	N	N
DELAWARE							
Roth	N	Y	Y	N	N	N	N
Biden	N	Y	Y	N	N	N	N
FLORIDA							
Mack	N	Y	Y	N	N	N	N
Graham	Y	N	Y	N	N	N	N
GEORGIA							
Coverdell	N	Y	Y	N	N	N	N
Cleland	N	Y	Y	N	N	N	N
HAWAII							
Akaka	N	Y	Y	N	N	N	N
Inouye	N	Y	Y	N	N	N	N
IDAHO							
Craig	N	Y	Y	Y	Y	Y	Y
Kempthorne	Y	Y	Y	Y	Y	Y	Y
ILLINOIS							
Durbin	N	Y	Y	N	N	N	N
Moseley-Braun	Y	?	+	N	N	N	N
INDIANA							
Coats	N	Y	Y	N	N	N	N
Lugar	N	Y	Y	N	N	N	N

	106	107	108	109	110	111	112
IOWA							
Grassley	N	Y	Y	N	Y	N	N
Harkin	Y	Y	Y	N	N	Y	Y
KANSAS							
Brownback	N	Y	Y	N	N	N	N
Roberts	N	N	Y	Y	Y	Y	N
KENTUCKY							
McConnell	N	Y	Y	N	N	N	N
Ford	N	Y	Y	N	N	N	N
LOUISIANA							
Breaux	N	Y	Y	N	N	N	N
Landrieu	N	Y	Y	N	N	N	N
MAINE							
Collins	N	Y	Y	N	N	N	N
Snowe	N	Y	Y	Y	N	N	Y
MARYLAND							
Mikulski	N	Y	Y	N	N	N	N
Sarbanes	N	N	Y	N	N	N	N
MASSACHUSETTS							
Kennedy	N	Y	Y	N	N	N	N
Kerry	N	Y	Y	N	N	N	N
MICHIGAN							
Abraham	N	Y	Y	N	N	N	N
Levin	N	Y	Y	N	N	N	N
MINNESOTA							
Grams	N	Y	Y	N	N	N	N
Wellstone	Y	N	Y	N	N	Y	Y
MISSISSIPPI							
Cochran	N	Y	Y	N	N	N	N
Lott	N	Y	Y	N	N	N	N
MISSOURI							
Ashcroft	Y	N	Y	Y	Y	Y	Y
Bond	Y	Y	?	Y	N	N	Y
MONTANA							
Burns	N	Y	Y	Y	Y	N	Y
Baucus	Y	Y	Y	N	N	N	N
NEBRASKA							
Hagel	N	Y	Y	N	N	N	N
Kerrey	N	Y	Y	N	N	N	N
NEVADA							
Bryan	N	Y	Y	N	N	N	N
Reid	N	Y	Y	N	N	N	Y

	106	107	108	109	110	111	112
NEW HAMPSHIRE							
Gregg	N	Y	Y	N	Y	N	N
Smith	Y	N	Y	Y	Y	Y	Y
NEW JERSEY							
Lautenberg	N	Y	Y	N	N	N	N
Torricelli	Y	Y	Y	N	N	Y	N
NEW MEXICO							
Domenici	N	Y	Y	N	N	N	N
Bingaman	N	N	Y	N	N	N	Y
NEW YORK							
D'Amato	N	Y	Y	N	N	N	N
Moynihan	Y	Y	Y	Y	N	Y	Y
NORTH CAROLINA							
Faircloth	N	Y	Y	N	N	N	N
Helms	N	Y	Y	Y	N	N	N
NORTH DAKOTA							
Conrad	Y	Y	Y	N	N	N	Y
Dorgan	Y	Y	Y	N	N	N	Y
OHIO							
DeWine	N	Y	Y	N	N	N	N
Glenn	N	Y	Y	N	N	N	N
OKLAHOMA							
Inhofe	N	Y	Y	Y	Y	N	N
Nickles	N	Y	Y	Y	N	N	Y
OREGON							
Smith	N	Y	Y	N	N	N	N
Wyden	Y	Y	Y	N	Y	N	Y
PENNSYLVANIA							
Santorum	N	Y	Y	N	N	N	N
Specter	N	Y	Y	Y	Y	Y	Y
RHODE ISLAND							
Chafee	N	Y	Y	N	N	N	Y
Reed	N	Y	Y	N	N	N	N
SOUTH CAROLINA							
Thurmond	N	Y	Y	Y	N	N	Y
Hollings	N	Y	Y	?	N	N	Y
SOUTH DAKOTA							
Daschle	N	Y	Y	N	N	N	N
Johnson	Y	Y	Y	N	N	N	N
TENNESSEE							
Frist	N	Y	Y	N	N	N	N
Thompson	N	Y	Y	N	N	N	N

Key

Y	Voted for (yea).
#	Paired for.
+	Announced for.
N	Voted against (nay).
X	Paired against.
–	Announced against.
P	Voted "present."
C	Voted "present" to avoid possible conflict of interest.
?	Did not vote or otherwise make a position known.

Democrats **Republicans**

	106	107	108	109	110	111	112
TEXAS							
Gramm	N	Y	Y	Y	Y	N	N
Hutchison	N	Y	Y	Y	Y	Y	Y
UTAH							
Bennett	N	Y	Y	Y	N	N	N
Hatch	N	Y	Y	Y	N	N	N
VERMONT							
Jeffords	Y	Y	Y	Y	Y	Y	Y
Leahy	Y	Y	Y	N	N	Y	Y
VIRGINIA							
Warner	Y	Y	Y	Y	Y	Y	Y
Robb	N	Y	Y	N	N	N	N
WASHINGTON							
Gorton	N	Y	Y	N	N	N	N
Murray	Y	Y	Y	N	N	Y	Y
WEST VIRGINIA							
Byrd	Y	N	Y	N	N	N	Y
Rockefeller	N	Y	?	N	N	N	N
WISCONSIN							
Feingold	Y	Y	Y	N	Y	N	N
Kohl	Y	Y	Y	N	N	N	Y
WYOMING							
Enzi	N	Y	Y	Y	N	N	Y
Thomas	N	Y	Y	Y	N	N	N

ND Northern Democrats   SD Southern Democrats

Southern states - Ala., Ark., Fla., Ga., Ky., La., Miss., N.C., Okla., S.C., Tenn., Texas, Va.

106. NATO Expansion/U.S. Costs. Harkin, D-Iowa, amendment to add language to the resolution of ratification that would limit U.S. support for so-called national expenses of new members to 25 percent of the total contributions made by all NATO nations. Rejected 24-76: R 7-48; D 17-28 (ND 15-22, SD 2-6). April 28, 1998. A "nay" was a vote in support of the president's position.

107. NATO Expansion/NATO Policy. Kyl, R-Ariz., amendment to add language to the resolution of ratification that would stipulate that the United States continues to support NATO policy as outlined in the 1991 Strategic Concept of NATO, which states that NATO is primarily a defensive military alliance, that strong U.S. leadership in NATO protects vital U.S. national interests and that the costs of defending Europe will be equitably shared by NATO members. Adopted 90-9: R 52-3; D 38-6 (ND 32-4, SD 6-2). April 28, 1998.

108. NATO Expansion/POW-MIAs. Smith, R-N.H., amendment to add language to the resolution of ratification that would require the president to certify to Congress before signing the treaty that the governments of Poland, Hungary and the Czech Republic are fully cooperating with U.S. efforts to recover soldiers captured or missing from past military conflicts or Cold War incidents. Adopted 97-0: R 54-0; D 43-0 (ND 35-0, SD 8-0). April 29, 1998.

109. NATO Expansion/Dispute Resolution. Hutchison, R-Texas, amendment to add language to the resolution of ratification that would direct the U.S. representative to NATO to propose a process through which NATO could resolve disputes involving one or more NATO members when military force is threatened. Rejected 37-62: R 32-23; D 5-39 (ND 4-33, SD 1-6). April 29, 1998. A "nay" was a vote in support of the president's position.

110. NATO Expansion/Troops in Bosnia. Craig, R-Idaho, amendment to add language to the resolution of ratification that would require Congress and the president to enact legislation specifically authorizing the continued deployment of U.S. troops in Bosnia before the United States ratifies the NATO expansion treaty. Rejected 20-80: R 19-36; D 1-44 (ND 1-36, SD 0-8). April 30, 1998. A "nay" was a vote in support of the president's position.

111. NATO Expansion/EU Membership. Moynihan, D-N.Y., amendment to add language to the resolution of ratification that would require Poland, Hungary and the Czech Republic to become members of the European Union before being admitted to NATO. Rejected 17-83: R 9-46; D 8-37 (ND 7-30, SD 1-7). April 30, 1998. A "nay" was a vote in support of the president's position.

112. NATO Expansion/Three Year Moratorium. Warner, R-Va., amendment to add language to the resolution of ratification that would require the president to certify to Congress that the United States will not support any further NATO expansion for three years from the date which Poland, Hungary and the Czech Republic join the alliance. Rejected 41-59: R 24-31; D 17-28 (ND 15-22, SD 2-6). April 30, 1998. A "nay" was a vote in support of the president's position.

	113	114	115	116	117	118	119
ALABAMA							
Sessions	N	N	Y	Y	Y	Y	Y
Shelby	N	Y	N	N	Y	Y	N
ALASKA							
Murkowski	N	Y	N	N	Y	Y	Y
Stevens	N	Y	N	N	Y	Y	Y
ARIZONA							
Kyl	N	Y	?	?	+	?	Y
McCain	N	Y	N	N	Y	Y	Y
ARKANSAS							
Hutchinson	N	N	Y	Y	Y	N	Y
Bumpers	Y	Y	Y	N	N	N	Y
CALIFORNIA							
Boxer	N	Y	N	N	Y	Y	Y
Feinstein	N	Y	N	N	Y	Y	Y
COLORADO							
Allard	N	Y	N	N	Y	Y	N
Campbell	N	Y	N	N	Y	Y	Y
CONNECTICUT							
Dodd	N	Y	N	N	Y	Y	Y
Lieberman	N	Y	N	N	Y	Y	Y
DELAWARE							
Roth	N	Y	N	N	Y	Y	Y
Biden	N	Y	N	N	Y	Y	Y
FLORIDA							
Mack	N	Y	N	N	Y	Y	Y
Graham	N	Y	Y	N	Y	Y	Y
GEORGIA							
Coverdell	N	Y	N	N	Y	Y	Y
Cleland	N	Y	N	N	Y	Y	Y
HAWAII							
Akaka	N	Y	N	N	Y	Y	Y
Inouye	N	Y	N	N	Y	Y	Y
IDAHO							
Craig	N	Y	N	Y	N	Y	Y
Kempthorne	N	N	Y	N	Y	N	Y
ILLINOIS							
Durbin	N	Y	N	N	Y	N	Y
Moseley-Braun	N	Y	N	N	Y	N	Y
INDIANA							
Coats	N	Y	N	N	Y	Y	Y
Lugar	N	Y	N	N	Y	Y	Y

	113	114	115	116	117	118	119
IOWA							
Grassley	N	N	N	Y	Y	Y	Y
Harkin	Y	Y	Y	N	N	N	Y
KANSAS							
Brownback	N	N	N	Y	Y	Y	N
Roberts	N	N	Y	Y	Y	Y	Y
KENTUCKY							
McConnell	N	Y	N	N	Y	Y	Y
Ford	N	Y	N	N	Y	Y	Y
LOUISIANA							
Breaux	N	Y	N	N	Y	Y	Y
Landrieu	N	Y	N	N	Y	Y	Y
MAINE							
Collins	N	Y	N	N	Y	Y	Y
Snowe	N	Y	N	N	Y	Y	Y
MARYLAND							
Mikulski	N	Y	N	N	Y	Y	Y
Sarbanes	N	Y	N	N	Y	Y	Y
MASSACHUSETTS							
Kennedy	Y	Y	N	N	Y	Y	Y
Kerry	Y	Y	N	N	Y	Y	Y
MICHIGAN							
Abraham	N	Y	N	N	Y	Y	Y
Levin	N	Y	N	N	Y	Y	Y
MINNESOTA							
Grams	N	N	N	N	Y	Y	Y
Wellstone	Y	Y	Y	N	N	Y	Y
MISSISSIPPI							
Cochran	N	Y	N	N	Y	Y	Y
Lott	N	Y	N	N	Y	Y	Y
MISSOURI							
Ashcroft	N	N	Y	N	Y	N	N
Bond	N	N	N	N	Y	Y	N
MONTANA							
Burns	N	Y	N	N	Y	Y	Y
Baucus	N	Y	N	N	Y	Y	Y
NEBRASKA							
Hagel	N	Y	N	N	Y	Y	Y
Kerrey	N	Y	N	N	Y	Y	Y
NEVADA							
Bryan	Y	Y	N	N	N	Y	Y
Reid	N	Y	N	N	N	Y	Y

	113	114	115	116	117	118	119
NEW HAMPSHIRE							
Gregg	N	Y	N	N	Y	Y	Y
Smith	N	N	Y	Y	N	N	N
NEW JERSEY							
Lautenberg	Y	Y	N	N	Y	Y	Y
Torricelli	N	Y	N	N	Y	Y	Y
NEW MEXICO							
Domenici	N	Y	N	N	Y	Y	Y
Bingaman	Y	Y	Y	N	Y	Y	Y
NEW YORK							
D'Amato	N	Y	N	N	Y	Y	Y
Moynihan	N	Y	N	N	N	Y	Y
NORTH CAROLINA							
Faircloth	N	N	N	N	Y	Y	?
Helms	N	N	N	N	Y	Y	?
NORTH DAKOTA							
Conrad	Y	Y	Y	N	N	Y	Y
Dorgan	Y	Y	Y	N	N	Y	Y
OHIO							
DeWine	N	Y	N	N	Y	Y	Y
Glenn	N	Y	N	N	Y	Y	Y
OKLAHOMA							
Inhofe	N	N	Y	Y	N	N	N
Nickles	N	N	N	N	Y	N	Y
OREGON							
Smith	N	Y	N	N	Y	Y	Y
Wyden	Y	Y	Y	N	N	Y	Y
PENNSYLVANIA							
Santorum	N	Y	N	N	Y	Y	Y
Specter	N	Y	N	Y	N	Y	Y
RHODE ISLAND							
Chafee	N	Y	N	N	Y	Y	Y
Reed	N	Y	N	N	Y	Y	Y
SOUTH CAROLINA							
Thurmond	N	N	N	N	Y	Y	Y
Hollings	N	Y	N	N	Y	Y	Y
SOUTH DAKOTA							
Daschle	N	Y	N	N	Y	Y	Y
Johnson	Y	Y	N	N	Y	Y	Y
TENNESSEE							
Frist	N	Y	N	N	Y	Y	Y
Thompson	N	Y	N	N	Y	Y	Y

	113	114	115	116	117	118	119
TEXAS							
Gramm	N	Y	N	N	Y	N	Y
Hutchison	N	N	Y	Y	Y	Y	Y
UTAH							
Bennett	N	Y	N	N	Y	Y	Y
Hatch	N	Y	N	N	Y	Y	Y
VERMONT							
Jeffords	Y	Y	N	N	Y	Y	Y
Leahy	Y	Y	N	N	Y	Y	Y
VIRGINIA							
Warner	N	Y	N	N	Y	Y	Y
Robb	N	Y	N	N	Y	Y	Y
WASHINGTON							
Gorton	N	Y	N	N	Y	Y	Y
Murray	Y	Y	Y	N	N	Y	Y
WEST VIRGINIA							
Byrd	N	Y	N	N	Y	Y	Y
Rockefeller	N	Y	N	N	Y	Y	Y
WISCONSIN							
Feingold	N	Y	N	N	Y	N	Y
Kohl	Y	Y	Y	N	Y	N	Y
WYOMING							
Enzi	N	Y	N	N	Y	Y	Y
Thomas	N	Y	N	N	Y	Y	Y

Key

Y	Voted for (yea).
#	Paired for.
+	Announced for.
N	Voted against (nay).
X	Paired against.
–	Announced against.
P	Voted "present."
C	Voted "present" to avoid possible conflict of interest.
?	Did not vote or otherwise make a position known.

● Democrats *Republicans*

ND Northern Democrats   SD Southern Democrats

Southern states - Ala., Ark., Fla., Ga., Ky., La., Miss., N.C., Okla., S.C., Tenn., Texas, Va.

113. NATO Expansion/Nuclear Weapon Dismantlement. Conrad, D-N.D., amendment to add language to the resolution of ratification that would require the president to certify to the Senate before signing the treaty that the United States has initiated discussions with Russia on a reduction in non-strategic nuclear weapons. Rejected 16-84: R 1-54; D 15-30 (ND 14-23, SD 1-7). April 30, 1998.

114. NATO Expansion/Defensive Alliance. Biden, D-Del., motion to table (kill) the Ashcroft, R-Mo., amendment to add language to the resolution of ratification that would require the president to certify to the Senate before signing the treaty that NATO's primary goal is to defend the territory of its member nations. Motion agreed to 82-18: R 37-18; D 45-0 (ND 37-0, SD 8-0). April 30, 1998.

115. NATO Expansion/NATO Strategic Statement. Bingaman, D-N.M., amendment to add language to the resolution of ratification that would require the president to certify to the Senate before signing the treaty that the United States will not support further expansion of NATO beyond Poland, Hungary and the Czech Republic until NATO agrees on a revised official statement of alliance strategy. Rejected 23-76: R 10-44; D 13-32 (ND 10-27, SD 3-5). April 30, 1998.

116. NATO Expansion/Bosnia Troop Deployment. Smith, R-N.H., amendment to add language to the resolution of ratification that would require both Houses of Congress to vote on legislation, prior to ratification of NATO expansion, that would authorize continued U.S. troop deployment in Bosnia. Rejected 16-83: R 15-39; D 1-44 (ND 1-36, SD 0-8). April 30, 1998.

117. NATO Expansion/Adoption. Adoption of the resolution of ratification of the protocol (Treaty Doc. 105-36) revising the 1949 North Atlantic Treaty to admit Poland, Hungary and the Czech Republic into the North Atlantic Treaty Organization. Adopted 80-19: R 45-9; D 35-10 (ND 28-9, SD 7-1). April 30, 1998. A two-thirds majority of those present and voting (66 in this case) is required for adoption of resolutions of ratification. A "yea" was a vote in support of the president's position.

118. HR 3579. Fiscal 1998 Emergency Supplemental Appropriations/Conference Report. Adoption of the conference report on the bill to appropriate $6.1 billion in supplemental spending, including $2.6 billion for disaster relief and $2.9 billion for military operations in Bosnia and the Middle East. Adopted (thus cleared for the president) 88-11: R 48-6; D 40-5 (ND 33-4, SD 7-1). April 30, 1998.

119. HR 1385. Job Training Program Consolidation/Passage. Passage of the bill to consolidate nearly 70 existing job training, vocational education and adult literacy programs into block grant programs to the states. The measure also would simplify eligibility requirements for vocational rehabilitation and job training programs; enable states to offer customized support, such as home training, for disabled individuals; and authorize random drug testing for participants in federally funded job training programs. Passed 91-7: R 46-7; D 45-0 (ND 37-0, SD 8-0). May 5, 1998. A "yea" was a vote in support of the president's position.

	120	121	122	123	124	125	126
ALABAMA							
Sessions	Y	N	Y	Y	Y	N	Y
Shelby	Y	Y	Y	Y	Y	N	Y
ALASKA							
Murkowski	Y	N	Y	Y	Y	N	Y
Stevens	Y	Y	N	N	N	N	Y
ARIZONA							
Kyl	Y	Y	Y	Y	Y	Y	Y
McCain	Y	Y	Y	Y	Y	Y	Y
ARKANSAS							
Hutchinson	Y	Y	Y	Y	Y	Y	Y
Bumpers	N	N	N	N	N	N	Y
CALIFORNIA							
Boxer	N	N	N	N	N	N	Y
Feinstein	N	N	N	N	N	N	Y
COLORADO							
Allard	Y	N	Y	Y	Y	N	Y
Campbell	Y	Y	N	Y	Y	Y	Y
CONNECTICUT							
Dodd	N	N	N	N	N	N	Y
Lieberman	N	N	N	N	N	N	Y
DELAWARE							
Roth	Y	N	Y	Y	Y	N	Y
Biden	Y	N	N	N	N	N	Y
FLORIDA							
Mack	Y	N	Y	Y	Y	N	Y
Graham	N	N	N	N	N	N	Y
GEORGIA							
Coverdell	Y	Y	Y	Y	Y	Y	Y
Cleland	N	N	N	N	N	N	Y
HAWAII							
Akaka	?	?	?	?	?	?	?
Inouye	N	N	N	N	N	N	Y
IDAHO							
Craig	Y	Y	Y	N	Y	Y	Y
Kempthorne	Y	Y	Y	N	Y	Y	Y
ILLINOIS							
Durbin	N	N	N	N	N	N	Y
Moseley-Braun	Y	N	N	N	N	N	Y
INDIANA							
Coats	Y	N	Y	N	Y	N	Y
Lugar	Y	N	Y	Y	N	Y	Y

	120	121	122	123	124	125	126
IOWA							
Grassley	Y	N	N	N	Y	N	Y
Harkin	N	N	N	N	N	N	Y
KANSAS							
Brownback	Y	N	Y	Y	Y	Y	Y
Roberts	Y	N	Y	Y	Y	N	Y
KENTUCKY							
McConnell	Y	Y	Y	Y	Y	Y	Y
Ford	N	N	N	N	N	N	Y
LOUISIANA							
Breaux	N	N	N	N	N	N	Y
Landrieu	N	N	N	N	N	N	Y
MAINE							
Collins	Y	N	Y	N	N	N	Y
Snowe	Y	N	N	N	N	N	Y
MARYLAND							
Mikulski	N	N	N	N	N	N	Y
Sarbanes	N	N	N	N	N	N	Y
MASSACHUSETTS							
Kennedy	N	N	N	N	N	N	Y
Kerry	N	N	N	N	N	N	Y
MICHIGAN							
Abraham	Y	Y	Y	Y	Y	Y	Y
Levin	N	N	N	N	N	N	Y
MINNESOTA							
Grams	Y	N	Y	Y	Y	N	Y
Wellstone	N	N	N	N	N	N	Y
MISSISSIPPI							
Cochran	Y	N	Y	N	Y	N	Y
Lott	Y	N	Y	Y	Y	Y	Y
MISSOURI							
Ashcroft	Y	Y	Y	Y	Y	Y	Y
Bond	Y	Y	Y	Y	Y	Y	Y
MONTANA							
Burns	Y	Y	Y	N	Y	Y	Y
Baucus	N	N	N	N	N	N	Y
NEBRASKA							
Hagel	Y	N	N	N	Y	N	Y
Kerrey	N	N	N	N	N	N	Y
NEVADA							
Bryan	N	N	N	N	N	N	Y
Reid	N	N	N	N	N	N	Y

	120	121	122	123	124	125	126
NEW HAMPSHIRE							
Gregg	Y	N	Y	Y	Y	Y	Y
Smith	Y	Y	Y	Y	Y	Y	Y
NEW JERSEY							
Lautenberg	N	N	N	N	N	N	Y
Torricelli	N	N	N	N	N	N	Y
NEW MEXICO							
Domenici	Y	N	N	N	N	N	Y
Bingaman	N	N	N	N	N	N	Y
NEW YORK							
D'Amato	Y	Y	N	N	N	N	Y
Moynihan	N	N	N	N	N	N	Y
NORTH CAROLINA							
Faircloth	Y	Y	Y	Y	Y	Y	Y
Helms	?	N	Y	Y	Y	Y	Y
NORTH DAKOTA							
Conrad	N	N	N	N	N	N	Y
Dorgan	N	N	N	N	N	N	Y
OHIO							
DeWine	Y	Y	N	Y	Y	Y	Y
Glenn	N	N	N	N	N	?	?
OKLAHOMA							
Inhofe	Y	Y	Y	N	Y	Y	Y
Nickles	Y	Y	Y	Y	Y	N	Y
OREGON							
Smith	Y	N	Y	Y	N	N	Y
Wyden	N	N	N	N	N	N	Y
PENNSYLVANIA							
Santorum	Y	N	N	N	N	N	Y
Specter	Y	N	Y	N	N	N	Y
RHODE ISLAND							
Chafee	Y	N	Y	N	N	N	Y
Reed	N	N	N	N	N	N	Y
SOUTH CAROLINA							
Thurmond	Y	Y	Y	Y	Y	+	+
Hollings	N	Y	N	N	N	N	Y
SOUTH DAKOTA							
Daschle	N	N	N	N	N	N	Y
Johnson	N	N	N	N	N	N	Y
TENNESSEE							
Frist	Y	Y	Y	Y	Y	Y	Y
Thompson	Y	N	Y	Y	Y	Y	Y

Key

Y	Voted for (yea).
#	Paired for.
+	Announced for.
N	Voted against (nay).
X	Paired against.
−	Announced against.
P	Voted "present."
C	Voted "present" to avoid possible conflict of interest.
?	Did not vote or otherwise make a position known.

Democrats · *Republicans*

	120	121	122	123	124	125	126
TEXAS							
Gramm	Y	Y	Y	Y	Y	N	Y
Hutchison	Y	N	Y	Y	Y	Y	Y
UTAH							
Bennett	Y	N	Y	N	N	Y	Y
Hatch	Y	N	N	N	Y	Y	Y
VERMONT							
Jeffords	Y	N	Y	N	N	N	Y
Leahy	N	N	N	N	N	N	Y
VIRGINIA							
Warner	Y	N	Y	N	N	N	Y
Robb	N	N	N	N	N	N	Y
WASHINGTON							
Gorton	Y	N	Y	N	N	N	Y
Murray	N	N	N	N	N	N	Y
WEST VIRGINIA							
Byrd	N	N	N	N	N	N	Y
Rockefeller	N	N	N	N	N	N	Y
WISCONSIN							
Feingold	N	N	N	N	N	N	Y
Kohl	N	N	N	N	N	N	Y
WYOMING							
Enzi	Y	N	Y	N	N	Y	Y
Thomas	Y	Y	Y	Y	Y	Y	Y

ND Northern Democrats   SD Southern Democrats

Southern states - Ala., Ark., Fla., Ga., Ky., La., Miss., N.C., Okla., S.C., Tenn., Texas, Va.

120. HR 2676. Internal Revenue Service Overhaul/Roth IRAs. Roth, R-Del., amendment to allow taxpayers who are older than 70 1/2 and whose incomes are more than $100,000 to convert their traditional Individual Retirement Accounts (IRAs) to so-called Roth IRAs, which allow individuals to withdraw both contributions and investment earnings tax-free upon retirement. The amendment would raise approximately $8 billion over fiscal years 2003-2007 because the money investors withdraw from traditional IRAs to shift funds to Roth IRAs would be taxed as income. Current law prohibits taxpayers with incomes of more than $100,000 from shifting their retirement funds to Roth IRAs. Adopted 56-42: R 54-0; D 2-42 (ND 2-34, SD 0-8). May 6, 1998.

121. HR 2676. Internal Revenue Service Overhaul/IRS Oversight Board. Bond, R-Mo., amendment to replace language that would establish a nine-member part-time IRS oversight board with provisions to create a five-member full-time IRS Board of Governors. Rejected 25-74: R 24-31; D 1-43 (ND 0-36, SD 1-7). May 6, 1998.

122. HR 2676. Internal Revenue Service Overhaul/Ethics Waiver. Thompson, R-Tenn., amendment to strike language in the bill that would provide a special waiver of government ethics laws governing conflicts-of-interest for the representative of IRS employees serving on the oversight board established in the bill. Rejected 42-57: R 42-13; D 0-44 (ND 0-36, SD 0-8). May 7, 1998.

123. HR 2676. Internal Revenue Service Overhaul/Union Representation. Faircloth, R-N.C., amendment to strike language allowing a representa-

tive of IRS employees to sit on the oversight board. Rejected 35-64: R 35-20; D 0-44 (ND 0-36, SD 0-8). May 7, 1998.

124. HR 2676. Internal Revenue Service Overhaul/Treasury Secretary. Mack, R-Fla., amendment to strike language that would give the secretary of the Treasury a seat on the IRS oversight board. Rejected 40-59: R 40-15; D 0-44 (ND 0-36, SD 0-8). May 7, 1998.

125. HR 2676. Internal Revenue Service Overhaul/Random Audits. Coverdell, R-Ga., motion to waive the Budget Act with respect to the Kerrey, D-Neb., point of order against the Coverdell amendment. The Coverdell amendment would prohibit the Internal Revenue Service from initiating random taxpayer audits. Motion rejected 37-60: R 37-17; D 0-43 (ND 0-35, SD 0-8). May 7, 1998. A three-fifths majority vote (60) of the total Senate is required to waive the Budget Act. (Subsequently, the chair upheld the point of order, and the amendment fell.)

126. HR 2676. Internal Revenue Service Overhaul/Passage. Passage of the bill to restructure the management of the Internal Revenue Service by establishing an oversight board to oversee the agency's operations. The bill would expand several taxpayer rights, including shifting the burden of proof from the taxpayer to the IRS, allowing more individuals to claim "innocent spouse" relief in cases when a tax debt is determined to be the responsibility of an ex-spouse and allowing taxpayers to sue the federal government for civil damages caused by IRS employees who negligently disregard tax laws. The measure would cost approximately $18.3 billion over 10 years. Passed 97-0: R 54-0; D 43-0 (ND 35-0, SD 8-0). May 7, 1998.

Senate Votes 127, 128, 129, 130, 131, 132, 133

	127	128	129	130	131	132	133
ALABAMA							
Sessions	Y	Y	N	Y	Y	Y	Y
Shelby	Y	Y	Y	Y	Y	Y	N
ALASKA							
Murkowski	Y	N	Y	N	Y	Y	Y
Stevens	Y	N	Y	N	Y	Y	Y
ARIZONA							
Kyl	Y	Y	N	Y	Y	Y	Y
McCain	Y	Y	Y	Y	Y	Y	P
ARKANSAS							
Hutchinson	Y	Y	Y	Y	Y	Y	Y
Bumpers	Y	N	Y	Y	N	Y	N
CALIFORNIA							
Boxer	Y	N	Y	N	Y	Y	Y
Feinstein	Y	N	Y	N	Y	N	Y
COLORADO							
Allard	Y	Y	Y	Y	Y	Y	Y
Campbell	Y	N	Y	Y	Y	Y	Y
CONNECTICUT							
Dodd	Y	N	Y	N	Y	N	Y
Lieberman	Y	N	Y	N	Y	N	Y
DELAWARE							
Roth	Y	N	Y	Y	Y	Y	Y
Biden	Y	N	Y	?	N	Y	N
FLORIDA							
Mack	Y	N	Y	Y	Y	Y	Y
Graham	Y	N	Y	N	Y	N	Y
GEORGIA							
Coverdell	Y	N	Y	Y	Y	Y	Y
Cleland	Y	N	Y	N	Y	N	Y
HAWAII							
Akaka	Y	N	Y	Y	Y	Y	N
Inouye	Y	N	Y	Y	Y	Y	N
IDAHO							
Craig	Y	N	Y	Y	Y	Y	Y
Kempthorne	Y	N	Y	Y	Y	Y	Y
ILLINOIS							
Durbin	Y	N	Y	Y	Y	N	N
Moseley-Braun	Y	N	Y	Y	N	Y	N
INDIANA							
Coats	Y	N	Y	Y	Y	Y	Y
Lugar	Y	N	Y	Y	Y	Y	Y

	127	128	129	130	131	132	133
IOWA							
Grassley	Y	N	Y	Y	Y	Y	Y
Harkin	Y	N	Y	N	Y	Y	Y
KANSAS							
Brownback	Y	N	Y	Y	Y	Y	Y
Roberts	Y	N	Y	Y	Y	Y	Y
KENTUCKY							
McConnell	Y	N	Y	Y	Y	Y	Y
Ford	Y	N	Y	N	Y	N	Y
LOUISIANA							
Breaux	Y	N	Y	N	Y	N	N
Landrieu	Y	N	Y	N	Y	N	N
MAINE							
Collins	Y	N	Y	Y	Y	Y	N
Snowe	Y	Y	Y	Y	Y	Y	N
MARYLAND							
Mikulski	Y	N	Y	N	Y	N	N
Sarbanes	Y	N	Y	N	Y	N	N
MASSACHUSETTS							
Kennedy	Y	N	Y	N	Y	N	N
Kerry	Y	N	Y	N	Y	N	Y
MICHIGAN							
Abraham	Y	Y	Y	Y	Y	Y	Y
Levin	Y	N	Y	N	Y	Y	N
MINNESOTA							
Grams	Y	N	Y	Y	Y	Y	Y
Wellstone	Y	N	Y	N	Y	N	Y
MISSISSIPPI							
Cochran	Y	N	Y	Y	Y	Y	Y
Lott	Y	Y	Y	Y	Y	Y	Y
MISSOURI							
Ashcroft	Y	Y	Y	Y	Y	Y	Y
Bond	Y	N	Y	Y	Y	Y	Y
MONTANA							
Burns	Y	N	Y	Y	Y	Y	Y
Baucus	Y	N	Y	Y	Y	Y	Y
NEBRASKA							
Hagel	Y	N	Y	Y	Y	Y	Y
Kerrey	Y	N	Y	Y	N	Y	N
NEVADA							
Bryan	Y	N	Y	Y	N	Y	N
Reid	Y	N	Y	N	Y	N	Y

	127	128	129	130	131	132	133
NEW HAMPSHIRE							
Gregg	Y	Y	N	Y	Y	Y	Y
Smith	Y	Y	N	Y	Y	Y	Y
NEW JERSEY							
Lautenberg	Y	N	Y	Y	N	Y	N
Torricelli	Y	N	Y	N	Y	Y	N
NEW MEXICO							
Domenici	Y	N	Y	Y	Y	Y	Y
Bingaman	Y	N	Y	Y	Y	Y	Y
NEW YORK							
D'Amato	Y	N	Y	Y	Y	Y	Y
Moynihan	Y	N	Y	Y	Y	N	N
NORTH CAROLINA							
Faircloth	Y	Y	Y	Y	Y	Y	Y
Helms	Y	Y	N	Y	Y	Y	Y
NORTH DAKOTA							
Conrad	Y	N	Y	N	Y	N	N
Dorgan	Y	N	Y	N	Y	N	N
OHIO							
DeWine	Y	N	Y	Y	Y	Y	Y
Glenn	Y	N	Y	N	Y	N	N
OKLAHOMA							
Inhofe	?	Y	N	Y	Y	Y	Y
Nickles	Y	Y	N	Y	Y	Y	Y
OREGON							
Smith	Y	N	Y	Y	Y	Y	Y
Wyden	Y	N	Y	N	Y	N	Y
PENNSYLVANIA							
Santorum	Y	N	Y	Y	Y	Y	Y
Specter	Y	N	Y	Y	Y	Y	N
RHODE ISLAND							
Chafee	Y	N	Y	Y	Y	Y	Y
Reed	Y	N	Y	N	Y	N	Y
SOUTH CAROLINA							
Thurmond	Y	Y	Y	Y	Y	Y	Y
Hollings	Y	Y	Y	Y	Y	Y	N
SOUTH DAKOTA							
Daschle	Y	N	Y	Y	Y	Y	Y
Johnson	Y	N	Y	N	Y	N	N
TENNESSEE							
Frist	Y	N	Y	Y	Y	Y	Y
Thompson	Y	Y	Y	Y	Y	Y	Y

	127	128	129	130	131	132	133
TEXAS							
Gramm	Y	Y	N	Y	Y	Y	Y
Hutchison	Y	Y	Y	Y	Y	Y	Y
UTAH							
Bennett	Y	N	Y	Y	Y	Y	Y
Hatch	Y	N	Y	Y	Y	Y	Y
VERMONT							
Jeffords	Y	N	Y	Y	Y	Y	Y
Leahy	Y	N	Y	N	Y	Y	Y
VIRGINIA							
Warner	Y	N	Y	Y	Y	Y	Y
Robb	Y	N	Y	N	Y	Y	Y
WASHINGTON							
Gorton	Y	N	Y	Y	Y	Y	Y
Murray	Y	N	Y	N	Y	Y	Y
WEST VIRGINIA							
Byrd	Y	N	Y	N	Y	N	N
Rockefeller	Y	N	Y	N	Y	N	N
WISCONSIN							
Feingold	Y	N	Y	Y	Y	Y	Y
Kohl	Y	N	Y	N	Y	Y	Y
WYOMING							
Enzi	Y	Y	Y	Y	Y	Y	Y
Thomas	Y	Y	Y	Y	Y	Y	Y

Key

Y	Voted for (yea).
#	Paired for.
+	Announced for.
N	Voted against (nay).
X	Paired against.
−	Announced against.
P	Voted "present."
C	Voted "present" to avoid possible conflict of interest.
?	Did not vote or otherwise make a position known.

Democrats   *Republicans*

ND Northern Democrats   SD Southern Democrats

Southern states - Ala., Ark., Fla., Ga., Ky., La., Miss., N.C., Okla., S.C., Tenn., Texas, Va.

127. HR 1273. National Science Foundation Reauthorization/Passage. Passage of the bill to reauthorize the National Science Foundation for three years. The bill would authorize $3.5 billion in fiscal 1998, $3.8 billion in fiscal 1999 and $3.9 billion in fiscal 2000. It also would prohibit any funds for the U.S. Man and the Biosphere Program and would require the National Science Foundation director to submit an annual plan to Congress on recommended upgrades to national research facilities. Passed 99-0: R 54-0; D 45-0 (ND 37-0, SD 8-0). May 12, 1998.

128. S 1150. Agriculture Research/Motion to Recommit. Gramm, R-Texas, motion to recommit the conference report to the conference committee with instructions that Senate conferees insist that the bill's expansion of food stamp eligibility only apply to refugees and asylees who were lawfully residing in the United States on August 22, 1996. The conference report would allow future refugees and asylees to qualify for the bill's language expanding food stamp eligibility from five to seven years. Motion rejected 23-77: R 22-33; D 1-44 (ND 0-37, SD 1-7). May 12, 1998. A "nay" was a vote in support of the president's position.

129. S 1150. Agriculture Research/Conference Report. Adoption of the conference report on the bill to reauthorize federal agriculture research programs. The measure would authorize $600 million in new mandatory spending over five years for expanded food safety, genetic engineering and other technology programs, $500 million in new crop insurance under the federal crop insurance program and $100 million for rural development and research programs. The bill also would authorize $818 million over five years to restore food stamp eligibility to 250,000 legal immigrants who lost benefits under the 1996 welfare law (PL 104-193). Adopted (thus sent to the House) 92-8: R 47-8; D 45-0 (ND 37-0, SD 8-0). May 12, 1998. A "yea" was a vote in support of the president's position.

130. S 1618. Long-Distance Phone Slamming/Passage. Passage of the bill that aims to reduce incidents of "slamming," which is the unauthorized change of a customer's long-distance telephone service, by requiring telephone companies to gain oral, written or electronic verification from consumers before switching their long-distance service and by establishing criminal penalties for individuals who engage in slamming. Passed 99-0: R 55-0; D 44-0 (ND 36-0, SD 8-0). May 12, 1998. A "yea" was a vote in support of the president's position.

131. S 1873. National Missile Defense/Cloture. Motion to invoke cloture (thus limiting debate) on the motion to proceed to the bill that would make it U.S. policy to implement a national missile defense shield. The measure would not establish a specific time frame, but would declare a national policy to deploy a system to protect U.S. territory from a limited number of incoming missiles "as soon as is technologically possible." Motion rejected 59-41: R 55-0; D 4-41 (ND 3-34, SD 1-7). May 13, 1998. Three-fifths of the total Senate (60) is required to invoke cloture. A "nay" was a vote in support of the president's position.

132. S 1244. Debtor Charitable Contributions/Passage. Passage of the bill to shield contributions of up to 15 percent of an individual who files for bankruptcy's income to religious groups or charitable, nonprofit groups. The measure also would allow bankruptcy filers to include future religious donations as part of their debt repayment plan. Passed 100-0: R 55-0; D 45-0 (ND 37-0, SD 8-0). May 13, 1998.

133. S 1260. Securities Lawsuits/Statute of Limitations. D'Amato, R-N.Y., motion to table (kill) the Sarbanes, D-Md., amendment to allow plaintiffs to file lawsuits under state statutes of limitations if the bill requires them to file their class actions suits in federal court instead of state court. Motion agreed to 69-30: R 50-4; D 19-26 (ND 17-20, SD 2-6). May 13, 1998.

Senate Votes 134, 135, 136, 137, 138, 139, 140

	134	135	136	137	138	139	140
ALABAMA							
Sessions	Y	Y	N	Y	Y	Y	Y
Shelby	N	N	N	Y	Y	Y	Y
ALASKA							
Murkowski	Y	Y	Y	Y	Y	Y	Y
Stevens	Y	Y	N	Y	Y	Y	Y
ARIZONA							
Kyl	Y	Y	N	Y	Y	Y	Y
McCain	P	N	N	Y	Y	Y	Y
ARKANSAS							
Hutchinson	Y	Y	N	Y	Y	Y	Y
Bumpers	N	N	N	Y	N	N	N
CALIFORNIA							
Boxer	Y	Y	N	Y	N	N	Y
Feinstein	Y	Y	N	Y	N	N	Y
COLORADO							
Allard	Y	Y	N	Y	Y	Y	N
Campbell	Y	Y	N	Y	N	N	Y
CONNECTICUT							
Dodd	Y	Y	N	Y	N	N	Y
Lieberman	Y	Y	N	Y	Y	Y	Y
DELAWARE							
Roth	Y	Y	N	Y	Y	Y	Y
Biden	N	N	Y	Y	N	N	N
FLORIDA							
Mack	Y	Y	N	Y	Y	Y	Y
Graham	N	Y	Y	Y	Y	Y	Y
GEORGIA							
Coverdell	Y	Y	N	Y	Y	Y	Y
Cleland	N	N	Y	Y	Y	Y	N
HAWAII							
Akaka	N	N	Y	N	N	N	Y
Inouye	N	N	Y	N	N	N	Y
IDAHO							
Craig	Y	Y	N	Y	Y	Y	Y
Kempthorne	Y	Y	N	Y	Y	Y	Y
ILLINOIS							
Durbin	N	N	N	Y	N	N	Y
Moseley-Braun	Y	Y	N	Y	N	N	Y
INDIANA							
Coats	Y	Y	N	Y	Y	Y	Y
Lugar	Y	Y	Y	Y	Y	Y	Y

	134	135	136	137	138	139	140
IOWA							
Grassley	Y	Y	N	Y	Y	Y	Y
Harkin	Y	Y	N	Y	N	N	N
KANSAS							
Brownback	Y	Y	N	Y	Y	Y	Y
Roberts	Y	Y	Y	Y	Y	Y	N
KENTUCKY							
McConnell	Y	Y	N	Y	Y	Y	Y
Ford	Y	Y	Y	Y	N	N	Y
LOUISIANA							
Breaux	Y	Y	N	Y	Y	Y	Y
Landrieu	Y	Y	N	Y	N	N	N
MAINE							
Collins	Y	Y	N	Y	Y	Y	Y
Snowe	Y	Y	N	Y	Y	Y	Y
MARYLAND							
Mikulski	Y	Y	N	Y	N	N	N
Sarbanes	N	N	N	Y	N	N	N
MASSACHUSETTS							
Kennedy	N	Y	N	Y	N	N	N
Kerry	N	Y	N	Y	N	N	N
MICHIGAN							
Abraham	Y	Y	N	Y	Y	Y	Y
Levin	N	N	Y	Y	–	–	–
MINNESOTA							
Grams	Y	Y	N	Y	Y	Y	Y
Wellstone	N	N	N	Y	N	N	N
MISSISSIPPI							
Cochran	Y	Y	N	Y	Y	Y	Y
Lott	Y	Y	N	Y	Y	Y	Y
MISSOURI							
Ashcroft	Y	Y	N	Y	Y	Y	Y
Bond	Y	Y	N	Y	Y	Y	Y
MONTANA							
Burns	Y	Y	N	Y	Y	Y	Y
Baucus	Y	Y	Y	Y	Y	Y	N
NEBRASKA							
Hagel	Y	Y	Y	Y	Y	Y	Y
Kerrey	Y	Y	Y	Y	N	N	N
NEVADA							
Bryan	N	N	N	Y	N	N	Y
Reid	Y	Y	N	Y	N	N	Y

	134	135	136	137	138	139	140
NEW HAMPSHIRE							
Gregg	Y	Y	N	?	Y	Y	Y
Smith	Y	Y	N	Y	Y	Y	Y
NEW JERSEY							
Lautenberg	N	N	N	Y	N	N	Y
Torricelli	N	N	N	Y	N	N	N
NEW MEXICO							
Domenici	Y	Y	N	Y	Y	Y	Y
Bingaman	Y	Y	Y	Y	Y	N	N
NEW YORK							
D'Amato	Y	Y	N	Y	Y	Y	Y
Moynihan	N	N	N	Y	N	N	N
NORTH CAROLINA							
Faircloth	Y	Y	N	Y	?	?	?
Helms	Y	Y	N	Y	Y	Y	Y
NORTH DAKOTA							
Conrad	N	N	N	Y	N	N	N
Dorgan	N	N	N	Y	N	N	N
OHIO							
DeWine	Y	Y	N	Y	Y	Y	Y
Glenn	N	N	Y	N	N	N	N
OKLAHOMA							
Inhofe	Y	Y	N	Y	Y	Y	Y
Nickles	Y	Y	N	Y	Y	Y	Y
OREGON							
Smith	Y	Y	N	Y	Y	Y	Y
Wyden	Y	Y	N	Y	N	N	N
PENNSYLVANIA							
Santorum	Y	Y	N	Y	Y	Y	Y
Specter	Y	Y	N	Y	Y	Y	Y
RHODE ISLAND							
Chafee	Y	Y	N	Y	Y	Y	Y
Reed	N	Y	Y	Y	N	N	N
SOUTH CAROLINA							
Thurmond	Y	Y	N	Y	Y	Y	Y
Hollings	N	Y	N	Y	N	N	N
SOUTH DAKOTA							
Daschle	Y	Y	N	Y	Y	Y	Y
Johnson	N	N	Y	Y	N	N	Y
TENNESSEE							
Frist	Y	Y	N	Y	Y	Y	Y
Thompson	N	Y	N	Y	Y	Y	Y

	134	135	136	137	138	139	140
TEXAS							
Gramm	Y	Y	N	Y	Y	Y	Y
Hutchison	Y	Y	N	Y	Y	Y	Y
UTAH							
Bennett	Y	Y	N	Y	Y	Y	Y
Hatch	Y	Y	N	Y	Y	Y	Y
VERMONT							
Jeffords	Y	Y	N	Y	Y	Y	Y
Leahy	Y	Y	N	Y	N	N	Y
VIRGINIA							
Warner	Y	Y	N	Y	Y	Y	Y
Robb	Y	Y	Y	Y	N	N	Y
WASHINGTON							
Gorton	Y	Y	N	Y	Y	Y	Y
Murray	Y	Y	N	Y	Y	Y	Y
WEST VIRGINIA							
Byrd	N	N	N	Y	N	N	Y
Rockefeller	N	Y	Y	N	N	N	Y
WISCONSIN							
Feingold	N	N	N	Y	N	N	N
Kohl	Y	Y	N	Y	Y	Y	Y
WYOMING							
Enzi	Y	Y	N	Y	Y	Y	Y
Thomas	Y	Y	N	Y	Y	Y	Y

Key

- **Y** Voted for (yea).
- **#** Paired for.
- **+** Announced for.
- **N** Voted against (nay).
- **X** Paired against.
- **–** Announced against.
- **P** Voted "present."
- **C** Voted "present" to avoid possible conflict of interest.
- **?** Did not vote or otherwise make a position known.

Democrats *Republicans*

ND Northern Democrats   SD Southern Democrats

Southern states - Ala., Ark., Fla., Ga., Ky., La., Miss., N.C., Okla., S.C., Tenn., Texas, Va.

134. S 1260. Securities Lawsuits/Consolidation of Suits. D'Amato, R-N.Y., motion to table (kill) the Sarbanes, D-Md., amendment to remove the bill's language that would allow state judges to lump together securities lawsuits against a common defendant and ship the consolidated case to federal court if more than 50 parties are involved. Motion agreed to 72-27: R 52-2; D 20-25 (ND 16-21, SD 4-4). May 13, 1998.

135. S 1260. Securities Lawsuits/Passage. Passage of the bill to require that all class-action securities lawsuits involving more than 50 parties be filed in federal court, where standards established in a 1995 securities law (PL 104-67) would apply. Passed 79-21: R 53-2; D 26-19 (ND 20-17, SD 6-2). May 13, 1998.

136. S 2057. Fiscal 1999 Defense Authorization/Chinese Commercial Fronts. Grams, R-Minn., motion to table (kill) the Hutchinson, R-Ark., amendment that would authorize the president to monitor, seize the assets of, and ban commercial fronts operating in the United States on behalf of the Chinese army — known as the People's Liberation Army (PLA). The amendment would direct the Defense Department and several law enforcement agencies to compile and publish a list of all people or organizations in the United States that are associated with or controlled by the Chinese military. It would authorize the president to invoke the International Emergency Economic Powers Act, which allows the president to impose an array of sanctions in response to a foreign threat, against groups on the list without consulting Congress. Motion rejected 24-76: R 6-49; D 18-27 (ND 13-24, SD 5-3). May 14, 1998. (Subsequently, the Hutchinson amendment as amended was adopted by voice vote.)

137. S 2037. Digital Copyright Protection/Passage. Passage of the bill to bring the United States into compliance with two international treaties that seek to improve protection for copyrighted digital works such as computer software and movies. The bill also would provide on-line service providers with some protection against liability for infringement that takes place without their knowledge. Passed 99-0: R 54-0; D 45-0 (ND 37-0, SD 8-0). May 14, 1998.

138. S 1723. Expanding Immigration for Skilled Workers/U.S. Worker Lay-Offs. Abraham, R-Mich., motion to table (kill) the Kennedy, D-Mass., amendment that would prohibit employers from sponsoring foreign workers if they had laid off U.S. workers with similar skills in the preceding six months. Motion agreed to 60-38: R 53-1; D 7-37 (ND 5-31, SD 2-6). May 18, 1998. A "nay" was a vote in support of the president's position.

139. S 1723. Expanding Immigration for Skilled Workers/U.S. Worker Recruitment. Abraham, R-Mich., motion to table (kill) the Kennedy, D-Mass., amendment that would require employers seeking to sponsor foreign workers to attest to having first launched a significant "good faith" recruitment effort to hire a U.S. worker. Motion agreed to 59-39: R 53-1; D 6-38 (ND 4-32, SD 2-6). May 18, 1998. A "nay" was a vote in support of the president's position.

140. S 1723. Expanding Immigration for Skilled Workers/Investor Temporary Residency. Abraham, R-Mich., motion to table (kill) the Bumpers, D-Ark., amendment that would repeal the so-called EB-5 visa program, which provides up to 10,000 immigrant visas per year to foreign investors that invest enough money in a U.S. enterprise to provide jobs for at least 10 U.S. citizens. Motion agreed to 74-24: R 50-4; D 24-20 (ND 20-16, SD 4-4). May 18, 1998.

	141	142	143	144	145	146	147
ALABAMA							
Sessions	Y	N	N	Y	Y	Y	Y
Shelby	Y	Y	N	Y	N	Y	Y
ALASKA							
Murkowski	Y	N	Y	Y	Y	?	?
Stevens	Y	Y	Y	Y	Y	Y	Y
ARIZONA							
Kyl	Y	N	N	Y	N	Y	N
McCain	Y	N	Y	Y	Y	?	–
ARKANSAS							
Hutchinson	N	N	N	Y	N	Y	Y
Bumpers	N	Y	Y	N	N	?	?
CALIFORNIA							
Boxer	Y	C	Y	N	C	Y	Y
Feinstein	Y	Y	Y	Y	Y	Y	Y
COLORADO							
Allard	Y	N	N	Y	N	Y	Y
Campbell	Y	N	Y	Y	N	Y	Y
CONNECTICUT							
Dodd	Y	Y	Y	N	Y	Y	Y
Lieberman	Y	Y	Y	N	Y	Y	Y
DELAWARE							
Roth	Y	Y	Y	Y	Y	Y	N
Biden	N	Y	Y	N	Y	N	Y
FLORIDA							
Mack	Y	N	Y	N	Y	Y	Y
Graham	Y	Y	Y	N	Y	Y	Y
GEORGIA							
Coverdell	Y	N	N	Y	N	Y	Y
Cleland	Y	Y	Y	Y	N	Y	Y
HAWAII							
Akaka	N	N	Y	N	Y	Y	Y
Inouye	Y	Y	Y	Y	Y	?	?
IDAHO							
Craig	Y	N	N	Y	N	Y	Y
Kempthorne	Y	N	N	Y	N	Y	Y
ILLINOIS							
Durbin	N	Y	Y	N	N	Y	Y
Moseley-Braun	N	Y	Y	N	N	Y	Y
INDIANA							
Coats	Y	N	N	Y	N	Y	Y
Lugar	Y	N	Y	N	N	N	Y

	141	142	143	144	145	146	147
IOWA							
Grassley	Y	N	Y	N	N	Y	Y
Harkin	N	Y	Y	N	Y	N	Y
KANSAS							
Brownback	Y	N	Y	Y	N	Y	Y
Roberts	Y	N	Y	Y	N	Y	Y
KENTUCKY							
McConnell	Y	N	N	Y	Y	Y	Y
Ford	Y	Y	Y	Y	Y	?	?
LOUISIANA							
Breaux	Y	Y	Y	N	Y	Y	Y
Landrieu	Y	Y	Y	N	Y	Y	Y
MAINE							
Collins	Y	Y	Y	N	Y	Y	Y
Snowe	Y	N	Y	N	N	Y	Y
MARYLAND							
Mikulski	N	Y	Y	N	N	Y	Y
Sarbanes	N	Y	Y	N	N	Y	Y
MASSACHUSETTS							
Kennedy	N	Y	Y	N	N	+	+
Kerry	N	Y	Y	N	Y	Y	Y
MICHIGAN							
Abraham	Y	N	Y	N	N	Y	Y
Levin	N	Y	Y	N	Y	Y	Y
MINNESOTA							
Grams	Y	N	N	Y	N	Y	Y
Wellstone	N	Y	Y	N	N	Y	N
MISSISSIPPI							
Cochran	Y	Y	N	Y	N	Y	Y
Lott	Y	C	C	C	C	Y	Y
MISSOURI							
Ashcroft	Y	N	N	Y	N	Y	Y
Bond	Y	N	Y	Y	N	Y	Y
MONTANA							
Burns	Y	N	N	Y	N	Y	Y
Baucus	Y	Y	Y	N	N	Y	Y
NEBRASKA							
Hagel	Y	N	N	Y	N	Y	Y
Kerrey	Y	Y	Y	N	Y	Y	Y
NEVADA							
Bryan	Y	Y	Y	N	Y	Y	Y
Reid	Y	Y	Y	N	Y	Y	Y

	141	142	143	144	145	146	147
NEW HAMPSHIRE							
Gregg	Y	N	Y	Y	N	Y	Y
Smith	Y	?	?	?	N	Y	Y
NEW JERSEY							
Lautenberg	Y	Y	Y	N	N	Y	Y
Torricelli	N	Y	Y	Y	N	Y	?
NEW MEXICO							
Domenici	Y	Y	N	Y	N	Y	Y
Bingaman	Y	Y	Y	N	N	Y	Y
NEW YORK							
D'Amato	?	Y	Y	Y	Y	Y	Y
Moynihan	N	Y	Y	N	N	Y	Y
NORTH CAROLINA							
Faircloth	?	N	N	Y	Y	Y	Y
Helms	Y	N	N	Y	N	Y	Y
NORTH DAKOTA							
Conrad	Y	Y	Y	N	N	Y	Y
Dorgan	Y	Y	Y	N	N	Y	Y
OHIO							
DeWine	Y	Y	Y	N	Y	Y	Y
Glenn	N	Y	Y	N	Y	Y	Y
OKLAHOMA							
Inhofe	Y	N	N	Y	N	Y	Y
Nickles	Y	N	N	Y	N	Y	Y
OREGON							
Smith	Y	Y	Y	N	Y	Y	Y
Wyden	Y	Y	Y	N	N	Y	Y
PENNSYLVANIA							
Santorum	Y	N	Y	Y	N	Y	Y
Specter	Y	Y	Y	N	Y	Y	N
RHODE ISLAND							
Chafee	Y	N	Y	N	Y	N	Y
Reed	Y	Y	Y	N	Y	Y	Y
SOUTH CAROLINA							
Thurmond	Y	N	Y	Y	N	Y	Y
Hollings	Y	Y	Y	Y	Y	Y	Y
SOUTH DAKOTA							
Daschle	Y	N	Y	N	Y	Y	Y
Johnson	Y	Y	Y	N	Y	Y	Y
TENNESSEE							
Frist	Y	N	Y	Y	Y	Y	Y
Thompson	Y	N	Y	Y	Y	Y	Y

	141	142	143	144	145	146	147
TEXAS							
Gramm	Y	N	N	Y	N	Y	Y
Hutchison	Y	N	N	Y	Y	Y	Y
UTAH							
Bennett	Y	Y	Y	Y	Y	Y	Y
Hatch	Y	Y	Y	Y	Y	Y	Y
VERMONT							
Jeffords	Y	Y	Y	N	Y	Y	Y
Leahy	Y	Y	Y	N	N	Y	Y
VIRGINIA							
Warner	Y	N	N	Y	N	Y	Y
Robb	Y	Y	Y	Y	Y	Y	Y
WASHINGTON							
Gorton	Y	Y	Y	Y	Y	Y	N
Murray	Y	Y	Y	N	N	Y	Y
WEST VIRGINIA							
Byrd	N	N	Y	N	Y	N	Y
Rockefeller	N	Y	Y	N	Y	N	Y
WISCONSIN							
Feingold	N	Y	Y	N	Y	Y	Y
Kohl	N	Y	Y	N	Y	Y	Y
WYOMING							
Enzi	Y	N	N	Y	N	Y	Y
Thomas	N	N	N	Y	N	Y	Y

ND Northern Democrats   SD Southern Democrats

Southern states - Ala., Ark., Fla., Ga., Ky., La., Miss., N.C., Okla., S.C., Tenn., Texas, Va.

Key

Y	Voted for (yea).
#	Paired for.
+	Announced for.
N	Voted against (nay).
X	Paired against.
–	Announced against.
P	Voted "present."
C	Voted "present" to avoid possible conflict of interest.
?	Did not vote or otherwise make a position known.

Democrats   *Republicans*

141. S 1723. Expanding Immigration for Skilled Workers/Passage. Passage of the bill to increase the number of so-called H-1B visas, which allow highly skilled immigrants to work in the United States for six years, from the current cap of 65,000 per year to 95,000 for the remainder of fiscal 1998. The measure also would increase the cap on the visas to 105,000 for fiscal 1999 and 115,000 for the following three fiscal years, but would sunset the cap to its original level at the end of fiscal 2002. The bill also would increase the authorization for certain educational grants, authorize funding for an Internet job bank and authorize funding to provide training opportunities in information technology. Passed 78-20: R 51-2; D 27-18 (ND 20-17, SD 7-1). May 18, 1998. A "nay" was a vote in support of the president's position.

142. S 1415. Tobacco Restrictions/Cap on Attorney's Fees. Hollings, D-S.C., motion to table (kill) the Faircloth, R-N.C., amendment to the modified Senate Commerce Committee substitute amendment. The Faircloth amendment would cap at $250 per hour the amount lawyers are allowed to charge for services in relation to tobacco-related lawsuits. The amendment would not exempt suits in which states have already settled with tobacco manufacturers and it would require attorneys seeking payment to provide Congress with a detailed time accounting of related work. Motion agreed to 58-39: R 15-38; D 43-1 (ND 35-1, SD 8-0). May 19, 1998.

143. S 1415. Tobacco Restrictions/Remove Tax Provisions. Kerry, D-Mass., motion to table (kill) the Ashcroft, R-Mo., amendment to the Kennedy, D-Mass., amendment to the modified Senate Commerce Committee substitute amendment. The Ashcroft amendment would strike all provisions from the bill concerning an increase of tobacco taxes. Motion agreed to 72-26: R 27-26; D 45-0 (ND 37-0, SD 8-0). May 20, 1998.

144. S 1415. Tobacco Restrictions/Cigarette Taxes. McCain, R-Ariz., motion to table (kill) the Kennedy, D-Mass., amendment to the modified Senate Commerce Committee substitute amendment. The Kennedy amendment would replace language in the bill that would raise the federal cigarette fees by $1.10 per pack with language to raise the fees by $1.50 per pack. Motion agreed to 58-40: R 45-8; D 13-32 (ND 8-29, SD 5-3). May 20, 1998.

145. S 1415. Tobacco Restrictions/Tobacco Industry Liability. McCain, R-Ariz., motion to table (kill) the Gregg, R-N.H., amendment that would eliminate the bill's $8 billion annual cap on legal damages that tobacco companies could be forced to pay. Motion rejected 37-61: R 17-37; D 20-24 (ND 14-22, SD 6-2). May 21, 1998. A "yea" was a vote in support of the president's position.

146. HR 2709. Iran Missile Sanctions/Passage. Passage of the bill to require economic sanctions against overseas companies and research institutes that have aided Iranian efforts to develop ballistic missiles that could reach Israel, U.S. forces in the Persian Gulf or Europe. The measure also contains provisions needed to implement a treaty banning chemical weapons that was approved by the Senate in 1997. Passed 90-4: R 51-2; D 39-2 (ND 33-2, SD 6-0). May 22, 1998. A "nay" was a vote in support of the president's position.

147. HR 2400. Surface Transportation Reauthorization/Conference Report. Adoption of the conference report on the bill to authorize approximately $216 billion over fiscal years 1998-2003 for federal transportation programs, including $41 billion for mass transit programs and $2 billion for highway safety. The report would offset some of the new spending by saving $15.5 billion by eliminating disability benefits for veterans with smoking-related illnesses that were not due to their military service. Adopted (thus sent to the House) 88-5: R 49-4; D 39-1 (ND 33-1, SD 6-0). May 22, 1998.

	148	149	150	151	152	153	154
ALABAMA							
Sessions	Y	N	N	Y	N	N	N
Shelby	Y	N	N	Y	N	N	N
ALASKA							
Murkowski	Y	N	N	Y	N	N	N
Stevens	Y	Y	N	Y	N	N	N
ARIZONA							
Kyl	Y	Y	N	Y	N	N	N
McCain	Y	Y	N	Y	Y	N	N
ARKANSAS							
Hutchinson	Y	N	N	Y	N	N	N
Bumpers	N	Y	Y	N	Y	Y	Y
CALIFORNIA							
Boxer	?	N	Y	N	Y	Y	Y
Feinstein	N	N	Y	N	Y	Y	Y
COLORADO							
Allard	Y	Y	N	Y	N	N	N
Campbell	Y	Y	N	Y	N	N	N
CONNECTICUT							
Dodd	N	N	Y	N	Y	Y	Y
Lieberman	N	N	Y	N	Y	Y	Y
DELAWARE							
Roth	Y	Y	N	Y	N	N	N
Biden	?	?	Y	N	Y	Y	?
FLORIDA							
Mack	Y	Y	N	Y	N	N	Y
Graham	N	N	Y	N	Y	Y	Y
GEORGIA							
Coverdell	Y	N	N	Y	N	N	N
Cleland	N	N	Y	N	Y	Y	Y
HAWAII							
Akaka	N	N	Y	N	Y	Y	Y
Inouye	N	?	?	?	?	Y	Y
IDAHO							
Craig	Y	N	N	Y	N	N	N
Kempthorne	Y	N	N	Y	N	N	N
ILLINOIS							
Durbin	N	N	Y	N	Y	Y	Y
Moseley-Braun	?	N	Y	N	Y	Y	Y
INDIANA							
Coats	Y	Y	N	Y	N	N	N
Lugar	Y	Y	N	Y	N	N	N
IOWA							
Grassley	Y	N	N	Y	N	N	N
Harkin	N	N	Y	N	Y	Y	Y
KANSAS							
Brownback	Y	N	N	Y	N	N	N
Roberts	Y	N	N	Y	N	N	N
KENTUCKY							
McConnell	Y	N	N	Y	N	N	N
Ford	N	Y	N	N	Y	N	Y
LOUISIANA							
Breaux	N	Y	Y	N	Y	Y	Y
Landrieu	N	N	Y	N	Y	Y	Y
MAINE							
Collins	Y	N	N	Y	N	N	N
Snowe	Y	N	N	Y	N	N	N
MARYLAND							
Mikulski	N	N	Y	N	Y	Y	Y
Sarbanes	N	N	Y	N	Y	Y	Y
MASSACHUSETTS							
Kennedy	N	N	Y	N	Y	Y	Y
Kerry	N	N	Y	N	Y	Y	Y
MICHIGAN							
Abraham	Y	N	N	Y	N	N	N
Levin	Y	N	Y	N	Y	Y	Y
MINNESOTA							
Grams	Y	N	N	Y	N	N	N
Wellstone	N	N	Y	N	Y	Y	Y
MISSISSIPPI							
Cochran	Y	Y	N	Y	N	N	N
Lott	Y	C	N	Y	N	N	N
MISSOURI							
Ashcroft	Y	N	N	Y	N	N	N
Bond	Y	N	N	Y	N	N	N
MONTANA							
Burns	Y	Y	N	Y	N	N	N
Baucus	N	N	Y	N	Y	Y	Y
NEBRASKA							
Hagel	Y	Y	N	Y	N	N	N
Kerrey	N	N	Y	N	Y	Y	Y
NEVADA							
Bryan	N	N	Y	N	Y	Y	Y
Reid	N	N	Y	N	Y	Y	Y
NEW HAMPSHIRE							
Gregg	Y	N	N	Y	N	?	N
Smith	Y	Y	N	Y	N	N	N
NEW JERSEY							
Lautenberg	N	N	Y	N	Y	Y	Y
Torricelli	N	N	Y	N	Y	Y	Y
NEW MEXICO							
Domenici	Y	N	N	Y	N	N	N
Bingaman	N	N	Y	N	Y	Y	Y
NEW YORK							
D'Amato	Y	N	N	Y	N	N	N
Moynihan	N	N	Y	N	Y	Y	Y
NORTH CAROLINA							
Faircloth	Y	Y	N	Y	N	N	N
Helms	Y	Y	N	Y	N	N	N
NORTH DAKOTA							
Conrad	N	N	Y	N	Y	Y	Y
Dorgan	N	N	Y	N	Y	Y	Y
OHIO							
DeWine	Y	N	N	Y	N	N	N
Glenn	N	N	Y	N	Y	Y	Y
OKLAHOMA							
Inhofe	?	N	N	Y	N	N	N
Nickles	Y	Y	N	Y	N	N	N
OREGON							
Smith	Y	N	N	Y	N	N	N
Wyden	N	N	Y	N	Y	Y	Y
PENNSYLVANIA							
Santorum	Y	N	N	Y	N	N	N
Specter	?	?	?	?	?	?	?
RHODE ISLAND							
Chafee	Y	N	N	N	N	N	Y
Reed	N	N	Y	N	Y	Y	Y
SOUTH CAROLINA							
Thurmond	Y	Y	N	Y	N	N	N
Hollings	Y	Y	N	Y	N	Y	N
SOUTH DAKOTA							
Daschle	N	N	Y	N	Y	Y	Y
Johnson	N	N	Y	N	Y	Y	Y
TENNESSEE							
Frist	Y	Y	N	Y	N	N	N
Thompson	Y	Y	N	Y	N	N	N
TEXAS							
Gramm	Y	N	N	Y	N	N	N
Hutchison	Y	N	N	Y	N	N	N
UTAH							
Bennett	Y	N	N	Y	N	N	N
Hatch	Y	+	N	Y	N	N	N
VERMONT							
Jeffords	Y	N	N	N	N	N	N
Leahy	N	N	Y	N	Y	Y	Y
VIRGINIA							
Warner	Y	Y	N	Y	N	N	N
Robb	Y	Y	N	N	N	N	Y
WASHINGTON							
Gorton	Y	Y	N	Y	N	N	N
Murray	N	N	Y	N	Y	Y	Y
WEST VIRGINIA							
Byrd	N	N	Y	N	Y	Y	Y
Rockefeller	N	N	Y	N	Y	Y	Y
WISCONSIN							
Feingold	N	N	Y	N	Y	Y	Y
Kohl	N	N	Y	N	Y	Y	Y
WYOMING							
Enzi	Y	Y	N	Y	N	N	N
Thomas	Y	Y	N	Y	N	N	N

Key

Y   Voted for (yea).
\#   Paired for.
\+   Announced for.
N   Voted against (nay).
X   Paired against.
–   Announced against.
P   Voted "present."
C   Voted "present" to avoid possible conflict of interest.
?   Did not vote or otherwise make a position known.

•
Democrats   *Republicans*

ND Northern Democrats   SD Southern Democrats

Southern states - Ala., Ark., Fla., Ga., Ky., La., Miss., N.C., Okla., S.C., Tenn., Texas, Va.

148. HR 1270. Temporary Nuclear Waste Repository/Cloture. Motion to invoke cloture (thus limiting debate) on the motion to proceed to the bill that would establish a temporary nuclear waste storage site at Yucca Mountain, Nev. Motion rejected 56-39: R 53-0; D 3-39 (ND 1-33, SD 2-6). June 2, 1998. Three-fifths of the total Senate (60) is required to invoke cloture. A "nay" was a vote in support of the president's position.

149. S 1415. Tobacco Restrictions/Look-Back Provisions. Lott, R-Miss., motion to table (kill) the Durbin, D-Ill., amendment to the Durbin amendment to the Gramm, R-Texas, motion to recommit the bill with instructions. The second-degree Durbin amendment, which is virtually identical to the underlying Durbin amendment, would toughen the bill's so-called look-back provisions, which would penalize the tobacco industry for failure to achieve targeted reductions in youth smoking. The amendment raises the underlying bill's 10-year reduction target from 60 percent to 67 percent and lifts the maximum annual penalties from $4 billion to $7 billion. Motion rejected 29-66: R 24-28; D 5-38 (ND 0-35, SD 5-3). June 4, 1998. (Subsequently, the second-degree Durbin amendment was adopted by voice vote.)

150. S 1415. Tobacco Restrictions/Cloture. Motion to invoke cloture (thus limiting debate) on the modified Senate Commerce Committee substitute amendment to the bill to increase tobacco restrictions. The substitute would require the tobacco industry to pay $516 billion over 25 years for anti-smoking, education and research programs, raise taxes on cigarettes by $1.10 per pack over five years, grant authority to the Food and Drug Administration to regulate nicotine and impose penalties on the tobacco industry if youth smoking does not decrease by 60 percent over 10 years. Motion rejected 42-56: R 0-54; D 42-2 (ND 36-0, SD 6-2). June 9, 1998.

151. S 1415. Tobacco Restrictions/Drug Prevention. Coverdell, R-Ga., amendment to the Durbin, D-Ill., amendment to the Gramm, R-Texas, motion to recommit the bill with instructions. The Coverdell amendment would authorize $16 billion over five years from the bill's tobacco revenues for drug prevention efforts. It would increase funding for border patrol, as well as anti-drug trafficking efforts of the FBI and the Drug Enforcement Administration, allow federal funds to be spent on school vouchers for public school children

who have been victims of violent crimes on school property, ban federal funding for needle-exchange programs and encourage states to establish voluntary drug testing programs for all first-time individuals seeking a driver's license. Adopted 52-46: R 52-2; D 0-44 (ND 0-36, SD 0-8). June 9, 1998.

152. S 1415. Tobacco Restrictions/Democratic Drug Prevention Alternative. Daschle, D-S.D., amendment to the Durbin, D-Ill., amendment to the Gramm, R-Texas, motion to recommit the bill with instructions. The Daschle amendment would replace the text of the previously adopted Coverdell, R-Ga., amendment with a Democratic substitute. The substitute would authorize new funding for drug prevention efforts in the Coverdell amendment, but would not take revenue from the tobacco trust funds to do so. It also would not allow federal funds to be spent on school vouchers for public school children and would attach a section designed to strengthen anti-money laundering laws. Rejected 45-53: R 1-53; D 44-0 (ND 36-0, SD 8-0). June 9, 1998.

153. S 1415. Tobacco Restrictions/Cloture. Motion to invoke cloture (thus limiting debate) on the modified Senate Commerce Committee substitute amendment to the bill to increase tobacco restrictions. The substitute would require the tobacco industry to pay $516 billion over 25 years for anti-smoking, education and research programs, raise taxes on cigarettes by $1.10 per pack over five years, grant authority to the Food and Drug Administration to regulate nicotine and impose penalties on the tobacco industry if youth smoking does not decrease by 60 percent over 10 years. Motion rejected 43-55: R 0-53; D 43-2 (ND 37-0, SD 6-2). June 10, 1998.

154. S 1415. Tobacco Restrictions/Marriage Penalty. Kerry, D-Mass., motion to table (kill) the Gramm, R-Texas, amendment to the Durbin, D-Ill., amendment to the Gramm motion to recommit the bill with instructions. The Gramm amendment would allow couples with combined incomes under $50,000 a year to claim an additional $3,300 income tax deduction, thus eliminating the so-called marriage penalty for those in that income bracket, at a cost of $46 billion over 10 years. The amendment also would allow self-employed individuals to deduct the full cost of their health insurance on their income taxes. Motion rejected 48-50: R 5-49; D 43-1 (ND 36-0, SD 7-1). June 10, 1998. (Subsequently, the Gramm amendment was adopted by voice vote.)

	155	156	157	158	159	160	161
ALABAMA							
Sessions	Y	N	Y	N	Y	Y	N
Shelby	Y	N	N	Y	Y	N	N
ALASKA							
Murkowski	Y	N	Y	N	Y	Y	N
Stevens	Y	N	Y	N	Y	Y	Y
ARIZONA							
Kyl	Y	N	Y	N	Y	Y	N
McCain	Y	N	Y	N	Y	Y	Y
ARKANSAS							
Hutchinson	Y	N	Y	N	Y	Y	N
Bumpers	N	Y	N	?	N	N	Y
CALIFORNIA							
Boxer	N	Y	N	C	N	C	Y
Feinstein	N	Y	N	Y	N	N	Y
COLORADO							
Allard	Y	N	Y	N	Y	Y	N
Campbell	Y	N	N	Y	Y	Y	N
CONNECTICUT							
Dodd	N	Y	N	N	N	Y	Y
Lieberman	N	Y	N	Y	N	N	Y
DELAWARE							
Roth	Y	N	Y	N	Y	N	Y
Biden	?	Y	N	Y	N	N	Y
FLORIDA							
Mack	Y	N	Y	N	Y	Y	N
Graham	N	Y	N	Y	N	N	Y
GEORGIA							
Coverdell	Y	N	N	N	Y	Y	N
Cleland	N	Y	N	Y	N	N	Y
HAWAII							
Akaka	N	Y	N	Y	N	N	Y
Inouye	N	Y	N	Y	N	N	Y
IDAHO							
Craig	Y	N	Y	N	Y	Y	N
Kempthorne	Y	N	Y	N	Y	Y	N
ILLINOIS							
Durbin	N	Y	N	Y	–	N	Y
Moseley-Braun	N	Y	N	Y	?	N	Y
INDIANA							
Coats	Y	N	Y	N	Y	Y	N
Lugar	Y	N	Y	N	Y	Y	N

	155	156	157	158	159	160	161
IOWA							
Grassley	Y	N	N	N	Y	Y	Y
Harkin	N	Y	N	Y	N	N	Y
KANSAS							
Brownback	Y	N	Y	N	Y	Y	N
Roberts	Y	N	Y	N	Y	Y	N
KENTUCKY							
McConnell	Y	N	Y	N	Y	Y	N
Ford	N	N	N	Y	Y	N	N
LOUISIANA							
Breaux	N	Y	N	Y	N	N	Y
Landrieu	N	Y	N	Y	N	N	Y
MAINE							
Collins	Y	N	Y	N	N	Y	Y
Snowe	Y	N	N	N	N	Y	Y
MARYLAND							
Mikulski	N	Y	N	Y	N	N	Y
Sarbanes	N	Y	N	Y	N	N	Y
MASSACHUSETTS							
Kennedy	N	Y	N	Y	N	N	Y
Kerry	N	Y	N	Y	N	N	Y
MICHIGAN							
Abraham	Y	N	N	N	Y	Y	Y
Levin	N	Y	N	Y	N	N	Y
MINNESOTA							
Grams	Y	N	N	Y	Y	Y	N
Wellstone	N	Y	N	N	N	N	Y
MISSISSIPPI							
Cochran	Y	N	Y	N	Y	Y	N
Lott	Y	N	Y	C	Y	C	N
MISSOURI							
Ashcroft	Y	N	Y	N	Y	Y	N
Bond	Y	N	N	N	Y	Y	N
MONTANA							
Burns	Y	N	N	N	?	Y	N
Baucus	N	Y	N	Y	N	N	Y
NEBRASKA							
Hagel	Y	N	Y	N	Y	Y	N
Kerrey	N	Y	N	Y	?	N	Y
NEVADA							
Bryan	N	Y	N	Y	N	N	Y
Reid	N	Y	N	Y	N	N	Y

	155	156	157	158	159	160	161
NEW HAMPSHIRE							
Gregg	Y	N	Y	N	Y	Y	Y
Smith	Y	N	Y	N	Y	Y	N
NEW JERSEY							
Lautenberg	N	Y	N	Y	N	N	Y
Torricelli	N	Y	N	Y	N	N	Y
NEW MEXICO							
Domenici	Y	N	N	N	Y	Y	N
Bingaman	N	Y	N	?	N	N	Y
NEW YORK							
D'Amato	Y	N	Y	N	Y	Y	N
Moynihan	N	Y	N	Y	N	N	Y
NORTH CAROLINA							
Faircloth	Y	N	N	N	Y	Y	N
Helms	Y	N	Y	N	Y	Y	N
NORTH DAKOTA							
Conrad	N	Y	N	N	N	N	Y
Dorgan	N	Y	N	N	N	N	Y
OHIO							
DeWine	Y	N	Y	N	Y	Y	N
Glenn	N	Y	N	Y	N	N	Y
OKLAHOMA							
Inhofe	Y	N	Y	N	?	Y	N
Nickles	Y	N	Y	N	Y	Y	N
OREGON							
Smith	Y	N	Y	N	Y	Y	N
Wyden	N	Y	N	Y	N	N	Y
PENNSYLVANIA							
Santorum	Y	N	Y	N	Y	Y	N
Specter	?	?	?	?	?	?	?
RHODE ISLAND							
Chafee	Y	N	N	N	N	Y	Y
Reed	N	Y	N	Y	N	N	Y
SOUTH CAROLINA							
Thurmond	Y	N	Y	N	Y	Y	N
Hollings	N	Y	N	Y	N	N	Y
SOUTH DAKOTA							
Daschle	N	Y	N	Y	N	N	Y
Johnson	N	Y	N	Y	N	N	Y
TENNESSEE							
Frist	Y	N	Y	N	Y	Y	N
Thompson	Y	N	Y	Y	Y	Y	N

	155	156	157	158	159	160	161
TEXAS							
Gramm	Y	N	Y	N	Y	Y	N
Hutchison	Y	N	N	Y	Y	Y	N
UTAH							
Bennett	Y	N	N	Y	Y	N	Y
Hatch	Y	N	Y	N	Y	Y	N
VERMONT							
Jeffords	Y	N	Y	N	Y	Y	N
Leahy	N	Y	N	Y	N	N	Y
VIRGINIA							
Warner	Y	N	Y	N	Y	Y	N
Robb	N	N	N	Y	N	N	N
WASHINGTON							
Gorton	Y	N	Y	N	Y	Y	N
Murray	N	Y	N	Y	N	N	Y
WEST VIRGINIA							
Byrd	N	Y	N	N	N	Y	Y
Rockefeller	N	Y	N	Y	N	N	Y
WISCONSIN							
Feingold	Y	Y	Y	N	Y	Y	N
Kohl	N	Y	N	Y	N	N	Y
WYOMING							
Enzi	Y	N	Y	N	Y	Y	N
Thomas	Y	N	Y	N	Y	Y	N

Key

Y Voted for (yea).
Paired for.
+ Announced for.
N Voted against (nay).
X Paired against.
– Announced against.
P Voted "present."
C Voted "present" to avoid possible conflict of interest.
? Did not vote or otherwise make a position known.

Democrats *Republicans*

ND Northern Democrats   SD Southern Democrats

Southern states - Ala., Ark., Fla., Ga., Ky., La., Miss., N.C., Okla., S.C., Tenn., Texas, Va.

155. S 1415. Tobacco Restrictions/Democratic Marriage Penalty Alternative. Lott, R-Miss., motion to table (kill) the Daschle, D-S.D., amendment to the Durbin, D-Ill., amendment to the Gramm, R-Texas, motion to recommit the bill with instructions. The Daschle amendment would strike the provisions of the previously adopted Gramm amendment and replace them with language to allow couples with combined incomes under $50,000 a year to deduct 20 percent of the income of the lesser-earning spouse on their income taxes, thus eliminating the so-called marriage penalty for those in that income bracket, at a cost of $31 billion over 10 years. The amendment also would allow self-employed individuals to deduct the full cost of their health insurance on their income taxes. Motion agreed to 55-43: R 54-0; D 1-43 (ND 1-35, SD 0-8). June 10, 1998.

156. S 1415. Tobacco Restrictions/Cloture. Motion to invoke cloture (thus limiting debate) on the modified Senate Commerce Committee substitute amendment to the bill to increase tobacco restrictions. The substitute would require the tobacco industry to pay $516 billion over 25 years for anti-smoking, education and research programs, raise taxes on cigarettes by $1.10 per pack over five years, grant authority to the Food and Drug Administration to regulate nicotine and impose penalties on the tobacco industry if youth smoking does not decrease by 60 percent over 10 years. Motion rejected 43-56: R 0-54; D 43-2 (ND 37-0, SD 6-2). June 11, 1998.

157. S 1415. Tobacco Restrictions/Child Care Block Grants. McCain, R-Ariz., motion to table (kill) the Kerry, D-Mass., amendment to the Durbin, D-Ill., amendment to the Gramm, R-Texas, motion to recommit the bill with instructions. The Kerry amendment would require states to spend at least 50 percent of the restricted-use tobacco revenue, which is 50 percent of the money states would receive, on the child care and development block grant programs. Motion rejected 33-66: R 33-21; D 0-45 (ND 0-37, SD 0-8). June 11, 1998. (Subsequently, the Kerry amendment, after being modified, was adopted by voice vote.)

158. S 1415. Tobacco Restrictions/Cap on Attorney's Fees. Kerry, D-Mass., motion to table (kill) the Faircloth, R-N.C., amendment to the Durbin, D-Ill., amendment to the Gramm, R-Texas, motion to recommit the bill with instructions. The Faircloth amendment would cap at $1,000 per hour the amount lawyers are allowed to charge for services in relation to any tobacco-related lawsuits. It would not exempt suits in which states have already settled with tobacco manufacturers. Motion agreed to 50-45: R 12-41; D 38-4 (ND 31-4, SD 7-0). June 11, 1998.

159. S 1415. Tobacco Restrictions/Advertising Tax Deductions. Gorton, R-Wash., motion to table (kill) the Reed, D-R.I., amendment to the Durbin, D-Ill., amendment to the Gramm, R-Texas, motion to recommit the bill with instructions. The Reed amendment would eliminate advertising tax deductions for those tobacco companies that the Food and Drug Administration determines are directing their advertisements at children. Motion rejected 47-47: R 43-9; D 4-38 (ND 2-32, SD 2-6). June 15, 1998.

160. S 1415. Tobacco Restrictions/Cap on Attorney's Fees. Gorton, R-Wash., amendment to the Durbin, D-Ill., amendment to the Gramm, R-Texas, motion to recommit the bill with instructions. The Gorton amendment would cap at $4,000 per hour the amount lawyers for plaintiffs are allowed to charge for services in relation to any tobacco-related lawsuits filed before Dec. 31, 1994. The amendment would cap the amount at $2,000 per hour for actions filed between Dec. 31, 1994, and March 31, 1997, $1,000 per hour for actions filed between April 1, 1997, and June 15, 1998, and $500 per hour for actions filed after June 15, 1998. The cap would not apply to any attorney who received payment before June 15, 1998, or attorneys for tobacco companies. Adopted 49-48: R 45-8; D 4-40 (ND 4-32, SD 0-8). June 16, 1998.

161. S 1415. Tobacco Restrictions/Cloture. Motion to invoke cloture (thus limiting debate) on the modified Senate Commerce, Science and Transportation Committee substitute amendment to the bill to increase tobacco restrictions. The substitute would require the tobacco industry to pay $516 billion over 25 years for anti-smoking, education and research programs, raise taxes on cigarettes by $1.10 per pack over five years, grant authority to the Food and Drug Administration to regulate nicotine and impose penalties on the tobacco industry if youth smoking does not decrease by 60 percent over 10 years. Motion rejected 57-42: R 14-40; D 43-2 (ND 37-0, SD 6-2). June 17, 1998. Three-fifths of the total Senate (60) is required to invoke cloture. A "yea" was a vote in support of the president's position.

Senate Votes 162, 163, 164, 165, 166, 167, 168

State / Senator	162	163	164	165	166	167	168
ALABAMA							
Sessions	N	Y	Y	Y	N	N	N
Shelby	N	Y	Y	Y	N	N	N
ALASKA							
Murkowski	N	Y	Y	Y	?	N	N
Stevens	N	Y	Y	Y	Y	Y	N
ARIZONA							
Kyl	N	Y	Y	Y	N	N	N
McCain	Y	Y	Y	Y	N	Y	N
ARKANSAS							
Hutchinson	N	Y	Y	Y	N	N	N
Bumpers	Y	Y	N	Y	Y	N	N
CALIFORNIA							
Boxer	Y	Y	N	Y	Y	N	N
Feinstein	Y	Y	N	Y	Y	N	N
COLORADO							
Allard	N	Y	Y	Y	N	N	N
Campbell	N	Y	Y	Y	N	N	N
CONNECTICUT							
Dodd	Y	Y	N	Y	Y	N	N
Lieberman	Y	Y	N	Y	Y	Y	N
DELAWARE							
Roth	Y	Y	N	Y	Y	N	N
Biden	Y	Y	N	Y	Y	N	N
FLORIDA							
Mack	N	Y	Y	Y	N	N	N
Graham	Y	Y	N	Y	Y	N	N
GEORGIA							
Coverdell	N	Y	Y	Y	N	N	N
Cleland	Y	Y	N	Y	Y	N	N
HAWAII							
Akaka	Y	Y	N	Y	Y	N	N
Inouye	Y	Y	N	Y	Y	N	N
IDAHO							
Craig	N	Y	Y	Y	N	N	N
Kempthorne	N	Y	Y	Y	N	N	N
ILLINOIS							
Durbin	Y	Y	N	Y	Y	N	N
Moseley-Braun	Y	Y	N	Y	?	N	N
INDIANA							
Coats	N	Y	Y	Y	N	N	N
Lugar	N	Y	Y	Y	Y	N	N
IOWA							
Grassley	Y	Y	Y	Y	N	N	N
Harkin	Y	Y	N	Y	Y	N	N
KANSAS							
Brownback	N	Y	Y	Y	N	N	N
Roberts	N	Y	Y	Y	N	N	N
KENTUCKY							
McConnell	N	Y	Y	Y	N	N	N
Ford	N	Y	N	Y	N	N	N
LOUISIANA							
Breaux	Y	N	N	Y	Y	N	N
Landrieu	Y	Y	N	Y	Y	N	N
MAINE							
Collins	Y	Y	Y	Y	N	N	N
Snowe	Y	Y	Y	Y	N	N	N
MARYLAND							
Mikulski	Y	Y	N	Y	Y	N	N
Sarbanes	Y	Y	N	Y	Y	N	N
MASSACHUSETTS							
Kennedy	Y	Y	N	Y	Y	N	N
Kerry	Y	Y	N	Y	Y	N	N
MICHIGAN							
Abraham	N	Y	Y	Y	N	N	N
Levin	Y	Y	N	Y	Y	N	N
MINNESOTA							
Grams	N	Y	Y	Y	N	Y	N
Wellstone	Y	Y	N	Y	Y	N	N
MISSISSIPPI							
Cochran	N	Y	Y	Y	Y	Y	N
Lott	N	Y	Y	Y	Y	N	N
MISSOURI							
Ashcroft	N	Y	Y	Y	N	N	N
Bond	N	N	Y	Y	N	N	N
MONTANA							
Burns	N	Y	Y	Y	N	N	N
Baucus	Y	Y	N	Y	Y	N	N
NEBRASKA							
Hagel	N	Y	Y	Y	N	N	N
Kerrey	Y	Y	N	Y	Y	N	N
NEVADA							
Bryan	Y	Y	N	Y	Y	N	N
Reid	Y	Y	N	Y	?	N	N
NEW HAMPSHIRE							
Gregg	N	Y	Y	Y	Y	N	N
Smith	N	Y	Y	Y	N	N	N
NEW JERSEY							
Lautenberg	Y	Y	N	Y	Y	N	N
Torricelli	Y	Y	N	Y	Y	N	N
NEW MEXICO							
Domenici	N	Y	Y	Y	?	?	?
Bingaman	Y	Y	N	Y	Y	N	N
NEW YORK							
D'Amato	Y	Y	Y	Y	?	N	N
Moynihan	Y	Y	N	Y	Y	N	N
NORTH CAROLINA							
Faircloth	N	?	?	Y	N	N	N
Helms	N	Y	Y	N	N	N	N
NORTH DAKOTA							
Conrad	Y	Y	N	Y	Y	N	N
Dorgan	Y	Y	N	Y	Y	N	N
OHIO							
DeWine	Y	Y	Y	Y	N	N	N
Glenn	Y	Y	N	Y	Y	N	N
OKLAHOMA							
Inhofe	N	Y	Y	Y	N	N	N
Nickles	N	Y	Y	Y	N	N	N
OREGON							
Smith	Y	Y	N	Y	Y	N	N
Wyden	Y	Y	N	Y	Y	N	N
PENNSYLVANIA							
Santorum	N	Y	Y	N	N	N	N
Specter	?	?	?	?	?	?	?
RHODE ISLAND							
Chafee	Y	Y	Y	Y	?	?	N
Reed	Y	Y	N	Y	Y	N	N
SOUTH CAROLINA							
Thurmond	N	Y	Y	Y	N	N	N
Hollings	N	Y	N	Y	N	N	N
SOUTH DAKOTA							
Daschle	Y	Y	N	Y	Y	N	N
Johnson	Y	Y	N	Y	Y	N	N
TENNESSEE							
Frist	N	Y	Y	Y	N	N	N
Thompson	N	Y	Y	Y	N	N	N
TEXAS							
Gramm	N	Y	Y	Y	N	N	N
Hutchison	N	Y	Y	Y	N	N	N
UTAH							
Bennett	Y	Y	Y	Y	?	?	?
Hatch	N	Y	Y	Y	Y	N	N
VERMONT							
Jeffords	Y	Y	Y	Y	Y	N	N
Leahy	Y	Y	N	Y	+	N	N
VIRGINIA							
Warner	N	Y	Y	Y	N	Y	N
Robb	N	Y	N	Y	Y	N	Y
WASHINGTON							
Gorton	N	Y	Y	Y	N	N	N
Murray	Y	Y	N	Y	Y	N	N
WEST VIRGINIA							
Byrd	Y	Y	Y	Y	N	N	N
Rockefeller	Y	Y	N	Y	Y	N	?
WISCONSIN							
Feingold	Y	Y	N	Y	Y	N	N
Kohl	Y	Y	N	Y	Y	N	N
WYOMING							
Enzi	N	Y	Y	Y	N	N	N
Thomas	N	Y	Y	Y	?	Y	N

ND Northern Democrats SD Southern Democrats

Southern states - Ala., Ark., Fla., Ga., Ky., La., Miss., N.C., Okla., S.C., Tenn., Texas, Va.

Key

Y   Voted for (yea).
\#   Paired for.
\+   Announced for.
N   Voted against (nay).
X   Paired against.
–   Announced against.
P   Voted "present."
C   Voted "present" to avoid possible conflict of interest.
?   Did not vote or otherwise make a position known.

Democrats   *Republicans*

162. S 1415. Tobacco Restrictions/Budget Act Waiver. Daschle, D-S.D., motion to waive the Budget Act with respect to the Stevens, R-Alaska, point of order against the bill to increase tobacco restrictions. The bill, as amended, would require the tobacco industry to pay $516 billion over 25 years for anti-smoking, education and research programs, raise taxes on cigarettes by $1.10 per pack over five years, grant authority to the Food and Drug Administration to regulate nicotine and impose penalties on the tobacco industry if youth smoking does not decrease by 60 percent over 10 years. Motion rejected 53-46: R 11-43; D 42-3 (ND 37-0, SD 5-3). June 17, 1998. A three-fifths majority vote (60) of the total Senate is required to waive the Budget Act. (Subsequently, the chair upheld the point of order, and the bill was returned to the Senate Commerce Committee.) A "yea" was a vote in support of the president's position.

163. Procedural Motion. Lott, R-Miss., motion to instruct the sergeant-at-arms to request the attendance of absent senators. Motion agreed to 96-2: R 52-1; D 44-1 (ND 37-0, SD 7-1). June 18, 1998.

164. S 2138. Fiscal 1999 Energy and Water Appropriations/Tobacco Restrictions. Lott, R-Miss., motion to table (kill) the Reid, D-Nev., motion to waive the Budget Act with respect to the Domenici, R-N.M., point of order against the Daschle, D-S.D., amendment. The Daschle amendment would require the tobacco industry to pay $516 billion over 25 years for anti-smoking, education and research programs, raise taxes on cigarettes by $1.10 per pack over five years, grant authority to the Food and Drug Administration to regulate nicotine and impose penalties on the tobacco industry if youth smoking does not decrease by 60 percent over 10 years. Motion agreed to 54-44: R 53-0; D 1-44 (ND 1-36, SD 0-8). June 18, 1998.

165. S 2138. Fiscal 1999 Energy and Water Development Appropria-tions/Passage. Passage of the bill to provide $21.4 billion in new budget authority for energy and water development programs in fiscal 1999. The bill provides $109 million more than provided in fiscal 1998 and $354 million less than requested by the Clinton administration. Passed 98-1: R 54-0; D 44-1 (ND 36-1, SD 8-0). June 18, 1998.

166. Mollway Nomination/Confirmation. Confirmation of President Clinton's nomination of Susan Oki Mollway of Hawaii to be U.S. District Judge for the District of Hawaii. Confirmed 56-34: R 14-34; D 42-0 (ND 34-0, SD 8-0). June 22, 1998. A "yea" was a vote in support of the president's position.

167. S 2057. Fiscal 1999 Defense Authorization/Chinese Forced Abortions. Warner, R-Va., motion to table (kill) the Warner-Hutchinson, R-Ark., amendment to the Warner perfecting amendment to the Warner motion to recommit the bill with instructions. The second-degree Warner-Hutchinson amendment would condemn various human rights violations of the Chinese government and would prohibit the issuing of U.S. visas to Chinese officials involved in forced abortions or forced sterilizations. Motion rejected 14-82: R 12-39; D 2-43 (ND 1-36, SD 1-7). June 23, 1998. (Subsequently, these amendments were withdrawn.)

168. S 2057. Fiscal 1999 Defense Authorization/Chinese Forced Abortions. Ashcroft, R-Mo., motion to table (kill) Division I of the Hutchinson, R-Ark., amendment to the Hutchinson amendment to the Warner, R-Va., motion to recommit the bill with instructions. Division I would prohibit U.S. visas to Chinese officials involved in forced abortions or forced sterilizations. The tabling motion was intended to test of Senate support for Division I , but opponents thwarted that intent by voting against the motion. Motion rejected 0-96: R 0-52; D 0-44 (ND 0-36, SD 0-8). June 23, 1998.

	169	170	171	172	173	174	175
ALABAMA							
Sessions	Y	Y	N	N	N	Y	N
Shelby	Y	Y	Y	N	N	Y	N
ALASKA							
Murkowski	Y	Y	Y	N	N	N	N
Stevens	Y	Y	Y	Y	N	N	N
ARIZONA							
Kyl	Y	Y	N	N	N	N	N
McCain	Y	Y	N	N	N	N	N
ARKANSAS							
Hutchinson	Y	Y	N	N	?	?	?
Bumpers	N	Y	Y	Y	Y	N	Y
CALIFORNIA							
Boxer	N	Y	Y	Y	Y	Y	Y
Feinstein	Y	Y	Y	Y	N	N	Y
COLORADO							
Allard	Y	Y	N	N	N	N	N
Campbell	Y	Y	Y	Y	N	Y	N
CONNECTICUT							
Dodd	N	N	Y	Y	N	Y	Y
Lieberman	Y	N	Y	Y	N	N	N
DELAWARE							
Roth	Y	Y	Y	?	?	?	?
Biden	Y	N	Y	Y	N	N	Y
FLORIDA							
Mack	Y	Y	Y	Y	N	Y	N
Graham	N	Y	Y	Y	N	Y	N
GEORGIA							
Coverdell	Y	Y	Y	N	N	Y	N
Cleland	Y	N	Y	N	Y	N	Y
HAWAII							
Akaka	?	?	?	?	?	?	?
Inouye	N	Y	Y	Y	N	N	Y
IDAHO							
Craig	Y	Y	N	N	N	Y	N
Kempthorne	Y	Y	N	Y	N	Y	N
ILLINOIS							
Durbin	N	Y	N	Y	Y	Y	Y
Moseley-Braun	N	Y	Y	Y	Y	Y	Y
INDIANA							
Coats	Y	Y	Y	N	N	N	N
Lugar	Y	Y	Y	N	N	N	N
IOWA							
Grassley	Y	Y	N	N	N	N	Y
Harkin	N	Y	Y	Y	Y	N	Y
KANSAS							
Brownback	Y	Y	N	N	N	Y	N
Roberts	Y	Y	N	N	N	Y	N
KENTUCKY							
McConnell	Y	Y	Y	N	N	Y	N
Ford	N	Y	Y	Y	Y	Y	Y
LOUISIANA							
Breaux	Y	Y	Y	N	N	Y	N
Landrieu	N	Y	Y	Y	N	Y	Y
MAINE							
Collins	Y	Y	Y	Y	N	Y	N
Snowe	Y	Y	N	Y	N	Y	N
MARYLAND							
Mikulski	N	Y	Y	Y	Y	Y	Y
Sarbanes	N	Y	Y	Y	Y	Y	Y
MASSACHUSETTS							
Kennedy	N	Y	Y	Y	Y	N	Y
Kerry	N	Y	Y	Y	Y	N	Y
MICHIGAN							
Abraham	Y	Y	Y	N	N	Y	N
Levin	N	Y	Y	Y	N	N	N
MINNESOTA							
Grams	Y	Y	N	N	N	Y	N
Wellstone	N	Y	Y	Y	Y	N	Y
MISSISSIPPI							
Cochran	Y	Y	Y	N	N	Y	N
Lott	Y	Y	N	N	N	N	N
MISSOURI							
Ashcroft	Y	Y	N	N	N	N	N
Bond	Y	Y	N	N	N	Y	N
MONTANA							
Burns	Y	Y	N	Y	N	Y	N
Baucus	?	?	?	?	?	?	?
NEBRASKA							
Hagel	Y	Y	Y	N	N	Y	N
Kerrey	N	Y	Y	Y	N	N	N
NEVADA							
Bryan	N	Y	Y	Y	N	N	Y
Reid	N	Y	Y	Y	N	N	Y
NEW HAMPSHIRE							
Gregg	Y	Y	N	N	N	N	N
Smith	Y	Y	N	N	N	N	N
NEW JERSEY							
Lautenberg	N	Y	Y	Y	Y	Y	Y
Torricelli	Y	Y	Y	Y	Y	Y	N
NEW MEXICO							
Domenici	+	?	Y	Y	N	Y	N
Bingaman	N	Y	Y	Y	N	N	N
NEW YORK							
D'Amato	Y	Y	Y	N	N	N	N
Moynihan	N	Y	Y	Y	N	N	N
NORTH CAROLINA							
Faircloth	Y	Y	N	N	N	Y	Y
Helms	Y	Y	N	–	?	Y	N
NORTH DAKOTA							
Conrad	N	Y	Y	N	N	Y	Y
Dorgan	N	Y	Y	Y	N	Y	Y
OHIO							
DeWine	Y	Y	Y	N	N	N	N
Glenn	N	Y	Y	?	?	?	?
OKLAHOMA							
Inhofe	Y	Y	N	N	N	Y	N
Nickles	Y	Y	N	N	N	Y	N
OREGON							
Smith	Y	Y	Y	N	N	N	N
Wyden	N	Y	Y	Y	Y	N	Y
PENNSYLVANIA							
Santorum	Y	Y	N	N	N	N	N
Specter	?	?	?	?	?	?	?
RHODE ISLAND							
Chafee	N	Y	Y	Y	N	N	N
Reed	N	Y	Y	Y	N	N	N
SOUTH CAROLINA							
Thurmond	Y	Y	Y	N	N	N	N
Hollings	N	Y	Y	N	N	N	N
SOUTH DAKOTA							
Daschle	N	Y	Y	Y	N	N	Y
Johnson	N	Y	Y	Y	N	N	Y
TENNESSEE							
Frist	Y	Y	N	N	N	Y	N
Thompson	Y	Y	N	N	N	N	N

	169	170	171	172	173	174	175
TEXAS							
Gramm	Y	Y	N	N	N	N	N
Hutchison	Y	Y	N	N	N	Y	N
UTAH							
Bennett	Y	Y	Y	Y	N	Y	N
Hatch	Y	Y	N	N	N	Y	N
VERMONT							
Jeffords	N	Y	Y	N	N	Y	N
Leahy	N	Y	Y	Y	N	N	Y
VIRGINIA							
Warner	Y	Y	N	N	N	N	N
Robb	N	N	Y	N	N	N	N
WASHINGTON							
Gorton	Y	Y	Y	N	N	Y	N
Murray	N	Y	Y	Y	Y	Y	Y
WEST VIRGINIA							
Byrd	Y	Y	Y	N	N	N	Y
Rockefeller	?	?	?	?	?	?	?
WISCONSIN							
Feingold	N	Y	N	Y	Y	N	Y
Kohl	Y	Y	Y	Y	Y	N	Y
WYOMING							
Enzi	Y	Y	N	N	N	Y	N
Thomas	Y	Y	N	Y	N	Y	N

Key

Y	Voted for (yea).
#	Paired for.
+	Announced for.
N	Voted against (nay).
X	Paired against.
–	Announced against.
P	Voted "present."
C	Voted "present" to avoid possible conflict of interest.
?	Did not vote or otherwise make a position known.

Democrats   *Republicans*

ND Northern Democrats   SD Southern Democrats

Southern states - Ala., Ark., Fla., Ga., Ky., La., Miss., N.C., Okla., S.C., Tenn., Texas, Va.

169. HR 2646. Expanding Education Savings Accounts/Conference Report. Adoption of the conference report on the bill to allow individuals to contribute up to $2,000 a year of after-tax funds in tax-sheltered savings accounts that may be used to pay for educational expenses. Adopted (thus cleared for the president) 59-36: R 51-2; D 8-34 (ND 6-28, SD 2-6). June 24, 1998. A "nay" was a vote in support of the president's position.

170. S 2057. Fiscal 1999 Defense Authorization/Troops in Bosnia. Thurmond, R-S.C., amendment to express the sense of Congress that U.S. ground forces should not remain in Bosnia indefinitely and that the president should work with NATO to withdraw U.S. forces "within a reasonable period of time." Adopted 90-5: R 53-0; D 37-5 (ND 31-3, SD 6-2). June 24, 1998.

171. S 2057. Fiscal 1999 Defense Authorization/Troops in Bosnia. McCain, R-Ariz., motion to table (kill) the Smith, R-N.H., amendment that would prohibit funding for U.S. ground troop deployment in Bosnia if both houses of Congress do not vote by March 31, 1999, on legislation that would authorize continued deployment in Bosnia. Motion agreed to 65-31: R 25-29; D 40-2 (ND 32-2, SD 8-0). June 24, 1998.

172. S 2057. Fiscal 1999 Defense Authorization/Separate Gender Barracks. Snowe, R-Maine, amendment to the Brownback, R-Kan., amendment. The Snowe amendment would replace the text of the Brownback amendment with language to prohibit the Defense Department from making any changes in its gender separation policies until a commission established in the fiscal 1998 defense authorization bill issues a report early next year. Adopted 56-37: R 18-34; D 38-3 (ND 31-2, SD 7-1). June 24,

1998. (Subsequently, the Brownback amendment as amended was adopted by voice vote.)

173. S 2057. Fiscal 1999 Defense Authorization/Child Development Program. Wellstone, D-Minn., amendment to authorize an additional $270 million over five years for the Defense Department's child development program. The amendment would pay for the increase with a 0.1 percent across-the-board cut to all other programs authorized by the bill. Rejected 18-74: R 1-50; D 17-24 (ND 15-18, SD 2-6). June 25, 1998.

174. S 2057. Fiscal 1999 Defense Authorization/Base Closures and Realignments. Inhofe, R-Okla., amendment that would reduce the Defense Department's authority to close or realign military installations without congressional approval. The amendment also would express the sense of Congress that Congress should not consider further base closings until activities related to previously authorized closings are complete and that the Defense Department should report to Congress on the effect closings and realignments have on the ability to mobilize U.S. forces. Adopted 48-45: R 31-21; D 17-24 (ND 12-21, SD 5-3). June 25, 1998.

175. S 2057. Fiscal 1999 Defense Authorization/Veterans' Health Care. Harkin, D-Iowa, amendment that would transfer $329 million from defense accounts to the Veterans Affairs Department for health care programs. The amendment would order the secretary of Defense to transfer the funds from defense programs that would result in the "least significant harm" to armed forces readiness and military personnel quality of life. Rejected 38-55: R 5-47; D 33-8 (ND 28-5, SD 5-3). June 25, 1998.

	176	177	178	179	180	181	182
ALABAMA							
Sessions	N	Y	N	N	Y	Y	Y
Shelby	N	Y	N	N	Y	Y	Y
ALASKA							
Murkowski	N	Y	N	N	Y	Y	Y
Stevens	Y	Y	N	N	Y	Y	?
ARIZONA							
Kyl	N	Y	N	N	Y	Y	?
McCain	N	Y	N	N	N	Y	?
ARKANSAS							
Hutchinson	–	?	?	?	?	?	?
Bumpers	Y	N	Y	Y	Y	N	Y
CALIFORNIA							
Boxer	Y	N	Y	N	Y	N	Y
Feinstein	Y	N	N	Y	N	Y	Y
COLORADO							
Allard	N	Y	N	N	Y	Y	Y
Campbell	N	Y	N	Y	Y	Y	Y
CONNECTICUT							
Dodd	Y	N	N	N	Y	Y	Y
Lieberman	Y	N	N	N	N	Y	Y
DELAWARE							
Roth	?	?	?	?	?	?	?
Biden	Y	N	Y	N	N	Y	Y
FLORIDA							
Mack	N	Y	N	N	N	Y	Y
Graham	Y	N	N	N	N	Y	Y
GEORGIA							
Coverdell	N	Y	N	N	Y	Y	Y
Cleland	Y	N	N	N	N	Y	Y
HAWAII							
Akaka	?	?	?	?	?	?	?
Inouye	Y	N	N	N	Y	Y	Y
IDAHO							
Craig	N	Y	N	N	Y	Y	Y
Kempthorne	N	Y	N	N	Y	Y	Y
ILLINOIS							
Durbin	Y	N	Y	Y	N	Y	Y
Moseley-Braun	Y	N	Y	Y	N	Y	Y
INDIANA							
Coats	N	Y	N	Y	Y	Y	Y
Lugar	N	Y	N	N	N	Y	Y
IOWA							
Grassley	N	Y	N	Y	Y	Y	Y
Harkin	Y	N	Y	N	N	N	?
KANSAS							
Brownback	N	Y	N	N	Y	Y	Y
Roberts	N	Y	N	N	Y	Y	Y
KENTUCKY							
McConnell	N	Y	N	N	Y	Y	Y
Ford	N	N	N	N	Y	Y	Y
LOUISIANA							
Breaux	N	N	N	N	N	Y	Y
Landrieu	Y	N	N	N	N	Y	Y
MAINE							
Collins	Y	Y	N	N	Y	Y	Y
Snowe	Y	Y	N	N	Y	Y	Y
MARYLAND							
Mikulski	Y	N	Y	N	N	Y	Y
Sarbanes	Y	N	Y	N	N	Y	Y
MASSACHUSETTS							
Kennedy	Y	N	Y	N	Y	N	Y
Kerry	Y	N	Y	N	Y	N	Y
MICHIGAN							
Abraham	N	Y	N	N	Y	Y	Y
Levin	Y	N	Y	N	N	Y	Y
MINNESOTA							
Grams	N	Y	N	Y	Y	Y	Y
Wellstone	Y	N	Y	Y	N	N	+
MISSISSIPPI							
Cochran	N	Y	N	N	Y	Y	Y
Lott	N	Y	N	N	Y	Y	Y
MISSOURI							
Ashcroft	N	Y	N	N	Y	Y	Y
Bond	N	Y	N	N	Y	Y	Y
MONTANA							
Burns	N	Y	N	N	Y	Y	Y
Baucus	?	?	?	?	?	?	?
NEBRASKA							
Hagel	N	Y	N	N	Y	Y	Y
Kerrey	Y	N	N	N	N	Y	Y
NEVADA							
Bryan	Y	N	Y	N	N	Y	Y
Reid	N	N	Y	N	N	Y	Y

	176	177	178	179	180	181	182
NEW HAMPSHIRE							
Gregg	N	Y	N	N	Y	Y	Y
Smith	N	Y	N	N	Y	Y	Y
NEW JERSEY							
Lautenberg	Y	N	Y	N	Y	N	Y
Torricelli	Y	N	N	N	Y	Y	Y
NEW MEXICO							
Domenici	N	Y	N	N	N	Y	Y
Bingaman	Y	N	N	N	N	Y	Y
NEW YORK							
D'Amato	N	Y	N	N	Y	Y	Y
Moynihan	Y	N	N	N	Y	Y	Y
NORTH CAROLINA							
Faircloth	N	Y	N	N	Y	Y	Y
Helms	N	Y	N	N	Y	Y	Y
NORTH DAKOTA							
Conrad	Y	N	N	N	Y	Y	Y
Dorgan	Y	N	N	N	N	Y	Y
OHIO							
DeWine	N	Y	N	N	Y	Y	Y
Glenn	?	?	?	?	?	?	?
OKLAHOMA							
Inhofe	N	Y	N	N	Y	Y	?
Nickles	N	Y	N	N	Y	Y	Y
OREGON							
Smith	N	N	N	N	N	Y	Y
Wyden	Y	N	+	+	–	+	+
PENNSYLVANIA							
Santorum	N	Y	N	N	Y	Y	Y
Specter	?	?	?	?	?	?	?
RHODE ISLAND							
Chafee	Y	Y	N	N	N	Y	Y
Reed	Y	N	N	N	Y	Y	Y
SOUTH CAROLINA							
Thurmond	N	Y	N	N	Y	Y	Y
Hollings	Y	N	N	N	Y	Y	Y
SOUTH DAKOTA							
Daschle	Y	N	Y	N	N	Y	Y
Johnson	Y	N	Y	Y	N	Y	Y
TENNESSEE							
Frist	N	Y	N	N	Y	Y	Y
Thompson	N	Y	N	N	N	Y	Y

	176	177	178	179	180	181	182
TEXAS							
Gramm	N	Y	N	N	N	Y	Y
Hutchison	N	Y	N	N	N	Y	Y
UTAH							
Bennett	N	N	N	N	Y	Y	?
Hatch	N	N	N	N	Y	Y	Y
VERMONT							
Jeffords	Y	Y	N	Y	N	Y	Y
Leahy	Y	N	Y	Y	N	Y	Y
VIRGINIA							
Warner	N	Y	N	N	Y	Y	Y
Robb	Y	N	N	N	N	Y	Y
WASHINGTON							
Gorton	Y	Y	N	N	Y	Y	Y
Murray	Y	N	N	N	N	Y	Y
WEST VIRGINIA							
Byrd	Y	N	Y	Y	Y	Y	Y
Rockefeller	?	?	?	?	?	?	?
WISCONSIN							
Feingold	Y	N	Y	Y	N	N	Y
Kohl	Y	N	Y	Y	N	Y	Y
WYOMING							
Enzi	N	Y	N	N	Y	Y	Y
Thomas	N	Y	N	N	N	Y	Y

ND Northern Democrats   SD Southern Democrats

Southern states - Ala., Ark., Fla., Ga., Ky., La., Miss., N.C., Okla., S.C., Tenn., Texas, Va.

Key

Y	Voted for (yea).
#	Paired for.
+	Announced for.
N	Voted against (nay).
X	Paired against.
–	Announced against.
P	Voted "present."
C	Voted "present" to avoid possible conflict of interest.
?	Did not vote or otherwise make a position known.

Democrats   *Republicans*

176. S 2057. Fiscal 1999 Defense Authorization/Overseas Military Hospital Abortions. Murray, D-Wash., amendment to repeal current law prohibiting overseas U.S. military hospitals and medical facilities from performing privately funded abortions for U.S. service members and their dependents. Rejected 44-49: R 6-46; D 38-3 (ND 32-1, SD 6-2). June 25, 1998. A "yea" was a vote in support of the president's position.

177. S 2057. Fiscal 1999 Defense Authorization/Idaho Air Force Base Expansion. Kempthorne, R-Idaho, motion to table (kill) the Reid, D-Nev., amendment that would strike language in the bill allowing the Air Force to expand training activities at the Mountain Home Air Force Base in Idaho. Motion agreed to 49-44: R 49-3; D 0-41 (ND 0-33, SD 0-8). June 25, 1998.

178. S 2057. Fiscal 1999 Defense Authorization/Navy Communications System. Feingold, D-Wis., amendment that would terminate the Navy's extremely low frequency communications system (ELF) and require that all savings from the termination be transferred to the operation and maintenance accounts of the National Guard. Rejected 20-72: R 0-52; D 20-20 (ND 19-13, SD 1-7). June 25, 1998.

179. S 2057. Fiscal 1999 Defense Authorization/F-22 Aircraft. Bumpers, D-Ark., amendment that would prohibit the Defense Department from purchasing any of the six previously ordered F-22 aircraft until 30 days after the secretary of Defense certifies that the Air Force has completed 601 hours of flight testing on the F-22. Rejected 19-73: R 3-49; D 16-24 (ND 15-17, SD 1-7). June 25, 1998.

180. S 2057. Fiscal 1999 Defense Authorization/Same-Sex Barracks and Training. Byrd, D-W.Va., amendment to the Gramm, R-Texas, amendment. The Byrd amendment would prohibit the armed forces from housing male and female recruits in the same barracks and would prohibit them from conducting gender-integrated basic training. The Gramm amendment would remove restrictions on recipients of Naval Reserve Officers' Training Corps scholarships. Rejected 39-53: R 31-21; D 8-32 (ND 5-27, SD 3-5). June 25, 1998. (Subsequently, the Gramm amendment was adopted by voice vote.) A "nay" was a vote in support of the president's position.

181. S 2057. Fiscal 1999 Defense Authorization/Passage. Passage of the bill to authorize $274 billion for defense-related activities in fiscal 1999, $462 million more than President Clinton's request. The bill also would authorize a 3.6 percent raise in military pay. Passed 88-4: R 52-0; D 36-4 (ND 29-3, SD 7-1). June 25, 1998.

182. Matz Nomination/Confirmation. Confirmation of President Clinton's nomination of A. Howard Matz of California to be U.S. district judge for the Central District of California. Confirmed 85-0: R 47-0; D 38-0 (ND 30-0, SD 8-0). June 26, 1998. A "yea" was a vote in support of the president's position.

	183	184	185	186	187	188	189
ALABAMA							
Sessions	Y	Y	N	Y	Y	Y	Y
Shelby	Y	N	N	Y	Y	N	Y
ALASKA							
Murkowski	Y	Y	N	Y	Y	Y	Y
Stevens	?	Y	N	Y	Y	Y	Y
ARIZONA							
Kyl	?	Y	N	?	?	+	+
McCain	?	Y	N	Y	N	Y	Y
ARKANSAS							
Hutchinson	?	Y	Y	Y	Y	Y	Y
Bumpers	Y	Y	Y	N	N	N	Y
CALIFORNIA							
Boxer	Y	N	N	Y	N	N	Y
Feinstein	Y	N	N	Y	N	N	Y
COLORADO							
Allard	Y	Y	N	Y	Y	Y	Y
Campbell	Y	Y	N	Y	Y	Y	Y
CONNECTICUT							
Dodd	Y	Y	N	Y	N	N	Y
Lieberman	Y	Y	N	Y	N	N	Y
DELAWARE							
Roth	?	N	N	Y	Y	N	Y
Biden	Y	N	N	Y	N	N	Y
FLORIDA							
Mack	Y	Y	N	Y	Y	Y	Y
Graham	Y	N	N	N	N	N	Y
GEORGIA							
Coverdell	Y	Y	N	Y	Y	Y	Y
Cleland	Y	N	N	N	N	N	Y
HAWAII							
Akaka	?	N	N	Y	N	N	Y
Inouye	Y	?	?	Y	N	N	Y
IDAHO							
Craig	Y	Y	N	Y	Y	Y	Y
Kempthorne	Y	Y	N	Y	Y	Y	Y
ILLINOIS							
Durbin	Y	N	Y	N	N	N	Y
Moseley-Braun	Y	N	N	Y	N	N	Y
INDIANA							
Coats	Y	Y	Y	Y	Y	Y	Y
Lugar	Y	Y	Y	Y	Y	Y	Y

	183	184	185	186	187	188	189
IOWA							
Grassley	Y	Y	N	Y	Y	Y	Y
Harkin	?	N	Y	N	N	N	Y
KANSAS							
Brownback	Y	Y	N	Y	Y	Y	Y
Roberts	Y	Y	N	Y	Y	Y	Y
KENTUCKY							
McConnell	Y	Y	N	Y	Y	Y	Y
Ford	Y	N	N	Y	N	N	Y
LOUISIANA							
Breaux	Y	N	N	Y	N	N	Y
Landrieu	Y	Y	N	Y	N	N	Y
MAINE							
Collins	Y	Y	N	Y	Y	Y	Y
Snowe	Y	Y	Y	Y	Y	Y	Y
MARYLAND							
Mikulski	Y	?	N	N	N	N	Y
Sarbanes	Y	?	N	N	N	N	Y
MASSACHUSETTS							
Kennedy	Y	N	N	N	N	N	Y
Kerry	Y	N	N	Y	N	N	Y
MICHIGAN							
Abraham	Y	Y	Y	Y	Y	Y	Y
Levin	Y	N	Y	N	N	N	Y
MINNESOTA							
Grams	Y	Y	N	Y	Y	Y	Y
Wellstone	+	N	Y	N	N	N	N
MISSISSIPPI							
Cochran	Y	Y	N	Y	Y	Y	Y
Lott	Y	Y	N	Y	Y	Y	Y
MISSOURI							
Ashcroft	Y	Y	Y	Y	Y	Y	Y
Bond	Y	Y	N	Y	N	Y	Y
MONTANA							
Burns	Y	Y	N	Y	Y	Y	Y
Baucus	?	N	Y	Y	Y	N	Y
NEBRASKA							
Hagel	Y	Y	N	Y	Y	Y	Y
Kerrey	Y	Y	N	Y	N	N	Y
NEVADA							
Bryan	Y	Y	Y	N	N	N	Y
Reid	Y	Y	N	Y	N	N	Y

	183	184	185	186	187	188	189
NEW HAMPSHIRE							
Gregg	Y	Y	N	Y	Y	Y	Y
Smith	Y	Y	N	Y	Y	Y	Y
NEW JERSEY							
Lautenberg	Y	Y	Y	Y	Y	N	Y
Torricelli	Y	N	N	Y	N	N	Y
NEW MEXICO							
Domenici	Y	Y	N	Y	Y	Y	Y
Bingaman	Y	Y	N	N	N	N	Y
NEW YORK							
D'Amato	Y	N	N	Y	N	Y	Y
Moynihan	Y	Y	Y	Y	Y	N	Y
NORTH CAROLINA							
Faircloth	Y	Y	N	Y	Y	Y	Y
Helms	Y	N	N	Y	Y	Y	Y
NORTH DAKOTA							
Conrad	Y	N	N	N	N	N	Y
Dorgan	Y	Y	Y	N	N	N	Y
OHIO							
DeWine	Y	Y	N	Y	Y	Y	Y
Glenn	?	N	N	N	N	N	Y
OKLAHOMA							
Inhofe	?	Y	N	Y	Y	Y	Y
Nickles	Y	Y	N	Y	Y	Y	Y
OREGON							
Smith	Y	Y	N	Y	Y	Y	Y
Wyden	+	Y	Y	Y	N	N	Y
PENNSYLVANIA							
Santorum	Y	Y	N	Y	Y	Y	Y
Specter	?	?	Y	Y	N	Y	Y
RHODE ISLAND							
Chafee	Y	Y	Y	Y	Y	N	Y
Reed	Y	Y	Y	N	N	N	Y
SOUTH CAROLINA							
Thurmond	Y	Y	N	Y	Y	Y	Y
Hollings	Y	N	N	N	N	N	Y
SOUTH DAKOTA							
Daschle	Y	Y	Y	N	N	N	Y
Johnson	Y	Y	N	N	N	N	Y
TENNESSEE							
Frist	Y	Y	N	Y	Y	Y	Y
Thompson	Y	Y	N	Y	Y	Y	Y

	183	184	185	186	187	188	189
TEXAS							
Gramm	Y	Y	N	Y	Y	Y	Y
Hutchison	Y	?	N	?	?	?	+
UTAH							
Bennett	?	Y	N	Y	Y	Y	Y
Hatch	Y	Y	N	Y	Y	Y	Y
VERMONT							
Jeffords	Y	Y	Y	Y	Y	Y	Y
Leahy	Y	Y	Y	Y	N	N	Y
VIRGINIA							
Warner	Y	Y	N	Y	Y	Y	Y
Robb	Y	Y	N	Y	N	N	Y
WASHINGTON							
Gorton	Y	Y	N	Y	Y	Y	Y
Murray	Y	N	N	N	N	N	Y
WEST VIRGINIA							
Byrd	Y	Y	Y	N	N	N	Y
Rockefeller	?	Y	N	N	N	N	N
WISCONSIN							
Feingold	Y	N	Y	N	N	N	Y
Kohl	Y	Y	Y	Y	N	N	Y
WYOMING							
Enzi	Y	Y	N	Y	Y	Y	Y
Thomas	Y	Y	Y	Y	Y	Y	Y

Key

Y	Voted for (yea).
#	Paired for.
+	Announced for.
N	Voted against (nay).
X	Paired against.
−	Announced against.
P	Voted "present."
C	Voted "present" to avoid possible conflict of interest.
?	Did not vote or otherwise make a position known.

Democrats   *Republicans*

ND Northern Democrats   SD Southern Democrats

Southern states - Ala., Ark., Fla., Ga., Ky., La., Miss., N.C., Okla., S.C., Tenn., Texas, Va.

183. Roberts Nomination/Confirmation. Confirmation of President Clinton's nomination of Victoria A. Roberts of Michigan to be U.S. district judge for the Eastern District of Michigan. Confirmed 85-0: R 47-0; D 38-0 (ND 30-0, SD 8-0). June 26, 1998. A "yea" was a vote in support of the president's position.

184. S 648. Product Liability Overhaul/Cloture. Motion to invoke cloture (thus limiting debate) on the motion to proceed to the bill that would overhaul U.S. product liability laws. As approved by the Senate Commerce Committee, the bill would cap punitive awards against both small businesses and large companies. Motion agreed to 71-24: R 50-3; D 21-21 (ND 18-16, SD 3-5). July 7, 1998. Three-fifths of the total Senate (60) is required to invoke cloture. (Subsequently, the motion to proceed was agreed to by voice vote.)

185. S 2168. Fiscal 1999 VA-HUD Appropriations/International Space Station. Bumpers, D-Ark., amendment that would eliminate the bill's $2.3 billion appropriation for the international space station. The amendment would provide $850 million to terminate the program, $1 billion for veterans' health care programs and $450 million for low-income housing. Rejected 33-66: R 12-43; D 21-23 (ND 19-17, SD 2-6). July 7, 1998.

186. HR 2676. Internal Revenue Service Overhaul/Capital Gains Holding Period. Roth, R-Del., motion to table (kill) the Dorgan, D-N.D., appeal of the ruling of the chair rejecting the Dorgan point of order against certain provisions in the conference report. Dorgan raised a point of order that language reducing from 18 months to 12 months the time a taxpayer must hold an investment before being eligible for the 20 percent tax rate on capital gains violates Senate rules because the provisions were not in either the House-passed or Senate-passed versions of the legislation. Motion agreed to 76-22: R 53-0; D 23-22 (ND 19-18, SD 4-4). July 8, 1998.

187. HR 2676. Internal Revenue Service Overhaul/Surface Transportation Corrections. Chafee, R-R.I., motion to table (kill) the Murray, D-Wash., appeal of the ruling of the chair rejecting the Murray point of order against certain provisions in the conference report. Murray raised a point of order that provisions to make technical and other changes to the recently enacted six-year surface transportation reauthorization (PL 105-178) violate Senate rules because they were not in either the House-passed or Senate-passed versions of HR2676. Motion agreed to 50-48: R 48-5; D 2-43 (ND 2-35, SD 0-8). July 8, 1998.

188. S 648. Product Liability Overhaul/Cloture. Motion to invoke cloture (thus limiting debate) on the Lott, R-Miss., substitute amendment to the bill that would overhaul U.S. product liability laws. The amendment would cap punitive awards against small businesses, but not large companies, at $250,000. Manufacturers of tobacco products and silicone breast implants would be exempt from the liability protections. Motion rejected 51-47: R 51-2; D 0-45 (ND 0-37, SD 0-8). July 9, 1998. Three-fifths of the total Senate (60) is required to invoke cloture.

189. HR 2676. Internal Revenue Service Overhaul/Conference Report. Adoption of the conference report on the bill to restructure the management of the Internal Revenue Service by establishing an oversight board to oversee the agency's operations. Along with expanding certain taxpayer rights, the conference report also reduces from 18 months to 12 months the time a taxpayer must hold an investment before being eligible for the 20 percent tax rate on capital gains, contains numerous technical and other changes to the recently enacted six-year surface transportation reauthorization (PL 105-178) and changes the term "most favored nation" in trade law to "normal trade relation." The measure's $12.9 billion cost over 10 years is offset by several revenue-raising provisions, including language to permit wealthy elderly individuals to convert traditional IRAs into the new Roth IRA and pay taxes on the converted money. Adopted (thus cleared for the president) 96-2: R 53-0; D 43-2 (ND 35-2, SD 8-0). July 9, 1998. A "yea" was a vote in support of the president's position.

	190	191	192	193	194	195	196
ALABAMA							
Sessions	Y	N	N	N	N	Y	Y
Shelby	Y	N	N	N	N	Y	Y
ALASKA							
Murkowski	Y	N	N	N	N	Y	Y
Stevens	Y	Y	N	N	N	Y	Y
ARIZONA							
Kyl	?	?	?	?	?	?	+
McCain	Y	N	N	N	N	Y	?
ARKANSAS							
Hutchinson	Y	N	N	N	N	Y	Y
Bumpers	Y	Y	Y	Y	Y	Y	Y
CALIFORNIA							
Boxer	Y	Y	Y	Y	Y	Y	Y
Feinstein	Y	Y	Y	Y	Y	Y	Y
COLORADO							
Allard	Y	N	N	N	N	Y	Y
Campbell	Y	N	N	N	N	Y	Y
CONNECTICUT							
Dodd	Y	Y	Y	N	Y	Y	Y
Lieberman	Y	Y	Y	N	Y	Y	Y
DELAWARE							
Roth	Y	N	N	N	N	Y	Y
Biden	Y	Y	Y	Y	Y	Y	Y
FLORIDA							
Mack	Y	N	N	N	N	Y	Y
Graham	Y	Y	Y	N	Y	Y	Y
GEORGIA							
Coverdell	Y	N	N	N	N	Y	Y
Cleland	Y	Y	Y	N	Y	Y	Y
HAWAII							
Akaka	Y	Y	Y	N	Y	Y	Y
Inouye	Y	Y	Y	N	Y	Y	Y
IDAHO							
Craig	Y	N	N	N	N	Y	Y
Kempthorne	Y	N	N	N	N	Y	Y
ILLINOIS							
Durbin	Y	Y	Y	N	Y	Y	Y
Moseley-Braun	Y	Y	Y	Y	Y	Y	Y
INDIANA							
Coats	Y	N	N	N	N	Y	Y
Lugar	Y	N	N	Y	N	Y	Y
IOWA							
Grassley	Y	N	N	N	N	Y	Y
Harkin	Y	Y	Y	Y	Y	Y	Y
KANSAS							
Brownback	Y	N	N	N	N	Y	Y
Roberts	Y	N	N	N	N	Y	Y
KENTUCKY							
McConnell	Y	N	N	N	N	Y	Y
Ford	Y	Y	N	Y	Y	Y	Y
LOUISIANA							
Breaux	Y	Y	Y	N	Y	Y	Y
Landrieu	Y	Y	Y	N	Y	Y	Y
MAINE							
Collins	Y	N	N	N	N	Y	Y
Snowe	Y	Y	N	N	N	Y	Y
MARYLAND							
Mikulski	Y	Y	Y	N	Y	Y	Y
Sarbanes	Y	Y	Y	N	Y	Y	Y
MASSACHUSETTS							
Kennedy	Y	Y	Y	N	Y	Y	Y
Kerry	Y	Y	Y	N	Y	Y	Y
MICHIGAN							
Abraham	Y	N	N	N	N	Y	Y
Levin	Y	Y	Y	Y	Y	Y	Y
MINNESOTA							
Grams	Y	N	N	N	N	Y	Y
Wellstone	Y	Y	Y	Y	Y	Y	Y
MISSISSIPPI							
Cochran	Y	N	N	N	N	Y	Y
Lott	Y	N	N	N	N	Y	Y
MISSOURI							
Ashcroft	Y	N	N	N	N	Y	?
Bond	Y	N	N	N	N	Y	Y
MONTANA							
Burns	Y	N	N	N	N	Y	Y
Baucus	Y	Y	N	N	Y	Y	Y
NEBRASKA							
Hagel	Y	N	N	N	N	Y	Y
Kerrey	Y	Y	N	Y	N	Y	Y
NEVADA							
Bryan	Y	Y	Y	Y	N	Y	Y
Reid	Y	Y	Y	Y	Y	Y	Y
NEW HAMPSHIRE							
Gregg	Y	N	N	N	N	Y	Y
Smith	Y	N	N	N	N	Y	Y
NEW JERSEY							
Lautenberg	Y	Y	Y	N	Y	Y	Y
Torricelli	Y	Y	Y	Y	Y	Y	Y
NEW MEXICO							
Domenici	Y	N	N	Y	N	Y	?
Bingaman	Y	Y	Y	Y	Y	Y	?
NEW YORK							
D'Amato	Y	Y	N	N	N	Y	Y
Moynihan	Y	Y	?	?	?	?	Y
NORTH CAROLINA							
Faircloth	Y	N	N	N	N	Y	Y
Helms	Y	N	N	N	N	N	Y
NORTH DAKOTA							
Conrad	Y	Y	Y	N	Y	Y	Y
Dorgan	Y	Y	Y	N	Y	Y	Y
OHIO							
DeWine	Y	N	N	N	N	Y	Y
Glenn	Y	Y	Y	N	Y	Y	Y
OKLAHOMA							
Inhofe	Y	N	N	N	N	Y	Y
Nickles	Y	N	N	N	N	Y	?
OREGON							
Smith	Y	N	N	N	Y	Y	?
Wyden	Y	Y	Y	N	Y	Y	Y
PENNSYLVANIA							
Santorum	Y	N	N	N	N	Y	Y
Specter	Y	Y	N	N	N	Y	Y
RHODE ISLAND							
Chafee	Y	N	N	N	N	Y	Y
Reed	Y	Y	Y	N	Y	Y	Y
SOUTH CAROLINA							
Thurmond	Y	N	N	N	N	Y	Y
Hollings	Y	Y	Y	Y	Y	Y	Y
SOUTH DAKOTA							
Daschle	Y	Y	Y	N	Y	Y	Y
Johnson	Y	Y	Y	N	Y	Y	Y
TENNESSEE							
Frist	Y	N	N	N	N	Y	Y
Thompson	Y	N	N	N	N	Y	Y
TEXAS							
Gramm	Y	N	N	N	N	Y	Y
Hutchison	?	?	?	?	?	?	+
UTAH							
Bennett	Y	N	N	N	N	Y	Y
Hatch	Y	Y	N	N	N	Y	Y
VERMONT							
Jeffords	Y	Y	N	N	N	Y	Y
Leahy	Y	Y	N	N	Y	Y	Y
VIRGINIA							
Warner	Y	N	N	N	N	Y	Y
Robb	Y	Y	Y	Y	Y	Y	Y
WASHINGTON							
Gorton	Y	N	N	N	N	Y	Y
Murray	Y	Y	Y	N	Y	Y	Y
WEST VIRGINIA							
Byrd	Y	Y	Y	N	Y	Y	Y
Rockefeller	Y	Y	Y	N	Y	Y	Y
WISCONSIN							
Feingold	Y	Y	Y	N	Y	Y	Y
Kohl	Y	Y	Y	N	Y	Y	Y
WYOMING							
Enzi	Y	N	N	N	N	Y	Y
Thomas	Y	N	N	N	N	Y	Y

Key

Y   Voted for (yea).
Paired for.
+   Announced for.
N   Voted against (nay).
X   Paired against.
−   Announced against.
P   Voted "present."
C   Voted "present" to avoid possible conflict of interest.
?   Did not vote or otherwise make a position known.

Democrats   *Republicans*

ND Northern Democrats   SD Southern Democrats

Southern states - Ala., Ark., Fla., Ga., Ky., La., Miss., N.C., Okla., S.C., Tenn., Texas, Va.

190. Agriculture Export Sanctions/Passage. Passage of the bill to revise the Arms Export Control Act to allow the Agriculture Department to provide credits, credit guarantees and financial assistance for the purchase of food or other agricultural commodities to previously non-nuclear nations such as India and Pakistan that the president determines have detonated a nuclear device. Under current law, the president must prohibit the department from providing credits to such nations. Passed 98-0: R 53-0; D 45-0 (ND 37-0, SD 8-0). July 9, 1998.

191. S 1882. Higher Education Act Reauthorization/Welfare Education. Wellstone, D-Minn., amendment that would allow states to count up to two years of post-secondary or vocational education toward work requirements for welfare parents under the 1996 welfare law (PL 104-193). Current law allows states to count up to one year of vocational education toward the requirement. The amendment also would prohibit states from counting teenage welfare parents' education toward the 30 percent education limitation imposed by the 1996 law. Adopted 56-42: R 11-42; D 45-0 (ND 37-0, SD 8-0). July 9, 1998.

192. S 1882. Higher Education Act Reauthorization/Market-Based Lending. Kennedy, D-Mass., amendment that would establish a pilot program to auction off the right to make student loans, thus letting the market, rather than the government, determine interest rates. Rejected 39-58: R 0-53; D 39-5 (ND 32-4, SD 7-1). July 9, 1998.

193. S 1882. Higher Education Act Reauthorization/Teacher Education. Bingaman, D-N.M., amendment that would require colleges that receive federal aid to establish, within three years of the bill's enactment, a policy that all undergraduate students preparing to be secondary school teachers complete an academic major in the academic area in which they plan to teach. Rejected 23-74: R 3-50; D 20-24 (ND 16-20, SD 4-4). July 9, 1998.

194. S 1882. Higher Education Act Reauthorization/Student Loan Fees. Harkin, D-Iowa, amendment that would reduce the federal student loan origination and insurance fee from 4 percent of the principal amount of the loan to 3 percent of the principal amount. The amendment would pay for the reduction by eliminating a subsidy to student loan insurance agencies. Rejected 41-56: R 1-52; D 40-4 (ND 32-4, SD 8-0). July 9, 1998.

195. HR 6. Higher Education Act Reauthorization/Passage. Passage of the bill to authorize $108 billion during the next five years for almost all federal higher education programs. The measure contains language that would cut interest rates on federally guaranteed student loans while providing special subsidies to banks. Passed 96-1: R 52-1; D 44-0 (ND 36-0, SD 8-0). July 9, 1998. (Before passage, the Senate struck all after the enacting clause and inserted the text of S1882 as amended.)

196. S Con Res 107. U.S. Support for Taiwan/Adoption. Adoption of the concurrent resolution to reaffirm U.S. support for Taiwan as stipulated in the Taiwan Relations Act (PL 96-8). The resolution would reaffirm that any effort to determine the future of Taiwan by other than peaceful means would be of "grave concern to the United States" and would urge President Clinton to seek a public renunciation by China of any use of force against Taiwan. Adopted 92-0: R 48-0; D 44-0 (ND 36-0, SD 8-0). July 10, 1998.

Senate Votes 197, 198, 199, 200, 201, 202, 203

ND Northern Democrats   SD Southern Democrats

	197	198	199	200	201	202	203
ALABAMA							
Sessions	Y	N	Y	Y	N	Y	Y
Shelby	Y	N	Y	Y	Y	Y	Y
ALASKA							
Murkowski	Y	N	Y	Y	N	Y	Y
Stevens	Y	N	Y	Y	Y	Y	Y
ARIZONA							
Kyl	Y	N	Y	Y	N	Y	N
McCain	Y	N	Y	Y	Y	N	Y
ARKANSAS							
Hutchinson	Y	N	Y	Y	Y	Y	Y
Bumpers	N	Y	Y	N	N	N	N
CALIFORNIA							
Boxer	N	Y	Y	N	Y	N	Y
Feinstein	N	Y	Y	N	Y	N	Y
COLORADO							
Allard	Y	N	Y	Y	N	N	N
Campbell	Y	N	Y	Y	Y	Y	Y
CONNECTICUT							
Dodd	N	Y	Y	N	N	Y	N
Lieberman	N	Y	Y	N	Y	Y	N
DELAWARE							
Roth	N	N	Y	Y	N	N	N
Biden	?	?	Y	N	N	Y	N
FLORIDA							
Mack	Y	N	Y	Y	N	Y	Y
Graham	N	Y	Y	N	Y	Y	Y
GEORGIA							
Coverdell	Y	N	Y	Y	N	Y	Y
Cleland	N	Y	Y	N	N	Y	N
HAWAII							
Akaka	N	Y	Y	N	Y	Y	N
Inouye	N	Y	Y	N	Y	Y	N
IDAHO							
Craig	Y	N	Y	Y	N	Y	N
Kempthorne	Y	N	Y	Y	N	Y	N
ILLINOIS							
Durbin	N	Y	Y	N	N	Y	N
Moseley-Braun	N	Y	Y	N	N	N	N
INDIANA							
Coats	Y	N	Y	Y	N	Y	N
Lugar	Y	N	Y	Y	N	Y	N
IOWA							
Grassley	Y	N	Y	Y	Y	Y	N
Harkin	N	Y	Y	N	Y	Y	N
KANSAS							
Brownback	Y	N	Y	Y	N	N	N
Roberts	Y	N	Y	Y	N	N	N
KENTUCKY							
McConnell	Y	N	Y	Y	Y	Y	Y
Ford	Y	Y	Y	N	Y	Y	Y
LOUISIANA							
Breaux	?	?	Y	Y	N	Y	Y
Landrieu	Y	Y	Y	N	N	Y	Y
MAINE							
Collins	N	N	Y	Y	Y	Y	N
Snowe	N	N	Y	Y	Y	Y	Y
MARYLAND							
Mikulski	N	Y	Y	N	Y	N	N
Sarbanes	N	Y	Y	N	Y	Y	N
MASSACHUSETTS							
Kennedy	N	Y	Y	N	Y	N	N
Kerry	N	Y	Y	N	Y	N	N
MICHIGAN							
Abraham	Y	N	Y	Y	N	N	N
Levin	N	Y	Y	N	Y	Y	Y
MINNESOTA							
Grams	Y	N	Y	Y	N	N	N
Wellstone	N	Y	Y	N	N	N	N
MISSISSIPPI							
Cochran	Y	N	Y	Y	N	Y	Y
Lott	Y	N	Y	Y	Y	Y	Y
MISSOURI							
Ashcroft	Y	N	Y	Y	N	Y	N
Bond	Y	N	Y	Y	N	Y	N
MONTANA							
Burns	Y	N	Y	Y	N	Y	N
Baucus	N	Y	Y	N	Y	N	Y
NEBRASKA							
Hagel	Y	N	Y	Y	N	Y	N
Kerrey	N	Y	Y	N	N	Y	N
NEVADA							
Bryan	N	Y	Y	N	Y	N	Y
Reid	Y	Y	Y	N	Y	N	Y
NEW HAMPSHIRE							
Gregg	N	N	Y	Y	N	N	Y
Smith	Y	N	Y	Y	Y	N	Y
NEW JERSEY							
Lautenberg	N	Y	Y	N	Y	N	Y
Torricelli	?	Y	Y	N	Y	N	Y
NEW MEXICO							
Domenici	Y	N	Y	Y	N	Y	N
Bingaman	N	Y	Y	N	Y	N	?
NEW YORK							
D'Amato	?	N	Y	Y	N	Y	N
Moynihan	N	Y	Y	N	N	N	N
NORTH CAROLINA							
Faircloth	Y	N	Y	Y	N	Y	Y
Helms	Y	N	Y	Y	Y	Y	Y
NORTH DAKOTA							
Conrad	Y	Y	Y	N	N	Y	N
Dorgan	Y	Y	Y	N	N	Y	N
OHIO							
DeWine	Y	N	Y	Y	Y	Y	N
Glenn	?	?	?	?	?	?	?
OKLAHOMA							
Inhofe	Y	N	Y	Y	N	N	N
Nickles	Y	N	Y	Y	N	N	N
OREGON							
Smith	N	Y	Y	N	Y	N	N
Wyden	N	Y	Y	N	Y	N	Y
PENNSYLVANIA							
Santorum	Y	N	Y	Y	N	Y	N
Specter	Y	Y	Y	Y	Y	Y	Y
RHODE ISLAND							
Chafee	N	N	Y	Y	N	Y	Y
Reed	N	Y	Y	N	Y	N	Y
SOUTH CAROLINA							
Thurmond	Y	N	Y	Y	N	Y	Y
Hollings	N	Y	Y	N	Y	N	Y
SOUTH DAKOTA							
Daschle	N	Y	Y	N	Y	N	Y
Johnson	N	Y	Y	N	Y	N	Y
TENNESSEE							
Frist	?	N	Y	Y	N	Y	Y
Thompson	Y	N	Y	Y	Y	N	Y
TEXAS							
Gramm	Y	N	Y	Y	N	Y	Y
Hutchison	Y	N	Y	Y	N	Y	N
UTAH							
Bennett	Y	N	Y	Y	Y	Y	N
Hatch	Y	N	Y	Y	Y	Y	N
VERMONT							
Jeffords	N	N	Y	Y	N	Y	Y
Leahy	N	Y	Y	N	Y	Y	Y
VIRGINIA							
Warner	Y	N	Y	Y	N	Y	N
Robb	N	Y	Y	N	N	N	N
WASHINGTON							
Gorton	Y	N	Y	Y	N	Y	N
Murray	N	Y	Y	N	Y	N	N
WEST VIRGINIA							
Byrd	N	N	Y	N	N	Y	N
Rockefeller	N	Y	Y	N	N	N	N
WISCONSIN							
Feingold	N	Y	Y	N	Y	Y	N
Kohl	N	Y	Y	N	Y	Y	Y
WYOMING							
Enzi	Y	N	Y	Y	N	Y	N
Thomas	Y	N	Y	Y	N	Y	N

Southern states - Ala., Ark., Fla., Ga., Ky., La., Miss., N.C., Okla., S.C., Tenn., Texas, Va.

Key

Y	Voted for (yea).
#	Paired for.
+	Announced for.
N	Voted against (nay).
X	Paired against.
–	Announced against.
P	Voted "present."
C	Voted "present" to avoid possible conflict of interest.
?	Did not vote or otherwise make a position known.

Democrats   ***Republicans***

197. S 2271. Private Property Rights/Cloture. Motion to invoke cloture (thus limiting debate) on the motion to proceed to the bill that would provide private property owners with new rights to challenge decisions of local zoning and planning boards in federal court. Motion rejected 52-42: R 47-6; D 5-36 (ND 3-31, SD 2-5). July 13, 1998. Three-fifths of the total Senate (60) is required to invoke cloture. A "nay" was a vote in support of the president's position.

198. S 2159. Fiscal 1999 Agriculture Appropriations/Tobacco Restrictions. Daschle, D-S.D., motion to waive the Budget Act with respect to the Lott, R-Miss., point of order against the Daschle amendment. The amendment would require the tobacco industry to pay $516 billion over 25 years for anti-smoking, education and research programs, raise taxes on cigarettes by $1.10 per pack over five years, codify Food and Drug Administration authority to regulate nicotine and impose penalties on the tobacco industry if youth smoking does not decrease by 60 percent over 10 years. Motion rejected 43-55: R 1-54; D 42-1 (ND 34-1, SD 8-0). July 14, 1998. A three-fifths majority vote (60) of the total Senate is required to waive the Budget Act. (Subsequently, the chair upheld the point of order, and the amendment fell.)

199. S 2159. Fiscal 1999 Agriculture Appropriations/Farming Difficulties. Daschle, D-S.D., amendment to express the sense of the Senate that Congress and the president should take immediate action to respond to the economic hardships facing agricultural producers. Adopted 99-0: R 55-0; D 44-0 (ND 36-0, SD 8-0). July 14, 1998.

200. S 2159. Fiscal 1999 Agriculture Appropriations/Agriculture Marketing Loans. Cochran, R-Miss., motion to table (kill) the Daschle, D-S.D., amendment that would lift the cap on agriculture commodity marketing loans imposed by the 1996 farm law (PL 104-127) for fiscal 1999. The new loan rate

would be based on 85 percent of the average price of the product for the past five years, not including the highest and lowest years. The amendment also would extend the marketing loan term from nine months to 15 months for fiscal 1999. Motion agreed to 56-43: R 55-0; D 1-43 (ND 1-35, SD 0-8). July 15, 1998.

201. S 2159. Fiscal 1999 Agriculture Appropriations/Unilateral Economic Sanctions. Stevens, R-Alaska, motion to table (kill) the Lugar, R-Ind., amendment that would revise the process the president and Congress use to impose unilateral economic sanctions by establishing guidelines for future sanctions and setting up procedures for consideration and implementation of sanctions proposals. The amendment would prohibit the president from implementing any unilateral economic sanction without 45 days' notice, and it would express the sense of Congress that all future unilateral sanctions end within two years of their enactment unless extended by law. Motion agreed to 53-46: R 27-28; D 26-18 (ND 22-14, SD 4-4). July 15, 1998.

202. S 2159. Fiscal 1999 Agriculture Appropriations/Overseas Market Promotion. Cochran, R-Miss., motion to table (kill) the Bryan, D-Nev., amendment that would eliminate the bill's funding for subsidized overseas market promotion programs. Motion agreed to 70-29: R 43-12; D 27-17 (ND 22-14, SD 5-3). July 15, 1998.

203. S 2159. Fiscal 1999 Agriculture Appropriations/Food and Medicine Sanctions. Stevens, R-Alaska, motion to table (kill) the Dodd, D-Conn., amendment that would prohibit the president from restricting exports of food, agricultural products, medicines or medicinal equipment as part of any current or future unilateral economic sanction. Motion rejected 38-60: R 26-29; D 12-31 (ND 7-28, SD 5-3). July 15, 1998. (Subsequently, the Dodd amendment was amended by a similar Roberts amendment.)

	204	205	206	207	208	209	210
ALABAMA							
Sessions	N	Y	N	N	N	Y	N
Shelby	N	Y	Y	Y	N	Y	N
ALASKA							
Murkowski	N	Y	Y	N	N	Y	N
Stevens	N	N	Y	Y	N	Y	N
ARIZONA							
Kyl	N	Y	N	N	N	N	N
McCain	N	Y	Y	Y	Y	Y	?
ARKANSAS							
Hutchinson	N	Y	N	N	N	Y	N
Bumpers	N	N	Y	Y	Y	Y	Y
CALIFORNIA							
Boxer	N	N	Y	Y	Y	Y	Y
Feinstein	N	N	Y	Y	Y	Y	Y
COLORADO							
Allard	N	Y	Y	N	N	Y	N
Campbell	N	Y	N	Y	N	Y	N
CONNECTICUT							
Dodd	Y	N	Y	Y	Y	Y	?
Lieberman	N	N	Y	Y	Y	Y	Y
DELAWARE							
Roth	N	Y	N	N	N	Y	N
Biden	N	N	Y	Y	Y	Y	Y
FLORIDA							
Mack	N	Y	N	Y	N	Y	N
Graham	N	Y	N	Y	N	Y	Y
GEORGIA							
Coverdell	N	Y	Y	Y	N	Y	Y
Cleland	Y	N	Y	Y	Y	Y	Y
HAWAII							
Akaka	Y	N	Y	Y	Y	Y	Y
Inouye	Y	N	Y	Y	Y	Y	?
IDAHO							
Craig	N	Y	Y	N	N	Y	N
Kempthorne	N	Y	Y	N	N	Y	N
ILLINOIS							
Durbin	Y	N	Y	Y	Y	Y	Y
Moseley-Braun	Y	N	Y	Y	Y	Y	Y
INDIANA							
Coats	N	Y	N	N	N	Y	N
Lugar	Y	Y	Y	Y	N	Y	N
IOWA							
Grassley	N	N	Y	Y	N	Y	N
Harkin	Y	N	Y	Y	Y	Y	Y
KANSAS							
Brownback	Y	Y	Y	Y	N	Y	N
Roberts	Y	Y	Y	N	N	Y	?
KENTUCKY							
McConnell	N	Y	Y	N	N	Y	N
Ford	N	N	Y	N	N	Y	Y
LOUISIANA							
Breaux	N	Y	Y	N	N	Y	Y
Landrieu	N	N	Y	Y	Y	Y	Y
MAINE							
Collins	N	Y	Y	N	Y	Y	Y
Snowe	N	Y	N	Y	Y	Y	Y
MARYLAND							
Mikulski	Y	N	N	Y	Y	Y	Y
Sarbanes	Y	N	N	Y	Y	Y	Y
MASSACHUSETTS							
Kennedy	Y	N	N	Y	Y	Y	Y
Kerry	N	N	Y	Y	Y	Y	Y
MICHIGAN							
Abraham	N	Y	Y	N	Y	Y	N
Levin	N	N	N	Y	Y	Y	Y
MINNESOTA							
Grams	Y	N	Y	Y	N	Y	N
Wellstone	Y	N	N	Y	Y	Y	Y
MISSISSIPPI							
Cochran	N	Y	Y	N	N	Y	N
Lott	N	Y	N	N	N	Y	N
MISSOURI							
Ashcroft	N	Y	N	N	N	Y	N
Bond	N	Y	Y	Y	Y	Y	Y
MONTANA							
Burns	N	N	Y	N	N	Y	N
Baucus	Y	N	Y	Y	Y	Y	N
NEBRASKA							
Hagel	Y	N	Y	Y	N	Y	N
Kerrey	Y	N	Y	Y	Y	Y	Y
NEVADA							
Bryan	N	N	Y	Y	Y	Y	Y
Reid	N	N	N	Y	Y	Y	Y
NEW HAMPSHIRE							
Gregg	N	Y	Y	N	N	Y	N
Smith	N	Y	N	N	N	Y	N
NEW JERSEY							
Lautenberg	N	N	N	Y	Y	Y	Y
Torricelli	N	N	N	Y	Y	Y	Y
NEW MEXICO							
Domenici	N	Y	Y	N	N	Y	N
Bingaman	?	?	Y	Y	Y	Y	Y
NEW YORK							
D'Amato	N	Y	Y	N	N	Y	N
Moynihan	Y	N	Y	Y	N	Y	Y
NORTH CAROLINA							
Faircloth	N	Y	N	N	N	Y	N
Helms	N	Y	N	N	N	Y	–
NORTH DAKOTA							
Conrad	Y	N	N	N	Y	Y	Y
Dorgan	Y	N	N	Y	Y	Y	Y
OHIO							
DeWine	N	Y	Y	Y	Y	Y	N
Glenn	?	?	?	?	?	?	?
OKLAHOMA							
Inhofe	N	Y	N	N	N	Y	N
Nickles	N	Y	N	N	N	Y	N
OREGON							
Smith	N	Y	Y	N	N	Y	N
Wyden	N	N	Y	Y	Y	Y	Y
PENNSYLVANIA							
Santorum	N	N	N	Y	N	N	N
Specter	N	Y	N	Y	Y	Y	Y
RHODE ISLAND							
Chafee	N	Y	Y	N	N	Y	N
Reed	Y	N	N	Y	Y	Y	Y
SOUTH CAROLINA							
Thurmond	N	Y	Y	N	N	Y	N
Hollings	N	N	N	N	N	Y	Y
SOUTH DAKOTA							
Daschle	Y	N	Y	Y	Y	Y	Y
Johnson	Y	N	Y	Y	Y	Y	Y
TENNESSEE							
Frist	N	Y	Y	N	Y	Y	N
Thompson	N	Y	N	N	N	Y	N
TEXAS							
Gramm	N	Y	Y	N	Y	N	N
Hutchison	N	Y	Y	Y	N	Y	Y
UTAH							
Bennett	N	Y	Y	N	N	Y	Y
Hatch	N	Y	Y	N	N	Y	N
VERMONT							
Jeffords	?	Y	Y	Y	N	Y	Y
Leahy	Y	N	Y	Y	Y	Y	Y
VIRGINIA							
Warner	Y	Y	Y	Y	N	Y	Y
Robb	N	N	Y	Y	Y	Y	Y
WASHINGTON							
Gorton	N	Y	Y	N	Y	N	N
Murray	N	N	Y	Y	Y	Y	Y
WEST VIRGINIA							
Byrd	Y	N	N	Y	Y	Y	Y
Rockefeller	Y	N	Y	Y	Y	Y	Y
WISCONSIN							
Feingold	N	N	Y	Y	Y	Y	Y
Kohl	N	N	Y	Y	Y	Y	Y
WYOMING							
Enzi	Y	N	Y	N	N	Y	N
Thomas	Y	N	Y	N	N	Y	N

ND Northern Democrats   SD Southern Democrats

Southern states - Ala., Ark., Fla., Ga., Ky., La., Miss., N.C., Okla., S.C., Tenn., Texas, Va.

Key

Y   Voted for (yea).
Paired for.
+   Announced for.
N   Voted against (nay).
X   Paired against.
–   Announced against.
P   Voted "present."
C   Voted "present" to avoid possible conflict of interest.
?   Did not vote or otherwise make a position known.

Democrats   *Republicans*

204. S 2159. Fiscal 1999 Agriculture Appropriations/Sanctions on Terrorist Nations. Dodd, D-Conn., motion to table (kill) the Torricelli, D-N.J., amendment to the Dodd amendment. The Torricelli amendment would allow the president to restrict exports of food and medicine to nations that have repeatedly provided support for acts of international terrorism. Motion rejected 30-67: R 8-46; D 22-21 (ND 21-14, SD 1-7). July 15, 1998. (Subsequently, the Torricelli amendment and the underlying Dodd amendment as amended were adopted by voice vote.)

205. S 2159. Fiscal 1999 Agriculture Appropriations/Livestock Price Reporting. Cochran, R-Miss., motion to table (kill) the Kerrey, D-Neb., amendment that would authorize a three-year pilot program to study the efficiency of requiring mandatory price reporting by livestock producers. Motion rejected 49-49: R 47-8; D 2-41 (ND 0-35, SD 2-6). July 15, 1998. (Subsequently, the Kerrey amendment was adopted by voice vote.)

206. S 2159. Fiscal 1999 Agriculture Appropriations/Relief for Farmers. Grassley, R-Iowa, amendment to express the sense of the Senate that Congress and the president should take actions to alleviate the economic effects of low commodity prices, including: reauthorizing fast-track trading authority for the president; fully funding the International Monetary Fund; overhauling the way economic sanctions are implemented; extending most-favored-nation trading status for China; revising capital gains and estate tax rates; reducing regulations on farmers; and allowing self-employed individuals to fully deduct the cost of their health insurance. Adopted 71-28: R 42-13; D 29-15 (ND 24-12, SD 5-3). July 16, 1998.

207. S 2159. Fiscal 1999 Agriculture Appropriations/Food Safety. Harkin, D-Iowa, amendment that would provide an additional $66 million for President Clinton's food safety initiative, which would increase inspections, expand research and increase consumer education programs. The amendment would offset the increased spending by reducing tobacco subsidies, Agriculture Department computer funding and Agricultural Research Service building construction funds. Adopted 65-34: R 25-30; D 40-4 (ND 35-1, SD 5-3). July 16, 1998.

208. S 2159. Fiscal 1999 Agriculture Appropriations/Teen Smoking. Harkin, D-Iowa, motion to waive the Budget Act with respect to the Domenici, R-N.M., point of order against the Harkin amendment. The Harkin amendment would increase funding for Food and Drug Administration teen anti-smoking programs by $100 million. The amendment would attempt to offset the increase in funding by imposing a fee on tobacco companies based on their share of the U.S. tobacco market. Motion rejected 49-50: R 9-46; D 40-4 (ND 35-1, SD 5-3). July 16, 1998. A three-fifths majority vote (60) of the total Senate is required to waive the Budget Act. (Subsequently, the chair upheld the point of order, and the amendment fell.)

209. HR 4101. Fiscal 1999 Agriculture Appropriations/Passage. Passage of the bill to provide $57.3 billion in new budget authority for the Agriculture Department (USDA), the Food and Drug Administration (FDA) and rural development programs in fiscal 1999. The bill provides $7.5 billion more than provided in fiscal 1998 and $500 million less than requested by President Clinton. Passed 97-2: R 53-2; D 44-0 (ND 36-0, SD 8-0). July 16, 1998. (Before passage, the Senate struck all after the enacting clause and inserted the text of S2159 as amended.)

210. S 2168. Fiscal 1999 VA-HUD Appropriations/Veterans' Tobacco-Related Illnesses. Wellstone, D-Minn., motion to waive the Budget Act with respect to the Domenici, R-N.M., point of order against the Wellstone amendment. The Wellstone amendment would repeal a provision in the six-year surface transportation reauthorization (PL 105-178) that prohibits compensation payments to veterans for tobacco-related illnesses. Motion rejected 54-40: R 13-39; D 41-1 (ND 33-1, SD 8-0). July 17, 1998. A three-fifths majority vote (60) of the total Senate is required to waive the Budget Act. (Subsequently, the chair upheld the point of order, and the amendment fell.)

	211	212	213	214	215	216	217
ALABAMA							
Sessions	Y	N	N	Y	Y	Y	Y
Shelby	Y	N	Y	Y	Y	Y	Y
ALASKA							
Murkowski	Y	N	Y	Y	Y	Y	Y
Stevens	Y	Y	Y	Y	Y	Y	Y
ARIZONA							
Kyl	N	N	N	Y	Y	Y	Y
McCain	?	?	N	Y	Y	Y	Y
ARKANSAS							
Hutchinson	Y	N	N	Y	Y	Y	Y
Bumpers	Y	Y	Y	Y	N	N	N
CALIFORNIA							
Boxer	Y	Y	Y	N	N	N	N
Feinstein	Y	Y	Y	Y	N	N	N
COLORADO							
Allard	N	Y	N	N	Y	Y	Y
Campbell	Y	Y	N	Y	Y	Y	Y
CONNECTICUT							
Dodd	Y	Y	Y	N	N	N	N
Lieberman	Y	Y	Y	Y	N	N	N
DELAWARE							
Roth	Y	N	Y	Y	Y	Y	Y
Biden	Y	Y	Y	Y	N	N	N
FLORIDA							
Mack	N	N	Y	Y	Y	Y	Y
Graham	Y	Y	Y	Y	Y	N	N
GEORGIA							
Coverdell	Y	N	Y	Y	Y	Y	Y
Cleland	Y	Y	Y	Y	N	N	N
HAWAII							
Akaka	Y	Y	Y	Y	N	N	N
Inouye	Y	Y	Y	Y	N	N	N
IDAHO							
Craig	N	N	Y	Y	Y	Y	Y
Kempthorne	N	N	N	Y	Y	Y	Y
ILLINOIS							
Durbin	Y	Y	Y	Y	N	N	N
Moseley-Braun	Y	Y	Y	Y	N	N	N
INDIANA							
Coats	Y	Y	N	Y	Y	Y	Y
Lugar	N	N	Y	Y	Y	Y	Y
IOWA							
Grassley	Y	Y	Y	Y	Y	Y	Y
Harkin	Y	Y	Y	Y	N	N	N
KANSAS							
Brownback	N	N	N	Y	Y	Y	Y
Roberts	?	?	Y	Y	Y	Y	Y
KENTUCKY							
McConnell	N	N	Y	Y	Y	Y	Y
Ford	Y	Y	Y	Y	Y	N	N
LOUISIANA							
Breaux	Y	Y	Y	Y	Y	Y	Y
Landrieu	Y	Y	Y	Y	N	N	N
MAINE							
Collins	Y	Y	Y	Y	Y	Y	Y
Snowe	Y	Y	Y	Y	Y	Y	Y
MARYLAND							
Mikulski	Y	Y	Y	Y	Y	N	N
Sarbanes	Y	Y	Y	Y	N	N	N
MASSACHUSETTS							
Kennedy	Y	Y	Y	Y	N	N	N
Kerry	Y	Y	Y	Y	N	N	N
MICHIGAN							
Abraham	Y	N	Y	Y	Y	Y	Y
Levin	Y	Y	Y	Y	N	N	N
MINNESOTA							
Grams	N	N	Y	Y	Y	Y	Y
Wellstone	Y	Y	N	Y	N	N	N
MISSISSIPPI							
Cochran	N	N	Y	Y	Y	Y	Y
Lott	N	N	Y	Y	Y	Y	Y
MISSOURI							
Ashcroft	N	N	N	N	Y	Y	Y
Bond	Y	Y	Y	Y	Y	Y	Y
MONTANA							
Burns	Y	N	Y	Y	Y	Y	Y
Baucus	Y	Y	Y	N	Y	Y	Y
NEBRASKA							
Hagel	N	N	Y	Y	Y	Y	Y
Kerrey	Y	Y	Y	Y	Y	N	Y
NEVADA							
Bryan	Y	Y	Y	Y	Y	Y	N
Reid	Y	?	Y	Y	Y	Y	Y
NEW HAMPSHIRE							
Gregg	N	Y	Y	Y	Y	Y	Y
Smith	N	N	N	N	Y	Y	Y
NEW JERSEY							
Lautenberg	Y	Y	Y	Y	N	N	N
Torricelli	Y	Y	Y	Y	N	N	N
NEW MEXICO							
Domenici	Y	Y	Y	Y	Y	Y	Y
Bingaman	Y	Y	Y	Y	Y	N	Y
NEW YORK							
D'Amato	Y	Y	Y	Y	Y	Y	Y
Moynihan	Y	Y	Y	Y	N	N	N
NORTH CAROLINA							
Faircloth	N	N	N	N	Y	Y	Y
Helms	?	?	N	Y	Y	Y	Y
NORTH DAKOTA							
Conrad	Y	Y	Y	Y	Y	Y	Y
Dorgan	Y	Y	Y	Y	Y	Y	Y
OHIO							
DeWine	N	N	N	Y	Y	Y	N
Glenn	?	?	Y	Y	N	N	N
OKLAHOMA							
Inhofe	N	N	?	?	Y	Y	Y
Nickles	N	N	Y	Y	Y	Y	Y
OREGON							
Smith	Y	N	Y	Y	Y	Y	Y
Wyden	Y	Y	Y	Y	N	N	N
PENNSYLVANIA							
Santorum	Y	Y	Y	Y	Y	Y	Y
Specter	Y	Y	Y	Y	Y	Y	Y
RHODE ISLAND							
Chafee	Y	Y	Y	Y	N	N	Y
Reed	Y	Y	Y	Y	N	N	N
SOUTH CAROLINA							
Thurmond	N	N	Y	Y	Y	Y	Y
Hollings	Y	Y	Y	Y	Y	Y	Y
SOUTH DAKOTA							
Daschle	Y	Y	Y	Y	Y	N	Y
Johnson	Y	Y	Y	Y	Y	N	Y
TENNESSEE							
Frist	Y	N	Y	Y	Y	Y	Y
Thompson	N	N	N	Y	Y	Y	Y
TEXAS							
Gramm	N	N	Y	N	Y	Y	Y
Hutchison	Y	N	Y	Y	Y	Y	Y
UTAH							
Bennett	Y	N	Y	Y	Y	Y	Y
Hatch	Y	N	Y	Y	Y	Y	Y
VERMONT							
Jeffords	Y	Y	Y	Y	Y	Y	Y
Leahy	Y	Y	Y	Y	Y	Y	Y
VIRGINIA							
Warner	N	Y	Y	Y	Y	Y	Y
Robb	Y	Y	Y	Y	N	Y	N
WASHINGTON							
Gorton	Y	N	Y	Y	Y	Y	Y
Murray	Y	Y	Y	Y	Y	N	Y
WEST VIRGINIA							
Byrd	Y	N	Y	Y	N	N	N
Rockefeller	Y	Y	Y	Y	N	N	Y
WISCONSIN							
Feingold	N	Y	Y	Y	N	Y	Y
Kohl	N	Y	Y	Y	N	N	N
WYOMING							
Enzi	N	N	Y	Y	Y	Y	Y
Thomas	N	N	Y	Y	Y	Y	Y

ND Northern Democrats   SD Southern Democrats

Southern states - Ala., Ark., Fla., Ga., Ky., La., Miss., N.C., Okla., S.C., Tenn., Texas, Va.

Key

Y	Voted for (yea).
#	Paired for.
+	Announced for.
N	Voted against (nay).
X	Paired against.
–	Announced against.
P	Voted "present."
C	Voted "present" to avoid possible conflict of interest.
?	Did not vote or otherwise make a position known.

Democrats   *Republicans*

---

211. S 2168. Fiscal 1999 VA-HUD Appropriations/Mortgage Lending. Bond, R-Mo., motion to table (kill) the Nickles, R-Okla., amendment that would strike language increasing from $170,362 to $197,620 the maximum value of home mortgages that the Federal Housing Administration (FHA) could insure in high-cost areas. The amendment also would increase Ginnie Mae National Mortgage Association fees from six basis points to 12. Motion agreed to 69-27: R 27-25; D 42-2 (ND 34-2, SD 8-0). July 17, 1998.

212. S 2168. Fiscal 1999 VA-HUD Appropriations/NASA Funding. Bond, R-Mo., motion to table (kill) the Sessions, R-Ala., amendment that would increase funding for NASA programs by $33 million, offset by reductions in the AmeriCorps national service program. The amendment would provide $20 million for aeronautics, space transportation and technology and $13 million for science and technology. Motion agreed to 58-37: R 16-36; D 42-1 (ND 34-1, SD 8-0). July 17, 1998. (Subsequently, the underlying $93.3 billion bill as amended was passed by voice vote.)

213. HR 4112. Fiscal 1999 Legislative Branch Appropriations/Cloture. Motion to invoke cloture (thus limiting debate) on the bill to provide $1.6 billion in new budget authority for Senate and other legislative branch operations in fiscal 1999. The bill, which excludes funds for internal House operations, would provide $51.5 million more than provided in fiscal 1998. Motion agreed to 83-16: R 39-15; D 44-1 (ND 36-1, SD 8-0). July 21, 1998. Three-fifths of the total Senate (60) is required to invoke cloture.

214. HR 4112. Fiscal 1999 Legislative Branch Appropriations/Passage. Passage of the bill to provide $1.6 billion in new budget authority for Senate and other legislative branch operations in fiscal 1999. The bill, which excludes funds for internal House operations, would provide $51.5

million more than provided in fiscal 1998 and $74.6 million less than requested by President Clinton. Passed 90-9: R 47-7; D 43-2 (ND 35-2, SD 8-0). July 21, 1998.

215. S 2260. Fiscal 1999 Commerce, Justice, State Appropriations/Gun Lock Availibility. Craig, R-Idaho, amendment that would require gun dealers to make safety devices, such as so-called trigger locks, "available" as a condition for receiving and keeping their licenses. The amendment also would establish a grant program to educate and train the public on the safe ownership, storage and use of firearms. Adopted 72-28: R 54-1; D 18-27 (ND 14-23, SD 4-4). July 21, 1998.

216. S 2260. Fiscal 1999 Commerce, Justice, State Appropriations/Gun Lock Requirement. Craig, R-Idaho, motion to table (kill) the Boxer, D-Calif., amendment that would require all gun dealers to sell so-called trigger locks with each handgun sold. The amendment would establish civil penalties for dealers that do not comply. Motion agreed to 61-39: R 52-3; D 9-36 (ND 6-31, SD 3-5). July 21, 1998.

217. S 2260. Fiscal 1999 Commerce, Justice, State Appropriations/Firearm Purchase Background Checks. Smith, R-N.H., amendment to the Smith amendment. Both amendments would prohibit the use of any taxes or fees to pay for the national instant background check required for new gun purchases under the Brady law (PL 103-159) and would require law enforcement agencies to immediately destroy any information on individuals allowed to purchase firearms after the check. Adopted 69-31: R 55-0; D 14-31 (ND 12-25, SD 2-6). July 21, 1998. (Subsequently, the underlying Smith amendment as amended was adopted by voice vote.)

	218	219	220	221	222	223	224
ALABAMA							
Sessions	N	N	N	Y	N	Y	Y
Shelby	N	N	N	Y	N	Y	Y
ALASKA							
Murkowski	N	N	N	Y	N	Y	Y
Stevens	N	N	Y	N	Y	N	N
ARIZONA							
Kyl	N	N	N	Y	N	Y	Y
McCain	N	N	N	Y	N	Y	Y
ARKANSAS							
Hutchinson	N	N	N	Y	N	Y	Y
Bumpers	Y	Y	Y	N	Y	N	N
CALIFORNIA							
Boxer	Y	Y	Y	N	Y	Y	N
Feinstein	N	Y	Y	N	Y	N	N
COLORADO							
Allard	N	Y	N	Y	N	Y	Y
Campbell	N	N	N	Y	N	Y	Y
CONNECTICUT							
Dodd	Y	Y	Y	N	Y	N	N
Lieberman	N	Y	Y	N	Y	N	N
DELAWARE							
Roth	N	N	N	Y	N	Y	Y
Biden	N	Y	Y	N	Y	N	N
FLORIDA							
Mack	Y	Y	N	Y	N	Y	Y
Graham	Y	Y	Y	N	Y	N	N
GEORGIA							
Coverdell	N	N	N	Y	N	Y	Y
Cleland	Y	Y	Y	N	Y	N	N
HAWAII							
Akaka	Y	Y	Y	N	Y	N	N
Inouye	Y	Y	Y	N	Y	N	N
IDAHO							
Craig	N	N	N	Y	N	Y	Y
Kempthorne	N	N	N	Y	N	Y	Y
ILLINOIS							
Durbin	Y	Y	Y	N	Y	N	N
Moseley-Braun	Y	Y	Y	N	Y	N	Y
INDIANA							
Coats	N	N	N	Y	N	Y	Y
Lugar	N	Y	N	Y	N	Y	Y

	218	219	220	221	222	223	224
IOWA							
Grassley	N	Y	Y	Y	N	Y	Y
Harkin	Y	Y	Y	N	Y	N	N
KANSAS							
Brownback	N	Y	N	Y	N	Y	Y
Roberts	N	N	N	Y	N	Y	Y
KENTUCKY							
McConnell	N	N	N	Y	N	N	Y
Ford	Y	Y	Y	N	Y	N	Y
LOUISIANA							
Breaux	Y	Y	Y	N	Y	N	Y
Landrieu	Y	Y	Y	N	Y	N	N
MAINE							
Collins	N	N	N	Y	N	Y	Y
Snowe	N	Y	Y	Y	Y	Y	Y
MARYLAND							
Mikulski	Y	Y	Y	N	Y	N	N
Sarbanes	Y	Y	Y	N	Y	N	N
MASSACHUSETTS							
Kennedy	Y	Y	Y	N	Y	N	N
Kerry	Y	Y	Y	N	Y	N	N
MICHIGAN							
Abraham	N	N	N	Y	N	Y	Y
Levin	Y	Y	Y	N	Y	N	N
MINNESOTA							
Grams	N	Y	N	Y	N	Y	Y
Wellstone	Y	Y	Y	N	Y	N	N
MISSISSIPPI							
Cochran	N	N	N	Y	N	Y	Y
Lott	N	N	N	Y	N	N	Y
MISSOURI							
Ashcroft	N	N	N	Y	N	Y	Y
Bond	N	N	N	Y	N	Y	Y
MONTANA							
Burns	N	N	N	Y	N	Y	Y
Baucus	Y	Y	Y	N	Y	N	Y
NEBRASKA							
Hagel	N	N	N	Y	N	Y	Y
Kerrey	Y	Y	Y	N	Y	N	Y
NEVADA							
Bryan	Y	Y	Y	N	Y	Y	Y
Reid	N	Y	Y	N	Y	Y	Y

	218	219	220	221	222	223	224
NEW HAMPSHIRE							
Gregg	N	N	Y	N	Y	N	N
Smith	N	N	N	Y	N	Y	Y
NEW JERSEY							
Lautenberg	Y	Y	Y	N	Y	N	N
Torricelli	Y	Y	Y	N	Y	N	N
NEW MEXICO							
Domenici	N	N	N	Y	N	N	Y
Bingaman	Y	Y	Y	N	Y	Y	Y
NEW YORK							
D'Amato	N	N	Y	N	Y	N	N
Moynihan	N	Y	Y	N	Y	N	N
NORTH CAROLINA							
Faircloth	N	N	N	Y	N	N	Y
Helms	N	N	N	Y	N	N	Y
NORTH DAKOTA							
Conrad	Y	Y	Y	N	Y	Y	Y
Dorgan	Y	Y	Y	N	Y	Y	Y
OHIO							
DeWine	N	Y	N	Y	N	Y	N
Glenn	Y	Y	Y	N	Y	N	N
OKLAHOMA							
Inhofe	N	Y	N	Y	N	N	Y
Nickles	N	Y	N	Y	N	N	Y
OREGON							
Smith	N	N	N	Y	N	Y	Y
Wyden	Y	Y	Y	N	Y	N	N
PENNSYLVANIA							
Santorum	N	N	N	Y	N	N	Y
Specter	Y	N	Y	Y	N	Y	Y
RHODE ISLAND							
Chafee	N	N	Y	Y	N	N	N
Reed	Y	Y	Y	N	Y	N	N
SOUTH CAROLINA							
Thurmond	N	N	N	Y	N	N	Y
Hollings	Y	Y	Y	N	Y	N	Y
SOUTH DAKOTA							
Daschle	Y	Y	Y	N	Y	N	Y
Johnson	Y	Y	Y	N	Y	N	Y
TENNESSEE							
Frist	N	N	N	Y	N	Y	Y
Thompson	N	N	N	Y	N	Y	Y

ND Northern Democrats   SD Southern Democrats

Key

Y	Voted for (yea).
#	Paired for.
+	Announced for.
N	Voted against (nay).
X	Paired against.
–	Announced against.
P	Voted "present."
C	Voted "present" to avoid possible conflict of interest.
?	Did not vote or otherwise make a position known.

Democrats   **Republicans**

	218	219	220	221	222	223	224
TEXAS							
Gramm	N	N	N	Y	N	Y	Y
Hutchison	Y	N	Y	N	Y	N	N
UTAH							
Bennett	N	N	Y	N	Y	N	N
Hatch	N	Y	N	Y	N	N	Y
VERMONT							
Jeffords	N	N	Y	N	Y	N	Y
Leahy	Y	Y	Y	N	Y	N	Y
VIRGINIA							
Warner	N	N	Y	N	Y	N	Y
Robb	Y	Y	Y	N	Y	N	N
WASHINGTON							
Gorton	N	N	N	Y	N	Y	Y
Murray	Y	N	Y	N	Y	N	Y
WEST VIRGINIA							
Byrd	N	Y	Y	N	Y	N	N
Rockefeller	Y	Y	Y	N	Y	N	Y
WISCONSIN							
Feingold	Y	Y	Y	N	Y	Y	Y
Kohl	N	Y	N	Y	Y	Y	N
WYOMING							
Enzi	N	N	N	Y	N	Y	Y
Thomas	N	N	N	Y	N	Y	Y

Southern states - Ala., Ark., Fla., Ga., Ky., La., Miss., N.C., Okla., S.C., Tenn., Texas, Va.

218. S 2260. Fiscal 1999 Commerce, Justice, State Appropriations/Grand Jury Witnesses. Bumpers, D-Ark., amendment that would allow witnesses testifying before a federal grand jury to have their attorney present in the grand jury room during questioning. Rejected 41-59: R 3-52; D 38-7 (ND 30-7, SD 8-0). July 22, 1998.

219. S 2260. Fiscal 1999 Commerce, Justice, State Appropriations/Law Enforcement and Rescue Flights. Graham, D-Fla., amendment that would allow local public agencies to recover costs incurred by operating aircraft to assist other jurisdictions in law enforcement operations, search and rescue missions or when responding to an "imminent threat" to property or natural resources. Adopted 56-44: R 12-43; D 44-1 (ND 36-1, SD 8-0). July 22, 1998.

220. S 2260. Fiscal 1999 Commerce, Justice, State Appropriations/Juvenile Justice. Gregg, R-N.H., motion to table (kill) the Sessions, R-Ala., amendment that would increase funding for juvenile accountability incentive block grants, for purposes such as hiring additional juvenile judges and prosecutors, from $100 million to $150 million. To pay for the increase, the amendment would decrease funding for juvenile delinquency prevention programs from $95 million to $45 million. Motion agreed to 64-36: R 19-36; D 45-0 (ND 37-0, SD 8-0). July 22, 1998.

221. S 2260. Fiscal 1999 Commerce, Justice, State Appropriations/Social Security and Tax Cuts. Gregg, R-N.H., amendment that would express the sense of the Senate that Congress and the president should: "save Social Security first" and then return any remaining budgetary surpluses to U.S. taxpayers; work together to balance the budget without counting Social Security trust fund surpluses; and enact bipartisan legislation to ensure the financial security of the Social Security system. Adopted 55-45: R 55-0; D 0-45 (ND 0-37, SD 0-8). July 22, 1998.

222. S 2260. Fiscal 1999 Commerce, Justice, State Appropriations/Social Security. Hollings, D-S.C., amendment that would express the sense of the Senate that Congress and the president should: "save Social Security first" by reserving any fiscal 1999 budget surplus for that purpose; work together to balance the budget without counting Social Security trust fund surpluses; and enact bipartisan legislation to ensure the financial security of the Social Security system. Rejected 47-53: R 2-53; D 45-0 (ND 37-0, SD 8-0). July 22, 1998.

223. S 2260. Fiscal 1999 Commerce, Justice, State Appropriations/Patent and Trademark Office Relocation. McCain, R-Ariz., amendment that would prohibit the Patent and Trademark Office from relocating its offices until 90 days after the General Services Administration issues a report on the benefits and costs of relocating. Rejected 47-53: R 36-19; D 11-34 (ND 10-27, SD 1-7). July 22, 1998.

224. S 2260. Fiscal 1999 Commerce, Justice, State Appropriations/Gun Owner Liability. Craig, R-Idaho, motion to table (kill) the Durbin, D-Ill., amendment that would provide for penalties of up to one year in prison and a $10,000 fine for adult gun owners if a juvenile obtains access to the firearm and uses it criminally to kill, wound or exhibit the gun in a public place if the adult had not secured the gun with a trigger lock, lock box or other "safety device." Motion agreed to 69-31: R 53-2; D 16-29 (ND 12-25, SD 4-4). July 22, 1998.

	225	226	227	228	229	230	231
ALABAMA							
Sessions	N	Y	Y	N	Y	Y	Y
Shelby	N	Y	Y	N	Y	Y	N
ALASKA							
Murkowski	N	Y	Y	N	Y	Y	N
Stevens	N	Y	Y	Y	N	Y	N
ARIZONA							
Kyl	N	Y	Y	N	Y	Y	N
McCain	N	Y	Y	N	Y	Y	N
ARKANSAS							
Hutchinson	Y	N	Y	N	Y	Y	Y
Bumpers	Y	N	N	N	Y	N	N
CALIFORNIA							
Boxer	Y	N	N	Y	Y	N	Y
Feinstein	Y	N	N	N	Y	N	N
COLORADO							
Allard	N	Y	Y	Y	Y	Y	Y
Campbell	N	Y	Y	Y	Y	Y	Y
CONNECTICUT							
Dodd	Y	N	N	N	Y	N	N
Lieberman	Y	N	N	N	Y	N	N
DELAWARE							
Roth	N	Y	Y	N	Y	Y	N
Biden	Y	N	N	Y	N	N	N
FLORIDA							
Mack	N	Y	P	N	Y	N	N
Graham	Y	N	N	N	Y	N	N
GEORGIA							
Coverdell	Y	Y	N	N	Y	Y	Y
Cleland	Y	N	N	N	Y	N	N
HAWAII							
Akaka	Y	N	N	Y	N	N	N
Inouye	Y	N	Y	Y	N	Y	N
IDAHO							
Craig	N	Y	Y	Y	N	Y	Y
Kempthorne	N	Y	Y	Y	Y	Y	Y
ILLINOIS							
Durbin	Y	N	N	N	Y	N	N
Moseley-Braun	Y	N	N	N	Y	N	Y
INDIANA							
Coats	Y	Y	Y	N	Y	N	N
Lugar	N	Y	Y	N	Y	Y	N

	225	226	227	228	229	230	231
IOWA							
Grassley	N	Y	Y	N	Y	Y	Y
Harkin	Y	N	N	Y	N	N	N
KANSAS							
Brownback	N	Y	Y	N	Y	N	Y
Roberts	N	Y	Y	N	Y	N	Y
KENTUCKY							
McConnell	N	Y	Y	N	Y	Y	N
Ford	Y	N	Y	N	Y	N	N
LOUISIANA							
Breaux	Y	N	Y	N	Y	Y	N
Landrieu	Y	N	Y	N	Y	N	N
MAINE							
Collins	N	Y	Y	N	Y	N	Y
Snowe	Y	N	Y	N	Y	Y	Y
MARYLAND							
Mikulski	Y	N	N	N	Y	N	N
Sarbanes	Y	N	N	N	Y	N	N
MASSACHUSETTS							
Kennedy	Y	N	N	N	Y	N	N
Kerry	Y	N	N	N	Y	N	N
MICHIGAN							
Abraham	N	Y	Y	N	Y	N	N
Levin	Y	N	N	N	Y	N	N
MINNESOTA							
Grams	N	Y	Y	N	Y	N	N
Wellstone	Y	N	N	Y	N	N	N
MISSISSIPPI							
Cochran	N	Y	Y	N	Y	Y	Y
Lott	N	Y	Y	N	Y	Y	Y
MISSOURI							
Ashcroft	N	Y	Y	N	Y	Y	Y
Bond	N	Y	Y	N	Y	Y	N
MONTANA							
Burns	N	Y	Y	N	Y	Y	Y
Baucus	Y	N	N	N	Y	N	N
NEBRASKA							
Hagel	N	Y	Y	N	Y	Y	Y
Kerrey	Y	N	Y	Y	Y	N	N
NEVADA							
Bryan	Y	N	Y	N	Y	N	N
Reid	Y	N	Y	N	Y	N	Y

	225	226	227	228	229	230	231
NEW HAMPSHIRE							
Gregg	N	Y	Y	N	Y	Y	Y
Smith	N	Y	Y	N	Y	Y	Y
NEW JERSEY							
Lautenberg	Y	N	N	N	Y	N	N
Torricelli	Y	N	Y	N	Y	N	N
NEW MEXICO							
Domenici	N	Y	Y	N	Y	N	Y
Bingaman	Y	N	Y	N	Y	N	N
NEW YORK							
D'Amato	N	Y	Y	N	Y	N	Y
Moynihan	N	N	Y	N	N	N	N
NORTH CAROLINA							
Faircloth	N	Y	Y	N	Y	Y	Y
Helms	N	Y	Y	N	Y	Y	Y
NORTH DAKOTA							
Conrad	Y	N	N	N	Y	N	N
Dorgan	Y	N	N	Y	N	Y	N
OHIO							
DeWine	N	Y	Y	Y	Y	N	N
Glenn	Y	N	N	N	Y	N	N
OKLAHOMA							
Inhofe	N	Y	Y	N	Y	Y	Y
Nickles	N	Y	Y	N	Y	Y	Y
OREGON							
Smith	N	Y	Y	N	Y	Y	N
Wyden	Y	N	N	N	Y	Y	N
PENNSYLVANIA							
Santorum	N	Y	Y	N	Y	Y	Y
Specter	N	Y	N	N	Y	N	N
RHODE ISLAND							
Chafee	Y	N	Y	N	Y	Y	N
Reed	Y	N	Y	N	Y	N	N
SOUTH CAROLINA							
Thurmond	N	Y	Y	N	Y	Y	Y
Hollings	Y	N	Y	N	Y	Y	N
SOUTH DAKOTA							
Daschle	Y	N	N	Y	N	Y	N
Johnson	Y	N	N	Y	N	Y	N
TENNESSEE							
Frist	N	Y	Y	N	Y	Y	Y
Thompson	N	Y	Y	N	Y	N	N

	225	226	227	228	229	230	231
TEXAS							
Gramm	N	Y	Y	N	Y	Y	Y
Hutchison	N	Y	Y	N	Y	Y	Y
UTAH							
Bennett	N	Y	Y	N	Y	Y	Y
Hatch	N	Y	Y	N	Y	N	Y
VERMONT							
Jeffords	Y	N	N	N	Y	Y	N
Leahy	Y	N	N	N	Y	N	N
VIRGINIA							
Warner	N	Y	Y	N	Y	N	N
Robb	Y	N	N	N	Y	N	N
WASHINGTON							
Gorton	N	Y	Y	N	Y	N	N
Murray	Y	N	N	N	Y	N	N
WEST VIRGINIA							
Byrd	Y	N	N	N	Y	Y	Y
Rockefeller	Y	N	N	N	Y	N	N
WISCONSIN							
Feingold	Y	N	N	N	N	N	N
Kohl	Y	N	N	N	Y	N	N
WYOMING							
Enzi	N	Y	Y	N	Y	Y	Y
Thomas	N	Y	Y	N	Y	Y	N

ND Northern Democrats   SD Southern Democrats

Southern states - Ala., Ark., Fla., Ga., Ky., La., Miss., N.C., Okla., S.C., Tenn., Texas, Va.

Key

Y   Voted for (yea).
Paired for.
+   Announced for.
N   Voted against (nay).
X   Paired against.
−   Announced against.
P   Voted "present."
C   Voted "present" to avoid possible conflict of interest.
?   Did not vote or otherwise make a position known.

Democrats   *Republicans*

225. S 2260. Fiscal 1999 Commerce, Justice, State Appropriations/Secret Phone Recordings. Bumpers, D-Ark., amendment that would prohibit the recording of any telephone conversation unless all parties agree to its recording or the conversation is being recorded as part of a criminal investigation. Rejected 50-50: R 6-49; D 44-1 (ND 36-1, SD 8-0). July 22, 1998.

226. S 2260. Fiscal 1999 Commerce, Justice, State Appropriations/Reconsider. Lott, R-Miss., motion to table (kill) the Lott motion to reconsider the vote on the Bumpers amendment. Motion agreed to 51-49: R 51-4; D 0-45 (ND 0-37, SD 0-8). July 22, 1998.

227. S 2260. Fiscal 1999 Commerce, Justice, State Appropriations/Cable Television Rates. McCain, R-Ariz., motion to table (kill) the Feingold, D-Wis., amendment that would require the Federal Communications Commission to issue a report examining whether the 1992 telecommunications law (PL 102-385) has been successful at increasing competition in the cable industry and lowering cable television rates. Motion agreed to 63-36: R 49-5; D 14-31 (ND 10-27, SD 4-4). July 22, 1998.

228. S 2260. Fiscal 1999 Commerce, Justice, State Appropriations/Indian Gaming. Craig, R-Idaho, amendment to the Kyl, R-Ariz., amendment. The Craig amendment would clarify that Indian gaming is regulated by the federal government under the Indian Gaming Regulatory Act and not the restrictions of the Kyl amendment. Rejected 18-82: R 9-46; D

9-36 (ND 9-28, SD 0-8). July 23, 1998.

229. S 2260. Fiscal 1999 Commerce, Justice, State Appropriations/Internet Gambling Ban. Kyl, R-Ariz., amendment that would ban Internet gambling by prohibiting any individual from knowingly using the Internet or any other interactive computer service to place, receive or otherwise make a bet or wager. The amendment would provide exemptions for multistate lotteries, securities trading, commodities trading and so-called fantasy rotisserie leagues. Adopted 90-10: R 52-3; D 38-7 (ND 30-7, SD 8-0). July 23, 1998.

230. S 2260. Fiscal 1999 Commerce, Justice, State Appropriations/Court-Appointed Attorney Fees. Nickles, R-Okla., amendment that would limit the amount of pay that court-appointed defense attorneys in federal death penalty cases could receive to the monthly amount allocated to U.S. attorneys in the district where the action is prosecuted. Adopted 53-47: R 45-10; D 8-37 (ND 6-31, SD 2-6). July 23, 1998.

231. S 2260. Fiscal 1999 Commerce, Justice, State Appropriations/Vietnam POW/MIAs. Gregg, R-N.H., motion to table (kill) the Kerry, D-Mass., amendment that would replace language in the bill strengthening the standard for certifying that Vietnam is cooperating with U.S. efforts to recover American POW/MIAs with language restating the current standard. Motion rejected 34-66: R 30-25; D 4-41 (ND 4-33, SD 0-8). July 23, 1998. (Subsequently, the amendment was adopted by voice vote.)

	232	233	234	235	236	237	238
ALABAMA							
Sessions	Y	Y	Y	Y	N	N	N
Shelby	Y	Y	Y	Y	N	N	N
ALASKA							
Murkowski	Y	Y	Y	Y	N	Y	N
Stevens	Y	Y	Y	?	N	Y	Y
ARIZONA							
Kyl	Y	Y	Y	N	N	N	N
McCain	Y	Y	Y	?	?	N	N
ARKANSAS							
Hutchinson	Y	Y	Y	Y	N	N	N
Bumpers	Y	Y	Y	?	N	Y	Y
CALIFORNIA							
Boxer	Y	N	Y	?	Y	Y	Y
Feinstein	Y	N	Y	Y	Y	Y	Y
COLORADO							
Allard	Y	Y	Y	Y	N	N	N
Campbell	Y	Y	Y	Y	N	Y	Y
CONNECTICUT							
Dodd	Y	N	Y	Y	Y	Y	Y
Lieberman	Y	N	Y	Y	Y	Y	Y
DELAWARE							
Roth	Y	Y	Y	Y	N	N	N
Biden	Y	Y	Y	Y	Y	Y	Y
FLORIDA							
Mack	Y	Y	Y	Y	N	N	N
Graham	Y	Y	Y	Y	Y	N	Y
GEORGIA							
Coverdell	Y	Y	Y	Y	N	Y	N
Cleland	Y	Y	Y	Y	Y	Y	Y
HAWAII							
Akaka	Y	N	Y	Y	Y	Y	Y
Inouye	Y	N	Y	Y	Y	Y	Y
IDAHO							
Craig	Y	Y	Y	Y	N	Y	N
Kempthorne	Y	Y	Y	?	N	Y	N
ILLINOIS							
Durbin	Y	N	Y	Y	Y	Y	Y
Moseley-Braun	Y	N	Y	Y	Y	Y	Y
INDIANA							
Coats	Y	Y	Y	Y	N	N	N
Lugar	Y	Y	Y	Y	N	N	Y
IOWA							
Grassley	Y	Y	Y	Y	N	Y	N
Harkin	Y	N	Y	Y	+	+	+
KANSAS							
Brownback	Y	Y	Y	Y	N	N	N
Roberts	Y	Y	Y	Y	N	N	N
KENTUCKY							
McConnell	Y	Y	Y	Y	N	N	N
Ford	Y	N	Y	Y	Y	Y	Y
LOUISIANA							
Breaux	Y	Y	Y	Y	N	N	N
Landrieu	Y	N	Y	Y	Y	Y	Y
MAINE							
Collins	Y	Y	Y	Y	N	Y	Y
Snowe	Y	Y	Y	Y	N	Y	Y
MARYLAND							
Mikulski	Y	N	Y	Y	Y	Y	Y
Sarbanes	Y	N	Y	Y	Y	Y	Y
MASSACHUSETTS							
Kennedy	Y	N	Y	Y	Y	Y	Y
Kerry	Y	N	Y	Y	Y	Y	Y
MICHIGAN							
Abraham	Y	Y	Y	Y	N	Y	N
Levin	Y	N	Y	Y	Y	Y	Y
MINNESOTA							
Grams	Y	Y	Y	Y	N	N	N
Wellstone	N	N	Y	Y	Y	Y	Y
MISSISSIPPI							
Cochran	Y	Y	Y	Y	N	N	N
Lott	Y	Y	Y	Y	N	N	N
MISSOURI							
Ashcroft	Y	Y	Y	Y	N	N	N
Bond	Y	Y	Y	Y	N	Y	N
MONTANA							
Burns	Y	Y	Y	+	N	Y	N
Baucus	Y	Y	Y	Y	Y	Y	Y
NEBRASKA							
Hagel	Y	Y	Y	Y	N	N	N
Kerrey	N	Y	Y	Y	Y	N	Y
NEVADA							
Bryan	Y	Y	Y	Y	N	Y	Y
Reid	Y	Y	Y	Y	Y	Y	Y

	232	233	234	235	236	237	238
NEW HAMPSHIRE							
Gregg	Y	Y	Y	Y	N	N	N
Smith	Y	Y	Y	Y	N	N	N
NEW JERSEY							
Lautenberg	Y	N	Y	Y	Y	Y	Y
Torricelli	Y	N	Y	Y	Y	Y	Y
NEW MEXICO							
Domenici	Y	Y	Y	Y	?	?	Y
Bingaman	Y	Y	Y	Y	?	?	Y
NEW YORK							
D'Amato	Y	Y	Y	Y	Y	Y	Y
Moynihan	Y	Y	Y	Y	Y	Y	Y
NORTH CAROLINA							
Faircloth	Y	Y	Y	Y	N	Y	N
Helms	Y	Y	Y	?	–	–	–
NORTH DAKOTA							
Conrad	Y	N	Y	Y	Y	Y	Y
Dorgan	Y	N	Y	Y	Y	Y	Y
OHIO							
DeWine	Y	Y	Y	Y	N	N	N
Glenn	Y	N	Y	Y	Y	Y	Y
OKLAHOMA							
Inhofe	Y	Y	Y	Y	N	N	N
Nickles	Y	Y	Y	Y	N	N	N
OREGON							
Smith	Y	Y	Y	Y	N	Y	N
Wyden	Y	Y	Y	Y	?	?	Y
PENNSYLVANIA							
Santorum	Y	Y	Y	Y	N	Y	Y
Specter	Y	?	?	Y	N	Y	Y
RHODE ISLAND							
Chafee	Y	Y	Y	Y	N	Y	Y
Reed	Y	N	Y	Y	Y	Y	Y
SOUTH CAROLINA							
Thurmond	Y	Y	Y	Y	N	N	N
Hollings	Y	Y	Y	Y	Y	Y	Y
SOUTH DAKOTA							
Daschle	Y	N	Y	Y	Y	Y	Y
Johnson	Y	N	Y	Y	Y	Y	Y
TENNESSEE							
Frist	Y	Y	Y	Y	N	N	N
Thompson	Y	Y	Y	Y	N	N	N

	232	233	234	235	236	237	238
TEXAS							
Gramm	Y	Y	Y	Y	N	N	N
Hutchison	Y	Y	Y	Y	N	N	N
UTAH							
Bennett	Y	Y	Y	?	N	N	N
Hatch	Y	Y	Y	Y	N	Y	N
VERMONT							
Jeffords	Y	Y	Y	Y	N	N	Y
Leahy	Y	N	Y	Y	Y	N	Y
VIRGINIA							
Warner	Y	Y	Y	Y	N	N	Y
Robb	Y	Y	Y	Y	Y	N	Y
WASHINGTON							
Gorton	Y	Y	Y	Y	N	Y	N
Murray	Y	N	Y	Y	Y	Y	Y
WEST VIRGINIA							
Byrd	Y	N	Y	Y	Y	N	Y
Rockefeller	Y	N	Y	Y	Y	N	Y
WISCONSIN							
Feingold	Y	N	Y	Y	Y	Y	Y
Kohl	Y	N	Y	Y	Y	Y	Y
WYOMING							
Enzi	Y	Y	Y	?	N	N	N
Thomas	Y	Y	Y	Y	N	N	N

Key

Y   Voted for (yea).
\#   Paired for.
\+   Announced for.
N   Voted against (nay).
X   Paired against.
–   Announced against.
P   Voted "present."
C   Voted "present" to avoid possible conflict of interest.
?   Did not vote or otherwise make a position known.

Democrats   *Republicans*

ND Northern Democrats   SD Southern Democrats

Southern states - Ala., Ark., Fla., Ga., Ky., La., Miss., N.C., Okla., S.C., Tenn., Texas, Va.

232. S 2260. Fiscal 1999 Commerce, Justice, State Appropriations/ Japanese Financial Problems. Lieberman, D-Conn., amendment that would express the sense of the Senate that the president should inform Japan that financial and market deregulation, along with restructuring "bad bank debt," are fundamental to Japan's economic recovery, and that the first priority of Japan's new prime minister and Cabinet should be to restore growth and promote stability in international financial markets. Adopted 98-2: R 55-0; D 43-2 (ND 35-2, SD 8-0). July 23, 1998.

233. S 2260. Fiscal 1999 Commerce, Justice, State Appropriations/ Temporary Farm Workers. Smith, R-Ore., amendment that would establish a registry of temporary agricultural workers to link U.S. farmworkers to agricultural jobs. If there are insufficient U.S. workers to fill the number of positions offered by a specific employer, the attorney general shall admit enough foreign workers to fill those positions. The amendment also would require that employers provide prevailing wages, housing and transportation reimbursements for the workers and would direct the attorney general to conduct a study on whether foreign workers depart the country upon completion of their authorized stay. Adopted 68-31: R 54-0; D 14-31 (ND 8-29, SD 6-2). July 23, 1998.

234. S 2260. Fiscal 1999 Commerce, Justice, State Appropriations/ Passage. Passage of the bill to provide $33.2 billion in new budget authority for the departments of Commerce, Justice and State and the federal judiciary in fiscal 1999. The bill provides $1.1 billion more than in fiscal 1998 and $3.6 billion less than requested by President Clinton. Passed 99-0: R 54-0; D 45-0 (ND 37-0, SD 8-0). July 23, 1998.

235. S 2307. Fiscal 1999 Transportation Appropriations/Passage. Passage of the bill to provide $47.1 billion in new budget authority for the Department of Transportation and related agencies in fiscal 1999. The bill would provide $4.4 billion more than in fiscal 1998 and $4.1 billion more than requested by Presi-

dent Clinton. Passed 90-1: R 47-1; D 43-0 (ND 36-0, SD 7-0). July 24, 1998.

236. HR 1151. Credit Union Membership Rules/Low-Income Loans. Sarbanes, D-Md., motion to table (kill) the Gramm, R-Texas, amendment that would strike the bill's provisions to apply to credit unions requirements similar to the 1977 Community Reinvestment Act (PL 95-128), which requires federal regulators to consider a bank's lending record to all areas in the community it serves when deciding whether to allow a branch, merger or other endeavor. The bill's language would require the National Credit Union Administration to review credit unions to ensure that they provide affordable services to individuals of modest means within the community. Motion rejected 44-50: R 3-49; D 41-1 (ND 34-0, SD 7-1). July 27, 1998. (Subsequently, the Gramm amendment was adopted by voice vote)

237. HR 1151. Credit Union Membership Rules/Business Loans. D'Amato, R-N.Y., motion to table (kill) the Hagel, R-Neb., amendment that would reduce the cap on commercial business loans to credit union members from 12.25 percent to 7 percent of their net worth for well-capitalized credit unions. The amendment would require credit unions to count loans of up to $50,000 as business loans and would require that credit unionpersonnel who make commercial loans have at least two years of experience. Motion agreed to 53-42: R 18-35; D 35-7 (ND 29-5, SD 6-2). July 27, 1998.

238. HR 1151. Credit Union Membership Rules/Small Bank Reinvestment Exemption. D'Amato, R-N.Y., motion to table (kill) the Shelby, R-Ala., amendment that would exempt banks with assets of less than $250 million from the 1977 Community Reinvestment Act (PL 95-128). The act requires federal regulators to consider a bank's lending record to all areas in the community it serves when deciding whether to allow a branch, merger or other endeavor. Motion agreed to 59-39: R 15-39; D 44-0 (ND 36-0, SD 8-0). July 28, 1998. A "yea" was a vote in support of the president's position.

	239	240	241	242	243	244	245
ALABAMA							
Sessions	Y	Y	Y	N	Y	N	N
Shelby	Y	Y	Y	N	Y	N	N
ALASKA							
Murkowski	Y	Y	Y	N	Y	N	Y
Stevens	Y	Y	N	Y	N	Y	N
ARIZONA							
Kyl	Y	Y	Y	N	Y	N	N
McCain	Y	Y	Y	N	Y	N	N
ARKANSAS							
Hutchinson	Y	Y	Y	N	Y	N	N
Bumpers	Y	N	N	Y	N	Y	N
CALIFORNIA							
Boxer	Y	N	N	Y	N	Y	N
Feinstein	Y	N	N	Y	N	Y	N
COLORADO							
Allard	Y	Y	Y	N	Y	N	N
Campbell	Y	Y	Y	N	Y	N	Y
CONNECTICUT							
Dodd	Y	N	N	Y	N	Y	N
Lieberman	Y	N	N	Y	N	Y	N
DELAWARE							
Roth	Y	Y	Y	N	Y	N	Y
Biden	Y	N	N	Y	N	Y	N
FLORIDA							
Mack	N	Y	Y	N	Y	N	N
Graham	Y	N	N	Y	N	Y	Y
GEORGIA							
Coverdell	Y	Y	Y	N	Y	N	N
Cleland	Y	N	N	Y	N	Y	Y
HAWAII							
Akaka	Y	N	N	Y	N	Y	N
Inouye	Y	N	N	Y	N	Y	N
IDAHO							
Craig	Y	Y	Y	N	Y	N	Y
Kempthorne	Y	Y	Y	N	Y	N	N
ILLINOIS							
Durbin	Y	N	N	Y	N	Y	N
Moseley-Braun	Y	N	Y	N	Y	N	N
INDIANA							
Coats	N	Y	Y	N	Y	N	?
Lugar	Y	N	Y	N	Y	N	Y
IOWA							
Grassley	Y	Y	N	N	Y	N	N
Harkin	+	−	−	Y	N	Y	N
KANSAS							
Brownback	Y	Y	Y	N	Y	N	N
Roberts	N	Y	N	N	Y	N	Y
KENTUCKY							
McConnell	Y	Y	Y	N	Y	N	N
Ford	Y	N	N	Y	N	Y	N
LOUISIANA							
Breaux	Y	N	Y	N	Y	N	Y
Landrieu	Y	N	N	Y	N	Y	N
MAINE							
Collins	Y	Y	Y	Y	Y	N	N
Snowe	Y	Y	Y	Y	Y	N	N
MARYLAND							
Mikulski	Y	N	N	Y	N	Y	N
Sarbanes	Y	N	N	Y	N	Y	N
MASSACHUSETTS							
Kennedy	Y	N	N	Y	N	Y	N
Kerry	Y	N	N	Y	N	Y	N
MICHIGAN							
Abraham	Y	Y	Y	N	Y	N	N
Levin	Y	N	N	Y	N	Y	N
MINNESOTA							
Grams	Y	Y	Y	N	Y	N	N
Wellstone	Y	N	N	Y	N	Y	N
MISSISSIPPI							
Cochran	Y	Y	N	N	Y	N	Y
Lott	Y	Y	Y	N	Y	N	N
MISSOURI							
Ashcroft	Y	Y	Y	N	Y	N	Y
Bond	Y	Y	Y	N	Y	N	N
MONTANA							
Burns	Y	Y	Y	N	Y	N	N
Baucus	Y	Y	N	Y	N	Y	N
NEBRASKA							
Hagel	N	Y	Y	N	Y	N	N
Kerrey	Y	N	N	Y	N	Y	N
NEVADA							
Bryan	Y	N	N	Y	N	Y	N
Reid	Y	N	Y	Y	N	Y	N
NEW HAMPSHIRE							
Gregg	Y	Y	Y	N	Y	N	Y
Smith	Y	Y	Y	N	Y	N	N
NEW JERSEY							
Lautenberg	Y	N	N	Y	N	Y	N
Torricelli	Y	N	N	Y	N	Y	N
NEW MEXICO							
Domenici	Y	Y	Y	N	Y	N	N
Bingaman	Y	Y	N	Y	N	Y	N
NEW YORK							
D'Amato	Y	N	N	Y	N	Y	N
Moynihan	Y	N	N	Y	Y	Y	Y
NORTH CAROLINA							
Faircloth	Y	Y	Y	N	Y	N	N
Helms	−	+	+	−	+	−	?
NORTH DAKOTA							
Conrad	Y	N	N	Y	N	Y	N
Dorgan	Y	N	N	Y	N	Y	N
OHIO							
DeWine	Y	N	Y	N	Y	N	N
Glenn	Y	N	N	Y	N	Y	N
OKLAHOMA							
Inhofe	N	Y	Y	N	Y	N	N
Nickles	N	Y	Y	N	Y	N	Y
OREGON							
Smith	Y	Y	Y	N	Y	N	N
Wyden	Y	N	N	Y	N	Y	N
PENNSYLVANIA							
Santorum	Y	Y	Y	N	Y	N	Y
Specter	Y	Y	Y	N	Y	N	N
RHODE ISLAND							
Chafee	Y	N	N	Y	N	Y	N
Reed	Y	N	N	Y	N	Y	N
SOUTH CAROLINA							
Thurmond	Y	Y	Y	N	Y	N	N
Hollings	Y	Y	N	N	Y	N	N
SOUTH DAKOTA							
Daschle	Y	N	N	Y	N	Y	N
Johnson	Y	N	N	Y	N	Y	N
TENNESSEE							
Frist	Y	Y	Y	Y	Y	N	Y
Thompson	Y	Y	Y	Y	Y	N	Y
TEXAS							
Gramm	Y	Y	Y	N	Y	N	Y
Hutchison	Y	Y	Y	N	Y	N	N
UTAH							
Bennett	Y	Y	Y	N	Y	N	N
Hatch	Y	Y	Y	N	Y	N	N
VERMONT							
Jeffords	Y	Y	N	Y	N	Y	N
Leahy	Y	N	N	Y	N	Y	N
VIRGINIA							
Warner	Y	Y	N	Y	Y	Y	N
Robb	Y	N	N	Y	Y	Y	N
WASHINGTON							
Gorton	Y	Y	Y	Y	Y	N	?
Murray	Y	N	N	Y	N	Y	N
WEST VIRGINIA							
Byrd	Y	N	N	Y	N	Y	N
Rockefeller	Y	N	N	Y	N	Y	N
WISCONSIN							
Feingold	Y	N	N	Y	N	Y	N
Kohl	Y	N	N	Y	N	Y	N
WYOMING							
Enzi	Y	Y	Y	N	Y	N	N
Thomas	Y	Y	Y	N	Y	N	N

Key

Y	Voted for (yea).
#	Paired for.
+	Announced for.
N	Voted against (nay).
X	Paired against.
−	Announced against.
P	Voted "present."
C	Voted "present" to avoid possible conflict of interest.
?	Did not vote or otherwise make a position known.

Democrats   *Republicans*

ND Northern Democrats   SD Southern Democrats

Southern states - Ala., Ark., Fla., Ga., Ky., La., Miss., N.C., Okla., S.C., Tenn., Texas, Va.

239. HR 1151. Credit Union Membership Rules/Passage. Passage of the bill to allow credit union members to keep their accounts and to permit credit unions to join unrelated groups as long as the groups would provide no more than 3,000 members. Passed 92-6: R 48-6; D 44-0 (ND 36-0, SD 8-0). July 28, 1998.

240. S 2312. Fiscal 1999 Treasury-Postal Service-General Government Appropriations/Large Capacity Ammunition Ban. Campbell, R-Colo., motion to table (kill) the Feinstein, D-Calif., amendment that would prohibit the importation of large capacity ammunition feeding devices. The devices are currently illegal in the United States. Motion agreed to 54-44: R 49-5; D 5-39 (ND 3-33, SD 2-6). July 28, 1998.

241. S 2312. Fiscal 1999 Treasury-Postal Service-General Government Appropriations/Tax Code Termination. Hutchinson, R-Ark., motion to waive the Budget Act with respect to the Kohl, D-Wis., point of order against the Hutchinson amendment. The Hutchinson amendment would abolish the current tax code by Dec. 31, 2002, and recommend that Congress approve a new tax code by July 4, 2002. Motion rejected 49-49: R 47-7; D 2-42 (ND 2-34, SD 0-8). July 28, 1998. A three-fifths majority vote (60) of the total Senate is required to waive the Budget Act. (Subsequently, the chair upheld the point of order, and the amendment fell.) A "nay" was a vote in support of the president's position.

242. S 2312. Fiscal 1999 Treasury-Postal Service-General Government Appropriations/Marriage Penalty. Roth, R-Del., motion to table (kill) the Brownback, R-Kan., amendment that would allow each spouse to claim one-half of the combined taxable income of both spouses as if unmarried, thus eliminating the so-called marriage penalty. Motion rejected 48-51: R 4-50; D 44-1 (ND 37-0, SD 7-1). July 29, 1998. (Subsequently, the Brownback amendment was withdrawn.)

243. S 2312. Fiscal 1999 Treasury-Postal Service-General Government Appropriations/Democratic Marriage Penalty Alternative. Campbell, R-Colo., motion to table (kill) the Daschle, D-S.D., amendment that would allow married couples with combined incomes below $50,000 a year to deduct 20 percent of the income of the lesser-earning spouse on their income taxes, thus eliminating the so-called marriage penalty for those in that income bracket. Motion agreed to 57-42: R 54-0; D 3-42 (ND 2-35, SD 1-7). July 29, 1998.

244. S 2312. Fiscal 1999 Treasury-Postal Service-General Government Appropriations/Child Labor. Harkin, D-Iowa, amendment to the Thompson, R-Tenn., amendment. The Harkin amendment would replace the text of the Thompson amendment with the bill's language regarding child labor with a few changes. That language would prohibit the government from buying products made by forced or indentured child labor and would require executive agencies to publish a list of products mined or manufactured with forced or indentured child labor. The Thompson amendment would strike all bill language concerning child labor except for a provision requiring revisions to federal acquisition regulations within 180 days of the bill's enactment. Rejected 46-53: R 1-53; D 45-0 (ND 37-0, SD 8-0). July 29, 1998. (Subsequently, the underlying Thompson amendment was adopted by voice vote.)

245. S 2312. Fiscal 1999 Treasury-Postal Service-General Government Appropriations/Post Office Closings. Cochran, R-Miss., motion to table (kill) the Baucus, D-Mont., amendment that would require the Postal Service to provide 60 days notice to the community, hold a hearing and abide by local zoning requirements before closing or relocating a post office in that community. Motion rejected 21-76: R 18-34; D 3-42 (ND 1-36, SD 2-6). July 29, 1998. (Subsequently, the Baucus amendment was adopted by voice vote.)

	246	247	248	249	250	251	252
ALABAMA							
Sessions	N	Y	N	N	Y	Y	Y
Shelby	N	Y	N	N	Y	Y	Y
ALASKA							
Murkowski	N	Y	N	N	Y	Y	Y
Stevens	N	Y	Y	N	Y	Y	Y
ARIZONA							
Kyl	N	Y	N	Y	Y	Y	Y
McCain	N	Y	N	Y	Y	Y	Y
ARKANSAS							
Hutchinson	N	Y	N	N	Y	Y	Y
Bumpers	Y	N	Y	Y	Y	Y	Y
CALIFORNIA							
Boxer	Y	Y	N	Y	N	Y	N
Feinstein	Y	Y	Y	Y	Y	Y	Y
COLORADO							
Allard	N	Y	N	N	Y	Y	Y
Campbell	N	Y	N	N	Y	Y	Y
CONNECTICUT							
Dodd	Y	Y	N	Y	Y	Y	Y
Lieberman	Y	Y	N	Y	Y	Y	Y
DELAWARE							
Roth	N	Y	N	Y	Y	Y	Y
Biden	Y	Y	N	Y	Y	N	Y
FLORIDA							
Mack	N	Y	N	Y	Y	Y	Y
Graham	Y	N	Y	N	Y	Y	Y
GEORGIA							
Coverdell	N	Y	N	Y	Y	Y	Y
Cleland	Y	Y	Y	Y	Y	Y	Y
HAWAII							
Akaka	Y	Y	Y	Y	Y	Y	Y
Inouye	Y	Y	Y	Y	Y	Y	Y
IDAHO							
Craig	N	Y	N	Y	Y	Y	Y
Kempthorne	N	Y	N	N	Y	Y	Y
ILLINOIS							
Durbin	Y	Y	N	Y	Y	N	Y
Moseley-Braun	Y	Y	N	Y	N	Y	Y
INDIANA							
Coats	N	Y	N	Y	Y	Y	Y
Lugar	N	Y	Y	Y	Y	Y	Y

	246	247	248	249	250	251	252
IOWA							
Grassley	N	Y	N	Y	Y	Y	Y
Harkin	Y	N	N	Y	Y	N	Y
KANSAS							
Brownback	N	Y	N	Y	Y	Y	Y
Roberts	N	Y	Y	Y	Y	Y	Y
KENTUCKY							
McConnell	N	Y	N	Y	Y	Y	Y
Ford	Y	Y	N	Y	Y	Y	Y
LOUISIANA							
Breaux	Y	N	N	Y	Y	Y	Y
Landrieu	Y	Y	Y	Y	Y	Y	Y
MAINE							
Collins	N	Y	N	Y	Y	Y	Y
Snowe	N	Y	N	Y	Y	Y	Y
MARYLAND							
Mikulski	Y	Y	N	Y	Y	Y	Y
Sarbanes	Y	Y	N	Y	Y	Y	Y
MASSACHUSETTS							
Kennedy	Y	Y	Y	Y	Y	N	Y
Kerry	Y	Y	N	Y	Y	Y	Y
MICHIGAN							
Abraham	N	Y	N	Y	Y	Y	Y
Levin	Y	Y	Y	Y	Y	Y	Y
MINNESOTA							
Grams	N	Y	N	Y	Y	Y	Y
Wellstone	Y	N	N	Y	Y	N	N
MISSISSIPPI							
Cochran	N	Y	N	Y	Y	Y	Y
Lott	N	Y	N	Y	Y	Y	Y
MISSOURI							
Ashcroft	N	Y	N	Y	Y	Y	Y
Bond	N	Y	Y	N	Y	Y	Y
MONTANA							
Burns	N	Y	N	Y	Y	Y	Y
Baucus	Y	Y	Y	Y	Y	Y	Y
NEBRASKA							
Hagel	N	Y	N	Y	Y	Y	Y
Kerrey	Y	N	N	Y	Y	Y	Y
NEVADA							
Bryan	Y	N	N	Y	Y	Y	Y
Reid	Y	N	Y	Y	Y	Y	Y

	246	247	248	249	250	251	252
NEW HAMPSHIRE							
Gregg	N	Y	N	N	Y	Y	Y
Smith	N	Y	N	N	Y	Y	Y
NEW JERSEY							
Lautenberg	Y	N	N	Y	Y	Y	Y
Torricelli	Y	Y	N	Y	Y	Y	Y
NEW MEXICO							
Domenici	N	Y	Y	Y	Y	Y	Y
Bingaman	Y	N	Y	Y	Y	N	Y
NEW YORK							
D'Amato	N	Y	N	Y	Y	Y	Y
Moynihan	Y	Y	Y	Y	Y	Y	Y
NORTH CAROLINA							
Faircloth	N	Y	N	N	Y	Y	Y
Helms	-	+	-	-	+	+	+
NORTH DAKOTA							
Conrad	Y	N	N	Y	Y	Y	Y
Dorgan	Y	Y	N	N	Y	Y	Y
OHIO							
DeWine	N	Y	N	N	Y	Y	Y
Glenn	Y	Y	Y	Y	Y	Y	Y
OKLAHOMA							
Inhofe	N	Y	N	N	Y	Y	Y
Nickles	N	Y	N	N	Y	Y	Y
OREGON							
Smith	N	Y	N	Y	Y	Y	Y
Wyden	Y	N	N	Y	Y	Y	Y
PENNSYLVANIA							
Santorum	N	Y	N	Y	Y	Y	Y
Specter	N	Y	N	Y	N	Y	Y
RHODE ISLAND							
Chafee	N	Y	Y	Y	Y	Y	Y
Reed	Y	Y	Y	Y	Y	Y	Y
SOUTH CAROLINA							
Thurmond	N	Y	N	Y	Y	Y	Y
Hollings	Y	Y	Y	Y	Y	N	Y
SOUTH DAKOTA							
Daschle	Y	N	N	Y	Y	Y	Y
Johnson	Y	N	N	Y	Y	N	Y
TENNESSEE							
Frist	N	Y	N	N	Y	Y	Y
Thompson	N	Y	N	N	Y	Y	Y

Key

Key

Y	Voted for (yea).
#	Paired for.
+	Announced for.
N	Voted against (nay).
X	Paired against.
–	Announced against.
P	Voted "present."
C	Voted "present" to avoid possible conflict of interest.
?	Did not vote or otherwise make a position known.

Democrats   *Republicans*

	246	247	248	249	250	251	252
TEXAS							
Gramm	N	Y	N	N	Y	Y	Y
Hutchison	N	Y	N	N	Y	N	Y
UTAH							
Bennett	N	Y	N	Y	Y	Y	Y
Hatch	N	Y	N	Y	Y	Y	Y
VERMONT							
Jeffords	N	N	Y	Y	Y	Y	Y
Leahy	Y	N	N	Y	Y	Y	Y
VIRGINIA							
Warner	N	Y	N	Y	Y	Y	Y
Robb	Y	Y	Y	Y	Y	Y	Y
WASHINGTON							
Gorton	N	Y	N	N	Y	Y	Y
Murray	Y	Y	Y	Y	Y	Y	Y
WEST VIRGINIA							
Byrd	Y	N	N	Y	N	Y	Y
Rockefeller	Y	N	Y	Y	Y	Y	Y
WISCONSIN							
Feingold	Y	N	N	N	Y	N	N
Kohl	Y	N	N	Y	Y	Y	Y
WYOMING							
Enzi	N	Y	N	Y	Y	Y	Y
Thomas	N	Y	Y	N	Y	Y	Y

ND Northern Democrats   SD Southern Democrats

Southern states - Ala., Ark., Fla., Ga., Ky., La., Miss., N.C., Okla., S.C., Tenn., Texas, Va.

246. S 2312. Fiscal 1999 Treasury-Postal Service-General Government Appropriations/FEC Term Limits. Glenn, D-Ohio, motion to table (kill) the McConnell, R-Ky., amendment that would impose four-year term limits on the staff director and the general counsel of the Federal Election Commission (FEC), though the officers could be elected to additional terms if four members of the six-member commission vote for reappointment. Motion rejected 45-54: R 0-54; D 45-0 (ND 37-0, SD 8-0). July 30, 1998. (Subsequently, the underlying bill, along with all pending amendments, were set aside.)

247. S 2132. Fiscal 1999 Defense Appropriations/Navy Aircraft Procurement. Stevens, R-Alaska, motion to table (kill) the Feingold, D-Wis., amendment that would reduce funding for the Navy's F/A-18 E and F aircraft procurement by $219.7 million (three planes) and redirect the funding to the operation and maintenance accounts of the National Guard. Motion agreed to 80-19: R 53-1; D 27-18 (ND 22-15, SD 5-3). July 30, 1998.

248. S 2132. Fiscal 1999 Defense Appropriations/Chinese Forced Abortions. Stevens, R-Alaska, motion to table (kill) the Hutchinson, R-Ark., amendment that would prohibit U.S. visas to Chinese officials involved in forced abortions, forced sterilizations or religious persecution. The president could waive the prohibition if he determines it is in the "national interest" to do so. Motion rejected 29-70: R 12-42; D 17-28 (ND 12-25, SD 5-3). July 30, 1998.

249. S 2132. Fiscal 1999 Defense Appropriations/Troops in Bosnia. McCain, R-Ariz., motion to table (kill) the Hutchison, R-Texas, amendment that would require the president to reduce U.S. combat forces in Bosnia to 6,500 by Feb. 2, 1999, and 5,000 by Oct. 1, 1999. Motion agreed to 68-31: R 26-28; D 42-3 (ND 34-3, SD 8-0). July 30, 1998. A "yea" was a vote in support of the president's position.

250. S 2132. Fiscal 1999 Defense Appropriations/Forced Abortions. Hutchinson, R-Ark., amendment to the Hutchinson amendment. The second-degree Hutchinson amendment would extend the underlying Hutchinson amendment to deny visas to officials of any country engaged in forced abortions, forced sterilizations or religious persecution. Adopted 99-0: R 54-0; D 45-0 (ND 37-0, SD 8-0). July 30, 1998. (Subsequently, the underlying Hutchinson amendment as amended was adopted by voice vote.)

251. S 2132. Fiscal 1999 Defense Appropriations/War Powers. Stevens, R-Alaska, motion to table (kill) the Durbin, D-Ill., amendment that would require that no funds be used to "initiate or conduct" U.S. military operations except in accordance with Article I, Section 8 of the Constitution, which vests in Congress the power to declare war and take other related actions. Motion agreed to 84-15: R 52-2; D 32-13 (ND 25-12, SD 7-1). July 30, 1998.

252. HR 4103. Fiscal 1999 Defense Appropriations/Passage. Passage of the bill to provide $252.4 billion in new budget authority for defense-related programs in fiscal 1999. The bill would provide $481 million less than requested by President Clinton and $4.7 billion more than provided in fiscal 1998. The bill would provide $48.6 billion for military procurement and $83.5 billion for Defense Department operations. Passed 97-2: R 54-0; D 43-2 (ND 35-2, SD 8-0). July 30, 1998. (Before passage, the Senate struck all after the enacting clause and inserted the text of S 2132 as amended.)

Key

Y	Voted for (yea).
#	Paired for.
+	Announced for.
N	Voted against (nay).
X	Paired against.
–	Announced against.
P	Voted "present."
C	Voted "present" to avoid possible conflict of interest.
?	Did not vote or otherwise make a position known.

Democrats   *Republicans*

State / Senator	253	254	255	256	257	258	259
ALABAMA							
Sessions	Y	N	Y	N	N	Y	Y
Shelby	Y	N	Y	N	N	Y	Y
ALASKA							
Murkowski	?	?	?	?	?	?	?
Stevens	Y	Y	Y	Y	N	Y	Y
ARIZONA							
Kyl	N	N	Y	N	N	Y	Y
McCain	N	N	Y	Y	N	Y	Y
ARKANSAS							
Hutchinson	Y	N	Y	N	N	Y	Y
Bumpers	Y	Y	Y	Y	N	N	Y
CALIFORNIA							
Boxer	Y	Y	N	Y	N	N	Y
Feinstein	Y	Y	Y	Y	N	N	Y
COLORADO							
Allard	Y	N	Y	N	N	Y	Y
Campbell	Y	Y	Y	N	N	Y	Y
CONNECTICUT							
Dodd	Y	Y	Y	Y	N	N	Y
Lieberman	Y	Y	Y	Y	Y	N	Y
DELAWARE							
Roth	Y	N	Y	N	N	Y	Y
Biden	Y	Y	Y	Y	Y	N	Y
FLORIDA							
Mack	Y	N	Y	N	N	Y	Y
Graham	Y	Y	Y	Y	N	N	Y
GEORGIA							
Coverdell	+	N	?	?	?	?	?
Cleland	Y	Y	Y	Y	N	Y	Y
HAWAII							
Akaka	Y	Y	N	Y	N	Y	N
Inouye	?	?	?	?	?	?	?
IDAHO							
Craig	Y	N	Y	Y	N	Y	Y
Kempthorne	Y	N	Y	Y	?	Y	Y
ILLINOIS							
Durbin	Y	Y	Y	Y	N	N	Y
Moseley-Braun	Y	Y	N	Y	N	N	Y
INDIANA							
Coats	Y	N	Y	N	N	Y	Y
Lugar	Y	N	Y	N	N	Y	Y
IOWA							
Grassley	Y	N	Y	N	N	Y	Y
Harkin	Y	Y	N	Y	N	N	Y
KANSAS							
Brownback	Y	N	Y	Y	–	Y	Y
Roberts	Y	N	Y	Y	N	Y	Y
KENTUCKY							
McConnell	Y	N	Y	N	N	Y	Y
Ford	Y	Y	Y	Y	N	N	Y
LOUISIANA							
Breaux	Y	Y	Y	Y	N	N	Y
Landrieu	Y	Y	Y	Y	N	N	Y
MAINE							
Collins	Y	N	Y	N	Y	N	Y
Snowe	Y	N	Y	N	Y	N	Y
MARYLAND							
Mikulski	Y	Y	Y	Y	N	N	Y
Sarbanes	Y	Y	Y	Y	N	N	Y
MASSACHUSETTS							
Kennedy	Y	Y	N	Y	N	N	Y
Kerry	Y	Y	N	Y	N	N	Y
MICHIGAN							
Abraham	Y	N	Y	Y	N	Y	Y
Levin	Y	Y	Y	Y	Y	N	Y
MINNESOTA							
Grams	Y	N	Y	N	N	Y	Y
Wellstone	Y	Y	N	Y	Y	N	Y
MISSISSIPPI							
Cochran	Y	N	Y	Y	N	Y	Y
Lott	Y	N	Y	Y	N	Y	Y
MISSOURI							
Ashcroft	Y	N	Y	N	N	N	Y
Bond	Y	N	Y	Y	N	Y	Y
MONTANA							
Burns	Y	N	Y	Y	N	Y	Y
Baucus	Y	Y	Y	Y	N	N	Y
NEBRASKA							
Hagel	Y	N	Y	Y	N	Y	Y
Kerrey	Y	Y	Y	Y	Y	N	Y
NEVADA							
Bryan	Y	Y	N	Y	N	N	Y
Reid	Y	Y	N	Y	N	N	Y
NEW HAMPSHIRE							
Gregg	Y	N	Y	Y	N	Y	Y
Smith	Y	N	Y	N	N	Y	Y
NEW JERSEY							
Lautenberg	Y	Y	N	Y	N	N	Y
Torricelli	Y	Y	N	Y	N	N	Y
NEW MEXICO							
Domenici	?	?	?	?	?	?	?
Bingaman	?	?	?	?	?	?	?
NEW YORK							
D'Amato	Y	Y	Y	Y	N	N	Y
Moynihan	Y	Y	Y	Y	N	N	Y
NORTH CAROLINA							
Faircloth	Y	N	Y	N	N	Y	N
Helms	+	–	+	–	–	+	–
NORTH DAKOTA							
Conrad	Y	Y	Y	Y	N	N	Y
Dorgan	Y	Y	Y	Y	N	N	Y
OHIO							
DeWine	Y	N	Y	N	N	Y	Y
Glenn	?	?	?	?	?	?	?
OKLAHOMA							
Inhofe	Y	N	Y	N	N	Y	Y
Nickles	Y	N	Y	N	N	Y	Y
OREGON							
Smith	Y	N	Y	N	N	Y	Y
Wyden	Y	Y	N	Y	N	N	Y
PENNSYLVANIA							
Santorum	Y	N	Y	N	N	Y	Y
Specter	Y	Y	Y	Y	N	Y	Y
RHODE ISLAND							
Chafee	Y	Y	Y	Y	Y	Y	Y
Reed	Y	Y	N	Y	N	N	Y
SOUTH CAROLINA							
Thurmond	Y	N	Y	Y	N	N	Y
Hollings	+	Y	Y	Y	N	N	Y
SOUTH DAKOTA							
Daschle	Y	Y	Y	Y	N	N	Y
Johnson	Y	Y	Y	Y	N	N	Y
TENNESSEE							
Frist	Y	N	Y	N	N	Y	Y
Thompson	Y	N	Y	N	N	Y	Y
TEXAS							
Gramm	?	?	Y	Y	N	Y	Y
Hutchison	Y	N	Y	N	N	Y	Y
UTAH							
Bennett	Y	Y	Y	N	Y	N	Y
Hatch	Y	N	Y	Y	N	Y	Y
VERMONT							
Jeffords	Y	Y	Y	Y	N	Y	Y
Leahy	Y	Y	Y	Y	Y	N	Y
VIRGINIA							
Warner	?	N	Y	Y	N	Y	Y
Robb	N	Y	Y	Y	N	N	Y
WASHINGTON							
Gorton	Y	N	Y	Y	N	Y	Y
Murray	Y	Y	Y	Y	N	N	Y
WEST VIRGINIA							
Byrd	Y	Y	Y	N	N	N	N
Rockefeller	Y	Y	Y	Y	N	N	Y
WISCONSIN							
Feingold	Y	Y	N	Y	N	N	Y
Kohl	Y	Y	Y	Y	Y	N	Y
WYOMING							
Enzi	Y	N	Y	N	N	Y	Y
Thomas	Y	N	Y	N	N	Y	Y

ND Northern Democrats   SD Southern Democrats

Southern states - Ala., Ark., Fla., Ga., Ky., La., Miss., N.C., Okla., S.C., Tenn., Texas, Va.

253. HR 4059. Fiscal 1999 Military Construction Appropriations/ Conference Report. Adoption of the conference report on the bill to provide $8.45 billion in new budget authority for military construction projects in fiscal 1999. It would provide $759 million less than provided in fiscal 1998 and $666 million more than requested by President Clinton. Adopted (thus cleared for the president) 87-3: R 47-2; D 40-1 (ND 34-0, SD 6-1). Sept. 1, 1998.

254. S 2334. Fiscal 1999 Foreign Operations Appropriations/Nuclear Test Ban Funding. Specter, R-Pa., amendment that would add $28.9 million for expenses related to the Comprehensive Nuclear Test Ban Treaty Preparatory Commission. The Senate has not yet ratified the test ban treaty (Treaty Doc. 105-28). Adopted 49-44: R 7-44; D 42-0 (ND 34-0, SD 8-0). Sept. 1, 1998. A "yea" was a vote in support of the president's position.

255. HR 629. Texas, Maine and Vermont Low-Level Radioactive Waste Compact/Conference Report. Adoption of the conference report on the bill that would allow Maine and Vermont to export low-level radioactive waste to Texas. Adopted (thus cleared for the president) 78-15: R 51-0; D 27-15 (ND 19-15, SD 8-0). Sept. 2, 1998.

256. S 2334. Fiscal 1999 Foreign Operations Appropriations/IMF Lending Requirements. Hagel, R-Neb., motion to table (kill) the Kyl, R-Ariz., amendment that would replace previously passed language in the bill regarding conditions on the International Monetary Fund's use of U.S. quota re-

sources with more restrictive language. Motion agreed to 74-19: R 33-18; D 41-1 (ND 33-1, SD 8-0). Sept. 2, 1998.

257. S 2334. Fiscal 1999 Foreign Operations Appropriations/North Korean Nuclear Development. McConnell, R-Ky., motion to table (kill) the McCain, R-Ariz., amendment that would restrict funds for the Korean Peninsula Energy Development Organization unless the president certifies that North Korea is not actively pursuing the acquisition or development of nuclear weapons. Motion rejected 11-80: R 1-48; D 10-32 (ND 9-25, SD 1-7). Sept. 2, 1998. (Subsequently, the McCain amendment as amended was adopted by voice vote.)

258. S 2334. Fiscal 1999 Foreign Operations Appropriations/ Guatemala and Honduras Human Rights Records Declassification. McConnell, R-Ky., motion to table (kill) the Dodd, D-Conn., amendment that would establish a procedure for the declassification of documents related to human rights violations in Guatemala and Honduras. Motion agreed to 50-43: R 50-1; D 0-42 (ND 0-34, SD 0-8). Sept. 2, 1998.

259. S 2334. Fiscal 1999 Foreign Operations Appropriations/Passage. Passage of the bill to provide $12.6 billion in new budget authority for foreign affairs programs in fiscal 1999, plus an additional $18 billion for the International Monetary Fund and $311 million in arrears to multilateral institutions. Passed 90-3: R 49-2; D 41-1 (ND 33-1, SD 8-0). Sept. 2, 1998.

ALABAMA	260	261	262	263	264	265	266
Sessions	Y	N	Y	Y	N	Y	Y
Shelby	Y	N	Y	Y	N	Y	Y
ALASKA							
Murkowski	?	N	Y	Y	N	Y	Y
Stevens	Y	N	Y	Y	N	Y	Y
ARIZONA							
Kyl	Y	N	Y	Y	N	Y	Y
McCain	Y	N	Y	Y	Y	Y	Y
ARKANSAS							
Hutchinson	N	N	Y	Y	N	Y	Y
Bumpers	Y	N	N	Y	Y	Y	N
CALIFORNIA							
Boxer	Y	N	N	Y	Y	Y	N
Feinstein	Y	?	N	Y	Y	Y	N
COLORADO							
Allard	Y	N	Y	Y	N	Y	Y
Campbell	Y	N	Y	Y	N	Y	Y
CONNECTICUT							
Dodd	Y	?	N	Y	Y	Y	N
Lieberman	Y	N	Y	Y	Y	Y	N
DELAWARE							
Roth	Y	N	Y	Y	N	Y	Y
Biden	Y	?	N	Y	Y	Y	N
FLORIDA							
Mack	Y	N	Y	Y	N	Y	Y
Graham	Y	N	N	Y	Y	Y	N
GEORGIA							
Coverdell	Y	N	Y	Y	N	Y	Y
Cleland	Y	N	Y	Y	Y	Y	N
HAWAII							
Akaka	Y	N	Y	Y	Y	Y	N
Inouye	?	N	Y	Y	Y	Y	N
IDAHO							
Craig	Y	N	Y	Y	N	Y	Y
Kempthorne	Y	?	Y	Y	N	Y	Y
ILLINOIS							
Durbin	Y	N	N	Y	Y	Y	N
Moseley-Braun	Y	?	N	Y	Y	?	?
INDIANA							
Coats	Y	N	Y	Y	N	Y	Y
Lugar	Y	N	Y	Y	N	Y	Y

IOWA	260	261	262	263	264	265	266
Grassley	Y	N	Y	Y	N	Y	Y
Harkin	Y	N	N	Y	Y	Y	Y
KANSAS							
Brownback	N	N	Y	N	N	Y	Y
Roberts	Y	N	Y	Y	N	Y	Y
KENTUCKY							
McConnell	Y	N	Y	Y	N	Y	Y
Ford	Y	N	N	Y	Y	Y	N
LOUISIANA							
Breaux	Y	N	N	Y	Y	Y	N
Landrieu	Y	?	N	Y	Y	Y	N
MAINE							
Collins	Y	N	Y	Y	Y	Y	Y
Snowe	Y	N	Y	Y	Y	Y	Y
MARYLAND							
Mikulski	Y	N	N	Y	Y	Y	?
Sarbanes	Y	N	N	Y	Y	Y	N
MASSACHUSETTS							
Kennedy	Y	?	N	Y	Y	Y	N
Kerry	Y	N	N	Y	Y	Y	N
MICHIGAN							
Abraham	Y	N	Y	Y	N	Y	Y
Levin	Y	N	N	Y	Y	Y	N
MINNESOTA							
Grams	Y	?	Y	Y	N	Y	Y
Wellstone	Y	N	N	Y	Y	Y	N
MISSISSIPPI							
Cochran	Y	N	Y	Y	N	Y	Y
Lott	Y	N	Y	Y	N	Y	Y
MISSOURI							
Ashcroft	N	N	Y	Y	N	Y	Y
Bond	Y	N	Y	Y	N	Y	Y
MONTANA							
Burns	Y	N	Y	Y	N	Y	Y
Baucus	Y	N	N	Y	Y	Y	N
NEBRASKA							
Hagel	Y	N	Y	Y	N	Y	Y
Kerrey	Y	N	N	Y	Y	?	N
NEVADA							
Bryan	Y	N	N	Y	Y	Y	N
Reid	Y	N	N	Y	Y	Y	N

NEW HAMPSHIRE	260	261	262	263	264	265	266
Gregg	Y	?	Y	Y	N	Y	Y
Smith	N	N	Y	Y	N	Y	Y
NEW JERSEY							
Lautenberg	Y	?	N	Y	Y	Y	N
Torricelli	Y	N	N	Y	Y	Y	?
NEW MEXICO							
Domenici	Y	N	Y	Y	N	Y	Y
Bingaman	?	N	N	Y	Y	Y	Y
NEW YORK							
D'Amato	Y	N	Y	Y	N	Y	?
Moynihan	Y	N	N	Y	Y	Y	N
NORTH CAROLINA							
Faircloth	Y	N	Y	Y	N	Y	Y
Helms	+	N	Y	N	Y	Y	
NORTH DAKOTA							
Conrad	Y	N	N	Y	Y	Y	N
Dorgan	Y	N	N	Y	Y	Y	N
OHIO							
DeWine	Y	N	Y	Y	N	Y	Y
Glenn	Y	N	N	Y	Y	Y	N
OKLAHOMA							
Inhofe	Y	N	Y	Y	N	Y	Y
Nickles	Y	N	Y	Y	N	Y	Y
OREGON							
Smith	Y	N	Y	Y	N	Y	Y
Wyden	Y	?	N	Y	Y	Y	N
PENNSYLVANIA							
Santorum	Y	?	Y	Y	N	Y	Y
Specter	Y	N	Y	Y	Y	Y	?
RHODE ISLAND							
Chafee	Y	?	Y	Y	N	Y	Y
Reed	Y	N	N	Y	Y	Y	N
SOUTH CAROLINA							
Thurmond	Y	N	Y	Y	N	Y	Y
Hollings	Y	?	Y	Y	Y	Y	?
SOUTH DAKOTA							
Daschle	Y	N	N	Y	Y	Y	N
Johnson	Y	N	N	Y	Y	Y	N
TENNESSEE							
Frist	Y	N	Y	Y	N	Y	Y
Thompson	Y	N	Y	Y	N	Y	Y

TEXAS	260	261	262	263	264	265	266
Gramm	Y	N	Y	Y	N	Y	Y
Hutchison	Y	?	Y	Y	N	Y	Y
UTAH							
Bennett	Y	N	Y	Y	N	Y	Y
Hatch	Y	N	Y	Y	N	Y	Y
VERMONT							
Jeffords	Y	N	Y	Y	Y	Y	Y
Leahy	Y	?	N	Y	Y	Y	N
VIRGINIA							
Warner	Y	N	Y	Y	N	Y	Y
Robb	Y	N	N	Y	Y	Y	N
WASHINGTON							
Gorton	Y	N	Y	Y	N	Y	Y
Murray	Y	?	N	Y	Y	Y	N
WEST VIRGINIA							
Byrd	Y	N	N	Y	Y	Y	N
Rockefeller	Y	N	N	Y	Y	?	N
WISCONSIN							
Feingold	N	N	N	Y	Y	Y	N
Kohl	Y	N	N	Y	Y	Y	N
WYOMING							
Enzi	Y	N	Y	Y	N	Y	Y
Thomas	Y	N	Y	Y	N	Y	Y

Key

Y   Voted for (yea).
Paired for.
+   Announced for.
N   Voted against (nay).
X   Paired against.
−   Announced against.
P   Voted "present."
C   Voted "present" to avoid possible conflict of interest.
?   Did not vote or otherwise make a position known.

Democrats   *Republicans*

ND Northern Democrats   SD Southern Democrats

Southern states - Ala., Ark., Fla., Ga., Ky., La., Miss., N.C., Okla., S.C., Tenn., Texas, Va.

260. HR 4104. Fiscal 1999 Treasury-Postal Service Appropriations/ Passage. Passage of the bill to provide $29.9 billion in new budget authority for the Treasury Department, the White House, postal subsidies and civil service benefits in fiscal 1999. The bill would provide $4.6 billion more than in fiscal 1998 and $3.1 billion more than requested by President Clinton. It would provide a 3.6 percent cost of living adjustment for federal workers. Passed 91-5: R 49-4; D 42-1 (ND 34-1, SD 8-0). Sept. 3, 1998. (Before passage, the Senate struck all after the enacting clause and inserted the text of S2312 as amended.)

261. S 2237. Fiscal 1999 Interior Appropriations/Civil War Battlefield Preservation. Gorton, R-Wash., motion to table (kill) the Jeffords, R-Vt., amendment that would provide up to $10 million for matching grants to states and localities for the preservation of Civil War battlefields. Motion rejected 0-83: R 0-49; D 0-34 (ND 0-28, SD 0-6). Sept. 8, 1998.

262. S 1873. National Missile Defense/Cloture. Motion to invoke cloture (thus limiting debate) on the motion to proceed to the bill that would make it U.S. policy to implement a national missile defense shield. The measure would not establish a specific time frame, but would declare a national policy to deploy a system to protect U.S. territory from a limited number of incoming missiles "as soon as is technologically possible." Motion rejected 59-41: R 55-0; D 4-41 (ND 3-34, SD 1-7). Sept. 9, 1998. Three-fifths of the total Senate (60) is required to invoke cloture. A "nay" was a vote in support of the president's position.

263. S 1301. Consumer Bankruptcy Revisions/Cloture. Motion to invoke cloture (thus limiting debate) on the motion to proceed to the bill that would revise the nation's bankruptcy laws by allowing a bankruptcy judge to dismiss any claim for Chapter 7 relief, or convert the claim to a Chapter 13 case, if the judge determines that the debtor has sufficient income to pay at least 20 percent of his unsecured debts. The bill also would allow creditors, in addition to bankruptcy trustees and judges, to challenge the validity of an individual's claim. Motion agreed to 99-1: R 54-1; D 45-0 (ND 37-0, SD 8-0). Sept. 9, 1998. Three-fifths of the total Senate (60) is required to invoke cloture. (Subsequently, the motion to proceed was agreed to by voice vote.)

264. S 2237. Fiscal 1999 Interior Appropriations/Campaign Finance Revisions — Cloture. Motion to invoke cloture (thus limiting debate) on the McCain, R-Ariz., amendment that would overhaul laws governing the financing of federal political campaigns. Motion rejected 52-48: R 7-48; D 45-0 (ND 37-0, SD 8-0). Sept. 10, 1998. Three-fifths of the total Senate (60) is required to invoke cloture. A "yea" was a vote in support of the president's position.

265. S 1645. Transporting Minors for an Abortion/Cloture. Motion to invoke cloture (thus limiting debate) on the motion to proceed to the bill that would make it a federal crime for anyone other than the parent to transport a minor across state lines with the intent to obtain an abortion. Motion agreed to 97-0: R 55-0; D 42-0 (ND 34-0, SD 8-0). Sept. 11, 1998. Three-fifths of the total Senate (60) is required to invoke cloture.

266. S 1981. Labor Union Organizing Curbs/Cloture. Motion to invoke cloture (thus limiting debate) on the motion to proceed to the bill that would permit employers to refuse to hire, or fire, individuals who seek employment with the primary intent of organizing workers to join a labor union. Motion rejected 52-42: R 52-1; D 0-41 (ND 0-34, SD 0-7). Sept. 14, 1998. Three-fifths of the total Senate (60) is required to invoke cloture. A "nay" was a vote in support of the president's position.

	267	268	269	270	271	272	273
ALABAMA							
Sessions	Y	Y	N	?	Y	Y	Y
Shelby	Y	Y	N	?	Y	Y	Y
ALASKA							
Murkowski	Y	Y	Y	Y	Y	Y	N
Stevens	Y	Y	N	Y	Y	Y	Y
ARIZONA							
Kyl	Y	Y	N	Y	Y	Y	Y
McCain	Y	Y	N	Y	Y	Y	Y
ARKANSAS							
Hutchinson	Y	Y	N	Y	Y	Y	Y
Bumpers	N	N	Y	?	Y	N	N
CALIFORNIA							
Boxer	N	N	Y	Y	Y	N	N
Feinstein	N	N	Y	Y	Y	N	N
COLORADO							
Allard	Y	Y	Y	Y	Y	Y	N
Campbell	Y	Y	Y	Y	Y	Y	N
CONNECTICUT							
Dodd	N	N	Y	Y	Y	N	N
Lieberman	N	N	Y	Y	Y	N	N
DELAWARE							
Roth	Y	N	N	Y	Y	Y	N
Biden	N	N	Y	Y	Y	N	N
FLORIDA							
Mack	Y	Y	N	Y	Y	Y	Y
Graham	N	N	Y	Y	Y	N	N
GEORGIA							
Coverdell	Y	Y	Y	Y	Y	Y	N
Cleland	N	Y	Y	Y	Y	N	N
HAWAII							
Akaka	N	N	Y	Y	Y	N	N
Inouye	N	Y	Y	Y	Y	N	N
IDAHO							
Craig	Y	Y	Y	Y	Y	Y	Y
Kempthorne	Y	Y	Y	Y	Y	Y	Y
ILLINOIS							
Durbin	N	N	Y	Y	Y	N	N
Moseley-Braun	–	N	Y	Y	Y	N	N
INDIANA							
Coats	Y	N	N	Y	Y	Y	Y
Lugar	Y	Y	Y	Y	Y	Y	Y

	267	268	269	270	271	272	273
IOWA							
Grassley	Y	Y	Y	Y	Y	Y	Y
Harkin	N	N	Y	Y	Y	N	N
KANSAS							
Brownback	Y	Y	N	Y	Y	Y	Y
Roberts	Y	Y	Y	Y	Y	Y	Y
KENTUCKY							
McConnell	Y	Y	N	Y	Y	Y	Y
Ford	N	Y	Y	Y	Y	N	N
LOUISIANA							
Breaux	N	Y	Y	N	N	N	N
Landrieu	N	N	Y	Y	Y	N	N
MAINE							
Collins	Y	Y	N	Y	Y	Y	Y
Snowe	Y	N	Y	Y	Y	Y	Y
MARYLAND							
Mikulski	?	?	?	Y	Y	N	N
Sarbanes	N	N	Y	Y	Y	N	N
MASSACHUSETTS							
Kennedy	N	N	Y	Y	Y	N	N
Kerry	N	N	Y	Y	Y	N	N
MICHIGAN							
Abraham	Y	N	Y	Y	Y	Y	Y
Levin	N	N	Y	Y	Y	N	N
MINNESOTA							
Grams	Y	Y	N	Y	Y	Y	Y
Wellstone	N	N	Y	Y	Y	N	N
MISSISSIPPI							
Cochran	Y	Y	N	Y	Y	Y	Y
Lott	Y	Y	N	Y	Y	Y	Y
MISSOURI							
Ashcroft	Y	Y	Y	Y	Y	Y	Y
Bond	Y	Y	Y	Y	Y	Y	N
MONTANA							
Burns	N	Y	Y	Y	Y	Y	Y
Baucus	N	Y	Y	Y	Y	N	N
NEBRASKA							
Hagel	Y	Y	N	Y	Y	Y	Y
Kerrey	N	N	Y	Y	Y	N	N
NEVADA							
Bryan	N	Y	Y	Y	Y	N	N
Reid	N	Y	Y	Y	Y	N	N

	267	268	269	270	271	272	273
NEW HAMPSHIRE							
Gregg	Y	N	Y	Y	Y	Y	Y
Smith	Y	Y	N	Y	Y	Y	Y
NEW JERSEY							
Lautenberg	N	N	Y	Y	Y	N	N
Torricelli	?	N	Y	Y	Y	N	N
NEW MEXICO							
Domenici	Y	Y	Y	Y	Y	Y	Y
Bingaman	N	Y	Y	Y	Y	N	N
NEW YORK							
D'Amato	?	Y	Y	Y	Y	Y	N
Moynihan	N	Y	Y	Y	Y	Y	N
NORTH CAROLINA							
Faircloth	Y	Y	N	Y	Y	Y	Y
Helms	Y	Y	N	?	?	?	Y
NORTH DAKOTA							
Conrad	N	Y	Y	Y	Y	N	N
Dorgan	N	Y	Y	Y	Y	N	N
OHIO							
DeWine	Y	Y	Y	Y	Y	Y	Y
Glenn	N	N	Y	Y	Y	N	N
OKLAHOMA							
Inhofe	Y	Y	N	Y	Y	Y	Y
Nickles	Y	Y	N	Y	Y	Y	Y
OREGON							
Smith	Y	Y	Y	Y	Y	Y	Y
Wyden	N	N	Y	Y	Y	N	N
PENNSYLVANIA							
Santorum	Y	Y	Y	Y	Y	Y	Y
Specter	?	N	Y	Y	Y	Y	N
RHODE ISLAND							
Chafee	Y	N	Y	Y	Y	Y	Y
Reed	N	N	Y	Y	Y	N	N
SOUTH CAROLINA							
Thurmond	Y	Y	Y	Y	Y	Y	Y
Hollings	?	?	?	?	?	?	?
SOUTH DAKOTA							
Daschle	N	Y	Y	Y	Y	N	N
Johnson	N	N	Y	Y	Y	N	N
TENNESSEE							
Frist	Y	Y	Y	Y	Y	Y	Y
Thompson	Y	Y	N	Y	Y	Y	Y

	267	268	269	270	271	272	273
TEXAS							
Gramm	Y	Y	N	Y	Y	Y	Y
Hutchison	Y	Y	Y	Y	Y	Y	N
UTAH							
Bennett	Y	Y	Y	Y	Y	Y	Y
Hatch	Y	Y	Y	Y	Y	Y	Y
VERMONT							
Jeffords	Y	N	Y	Y	Y	Y	N
Leahy	N	N	Y	Y	Y	N	N
VIRGINIA							
Warner	Y	N	Y	Y	Y	Y	N
Robb	N	N	Y	Y	Y	N	N
WASHINGTON							
Gorton	Y	Y	Y	Y	Y	Y	Y
Murray	N	N	Y	Y	Y	N	N
WEST VIRGINIA							
Byrd	N	Y	Y	Y	Y	N	N
Rockefeller	N	N	Y	Y	Y	N	N
WISCONSIN							
Feingold	Y	N	Y	Y	Y	N	N
Kohl	N	N	Y	Y	Y	N	N
WYOMING							
Enzi	Y	Y	Y	Y	Y	Y	Y
Thomas	Y	Y	Y	Y	Y	Y	Y

Key

Y	Voted for (yea).
#	Paired for.
+	Announced for.
N	Voted against (nay).
X	Paired against.
–	Announced against.
P	Voted "present."
C	Voted "present" to avoid possible conflict of interest.
?	Did not vote or otherwise make a position known.

Democrats   *Republicans*

ND Northern Democrats   SD Southern Democrats

Southern states - Ala., Ark., Fla., Ga., Ky., La., Miss., N.C., Okla., S.C., Tenn., Texas, Va.

267. S 2237. Fiscal 1999 Interior Appropriations/Agriculture Marketing Loans. Lugar, R-Ind., motion to table (kill) the Daschle, D-S.D., amendment that would lift the cap on agriculture commodity marketing loans imposed by the 1996 farm law (PL 104-127) for one year. The new loan rate would be based on 85 percent of the average price of the product for the past five years, not including the highest and lowest years. The amendment also would give the Agriculture Department authority to extend the marketing loan term from nine months to 15 months for one year. Motion agreed to 53-41: R 52-1; D 1-40 (ND 1-33, SD 0-7). Sept. 14, 1998.

268. S 2237. Fiscal 1999 Interior Appropriations/Mining Regulations. Murkowski, R-Alaska, motion to table (kill) the Bumpers, D-Ark., amendment to remove language in the bill that would prohibit the Interior Department from implementing proposed mining regulations until the National Academy of Sciences conducts a study of existing regulations governing mining on public lands. Motion agreed to 58-40: R 45-10; D 13-30 (ND 10-26, SD 3-4). Sept. 15, 1998.

269. S 2237. Fiscal 1999 Interior Appropriations/NEA Funding. Gorton, R-Wash., motion to table (kill) the Ashcroft, R-Mo., amendment that would eliminate funding for programs and activities carried out by the National Endowment for the Arts and transfer the $100 million taken from the NEA to the National Park Service. Motion agreed to 76-22: R 33-22; D 43-0 (ND 36-0, SD 7-0). Sept. 15, 1998.

270. Procedural Motion. Lott, R-Miss., motion to instruct the sergeant-at-arms to request the attendance of absent senators. Motion agreed to 94-1: R 52-0; D 42-1 (ND 37-0, SD 5-1). Sept. 16, 1998.

271. Procedural Motion. Lott, R-Miss., motion to instruct the sergeant-at-arms to request the attendance of absent senators. Motion agreed to 97-1: R 54-0; D 43-1 (ND 37-0, SD 6-1). Sept. 16, 1998.

272. Procedural Motion/Adjourn. Lott, R-Miss., motion to adjourn. Motion agreed to 55-43: R 54-0; D 1-43 (ND 1-36, SD 0-7). Sept. 16, 1998.

273. S 1301. Consumer Bankruptcy Revisions/Credit Card Finance Charges. Grassley, R-Iowa, motion to table (kill) the Reed, D-R.I., amendment that would prohibit credit card companies from terminating or refusing to renew credit to consumers who avoid finance charges by paying off their balances. The amendment also would prohibit creditors from charging such consumers a fee in lieu of finance charges. Motion rejected 47-52: R 47-8; D 0-44 (ND 0-37, SD 0-7). Sept. 17, 1998. (Subsequently, the amendment was adopted by voice vote.)

	274	275	276	277	278	279	280
ALABAMA							
Sessions	Y	Y	?	Y	Y	Y	Y
Shelby	Y	Y	?	Y	Y	N	Y
ALASKA							
Murkowski	Y	Y	Y	Y	Y	Y	Y
Stevens	Y	Y	Y	Y	Y	Y	Y
ARIZONA							
Kyl	Y	Y	Y	Y	Y	Y	Y
McCain	Y	N	Y	Y	Y	Y	Y
ARKANSAS							
Hutchinson	Y	Y	Y	Y	Y	Y	Y
Bumpers	N	N	Y	N	N	N	N
CALIFORNIA							
Boxer	N	N	Y	N	N	N	N
Feinstein	N	N	Y	N	N	N	N
COLORADO							
Allard	Y	Y	Y	Y	Y	Y	Y
Campbell	Y	Y	Y	Y	Y	Y	Y
CONNECTICUT							
Dodd	N	N	Y	N	N	N	N
Lieberman	N	N	Y	N	N	N	N
DELAWARE							
Roth	Y	Y	Y	Y	Y	Y	Y
Biden	Y	Y	Y	Y	N	N	N
FLORIDA							
Mack	Y	Y	Y	Y	Y	Y	Y
Graham	N	Y	Y	N	Y	N	N
GEORGIA							
Coverdell	?	?	Y	Y	Y	Y	Y
Cleland	N	Y	Y	N	N	N	N
HAWAII							
Akaka	N	Y	N	N	N	N	N
Inouye	N	Y	?	N	N	N	N
IDAHO							
Craig	Y	Y	Y	Y	Y	Y	Y
Kempthorne	Y	Y	Y	Y	Y	Y	Y
ILLINOIS							
Durbin	N	N	Y	N	N	N	N
Moseley-Braun	N	N	Y	N	N	N	N
INDIANA							
Coats	N	Y	?	Y	Y	Y	Y
Lugar	Y	Y	Y	Y	Y	Y	Y
IOWA							
Grassley	Y	Y	Y	Y	Y	Y	Y
Harkin	N	N	Y	N	N	N	N
KANSAS							
Brownback	Y	Y	Y	Y	Y	Y	Y
Roberts	Y	Y	Y	Y	Y	Y	Y
KENTUCKY							
McConnell	Y	Y	Y	Y	Y	Y	Y
Ford	N	Y	Y	N	N	N	N
LOUISIANA							
Breaux	N	Y	Y	Y	N	Y	N
Landrieu	N	Y	Y	Y	N	N	N
MAINE							
Collins	Y	Y	Y	N	Y	Y	N
Snowe	Y	Y	Y	N	Y	Y	N
MARYLAND							
Mikulski	N	N	Y	N	N	N	N
Sarbanes	N	N	Y	N	N	N	N
MASSACHUSETTS							
Kennedy	N	N	?	N	N	N	N
Kerry	N	N	?	N	N	N	N
MICHIGAN							
Abraham	Y	Y	Y	Y	Y	Y	Y
Levin	N	N	?	N	N	N	N
MINNESOTA							
Grams	Y	Y	Y	Y	Y	Y	Y
Wellstone	N	N	Y	N	N	N	N
MISSISSIPPI							
Cochran	Y	Y	Y	Y	Y	Y	Y
Lott	Y	Y	Y	Y	Y	Y	Y
MISSOURI							
Ashcroft	Y	Y	Y	Y	Y	Y	Y
Bond	Y	Y	Y	Y	Y	Y	Y
MONTANA							
Burns	Y	Y	Y	Y	Y	Y	Y
Baucus	N	Y	Y	N	N	N	N
NEBRASKA							
Hagel	Y	Y	Y	Y	Y	Y	Y
Kerrey	N	Y	Y	N	N	N	N
NEVADA							
Bryan	N	N	Y	N	N	Y	N
Reid	Y	Y	Y	Y	N	Y	N
NEW HAMPSHIRE							
Gregg	Y	Y	Y	Y	Y	Y	Y
Smith	Y	Y	Y	Y	Y	Y	Y
NEW JERSEY							
Lautenberg	N	N	Y	N	N	N	N
Torricelli	N	N	Y	N	N	N	N
NEW MEXICO							
Domenici	Y	Y	Y	Y	Y	Y	N
Bingaman	N	N	Y	N	N	N	N
NEW YORK							
D'Amato	N	N	Y	N	N	N	N
Moynihan	N	N	+	Y	N	N	N
NORTH CAROLINA							
Faircloth	Y	Y	Y	Y	Y	Y	Y
Helms	Y	Y	?	Y	Y	Y	Y
NORTH DAKOTA							
Conrad	N	Y	Y	N	Y	N	N
Dorgan	N	Y	Y	N	Y	N	N
OHIO							
DeWine	Y	Y	Y	Y	Y	Y	Y
Glenn	Y	N	Y	N	?	?	?
OKLAHOMA							
Inhofe	Y	Y	Y	Y	Y	Y	Y
Nickles	Y	Y	Y	Y	Y	Y	Y
OREGON							
Smith	N	Y	Y	N	N	N	N
Wyden	N	Y	Y	N	N	N	N
PENNSYLVANIA							
Santorum	Y	Y	Y	Y	Y	Y	Y
Specter	Y	Y	Y	N	N	N	N
RHODE ISLAND							
Chafee	Y	N	Y	N	Y	N	N
Reed	N	N	Y	N	N	N	N
SOUTH CAROLINA							
Thurmond	Y	Y	Y	Y	Y	Y	Y
Hollings	?	?	?	Y	Y	N	Y
SOUTH DAKOTA							
Daschle	N	Y	Y	N	N	N	N
Johnson	Y	Y	Y	N	N	N	N
TENNESSEE							
Frist	Y	Y	Y	Y	Y	Y	Y
Thompson	Y	Y	Y	Y	Y	Y	Y
TEXAS							
Gramm	Y	Y	Y	Y	Y	Y	Y
Hutchison	Y	Y	Y	Y	Y	Y	Y
UTAH							
Bennett	Y	Y	Y	Y	Y	Y	Y
Hatch	Y	Y	Y	Y	Y	Y	Y
VERMONT							
Jeffords	Y	Y	Y	N	Y	N	Y
Leahy	N	Y	Y	N	N	N	N
VIRGINIA							
Warner	Y	Y	Y	N	N	N	N
Robb	Y	Y	Y	N	N	N	N
WASHINGTON							
Gorton	Y	Y	Y	Y	Y	Y	Y
Murray	N	N	Y	N	N	N	N
WEST VIRGINIA							
Byrd	N	Y	Y	Y	N	Y	N
Rockefeller	N	Y	Y	Y	N	N	N
WISCONSIN							
Feingold	Y	N	Y	N	N	N	N
Kohl	Y	N	Y	N	N	N	N
WYOMING							
Enzi	Y	Y	?	Y	Y	Y	Y
Thomas	Y	Y	Y	Y	Y	Y	Y

Key

Y	Voted for (yea).
#	Paired for.
+	Announced for.
N	Voted against (nay).
X	Paired against.
−	Announced against.
P	Voted "present."
C	Voted "present" to avoid possible conflict of interest.
?	Did not vote or otherwise make a position known.

Democrats   *Republicans*

ND Northern Democrats   SD Southern Democrats

Southern states - Ala., Ark., Fla., Ga., Ky., La., Miss., N.C., Okla., S.C., Tenn., Texas, Va.

274. S 1301. Consumer Bankruptcy Revisions/College-Age Credit Card Consumers. Grassley, R-Iowa, motion to table (kill) the Dodd, D-Conn., amendment that would prohibit credit card issuers from issuing a card to any consumer under age 21 unless the consumer provides either parental consent or financial information indicating an independent means of repaying debt that may arise from the issuance. Motion agreed to 58-40: R 51-3; D 7-37 (ND 6-31, SD 1-6). Sept. 17, 1998.

275. S 1301. Consumer Bankruptcy Revisions/ATM Surcharges. Grassley, R-Iowa, motion to table (kill) the D'Amato, R-N.Y., amendment that would prohibit financial institutions from imposing a surcharge — a charge in addition to the interchange fee — for the use of their automated teller machines (ATMs). Motion agreed to 72-26: R 51-3; D 21-23 (ND 15-22, SD 6-1). Sept. 17, 1998.

276. S 1301. Consumer Bankruptcy Revisions/IRA Protections. Hatch, R-Utah, amendment that would provide that all funds contributed to IRS-qualified retirement plans, such as Roth IRAs, are exempt from bankruptcy proceedings. Under current law, only retirement savings held in 401(k) plans are exempt. Adopted 89-0: R 50-0; D 39-0 (ND 32-0, SD 7-0). Sept. 17, 1998.

277. HR 1122. Abortion Procedure Ban/Veto Override. Passage, over President Clinton's Oct. 10, 1997, veto, of the bill to ban a certain late-term abortion procedure, in which the physician partially delivers the fetus before completing the abortion. Anyone convicted of performing such an abortion would be subject to a fine and up to two years in prison. Rejected 64-36: R 51-4; D 13-32 (ND 9-28, SD 4-4). Sept. 18, 1998. A two-thirds majority of those present and voting (67 in this case) of both houses is required to override a veto. A "nay" was a vote in support of the president's position.

278. S 1301. Consumer Bankruptcy Revisions/Minimum Wage Increase. Lott, R-Miss., motion to table (kill) the Kennedy, D-Mass., amendment that would increase the minimum wage by 50 cents in 1999 and 50 cents in 2000, raising it from $5.15 an hour to $6.15 an hour. Motion agreed to 55-44: R 53-2; D 2-42 (ND 0-36, SD 2-6). Sept. 22, 1998. A "nay" was a vote in support of the president's position.

279. S 1301. Consumer Bankruptcy Revisions/Bankruptcy Attorneys. Grassley, R-Iowa, motion to table (kill) the Feingold, D-Wis., amendment that would replace language requiring a debtor's attorney to pay for the costs of the trustee if the attorney is found to have not been "substantially justified" in filing a Chapter 7 bankruptcy claim with language making debtors responsible for the costs of the trustee if their filing is dismissed or converted to Chapter 13. Motion agreed to 57-42: R 53-2; D 4-40 (ND 3-33, SD 1-7). Sept. 22, 1998.

280. S 1301. Consumer Bankruptcy Revisions/Filing Fee Waiver. Grassley, R-Iowa, motion to table (kill) the Feingold, D-Wis., amendment that would allow the court to waive the filing fee for an individual debtor if the court determines that the debtor is unable to pay the fee in installments. Motion rejected 47-52: R 47-8; D 0-44 (ND 0-36, SD 0-8). Sept. 22, 1998. (Subsequently, the Feingold amendment was adopted by voice vote.)

	281	282	283	284	285	286	287
ALABAMA							
Sessions	Y	Y	Y	Y	Y	Y	Y
Shelby	Y	Y	Y	Y	Y	Y	Y
ALASKA							
Murkowski	Y	Y	Y	Y	Y	Y	Y
Stevens	Y	Y	Y	Y	Y	Y	Y
ARIZONA							
Kyl	Y	Y	Y	Y	Y	Y	Y
McCain	Y	Y	Y	Y	Y	Y	N
ARKANSAS							
Hutchinson	Y	Y	Y	Y	Y	Y	Y
Bumpers	N	N	N	Y	N	Y	N
CALIFORNIA							
Boxer	N	N	N	Y	Y	N	N
Feinstein	N	N	Y	Y	Y	N	N
COLORADO							
Allard	Y	Y	Y	Y	Y	Y	Y
Campbell	Y	Y	Y	Y	Y	Y	Y
CONNECTICUT							
Dodd	N	N	Y	Y	Y	N	N
Lieberman	Y	N	N	Y	Y	N	N
DELAWARE							
Roth	Y	Y	Y	Y	Y	N	Y
Biden	Y	N	Y	Y	Y	N	Y
FLORIDA							
Mack	Y	Y	Y	Y	Y	Y	Y
Graham	Y	N	N	Y	Y	N	Y
GEORGIA							
Coverdell	Y	Y	Y	Y	Y	Y	Y
Cleland	N	N	N	Y	Y	N	Y
HAWAII							
Akaka	N	N	N	Y	Y	N	Y
Inouye	N	N	N	Y	Y	N	Y
IDAHO							
Craig	Y	Y	Y	Y	Y	Y	Y
Kempthorne	Y	Y	Y	Y	Y	Y	Y
ILLINOIS							
Durbin	N	N	Y	Y	N	N	N
Moseley-Braun	N	N	Y	Y	?	?	?
INDIANA							
Coats	Y	Y	Y	Y	Y	Y	Y
Lugar	Y	Y	Y	Y	Y	Y	Y
IOWA							
Grassley	Y	Y	Y	Y	Y	Y	Y
Harkin	N	N	N	Y	Y	N	Y
KANSAS							
Brownback	Y	Y	Y	Y	Y	Y	Y
Roberts	Y	Y	Y	Y	Y	Y	Y
KENTUCKY							
McConnell	Y	Y	Y	Y	Y	Y	Y
Ford	N	N	N	Y	Y	N	Y
LOUISIANA							
Breaux	Y	N	Y	Y	Y	Y	Y
Landrieu	Y	N	Y	Y	Y	N	Y
MAINE							
Collins	Y	Y	Y	Y	Y	Y	Y
Snowe	Y	Y	Y	Y	Y	Y	Y
MARYLAND							
Mikulski	N	N	N	Y	Y	N	N
Sarbanes	N	N	N	Y	Y	N	N
MASSACHUSETTS							
Kennedy	N	N	N	Y	Y	N	N
Kerry	N	N	Y	Y	Y	N	N
MICHIGAN							
Abraham	Y	Y	Y	Y	Y	Y	Y
Levin	N	N	N	Y	Y	N	N
MINNESOTA							
Grams	Y	Y	Y	Y	Y	Y	Y
Wellstone	N	N	N	N	+	−	−
MISSISSIPPI							
Cochran	Y	Y	Y	Y	Y	Y	Y
Lott	Y	Y	Y	Y	Y	Y	Y
MISSOURI							
Ashcroft	Y	Y	Y	Y	Y	Y	Y
Bond	Y	Y	Y	Y	Y	Y	Y
MONTANA							
Burns	Y	Y	Y	Y	Y	Y	Y
Baucus	N	N	N	Y	Y	N	Y
NEBRASKA							
Hagel	Y	Y	Y	Y	Y	N	Y
Kerrey	N	N	N	Y	Y	N	Y
NEVADA							
Bryan	N	N	N	Y	Y	N	Y
Reid	Y	Y	N	Y	Y	N	N
NEW HAMPSHIRE							
Gregg	Y	Y	Y	Y	Y	N	Y
Smith	Y	Y	Y	Y	Y	Y	Y
NEW JERSEY							
Lautenberg	N	N	N	Y	Y	N	N
Torricelli	N	N	N	Y	Y	N	N
NEW MEXICO							
Domenici	Y	Y	Y	Y	Y	Y	Y
Bingaman	N	N	N	Y	N	Y	N
NEW YORK							
D'Amato	Y	Y	Y	Y	Y	N	N
Moynihan	N	N	Y	Y	Y	N	N
NORTH CAROLINA							
Faircloth	Y	Y	Y	Y	Y	Y	Y
Helms	Y	Y	Y	Y	Y	Y	Y
NORTH DAKOTA							
Conrad	N	N	N	Y	Y	N	Y
Dorgan	N	N	N	Y	Y	N	Y
OHIO							
DeWine	Y	Y	Y	Y	Y	N	Y
Glenn	?	?	?	?	?	?	?
OKLAHOMA							
Inhofe	Y	Y	Y	Y	Y	Y	Y
Nickles	Y	Y	Y	Y	Y	Y	Y
OREGON							
Smith	Y	Y	Y	Y	Y	Y	Y
Wyden	N	N	Y	Y	Y	N	Y
PENNSYLVANIA							
Santorum	Y	Y	Y	Y	Y	Y	Y
Specter	Y	N	Y	Y	Y	Y	N
RHODE ISLAND							
Chafee	Y	N	Y	Y	Y	Y	Y
Reed	N	N	N	Y	Y	N	N
SOUTH CAROLINA							
Thurmond	Y	Y	Y	Y	Y	Y	Y
Hollings	N	Y	N	Y	Y	N	?
SOUTH DAKOTA							
Daschle	N	N	N	Y	Y	N	Y
Johnson	Y	N	N	Y	Y	N	N
TENNESSEE							
Frist	Y	Y	Y	Y	Y	Y	Y
Thompson	Y	Y	Y	Y	Y	N	Y
TEXAS							
Gramm	Y	Y	Y	Y	Y	N	Y
Hutchison	Y	Y	Y	Y	Y	Y	N
UTAH							
Bennett	Y	Y	Y	Y	Y	Y	Y
Hatch	Y	Y	Y	Y	Y	Y	Y
VERMONT							
Jeffords	N	N	Y	Y	Y	N	N
Leahy	N	N	Y	Y	Y	N	N
VIRGINIA							
Warner	Y	Y	?	?	Y	Y	Y
Robb	Y	N	Y	Y	Y	N	N
WASHINGTON							
Gorton	Y	Y	N	Y	Y	N	Y
Murray	N	N	Y	Y	Y	N	Y
WEST VIRGINIA							
Byrd	N	N	Y	Y	N	N	N
Rockefeller	N	N	Y	Y	Y	N	Y
WISCONSIN							
Feingold	N	N	N	Y	Y	N	N
Kohl	Y	N	Y	Y	Y	N	Y
WYOMING							
Enzi	Y	Y	Y	Y	Y	Y	Y
Thomas	Y	Y	Y	Y	Y	Y	Y

Key

Y	Voted for (yea).
#	Paired for.
+	Announced for.
N	Voted against (nay).
X	Paired against.
−	Announced against.
P	Voted "present."
C	Voted "present" to avoid possible conflict of interest.
?	Did not vote or otherwise make a position known.

Democrats   *Republicans*

ND Northern Democrats   SD Southern Democrats

Southern states - Ala., Ark., Fla., Ga., Ky., La., Miss., N.C., Okla., S.C., Tenn., Texas, Va.

281. S 1301. Consumer Bankruptcy Revisions/Creditor Good Faith. Hatch, R-Utah, motion to table (kill) the Reed, D-R.I., amendment that would allow the court to consider whether a creditor who moves for dismissal or conversion of a Chapter 7 bankruptcy case has "dealt in good faith" with the debtor. Motion agreed to 63-36: R 54-1; D 9-35 (ND 5-31, SD 4-4). Sept. 22, 1998.

282. S 1645. Transporting Minors for an Abortion/Cloture. Motion to invoke cloture (thus limiting debate) on the substitute amendment to the bill that would make it a federal crime for anyone other than a parent to transport a minor across state lines with the intent to obtain an abortion. Motion rejected 54-45: R 52-3; D 2-42 (ND 1-35, SD 1-7). Sept. 22, 1998. Three-fifths of the total Senate (60) is required to invoke cloture.

283. S 1301. Consumer Bankruptcy Revisions/Federal Reserve Interest Rates. Domenici, R-N.M., motion to table (kill) the Harkin, D-Iowa, amendment that would express the sense of Congress that the Federal Reserve should decrease the Federal Funds interest rate. Motion agreed to 71-27: R 53-1; D 18-26 (ND 14-22, SD 4-4). Sept. 23, 1998.

284. HR 3150. Consumer Bankruptcy Revisions/Passage. Passage of the bill to revise the nation's bankruptcy laws by allowing a bankruptcy judge to dismiss any claim for Chapter 7 relief, or convert the claim to a Chapter 13 case, if the judge determines that the debtor has is able to pay at least 30 percent of his unsecured debt. Passed 97-1: R 54-0; D 43-1 (ND 35-1, SD 8-0). Sept. 23, 1998. A "yea" was a vote in support of the president's position. (Before passage, the Senate struck all after the enacting clause and inserted the text of S 1301.)

285. S 2176. Acting Presidential Appointments/Cloture. Motion to invoke cloture (thus limiting debate) on the motion to proceed to the bill that would clarify that all executive branch positions that are not explicitly governed by other federal statutes fall under the "Vacancies Act," which prohibits the president from appointing individuals on an "acting" basis for more than 120 days to executive branch positions that require Senate confirmation. The bill also would extend from 120 days to 150 days the length of time a department's top deputy may fill a vacancy on an "acting" basis. Motion agreed to 96-1: R 55-0; D 41-1 (ND 33-1, SD 8-0). Sept. 24, 1998. Three-fifths of the total Senate (60) is required to invoke cloture. (Subsequently, the motion to proceed was agreed to by voice vote.)

286. S 2279. Federal Aviation Administration Reauthorization/Pilot License Revocation. Inhofe, R-Okla., amendment that would allow any pilot who has had his license revoked for safety reasons by emergency action of the Federal Aviation Administration (FAA) to appeal the decision within 48 hours to the National Transportation Safety Board (NTSB). The amendment would require the NTSB to rule within five days of the appeal whether the FAA has proven the existence of an emergency that requires the immediate revocation of the license in the interest of air safety. If the NTSB rules that there is no emergency, the license is returned to the pilot while the FAA pursues its case. Rejected 46-51: R 45-10; D 1-41 (ND 0-34, SD 1-7). Sept. 24, 1998.

287. S 2279. Federal Aviation Administration Reauthorization/Noise Control. McCain, R-Ariz., motion to table (kill) the Torricelli, D-N.J., amendment that would reestablish the Environmental Protection Agency's Office of Noise Abatement and Control and would require an EPA study on airport noise. Motion agreed to 69-27: R 50-5; D 19-22 (ND 14-20, SD 5-2). Sept. 24, 1998.

	288	289	290	291	292	293	294
ALABAMA							
Sessions	Y	?	?	?	?	Y	Y
Shelby	Y	Y	Y	Y	Y	Y	Y
ALASKA							
Murkowski	Y	Y	Y	Y	Y	Y	Y
Stevens	Y	Y	Y	Y	Y	Y	Y
ARIZONA							
Kyl	Y	Y	Y	Y	Y	Y	Y
McCain	Y	Y	Y	Y	Y	Y	Y
ARKANSAS							
Hutchinson	Y	Y	Y	Y	Y	Y	Y
Bumpers	Y	N	Y	N	Y	N	N
CALIFORNIA							
Boxer	?	N	Y	Y	?	Y	N
Feinstein	Y	N	Y	Y	Y	Y	N
COLORADO							
Allard	Y	Y	Y	Y	Y	Y	Y
Campbell	Y	Y	Y	Y	Y	Y	Y
CONNECTICUT							
Dodd	Y	N	Y	Y	Y	Y	N
Lieberman	Y	N	Y	Y	Y	Y	N
DELAWARE							
Roth	Y	Y	Y	Y	Y	Y	Y
Biden	Y	N	Y	Y	Y	Y	N
FLORIDA							
Mack	Y	Y	Y	Y	Y	Y	Y
Graham	Y	N	Y	N	Y	N	N
GEORGIA							
Coverdell	Y	Y	Y	Y	Y	Y	Y
Cleland	Y	N	Y	Y	N	Y	N
HAWAII							
Akaka	Y	N	Y	Y	Y	Y	Y
Inouye	Y	N	Y	Y	Y	Y	Y
IDAHO							
Craig	Y	Y	Y	Y	Y	Y	Y
Kempthorne	?	Y	Y	Y	Y	Y	Y
ILLINOIS							
Durbin	Y	N	Y	Y	Y	Y	N
Moseley-Braun	?	?	+	+	?	?	–
INDIANA							
Coats	Y	Y	Y	Y	Y	Y	Y
Lugar	Y	Y	Y	Y	Y	Y	Y

	288	289	290	291	292	293	294
IOWA							
Grassley	Y	Y	Y	Y	Y	Y	Y
Harkin	Y	N	Y	Y	Y	Y	N
KANSAS							
Brownback	Y	Y	Y	Y	Y	Y	Y
Roberts	Y	Y	Y	Y	Y	Y	Y
KENTUCKY							
McConnell	Y	Y	Y	Y	Y	Y	Y
Ford	Y	N	Y	Y	Y	Y	Y
LOUISIANA							
Breaux	Y	N	Y	Y	Y	Y	Y
Landrieu	Y	N	Y	Y	Y	Y	Y
MAINE							
Collins	Y	Y	Y	Y	Y	Y	Y
Snowe	Y	Y	Y	Y	Y	Y	Y
MARYLAND							
Mikulski	Y	N	Y	Y	Y	Y	N
Sarbanes	Y	N	Y	Y	Y	Y	N
MASSACHUSETTS							
Kennedy	Y	?	Y	Y	Y	Y	N
Kerry	Y	N	Y	Y	Y	Y	N
MICHIGAN							
Abraham	Y	Y	Y	Y	Y	Y	N
Levin	Y	N	Y	Y	Y	Y	N
MINNESOTA							
Grams	Y	Y	Y	Y	Y	Y	Y
Wellstone	+	N	Y	N	Y	N	N
MISSISSIPPI							
Cochran	Y	Y	Y	Y	Y	Y	Y
Lott	Y	Y	Y	Y	Y	Y	Y
MISSOURI							
Ashcroft	?	Y	Y	Y	Y	Y	Y
Bond	Y	?	Y	Y	Y	Y	Y
MONTANA							
Burns	Y	Y	Y	Y	Y	Y	Y
Baucus	Y	N	Y	Y	Y	Y	N
NEBRASKA							
Hagel	Y	Y	?	?	?	Y	Y
Kerrey	Y	N	Y	Y	Y	Y	N
NEVADA							
Bryan	Y	N	Y	Y	Y	Y	N
Reid	Y	–	Y	Y	Y	Y	N

	288	289	290	291	292	293	294
NEW HAMPSHIRE							
Gregg	Y	Y	Y	Y	Y	Y	?
Smith	Y	Y	Y	Y	Y	Y	Y
NEW JERSEY							
Lautenberg	Y	N	Y	Y	Y	Y	N
Torricelli	Y	?	Y	Y	Y	Y	Y
NEW MEXICO							
Domenici	Y	Y	Y	Y	Y	Y	Y
Bingaman	Y	N	Y	Y	Y	Y	Y
NEW YORK							
D'Amato	Y	?	Y	Y	Y	Y	Y
Moynihan	Y	N	Y	Y	Y	Y	N
NORTH CAROLINA							
Faircloth	Y	Y	Y	Y	Y	Y	Y
Helms	Y	Y	Y	Y	Y	Y	Y
NORTH DAKOTA							
Conrad	Y	N	Y	Y	Y	Y	N
Dorgan	Y	N	Y	Y	Y	Y	N
OHIO							
DeWine	Y	Y	Y	Y	Y	Y	Y
Glenn	?	N	Y	Y	Y	?	?
OKLAHOMA							
Inhofe	Y	Y	Y	Y	Y	Y	Y
Nickles	Y	Y	Y	Y	Y	Y	Y
OREGON							
Smith	Y	Y	Y	Y	Y	Y	Y
Wyden	Y	?	Y	Y	Y	Y	N
PENNSYLVANIA							
Santorum	Y	Y	Y	Y	Y	Y	Y
Specter	Y	Y	Y	Y	Y	Y	N
RHODE ISLAND							
Chafee	Y	Y	Y	Y	Y	Y	Y
Reed	Y	N	Y	Y	Y	Y	N
SOUTH CAROLINA							
Thurmond	Y	Y	Y	Y	Y	Y	Y
Hollings	?	?	?	?	?	Y	Y
SOUTH DAKOTA							
Daschle	Y	N	Y	Y	Y	Y	N
Johnson	Y	N	Y	Y	Y	Y	N
TENNESSEE							
Frist	Y	Y	Y	Y	Y	Y	Y
Thompson	Y	Y	Y	Y	Y	Y	Y

Key

Y   Voted for (yea).
\#   Paired for.
\+   Announced for.
N   Voted against (nay).
X   Paired against.
–   Announced against.
P   Voted "present."
C   Voted "present" to avoid possible conflict of interest.
?   Did not vote or otherwise make a position known.

Democrats   *Republicans*

	288	289	290	291	292	293	294
TEXAS							
Gramm	Y	Y	Y	Y	Y	Y	Y
Hutchison	Y	Y	Y	Y	Y	Y	Y
UTAH							
Bennett	Y	Y	Y	Y	N	Y	Y
Hatch	Y	Y	Y	Y	Y	Y	Y
VERMONT							
Jeffords	Y	Y	Y	Y	Y	Y	Y
Leahy	Y	N	Y	Y	Y	Y	N
VIRGINIA							
Warner	Y	Y	Y	Y	Y	Y	Y
Robb	N	N	Y	Y	Y	Y	N
WASHINGTON							
Gorton	Y	Y	Y	Y	N	Y	Y
Murray	Y	N	Y	Y	Y	Y	N
WEST VIRGINIA							
Byrd	Y	Y	Y	Y	Y	Y	Y
Rockefeller	Y	N	Y	Y	Y	Y	N
WISCONSIN							
Feingold	Y	N	Y	N	Y	N	N
Kohl	Y	N	Y	Y	Y	Y	N
WYOMING							
Enzi	Y	Y	Y	Y	N	Y	Y
Thomas	Y	Y	Y	Y	Y	Y	Y

ND Northern Democrats   SD Southern Democrats

Southern states - Ala., Ark., Fla., Ga., Ky., La., Miss., N.C., Okla., S.C., Tenn., Texas, Va.

288. HR 4057. Federal Aviation Administration Reauthorization/Passage. Passage of the bill to reauthorize the Federal Aviation Administration for two years, including operations, facilities and equipment, as well as the Airport Improvement Program and funding for aviation safety and security improvements. The bill also would increase slot exemptions at New York's LaGuardia and John F. Kennedy airports, Chicago's O'Hare and Washington's Reagan National Airport, and would authorize exemptions to the so-called perimeter rule at Reagan National, which prohibits nonstop flights over a certain mileage. Passed 92-1: R 53-0; D 39-1 (ND 33-0, SD 6-1). Sept. 25, 1998. (Before passage, the Senate struck all after the enacting clause and inserted the text of S 2279 as amended.)

289. S 2176. Acting Presidential Appointments/Cloture. Motion to invoke cloture (thus limiting debate) on the bill that would clarify that all executive branch positions that are not explicitly governed by other federal statutes fall under the "Vacancies Act," which prohibits the president from appointing individuals on an "acting" basis for more than 120 days to executive branch positions that require Senate confirmation. The bill also would extend from 120 days to 150 days the length of time a department's top deputy may fill a vacancy on an "acting" basis. Motion rejected 53-38: R 52-0; D 1-38 (ND 1-31, SD 0-7). Sept. 28, 1998. Three-fifths of the total Senate (60) is required to invoke cloture.

290. HR 6. Higher Education Act Reauthorization/Conference Report. Adoption of the conference report on the bill to reauthorize higher education programs for five years. The measure would cut interest rates on federally guaranteed student loans while providing special subsidies to banks. Adopted (thus cleared for the president) 96-0: R 53-0; D 43-0 (ND 36-0, SD 7-0). Sept. 29, 1998. A "yea" was a vote in support of the president's position.

291. HR 4103. Fiscal 1999 Defense Appropriations/Conference Report. Adoption of the conference report on the bill to provide $250.5 billion in new budget authority for defense-related programs for fiscal 1999. The bill

would provide $485 million less than requested by President Clinton and $2.8 billion more than provided in fiscal 1998. Adopted (thus cleared for the president) 94-2: R 53-0; D 41-2 (ND 34-2, SD 7-0). Sept. 29, 1998.

292. S 442. Internet Tax Moratorium/Cloture. Motion to invoke cloture (thus limiting debate) on the motion to proceed to the bill that would impose a two-year moratorium on state Internet taxation to allow state, local and federal officials and industry representatives to negotiate what type of tax treatment should be applied to Internet access and commerce. Motion agreed to 89-6: R 50-3; D 39-3 (ND 35-0, SD 4-3). Sept. 29, 1998. Three-fifths of the total Senate (60) is required to invoke cloture.

293. HR 3616. Fiscal 1999 Defense Authorization/Conference Report. Adoption of the conference report on the bill to authorize $270.5 billion in new budget authority for defense-related activities in fiscal 1999, which is $406 million less than requested by President Clinton. The bill would authorize an additional $1.86 billion, designated as emergency spending, for U.S. troop operations in Bosnia during fiscal 1999. It also would authorize a 3.6 percent raise in military pay. Adopted (thus cleared for the president) 96-2: R 55-0; D 41-2 (ND 33-2, SD 8-0). Oct. 1, 1998.

294. S 1092. King Cove Land Transfer/Passage. Passage of the bill to require the Interior Department to transfer a perpetual 100-foot-wide, 30-mile right-of-way through the Izembek National Wildlife Refuge in Alaska to the Aleutians East Borough for the purpose of constructing a gravel, one-lane public road from the remote Alaska town of King Cove to Cold Bay, which has an all-weather airport. The measure would require the King Cove Corporation, an Alaskan Native group that along with the federal government owns most of the surrounding land, to transfer 664 acres of lands south of Cold Bay to the Interior Department in exchange for the road land. Passed 59-38: R 51-3; D 8-35 (ND 4-31, SD 4-4). Oct. 01, 1998. A "nay" was a vote in support of the president's position.

	295	296	297	298	299	300	301
ALABAMA							
Sessions	N	Y	Y	Y	Y	Y	N
Shelby	N	Y	Y	Y	Y	Y	N
ALASKA							
Murkowski	Y	Y	Y	Y	Y	Y	Y
Stevens	Y	Y	Y	Y	Y	Y	Y
ARIZONA							
Kyl	N	Y	N	Y	Y	Y	Y
McCain	N	Y	N	Y	Y	Y	Y
ARKANSAS							
Hutchinson	N	Y	Y	Y	Y	Y	Y
Bumpers	Y	N	Y	N	N	N	N
CALIFORNIA							
Boxer	Y	Y	?	Y	Y	Y	Y
Feinstein	Y	Y	Y	Y	Y	Y	Y
COLORADO							
Allard	N	Y	Y	Y	Y	Y	Y
Campbell	Y	Y	Y	Y	Y	Y	Y
CONNECTICUT							
Dodd	Y	Y	Y	N	Y	Y	Y
Lieberman	Y	Y	Y	Y	Y	Y	Y
DELAWARE							
Roth	Y	Y	Y	Y	Y	Y	Y
Biden	Y	Y	Y	N	Y	Y	Y
FLORIDA							
Mack	Y	Y	Y	Y	Y	Y	Y
Graham	Y	N	Y	N	N	N	Y
GEORGIA							
Coverdell	N	Y	Y	Y	Y	Y	Y
Cleland	Y	N	Y	N	N	N	Y
HAWAII							
Akaka	Y	N	Y	N	Y	N	Y
Inouye	Y	N	Y	N	Y	N	Y
IDAHO							
Craig	N	Y	Y	Y	Y	Y	Y
Kempthorne	N	Y	Y	Y	Y	Y	Y
ILLINOIS							
Durbin	Y	Y	?	N	Y	N	Y
Moseley-Braun	?	?	Y	N	Y	Y	Y
INDIANA							
Coats	Y	Y	Y	Y	Y	Y	Y
Lugar	Y	Y	Y	Y	Y	Y	Y

	295	296	297	298	299	300	301
IOWA							
Grassley	N	Y	Y	Y	Y	Y	Y
Harkin	Y	N	Y	N	Y	N	Y
KANSAS							
Brownback	N	Y	Y	Y	Y	Y	Y
Roberts	N	N	Y	Y	Y	Y	N
KENTUCKY							
McConnell	N	Y	Y	Y	Y	Y	Y
Ford	Y	N	Y	N	N	N	Y
LOUISIANA							
Breaux	Y	N	Y	Y	N	N	Y
Landrieu	Y	N	Y	Y	N	N	Y
MAINE							
Collins	Y	Y	Y	Y	Y	Y	Y
Snowe	Y	Y	Y	Y	Y	Y	Y
MARYLAND							
Mikulski	Y	N	Y	N	Y	N	N
Sarbanes	Y	N	Y	N	Y	N	Y
MASSACHUSETTS							
Kennedy	Y	N	Y	N	N	N	Y
Kerry	Y	Y	Y	N	Y	Y	Y
MICHIGAN							
Abraham	N	Y	Y	Y	Y	Y	Y
Levin	Y	N	Y	N	N	N	Y
MINNESOTA							
Grams	Y	Y	Y	Y	Y	Y	Y
Wellstone	Y	N	Y	N	N	N	N
MISSISSIPPI							
Cochran	Y	N	Y	N	Y	Y	Y
Lott	N	Y	Y	Y	Y	Y	Y
MISSOURI							
Ashcroft	Y	Y	Y	Y	Y	Y	Y
Bond	?	?	Y	Y	Y	Y	Y
MONTANA							
Burns	N	Y	N	Y	Y	Y	Y
Baucus	Y	Y	Y	N	Y	Y	Y
NEBRASKA							
Hagel	N	Y	Y	Y	Y	Y	Y
Kerrey	Y	?	Y	N	Y	Y	Y
NEVADA							
Bryan	Y	N	Y	N	Y	N	Y
Reid	Y	Y	Y	N	Y	Y	Y

	295	296	297	298	299	300	301
NEW HAMPSHIRE							
Gregg	Y	Y	Y	N	Y	Y	Y
Smith	N	Y	Y	Y	Y	Y	Y
NEW JERSEY							
Lautenberg	Y	Y	Y	N	Y	Y	Y
Torricelli	Y	Y	Y	N	Y	Y	Y
NEW MEXICO							
Domenici	Y	Y	Y	Y	Y	Y	Y
Bingaman	Y	N	Y	N	Y	Y	Y
NEW YORK							
D'Amato	Y	Y	Y	Y	Y	Y	Y
Moynihan	Y	N	+	+	?	?	Y
NORTH CAROLINA							
Faircloth	N	Y	Y	Y	Y	Y	Y
Helms	Y	Y	Y	Y	Y	Y	Y
NORTH DAKOTA							
Conrad	Y	N	Y	N	Y	N	N
Dorgan	Y	N	Y	N	N	N	N
OHIO							
DeWine	Y	Y	Y	Y	Y	Y	Y
Glenn	?	?	?	?	?	?	?
OKLAHOMA							
Inhofe	N	Y	Y	Y	N	N	Y
Nickles	N	Y	Y	Y	Y	Y	Y
OREGON							
Smith	Y	Y	Y	N	Y	Y	Y
Wyden	Y	Y	Y	N	Y	Y	Y
PENNSYLVANIA							
Santorum	Y	Y	?	N	Y	Y	Y
Specter	Y	N	Y	N	Y	Y	Y
RHODE ISLAND							
Chafee	Y	Y	Y	Y	Y	Y	Y
Reed	Y	N	Y	N	Y	N	Y
SOUTH CAROLINA							
Thurmond	N	Y	Y	Y	Y	Y	Y
Hollings	?	?	?	N	N	N	Y
SOUTH DAKOTA							
Daschle	Y	Y	Y	N	Y	Y	Y
Johnson	Y	N	Y	N	Y	N	Y
TENNESSEE							
Frist	Y	Y	Y	Y	Y	Y	Y
Thompson	N	Y	Y	Y	Y	Y	Y

	295	296	297	298	299	300	301
TEXAS							
Gramm	N	Y	Y	Y	Y	Y	N
Hutchison	N	Y	Y	Y	Y	Y	N
UTAH							
Bennett	Y	N	Y	Y	Y	N	Y
Hatch	Y	Y	?	Y	Y	Y	Y
VERMONT							
Jeffords	Y	Y	Y	Y	Y	Y	Y
Leahy	Y	Y	Y	Y	Y	Y	Y
VIRGINIA							
Warner	Y	Y	Y	Y	Y	Y	Y
Robb	Y	Y	Y	N	Y	Y	Y
WASHINGTON							
Gorton	N	N	Y	Y	Y	N	N
Murray	Y	Y	Y	N	Y	Y	Y
WEST VIRGINIA							
Byrd	Y	N	Y	N	N	N	Y
Rockefeller	Y	N	Y	N	Y	N	Y
WISCONSIN							
Feingold	Y	Y	Y	N	Y	N	N
Kohl	Y	Y	Y	N	Y	Y	Y
WYOMING							
Enzi	N	N	Y	Y	Y	Y	Y
Thomas	N	Y	N	Y	Y	Y	Y

Key

Y	Voted for (yea).
#	Paired for.
+	Announced for.
N	Voted against (nay).
X	Paired against.
−	Announced against.
P	Voted "present."
C	Voted "present" to avoid possible conflict of interest.
?	Did not vote or otherwise make a position known.

Democrats   *Republicans*

ND Northern Democrats   SD Southern Democrats

Southern states - Ala., Ark., Fla., Ga., Ky., La., Miss., N.C., Okla., S.C., Tenn., Texas, Va.

295. Sotomayor Nomination/Confirmation. Confirmation of President Clinton's nomination of Sonia Sotomayor of New York to be a judge for the 2nd U.S. Circuit Court of Appeals. Confirmed 67-29: R 25-29; D 42-0 (ND 35-0, SD 7-0). Oct. 2, 1998. A "yea" was a vote in support of the president's position.

296. S 442. Internet Tax Moratorium/Catalog Sales. McCain, R-Ariz., motion to table (kill) the Bumpers, D-Ark., amendment that would allow states to require companies selling goods through the Internet, phone or mail, such as catalog goods, to collect state or local taxes on the transaction. Motion agreed to 66-29: R 48-6; D 18-23 (ND 17-17, SD 1-6). Oct. 2, 1998.

297. HR 10. Financial Services Overhaul/Cloture. Motion to invoke cloture (thus limiting debate) on the motion to proceed to the bill that would eliminate current barriers erected by the 1933 Glass-Steagall Act and other laws that impede affiliations between banking, securities, insurance and other firms. Motion agreed to 93-0: R 53-0; D 40-0 (ND 33-0, SD 7-0). Oct. 5, 1998. Three-fifths of the total Senate (60) is required to invoke cloture.

298. HR 4101. Fiscal 1999 Agriculture Appropriations/Conference Report. Adoption of the conference report on the bill to provide $55.9 billion in new budget authority for the Agriculture Department, the Food and Drug Administration and rural development programs in fiscal 1999. The bill would provide approximately $6 billion more than provided in fiscal 1998 and $1.9 billion less than requested by President Clinton. The conference report also includes an additional $4.2 billion in emergency funding for farmers and others who have suffered financial hardship due to natural disasters or poor export markets. Adopted (thus cleared for the president) 55-43: R 50-5; D 5-38 (ND 3-32, SD 2-6). Oct. 6, 1998. A "nay" was a vote in support of the president's position.

299. S 442. Internet Tax Moratorium/Moratorium Extension. McCain, R-Ariz., motion to table (kill) the Graham, D-Fla., amendment that would require a three-fifths "supermajority" vote of each chamber of Congress in order to extend the two-year Internet tax moratorium that the bill would impose. Motion agreed to 83-15: R 53-2; D 30-13 (ND 29-6, SD 1-7). Oct. 6, 1998.

300. S 442. Internet Tax Moratorium/Sales Tax Disclosure. Gregg, R-N.H., motion to table (kill) the Bumpers, D-Ark., amendment that would require businesses selling goods over the Internet to disclose to potential customers that they may be subject to state or local sales and use taxes on their purchases depending on where they reside. Motion agreed to 71-27: R 52-3; D 19-24 (ND 18-17, SD 1-7). Oct. 6, 1998.

301. HR 10. Financial Services Overhaul/Motion to Proceed. Motion to proceed to the bill that would eliminate current barriers erected by the 1933 Glass-Steagall Act and other laws that impede affiliations between banking, securities, insurance and other firms. Motion agreed to 88-11: R 49-6; D 39-5 (ND 32-4, SD 7-1). Oct. 7, 1998.

	302	303	304	305	306	307	308
ALABAMA							
Sessions	Y	Y	N	N	N	Y	Y
Shelby	Y	Y	Y	Y	Y	Y	Y
ALASKA							
Murkowski	Y	Y	N	Y	Y	Y	Y
Stevens	Y	Y	Y	Y	Y	Y	Y
ARIZONA							
Kyl	Y	Y	Y	Y	N	N	Y
McCain	Y	Y	Y	Y	N	Y	Y
ARKANSAS							
Hutchinson	Y	Y	N	N	Y	Y	Y
Bumpers	N	Y	N	N	N	Y	N
CALIFORNIA							
Boxer	Y	Y	N	Y	N	Y	Y
Feinstein	Y	Y	N	N	N	Y	Y
COLORADO							
Allard	Y	Y	N	Y	N	Y	Y
Campbell	Y	Y	Y	Y	N	Y	Y
CONNECTICUT							
Dodd	Y	Y	Y	Y	N	Y	Y
Lieberman	Y	Y	Y	Y	Y	N	Y
DELAWARE							
Roth	Y	Y	N	Y	N	Y	Y
Biden	Y	Y	N	N	N	Y	Y
FLORIDA							
Mack	Y	Y	N	Y	N	Y	Y
Graham	Y	Y	N	N	N	Y	Y
GEORGIA							
Coverdell	Y	Y	N	Y	Y	Y	Y
Cleland	Y	Y	N	N	N	Y	Y
HAWAII							
Akaka	Y	Y	N	Y	N	Y	Y
Inouye	Y	Y	Y	Y	N	Y	Y
IDAHO							
Craig	Y	Y	Y	Y	N	Y	Y
Kempthorne	Y	Y	Y	N	Y	Y	Y
ILLINOIS							
Durbin	Y	Y	Y	Y	N	Y	Y
Moseley-Braun	Y	Y	Y	N	Y	Y	Y
INDIANA							
Coats	Y	Y	Y	Y	N	Y	Y
Lugar	Y	Y	N	Y	N	Y	Y
IOWA							
Grassley	Y	Y	N	Y	Y	Y	Y
Harkin	Y	Y	N	N	N	Y	Y
KANSAS							
Brownback	Y	Y	N	N	N	Y	Y
Roberts	Y	Y	N	N	N	Y	Y
KENTUCKY							
McConnell	Y	Y	Y	Y	Y	Y	Y
Ford	Y	Y	N	N	N	Y	Y
LOUISIANA							
Breaux	Y	Y	N	N	N	Y	Y
Landrieu	Y	Y	N	N	N	Y	Y
MAINE							
Collins	Y	Y	N	Y	N	Y	Y
Snowe	Y	Y	Y	N	N	Y	Y
MARYLAND							
Mikulski	Y	Y	N	N	N	Y	Y
Sarbanes	Y	Y	N	N	N	Y	Y
MASSACHUSETTS							
Kennedy	Y	Y	N	N	N	Y	Y
Kerry	Y	Y	Y	Y	N	Y	Y
MICHIGAN							
Abraham	Y	Y	N	Y	N	Y	Y
Levin	Y	Y	N	N	N	Y	Y
MINNESOTA							
Grams	Y	Y	N	Y	N	Y	Y
Wellstone	Y	Y	N	N	N	Y	Y
MISSISSIPPI							
Cochran	Y	Y	N	Y	Y	Y	Y
Lott	Y	Y	N	Y	Y	Y	Y
MISSOURI							
Ashcroft	Y	Y	N	Y	N	Y	Y
Bond	Y	Y	N	N	N	Y	Y
MONTANA							
Burns	Y	Y	Y	Y	N	Y	Y
Baucus	Y	Y	N	Y	N	Y	Y
NEBRASKA							
Hagel	Y	Y	Y	Y	N	Y	Y
Kerrey	Y	Y	N	N	N	Y	Y
NEVADA							
Bryan	Y	Y	N	N	N	Y	Y
Reid	Y	Y	N	N	N	Y	Y
NEW HAMPSHIRE							
Gregg	Y	Y	Y	Y	Y	Y	Y
Smith	Y	Y	Y	Y	Y	Y	Y
NEW JERSEY							
Lautenberg	Y	Y	Y	Y	N	Y	Y
Torricelli	Y	Y	Y	Y	Y	Y	Y
NEW MEXICO							
Domenici	Y	Y	N	Y	N	Y	Y
Bingaman	Y	Y	N	N	N	Y	Y
NEW YORK							
D'Amato	Y	Y	N	Y	Y	Y	Y
Moynihan	Y	Y	N	N	N	Y	Y
NORTH CAROLINA							
Faircloth	Y	Y	Y	Y	Y	Y	Y
Helms	Y	Y	N	N	Y	?	Y
NORTH DAKOTA							
Conrad	Y	Y	N	N	N	Y	Y
Dorgan	N	Y	N	N	N	Y	Y
OHIO							
DeWine	Y	Y	N	Y	N	Y	Y
Glenn	?	?	?	?	?	?	?
OKLAHOMA							
Inhofe	Y	Y	N	N	N	Y	Y
Nickles	Y	Y	N	Y	Y	Y	Y
OREGON							
Smith	Y	Y	Y	Y	N	Y	Y
Wyden	Y	Y	Y	Y	Y	Y	Y
PENNSYLVANIA							
Santorum	Y	Y	N	Y	N	Y	Y
Specter	Y	Y	N	?	?	Y	Y
RHODE ISLAND							
Chafee	Y	Y	N	N	N	Y	Y
Reed	Y	Y	N	N	N	Y	Y
SOUTH CAROLINA							
Thurmond	Y	Y	N	N	N	Y	Y
Hollings	N	Y	?	?	?	?	?
SOUTH DAKOTA							
Daschle	Y	Y	N	N	N	Y	Y
Johnson	Y	Y	N	N	N	Y	Y
TENNESSEE							
Frist	Y	Y	N	N	N	Y	Y
Thompson	Y	Y	Y	N	N	Y	Y
TEXAS							
Gramm	Y	Y	N	N	Y	Y	Y
Hutchison	Y	Y	N	N	Y	Y	Y
UTAH							
Bennett	Y	Y	N	Y	N	Y	Y
Hatch	Y	Y	N	Y	N	Y	Y
VERMONT							
Jeffords	?	Y	N	N	Y	Y	Y
Leahy	Y	N	N	Y	N	Y	Y
VIRGINIA							
Warner	Y	Y	N	Y	N	Y	Y
Robb	Y	Y	N	Y	N	Y	Y
WASHINGTON							
Gorton	N	Y	N	N	N	Y	N
Murray	Y	Y	Y	N	N	Y	Y
WEST VIRGINIA							
Byrd	Y	Y	N	N	N	Y	Y
Rockefeller	Y	Y	N	N	N	Y	Y
WISCONSIN							
Feingold	Y	Y	N	N	N	Y	Y
Kohl	Y	Y	Y	N	N	Y	Y
WYOMING							
Enzi	Y	Y	N	Y	N	Y	Y
Thomas	Y	Y	N	N	Y	Y	Y

Key

Y Voted for (yea).
Paired for.
+ Announced for.
N Voted against (nay).
X Paired against.
− Announced against.
P Voted "present."
C Voted "present" to avoid possible conflict of interest.
? Did not vote or otherwise make a position known.

• Democrats   *Republicans*

ND Northern Democrats   SD Southern Democrats

Southern states - Ala., Ark., Fla., Ga., Ky., La., Miss., N.C., Okla., S.C., Tenn., Texas, Va.

302. S 442. Internet Tax Moratorium/Cloture. Motion to invoke cloture (thus limiting debate) on the bill that would impose a two-year moratorium on state and local Internet taxation to allow state, local and federal officials and industry representatives to negotiate what type of tax treatment should be applied to Internet commerce. Motion agreed to 94-4: R 53-1; D 41-3 (ND 35-1, SD 6-2). Oct. 7, 1998. Three-fifths of the total Senate (60) is required to invoke cloture.

303. S 442. Internet Tax Moratorium/Indecent Material. Coats, R-Ind., amendment that would exempt individuals or businesses that transfer or sell indecent sexual material over the Internet from the tax moratorium unless they restrict minors' access to the material by requiring a credit card number or other adult information for access. The amendment also would exempt Internet access providers from the moratorium unless they offer customers screening software designed to allow the customer to limit minors' access to the material. Adopted 98-1: R 55-0; D 43-1 (ND 35-1, SD 8-0). Oct. 7, 1998.

304. S 442. Internet Tax Moratorium/Interstate Taxation Review. McCain, R-Ariz., motion to table (kill) the Hutchinson, R-Ark., amendment to the McCain amendment. The Hutchinson amendment would require the commission established by the bill to examine the effect taxation on interstate sales transactions, including Internet transactions, has on retail businesses and state and local governments. The underlying McCain amendment would direct the commission to study model state legislation governing Internet taxes. Motion rejected 30-68: R 20-35; D 10-33 (ND 10-26, SD 0-7). Oct. 7, 1998. (Subsequently, the Hutchinson amendment and the underlying McCain amendment as amended were adopted by voice vote.)

305. S 442. Internet Tax Moratorium/Four-Year Moratorium. McCain, R-Ariz., amendment to the McCain amendment. The second-degree amendment would extend the moratorium from three years to four. The underlying amendment would extend the moratorium from the bill's language of two years to three years. Rejected 45-52: R 32-22; D 13-30 (ND 12-24, SD 1-6). Oct. 7, 1998.

306. S 442. Internet Tax Moratorium/Three-Year Moratorium and Current Tax Allowance. Murkowski, R-Alaska, motion to table (kill) the McCain, R-Ariz., amendment that would extend the moratorium from two years to three years and allow states that currently impose taxes on Internet access to continue doing so after the moratorium takes effect. Motion rejected 28-69: R 27-27; D 1-42 (ND 1-35, SD 0-7). Oct. 7, 1998.

307. HR 4194. Fiscal 1999 VA-HUD Appropriations/Conference Report. Adoption of the conference report on the bill to provide $93.4 billion in new budget authority for veterans, housing, space and science programs and agencies in fiscal 1999. The bill includes legislation to overhaul the nation's public housing system. Adopted (thus cleared for the president) 96-1: R 53-1; D 43-0 (ND 36-0, SD 7-0). Oct. 8, 1998.

308. S 442. Internet Tax Moratorium/Passage. Passage of the bill to impose a three-year moratorium on state and local Internet taxation to allow state, local and federal officials and industry representatives to negotiate what type of tax treatment should be applied to Internet access and commerce. The bill would allow states that currently impose taxes on Internet access to continue to do so. Passed 96-2: R 54-1; D 42-1 (ND 36-0, SD 6-1). Oct. 8, 1998.

Key

Y	Voted for (yea).
#	Paired for.
+	Announced for.
N	Voted against (nay).
X	Paired against.
−	Announced against.
P	Voted "present."
C	Voted "present" to avoid possible conflict of interest.
?	Did not vote or otherwise make a position known.

• Democrats   *Republicans*

	309	310	311	312	313	314
ALABAMA						
Sessions	N	Y	Y	Y	Y	N
Shelby	N	Y	Y	Y	Y	Y
ALASKA						
Murkowski	N	Y	Y	Y	Y	?
Stevens	Y	Y	Y	Y	Y	Y
ARIZONA						
Kyl	N	Y	Y	Y	Y	N
McCain	N	Y	Y	Y	Y	N
ARKANSAS						
Hutchinson	N	Y	Y	Y	Y	Y
Bumpers	Y	Y	N	Y	Y	?
CALIFORNIA						
Boxer	Y	Y	N	N	Y	Y
Feinstein	Y	Y	N	N	Y	Y
COLORADO						
Allard	N	Y	Y	Y	Y	N
Campbell	N	Y	Y	Y	Y	Y
CONNECTICUT						
Dodd	Y	Y	N	N	Y	Y
Lieberman	Y	Y	N	N	Y	Y
DELAWARE						
Roth	Y	Y	Y	Y	Y	Y
Biden	Y	Y	N	N	Y	Y
FLORIDA						
Mack	Y	Y	Y	Y	Y	Y
Graham	Y	Y	N	Y	Y	Y
GEORGIA						
Coverdell	N	Y	Y	Y	N	Y
Cleland	Y	Y	N	N	Y	Y
HAWAII						
Akaka	Y	Y	N	N	Y	Y
Inouye	Y	Y	N	N	Y	?
IDAHO						
Craig	N	Y	Y	Y	Y	Y
Kempthorne	N	Y	Y	Y	Y	Y
ILLINOIS						
Durbin	Y	Y	N	N	Y	Y
Moseley-Braun	Y	Y	N	N	Y	Y
INDIANA						
Coats	N	Y	Y	Y	Y	N
Lugar	Y	Y	Y	Y	Y	N

	309	310	311	312	313	314
IOWA						
Grassley	N	Y	N	N	N	Y
Harkin	Y	Y	N	N	N	Y
KANSAS						
Brownback	N	Y	Y	Y	Y	Y
Roberts	N	Y	Y	Y	Y	Y
KENTUCKY						
McConnell	N	Y	?	Y	Y	Y
Ford	Y	Y	N	Y	N	Y
LOUISIANA						
Breaux	Y	Y	N	N	Y	Y
Landrieu	Y	Y	N	N	Y	Y
MAINE						
Collins	Y	Y	Y	N	Y	Y
Snowe	N	Y	Y	N	Y	N
MARYLAND						
Mikulski	Y	Y	N	N	Y	Y
Sarbanes	Y	Y	N	N	Y	Y
MASSACHUSETTS						
Kennedy	Y	Y	N	N	Y	Y
Kerry	Y	Y	N	N	Y	Y
MICHIGAN						
Abraham	N	Y	Y	Y	Y	Y
Levin	Y	Y	N	N	Y	Y
MINNESOTA						
Grams	N	Y	Y	Y	Y	N
Wellstone	Y	Y	N	−	+	N
MISSISSIPPI						
Cochran	N	Y	Y	Y	Y	N
Lott	N	Y	Y	Y	Y	Y
MISSOURI						
Ashcroft	N	Y	Y	Y	Y	N
Bond	N	Y	N	Y	?	Y
MONTANA						
Burns	N	Y	Y	Y	Y	N
Baucus	Y	Y	N	N	Y	N
NEBRASKA						
Hagel	N	Y	Y	Y	Y	N
Kerrey	Y	Y	N	N	Y	N
NEVADA						
Bryan	Y	Y	N	N	Y	Y
Reid	Y	Y	N	N	Y	N

	309	310	311	312	313	314
NEW HAMPSHIRE						
Gregg	N	Y	Y	Y	Y	Y
Smith	N	Y	Y	Y	Y	N
NEW JERSEY						
Lautenberg	Y	Y	N	N	Y	Y
Torricelli	Y	Y	N	N	Y	Y
NEW MEXICO						
Domenici	Y	Y	Y	Y	Y	Y
Bingaman	Y	Y	N	N	Y	Y
NEW YORK						
D'Amato	Y	Y	N	Y	Y	Y
Moynihan	Y	Y	N	N	Y	N
NORTH CAROLINA						
Faircloth	N	N	Y	Y	Y	Y
Helms	N	Y	Y	Y	Y	?
NORTH DAKOTA						
Conrad	Y	Y	N	N	Y	Y
Dorgan	Y	Y	N	N	Y	Y
OHIO						
DeWine	N	Y	Y	Y	Y	Y
Glenn	?	?	?	?	?	?
OKLAHOMA						
Inhofe	N	Y	Y	Y	Y	N
Nickles	N	Y	Y	Y	Y	N
OREGON						
Smith	N	Y	Y	Y	Y	Y
Wyden	Y	Y	N	N	Y	Y
PENNSYLVANIA						
Santorum	N	Y	Y	Y	Y	N
Specter	Y	Y	N	Y	Y	N
RHODE ISLAND						
Chafee	Y	Y	Y	Y	Y	Y
Reed	Y	Y	N	N	Y	Y
SOUTH CAROLINA						
Thurmond	N	Y	Y	Y	Y	Y
Hollings	?	?	−	?	?	?
SOUTH DAKOTA						
Daschle	Y	Y	N	N	Y	Y
Johnson	Y	Y	N	N	Y	Y
TENNESSEE						
Frist	N	Y	Y	Y	Y	N
Thompson	N	Y	Y	Y	Y	Y

	309	310	311	312	313	314
TEXAS						
Gramm	N	Y	Y	Y	Y	N
Hutchison	N	Y	Y	Y	Y	Y
UTAH						
Bennett	Y	Y	Y	Y	Y	Y
Hatch	Y	Y	Y	Y	Y	Y
VERMONT						
Jeffords	Y	Y	Y	Y	Y	Y
Leahy	Y	Y	N	N	Y	Y
VIRGINIA						
Warner	N	Y	Y	N	Y	Y
Robb	Y	Y	N	N	Y	Y
WASHINGTON						
Gorton	Y	Y	Y	Y	Y	Y
Murray	Y	Y	N	N	Y	Y
WEST VIRGINIA						
Byrd	Y	Y	N	Y	Y	N
Rockefeller	Y	Y	N	N	Y	Y
WISCONSIN						
Feingold	Y	Y	N	N	Y	N
Kohl	Y	Y	N	Y	N	N
WYOMING						
Enzi	N	Y	Y	Y	Y	N
Thomas	N	Y	Y	Y	Y	N

ND Northern Democrats   SD Southern Democrats

Southern states - Ala., Ark., Fla., Ga., Ky., La., Miss., N.C., Okla., S.C., Tenn., Texas, Va.

309. Fletcher Nomination/Confirmation. Confirmation of President Clinton's nomination of William A. Fletcher of California to be a judge for the 9th U.S. Circuit Court of Appeals. Confirmed 57-41: R 14-41; D 43-0 (ND 36-0, SD 7-0). Oct. 8, 1998. A "yea" was a vote in support of the president's position.

310. HR 2431. Religious Persecution Overseas/Passage. Passage of the bill to require the State Department to produce an annual report on religious persecution abroad and require the president to impose sanctions ranging from diplomatic protests to cutting off U.S. aid to nations that engage in religious persecution. Passed 98-0: R 55-0; D 43-0 (ND 36-0, SD 7-0). Oct. 9, 1998.

311. HR 4250. Revamp Medical Insurance Regulations/Motion to Proceed. Lott, R-Miss., motion to table (kill) the Daschle, D-S.D., motion to proceed to the bill that would revise managed care and medical insurance regulations. The bill would provide a range of patient protections, create a two-step appeals process for challenging a health plan administrator's decisions and expand the availability of medical savings accounts. Motion agreed to 50-47: R 50-4; D 0-43 (ND 0-36, SD 0-7). Oct. 9, 1998.

312. HR 4104. Fiscal 1999 Treasury-Postal Service Appropriations/Motion to Proceed. Motion to proceed to the conference report on the bill to provide about $27 billion in new budget authority for the Treasury Department, the White House, postal subsidies and civil service benefits in fiscal 1999. Motion agreed to 58-39: R 54-1; D 4-38 (ND 2-33, SD 2-5). Oct. 9, 1998. (Subsequently, Lott, R-Miss., pulled the bill from consideration.)

313. HR 3150. Consumer Bankruptcy Revisions/Motion to Pro-

ceed. Motion to proceed to the conference report on the bill to revise the nation's bankruptcy laws by forcing most debtors to file for relief under Chapter 13, instead of Chapter 7, if they have an above-median income and the ability to pay off at least 25 percent of their debts over five years. Motion agreed to 94-2: R 54-0; D 40-2 (ND 33-2, SD 7-0). Oct. 9, 1998. (Subsequently, the Senate moved into morning business and off consideration of the bill.)

314. HR 4328. Fiscal 1999 Omnibus Appropriations/Conference Report. Adoption of the conference report on the bill to provide almost $500 billion in new budget authority for those Cabinet departments and federal agencies whose fiscal 1999 appropriations bills were never enacted. The measure incorporates eight previously separate appropriations bills: Labor-HHS-Education, Interior, Treasury-Postal, Foreign Operations, Commerce-Justice-State, District of Columbia, Agriculture and Transportation. In addition, the bill provides $20.8 billion in "emergency" supplemental spending, including $6.8 billion for military spending ($1.9 billion of it for Bosnia operations), $5.9 billion for relief to farmers, $2.4 billion for anti-terrorism programs, $3.35 billion to address Year 2000 computer problems and $1.55 billion for disaster relief from Hurricane Georges. The measure also contains language to extend expiring tax provisions (at a cost of $9.7 billion over nine years), increase the number of H-1B visas for high-tech foreign workers, impose a three-year moratorium on new taxes on Internet access, implement the Chemical Weapons Convention and extend for six months Chapter 12 of the bankruptcy code, which is designed to help struggling farmers. Adopted (thus cleared for the president) 65-29: R 33-20; D 32-9 (ND 26-9, SD 6-0). Oct. 21, 1998. (HR 4328 was originally the fiscal 1999 Transportation appropriations bill.) A "yea" was a vote in support of the president's position.

Senate Roll Call Votes By Subject

HOUSE ROLL CALL VOTES

House Roll Call Votes
By Bill Number

House Bills

H Con Res 152, H-18
H Con Res 185, H-122
H Con Res 202, H-6
H Con Res 206, H-14
H Con Res 208, H-86
H Con Res 213, H-108
H Con Res 218, H-32
H Con Res 220, H-38
H Con Res 227, H-18
H Con Res 235, H-18
H Con Res 254, H-122
H Con Res 270, H-62
H Con Res 284, H-60, H-62
H Con Res 285, H-60
H Con Res 288, H-74
H Con Res 301, H-86
H Con Res 304, H-122
H Con Res 311, H-98
H Con Res 315, H-130
H Con Res 320, H-146
H Con Res 331, H-144
H Con Res 334, H-146

H J Res 78, H-58
H J Res 102, H-34
H J Res 107, H-4
H J Res 111, H-30
H J Res 117, H-124
H J Res 119, H-66
H J Res 120, H-100
H J Res 121, H-92
H J Res 128, H-126

H Res 144, H-128
H Res 267, H-38
H Res 352, H-6
H Res 355, H-6
H Res 361, H-18
H Res 364, H-18
H Res 392, H-86
H Res 401, H-68
H Res 414, H-36
H Res 417, H-62
H Res 422, H-42
H Res 423, H-40
H Res 432, H-52
H Res 433, H-52
H Res 440, H-48
H Res 447, H-62
H Res 452, H-74
H Res 459, H-118
H Res 463, H-70
H Res 494, H-148
H Res 505, H-130
H Res 507, H-102
H Res 525, H-120
H Res 545, H-128
H Res 552, H-130, H-132
H Res 557, H-144
H Res 565, H-144
H Res 575, H-138

H Res 581, H-140, H-142
H Res 598, H-150
H Res 604, H-152
H Res 611, H-154, H-156

HR 6, H-36, H-38, H-40
HR 10, H-42, H-44
HR 34, H-26
HR 217, H-10
HR 424, H-8
HR 559, H-150
HR 629, H-98
HR 678, H-118
HR 856, H-10, H-12
HR 992, H-16
HR 1122, H-92, H-94
HR 1151, H-28
HR 1154, H-136
HR 1252, H-30, H-32
HR 1260, H-150
HR 1428, H-8
HR 1432, H-14, H-16
HR 1544, H-8, H-10
HR 1560, H-118
HR 1635, H-62
HR 1689, H-92
HR 1722, H-150
HR 1754, H-150
HR 1757, H-24
HR 1847, H-68
HR 1872, H-38
HR 2181, H-8
HR 2183, H-54, H-70, H-72, H-80, H-86, H-88, H-102, H-104, H-106, H-108, H-114
HR 2348, H-140
HR 2369, H-12
HR 2400, H-28, H-30, H-52, H-54, H-56
HR 2431, H-46
HR 2460, H-10
HR 2515, H-24
HR 2538, H-120
HR 2578, H-22
HR 2589, H-22
HR 2608, H-26
HR 2616, H-148
HR 2621, H-132
HR 2625, H-4
HR 2631, H-6
HR 2646, H-40, H-68, H-70
HR 2676, H-56, H-78, H-80
HR 2709, H-62
HR 2829, H-42
HR 2846, H-4, H-6
HR 2863, H-120
HR 2870, H-18, H-20
HR 2883, H-16
HR 2888, H-66
HR 3039, H-48
HR 3096, H-22
HR 3097, H-68, H-70
HR 3130, H-14

HR 3150, H-64, H-66, H-134, H-144
HR 3211, H-20
HR 3246, H-24
HR 3248, H-128
HR 3267, H-82
HR 3310, H-22, H-24
HR 3412, H-20
HR 3433, H-58
HR 3494, H-66, H-68, H-148
HR 3528, H-30
HR 3534, H-46, H-48
HR 3546, H-34
HR 3565, H-30
HR 3579, H-26, H-28, H-32, H-36
HR 3616, H-48, H-50, H-52, H-54, H-92, H-130
HR 3630, H-58
HR 3682, H-80
HR 3694, H-40, H-138
HR 3717, H-34
HR 3718, H-48
HR 3731, H-84
HR 3736, H-130
HR 3743, H-106
HR 3808, H-56
HR 3809, H-48
HR 3811, H-42
HR 3853, H-74
HR 3874, H-86
HR 3875, H-144
HR 3891, H-134
HR 3892, H-120
HR 3963, H-150
HR 3989, H-60
HR 4059, H-72, H-74, H-100
HR 4060, H-72, H-74, H-134
HR 4101, H-74, H-76, H-122, H-136
HR 4103, H-76, H-122, H-134
HR 4104, H-78, H-82, H-84, H-134, H-140
HR 4110, H-146
HR 4112, H-78, H-130
HR 4193, H-90, H-92, H-94
HR 4194, H-82, H-86, H-96, H-98, H-100, H-124, H-138
HR 4250, H-96
HR 4259, H-138
HR 4274, H-136, H-142
HR 4276, H-108, H-110, H-112, H-114
HR 4300, H-124, H-126
HR 4328, H-100, H-122, H-152
HR 4380, H-116, H-118
HR 4382, H-124
HR 4550, H-126
HR 4567, H-146
HR 4569, H-126, H-128
HR 4570, H-138
HR 4578, H-132
HR 4579, H-132, H-134
HR 4614, H-136

HR 4616, H-140
HR 4655, H-136
HR 4756, H-150

Senate Bills

S 419, H-14
S 852, H-148
S 1132, H-152
S 1150, H-56, H-60
S 1364, H-148
S 1502, H-34, H-36
S 1733, H-152
S 2073, H-124, H-134
S 2095, H-148
S 2133, H-152
S 2206, H-120

S Con Res 37, H-34

S J Res 54, H-108

1. Quorum Call.* 364 Responded. Jan. 27, 1998.

2. Robert K. Dornan Election Challenge/Motion To Table. Solomon, R-N.Y., motion to table the Gephardt, D-Mo., privileged resolution to dismiss the complaint by former Rep. Robert K. Dornan, R-Calif., contesting the election of Loretta Sanchez, D-Calif. Motion agreed to 214-189: R 213-1; D 1-187 (ND 1-136, SD 0-51); I 0-1. Jan. 28, 1998.

3. HR 2625. Renaming National Airport/Previous Question. Solomon, R-N.Y., motion to order the previous question (thus ending debate and the possibility of amendment) on adoption of the rule (H Res 344) to provide for House floor consideration of the bill to rename Washington National Airport the Ronald Reagan National Airport. Motion agreed to 227-189: R 222-0; D 5-188 (ND 3-136, SD 2-52); I 0-1. Feb. 4, 1998.

4. HR 2625. Renaming National Airport/Local Authority. Davis, R-Va., amendment to make renaming Washington National Airport located in Virginia the Ronald Reagan National Airport contingent on the approval of the Metropolitan Washington Airports Authority. Rejected 206-215: R 10-214; D 195-1 (ND 141-1, SD 54-0); I 1-0. Feb. 4, 1998.

5. HR 2625. Renaming National Airport/Recommit. Oberstar, D-Minn., motion to recommit the bill to the Transportation and Infrastructure Committee with instructions to report it back with an amendment to name the terminal at Washington National Airport, instead of the airport itself, after Ronald Reagan. Motion rejected 186-237: R 0-223; D 185-14 (ND 136-9, SD 49-5); I 1-0. Feb. 4, 1998.

6. HR 2625. Renaming National Airport/Passage. Passage of the bill to rename Washington National Airport located in Virginia the Ronald Reagan National Airport. Passed 240-186: R 222-3; D 18-182 (ND 14-132, SD 4-50); I 0-1. Feb. 4, 1998.

7. H J Res 107. Health Care Task Force Sanctions/Passage. Passage of the joint resolution to express the sense of Congress that public funds should not be used to pay a $285,865 sanction a federal judge imposed after ruling that Clinton Administration officials misled the courts regarding the makeup of a 1993 health care reform task force. Passed 273-126: R 209-3; D 64-122 (ND 41-93, SD 23-29); I 0-1. Feb. 4, 1998.

8. HR 2846. National Education Testing Curbs/Previous Question. Linder, R-Ga., motion to order the previous question (thus ending debate and the possibility of amendment) on adoption of the rule (H Res 348) to provide for House floor consideration of the bill to prohibit the use of federal education funds for any federally-sponsored national test in reading, math, or any other subject that is not specifically authorized by federal statute. Motion agreed to 220-185: R 214-0; D 6-184 (ND 3-134, SD 3-50); I 0-1. Feb. 5, 1998.

* CQ does not include quorum calls in its vote charts.

Key

Y	Voted for (yea).
#	Paired for.
+	Announced for.
N	Voted against (nay).
X	Paired against.
–	Announced against.
P	Voted "present."
C	Voted "present" to avoid possible conflict of interest.
?	Did not vote or otherwise make a position known.

Democrats **Republicans**
Independent

	2	3	4	5	6	7	8
ALABAMA							
1 *Callahan*	Y	Y	N	N	Y	Y	Y
2 *Everett*	Y	Y	N	N	Y	Y	Y
3 *Riley*	Y	Y	N	N	Y	Y	Y
4 *Aderholt*	Y	Y	N	N	Y	+	Y
5 Cramer	N	N	Y	N	Y	N	N
6 *Bachus*	Y	Y	N	N	Y	Y	Y
7 Hilliard	N	N	Y	Y	N	N	N
ALASKA							
AL *Young*	?	Y	N	N	Y	Y	Y
ARIZONA							
1 *Salmon*	Y	Y	N	N	Y	Y	Y
2 Pastor	N	N	Y	Y	N	N	N
3 *Stump*	Y	Y	N	N	Y	Y	Y
4 *Shadegg*	Y	Y	N	N	Y	Y	Y
5 *Kolbe*	Y	Y	N	N	Y	Y	Y
6 *Hayworth*	Y	Y	N	N	Y	Y	Y
ARKANSAS							
1 Berry	N	N	Y	Y	N	N	N
2 Snyder	N	N	Y	Y	N	Y	N
3 *Hutchinson*	?	Y	N	N	Y	Y	Y
4 *Dickey*	Y	Y	N	N	Y	Y	Y
CALIFORNIA							
1 *Riggs*	Y	?	N	N	Y	Y	?
2 *Herger*	Y	?	?	?	?	?	?
3 Fazio	N	N	Y	N	N	N	N
4 *Doolittle*	Y	Y	N	N	Y	Y	Y
5 Matsui	N	N	Y	N	N	N	N
6 Woolsey	N	N	Y	Y	N	N	N
7 Miller	N	N	Y	Y	N	N	N
8 Pelosi	N	N	Y	Y	N	N	N
9 Dellums	N	N	Y	N	Y	?	N
10 Tauscher	N	N	Y	Y	N	N	N
11 *Pombo*	Y	Y	N	N	Y	Y	Y
12 Lantos	N	N	Y	N	N	N	N
13 Stark	N	N	Y	N	N	N	N
14 Eshoo	N	?	?	?	?	?	?
15 *Campbell*	Y	Y	N	N	Y	N	Y
16 Lofgren	N	N	Y	N	N	N	N
17 Farr	N	N	Y	N	N	?	N
18 Condit	N	N	Y	N	N	N	N
19 *Radanovich*	Y	Y	N	N	Y	Y	?
20 Dooley	?	N	Y	N	N	N	N
21 *Thomas*	Y	Y	N	N	Y	Y	Y
22 Vacant							
23 *Gallegly*	?	Y	N	N	Y	Y	Y
24 Sherman	N	N	Y	Y	N	N	N
25 *McKeon*	Y	Y	N	N	Y	+	+
26 Berman	?	N	Y	N	N	N	N
27 *Rogan*	Y	Y	N	N	Y	Y	?
28 *Dreier*	Y	Y	N	N	Y	Y	Y
29 Waxman	N	N	Y	Y	N	N	N
30 Becerra	–	–	+	+	N	–	–
31 Martinez	N	N	Y	N	N	N	N
32 Dixon	N	N	Y	N	N	N	N
33 Roybal-Allard	N	N	Y	N	N	N	N
34 Torres	N	?	?	Y	N	N	N
35 Waters	N	N	Y	N	N	N	N
36 Harman	N	N	Y	Y	N	N	N
37 Millender-McD.	N	N	Y	N	N	N	N

	2	3	4	5	6	7	8
38 *Horn*	Y	Y	N	N	Y	Y	Y
39 *Royce*	Y	Y	N	N	Y	Y	Y
40 *Lewis*	Y	Y	N	N	Y	Y	Y
41 *Kim*	Y	Y	N	N	Y	Y	Y
42 Brown	N	N	Y	N	N	N	N
43 *Calvert*	Y	Y	N	N	Y	Y	Y
44 Vacant							
45 *Rohrabacher*	Y	Y	N	N	Y	Y	Y
46 Sanchez	N	N	Y	Y	N	+	N
47 *Cox*	Y	Y	N	N	Y	Y	Y
48 *Packard*	Y	Y	N	N	Y	Y	Y
49 *Bilbray*	Y	Y	N	N	Y	Y	Y
50 Filner	N	N	Y	N	N	N	N
51 *Cunningham*	Y	Y	N	N	Y	Y	Y
52 *Hunter*	Y	Y	N	N	Y	Y	Y
COLORADO							
1 DeGette	?	N	Y	Y	N	N	N
2 Skaggs	N	N	Y	Y	N	N	N
3 *McInnis*	Y	Y	N	N	Y	Y	Y
4 *Schaffer*	Y	Y	N	N	Y	Y	Y
5 *Hefley*	Y	Y	N	N	Y	Y	Y
6 *Schaefer*	Y	Y	N	N	Y	Y	Y
CONNECTICUT							
1 Kennelly	?	N	Y	Y	Y	N	N
2 Gejdenson	N	N	Y	Y	N	N	N
3 DeLauro	N	N	Y	Y	N	N	N
4 *Shays*	Y	Y	N	N	Y	Y	Y
5 Maloney	N	N	Y	Y	N	Y	N
6 *Johnson*	?	Y	N	N	Y	Y	Y
DELAWARE							
AL *Castle*	Y	Y	N	N	Y	Y	Y
FLORIDA							
1 *Scarborough*	?	Y	N	N	Y	Y	Y
2 Boyd	N	N	Y	Y	N	Y	N
3 Brown	N	N	Y	N	N	N	N
4 *Fowler*	Y	Y	N	N	Y	Y	Y
5 Thurman	N	N	Y	N	N	N	N
6 *Stearns*	Y	Y	N	N	Y	Y	Y
7 *Mica*	Y	Y	N	N	Y	Y	Y
8 *McCollum*	Y	Y	N	N	Y	Y	Y
9 *Bilirakis*	Y	Y	N	N	Y	Y	Y
10 *Young*	Y	Y	N	N	Y	Y	Y
11 Davis	N	N	Y	N	N	N	N
12 *Canady*	Y	Y	N	N	Y	Y	Y
13 *Miller*	Y	Y	N	N	Y	Y	Y
14 *Goss*	Y	Y	N	N	Y	Y	Y
15 *Weldon*	Y	Y	N	N	Y	Y	Y
16 *Foley*	Y	Y	N	N	Y	Y	Y
17 Meek	N	N	Y	N	N	N	N
18 *Ros-Lehtinen*	?	Y	N	N	Y	Y	Y
19 Wexler	N	N	Y	N	N	N	N
20 Deutsch	N	N	Y	N	N	N	N
21 *Diaz-Balart*	Y	Y	N	N	Y	Y	Y
22 *Shaw*	Y	Y	N	N	Y	Y	Y
23 Hastings	N	N	Y	N	N	N	N
GEORGIA							
1 *Kingston*	Y	Y	N	N	Y	Y	Y
2 Bishop	N	N	Y	Y	N	N	N
3 *Collins*	Y	Y	N	N	Y	Y	Y
4 McKinney	N	N	Y	Y	N	N	N
5 Lewis	N	N	Y	Y	N	N	N
6 *Gingrich*			N	N	Y	I	
7 *Barr*	Y	Y	N	N	Y	Y	Y
8 *Chambliss*	Y	Y	N	N	Y	Y	Y
9 *Deal*	?	Y	N	N	Y	Y	Y
10 *Norwood*	Y	Y	N	N	Y	Y	Y
11 *Linder*	Y	Y	N	N	Y	Y	Y
HAWAII							
1 Abercrombie	N	N	?	N	N	?	N
2 Mink	N	N	Y	Y	N	Y	N
IDAHO							
1 *Chenoweth*	Y	Y	N	N	Y	Y	?
2 *Crapo*	Y	Y	N	N	Y	Y	Y
ILLINOIS							
1 Rush	N	N	Y	Y	N	N	N
2 Jackson	N	N	Y	Y	N	N	N
3 Lipinski	?	N	Y	N	Y	N	N
4 Gutierrez	N	N	Y	Y	N	N	N
5 Blagojevich	N	N	Y	Y	N	N	N
6 *Hyde*	Y	Y	N	N	Y	Y	Y
7 Davis	N	N	Y	Y	N	N	N
8 *Crane*	Y	Y	N	N	Y	Y	Y
9 Yates	N	N	Y	Y	N	?	N
10 *Porter*	Y	Y	N	N	Y	Y	Y
11 *Weller*	Y	Y	N	N	Y	Y	Y
12 Costello	N	N	Y	Y	N	N	N

ND Northern Democrats   **SD** Southern Democrats

	2	3	4	5	6	7	8
13 ***Fawell***	Y	Y	N	N	Y	Y	Y
14 ***Hastert***	Y	Y	N	N	Y	Y	Y
15 ***Ewing***	?	Y	N	N	Y	Y	Y
16 ***Manzullo***	Y	Y	N	N	Y	Y	Y
17 Evans	N	Y	Y	N	Y	Y	N
18 ***LaHood***	Y	Y	N	N	Y	Y	Y
19 Poshard	N	N	Y	Y	N	Y	N
20 ***Shimkus***	Y	Y	N	N	Y	Y	Y
INDIANA							
1 Visclosky	N	N	Y	Y	N	Y	?
2 ***McIntosh***	Y	Y	N	N	Y	Y	Y
3 Roemer	N	N	Y	Y	N	Y	N
4 ***Souder***	Y	Y	N	N	Y	?	Y
5 ***Buyer***	Y	Y	N	N	Y	Y	Y
6 ***Burton***	Y	Y	N	N	Y	Y	+
7 ***Pease***	Y	Y	N	N	Y	Y	Y
8 ***Hostettler***	Y	Y	N	N	Y	Y	Y
9 Hamilton	N	N	Y	Y	N	Y	N
10 Carson	N	N	Y	Y	N	N	N
IOWA							
1 ***Leach***	Y	Y	?	N	Y	Y	Y
2 ***Nussle***	Y	Y	Y	N	Y	Y	Y
3 Boswell	N	N	Y	Y	N	Y	N
4 ***Ganske***	Y	Y	N	N	Y	Y	Y
5 ***Latham***	Y	Y	N	N	Y	Y	Y
KANSAS							
1 ***Moran***	Y	Y	N	N	Y	Y	Y
2 ***Ryun***	Y	Y	N	N	Y	Y	Y
3 ***Snowbarger***	Y	Y	N	N	Y	Y	Y
4 ***Tiahrt***	Y	Y	N	N	Y	Y	Y
KENTUCKY							
1 ***Whitfield***	Y	Y	N	N	Y	?	Y
2 ***Lewis***	Y	Y	N	N	Y	Y	Y
3 ***Northup***	Y	Y	N	N	Y	Y	Y
4 ***Bunning***	Y	Y	N	N	Y	Y	Y
5 ***Rogers***	Y	Y	N	N	Y	Y	Y
6 Baesler	N	N	Y	N	Y	Y	N
LOUISIANA							
1 ***Livingston***	Y	Y	N	N	Y	Y	Y
2 Jefferson	N	N	Y	Y	N	N	N
3 ***Tauzin***	Y	Y	N	N	Y	Y	Y
4 ***McCrery***	Y	Y	N	N	Y	Y	Y
5 ***Cooksey***	Y	Y	N	N	Y	Y	Y
6 ***Baker***	Y	Y	N	N	Y	Y	Y
7 John	N	N	Y	Y	N	Y	N
MAINE							
1 Allen	N	N	Y	Y	N	N	N
2 Baldacci	N	N	Y	Y	N	Y	N
MARYLAND							
1 ***Gilchrest***	Y	Y	Y	N	Y	Y	Y
2 ***Ehrlich***	Y	Y	N	N	Y	Y	Y
3 Cardin	N	N	Y	Y	N	N	N
4 Wynn	N	N	Y	Y	N	Y	N
5 Hoyer	N	N	Y	?	N	N	N
6 ***Bartlett***	Y	Y	N	N	Y	?	Y
7 Cummings	N	N	Y	Y	N	N	N
8 ***Morella***	?	Y	Y	N	N	Y	Y
MASSACHUSETTS							
1 Olver	N	N	Y	Y	N	N	N
2 Neal	N	N	Y	Y	N	N	?
3 McGovern	N	N	Y	Y	N	N	N
4 Frank	N	N	Y	Y	N	?	N
5 Meehan	N	N	Y	Y	Y	N	N
6 Tierney	N	N	Y	Y	N	N	N
7 Markey	N	N	Y	Y	N	N	?
8 Kennedy	N	N	Y	Y	Y	N	N
9 Moakley	N	N	Y	Y	N	N	N
10 Delahunt	N	N	Y	Y	N	?	N
MICHIGAN							
1 Stupak	N	N	Y	Y	N	N	?
2 ***Hoekstra***	Y	Y	N	N	Y	Y	Y
3 ***Ehlers***	Y	Y	N	?	Y	Y	Y
4 ***Camp***	Y	Y	N	N	Y	Y	Y
5 Barcia	N	N	?	Y	N	Y	N
6 ***Upton***	Y	Y	N	N	Y	Y	Y
7 ***Smith***	Y	Y	N	N	Y	Y	Y
8 Stabenow	N	N	Y	Y	N	Y	N
9 Kildee	N	N	Y	Y	N	Y	N
10 Bonior	N	N	Y	Y	N	?	N
11 ***Knollenberg***	Y	Y	N	N	Y	Y	Y
12 Levin	N	N	Y	Y	N	N	N
13 Rivers	N	N	Y	Y	N	Y	N
14 Conyers	N	N	Y	Y	N	N	N
15 Kilpatrick	N	N	Y	Y	N	N	N
16 Dingell	N	N	Y	Y	N	N	N

	2	3	4	5	6	7	8
MINNESOTA							
1 ***Gutknecht***	Y	Y	N	N	Y	Y	Y
2 Minge	N	N	Y	Y	N	Y	N
3 ***Ramstad***	Y	Y	N	N	Y	Y	Y
4 Vento	N	N	Y	Y	Y	N	N
5 Sabo	N	N	Y	Y	N	N	Y
6 Luther	–	–	Y	Y	N	Y	N
7 Peterson	N	N	Y	Y	N	Y	N
8 Oberstar	N	N	Y	Y	N	N	N
MISSISSIPPI							
1 ***Wicker***	Y	Y	N	N	Y	Y	Y
2 Thompson	N	N	Y	Y	N	N	N
3 ***Pickering***	Y	Y	N	N	Y	?	Y
4 ***Parker***	Y	Y	N	N	Y	Y	Y
5 Taylor	N	N	Y	N	Y	Y	N
MISSOURI							
1 Clay	N	N	Y	Y	N	N	N
2 ***Talent***	Y	Y	N	N	Y	?	Y
3 Gephardt	N	N	Y	Y	N	N	N
4 Skelton	N	N	Y	Y	N	Y	Y
5 McCarthy	N	–	Y	Y	N	N	N
6 Danner	N	N	Y	Y	N	Y	N
7 ***Blunt***	Y	Y	N	N	Y	Y	Y
8 ***Emerson***	Y	Y	N	N	Y	Y	Y
9 ***Hulshof***	Y	Y	N	N	Y	Y	Y
MONTANA							
AL ***Hill***	Y	Y	N	N	Y	Y	Y
NEBRASKA							
1 ***Bereuter***	Y	Y	N	N	Y	?	Y
2 ***Christensen***	Y	Y	N	N	Y	Y	Y
3 ***Barrett***	Y	Y	Y	N	Y	Y	Y
NEVADA							
1 ***Ensign***	Y	Y	N	N	Y	Y	Y
2 ***Gibbons***	Y	Y	N	N	Y	Y	Y
NEW HAMPSHIRE							
1 ***Sununu***	Y	Y	N	N	Y	Y	Y
2 ***Bass***	Y	Y	N	N	Y	Y	Y
NEW JERSEY							
1 Andrews	N	N	Y	Y	N	N	N
2 ***LoBiondo***	Y	Y	N	N	Y	Y	Y
3 ***Saxton***	Y	Y	N	N	Y	Y	Y
4 ***Smith***	Y	Y	N	N	Y	Y	Y
5 ***Roukema***	Y	Y	N	N	Y	Y	Y
6 Pallone	N	N	Y	Y	N	N	N
7 ***Franks***	Y	?	N	N	Y	Y	Y
8 Pascrell	N	N	Y	Y	N	Y	N
9 Rothman	N	N	Y	Y	N	N	N
10 Payne	N	?	Y	Y	N	N	N
11 ***Frelinghuysen***	Y	Y	N	N	Y	Y	Y
12 ***Pappas***	Y	Y	N	N	Y	Y	Y
13 Menendez	N	N	Y	Y	N	N	N
NEW MEXICO							
1 ***Schiff***	?	?	?	?	?	?	?
2 ***Skeen***	Y	Y	N	N	Y	Y	Y
3 ***Redmond***	Y	Y	N	N	Y	Y	Y
NEW YORK							
1 ***Forbes***	N	Y	Y	N	Y	Y	Y
2 ***Lazio***	Y	Y	N	N	Y	Y	Y
3 ***King***	Y	Y	N	N	Y	N	?
4 McCarthy	N	N	Y	Y	Y	Y	N
5 Ackerman	N	N	Y	Y	N	N	N
6 Vacant							
7 Manton	N	N	Y	Y	N	N	N
8 Nadler	N	N	Y	Y	N	N	N
9 Schumer	N	N	Y	Y	N	N	N
10 Towns	N	N	Y	Y	N	N	N
11 Owens	N	N	Y	Y	N	N	N
12 Velázquez	N	N	Y	Y	N	N	N
13 ***Fossella***	Y	Y	N	N	Y	Y	Y
14 Maloney	N	N	Y	Y	N	Y	N
15 Rangel	N	N	Y	Y	N	N	N
16 Serrano	N	N	Y	Y	N	N	N
17 Engel	N	N	Y	Y	N	N	?
18 Lowey	N	N	Y	Y	N	N	N
19 ***Kelly***	Y	Y	N	N	Y	Y	Y
20 ***Gilman***	Y	Y	N	N	Y	Y	Y
21 McNulty	N	N	Y	Y	N	N	N
22 ***Solomon***	Y	Y	N	N	Y	Y	Y
23 ***Boehlert***	Y	Y	N	N	Y	Y	Y
24 ***McHugh***	Y	Y	N	N	Y	Y	Y
25 ***Walsh***	Y	Y	N	N	Y	Y	Y
26 Hinchey	N	N	Y	Y	N	N	N
27 ***Paxon***	Y	Y	N	N	Y	Y	Y
28 Slaughter	N	N	Y	Y	N	N	N
29 LaFalce	N	N	Y	Y	N	N	N

	2	3	4	5	6	7	8
30 ***Quinn***	Y	Y	N	N	Y	Y	Y
31 ***Houghton***	Y	Y	N	N	Y	N	Y
NORTH CAROLINA							
1 Clayton	N	N	Y	Y	N	N	N
2 Etheridge	N	N	Y	Y	N	Y	N
3 ***Jones***	Y	Y	N	N	Y	Y	Y
4 Price	N	N	Y	Y	N	Y	N
5 ***Burr***	Y	Y	N	N	Y	Y	Y
6 ***Coble***	Y	Y	N	N	Y	Y	Y
7 McIntyre	N	N	Y	Y	N	Y	N
8 Hefner	?	N	Y	Y	N	N	N
9 ***Myrick***	Y	Y	N	N	Y	Y	Y
10 ***Ballenger***	Y	Y	N	N	Y	Y	Y
11 ***Taylor***	Y	Y	N	N	Y	Y	?
12 Watt	N	N	Y	Y	N	N	N
NORTH DAKOTA							
AL Pomeroy	N	N	Y	Y	N	N	?
OHIO							
1 ***Chabot***	Y	Y	N	N	Y	Y	Y
2 ***Portman***	Y	Y	N	N	Y	Y	Y
3 Hall	N	N	Y	Y	N	?	–
4 ***Oxley***	Y	Y	N	N	Y	Y	Y
5 ***Gillmor***	Y	Y	N	N	Y	Y	Y
6 Strickland	N	N	Y	Y	N	Y	N
7 ***Hobson***	Y	Y	N	N	Y	Y	Y
8 ***Boehner***	Y	Y	N	N	Y	Y	Y
9 Kaptur	N	N	Y	Y	N	N	N
10 Kucinich	N	N	Y	Y	N	N	N
11 Stokes	N	?	Y	Y	N	N	N
12 ***Kasich***	Y	Y	N	N	Y	Y	Y
13 Brown	N	N	Y	Y	N	N	N
14 Sawyer	N	N	Y	Y	N	N	N
15 ***Pryce***	Y	Y	N	N	Y	Y	Y
16 ***Regula***	Y	Y	N	N	Y	Y	Y
17 Traficant	Y	Y	N	N	Y	Y	Y
18 ***Ney***	Y	Y	N	?	Y	?	Y
19 ***LaTourette***	Y	Y	N	N	Y	Y	Y
OKLAHOMA							
1 ***Largent***	Y	Y	N	N	Y	Y	?
2 ***Coburn***	Y	Y	N	N	Y	Y	Y
3 ***Watkins***	Y	Y	N	N	Y	Y	Y
4 ***Watts***	Y	Y	N	N	Y	Y	Y
5 ***Istook***	Y	Y	N	N	Y	Y	Y
6 ***Lucas***	Y	Y	N	N	Y	Y	Y
OREGON							
1 Furse	N	N	Y	Y	N	N	N
2 ***Smith***	?	Y	N	N	Y	Y	Y
3 Blumenauer	N	N	Y	Y	N	N	?
4 DeFazio	N	N	Y	Y	N	N	N
5 Hooley	N	N	Y	Y	N	Y	N
PENNSYLVANIA							
1 Vacant							
2 Fattah	N	?	?	Y	N	?	N
3 Borski	?	N	Y	Y	N	?	N
4 Klink	N	N	Y	Y	N	Y	?
5 ***Peterson***	Y	Y	N	N	Y	Y	Y
6 Holden	N	N	Y	Y	Y	Y	N
7 ***Weldon***	Y	Y	N	N	Y	Y	Y
8 ***Greenwood***	Y	Y	N	N	Y	Y	Y
9 ***Shuster***	Y	Y	N	N	Y	Y	Y
10 ***McDade***	?	Y	N	N	Y	Y	Y
11 Kanjorski	N	N	Y	Y	N	N	N
12 Murtha	N	N	Y	Y	N	Y	N
13 ***Fox***	Y	Y	N	N	Y	Y	Y
14 Coyne	N	N	Y	Y	N	N	N
15 McHale	N	N	Y	Y	N	N	N
16 ***Pitts***	Y	Y	N	N	Y	Y	Y
17 ***Gekas***	Y	Y	N	N	Y	?	Y
18 Doyle	N	N	Y	Y	Y	Y	N
19 ***Goodling***	Y	Y	N	N	Y	+	Y
20 Mascara	N	N	Y	Y	N	Y	N
21 ***English***	Y	Y	N	N	Y	Y	Y
RHODE ISLAND							
1 Kennedy	N	N	Y	Y	Y	N	N
2 Weygand	N	N	Y	Y	N	N	N
SOUTH CAROLINA							
1 ***Sanford***	Y	Y	Y	N	N	Y	Y
2 ***Spence***	Y	Y	N	N	Y	Y	Y
3 ***Graham***	Y	Y	N	N	Y	Y	Y
4 ***Inglis***	Y	Y	N	N	Y	Y	Y
5 Spratt	N	N	Y	Y	N	?	N
6 Clyburn	N	N	Y	Y	N	N	N
SOUTH DAKOTA							
AL ***Thune***	Y	Y	N	N	Y	Y	Y

	2	3	4	5	6	7	8
TENNESSEE							
1 ***Jenkins***	Y	Y	N	N	Y	Y	Y
2 ***Duncan***	Y	Y	N	N	Y	Y	Y
3 ***Wamp***	Y	Y	N	N	Y	Y	Y
4 ***Hilleary***	Y	Y	N	N	Y	Y	Y
5 Clement	N	N	Y	Y	N	Y	N
6 Gordon	N	N	Y	Y	N	N	N
7 ***Bryant***	Y	Y	N	N	Y	Y	Y
8 Tanner	?	N	Y	Y	N	Y	N
9 Ford	N	N	Y	Y	N	N	N
TEXAS							
1 Sandlin	N	N	Y	Y	N	N	N
2 Turner	N	Y	Y	N	Y	Y	Y
3 ***Johnson, Sam***	Y	Y	N	N	Y	Y	?
4 Hall	N	Y	Y	N	Y	Y	Y
5 ***Sessions***	Y	Y	N	N	Y	Y	Y
6 ***Barton***	Y	Y	N	N	Y	Y	Y
7 ***Archer***	Y	Y	N	N	Y	Y	Y
8 ***Brady***	Y	Y	N	N	Y	Y	Y
9 Lampson	N	N	Y	Y	N	N	N
10 Doggett	N	N	Y	Y	N	N	?
11 Edwards	N	N	Y	Y	N	Y	N
12 ***Granger***	Y	Y	N	N	Y	Y	Y
13 ***Thornberry***	Y	Y	N	N	Y	Y	Y
14 ***Paul***	Y	Y	Y	N	N	Y	Y
15 Hinojosa	N	N	Y	Y	N	?	N
16 Reyes	N	N	Y	Y	N	N	N
17 Stenholm	N	N	Y	Y	N	Y	N
18 Jackson-Lee	N	N	Y	Y	N	N	N
19 ***Combest***	Y	Y	N	N	Y	Y	Y
20 Gonzalez	?	?	?	?	?	?	?
21 ***Smith***	Y	Y	N	N	Y	Y	Y
22 ***DeLay***	Y	Y	N	N	Y	Y	Y
23 ***Bonilla***	Y	Y	N	N	Y	Y	Y
24 Frost	N	N	Y	Y	N	N	N
25 Bentsen	N	N	Y	Y	N	N	N
26 ***Armey***	Y	Y	N	N	Y	Y	Y
27 Ortiz	?	N	Y	Y	N	Y	N
28 Rodriguez	N	N	Y	Y	N	Y	N
29 Green	N	N	Y	Y	N	Y	N
30 Johnson, E.B.	N	N	Y	Y	N	N	N
UTAH							
1 ***Hansen***	Y	Y	N	N	Y	Y	Y
2 ***Cook***	Y	Y	N	N	Y	Y	Y
3 ***Cannon***	Y	Y	N	N	Y	Y	Y
VERMONT							
AL *Sanders*	N	N	Y	Y	N	N	N
VIRGINIA							
1 ***Bateman***	Y	Y	N	N	Y	Y	Y
2 Pickett	N	N	Y	Y	N	Y	N
3 Scott	N	N	Y	Y	N	N	N
4 Sisisky	N	N	Y	Y	N	Y	N
5 Goode	N	N	Y	Y	N	Y	Y
6 ***Goodlatte***	Y	Y	N	N	Y	Y	Y
7 ***Bliley***	Y	Y	N	N	Y	Y	Y
8 Moran	N	N	Y	Y	N	N	N
9 Boucher	N	N	Y	Y	N	N	N
10 ***Wolf***	Y	Y	Y	N	Y	Y	Y
11 ***Davis***	Y	Y	Y	N	Y	Y	Y
WASHINGTON							
1 ***White***	Y	Y	N	N	Y	Y	Y
2 ***Metcalf***	Y	Y	N	N	Y	Y	Y
3 ***Smith, Linda***	Y	Y	N	N	Y	Y	Y
4 ***Hastings***	Y	Y	N	N	Y	Y	Y
5 ***Nethercutt***	Y	Y	N	N	Y	?	Y
6 Dicks	N	Y	Y	Y	N	?	N
7 McDermott	N	N	Y	Y	N	N	N
8 ***Dunn***	Y	Y	N	N	Y	Y	Y
9 Smith, Adam	N	N	Y	Y	N	N	N
WEST VIRGINIA							
1 Mollohan	?	?	Y	Y	N	N	N
2 Wise	?	N	Y	Y	N	Y	N
3 Rahall	N	N	Y	Y	N	Y	N
WISCONSIN							
1 ***Neumann***	Y	Y	N	N	Y	Y	Y
2 ***Klug***	Y	Y	N	N	Y	Y	Y
3 Kind	?	N	Y	Y	N	Y	N
4 Kleczka	N	N	Y	Y	N	Y	N
5 Barrett	N	N	Y	Y	N	Y	N
6 ***Petri***	Y	Y	N	N	Y	Y	Y
7 Obey	N	N	Y	Y	N	Y	N
8 Johnson	N	N	Y	Y	N	Y	N
9 ***Sensenbrenner***	Y	Y	N	N	Y	Y	Y
WYOMING							
AL ***Cubin***	Y	Y	N	N	Y	Y	Y

Southern states - Ala., Ark., Fla., Ga., Ky., La., Miss., N.C., Okla., S.C., Tenn., Texas, Va.

9. HR 2846. National Education Testing Curbs/Passage. Passage of the bill to prohibit the use of federal education funds for any federally-sponsored national test in reading, math, or any other subject that is not specifically authorized by federal statute. Passed 242-174: R 217-2; D 25-171 (ND 16-126, SD 9-45); I 0-1. Feb. 5, 1998. A "nay" was a vote in support of the president's position.

10. HR 2631. Military Construction Line-Item Veto Disapproval/Veto Override. Passage, over President Clinton's Nov. 13, 1997, veto, of the bill to disapprove Clinton's line-item vetoes of 38 projects, totaling $287 million, in the fiscal 1998 military construction appropriations bill (HR2016 — PL105-45). Passed 347-69: R 197-23; D 149-46 (ND 100-41, SD 49-5); I 1-0. Feb. 5, 1998. A two-thirds majority of those present and voting (277 in this case) of both chambers is required to override a veto. A "nay" was a vote in support of the president's position.

11. Quorum Call.* 356 Responded. Feb. 5, 1998.

12. H Res 352. Suspension of the Rules/Rule. Adoption of the rule (H Res 352) to provide for House floor consideration of bills on Wednesday, February 11 and Thursday, February 12 under suspension of the rules. Adopted 217-191: R 213-0; D 4-190 (ND 2-138, SD 2-52); I 0-1. Feb. 11, 1998.

13. H Con Res 202. Child Care Funds for Parents Staying Home/Adoption. Goodling, R-Pa., motion to suspend the rules and adopt the concurrent resolution to express the sense of Congress recognizing the importance of parents who forgo a second income to stay at home to raise children, and that Congress should not discriminate against these families. Motion agreed to 409-0: R 219-0; D 189-0 (ND 135-0, SD 54-0); I 1-0. Feb. 11, 1998. A two-thirds majority of those present and voting (273 in this case) is required for adoption under suspension of the rules.

14. Procedural Motion/Journal. Approval of the House Journal of Wednesday, Feb. 11, 1998. Approved 353-43: R 198-12; D 154-31 (ND 114-22, SD 40-9); I 1-0. Feb. 12, 1998.

15. H Res 355. Dornan Election Challenge/Recommit. Hoyer, D-Md., motion to recommit the privileged resolution to the House Oversight Committee with instructions to report it back with an amendment to include only the dismissal of the complaint by former Rep. Robert K. Dornan, R-Calif., contesting the election of Loretta Sanchez, D-Calif. Motion rejected 194-215: R 1-214; D 192-1 (ND 140-1, SD 52-0); I 1-0. Feb. 12, 1998.

16. H Res 355. Dornan Election Challenge/Adoption. Adoption of the privileged resolution to dismiss the complaint by former Rep. Robert K. Dornan, R-Calif., contesting the election of Loretta Sanchez, D-Calif. Adopted 378-33: R 184-33; D 193-0 (ND 141-0, SD 52-0); I 1-0. Feb. 12, 1998.

* CQ does not include quorum calls in its vote charts.

[1] Ronald V. Dellums, D-Calif., resigned Feb. 6.

[2] Gregory W. Meeks, D-N.Y., was sworn in Feb. 5, replacing Floyd H. Flake, D-N.Y., who resigned Nov. 15, 1997.

Key

Y	Voted for (yea).
#	Paired for.
+	Announced for.
N	Voted against (nay).
X	Paired against.
–	Announced against.
P	Voted "present."
C	Voted "present" to avoid possible conflict of interest.
?	Did not vote or otherwise make a position known.

Democrats **Republicans** *Independent*

	9	10	12	13	14	15	16
ALABAMA							
1 *Callahan*	Y	Y	?	?	?	?	?
2 *Everett*	Y	Y	Y	Y	Y	N	Y
3 *Riley*	Y	Y	Y	Y	Y	N	Y
4 *Aderholt*	Y	Y	Y	Y	Y	N	Y
5 Cramer	N	Y	N	Y	Y	Y	Y
6 *Bachus*	Y	Y	Y	Y	Y	N	Y
7 Hilliard	N	Y	N	Y	N	Y	Y
ALASKA							
AL *Young*	Y	Y	Y	Y	?	N	Y
ARIZONA							
1 *Salmon*	Y	N	Y	Y	Y	N	Y
2 Pastor	N	Y	N	Y	Y	Y	Y
3 *Stump*	Y	Y	Y	Y	Y	N	N
4 *Shadegg*	Y	Y	Y	Y	Y	N	Y
5 *Kolbe*	Y	Y	Y	Y	Y	N	Y
6 *Hayworth*	Y	Y	Y	Y	Y	N	Y
ARKANSAS							
1 Berry	N	Y	N	Y	?	Y	Y
2 Snyder	N	Y	N	Y	Y	Y	Y
3 *Hutchinson*	Y	Y	Y	Y	Y	N	Y
4 *Dickey*	N	Y	N	Y	Y	Y	Y
CALIFORNIA							
1 *Riggs*	Y	Y	Y	Y	?	?	?
2 *Herger*	?	?	Y	Y	Y	N	N
3 Fazio	N	Y	N	Y	Y	Y	Y
4 *Doolittle*	Y	Y	?	?	Y	N	N
5 Matsui	N	Y	N	Y	Y	Y	Y
6 Woolsey	N	N	N	Y	Y	Y	Y
7 Miller	N	Y	N	Y	Y	Y	Y
8 Pelosi	Y	Y	N	Y	Y	Y	Y
9 Dellums[1]	?	?					
10 Tauscher	N	Y	N	Y	Y	Y	Y
11 *Pombo*	Y	Y	Y	Y	Y	N	N
12 Lantos	N	Y	?	?	?	?	?
13 Stark	N	N	N	Y	Y	Y	Y
14 Eshoo	?	?	?	?	?	?	?
15 *Campbell*	Y	Y	Y	Y	Y	N	Y
16 Lofgren	N	N	N	Y	Y	Y	Y
17 Farr	N	Y	N	Y	Y	Y	Y
18 Condit	Y	Y	N	Y	Y	Y	Y
19 *Radanovich*	Y	Y	Y	Y	Y	N	Y
20 Dooley	N	N	N	Y	Y	Y	Y
21 *Thomas*	Y	Y	Y	Y	Y	N	Y
22 Vacant							
23 *Gallegly*	Y	Y	Y	Y	Y	N	Y
24 Sherman	N	N	N	Y	Y	Y	Y
25 *McKeon*	+	+	Y	Y	Y	N	Y
26 Berman	N	Y	N	Y	Y	Y	Y
27 *Rogan*	Y	Y	Y	Y	Y	N	Y
28 *Dreier*	Y	Y	Y	Y	Y	N	N
29 Waxman	N	N	N	Y	Y	Y	Y
30 Becerra	–	+	N	Y	N	Y	Y
31 Martinez	N	N	N	P	Y	Y	Y
32 Dixon	N	Y	N	Y	Y	Y	Y
33 Roybal-Allard	N	Y	N	Y	Y	Y	Y
34 Torres	N	Y	N	Y	?	Y	Y
35 Waters	N	Y	?	?	Y	Y	Y
36 Harman	N	N	?	?	?	?	?
37 Millender-McD.	N	Y	N	Y	Y	Y	Y

	9	10	12	13	14	15	16
38 *Horn*	Y	Y	Y	Y	Y	N	Y
39 *Royce*	Y	N	Y	Y	Y	N	N
40 *Lewis*	Y	Y	Y	Y	Y	N	Y
41 *Kim*	Y	Y	Y	Y	Y	N	Y
42 Brown	N	Y	N	Y	Y	Y	Y
43 *Calvert*	Y	Y	Y	Y	Y	N	Y
44 Vacant							
45 *Rohrabacher*	Y	N	Y	Y	Y	N	N
46 Sanchez	N	N	N	Y	Y	Y	Y
47 *Cox*	Y	Y	Y	Y	Y	N	Y
48 *Packard*	Y	Y	Y	Y	Y	N	Y
49 *Bilbray*	Y	Y	Y	Y	Y	N	Y
50 Filner	N	N	N	Y	Y	Y	Y
51 *Cunningham*	Y	Y	Y	Y	Y	N	Y
52 *Hunter*	Y	Y	Y	Y	?	N	N
COLORADO							
1 DeGette	N	N	N	Y	Y	Y	Y
2 Skaggs	N	N	N	Y	Y	Y	Y
3 *McInnis*	Y	Y	Y	Y	Y	N	Y
4 *Schaffer*	Y	Y	Y	Y	N	N	N
5 *Hefley*	Y	Y	Y	Y	N	N	Y
6 *Schaefer*	Y	Y	Y	Y	Y	N	Y
CONNECTICUT							
1 Kennelly	N	Y	N	Y	Y	Y	Y
2 Gejdenson	N	Y	N	Y	Y	Y	Y
3 DeLauro	N	Y	N	Y	Y	Y	Y
4 *Shays*	Y	N	Y	Y	Y	N	Y
5 Maloney	N	Y	N	Y	Y	Y	Y
6 *Johnson*	N	Y	Y	Y	Y	N	Y
DELAWARE							
AL *Castle*	Y	Y	Y	Y	Y	N	Y
FLORIDA							
1 *Scarborough*	Y	Y	Y	Y	Y	?	Y
2 Boyd	Y	N	N	Y	Y	Y	Y
3 Brown	N	Y	N	Y	Y	Y	Y
4 *Fowler*	Y	Y	Y	Y	Y	N	Y
5 Thurman	N	Y	N	Y	Y	Y	Y
6 *Stearns*	Y	Y	Y	Y	N	N	N
7 *Mica*	Y	Y	Y	Y	Y	N	N
8 *McCollum*	Y	Y	Y	Y	Y	N	Y
9 *Bilirakis*	Y	Y	Y	Y	Y	N	Y
10 *Young*	Y	Y	Y	Y	Y	N	Y
11 Davis	N	N	N	Y	Y	Y	Y
12 *Canady*	Y	Y	Y	Y	Y	N	Y
13 *Miller*	Y	N	?	?	?	?	?
14 *Goss*	Y	Y	Y	Y	Y	N	Y
15 *Weldon*	Y	Y	Y	Y	Y	N	Y
16 *Foley*	N	Y	N	Y	Y	Y	Y
17 Meek	N	Y	N	Y	Y	Y	Y
18 *Ros-Lehtinen*	Y	Y	+	Y	Y	N	Y
19 Wexler	N	N	N	Y	Y	Y	Y
20 Deutsch	N	N	N	Y	Y	Y	Y
21 *Diaz-Balart*	Y	Y	N	Y	Y	N	Y
22 *Shaw*	Y	Y	Y	Y	Y	N	Y
23 Hastings	N	Y	N	Y	Y	Y	Y
GEORGIA							
1 *Kingston*	Y	Y	Y	Y	Y	N	N
2 Bishop	N	Y	N	Y	Y	Y	Y
3 *Collins*	Y	Y	Y	Y	Y	N	Y
4 McKinney	N	N	N	Y	Y	Y	Y
5 Lewis	N	Y	N	Y	Y	Y	Y
6 *Gingrich*							
7 *Barr*	Y	Y	Y	Y	Y	N	N
8 *Chambliss*	Y	Y	Y	Y	Y	N	Y
9 *Deal*	Y	Y	Y	Y	Y	N	Y
10 *Norwood*	Y	Y	Y	Y	?	N	N
11 *Linder*	Y	Y	?	?	Y	N	Y
HAWAII							
1 Abercrombie	N	Y	N	Y	N	Y	Y
2 Mink	N	Y	–	+	+	+	Y
IDAHO							
1 *Chenoweth*	Y	Y	Y	Y	Y	N	N
2 *Crapo*	Y	Y	Y	Y	?	N	Y
ILLINOIS							
1 Rush	N	Y	N	Y	?	Y	Y
2 Jackson	N	Y	N	Y	Y	Y	Y
3 Lipinski	Y	Y	N	Y	Y	N	Y
4 Gutierrez	N	N	N	Y	Y	Y	Y
5 Blagojevich	N	Y	N	Y	Y	Y	Y
6 *Hyde*	N	Y	N	Y	?	N	Y
7 Davis	N	Y	N	Y	?	Y	Y
8 *Crane*	Y	Y	Y	Y	?	?	N
9 Yates	N	N	N	Y	?	Y	Y
10 *Porter*	Y	+	Y	Y	Y	N	Y
11 *Weller*	Y	Y	Y	Y	Y	N	Y
12 Costello	N	Y	N	Y	N	Y	Y

ND Northern Democrats   SD Southern Democrats

	9	10	12	13	14	15	16
13 **Fawell**	Y	Y	Y	Y	Y	N	Y
14 **Hastert**	Y	Y	Y	Y	Y	N	Y
15 **Ewing**	Y	N	Y	Y	Y	N	Y
16 **Manzullo**	Y	Y	Y	Y	Y	N	Y
17 Evans	Y	Y	N	Y	Y	Y	Y
18 **LaHood**	Y	Y	Y	Y	Y	N	Y
19 Poshard	N	Y	?	?	N	Y	Y
20 **Shimkus**	Y	Y	Y	Y	Y	N	Y
INDIANA							
1 Visclosky	N	Y	N	Y	N	Y	Y
2 **McIntosh**	Y	Y	Y	Y	Y	N	N
3 Roemer	Y	Y	N	Y	Y	Y	Y
4 **Souder**	Y	Y	Y	Y	Y	N	Y
5 **Buyer**	Y	Y	Y	Y	Y	?	?
6 **Burton**	+	+	Y	Y	Y	N	N
7 **Pease**	Y	Y	Y	Y	Y	N	Y
8 **Hostettler**	Y	Y	Y	Y	Y	N	N
9 Hamilton	Y	Y	Y	Y	Y	Y	Y
10 Carson	N	N	N	Y	Y	Y	Y
IOWA							
1 **Leach**	Y	N	Y	Y	Y	N	Y
2 **Nussle**	Y	N	Y	Y	Y	N	Y
3 Boswell	N	N	N	Y	Y	Y	Y
4 **Ganske**	Y	N	Y	Y	Y	N	Y
5 **Latham**	Y	Y	Y	Y	Y	N	Y
KANSAS							
1 **Moran**	Y	Y	Y	Y	N	N	Y
2 **Ryun**	Y	Y	Y	Y	Y	N	Y
3 **Snowbarger**	Y	Y	Y	Y	?	N	Y
4 **Tiahrt**	Y	Y	Y	Y	Y	N	N
KENTUCKY							
1 **Whitfield**	Y	Y	Y	Y	Y	N	Y
2 **Lewis**	Y	Y	Y	Y	Y	N	N
3 **Northup**	Y	Y	Y	Y	Y	N	Y
4 **Bunning**	Y	Y	Y	Y	Y	N	Y
5 **Rogers**	Y	Y	Y	Y	Y	N	Y
6 Baesler	N	Y	N	Y	Y	Y	Y
LOUISIANA							
1 **Livingston**	Y	Y	Y	Y	Y	N	?
2 Jefferson	N	Y	N	Y	Y	Y	Y
3 **Tauzin**	Y	Y	Y	Y	Y	N	Y
4 **McCrery**	Y	Y	Y	Y	Y	N	Y
5 **Cooksey**	Y	Y	Y	Y	Y	N	Y
6 **Baker**	Y	Y	Y	Y	Y	N	Y
7 John	Y	Y	N	Y	?	Y	Y
MAINE							
1 Allen	N	Y	N	Y	Y	Y	Y
2 Baldacci	N	Y	N	Y	N	Y	Y
MARYLAND							
1 **Gilchrest**	Y	Y	Y	Y	Y	N	Y
2 **Ehrlich**	Y	Y	Y	Y	Y	N	Y
3 Cardin	N	Y	N	Y	Y	Y	Y
4 Wynn	N	?	N	Y	Y	Y	Y
5 Hoyer	N	Y	N	Y	Y	Y	Y
6 **Bartlett**	Y	Y	Y	Y	Y	N	N
7 Cummings	N	Y	N	Y	Y	Y	Y
8 **Morella**	Y	Y	Y	Y	Y	N	Y
MASSACHUSETTS							
1 Olver	N	Y	N	Y	N	Y	Y
2 Neal	N	Y	N	Y	Y	Y	Y
3 McGovern	N	Y	N	Y	Y	Y	Y
4 Frank	N	N	N	P	Y	Y	Y
5 Meehan	N	N	N	Y	Y	Y	Y
6 Tierney	N	Y	N	Y	Y	Y	Y
7 Markey	N	N	N	Y	Y	Y	Y
8 Kennedy	N	Y	N	Y	Y	Y	Y
9 Moakley	N	Y	N	Y	Y	Y	Y
10 Delahunt	N	Y	N	Y	Y	Y	Y
MICHIGAN							
1 Stupak	N	N	N	Y	N	Y	Y
2 **Hoekstra**	Y	Y	Y	Y	Y	N	Y
3 **Ehlers**	Y	Y	Y	Y	Y	N	Y
4 **Camp**	Y	Y	Y	Y	Y	N	Y
5 Barcia	N	Y	N	Y	Y	Y	Y
6 **Upton**	Y	N	Y	Y	Y	N	Y
7 **Smith**	Y	N	Y	Y	Y	N	Y
8 Stabenow	N	Y	N	Y	Y	Y	Y
9 Kildee	N	Y	N	Y	Y	Y	Y
10 Bonior	N	Y	N	Y	Y	Y	Y
11 **Knollenberg**	Y	Y	Y	Y	Y	N	Y
12 Levin	N	Y	N	Y	Y	Y	Y
13 Rivers	N	N	N	Y	Y	Y	Y
14 Conyers	N	N	N	?	Y	?	Y
15 Kilpatrick	?	Y	N	Y	Y	Y	Y
16 Dingell	N	Y	N	Y	Y	Y	Y
MINNESOTA							
1 **Gutknecht**	Y	Y	Y	Y	N	N	N
2 Minge	N	N	N	Y	Y	Y	Y
3 **Ramstad**	Y	N	Y	Y	N	N	Y
4 Vento	N	N	N	Y	?	Y	Y
5 Sabo	N	Y	N	Y	Y	Y	Y
6 Luther	N	N	N	Y	Y	Y	Y
7 Peterson	Y	Y	N	Y	Y	Y	Y
8 Oberstar	N	Y	N	Y	?	Y	Y
MISSISSIPPI							
1 **Wicker**	Y	Y	Y	Y	Y	N	Y
2 Thompson	N	Y	N	Y	N	Y	Y
3 **Pickering**	?	Y	Y	Y	Y	N	Y
4 **Parker**	Y	Y	Y	Y	Y	N	Y
5 Taylor	Y	Y	N	Y	N	Y	Y
MISSOURI							
1 Clay	N	Y	N	Y	N	Y	Y
2 **Talent**	Y	Y	Y	Y	?	N	Y
3 Gephardt	N	Y	N	Y	N	Y	Y
4 Skelton	N	Y	N	Y	Y	Y	Y
5 McCarthy	N	N	N	Y	Y	Y	Y
6 Danner	Y	Y	N	Y	Y	Y	Y
7 **Blunt**	Y	Y	Y	Y	Y	N	Y
8 **Emerson**	Y	Y	Y	Y	Y	N	Y
9 **Hulshof**	Y	Y	Y	Y	Y	N	Y
MONTANA							
AL **Hill**	Y	Y	Y	Y	Y	N	Y
NEBRASKA							
1 **Bereuter**	Y	Y	Y	Y	Y	N	Y
2 **Christensen**	Y	Y	Y	Y	Y	N	Y
3 **Barrett**	Y	Y	Y	Y	Y	N	Y
NEVADA							
1 **Ensign**	Y	N	Y	Y	?	?	Y
2 **Gibbons**	Y	Y	Y	Y	N	N	Y
NEW HAMPSHIRE							
1 **Sununu**	Y	Y	Y	Y	Y	N	Y
2 **Bass**	Y	Y	Y	Y	Y	N	Y
NEW JERSEY							
1 Andrews	N	N	N	Y	Y	Y	Y
2 **LoBiondo**	Y	Y	Y	Y	N	N	Y
3 **Saxton**	Y	Y	Y	Y	Y	N	Y
4 **Smith**	Y	Y	Y	Y	Y	N	Y
5 **Roukema**	Y	Y	Y	Y	Y	N	Y
6 Pallone	N	Y	N	Y	Y	Y	Y
7 **Franks**	Y	N	Y	Y	Y	N	Y
8 Pascrell	N	Y	N	Y	N	Y	Y
9 Rothman	N	N	N	Y	Y	Y	Y
10 Payne	N	N	N	P	Y	Y	Y
11 **Frelinghuysen**	Y	Y	Y	Y	Y	N	Y
12 **Pappas**	Y	Y	Y	Y	Y	N	Y
13 Menendez	N	Y	N	Y	N	Y	Y
NEW MEXICO							
1 **Schiff**	?	?	?	?	?	?	?
2 **Skeen**	Y	Y	Y	Y	Y	N	Y
3 **Redmond**	Y	Y	Y	Y	Y	N	Y
NEW YORK							
1 **Forbes**	N	Y	Y	Y	Y	Y	Y
2 **Lazio**	Y	Y	Y	Y	Y	N	Y
3 **King**	Y	Y	Y	Y	Y	N	Y
4 McCarthy	N	N	N	Y	Y	Y	Y
5 Ackerman	N	N	N	Y	Y	Y	Y
6 Meeks [2]			N	Y	Y	Y	Y
7 Manton	N	N	N	Y	Y	Y	Y
8 Nadler	N	Y	?	?	?	Y	Y
9 Schumer	N	Y	N	Y	Y	Y	Y
10 Towns	N	N	N	Y	Y	Y	Y
11 Owens	N	N	N	Y	Y	Y	Y
12 Velázquez	N	Y	N	Y	N	Y	Y
13 **Fossella**	Y	Y	Y	Y	Y	N	Y
14 Maloney	N	Y	N	Y	Y	Y	Y
15 Rangel	N	N	N	Y	Y	Y	Y
16 Serrano	N	Y	N	Y	Y	Y	Y
17 Engel	N	N	N	Y	Y	Y	Y
18 Lowey	N	Y	N	Y	Y	Y	Y
19 **Kelly**	Y	Y	Y	Y	Y	N	Y
20 **Gilman**	Y	Y	Y	Y	Y	N	Y
21 McNulty	N	Y	N	Y	N	Y	Y
22 **Solomon**	Y	Y	Y	Y	Y	?	?
23 **Boehlert**	Y	Y	Y	Y	Y	N	Y
24 **McHugh**	Y	Y	Y	Y	Y	N	Y
25 **Walsh**	Y	Y	Y	Y	Y	N	Y
26 Hinchey	N	Y	N	Y	N	Y	Y
27 **Paxon**	Y	Y	Y	Y	Y	N	Y
28 Slaughter	N	Y	N	Y	Y	Y	Y
29 LaFalce	N	Y	N	Y	Y	Y	Y
30 **Quinn**	Y	Y	Y	Y	Y	N	Y
31 **Houghton**	Y	Y	Y	Y	Y	N	Y
NORTH CAROLINA							
1 Clayton	N	Y	N	Y	Y	Y	Y
2 Etheridge	N	Y	N	Y	Y	Y	Y
3 **Jones**	Y	Y	Y	Y	Y	N	N
4 Price	N	Y	N	Y	Y	Y	Y
5 **Burr**	Y	Y	Y	Y	Y	N	Y
6 **Coble**	Y	Y	Y	Y	Y	N	Y
7 McIntyre	N	Y	N	Y	Y	Y	Y
8 Hefner	N	Y	N	Y	Y	Y	Y
9 **Myrick**	Y	Y	?	?	Y	N	Y
10 **Ballenger**	Y	Y	Y	Y	Y	N	N
11 **Taylor**	Y	Y	Y	Y	Y	N	N
12 Watt	N	Y	N	Y	Y	Y	Y
NORTH DAKOTA							
AL Pomeroy	N	Y	N	Y	Y	Y	Y
OHIO							
1 **Chabot**	Y	N	Y	Y	Y	N	N
2 **Portman**	Y	Y	Y	Y	Y	N	Y
3 Hall	–	+	N	Y	Y	Y	Y
4 **Oxley**	Y	Y	Y	Y	Y	N	Y
5 **Gillmor**	Y	Y	Y	Y	Y	N	Y
6 Strickland	Y	N	N	Y	Y	Y	Y
7 **Hobson**	Y	Y	Y	Y	Y	N	Y
8 **Boehner**	Y	Y	Y	Y	Y	N	Y
9 Kaptur	Y	Y	N	Y	Y	Y	Y
10 Kucinich	N	Y	N	Y	N	Y	Y
11 Stokes	N	Y	N	Y	Y	Y	Y
12 **Kasich**	Y	Y	Y	Y	Y	N	Y
13 Brown	N	N	N	Y	Y	Y	Y
14 Sawyer	N	Y	?	Y	Y	Y	Y
15 **Pryce**	Y	Y	Y	Y	Y	N	Y
16 **Regula**	Y	Y	Y	Y	Y	N	Y
17 Traficant	Y	Y	Y	Y	Y	N	Y
18 **Ney**	Y	Y	Y	Y	Y	N	Y
19 **LaTourette**	Y	Y	Y	Y	Y	N	Y
OKLAHOMA							
1 **Largent**	Y	Y	Y	Y	Y	N	Y
2 **Coburn**	Y	Y	Y	Y	Y	N	Y
3 **Watkins**	Y	Y	Y	Y	Y	N	Y
4 **Watts**	Y	Y	Y	Y	Y	N	Y
5 **Istook**	+	Y	Y	Y	Y	N	Y
6 **Lucas**	Y	Y	Y	Y	Y	N	Y
OREGON							
1 Furse	N	?	N	Y	?	?	?
2 **Smith**	Y	Y	?	?	?	?	?
3 Blumenauer	N	Y	N	Y	Y	Y	Y
4 DeFazio	Y	N	N	Y	N	Y	Y
5 Hooley	N	Y	N	Y	Y	Y	Y
PENNSYLVANIA							
1 Vacant							
2 Fattah	N	Y	N	Y	Y	Y	Y
3 Borski	N	Y	N	Y	N	Y	Y
4 Klink	?	?	N	Y	Y	Y	Y
5 **Peterson**	Y	Y	Y	Y	Y	?	Y
6 Holden	Y	Y	N	Y	Y	Y	Y
7 **Weldon**	Y	Y	Y	Y	?	N	Y
8 **Greenwood**	Y	N	Y	Y	Y	N	Y
9 **Shuster**	Y	Y	Y	Y	Y	N	Y
10 **McDade**	Y	Y	Y	Y	?	N	Y
11 Kanjorski	N	N	N	Y	Y	Y	Y
12 Murtha	N	Y	N	Y	Y	Y	Y
13 **Fox**	Y	Y	Y	Y	N	N	Y
14 Coyne	N	Y	N	Y	Y	Y	Y
15 McHale	N	Y	N	Y	Y	Y	Y
16 **Pitts**	Y	Y	Y	Y	Y	N	Y
17 **Gekas**	Y	Y	Y	Y	Y	N	N
18 Doyle	Y	Y	N	Y	Y	Y	Y
19 **Goodling**	Y	Y	Y	Y	Y	N	Y
20 Mascara	N	Y	N	Y	Y	Y	Y
21 **English**	Y	Y	Y	Y	N	N	Y
RHODE ISLAND							
1 Kennedy	N	Y	N	Y	Y	Y	Y
2 Weygand	N	Y	N	Y	Y	Y	Y
SOUTH CAROLINA							
1 **Sanford**	Y	N	Y	Y	Y	N	Y
2 **Spence**	Y	Y	Y	Y	Y	N	N
3 **Graham**	Y	Y	Y	Y	Y	N	Y
4 **Inglis**	Y	Y	Y	Y	Y	N	Y
5 Spratt	N	Y	N	Y	P	Y	Y
6 Clyburn	N	Y	N	Y	N	Y	Y
SOUTH DAKOTA							
AL **Thune**	Y	Y	Y	Y	Y	N	Y
TENNESSEE							
1 **Jenkins**	Y	Y	Y	Y	Y	N	Y
2 **Duncan**	Y	N	Y	Y	Y	N	Y
3 **Wamp**	Y	Y	Y	Y	Y	N	Y
4 **Hilleary**	Y	Y	Y	Y	N	N	Y
5 Clement	N	Y	N	Y	+	+	+
6 Gordon	N	Y	N	Y	Y	Y	Y
7 **Bryant**	Y	Y	Y	Y	Y	N	Y
8 Tanner	N	Y	N	Y	Y	Y	Y
9 Ford	N	Y	N	Y	Y	Y	Y
TEXAS							
1 Sandlin	N	Y	N	Y	Y	Y	Y
2 Turner	Y	Y	N	Y	Y	Y	Y
3 **Johnson, Sam**	Y	Y	Y	Y	Y	N	Y
4 Hall	Y	Y	Y	Y	Y	Y	Y
5 **Sessions**	Y	Y	Y	Y	N	N	Y
6 **Barton**	Y	Y	Y	Y	Y	N	Y
7 **Archer**	Y	Y	Y	Y	Y	N	Y
8 **Brady**	Y	Y	Y	Y	Y	N	Y
9 Lampson	N	Y	N	Y	Y	Y	Y
10 Doggett	N	N	N	Y	Y	Y	Y
11 Edwards	N	Y	N	Y	?	Y	?
12 **Granger**	Y	Y	Y	Y	Y	N	Y
13 **Thornberry**	Y	Y	Y	Y	Y	N	Y
14 **Paul**	Y	Y	Y	Y	Y	N	N
15 Hinojosa	N	Y	N	Y	Y	Y	Y
16 Reyes	N	Y	N	Y	Y	Y	Y
17 Stenholm	Y	Y	N	Y	Y	Y	Y
18 Jackson-Lee	N	Y	N	Y	Y	Y	Y
19 **Combest**	Y	Y	Y	Y	Y	N	Y
20 Gonzalez	?	?	?	?	?	?	?
21 **Smith**	Y	Y	Y	Y	Y	N	Y
22 **DeLay**	Y	Y	Y	Y	Y	N	Y
23 **Bonilla**	Y	Y	Y	Y	Y	N	Y
24 Frost	N	Y	N	Y	Y	Y	Y
25 Bentsen	N	Y	N	Y	Y	Y	Y
26 **Armey**	Y	?	Y	Y	Y	N	Y
27 Ortiz	N	Y	N	Y	Y	Y	Y
28 Rodriguez	N	Y	N	Y	Y	?	Y
29 Green	N	Y	N	Y	N	Y	Y
30 Johnson, E.B.	N	Y	N	Y	Y	Y	Y
UTAH							
1 **Hansen**	Y	Y	Y	Y	Y	N	Y
2 **Cook**	Y	Y	Y	Y	Y	N	Y
3 **Cannon**	?	Y	Y	Y	Y	N	Y
VERMONT							
AL *Sanders*	N	Y	N	Y	Y	Y	Y
VIRGINIA							
1 **Bateman**	Y	Y	Y	Y	Y	N	Y
2 Pickett	Y	Y	N	Y	N	Y	Y
3 Scott	N	Y	N	Y	N	Y	Y
4 Sisisky	Y	Y	N	Y	Y	Y	Y
5 Goode	Y	Y	Y	Y	Y	Y	Y
6 **Goodlatte**	Y	Y	Y	Y	Y	N	Y
7 **Bliley**	Y	Y	Y	Y	Y	N	Y
8 Moran	N	Y	N	Y	Y	Y	Y
9 Boucher	N	Y	N	Y	Y	Y	Y
10 **Wolf**	Y	Y	Y	Y	Y	N	Y
11 **Davis**	Y	Y	Y	Y	Y	N	Y
WASHINGTON							
1 **White**	Y	Y	?	Y	Y	N	Y
2 **Metcalf**	Y	Y	Y	Y	Y	N	Y
3 **Smith, Linda**	Y	Y	?	Y	Y	N	?
4 **Hastings**	Y	Y	Y	Y	Y	N	Y
5 **Nethercutt**	Y	Y	Y	Y	Y	N	Y
6 Dicks	N	Y	N	Y	Y	Y	Y
7 McDermott	N	N	N	Y	N	Y	Y
8 **Dunn**	Y	Y	Y	Y	Y	N	Y
9 Smith, Adam	N	Y	N	Y	Y	Y	Y
WEST VIRGINIA							
1 Mollohan	Y	Y	N	Y	Y	Y	Y
2 Wise	N	Y	N	+	Y	Y	?
3 Rahall	N	Y	N	Y	Y	Y	Y
WISCONSIN							
1 **Neumann**	Y	N	Y	Y	Y	N	Y
2 **Klug**	Y	N	Y	Y	Y	N	Y
3 Kind	N	N	N	Y	Y	Y	Y
4 Kleczka	Y	N	Y	Y	Y	Y	Y
5 Barrett	N	N	N	Y	Y	Y	Y
6 **Petri**	Y	N	Y	Y	Y	N	Y
7 Obey	N	Y	N	?	N	Y	Y
8 Johnson	N	N	N	Y	?	?	?
9 **Sensenbrenner**	Y	N	?	Y	Y	N	N
WYOMING							
AL **Cubin**	Y	Y	Y	Y	Y	N	N

Southern states - Ala., Ark., Fla., Ga., Ky., La., Miss., N.C., Okla., S.C., Tenn., Texas, Va.

17. HR 1428. Voter Eligibility Verification/Passage. Pease, R-Ind., motion to suspend the rules and pass, as amended, the bill to establish a pilot program in the five largest states, under which state and local officials could require Social Security numbers from voting applicants. It also directs the Justice Department, in consultation with the Social Security Administration and the Immigration and Naturalization Service, to set up a system in which local officials could seek verification of the citizenship of those attempting to vote. Motion rejected 210-200: R 203-13; D 7-186 (ND 1-140, SD 6-46); I 0-1. Feb. 12, 1998. A two-thirds majority of those present and voting (273 in this case) is required for passage under suspension of the rules.

18. HR 424. Mandatory Minimum Sentences for Gun Crimes/Passage. McCollum, R-Fla., motion to suspend the rules and pass the bill to impose mandatory minimum sentences for possession of a gun while committing a violent crime or drug trafficking offense. Motion agreed to 350-59: R 219-4; D 130-55 (ND 91-45, SD 39-10); I 1-0. Feb. 24, 1998. A two-thirds majority of those present and voting (273 in this case) is required for passage under suspension of the rules.

19. HR 1544. Federal Agency Compliance/Internal Revenue Service. Nadler, D-N.Y., amendment to limit the bill to require federal agencies to follow appellate court precedents to affect only the Internal Revenue Service, and those agencies dealing with benefits. Rejected 172-238: R 8-212; D 163-26 (ND 128-11, SD 35-15); I 1-0. Feb. 25, 1998.

20. HR 2181. Witness Protection/Death Penalty. Conyers, D-Mich., amendment to give courts the ability to reduce death penalty sentences that are provided in the bill to make it a federal offense to travel across state or international borders to intimidate a witness in a state criminal proceeding. Rejected 113-300: R 7-214; D 105-86 (ND 91-49, SD 14-37); I 1-0. Feb. 25, 1998.

21. HR 2181. Witness Protection/Passage. Passage of the bill to make it a federal offense to travel across state or international borders to intimidate a witness in a state criminal proceeding. Passed 366-49: R 221-2; D 144-47 (ND 101-38, SD 43-9); I 1-0. Feb. 25, 1998.

22. HR 1544. Federal Agency Compliance/Civil Rights. Jackson-Lee, D-Texas, amendment to prevent the bill to require federal agencies to follow appellate court precedents from applying to issues dealing with civil, labor and environmental rights. Rejected 164-253: R 2-220; D 161-33 (ND 128-15, SD 33-18); I 1-0. Feb. 25, 1998.

23. HR 1544. Federal Agency Compliance/Foreign Entities. Jackson-Lee, D-Texas, amendment to prevent the bill to require federal agencies to follow appellate court precedents from applying to cases involving foreign entities. Rejected 154-258: R 1-217; D 152-41 (ND 119-22, SD 33-19); I 1-0. Feb. 25, 1998.

Key

Y	Voted for (yea).
#	Paired for.
+	Announced for.
N	Voted against (nay).
X	Paired against.
–	Announced against.
P	Voted "present."
C	Voted "present" to avoid possible conflict of interest.
?	Did not vote or otherwise make a position known.

Democrats **Republicans**
Independent

	17	18	19	20	21	22	23
ALABAMA							
1 *Callahan*	?	Y	N	N	Y	N	N
2 *Everett*	?	Y	N	N	Y	N	N
3 *Riley*	Y	Y	N	N	Y	N	N
4 *Aderholt*	Y	Y	N	N	Y	N	N
5 Cramer	N	Y	N	N	Y	N	N
6 *Bachus*	Y	Y	N	N	Y	N	N
7 Hilliard	N	N	Y	N	Y	Y	Y
ALASKA							
AL *Young*	?	?	N	N	Y	N	N
ARIZONA							
1 *Salmon*	Y	Y	N	N	Y	N	N
2 Pastor	N	Y	Y	N	Y	Y	Y
3 *Stump*	Y	Y	N	N	Y	N	N
4 *Shadegg*	?	Y	N	N	Y	N	N
5 *Kolbe*	Y	Y	N	N	Y	N	N
6 *Hayworth*	Y	Y	N	N	Y	N	N
ARKANSAS							
1 Berry	N	Y	N	N	Y	N	Y
2 Snyder	N	Y	Y	N	Y	N	N
3 *Hutchinson*	N	Y	N	N	Y	N	N
4 *Dickey*	Y	Y	N	N	Y	N	N
CALIFORNIA							
1 *Riggs*	?	Y	–	–	Y	N	–
2 *Herger*	Y	Y	N	N	Y	N	N
3 Fazio	N	N	Y	N	Y	Y	Y
4 *Doolittle*	Y	Y	N	N	Y	N	N
5 Matsui	N	Y	N	N	Y	N	Y
6 Woolsey	N	N	Y	N	Y	Y	Y
7 Miller	N	Y	?	?	?	?	?
8 Pelosi	N	?	?	?	?	?	?
9 Vacant							
10 Tauscher	N	Y	N	Y	Y	N	N
11 *Pombo*	Y	Y	N	N	Y	N	N
12 Lantos	?	?	Y	N	Y	Y	Y
13 Stark	N	Y	Y	Y	Y	Y	Y
14 Eshoo	N	Y	Y	N	Y	Y	Y
15 *Campbell*	Y	Y	N	N	Y	N	N
16 Lofgren	N	N	Y	N	Y	Y	Y
17 Farr	N	Y	Y	N	Y	Y	Y
18 Condit	N	Y	N	N	Y	N	N
19 *Radanovich*	Y	Y	N	N	Y	N	N
20 Dooley	N	Y	N	N	Y	N	N
21 *Thomas*	Y	Y	N	N	Y	N	N
22 Vacant							
23 *Gallegly*	Y	Y	N	N	Y	N	N
24 Sherman	N	Y	Y	N	Y	Y	Y
25 *McKeon*	Y	Y	N	N	Y	N	N
26 Berman	N	N	Y	Y	Y	Y	N
27 *Rogan*	Y	Y	N	N	Y	N	N
28 *Dreier*	Y	Y	N	N	Y	N	N
29 Waxman	N	N	Y	Y	Y	Y	Y
30 Becerra	N	Y	Y	Y	Y	Y	Y
31 Martinez	N	N	Y	N	Y	Y	Y
32 Dixon	N	N	Y	Y	Y	Y	Y
33 Roybal-Allard	N	N	Y	Y	Y	Y	Y
34 Torres	N	Y	Y	Y	Y	Y	Y
35 Waters	N	N	Y	Y	Y	Y	Y
36 Harman	?	?	Y	N	Y	Y	Y
37 Millender-McD.	N	N	Y	Y	Y	Y	Y

	17	18	19	20	21	22	23
38 *Horn*	Y	Y	N	N	Y	N	N
39 *Royce*	Y	Y	N	N	Y	N	N
40 *Lewis*	Y	Y	N	N	Y	N	N
41 *Kim*	Y	Y	N	N	Y	N	N
42 Brown	N	?	Y	Y	N	Y	Y
43 *Calvert*	Y	Y	N	N	Y	N	N
44 Vacant							
45 *Rohrabacher*	Y	Y	N	N	Y	N	N
46 Sanchez	N	Y	Y	N	+	Y	Y
47 *Cox*	Y	Y	N	N	Y	N	N
48 *Packard*	Y	Y	N	N	Y	N	N
49 *Bilbray*	Y	Y	N	N	Y	N	N
50 Filner	N	N	Y	Y	Y	Y	Y
51 *Cunningham*	Y	Y	N	N	Y	N	N
52 *Hunter*	Y	Y	N	N	Y	N	N
COLORADO							
1 DeGette	N	N	Y	N	Y	Y	Y
2 Skaggs	N	N	Y	Y	Y	Y	Y
3 *McInnis*	Y	Y	N	N	Y	N	N
4 *Schaffer*	Y	Y	N	N	Y	N	N
5 *Hefley*	Y	Y	N	N	Y	N	N
6 *Schaefer*	Y	Y	N	N	Y	N	N
CONNECTICUT							
1 Kennelly	N	Y	?	?	Y	Y	Y
2 Gejdenson	N	Y	+	+	Y	Y	Y
3 DeLauro	N	Y	?	?	Y	Y	Y
4 *Shays*	N	Y	N	Y	Y	Y	Y
5 Maloney	N	Y	Y	N	Y	Y	Y
6 *Johnson*	Y	Y	N	N	Y	N	N
DELAWARE							
AL *Castle*	Y	Y	N	N	Y	N	N
FLORIDA							
1 *Scarborough*	Y	Y	N	N	Y	N	N
2 Boyd	N	Y	N	N	Y	N	N
3 Brown	N	N	+	+	+	+	+
4 *Fowler*	Y	Y	N	N	Y	N	N
5 Thurman	N	Y	Y	Y	Y	Y	Y
6 *Stearns*	Y	Y	N	N	Y	N	N
7 *Mica*	Y	Y	–	–	+	–	–
8 *McCollum*	Y	Y	N	N	Y	N	N
9 *Bilirakis*	Y	Y	N	N	Y	N	Y
10 *Young*	Y	Y	N	N	Y	N	N
11 Davis	N	Y	N	N	Y	N	N
12 *Canady*	Y	Y	N	N	Y	N	N
13 *Miller*	?	Y	N	N	Y	N	N
14 *Goss*	Y	Y	N	N	Y	N	N
15 *Weldon*	Y	Y	N	N	Y	N	N
16 *Foley*	Y	Y	N	N	Y	N	N
17 Meek	N	N	Y	N	Y	Y	Y
18 *Ros-Lehtinen*	N	Y	N	N	Y	N	N
19 Wexler	N	Y	Y	Y	Y	Y	Y
20 Deutsch	N	Y	Y	Y	Y	Y	Y
21 *Diaz-Balart*	N	Y	N	N	Y	N	N
22 *Shaw*	Y	Y	N	N	Y	N	N
23 Hastings	N	N	Y	Y	N	Y	Y
GEORGIA							
1 *Kingston*	Y	Y	N	N	Y	N	N
2 Bishop	N	Y	N	N	Y	N	N
3 *Collins*	Y	Y	N	N	Y	N	N
4 McKinney	N	N	Y	Y	Y	Y	Y
5 Lewis	N	N	Y	Y	N	Y	Y
6 *Gingrich*	Y						
7 *Barr*	Y	Y	N	N	Y	N	N
8 *Chambliss*	Y	Y	N	N	Y	N	N
9 *Deal*	Y	Y	N	N	Y	N	N
10 *Norwood*	Y	Y	N	N	Y	N	N
11 *Linder*	Y	Y	N	N	Y	N	N
HAWAII							
1 Abercrombie	N	Y	Y	Y	Y	Y	Y
2 Mink	–	N	Y	Y	N	Y	Y
IDAHO							
1 *Chenoweth*	Y	Y	N	N	Y	N	N
2 *Crapo*	Y	Y	N	N	Y	N	N
ILLINOIS							
1 Rush	N	?	Y	Y	N	Y	Y
2 Jackson	N	N	Y	N	Y	Y	Y
3 Lipinski	Y	?	N	N	Y	N	N
4 Gutierrez	N	?	Y	Y	Y	Y	Y
5 Blagojevich	N	Y	Y	N	Y	Y	Y
6 *Hyde*	Y	Y	N	N	Y	N	N
7 Davis	N	N	Y	N	Y	Y	Y
8 *Crane*	Y	Y	N	N	Y	N	N
9 Yates	N	N	Y	N	Y	N	Y
10 *Porter*	Y	Y	N	N	Y	N	N
11 *Weller*	Y	Y	N	N	Y	N	N
12 Costello	N	Y	N	N	Y	N	N

ND Northern Democrats   SD Southern Democrats

	17	18	19	20	21	22	23
13 ***Fawell***	Y	Y	N	N	Y	N	N
14 ***Hastert***	Y	Y	N	N	Y	N	N
15 ***Ewing***	Y	Y	N	N	Y	N	N
16 ***Manzullo***	Y	Y	N	N	Y	N	N
17 Evans	N	Y	Y	Y	Y	Y	Y
18 ***LaHood***	Y	Y	N	N	Y	N	N
19 Poshard	N	?	?	?	?	?	?
20 ***Shimkus***	Y	Y	N	N	Y	N	N
INDIANA							
1 Visclosky	N	Y	Y	N	Y	Y	N
2 ***McIntosh***	Y	Y	N	N	Y	N	N
3 Roemer	N	Y	N	N	Y	N	N
4 ***Souder***	Y	Y	N	N	Y	N	N
5 ***Buyer***	?	Y	N	N	Y	N	N
6 ***Burton***	Y	Y	N	N	Y	N	N
7 ***Pease***	Y	Y	N	N	Y	N	N
8 ***Hostettler***	Y	Y	N	N	Y	N	N
9 Hamilton	N	Y	Y	Y	Y	Y	N
10 Carson	N	N	Y	Y	Y	Y	Y
IOWA							
1 ***Leach***	Y	Y	N	N	Y	N	N
2 ***Nussle***	Y	Y	N	N	Y	N	N
3 Boswell	N	Y	N	N	Y	N	N
4 ***Ganske***	Y	Y	N	N	Y	N	N
5 ***Latham***	Y	Y	N	N	Y	N	N
KANSAS							
1 ***Moran***	Y	Y	N	N	Y	N	N
2 ***Ryun***	Y	Y	N	N	Y	N	N
3 ***Snowbarger***	Y	Y	N	N	Y	N	N
4 ***Tiahrt***	Y	Y	N	N	Y	N	N
KENTUCKY							
1 ***Whitfield***	Y	Y	N	N	Y	N	N
2 ***Lewis***	Y	Y	?	N	Y	N	N
3 ***Northup***	Y	Y	N	N	Y	N	N
4 ***Bunning***	Y	Y	N	N	Y	N	N
5 ***Rogers***	Y	Y	N	N	Y	N	N
6 Baesler	N	Y	Y	N	Y	Y	Y
LOUISIANA							
1 ***Livingston***	Y	Y	N	N	Y	N	N
2 Jefferson	?	Y	Y	N	Y	Y	Y
3 ***Tauzin***	Y	Y	N	N	Y	N	N
4 ***McCrery***	Y	Y	N	N	Y	N	N
5 ***Cooksey***	Y	Y	N	N	Y	N	N
6 ***Baker***	Y	Y	N	N	Y	N	N
7 John	N	Y	N	N	Y	N	N
MAINE							
1 Allen	N	Y	Y	Y	Y	Y	Y
2 Baldacci	N	Y	Y	Y	Y	Y	Y
MARYLAND							
1 ***Gilchrest***	Y	Y	N	N	Y	N	N
2 ***Ehrlich***	Y	Y	N	N	Y	N	N
3 Cardin	N	Y	Y	N	Y	Y	Y
4 Wynn	N	N	Y	N	Y	Y	Y
5 Hoyer	N	Y	Y	N	Y	Y	Y
6 ***Bartlett***	Y	Y	N	N	Y	N	N
7 Cummings	N	N	Y	Y	N	N	Y
8 ***Morella***	N	Y	Y	N	Y	N	N
MASSACHUSETTS							
1 Olver	N	N	Y	Y	Y	Y	Y
2 Neal	N	Y	Y	Y	Y	Y	Y
3 McGovern	N	Y	Y	Y	N	Y	Y
4 Frank	N	Y	Y	Y	Y	Y	N
5 Meehan	N	Y	Y	Y	Y	Y	Y
6 Tierney	N	Y	Y	Y	Y	Y	Y
7 Markey	N	Y	Y	Y	Y	Y	Y
8 Kennedy	N	Y	Y	Y	Y	Y	Y
9 Moakley	N	N	Y	Y	Y	Y	Y
10 Delahunt	N	N	Y	Y	N	Y	Y
MICHIGAN							
1 Stupak	N	?	Y	Y	Y	Y	Y
2 ***Hoekstra***	Y	Y	N	Y	Y	N	N
3 ***Ehlers***	Y	Y	N	Y	Y	N	N
4 ***Camp***	Y	Y	N	N	Y	N	N
5 Barcia	N	Y	Y	N	Y	Y	Y
6 ***Upton***	Y	Y	N	N	Y	N	N
7 ***Smith***	Y	Y	N	N	Y	N	N
8 Stabenow	N	Y	Y	Y	N	Y	Y
9 Kildee	N	Y	Y	Y	Y	Y	Y
10 Bonior	N	N	Y	Y	N	Y	Y
11 ***Knollenberg***	Y	Y	N	N	Y	N	N
12 Levin	N	Y	Y	Y	Y	Y	Y
13 Rivers	N	Y	Y	Y	N	Y	Y
14 Conyers	N	N	Y	Y	N	Y	?
15 Kilpatrick	N	N	Y	Y	N	Y	Y
16 Dingell	N	Y	Y	N	Y	Y	Y
MINNESOTA							
1 ***Gutknecht***	Y	Y	N	Y	Y	N	N
2 Minge	N	N	N	Y	Y	N	N
3 ***Ramstad***	Y	Y	N	N	Y	N	N
4 Vento	N	N	Y	Y	Y	Y	Y
5 Sabo	N	N	Y	Y	N	N	Y
6 Luther	N	Y	–	+	+	–	–
7 Peterson	N	N	N	N	Y	N	N
8 Oberstar	N	N	Y	Y	N	Y	Y
MISSISSIPPI							
1 ***Wicker***	Y	Y	N	N	Y	N	N
2 Thompson	N	Y	Y	Y	Y	N	Y
3 ***Pickering***	Y	Y	N	N	Y	N	N
4 ***Parker***	Y	Y	N	N	Y	N	N
5 Taylor	Y	Y	N	N	Y	N	N
MISSOURI							
1 Clay	N	N	Y	Y	N	Y	Y
2 ***Talent***	Y	Y	N	N	Y	N	N
3 Gephardt	N	Y	?	N	Y	Y	Y
4 Skelton	N	Y	Y	N	Y	N	N
5 McCarthy	N	+	Y	Y	Y	Y	Y
6 Danner	N	Y	Y	N	Y	Y	Y
7 ***Blunt***	Y	Y	N	N	Y	N	N
8 ***Emerson***	Y	Y	N	N	Y	N	N
9 ***Hulshof***	Y	Y	N	N	Y	N	N
MONTANA							
AL ***Hill***	Y	Y	N	N	Y	N	N
NEBRASKA							
1 ***Bereuter***	Y	Y	N	N	Y	N	N
2 ***Christensen***	Y	Y	N	N	Y	N	N
3 ***Barrett***	Y	Y	N	N	Y	N	N
NEVADA							
1 ***Ensign***	Y	Y	N	N	Y	N	N
2 ***Gibbons***	Y	Y	N	N	Y	N	N
NEW HAMPSHIRE							
1 ***Sununu***	Y	Y	N	N	Y	N	N
2 ***Bass***	Y	Y	N	N	Y	N	N
NEW JERSEY							
1 Andrews	N	Y	Y	N	Y	Y	Y
2 ***LoBiondo***	Y	Y	Y	N	Y	N	N
3 ***Saxton***	Y	Y	N	N	Y	N	N
4 ***Smith***	Y	Y	N	?	Y	N	?
5 ***Roukema***	Y	Y	N	N	Y	N	N
6 Pallone	N	Y	Y	N	Y	Y	Y
7 ***Franks***	Y	Y	N	N	Y	N	N
8 Pascrell	N	Y	Y	N	Y	Y	Y
9 Rothman	N	Y	Y	N	Y	Y	Y
10 Payne	N	N	Y	Y	N	Y	Y
11 ***Frelinghuysen***	Y	Y	N	N	Y	N	?
12 ***Pappas***	Y	Y	N	Y	Y	N	N
13 Menendez	N	Y	Y	N	Y	Y	Y
NEW MEXICO							
1 ***Schiff***	?	?	?	?	?	?	?
2 ***Skeen***	Y	Y	N	N	Y	N	N
3 ***Redmond***	Y	Y	–	N	Y	N	N
NEW YORK							
1 ***Forbes***	N	Y	N	N	Y	N	N
2 ***Lazio***	Y	Y	N	N	Y	N	N
3 ***King***	Y	Y	N	N	Y	N	N
4 McCarthy	N	Y	Y	Y	Y	Y	Y
5 Ackerman	N	Y	Y	Y	Y	Y	Y
6 Meeks	N	N	Y	Y	N	Y	Y
7 Manton	N	Y	Y	N	Y	Y	N
8 Nadler	N	N	Y	Y	?	Y	Y
9 Schumer	N	Y	Y	N	Y	Y	Y
10 Towns	?	Y	Y	Y	N	Y	Y
11 Owens	N	Y	Y	Y	N	Y	Y
12 Velázquez	N	Y	Y	Y	Y	Y	Y
13 ***Fossella***	Y	Y	N	N	Y	N	N
14 Maloney	N	Y	Y	Y	Y	Y	Y
15 Rangel	N	N	Y	Y	N	Y	Y
16 Serrano	N	N	Y	Y	N	Y	Y
17 Engel	N	Y	Y	Y	Y	Y	Y
18 Lowey	N	Y	Y	Y	Y	Y	Y
19 ***Kelly***	Y	Y	N	N	Y	N	N
20 ***Gilman***	Y	?	Y	N	Y	N	N
21 McNulty	N	N	Y	Y	Y	Y	Y
22 ***Solomon***	Y	Y	N	N	Y	N	N
23 ***Boehlert***	N	Y	N	N	Y	N	N
24 ***McHugh***	Y	Y	Y	N	Y	N	N
25 ***Walsh***	N	Y	Y	N	Y	N	N
26 Hinchey	N	N	Y	Y	Y	Y	Y
27 ***Paxon***	Y	Y	?	?	?	?	?
28 Slaughter	N	Y	Y	Y	Y	Y	Y
29 LaFalce	N	N	Y	Y	N	Y	Y
30 ***Quinn***	Y	Y	Y	N	Y	N	N
31 ***Houghton***	N	Y	N	N	Y	N	N
NORTH CAROLINA							
1 Clayton	N	N	Y	Y	N	Y	Y
2 Etheridge	N	Y	Y	N	Y	Y	Y
3 ***Jones***	Y	Y	N	N	Y	N	N
4 Price	N	Y	Y	N	Y	Y	Y
5 ***Burr***	Y	Y	N	N	Y	N	N
6 ***Coble***	Y	Y	N	N	Y	N	N
7 McIntyre	N	?	Y	N	Y	Y	Y
8 Hefner	N	?	Y	Y	Y	Y	Y
9 ***Myrick***	Y	Y	N	N	Y	N	N
10 ***Ballenger***	Y	Y	N	N	Y	N	N
11 ***Taylor***	Y	Y	N	N	Y	N	N
12 Watt	N	N	Y	Y	N	Y	Y
NORTH DAKOTA							
AL Pomeroy	N	Y	Y	N	Y	Y	Y
OHIO							
1 ***Chabot***	N	Y	N	N	Y	N	N
2 ***Portman***	Y	Y	N	N	Y	N	N
3 Hall	N	Y	Y	Y	?	N	N
4 ***Oxley***	?	Y	N	N	Y	N	N
5 ***Gillmor***	Y	Y	N	N	Y	N	N
6 Strickland	N	Y	Y	N	Y	Y	Y
7 ***Hobson***	Y	Y	N	N	Y	N	?
8 ***Boehner***	Y	Y	N	N	Y	N	N
9 Kaptur	N	Y	Y	N	Y	Y	Y
10 Kucinich	N	Y	Y	Y	P	Y	Y
11 Stokes	N	N	Y	Y	N	Y	?
12 ***Kasich***	Y	Y	N	N	Y	N	N
13 Brown	N	?	Y	Y	N	Y	Y
14 Sawyer	N	N	Y	Y	Y	Y	Y
15 ***Pryce***	Y	Y	N	N	Y	N	N
16 ***Regula***	Y	Y	N	N	Y	N	N
17 Traficant	N	Y	N	N	Y	N	Y
18 ***Ney***	Y	Y	N	N	Y	N	N
19 ***LaTourette***	Y	Y	N	N	Y	N	N
OKLAHOMA							
1 ***Largent***	?	Y	N	N	Y	N	N
2 ***Coburn***	Y	Y	N	N	Y	N	N
3 ***Watkins***	Y	Y	N	N	Y	N	N
4 ***Watts***	Y	N	N	N	Y	N	N
5 ***Istook***	Y	Y	N	N	Y	N	N
6 ***Lucas***	Y	Y	N	N	Y	N	N
OREGON							
1 Furse	?	?	Y	Y	N	Y	Y
2 ***Smith***	?	Y	N	N	Y	N	N
3 Blumenauer	N	Y	Y	Y	Y	Y	Y
4 DeFazio	N	Y	Y	Y	Y	Y	Y
5 Hooley	N	Y	Y	Y	Y	Y	Y
PENNSYLVANIA							
1 Vacant							
2 Fattah	N	N	Y	Y	N	Y	Y
3 Borski	N	Y	Y	N	Y	Y	Y
4 Klink	N	?	?	?	?	?	?
5 ***Peterson***	Y	Y	N	N	Y	N	N
6 Holden	N	Y	Y	N	Y	Y	Y
7 ***Weldon***	Y	Y	N	N	Y	N	N
8 ***Greenwood***	Y	Y	N	N	Y	Y	N
9 ***Shuster***	Y	Y	N	N	Y	N	N
10 ***McDade***	Y	Y	N	N	Y	N	N
11 Kanjorski	N	Y	Y	N	Y	N	N
12 Murtha	N	Y	Y	N	Y	N	N
13 ***Fox***	Y	Y	Y	N	Y	Y	N
14 Coyne	N	N	Y	Y	Y	Y	Y
15 McHale	N	Y	Y	N	Y	Y	Y
16 ***Pitts***	Y	Y	N	N	Y	N	N
17 ***Gekas***	Y	Y	N	N	Y	N	N
18 Doyle	N	Y	Y	N	Y	Y	Y
19 ***Goodling***	Y	Y	N	Y	Y	N	N
20 Mascara	N	Y	Y	N	Y	Y	Y
21 ***English***	Y	Y	N	N	Y	N	N
RHODE ISLAND							
1 Kennedy	N	Y	Y	Y	N	Y	Y
2 Weygand	N	Y	Y	Y	N	Y	Y
SOUTH CAROLINA							
1 ***Sanford***	Y	Y	N	N	Y	N	N
2 ***Spence***	Y	Y	N	N	Y	N	N
3 ***Graham***	Y	Y	N	N	Y	N	?
4 ***Inglis***	Y	Y	N	N	Y	N	N
5 Spratt	N	Y	Y	N	Y	Y	N
6 Clyburn	N	Y	Y	Y	N	Y	Y
SOUTH DAKOTA							
AL ***Thune***	Y	Y	N	N	Y	N	N
TENNESSEE							
1 ***Jenkins***	Y	Y	N	N	Y	N	N
2 ***Duncan***	Y	Y	N	N	Y	N	N
3 ***Wamp***	Y	Y	N	N	Y	N	N
4 ***Hilleary***	Y	Y	N	N	Y	N	N
5 Clement	–	Y	N	N	Y	N	N
6 Gordon	N	Y	N	N	Y	N	N
7 ***Bryant***	Y	Y	N	N	Y	N	N
8 Tanner	N	Y	N	N	Y	N	N
9 Ford	N	?	?	?	?	?	?
TEXAS							
1 Sandlin	N	Y	Y	N	Y	Y	Y
2 Turner	Y	Y	Y	N	Y	N	N
3 ***Johnson, Sam***	Y	Y	N	N	Y	N	N
4 Hall	Y	Y	N	N	Y	N	N
5 ***Sessions***	Y	Y	N	N	Y	N	N
6 ***Barton***	Y	Y	N	N	Y	N	N
7 ***Archer***	Y	Y	N	N	Y	N	N
8 ***Brady***	Y	Y	N	N	Y	–	N
9 Lampson	N	+	Y	N	Y	Y	Y
10 Doggett	N	Y	Y	N	Y	Y	N
11 Edwards	N	Y	Y	N	Y	Y	Y
12 ***Granger***	Y	Y	N	N	Y	N	N
13 ***Thornberry***	Y	Y	N	N	Y	N	N
14 ***Paul***	N	N	N	Y	N	N	N
15 Hinojosa	N	Y	Y	N	Y	Y	Y
16 Reyes	N	Y	Y	N	Y	Y	Y
17 Stenholm	N	Y	N	N	Y	N	N
18 Jackson-Lee	N	?	Y	Y	Y	Y	Y
19 ***Combest***	Y	Y	N	N	Y	N	N
20 Gonzalez	?	?	?	?	?	?	?
21 ***Smith***	Y	Y	N	N	Y	N	N
22 ***DeLay***	Y	Y	N	N	Y	N	N
23 ***Bonilla***	Y	Y	N	N	Y	N	N
24 Frost	N	Y	Y	N	Y	+	Y
25 Bentsen	N	Y	Y	N	Y	Y	N
26 ***Armey***	Y	Y	N	N	Y	N	N
27 Ortiz	N	Y	Y	N	Y	Y	Y
28 Rodriguez	N	Y	?	?	Y	Y	Y
29 Green	N	Y	Y	N	Y	Y	Y
30 Johnson, E.B.	N	Y	Y	Y	Y	Y	Y
UTAH							
1 ***Hansen***	Y	Y	N	N	Y	N	N
2 ***Cook***	Y	Y	N	N	Y	N	N
3 ***Cannon***	Y	Y	N	N	Y	N	N
VERMONT							
AL *Sanders*	N	Y	Y	Y	Y	Y	Y
VIRGINIA							
1 ***Bateman***	Y	Y	N	N	Y	N	N
2 Pickett	Y	Y	N	N	Y	N	N
3 Scott	N	N	Y	Y	N	Y	Y
4 Sisisky	N	Y	N	N	Y	N	N
5 Goode	Y	N	N	N	Y	N	N
6 ***Goodlatte***	Y	Y	N	N	Y	N	N
7 ***Bliley***	Y	Y	N	N	Y	N	N
8 Moran	N	Y	Y	N	Y	Y	Y
9 Boucher	N	Y	?	N	Y	Y	Y
10 ***Wolf***	Y	Y	N	N	Y	N	N
11 ***Davis***	Y	Y	N	N	Y	N	N
WASHINGTON							
1 ***White***	Y	Y	N	N	Y	N	N
2 ***Metcalf***	Y	Y	N	N	Y	N	N
3 ***Smith, Linda***	N	N	N	N	Y	N	N
4 ***Hastings***	Y	Y	N	N	Y	N	N
5 ***Nethercutt***	Y	Y	N	N	Y	N	N
6 Dicks	N	Y	Y	N	Y	Y	N
7 McDermott	N	N	Y	Y	N	Y	Y
8 ***Dunn***	Y	Y	N	N	Y	N	N
9 Smith, Adam	N	Y	N	N	Y	N	N
WEST VIRGINIA							
1 Mollohan	N	N	Y	Y	N	Y	Y
2 Wise	N	Y	Y	Y	Y	Y	Y
3 Rahall	N	Y	Y	Y	Y	Y	Y
WISCONSIN							
1 ***Neumann***	Y	Y	N	N	Y	N	N
2 ***Klug***	Y	Y	N	Y	Y	N	N
3 Kind	N	Y	Y	Y	Y	Y	Y
4 Kleczka	N	Y	Y	Y	Y	Y	Y
5 Barrett	N	Y	Y	Y	N	Y	Y
6 ***Petri***	Y	Y	Y	N	Y	N	N
7 Obey	N	Y	Y	Y	Y	Y	Y
8 Johnson	?	Y	Y	Y	Y	Y	Y
9 ***Sensenbrenner***	Y	Y	N	N	Y	N	N
WYOMING							
AL ***Cubin***	Y	Y	N	N	Y	N	N

Southern states - Ala., Ark., Fla., Ga., Ky., La., Miss., N.C., Okla., S.C., Tenn., Texas, Va.

24. HR 1544. Federal Agency Compliance/Passage. Passage of the bill to require federal agencies to follow appellate court precedents when administering policies or regulations. Passed 241-176: R 191-31; D 50-144 (ND 29-114, SD 21-30); I 0-1. Feb. 25, 1998. A "nay" was a vote in support of the president's position.

25. HR 2460. Wireless Telephone Protection/Passage. Passage of the bill to prohibit the production, trafficking in and possession of devices used to reprogram cellular telephones with unauthorized identification numbers, and could impose a penalty of 15 years imprisonment if convicted. Passed 414-1: R 220-1; D 194-0 (ND 142-0, SD 52-0); I 0-0. Feb. 26, 1998. Subsequently, S493, a similar Senate-passed bill was passed in lieu after being amended to contain the text of HR2460 as passed by the House; HR2460 was laid on the table. A "yea" was a vote in support of the president's position.

26. HR 217. Homeless Housing Programs Consolidation/Passage. Lazio, R-N.Y., motion to suspend the rules and pass the bill to consolidate into a single block grant program seven homeless housing programs authorizing $1 billion a year through fiscal 2002. Motion agreed to 386-23: R 195-19; D 190-4 (ND 137-4, SD 53-0); I 1-0. March 3, 1998. A two-thirds majority of those present and voting (273 in this case) is required for passage under suspension of the rules.

27. HR 856. Puerto Rico Political Status/Rule. Adoption of the rule (H Res 376) to provide for House floor consideration of the bill to establish a process to determine and implement a permanent political status for Puerto Rico, including referenda in Puerto Rico and subsequent action by Congress. Adopted 370-41: R 180-36; D 189-5 (ND 137-3, SD 52-2); I 1-0. March 4, 1998.

28. HR 856. Puerto Rico Political Status/Spanish Language. Gutierrez, D-Ill., amendment to the Solomon, R-N.Y., amendment to maintain Spanish as an official language in Puerto Rico. The Solomon amendment would establish that English is the official language of the United States, and that if Puerto Rico chooses statehood, English would be the sole official language of all federal government activities in Puerto Rico. Rejected 13-406: R 0-223; D 13-182 (ND 12-129, SD 1-53); I 0-1. March 4, 1998.

29. HR 856. Puerto Rico Political Status/Languages. Burton, R-Ind., amendment to the Solomon, R-N.Y., amendment to treat Puerto Rico the same as the states and recognize the primary role of English in national affairs, but not preclude the use of other languages in government functions when appropriate. The Solomon amendment would establish that English is the official language of the United States, and that if Puerto Rico chooses statehood English would be the sole official language of all federal government activities in Puerto Rico. Adopted 238-182: R 55-168; D 182-14 (ND 134-8, SD 48-6); I 1-0. March 4, 1998.

30. HR 856. Puerto Rico Political Status/English Language. Solomon, R-N.Y., amendment to treat Puerto Rico the same as the states, recognizing the primary role of English in national affairs, but not preclude the use of other languages in government functions when appropriate. Adopted 265-153: R 85-138; D 179-15 (ND 132-8, SD 47-7); I 1-0. March 4, 1998.

Key

Y	Voted for (yea).
#	Paired for.
+	Announced for.
N	Voted against (nay).
X	Paired against.
−	Announced against.
P	Voted "present."
C	Voted "present" to avoid possible conflict of interest.
?	Did not vote or otherwise make a position known.

Democrats   **Republicans**
Independent

	24	25	26	27	28	29	30
ALABAMA							
1 *Callahan*	Y	Y	Y	Y	N	N	N
2 *Everett*	Y	Y	Y	Y	N	N	N
3 *Riley*	Y	Y	Y	N	N	N	N
4 *Aderholt*	Y	Y	Y	N	N	N	N
5 Cramer	Y	Y	Y	Y	N	Y	Y
6 *Bachus*	Y	Y	N	N	N	N	N
7 Hilliard	N	Y	Y	Y	N	Y	Y
ALASKA							
AL *Young*	Y	Y	Y	Y	N	Y	Y
ARIZONA							
1 *Salmon*	N	Y	?	N	N	N	N
2 Pastor	N	Y	Y	Y	Y	Y	Y
3 *Stump*	Y	Y	Y	N	N	N	N
4 *Shadegg*	N	Y	N	N	N	N	N
5 *Kolbe*	Y	Y	Y	Y	N	Y	Y
6 *Hayworth*	N	Y	Y	N	N	N	N
ARKANSAS							
1 Berry	Y	Y	Y	Y	N	Y	Y
2 Snyder	Y	Y	Y	Y	N	Y	Y
3 *Hutchinson*	Y	Y	Y	N	N	N	N
4 Dickey	Y	Y	Y	N	N	N	N
CALIFORNIA							
1 *Riggs*	N	Y	Y	Y	N	N	N
2 *Herger*	N	Y	Y	N	N	N	N
3 Fazio	Y	Y	Y	Y	N	Y	Y
4 *Doolittle*	N	Y	?	?	?	?	?
5 Matsui	Y	Y	Y	Y	N	Y	Y
6 Woolsey	N	Y	Y	Y	N	Y	Y
7 Miller	?	?	Y	Y	N	Y	Y
8 Pelosi	?	?	Y	Y	N	Y	Y
9 Vacant							
10 Tauscher	Y	Y	Y	Y	N	Y	Y
11 *Pombo*	N	Y	Y	N	N	Y	Y
12 Lantos	N	Y	Y	Y	N	Y	Y
13 Stark	N	Y	Y	Y	N	Y	Y
14 Eshoo	N	Y	Y	Y	N	Y	Y
15 *Campbell*	N	?	Y	Y	N	Y	Y
16 Lofgren	N	Y	Y	Y	N	Y	Y
17 Farr	Y	Y	Y	Y	N	Y	Y
18 Condit	Y	Y	Y	Y	N	Y	Y
19 *Radanovich*	N	Y	Y	Y	N	N	N
20 Dooley	Y	Y	Y	Y	N	Y	Y
21 *Thomas*	N	Y	Y	Y	N	N	Y
22 Vacant							
23 *Gallegly*	Y	Y	Y	Y	N	Y	Y
24 Sherman	Y	Y	Y	Y	N	Y	Y
25 *McKeon*	Y	Y	Y	Y	N	Y	Y
26 Berman	Y	Y	Y	Y	N	Y	?
27 *Rogan*	N	Y	Y	+	N	N	N
28 *Dreier*	N	Y	Y	Y	N	N	N
29 Waxman	N	Y	Y	Y	N	Y	Y
30 Becerra	N	Y	Y	Y	N	Y	Y
31 Martinez	N	Y	Y	Y	N	Y	Y
32 Dixon	N	Y	Y	Y	N	Y	Y
33 Roybal-Allard	N	Y	Y	Y	N	Y	Y
34 Torres	N	Y	?	?	?	?	?
35 Waters	N	Y	Y	Y	P	Y	Y
36 Harman	Y	Y	?	?	?	?	?
37 Millender-McD.	N	Y	Y	Y	N	Y	Y

	24	25	26	27	28	29	30
38 *Horn*	Y	Y	Y	Y	N	N	N
39 *Royce*	N	Y	N	N	N	N	N
40 *Lewis*	Y	Y	Y	N	N	N	N
41 *Kim*	Y	Y	Y	Y	N	Y	Y
42 Brown	N	Y	Y	Y	N	Y	Y
43 *Calvert*	Y	Y	Y	N	N	N	N
44 Vacant							
45 *Rohrabacher*	N	Y	Y	N	N	N	N
46 Sanchez	Y	Y	Y	Y	N	Y	Y
47 *Cox*	N	Y	N	N	N	N	N
48 *Packard*	Y	Y	Y	N	N	N	N
49 *Bilbray*	N	Y	Y	Y	N	N	N
50 Filner	N	Y	Y	Y	N	Y	Y
51 *Cunningham*	Y	Y	Y	N	N	N	N
52 *Hunter*	Y	Y	Y	N	N	N	Y
COLORADO							
1 DeGette	N	Y	Y	Y	N	Y	Y
2 Skaggs	N	Y	Y	Y	N	Y	Y
3 *McInnis*	Y	?	Y	Y	N	Y	Y
4 *Schaffer*	Y	Y	Y	N	N	N	N
5 *Hefley*	Y	Y	Y	N	N	N	N
6 *Schaefer*	Y	Y	Y	Y	N	N	N
CONNECTICUT							
1 Kennelly	N	Y	Y	Y	N	Y	Y
2 Gejdenson	N	Y	Y	Y	N	Y	Y
3 DeLauro	N	Y	Y	Y	N	Y	Y
4 *Shays*	Y	Y	Y	Y	N	N	N
5 Maloney	N	Y	?	Y	N	Y	Y
6 *Johnson*	Y	Y	Y	Y	N	N	N
DELAWARE							
AL *Castle*	Y	Y	Y	Y	N	Y	N
FLORIDA							
1 *Scarborough*	N	?	?	?	N	N	N
2 Boyd	Y	Y	Y	Y	N	Y	Y
3 Brown	−	?	Y	Y	N	Y	Y
4 *Fowler*	Y	Y	Y	N	N	N	N
5 Thurman	Y	Y	Y	Y	N	Y	Y
6 *Stearns*	Y	Y	Y	N	N	N	N
7 *Mica*	+	Y	Y	Y	N	Y	Y
8 *McCollum*	Y	Y	Y	Y	N	Y	N
9 *Bilirakis*	Y	Y	Y	N	N	N	N
10 *Young*	Y	Y	Y	N	N	N	N
11 Davis	Y	Y	Y	Y	N	Y	Y
12 *Canady*	Y	Y	Y	N	N	N	N
13 *Miller*	Y	Y	N	N	N	N	N
14 *Goss*	Y	Y	N	N	N	N	N
15 *Weldon*	Y	Y	Y	N	N	N	N
16 *Foley*	Y	Y	Y	Y	N	N	N
17 Meek	N	Y	Y	Y	N	Y	Y
18 *Ros-Lehtinen*	Y	Y	?	N	Y	Y	Y
19 Wexler	N	Y	Y	Y	N	Y	Y
20 Deutsch	N	Y	Y	Y	N	Y	Y
21 *Diaz-Balart*	Y	N	Y	N	Y	Y	Y
22 *Shaw*	Y	Y	Y	Y	N	Y	Y
23 Hastings	N	Y	Y	Y	N	Y	Y
GEORGIA							
1 *Kingston*	N	Y	Y	N	N	N	Y
2 Bishop	Y	Y	Y	Y	N	Y	Y
3 *Collins*	Y	Y	Y	N	N	N	N
4 McKinney	N	Y	Y	Y	Y	Y	Y
5 Lewis	N	Y	Y	Y	N	Y	Y
6 *Gingrich*							
7 *Barr*	N	Y	Y	N	N	N	N
8 *Chambliss*	Y	Y	Y	N	N	N	N
9 *Deal*	Y	Y	Y	N	N	N	N
10 *Norwood*	Y	Y	Y	N	N	N	N
11 *Linder*	Y	Y	Y	N	N	N	N
HAWAII							
1 Abercrombie	N	Y	Y	Y	N	Y	Y
2 Mink	N	Y	Y	Y	N	Y	Y
IDAHO							
1 *Chenoweth*	Y	Y	N	?	N	N	N
2 *Crapo*	Y	Y	Y	N	N	N	N
ILLINOIS							
1 Rush	N	Y	?	Y	Y	Y	Y
2 Jackson	N	Y	Y	Y	N	Y	Y
3 Lipinski	Y	Y	Y	N	N	N	N
4 Gutierrez	N	Y	Y	Y	N	N	N
5 Blagojevich	N	Y	Y	Y	N	Y	Y
6 *Hyde*	Y	Y	Y	Y	N	N	N
7 Davis	N	Y	Y	Y	Y	Y	Y
8 *Crane*	Y	Y	N	N	N	N	N
9 Yates	N	Y	Y	Y	N	Y	Y
10 *Porter*	Y	Y	Y	N	N	N	N
11 *Weller*	Y	Y	Y	N	N	N	N
12 Costello	Y	Y	Y	Y	N	Y	Y

ND Northern Democrats   SD Southern Democrats

Southern states - Ala., Ark., Fla., Ga., Ky., La., Miss., N.C., Okla., S.C., Tenn., Texas, Va.

31. Quorum Call.* 405 Responded. March 4, 1998.

32. HR 856. Puerto Rico Political Status/Voter Eligibility. Serrano, D-N.Y., amendment to permit individuals who were born in Puerto Rico, but who do not currently reside on the island, to vote in the referenda authorized by the bill. Rejected 57-356: R 9-208; D 47-148 (ND 42-99, SD 5-49); I 1-0. March 4, 1998.

33. HR 856. Puerto Rico Political Status/Second Referendum. Stearns, R-Fla., amendment to strike the provision authorizing a referendum every 10 years if the voters fail to approve statehood or independence by a majority, and instead authorize a second referendum no later than 90 days after the initial ballot to vote on the two status options that received the most votes in the first referendum. Rejected 28-384: R 26-190; D 2-193 (ND 2-139, SD 0-54); I 0-1. March 4, 1998.

34. HR 856. Puerto Rico Political Status/Supermajority. Barr, R-Ga., amendment to require a 75 percent supermajority in the third referendum that would be held to approve or disapprove a statehood or independence plan enacted by Congress. Rejected 131-282: R 124-95; D 7-186 (ND 3-137, SD 4-49); I 0-1. March 4, 1998.

35. HR 856. Puerto Rico Political Status/Olympics. Gutierrez, D-Ill., amendment to permit Puerto Rico to compete as an independent nation in the Olympics even if it becomes a state. Rejected 2-413: R 0-219; D 2-193 (ND 2-139, SD 0-54); I 0-1. March 4, 1998.

36. HR 856. Puerto Rico Political Status/English Language. Separate vote at the request of Solomon, R-N.Y., on the Solomon amendment, as amended, to treat Puerto Rico the same as the states with regard to language, recognizing the primary role of English in national affairs, but not preclude the use of other languages in government functions when appropriate. Adopted 240-177: R 56-164; D 183-13 (ND 135-7, SD 48-6); I 1-0. March 4, 1998.

37. HR 856. Puerto Rico Political Status/Passage. Passage of the bill to establish a process for determining and implementing a permanent political status for Puerto Rico, including referenda in Puerto Rico and subsequent action by Congress. Passed 209-208: R 43-177; D 165-31 (ND 121-21, SD 44-10); I 1-0. March 4, 1998. A "yea" was a vote in support of the president's position.

38. HR 2369. Wireless Privacy/Passage. Passage of the bill to require the Federal Communications Commission to step up enforcement against violators of wireless telephone privacy, and make illegal any modification of scanners to receive private wireless communications. Passed 414-1: R 219-1; D 194-0 (ND 143-0, SD 51-0); I 1-0. March 5, 1998. A "yea" was a vote in support of the president's position.

* CQ does not include quorum calls in its vote charts.

Key

Y	Voted for (yea).
#	Paired for.
+	Announced for.
N	Voted against (nay).
X	Paired against.
−	Announced against.
P	Voted "present."
C	Voted "present" to avoid possible conflict of interest.
?	Did not vote or otherwise make a position known.

Democrats   **Republicans**
Independent

	32	33	34	35	36	37	38
ALABAMA							
1 *Callahan*	N	N	Y	N	N	N	Y
2 *Everett*	N	N	Y	N	N	N	Y
3 *Riley*	N	N	N	N	N	N	Y
4 *Aderholt*	N	N	Y	N	N	N	Y
5 Cramer	N	N	N	N	Y	N	Y
6 *Bachus*	N	Y	N	N	N	N	Y
7 Hilliard	N	N	N	N	Y	Y	Y
ALASKA							
AL *Young*	Y	N	N	N	Y	Y	Y
ARIZONA							
1 *Salmon*	N	Y	N	Y	N	N	Y
2 Pastor	Y	N	N	N	Y	Y	Y
3 *Stump*	N	N	Y	N	N	N	Y
4 *Shadegg*	N	Y	N	Y	N	N	Y
5 *Kolbe*	N	N	N	N	Y	Y	Y
6 *Hayworth*	N	N	Y	N	N	N	Y
ARKANSAS							
1 Berry	N	N	N	N	N	Y	N
2 Snyder	N	N	N	N	Y	Y	Y
3 *Hutchinson*	N	N	N	N	N	N	Y
4 *Dickey*	N	N	Y	N	N	N	Y
CALIFORNIA							
1 *Riggs*	N	?	?	?	?	X	Y
2 *Herger*	N	Y	Y	N	N	N	Y
3 Fazio	N	N	N	N	Y	Y	Y
4 *Doolittle*	?	?	?	?	?	?	?
5 Matsui	N	N	N	N	Y	Y	Y
6 Woolsey	N	N	N	N	Y	Y	Y
7 Miller	Y	N	N	N	Y	Y	Y
8 Pelosi	N	N	N	N	Y	Y	Y
9 Vacant							
10 Tauscher	N	N	N	N	Y	Y	Y
11 *Pombo*	N	N	N	N	N	N	Y
12 Lantos	N	N	N	N	Y	Y	Y
13 Stark	N	N	N	N	Y	Y	Y
14 Eshoo	N	N	N	N	Y	Y	Y
15 *Campbell*	N	Y	N	N	N	Y	N
16 Lofgren	N	N	N	N	Y	Y	+
17 Farr	N	N	?	N	Y	Y	Y
18 Condit	N	N	N	N	Y	Y	Y
19 *Radanovich*	N	Y	N	N	Y	N	Y
20 Dooley	N	N	N	N	Y	Y	Y
21 *Thomas*	N	N	N	N	N	N	Y
22 Vacant							
23 *Gallegly*	N	N	N	N	Y	Y	Y
24 Sherman	N	Y	Y	N	Y	N	Y
25 *McKeon*	N	N	N	N	Y	Y	Y
26 Berman	N	?	?	?	?	?	Y
27 *Rogan*	N	Y	N	N	N	N	Y
28 *Dreier*	N	N	Y	N	N	N	Y
29 Waxman	N	N	N	N	Y	Y	Y
30 Becerra	N	N	N	N	Y	Y	Y
31 Martinez	N	N	N	N	Y	Y	Y
32 Dixon	N	N	N	N	Y	Y	Y
33 Roybal-Allard	N	N	N	N	Y	Y	Y
34 Torres	?	?	?	N	Y	Y	Y
35 Waters	N	N	N	P	Y	Y	Y
36 Harman	?	?	?	?	?	?	Y
37 Millender-McD.	N	N	N	N	Y	Y	Y

	32	33	34	35	36	37	38
38 *Horn*	N	Y	Y	N	N	N	Y
39 *Royce*	N	N	Y	N	N	N	Y
40 *Lewis*	N	N	N	N	N	N	Y
41 *Kim*	N	N	N	N	Y	Y	Y
42 Brown	Y	N	N	N	Y	Y	Y
43 *Calvert*	N	N	N	N	N	Y	Y
44 Vacant							
45 *Rohrabacher*	Y	Y	Y	N	N	N	Y
46 Sanchez	N	N	N	N	Y	Y	Y
47 *Cox*	Y	N	N	N	N	N	Y
48 *Packard*	N	N	N	N	N	N	Y
49 *Bilbray*	N	?	N	N	N	N	Y
50 Filner	N	N	N	N	Y	Y	Y
51 *Cunningham*	N	N	N	N	N	N	Y
52 *Hunter*	N	Y	N	N	N	N	Y
COLORADO							
1 DeGette	N	N	N	N	Y	Y	Y
2 Skaggs	N	N	N	N	Y	Y	Y
3 *McInnis*	N	N	N	N	N	N	Y
4 *Schaffer*	N	Y	N	N	N	N	Y
5 *Hefley*	N	N	N	N	N	N	Y
6 *Schaefer*	?	?	?	?	?	?	?
CONNECTICUT							
1 Kennelly	Y	N	N	N	Y	Y	Y
2 Gejdenson	Y	N	N	N	Y	Y	Y
3 DeLauro	Y	N	N	N	Y	Y	Y
4 *Shays*	Y	N	N	N	N	N	Y
5 Maloney	Y	N	N	N	Y	Y	Y
6 *Johnson*	Y	N	N	N	N	N	Y
DELAWARE							
AL *Castle*	N	N	Y	N	Y	N	Y
FLORIDA							
1 *Scarborough*	N	N	N	N	Y	Y	Y
2 Boyd	N	N	N	N	Y	Y	Y
3 Brown	N	N	N	N	Y	Y	Y
4 *Fowler*	N	N	N	N	Y	N	Y
5 Thurman	N	N	N	N	Y	Y	Y
6 *Stearns*	N	N	N	N	N	N	Y
7 *Mica*	N	N	N	N	Y	Y	Y
8 *McCollum*	N	N	N	N	Y	Y	Y
9 *Bilirakis*	N	N	N	N	N	N	Y
10 *Young*	N	N	N	N	N	N	Y
11 Davis	N	N	N	N	Y	Y	Y
12 *Canady*	N	N	Y	N	N	N	Y
13 *Miller*	N	N	N	N	N	N	Y
14 *Goss*	N	N	N	N	N	N	Y
15 *Weldon*	N	N	N	N	N	N	Y
16 *Foley*	N	?	N	N	Y	Y	Y
17 Meek	N	N	N	N	Y	Y	Y
18 *Ros-Lehtinen*	Y	N	N	N	Y	Y	+
19 Wexler	N	N	N	N	Y	Y	Y
20 Deutsch	N	N	N	N	Y	Y	Y
21 *Diaz-Balart*	Y	N	N	N	Y	Y	Y
22 *Shaw*	N	N	Y	N	N	N	Y
23 Hastings	N	N	N	N	Y	Y	Y
GEORGIA							
1 *Kingston*	N	Y	Y	N	N	N	Y
2 Bishop	N	N	N	N	Y	Y	Y
3 *Collins*	N	N	Y	N	N	N	Y
4 McKinney	Y	N	N	N	Y	Y	Y
5 Lewis	Y	N	N	N	Y	Y	Y
6 *Gingrich*							
7 *Barr*	N	N	Y	N	N	N	Y
8 *Chambliss*	N	N	N	N	Y	Y	Y
9 *Deal*	N	N	Y	N	N	N	Y
10 *Norwood*	N	N	N	N	Y	Y	Y
11 *Linder*	N	N	Y	N	N	N	Y
HAWAII							
1 Abercrombie	N	N	N	N	Y	Y	Y
2 Mink	N	N	N	N	Y	Y	Y
IDAHO							
1 *Chenoweth*	N	N	Y	N	N	N	Y
2 *Crapo*	N	N	Y	N	N	N	Y
ILLINOIS							
1 Rush	Y	N	N	N	Y	N	Y
2 Jackson	Y	N	N	N	Y	N	Y
3 Lipinski	N	N	Y	N	N	N	Y
4 Gutierrez	Y	N	N	N	N	N	Y
5 Blagojevich	N	N	N	N	Y	Y	Y
6 *Hyde*	N	N	N	N	N	N	Y
7 Davis	Y	N	N	N	Y	N	Y
8 *Crane*	N	N	Y	N	N	N	Y
9 Yates	N	?	?	?	?	?	Y
10 *Porter*	N	N	N	N	Y	N	Y
11 *Weller*	N	N	Y	N	N	N	Y
12 Costello	N	N	N	N	Y	N	Y

ND Northern Democrats   SD Southern Democrats

	32	33	34	35	36	37	38
13 ***Fawell***	N	N	Y	N	N	N	Y
14 ***Hastert***	N	N	N	N	N	N	Y
15 ***Ewing***	N	N	Y	N	Y	N	Y
16 ***Manzullo***	N	N	N	N	N	N	Y
17 Evans	N	N	N	N	Y	Y	Y
18 ***LaHood***	N	N	N	N	N	N	Y
19 Poshard	?	?	?	?	?	?	?
20 ***Shimkus***	?	?	?	?	?	?	?
INDIANA							
1 Visclosky	N	N	N	N	Y	Y	Y
2 ***McIntosh***	N	Y	Y	N	N	N	Y
3 Roemer	N	N	N	N	Y	Y	Y
4 ***Souder***	N	Y	Y	N	N	N	Y
5 ***Buyer***	N	N	N	N	N	Y	Y
6 ***Burton***	N	N	N	N	Y	Y	Y
7 ***Pease***	N	N	Y	N	N	N	Y
8 ***Hostettler***	N	N	Y	N	Y	N	Y
9 Hamilton	N	N	N	N	Y	Y	Y
10 Carson	Y	Y	N	N	Y	Y	Y
IOWA							
1 ***Leach***	N	N	N	N	Y	Y	Y
2 ***Nussle***	N	N	N	N	Y	N	Y
3 Boswell	N	N	N	N	Y	Y	Y
4 ***Ganske***	N	N	N	N	N	N	Y
5 ***Latham***	N	N	N	N	N	N	Y
KANSAS							
1 ***Moran***	N	Y	N	N	N	N	Y
2 ***Ryun***	N	N	Y	N	N	N	Y
3 ***Snowbarger***	N	Y	Y	N	N	N	Y
4 ***Tiahrt***	N	N	Y	N	N	N	Y
KENTUCKY							
1 ***Whitfield***	N	N	N	N	N	N	Y
2 ***Lewis***	N	N	Y	N	N	N	Y
3 ***Northup***	N	N	Y	N	N	N	Y
4 ***Bunning***	N	N	Y	N	N	N	Y
5 ***Rogers***	N	N	Y	N	N	N	Y
6 Baesler	N	N	N	N	N	N	Y
LOUISIANA							
1 ***Livingston***	N	N	Y	N	N	N	Y
2 Jefferson	Y	N	N	N	Y	Y	Y
3 ***Tauzin***	N	N	N	N	Y	Y	Y
4 ***McCrery***	N	N	Y	N	N	N	Y
5 ***Cooksey***	N	N	N	N	N	Y	Y
6 ***Baker***	N	N	N	N	N	N	Y
7 John	N	N	N	N	Y	Y	Y
MAINE							
1 Allen	N	N	N	N	Y	Y	Y
2 Baldacci	N	N	N	N	Y	Y	Y
MARYLAND							
1 ***Gilchrest***	N	N	Y	N	Y	Y	Y
2 ***Ehrlich***	N	N	N	N	Y	N	Y
3 Cardin	N	N	N	N	Y	Y	Y
4 Wynn	Y	N	N	N	Y	Y	Y
5 Hoyer	Y	N	N	N	Y	Y	Y
6 ***Bartlett***	N	N	Y	N	N	N	Y
7 Cummings	N	N	N	N	Y	Y	Y
8 ***Morella***	N	N	N	N	Y	Y	Y
MASSACHUSETTS							
1 Olver	Y	N	N	N	Y	Y	Y
2 Neal	Y	N	N	N	Y	Y	Y
3 McGovern	Y	N	N	N	Y	Y	Y
4 Frank	N	N	N	N	Y	Y	Y
5 Meehan	Y	N	N	N	Y	Y	Y
6 Tierney	Y	N	N	N	Y	Y	Y
7 Markey	Y	N	N	N	Y	Y	Y
8 Kennedy	Y	N	N	N	Y	Y	Y
9 Moakley	Y	N	N	N	Y	Y	Y
10 Delahunt	Y	N	N	N	Y	Y	Y
MICHIGAN							
1 Stupak	N	N	N	N	Y	Y	Y
2 ***Hoekstra***	N	N	Y	N	N	N	Y
3 ***Ehlers***	N	N	N	N	Y	Y	Y
4 ***Camp***	N	N	N	N	N	N	Y
5 Barcia	N	N	N	N	Y	Y	Y
6 ***Upton***	N	N	Y	N	N	N	Y
7 ***Smith***	N	N	Y	N	N	N	Y
8 Stabenow	N	N	N	N	Y	N	Y
9 Kildee	N	N	N	N	Y	Y	Y
10 Bonior	Y	N	N	N	Y	Y	Y
11 ***Knollenberg***	N	N	Y	N	N	N	Y
12 Levin	N	N	N	N	Y	Y	Y
13 Rivers	N	N	N	N	Y	N	Y
14 Conyers	N	N	N	N	Y	Y	Y
15 Kilpatrick	–	–	–	?	+	+	+
16 Dingell	?	N	N	N	Y	Y	Y
MINNESOTA							
1 ***Gutknecht***	N	N	Y	N	N	N	Y
2 Minge	N	N	N	N	Y	Y	Y
3 ***Ramstad***	N	N	N	N	N	N	Y
4 Vento	N	N	N	N	Y	Y	Y
5 Sabo	N	N	N	N	Y	Y	Y
6 Luther	–	–	–	?	+	+	+
7 Peterson	N	N	N	N	Y	N	Y
8 Oberstar	N	N	N	N	Y	Y	Y
MISSISSIPPI							
1 ***Wicker***	N	N	Y	N	N	N	Y
2 Thompson	N	N	N	N	Y	Y	Y
3 ***Pickering***	N	N	N	N	N	N	Y
4 ***Parker***	N	N	N	N	N	Y	Y
5 Taylor	N	N	N	N	Y	Y	Y
MISSOURI							
1 Clay	N	N	N	N	Y	Y	Y
2 ***Talent***	N	N	N	N	N	N	Y
3 Gephardt	N	N	N	N	Y	Y	Y
4 Skelton	N	N	N	N	Y	N	Y
5 McCarthy	N	N	N	N	Y	Y	Y
6 Danner	N	N	Y	N	Y	N	Y
7 ***Blunt***	N	N	N	N	N	N	Y
8 ***Emerson***	N	N	Y	N	N	N	Y
9 ***Hulshof***	N	N	N	N	Y	N	Y
MONTANA							
AL ***Hill***	N	N	Y	N	N	N	Y
NEBRASKA							
1 ***Bereuter***	N	N	Y	N	Y	N	Y
2 ***Christensen***	N	N	Y	N	Y	N	Y
3 ***Barrett***	N	N	Y	N	Y	N	Y
NEVADA							
1 ***Ensign***	N	N	N	N	N	N	Y
2 ***Gibbons***	N	N	Y	N	N	N	Y
NEW HAMPSHIRE							
1 ***Sununu***	N	N	Y	N	N	N	Y
2 ***Bass***	N	N	N	N	N	N	Y
NEW JERSEY							
1 Andrews	N	N	N	N	Y	Y	Y
2 ***LoBiondo***	N	N	N	N	N	N	Y
3 ***Saxton***	N	N	N	N	Y	Y	Y
4 ***Smith***	N	N	N	N	Y	Y	Y
5 ***Roukema***	N	N	N	N	N	N	Y
6 Pallone	Y	N	N	N	Y	Y	Y
7 ***Franks***	?	N	N	N	N	Y	Y
8 Pascrell	N	N	N	N	Y	Y	Y
9 Rothman	N	N	N	N	Y	Y	Y
10 Payne	Y	N	N	N	Y	Y	Y
11 ***Frelinghuysen***	N	N	N	N	N	Y	Y
12 ***Pappas***	N	N	N	N	N	N	Y
13 Menendez	Y	N	N	N	N	N	Y
NEW MEXICO							
1 ***Schiff***	?	?	?	?	?	?	?
2 ***Skeen***	N	N	N	N	Y	Y	Y
3 ***Redmond***	N	N	N	N	Y	Y	Y
NEW YORK							
1 ***Forbes***	N	N	N	N	Y	Y	Y
2 ***Lazio***	N	N	Y	N	Y	Y	Y
3 ***King***	N	N	N	N	Y	Y	Y
4 McCarthy	N	N	N	N	Y	Y	Y
5 Ackerman	Y	N	N	N	Y	Y	Y
6 Meeks	Y	N	N	N	Y	Y	Y
7 Manton	N	N	N	N	Y	Y	Y
8 Nadler	Y	N	N	N	Y	Y	Y
9 Schumer	+	N	N	N	Y	Y	Y
10 Towns	Y	N	N	N	N	N	Y
11 Owens	Y	N	N	N	Y	Y	Y
12 Velázquez	Y	N	N	Y	N	N	Y
13 ***Fossella***	N	N	Y	N	Y	N	Y
14 Maloney	N	N	N	N	Y	Y	Y
15 Rangel	Y	N	N	N	Y	Y	Y
16 Serrano	Y	N	N	N	Y	Y	Y
17 Engel	Y	N	N	N	Y	Y	Y
18 Lowey	N	N	N	N	Y	Y	Y
19 ***Kelly***	N	N	N	N	Y	Y	Y
20 ***Gilman***	Y	N	N	N	Y	Y	Y
21 McNulty	Y	N	N	N	Y	Y	Y
22 ***Solomon***	N	N	Y	N	N	N	Y
23 ***Boehlert***	N	N	N	N	Y	Y	Y
24 ***McHugh***	N	N	Y	N	Y	N	Y
25 ***Walsh***	N	N	N	N	Y	Y	Y
26 Hinchey	Y	N	N	N	Y	Y	Y
27 ***Paxon***	N	N	Y	N	N	N	Y
28 Slaughter	N	N	N	N	Y	Y	Y
29 LaFalce	N	N	N	N	Y	Y	Y
30 ***Quinn***	N	N	N	N	Y	Y	?
31 ***Houghton***	N	N	N	N	Y	N	?
NORTH CAROLINA							
1 Clayton	N	N	N	N	Y	Y	Y
2 Etheridge	N	N	N	N	Y	Y	Y
3 ***Jones***	N	Y	Y	N	N	N	Y
4 Price	N	N	N	N	Y	Y	Y
5 ***Burr***	N	N	N	N	N	N	Y
6 ***Coble***	N	N	Y	N	N	N	Y
7 McIntyre	N	N	N	N	Y	N	Y
8 Hefner	N	N	N	N	Y	Y	Y
9 ***Myrick***	N	N	Y	N	N	N	Y
10 ***Ballenger***	N	N	Y	N	N	N	Y
11 ***Taylor***	N	Y	Y	N	N	N	Y
12 Watt	N	N	N	N	Y	Y	Y
NORTH DAKOTA							
AL Pomeroy	N	N	N	N	Y	Y	Y
OHIO							
1 ***Chabot***	N	N	N	N	N	N	Y
2 ***Portman***	?	N	Y	N	N	N	Y
3 Hall	N	N	N	N	Y	Y	Y
4 ***Oxley***	N	N	Y	N	Y	N	Y
5 ***Gillmor***	N	N	N	N	Y	N	Y
6 Strickland	N	N	N	N	Y	N	Y
7 ***Hobson***	N	N	Y	N	N	N	Y
8 ***Boehner***	N	N	Y	N	N	N	Y
9 Kaptur	N	N	N	N	Y	N	Y
10 Kucinich	N	N	N	N	Y	Y	Y
11 Stokes	N	N	N	N	Y	Y	Y
12 ***Kasich***	N	N	N	N	N	N	Y
13 Brown	N	N	N	N	Y	Y	Y
14 Sawyer	N	N	N	N	Y	Y	Y
15 ***Pryce***	N	N	Y	N	N	N	Y
16 ***Regula***	N	N	Y	N	N	N	Y
17 Traficant	N	N	N	N	N	N	Y
18 ***Ney***	N	N	Y	N	N	N	Y
19 ***LaTourette***	?	N	N	N	N	N	Y
OKLAHOMA							
1 ***Largent***	N	N	N	N	N	N	Y
2 ***Coburn***	N	N	Y	N	N	N	Y
3 ***Watkins***	N	N	N	N	N	N	Y
4 ***Watts***	N	N	N	N	N	N	Y
5 ***Istook***	N	Y	Y	N	N	N	Y
6 ***Lucas***	N	N	N	N	N	N	Y
OREGON							
1 Furse	Y	N	N	N	Y	Y	Y
2 ***Smith***	N	?	?	?	N	N	Y
3 Blumenauer	N	N	N	N	Y	Y	Y
4 DeFazio	N	N	N	N	Y	Y	Y
5 Hooley	N	N	N	N	Y	Y	Y
PENNSYLVANIA							
1 Vacant							
2 Fattah	N	N	N	N	Y	Y	Y
3 Borski	N	N	N	N	Y	Y	Y
4 Klink	N	N	N	N	Y	Y	Y
5 ***Peterson***	?	N	Y	N	N	Y	Y
6 Holden	N	N	N	N	N	Y	Y
7 ***Weldon***	N	N	Y	N	N	N	Y
8 ***Greenwood***	N	N	Y	N	Y	N	Y
9 ***Shuster***	N	N	Y	N	N	N	Y
10 ***McDade***	N	?	?	?	?	#	Y
11 Kanjorski	N	N	N	N	Y	Y	Y
12 Murtha	N	N	N	N	Y	Y	Y
13 ***Fox***	N	N	N	N	Y	N	Y
14 Coyne	N	N	N	N	Y	Y	Y
15 McHale	N	N	N	N	Y	Y	Y
16 ***Pitts***	N	N	Y	N	N	N	Y
17 ***Gekas***	?	N	N	N	Y	Y	Y
18 Doyle	N	N	N	N	Y	Y	Y
19 ***Goodling***	N	N	Y	N	N	N	Y
20 Mascara	N	N	N	N	Y	Y	Y
21 ***English***	N	N	N	N	Y	Y	Y
RHODE ISLAND							
1 Kennedy	N	N	N	N	Y	Y	Y
2 Weygand	N	N	N	N	Y	Y	Y
SOUTH CAROLINA							
1 ***Sanford***	N	Y	Y	N	N	N	Y
2 ***Spence***	N	N	Y	N	N	N	Y
3 ***Graham***	N	N	Y	N	N	N	Y
4 ***Inglis***	N	N	Y	N	N	N	Y
5 Spratt	N	N	Y	N	Y	Y	Y
6 Clyburn	N	N	N	N	Y	Y	Y
SOUTH DAKOTA							
AL ***Thune***	N	N	N	N	N	N	Y
TENNESSEE							
1 ***Jenkins***	N	N	Y	N	N	N	Y
2 ***Duncan***	N	Y	Y	N	N	N	Y
3 ***Wamp***	N	N	Y	N	N	N	Y
4 ***Hilleary***	N	N	Y	N	N	N	Y
5 Clement	N	N	N	N	Y	Y	Y
6 Gordon	N	N	N	N	Y	N	Y
7 ***Bryant***	N	N	Y	N	N	N	Y
8 Tanner	N	N	N	N	Y	N	Y
9 Ford	N	N	N	N	Y	Y	Y
TEXAS							
1 Sandlin	N	N	N	N	Y	Y	Y
2 Turner	N	N	N	N	Y	Y	Y
3 ***Johnson, Sam***	N	N	Y	N	N	N	Y
4 Hall	N	N	Y	N	N	N	Y
5 ***Sessions***	N	N	N	N	N	N	Y
6 ***Barton***	N	N	Y	N	Y	N	Y
7 ***Archer***	N	N	Y	N	N	N	Y
8 ***Brady***	N	N	Y	N	N	N	Y
9 Lampson	N	N	N	N	Y	Y	Y
10 Doggett	N	N	N	N	Y	Y	Y
11 Edwards	N	N	N	N	Y	Y	Y
12 ***Granger***	N	?	Y	N	Y	Y	Y
13 ***Thornberry***	N	N	Y	N	N	N	Y
14 ***Paul***	N	Y	Y	N	N	N	N
15 Hinojosa	N	N	N	N	Y	Y	Y
16 Reyes	N	N	N	N	Y	Y	Y
17 Stenholm	N	N	N	N	N	Y	Y
18 Jackson-Lee	Y	N	N	N	Y	Y	+
19 ***Combest***	N	Y	Y	N	N	N	Y
20 Gonzalez	?	?	?	?	?	?	?
21 ***Smith***	N	N	Y	N	Y	N	Y
22 ***DeLay***	N	N	N	N	N	Y	Y
23 ***Bonilla***	N	N	N	N	Y	Y	Y
24 Frost	N	N	?	N	Y	Y	Y
25 Bentsen	N	N	N	N	Y	Y	Y
26 ***Armey***	N	N	Y	N	N	N	Y
27 Ortiz	N	N	N	N	Y	Y	Y
28 Rodriguez	N	N	N	N	Y	Y	?
29 Green	N	N	N	N	Y	Y	Y
30 Johnson, E.B.	Y	N	N	N	Y	Y	+
UTAH							
1 ***Hansen***	N	N	N	N	N	N	Y
2 ***Cook***	N	N	N	N	Y	N	Y
3 ***Cannon***	N	N	N	N	Y	Y	Y
VERMONT							
AL *Sanders*	Y	N	N	N	Y	Y	Y
VIRGINIA							
1 ***Bateman***	N	N	Y	N	N	N	Y
2 Pickett	N	N	N	N	N	N	Y
3 Scott	N	N	N	N	Y	Y	Y
4 Sisisky	N	N	Y	N	N	N	Y
5 Goode	N	N	Y	N	N	N	Y
6 ***Goodlatte***	N	N	Y	N	N	N	Y
7 ***Bliley***	N	N	N	N	N	N	Y
8 Moran	N	N	N	N	Y	Y	Y
9 Boucher	N	N	N	N	Y	Y	Y
10 ***Wolf***	N	N	Y	N	N	N	Y
11 ***Davis***	N	N	N	N	N	Y	Y
WASHINGTON							
1 ***White***	N	N	N	N	N	N	Y
2 ***Metcalf***	N	N	Y	N	N	N	Y
3 ***Smith, Linda***	N	Y	N	N	N	N	Y
4 ***Hastings***	N	N	Y	N	N	N	Y
5 ***Nethercutt***	N	N	N	N	N	N	Y
6 Dicks	N	N	N	N	Y	Y	Y
7 McDermott	N	N	N	N	Y	Y	Y
8 ***Dunn***	N	N	N	N	N	N	Y
9 Smith, Adam	N	N	N	N	Y	Y	Y
WEST VIRGINIA							
1 Mollohan	N	N	N	N	Y	Y	Y
2 Wise	N	N	N	N	Y	Y	Y
3 Rahall	N	N	N	N	Y	Y	Y
WISCONSIN							
1 ***Neumann***	N	N	Y	N	N	N	Y
2 ***Klug***	N	N	Y	N	N	N	Y
3 Kind	N	N	N	N	Y	N	Y
4 Kleczka	N	N	N	N	Y	N	Y
5 Barrett	N	N	N	N	Y	Y	Y
6 ***Petri***	N	Y	Y	N	N	N	Y
7 Obey	Y	N	N	N	Y	N	Y
8 Johnson	N	N	N	N	Y	N	Y
9 ***Sensenbrenner***	N	Y	Y	N	N	N	Y
WYOMING							
AL ***Cubin***	N	Y	Y	N	N	N	Y

Southern states - Ala., Ark., Fla., Ga., Ky., La., Miss., N.C., Okla., S.C., Tenn., Texas, Va.

Key

Y	Voted for (yea).
#	Paired for.
+	Announced for.
N	Voted against (nay).
X	Paired against.
−	Announced against.
P	Voted "present."
C	Voted "present" to avoid possible conflict of interest.
?	Did not vote or otherwise make a position known.

Democrats   **Republicans**
Independent

39. HR 3130. Child Support Performance/Passage. Passage of the bill to establish a new alternative penalty for states failing to meet the October 1, 1997 deadline to establish a computer system to assist in child support enforcement. The bill also would create a new federal incentive system to reward states with effective child support enforcement programs. Passed 414-1: R 218-1; D 195-0 (ND 141-0, SD 54-0); I 1-0. March 5, 1998. A "yea" was a vote in support of the president's position.

40. Procedural Motion/Journal. Approval of the House Journal of Monday, March 9, 1998. Approved 365-39: R 196-19; D 168-20 (ND 124-14, SD 44-6); I 1-0. March 10, 1998.

41. H Con Res 206. Use of Rotunda for Holocaust Remembrance/Passage. Thomas, R-Calif., motion to suspend the rules and adopt the resolution to permit the use of the Capitol Rotunda for a ceremony as part of the commemoration to remember victims of the Holocaust. Motion agreed to 406-0: R 215-0; D 190-0 (ND 140-0, SD 50-0); I 1-0. March 10, 1998. A two-thirds majority of those present and voting (271 in this case) is required for adoption under suspension of the rules.

42. S 419. Birth Defects Prevention/Passage. Bilirakis, R-Fla., motion to suspend the rules and pass the bill to authorize $30 million in fiscal 1998, $40 million in fiscal 1999, and such sums as may be necessary in fiscal 2000 and 2001 for programs intended to collect data on birth defects and prevention, conduct research on birth defects and broaden public awareness of birth defects. Motion agreed to 405-2: R 213-2; D 191-0 (ND 140-0, SD 51-0); I 1-0. March 10, 1998. A two-thirds majority of those present and voting (272 in this case) is required for passage under suspension of the rules.

43. HR 1432. Trade with sub-Saharan Africa/Rule. Adoption of the rule (H Res 383) to provide floor consideration of the bill to set a new trade and investment policy toward the countries of sub-Saharan Africa. Adopted 227-190: R 172-48; D 55-141 (ND 43-100, SD 12-41); I 0-1. March 11, 1998.

44. HR 1432. Trade with sub-Saharan Africa/Eligibility. Waters, D-Calif., amendment to clarify the eligibility provisions to state that countries need not meet every one of the bill's enumerated requirements. Rejected 81-334: R 3-218; D 77-116 (ND 58-84, SD 19-32); I 1-0. March 11, 1998.

45. HR 1432. Trade with sub-Saharan Africa/Morocco. Bereuter, R-Neb., amendment that would give the president discretion, subject to congressional approval, to designate Morocco as eligible to participate in the programs established by the bill if the country otherwise meets the eligibility requirements and if that designation is in the national interest of the United States. Rejected 156-258: R 131-91; D 25-166 (ND 19-122, SD 6-44); I 0-1. March 11, 1998.

	39	40	41	42	43	44	45
ALABAMA							
1 *Callahan*	Y	Y	Y	Y	Y	N	N
2 *Everett*	Y	Y	Y	Y	N	N	N
3 *Riley*	Y	Y	Y	Y	N	N	N
4 *Aderholt*	Y	Y	Y	Y	N	N	N
5 Cramer	Y	Y	Y	Y	N	N	N
6 *Bachus*	Y	Y	Y	Y	N	N	N
7 Hilliard	Y	N	Y	Y	N	Y	N
ALASKA							
AL *Young*	Y	Y	Y	Y	N	N	Y
ARIZONA							
1 *Salmon*	Y	Y	Y	Y	N	Y	N
2 Pastor	Y	Y	Y	Y	N	Y	N
3 *Stump*	Y	Y	Y	Y	Y	N	N
4 *Shadegg*	Y	Y	Y	Y	N	Y	N
5 *Kolbe*	Y	Y	Y	Y	Y	N	N
6 *Hayworth*	Y	Y	Y	Y	Y	N	Y
ARKANSAS							
1 Berry	Y	Y	Y	Y	N	N	N
2 Snyder	Y	Y	Y	Y	N	N	Y
3 *Hutchinson*	Y	Y	Y	Y	N	N	N
4 Dickey	Y	N	Y	Y	N	N	N
CALIFORNIA							
1 *Riggs*	Y	?	?	?	?	N	N
2 *Herger*	Y	Y	Y	Y	N	N	N
3 Fazio	Y	N	Y	Y	N	N	N
4 *Doolittle*	?	Y	Y	Y	N	Y	N
5 Matsui	Y	Y	Y	Y	Y	N	Y
6 Woolsey	Y	Y	Y	Y	N	N	N
7 Miller	Y	Y	Y	Y	N	N	N
8 Pelosi	Y	Y	Y	Y	N	Y	N
9 Vacant							
10 Tauscher	Y	Y	Y	Y	Y	N	N
11 *Pombo*	Y	Y	Y	Y	N	N	N
12 Lantos	Y	Y	Y	Y	N	N	N
13 Stark	Y	Y	Y	Y	N	Y	?
14 Eshoo	Y	Y	Y	Y	N	Y	N
15 *Campbell*	Y	Y	Y	Y	Y	Y	Y
16 Lofgren	Y	Y	Y	Y	N	N	N
17 Farr	Y	Y	Y	Y	N	Y	N
18 Condit	Y	Y	Y	Y	N	N	N
19 *Radanovich*	Y	Y	Y	Y	Y	?	?
20 Dooley	Y	Y	Y	Y	Y	N	N
21 *Thomas*	?	Y	Y	Y	N	N	N
23 *Gallegly*	Y	Y	Y	Y	N	N	N
24 Sherman	Y	Y	Y	Y	N	N	Y
25 *McKeon*	Y	Y	Y	Y	N	N	N
26 Berman	Y	Y	Y	Y	N	Y	Y
27 *Rogan*	Y	Y	Y	Y	N	N	Y
28 *Dreier*	Y	Y	Y	Y	N	N	Y
29 Waxman	Y	Y	Y	N	N	?	?
30 Becerra	Y	N	Y	Y	N	N	N
31 Martinez	Y	Y	Y	Y	Y	N	N
32 Dixon	Y	Y	Y	Y	N	Y	N
33 Roybal-Allard	Y	Y	Y	Y	N	Y	N
34 Torres	Y	Y	Y	Y	N	?	N
35 Waters	Y	N	Y	Y	N	Y	N
36 Harman	?	?	?	?	?	?	?
37 Millender-McD.	Y	Y	Y	Y	N	Y	N
38 *Horn*	Y	Y	Y	Y	Y	N	Y

	39	40	41	42	43	44	45
39 *Royce*	Y	Y	Y	Y	Y	N	N
40 *Lewis*	Y	Y	Y	Y	Y	N	Y
41 *Kim*	Y	Y	Y	Y	Y	N	N
42 Brown	Y	N	Y	Y	N	Y	Y
43 *Calvert*	Y	Y	Y	Y	Y	N	Y
44 Vacant							
45 *Rohrabacher*	Y	Y	Y	Y	Y	N	N
46 Sanchez	Y	Y	Y	Y	Y	N	N
47 *Cox*	Y	Y	Y	Y	Y	N	N
48 *Packard*	Y	Y	Y	Y	Y	N	N
49 *Bilbray*	Y	Y	Y	Y	Y	N	Y
50 Filner	Y	N	Y	Y	N	Y	N
51 *Cunningham*	Y	Y	Y	Y	N	N	N
52 *Hunter*	Y	Y	Y	Y	N	N	N
COLORADO							
1 DeGette	Y	Y	Y	Y	N	N	N
2 Skaggs	Y	Y	Y	Y	N	Y	N
3 *McInnis*	Y	Y	Y	Y	N	N	N
4 *Schaffer*	Y	N	Y	Y	N	N	Y
5 *Hefley*	Y	N	Y	Y	N	N	N
6 *Schaefer*	Y	?	?	?	Y	N	Y
CONNECTICUT							
1 Kennelly	Y	Y	Y	N	N	N	N
2 Gejdenson	Y	Y	Y	N	Y	Y	Y
3 DeLauro	Y	Y	Y	Y	N	Y	N
4 *Shays*	Y	Y	Y	Y	Y	N	N
5 Maloney	Y	Y	Y	N	Y	Y	Y
6 *Johnson*	Y	Y	Y	Y	Y	N	Y
DELAWARE							
AL *Castle*	Y	Y	Y	Y	Y	N	N
FLORIDA							
1 *Scarborough*	Y	Y	Y	Y	N	N	Y
2 Boyd	Y	Y	Y	N	N	N	N
3 Brown	Y	Y	Y	Y	N	N	N
4 *Fowler*	Y	Y	Y	N	N	N	N
5 Thurman	Y	Y	Y	Y	N	Y	N
6 *Stearns*	Y	Y	Y	Y	N	N	N
7 *Mica*	Y	Y	Y	Y	N	N	Y
8 *McCollum*	Y	Y	Y	Y	N	Y	Y
9 *Bilirakis*	?	Y	Y	Y	N	Y	Y
10 *Young*	Y	?	?	?	N	N	N
11 Davis	Y	Y	Y	Y	N	N	N
12 *Canady*	Y	Y	Y	Y	N	N	N
13 *Miller*	Y	Y	Y	Y	N	N	Y
14 *Goss*	Y	Y	Y	Y	N	N	N
15 *Weldon*	Y	Y	Y	Y	N	N	N
16 *Foley*	Y	Y	Y	Y	N	N	Y
17 Meek	Y	Y	Y	Y	Y	Y	?
18 *Ros-Lehtinen*	Y	Y	Y	Y	N	N	Y
19 Wexler	Y	Y	Y	Y	N	N	Y
20 Deutsch	Y	Y	Y	Y	N	−	−
21 *Diaz-Balart*	Y	Y	Y	Y	N	N	Y
22 *Shaw*	Y	Y	Y	Y	N	N	N
23 Hastings	Y	N	Y	Y	Y	Y	N
GEORGIA							
1 *Kingston*	Y	N	Y	Y	N	Y	N
2 Bishop	Y	Y	Y	Y	N	Y	N
3 *Collins*	Y	Y	Y	Y	N	N	N
4 McKinney	Y	Y	Y	Y	N	Y	N
5 Lewis	Y	N	Y	Y	N	Y	N
6 *Gingrich*							
7 *Barr*	Y	Y	Y	Y	N	N	Y
8 *Chambliss*	Y	Y	Y	Y	N	N	N
9 *Deal*	Y	Y	Y	Y	N	N	N
10 *Norwood*	Y	Y	Y	Y	N	N	N
11 *Linder*	Y	Y	Y	Y	N	N	N
HAWAII							
1 Abercrombie	Y	Y	Y	Y	N	N	N
2 Mink	Y	Y	Y	Y	N	Y	N
IDAHO							
1 *Chenoweth*	Y	N	Y	Y	Y	?	?
2 *Crapo*	Y	Y	Y	Y	N	N	N
ILLINOIS							
1 Rush	Y	?	Y	Y	Y	N	N
2 Jackson	Y	Y	Y	N	N	N	N
3 Lipinski	Y	Y	Y	Y	N	N	N
4 Gutierrez	Y	Y	Y	N	N	Y	Y
5 Blagojevich	Y	?	?	?	N	N	Y
6 *Hyde*	Y	Y	Y	Y	N	N	N
7 Davis	Y	Y	Y	N	N	Y	N
8 *Crane*	Y	N	Y	Y	Y	Y	N
9 Yates	Y	Y	Y	Y	N	N	N
10 *Porter*	Y	Y	Y	Y	N	N	Y
11 *Weller*	Y	?	?	?	N	N	N
12 Costello	Y	N	Y	Y	N	N	N
13 *Fawell*	Y	Y	Y	Y	N	N	Y

ND Northern Democrats   SD Southern Democrats

	39	40	41	42	43	44	45
14 **Hastert**	Y	Y	Y	Y	Y	N	Y
15 **Ewing**	Y	Y	Y	Y	Y	N	Y
16 **Manzullo**	Y	Y	Y	Y	Y	N	Y
17 Evans	Y	Y	Y	Y	N	N	N
18 **LaHood**	Y	Y	Y	Y	Y	N	Y
19 Poshard	?	?	?	?	?	?	?
20 **Shimkus**	?	Y	Y	Y	Y	N	Y
INDIANA							
1 Visclosky	Y	Y	Y	Y	N	N	N
2 **McIntosh**	Y	Y	Y	Y	Y	N	Y
3 Roemer	Y	Y	Y	Y	Y	N	N
4 **Souder**	Y	Y	Y	Y	Y	N	N
5 **Buyer**	Y	?	?	?	Y	N	Y
6 **Burton**	Y	Y	Y	Y	Y	N	N
7 **Pease**	Y	Y	Y	Y	Y	N	Y
8 **Hostettler**	Y	Y	Y	Y	N	N	Y
9 Hamilton	Y	Y	Y	Y	Y	N	Y
10 Carson	Y	Y	Y	Y	N	Y	N
IOWA							
1 **Leach**	Y	Y	Y	Y	Y	N	Y
2 **Nussle**	Y	N	Y	Y	Y	N	N
3 Boswell	Y	Y	Y	Y	N	N	N
4 **Ganske**	?	N	Y	Y	Y	N	N
5 **Latham**	Y	Y	Y	Y	Y	N	Y
KANSAS							
1 **Moran**	Y	N	Y	Y	N	N	Y
2 **Ryun**	Y	Y	Y	Y	Y	N	Y
3 **Snowbarger**	Y	Y	Y	Y	Y	N	Y
4 **Tiahrt**	Y	Y	Y	Y	Y	N	Y
KENTUCKY							
1 **Whitfield**	Y	Y	Y	Y	Y	N	Y
2 **Lewis**	Y	Y	Y	Y	N	N	N
3 **Northup**	Y	Y	Y	Y	Y	N	Y
4 **Bunning**	Y	Y	Y	Y	N	N	N
5 **Rogers**	Y	Y	Y	Y	N	N	N
6 Baesler	Y	Y	Y	Y	N	N	N
LOUISIANA							
1 **Livingston**	Y	Y	Y	Y	Y	N	N
2 Jefferson	Y	Y	Y	Y	Y	Y	N
3 **Tauzin**	Y	Y	Y	Y	Y	N	N
4 **McCrery**	Y	Y	Y	Y	Y	N	N
5 **Cooksey**	Y	Y	Y	Y	N	N	Y
6 **Baker**	Y	Y	Y	Y	Y	N	N
7 John	Y	Y	Y	Y	N	?	?
MAINE							
1 Allen	Y	Y	Y	Y	Y	N	N
2 Baldacci	Y	Y	Y	Y	N	N	N
MARYLAND							
1 **Gilchrest**	Y	?	?	?	Y	N	Y
2 **Ehrlich**	Y	Y	Y	Y	N	N	Y
3 Cardin	Y	Y	Y	Y	Y	N	N
4 Wynn	Y	Y	Y	Y	Y	Y	N
5 Hoyer	Y	Y	Y	Y	N	Y	Y
6 **Bartlett**	Y	Y	Y	Y	Y	N	N
7 Cummings	Y	Y	Y	Y	N	Y	N
8 **Morella**	Y	Y	Y	Y	Y	N	Y
MASSACHUSETTS							
1 Olver	Y	Y	Y	Y	N	Y	N
2 Neal	Y	Y	Y	Y	N	N	N
3 McGovern	Y	Y	Y	Y	N	N	N
4 Frank	Y	Y	Y	Y	N	Y	N
5 Meehan	Y	Y	Y	Y	N	Y	N
6 Tierney	Y	Y	Y	Y	N	Y	N
7 Markey	Y	Y	Y	Y	Y	Y	N
8 Kennedy	Y	?	?	?	N	Y	N
9 Moakley	Y	Y	Y	Y	N	N	N
10 Delahunt	Y	Y	Y	Y	N	Y	N
MICHIGAN							
1 Stupak	Y	Y	Y	Y	N	N	N
2 **Hoekstra**	Y	Y	Y	Y	Y	N	Y
3 **Ehlers**	Y	Y	Y	Y	Y	N	Y
4 **Camp**	Y	Y	Y	Y	Y	N	Y
5 Barcia	Y	Y	Y	Y	N	N	N
6 **Upton**	Y	Y	Y	Y	Y	N	N
7 **Smith**	Y	Y	Y	Y	Y	N	Y
8 Stabenow	Y	Y	Y	Y	N	N	N
9 Kildee	Y	Y	Y	Y	N	Y	N
10 Bonior	Y	N	Y	Y	N	Y	N
11 **Knollenberg**	Y	Y	Y	Y	Y	N	Y
12 Levin	Y	Y	Y	Y	Y	N	N
13 Rivers	Y	Y	Y	Y	N	Y	Y
14 Conyers	Y	Y	Y	Y	N	Y	N
15 Kilpatrick	+	Y	Y	Y	Y	Y	N
16 Dingell	?	Y	Y	Y	N	N	N

	39	40	41	42	43	44	45
MINNESOTA							
1 **Gutknecht**	Y	N	Y	Y	N	N	Y
2 Minge	Y	Y	Y	Y	N	N	Y
3 **Ramstad**	Y	N	Y	Y	Y	N	Y
4 Vento	Y	Y	Y	Y	Y	N	N
5 Sabo	Y	N	Y	Y	N	N	N
6 Luther	+	+	Y	Y	N	N	Y
7 Peterson	Y	Y	Y	Y	N	N	?
8 Oberstar	Y	Y	Y	Y	N	N	N
MISSISSIPPI							
1 **Wicker**	Y	N	Y	Y	N	N	Y
2 Thompson	Y	N	Y	Y	N	Y	N
3 **Pickering**	Y	Y	Y	Y	N	N	N
4 **Parker**	Y	Y	Y	Y	Y	N	N
5 Taylor	Y	N	Y	Y	N	N	N
MISSOURI							
1 Clay	Y	N	Y	Y	N	Y	N
2 **Talent**	Y	Y	Y	Y	N	N	Y
3 Gephardt	Y	N	Y	Y	N	Y	N
4 Skelton	Y	Y	Y	Y	Y	N	N
5 McCarthy	Y	Y	Y	Y	N	N	N
6 Danner	Y	Y	Y	Y	N	N	N
7 **Blunt**	Y	Y	Y	Y	Y	N	N
8 **Emerson**	Y	Y	Y	Y	N	N	N
9 **Hulshof**	Y	Y	Y	Y	Y	N	N
MONTANA							
AL **Hill**	Y	Y	Y	Y	Y	N	Y
NEBRASKA							
1 **Bereuter**	Y	Y	Y	Y	Y	N	Y
2 **Christensen**	Y	Y	Y	Y	Y	N	Y
3 **Barrett**	Y	Y	Y	Y	Y	N	Y
NEVADA							
1 **Ensign**	Y	N	Y	Y	Y	N	N
2 **Gibbons**	Y	Y	Y	Y	Y	N	Y
NEW HAMPSHIRE							
1 **Sununu**	Y	Y	Y	Y	Y	N	Y
2 **Bass**	Y	Y	Y	Y	Y	N	Y
NEW JERSEY							
1 Andrews	Y	Y	Y	Y	N	N	N
2 **LoBiondo**	Y	N	Y	Y	N	N	N
3 **Saxton**	Y	Y	Y	Y	Y	N	Y
4 **Smith**	Y	Y	Y	Y	Y	N	Y
5 **Roukema**	Y	Y	Y	Y	Y	N	Y
6 Pallone	Y	Y	Y	Y	N	N	N
7 **Franks**	Y	Y	Y	Y	Y	N	Y
8 Pascrell	Y	Y	Y	Y	?	N	N
9 Rothman	Y	Y	Y	Y	N	N	N
10 Payne	Y	Y	Y	Y	Y	Y	N
11 **Frelinghuysen**	Y	Y	Y	Y	Y	N	Y
12 **Pappas**	Y	Y	Y	Y	Y	N	Y
13 Menendez	Y	Y	Y	Y	Y	N	N
NEW MEXICO							
1 **Schiff**	?	?	?	?	?	?	?
2 **Skeen**	Y	Y	Y	Y	Y	N	Y
3 **Redmond**	Y	Y	Y	Y	+	–	+
NEW YORK							
1 **Forbes**	Y	Y	Y	Y	Y	N	Y
2 **Lazio**	Y	Y	Y	Y	Y	N	Y
3 **King**	Y	Y	Y	Y	Y	N	Y
4 McCarthy	Y	+	+	+	Y	N	N
5 Ackerman	Y	Y	Y	Y	Y	N	N
6 Meeks	Y	Y	Y	Y	Y	Y	N
7 Manton	Y	Y	Y	Y	N	?	?
8 Nadler	Y	Y	Y	Y	N	Y	N
9 Schumer	Y	?	?	?	N	N	N
10 Towns	Y	Y	Y	Y	Y	Y	N
11 Owens	Y	Y	Y	Y	N	Y	Y
12 Velázquez	Y	Y	Y	Y	N	Y	N
13 **Fossella**	Y	Y	Y	Y	Y	N	Y
14 Maloney	Y	Y	Y	Y	N	N	N
15 Rangel	Y	Y	Y	Y	Y	Y	N
16 Serrano	Y	Y	Y	Y	N	Y	N
17 Engel	Y	Y	Y	Y	Y	Y	N
18 Lowey	Y	Y	Y	Y	Y	N	N
19 **Kelly**	Y	Y	Y	Y	Y	N	Y
20 **Gilman**	Y	Y	Y	Y	N	N	Y
21 McNulty	Y	Y	Y	Y	Y	N	N
22 **Solomon**	Y	Y	Y	Y	Y	N	Y
23 **Boehlert**	Y	Y	Y	Y	Y	N	Y
24 **McHugh**	Y	Y	Y	Y	Y	N	Y
25 **Walsh**	Y	Y	Y	Y	Y	N	Y
26 Hinchey	Y	N	Y	Y	N	N	N
27 **Paxon**	Y	Y	Y	Y	Y	N	Y
28 Slaughter	Y	Y	Y	Y	N	N	N
29 LaFalce	Y	Y	Y	Y	N	N	Y

	39	40	41	42	43	44	45
30 **Quinn**	?	Y	Y	Y	Y	N	Y
31 **Houghton**	Y	Y	Y	Y	Y	N	Y
NORTH CAROLINA							
1 Clayton	Y	Y	Y	Y	N	Y	N
2 Etheridge	Y	Y	Y	Y	N	N	N
3 **Jones**	Y	Y	Y	Y	N	N	N
4 Price	Y	Y	Y	Y	N	N	N
5 **Burr**	Y	Y	Y	Y	Y	N	N
6 **Coble**	Y	Y	Y	Y	N	N	N
7 McIntyre	Y	Y	Y	Y	N	N	N
8 Hefner	Y	?	?	?	N	Y	N
9 **Myrick**	Y	Y	Y	Y	N	N	N
10 **Ballenger**	Y	Y	Y	Y	N	N	N
11 **Taylor**	Y	Y	Y	Y	N	N	N
12 Watt	Y	Y	Y	Y	N	Y	N
NORTH DAKOTA							
AL Pomeroy	Y	Y	Y	Y	Y	N	Y
OHIO							
1 **Chabot**	Y	Y	Y	Y	Y	N	Y
2 **Portman**	Y	Y	Y	Y	Y	N	Y
3 Hall	Y	Y	Y	Y	Y	N	Y
4 **Oxley**	Y	Y	Y	Y	Y	N	Y
5 **Gillmor**	Y	Y	Y	Y	Y	N	Y
6 Strickland	Y	Y	Y	Y	N	N	N
7 **Hobson**	Y	Y	Y	Y	Y	N	Y
8 **Boehner**	Y	Y	Y	Y	Y	N	Y
9 Kaptur	Y	Y	Y	Y	N	Y	N
10 Kucinich	Y	N	Y	Y	N	Y	N
11 Stokes	Y	Y	Y	Y	N	Y	N
12 **Kasich**	Y	Y	Y	Y	Y	N	Y
13 Brown	Y	Y	Y	Y	N	Y	N
14 Sawyer	Y	Y	Y	Y	N	N	N
15 **Pryce**	Y	Y	Y	Y	Y	N	Y
16 **Regula**	Y	Y	Y	Y	Y	N	N
17 Traficant	Y	Y	Y	Y	N	N	N
18 **Ney**	Y	Y	Y	Y	N	N	N
19 **LaTourette**	Y	Y	Y	Y	Y	N	Y
OKLAHOMA							
1 **Largent**	Y	Y	Y	Y	Y	N	N
2 **Coburn**	Y	Y	Y	Y	N	N	Y
3 **Watkins**	Y	Y	Y	Y	Y	N	Y
4 **Watts**	Y	N	Y	Y	Y	N	N
5 **Istook**	Y	Y	Y	Y	N	N	N
6 **Lucas**	Y	Y	Y	Y	Y	N	Y
OREGON							
1 Furse	Y	?	?	?	?	?	?
2 **Smith**	Y	Y	Y	Y	Y	N	Y
3 Blumenauer	Y	Y	Y	Y	Y	Y	N
4 DeFazio	Y	N	Y	Y	N	Y	N
5 Hooley	Y	Y	Y	Y	N	N	N
PENNSYLVANIA							
1 Vacant							
2 Fattah	Y	?	?	?	?	Y	N
3 Borski	Y	N	Y	Y	N	N	N
4 Klink	?	Y	Y	Y	N	N	N
5 **Peterson**	Y	Y	Y	Y	Y	N	Y
6 Holden	Y	Y	Y	Y	N	N	N
7 **Weldon**	Y	Y	Y	Y	?	N	N
8 **Greenwood**	Y	Y	Y	Y	Y	N	Y
9 **Shuster**	Y	Y	Y	Y	Y	N	Y
10 **McDade**	Y	Y	Y	Y	Y	N	Y
11 Kanjorski	Y	Y	Y	Y	N	N	N
12 Murtha	Y	Y	Y	Y	N	N	N
13 **Fox**	Y	N	Y	Y	Y	N	Y
14 Coyne	Y	Y	Y	Y	N	Y	N
15 McHale	Y	Y	Y	Y	N	N	N
16 **Pitts**	Y	Y	Y	Y	Y	N	Y
17 **Gekas**	Y	Y	Y	Y	?	N	Y
18 Doyle	Y	Y	Y	Y	N	N	N
19 **Goodling**	Y	Y	Y	Y	Y	N	N
20 Mascara	Y	Y	Y	Y	N	N	N
21 **English**	Y	N	Y	Y	Y	N	Y
RHODE ISLAND							
1 Kennedy	Y	Y	Y	Y	N	Y	N
2 Weygand	Y	Y	Y	Y	N	N	N
SOUTH CAROLINA							
1 **Sanford**	Y	Y	Y	Y	N	N	N
2 **Spence**	Y	Y	Y	Y	N	?	N
3 **Graham**	Y	Y	Y	Y	N	N	Y
4 **Inglis**	Y	?	?	?	N	N	N
5 Spratt	Y	Y	Y	Y	N	N	N
6 Clyburn	Y	N	Y	Y	N	Y	N
SOUTH DAKOTA							
AL **Thune**	Y	Y	Y	Y	Y	N	Y

	39	40	41	42	43	44	45
TENNESSEE							
1 **Jenkins**	Y	Y	Y	Y	Y	N	N
2 **Duncan**	Y	Y	Y	Y	N	N	N
3 **Wamp**	Y	Y	Y	Y	Y	N	N
4 **Hilleary**	Y	N	Y	Y	N	N	N
5 Clement	Y	Y	Y	Y	N	N	Y
6 Gordon	Y	Y	Y	Y	N	N	N
7 **Bryant**	Y	Y	Y	Y	Y	N	N
8 Tanner	Y	Y	Y	Y	N	N	N
9 Ford	Y	Y	Y	Y	Y	Y	N
TEXAS							
1 Sandlin	Y	Y	Y	Y	N	N	N
2 Turner	Y	Y	Y	Y	N	N	N
3 **Johnson, Sam**	Y	Y	Y	N	Y	N	N
4 Hall	Y	Y	Y	Y	N	N	N
5 **Sessions**	Y	N	Y	Y	Y	N	Y
6 **Barton**	Y	?	?	?	?	N	N
7 **Archer**	Y	Y	Y	Y	Y	N	N
8 **Brady**	Y	+	+	+	+	N	N
9 Lampson	Y	Y	Y	Y	N	N	N
10 Doggett	Y	Y	Y	?	Y	N	Y
11 Edwards	Y	Y	Y	Y	N	N	N
12 **Granger**	Y	Y	Y	Y	Y	N	N
13 **Thornberry**	Y	Y	Y	Y	N	N	N
14 **Paul**	N	Y	Y	N	Y	N	N
15 Hinojosa	Y	+	+	Y	N	N	N
16 Reyes	Y	Y	Y	Y	N	N	N
17 Stenholm	Y	Y	Y	Y	N	N	N
18 Jackson-Lee	Y	Y	Y	Y	Y	Y	N
19 **Combest**	Y	Y	Y	Y	N	N	N
20 Gonzalez	?	?	?	?	?	?	?
21 **Smith**	Y	Y	Y	Y	Y	N	Y
22 **DeLay**	Y	Y	Y	Y	Y	N	Y
23 **Bonilla**	Y	Y	Y	Y	N	N	N
24 Frost	Y	Y	Y	Y	N	N	N
25 Bentsen	Y	Y	Y	Y	N	N	N
26 **Armey**	Y	Y	Y	Y	Y	N	Y
27 Ortiz	Y	Y	Y	Y	N	N	N
28 Rodriguez	Y	?	?	?	?	?	?
29 Green	Y	Y	Y	Y	N	N	N
30 Johnson, E.B.	Y	Y	Y	Y	Y	Y	N
UTAH							
1 **Hansen**	Y	Y	Y	Y	Y	N	N
2 **Cook**	Y	Y	Y	Y	Y	N	N
3 **Cannon**	Y	Y	Y	Y	Y	N	Y
VERMONT							
AL Sanders	Y	Y	Y	Y	N	Y	N
VIRGINIA							
1 **Bateman**	Y	Y	Y	Y	Y	N	Y
2 Pickett	Y	?	?	Y	N	N	Y
3 Scott	Y	Y	Y	Y	N	Y	N
4 Sisisky	Y	Y	Y	Y	N	N	N
5 Goode	Y	Y	Y	Y	N	N	N
6 **Goodlatte**	Y	Y	Y	Y	Y	N	Y
7 **Bliley**	Y	Y	Y	Y	Y	N	Y
8 Moran	Y	Y	Y	Y	Y	Y	Y
9 Boucher	Y	Y	Y	Y	N	N	N
10 **Wolf**	Y	Y	Y	Y	Y	N	N
11 **Davis**	Y	?	?	?	Y	Y	Y
WASHINGTON							
1 **White**	Y	Y	Y	Y	Y	N	Y
2 **Metcalf**	Y	Y	Y	Y	N	N	N
3 **Smith, Linda**	Y	Y	Y	Y	N	N	N
4 **Hastings**	Y	Y	Y	Y	Y	N	Y
5 **Nethercutt**	Y	Y	Y	Y	Y	N	Y
6 Dicks	Y	Y	Y	Y	Y	N	N
7 McDermott	+	Y	Y	Y	Y	N	N
8 **Dunn**	Y	Y	Y	Y	Y	N	Y
9 Smith, Adam	Y	Y	Y	Y	Y	N	N
WEST VIRGINIA							
1 Mollohan	Y	Y	Y	Y	N	N	N
2 Wise	Y	Y	Y	Y	N	N	N
3 Rahall	Y	Y	Y	Y	N	N	N
WISCONSIN							
1 **Neumann**	Y	Y	Y	Y	Y	N	Y
2 **Klug**	Y	Y	Y	Y	Y	N	Y
3 Kind	Y	Y	Y	Y	Y	N	Y
4 Kleczka	Y	Y	Y	Y	Y	N	N
5 Barrett	Y	Y	Y	Y	N	N	N
6 **Petri**	Y	Y	Y	Y	Y	N	Y
7 Obey	Y	Y	Y	Y	N	N	N
8 Johnson	Y	Y	Y	Y	N	N	N
9 **Sensenbrenner**	Y	Y	Y	Y	Y	N	Y
WYOMING							
AL **Cubin**	Y	Y	Y	Y	Y	N	N

Southern states - Ala., Ark., Fla., Ga., Ky., La., Miss., N.C., Okla., S.C., Tenn., Texas, Va.

Key

Y	Voted for (yea).
#	Paired for.
+	Announced for.
N	Voted against (nay).
X	Paired against.
−	Announced against.
P	Voted "present."
C	Voted "present" to avoid possible conflict of interest.
?	Did not vote or otherwise make a position known.

Democrats **Republicans** *Independent*

46. HR 1432. Trade with sub-Saharan Africa/Recommit. Bishop, D-Ga., motion to recommit the bill to the Ways and Means Committee with instructions to declare that the president should investigate, rather than develop, the establishment of a free trade area, and that the access program established by the president should be modeled on the program now in effect for the countries of the Caribbean. Motion rejected 193-224: R 66-157; D 126-67 (ND 98-44, SD 28-23); I 1-0. March 11, 1998.

47. HR 1432. Trade with sub-Saharan Africa/Passage. Passage of the bill to set a new trade and investment policy towards the countries of sub-Saharan Africa, including authorizing the president to grant duty-free treatment to, and requiring the development of, a plan to enter into one or more free trade agreements with eligible sub-Saharan African countries. The bill also would strengthen punishment against countries that attempt to illegally transship textile and apparel through sub-Saharan Africa to avoid U.S. quotas. Passed 233-186: R 141-84; D 92-101 (ND 68-74, SD 24-27); I 0-1. March 11, 1998. A "yea" was a vote in support of the president's position.

48. HR 2883. Government Performance and Results/Rule. Adoption of the rule (HRes 384) to provide for House floor consideration of the bill to require federal agencies to revise and resubmit to Congress, by the end of fiscal 1998, their "strategic plans" to outline their mission, general goals and objectives, and describe how those goals and objectives will be achieved. Adopted 412-0: R 218-0; D 193-0 (ND 141-0, SD 52-0); I 1-0. March 12, 1998.

49. Procedural Motion/Journal. Approval of the House Journal of Wednesday, March 11, 1998. Approved 368-43: R 205-14; D 162-29 (ND 118-22, SD 44-7); I 1-0. March 12, 1998.

50. HR 2883. Government Performance and Results/Passage. Passage of the bill to require federal agencies to revise and resubmit to Congress, by the end of fiscal 1998, their "strategic plans" to outline their mission, general goals and objectives, and describe how those goals and objectives will be achieved. The bill also requires agency inspectors general to annually audit agency performance reports and submit the results to Congress. Passed 242-168: R 221-0; D 21-167 (ND 10-127, SD 11-40); I 0-1. March 12, 1998.

51. HR 992. Private Property Rights/U.S. District Courts. Watt, D-N.C., amendment to grant the U.S. District Courts jurisdiction to determine all claims arising out of disputes over government seizure of private property. Rejected 206-206: R 36-185; D 169-21 (ND 128-10, SD 41-11); I 1-0. March 12, 1998.

52. HR 992. Private Property Rights/Passage. Passage of the bill to give landowners greater leeway in suing the federal government for disputes over government seizure of private property, by allowing such suits to be heard either in the U.S. District Court or the U.S. Court of Federal Claims. Passed 230-180: R 184-36; D 46-143 (ND 21-116, SD 25-27); I 0-1. March 12, 1998. A "nay" was a vote in support of the president's position.

	46	47	48	49	50	51	52
ALABAMA							
1 *Callahan*	Y	N	Y	Y	Y	N	Y
2 *Everett*	Y	N	Y	Y	Y	N	Y
3 *Riley*	Y	N	Y	Y	Y	N	Y
4 *Aderholt*	Y	N	Y	Y	Y	N	Y
5 Cramer	Y	N	Y	Y	Y	N	Y
6 *Bachus*	Y	N	Y	Y	Y	N	Y
7 Hilliard	N	Y	Y	N	N	Y	N
ALASKA							
AL *Young*	N	N	Y	Y	Y	N	Y
ARIZONA							
1 *Salmon*	N	Y	Y	Y	Y	N	Y
2 Pastor	Y	N	Y	Y	N	Y	N
3 *Stump*	Y	N	Y	Y	Y	N	Y
4 *Shadegg*	N	Y	Y	Y	Y	N	Y
5 *Kolbe*	N	Y	Y	Y	Y	Y	Y
6 *Hayworth*	Y	Y	Y	Y	Y	N	Y
ARKANSAS							
1 Berry	Y	N	Y	Y	N	N	Y
2 Snyder	N	Y	Y	Y	N	Y	N
3 *Hutchinson*	N	Y	Y	Y	?	N	Y
4 *Dickey*	N	Y	Y	Y	Y	N	Y
CALIFORNIA							
1 *Riggs*	N	Y	Y	Y	Y	N	Y
2 *Herger*	N	Y	Y	Y	Y	N	Y
3 Fazio	N	Y	Y	Y	N	N	Y
4 *Doolittle*	N	Y	Y	Y	Y	N	Y
5 Matsui	N	Y	Y	Y	N	N	N
6 Woolsey	Y	N	Y	Y	N	Y	N
7 Miller	Y	N	N	N	N	Y	N
8 Pelosi	Y	Y	Y	Y	N	Y	N
9 Vacant							
10 Tauscher	N	Y	Y	Y	N	Y	N
11 *Pombo*	N	Y	Y	Y	Y	N	Y
12 Lantos	Y	N	Y	Y	N	Y	N
13 Stark	Y	N	Y	N	N	Y	N
14 Eshoo	N	Y	Y	Y	N	Y	N
15 *Campbell*	N	Y	Y	Y	Y	Y	Y
16 Lofgren	N	Y	?	?	?	?	?
17 Farr	Y	N	Y	Y	N	Y	N
18 Condit	Y	N	Y	Y	N	N	Y
19 *Radanovich*	N	Y	Y	Y	Y	N	Y
20 Dooley	N	Y	Y	Y	N	Y	N
21 *Thomas*	N	Y	Y	Y	N	N	Y
23 *Gallegly*	N	Y	Y	Y	Y	N	Y
24 Sherman	N	Y	Y	Y	N	Y	N
25 *McKeon*	N	Y	Y	Y	Y	N	Y
26 Berman	N	Y	Y	?	?	?	?
27 *Rogan*	N	Y	Y	N	Y	N	Y
28 *Dreier*	N	Y	Y	Y	Y	N	Y
29 Waxman	N	Y	Y	Y	Y	N	N
30 Becerra	Y	Y	Y	N	N	Y	N
31 Martinez	Y	Y	Y	Y	N	N	Y
32 Dixon	N	Y	Y	Y	N	Y	N
33 Roybal-Allard	Y	N	Y	Y	N	Y	?
34 Torres	Y	N	Y	Y	N	Y	?
35 Waters	Y	Y	Y	N	N	Y	N
36 Harman	?	?	?	?	?	?	?
37 Millender-McD.	N	Y	Y	Y	Y	Y	Y
38 Horn	N	Y	Y	Y	Y	Y	Y

	46	47	48	49	50	51	52
39 *Royce*	N	Y	Y	Y	Y	N	Y
40 *Lewis*	N	Y	Y	Y	Y	N	Y
41 *Kim*	N	Y	Y	Y	Y	N	Y
42 Brown	Y	N	Y	N	?	?	?
43 *Calvert*	N	Y	Y	Y	Y	N	Y
44 Vacant							
45 *Rohrabacher*	Y	N	Y	Y	Y	N	Y
46 Sanchez	Y	?	?	?	?	?	?
47 *Cox*	N	Y	Y	Y	Y	N	Y
48 *Packard*	N	Y	Y	Y	Y	N	Y
49 *Bilbray*	N	Y	Y	Y	Y	Y	N
50 Filner	Y	N	Y	N	N	N	N
51 *Cunningham*	Y	N	Y	Y	Y	N	Y
52 *Hunter*	Y	N	Y	Y	Y	N	Y
COLORADO							
1 DeGette	N	Y	Y	Y	N	Y	N
2 Skaggs	N	Y	Y	Y	N	Y	N
3 *McInnis*	N	Y	Y	Y	N	N	Y
4 *Schaffer*	N	N	Y	Y	N	N	Y
5 *Hefley*	N	N	Y	N	Y	N	Y
6 *Schaefer*	N	N	Y	Y	?	Y	Y
CONNECTICUT							
1 Kennelly	Y	Y	Y	Y	N	Y	N
2 Gejdenson	Y	N	Y	Y	N	Y	N
3 DeLauro	Y	N	Y	Y	N	Y	N
4 *Shays*	N	Y	Y	Y	Y	Y	N
5 Maloney	Y	N	Y	Y	N	Y	N
6 *Johnson*	N	Y	?	?	Y	Y	N
DELAWARE							
AL *Castle*	N	Y	Y	Y	Y	Y	N
FLORIDA							
1 *Scarborough*	N	Y	Y	?	Y	N	Y
2 Boyd	Y	N	Y	N	Y	N	Y
3 Brown	N	Y	Y	Y	N	Y	N
4 *Fowler*	Y	N	Y	Y	Y	N	Y
5 Thurman	N	Y	Y	Y	Y	Y	Y
6 *Stearns*	N	Y	Y	Y	Y	N	Y
7 *Mica*	N	N	Y	Y	Y	N	Y
8 *McCollum*	N	Y	Y	Y	Y	N	Y
9 *Bilirakis*	N	N	Y	Y	Y	N	Y
10 *Young*	N	Y	Y	Y	Y	N	Y
11 Davis	N	Y	?	Y	N	Y	N
12 *Canady*	N	Y	Y	Y	Y	N	Y
13 *Miller*	N	Y	Y	Y	Y	N	N
14 *Goss*	N	Y	Y	Y	+	−	+
15 *Weldon*	N	Y	Y	Y	Y	N	Y
16 *Foley*	N	Y	Y	Y	Y	N	Y
17 Meek	N	Y	Y	N	Y	Y	N
18 *Ros-Lehtinen*	N	Y	Y	Y	Y	N	Y
19 Wexler	N	Y	Y	Y	Y	N	N
20 Deutsch	+	+	Y	Y	N	Y	N
21 *Diaz-Balart*	N	N	Y	Y	Y	N	Y
22 *Shaw*	N	Y	Y	Y	Y	N	Y
23 Hastings	N	Y	Y	N	N	Y	N
GEORGIA							
1 *Kingston*	Y	N	Y	Y	Y	N	Y
2 Bishop	Y	N	Y	Y	N	Y	Y
3 *Collins*	Y	N	Y	Y	Y	N	Y
4 McKinney	N	Y	Y	Y	N	Y	N
5 Lewis	Y	Y	Y	N	Y	N	N
6 *Gingrich*	Y						N
7 *Barr*	Y	N	Y	Y	Y	N	Y
8 *Chambliss*	Y	N	Y	Y	Y	N	Y
9 *Deal*	Y	N	Y	Y	Y	N	Y
10 *Norwood*	Y	N	Y	Y	Y	N	Y
11 *Linder*	N	Y	Y	Y	Y	N	Y
HAWAII							
1 Abercrombie	Y	N	Y	N	N	Y	N
2 Mink	Y	N	Y	N	N	Y	N
IDAHO							
1 *Chenoweth*	N	N	Y	Y	Y	N	Y
2 *Crapo*	N	N	Y	Y	Y	N	Y
ILLINOIS							
1 Rush	Y	N	Y	N	Y	N	N
2 Jackson	N	N	Y	Y	N	Y	N
3 Lipinski	N	N	Y	Y	N	N	Y
4 Gutierrez	N	Y	N	N	N	Y	N
5 Blagojevich	Y	Y	Y	Y	N	Y	Y
6 *Hyde*	N	Y	Y	Y	N	Y	Y
7 Davis	N	N	Y	N	N	Y	N
8 *Crane*	N	?	Y	Y	N	Y	N
9 Yates	Y	Y	Y	Y	N	Y	N
10 *Porter*	N	Y	Y	Y	N	Y	N
11 *Weller*	N	Y	Y	Y	N	Y	?
12 Costello	N	Y	Y	Y	N	Y	N
13 *Fawell*	N	Y	Y	Y	Y	N	Y

ND Northern Democrats   SD Southern Democrats

	46	47	48	49	50	51	52
14 ***Hastert***	N	Y	Y	Y	Y	?	Y
15 ***Ewing***	N	Y	Y	Y	Y	Y	Y
16 ***Manzullo***	N	Y	Y	Y	Y	N	Y
17 Evans	Y	N	Y	Y	N	Y	N
18 ***LaHood***	N	Y	Y	Y	Y	Y	Y
19 Poshard	?	?	?	?	?	?	?
20 ***Shimkus***	N	Y	Y	Y	Y	N	Y
INDIANA							
1 Visclosky	N	N	Y	N	N	Y	N
2 ***McIntosh***	Y	Y	Y	Y	Y	N	Y
3 Roemer	N	Y	Y	Y	N	N	Y
4 ***Souder***	N	N	?	Y	Y	N	Y
5 ***Buyer***	N	N	Y	Y	Y	N	Y
6 ***Burton***	Y	N	Y	Y	Y	N	Y
7 ***Pease***	N	Y	Y	Y	Y	N	Y
8 ***Hostettler***	N	N	Y	Y	Y	N	Y
9 Hamilton	N	Y	Y	Y	N	Y	N
10 Carson	Y	N	Y	Y	N	Y	N
IOWA							
1 ***Leach***	N	Y	Y	Y	Y	Y	N
2 ***Nussle***	N	Y	Y	N	Y	N	Y
3 Boswell	Y	Y	Y	Y	N	N	Y
4 ***Ganske***	Y	Y	Y	Y	Y	N	Y
5 ***Latham***	N	Y	Y	Y	Y	N	Y
KANSAS							
1 ***Moran***	Y	N	Y	N	Y	N	Y
2 ***Ryun***	N	Y	Y	Y	Y	N	Y
3 ***Snowbarger***	N	Y	Y	Y	Y	N	Y
4 ***Tiahrt***	N	Y	Y	Y	Y	N	Y
KENTUCKY							
1 ***Whitfield***	N	N	Y	Y	Y	N	Y
2 ***Lewis***	Y	N	Y	Y	Y	N	Y
3 ***Northup***	N	Y	Y	Y	Y	N	Y
4 ***Bunning***	Y	N	Y	Y	?	?	Y
5 ***Rogers***	Y	N	Y	Y	Y	N	Y
6 Baesler	Y	N	Y	Y	Y	Y	Y
LOUISIANA							
1 ***Livingston***	N	Y	?	?	Y	N	Y
2 Jefferson	N	Y	Y	Y	N	Y	N
3 ***Tauzin***	Y	Y	Y	Y	Y	N	Y
4 ***McCrery***	N	Y	Y	Y	Y	N	Y
5 ***Cooksey***	Y	N	Y	Y	Y	N	Y
6 ***Baker***	Y	Y	Y	Y	Y	N	Y
7 John	?	?	?	?	?	?	?
MAINE							
1 Allen	N	Y	Y	Y	N	Y	N
2 Baldacci	Y	N	Y	Y	N	Y	N
MARYLAND							
1 ***Gilchrest***	N	Y	Y	Y	Y	Y	N
2 ***Ehrlich***	N	Y	Y	Y	Y	N	Y
3 Cardin	Y	Y	Y	Y	N	Y	N
4 Wynn	N	Y	Y	Y	N	Y	N
5 Hoyer	N	Y	Y	Y	N	Y	N
6 ***Bartlett***	N	N	Y	Y	Y	N	Y
7 Cummings	N	Y	Y	P	–	Y	N
8 ***Morella***	N	Y	Y	Y	Y	Y	N
MASSACHUSETTS							
1 Olver	Y	N	Y	Y	N	Y	N
2 Neal	Y	Y	Y	Y	N	Y	N
3 McGovern	Y	N	Y	Y	N	Y	N
4 Frank	Y	N	Y	Y	N	Y	N
5 Meehan	Y	Y	Y	Y	N	Y	N
6 Tierney	Y	N	Y	Y	N	Y	N
7 Markey	Y	Y	Y	Y	N	Y	?
8 Kennedy	Y	Y	Y	Y	N	Y	N
9 Moakley	Y	N	Y	Y	N	Y	N
10 Delahunt	Y	N	Y	Y	N	Y	N
MICHIGAN							
1 Stupak	Y	N	Y	N	N	Y	N
2 ***Hoekstra***	N	Y	Y	Y	Y	N	Y
3 ***Ehlers***	N	Y	Y	Y	Y	Y	N
4 ***Camp***	N	Y	Y	Y	Y	N	Y
5 Barcia	Y	N	Y	Y	N	N	Y
6 ***Upton***	N	Y	Y	Y	Y	Y	N
7 ***Smith***	N	Y	Y	Y	Y	N	Y
8 Stabenow	+	Y	Y	Y	Y	Y	N
9 Kildee	Y	N	Y	Y	N	Y	N
10 Bonior	Y	N	Y	Y	N	Y	N
11 ***Knollenberg***	N	Y	Y	Y	Y	N	Y
12 Levin	N	Y	Y	Y	N	Y	N
13 Rivers	Y	Y	Y	Y	Y	Y	N
14 Conyers	Y	N	Y	Y	N	Y	N
15 Kilpatrick	N	Y	Y	Y	N	Y	N
16 Dingell	Y	N	Y	Y	N	Y	N

	46	47	48	49	50	51	52
MINNESOTA							
1 ***Gutknecht***	N	Y	Y	Y	Y	N	Y
2 Minge	N	Y	Y	Y	N	Y	Y
3 ***Ramstad***	N	Y	Y	N	Y	Y	N
4 Vento	Y	Y	Y	Y	N	Y	N
5 Sabo	N	Y	Y	N	N	Y	N
6 Luther	Y	Y	Y	Y	Y	Y	N
7 Peterson	Y	N	Y	N	N	N	Y
8 Oberstar	Y	N	Y	N	N	Y	N
MISSISSIPPI							
1 ***Wicker***	Y	N	Y	Y	Y	N	Y
2 Thompson	Y	N	Y	N	N	Y	N
3 ***Pickering***	Y	N	Y	Y	Y	N	Y
4 ***Parker***	N	Y	Y	Y	Y	N	?
5 Taylor	Y	N	Y	N	Y	N	Y
MISSOURI							
1 Clay	Y	N	Y	N	N	Y	N
2 ***Talent***	Y	N	Y	Y	Y	N	Y
3 Gephardt	Y	Y	Y	N	?	?	N
4 Skelton	Y	N	Y	Y	Y	Y	Y
5 McCarthy	Y	Y	Y	Y	Y	Y	N
6 Danner	Y	N	Y	Y	Y	N	Y
7 ***Blunt***	N	N	Y	Y	Y	N	Y
8 ***Emerson***	Y	N	Y	Y	Y	N	Y
9 ***Hulshof***	N	Y	Y	Y	Y	N	Y
MONTANA							
AL ***Hill***	N	Y	Y	Y	Y	N	Y
NEBRASKA							
1 ***Bereuter***	N	Y	Y	Y	Y	N	Y
2 ***Christensen***	N	Y	Y	Y	Y	N	Y
3 ***Barrett***	N	Y	Y	Y	Y	N	Y
NEVADA							
1 ***Ensign***	N	N	Y	N	Y	N	Y
2 ***Gibbons***	Y	N	Y	N	Y	N	Y
NEW HAMPSHIRE							
1 ***Sununu***	N	Y	Y	Y	Y	N	Y
2 ***Bass***	Y	Y	Y	Y	Y	Y	N
NEW JERSEY							
1 Andrews	Y	N	Y	Y	N	Y	N
2 ***LoBiondo***	N	N	Y	N	Y	Y	N
3 ***Saxton***	N	N	?	Y	Y	Y	N
4 ***Smith***	N	N	Y	Y	Y	Y	N
5 ***Roukema***	N	Y	Y	Y	Y	Y	N
6 Pallone	Y	N	Y	Y	N	Y	N
7 ***Franks***	N	Y	Y	Y	Y	N	N
8 Pascrell	Y	N	Y	N	N	Y	N
9 Rothman	N	Y	Y	Y	N	Y	N
10 Payne	N	Y	Y	Y	N	Y	N
11 ***Frelinghuysen***	N	Y	Y	Y	Y	Y	N
12 ***Pappas***	Y	N	Y	Y	Y	Y	N
13 Menendez	N	Y	Y	Y	N	Y	N
NEW MEXICO							
1 ***Schiff***	?	?	?	?	?	?	?
2 ***Skeen***	N	Y	Y	Y	Y	N	Y
3 ***Redmond***	–	+	+	+	+	–	+
NEW YORK							
1 ***Forbes***	Y	N	Y	Y	Y	Y	N
2 ***Lazio***	N	Y	Y	Y	Y	N	N
3 ***King***	N	Y	Y	Y	Y	N	Y
4 McCarthy	N	Y	Y	Y	N	Y	N
5 Ackerman	Y	Y	?	?	N	Y	N
6 Meeks	N	Y	Y	Y	N	Y	N
7 Manton	?	?	Y	N	N	Y	N
8 Nadler	Y	N	Y	Y	?	?	?
9 Schumer	?	?	?	Y	N	Y	N
10 Towns	N	Y	Y	Y	N	Y	N
11 Owens	N	Y	Y	Y	N	Y	N
12 Velázquez	Y	N	Y	Y	N	Y	N
13 ***Fossella***	N	Y	Y	Y	Y	N	Y
14 Maloney	Y	Y	Y	Y	N	Y	N
15 Rangel	N	Y	Y	Y	N	?	N
16 Serrano	Y	N	Y	Y	N	Y	N
17 Engel	Y	Y	Y	Y	N	Y	N
18 Lowey	N	Y	Y	Y	N	Y	N
19 ***Kelly***	N	Y	Y	Y	Y	Y	N
20 ***Gilman***	N	Y	Y	Y	Y	Y	N
21 McNulty	Y	Y	Y	Y	N	Y	N
22 ***Solomon***	?	N	Y	Y	Y	N	Y
23 ***Boehlert***	N	Y	Y	Y	Y	Y	N
24 ***McHugh***	Y	N	?	?	Y	N	Y
25 ***Walsh***	N	N	Y	Y	Y	Y	N
26 Hinchey	Y	Y	Y	N	N	Y	N
27 ***Paxon***	N	Y	Y	Y	Y	N	Y
28 Slaughter	Y	N	Y	Y	N	Y	N
29 LaFalce	Y	N	Y	Y	N	Y	N

	46	47	48	49	50	51	52
30 ***Quinn***	N	N	Y	Y	Y	N	N
31 ***Houghton***	N	Y	Y	Y	Y	N	Y
NORTH CAROLINA							
1 Clayton	Y	N	Y	Y	N	Y	N
2 Etheridge	Y	N	Y	Y	N	Y	N
3 ***Jones***	Y	N	Y	Y	Y	N	Y
4 Price	Y	N	Y	Y	N	Y	N
5 ***Burr***	Y	N	Y	Y	Y	N	Y
6 ***Coble***	Y	N	Y	Y	Y	N	Y
7 McIntyre	Y	N	Y	Y	Y	Y	Y
8 Hefner	Y	N	Y	Y	N	Y	N
9 ***Myrick***	Y	N	Y	Y	Y	N	Y
10 ***Ballenger***	Y	N	Y	Y	Y	N	Y
11 ***Taylor***	N	N	Y	Y	Y	N	Y
12 Watt	Y	N	Y	Y	N	Y	N
NORTH DAKOTA							
AL Pomeroy	Y	Y	Y	Y	N	Y	N
OHIO							
1 ***Chabot***	N	Y	Y	Y	Y	N	Y
2 ***Portman***	N	Y	Y	Y	Y	N	N
3 Hall	N	Y	Y	Y	Y	Y	Y
4 ***Oxley***	N	Y	Y	Y	Y	N	Y
5 ***Gillmor***	N	Y	Y	N	Y	N	Y
6 Strickland	Y	N	Y	Y	N	Y	N
7 ***Hobson***	N	Y	Y	Y	Y	N	Y
8 ***Boehner***	N	Y	Y	Y	Y	N	Y
9 Kaptur	Y	N	Y	Y	N	Y	N
10 Kucinich	Y	N	Y	N	N	Y	N
11 Stokes	Y	N	Y	Y	N	Y	N
12 ***Kasich***	N	Y	Y	Y	Y	N	Y
13 Brown	Y	N	Y	Y	N	Y	N
14 Sawyer	Y	Y	Y	Y	N	Y	N
15 ***Pryce***	N	Y	Y	Y	Y	N	Y
16 ***Regula***	N	Y	Y	Y	Y	N	N
17 Traficant	Y	N	Y	Y	Y	N	Y
18 ***Ney***	Y	N	Y	Y	Y	N	Y
19 ***LaTourette***	N	Y	Y	Y	Y	N	N
OKLAHOMA							
1 ***Largent***	Y	Y	Y	Y	Y	N	Y
2 ***Coburn***	Y	N	Y	Y	Y	N	Y
3 ***Watkins***	Y	Y	Y	Y	Y	N	Y
4 ***Watts***	Y	Y	Y	Y	Y	N	Y
5 ***Istook***	N	Y	Y	Y	Y	N	Y
6 ***Lucas***	Y	N	Y	Y	Y	N	Y
OREGON							
1 Furse	?	?	?	?	?	?	?
2 ***Smith***	N	N	Y	Y	Y	N	Y
3 Blumenauer	N	Y	Y	Y	N	Y	N
4 DeFazio	Y	N	Y	N	N	Y	N
5 Hooley	N	Y	Y	Y	N	Y	N
PENNSYLVANIA							
1 Vacant							
2 Fattah	N	Y	Y	Y	N	Y	N
3 Borski	Y	N	Y	N	N	Y	N
4 Klink	Y	N	Y	Y	N	Y	N
5 ***Peterson***	N	Y	Y	Y	Y	N	Y
6 Holden	Y	N	Y	Y	N	Y	Y
7 ***Weldon***	N	N	Y	Y	Y	Y	N
8 ***Greenwood***	N	N	Y	Y	Y	Y	N
9 ***Shuster***	N	Y	Y	Y	Y	N	Y
10 ***McDade***	Y	Y	Y	Y	Y	N	Y
11 Kanjorski	Y	N	Y	Y	N	Y	N
12 Murtha	Y	N	Y	?	N	Y	N
13 ***Fox***	N	Y	Y	N	Y	Y	N
14 Coyne	Y	Y	Y	Y	N	Y	N
15 McHale	Y	N	Y	Y	N	Y	N
16 ***Pitts***	N	Y	Y	Y	Y	N	Y
17 ***Gekas***	N	Y	Y	Y	Y	N	Y
18 Doyle	Y	N	Y	Y	?	Y	Y
19 ***Goodling***	Y	N	Y	Y	Y	N	Y
20 Mascara	Y	N	Y	Y	N	Y	Y
21 ***English***	N	Y	Y	N	Y	N	Y
RHODE ISLAND							
1 Kennedy	Y	N	Y	Y	N	Y	N
2 Weygand	Y	N	Y	Y	N	Y	Y
SOUTH CAROLINA							
1 ***Sanford***	Y	N	Y	Y	Y	Y	N
2 ***Spence***	Y	N	Y	Y	Y	N	Y
3 ***Graham***	Y	N	Y	Y	Y	N	Y
4 ***Inglis***	Y	N	Y	Y	Y	Y	N
5 Spratt	Y	N	Y	Y	N	Y	N
6 Clyburn	Y	N	Y	N	N	Y	N
SOUTH DAKOTA							
AL ***Thune***	N	Y	Y	Y	Y	N	Y

	46	47	48	49	50	51	52
TENNESSEE							
1 ***Jenkins***	Y	N	Y	Y	Y	N	Y
2 ***Duncan***	Y	N	Y	Y	Y	N	Y
3 ***Wamp***	Y	N	Y	Y	Y	N	Y
4 ***Hilleary***	Y	N	Y	N	Y	N	Y
5 Clement	Y	N	Y	Y	N	N	Y
6 Gordon	Y	N	Y	Y	N	Y	Y
7 ***Bryant***	Y	N	Y	Y	Y	N	Y
8 Tanner	Y	N	?	?	?	?	?
9 Ford	N	Y	Y	Y	N	Y	Y
TEXAS							
1 Sandlin	N	Y	Y	Y	N	Y	Y
2 Turner	N	Y	Y	Y	N	N	Y
3 ***Johnson, Sam***	N	Y	Y	Y	Y	N	Y
4 Hall	Y	N	Y	Y	Y	N	Y
5 ***Sessions***	N	Y	Y	N	Y	N	Y
6 ***Barton***	N	Y	Y	Y	Y	N	Y
7 ***Archer***	N	Y	Y	Y	Y	N	Y
8 ***Brady***	N	Y	Y	Y	Y	N	Y
9 Lampson	N	Y	Y	Y	N	Y	N
10 Doggett	N	Y	Y	Y	Y	Y	N
11 Edwards	N	Y	Y	Y	N	N	Y
12 ***Granger***	N	Y	Y	Y	Y	N	Y
13 ***Thornberry***	Y	N	Y	Y	Y	N	Y
14 ***Paul***	N	N	Y	Y	Y	N	Y
15 Hinojosa	N	Y	Y	Y	–	Y	Y
16 Reyes	Y	N	Y	Y	N	Y	Y
17 Stenholm	Y	N	Y	Y	Y	N	Y
18 Jackson-Lee	N	Y	Y	Y	N	Y	N
19 ***Combest***	Y	N	Y	Y	Y	N	Y
20 Gonzalez	?	?	?	?	?	?	?
21 ***Smith***	N	Y	Y	Y	Y	N	Y
22 ***DeLay***	N	Y	Y	Y	Y	N	Y
23 ***Bonilla***	Y	N	Y	Y	Y	N	Y
24 Frost	N	Y	Y	Y	N	Y	Y
25 Bentsen	N	Y	Y	Y	N	Y	N
26 ***Armey***	N	Y	Y	Y	Y	N	Y
27 Ortiz	Y	N	Y	Y	N	Y	Y
28 Rodriguez	?	?	Y	Y	N	Y	N
29 Green	Y	N	Y	Y	Y	Y	Y
30 Johnson, E.B.	N	Y	Y	Y	N	Y	N
UTAH							
1 ***Hansen***	N	Y	Y	Y	Y	N	Y
2 ***Cook***	N	Y	Y	Y	Y	N	Y
3 ***Cannon***	N	Y	Y	Y	Y	N	Y
VERMONT							
AL *Sanders*	Y	N	Y	Y	N	Y	N
VIRGINIA							
1 ***Bateman***	N	Y	Y	Y	Y	N	Y
2 Pickett	Y	N	Y	N	Y	N	Y
3 Scott	N	Y	Y	Y	N	Y	N
4 Sisisky	Y	N	Y	Y	Y	N	Y
5 Goode	Y	N	Y	Y	Y	N	Y
6 ***Goodlatte***	Y	Y	Y	Y	Y	N	Y
7 ***Bliley***	N	Y	Y	Y	Y	N	Y
8 Moran	N	Y	Y	Y	N	Y	N
9 Boucher	Y	N	Y	Y	N	Y	N
10 ***Wolf***	N	Y	Y	Y	Y	N	Y
11 ***Davis***	N	Y	Y	Y	Y	N	Y
WASHINGTON							
1 ***White***	N	Y	Y	Y	Y	N	Y
2 ***Metcalf***	N	N	Y	Y	Y	N	Y
3 ***Smith, Linda***	N	Y	Y	Y	Y	N	Y
4 ***Hastings***	N	Y	Y	Y	Y	N	Y
5 ***Nethercutt***	N	Y	Y	Y	Y	N	Y
6 Dicks	N	Y	Y	Y	N	Y	N
7 McDermott	N	Y	Y	Y	N	Y	N
8 ***Dunn***	N	Y	Y	Y	Y	N	Y
9 Smith, Adam	N	Y	Y	Y	N	Y	N
WEST VIRGINIA							
1 Mollohan	Y	N	Y	Y	N	Y	N
2 Wise	N	Y	Y	Y	N	Y	N
3 Rahall	Y	N	Y	Y	N	Y	N
WISCONSIN							
1 ***Neumann***	N	N	Y	Y	Y	N	Y
2 ***Klug***	N	Y	Y	Y	Y	Y	N
3 Kind	N	Y	Y	Y	N	Y	Y
4 Kleczka	Y	N	Y	Y	N	Y	N
5 Barrett	Y	Y	Y	Y	Y	Y	N
6 ***Petri***	N	Y	Y	Y	Y	N	Y
7 Obey	Y	N	Y	Y	N	Y	N
8 Johnson	Y	N	Y	Y	N	Y	N
9 ***Sensenbrenner***	N	N	Y	Y	Y	N	Y
WYOMING							
AL ***Cubin***	N	Y	Y	Y	Y	N	Y

Southern states - Ala., Ark., Fla., Ga., Ky., La., Miss., N.C., Okla., S.C., Tenn., Texas, Va.

53. Procedural Motion/Journal. Approval of the House Journal of Monday, March 16, 1998. Approved 359-38: R 194-15; D 164-23 (ND 121-13, SD 43-10); I 1-0. March 17, 1998.

54. H Res 364. Human Rights in China/Passage. Smith, R-N.J., motion to suspend the rules and adopt the resolution to urge President Clinton to initiate a resolution in the United Nations to condemn human rights violations in China. Motion agreed to 397-0: R 209-0; D 187-0 (ND 134-0, SD 53-0); I 1-0. March 17, 1998. A two-thirds majority of those present and voting (265 in this case) is required for adoption under suspension of the rules.

55. H Res 361. Human Rights in Cambodia/Passage. Bereuter, R-Neb., motion to suspend the rules and adopt the resolution to call upon the government in Cambodia to enforce the rule of law, protect human rights, and allow exiled opposition leaders to return to with full political rights. Motion agreed to 393-1: R 205-1; D 187-0 (ND 134-0, SD 53-0); I 1-0. March 17, 1998. A two-thirds majority of those present and voting (263 in this case) is required for adoption under suspension of the rules.

56. H Con Res 152. Northern Ireland Peace Talks/Passage. Smith, R-N.J., motion to suspend the rules and adopt the resolution to call on all parties in the Northern Ireland peace talks to condemn violence and address outstanding human rights violations as part of the peace process. Motion agreed to 407-2: R 213-2; D 193-0 (ND 141-0, SD 52-0); I 1-0. March 18, 1998. A two-thirds majority of those present and voting (274 in this case) is required for adoption under suspension of the rules.

57. H Con Res 235. Violence in Kosovo/Passage. Gilman, R-N.Y., motion to suspend the rules and adopt the resolution to condemn violence against ethnic Albanians in Kosovo by Serbian authorities, and call for a dialogue between the Serbian government and the leaders of the ethnic Albanians in Kosovo to end the violence by all parties. Motion agreed to 406-1: R 211-1; D 194-0 (ND 142-0, SD 52-0); I 1-0. March 18, 1998. A two-thirds majority of those present and voting (272 in this case) is required for adoption under suspension of the rules.

58. H Con Res 227. Withdrawal of U.S. Forces from Bosnia/Adoption. Adoption of the concurrent resolution to invoke the authority granted by the War Powers Resolution of 1973 to direct the president to remove U.S. armed forces from the Republic of Bosnia and Herzegovina within 60 days after a final court judgment is entered determining the constitutional validity of the concurrent resolution, unless a declaration of war or specific authorization for such use of U.S. armed forces has been enacted. Rejected 193-225: R 180-43; D 13-181 (ND 10-131, SD 3-50); I 0-1. March 18, 1998. A "nay" was a vote in support of the president's position.

59. HR 2870. Tropical Forest Conservation/Rule. Adoption of the rule (H Res 388) to provide for floor consideration of the bill to authorize the president to forgive or reduce debts of developing countries to the United States in exchange for protection of tropical forests in those countries. Adopted 411-0: R 216-0; D 194-0 (ND 143-0, SD 51-0); I 1-0. March 19, 1998.

---

[1] Lois Capps, D-Calif., was sworn in March 17, replacing Walter Capps, D. Calif., who died Oct. 28, 1997.

Key

Y	Voted for (yea).
#	Paired for.
+	Announced for.
N	Voted against (nay).
X	Paired against.
−	Announced against.
P	Voted "present."
C	Voted "present" to avoid possible conflict of interest.
?	Did not vote or otherwise make a position known.

Democrats **Republicans**
Independent

	53	54	55	56	57	58	59
ALABAMA							
1 *Callahan*	Y	Y	Y	Y	Y	N	Y
2 *Everett*	Y	Y	Y	Y	Y	Y	Y
3 *Riley*	Y	Y	Y	Y	Y	Y	Y
4 *Aderholt*	Y	Y	Y	Y	Y	Y	Y
5 Cramer	Y	Y	Y	Y	Y	N	Y
6 *Bachus*	Y	Y	Y	Y	Y	Y	Y
7 Hilliard	N	Y	Y	Y	Y	N	Y
ALASKA							
AL *Young*	Y	Y	Y	Y	Y	N	?
ARIZONA							
1 *Salmon*	?	?	?	Y	Y	Y	Y
2 Pastor	Y	Y	Y	Y	Y	N	Y
3 *Stump*	Y	Y	Y	Y	Y	Y	Y
4 *Shadegg*	Y	Y	Y	Y	Y	N	Y
5 *Kolbe*	Y	Y	Y	Y	Y	N	Y
6 *Hayworth*	Y	Y	Y	Y	Y	Y	Y
ARKANSAS							
1 Berry	Y	Y	Y	Y	Y	N	Y
2 Snyder	Y	Y	Y	Y	Y	N	Y
3 *Hutchinson*	Y	Y	?	Y	Y	Y	Y
4 *Dickey*	N	Y	Y	Y	?	Y	Y
CALIFORNIA							
1 *Riggs*	Y	Y	Y	Y	Y	Y	?
2 *Herger*	Y	Y	?	Y	Y	Y	Y
3 Fazio	N	Y	Y	Y	Y	N	Y
4 *Doolittle*	?	Y	Y	?	Y	Y	Y
5 Matsui	Y	Y	Y	Y	Y	N	Y
6 Woolsey	Y	Y	Y	Y	Y	N	Y
7 Miller	Y	Y	Y	Y	Y	N	Y
8 Pelosi	Y	Y	Y	Y	Y	N	Y
9 Vacant							
10 Tauscher	Y	Y	Y	Y	Y	N	Y
11 *Pombo*	Y	Y	Y	Y	Y	N	Y
12 Lantos	Y	Y	Y	Y	Y	N	Y
13 Stark	Y	Y	Y	Y	Y	N	Y
14 Eshoo	Y	Y	Y	Y	Y	N	Y
15 *Campbell*	Y	Y	Y	Y	Y	Y	Y
16 Lofgren	Y	Y	Y	Y	Y	N	Y
17 Farr	Y	Y	Y	Y	Y	N	Y
18 Condit	Y	Y	Y	Y	Y	N	Y
19 *Radanovich*	Y	Y	Y	Y	Y	Y	Y
20 Dooley	Y	Y	Y	Y	Y	N	Y
21 *Thomas*	Y	Y	Y	Y	Y	Y	Y
22 Capps, L.[1]	Y	Y	Y	Y	Y	N	Y
23 *Gallegly*	Y	Y	Y	Y	Y	Y	?
24 Sherman	Y	Y	Y	Y	Y	N	Y
25 *McKeon*	Y	Y	Y	Y	Y	Y	Y
26 Berman	Y	Y	Y	Y	Y	N	Y
27 *Rogan*	N	Y	Y	Y	Y	N	Y
28 *Dreier*	Y	Y	Y	Y	Y	Y	Y
29 Waxman	Y	Y	Y	Y	Y	N	Y
30 Becerra	Y	Y	Y	Y	Y	N	Y
31 Martinez	?	?	?	?	?	?	?
32 Dixon	Y	Y	Y	Y	Y	N	Y
33 Roybal-Allard	Y	Y	Y	Y	Y	N	Y
34 Torres	Y	Y	Y	Y	Y	N	Y
35 Waters	N	Y	Y	?	Y	N	Y
36 Harman	Y	Y	Y	Y	Y	N	Y
37 Millender-McD.	Y	Y	Y	Y	Y	N	Y

	53	54	55	56	57	58	59
38 *Horn*	Y	Y	Y	Y	Y	N	Y
39 *Royce*	Y	Y	Y	Y	Y	Y	Y
40 *Lewis*	Y	Y	Y	Y	Y	N	Y
41 *Kim*	Y	Y	Y	Y	Y	N	Y
42 Brown	N	Y	Y	Y	Y	N	Y
43 *Calvert*	Y	Y	Y	Y	Y	Y	Y
44 Vacant							
45 *Rohrabacher*	Y	Y	Y	Y	Y	Y	Y
46 Sanchez	Y	Y	Y	Y	Y	N	Y
47 *Cox*	Y	Y	Y	Y	Y	N	Y
48 *Packard*	Y	Y	Y	Y	Y	Y	Y
49 *Bilbray*	?	?	?	Y	?	Y	Y
50 Filner	N	Y	Y	Y	Y	N	Y
51 *Cunningham*	Y	Y	Y	Y	Y	Y	?
52 *Hunter*	?	?	?	Y	Y	N	Y
COLORADO							
1 DeGette	Y	Y	Y	Y	Y	N	Y
2 Skaggs	Y	Y	Y	Y	Y	N	Y
3 *McInnis*	?	?	Y	Y	Y	Y	Y
4 *Schaffer*	N	Y	Y	Y	Y	Y	Y
5 *Hefley*	N	Y	Y	Y	Y	Y	Y
6 *Schaefer*	Y	Y	Y	Y	Y	Y	Y
CONNECTICUT							
1 Kennelly	Y	Y	Y	Y	Y	N	Y
2 Gejdenson	Y	Y	Y	Y	Y	N	Y
3 DeLauro	Y	Y	Y	Y	Y	N	Y
4 *Shays*	Y	Y	Y	Y	Y	Y	Y
5 Maloney	Y	Y	Y	Y	Y	N	Y
6 *Johnson*	Y	Y	Y	Y	Y	Y	Y
DELAWARE							
AL *Castle*	Y	Y	Y	Y	Y	N	Y
FLORIDA							
1 *Scarborough*	Y	Y	Y	Y	+	Y	Y
2 Boyd	Y	Y	Y	Y	Y	N	Y
3 Brown	Y	Y	Y	Y	Y	N	Y
4 *Fowler*	Y	Y	Y	Y	Y	N	Y
5 Thurman	Y	Y	Y	Y	Y	N	Y
6 *Stearns*	Y	Y	Y	Y	Y	Y	Y
7 *Mica*	Y	Y	Y	Y	Y	Y	Y
8 *McCollum*	Y	Y	Y	Y	Y	Y	Y
9 *Bilirakis*	Y	Y	Y	Y	Y	Y	Y
10 *Young*	Y	Y	Y	Y	Y	N	Y
11 Davis	Y	Y	Y	Y	Y	N	Y
12 *Canady*	Y	Y	Y	Y	Y	Y	Y
13 *Miller*	Y	Y	Y	Y	Y	Y	Y
14 *Goss*	Y	Y	Y	Y	Y	Y	Y
15 *Weldon*	Y	Y	Y	Y	Y	Y	Y
16 *Foley*	Y	Y	Y	Y	Y	Y	Y
17 Meek	Y	Y	Y	Y	Y	N	Y
18 *Ros-Lehtinen*	Y	Y	Y	Y	Y	Y	Y
19 Wexler	Y	Y	Y	Y	Y	N	Y
20 Deutsch	Y	Y	Y	Y	Y	N	Y
21 *Diaz-Balart*	?	+	+	Y	Y	N	Y
22 *Shaw*	Y	Y	Y	Y	Y	Y	Y
23 Hastings	N	Y	Y	Y	Y	N	Y
GEORGIA							
1 *Kingston*	Y	Y	Y	Y	Y	N	Y
2 Bishop	Y	Y	Y	Y	Y	N	Y
3 *Collins*	Y	?	?	Y	Y	Y	Y
4 McKinney	Y	Y	Y	Y	Y	N	Y
5 Lewis	N	Y	Y	Y	N	Y	?
6 *Gingrich*							
7 *Barr*	Y	Y	Y	P	P	Y	Y
8 *Chambliss*	Y	Y	Y	Y	Y	N	Y
9 *Deal*	Y	Y	Y	Y	Y	Y	Y
10 *Norwood*	Y	Y	Y	Y	Y	Y	Y
11 *Linder*	Y	Y	Y	Y	Y	Y	Y
HAWAII							
1 Abercrombie	Y	Y	Y	Y	Y	N	Y
2 Mink	Y	Y	Y	Y	Y	N	Y
IDAHO							
1 *Chenoweth*	Y	Y	Y	Y	Y	N	Y
2 *Crapo*	Y	Y	Y	Y	Y	Y	Y
ILLINOIS							
1 Rush	?	?	?	Y	N	N	Y
2 Jackson	Y	Y	Y	Y	Y	N	Y
3 Lipinski	?	?	?	?	?	?	Y
4 Gutierrez	?	?	?	?	?	?	Y
5 Blagojevich	?	?	?	?	?	?	Y
6 *Hyde*	Y	Y	Y	Y	Y	Y	?
7 Davis	?	?	?	?	?	?	Y
8 *Crane*	?	+	?	?	Y	Y	?
9 Yates	?	?	?	Y	N	Y	?
10 *Porter*	Y	Y	?	Y	Y	Y	Y
11 *Weller*	Y	Y	Y	Y	Y	Y	Y
12 Costello	?	?	Y	Y	Y	N	Y

ND Northern Democrats   SD Southern Democrats

	53	54	55	56	57	58	59
13 ***Fawell***	?	?	?	Y	?	N	Y
14 ***Hastert***	+	+	+	Y	Y	Y	Y
15 ***Ewing***	Y	Y	Y	?	Y	Y	Y
16 ***Manzullo***	Y	Y	Y	Y	Y	Y	Y
17 Evans	Y	Y	Y	Y	Y	N	Y
18 ***LaHood***	Y	Y	Y	Y	Y	Y	Y
19 Poshard	?	?	?	?	?	?	?
20 ***Shimkus***	Y	Y	Y	Y	Y	Y	Y
INDIANA							
1 Visclosky	N	Y	Y	Y	Y	N	Y
2 ***McIntosh***	Y	Y	Y	?	Y	Y	Y
3 Roemer	Y	Y	Y	Y	Y	N	Y
4 ***Souder***	Y	Y	Y	Y	Y	Y	Y
5 ***Buyer***	Y	Y	Y	Y	Y	N	Y
6 ***Burton***	Y	Y	Y	Y	Y	Y	Y
7 ***Pease***	Y	Y	Y	Y	Y	Y	Y
8 ***Hostettler***	Y	Y	Y	Y	Y	N	Y
9 Hamilton	Y	Y	Y	Y	Y	N	Y
10 Carson	Y	Y	Y	Y	Y	N	Y
IOWA							
1 ***Leach***	Y	Y	Y	Y	Y	N	Y
2 ***Nussle***	Y	Y	Y	Y	Y	Y	Y
3 Boswell	Y	Y	Y	Y	Y	N	Y
4 ***Ganske***	Y	Y	Y	Y	Y	Y	Y
5 ***Latham***	Y	Y	Y	Y	Y	Y	Y
KANSAS							
1 ***Moran***	N	Y	Y	Y	Y	Y	Y
2 ***Ryun***	Y	Y	Y	Y	Y	Y	Y
3 ***Snowbarger***	Y	Y	Y	Y	Y	Y	Y
4 ***Tiahrt***	Y	Y	Y	Y	Y	N	Y
KENTUCKY							
1 ***Whitfield***	Y	Y	Y	Y	Y	Y	Y
2 ***Lewis***	Y	Y	Y	Y	Y	Y	Y
3 ***Northup***	Y	Y	Y	Y	Y	N	Y
4 ***Bunning***	Y	Y	Y	Y	Y	Y	Y
5 ***Rogers***	Y	Y	Y	Y	Y	Y	Y
6 Baesler	Y	Y	Y	Y	Y	N	Y
LOUISIANA							
1 ***Livingston***	Y	Y	Y	Y	Y	Y	?
2 Jefferson	N	Y	Y	Y	Y	N	Y
3 ***Tauzin***	Y	Y	Y	Y	Y	Y	Y
4 ***McCrery***	Y	Y	Y	Y	Y	Y	Y
5 ***Cooksey***	Y	Y	Y	Y	Y	Y	Y
6 ***Baker***	Y	Y	Y	Y	Y	Y	Y
7 John	Y	Y	Y	Y	Y	N	Y
MAINE							
1 Allen	Y	Y	Y	Y	Y	N	Y
2 Baldacci	Y	Y	Y	Y	Y	N	Y
MARYLAND							
1 ***Gilchrest***	Y	Y	Y	Y	Y	N	Y
2 ***Ehrlich***	Y	Y	Y	Y	Y	Y	Y
3 Cardin	Y	Y	Y	Y	Y	N	Y
4 Wynn	Y	Y	Y	Y	Y	N	Y
5 Hoyer	Y	Y	Y	Y	Y	N	Y
6 ***Bartlett***	Y	Y	Y	Y	Y	Y	Y
7 Cummings	Y	Y	Y	Y	Y	N	Y
8 ***Morella***	Y	Y	Y	Y	Y	N	Y
MASSACHUSETTS							
1 Olver	Y	Y	Y	Y	Y	N	Y
2 Neal	Y	Y	Y	Y	Y	N	Y
3 McGovern	Y	Y	Y	Y	Y	N	Y
4 Frank	Y	Y	Y	Y	Y	Y	Y
5 Meehan	Y	Y	Y	Y	Y	N	Y
6 Tierney	Y	Y	Y	Y	Y	?	Y
7 Markey	Y	Y	Y	Y	Y	Y	Y
8 Kennedy	?	?	?	Y	Y	N	Y
9 Moakley	?	?	?	Y	Y	N	Y
10 Delahunt	Y	Y	Y	Y	Y	N	Y
MICHIGAN							
1 Stupak	?	?	?	?	?	?	Y
2 ***Hoekstra***	Y	Y	Y	Y	Y	Y	Y
3 ***Ehlers***	Y	Y	Y	Y	Y	Y	Y
4 ***Camp***	Y	Y	Y	Y	Y	Y	Y
5 Barcia	Y	Y	Y	Y	Y	N	Y
6 ***Upton***	Y	Y	Y	Y	Y	Y	Y
7 ***Smith***	Y	Y	Y	Y	Y	Y	Y
8 Stabenow	Y	Y	Y	Y	Y	N	Y
9 Kildee	Y	Y	Y	Y	Y	N	Y
10 Bonior	Y	Y	Y	Y	Y	N	Y
11 ***Knollenberg***	Y	Y	Y	Y	Y	N	Y
12 Levin	Y	Y	Y	Y	Y	N	Y
13 Rivers	Y	Y	Y	Y	Y	N	Y
14 Conyers	Y	Y	Y	Y	Y	N	Y
15 Kilpatrick	Y	Y	Y	Y	Y	N	Y
16 Dingell	Y	Y	Y	Y	Y	N	Y

	53	54	55	56	57	58	59
MINNESOTA							
1 ***Gutknecht***	Y	Y	Y	Y	Y	Y	?
2 Minge	Y	Y	Y	Y	Y	N	Y
3 ***Ramstad***	N	Y	Y	Y	Y	Y	Y
4 Vento	Y	Y	Y	Y	Y	N	Y
5 Sabo	N	Y	Y	Y	Y	N	Y
6 Luther	Y	Y	Y	Y	Y	N	Y
7 Peterson	Y	Y	Y	Y	Y	Y	Y
8 Oberstar	N	Y	Y	Y	Y	N	Y
MISSISSIPPI							
1 ***Wicker***	Y	Y	Y	Y	Y	N	Y
2 Thompson	N	Y	Y	Y	Y	N	Y
3 ***Pickering***	?	Y	Y	Y	Y	Y	Y
4 ***Parker***	?	?	?	?	?	?	?
5 Taylor	N	Y	Y	Y	Y	N	Y
MISSOURI							
1 Clay	N	Y	Y	Y	Y	N	Y
2 ***Talent***	Y	Y	Y	Y	Y	Y	Y
3 Gephardt	Y	Y	Y	?	?	?	?
4 Skelton	Y	Y	Y	Y	Y	N	Y
5 McCarthy	Y	Y	Y	Y	Y	N	Y
6 Danner	Y	Y	Y	Y	Y	Y	Y
7 ***Blunt***	Y	Y	Y	Y	Y	Y	Y
8 ***Emerson***	Y	Y	Y	Y	Y	Y	Y
9 ***Hulshof***	Y	Y	Y	Y	Y	Y	Y
MONTANA							
AL ***Hill***	Y	Y	Y	Y	Y	Y	Y
NEBRASKA							
1 ***Bereuter***	Y	Y	Y	Y	Y	Y	Y
2 ***Christensen***	Y	Y	Y	Y	Y	Y	Y
3 ***Barrett***	Y	Y	Y	Y	Y	Y	Y
NEVADA							
1 ***Ensign***	N	Y	Y	Y	Y	Y	Y
2 ***Gibbons***	Y	Y	Y	Y	Y	Y	Y
NEW HAMPSHIRE							
1 ***Sununu***	Y	Y	Y	Y	Y	Y	Y
2 ***Bass***	Y	Y	Y	Y	Y	Y	Y
NEW JERSEY							
1 Andrews	?	?	?	Y	Y	N	Y
2 ***LoBiondo***	N	Y	Y	Y	Y	Y	Y
3 ***Saxton***	Y	Y	Y	Y	Y	Y	Y
4 ***Smith***	Y	Y	Y	Y	Y	N	Y
5 ***Roukema***	Y	Y	Y	Y	Y	Y	Y
6 Pallone	Y	Y	Y	Y	Y	N	Y
7 ***Franks***	Y	Y	Y	Y	Y	Y	Y
8 Pascrell	Y	Y	Y	Y	Y	N	Y
9 Rothman	Y	Y	Y	Y	Y	N	Y
10 Payne	Y	Y	Y	Y	Y	N	Y
11 ***Frelinghuysen***	Y	Y	Y	Y	Y	Y	Y
12 ***Pappas***	Y	Y	Y	Y	Y	Y	Y
13 Menendez	Y	Y	Y	Y	Y	N	Y
NEW MEXICO							
1 ***Schiff***	?	?	?	?	?	?	?
2 ***Skeen***	Y	Y	Y	Y	Y	Y	Y
3 ***Redmond***	Y	Y	Y	Y	Y	Y	Y
NEW YORK							
1 ***Forbes***	Y	Y	Y	Y	Y	Y	Y
2 ***Lazio***	Y	Y	Y	Y	Y	N	Y
3 ***King***	Y	Y	Y	Y	Y	Y	Y
4 McCarthy	Y	Y	Y	Y	Y	N	Y
5 Ackerman	Y	Y	Y	Y	Y	N	Y
6 Meeks	Y	Y	Y	Y	Y	N	Y
7 Manton	Y	Y	Y	Y	Y	N	Y
8 Nadler	Y	Y	Y	Y	Y	N	Y
9 Schumer	Y	Y	Y	Y	Y	N	Y
10 Towns	Y	Y	Y	Y	Y	N	Y
11 Owens	Y	Y	Y	Y	Y	N	Y
12 Velázquez	Y	Y	Y	Y	Y	N	Y
13 ***Fossella***	Y	Y	Y	Y	Y	Y	Y
14 Maloney	Y	Y	Y	Y	Y	N	Y
15 Rangel	Y	Y	Y	Y	Y	N	?
16 Serrano	Y	Y	Y	Y	Y	N	Y
17 Engel	Y	Y	Y	Y	Y	N	?
18 Lowey	Y	Y	Y	Y	Y	N	Y
19 ***Kelly***	Y	Y	Y	Y	Y	Y	Y
20 ***Gilman***	Y	Y	Y	Y	Y	N	Y
21 McNulty	+	+	+	Y	Y	N	Y
22 ***Solomon***	Y	Y	Y	Y	Y	N	Y
23 ***Boehlert***	Y	Y	Y	Y	Y	N	Y
24 ***McHugh***	Y	Y	Y	Y	Y	Y	Y
25 ***Walsh***	Y	Y	Y	Y	Y	Y	Y
26 Hinchey	N	Y	Y	Y	Y	N	Y
27 ***Paxon***	Y	Y	Y	Y	Y	Y	Y
28 Slaughter	Y	Y	Y	Y	Y	N	Y
29 LaFalce	Y	Y	Y	Y	Y	N	Y

	53	54	55	56	57	58	59
30 ***Quinn***	Y	Y	Y	Y	Y	N	Y
31 ***Houghton***	Y	Y	Y	N	Y	N	Y
NORTH CAROLINA							
1 Clayton	Y	Y	Y	Y	Y	N	Y
2 Etheridge	Y	Y	Y	Y	Y	N	Y
3 ***Jones***	Y	Y	Y	Y	Y	Y	Y
4 Price	Y	Y	Y	Y	Y	N	Y
5 ***Burr***	Y	Y	Y	Y	Y	Y	Y
6 ***Coble***	Y	Y	Y	Y	Y	Y	Y
7 McIntyre	Y	Y	Y	Y	Y	N	Y
8 Hefner	Y	Y	Y	?	?	?	?
9 ***Myrick***	Y	Y	Y	Y	Y	Y	Y
10 ***Ballenger***	Y	Y	Y	Y	Y	Y	Y
11 ***Taylor***	Y	Y	Y	Y	Y	Y	Y
12 Watt	Y	Y	Y	Y	Y	N	Y
NORTH DAKOTA							
AL Pomeroy	Y	Y	Y	Y	Y	N	Y
OHIO							
1 ***Chabot***	Y	Y	Y	Y	Y	Y	Y
2 ***Portman***	Y	Y	Y	Y	Y	N	Y
3 Hall	Y	Y	Y	Y	Y	N	Y
4 ***Oxley***	Y	Y	Y	Y	Y	N	Y
5 ***Gillmor***	N	Y	Y	Y	Y	N	Y
6 Strickland	Y	Y	Y	Y	Y	N	?
7 ***Hobson***	Y	Y	Y	Y	?	Y	Y
8 ***Boehner***	Y	Y	Y	Y	Y	N	Y
9 Kaptur	Y	Y	Y	Y	Y	N	Y
10 Kucinich	N	Y	Y	Y	Y	N	Y
11 Stokes	Y	Y	Y	Y	Y	N	Y
12 ***Kasich***	Y	Y	Y	Y	Y	Y	Y
13 Brown	Y	Y	Y	Y	Y	N	Y
14 Sawyer	Y	Y	Y	Y	Y	N	Y
15 ***Pryce***	Y	Y	Y	Y	Y	Y	Y
16 ***Regula***	Y	Y	Y	Y	Y	Y	Y
17 Traficant	Y	Y	Y	Y	Y	Y	Y
18 ***Ney***	Y	Y	Y	Y	Y	Y	Y
19 ***LaTourette***	Y	Y	Y	Y	Y	N	Y
OKLAHOMA							
1 ***Largent***	Y	Y	?	Y	Y	N	Y
2 ***Coburn***	Y	Y	Y	Y	Y	Y	Y
3 ***Watkins***	Y	Y	Y	Y	Y	Y	Y
4 ***Watts***	N	Y	Y	Y	Y	Y	Y
5 ***Istook***	Y	Y	Y	Y	Y	Y	Y
6 ***Lucas***	Y	Y	Y	Y	Y	Y	Y
OREGON							
1 Furse	Y	Y	Y	Y	Y	N	Y
2 ***Smith***	Y	Y	Y	Y	Y	Y	Y
3 Blumenauer	Y	Y	Y	Y	Y	N	Y
4 DeFazio	N	Y	Y	Y	Y	Y	Y
5 Hooley	Y	Y	Y	Y	Y	N	Y
PENNSYLVANIA							
1 Vacant							
2 Fattah	Y	Y	Y	Y	Y	N	Y
3 Borski	?	?	?	Y	Y	N	Y
4 Klink	Y	Y	Y	Y	Y	N	Y
5 ***Peterson***	Y	Y	Y	Y	Y	Y	Y
6 Holden	Y	Y	Y	Y	Y	N	Y
7 ***Weldon***	Y	Y	Y	Y	Y	Y	Y
8 ***Greenwood***	Y	Y	Y	Y	Y	Y	Y
9 ***Shuster***	Y	Y	Y	Y	Y	Y	Y
10 ***McDade***	?	?	?	?	?	?	Y
11 Kanjorski	Y	Y	Y	Y	Y	N	Y
12 Murtha	Y	Y	Y	Y	Y	N	Y
13 ***Fox***	N	Y	Y	Y	Y	N	Y
14 Coyne	Y	Y	Y	Y	Y	N	Y
15 McHale	Y	Y	Y	Y	Y	N	Y
16 ***Pitts***	Y	Y	Y	Y	Y	Y	Y
17 ***Gekas***	Y	Y	Y	Y	?	Y	Y
18 Doyle	Y	Y	Y	Y	Y	N	Y
19 ***Goodling***	Y	Y	Y	Y	Y	Y	Y
20 Mascara	Y	Y	Y	Y	Y	N	Y
21 ***English***	N	?	Y	Y	Y	Y	Y
RHODE ISLAND							
1 Kennedy	Y	Y	Y	Y	Y	N	Y
2 Weygand	Y	Y	Y	Y	Y	N	Y
SOUTH CAROLINA							
1 ***Sanford***	?	?	?	Y	Y	Y	Y
2 ***Spence***	Y	Y	Y	Y	Y	Y	Y
3 ***Graham***	Y	Y	Y	Y	?	Y	Y
4 ***Inglis***	?	?	?	?	?	Y	Y
5 Spratt	Y	Y	Y	Y	Y	N	Y
6 Clyburn	N	Y	Y	Y	Y	N	Y
SOUTH DAKOTA							
AL ***Thune***	Y	Y	Y	Y	Y	Y	Y

	53	54	55	56	57	58	59
TENNESSEE							
1 ***Jenkins***	Y	Y	Y	Y	Y	Y	Y
2 ***Duncan***	Y	Y	Y	Y	Y	Y	Y
3 ***Wamp***	Y	Y	Y	Y	Y	Y	Y
4 ***Hilleary***	N	Y	Y	Y	Y	Y	Y
5 Clement	Y	Y	Y	Y	Y	N	Y
6 Gordon	Y	Y	Y	Y	Y	N	Y
7 ***Bryant***	Y	Y	Y	Y	Y	Y	Y
8 Tanner	Y	Y	Y	Y	Y	N	Y
9 Ford	Y	Y	Y	Y	Y	N	Y
TEXAS							
1 Sandlin	Y	Y	Y	Y	Y	N	Y
2 Turner	?	?	?	?	?	N	Y
3 ***Johnson, Sam***	Y	Y	Y	Y	Y	Y	Y
4 Hall	Y	Y	Y	Y	Y	Y	Y
5 ***Sessions***	N	Y	Y	Y	Y	Y	Y
6 ***Barton***	Y	Y	Y	Y	Y	Y	Y
7 ***Archer***	Y	Y	Y	Y	Y	Y	Y
8 ***Brady***	Y	Y	Y	Y	Y	Y	Y
9 Lampson	Y	Y	Y	Y	Y	N	Y
10 Doggett	Y	Y	Y	Y	Y	Y	Y
11 Edwards	Y	Y	Y	Y	Y	N	Y
12 ***Granger***	Y	Y	Y	Y	Y	Y	Y
13 ***Thornberry***	Y	Y	Y	Y	Y	N	Y
14 ***Paul***	Y	Y	N	N	N	Y	Y
15 Hinojosa	Y	Y	Y	Y	Y	N	Y
16 Reyes	Y	Y	Y	Y	Y	N	Y
17 Stenholm	N	Y	Y	Y	Y	N	Y
18 Jackson-Lee	Y	Y	Y	Y	Y	N	Y
19 ***Combest***	Y	Y	Y	Y	Y	Y	Y
20 Gonzalez	?	?	?	?	?	?	?
21 ***Smith***	Y	Y	Y	Y	Y	Y	Y
22 ***DeLay***	Y	Y	Y	Y	Y	Y	Y
23 ***Bonilla***	Y	Y	Y	Y	Y	Y	Y
24 Frost	Y	Y	Y	Y	Y	N	?
25 Bentsen	Y	Y	Y	Y	Y	N	Y
26 ***Armey***	Y	Y	Y	?	Y	Y	Y
27 Ortiz	Y	Y	Y	Y	Y	N	Y
28 Rodriguez	Y	Y	Y	Y	Y	N	Y
29 Green	Y	Y	Y	Y	Y	N	Y
30 Johnson, E.B.	N	Y	Y	Y	Y	N	Y
UTAH							
1 ***Hansen***	Y	Y	Y	Y	Y	Y	Y
2 ***Cook***	Y	Y	Y	Y	Y	Y	Y
3 ***Cannon***	?	?	?	Y	Y	Y	Y
VERMONT							
AL *Sanders*	Y	Y	Y	Y	Y	N	Y
VIRGINIA							
1 ***Bateman***	Y	Y	Y	Y	Y	N	Y
2 Pickett	N	Y	Y	Y	Y	N	Y
3 Scott	Y	Y	Y	Y	Y	N	Y
4 Sisisky	Y	Y	Y	Y	Y	N	Y
5 Goode	Y	Y	Y	Y	Y	Y	Y
6 ***Goodlatte***	Y	Y	Y	Y	Y	Y	Y
7 ***Bliley***	Y	Y	Y	Y	Y	N	Y
8 Moran	Y	Y	Y	Y	Y	N	Y
9 Boucher	Y	Y	Y	Y	Y	N	Y
10 ***Wolf***	Y	Y	Y	Y	Y	N	Y
11 ***Davis***	Y	Y	Y	Y	Y	N	Y
WASHINGTON							
1 ***White***	Y	Y	Y	Y	Y	Y	Y
2 ***Metcalf***	Y	Y	Y	Y	Y	Y	Y
3 ***Smith, Linda***	Y	Y	Y	Y	Y	Y	Y
4 ***Hastings***	Y	Y	Y	?	Y	N	Y
5 ***Nethercutt***	Y	Y	Y	Y	Y	Y	Y
6 Dicks	Y	Y	Y	Y	Y	N	Y
7 McDermott	N	Y	Y	Y	Y	N	Y
8 ***Dunn***	?	?	?	Y	Y	N	Y
9 Smith, Adam	Y	Y	Y	Y	Y	N	Y
WEST VIRGINIA							
1 Mollohan	Y	Y	Y	Y	Y	N	Y
2 Wise	Y	Y	Y	Y	Y	N	Y
3 Rahall	Y	Y	Y	Y	Y	N	Y
WISCONSIN							
1 ***Neumann***	Y	Y	Y	Y	Y	Y	Y
2 ***Klug***	Y	Y	Y	Y	Y	Y	Y
3 Kind	Y	Y	Y	Y	Y	N	Y
4 Kleczka	Y	Y	Y	Y	Y	N	Y
5 Barrett	Y	Y	Y	Y	Y	N	Y
6 ***Petri***	Y	Y	Y	Y	Y	Y	Y
7 Obey	Y	Y	?	Y	Y	N	Y
8 Johnson	Y	Y	Y	Y	Y	N	Y
9 ***Sensenbrenner***	Y	Y	Y	Y	Y	Y	Y
WYOMING							
AL ***Cubin***	Y	Y	Y	Y	Y	Y	Y

Southern states - Ala., Ark., Fla., Ga., Ky., La., Miss., N.C., Okla., S.C., Tenn., Texas, Va.

Key

Y	Voted for (yea).
#	Paired for.
+	Announced for.
N	Voted against (nay).
X	Paired against.
−	Announced against.
P	Voted "present."
C	Voted "present" to avoid possible conflict of interest.
?	Did not vote or otherwise make a position known.

Democrats **Republicans**
Independent

60. Procedural Motion/Journal. Approval of the House Journal of Wednesday, March 18, 1998. Approved 359-49: R 194-19; D 164-30 (ND 120-23, SD 44-7); I 1-0. March 19, 1998.

61. HR 2870. Tropical Forest Conservation/Notification. Gilman, R-N.Y., amendment to require the Clinton administration to notify Congress prior to finalizing any debt reduction transaction. Adopted 416-1: R 220-0; D 195-1 (ND 144-0, SD 51-1); I 1-0. March 19, 1998.

62. HR 2870. Tropical Forest Conservation/Medicinal Uses. Vento, D-Minn., amendment to expand the list of activities that could be supported with tropical forest protection funds to include research and identification of medical uses of tropical forest plant life, and require that indigenous leaders be consulted. Adopted 335-79: R 139-79; D 195-0 (ND 143-0, SD 52-0); I 1-0. March 19, 1998.

63. HR 2870. Tropical Forest Conservation/Passage. Passage of the bill to authorize the president to forgive or reduce debts of developing countries in exchange for protection of tropical forests in those countries. The bill would authorize the president to forgive up to $325 million of debt over the next three years for such projects and target debts to the United States incurred through the Agency for International Development and the Agriculture Department. Passed 356-61: R 161-60; D 194-1 (ND 142-1, SD 52-0); I 1-0. March 19, 1998. A "yea" was a vote in support of the president's position.

64. Procedural Motion/Journal. Approval of the House Journal of Monday, March 23, 1998. Approved 368-40: R 200-16; D 167-24 (ND 122-17, SD 45-7); I 1-0. March 24, 1998.

65. HR 3211. Arlington Cemetery Burials/Passage. Stump, R-Ariz., motion to suspend the rules and pass the bill to codify eligibility criteria for burial at Arlington National Cemetery to include individuals in the military who die on active duty, and most retired members of the armed forces. Motion agreed to 412-0: R 220-0; D 191-0 (ND 139-0, SD 52-0); I 1-0. March 24, 1998. A two-thirds majority of those present and voting (275 in this case) is required for passage under suspension of the rules.

66. HR 3412. Small Business Loans/Passage. Talent, R-Mo., motion to suspend the rules and pass the bill to reauthorize the activities of the Small Business Investment Companies program, which uses Small Business Administration guarantees to leverage private capital for investment in small businesses. Motion agreed to 407-0: R 215-0; D 191-0 (ND 139-0, SD 52-0); I 1-0. March 24, 1998. A two-thirds majority of those present and voting (272 in this case) is required for passage under suspension of the rules.

	60	61	62	63	64	65	66
ALABAMA							
1 *Callahan*	Y	Y	N	Y	Y	Y	Y
2 *Everett*	Y	Y	N	N	Y	Y	Y
3 *Riley*	Y	Y	N	N	Y	Y	Y
4 *Aderholt*	Y	Y	N	N	Y	Y	Y
5 Cramer	Y	Y	Y	Y	Y	Y	Y
6 *Bachus*	Y	Y	N	Y	Y	Y	Y
7 Hilliard	N	N	Y	N	Y	N	Y
ALASKA							
AL *Young*	?	Y	N	N	Y	Y	Y
ARIZONA							
1 *Salmon*	Y	Y	N	N	Y	Y	Y
2 Pastor	Y	Y	Y	Y	Y	Y	Y
3 *Stump*	Y	Y	N	N	Y	Y	Y
4 *Shadegg*	Y	Y	N	N	Y	Y	Y
5 *Kolbe*	Y	Y	Y	Y	Y	Y	Y
6 *Hayworth*	Y	Y	N	Y	Y	Y	Y
ARKANSAS							
1 Berry	Y	Y	Y	Y	Y	Y	Y
2 Snyder	Y	Y	Y	Y	Y	Y	Y
3 *Hutchinson*	?	Y	N	Y	Y	Y	Y
4 *Dickey*	N	Y	Y	Y	Y	Y	Y
CALIFORNIA							
1 *Riggs*	?	?	?	?	Y	Y	Y
2 *Herger*	N	Y	N	N	Y	Y	?
3 Fazio	N	Y	Y	Y	N	Y	Y
4 *Doolittle*	Y	Y	N	N	Y	Y	Y
5 Matsui	Y	Y	Y	Y	Y	Y	Y
6 Woolsey	Y	Y	Y	Y	Y	Y	Y
7 Miller	N	Y	Y	Y	Y	Y	Y
8 Pelosi	Y	Y	Y	Y	Y	Y	Y
9 Vacant							
10 Tauscher	Y	Y	Y	Y	Y	Y	Y
11 *Pombo*	Y	Y	N	N	Y	Y	Y
12 Lantos	Y	Y	Y	Y	Y	Y	Y
13 Stark	N	Y	Y	Y	?	?	?
14 Eshoo	Y	Y	Y	Y	Y	Y	Y
15 *Campbell*	Y	Y	Y	Y	Y	Y	Y
16 Lofgren	Y	Y	Y	Y	Y	Y	Y
17 Farr	Y	Y	Y	Y	Y	Y	Y
18 Condit	Y	Y	Y	Y	Y	Y	Y
19 *Radanovich*	Y	Y	N	N	Y	Y	Y
20 Dooley	Y	Y	Y	Y	Y	Y	Y
21 *Thomas*	Y	Y	N	Y	Y	Y	Y
22 Capps, L.	Y	Y	Y	Y	+	+	Y
23 *Gallegly*	?	?	?	?	Y	Y	Y
24 Sherman	Y	Y	Y	Y	Y	Y	Y
25 *McKeon*	Y	Y	N	Y	Y	Y	Y
26 Berman	Y	Y	Y	Y	Y	Y	Y
27 *Rogan*	N	Y	N	Y	N	Y	Y
28 *Dreier*	Y	Y	Y	Y	Y	Y	Y
29 Waxman	Y	Y	Y	Y	Y	Y	Y
30 Becerra	N	Y	Y	N	Y	Y	Y
31 Martinez	?	?	?	?	Y	Y	Y
32 Dixon	Y	Y	Y	Y	Y	Y	Y
33 Roybal-Allard	Y	Y	Y	Y	Y	Y	Y
34 Torres	Y	Y	Y	Y	Y	Y	Y
35 Waters	N	Y	Y	Y	?	?	Y
36 Harman	Y	Y	Y	Y	?	?	Y
37 Millender-McD.	Y	Y	Y	Y	Y	Y	Y

	60	61	62	63	64	65	66
38 *Horn*	Y	Y	Y	Y	Y	Y	Y
39 *Royce*	Y	Y	Y	?	Y	?	?
40 *Lewis*	Y	Y	Y	Y	Y	Y	Y
41 *Kim*	Y	Y	Y	Y	Y	Y	Y
42 Brown	N	Y	Y	Y	N	Y	Y
43 *Calvert*	?	Y	Y	Y	Y	Y	Y
44 Vacant							
45 *Rohrabacher*	Y	Y	Y	Y	Y	Y	Y
46 Sanchez	Y	Y	Y	Y	Y	Y	Y
47 *Cox*	Y	Y	Y	Y	Y	Y	Y
48 *Packard*	Y	Y	Y	Y	Y	Y	Y
49 *Bilbray*	Y	Y	Y	Y	Y	Y	Y
50 Filner	N	Y	Y	N	Y	N	Y
51 *Cunningham*	Y	Y	Y	Y	Y	Y	Y
52 *Hunter*	Y	Y	Y	Y	Y	Y	Y
COLORADO							
1 DeGette	Y	Y	Y	Y	Y	Y	Y
2 Skaggs	Y	Y	Y	Y	Y	Y	Y
3 *McInnis*	Y	Y	Y	Y	Y	Y	Y
4 *Schaffer*	N	Y	N	N	N	Y	Y
5 *Hefley*	Y	Y	Y	Y	Y	Y	Y
6 *Schaefer*	Y	Y	Y	N	Y	Y	Y
CONNECTICUT							
1 Kennelly	Y	Y	Y	Y	Y	Y	Y
2 Gejdenson	Y	Y	Y	Y	Y	Y	Y
3 DeLauro	Y	Y	Y	Y	Y	Y	Y
4 *Shays*	Y	Y	Y	Y	Y	Y	Y
5 Maloney	Y	Y	Y	Y	Y	Y	Y
6 *Johnson*	Y	Y	Y	Y	Y	Y	Y
DELAWARE							
AL *Castle*	Y	Y	Y	Y	Y	Y	Y
FLORIDA							
1 *Scarborough*	Y	Y	Y	Y	Y	Y	Y
2 Boyd	Y	Y	Y	Y	Y	Y	Y
3 Brown	Y	Y	?	Y	Y	Y	Y
4 *Fowler*	Y	Y	Y	Y	Y	Y	Y
5 Thurman	Y	Y	Y	Y	Y	Y	Y
6 *Stearns*	Y	Y	N	N	Y	Y	Y
7 *Mica*	Y	Y	N	Y	Y	Y	Y
8 *McCollum*	Y	Y	N	Y	Y	Y	Y
9 *Bilirakis*	Y	Y	Y	Y	Y	Y	Y
10 *Young*	Y	Y	Y	Y	Y	Y	?
11 Davis	Y	Y	Y	Y	Y	Y	Y
12 *Canady*	Y	Y	Y	Y	Y	Y	Y
13 *Miller*	Y	Y	Y	Y	Y	Y	Y
14 *Goss*	Y	Y	Y	Y	Y	Y	Y
15 *Weldon*	Y	Y	Y	Y	Y	Y	Y
16 *Foley*	Y	+	+	Y	Y	Y	Y
17 Meek	Y	Y	Y	Y	Y	Y	Y
18 *Ros-Lehtinen*	Y	Y	Y	Y	Y	Y	Y
19 Wexler	Y	Y	Y	Y	Y	Y	Y
20 Deutsch	Y	Y	Y	Y	Y	Y	Y
21 *Diaz-Balart*	Y	Y	Y	Y	?	Y	Y
22 *Shaw*	Y	Y	Y	Y	Y	Y	Y
23 Hastings	N	Y	Y	Y	Y	Y	Y
GEORGIA							
1 *Kingston*	Y	Y	Y	Y	Y	Y	Y
2 Bishop	Y	Y	Y	Y	Y	Y	Y
3 *Collins*	Y	Y	N	N	Y	Y	Y
4 McKinney	Y	Y	Y	Y	Y	Y	Y
5 Lewis	?	?	?	?	N	Y	Y
6 *Gingrich*							
7 *Barr*	Y	Y	N	N	Y	Y	Y
8 *Chambliss*	Y	Y	Y	Y	Y	Y	Y
9 *Deal*	Y	Y	Y	?	Y	Y	Y
10 *Norwood*	Y	Y	Y	Y	Y	Y	Y
11 *Linder*	Y	Y	Y	Y	Y	Y	Y
HAWAII							
1 Abercrombie	N	Y	Y	Y	Y	Y	Y
2 Mink	Y	Y	Y	Y	Y	Y	Y
IDAHO							
1 *Chenoweth*	N	Y	N	N	+	+	+
2 *Crapo*	Y	Y	N	Y	Y	Y	Y
ILLINOIS							
1 Rush	Y	Y	Y	Y	Y	Y	Y
2 Jackson	Y	Y	Y	Y	Y	Y	Y
3 Lipinski	Y	Y	Y	Y	Y	Y	Y
4 Gutierrez	Y	Y	Y	Y	N	Y	Y
5 Blagojevich	Y	Y	Y	Y	Y	Y	Y
6 *Hyde*	Y	Y	Y	Y	Y	Y	Y
7 Davis	Y	Y	Y	Y	Y	Y	Y
8 *Crane*	?	Y	N	N	N	Y	Y
9 Yates	N	Y	Y	Y	?	?	?
10 *Porter*	Y	Y	Y	Y	Y	Y	Y
11 *Weller*	N	Y	Y	Y	Y	Y	Y
12 Costello	N	Y	Y	N	Y	Y	Y

ND Northern Democrats SD Southern Democrats

Vote columns: **60 61 62 63 64 65 66**

ILLINOIS

District	Member	60	61	62	63	64	65	66
13	*Fawell*	N	Y	Y	Y	Y	Y	Y
14	*Hastert*	Y	Y	Y	Y	Y	Y	Y
15	*Ewing*	Y	Y	Y	Y	Y	Y	Y
16	*Manzullo*	?	Y	Y	Y	?	?	?
17	Evans	Y	Y	Y	Y	Y	Y	Y
18	*LaHood*	Y	Y	Y	Y	Y	Y	Y
19	Poshard	?	?	?	?	Y	Y	Y
20	*Shimkus*	Y	Y	Y	Y	Y	Y	Y

INDIANA

District	Member	60	61	62	63	64	65	66
1	Visclosky	N	Y	Y	Y	Y	Y	Y
2	*McIntosh*	Y	Y	Y	Y	Y	Y	Y
3	Roemer	Y	Y	Y	Y	Y	Y	Y
4	*Souder*	Y	Y	N	Y	Y	Y	Y
5	*Buyer*	Y	Y	Y	Y	?	Y	Y
6	*Burton*	Y	Y	N	N	Y	Y	Y
7	*Pease*	Y	Y	Y	Y	Y	Y	Y
8	*Hostettler*	Y	Y	N	Y	Y	Y	Y
9	Hamilton	Y	Y	Y	Y	Y	Y	Y
10	Carson	N	Y	Y	Y	Y	Y	Y

IOWA

District	Member	60	61	62	63	64	65	66
1	*Leach*	Y	Y	Y	Y	Y	Y	Y
2	*Nussle*	Y	Y	Y	Y	Y	Y	Y
3	Boswell	Y	Y	Y	Y	Y	Y	Y
4	*Ganske*	Y	Y	Y	Y	Y	Y	Y
5	*Latham*	Y	Y	Y	Y	Y	Y	Y

KANSAS

District	Member	60	61	62	63	64	65	66
1	*Moran*	N	Y	N	Y	N	Y	Y
2	*Ryun*	Y	Y	N	Y	Y	Y	Y
3	*Snowbarger*	Y	Y	N	N	Y	Y	Y
4	*Tiahrt*	Y	Y	N	N	Y	Y	Y

KENTUCKY

District	Member	60	61	62	63	64	65	66
1	*Whitfield*	Y	Y	Y	Y	Y	Y	Y
2	*Lewis*	Y	Y	–	N	Y	Y	Y
3	*Northup*	Y	Y	Y	Y	Y	Y	Y
4	*Bunning*	Y	Y	N	Y	Y	Y	Y
5	*Rogers*	Y	Y	Y	Y	Y	Y	Y
6	Baesler	Y	Y	Y	Y	Y	Y	Y

LOUISIANA

District	Member	60	61	62	63	64	65	66
1	*Livingston*	?	Y	Y	Y	Y	Y	Y
2	Jefferson	Y	Y	Y	Y	?	?	?
3	*Tauzin*	Y	Y	Y	Y	Y	Y	Y
4	*McCrery*	Y	Y	Y	Y	Y	Y	Y
5	*Cooksey*	Y	Y	Y	Y	?	Y	Y
6	*Baker*	Y	Y	N	Y	Y	Y	Y
7	John	Y	Y	Y	Y	Y	Y	Y

MAINE

District	Member	60	61	62	63	64	65	66
1	Allen	Y	Y	Y	Y	Y	Y	Y
2	Baldacci	Y	Y	Y	Y	Y	Y	Y

MARYLAND

District	Member	60	61	62	63	64	65	66
1	*Gilchrest*	Y	Y	Y	Y	Y	Y	Y
2	*Ehrlich*	Y	Y	Y	Y	N	Y	Y
3	Cardin	Y	Y	Y	Y	Y	Y	Y
4	Wynn	Y	Y	Y	Y	Y	Y	Y
5	Hoyer	?	Y	Y	Y	Y	Y	Y
6	*Bartlett*	Y	Y	N	N	Y	Y	Y
7	Cummings	Y	Y	Y	Y	Y	Y	Y
8	*Morella*	Y	Y	Y	Y	Y	Y	Y

MASSACHUSETTS

District	Member	60	61	62	63	64	65	66
1	Olver	Y	Y	Y	Y	Y	Y	Y
2	Neal	Y	Y	Y	Y	Y	Y	Y
3	McGovern	Y	Y	Y	Y	Y	Y	Y
4	Frank	Y	Y	Y	Y	Y	Y	Y
5	Meehan	Y	Y	Y	Y	Y	Y	Y
6	Tierney	Y	Y	Y	Y	Y	Y	Y
7	Markey	Y	Y	Y	Y	Y	Y	Y
8	Kennedy	Y	Y	Y	Y	Y	Y	Y
9	Moakley	Y	Y	Y	Y	Y	Y	Y
10	Delahunt	Y	Y	Y	Y	Y	Y	Y

MICHIGAN

District	Member	60	61	62	63	64	65	66
1	Stupak	N	Y	Y	Y	N	Y	Y
2	*Hoekstra*	Y	Y	N	Y	Y	Y	Y
3	*Ehlers*	Y	Y	Y	Y	Y	Y	Y
4	*Camp*	Y	Y	Y	Y	Y	Y	Y
5	Barcia	Y	Y	Y	Y	Y	Y	Y
6	*Upton*	Y	Y	Y	Y	Y	Y	Y
7	*Smith*	Y	Y	Y	Y	Y	Y	Y
8	Stabenow	Y	Y	Y	Y	Y	Y	Y
9	Kildee	Y	Y	Y	Y	Y	Y	Y
10	Bonior	Y	Y	Y	?	Y	Y	Y
11	*Knollenberg*	Y	Y	Y	Y	Y	Y	Y
12	Levin	Y	Y	Y	Y	Y	Y	Y
13	Rivers	Y	Y	Y	Y	Y	Y	Y
14	Conyers	Y	Y	Y	Y	Y	Y	Y
15	Kilpatrick	Y	Y	Y	Y	Y	Y	Y
16	Dingell	Y	Y	Y	Y	Y	Y	Y

MINNESOTA

District	Member	60	61	62	63	64	65	66
1	*Gutknecht*	?	Y	Y	Y	N	Y	Y
2	Minge	Y	Y	Y	Y	Y	Y	Y
3	*Ramstad*	N	Y	Y	Y	N	Y	Y
4	Vento	Y	Y	Y	Y	Y	Y	Y
5	Sabo	N	Y	Y	Y	N	Y	Y
6	Luther	Y	Y	Y	Y	Y	Y	Y
7	Peterson	Y	Y	Y	Y	Y	Y	Y
8	Oberstar	N	Y	Y	Y	N	Y	Y

MISSISSIPPI

District	Member	60	61	62	63	64	65	66
1	*Wicker*	N	Y	N	Y	N	Y	Y
2	Thompson	N	Y	Y	Y	N	Y	Y
3	*Pickering*	Y	Y	Y	Y	N	Y	Y
4	*Parker*	?	?	N	N	Y	Y	Y
5	Taylor	N	Y	Y	Y	N	Y	Y

MISSOURI

District	Member	60	61	62	63	64	65	66
1	Clay	N	Y	N	Y	N	Y	Y
2	*Talent*	Y	Y	Y	Y	Y	Y	Y
3	Gephardt	?	?	?	?	Y	Y	Y
4	Skelton	Y	Y	Y	Y	Y	Y	Y
5	McCarthy	Y	Y	Y	Y	Y	Y	Y
6	Danner	Y	Y	Y	N	Y	Y	Y
7	*Blunt*	Y	Y	Y	Y	Y	Y	Y
8	*Emerson*	Y	Y	N	N	Y	Y	Y
9	*Hulshof*	Y	Y	Y	Y	Y	Y	Y

MONTANA

District	Member	60	61	62	63	64	65	66
AL	*Hill*	Y	Y	Y	Y	N	Y	Y

NEBRASKA

District	Member	60	61	62	63	64	65	66
1	*Bereuter*	Y	Y	Y	Y	Y	Y	Y
2	*Christensen*	Y	Y	Y	Y	Y	Y	Y
3	*Barrett*	Y	Y	Y	Y	Y	Y	Y

NEVADA

District	Member	60	61	62	63	64	65	66
1	*Ensign*	N	Y	Y	Y	N	Y	Y
2	*Gibbons*	N	Y	N	Y	Y	Y	Y

NEW HAMPSHIRE

District	Member	60	61	62	63	64	65	66
1	*Sununu*	Y	Y	N	Y	Y	Y	Y
2	*Bass*	Y	Y	Y	Y	Y	Y	?

NEW JERSEY

District	Member	60	61	62	63	64	65	66
1	Andrews	Y	Y	Y	Y	Y	Y	Y
2	*LoBiondo*	N	Y	Y	Y	N	Y	Y
3	*Saxton*	Y	Y	Y	Y	Y	Y	Y
4	*Smith*	Y	Y	Y	Y	Y	Y	Y
5	*Roukema*	Y	Y	Y	Y	Y	Y	Y
6	Pallone	Y	Y	Y	Y	Y	Y	Y
7	*Franks*	Y	Y	Y	Y	Y	Y	Y
8	Pascrell	Y	Y	Y	Y	Y	Y	Y
9	Rothman	Y	Y	Y	Y	Y	Y	Y
10	Payne	Y	Y	Y	Y	?	?	?
11	*Frelinghuysen*	Y	Y	Y	Y	Y	Y	Y
12	*Pappas*	Y	Y	Y	Y	Y	Y	Y
13	Menendez	Y	Y	Y	Y	N	Y	Y

NEW MEXICO

District	Member	60	61	62	63	64	65	66
1	*Schiff*	?	?	?	?	?	?	?
2	*Skeen*	Y	Y	Y	Y	Y	Y	Y
3	*Redmond*	Y	Y	Y	Y	Y	Y	Y

NEW YORK

District	Member	60	61	62	63	64	65	66
1	*Forbes*	Y	Y	Y	Y	Y	Y	Y
2	*Lazio*	Y	Y	Y	Y	Y	Y	Y
3	*King*	Y	Y	Y	Y	Y	Y	Y
4	McCarthy	Y	Y	Y	Y	Y	Y	Y
5	Ackerman	Y	Y	Y	Y	Y	Y	Y
6	Meeks	Y	Y	Y	Y	Y	Y	Y
7	Manton	Y	Y	Y	Y	Y	Y	Y
8	Nadler	Y	Y	Y	Y	Y	Y	Y
9	Schumer	Y	Y	Y	Y	?	?	?
10	Towns	Y	Y	Y	Y	Y	Y	Y
11	Owens	N	Y	Y	Y	Y	Y	Y
12	Velázquez	Y	Y	Y	Y	Y	Y	Y
13	*Fossella*	Y	Y	N	N	Y	Y	Y
14	Maloney	Y	Y	Y	Y	N	Y	Y
15	Rangel	?	?	?	?	?	?	?
16	Serrano	Y	Y	Y	Y	Y	Y	Y
17	Engel	?	Y	Y	Y	Y	Y	Y
18	Lowey	Y	Y	Y	Y	Y	Y	Y
19	*Kelly*	Y	Y	Y	Y	Y	Y	Y
20	*Gilman*	Y	Y	Y	Y	Y	Y	Y
21	McNulty	N	Y	Y	Y	N	Y	Y
22	*Solomon*	Y	Y	N	N	Y	Y	Y
23	*Boehlert*	Y	Y	Y	Y	Y	Y	Y
24	*McHugh*	Y	Y	Y	Y	Y	Y	Y
25	*Walsh*	Y	Y	Y	Y	Y	Y	Y
26	Hinchey	N	Y	Y	Y	Y	Y	Y
27	*Paxon*	Y	Y	Y	Y	Y	Y	Y
28	Slaughter	Y	Y	Y	Y	N	Y	Y
29	LaFalce	Y	Y	Y	Y	Y	Y	Y
30	Quinn	Y	Y	Y	Y	Y	Y	Y
31	Houghton	Y	Y	?	Y	Y	Y	Y

NORTH CAROLINA

District	Member	60	61	62	63	64	65	66
1	Clayton	Y	Y	Y	Y	Y	Y	Y
2	Etheridge	Y	Y	Y	Y	Y	Y	Y
3	*Jones*	Y	Y	N	N	Y	Y	Y
4	Price	Y	Y	Y	Y	Y	Y	Y
5	*Burr*	Y	Y	Y	Y	Y	Y	Y
6	*Coble*	Y	Y	N	N	Y	Y	Y
7	McIntyre	Y	Y	Y	Y	Y	Y	Y
8	Hefner	?	Y	Y	Y	Y	Y	Y
9	*Myrick*	Y	Y	N	Y	Y	Y	Y
10	*Ballenger*	Y	Y	N	Y	Y	Y	Y
11	*Taylor*	Y	Y	N	Y	Y	Y	Y
12	Watt	Y	Y	Y	Y	Y	Y	Y

NORTH DAKOTA

District	Member	60	61	62	63	64	65	66
AL	Pomeroy	Y	Y	Y	Y	Y	Y	Y

OHIO

District	Member	60	61	62	63	64	65	66
1	*Chabot*	Y	Y	N	Y	Y	Y	Y
2	*Portman*	Y	Y	Y	Y	Y	Y	Y
3	Hall	Y	Y	Y	Y	Y	Y	Y
4	*Oxley*	Y	Y	Y	Y	Y	Y	Y
5	*Gillmor*	Y	Y	Y	Y	Y	Y	Y
6	Strickland	Y	Y	Y	Y	Y	Y	Y
7	*Hobson*	Y	Y	Y	Y	Y	Y	Y
8	*Boehner*	Y	Y	Y	Y	Y	Y	Y
9	Kaptur	Y	Y	Y	Y	Y	Y	Y
10	Kucinich	N	Y	Y	Y	N	Y	Y
11	Stokes	Y	Y	Y	Y	Y	Y	Y
12	*Kasich*	?	Y	Y	Y	Y	Y	Y
13	Brown	Y	Y	Y	Y	Y	Y	Y
14	Sawyer	Y	Y	Y	Y	Y	Y	Y
15	*Pryce*	Y	Y	Y	Y	Y	Y	Y
16	*Regula*	Y	Y	Y	Y	Y	Y	Y
17	Traficant	Y	Y	Y	Y	Y	Y	Y
18	*Ney*	Y	Y	Y	N	Y	Y	Y
19	*LaTourette*	Y	Y	Y	Y	Y	Y	Y

OKLAHOMA

District	Member	60	61	62	63	64	65	66
1	*Largent*	Y	Y	Y	Y	Y	Y	Y
2	*Coburn*	Y	Y	N	N	Y	Y	?
3	*Watkins*	Y	Y	Y	N	Y	Y	Y
4	*Watts*	Y	Y	Y	N	Y	Y	Y
5	*Istook*	Y	Y	Y	Y	Y	Y	Y
6	*Lucas*	Y	Y	Y	N	Y	Y	Y

OREGON

District	Member	60	61	62	63	64	65	66
1	Furse	Y	?	?	Y	Y	Y	Y
2	*Smith*	Y	Y	N	N	Y	Y	?
3	Blumenauer	Y	Y	Y	Y	Y	Y	Y
4	DeFazio	N	Y	Y	N	Y	Y	Y
5	Hooley	Y	Y	Y	Y	+	+	+

PENNSYLVANIA

District	Member	60	61	62	63	64	65	66
1	Vacant							
2	Fattah	Y	Y	Y	Y	Y	Y	Y
3	Borski	N	Y	Y	Y	N	Y	Y
4	Klink	Y	Y	Y	Y	Y	Y	Y
5	*Peterson*	Y	Y	N	Y	Y	Y	Y
6	Holden	Y	Y	Y	Y	Y	Y	Y
7	*Weldon*	?	Y	Y	Y	Y	Y	Y
8	*Greenwood*	Y	Y	Y	Y	Y	Y	Y
9	*Shuster*	Y	Y	Y	Y	Y	Y	Y
10	*McDade*	Y	Y	Y	Y	Y	Y	Y
11	Kanjorski	Y	Y	Y	Y	Y	Y	Y
12	Murtha	Y	Y	Y	Y	Y	Y	Y
13	*Fox*	N	Y	N	Y	N	Y	Y
14	Coyne	Y	Y	Y	Y	Y	Y	Y
15	McHale	Y	Y	Y	Y	Y	Y	Y
16	*Pitts*	Y	Y	Y	Y	Y	Y	Y
17	*Gekas*	Y	?	?	N	Y	Y	Y
18	Doyle	Y	Y	Y	Y	Y	Y	Y
19	*Goodling*	Y	Y	?	?	Y	Y	Y
20	Mascara	Y	Y	Y	Y	Y	Y	Y
21	*English*	N	Y	Y	Y	Y	Y	Y

RHODE ISLAND

District	Member	60	61	62	63	64	65	66
1	Kennedy	Y	Y	Y	Y	Y	Y	Y
2	Weygand	Y	Y	Y	Y	Y	Y	Y

SOUTH CAROLINA

District	Member	60	61	62	63	64	65	66
1	*Sanford*	Y	Y	N	Y	Y	Y	Y
2	*Spence*	Y	Y	N	N	Y	Y	Y
3	*Graham*	Y	Y	N	Y	Y	Y	Y
4	*Inglis*	Y	Y	N	Y	?	?	?
5	Spratt	Y	Y	Y	Y	?	?	?
6	Clyburn	N	Y	Y	Y	N	Y	Y

SOUTH DAKOTA

District	Member	60	61	62	63	64	65	66
AL	*Thune*	Y	Y	Y	Y	Y	Y	Y

TENNESSEE

District	Member	60	61	62	63	64	65	66
1	*Jenkins*	Y	Y	N	N	Y	Y	Y
2	*Duncan*	Y	Y	N	N	Y	Y	Y
3	*Wamp*	Y	Y	N	N	Y	Y	Y
4	*Hilleary*	N	Y	N	N	N	Y	Y
5	Clement	Y	Y	Y	Y	Y	Y	Y
6	Gordon	Y	Y	Y	Y	Y	Y	Y
7	*Bryant*	Y	Y	Y	Y	Y	Y	Y
8	Tanner	Y	Y	Y	Y	Y	Y	Y
9	Ford	N	Y	Y	Y	Y	Y	Y

TEXAS

District	Member	60	61	62	63	64	65	66
1	Sandlin	Y	Y	Y	Y	Y	Y	Y
2	Turner	Y	Y	Y	Y	Y	Y	Y
3	*Johnson, Sam*	Y	Y	N	Y	Y	Y	Y
4	Hall	Y	Y	Y	Y	Y	Y	Y
5	*Sessions*	N	Y	N	N	Y	Y	Y
6	*Barton*	Y	Y	N	Y	Y	Y	Y
7	*Archer*	Y	Y	Y	Y	Y	Y	Y
8	*Brady*	N	Y	N	N	Y	Y	Y
9	Lampson	Y	Y	Y	Y	Y	Y	Y
10	Doggett	Y	Y	Y	Y	Y	Y	Y
11	Edwards	Y	Y	Y	Y	Y	Y	Y
12	*Granger*	Y	Y	Y	Y	Y	Y	Y
13	*Thornberry*	Y	Y	N	N	Y	Y	Y
14	*Paul*	Y	Y	N	N	Y	Y	Y
15	Hinojosa	Y	Y	Y	Y	Y	Y	Y
16	Reyes	Y	Y	Y	Y	Y	Y	Y
17	Stenholm	Y	Y	Y	Y	Y	Y	Y
18	Jackson-Lee	Y	Y	Y	Y	Y	Y	Y
19	*Combest*	Y	Y	Y	Y	Y	Y	Y
20	Gonzalez	?	?	?	?	?	?	?
21	*Smith*	Y	Y	Y	Y	Y	Y	Y
22	*DeLay*	N	Y	N	N	Y	Y	Y
23	*Bonilla*	Y	Y	N	N	Y	Y	Y
24	Frost	?	?	?	?	Y	Y	Y
25	Bentsen	Y	Y	Y	Y	Y	Y	Y
26	*Armey*	Y	Y	N	Y	Y	Y	Y
27	Ortiz	Y	Y	Y	Y	Y	Y	Y
28	Rodriguez	Y	Y	Y	Y	Y	Y	Y
29	Green	Y	Y	Y	Y	Y	Y	Y
30	Johnson, E.B.	Y	Y	Y	Y	N	Y	Y

UTAH

District	Member	60	61	62	63	64	65	66
1	*Hansen*	Y	Y	N	N	Y	Y	Y
2	*Cook*	Y	Y	Y	Y	Y	Y	Y
3	*Cannon*	Y	Y	N	N	?	?	?

VERMONT

District	Member	60	61	62	63	64	65	66
AL	Sanders	Y	Y	Y	Y	Y	Y	Y

VIRGINIA

District	Member	60	61	62	63	64	65	66
1	*Bateman*	Y	Y	Y	Y	Y	Y	Y
2	Pickett	N	Y	Y	N	Y	Y	Y
3	Scott	Y	Y	Y	Y	Y	Y	Y
4	Sisisky	Y	Y	Y	Y	Y	Y	Y
5	Goode	Y	Y	Y	Y	Y	Y	Y
6	*Goodlatte*	Y	Y	Y	Y	Y	Y	Y
7	*Bliley*	Y	Y	Y	Y	Y	Y	Y
8	Moran	Y	Y	Y	Y	Y	Y	Y
9	Boucher	Y	Y	Y	Y	Y	Y	Y
10	*Wolf*	Y	Y	Y	Y	Y	Y	Y
11	*Davis*	Y	Y	Y	Y	Y	Y	Y

WASHINGTON

District	Member	60	61	62	63	64	65	66
1	*White*	Y	Y	Y	?	Y	Y	Y
2	*Metcalf*	Y	Y	Y	Y	Y	Y	Y
3	*Smith, Linda*	Y	Y	Y	?	Y	Y	Y
4	*Hastings*	Y	Y	N	Y	Y	Y	Y
5	*Nethercutt*	Y	Y	N	Y	Y	Y	Y
6	Dicks	Y	Y	Y	Y	Y	Y	Y
7	McDermott	N	Y	Y	Y	+	+	+
8	*Dunn*	Y	Y	Y	Y	Y	Y	Y
9	Smith, Adam	Y	Y	Y	Y	Y	Y	Y

WEST VIRGINIA

District	Member	60	61	62	63	64	65	66
1	Mollohan	Y	Y	Y	Y	Y	Y	Y
2	Wise	Y	Y	Y	Y	Y	Y	Y
3	Rahall	Y	Y	Y	Y	Y	Y	Y

WISCONSIN

District	Member	60	61	62	63	64	65	66
1	*Neumann*	Y	Y	N	N	Y	Y	Y
2	*Klug*	Y	Y	Y	Y	Y	Y	Y
3	Kind	Y	Y	Y	Y	Y	Y	Y
4	Kleczka	Y	Y	Y	Y	Y	Y	Y
5	Barrett	Y	Y	Y	Y	Y	Y	Y
6	*Petri*	Y	Y	N	N	Y	Y	Y
7	Obey	Y	Y	Y	Y	Y	Y	Y
8	Johnson	Y	Y	Y	Y	Y	Y	Y
9	*Sensenbrenner*	Y	Y	N	N	Y	Y	Y

WYOMING

District	Member	60	61	62	63	64	65	66
AL	*Cubin*	Y	Y	N	N	Y	Y	Y

Southern states - Ala., Ark., Fla., Ga., Ky., La., Miss., N.C., Okla., S.C., Tenn., Texas, Va.

67. HR 3096. Fraudulent Disability Claims Correction/Passage. Greenwood, R-Pa., motion to suspend the rules and pass the bill to correct current law to clarify that a person convicted of fraud in the initial application for federal employees' workers compensation benefits, or in any subsequent application for continuation of benefits, would lose those benefits. Motion agreed to 408-0: R 216-0; D 191-0 (ND 140-0, SD 51-0); I 1-0. March 24, 1998. Bills on the corrections calendar require a three-fifths majority of those present and voting (245 in this case) for passage.

68. HR 2589. Copyright Term Extension/Small Business. McCollum, R-Fla., amendment to the Sensenbrenner, R-Wis., amendment to limit the exemption from music licensing fees to cover restaurants of 3,500 square feet or less which play radio or television broadcasts. The Sensenbrenner amendment would exempt restaurants, bars, and coffee shops from having to pay licensing fees for retransmission of radio and television broadcasts. Rejected 150-259: R 34-187; D 115-72 (ND 97-41, SD 18-31); I 1-0. March 25, 1998.

69. HR 2589. Copyright Term Extension/Music Licensing Fees. Sensenbrenner, R-Wis., amendment to exempt restaurants, bars, and coffee shops from having to pay licensing fees for retransmission of radio and television broadcasts. Adopted 297-112: R 205-16; D 92-95 (ND 57-81, SD 35-14); I 0-1. March 25, 1998. Subsequently, HR2589 was passed by voice vote.

70. HR 2578. Traveler Visa Waivers/Greece and Portugal. Pombo, R-Calif., amendment to increase the visa refusal rate (the number of citizens refused visas to the United States from their home consulates) from 2 percent to 3 percent to allow citizens of Portugal and Greece to take part with the other Europeans Union countries in the tourist visa waiver program. Adopted 360-46: R 179-41; D 180-5 (ND 136-0, SD 44-5); I 1-0. March 25, 1998.

71. HR 2578. Traveler Visa Waivers/Passage. Passage of the bill to extend through April 2000 the visa waiver pilot program which allows most Western Europeans, Japanese and Australians to travel to the United States for 90 days without a visa. Passed 407-0: R 221-0; D 185-0 (ND 136-0, SD 49-0); I 1-0. March 25, 1998. A "yea" was a vote in support of the president's position.

72. HR 3310. Small Business Paperwork Reduction/Agency Discretion. Kucinich, D-Ohio., amendment to require agencies to establish policies to waive, delay or reduce civil penalties for first-time violations in appropriate circumstances, including whether the business has been acting in good faith to comply, and whether the business has obtained significant economic benefit from the violation. Rejected 183-221: R 7-209; D 175-12 (ND 135-4, SD 40-8); I 1-0. March 26, 1998.

73. HR 3310. Small Business Paperwork Reduction/State-Run Federal Programs. McIntosh, R-Ind., amendment to apply the bill's suspension of fines provision to state-run federal enforcement programs. Adopted 224-179: R 203-12; D 21-167 (ND 7-132, SD 14-35); I 0-0. March 26, 1998.

[1] *Stephen H. Schiff, R-N.M., died March 25.*

Key

Y	Voted for (yea).
#	Paired for.
+	Announced for.
N	Voted against (nay).
X	Paired against.
−	Announced against.
P	Voted "present."
C	Voted "present" to avoid possible conflict of interest.
?	Did not vote or otherwise make a position known.

Democrats   **Republicans**
Independent

	67	68	69	70	71	72	73
ALABAMA							
1 *Callahan*	Y	Y	Y	Y	Y	N	Y
2 *Everett*	Y	N	Y	Y	Y	N	Y
3 *Riley*	Y	N	Y	Y	Y	N	Y
4 *Aderholt*	Y	N	Y	N	Y	N	Y
5 Cramer	Y	N	Y	Y	Y	Y	Y
6 *Bachus*	Y	N	Y	Y	Y	N	Y
7 Hilliard	Y	N	N	Y	Y	Y	N
ALASKA							
AL *Young*	Y	N	Y	Y	Y	N	Y
ARIZONA							
1 *Salmon*	Y	N	Y	Y	Y	N	Y
2 Pastor	Y	Y	N	Y	Y	Y	N
3 *Stump*	Y	N	Y	N	Y	N	Y
4 *Shadegg*	Y	N	Y	N	Y	N	Y
5 *Kolbe*	Y	N	Y	Y	Y	N	Y
6 *Hayworth*	Y	N	Y	Y	Y	N	Y
ARKANSAS							
1 Berry	?	N	Y	N	Y	Y	N
2 Snyder	Y	N	Y	Y	Y	Y	N
3 *Hutchinson*	Y	Y	Y	Y	Y	N	Y
4 *Dickey*	Y	N	Y	Y	Y	N	Y
CALIFORNIA							
1 *Riggs*	Y	−	+	Y	Y	?	?
2 *Herger*	?	N	Y	Y	Y	N	Y
3 Fazio	Y	Y	N	Y	Y	Y	N
4 *Doolittle*	Y	N	Y	Y	Y	N	Y
5 Matsui	Y	Y	N	Y	Y	Y	N
6 Woolsey	Y	N	N	Y	Y	Y	N
7 Miller	Y	Y	N	Y	Y	Y	N
8 Pelosi	Y	N	N	Y	Y	Y	N
9 Vacant							
10 Tauscher	Y	N	Y	Y	Y	Y	N
11 *Pombo*	Y	N	N	Y	Y	N	Y
12 Lantos	Y	Y	N	Y	Y	Y	N
13 Stark	?	?	?	Y	Y	Y	N
14 Eshoo	Y	N	N	Y	Y	Y	N
15 *Campbell*	Y	N	Y	N	Y	N	Y
16 Lofgren	Y	Y	N	Y	Y	Y	N
17 Farr	Y	N	Y	Y	Y	Y	N
18 Condit	Y	N	Y	Y	Y	Y	N
19 *Radanovich*	Y	N	Y	Y	Y	N	Y
20 Dooley	Y	N	Y	Y	Y	Y	N
21 *Thomas*	Y	Y	Y	Y	Y	N	Y
22 Capps, L.	Y	Y	N	Y	Y	Y	N
23 *Gallegly*	Y	N	Y	N	Y	N	Y
24 Sherman	Y	Y	N	Y	Y	Y	N
25 *McKeon*	Y	N	Y	Y	Y	N	Y
26 Berman	Y	Y	N	Y	Y	Y	N
27 *Rogan*	Y	Y	Y	Y	Y	N	Y
28 *Dreier*	Y	N	Y	Y	Y	N	Y
29 Waxman	Y	Y	N	Y	Y	Y	N
30 Becerra	Y	Y	N	Y	Y	?	?
31 Martinez	Y	N	Y	Y	Y	Y	N
32 Dixon	Y	Y	N	Y	Y	Y	N
33 Roybal-Allard	Y	Y	N	Y	Y	Y	N
34 Torres	Y	Y	Y	Y	Y	Y	N
35 Waters	?	?	?	?	?	?	?
36 Harman	?	?	?	?	?	?	?
37 Millender-McD.	Y	?	?	?	?	?	?

	67	68	69	70	71	72	73
38 *Horn*	Y	N	Y	Y	Y	N	Y
39 *Royce*	?	?	?	?	?	?	?
40 *Lewis*	Y	N	Y	Y	Y	N	Y
41 *Kim*	Y	Y	Y	N	Y	N	Y
42 Brown	Y	Y	N	Y	Y	Y	N
43 *Calvert*	Y	N	Y	Y	Y	N	Y
44 Vacant							
45 *Rohrabacher*	Y	N	Y	Y	Y	N	Y
46 Sanchez	Y	Y	N	Y	Y	Y	N
47 *Cox*	Y	N	Y	Y	Y	N	Y
48 *Packard*	Y	N	Y	Y	Y	N	Y
49 *Bilbray*	Y	N	Y	Y	Y	N	Y
50 Filner	Y	Y	N	Y	Y	Y	N
51 *Cunningham*	Y	N	Y	Y	Y	N	Y
52 *Hunter*	Y	Y	Y	Y	Y	N	Y
COLORADO							
1 DeGette	Y	Y	N	Y	Y	Y	N
2 Skaggs	Y	Y	N	Y	Y	Y	N
3 *McInnis*	Y	N	Y	Y	Y	N	Y
4 *Schaffer*	Y	N	Y	Y	Y	N	Y
5 *Hefley*	Y	N	Y	Y	Y	N	Y
6 *Schaefer*	Y	N	Y	Y	Y	N	Y
CONNECTICUT							
1 Kennelly	Y	Y	N	Y	Y	Y	N
2 Gejdenson	Y	Y	N	Y	Y	Y	N
3 DeLauro	Y	Y	N	Y	Y	Y	N
4 *Shays*	Y	Y	N	Y	Y	N	Y
5 Maloney	Y	N	Y	Y	Y	Y	N
6 *Johnson*	Y	N	Y	Y	Y	N	N
DELAWARE							
AL *Castle*	Y	N	Y	Y	Y	N	Y
FLORIDA							
1 *Scarborough*	Y	Y	N	Y	Y	N	Y
2 Boyd	Y	N	Y	Y	Y	N	Y
3 Brown	Y	+	−	Y	+	+	−
4 *Fowler*	Y	N	Y	Y	Y	N	Y
5 Thurman	Y	Y	Y	Y	Y	Y	N
6 *Stearns*	Y	N	Y	Y	Y	N	Y
7 *Mica*	Y	N	Y	Y	Y	N	Y
8 *McCollum*	Y	Y	N	N	Y	N	Y
9 *Bilirakis*	Y	N	Y	Y	Y	N	Y
10 *Young*	?	N	Y	Y	Y	N	Y
11 Davis	Y	N	Y	Y	Y	Y	N
12 *Canady*	Y	N	Y	Y	Y	N	Y
13 *Miller*	Y	N	Y	Y	Y	N	Y
14 *Goss*	Y	N	Y	Y	Y	N	Y
15 *Weldon*	Y	N	Y	Y	Y	N	Y
16 *Foley*	Y	Y	Y	Y	Y	N	Y
17 Meek	Y	N	Y	Y	Y	Y	N
18 *Ros-Lehtinen*	N	Y	Y	Y	Y	N	Y
19 Wexler	Y	Y	N	Y	Y	Y	N
20 Deutsch	Y	Y	N	Y	Y	Y	N
21 *Diaz-Balart*	N	Y	Y	Y	Y	N	Y
22 *Shaw*	Y	N	Y	Y	Y	N	Y
23 Hastings	Y	Y	N	Y	Y	Y	N
GEORGIA							
1 *Kingston*	Y	N	Y	Y	Y	N	Y
2 Bishop	Y	N	Y	Y	Y	N	Y
3 *Collins*	Y	N	Y	N	Y	N	Y
4 McKinney	Y	Y	N	Y	Y	Y	N
5 Lewis	Y	Y	N	Y	Y	Y	N
6 *Gingrich*							
7 *Barr*	Y	N	Y	N	Y	N	Y
8 *Chambliss*	Y	N	Y	Y	Y	N	Y
9 *Deal*	Y	N	Y	N	Y	N	Y
10 *Norwood*	Y	N	Y	Y	Y	N	Y
11 *Linder*	Y	N	Y	Y	Y	N	Y
HAWAII							
1 Abercrombie	Y	N	Y	Y	Y	Y	N
2 Mink	Y	Y	N	Y	Y	Y	N
IDAHO							
1 *Chenoweth*	+	N	Y	Y	Y	N	Y
2 *Crapo*	Y	N	Y	Y	Y	?	?
ILLINOIS							
1 Rush	Y	Y	Y	Y	Y	Y	N
2 Jackson	Y	Y	Y	Y	Y	Y	N
3 Lipinski	Y	Y	Y	Y	Y	Y	N
4 Gutierrez	Y	Y	N	Y	Y	Y	N
5 Blagojevich	Y	Y	N	Y	Y	Y	N
6 *Hyde*	Y	N	Y	N	Y	N	Y
7 Davis	Y	Y	Y	Y	Y	Y	N
8 *Crane*	Y	N	Y	Y	Y	N	Y
9 Yates	?	Y	N	?	?	N	Y
10 *Porter*	Y	N	Y	Y	Y	N	Y
11 *Weller*	Y	N	Y	Y	Y	N	Y
12 Costello	Y	Y	Y	Y	Y	Y	N

ND Northern Democrats   SD Southern Democrats

	67	68	69	70	71	72	73
13 **Fawell**	Y	N	Y	N	Y	N	Y
14 **Hastert**	Y	N	Y	Y	Y	N	Y
15 **Ewing**	Y	N	Y	Y	Y	N	Y
16 **Manzullo**	?	N	Y	Y	Y	N	Y
17 Evans	Y	Y	Y	Y	Y	Y	N
18 **LaHood**	Y	Y	N	Y	Y	N	Y
19 Poshard	Y	Y	Y	Y	Y	Y	N
20 **Shimkus**	Y	N	Y	Y	Y	N	Y
INDIANA							
1 Visclosky	Y	N	Y	Y	Y	Y	N
2 **McIntosh**	Y	N	Y	Y	Y	N	Y
3 Roemer	Y	N	Y	Y	Y	N	N
4 **Souder**	Y	N	Y	Y	Y	N	Y
5 **Buyer**	Y	N	Y	Y	Y	N	Y
6 **Burton**	Y	N	Y	Y	Y	N	Y
7 **Pease**	Y	Y	N	N	Y	N	Y
8 **Hostettler**	Y	N	Y	Y	Y	N	Y
9 Hamilton	Y	N	Y	Y	Y	N	N
10 Carson	Y	Y	Y	Y	Y	Y	N
IOWA							
1 **Leach**	Y	N	Y	Y	Y	N	Y
2 **Nussle**	Y	N	Y	Y	Y	N	Y
3 Boswell	Y	N	Y	Y	Y	Y	N
4 **Ganske**	Y	N	Y	Y	Y	N	Y
5 **Latham**	Y	N	Y	Y	Y	N	Y
KANSAS							
1 **Moran**	Y	N	Y	Y	Y	N	Y
2 **Ryun**	Y	N	Y	Y	Y	N	Y
3 **Snowbarger**	Y	N	Y	N	Y	N	Y
4 **Tiahrt**	Y	N	Y	Y	Y	N	Y
KENTUCKY							
1 **Whitfield**	Y	N	Y	Y	Y	N	Y
2 **Lewis**	Y	N	Y	N	Y	N	Y
3 **Northup**	Y	N	Y	Y	Y	N	Y
4 **Bunning**	Y	N	Y	N	Y	N	Y
5 **Rogers**	Y	N	Y	N	Y	N	Y
6 Baesler	Y	N	Y	N	Y	Y	N
LOUISIANA							
1 **Livingston**	Y	Y	Y	Y	Y	N	Y
2 Jefferson	?	?	?	?	?	?	?
3 **Tauzin**	Y	N	Y	Y	Y	N	Y
4 **McCrery**	Y	N	Y	Y	Y	N	Y
5 **Cooksey**	Y	N	Y	Y	Y	N	Y
6 **Baker**	Y	N	Y	N	Y	N	Y
7 John	Y	N	Y	Y	Y	Y	Y
MAINE							
1 Allen	Y	Y	N	Y	Y	Y	N
2 Baldacci	Y	Y	Y	Y	Y	Y	N
MARYLAND							
1 **Gilchrest**	Y	Y	Y	N	Y	Y	Y
2 **Ehrlich**	Y	Y	Y	Y	Y	N	Y
3 Cardin	Y	?	?	?	?	?	?
4 Wynn	Y	N	Y	Y	Y	Y	N
5 Hoyer	Y	Y	N	Y	Y	Y	N
6 **Bartlett**	Y	N	Y	Y	Y	N	Y
7 Cummings	Y	N	N	Y	Y	Y	N
8 **Morella**	Y	Y	N	Y	Y	Y	N
MASSACHUSETTS							
1 Olver	Y	Y	N	Y	Y	?	?
2 Neal	Y	Y	Y	Y	Y	Y	N
3 McGovern	Y	Y	N	Y	Y	Y	N
4 Frank	Y	Y	N	Y	Y	Y	N
5 Meehan	Y	Y	N	Y	Y	Y	N
6 Tierney	Y	Y	N	Y	Y	Y	N
7 Markey	Y	Y	N	Y	Y	Y	N
8 Kennedy	Y	Y	N	Y	Y	Y	N
9 Moakley	Y	Y	N	Y	Y	Y	N
10 Delahunt	Y	Y	N	Y	Y	Y	N
MICHIGAN							
1 Stupak	Y	Y	N	Y	Y	Y	N
2 **Hoekstra**	Y	N	Y	Y	Y	N	Y
3 **Ehlers**	Y	N	Y	Y	Y	N	Y
4 **Camp**	Y	N	Y	Y	Y	N	Y
5 Barcia	Y	N	Y	Y	Y	Y	N
6 **Upton**	Y	N	Y	Y	Y	N	Y
7 **Smith**	Y	N	Y	Y	Y	N	Y
8 Stabenow	Y	N	Y	Y	Y	Y	N
9 Kildee	Y	Y	N	Y	Y	Y	N
10 Bonior	Y	Y	N	Y	Y	Y	N
11 **Knollenberg**	Y	N	Y	Y	Y	N	Y
12 Levin	Y	Y	N	Y	Y	Y	N
13 Rivers	Y	Y	N	Y	Y	Y	N
14 Conyers	Y	+	−	+	+	+	−
15 Kilpatrick	Y	Y	N	Y	Y	Y	N
16 Dingell	Y	Y	N	Y	Y	Y	N

	67	68	69	70	71	72	73
MINNESOTA							
1 **Gutknecht**	Y	N	Y	Y	Y	N	Y
2 Minge	Y	N	Y	Y	Y	Y	Y
3 **Ramstad**	Y	N	Y	Y	Y	N	Y
4 Vento	Y	Y	N	Y	Y	Y	N
5 Sabo	Y	Y	N	Y	Y	Y	N
6 Luther	Y	Y	N	Y	Y	Y	N
7 Peterson	Y	N	Y	Y	Y	Y	N
8 Oberstar	Y	Y	N	Y	Y	Y	N
MISSISSIPPI							
1 **Wicker**	Y	N	Y	Y	Y	N	Y
2 Thompson	Y	N	Y	Y	Y	Y	N
3 **Pickering**	Y	N	Y	Y	Y	N	Y
4 **Parker**	Y	N	Y	Y	Y	N	Y
5 Taylor	Y	N	Y	N	Y	N	Y
MISSOURI							
1 Clay	Y	Y	N	Y	Y	Y	N
2 **Talent**	Y	N	Y	Y	Y	N	Y
3 Gephardt	Y	Y	N	Y	Y	Y	N
4 Skelton	Y	N	Y	Y	Y	Y	Y
5 McCarthy	Y	Y	N	Y	Y	Y	N
6 Danner	Y	N	Y	Y	Y	Y	Y
7 **Blunt**	Y	N	Y	N	Y	N	Y
8 **Emerson**	Y	N	Y	N	Y	N	Y
9 **Hulshof**	Y	N	Y	Y	Y	N	Y
MONTANA							
AL **Hill**	Y	N	Y	Y	Y	N	Y
NEBRASKA							
1 **Bereuter**	Y	N	Y	Y	Y	N	Y
2 **Christensen**	Y	N	Y	Y	Y	N	Y
3 **Barrett**	Y	N	Y	Y	Y	N	Y
NEVADA							
1 **Ensign**	Y	N	Y	Y	Y	N	Y
2 **Gibbons**	Y	N	Y	Y	Y	N	Y
NEW HAMPSHIRE							
1 **Sununu**	Y	N	Y	Y	Y	N	Y
2 **Bass**	Y	N	Y	Y	Y	N	Y
NEW JERSEY							
1 Andrews	Y	N	Y	Y	Y	Y	N
2 **LoBiondo**	Y	N	Y	Y	Y	N	N
3 **Saxton**	Y	N	Y	?	?	N	N
4 **Smith**	Y	N	Y	Y	Y	N	N
5 **Roukema**	Y	N	Y	N	Y	N	Y
6 Pallone	Y	N	Y	Y	Y	Y	N
7 **Franks**	Y	N	Y	Y	Y	N	N
8 Pascrell	Y	Y	Y	Y	Y	Y	N
9 Rothman	Y	?	?	?	?	Y	N
10 Payne	?	?	?	?	?	?	?
11 **Frelinghuysen**	Y	N	Y	Y	Y	N	?
12 **Pappas**	Y	N	Y	Y	Y	N	Y
13 Menendez	Y	Y	N	Y	Y	Y	N
NEW MEXICO							
1 **Schiff**[1]	?	?	?	?			
2 **Skeen**	Y	N	Y	Y	Y	N	Y
3 **Redmond**	Y	N	Y	Y	Y	Y	Y
NEW YORK							
1 **Forbes**	Y	Y	N	Y	Y	N	N
2 **Lazio**	Y	Y	Y	Y	Y	Y	Y
3 **King**	Y	N	Y	Y	Y	N	N
4 McCarthy	Y	Y	N	Y	Y	Y	N
5 Ackerman	Y	Y	N	Y	Y	Y	N
6 Meeks	Y	Y	N	Y	Y	Y	N
7 Manton	Y	Y	N	Y	Y	Y	N
8 Nadler	Y	Y	N	Y	Y	Y	N
9 Schumer	?	Y	N	?	?	Y	N
10 Towns	Y	Y	N	?	?	Y	N
11 Owens	Y	Y	N	Y	Y	Y	N
12 Velázquez	Y	Y	N	Y	Y	Y	N
13 **Fossella**	Y	N	Y	Y	Y	N	Y
14 Maloney	Y	Y	N	Y	Y	Y	N
15 Rangel	?	X	?	?	?	?	?
16 Serrano	Y	Y	N	Y	Y	Y	N
17 Engel	Y	Y	N	Y	Y	Y	N
18 Lowey	Y	Y	N	Y	Y	Y	N
19 **Kelly**	Y	Y	N	Y	Y	N	Y
20 **Gilman**	Y	Y	N	Y	Y	N	Y
21 McNulty	Y	N	Y	Y	Y	Y	N
22 **Solomon**	Y	N	Y	N	Y	N	Y
23 **Boehlert**	Y	N	Y	Y	Y	Y	N
24 **McHugh**	Y	N	Y	Y	Y	N	Y
25 **Walsh**	Y	N	Y	Y	Y	N	Y
26 Hinchey	Y	Y	N	Y	Y	Y	N
27 **Paxon**	Y	N	Y	Y	Y	?	?
28 Slaughter	Y	Y	N	Y	Y	Y	N
29 LaFalce	Y	Y	N	Y	Y	Y	N

	67	68	69	70	71	72	73
30 **Quinn**	Y	N	Y	Y	Y	N	Y
31 **Houghton**	Y	?	?	?	?	?	?
NORTH CAROLINA							
1 Clayton	Y	Y	Y	Y	Y	Y	N
2 Etheridge	Y	N	Y	Y	Y	Y	N
3 **Jones**	Y	N	Y	Y	Y	N	Y
4 Price	Y	N	Y	Y	Y	Y	N
5 **Burr**	Y	N	Y	Y	Y	N	Y
6 **Coble**	Y	Y	N	Y	Y	N	Y
7 McIntyre	Y	N	Y	Y	Y	Y	N
8 Hefner	Y	Y	Y	Y	Y	Y	N
9 **Myrick**	Y	N	Y	Y	Y	N	Y
10 **Ballenger**	Y	N	Y	N	Y	N	Y
11 **Taylor**	Y	N	Y	Y	Y	N	Y
12 Watt	Y	Y	N	Y	Y	Y	N
NORTH DAKOTA							
AL Pomeroy	Y	N	Y	Y	Y	Y	N
OHIO							
1 **Chabot**	Y	N	Y	Y	Y	N	Y
2 **Portman**	Y	N	Y	Y	Y	N	Y
3 Hall	Y	Y	Y	Y	Y	Y	N
4 **Oxley**	Y	N	Y	Y	Y	N	Y
5 **Gillmor**	Y	N	Y	Y	Y	?	?
6 Strickland	Y	N	Y	Y	Y	Y	N
7 **Hobson**	Y	N	Y	Y	Y	N	Y
8 **Boehner**	Y	N	Y	Y	Y	N	Y
9 Kaptur	Y	Y	Y	Y	Y	Y	N
10 Kucinich	Y	Y	Y	Y	Y	Y	N
11 Stokes	Y	Y	N	Y	Y	Y	N
12 **Kasich**	Y	N	Y	Y	Y	N	Y
13 Brown	Y	Y	N	Y	Y	Y	N
14 Sawyer	Y	Y	N	Y	Y	Y	N
15 **Pryce**	Y	N	Y	Y	Y	N	Y
16 **Regula**	Y	N	Y	Y	Y	N	Y
17 Traficant	Y	N	Y	Y	Y	Y	Y
18 **Ney**	Y	N	Y	Y	Y	N	Y
19 **LaTourette**	Y	N	Y	Y	Y	N	Y
OKLAHOMA							
1 **Largent**	Y	N	Y	Y	Y	N	Y
2 **Coburn**	Y	N	Y	Y	Y	N	Y
3 **Watkins**	Y	N	Y	Y	Y	N	Y
4 **Watts**	Y	N	Y	N	Y	N	Y
5 **Istook**	Y	N	Y	N	Y	N	Y
6 **Lucas**	Y	N	Y	Y	Y	N	Y
OREGON							
1 Furse	Y	Y	N	Y	Y	Y	N
2 **Smith**	Y	N	Y	Y	Y	N	Y
3 Blumenauer	Y	N	Y	Y	Y	Y	N
4 DeFazio	Y	Y	N	Y	Y	Y	N
5 Hooley	+	N	Y	Y	Y	Y	N
PENNSYLVANIA							
1 Vacant							
2 Fattah	Y	Y	N	Y	Y	Y	N
3 Borski	Y	Y	Y	Y	Y	Y	N
4 Klink	Y	N	Y	Y	Y	Y	N
5 **Peterson**	Y	N	Y	Y	Y	N	Y
6 Holden	Y	N	Y	Y	Y	Y	Y
7 **Weldon**	Y	N	Y	Y	Y	N	N
8 **Greenwood**	Y	N	Y	Y	Y	N	N
9 **Shuster**	Y	N	Y	Y	Y	N	Y
10 **McDade**	Y	Y	Y	?	Y	N	Y
11 Kanjorski	Y	N	Y	Y	Y	Y	N
12 Murtha	Y	N	Y	Y	Y	Y	Y
13 **Fox**	Y	N	Y	Y	Y	N	Y
14 Coyne	Y	Y	N	Y	Y	Y	N
15 McHale	Y	N	Y	Y	Y	Y	N
16 **Pitts**	Y	N	Y	Y	Y	N	Y
17 **Gekas**	Y	N	Y	Y	Y	N	Y
18 Doyle	Y	N	Y	Y	Y	Y	N
19 **Goodling**	Y	N	Y	N	Y	N	Y
20 Mascara	Y	N	Y	Y	Y	Y	N
21 **English**	Y	N	Y	Y	Y	N	Y
RHODE ISLAND							
1 Kennedy	Y	Y	N	Y	Y	Y	N
2 Weygand	Y	N	Y	Y	Y	Y	N
SOUTH CAROLINA							
1 **Sanford**	Y	N	Y	N	Y	N	Y
2 **Spence**	Y	N	Y	Y	Y	N	Y
3 **Graham**	Y	N	Y	Y	Y	N	Y
4 **Inglis**	?	N	Y	Y	Y	N	Y
5 Spratt	?	N	Y	Y	Y	Y	N
6 Clyburn	Y	N	Y	Y	Y	Y	N
SOUTH DAKOTA							
AL **Thune**	Y	N	Y	Y	Y	N	Y

	67	68	69	70	71	72	73
TENNESSEE							
1 **Jenkins**	Y	Y	Y	Y	Y	N	Y
2 **Duncan**	Y	N	Y	Y	Y	N	Y
3 **Wamp**	Y	Y	Y	Y	Y	N	Y
4 **Hilleary**	Y	Y	Y	Y	Y	N	Y
5 Clement	Y	Y	N	Y	Y	Y	Y
6 Gordon	Y	Y	N	Y	Y	Y	Y
7 **Bryant**	Y	Y	Y	N	Y	N	Y
8 Tanner	Y	Y	N	Y	Y	Y	Y
9 Ford	Y	+	−	+	+	+	−
TEXAS							
1 Sandlin	Y	N	Y	Y	Y	Y	N
2 Turner	Y	N	Y	Y	Y	N	Y
3 **Johnson, Sam**	Y	N	Y	N	Y	N	Y
4 Hall	Y	N	Y	N	Y	N	Y
5 **Sessions**	Y	N	Y	Y	Y	N	Y
6 **Barton**	?	N	Y	N	Y	N	Y
7 **Archer**	Y	N	Y	Y	Y	N	Y
8 **Brady**	Y	N	Y	N	Y	N	Y
9 Lampson	Y	Y	N	Y	Y	Y	N
10 Doggett	Y	Y	N	Y	Y	Y	N
11 Edwards	Y	N	Y	Y	Y	Y	N
12 **Granger**	Y	N	Y	N	Y	N	Y
13 **Thornberry**	Y	N	Y	Y	Y	N	Y
14 **Paul**	Y	Y	N	Y	Y	N	Y
15 Hinojosa	Y	N	Y	Y	Y	Y	N
16 Reyes	Y	N	Y	Y	Y	?	N
17 Stenholm	Y	N	Y	Y	Y	N	Y
18 Jackson-Lee	Y	?	?	?	?	?	?
19 **Combest**	Y	N	Y	N	Y	N	Y
20 Gonzalez	?	?	?	?	?	?	?
21 **Smith**	Y	N	Y	N	Y	N	Y
22 **DeLay**	Y	N	Y	Y	Y	?	Y
23 **Bonilla**	Y	N	Y	Y	Y	N	?
24 Frost	Y	Y	Y	Y	Y	Y	N
25 Bentsen	Y	N	Y	Y	Y	Y	N
26 **Armey**	?	N	Y	Y	Y	N	Y
27 Ortiz	Y	Y	N	Y	Y	Y	N
28 Rodriguez	Y	N	Y	Y	Y	Y	N
29 Green	Y	N	Y	N	Y	Y	N
30 Johnson, E.B.	Y	?	?	?	?	?	?
UTAH							
1 **Hansen**	Y	Y	Y	Y	Y	N	Y
2 **Cook**	Y	N	Y	Y	Y	−	+
3 **Cannon**	?	?	?	?	?	?	?
VERMONT							
AL *Sanders*	Y	Y	N	Y	Y	Y	?
VIRGINIA							
1 **Bateman**	Y	N	Y	Y	Y	N	Y
2 Pickett	Y	N	Y	Y	Y	N	Y
3 Scott	Y	N	Y	Y	Y	Y	N
4 Sisisky	Y	N	Y	Y	Y	N	Y
5 Goode	Y	N	Y	Y	Y	N	Y
6 **Goodlatte**	Y	Y	Y	N	Y	N	Y
7 **Bliley**	Y	Y	Y	Y	Y	N	Y
8 Moran	Y	N	Y	Y	Y	Y	N
9 Boucher	Y	Y	Y	Y	Y	Y	N
10 **Wolf**	Y	N	Y	Y	Y	N	Y
11 **Davis**	Y	N	Y	Y	Y	N	Y
WASHINGTON							
1 **White**	Y	N	Y	N	Y	N	Y
2 **Metcalf**	Y	N	Y	Y	Y	N	Y
3 **Smith, Linda**	Y	N	Y	Y	Y	N	Y
4 **Hastings**	Y	N	Y	N	Y	N	Y
5 **Nethercutt**	Y	N	Y	Y	Y	N	Y
6 Dicks	Y	N	Y	Y	Y	Y	N
7 McDermott	+	#	X	+	+	+	−
8 **Dunn**	Y	N	Y	Y	Y	N	Y
9 Smith, Adam	Y	N	Y	Y	Y	Y	N
WEST VIRGINIA							
1 Mollohan	Y	Y	Y	Y	Y	N	Y
2 Wise	Y	Y	Y	Y	Y	Y	N
3 Rahall	Y	Y	Y	Y	Y	Y	N
WISCONSIN							
1 **Neumann**	Y	N	Y	Y	Y	N	Y
2 **Klug**	Y	N	Y	Y	Y	N	Y
3 Kind	Y	N	Y	Y	Y	Y	N
4 Kleczka	Y	−	#	+	+	Y	N
5 Barrett	Y	Y	Y	Y	Y	Y	N
6 **Petri**	Y	N	Y	Y	Y	N	Y
7 Obey	Y	Y	Y	Y	Y	Y	N
8 Johnson	Y	Y	Y	Y	Y	Y	N
9 **Sensenbrenner**	Y	N	Y	Y	Y	N	Y
WYOMING							
AL **Cubin**	Y	N	Y	Y	Y	N	Y

Southern states - Ala., Ark., Fla., Ga., Ky., La., Miss., N.C., Okla., S.C., Tenn., Texas, Va.

74. HR 3310. Small Business Paperwork Reduction/Passage. Passage of the bill to suspend most civil fines on small-businesses for first-time paperwork violations. Under the bill, the federal regulating agency could choose to suspend the fine if the violation had not caused actual harm to the public health or safety, and the business corrects the violation within six months. Passed 267-140: R 213-4; D 54-135 (ND 27-113, SD 27-22); I 0-1. March 26, 1998. A "nay" was a vote in support of the president's position.

75. HR 1757. Fiscal 1998 State Department Authorization/Rule. Adoption of the rule (H Res 385) to provide for floor consideration of the conference report on the bill to authorize $1.75 billion in fiscal 1998 and $1.69 billion in fiscal 1999 for State Department diplomatic and consular functions, authorize $819 million over fiscal years 1998 through 2000 to pay back U.S. dues to the United Nations, codify restrictions on U.S. funds for international family planning and reorganize U.S. foreign policy agencies. Adopted 234-172: R 215-4; D 19-167 (ND 14-124, SD 5-43); I 0-1. March 26, 1998. (Subsequently, the conference report was adopted by voice vote.)

76. HR 3246. Labor Union Organizing Curbs/Rule. Adoption of the rule (H Res 393) to provide for floor consideration of the bill to permit employers to refuse to hire, or fire, those who seek employment with the primary intent of organizing workers to join a union. Adopted 220-185: R 216-1; D 4-183 (ND 1-137, SD 3-46); I 0-1. March 26, 1998.

77. HR 3246. Labor Union Organizing Curbs/Bona Fide Applicants. Goodling, R-Pa., amendment to clarify that any "bona fide" applicant would continue to enjoy every right provided by the National Labor Relations Act, including the right to form, join, or assist labor organizations. Adopted 398-0: R 214-0; D 183-0 (ND 135-0, SD 48-0); I 1-0. March 26, 1998.

78. HR 3246. Labor Union Organizing Curbs/Passage. Passage of the bill to permit employers to refuse to hire, or fire, those who seek employment to organize workers to join a union. Passed 202-200: R 194-20; D 8-179 (ND 0-138, SD 8-41); I 0-1. March 26, 1998. A "nay" was a vote in support of the president's position.

79. HR 2515. Forest Recovery/Road Construction. Boehlert, R-N.Y., amendment to the Smith, R-Ore., amendment to prohibit the building of roads under the bill in roadless areas. The Smith amendment would prohibit the construction of roads under the bill that are not allowed under current law. Adopted 200-187: R 52-156; D 147-31 (ND 117-17, SD 30-14); I 1-0. March 27, 1998. (Subsequently, the Smith amendment, as amended, was rejected by voice vote).

80. HR 2515. Forest Recovery/Passage. Passage of the bill to direct the Agriculture Department to establish a five-year nationwide program to restore and protect public forests from fire, disease and infestation through forest recovery projects. Rejected 181-201: R 153-51; D 28-149 (ND 12-123, SD 16-26); I 0-1. March 27, 1998. A "nay" was a vote in support of the president's position.

Key

Y	Voted for (yea).
#	Paired for.
+	Announced for.
N	Voted against (nay).
X	Paired against.
–	Announced against.
P	Voted "present."
C	Voted "present" to avoid possible conflict of interest.
?	Did not vote or otherwise make a position known.

● Democrats **Republicans**
Independent

	74	75	76	77	78	79	80
ALABAMA							
1 *Callahan*	Y	Y	Y	Y	Y	N	Y
2 *Everett*	Y	Y	Y	Y	Y	N	Y
3 *Riley*	Y	Y	Y	Y	Y	N	Y
4 *Aderholt*	Y	Y	Y	Y	Y	N	Y
5 Cramer	Y	N	N	Y	N	N	Y
6 *Bachus*	Y	Y	Y	Y	Y	N	Y
7 Hilliard	N	N	N	Y	N	N	Y
ALASKA							
AL *Young*	Y	Y	Y	Y	N	?	?
ARIZONA							
1 *Salmon*	Y	Y	Y	Y	Y	N	Y
2 Pastor	N	N	N	Y	N	Y	N
3 *Stump*	Y	Y	Y	Y	Y	N	Y
4 *Shadegg*	Y	Y	Y	Y	Y	N	Y
5 *Kolbe*	Y	Y	Y	Y	Y	N	Y
6 *Hayworth*	Y	Y	Y	Y	Y	N	Y
ARKANSAS							
1 Berry	Y	Y	N	Y	N	–	+
2 Snyder	N	N	N	Y	N	Y	N
3 *Hutchinson*	Y	Y	Y	Y	Y	N	Y
4 *Dickey*	Y	Y	Y	Y	Y	N	Y
CALIFORNIA							
1 *Riggs*	Y	Y	Y	Y	Y	N	Y
2 *Herger*	Y	Y	Y	Y	Y	N	Y
3 Fazio	N	N	N	Y	N	Y	N
4 *Doolittle*	Y	Y	Y	Y	Y	N	Y
5 Matsui	N	N	N	Y	N	Y	N
6 Woolsey	N	N	N	Y	N	Y	N
7 Miller	N	N	N	Y	N	Y	N
8 Pelosi	N	N	N	Y	N	Y	N
9 Vacant							
10 Tauscher	Y	N	N	Y	N	Y	N
11 *Pombo*	Y	Y	Y	Y	Y	N	Y
12 Lantos	N	N	N	Y	N	Y	N
13 Stark	N	N	N	Y	N	Y	N
14 Eshoo	N	N	N	Y	N	Y	N
15 *Campbell*	Y	Y	Y	Y	N	N	N
16 Lofgren	N	N	N	Y	N	Y	N
17 Farr	N	N	N	Y	N	Y	N
18 Condit	Y	N	N	Y	N	N	N
19 *Radanovich*	Y	Y	Y	Y	Y	N	Y
20 Dooley	Y	N	N	Y	N	N	N
21 *Thomas*	Y	N	N	Y	N	Y	N
22 Capps, L.	Y	N	N	Y	N	Y	N
23 *Gallegly*	Y	Y	Y	Y	Y	N	Y
24 Sherman	N	N	N	+	N	Y	N
25 *McKeon*	Y	Y	Y	Y	Y	N	Y
26 Berman	N	N	N	Y	N	Y	N
27 *Rogan*	Y	Y	Y	Y	Y	N	Y
28 *Dreier*	Y	Y	Y	Y	Y	N	Y
29 Waxman	N	N	N	Y	N	Y	N
30 Becerra	?	N	N	Y	N	+	–
31 Martinez	N	N	N	Y	N	Y	N
32 Dixon	N	N	N	Y	N	Y	N
33 Roybal-Allard	N	N	N	Y	N	Y	N
34 Torres	N	N	N	Y	N	Y	N
35 Waters	?	?	?	?	?	?	?
36 Harman	?	?	?	?	?	?	?
37 Millender-McD.	?	?	?	?	?	?	?
38 *Horn*	Y	Y	Y	Y	Y	Y	N
39 *Royce*	#	?	?	?	?	?	?
40 *Lewis*	Y	Y	Y	Y	Y	N	Y
41 *Kim*	Y	Y	Y	Y	Y	N	Y
42 Brown	N	N	N	Y	N	Y	N
43 *Calvert*	Y	Y	Y	Y	Y	N	Y
44 Vacant							
45 *Rohrabacher*	Y	Y	Y	Y	Y	N	Y
46 Sanchez	Y	N	N	Y	N	+	–
47 *Cox*	Y	Y	Y	Y	Y	N	Y
48 *Packard*	Y	Y	Y	Y	Y	N	Y
49 *Bilbray*	Y	Y	Y	Y	Y	N	Y
50 Filner	N	N	N	Y	N	Y	N
51 *Cunningham*	Y	Y	Y	Y	Y	N	?
52 *Hunter*	Y	Y	Y	?	Y	N	Y
COLORADO							
1 DeGette	N	N	N	Y	N	Y	N
2 Skaggs	N	N	N	Y	N	Y	N
3 *McInnis*	Y	Y	Y	Y	Y	N	Y
4 *Schaffer*	Y	Y	Y	Y	Y	N	Y
5 *Hefley*	Y	Y	Y	Y	Y	N	Y
6 *Schaefer*	Y	Y	Y	Y	Y	N	Y
CONNECTICUT							
1 Kennelly	N	N	N	Y	N	Y	N
2 Gejdenson	N	N	N	Y	N	Y	N
3 DeLauro	N	N	N	Y	N	Y	N
4 *Shays*	N	Y	Y	Y	N	Y	N
5 Maloney	Y	N	N	Y	N	Y	N
6 *Johnson*	Y	Y	Y	Y	Y	N	Y
DELAWARE							
AL *Castle*	Y	N	Y	Y	Y	Y	N
FLORIDA							
1 *Scarborough*	Y	Y	Y	Y	Y	N	Y
2 Boyd	Y	N	N	Y	N	Y	N
3 Brown	–	–	–	+	N	+	N
4 *Fowler*	Y	Y	Y	Y	Y	N	Y
5 Thurman	N	N	N	Y	N	N	N
6 *Stearns*	Y	Y	Y	Y	Y	N	Y
7 *Mica*	Y	Y	Y	Y	Y	N	Y
8 *McCollum*	Y	Y	Y	Y	?	?	?
9 *Bilirakis*	Y	Y	Y	Y	Y	N	Y
10 *Young*	Y	Y	Y	Y	Y	N	Y
11 Davis	Y	N	N	Y	N	Y	N
12 *Canady*	Y	Y	Y	Y	Y	N	Y
13 *Miller*	Y	Y	Y	Y	Y	Y	?
14 *Goss*	Y	Y	Y	Y	Y	N	Y
15 *Weldon*	Y	Y	Y	Y	Y	N	Y
16 *Foley*	Y	Y	Y	Y	Y	N	N
17 Meek	N	N	N	Y	N	Y	N
18 *Ros-Lehtinen*	N	Y	Y	Y	–	Y	Y
19 Wexler	N	N	N	Y	N	Y	N
20 Deutsch	N	N	N	Y	N	Y	N
21 *Diaz-Balart*	Y	Y	?	Y	N	Y	Y
22 *Shaw*	Y	Y	Y	Y	Y	Y	Y
23 Hastings	N	N	N	Y	N	Y	N
GEORGIA							
1 *Kingston*	Y	N	Y	Y	Y	N	Y
2 Bishop	Y	N	N	Y	N	N	Y
3 *Collins*	Y	Y	Y	Y	Y	N	Y
4 McKinney	N	N	N	Y	N	Y	N
5 Lewis	N	N	N	Y	N	Y	N
6 *Gingrich*				Y			
7 *Barr*	Y	Y	Y	Y	Y	N	Y
8 *Chambliss*	Y	Y	Y	Y	Y	N	Y
9 *Deal*	Y	Y	Y	Y	Y	N	Y
10 *Norwood*	Y	Y	Y	Y	Y	N	Y
11 *Linder*	Y	Y	Y	Y	Y	N	Y
HAWAII							
1 Abercrombie	N	N	N	Y	N	Y	N
2 Mink	N	N	N	Y	N	Y	N
IDAHO							
1 *Chenoweth*	Y	Y	Y	Y	Y	N	N
2 *Crapo*	?	?	?	?	?	N	N
ILLINOIS							
1 Rush	N	N	N	Y	N	Y	N
2 Jackson	N	N	N	Y	N	Y	N
3 Lipinski	N	Y	N	Y	N	?	?
4 Gutierrez	N	N	N	Y	N	Y	N
5 Blagojevich	N	N	N	Y	N	Y	N
6 *Hyde*	Y	Y	Y	Y	Y	N	Y
7 Davis	N	N	N	Y	N	Y	N
8 *Crane*	Y	Y	Y	Y	Y	N	Y
9 Yates	N	N	?	?	Y	N	Y
10 *Porter*	Y	Y	Y	Y	Y	N	Y
11 *Weller*	Y	Y	Y	Y	Y	N	Y
12 Costello	N	Y	N	Y	N	N	Y

ND Northern Democrats   SD Southern Democrats

ILLINOIS	74	75	76	77	78	79	80
13 Fawell	Y	Y	Y	Y	Y	Y	N
14 Hastert	Y	Y	Y	Y	Y	Y	N
15 Ewing	Y	Y	Y	Y	Y	Y	N
16 Manzullo	Y	Y	Y	Y	Y	Y	N
17 Evans	N	N	N	Y	N	Y	N
18 LaHood	Y	Y	Y	Y	Y	N	Y
19 Poshard	N	Y	N	Y	N	N	N
20 Shimkus	Y	Y	Y	Y	N	N	Y

INDIANA	74	75	76	77	78	79	80
1 Visclosky	N	N	N	Y	N	Y	N
2 McIntosh	Y	Y	Y	Y	Y	Y	N
3 Roemer	Y	N	N	Y	N	Y	N
4 Souder	Y	Y	Y	Y	Y	Y	N
5 Buyer	Y	Y	Y	Y	Y	Y	N
6 Burton	Y	Y	Y	Y	Y	Y	N
7 Pease	Y	Y	Y	Y	Y	Y	N
8 Hostettler	Y	Y	Y	Y	Y	Y	N
9 Hamilton	Y	N	N	Y	N	Y	N
10 Carson	N	N	N	Y	N	Y	N

IOWA	74	75	76	77	78	79	80
1 Leach	Y	N	Y	Y	Y	Y	N
2 Nussle	Y	Y	Y	Y	Y	Y	Y
3 Boswell	Y	N	N	Y	N	Y	N
4 Ganske	Y	Y	Y	Y	Y	Y	N
5 Latham	Y	Y	Y	Y	Y	N	Y

KANSAS	74	75	76	77	78	79	80
1 Moran	Y	Y	Y	Y	Y	N	Y
2 Ryun	Y	Y	Y	Y	Y	N	Y
3 Snowbarger	Y	Y	Y	Y	Y	N	Y
4 Tiahrt	Y	Y	Y	Y	Y	N	Y

KENTUCKY	74	75	76	77	78	79	80
1 Whitfield	Y	Y	Y	Y	Y	N	Y
2 Lewis	Y	Y	Y	Y	Y	N	Y
3 Northup	Y	Y	Y	Y	Y	N	Y
4 Bunning	Y	Y	Y	Y	Y	N	Y
5 Rogers	Y	Y	Y	?	?	?	?
6 Baesler	N	N	N	Y	N	Y	

LOUISIANA	74	75	76	77	78	79	80
1 Livingston	Y	Y	Y	Y	Y	N	Y
2 Jefferson	?	?	?	?	?	?	?
3 Tauzin	Y	Y	Y	Y	Y	N	Y
4 McCrery	Y	Y	Y	Y	Y	N	Y
5 Cooksey	Y	Y	+	+	+	-	+
6 Baker	Y	Y	Y	Y	Y	N	Y
7 John	Y	Y	N	Y	N	Y	N

MAINE	74	75	76	77	78	79	80
1 Allen	N	N	N	Y	N	Y	N
2 Baldacci	N	N	N	Y	N	Y	N

MARYLAND	74	75	76	77	78	79	80
1 Gilchrest	Y	Y	Y	Y	Y	Y	Y
2 Ehrlich	Y	Y	Y	Y	Y	N	Y
3 Cardin	?	?	?	?	?	?	?
4 Wynn	N	N	N	Y	N	Y	N
5 Hoyer	N	N	N	Y	N	Y	N
6 Bartlett	Y	Y	Y	Y	Y	N	Y
7 Cummings	N	N	N	Y	N	Y	N
8 Morella	Y	Y	Y	Y	Y	Y	N

MASSACHUSETTS	74	75	76	77	78	79	80
1 Olver	N	N	N	Y	N	Y	N
2 Neal	N	N	N	Y	N	Y	N
3 McGovern	N	?	N	Y	N	Y	N
4 Frank	N	N	N	Y	N	Y	N
5 Meehan	N	N	N	Y	N	Y	N
6 Tierney	N	N	N	Y	N	Y	N
7 Markey	N	N	N	?	N	Y	N
8 Kennedy	N	N	N	Y	N	Y	N
9 Moakley	N	?	N	Y	N	Y	N
10 Delahunt	N	N	N	Y	N	N	N

MICHIGAN	74	75	76	77	78	79	80
1 Stupak	N	Y	N	Y	N	N	Y
2 Hoekstra	Y	Y	Y	Y	Y	Y	N
3 Ehlers	Y	Y	Y	Y	Y	Y	N
4 Camp	Y	Y	Y	Y	Y	Y	N
5 Barcia	N	Y	N	Y	N	Y	N
6 Upton	Y	Y	Y	Y	Y	Y	N
7 Smith	Y	Y	Y	Y	Y	Y	N
8 Stabenow	Y	N	N	Y	N	Y	N
9 Kildee	N	Y	N	Y	N	Y	N
10 Bonior	N	N	N	Y	N	Y	N
11 Knollenberg	Y	Y	Y	Y	Y	Y	N
12 Levin	N	N	N	Y	N	Y	N
13 Rivers	N	N	N	Y	N	Y	N
14 Conyers	-	-	-	+	-	+	-
15 Kilpatrick	N	N	N	Y	N	Y	N
16 Dingell	N	N	N	Y	N	Y	N

MINNESOTA	74	75	76	77	78	79	80
1 Gutknecht	Y	Y	Y	Y	Y	N	Y
2 Minge	Y	N	N	Y	N	N	N
3 Ramstad	Y	Y	Y	Y	Y	Y	N
4 Vento	N	N	N	Y	N	Y	N
5 Sabo	N	N	N	Y	N	Y	N
6 Luther	Y	N	N	Y	N	Y	N
7 Peterson	N	Y	N	Y	N	N	N
8 Oberstar	N	Y	N	Y	N	Y	N

MISSISSIPPI	74	75	76	77	78	79	80
1 Wicker	Y	Y	Y	Y	Y	?	?
2 Thompson	N	N	N	Y	N	Y	N
3 Pickering	Y	Y	Y	Y	Y	N	Y
4 Parker	Y	Y	Y	Y	Y	N	?
5 Taylor	Y	Y	N	Y	Y	Y	Y

MISSOURI	74	75	76	77	78	79	80
1 Clay	N	N	N	Y	N	?	?
2 Talent	Y	Y	Y	Y	Y	N	Y
3 Gephardt	N	N	N	Y	N	Y	N
4 Skelton	Y	N	N	Y	N	Y	Y
5 McCarthy	N	N	N	Y	N	Y	N
6 Danner	Y	N	N	Y	N	N	Y
7 Blunt	Y	Y	Y	Y	Y	N	Y
8 Emerson	Y	Y	Y	Y	Y	N	Y
9 Hulshof	Y	Y	Y	Y	Y	N	Y

MONTANA	74	75	76	77	78	79	80
AL Hill	Y	Y	Y	Y	Y	N	Y

NEBRASKA	74	75	76	77	78	79	80
1 Bereuter	Y	Y	Y	Y	Y	N	Y
2 Christensen	Y	Y	Y	Y	Y	?	?
3 Barrett	Y	Y	Y	Y	Y	N	Y

NEVADA	74	75	76	77	78	79	80
1 Ensign	Y	Y	Y	Y	Y	N	Y
2 Gibbons	Y	Y	Y	Y	Y	N	Y

NEW HAMPSHIRE	74	75	76	77	78	79	80
1 Sununu	Y	Y	Y	Y	Y	Y	Y
2 Bass	Y	Y	Y	Y	Y	Y	N

NEW JERSEY	74	75	76	77	78	79	80
1 Andrews	N	N	N	Y	N	Y	N
2 LoBiondo	Y	Y	Y	Y	Y	Y	N
3 Saxton	Y	Y	Y	Y	Y	Y	N
4 Smith	N	Y	Y	Y	Y	Y	N
5 Roukema	Y	Y	Y	Y	Y	Y	N
6 Pallone	N	N	N	Y	N	Y	N
7 Franks	Y	Y	Y	Y	Y	Y	N
8 Pascrell	N	N	N	Y	N	Y	N
9 Rothman	N	N	N	Y	N	Y	N
10 Payne	?	?	?	?	?	?	?
11 Frelinghuysen	Y	Y	Y	Y	Y	Y	N
12 Pappas	Y	Y	Y	Y	Y	Y	N
13 Menendez	N	N	N	Y	N	Y	N

NEW MEXICO	74	75	76	77	78	79	80
1 Vacant							
2 Skeen	Y	Y	Y	Y	Y	N	Y
3 Redmond	Y	Y	Y	Y	Y	N	Y

NEW YORK	74	75	76	77	78	79	80
1 Forbes	Y	Y	N	Y	N	Y	N
2 Lazio	Y	Y	Y	Y	N	Y	N
3 King	Y	Y	Y	Y	N	N	Y
4 McCarthy	N	N	N	Y	N	Y	N
5 Ackerman	N	N	N	Y	N	Y	N
6 Meeks	N	N	N	Y	N	Y	N
7 Manton	N	N	N	Y	N	Y	N
8 Nadler	N	N	N	Y	N	Y	N
9 Schumer	N	N	N	Y	N	Y	N
10 Towns	N	N	N	Y	N	Y	N
11 Owens	N	N	N	Y	N	Y	N
12 Velázquez	N	N	N	Y	N	Y	N
13 Fossella	Y	Y	Y	Y	-	Y	N
14 Maloney	N	N	N	Y	N	?	N
15 Rangel	X	?	?	?	?	?	?
16 Serrano	N	N	N	Y	N	Y	N
17 Engel	N	N	-	+	-	Y	N
18 Lowey	N	N	N	Y	N	Y	N
19 Kelly	Y	Y	Y	Y	N	Y	N
20 Gilman	Y	Y	Y	Y	-	Y	N
21 McNulty	N	-	-	+	-	+	-
22 Solomon	Y	Y	Y	Y	?	N	Y
23 Boehlert	N	Y	Y	Y	N	Y	N
24 McHugh	Y	Y	Y	Y	N	N	Y
25 Walsh	Y	Y	Y	Y	Y	N	Y
26 Hinchey	N	N	N	Y	N	Y	N
27 Paxon	Y	Y	Y	Y	Y	?	Y
28 Slaughter	N	N	N	Y	N	Y	N
29 LaFalce	N	N	N	Y	N	Y	N
30 Quinn	Y	Y	Y	Y	N	Y	N
31 Houghton	?	?	?	?	?	?	?

NORTH CAROLINA	74	75	76	77	78	79	80
1 Clayton	Y	N	N	Y	N	Y	N
2 Etheridge	Y	N	N	Y	N	Y	N
3 Jones	Y	Y	Y	Y	Y	Y	N
4 Price	Y	N	N	Y	N	Y	N
5 Burr	Y	Y	Y	Y	Y	N	Y
6 Coble	Y	Y	Y	Y	Y	N	Y
7 McIntyre	Y	N	N	Y	N	Y	N
8 Hefner	N	N	N	?	N	Y	N
9 Myrick	Y	Y	Y	Y	Y	N	Y
10 Ballenger	Y	Y	Y	Y	Y	N	+
11 Taylor	Y	Y	Y	Y	Y	N	Y
12 Watt	N	N	N	Y	N	?	?

NORTH DAKOTA	74	75	76	77	78	79	80
AL Pomeroy	Y	N	N	Y	N	?	?

OHIO	74	75	76	77	78	79	80
1 Chabot	Y	Y	Y	Y	Y	Y	N
2 Portman	Y	Y	Y	Y	Y	N	N
3 Hall	Y	N	Y	N	Y	N	Y
4 Oxley	Y	Y	Y	Y	Y	N	Y
5 Gillmor	?	?	?	Y	Y	Y	N
6 Strickland	N	N	N	Y	N	Y	N
7 Hobson	Y	Y	Y	Y	Y	N	Y
8 Boehner	Y	Y	Y	Y	Y	N	Y
9 Kaptur	N	N	N	Y	N	Y	N
10 Kucinich	N	N	N	Y	N	Y	N
11 Stokes	N	N	N	Y	N	Y	N
12 Kasich	?	Y	Y	Y	Y	N	Y
13 Brown	N	N	N	Y	N	Y	N
14 Sawyer	N	N	N	Y	N	Y	N
15 Pryce	Y	Y	Y	Y	Y	N	Y
16 Regula	Y	Y	Y	Y	Y	N	Y
17 Traficant	Y	Y	Y	Y	Y	N	Y
18 Ney	Y	Y	Y	Y	Y	N	Y
19 LaTourette	Y	Y	Y	Y	N	N	N

OKLAHOMA	74	75	76	77	78	79	80
1 Largent	Y	Y	Y	Y	Y	N	Y
2 Coburn	Y	Y	Y	Y	Y	?	?
3 Watkins	Y	Y	Y	Y	Y	?	?
4 Watts	Y	Y	Y	Y	Y	N	Y
5 Istook	Y	Y	Y	Y	Y	N	Y
6 Lucas	Y	Y	Y	Y	Y	N	Y

OREGON	74	75	76	77	78	79	80
1 Furse	N	N	N	Y	N	Y	N
2 Smith	Y	Y	Y	?	Y	Y	N
3 Blumenauer	N	N	N	Y	N	Y	N
4 DeFazio	N	N	N	Y	N	Y	N
5 Hooley	N	N	N	Y	N	Y	N

PENNSYLVANIA	74	75	76	77	78	79	80
1 Vacant							
2 Fattah	N	N	N	Y	N	Y	N
3 Borski	N	N	N	Y	N	Y	N
4 Klink	Y	N	N	Y	N	N	N
5 Peterson	Y	Y	Y	Y	Y	N	Y
6 Holden	Y	N	N	Y	N	Y	N
7 Weldon	Y	Y	Y	Y	Y	Y	N
8 Greenwood	Y	Y	Y	Y	Y	Y	N
9 Shuster	Y	Y	Y	Y	Y	N	Y
10 McDade	Y	Y	Y	?	N	Y	N
11 Kanjorski	N	N	N	Y	N	Y	N
12 Murtha	Y	N	N	Y	N	Y	N
13 Fox	Y	Y	Y	Y	Y	Y	N
14 Coyne	N	N	N	Y	N	Y	N
15 McHale	Y	N	N	Y	N	Y	N
16 Pitts	Y	Y	Y	Y	Y	Y	N
17 Gekas	Y	Y	Y	Y	Y	N	Y
18 Doyle	Y	N	N	Y	N	Y	N
19 Goodling	Y	Y	Y	Y	Y	Y	N
20 Mascara	N	N	N	Y	N	Y	N
21 English	Y	Y	Y	Y	Y	Y	Y

RHODE ISLAND	74	75	76	77	78	79	80
1 Kennedy	N	N	N	Y	N	Y	N
2 Weygand	Y	N	N	Y	N	Y	N

SOUTH CAROLINA	74	75	76	77	78	79	80
1 Sanford	Y	Y	Y	Y	Y	N	Y
2 Spence	Y	Y	Y	Y	Y	N	Y
3 Graham	Y	Y	Y	Y	Y	N	Y
4 Inglis	Y	Y	Y	Y	Y	N	Y
5 Spratt	Y	N	N	Y	N	Y	N
6 Clyburn	N	N	N	Y	N	Y	N

SOUTH DAKOTA	74	75	76	77	78	79	80
AL Thune	Y	Y	Y	Y	Y	N	Y

TENNESSEE	74	75	76	77	78	79	80
1 Jenkins	Y	Y	Y	Y	Y	N	Y
2 Duncan	Y	Y	Y	Y	Y	N	Y
3 Wamp	Y	Y	Y	Y	Y	N	N
4 Hilleary	Y	Y	Y	Y	Y	N	N
5 Clement	Y	N	N	Y	N	Y	N
6 Gordon	Y	N	N	Y	N	Y	N
7 Bryant	Y	Y	Y	Y	Y	?	?
8 Tanner	Y	N	N	Y	N	Y	N
9 Ford	-	-	-	+	-	+	-

TEXAS	74	75	76	77	78	79	80
1 Sandlin	Y	N	N	Y	N	N	Y
2 Turner	Y	N	N	Y	N	N	Y
3 Johnson, Sam	Y	Y	Y	Y	Y	N	Y
4 Hall	Y	Y	Y	Y	Y	N	Y
5 Sessions	Y	Y	Y	Y	Y	N	Y
6 Barton	Y	Y	Y	Y	Y	N	Y
7 Archer	?	Y	Y	Y	Y	N	Y
8 Brady	Y	Y	Y	Y	Y	N	Y
9 Lampson	N	N	N	Y	N	Y	N
10 Doggett	N	N	N	Y	N	Y	N
11 Edwards	N	?	N	Y	N	N	?
12 Granger	Y	Y	Y	Y	Y	N	Y
13 Thornberry	Y	Y	Y	Y	Y	N	Y
14 Paul	Y	Y	Y	Y	Y	N	N
15 Hinojosa	N	N	N	Y	N	?	?
16 Reyes	N	N	N	Y	N	Y	N
17 Stenholm	Y	N	N	Y	N	Y	N
18 Jackson-Lee	?	?	?	?	?	?	?
19 Combest	Y	Y	Y	Y	Y	N	Y
20 Gonzalez	?	?	?	?	?	?	?
21 Smith	Y	Y	Y	?	?	?	?
22 DeLay	Y	Y	Y	Y	Y	N	?
23 Bonilla	#	?	?	?	?	?	?
24 Frost	Y	N	N	Y	N	?	?
25 Bentsen	N	N	N	Y	N	Y	N
26 Armey	Y	Y	Y	Y	Y	N	Y
27 Ortiz	N	N	N	Y	N	Y	N
28 Rodriguez	N	N	N	Y	N	Y	N
29 Green	N	N	N	Y	N	Y	?
30 Johnson, E.B.	?	?	?	?	?	?	?

UTAH	74	75	76	77	78	79	80
1 Hansen	Y	Y	Y	Y	Y	?	?
2 Cook	Y	Y	Y	Y	Y	?	?
3 Cannon	?	?	?	?	?	?	?

VERMONT	74	75	76	77	78	79	80
AL Sanders	N	N	N	Y	N	Y	N

VIRGINIA	74	75	76	77	78	79	80
1 Bateman	Y	Y	Y	Y	Y	N	Y
2 Pickett	Y	N	N	Y	N	N	Y
3 Scott	N	N	N	Y	N	Y	N
4 Sisisky	Y	N	N	Y	N	Y	N
5 Goode	Y	Y	Y	Y	Y	N	Y
6 Goodlatte	Y	Y	Y	Y	Y	N	Y
7 Bliley	Y	Y	Y	Y	Y	N	Y
8 Moran	Y	N	N	Y	N	Y	N
9 Boucher	N	N	N	Y	N	Y	?
10 Wolf	Y	Y	Y	Y	Y	N	Y
11 Davis	Y	Y	Y	Y	Y	Y	N

WASHINGTON	74	75	76	77	78	79	80
1 White	Y	Y	Y	Y	Y	Y	N
2 Metcalf	Y	Y	Y	Y	Y	N	Y
3 Smith, Linda	Y	Y	Y	Y	Y	N	Y
4 Hastings	Y	Y	Y	Y	Y	N	Y
5 Nethercutt	Y	Y	Y	Y	Y	N	Y
6 Dicks	N	N	N	Y	N	N	N
7 McDermott	X	-	-	-	-	+	-
8 Dunn	Y	Y	Y	Y	Y	N	Y
9 Smith, Adam	Y	N	N	Y	N	Y	N

WEST VIRGINIA	74	75	76	77	78	79	80
1 Mollohan	Y	Y	Y	N	N	N	N
2 Wise	N	N	N	Y	N	N	Y
3 Rahall	N	Y	N	Y	N	N	Y

WISCONSIN	74	75	76	77	78	79	80
1 Neumann	Y	Y	Y	Y	Y	N	N
2 Klug	Y	Y	Y	Y	Y	Y	N
3 Kind	Y	N	N	Y	N	Y	N
4 Kleczka	N	N	N	Y	N	Y	N
5 Barrett	N	N	N	Y	N	Y	N
6 Petri	Y	Y	Y	Y	Y	Y	N
7 Obey	N	N	N	Y	N	Y	N
8 Johnson	Y	N	N	?	N	Y	N
9 Sensenbrenner	Y	Y	Y	Y	Y	Y	N

WYOMING	74	75	76	77	78	79	80
AL Cubin	Y	Y	Y	Y	Y	N	Y

Southern states - Ala., Ark., Fla., Ga., Ky., La., Miss., N.C., Okla., S.C., Tenn., Texas, Va.

81. Campaign Finance Overhaul/Passage. Thomas, R-Calif., motion to suspend the rules and pass the bill to ban raising or spending "soft money" contributions by federal candidates and state and national political parties, require unions to obtain written consent from workers before they spend dues revenue, and to establish a voter eligibility confirmation pilot program. Motion rejected 74-337: R 74-140; D 0-196 (ND 0-143, SD 0-53); I 0-1. March 30, 1998. A two-thirds majority of those present and voting (275 in this case) is required for passage under suspension of the rules.

82. HR 34. Non-Citizens Contributions Ban/Passage. Thomas, R-Calif., motion to suspend the rules and pass the bill to clarify that non-citizens are prohibited from contributing to federal campaigns. Motion agreed to 369-43: R 209-6; D 159-37 (ND 112-31, SD 47-6); I 1-0. March 30, 1998. A two-thirds majority of those present and voting (276 in this case) is required for passage under suspension of the rules.

83. HR 2608. Involuntary Contributions Ban/Passage. Thomas, R-Calif., motion to suspend the rules and pass the bill to prohibit involuntary use of funds of employees and shareholders of corporations, and of labor union members, for political activities. Motion rejected 166-246: R 163-52; D 3-193 (ND 0-143, SD 3-50); I 0-1. March 30, 1998. A two-thirds majority of those present and voting (276 in this case) is required for passage under suspension of the rules.

84. Campaign Reporting and Disclosure/Passage. Thomas, R-Calif., motion to suspend the rules and pass the bill to overhaul the reporting of campaign contribution information to the Federal Election Commission by tightening reporting requirements and expanding the type of information reported. Motion agreed to 405-6: R 213-1; D 191-5 (ND 138-5, SD 53-0); I 1-0. March 30, 1998. A two-thirds majority of those present and voting (275 in this case) is required for passage under suspension of the rules.

85. HR 3579. Fiscal 1998 Supplemental Appropriations/Rule. Adoption of the rule (H Res 402) to provide for floor consideration of the bill to provide $2.9 billion in supplemental appropriations, including $2.3 billion for the military, primarily to support military operations in Iraq and Bosnia, and $575 million for disaster relief. Adopted 220-199: R 218-3; D 2-195 (ND 0-145, SD 2-50); I 0-1. March 31, 1998.

86. Procedural Motion/Secret Session. Obey, D-Wis., motion that the House resolve into secret session to discuss intelligence budget issues relating to HR3579, which provides supplemental appropriations for the military and disaster relief. Motion rejected 194-227: R 0-223; D 193-4 (ND 143-1, SD 50-3); I 1-0. March 31, 1998.

87. HR 3579. Fiscal 1998 Supplemental Appropriations/Recommit. Murtha, D-Pa., motion to recommit the bill to the House Appropriations Committee with instructions to report it back with an amendment to strike the bill's offsets of $2.9 billion. Motion rejected 195-224: R 0-220; D 194-4 (ND 146-0, SD 48-4); I 1-0. March 31, 1998.

Key

Y	Voted for (yea).
#	Paired for.
+	Announced for.
N	Voted against (nay).
X	Paired against.
−	Announced against.
P	Voted "present."
C	Voted "present" to avoid possible conflict of interest.
?	Did not vote or otherwise make a position known.

Democrats **Republicans**
Independent

	81	82	83	84	85	86	87
ALABAMA							
1 *Callahan*	N	Y	Y	Y	Y	N	N
2 *Everett*	N	Y	Y	Y	Y	N	N
3 *Riley*	N	Y	Y	Y	Y	N	N
4 *Aderholt*	N	Y	Y	Y	Y	N	N
5 Cramer	N	Y	N	Y	N	Y	Y
6 *Bachus*	Y	Y	N	Y	Y	N	N
7 Hilliard	N	Y	N	Y	N	Y	Y
ALASKA							
AL *Young*	N	Y	N	Y	Y	N	N
ARIZONA							
1 *Salmon*	Y	Y	Y	Y	Y	N	N
2 Pastor	N	Y	N	Y	N	Y	Y
3 *Stump*	N	Y	Y	Y	Y	N	N
4 *Shadegg*	Y	Y	N	Y	Y	N	N
5 *Kolbe*	Y	Y	Y	Y	Y	N	N
6 *Hayworth*	Y	Y	Y	Y	Y	N	N
ARKANSAS							
1 Berry	N	Y	N	Y	N	Y	+
2 Snyder	N	Y	N	Y	N	Y	Y
3 *Hutchinson*	Y	Y	Y	Y	Y	N	N
4 *Dickey*	N	Y	Y	Y	Y	N	N
CALIFORNIA							
1 *Riggs*	−	+	+	+	+	−	−
2 *Herger*	Y	Y	Y	Y	Y	N	N
3 Fazio	N	N	N	Y	N	Y	Y
4 *Doolittle*	N	N	Y	Y	Y	N	N
5 Matsui	N	Y	N	Y	N	Y	Y
6 Woolsey	N	Y	N	Y	N	Y	Y
7 Miller	N	Y	N	Y	N	Y	Y
8 Pelosi	N	N	N	Y	N	Y	Y
9 Vacant							
10 Tauscher	N	Y	N	Y	N	Y	Y
11 *Pombo*	N	N	Y	Y	Y	N	N
12 Lantos	N	Y	N	Y	N	Y	Y
13 Stark	N	Y	N	Y	N	Y	Y
14 Eshoo	N	Y	N	Y	N	Y	Y
15 *Campbell*	Y	Y	N	Y	N	N	N
16 Lofgren	N	N	N	Y	N	Y	Y
17 Farr	N	N	N	Y	N	Y	Y
18 Condit	N	Y	N	Y	N	Y	Y
19 *Radanovich*	Y	Y	Y	Y	Y	N	N
20 Dooley	N	Y	N	Y	N	Y	Y
21 *Thomas*	Y	Y	Y	Y	Y	N	N
22 Capps, L.	N	Y	N	Y	N	Y	Y
23 *Gallegly*	N	Y	Y	Y	Y	N	N
24 Sherman	N	Y	N	Y	N	Y	Y
25 *McKeon*	Y	Y	Y	Y	Y	N	N
26 Berman	N	N	N	Y	N	Y	Y
27 *Rogan*	N	Y	Y	Y	Y	N	N
28 *Dreier*	N	Y	Y	Y	Y	N	N
29 Waxman	N	N	N	Y	N	Y	Y
30 Becerra	N	N	N	Y	N	?	Y
31 Martinez	N	N	N	Y	N	Y	Y
32 Dixon	N	N	N	Y	N	Y	Y
33 Roybal-Allard	N	N	N	Y	N	Y	Y
34 Torres	N	N	N	Y	N	Y	Y
35 Waters	?	?	?	?	?	?	?
36 Harman	N	Y	N	Y	N	Y	Y
37 Millender-McD.	N	Y	N	Y	N	Y	Y

	81	82	83	84	85	86	87
38 *Horn*	Y	Y	N	Y	Y	N	N
39 *Royce*	?	?	?	?	?	?	?
40 *Lewis*	N	Y	Y	Y	Y	N	N
41 *Kim*	P	P	P	P	Y	N	N
42 Brown	N	Y	N	Y	N	Y	Y
43 *Calvert*	N	Y	N	Y	Y	N	N
44 Vacant							
45 *Rohrabacher*	Y	Y	Y	Y	Y	N	N
46 Sanchez	N	Y	N	Y	N	Y	Y
47 *Cox*	?	Y	Y	Y	Y	N	N
48 *Packard*	N	Y	Y	Y	Y	N	N
49 *Bilbray*	N	Y	N	Y	Y	N	N
50 Filner	N	N	N	Y	N	Y	Y
51 *Cunningham*	N	Y	Y	Y	Y	N	N
52 *Hunter*	?	?	?	?	Y	N	N
COLORADO							
1 DeGette	N	Y	N	Y	N	Y	Y
2 Skaggs	N	N	N	Y	N	Y	Y
3 *McInnis*	N	Y	Y	Y	Y	N	N
4 *Schaffer*	N	Y	Y	Y	Y	N	N
5 *Hefley*	N	Y	Y	Y	Y	N	N
6 *Schaefer*	Y	Y	Y	Y	Y	N	N
CONNECTICUT							
1 Kennelly	N	Y	N	Y	N	Y	Y
2 Gejdenson	N	Y	N	Y	N	Y	Y
3 DeLauro	N	Y	N	Y	N	Y	Y
4 *Shays*	N	Y	Y	Y	Y	N	N
5 Maloney	N	Y	N	Y	N	Y	Y
6 *Johnson*	N	Y	N	Y	Y	N	N
DELAWARE							
AL *Castle*	Y	Y	N	Y	Y	N	N
FLORIDA							
1 *Scarborough*	Y	Y	Y	Y	Y	N	N
2 Boyd	N	Y	N	Y	N	Y	Y
3 Brown	N	Y	N	Y	N	Y	Y
4 *Fowler*	Y	Y	Y	Y	Y	N	N
5 Thurman	N	Y	N	Y	N	Y	Y
6 *Stearns*	Y	Y	Y	Y	Y	N	N
7 *Mica*	Y	Y	Y	Y	Y	N	N
8 *McCollum*	N	Y	Y	Y	Y	N	N
9 *Bilirakis*	N	Y	Y	Y	Y	N	N
10 *Young*	N	Y	Y	Y	Y	N	N
11 Davis	N	Y	N	Y	N	Y	Y
12 *Canady*	N	Y	Y	Y	Y	N	N
13 *Miller*	Y	Y	Y	Y	Y	N	N
14 *Goss*	Y	Y	Y	Y	Y	N	N
15 *Weldon*	N	Y	Y	Y	Y	N	N
16 *Foley*	N	Y	N	Y	Y	N	N
17 Meek	N	N	N	Y	N	Y	Y
18 *Ros-Lehtinen*	N	N	N	Y	N	N	N
19 Wexler	N	Y	N	Y	N	Y	Y
20 Deutsch	N	Y	N	Y	N	Y	Y
21 *Diaz-Balart*	N	N	N	Y	N	N	N
22 *Shaw*	N	Y	Y	Y	Y	N	N
23 Hastings	N	Y	N	Y	N	Y	Y
GEORGIA							
1 *Kingston*	Y	Y	Y	Y	Y	N	N
2 Bishop	N	Y	N	Y	N	Y	Y
3 *Collins*	N	Y	Y	Y	Y	N	N
4 McKinney	N	N	N	Y	N	Y	Y
5 Lewis	N	Y	N	Y	N	Y	Y
6 *Gingrich*		Y		N			
7 *Barr*	Y	Y	Y	Y	Y	N	N
8 *Chambliss*	Y	Y	Y	Y	Y	N	N
9 *Deal*	N	Y	Y	Y	Y	N	N
10 *Norwood*	N	Y	Y	Y	Y	N	N
11 *Linder*	Y	Y	Y	Y	Y	N	N
HAWAII							
1 Abercrombie	N	Y	N	Y	N	Y	Y
2 Mink	N	N	N	Y	N	Y	Y
IDAHO							
1 *Chenoweth*	N	Y	N	Y	Y	N	N
2 *Crapo*	N	Y	N	Y	Y	N	N
ILLINOIS							
1 Rush	N	Y	N	Y	N	Y	Y
2 Jackson	N	Y	N	Y	N	Y	Y
3 Lipinski	N	Y	N	Y	N	Y	Y
4 Gutierrez	N	N	N	Y	N	Y	Y
5 Blagojevich	N	Y	N	Y	N	Y	Y
6 *Hyde*	N	Y	Y	Y	Y	N	N
7 Davis	N	N	N	Y	N	?	Y
8 *Crane*	N	Y	Y	Y	Y	N	N
9 Yates	?	?	?	?	N	Y	Y
10 *Porter*	Y	Y	Y	Y	Y	N	N
11 *Weller*	N	Y	Y	Y	Y	N	N
12 Costello	N	Y	N	Y	N	Y	Y

ND Northern Democrats   SD Southern Democrats

	81	82	83	84	85	86	87
13 ***Fawell***	Y	Y	Y	Y	Y	N	?
14 ***Hastert***	N	Y	Y	Y	Y	N	N
15 ***Ewing***	Y	Y	Y	Y	Y	N	N
16 ***Manzullo***	N	Y	Y	Y	Y	N	N
17 Evans	N	Y	N	Y	N	Y	Y
18 ***LaHood***	N	Y	N	Y	Y	N	N
19 Poshard	N	Y	N	Y	N	Y	Y
20 ***Shimkus***	Y	Y	N	Y	Y	N	N
INDIANA							
1 Visclosky	N	Y	N	Y	N	Y	Y
2 ***McIntosh***	N	Y	Y	Y	Y	N	N
3 Roemer	N	Y	N	Y	N	Y	Y
4 ***Souder***	Y	Y	Y	Y	Y	N	N
5 ***Buyer***	Y	Y	Y	Y	Y	N	N
6 ***Burton***	N	Y	Y	Y	Y	N	N
7 ***Pease***	N	Y	N	Y	Y	N	N
8 ***Hostettler***	N	Y	Y	Y	Y	N	N
9 Hamilton	N	Y	N	Y	N	Y	Y
10 Carson	N	Y	N	Y	N	Y	Y
IOWA							
1 ***Leach***	N	Y	N	Y	Y	N	N
2 ***Nussle***	N	Y	Y	Y	Y	N	N
3 Boswell	N	Y	N	Y	N	Y	Y
4 ***Ganske***	N	Y	Y	Y	Y	N	N
5 ***Latham***	N	Y	Y	Y	Y	N	N
KANSAS							
1 ***Moran***	N	Y	Y	Y	Y	N	N
2 ***Ryun***	N	Y	Y	Y	Y	N	N
3 ***Snowbarger***	N	Y	Y	Y	Y	N	N
4 ***Tiahrt***	N	Y	Y	Y	Y	N	N
KENTUCKY							
1 ***Whitfield***	N	Y	N	Y	Y	N	N
2 ***Lewis***	N	Y	Y	Y	Y	N	N
3 ***Northup***	N	Y	N	Y	Y	N	N
4 ***Bunning***	N	Y	Y	Y	Y	N	N
5 ***Rogers***	N	Y	Y	Y	Y	N	N
6 Baesler	N	Y	N	Y	?	Y	Y
LOUISIANA							
1 ***Livingston***	Y	Y	Y	Y	Y	N	N
2 Jefferson	?	?	?	?	?	?	?
3 ***Tauzin***	Y	Y	Y	Y	Y	N	N
4 ***McCrery***	N	Y	Y	Y	Y	N	N
5 ***Cooksey***	–	+	+	+	Y	N	N
6 ***Baker***	N	Y	Y	Y	Y	N	N
7 John	N	Y	N	Y	N	Y	Y
MAINE							
1 Allen	N	Y	N	Y	N	Y	Y
2 Baldacci	N	Y	N	Y	N	Y	Y
MARYLAND							
1 ***Gilchrest***	Y	Y	Y	Y	Y	N	N
2 ***Ehrlich***	Y	Y	Y	Y	Y	N	N
3 Cardin	?	?	?	?	N	Y	Y
4 Wynn	N	N	N	Y	N	Y	Y
5 Hoyer	N	N	N	Y	N	?	Y
6 ***Bartlett***	Y	Y	Y	Y	Y	N	N
7 Cummings	N	Y	N	Y	N	Y	Y
8 ***Morella***	N	N	N	Y	N	N	N
MASSACHUSETTS							
1 Olver	N	Y	N	Y	N	Y	Y
2 Neal	N	Y	N	Y	N	Y	Y
3 McGovern	N	Y	N	Y	N	Y	Y
4 Frank	N	Y	N	Y	N	Y	Y
5 Meehan	N	Y	N	Y	N	Y	Y
6 Tierney	N	Y	N	Y	N	Y	Y
7 Markey	N	Y	N	Y	N	Y	Y
8 Kennedy	N	Y	N	Y	N	Y	Y
9 Moakley	N	Y	N	Y	N	Y	Y
10 Delahunt	N	Y	N	Y	N	Y	Y
MICHIGAN							
1 Stupak	N	Y	N	Y	N	Y	Y
2 ***Hoekstra***	N	Y	Y	Y	Y	N	N
3 ***Ehlers***	N	N	N	Y	Y	N	N
4 ***Camp***	Y	Y	Y	Y	Y	N	N
5 Barcia	N	Y	N	Y	N	Y	Y
6 ***Upton***	Y	Y	Y	Y	Y	N	N
7 ***Smith***	Y	Y	Y	Y	Y	N	N
8 Stabenow	N	Y	N	Y	N	Y	Y
9 Kildee	N	Y	N	Y	N	Y	Y
10 Bonior	N	Y	N	Y	N	Y	Y
11 ***Knollenberg***	N	Y	Y	Y	Y	N	N
12 Levin	N	Y	N	Y	N	Y	Y
13 Rivers	N	Y	N	Y	N	Y	Y
14 Conyers	N	Y	N	Y	N	Y	Y
15 Kilpatrick	N	Y	N	Y	N	Y	Y
16 Dingell	N	N	N	N	N	Y	Y

	81	82	83	84	85	86	87
MINNESOTA							
1 ***Gutknecht***	Y	Y	Y	Y	Y	N	N
2 Minge	N	Y	N	Y	N	Y	Y
3 ***Ramstad***	N	Y	Y	Y	Y	N	N
4 Vento	N	Y	N	Y	N	Y	Y
5 Sabo	N	N	N	N	N	Y	Y
6 Luther	N	Y	N	Y	N	Y	Y
7 Peterson	N	Y	N	Y	N	Y	Y
8 Oberstar	N	N	N	Y	N	Y	Y
MISSISSIPPI							
1 ***Wicker***	N	Y	Y	Y	Y	N	N
2 Thompson	N	Y	N	Y	N	Y	Y
3 ***Pickering***	N	Y	Y	Y	Y	N	N
4 ***Parker***	N	Y	Y	Y	Y	N	N
5 Taylor	N	Y	Y	Y	Y	N	N
MISSOURI							
1 Clay	N	Y	N	Y	N	Y	Y
2 ***Talent***	N	Y	Y	Y	Y	N	N
3 Gephardt	N	Y	N	Y	N	Y	Y
4 Skelton	N	Y	N	Y	N	Y	Y
5 McCarthy	–	+	–	+	N	Y	Y
6 Danner	N	Y	N	Y	N	Y	Y
7 ***Blunt***	N	Y	Y	Y	Y	N	N
8 ***Emerson***	N	Y	Y	Y	Y	N	N
9 ***Hulshof***	Y	Y	Y	Y	Y	N	N
MONTANA							
AL ***Hill***	Y	Y	Y	Y	Y	N	N
NEBRASKA							
1 ***Bereuter***	?	?	?	?	Y	N	N
2 ***Christensen***	N	Y	Y	Y	Y	N	N
3 ***Barrett***	N	Y	Y	Y	Y	N	N
NEVADA							
1 ***Ensign***	N	Y	Y	Y	Y	N	N
2 ***Gibbons***	N	Y	Y	Y	Y	N	N
NEW HAMPSHIRE							
1 ***Sununu***	Y	Y	Y	Y	Y	N	N
2 ***Bass***	Y	Y	N	Y	Y	N	N
NEW JERSEY							
1 Andrews	N	Y	N	Y	N	Y	Y
2 ***LoBiondo***	N	Y	N	Y	Y	N	N
3 ***Saxton***	N	Y	N	Y	Y	N	N
4 ***Smith***	N	Y	N	Y	Y	N	N
5 ***Roukema***	Y	Y	Y	Y	Y	N	N
6 Pallone	N	Y	N	Y	N	Y	Y
7 ***Franks***	N	Y	N	Y	Y	N	N
8 Pascrell	N	Y	N	Y	N	Y	Y
9 Rothman	N	Y	N	Y	N	Y	Y
10 Payne	?	?	?	?	?	?	?
11 ***Frelinghuysen***	Y	Y	Y	Y	Y	N	N
12 ***Pappas***	N	Y	N	Y	Y	N	N
13 Menendez	N	Y	N	Y	N	Y	Y
NEW MEXICO							
1 Vacant							
2 ***Skeen***	N	Y	Y	Y	Y	N	N
3 ***Redmond***	N	Y	Y	Y	Y	N	N
NEW YORK							
1 ***Forbes***	N	Y	N	Y	Y	N	N
2 ***Lazio***	N	Y	N	Y	Y	N	N
3 ***King***	N	Y	N	Y	Y	N	N
4 McCarthy	N	Y	N	Y	N	Y	Y
5 Ackerman	N	Y	N	Y	N	Y	Y
6 Meeks	N	N	N	Y	N	Y	Y
7 Manton	N	Y	N	Y	N	Y	Y
8 Nadler	N	Y	N	Y	N	Y	Y
9 Schumer	N	Y	N	Y	N	Y	Y
10 Towns	N	N	N	Y	N	Y	Y
11 Owens	N	Y	N	Y	N	Y	Y
12 Velázquez	N	N	N	Y	N	Y	Y
13 ***Fossella***	N	Y	Y	Y	Y	N	N
14 Maloney	N	Y	N	Y	N	Y	Y
15 Rangel	?	?	?	?	?	?	?
16 Serrano	N	N	N	Y	N	Y	Y
17 Engel	N	Y	N	Y	N	Y	Y
18 Lowey	N	Y	N	Y	N	Y	Y
19 ***Kelly***	N	Y	N	Y	Y	N	N
20 ***Gilman***	N	Y	N	Y	Y	N	N
21 McNulty	N	Y	N	Y	N	Y	Y
22 ***Solomon***	?	?	?	?	Y	N	N
23 ***Boehlert***	N	Y	N	Y	Y	N	N
24 ***McHugh***	N	Y	N	Y	Y	N	N
25 ***Walsh***	N	Y	N	Y	Y	N	N
26 Hinchey	N	Y	N	Y	N	Y	Y
27 ***Paxon***	N	Y	Y	Y	?	N	N
28 Slaughter	N	Y	N	Y	N	Y	Y
29 LaFalce	N	Y	N	Y	N	Y	Y

	81	82	83	84	85	86	87
30 ***Quinn***	N	Y	N	Y	N	N	N
31 ***Houghton***	N	Y	N	Y	Y	N	N
NORTH CAROLINA							
1 Clayton	N	Y	N	Y	N	Y	Y
2 Etheridge	N	Y	N	Y	N	Y	Y
3 ***Jones***	N	Y	Y	Y	Y	N	N
4 Price	N	Y	N	Y	N	Y	Y
5 ***Burr***	N	Y	Y	Y	Y	N	N
6 ***Coble***	+	+	+	+	Y	N	N
7 McIntyre	N	Y	N	Y	N	Y	Y
8 Hefner	N	Y	N	Y	N	Y	Y
9 ***Myrick***	N	Y	Y	Y	Y	N	N
10 ***Ballenger***	Y	Y	Y	Y	Y	N	N
11 ***Taylor***	Y	Y	N	Y	Y	N	N
12 Watt	N	N	N	Y	N	Y	Y
NORTH DAKOTA							
AL Pomeroy	N	Y	N	Y	N	Y	Y
OHIO							
1 ***Chabot***	N	Y	Y	Y	Y	N	N
2 ***Portman***	N	Y	Y	Y	Y	N	N
3 Hall	N	Y	N	Y	N	Y	Y
4 ***Oxley***	N	Y	Y	Y	Y	N	N
5 ***Gillmor***	Y	Y	Y	Y	Y	N	N
6 Strickland	N	Y	N	Y	N	Y	Y
7 ***Hobson***	N	Y	Y	Y	Y	N	N
8 ***Boehner***	N	Y	Y	Y	Y	N	N
9 Kaptur	N	N	N	Y	N	Y	Y
10 Kucinich	N	Y	N	Y	N	Y	Y
11 Stokes	N	Y	N	Y	N	Y	Y
12 ***Kasich***	Y	Y	Y	Y	Y	N	N
13 Brown	N	Y	N	Y	N	Y	Y
14 Sawyer	N	Y	N	Y	N	Y	Y
15 ***Pryce***	Y	Y	Y	Y	Y	N	N
16 ***Regula***	N	Y	N	Y	Y	N	N
17 Traficant	N	Y	N	Y	N	N	Y
18 ***Ney***	N	Y	N	Y	Y	N	N
19 ***LaTourette***	N	Y	N	Y	Y	N	N
OKLAHOMA							
1 ***Largent***	N	Y	Y	Y	Y	N	N
2 ***Coburn***	Y	Y	N	Y	Y	N	N
3 ***Watkins***	Y	Y	Y	Y	Y	N	N
4 ***Watts***	N	Y	Y	Y	Y	N	N
5 ***Istook***	N	Y	Y	Y	Y	N	N
6 ***Lucas***	Y	Y	Y	Y	Y	N	N
OREGON							
1 Furse	N	Y	N	Y	N	Y	Y
2 ***Smith***	N	Y	Y	Y	Y	N	N
3 Blumenauer	N	Y	N	Y	N	Y	Y
4 DeFazio	N	Y	N	Y	N	Y	Y
5 Hooley	N	Y	N	Y	N	Y	Y
PENNSYLVANIA							
1 Vacant							
2 Fattah	N	N	N	Y	N	Y	Y
3 Borski	N	Y	N	Y	N	Y	Y
4 Klink	N	Y	N	Y	N	Y	Y
5 ***Peterson***	N	Y	Y	Y	Y	N	N
6 Holden	N	Y	N	Y	N	Y	Y
7 ***Weldon***	Y	Y	N	Y	Y	N	N
8 ***Greenwood***	Y	Y	N	Y	Y	N	N
9 ***Shuster***	Y	Y	Y	Y	Y	N	N
10 ***McDade***	N	Y	N	Y	Y	N	N
11 Kanjorski	N	Y	N	Y	N	Y	Y
12 Murtha	N	N	N	N	N	Y	Y
13 ***Fox***	Y	Y	N	Y	Y	N	N
14 Coyne	N	Y	N	Y	N	Y	Y
15 McHale	N	Y	N	Y	N	Y	Y
16 ***Pitts***	N	Y	Y	Y	Y	N	N
17 ***Gekas***	N	Y	?	Y	Y	N	N
18 Doyle	N	Y	N	Y	N	Y	Y
19 ***Goodling***	N	Y	Y	Y	Y	N	N
20 Mascara	N	Y	N	Y	N	Y	Y
21 ***English***	Y	Y	N	Y	Y	N	N
RHODE ISLAND							
1 Kennedy	N	N	N	Y	N	Y	Y
2 Weygand	N	Y	N	Y	N	Y	Y
SOUTH CAROLINA							
1 ***Sanford***	Y	Y	Y	Y	Y	N	N
2 ***Spence***	Y	Y	Y	Y	Y	N	N
3 ***Graham***	N	Y	Y	Y	Y	N	N
4 ***Inglis***	N	Y	Y	Y	Y	N	N
5 Spratt	N	Y	N	Y	N	Y	Y
6 Clyburn	N	Y	N	Y	N	Y	Y
SOUTH DAKOTA							
AL ***Thune***	N	Y	Y	Y	Y	N	N

	81	82	83	84	85	86	87
TENNESSEE							
1 ***Jenkins***	N	Y	Y	Y	Y	N	N
2 ***Duncan***	Y	Y	Y	Y	Y	N	N
3 ***Wamp***	N	Y	Y	Y	Y	N	N
4 ***Hilleary***	Y	Y	Y	Y	Y	N	N
5 Clement	N	Y	N	Y	N	Y	Y
6 Gordon	N	Y	N	Y	N	Y	Y
7 ***Bryant***	Y	Y	Y	Y	Y	N	N
8 Tanner	N	Y	N	Y	N	Y	Y
9 Ford	N	Y	N	Y	N	Y	Y
TEXAS							
1 Sandlin	N	Y	N	Y	N	Y	Y
2 Turner	N	Y	N	Y	N	Y	Y
3 ***Johnson, Sam***	N	Y	Y	Y	Y	N	?
4 Hall	N	Y	Y	Y	Y	N	N
5 ***Sessions***	N	Y	Y	Y	Y	N	N
6 ***Barton***	N	Y	Y	Y	Y	N	N
7 ***Archer***	Y	Y	Y	?	Y	N	N
8 ***Brady***	N	Y	Y	Y	Y	N	N
9 Lampson	N	Y	N	Y	N	Y	Y
10 Doggett	N	Y	N	Y	N	Y	Y
11 Edwards	N	Y	N	Y	N	Y	Y
12 ***Granger***	Y	Y	Y	Y	Y	N	N
13 ***Thornberry***	Y	Y	Y	Y	Y	N	N
14 ***Paul***	N	Y	N	Y	Y	N	N
15 Hinojosa	N	Y	N	Y	N	Y	Y
16 Reyes	N	Y	N	Y	N	Y	Y
17 Stenholm	N	Y	N	Y	N	Y	N
18 Jackson-Lee	N	N	N	Y	N	Y	Y
19 ***Combest***	N	Y	Y	Y	Y	N	N
20 Gonzalez	?	?	?	?	?	?	?
21 ***Smith***	N	Y	Y	Y	Y	N	N
22 ***DeLay***	N	Y	Y	Y	Y	N	N
23 ***Bonilla***	N	Y	Y	Y	Y	N	N
24 Frost	N	Y	N	Y	N	Y	Y
25 Bentsen	N	Y	N	Y	N	Y	Y
26 ***Armey***	N	Y	Y	Y	Y	N	N
27 Ortiz	N	Y	N	Y	N	Y	Y
28 Rodriguez	N	Y	N	Y	N	Y	Y
29 Green	N	Y	N	Y	N	Y	Y
30 Johnson, E.B.	N	N	N	Y	N	Y	Y
UTAH							
1 ***Hansen***	Y	Y	Y	Y	Y	N	N
2 ***Cook***	Y	Y	Y	Y	Y	N	N
3 ***Cannon***	?	?	?	?	?	?	?
VERMONT							
AL *Sanders*	N	Y	N	Y	N	Y	Y
VIRGINIA							
1 ***Bateman***	N	Y	Y	Y	Y	N	N
2 Pickett	N	Y	N	Y	N	Y	Y
3 Scott	N	N	N	Y	N	Y	Y
4 Sisisky	N	Y	N	Y	N	Y	Y
5 Goode	N	Y	Y	Y	N	N	N
6 ***Goodlatte***	N	Y	Y	Y	Y	N	N
7 ***Bliley***	?	?	?	?	Y	N	N
8 Moran	N	Y	N	Y	N	Y	Y
9 Boucher	N	Y	N	Y	N	Y	Y
10 ***Wolf***	N	Y	Y	Y	Y	N	N
11 ***Davis***	N	Y	N	Y	Y	N	N
WASHINGTON							
1 ***White***	Y	Y	Y	Y	Y	N	N
2 ***Metcalf***	Y	Y	N	Y	Y	N	N
3 ***Smith, Linda***	N	Y	Y	Y	Y	N	N
4 ***Hastings***	N	Y	Y	Y	Y	N	N
5 ***Nethercutt***	N	Y	Y	Y	Y	N	N
6 Dicks	N	Y	N	Y	N	Y	Y
7 McDermott	N	N	N	Y	N	Y	Y
8 ***Dunn***	N	Y	Y	Y	Y	N	N
9 Smith, Adam	N	Y	N	Y	N	Y	Y
WEST VIRGINIA							
1 Mollohan	N	N	N	N	N	Y	Y
2 Wise	N	Y	N	Y	N	Y	Y
3 Rahall	N	Y	N	Y	N	Y	Y
WISCONSIN							
1 ***Neumann***	N	Y	N	Y	Y	N	N
2 ***Klug***	N	Y	Y	Y	Y	N	N
3 Kind	N	Y	N	Y	N	Y	Y
4 Kleczka	N	Y	N	Y	N	Y	Y
5 Barrett	N	Y	N	Y	N	Y	Y
6 ***Petri***	Y	Y	N	Y	Y	N	N
7 Obey	N	Y	N	Y	N	Y	Y
8 Johnson	N	Y	N	Y	N	Y	Y
9 ***Sensenbrenner***	Y	Y	Y	Y	Y	N	N
WYOMING							
AL ***Cubin***	N	Y	Y	Y	Y	N	N

Southern states - Ala., Ark., Fla., Ga., Ky., La., Miss., N.C., Okla., S.C., Tenn., Texas, Va.

88. HR 3579. Fiscal 1998 Supplemental Appropriations/Passage. Passage of the bill to provide $2.9 billion in supplemental appropriations, including $2.3 billion for the military, primarily to support military operations in Iraq and Bosnia, and $575 million for disaster relief. Passed 212-208: R 205-17; D 7-190 (ND 2-143, SD 5-47); I 0-1. March 31, 1998. A "nay" was a vote in support of the president's position.

89. Quorum Call.* 387 Responded. March 31, 1998.

90. HR 2400. Surface Transportation Reauthorization/Rule. Adoption of the rule (H Res 405) to provide for floor consideration of the bill to authorize $218.3 billion over six years for federal highway and mass transit programs. Adopted 357-61: R 203-16; D 153-45 (ND 118-27, SD 35-18); I 1-0. April 1, 1998.

91. Adjournment Resolution/Adoption. Adoption of the concurrent resolution to adjourn the House from April 1, 1998 until 12:30 p.m. on April 21, 1998, and the Senate until noon on April 20, 1998. Adopted 223-187: R 212-2; D 11-184 (ND 9-134, SD 2-50); I 0-1. April 1, 1998.

92. HR 1151. Credit Union Membership Rules/Passage. Leach, R-Iowa, motion to suspend the rules and pass the bill to allow credit unions to expand beyond their original membership base. Motion agreed to 411-8: R 213-8; D 197-0 (ND 144-0, SD 53-0); I 1-0. April 1, 1998. A two-thirds majority of those present and voting (280 in this case) is required for passage under suspension of the rules.

93. HR 2400. Surface Transportation Reauthorization/Affirmative Action. Roukema, R-N.J., amendment to end the Transportation Department's program that sets a goal of providing at least 10 percent of transportation contracts to small businesses owned by women and minorities and replace it with a program encouraging affirmative action and discouraging preferential treatment in relation to government transportation contracts. Rejected 194-225: R 191-29; D 3-195 (ND 0-145, SD 3-50); I 0-1. April 1, 1998.

94. HR 2400. Surface Transportation Reauthorization/Welfare to Work Transportation. Davis, D-Ill., amendment to increase from $42 million to $150 million per year the authorization for a new welfare-to-work transportation program, which would finance services that transport current and former welfare recipients to and from jobs, and job-related activities. Adopted 242-175: R 48-171; D 193-4 (ND 145-0, SD 48-4); I 1-0. April 1, 1998.

95. HR 2400. Surface Transportation Reauthorization/Specified Projects. Graham, R-S.C., amendment to strike provisions that provide funds for specified projects, including about $9 billion for highway projects, and other funding for specified transit and bus projects. Rejected 79-337: R 67-152; D 12-184 (ND 6-137, SD 6-47); I 0-1. April 1, 1998.

* CQ does not include quorum calls in its vote charts.

Key

Y	Voted for (yea).
#	Paired for.
+	Announced for.
N	Voted against (nay).
X	Paired against.
–	Announced against.
P	Voted "present."
C	Voted "present" to avoid possible conflict of interest.
?	Did not vote or otherwise make a position known.

•
Democrats   ***Republicans***
Independent

	88	90	91	92	93	94	95
ALABAMA							
1 *Callahan*	Y	Y	Y	Y	Y	N	N
2 *Everett*	Y	Y	Y	Y	Y	N	N
3 *Riley*	Y	Y	Y	Y	Y	N	N
4 *Aderholt*	Y	Y	Y	Y	Y	N	N
5 Cramer	N	N	N	N	Y	N	N
6 *Bachus*	Y	Y	Y	N	Y	N	N
7 Hilliard	N	Y	N	Y	N	Y	N
ALASKA							
AL *Young*	Y	Y	Y	Y	Y	N	N
ARIZONA							
1 *Salmon*	Y	N	Y	Y	Y	N	Y
2 Pastor	N	Y	N	Y	N	Y	N
3 *Stump*	Y	Y	Y	Y	Y	N	Y
4 *Shadegg*	Y	N	Y	Y	Y	N	Y
5 *Kolbe*	Y	Y	Y	Y	Y	N	Y
6 *Hayworth*	Y	Y	Y	Y	Y	N	Y
ARKANSAS							
1 Berry	–	Y	N	Y	N	Y	N
2 Snyder	N	Y	N	Y	N	Y	N
3 *Hutchinson*	Y	Y	Y	Y	?	Y	N
4 *Dickey*	Y	Y	Y	Y	Y	Y	N
CALIFORNIA							
1 *Riggs*	+	+	+	Y	Y	N	N
2 *Herger*	Y	Y	Y	Y	Y	N	N
3 Fazio	N	N	N	N	Y	N	N
4 *Doolittle*	Y	Y	Y	Y	N	N	N
5 Matsui	N	Y	N	Y	N	Y	N
6 Woolsey	N	Y	N	Y	N	Y	N
7 Miller	N	Y	N	Y	N	Y	N
8 Pelosi	N	N	N	N	Y	N	N
9 Vacant							
10 Tauscher	N	N	Y	N	Y	N	N
11 *Pombo*	Y	Y	Y	Y	Y	Y	N
12 Lantos	N	Y	N	Y	N	Y	N
13 Stark	N	N	N	Y	N	Y	N
14 Eshoo	N	Y	N	Y	N	Y	N
15 *Campbell*	N	Y	Y	Y	N	Y	N
16 Lofgren	N	Y	N	Y	N	Y	P
17 Farr	N	Y	N	Y	N	Y	N
18 Condit	N	Y	N	+	N	Y	N
19 *Radanovich*	Y	Y	Y	P	N	N	N
20 Dooley	N	N	N	N	Y	N	N
21 *Thomas*	N	Y	Y	Y	N	Y	N
22 Capps, L.	N	Y	N	Y	N	Y	N
23 *Gallegly*	Y	Y	Y	Y	Y	N	N
24 Sherman	N	Y	N	Y	N	Y	N
25 *McKeon*	Y	Y	Y	Y	Y	N	N
26 Berman	N	Y	N	Y	N	Y	N
27 *Rogan*	Y	Y	Y	Y	Y	Y	N
28 *Dreier*	Y	Y	Y	Y	Y	N	N
29 Waxman	N	Y	N	Y	N	Y	N
30 Becerra	N	N	N	Y	N	Y	N
31 Martinez	N	Y	N	Y	N	Y	N
32 Dixon	N	Y	N	Y	N	Y	N
33 Roybal-Allard	N	N	N	Y	N	Y	N
34 Torres	N	N	N	Y	N	Y	?
35 Waters	?	?	?	?	?	?	?
36 Harman	N	Y	N	Y	N	Y	N
37 Millender-McD.	N	Y	N	Y	N	Y	N

	88	90	91	92	93	94	95
38 *Horn*	Y	Y	Y	Y	Y	Y	N
39 *Royce*	?	?	?	?	?	?	?
40 *Lewis*	Y	Y	Y	Y	Y	N	N
41 *Kim*	Y	Y	Y	Y	N	N	N
42 Brown	N	Y	N	Y	N	Y	N
43 *Calvert*	Y	Y	Y	Y	Y	Y	N
44 Vacant							
45 *Rohrabacher*	N	Y	Y	Y	Y	N	N
46 Sanchez	N	Y	N	Y	N	Y	N
47 *Cox*	Y	?	?	Y	Y	Y	N
48 *Packard*	Y	Y	Y	Y	Y	N	N
49 *Bilbray*	Y	Y	Y	Y	Y	N	N
50 Filner	N	Y	N	Y	N	Y	N
51 *Cunningham*	Y	Y	Y	Y	Y	N	N
52 *Hunter*	Y	Y	Y	Y	Y	N	Y
COLORADO							
1 DeGette	N	Y	N	Y	N	Y	N
2 Skaggs	N	N	N	Y	N	Y	N
3 *McInnis*	Y	Y	Y	Y	Y	N	N
4 *Schaffer*	Y	Y	Y	Y	Y	N	Y
5 *Hefley*	Y	Y	Y	Y	Y	N	N
6 *Schaefer*	Y	Y	Y	N	Y	N	N
CONNECTICUT							
1 Kennelly	N	Y	N	Y	N	Y	N
2 Gejdenson	N	Y	N	Y	N	Y	N
3 DeLauro	N	Y	N	Y	N	Y	N
4 *Shays*	N	N	Y	N	Y	Y	N
5 Maloney	N	Y	N	Y	N	Y	N
6 *Johnson*	Y	Y	Y	Y	Y	Y	N
DELAWARE							
AL *Castle*	N	N	Y	Y	N	N	Y
FLORIDA							
1 *Scarborough*	Y	Y	Y	Y	Y	?	Y
2 Boyd	N	Y	N	Y	N	Y	N
3 Brown	N	Y	N	Y	N	Y	N
4 *Fowler*	Y	Y	Y	Y	Y	N	N
5 Thurman	N	Y	N	Y	N	Y	N
6 *Stearns*	Y	Y	Y	Y	Y	N	N
7 *Mica*	Y	Y	Y	Y	Y	N	N
8 *McCollum*	Y	Y	Y	Y	Y	N	N
9 *Bilirakis*	Y	Y	Y	Y	Y	N	N
10 *Young*	Y	Y	Y	Y	Y	N	N
11 Davis	N	N	N	Y	N	Y	N
12 *Canady*	N	Y	Y	Y	N	N	N
13 *Miller*	N	Y	Y	Y	N	Y	N
14 *Goss*	Y	Y	Y	Y	Y	N	N
15 *Weldon*	Y	Y	Y	Y	Y	N	N
16 *Foley*	Y	Y	Y	Y	Y	Y	N
17 Meek	N	N	N	Y	N	Y	N
18 *Ros-Lehtinen*	Y	Y	Y	?	?	?	?
19 Wexler	N	N	N	N	Y	N	N
20 Deutsch	N	N	N	Y	N	Y	N
21 *Diaz-Balart*	Y	Y	Y	Y	Y	N	N
22 *Shaw*	Y	Y	Y	Y	Y	Y	N
23 Hastings	N	N	N	N	Y	N	N
GEORGIA							
1 *Kingston*	Y	Y	Y	Y	Y	Y	Y
2 Bishop	Y	Y	Y	Y	Y	Y	N
3 *Collins*	Y	Y	Y	Y	N	N	N
4 McKinney	N	Y	N	Y	N	Y	N
5 Lewis	N	N	N	Y	N	Y	N
6 *Gingrich*					Y		
7 *Barr*	Y	Y	Y	Y	Y	N	N
8 *Chambliss*	Y	Y	Y	Y	Y	N	N
9 *Deal*	Y	Y	Y	Y	Y	N	Y
10 *Norwood*	Y	Y	Y	Y	Y	N	N
11 *Linder*	Y	Y	?	Y	Y	N	N
HAWAII							
1 Abercrombie	N	Y	N	Y	N	Y	N
2 Mink	N	Y	N	Y	N	Y	N
IDAHO							
1 *Chenoweth*	N	Y	Y	Y	Y	N	N
2 *Crapo*	N	Y	Y	Y	Y	N	N
ILLINOIS							
1 Rush	N	Y	N	Y	N	Y	N
2 Jackson	N	Y	N	Y	N	Y	N
3 Lipinski	N	Y	N	Y	N	Y	N
4 Gutierrez	N	Y	N	Y	N	Y	N
5 Blagojevich	N	Y	N	Y	N	Y	N
6 *Hyde*	Y	Y	Y	Y	Y	N	Y
7 Davis	N	Y	N	Y	N	Y	N
8 *Crane*	Y	Y	Y	Y	Y	N	N
9 Yates	N	N	Y	Y	N	Y	?
10 *Porter*	Y	N	Y	Y	N	Y	N
11 *Weller*	Y	Y	Y	Y	Y	N	N
12 Costello	N	Y	N	Y	N	Y	N

ND Northern Democrats   SD Southern Democrats

	88	90	91	92	93	94	95
13 ***Fawell***	Y	Y	?	Y	Y	Y	N
14 ***Hastert***	Y	Y	Y	Y	Y	N	N
15 ***Ewing***	Y	Y	Y	Y	Y	N	N
16 ***Manzullo***	Y	Y	Y	Y	Y	N	N
17 Evans	N	Y	N	Y	N	Y	N
18 ***LaHood***	Y	Y	Y	Y	N	Y	N
19 Poshard	N	Y	N	Y	N	Y	N
20 ***Shimkus***	Y	Y	Y	Y	Y	Y	N
INDIANA							
1 Visclosky	N	Y	N	Y	N	Y	N
2 ***McIntosh***	Y	Y	Y	Y	Y	N	?
3 Roemer	N	Y	N	Y	N	Y	N
4 ***Souder***	N	Y	Y	Y	N	Y	Y
5 ***Buyer***	Y	Y	Y	Y	Y	N	N
6 ***Burton***	Y	Y	Y	Y	Y	N	N
7 ***Pease***	Y	Y	Y	Y	Y	N	N
8 ***Hostettler***	Y	Y	Y	N	Y	N	N
9 Hamilton	N	Y	N	Y	N	Y	N
10 Carson	N	Y	Y	Y	N	Y	N
IOWA							
1 ***Leach***	Y	Y	Y	Y	N	Y	Y
2 ***Nussle***	N	Y	Y	Y	Y	Y	N
3 Boswell	N	Y	Y	Y	N	Y	N
4 ***Ganske***	Y	Y	Y	Y	Y	N	N
5 ***Latham***	Y	Y	Y	Y	Y	N	N
KANSAS							
1 ***Moran***	N	Y	Y	Y	Y	N	N
2 ***Ryun***	Y	Y	Y	Y	Y	N	N
3 ***Snowbarger***	Y	Y	Y	Y	Y	N	N
4 ***Tiahrt***	Y	Y	Y	Y	Y	N	N
KENTUCKY							
1 ***Whitfield***	Y	Y	Y	Y	Y	N	N
2 ***Lewis***	Y	Y	Y	Y	Y	N	N
3 ***Northup***	Y	Y	Y	Y	Y	N	N
4 ***Bunning***	Y	Y	Y	Y	Y	N	N
5 ***Rogers***	Y	Y	Y	Y	Y	Y	N
6 Baesler	N	Y	N	Y	N	Y	N
LOUISIANA							
1 ***Livingston***	Y	Y	Y	Y	Y	N	N
2 Jefferson	?	?	?	?	?	?	?
3 ***Tauzin***	Y	Y	Y	Y	Y	N	N
4 ***McCrery***	Y	Y	Y	Y	Y	N	P
5 ***Cooksey***	Y	Y	Y	Y	Y	N	N
6 ***Baker***	Y	Y	Y	Y	Y	N	N
7 John	N	Y	N	Y	N	Y	N
MAINE							
1 Allen	Y	Y	N	Y	N	Y	N
2 Baldacci	Y	Y	N	Y	N	Y	N
MARYLAND							
1 ***Gilchrest***	Y	?	?	Y	N	Y	N
2 ***Ehrlich***	Y	Y	Y	Y	Y	N	Y
3 Cardin	N	N	N	Y	N	Y	N
4 Wynn	N	Y	N	Y	N	Y	N
5 Hoyer	N	N	N	Y	N	Y	N
6 ***Bartlett***	Y	Y	Y	Y	Y	Y	N
7 Cummings	N	Y	N	Y	N	Y	N
8 ***Morella***	N	N	Y	Y	N	Y	Y
MASSACHUSETTS							
1 Olver	N	Y	N	Y	N	Y	N
2 Neal	N	Y	N	Y	N	Y	N
3 McGovern	N	Y	N	Y	N	Y	N
4 Frank	N	Y	N	Y	N	Y	N
5 Meehan	N	Y	N	Y	N	Y	N
6 Tierney	N	Y	N	Y	N	Y	N
7 Markey	N	Y	N	Y	N	Y	N
8 Kennedy	N	?	?	?	N	Y	N
9 Moakley	N	Y	N	Y	N	Y	N
10 Delahunt	N	Y	N	Y	N	Y	N
MICHIGAN							
1 Stupak	N	Y	N	Y	N	Y	N
2 ***Hoekstra***	Y	Y	Y	Y	Y	N	Y
3 ***Ehlers***	Y	Y	Y	Y	Y	N	N
4 ***Camp***	Y	Y	Y	Y	Y	N	N
5 Barcia	N	Y	N	Y	N	Y	N
6 ***Upton***	N	Y	Y	Y	Y	Y	N
7 ***Smith***	Y	Y	Y	Y	Y	?	Y
8 Stabenow	N	Y	N	Y	N	Y	N
9 Kildee	N	Y	N	Y	N	Y	N
10 Bonior	N	Y	N	Y	N	Y	N
11 ***Knollenberg***	Y	Y	Y	Y	Y	N	N
12 Levin	N	Y	N	Y	N	Y	N
13 Rivers	N	Y	N	Y	N	Y	N
14 Conyers	N	N	N	Y	N	Y	N
15 Kilpatrick	N	Y	N	Y	N	Y	N
16 Dingell	N	Y	N	Y	N	Y	N

	88	90	91	92	93	94	95
MINNESOTA							
1 ***Gutknecht***	Y	Y	Y	Y	Y	N	Y
2 Minge	N	N	N	Y	N	Y	Y
3 ***Ramstad***	Y	Y	Y	Y	Y	N	N
4 Vento	N	Y	N	Y	N	Y	N
5 Sabo	N	N	N	Y	N	Y	N
6 Luther	N	N	N	Y	N	Y	N
7 Peterson	N	Y	N	Y	N	Y	N
8 Oberstar	N	Y	N	Y	N	Y	N
MISSISSIPPI							
1 ***Wicker***	Y	Y	Y	Y	Y	N	N
2 Thompson	N	Y	N	Y	N	Y	N
3 ***Pickering***	Y	Y	Y	Y	Y	N	N
4 ***Parker***	Y	Y	Y	Y	Y	N	Y
5 Taylor	Y	Y	N	Y	Y	N	N
MISSOURI							
1 Clay	N	Y	N	Y	N	Y	N
2 ***Talent***	Y	Y	Y	Y	Y	N	N
3 Gephardt	N	N	N	Y	N	Y	N
4 Skelton	N	Y	N	Y	N	Y	N
5 McCarthy	N	Y	N	Y	N	Y	N
6 Danner	N	Y	N	Y	N	Y	N
7 ***Blunt***	Y	Y	Y	Y	Y	N	N
8 ***Emerson***	Y	Y	Y	Y	Y	Y	N
9 ***Hulshof***	Y	Y	Y	Y	Y	Y	N
MONTANA							
AL ***Hill***	Y	Y	Y	Y	Y	N	Y
NEBRASKA							
1 ***Bereuter***	Y	Y	Y	Y	Y	N	N
2 ***Christensen***	Y	N	Y	Y	Y	N	Y
3 ***Barrett***	Y	N	Y	Y	Y	N	Y
NEVADA							
1 ***Ensign***	Y	Y	Y	Y	Y	Y	N
2 ***Gibbons***	Y	Y	Y	Y	N	N	N
NEW HAMPSHIRE							
1 ***Sununu***	Y	Y	Y	Y	Y	N	N
2 ***Bass***	Y	Y	Y	Y	Y	N	N
NEW JERSEY							
1 Andrews	N	Y	?	Y	N	Y	N
2 ***LoBiondo***	Y	Y	Y	Y	Y	Y	N
3 ***Saxton***	Y	Y	Y	Y	Y	N	N
4 ***Smith***	Y	Y	Y	Y	Y	Y	N
5 ***Roukema***	Y	Y	Y	Y	Y	N	N
6 Pallone	N	Y	N	Y	N	Y	N
7 ***Franks***	Y	Y	Y	Y	Y	Y	N
8 Pascrell	N	Y	N	Y	N	Y	N
9 Rothman	N	Y	N	Y	N	Y	N
10 Payne	?	?	?	?	?	?	?
11 ***Frelinghuysen***	Y	Y	Y	Y	Y	N	Y
12 ***Pappas***	Y	Y	Y	Y	Y	Y	Y
13 Menendez	N	Y	N	Y	N	Y	N
NEW MEXICO							
1 Vacant							
2 ***Skeen***	Y	Y	Y	Y	Y	Y	N
3 ***Redmond***	Y	Y	Y	Y	Y	Y	N
NEW YORK							
1 ***Forbes***	Y	Y	Y	Y	N	Y	N
2 ***Lazio***	Y	Y	Y	Y	N	Y	N
3 ***King***	Y	Y	Y	Y	Y	N	N
4 McCarthy	N	Y	N	Y	N	Y	N
5 Ackerman	N	Y	N	Y	N	Y	N
6 Meeks	N	Y	N	Y	N	Y	N
7 Manton	N	Y	N	Y	N	Y	N
8 Nadler	N	Y	N	Y	N	Y	N
9 Schumer	?	N	N	Y	N	Y	N
10 Towns	N	Y	N	Y	N	Y	N
11 Owens	N	Y	N	Y	N	Y	N
12 Velázquez	N	Y	N	Y	N	Y	N
13 ***Fossella***	Y	Y	Y	Y	Y	N	N
14 Maloney	N	N	N	Y	N	Y	N
15 Rangel	?	?	?	?	?	?	?
16 Serrano	N	Y	N	Y	N	Y	N
17 Engel	N	Y	N	Y	N	Y	N
18 Lowey	N	N	N	Y	N	Y	N
19 ***Kelly***	Y	Y	Y	Y	N	Y	N
20 ***Gilman***	Y	Y	Y	Y	N	Y	N
21 McNulty	N	Y	N	Y	N	Y	N
22 ***Solomon***	Y	Y	Y	Y	Y	N	N
23 ***Boehlert***	Y	Y	Y	Y	N	Y	N
24 ***McHugh***	Y	Y	Y	Y	Y	Y	N
25 ***Walsh***	Y	Y	Y	Y	N	Y	N
26 Hinchey	N	Y	N	Y	N	Y	N
27 ***Paxon***	Y	Y	Y	N	Y	N	N
28 Slaughter	N	Y	N	Y	N	Y	N
29 LaFalce	N	N	N	Y	?	?	N

	88	90	91	92	93	94	95
30 ***Quinn***	Y	Y	Y	Y	N	Y	N
31 ***Houghton***	Y	Y	Y	Y	N	Y	N
NORTH CAROLINA							
1 Clayton	N	N	N	Y	N	Y	N
2 Etheridge	N	N	N	Y	N	Y	N
3 ***Jones***	Y	Y	Y	Y	Y	N	Y
4 Price	N	N	N	Y	N	Y	N
5 ***Burr***	Y	Y	Y	Y	Y	N	Y
6 ***Coble***	Y	Y	Y	Y	Y	N	N
7 McIntyre	N	Y	N	Y	N	Y	N
8 Hefner	N	Y	N	Y	N	Y	N
9 ***Myrick***	Y	N	Y	Y	Y	N	Y
10 ***Ballenger***	Y	Y	Y	Y	Y	N	Y
11 ***Taylor***	Y	Y	Y	Y	Y	N	Y
12 Watt	N	N	N	Y	N	Y	N
NORTH DAKOTA							
AL Pomeroy	N	N	N	Y	N	Y	Y
OHIO							
1 ***Chabot***	Y	Y	Y	Y	Y	N	Y
2 ***Portman***	Y	Y	Y	Y	Y	N	N
3 Hall	N	Y	N	Y	N	Y	N
4 ***Oxley***	Y	Y	Y	Y	Y	N	N
5 ***Gillmor***	Y	Y	Y	N	Y	Y	N
6 Strickland	N	Y	N	Y	N	Y	N
7 ***Hobson***	Y	Y	Y	Y	Y	N	Y
8 ***Boehner***	Y	Y	Y	Y	Y	N	Y
9 Kaptur	N	Y	N	Y	N	Y	N
10 Kucinich	N	Y	N	Y	N	Y	N
11 Stokes	N	Y	N	Y	N	Y	N
12 ***Kasich***	Y	Y	Y	Y	Y	N	Y
13 Brown	N	N	N	Y	N	Y	N
14 Sawyer	N	Y	N	Y	N	Y	N
15 ***Pryce***	Y	Y	Y	Y	Y	N	N
16 ***Regula***	Y	Y	Y	Y	Y	N	N
17 Traficant	N	Y	Y	Y	N	Y	N
18 ***Ney***	Y	Y	Y	Y	Y	N	N
19 ***LaTourette***	Y	Y	Y	Y	N	N	N
OKLAHOMA							
1 ***Largent***	Y	Y	Y	Y	Y	N	Y
2 ***Coburn***	Y	Y	P	Y	Y	N	Y
3 ***Watkins***	Y	Y	Y	N	Y	N	N
4 ***Watts***	Y	Y	Y	Y	N	N	N
5 ***Istook***	Y	Y	Y	Y	Y	N	Y
6 ***Lucas***	Y	Y	Y	Y	Y	N	N
OREGON							
1 Furse	N	Y	N	Y	N	Y	N
2 ***Smith***	Y	Y	Y	?	N	Y	N
3 Blumenauer	N	Y	N	Y	N	Y	N
4 DeFazio	N	Y	N	Y	N	Y	N
5 Hooley	N	Y	N	Y	N	Y	N
PENNSYLVANIA							
1 Vacant							
2 Fattah	N	Y	N	Y	N	Y	N
3 Borski	N	Y	?	Y	N	Y	N
4 Klink	N	Y	N	Y	N	Y	N
5 ***Peterson***	Y	Y	Y	Y	Y	N	N
6 Holden	N	Y	Y	Y	N	Y	N
7 ***Weldon***	Y	Y	Y	Y	Y	Y	N
8 ***Greenwood***	Y	Y	?	Y	Y	N	N
9 ***Shuster***	Y	Y	Y	Y	N	N	N
10 ***McDade***	Y	Y	Y	Y	N	N	N
11 Kanjorski	N	Y	N	Y	N	Y	N
12 Murtha	N	Y	Y	Y	N	Y	N
13 ***Fox***	Y	Y	Y	Y	N	Y	N
14 Coyne	N	Y	N	Y	N	Y	N
15 McHale	N	Y	N	Y	N	Y	N
16 ***Pitts***	Y	Y	Y	Y	Y	N	N
17 ***Gekas***	Y	Y	Y	Y	Y	N	N
18 Doyle	N	Y	Y	Y	N	Y	N
19 ***Goodling***	Y	Y	Y	Y	Y	N	N
20 Mascara	N	Y	Y	Y	N	Y	N
21 ***English***	Y	Y	Y	Y	N	Y	N
RHODE ISLAND							
1 Kennedy	N	Y	N	Y	N	Y	N
2 Weygand	N	Y	N	Y	N	Y	N
SOUTH CAROLINA							
1 ***Sanford***	Y	N	Y	Y	Y	N	Y
2 ***Spence***	Y	Y	Y	Y	Y	N	N
3 ***Graham***	Y	N	Y	Y	Y	N	Y
4 ***Inglis***	Y	N	Y	Y	Y	N	Y
5 Spratt	N	N	N	Y	N	?	N
6 Clyburn	N	Y	N	Y	N	Y	N
SOUTH DAKOTA							
AL ***Thune***	Y	Y	Y	Y	Y	N	N

	88	90	91	92	93	94	95
TENNESSEE							
1 ***Jenkins***	Y	Y	Y	Y	Y	N	N
2 ***Duncan***	N	Y	Y	Y	Y	N	N
3 ***Wamp***	Y	Y	Y	Y	Y	N	Y
4 ***Hilleary***	Y	Y	Y	Y	Y	N	Y
5 Clement	N	Y	N	Y	N	Y	N
6 Gordon	N	Y	N	Y	N	Y	N
7 ***Bryant***	Y	Y	Y	Y	Y	N	N
8 Tanner	N	N	N	Y	N	Y	N
9 Ford	N	N	N	Y	N	Y	N
TEXAS							
1 Sandlin	N	Y	N	Y	N	Y	N
2 Turner	N	Y	N	Y	N	Y	N
3 ***Johnson, Sam***	Y	Y	Y	Y	Y	N	Y
4 Hall	Y	Y	N	Y	Y	N	Y
5 ***Sessions***	Y	Y	Y	Y	Y	N	Y
6 ***Barton***	Y	Y	Y	N	Y	N	Y
7 ***Archer***	Y	Y	Y	Y	Y	N	Y
8 ***Brady***	Y	Y	Y	Y	Y	N	N
9 Lampson	N	Y	N	Y	N	Y	N
10 Doggett	N	Y	N	Y	N	Y	N
11 Edwards	N	N	N	Y	N	Y	Y
12 ***Granger***	Y	Y	Y	Y	Y	N	N
13 ***Thornberry***	Y	Y	Y	Y	Y	N	Y
14 ***Paul***	N	Y	Y	N	Y	N	N
15 Hinojosa	N	Y	N	Y	N	Y	N
16 Reyes	N	Y	N	Y	N	Y	N
17 Stenholm	N	N	N	Y	Y	Y	Y
18 Jackson-Lee	N	Y	N	Y	N	Y	N
19 ***Combest***	Y	Y	Y	Y	Y	N	N
20 Gonzalez	?	?	?	?	?	?	?
21 ***Smith***	Y	Y	Y	Y	Y	Y	N
22 ***DeLay***	Y	Y	Y	Y	Y	N	Y
23 ***Bonilla***	Y	Y	Y	Y	Y	N	Y
24 Frost	N	Y	N	Y	N	Y	N
25 Bentsen	N	N	N	Y	N	Y	N
26 ***Armey***	Y	Y	Y	Y	Y	N	N
27 Ortiz	N	Y	N	Y	N	Y	N
28 Rodriguez	N	Y	N	Y	N	Y	N
29 Green	N	Y	N	Y	N	Y	N
30 Johnson, E.B.	N	Y	N	Y	N	Y	N
UTAH							
1 ***Hansen***	Y	Y	Y	Y	Y	N	N
2 ***Cook***	Y	Y	Y	Y	Y	N	N
3 ***Cannon***	?	?	?	?	?	?	?
VERMONT							
AL *Sanders*	N	Y	N	Y	N	Y	N
VIRGINIA							
1 ***Bateman***	Y	Y	Y	Y	Y	N	N
2 Pickett	Y	Y	Y	Y	N	Y	N
3 Scott	N	Y	N	Y	N	Y	N
4 Sisisky	N	Y	N	Y	N	Y	N
5 Goode	Y	Y	?	Y	N	N	N
6 ***Goodlatte***	Y	Y	Y	Y	Y	N	N
7 ***Bliley***	Y	Y	Y	Y	Y	N	N
8 Moran	N	N	N	Y	N	Y	N
9 Boucher	N	Y	Y	Y	N	Y	N
10 ***Wolf***	Y	N	Y	Y	Y	N	Y
11 ***Davis***	Y	Y	Y	Y	N	N	N
WASHINGTON							
1 ***White***	Y	Y	Y	Y	Y	N	Y
2 ***Metcalf***	Y	Y	Y	Y	Y	N	N
3 ***Smith, Linda***	Y	Y	Y	Y	Y	Y	N
4 ***Hastings***	Y	Y	Y	Y	Y	N	N
5 ***Nethercutt***	Y	Y	Y	Y	Y	N	Y
6 Dicks	N	Y	N	Y	N	Y	N
7 McDermott	N	N	N	Y	N	Y	N
8 ***Dunn***	Y	Y	Y	Y	Y	N	N
9 Smith, Adam	N	N	N	Y	N	Y	N
WEST VIRGINIA							
1 Mollohan	N	Y	N	Y	N	Y	N
2 Wise	N	Y	N	Y	N	Y	N
3 Rahall	N	Y	N	Y	N	Y	N
WISCONSIN							
1 ***Neumann***	Y	Y	Y	Y	Y	N	Y
2 ***Klug***	N	?	?	?	?	?	?
3 Kind	N	N	N	Y	N	Y	Y
4 Kleczka	N	Y	N	Y	N	Y	N
5 Barrett	N	N	N	Y	N	Y	Y
6 ***Petri***	N	Y	?	Y	N	N	N
7 Obey	N	N	N	Y	N	Y	N
8 Johnson	N	Y	N	Y	N	Y	N
9 ***Sensenbrenner***	N	Y	Y	Y	Y	N	Y
WYOMING							
AL ***Cubin***	Y	Y	Y	Y	Y	N	Y

Southern states - Ala., Ark., Fla., Ga., Ky., La., Miss., N.C., Okla., S.C., Tenn., Texas, Va.

96. HR 2400. Surface Transportation Reauthorization/Extend ISTEA. Spratt, D-S.C., amendment to eliminate all the bill's provisions and instead extend the existing short-term ISTEA reauthorization until July 1, 1998. Rejected 106-312: R 51-169; D 55-142 (ND 32-112, SD 23-30); I 0-1. April 1, 1998. A "yea" was a vote in support of the president's position.

97. HR 2400. Surface Transportation Reauthorization/State Transition. Kasich, R-Ohio, amendment to eliminate all of the bill's provisions, and instead turn over more control of transportation projects to the states and reduce the federal gas tax over a four-year period. Rejected 98-318: R 82-138; D 16-179 (ND 8-134, SD 8-45); I 0-1. April 1, 1998.

98. HR 2400. Surface Transportation Reauthorization/Passage. Passage of the bill to authorize $219 billion over six years for federal highway and mass transit programs. The bill's transportation funding represents a 40 percent increase in spending over the next six years. The bill also modifies highway funding formulas. Passed 337-80: R 165-54; D 171-26 (ND 129-15, SD 42-11); I 1-0. April 1, 1998.

99. Quorum Call.* 389 Responded. April 21, 1998.

100. HR 3565. Assistance for Police Survivors/Passage. McCollum, R-Fla., motion to suspend the rules and pass the bill to authorize the Bureau of Justice Assistance to spend no less than $150,000 each year to provide counseling and peer support programs for families of public safety officers killed in the line of duty. Motion agreed to 403-8: R 208-8; D 194-0 (ND 142-0, SD 52-0); I 1-0. April 21, 1998. A two-thirds majority of those present and voting (274 in this case) is required for passage under suspension of the rules. A "yea" was a vote in support of the president's position.

101. HR 3528. Dispute Resolution Alternatives/Passage. Coble, R-N.C., motion to suspend the rules and pass the bill to direct federal district courts to devise and implement their own alternative dispute resolution programs or to examine and improve any such existing programs. Motion agreed to 405-2: R 211-1; D 193-1 (ND 142-1, SD 51-0); I 1-0. April 21, 1998. A two-thirds majority of those present and voting (272 in this case) is required for passage under suspension of the rules. A "yea" was a vote in support of the president's position.

102. H J Res 111. Tax Limitation Constitutional Amendment/Passage. Passage of the joint resolution proposing a constitutional amendment requiring a two-thirds majority vote in both the House and the Senate in order to raise taxes. Rejected 238-186: R 213-12; D 25-173 (ND 14-133, SD 11-40); I 0-1. April 22, 1998. A two-thirds majority of those present and voting (283 in this case) is required to pass a joint resolution proposing an amendment to the Constitution. A "nay" was a vote in support of the president's position.

103. HR 1252. Limits on Federal Judges' Power/Tax Increases. Delahunt, D-Mass., amendment to provide that the limitation on judicial imposition of remedies that require a tax increase shall apply only where the court "expressly directs" that a tax be imposed. Adopted 230-181: R 47-168; D 182-13 (ND 140-4, SD 42-9); I 1-0. April 23, 1998. (Subsequently, the section containing this provision was removed by unanimous consent.)

* CQ does not include quorum calls in its vote charts.

[1] Barbara Lee, D-Calif., was sworn in April 21, replacing Ronald V. Dellums, D-Calif., who resigned Feb. 6.

[2] Mary Bono, R-Calif., was sworn in April 21, replacing Sonny Bono, R-Calif., who died Jan. 5.

Key

Y	Voted for (yea).
#	Paired for.
+	Announced for.
N	Voted against (nay).
X	Paired against.
−	Announced against.
P	Voted "present."
C	Voted "present" to avoid possible conflict of interest.
?	Did not vote or otherwise make a position known.

Democrats **Republicans**
Independent

	96	97	98	100	101	102	103
ALABAMA							
1 *Callahan*	N	N	Y	Y	Y	Y	N
2 *Everett*	N	N	Y	Y	Y	Y	N
3 *Riley*	N	N	Y	Y	Y	Y	N
4 *Aderholt*	N	N	Y	Y	Y	Y	N
5 Cramer	N	N	Y	Y	Y	Y	N
6 *Bachus*	N	Y	Y	Y	Y	Y	N
7 Hilliard	N	N	Y	Y	Y	N	N
ALASKA							
AL *Young*	N	N	Y	Y	Y	Y	N
ARIZONA							
1 *Salmon*	Y	Y	N	Y	Y	Y	N
2 Pastor	N	N	Y	Y	Y	N	Y
3 *Stump*	N	Y	N	Y	Y	Y	N
4 *Shadegg*	Y	Y	N	Y	Y	Y	N
5 *Kolbe*	Y	Y	Y	Y	Y	Y	N
6 *Hayworth*	Y	Y	N	Y	Y	Y	N
ARKANSAS							
1 Berry	N	N	Y	Y	Y	Y	Y
2 Snyder	Y	N	Y	Y	Y	N	Y
3 *Hutchinson*	N	N	Y	Y	Y	Y	N
4 *Dickey*	N	N	Y	Y	Y	Y	N
CALIFORNIA							
1 *Riggs*	N	N	Y	Y	Y	Y	N
2 *Herger*	N	Y	N	Y	Y	Y	N
3 Fazlo	Y	N	Y	Y	Y	N	Y
4 *Doolittle*	N	N	Y	Y	Y	Y	N
5 Matsui	N	N	Y	Y	Y	Y	?
6 Woolsey	N	N	Y	Y	Y	N	Y
7 Miller	N	Y	Y	Y	Y	N	Y
8 Pelosi	N	N	Y	Y	Y	N	Y
9 Lee [1]			Y	Y	Y	N	Y
10 Tauscher	N	N	Y	Y	Y	N	Y
11 *Pombo*	N	Y	Y	Y	Y	Y	N
12 Lantos	N	N	Y	Y	Y	N	Y
13 Stark	Y	Y	N	Y	Y	N	Y
14 Eshoo	Y	N	Y	Y	Y	N	Y
15 *Campbell*	Y	Y	N	Y	N	N	N
16 Lofgren	Y	P	P	Y	Y	N	Y
17 Farr	Y	Y	Y	Y	Y	Y	N
18 Condit	Y	Y	Y	Y	Y	Y	N
19 *Radanovich*	N	Y	Y	Y	Y	Y	?
20 Dooley	Y	Y	N	Y	Y	N	Y
21 *Thomas*	N	N	Y	Y	Y	Y	N
22 Capps, L.	N	N	Y	Y	Y	N	Y
23 *Gallegly*	N	N	Y	Y	Y	Y	N
24 Sherman	N	N	Y	Y	Y	Y	Y
25 *McKeon*	N	N	Y	Y	Y	Y	N
26 Berman	Y	N	Y	Y	Y	N	Y
27 *Rogan*	Y	Y	Y	Y	Y	Y	N
28 *Dreier*	N	N	Y	Y	Y	Y	N
29 Waxman	Y	N	Y	Y	Y	N	Y
30 Becerra	Y	Y	N	Y	Y	N	Y
31 Martinez	N	N	Y	Y	Y	N	Y
32 Dixon	N	N	Y	?	?	?	?
33 Roybal-Allard	N	N	Y	Y	Y	N	Y
34 Torres	?	?	Y	Y	Y	N	Y
35 Waters	?	?	Y	Y	Y	N	Y
36 Harman	N	N	Y	Y	Y	Y	Y
37 Millender-McD.	N	N	Y	Y	Y	N	Y

	96	97	98	100	101	102	103
38 *Horn*	N	N	Y	Y	Y	Y	Y
39 *Royce*	?	?	?	Y	Y	Y	N
40 *Lewis*	N	N	Y	Y	Y	Y	N
41 *Kim*	N	N	Y	Y	Y	Y	N
42 Brown	N	Y	Y	?	?	?	Y
43 *Calvert*	N	N	Y	Y	Y	Y	N
44 *Bono, M.* [2]			Y	Y	Y	Y	N
45 *Rohrabacher*	Y	Y	N	Y	Y	Y	N
46 Sanchez	Y	N	Y	Y	Y	Y	Y
47 *Cox*	Y	Y	N	Y	Y	Y	N
48 *Packard*	N	N	Y	Y	Y	Y	N
49 *Bilbray*	N	N	Y	Y	Y	Y	N
50 Filner	N	N	Y	Y	Y	N	Y
51 *Cunningham*	N	Y	Y	Y	Y	Y	N
52 *Hunter*	N	Y	Y	Y	Y	Y	N
COLORADO							
1 DeGette	N	N	Y	Y	Y	N	Y
2 Skaggs	Y	N	Y	Y	Y	N	Y
3 *McInnis*	N	N	Y	Y	Y	Y	N
4 *Schaffer*	N	Y	N	Y	Y	Y	N
5 *Hefley*	N	Y	P	Y	Y	Y	N
6 *Schaefer*	N	N	Y	Y	Y	Y	N
CONNECTICUT							
1 Kennelly	N	N	Y	Y	Y	N	Y
2 Gejdenson	N	N	Y	Y	Y	N	Y
3 DeLauro	N	N	Y	Y	Y	N	Y
4 *Shays*	Y	N	Y	Y	Y	Y	Y
5 Maloney	N	N	Y	Y	Y	N	Y
6 *Johnson*	N	N	Y	Y	Y	N	Y
DELAWARE							
AL *Castle*	Y	N	N	Y	Y	Y	N
FLORIDA							
1 *Scarborough*	Y	Y	N	N	Y	N	Y
2 Boyd	Y	Y	Y	Y	Y	N	?
3 Brown	N	N	Y	Y	Y	N	Y
4 *Fowler*	N	N	Y	Y	Y	Y	N
5 Thurman	N	N	Y	Y	Y	N	Y
6 *Stearns*	N	N	Y	Y	Y	Y	N
7 *Mica*	N	N	Y	Y	Y	Y	N
8 *McCollum*	N	Y	Y	Y	Y	Y	N
9 *Bilirakis*	N	N	Y	Y	Y	Y	N
10 *Young*	N	Y	Y	?	?	Y	N
11 Davis	Y	N	N	Y	N	Y	N
12 *Canady*	N	Y	Y	Y	Y	Y	N
13 *Miller*	Y	Y	N	Y	Y	Y	N
14 *Goss*	N	Y	Y	Y	Y	Y	N
15 *Weldon*	N	N	Y	?	Y	Y	N
16 *Foley*	N	Y	Y	Y	Y	Y	N
17 Meek	N	N	Y	Y	Y	N	Y
18 *Ros-Lehtinen*	?	?	#	Y	Y	Y	N
19 Wexler	Y	Y	N	Y	Y	N	Y
20 Deutsch	Y	N	Y	Y	Y	N	Y
21 *Diaz-Balart*	N	N	Y	Y	Y	Y	N
22 *Shaw*	N	N	Y	Y	Y	N	N
23 Hastings	Y	N	N	Y	?	?	?
GEORGIA							
1 *Kingston*	Y	Y	N	N	Y	Y	N
2 Bishop	N	N	Y	Y	Y	N	Y
3 *Collins*	N	N	Y	Y	Y	Y	N
4 McKinney	N	N	Y	Y	Y	N	Y
5 Lewis	Y	N	N	Y	N	Y	N
6 *Gingrich*						Y	
7 *Barr*	Y	Y	N	Y	Y	Y	?
8 *Chambliss*	N	N	Y	Y	Y	Y	N
9 *Deal*	Y	Y	N	Y	Y	Y	N
10 *Norwood*	N	N	Y	Y	Y	Y	N
11 *Linder*	N	Y	Y	Y	Y	Y	N
HAWAII							
1 Abercrombie	N	N	Y	Y	Y	N	Y
2 Mink	N	N	Y	Y	Y	N	Y
IDAHO							
1 *Chenoweth*	N	Y	Y	N	Y	Y	N
2 *Crapo*	N	Y	Y	Y	Y	Y	N
ILLINOIS							
1 Rush	N	N	Y	?	?	N	Y
2 Jackson	N	N	Y	Y	Y	N	Y
3 Lipinski	N	N	Y	Y	Y	N	Y
4 Gutierrez	N	N	Y	Y	Y	N	Y
5 Blagojevich	N	N	Y	Y	Y	N	Y
6 *Hyde*	N	N	Y	Y	Y	Y	N
7 Davis	N	N	Y	Y	Y	N	Y
8 *Crane*	Y	Y	N	Y	Y	Y	N
9 Yates	?	?	X	Y	Y	N	Y
10 *Porter*	Y	N	Y	Y	Y	Y	N
11 *Weller*	N	N	Y	Y	Y	Y	N
12 Costello	N	N	Y	Y	Y	N	Y

ND Northern Democrats   SD Southern Democrats

	96	97	98	100	101	102	103
13 ***Fawell***	N	N	Y	Y	Y	Y	Y
14 ***Hastert***	N	N	Y	Y	Y	Y	N
15 ***Ewing***	N	N	Y	Y	Y	Y	Y
16 ***Manzullo***	N	N	Y	Y	Y	Y	N
17 Evans	N	N	Y	Y	Y	N	Y
18 ***LaHood***	N	N	Y	Y	Y	Y	Y
19 Poshard	N	N	Y	Y	Y	N	Y
20 ***Shimkus***	N	N	Y	Y	Y	Y	N
INDIANA							
1 Visclosky	N	N	Y	Y	Y	N	Y
2 ***McIntosh***	N	Y	Y	Y	Y	Y	N
3 Roemer	Y	N	Y	Y	Y	Y	Y
4 ***Souder***	Y	Y	N	Y	Y	Y	N
5 ***Buyer***	N	N	Y	Y	Y	Y	N
6 ***Burton***	N	N	Y	Y	Y	Y	N
7 ***Pease***	N	N	Y	Y	Y	Y	N
8 ***Hostettler***	N	N	Y	Y	Y	N	N
9 Hamilton	N	N	Y	Y	Y	N	Y
10 Carson	N	N	Y	Y	Y	N	Y
IOWA							
1 ***Leach***	N	N	Y	Y	Y	Y	Y
2 ***Nussle***	N	N	Y	Y	Y	Y	N
3 Boswell	N	N	Y	Y	Y	Y	Y
4 ***Ganske***	N	N	Y	Y	Y	Y	Y
5 ***Latham***	N	N	Y	Y	Y	Y	N
KANSAS							
1 ***Moran***	N	N	Y	Y	Y	Y	N
2 ***Ryun***	N	N	Y	Y	Y	Y	N
3 ***Snowbarger***	N	N	Y	Y	Y	Y	N
4 ***Tiahrt***	N	N	Y	Y	Y	Y	N
KENTUCKY							
1 ***Whitfield***	Y	N	Y	Y	Y	Y	Y
2 ***Lewis***	N	N	Y	Y	Y	Y	N
3 ***Northup***	N	N	Y	Y	Y	Y	N
4 ***Bunning***	N	N	Y	Y	Y	Y	?
5 ***Rogers***	N	N	Y	Y	Y	Y	N
6 Baesler	N	N	Y	Y	Y	N	Y
LOUISIANA							
1 ***Livingston***	Y	Y	Y	Y	Y	Y	N
2 Jefferson	?	?	?	Y	Y	N	Y
3 ***Tauzin***	N	N	Y	Y	Y	Y	N
4 ***McCrery***	P	P	P	Y	?	Y	N
5 ***Cooksey***	N	N	Y	Y	Y	Y	?
6 ***Baker***	N	N	Y	Y	Y	Y	N
7 John	N	N	Y	?	?	Y	Y
MAINE							
1 Allen	N	N	Y	Y	Y	N	Y
2 Baldacci	N	N	Y	Y	Y	N	Y
MARYLAND							
1 ***Gilchrest***	N	N	Y	Y	Y	Y	Y
2 ***Ehrlich***	N	N	Y	Y	Y	Y	N
3 Cardin	Y	N	N	Y	Y	N	Y
4 Wynn	N	N	Y	Y	Y	N	Y
5 Hoyer	Y	N	N	Y	Y	N	Y
6 ***Bartlett***	Y	Y	Y	Y	Y	Y	N
7 Cummings	N	N	Y	Y	Y	N	Y
8 ***Morella***	N	N	N	Y	Y	N	Y
MASSACHUSETTS							
1 Olver	N	N	Y	Y	Y	N	?
2 Neal	N	N	Y	Y	Y	N	Y
3 McGovern	N	N	Y	Y	Y	N	Y
4 Frank	N	N	Y	Y	Y	N	Y
5 Meehan	N	N	Y	?	?	N	Y
6 Tierney	N	N	Y	Y	Y	N	Y
7 Markey	N	N	Y	Y	Y	N	Y
8 Kennedy	N	N	Y	?	?	N	Y
9 Moakley	N	N	Y	Y	Y	N	Y
10 Delahunt	N	N	Y	Y	Y	N	Y
MICHIGAN							
1 Stupak	N	N	Y	Y	Y	N	Y
2 ***Hoekstra***	N	Y	N	Y	Y	Y	N
3 ***Ehlers***	N	N	Y	Y	Y	Y	Y
4 ***Camp***	N	N	Y	Y	Y	Y	Y
5 Barcia	N	N	Y	Y	Y	Y	Y
6 ***Upton***	N	N	Y	Y	Y	Y	Y
7 ***Smith***	N	Y	Y	Y	Y	Y	N
8 Stabenow	N	N	Y	Y	Y	N	Y
9 Kildee	N	N	Y	Y	Y	N	Y
10 Bonior	N	N	Y	Y	Y	N	Y
11 ***Knollenberg***	N	N	Y	Y	Y	Y	N
12 Levin	N	N	Y	Y	Y	N	Y
13 Rivers	N	N	Y	Y	Y	N	Y
14 Conyers	N	N	Y	Y	?	N	Y
15 Kilpatrick	N	N	Y	Y	Y	N	Y
16 Dingell	N	N	Y	Y	Y	N	Y
MINNESOTA							
1 ***Gutknecht***	N	N	Y	Y	Y	Y	Y
2 Minge	Y	N	N	Y	Y	N	Y
3 ***Ramstad***	N	N	Y	Y	Y	Y	Y
4 Vento	N	N	Y	Y	Y	N	Y
5 Sabo	Y	N	N	Y	Y	N	Y
6 Luther	Y	N	Y	Y	Y	N	Y
7 Peterson	Y	N	Y	Y	Y	N	N
8 Oberstar	N	N	Y	Y	Y	N	Y
MISSISSIPPI							
1 ***Wicker***	N	N	Y	Y	Y	Y	N
2 Thompson	N	N	Y	Y	Y	N	Y
3 ***Pickering***	N	N	Y	Y	Y	Y	N
4 ***Parker***	Y	Y	N	Y	Y	Y	N
5 Taylor	Y	N	Y	Y	Y	Y	N
MISSOURI							
1 Clay	N	N	Y	Y	Y	N	?
2 ***Talent***	N	N	Y	Y	Y	Y	N
3 Gephardt	N	N	Y	Y	Y	N	Y
4 Skelton	N	N	Y	Y	Y	Y	Y
5 McCarthy	N	N	Y	Y	Y	N	Y
6 Danner	N	N	Y	Y	Y	Y	N
7 ***Blunt***	N	N	Y	Y	Y	Y	N
8 ***Emerson***	N	N	Y	Y	Y	Y	N
9 ***Hulshof***	N	N	Y	Y	Y	Y	N
MONTANA							
AL ***Hill***	Y	N	N	Y	Y	N	N
NEBRASKA							
1 ***Bereuter***	N	N	Y	Y	Y	N	N
2 ***Christensen***	Y	Y	N	?	?	Y	N
3 ***Barrett***	Y	Y	N	Y	Y	Y	N
NEVADA							
1 ***Ensign***	N	N	Y	Y	Y	Y	N
2 ***Gibbons***	N	N	Y	Y	Y	Y	N
NEW HAMPSHIRE							
1 ***Sununu***	Y	N	Y	Y	Y	Y	Y
2 ***Bass***	N	N	Y	Y	Y	Y	Y
NEW JERSEY							
1 Andrews	N	N	Y	Y	Y	Y	Y
2 ***LoBiondo***	N	N	Y	Y	Y	Y	Y
3 ***Saxton***	N	N	Y	Y	Y	Y	Y
4 ***Smith***	N	N	Y	Y	Y	Y	Y
5 ***Roukema***	N	N	Y	Y	Y	Y	Y
6 Pallone	N	N	Y	Y	Y	Y	Y
7 ***Franks***	N	N	Y	Y	Y	Y	Y
8 Pascrell	N	N	Y	Y	Y	N	Y
9 Rothman	N	N	Y	Y	Y	N	Y
10 Payne	?	?	?	Y	Y	N	Y
11 ***Frelinghuysen***	N	N	Y	Y	Y	Y	N
12 ***Pappas***	N	N	Y	Y	Y	Y	Y
13 Menendez	N	N	Y	Y	Y	N	Y
NEW MEXICO							
1 Vacant							
2 ***Skeen***	N	N	Y	Y	Y	Y	N
3 ***Redmond***	N	N	Y	Y	?	Y	N
NEW YORK							
1 ***Forbes***	N	N	Y	Y	Y	Y	Y
2 ***Lazio***	N	N	Y	Y	Y	Y	Y
3 ***King***	N	N	Y	Y	Y	Y	N
4 McCarthy	N	?	Y	Y	Y	Y	Y
5 Ackerman	N	N	Y	?	?	N	Y
6 Meeks	N	N	Y	Y	Y	N	Y
7 Manton	N	N	Y	Y	Y	N	Y
8 Nadler	N	N	Y	Y	Y	N	Y
9 Schumer	N	N	Y	Y	Y	?	Y
10 Towns	N	N	Y	?	Y	N	Y
11 Owens	N	N	Y	Y	Y	N	Y
12 Velázquez	N	N	Y	Y	Y	N	Y
13 ***Fossella***	N	N	Y	Y	Y	Y	N
14 Maloney	Y	N	Y	?	Y	N	Y
15 Rangel	?	?	?	Y	Y	N	Y
16 Serrano	N	N	Y	Y	Y	N	Y
17 Engel	N	N	Y	Y	Y	N	Y
18 Lowey	N	N	Y	Y	Y	N	Y
19 ***Kelly***	N	N	Y	Y	Y	Y	Y
20 ***Gilman***	N	N	Y	Y	Y	Y	Y
21 McNulty	N	N	Y	Y	Y	N	Y
22 ***Solomon***	N	N	Y	Y	Y	Y	N
23 ***Boehlert***	N	N	Y	Y	N	N	Y
24 ***McHugh***	N	N	Y	Y	Y	Y	N
25 ***Walsh***	N	N	Y	Y	Y	N	Y
26 Hinchey	N	N	Y	Y	Y	N	Y
27 ***Paxon***	N	N	Y	?	?	Y	?
28 Slaughter	N	N	Y	Y	N	N	Y
29 LaFalce	Y	N	N	Y	Y	N	Y
30 ***Quinn***	N	N	Y	Y	Y	Y	Y
31 ***Houghton***	N	N	Y	Y	Y	N	Y
NORTH CAROLINA							
1 Clayton	Y	N	Y	Y	Y	N	Y
2 Etheridge	Y	N	Y	Y	Y	Y	Y
3 ***Jones***	Y	Y	N	Y	Y	Y	N
4 Price	Y	N	Y	Y	Y	N	Y
5 ***Burr***	Y	Y	N	Y	Y	Y	Y
6 ***Coble***	N	N	Y	Y	Y	Y	N
7 McIntyre	N	N	Y	Y	Y	Y	Y
8 Hefner	N	N	Y	?	?	?	Y
9 ***Myrick***	Y	Y	N	Y	Y	Y	N
10 ***Ballenger***	Y	Y	N	Y	Y	Y	N
11 ***Taylor***	N	Y	Y	Y	Y	Y	N
12 Watt	Y	N	Y	Y	Y	N	Y
NORTH DAKOTA							
AL Pomeroy	Y	N	N	Y	Y	N	Y
OHIO							
1 ***Chabot***	Y	Y	N	Y	Y	Y	N
2 ***Portman***	Y	Y	N	Y	Y	Y	N
3 Hall	N	N	Y	Y	Y	N	Y
4 ***Oxley***	N	N	Y	Y	Y	Y	N
5 ***Gillmor***	Y	N	Y	Y	Y	N	N
6 Strickland	N	N	Y	Y	Y	N	Y
7 ***Hobson***	Y	Y	N	Y	Y	Y	Y
8 ***Boehner***	Y	Y	N	Y	Y	Y	N
9 Kaptur	N	N	Y	Y	Y	N	Y
10 Kucinich	N	N	Y	Y	Y	N	Y
11 Stokes	N	N	Y	Y	Y	N	Y
12 ***Kasich***	Y	Y	N	Y	Y	Y	N
13 Brown	Y	Y	N	Y	Y	N	Y
14 Sawyer	Y	N	Y	Y	Y	N	Y
15 ***Pryce***	N	Y	Y	Y	Y	Y	Y
16 ***Regula***	N	N	Y	Y	Y	Y	Y
17 Traficant	N	N	Y	Y	Y	Y	N
18 ***Ney***	N	N	Y	Y	Y	Y	Y
19 ***LaTourette***	N	N	Y	Y	Y	Y	Y
OKLAHOMA							
1 ***Largent***	Y	Y	N	Y	Y	Y	N
2 ***Coburn***	Y	Y	N	N	Y	Y	N
3 ***Watkins***	N	Y	Y	?	?	Y	?
4 ***Watts***	N	N	Y	Y	Y	Y	N
5 ***Istook***	N	Y	Y	?	?	+	?
6 ***Lucas***	N	Y	Y	Y	Y	Y	N
OREGON							
1 Furse	N	N	Y	Y	Y	N	Y
2 ***Smith***	N	N	Y	?	?	Y	N
3 Blumenauer	N	N	Y	Y	Y	N	Y
4 DeFazio	N	N	Y	Y	Y	N	Y
5 Hooley	N	N	Y	Y	Y	N	Y
PENNSYLVANIA							
1 Vacant							
2 Fattah	N	N	Y	Y	Y	N	Y
3 Borski	N	N	Y	Y	Y	N	Y
4 Klink	N	N	Y	Y	Y	N	Y
5 ***Peterson***	N	N	Y	Y	Y	Y	N
6 Holden	N	N	Y	Y	Y	N	Y
7 ***Weldon***	N	N	Y	Y	Y	Y	?
8 ***Greenwood***	N	N	Y	?	?	Y	Y
9 ***Shuster***	N	N	Y	Y	Y	Y	N
10 ***McDade***	N	N	Y	Y	Y	Y	Y
11 Kanjorski	N	N	Y	Y	Y	N	Y
12 Murtha	N	N	Y	Y	Y	N	Y
13 ***Fox***	N	N	Y	Y	Y	Y	Y
14 Coyne	N	N	Y	Y	Y	N	Y
15 McHale	N	N	Y	Y	Y	N	Y
16 ***Pitts***	N	N	Y	Y	Y	Y	N
17 ***Gekas***	N	N	Y	Y	Y	Y	N
18 Doyle	N	N	Y	Y	Y	N	Y
19 ***Goodling***	N	N	Y	Y	Y	Y	N
20 Mascara	N	N	Y	Y	Y	N	Y
21 ***English***	N	N	Y	Y	Y	Y	N
RHODE ISLAND							
1 Kennedy	Y	N	Y	Y	Y	N	Y
2 Weygand	Y	N	Y	Y	Y	N	Y
SOUTH CAROLINA							
1 ***Sanford***	Y	Y	N	N	Y	Y	N
2 ***Spence***	N	N	Y	Y	Y	Y	N
3 ***Graham***	Y	Y	N	Y	Y	Y	N
4 ***Inglis***	Y	Y	N	?	?	Y	N
5 Spratt	Y	N	N	Y	Y	N	Y
6 Clyburn	N	N	Y	Y	Y	N	Y
SOUTH DAKOTA							
AL ***Thune***	N	N	Y	Y	Y	Y	N
TENNESSEE							
1 ***Jenkins***	N	N	Y	Y	Y	Y	N
2 ***Duncan***	N	N	Y	Y	Y	Y	N
3 ***Wamp***	N	Y	Y	N	Y	Y	N
4 ***Hilleary***	N	Y	Y	Y	Y	Y	N
5 Clement	N	N	Y	Y	Y	N	Y
6 Gordon	N	N	Y	Y	Y	Y	Y
7 ***Bryant***	N	N	Y	Y	Y	Y	N
8 Tanner	Y	N	Y	Y	Y	?	?
9 Ford	N	N	Y	Y	?	N	Y
TEXAS							
1 Sandlin	N	N	Y	Y	Y	Y	Y
2 Turner	N	N	Y	Y	Y	N	N
3 ***Johnson, Sam***	N	Y	N	Y	Y	Y	N
4 Hall	Y	Y	N	Y	Y	Y	N
5 ***Sessions***	Y	Y	N	Y	Y	Y	N
6 ***Barton***	Y	Y	N	Y	Y	Y	N
7 ***Archer***	N	Y	Y	Y	Y	Y	N
8 ***Brady***	N	Y	Y	Y	Y	Y	N
9 Lampson	N	N	Y	Y	Y	N	Y
10 Doggett	Y	N	Y	Y	Y	N	Y
11 Edwards	Y	N	N	Y	Y	N	Y
12 ***Granger***	N	N	Y	Y	Y	Y	N
13 ***Thornberry***	Y	Y	N	Y	Y	Y	N
14 ***Paul***	Y	Y	N	N	Y	Y	N
15 Hinojosa	N	N	Y	Y	Y	N	Y
16 Reyes	N	N	Y	Y	Y	N	Y
17 Stenholm	Y	Y	N	Y	Y	N	N
18 Jackson-Lee	N	N	Y	Y	Y	N	Y
19 ***Combest***	N	N	Y	Y	Y	Y	N
20 Gonzalez	?	?	?	?	?	?	?
21 ***Smith***	N	N	Y	Y	Y	Y	N
22 ***DeLay***	N	Y	Y	Y	Y	Y	N
23 ***Bonilla***	Y	Y	N	Y	Y	Y	N
24 Frost	N	N	Y	Y	Y	N	Y
25 Bentsen	Y	N	N	Y	Y	N	Y
26 ***Armey***	N	Y	Y	Y	Y	Y	N
27 Ortiz	N	N	Y	Y	Y	N	Y
28 Rodriguez	N	N	Y	Y	Y	N	Y
29 Green	N	N	Y	Y	Y	Y	Y
30 Johnson, E.B.	N	N	Y	Y	Y	N	Y
UTAH							
1 ***Hansen***	N	N	Y	Y	Y	Y	N
2 ***Cook***	N	N	Y	Y	Y	Y	?
3 ***Cannon***	?	?	?	?	?	Y	N
VERMONT							
AL *Sanders*	N	N	Y	Y	Y	N	Y
VIRGINIA							
1 ***Bateman***	N	N	Y	+	+	–	–
2 Pickett	N	N	Y	Y	Y	N	N
3 Scott	Y	N	Y	Y	Y	N	Y
4 Sisisky	Y	Y	Y	Y	Y	N	N
5 Goode	N	N	Y	Y	Y	Y	N
6 ***Goodlatte***	N	Y	Y	Y	Y	Y	N
7 ***Bliley***	N	N	Y	Y	Y	Y	N
8 Moran	Y	Y	N	Y	Y	N	Y
9 Boucher	N	N	Y	Y	Y	N	Y
10 ***Wolf***	Y	Y	N	Y	Y	Y	N
11 ***Davis***	N	N	Y	Y	?	Y	N
WASHINGTON							
1 ***White***	Y	Y	N	Y	Y	Y	Y
2 ***Metcalf***	N	N	Y	Y	Y	Y	N
3 ***Smith, Linda***	N	N	Y	Y	Y	Y	N
4 ***Hastings***	N	Y	Y	Y	Y	Y	N
5 ***Nethercutt***	Y	N	N	Y	Y	Y	N
6 Dicks	Y	N	Y	Y	Y	N	Y
7 McDermott	N	N	Y	Y	Y	N	Y
8 ***Dunn***	N	N	Y	Y	Y	Y	N
9 Smith, Adam	Y	N	N	Y	Y	N	Y
WEST VIRGINIA							
1 Mollohan	N	N	Y	Y	Y	N	Y
2 Wise	N	N	Y	Y	Y	N	Y
3 Rahall	N	N	Y	Y	Y	N	Y
WISCONSIN							
1 ***Neumann***	Y	Y	Y	Y	Y	Y	N
2 ***Klug***	?	?	?	Y	Y	Y	Y
3 Kind	Y	Y	N	Y	Y	N	Y
4 Kleczka	N	N	Y	Y	Y	N	Y
5 Barrett	Y	N	N	Y	Y	N	Y
6 ***Petri***	N	N	Y	Y	Y	Y	?
7 Obey	Y	Y	N	Y	Y	N	Y
8 Johnson	N	N	Y	Y	Y	N	Y
9 ***Sensenbrenner***	N	Y	N	Y	Y	Y	N
WYOMING							
AL ***Cubin***	N	N	N	Y	Y	Y	N

Southern states - Ala., Ark., Fla., Ga., Ky., La., Miss., N.C., Okla., S.C., Tenn., Texas, Va.

Key

Y	Voted for (yea).
#	Paired for.
+	Announced for.
N	Voted against (nay).
X	Paired against.
–	Announced against.
P	Voted "present."
C	Voted "present" to avoid possible conflict of interest.
?	Did not vote or otherwise make a position known.

Democrats **Republicans**
Independent

104. HR 1252. Limits on Federal Judges' Power/Restricting Disclosure. Jackson-Lee, D-Texas, amendment to permit a federal court to enter an order restricting the disclosure of information obtained through discovery or an order restricting access to court records in a civil case only after making a finding of fact that such an order would not restrict the disclosure of information that is relevant to protecting the public health or safety. Rejected 177-242: R 9-211; D 167-31 (ND 129-18, SD 38-13); I 1-0. April 23, 1998.

105. HR 1252. Limits on Federal Judges' Power/Prisoner Release. DeLay, R-Texas, amendment to prohibit federal judges from allowing the early release from prison of any prisoner on the basis of prison conditions. Adopted 367-52: R 220-2; D 147-49 (ND 104-42, SD 43-7); I 0-1. April 23, 1998.

106. HR 1252. Limits on Federal Judges' Power/Parent Testimony. Lofgren, D-Calif., amendment to establish a privilege under the Federal Rules of Evidence to prevent parents and children from being compelled to testify against one another. Rejected 162-256: R 10-211; D 151-45 (ND 118-29, SD 33-16); I 1-0. April 23, 1998.

107. HR 1252. Limits on Federal Judges' Power/Jurisdiction. Conyers, D-Mich., amendment to provide for jurisdiction, service of process and discovery in civil actions brought against defendants located outside the United States. Rejected 200-216: R 18-201; D 181-15 (ND 142-4, SD 39-11); I 1-0. April 23, 1998.

108. HR 1252. Limits on Federal Judges' Power/Disburse Funds. Aderholt, R-Ala., amendment to prohibit federal judges from ordering state and local governments to disburse any funds to enforce a federal or state law. Rejected 174-236: R 162-53; D 12-182 (ND 4-140, SD 8-42); I 0-1. April 23, 1998. (Subsequently, the bill passed by voice vote).

109. HR 3579. Fiscal 1998 Supplemental Appropriations/Motion to Instruct. Obey, D-Wis., motion to instruct the House conferees to support the Clinton administration's request for $18 billion for the International Monetary Fund. Rejected 186-222: R 22-193; D 164-28 (ND 123-20, SD 41-8); I 0-1. April 23, 1998.

110. H Con Res 218. Cease Fire in Afghanistan/Adoption. Bereuter, R-Neb., motion to suspend the rules and adopt the concurrent resolution to express the sense of Congress to call upon all warring factions and national powers in Afghanistan to participate in a dialogue and to actively cooperate in the acceleration of endeavors for peace. Motion agreed to 391-1: R 205-1; D 185-0 (ND 136-0, SD 49-0); I 1-0. April 28, 1998. A two-thirds majority of those present and voting (262 in this case) is required for adoption under suspension of the rules.

	104	105	106	107	108	109	110
ALABAMA							
1 *Callahan*	N	Y	N	N	Y	N	Y
2 *Everett*	N	Y	N	N	Y	N	Y
3 *Riley*	N	Y	N	N	Y	N	+
4 *Aderholt*	N	Y	N	N	Y	N	Y
5 Cramer	N	Y	N	N	Y	Y	Y
6 *Bachus*	N	Y	N	N	Y	N	Y
7 Hilliard	Y	N	Y	N	N	Y	Y
ALASKA							
AL *Young*	N	Y	N	N	Y	N	Y
ARIZONA							
1 *Salmon*	N	Y	N	Y	Y	N	Y
2 Pastor	Y	Y	Y	Y	N	Y	Y
3 *Stump*	N	Y	N	N	Y	N	Y
4 *Shadegg*	N	Y	N	N	N	Y	Y
5 *Kolbe*	N	Y	N	N	Y	Y	Y
6 *Hayworth*	N	Y	N	N	Y	N	Y
ARKANSAS							
1 Berry	Y	Y	Y	Y	N	N	Y
2 Snyder	N	Y	N	Y	N	Y	Y
3 *Hutchinson*	N	Y	N	N	Y	N	Y
4 *Dickey*	N	Y	N	N	Y	N	Y
CALIFORNIA							
1 *Riggs*	N	Y	N	?	?	N	?
2 *Herger*	N	Y	N	N	Y	N	Y
3 Fazio	Y	Y	Y	Y	N	Y	Y
4 *Doolittle*	N	Y	N	N	Y	N	Y
5 Matsui	N	Y	N	N	Y	N	Y
6 Woolsey	Y	Y	Y	Y	N	Y	Y
7 Miller	Y	N	Y	Y	N	N	Y
8 Pelosi	Y	N	Y	Y	N	Y	Y
9 Lee	Y	Y	Y	Y	N	Y	Y
10 Tauscher	Y	Y	Y	Y	N	Y	Y
11 *Pombo*	N	Y	N	N	Y	N	Y
12 Lantos	Y	Y	Y	Y	N	Y	Y
13 Stark	Y	N	Y	Y	N	?	Y
14 Eshoo	Y	Y	Y	Y	N	Y	Y
15 *Campbell*	Y	Y	N	N	N	N	Y
16 Lofgren	N	Y	Y	Y	N	Y	+
17 Farr	Y	Y	Y	Y	N	Y	Y
18 Condit	N	Y	Y	Y	N	Y	Y
19 *Radanovich*	N	Y	N	N	Y	N	Y
20 Dooley	N	Y	Y	Y	N	Y	Y
21 *Thomas*	N	Y	N	N	Y	N	Y
22 Capps, L.	Y	Y	Y	Y	N	Y	Y
23 *Gallegly*	N	Y	N	N	Y	N	Y
24 Sherman	Y	Y	Y	Y	N	Y	Y
25 *McKeon*	N	Y	N	N	Y	N	Y
26 Berman	Y	Y	Y	Y	N	Y	Y
27 *Rogan*	N	Y	N	N	Y	N	Y
28 *Dreier*	N	Y	N	N	Y	N	Y
29 Waxman	Y	N	Y	Y	N	Y	Y
30 Becerra	Y	N	Y	Y	N	Y	Y
31 Martinez	Y	N	Y	Y	N	Y	?
32 Dixon	?	?	?	?	?	?	?
33 Roybal-Allard	Y	Y	Y	Y	N	Y	Y
34 Torres	Y	Y	Y	Y	N	Y	Y
35 Waters	Y	N	Y	Y	N	Y	Y
36 Harman	Y	Y	Y	Y	N	Y	+
37 Millender-McD.	Y	N	Y	Y	N	Y	+

	104	105	106	107	108	109	110
38 *Horn*	Y	Y	N	N	N	N	Y
39 *Royce*	N	Y	N	N	Y	N	Y
40 *Lewis*	N	Y	N	N	Y	N	Y
41 *Kim*	N	Y	N	N	Y	N	Y
42 Brown	Y	N	Y	N	Y	N	Y
43 *Calvert*	N	Y	N	N	Y	N	Y
44 *Bono, M.*	N	Y	N	N	Y	N	Y
45 *Rohrabacher*	Y	Y	N	N	Y	N	?
46 Sanchez	Y	Y	Y	Y	N	Y	Y
47 *Cox*	N	Y	N	N	?	N	Y
48 *Packard*	N	Y	N	N	Y	N	Y
49 *Bilbray*	N	Y	N	N	N	N	Y
50 Filner	Y	N	Y	N	Y	N	Y
51 *Cunningham*	N	Y	N	N	Y	N	Y
52 *Hunter*	N	Y	N	N	Y	N	Y
COLORADO							
1 DeGette	Y	N	Y	N	Y	N	Y
2 Skaggs	N	N	N	N	N	Y	Y
3 *McInnis*	N	Y	N	N	Y	N	Y
4 *Schaffer*	N	Y	N	N	Y	N	Y
5 *Hefley*	N	Y	N	N	Y	N	Y
6 *Schaefer*	N	Y	N	N	Y	N	Y
CONNECTICUT							
1 Kennelly	Y	Y	Y	Y	N	Y	Y
2 Gejdenson	Y	Y	Y	Y	N	Y	?
3 DeLauro	Y	Y	Y	Y	N	Y	Y
4 *Shays*	Y	Y	N	N	Y	N	Y
5 Maloney	Y	Y	Y	Y	N	Y	Y
6 *Johnson*	N	Y	N	N	N	N	Y
DELAWARE							
AL *Castle*	N	Y	N	N	N	N	Y
FLORIDA							
1 *Scarborough*	N	Y	N	N	N	N	Y
2 Boyd	N	Y	N	N	N	Y	Y
3 Brown	Y	Y	Y	Y	N	Y	Y
4 *Fowler*	N	Y	N	N	Y	N	Y
5 Thurman	N	Y	N	N	Y	Y	Y
6 *Stearns*	N	Y	N	N	Y	N	Y
7 *Mica*	N	Y	N	N	Y	N	Y
8 *McCollum*	N	Y	N	N	Y	N	Y
9 *Bilirakis*	N	Y	N	N	Y	N	Y
10 *Young*	N	Y	N	N	Y	N	Y
11 Davis	Y	Y	+	Y	N	Y	Y
12 *Canady*	N	Y	N	N	Y	N	Y
13 *Miller*	?	?	?	?	?	?	Y
14 *Goss*	N	Y	N	N	Y	N	Y
15 *Weldon*	N	Y	N	N	Y	N	?
16 *Foley*	N	Y	N	N	Y	N	?
17 Meek	?	?	?	?	?	?	Y
18 *Ros-Lehtinen*	Y	Y	N	N	Y	N	Y
19 Wexler	Y	Y	Y	Y	N	Y	Y
20 Deutsch	Y	Y	Y	Y	N	Y	Y
21 *Diaz-Balart*	N	Y	N	N	Y	N	Y
22 *Shaw*	N	Y	N	N	Y	N	Y
23 Hastings	?	?	?	?	?	?	Y
GEORGIA							
1 *Kingston*	N	Y	N	N	Y	N	Y
2 Bishop	Y	Y	Y	Y	N	Y	Y
3 *Collins*	N	Y	N	N	Y	N	Y
4 McKinney	Y	Y	Y	Y	N	Y	Y
5 Lewis	Y	N	Y	Y	N	Y	Y
6 *Gingrich*							
7 *Barr*	N	Y	N	N	Y	N	?
8 *Chambliss*	N	Y	N	N	Y	N	Y
9 *Deal*	N	Y	N	N	Y	N	Y
10 *Norwood*	N	Y	N	N	Y	N	Y
11 *Linder*	N	Y	N	N	Y	N	Y
HAWAII							
1 Abercrombie	Y	Y	Y	Y	N	Y	Y
2 Mink	Y	Y	Y	Y	N	Y	Y
IDAHO							
1 *Chenoweth*	N	Y	N	N	Y	N	Y
2 *Crapo*	N	Y	N	N	Y	N	Y
ILLINOIS							
1 Rush	Y	N	Y	Y	N	Y	Y
2 Jackson	Y	N	Y	Y	N	Y	Y
3 Lipinski	Y	Y	N	N	N	N	Y
4 Gutierrez	?	Y	Y	Y	N	Y	Y
5 Blagojevich	Y	Y	Y	Y	N	Y	Y
6 *Hyde*	N	Y	N	N	Y	N	?
7 Davis	Y	N	Y	Y	N	?	Y
8 *Crane*	N	Y	N	N	Y	N	Y
9 Yates	Y	N	Y	Y	N	?	?
10 *Porter*	N	Y	N	N	Y	N	Y
11 *Weller*	N	Y	N	N	Y	N	Y
12 Costello	Y	Y	Y	Y	N	N	Y

ND Northern Democrats   SD Southern Democrats

	104	105	106	107	108	109	110
13 ***Fawell***	N	N	N	N	N	Y	Y
14 ***Hastert***	N	Y	N	N	Y	?	Y
15 ***Ewing***	N	Y	N	N	N	N	Y
16 ***Manzullo***	N	Y	N	N	Y	N	Y
17 Evans	Y	N	Y	Y	N	N	Y
18 ***LaHood***	N	Y	N	N	N	Y	Y
19 Poshard	Y	Y	Y	?	?	?	?
20 ***Shimkus***	N	Y	N	N	Y	N	Y
INDIANA							
1 Visclosky	Y	Y	Y	Y	N	Y	Y
2 ***McIntosh***	N	Y	N	N	Y	N	Y
3 Roemer	N	Y	N	Y	N	Y	Y
4 ***Souder***	N	Y	N	N	?	N	Y
5 ***Buyer***	N	Y	N	N	?	N	Y
6 ***Burton***	N	Y	N	N	Y	N	Y
7 ***Pease***	N	Y	N	N	Y	N	Y
8 ***Hostettler***	N	Y	N	N	Y	N	Y
9 Hamilton	N	Y	N	Y	N	Y	Y
10 Carson	Y	N	Y	Y	N	N	Y
IOWA							
1 ***Leach***	Y	Y	Y	N	N	Y	Y
2 ***Nussle***	N	Y	N	N	Y	Y	Y
3 Boswell	Y	Y	N	Y	N	Y	Y
4 ***Ganske***	N	Y	N	N	N	N	?
5 ***Latham***	N	Y	N	N	Y	Y	Y
KANSAS							
1 ***Moran***	N	Y	N	N	Y	N	Y
2 ***Ryun***	N	Y	N	N	Y	N	+
3 ***Snowbarger***	N	Y	?	N	Y	N	Y
4 ***Tiahrt***	N	Y	N	N	Y	N	Y
KENTUCKY							
1 ***Whitfield***	N	Y	N	N	N	N	Y
2 ***Lewis***	N	Y	N	N	Y	N	Y
3 ***Northup***	N	Y	N	N	Y	N	Y
4 ***Bunning***	N	Y	N	N	Y	N	Y
5 ***Rogers***	N	Y	N	N	Y	N	Y
6 Baesler	Y	Y	Y	Y	N	Y	?
LOUISIANA							
1 ***Livingston***	N	Y	N	N	Y	N	Y
2 Jefferson	Y	Y	Y	Y	N	?	?
3 ***Tauzin***	N	Y	N	N	Y	N	Y
4 ***McCrery***	?	Y	N	N	Y	N	Y
5 ***Cooksey***	N	Y	N	N	Y	N	Y
6 ***Baker***	N	Y	N	N	Y	N	Y
7 John	N	Y	N	Y	N	Y	Y
MAINE							
1 Allen	Y	Y	N	Y	N	Y	Y
2 Baldacci	Y	Y	Y	Y	N	Y	Y
MARYLAND							
1 ***Gilchrest***	N	Y	N	N	N	Y	Y
2 ***Ehrlich***	N	Y	N	Y	Y	N	Y
3 Cardin	Y	Y	N	Y	N	Y	Y
4 Wynn	Y	Y	Y	Y	N	Y	Y
5 Hoyer	Y	Y	N	Y	N	Y	Y
6 ***Bartlett***	N	Y	N	N	Y	N	Y
7 Cummings	Y	Y	Y	Y	N	Y	Y
8 ***Morella***	Y	Y	N	Y	N	?	Y
MASSACHUSETTS							
1 Olver	Y	N	Y	Y	N	Y	Y
2 Neal	Y	Y	Y	Y	N	Y	Y
3 McGovern	Y	Y	N	Y	N	Y	Y
4 Frank	Y	N	N	Y	N	Y	Y
5 Meehan	Y	N	Y	Y	N	Y	Y
6 Tierney	Y	N	N	Y	N	Y	Y
7 Markey	Y	Y	Y	Y	N	Y	Y
8 Kennedy	Y	N	Y	Y	N	Y	Y
9 Moakley	Y	Y	N	Y	N	Y	Y
10 Delahunt	Y	N	Y	Y	N	Y	Y
MICHIGAN							
1 Stupak	Y	Y	Y	Y	N	Y	Y
2 ***Hoekstra***	N	Y	N	N	Y	N	Y
3 ***Ehlers***	N	Y	N	N	N	N	Y
4 ***Camp***	N	Y	N	N	–	N	Y
5 Barcia	Y	Y	Y	Y	N	N	Y
6 ***Upton***	N	Y	N	N	N	N	Y
7 ***Smith***	N	Y	N	Y	Y	N	Y
8 Stabenow	Y	Y	Y	Y	N	Y	Y
9 Kildee	Y	Y	Y	Y	N	Y	Y
10 Bonior	Y	N	Y	Y	N	Y	Y
11 ***Knollenberg***	N	Y	N	N	Y	N	Y
12 Levin	Y	Y	N	Y	N	Y	Y
13 Rivers	Y	Y	N	Y	N	Y	Y
14 Conyers	Y	N	Y	Y	N	N	Y
15 Kilpatrick	Y	N	Y	Y	N	Y	Y
16 Dingell	Y	Y	N	Y	N	Y	Y

	104	105	106	107	108	109	110
MINNESOTA							
1 ***Gutknecht***	N	Y	N	N	N	N	Y
2 Minge	Y	Y	Y	Y	N	Y	Y
3 ***Ramstad***	N	Y	N	N	N	N	Y
4 Vento	Y	Y	Y	Y	N	Y	Y
5 Sabo	Y	N	Y	Y	N	Y	Y
6 Luther	Y	Y	Y	Y	N	Y	Y
7 Peterson	N	Y	Y	N	Y	N	Y
8 Oberstar	Y	N	Y	Y	N	Y	Y
MISSISSIPPI							
1 ***Wicker***	N	Y	N	N	Y	N	Y
2 Thompson	Y	N	Y	Y	N	N	Y
3 ***Pickering***	N	Y	N	N	Y	N	Y
4 ***Parker***	N	Y	N	N	Y	N	Y
5 Taylor	N	Y	Y	Y	N	N	Y
MISSOURI							
1 Clay	?	?	?	?	?	?	Y
2 ***Talent***	N	Y	N	N	Y	N	Y
3 Gephardt	Y	Y	Y	Y	N	Y	Y
4 Skelton	N	Y	Y	Y	N	Y	Y
5 McCarthy	Y	Y	N	Y	N	Y	Y
6 Danner	N	Y	N	Y	Y	N	Y
7 ***Blunt***	N	Y	N	N	Y	N	?
8 ***Emerson***	Y	Y	N	N	Y	N	Y
9 ***Hulshof***	N	Y	N	N	Y	N	Y
MONTANA							
AL ***Hill***	N	Y	N	N	Y	N	Y
NEBRASKA							
1 ***Bereuter***	Y	Y	N	N	Y	Y	Y
2 ***Christensen***	N	Y	N	N	Y	Y	?
3 ***Barrett***	N	Y	N	N	Y	Y	Y
NEVADA							
1 ***Ensign***	N	Y	N	Y	Y	N	?
2 ***Gibbons***	N	Y	N	N	Y	N	Y
NEW HAMPSHIRE							
1 ***Sununu***	N	Y	N	N	N	N	Y
2 ***Bass***	N	Y	N	N	N	N	Y
NEW JERSEY							
1 Andrews	Y	Y	Y	Y	N	Y	Y
2 ***LoBiondo***	N	Y	Y	Y	N	N	Y
3 ***Saxton***	N	Y	N	N	N	N	Y
4 ***Smith***	N	Y	N	N	N	N	Y
5 ***Roukema***	N	Y	N	N	N	Y	Y
6 Pallone	Y	Y	Y	Y	N	Y	Y
7 ***Franks***	N	Y	N	Y	N	N	Y
8 Pascrell	Y	Y	Y	Y	N	Y	Y
9 Rothman	N	Y	Y	N	N	Y	Y
10 Payne	Y	N	Y	Y	N	Y	Y
11 ***Frelinghuysen***	N	Y	N	N	N	N	Y
12 ***Pappas***	N	Y	N	Y	N	N	Y
13 Menendez	Y	Y	Y	Y	N	Y	Y
NEW MEXICO							
1 Vacant							
2 ***Skeen***	N	Y	N	N	Y	Y	Y
3 ***Redmond***	N	Y	N	N	Y	N	Y
NEW YORK							
1 ***Forbes***	N	Y	N	N	N	?	Y
2 ***Lazio***	N	Y	N	N	N	Y	Y
3 ***King***	N	Y	Y	N	Y	N	Y
4 McCarthy	Y	Y	Y	Y	N	Y	Y
5 Ackerman	Y	Y	Y	Y	N	Y	Y
6 Meeks	Y	N	Y	Y	N	Y	+
7 Manton	Y	Y	N	Y	N	Y	Y
8 Nadler	Y	Y	Y	Y	N	Y	Y
9 Schumer	Y	Y	Y	Y	N	Y	Y
10 Towns	Y	N	N	Y	N	Y	?
11 Owens	Y	N	Y	Y	N	Y	Y
12 Velázquez	Y	N	Y	Y	N	Y	Y
13 ***Fossella***	N	Y	N	N	Y	N	Y
14 Maloney	N	Y	Y	Y	N	Y	?
15 Rangel	Y	N	Y	Y	N	Y	?
16 Serrano	Y	N	Y	Y	N	Y	?
17 Engel	Y	Y	Y	Y	N	Y	+
18 Lowey	Y	Y	Y	Y	N	Y	Y
19 ***Kelly***	N	Y	N	N	N	N	Y
20 ***Gilman***	N	Y	N	N	N	Y	Y
21 McNulty	Y	Y	Y	Y	N	Y	Y
22 ***Solomon***	N	Y	N	N	Y	N	Y
23 ***Boehlert***	N	Y	N	N	N	N	Y
24 ***McHugh***	N	Y	N	Y	Y	N	Y
25 ***Walsh***	N	Y	N	N	N	N	Y
26 Hinchey	Y	N	Y	Y	N	Y	Y
27 ***Paxon***	?	?	?	?	?	?	Y
28 Slaughter	Y	Y	Y	Y	N	Y	Y
29 LaFalce	Y	Y	Y	Y	N	Y	Y

	104	105	106	107	108	109	110
30 ***Quinn***	N	Y	N	N	N	N	Y
31 ***Houghton***	N	Y	N	N	N	Y	Y
NORTH CAROLINA							
1 Clayton	Y	Y	Y	Y	N	Y	Y
2 Etheridge	Y	Y	Y	Y	N	Y	Y
3 ***Jones***	N	Y	N	N	Y	N	Y
4 Price	Y	Y	Y	Y	N	Y	Y
5 ***Burr***	N	Y	N	N	Y	?	Y
6 ***Coble***	N	Y	N	?	?	?	Y
7 McIntyre	Y	Y	N	Y	Y	Y	Y
8 Hefner	Y	Y	Y	Y	Y	Y	Y
9 ***Myrick***	N	Y	N	N	Y	N	Y
10 ***Ballenger***	N	Y	N	Y	Y	N	Y
11 ***Taylor***	N	Y	N	N	Y	N	+
12 Watt	N	N	Y	Y	N	Y	Y
NORTH DAKOTA							
AL Pomeroy	N	Y	Y	Y	N	Y	Y
OHIO							
1 ***Chabot***	N	Y	N	Y	Y	N	Y
2 ***Portman***	N	Y	N	N	Y	N	Y
3 Hall	Y	Y	Y	Y	N	Y	Y
4 ***Oxley***	N	Y	N	N	N	N	Y
5 ***Gillmor***	N	Y	N	N	Y	N	Y
6 Strickland	Y	Y	Y	Y	N	N	Y
7 ***Hobson***	N	Y	N	N	N	N	Y
8 ***Boehner***	N	Y	N	N	Y	?	Y
9 Kaptur	Y	Y	Y	Y	?	?	Y
10 Kucinich	Y	Y	N	Y	N	N	Y
11 Stokes	Y	N	Y	Y	N	Y	Y
12 ***Kasich***	N	Y	N	N	Y	N	Y
13 Brown	Y	Y	Y	Y	N	N	Y
14 Sawyer	Y	Y	N	Y	N	Y	Y
15 ***Pryce***	N	Y	N	N	N	N	Y
16 ***Regula***	N	Y	N	N	N	N	Y
17 Traficant	N	Y	Y	Y	Y	N	Y
18 ***Ney***	N	Y	N	N	N	Y	Y
19 ***LaTourette***	N	Y	N	N	N	Y	Y
OKLAHOMA							
1 ***Largent***	N	Y	N	N	Y	N	Y
2 ***Coburn***	N	Y	N	N	Y	N	Y
3 ***Watkins***	N	Y	N	N	Y	N	Y
4 ***Watts***	N	Y	N	N	Y	N	Y
5 ***Istook***	?	?	?	?	?	–	Y
6 ***Lucas***	N	Y	N	N	Y	N	Y
OREGON							
1 Furse	Y	N	Y	Y	N	Y	Y
2 ***Smith***	N	Y	N	N	Y	N	?
3 Blumenauer	Y	Y	Y	Y	N	Y	Y
4 DeFazio	Y	Y	Y	Y	N	N	Y
5 Hooley	Y	Y	Y	Y	N	Y	Y
PENNSYLVANIA							
1 Vacant							
2 Fattah	Y	?	?	?	?	?	Y
3 Borski	Y	Y	Y	Y	N	Y	Y
4 Klink	Y	Y	Y	Y	N	N	Y
5 ***Peterson***	N	Y	N	N	Y	N	Y
6 Holden	Y	Y	N	Y	N	Y	Y
7 ***Weldon***	N	Y	N	N	N	N	Y
8 ***Greenwood***	N	Y	N	N	N	N	?
9 ***Shuster***	N	Y	N	N	Y	N	Y
10 ***McDade***	N	Y	Y	N	N	N	Y
11 Kanjorski	N	Y	Y	Y	N	Y	Y
12 Murtha	N	Y	Y	N	N	Y	Y
13 ***Fox***	Y	Y	Y	?	?	?	Y
14 Coyne	Y	Y	Y	Y	N	Y	Y
15 McHale	Y	Y	N	Y	N	Y	Y
16 ***Pitts***	N	Y	N	N	Y	N	Y
17 ***Gekas***	N	Y	N	N	Y	N	Y
18 Doyle	N	Y	Y	Y	N	N	Y
19 ***Goodling***	N	Y	N	N	Y	N	Y
20 Mascara	Y	Y	Y	Y	N	Y	Y
21 ***English***	N	Y	N	Y	N	N	Y
RHODE ISLAND							
1 Kennedy	Y	N	Y	Y	N	Y	Y
2 Weygand	Y	Y	Y	Y	N	Y	Y
SOUTH CAROLINA							
1 ***Sanford***	N	Y	Y	N	Y	N	Y
2 ***Spence***	N	Y	N	N	Y	N	Y
3 ***Graham***	N	Y	N	N	Y	N	Y
4 ***Inglis***	N	Y	N	N	Y	N	?
5 Spratt	Y	?	?	Y	N	Y	Y
6 Clyburn	Y	N	Y	Y	N	Y	Y
SOUTH DAKOTA							
AL ***Thune***	N	Y	N	N	Y	N	Y

	104	105	106	107	108	109	110
TENNESSEE							
1 ***Jenkins***	N	Y	N	N	Y	N	Y
2 ***Duncan***	N	Y	N	Y	Y	N	Y
3 ***Wamp***	N	Y	N	Y	Y	N	Y
4 ***Hilleary***	N	Y	N	Y	Y	N	Y
5 Clement	Y	Y	Y	Y	N	Y	Y
6 Gordon	N	Y	Y	N	N	Y	Y
7 ***Bryant***	N	Y	N	N	Y	N	Y
8 Tanner	?	?	?	?	?	?	?
9 Ford	Y	Y	Y	Y	N	Y	Y
TEXAS							
1 Sandlin	N	Y	Y	Y	N	Y	?
2 Turner	N	Y	N	N	N	Y	Y
3 ***Johnson, Sam***	N	Y	N	N	Y	N	Y
4 Hall	?	Y	N	N	Y	N	Y
5 ***Sessions***	N	Y	N	N	Y	N	Y
6 ***Barton***	N	Y	N	N	Y	N	Y
7 ***Archer***	N	Y	N	N	Y	N	Y
8 ***Brady***	N	Y	N	N	Y	N	Y
9 Lampson	Y	Y	Y	Y	N	Y	Y
10 Doggett	Y	Y	N	Y	N	Y	Y
11 Edwards	Y	Y	Y	Y	N	Y	Y
12 ***Granger***	N	Y	N	N	Y	N	Y
13 ***Thornberry***	N	Y	N	N	Y	N	Y
14 ***Paul***	N	Y	Y	N	Y	N	N
15 Hinojosa	Y	Y	Y	+	–	Y	Y
16 Reyes	Y	Y	Y	Y	N	?	Y
17 Stenholm	N	Y	N	N	Y	Y	Y
18 Jackson-Lee	Y	N	Y	Y	N	Y	Y
19 ***Combest***	N	Y	N	N	Y	N	Y
20 Gonzalez	?	?	?	?	?	?	?
21 ***Smith***	N	Y	N	N	Y	N	Y
22 ***DeLay***	N	Y	N	N	Y	N	Y
23 ***Bonilla***	N	Y	N	N	Y	N	Y
24 Frost	Y	Y	Y	Y	N	Y	Y
25 Bentsen	Y	Y	N	Y	N	Y	Y
26 ***Armey***	N	Y	N	N	Y	N	Y
27 Ortiz	Y	Y	Y	Y	N	N	Y
28 Rodriguez	Y	Y	Y	Y	N	Y	Y
29 Green	Y	Y	Y	Y	N	Y	Y
30 Johnson, E.B.	Y	Y	Y	Y	N	Y	Y
UTAH							
1 ***Hansen***	N	Y	N	N	Y	N	Y
2 ***Cook***	?	Y	N	N	Y	N	?
3 ***Cannon***	N	Y	N	N	Y	N	Y
VERMONT							
AL *Sanders*	Y	N	Y	Y	N	N	Y
VIRGINIA							
1 ***Bateman***	–	–	–	+	+	–	+
2 Pickett	N	Y	N	N	Y	Y	Y
3 Scott	Y	N	N	Y	N	Y	Y
4 Sisisky	N	Y	N	N	Y	Y	Y
5 Goode	N	Y	N	N	Y	N	?
6 ***Goodlatte***	N	Y	N	N	Y	N	Y
7 ***Bliley***	N	Y	N	N	Y	N	Y
8 Moran	Y	Y	N	Y	N	Y	Y
9 Boucher	Y	Y	Y	Y	N	Y	Y
10 ***Wolf***	N	Y	N	N	Y	N	Y
11 ***Davis***	N	Y	N	N	N	Y	Y
WASHINGTON							
1 ***White***	N	Y	N	N	N	N	?
2 ***Metcalf***	N	Y	N	N	Y	N	Y
3 ***Smith, Linda***	N	Y	N	N	Y	N	Y
4 ***Hastings***	N	Y	N	N	Y	N	Y
5 ***Nethercutt***	N	Y	N	N	Y	N	Y
6 Dicks	N	Y	N	Y	N	Y	Y
7 McDermott	Y	N	Y	Y	N	Y	Y
8 ***Dunn***	N	Y	N	N	Y	N	Y
9 Smith, Adam	Y	Y	N	Y	N	Y	Y
WEST VIRGINIA							
1 Mollohan	Y	Y	Y	Y	N	N	Y
2 Wise	Y	Y	N	Y	N	Y	Y
3 Rahall	Y	Y	Y	Y	N	N	Y
WISCONSIN							
1 ***Neumann***	N	Y	N	N	Y	N	Y
2 ***Klug***	N	Y	N	N	N	N	Y
3 Kind	Y	Y	Y	Y	N	Y	Y
4 Kleczka	Y	Y	N	Y	N	Y	Y
5 Barrett	Y	N	N	Y	N	Y	Y
6 ***Petri***	N	Y	N	N	N	N	Y
7 Obey	Y	?	Y	Y	N	Y	Y
8 Johnson	Y	Y	Y	Y	N	Y	Y
9 ***Sensenbrenner***	N	Y	N	N	Y	N	Y
WYOMING							
AL ***Cubin***	N	Y	N	N	Y	N	Y

Southern states - Ala., Ark., Fla., Ga., Ky., La., Miss., N.C., Okla., S.C., Tenn., Texas, Va.

Key

Y	Voted for (yea).
#	Paired for.
+	Announced for.
N	Voted against (nay).
X	Paired against.
−	Announced against.
P	Voted "present."
C	Voted "present" to avoid possible conflict of interest.
?	Did not vote or otherwise make a position known.

● Democrats **Republicans** *Independent*

111. S Con Res 37. International Character of Little League Baseball, Inc/Adoption. Smith, R-N.J., motion to suspend the rules and adopt the concurrent resolution to express the sense of Congress that Little League Baseball, Inc. was established to support and develop Little League Baseball worldwide. Motion agreed to 398-0: R 210-0; D 187-0 (ND 137-0, SD 50-0); I 1-0. April 28, 1998. A two-thirds majority of those present and voting (266 in this case) is required for adoption under suspension of the rules.

112. H J Res 102. 50th Anniversary of Modern State of Israel/Adoption. Gilman, R-N.Y., motion to suspend the rules and adopt the joint resolution to commend the people of Israel for their achievements in building a new state and a pluralistic democratic society in the Middle East, and reaffirm the bonds of friendship which have existed between the United States and Israel for the past half-century. Motion agreed to 402-0: R 211-0; D 190-0 (ND 139-0, SD 51-0); I 1-0. April 28, 1998. A two-thirds majority of those present and voting (268 in this case) is required for adoption under suspension of the rules.

113. HR 3717. Needle Distribution Programs/Recommit. Pelosi, D-Calif., motion to recommit the bill to the Commerce Committee with instructions to report it back with an amendment to allow lifting the ban on federal funds for needle distribution in cases where state or municipal health officials certify that needle distribution reduces the spread of AIDS, does not increase illegal drug use and is acceptable to the locality involved. Motion rejected 149-277: R 7-216; D 141-61 (ND 115-34, SD 26-27); I 1-0. April 29, 1998.

114. HR 3717. Needle Distribution Programs/Passage. Passage of the bill to prohibit the use of federal funds for needle distribution programs. Passed 287-140: R 213-11; D 74-128 (ND 42-107, SD 32-21); I 0-1. April 29, 1998. A "nay" was a vote in support of the president's position.

115. HR 3546. National Dialogue on Social Security/Recommit. Pomeroy, D-N.D., motion to recommit the bill to the Ways and Means Committee with instructions to report it back with an amendment to reserve the budget surplus until Congress has taken comprehensive action to assure that Social Security is solvent for the future. Motion rejected 197-223: R 0-223; D 196-0 (ND 144-0, SD 52-0); I 1-0. April 29, 1998.

116. HR 3546. National Dialogue on Social Security/Passage. Passage of the bill to create an eight-member bipartisan panel to recommend long-range changes to keep Social Security from going bankrupt, and direct the president and Congress to convene a national dialogue on the future of Social Security with help from members of private public interest groups. Passed 413-8: R 222-1; D 191-6 (ND 139-6, SD 52-0); I 0-1. April 29, 1998.

117. S 1502. District of Columbia Student Scholarships/Rule. Adoption of the rule (H Res 413) to provide for House floor consideration of the bill to create a $7 million school scholarship program for low-income elementary and secondary students living in Washington, D.C. Adopted 224-199: R 223-1; D 1-197 (ND 1-147, SD 0-50); I 0-1. April 30, 1998.

	111	112	113	114	115	116	117
ALABAMA							
1 *Callahan*	N	Y	N	Y	N	Y	Y
2 *Everett*	N	Y	N	N	Y	N	Y
3 *Riley*	N	Y	N	N	Y	N	+
4 *Aderholt*	N	Y	N	N	Y	N	Y
5 Cramer	N	Y	N	Y	Y	Y	Y
6 *Bachus*	N	Y	N	N	Y	N	Y
7 Hilliard	Y	Y	Y	N	Y	N	Y
ALASKA							
AL *Young*	N	N	N	N	Y	N	Y
ARIZONA							
1 *Salmon*	N	Y	N	Y	Y	N	Y
2 Pastor	Y	Y	Y	N	Y	Y	Y
3 *Stump*	N	Y	N	N	Y	N	Y
4 *Shadegg*	N	Y	N	N	Y	N	Y
5 *Kolbe*	N	Y	N	Y	Y	N	Y
6 *Hayworth*	N	Y	N	N	Y	N	Y
ARKANSAS							
1 Berry	Y	Y	Y	Y	N	N	Y
2 Snyder	N	Y	N	Y	N	Y	Y
3 *Hutchinson*	N	Y	N	N	Y	N	Y
4 *Dickey*	N	Y	N	N	Y	N	Y
CALIFORNIA							
1 *Riggs*	N	Y	N	?	?	N	?
2 *Herger*	N	Y	N	N	Y	N	Y
3 Fazlo	Y	Y	Y	Y	N	Y	Y
4 *Doolittle*	N	Y	N	N	Y	N	Y
5 Matsui	N	Y	N	Y	Y	Y	Y
6 Woolsey	Y	Y	Y	Y	N	Y	Y
7 Miller	Y	N	Y	N	Y	Y	Y
8 Pelosi	Y	N	Y	N	Y	Y	Y
9 Lee	Y	N	Y	N	Y	Y	Y
10 Tauscher	Y	Y	Y	Y	N	Y	Y
11 *Pombo*	N	Y	N	N	Y	N	Y
12 Lantos	Y	Y	Y	Y	N	Y	Y
13 Stark	Y	N	Y	N	Y	?	Y
14 Eshoo	Y	Y	Y	Y	N	Y	+
15 *Campbell*	N	Y	Y	Y	N	N	N
16 Lofgren	N	Y	Y	Y	N	Y	+
17 Farr	Y	Y	Y	Y	N	Y	Y
18 Condit	N	Y	Y	Y	Y	N	Y
19 *Radanovich*	N	N	N	N	Y	N	Y
20 Dooley	Y	Y	Y	Y	N	Y	Y
21 *Thomas*	N	Y	N	N	Y	N	Y
22 Capps, L.	Y	Y	Y	Y	N	Y	Y
23 *Gallegly*	N	Y	N	N	Y	N	Y
24 Sherman	Y	Y	Y	Y	N	Y	Y
25 *McKeon*	N	Y	N	N	Y	N	Y
26 Berman	Y	Y	Y	Y	N	Y	Y
27 *Rogan*	N	Y	N	N	Y	N	Y
28 *Dreier*	N	Y	N	N	Y	N	Y
29 Waxman	N	Y	Y	Y	N	Y	Y
30 Becerra	Y	Y	Y	Y	N	Y	Y
31 Martinez	Y	N	Y	Y	Y	?	Y
32 Dixon	?	?	?	?	?	?	?
33 Roybal-Allard	Y	Y	Y	Y	N	Y	Y
34 Torres	Y	Y	Y	Y	N	Y	Y
35 Waters	Y	N	Y	N	Y	N	Y
36 Harman	Y	Y	Y	Y	N	Y	+
37 Millender-McD.	Y	N	Y	N	Y	N	+

	111	112	113	114	115	116	117
38 *Horn*	Y	Y	N	N	N	N	Y
39 *Royce*	N	Y	N	N	Y	N	Y
40 *Lewis*	N	Y	N	N	Y	N	Y
41 *Kim*	N	Y	N	N	Y	N	Y
42 Brown	Y	N	Y	N	Y	Y	Y
43 *Calvert*	N	Y	N	N	Y	N	Y
44 *Bono, M.*	N	Y	N	N	Y	N	Y
45 *Rohrabacher*	Y	Y	N	N	Y	N	?
46 Sanchez	Y	Y	Y	Y	N	Y	Y
47 *Cox*	N	Y	N	N	?	N	Y
48 *Packard*	N	Y	N	N	Y	N	Y
49 *Bilbray*	Y	Y	N	N	Y	N	?
50 Filner	Y	N	Y	N	Y	N	Y
51 *Cunningham*	N	Y	N	N	Y	N	Y
52 *Hunter*	N	Y	N	N	Y	N	Y
COLORADO							
1 DeGette	Y	N	Y	N	Y	Y	Y
2 Skaggs	N	N	N	Y	N	Y	Y
3 *McInnis*	N	Y	N	N	Y	N	Y
4 *Schaffer*	N	Y	N	N	Y	N	Y
5 *Hefley*	N	Y	N	N	Y	N	Y
6 *Schaefer*	N	Y	N	N	Y	N	Y
CONNECTICUT							
1 Kennelly	Y	Y	Y	Y	N	Y	Y
2 *Gejdenson*	Y	Y	Y	Y	N	Y	?
3 DeLauro	Y	Y	Y	Y	N	Y	Y
4 *Shays*	Y	Y	N	N	Y	N	Y
5 Maloney	Y	Y	Y	Y	N	Y	Y
6 *Johnson*	N	Y	N	N	Y	Y	Y
DELAWARE							
AL *Castle*	N	Y	N	N	N	N	Y
FLORIDA							
1 *Scarborough*	N	Y	N	N	N	N	Y
2 Boyd	N	Y	N	N	N	Y	Y
3 Brown	Y	Y	Y	Y	N	Y	Y
4 *Fowler*	Y	Y	Y	N	Y	N	Y
5 Thurman	Y	Y	Y	Y	N	Y	Y
6 *Stearns*	N	Y	N	N	Y	N	Y
7 *Mica*	N	Y	N	N	Y	N	Y
8 *McCollum*	N	Y	N	N	Y	N	Y
9 *Bilirakis*	N	Y	N	N	Y	N	Y
10 *Young*	N	Y	N	N	Y	N	Y
11 Davis	Y	Y	+	Y	N	Y	Y
12 *Canady*	N	Y	N	N	Y	N	Y
13 *Miller*	?	?	?	?	?	?	?
14 *Goss*	N	Y	N	N	Y	N	Y
15 *Weldon*	N	Y	N	N	Y	N	?
16 *Foley*	N	Y	N	N	Y	N	Y
17 Meek	Y	?	?	?	?	?	Y
18 *Ros-Lehtinen*	N	Y	N	N	N	N	Y
19 Wexler	Y	Y	Y	Y	N	Y	Y
20 Deutsch	Y	Y	Y	Y	Y	Y	Y
21 *Diaz-Balart*	Y	Y	N	N	N	N	Y
22 *Shaw*	N	Y	N	N	Y	N	Y
23 Hastings	?	?	?	?	?	?	?
GEORGIA							
1 *Kingston*	N	Y	N	N	Y	N	Y
2 Bishop	Y	Y	Y	Y	N	N	Y
3 *Collins*	N	Y	N	N	Y	N	Y
4 McKinney	Y	Y	Y	N	Y	N	Y
5 Lewis	Y	N	Y	N	Y	Y	Y
6 *Gingrich*							
7 *Barr*	N	Y	N	N	Y	N	?
8 *Chambliss*	N	Y	N	N	Y	N	Y
9 *Deal*	N	Y	N	Y	Y	N	Y
10 *Norwood*	N	Y	N	N	Y	N	Y
11 *Linder*	N	Y	N	N	Y	N	Y
HAWAII							
1 Abercrombie	Y	Y	Y	Y	N	Y	Y
2 Mink	Y	Y	Y	Y	N	Y	Y
IDAHO							
1 *Chenoweth*	N	Y	N	N	Y	N	Y
2 *Crapo*	N	Y	N	N	Y	N	Y
ILLINOIS							
1 Rush	Y	N	Y	N	Y	Y	Y
2 Jackson	N	Y	Y	Y	N	Y	Y
3 Lipinski	Y	N	N	N	N	N	Y
4 Gutierrez	?	Y	Y	Y	N	Y	Y
5 Blagojevich	Y	Y	Y	Y	N	Y	Y
6 *Hyde*	N	Y	N	N	Y	N	?
7 Davis	Y	N	Y	?	Y	Y	Y
8 *Crane*	N	Y	N	N	Y	N	Y
9 Yates	Y	N	Y	N	Y	?	Y
10 *Porter*	N	Y	N	N	N	N	Y
11 *Weller*	N	Y	N	N	Y	N	Y
12 Costello	Y	Y	Y	Y	N	Y	Y

ND Northern Democrats   SD Southern Democrats

	111	112	113	114	115	116	117
13 ***Fawell***	N	N	N	N	N	Y	Y
14 ***Hastert***	N	Y	N	N	Y	?	Y
15 ***Ewing***	N	Y	N	N	N	N	Y
16 ***Manzullo***	N	Y	N	N	Y	N	Y
17 Evans	Y	N	Y	Y	N	N	Y
18 ***LaHood***	N	Y	N	N	N	Y	Y
19 Poshard	Y	Y	Y	?	?	?	?
20 ***Shimkus***	N	Y	N	N	Y	N	Y
INDIANA							
1 Visclosky	Y	Y	Y	Y	N	Y	Y
2 ***McIntosh***	N	Y	N	N	Y	N	Y
3 Roemer	N	Y	N	Y	N	Y	Y
4 ***Souder***	N	Y	N	N	?	N	Y
5 ***Buyer***	N	Y	N	N	?	N	Y
6 ***Burton***	N	Y	N	N	Y	N	Y
7 ***Pease***	N	Y	N	N	Y	N	Y
8 ***Hostettler***	N	Y	N	N	Y	N	Y
9 Hamilton	N	Y	N	Y	N	Y	Y
10 Carson	Y	N	Y	Y	N	N	Y
IOWA							
1 ***Leach***	Y	Y	Y	N	N	Y	Y
2 ***Nussle***	N	Y	N	N	Y	Y	Y
3 Boswell	Y	Y	N	Y	N	Y	Y
4 ***Ganske***	N	Y	N	N	N	N	?
5 ***Latham***	N	Y	N	N	Y	Y	Y
KANSAS							
1 ***Moran***	N	Y	N	N	Y	N	Y
2 ***Ryun***	N	Y	N	N	Y	N	+
3 ***Snowbarger***	N	Y	?	N	Y	N	Y
4 ***Tiahrt***	N	Y	N	N	Y	N	Y
KENTUCKY							
1 ***Whitfield***	N	Y	N	N	N	N	Y
2 ***Lewis***	N	Y	N	N	Y	N	Y
3 ***Northup***	N	Y	N	N	Y	N	Y
4 ***Bunning***	N	Y	N	N	Y	N	Y
5 ***Rogers***	N	Y	N	N	Y	N	Y
6 Baesler	Y	Y	Y	Y	N	Y	?
LOUISIANA							
1 ***Livingston***	N	Y	N	N	Y	N	Y
2 Jefferson	Y	Y	Y	Y	N	?	?
3 ***Tauzin***	N	Y	N	N	Y	N	Y
4 ***McCrery***	?	Y	N	N	Y	N	Y
5 ***Cooksey***	N	Y	N	N	Y	N	Y
6 ***Baker***	N	Y	N	N	Y	N	Y
7 John	N	Y	N	Y	N	Y	Y
MAINE							
1 Allen	Y	Y	N	Y	N	Y	Y
2 Baldacci	Y	Y	Y	Y	N	Y	Y
MARYLAND							
1 ***Gilchrest***	N	Y	N	N	N	Y	Y
2 ***Ehrlich***	N	Y	N	Y	Y	N	Y
3 Cardin	Y	Y	N	Y	N	Y	Y
4 Wynn	Y	Y	Y	Y	N	Y	Y
5 Hoyer	Y	Y	N	Y	N	Y	Y
6 ***Bartlett***	N	Y	N	N	Y	N	Y
7 Cummings	Y	Y	Y	Y	N	Y	Y
8 ***Morella***	Y	Y	N	Y	N	?	Y
MASSACHUSETTS							
1 Olver	Y	N	Y	Y	N	Y	Y
2 Neal	Y	Y	Y	Y	N	Y	Y
3 McGovern	Y	Y	N	Y	N	Y	Y
4 Frank	Y	N	N	Y	N	Y	Y
5 Meehan	Y	N	Y	Y	N	Y	Y
6 Tierney	Y	N	N	Y	N	Y	Y
7 Markey	Y	Y	Y	Y	N	Y	Y
8 Kennedy	Y	N	Y	Y	N	Y	Y
9 Moakley	Y	Y	N	Y	N	Y	Y
10 Delahunt	Y	N	Y	Y	N	Y	Y
MICHIGAN							
1 Stupak	Y	Y	Y	Y	N	Y	Y
2 ***Hoekstra***	N	Y	N	N	Y	N	Y
3 ***Ehlers***	N	Y	N	N	N	N	Y
4 ***Camp***	N	Y	N	N	–	N	Y
5 Barcia	Y	Y	Y	Y	N	N	Y
6 ***Upton***	N	Y	N	N	N	N	Y
7 ***Smith***	N	Y	N	Y	Y	N	Y
8 Stabenow	Y	Y	Y	Y	N	Y	Y
9 Kildee	Y	Y	Y	Y	N	Y	Y
10 Bonior	Y	N	Y	Y	N	Y	Y
11 ***Knollenberg***	N	Y	N	N	Y	N	Y
12 Levin	Y	Y	N	Y	N	Y	Y
13 Rivers	Y	Y	N	Y	N	Y	Y
14 Conyers	Y	N	Y	Y	N	N	Y
15 Kilpatrick	Y	N	Y	Y	N	Y	Y
16 Dingell	Y	Y	N	Y	N	Y	Y
MINNESOTA							
1 ***Gutknecht***	N	Y	N	N	N	N	Y
2 Minge	Y	Y	Y	Y	N	Y	Y
3 ***Ramstad***	N	Y	N	N	N	N	Y
4 Vento	Y	Y	Y	Y	N	Y	Y
5 Sabo	Y	N	Y	Y	N	Y	Y
6 Luther	Y	Y	Y	Y	N	Y	Y
7 Peterson	N	Y	Y	N	Y	N	Y
8 Oberstar	Y	N	Y	Y	N	Y	Y
MISSISSIPPI							
1 ***Wicker***	N	Y	N	N	Y	N	Y
2 Thompson	Y	N	Y	Y	N	N	Y
3 ***Pickering***	N	Y	N	N	Y	N	Y
4 ***Parker***	N	Y	N	N	Y	N	Y
5 Taylor	N	Y	Y	Y	N	N	Y
MISSOURI							
1 Clay	?	?	?	?	?	?	Y
2 ***Talent***	N	Y	N	N	Y	N	Y
3 Gephardt	Y	Y	Y	Y	N	Y	Y
4 Skelton	N	Y	Y	Y	N	Y	Y
5 McCarthy	Y	Y	N	Y	N	Y	Y
6 Danner	N	Y	N	Y	Y	N	Y
7 ***Blunt***	N	Y	N	N	Y	N	?
8 ***Emerson***	Y	Y	N	N	Y	N	Y
9 ***Hulshof***	N	Y	N	N	Y	N	Y
MONTANA							
AL ***Hill***	N	Y	N	N	Y	N	Y
NEBRASKA							
1 ***Bereuter***	Y	Y	N	N	Y	Y	Y
2 ***Christensen***	N	Y	N	N	Y	Y	?
3 ***Barrett***	N	Y	N	N	Y	Y	Y
NEVADA							
1 ***Ensign***	N	Y	N	Y	Y	N	?
2 ***Gibbons***	N	Y	N	N	Y	N	Y
NEW HAMPSHIRE							
1 ***Sununu***	N	Y	N	N	N	N	Y
2 ***Bass***	N	Y	N	N	N	N	Y
NEW JERSEY							
1 Andrews	Y	Y	Y	Y	N	Y	Y
2 ***LoBiondo***	N	Y	Y	Y	N	N	Y
3 ***Saxton***	N	Y	N	N	N	N	Y
4 ***Smith***	N	Y	N	N	N	N	Y
5 ***Roukema***	N	Y	N	N	N	Y	Y
6 Pallone	Y	Y	Y	Y	N	Y	Y
7 ***Franks***	N	Y	N	Y	N	N	Y
8 Pascrell	Y	Y	Y	Y	N	Y	Y
9 Rothman	N	Y	Y	N	N	Y	Y
10 Payne	Y	N	Y	Y	N	Y	Y
11 ***Frelinghuysen***	N	Y	N	N	N	N	Y
12 ***Pappas***	N	Y	N	Y	N	N	Y
13 Menendez	Y	Y	Y	Y	N	Y	Y
NEW MEXICO							
1 Vacant							
2 ***Skeen***	N	Y	N	N	Y	Y	Y
3 ***Redmond***	N	Y	N	N	Y	N	Y
NEW YORK							
1 ***Forbes***	N	Y	N	N	N	?	Y
2 ***Lazio***	N	Y	N	N	N	Y	Y
3 ***King***	N	Y	Y	N	Y	N	Y
4 McCarthy	Y	Y	Y	Y	N	Y	Y
5 Ackerman	Y	Y	Y	Y	N	Y	Y
6 Meeks	Y	N	Y	Y	N	Y	+
7 Manton	Y	Y	N	Y	N	Y	Y
8 Nadler	Y	Y	Y	Y	N	Y	Y
9 Schumer	Y	Y	Y	Y	N	Y	Y
10 Towns	Y	N	N	Y	N	Y	?
11 Owens	Y	N	Y	Y	N	Y	Y
12 Velázquez	Y	N	Y	Y	N	Y	Y
13 ***Fossella***	N	Y	N	N	Y	N	Y
14 Maloney	N	Y	Y	Y	N	Y	?
15 Rangel	Y	N	Y	Y	N	Y	?
16 Serrano	Y	N	Y	Y	N	Y	?
17 Engel	Y	Y	Y	Y	N	Y	+
18 Lowey	Y	Y	Y	Y	N	Y	Y
19 ***Kelly***	N	Y	N	N	N	N	Y
20 ***Gilman***	N	Y	N	N	N	Y	Y
21 McNulty	Y	Y	Y	Y	N	Y	Y
22 ***Solomon***	N	Y	N	N	Y	N	Y
23 ***Boehlert***	N	Y	N	N	N	N	Y
24 ***McHugh***	N	Y	N	Y	Y	N	Y
25 ***Walsh***	N	Y	N	N	N	N	Y
26 Hinchey	Y	N	Y	Y	N	Y	Y
27 ***Paxon***	?	?	?	?	?	?	Y
28 Slaughter	Y	Y	Y	Y	N	Y	Y
29 LaFalce	Y	Y	Y	Y	N	Y	Y
30 ***Quinn***	N	Y	N	N	N	N	Y
31 ***Houghton***	N	Y	N	N	N	Y	Y
NORTH CAROLINA							
1 Clayton	Y	Y	Y	Y	N	Y	Y
2 Etheridge	Y	Y	Y	Y	N	Y	Y
3 ***Jones***	N	Y	N	N	Y	N	Y
4 Price	Y	Y	Y	Y	N	Y	Y
5 ***Burr***	N	Y	N	N	Y	?	Y
6 ***Coble***	N	Y	N	?	?	?	Y
7 McIntyre	Y	Y	N	Y	Y	Y	Y
8 Hefner	Y	Y	Y	Y	Y	Y	Y
9 ***Myrick***	N	Y	N	N	Y	N	Y
10 ***Ballenger***	N	Y	N	Y	Y	N	Y
11 ***Taylor***	N	Y	N	N	Y	N	+
12 Watt	N	N	Y	Y	N	Y	Y
NORTH DAKOTA							
AL Pomeroy	N	Y	Y	Y	N	Y	Y
OHIO							
1 ***Chabot***	N	Y	N	Y	Y	N	Y
2 ***Portman***	N	Y	N	N	Y	N	Y
3 Hall	Y	Y	Y	Y	N	Y	Y
4 ***Oxley***	N	Y	N	N	N	N	Y
5 ***Gillmor***	N	Y	N	N	Y	N	Y
6 Strickland	Y	Y	Y	Y	N	N	Y
7 ***Hobson***	N	Y	N	N	N	N	Y
8 ***Boehner***	N	Y	N	N	Y	?	Y
9 Kaptur	Y	Y	Y	Y	?	?	Y
10 Kucinich	Y	Y	N	Y	N	N	Y
11 Stokes	Y	N	Y	Y	N	Y	Y
12 ***Kasich***	N	Y	N	N	Y	N	Y
13 Brown	Y	Y	Y	Y	N	N	Y
14 Sawyer	Y	Y	N	Y	N	Y	Y
15 ***Pryce***	N	Y	N	N	N	N	Y
16 ***Regula***	N	Y	N	N	N	N	Y
17 Traficant	N	Y	Y	Y	Y	N	Y
18 ***Ney***	N	Y	N	N	N	Y	Y
19 ***LaTourette***	N	Y	N	N	N	Y	Y
OKLAHOMA							
1 ***Largent***	N	Y	N	N	Y	N	Y
2 ***Coburn***	N	Y	N	N	Y	N	Y
3 ***Watkins***	N	Y	N	N	Y	N	Y
4 ***Watts***	N	Y	N	N	Y	N	Y
5 ***Istook***	?	?	?	?	?	–	Y
6 ***Lucas***	N	Y	N	N	Y	N	Y
OREGON							
1 Furse	Y	N	Y	Y	N	Y	Y
2 ***Smith***	N	Y	N	N	Y	N	?
3 Blumenauer	Y	Y	Y	Y	N	Y	Y
4 DeFazio	Y	Y	Y	Y	N	N	Y
5 Hooley	Y	Y	Y	Y	N	Y	Y
PENNSYLVANIA							
1 Vacant							
2 Fattah	Y	?	?	?	?	?	Y
3 Borski	Y	Y	Y	Y	N	Y	Y
4 Klink	Y	Y	Y	Y	N	N	Y
5 ***Peterson***	N	Y	N	N	Y	N	Y
6 Holden	Y	Y	N	Y	N	Y	Y
7 ***Weldon***	N	Y	N	N	N	N	Y
8 ***Greenwood***	N	Y	N	N	N	N	?
9 ***Shuster***	N	Y	N	N	Y	N	Y
10 ***McDade***	N	Y	Y	N	N	N	Y
11 Kanjorski	N	Y	Y	Y	N	Y	Y
12 Murtha	N	Y	Y	N	N	Y	Y
13 ***Fox***	Y	Y	Y	?	?	?	Y
14 Coyne	Y	Y	Y	Y	N	Y	Y
15 McHale	Y	Y	N	Y	N	Y	Y
16 ***Pitts***	N	Y	N	N	Y	N	Y
17 ***Gekas***	N	Y	N	N	Y	N	Y
18 Doyle	N	Y	Y	Y	N	N	Y
19 ***Goodling***	N	Y	N	N	Y	N	Y
20 Mascara	Y	Y	Y	Y	N	Y	Y
21 ***English***	N	Y	N	Y	N	N	Y
RHODE ISLAND							
1 Kennedy	Y	N	Y	Y	N	Y	Y
2 Weygand	Y	Y	Y	Y	N	Y	Y
SOUTH CAROLINA							
1 ***Sanford***	N	Y	Y	N	Y	N	Y
2 ***Spence***	N	Y	N	N	Y	N	Y
3 ***Graham***	N	Y	N	N	Y	N	Y
4 ***Inglis***	N	Y	N	N	Y	N	?
5 Spratt	Y	?	?	Y	N	Y	Y
6 Clyburn	Y	N	Y	Y	N	Y	Y
SOUTH DAKOTA							
AL ***Thune***	N	Y	N	N	Y	N	Y
TENNESSEE							
1 ***Jenkins***	N	Y	N	N	Y	N	Y
2 ***Duncan***	N	Y	N	Y	Y	N	Y
3 ***Wamp***	N	Y	N	Y	Y	N	Y
4 ***Hilleary***	N	Y	N	Y	Y	N	Y
5 Clement	Y	Y	Y	Y	N	Y	Y
6 Gordon	N	Y	Y	N	N	Y	Y
7 ***Bryant***	N	Y	N	N	Y	N	Y
8 Tanner	?	?	?	?	?	?	?
9 Ford	Y	Y	Y	Y	N	Y	Y
TEXAS							
1 Sandlin	N	Y	Y	Y	N	Y	?
2 Turner	N	Y	N	N	N	Y	Y
3 ***Johnson, Sam***	N	Y	N	N	Y	N	Y
4 Hall	?	Y	N	N	Y	N	Y
5 ***Sessions***	N	Y	N	N	Y	N	Y
6 ***Barton***	N	Y	N	N	Y	N	Y
7 ***Archer***	N	Y	N	N	Y	N	Y
8 ***Brady***	N	Y	N	N	Y	N	Y
9 Lampson	Y	Y	Y	Y	N	Y	Y
10 Doggett	Y	Y	N	Y	N	Y	Y
11 Edwards	Y	Y	Y	Y	N	Y	Y
12 ***Granger***	N	Y	N	N	Y	N	Y
13 ***Thornberry***	N	Y	N	N	Y	N	Y
14 ***Paul***	N	Y	Y	N	Y	N	N
15 Hinojosa	Y	Y	Y	+	–	Y	Y
16 Reyes	Y	Y	Y	Y	N	?	Y
17 Stenholm	N	Y	N	N	Y	Y	Y
18 Jackson-Lee	Y	N	Y	Y	N	Y	Y
19 ***Combest***	N	Y	N	N	Y	N	Y
20 Gonzalez	?	?	?	?	?	?	?
21 ***Smith***	N	Y	N	N	Y	N	Y
22 ***DeLay***	N	Y	N	N	Y	N	Y
23 ***Bonilla***	N	Y	N	N	Y	N	Y
24 Frost	Y	Y	Y	Y	N	Y	Y
25 Bentsen	Y	Y	N	Y	N	Y	Y
26 ***Armey***	N	Y	N	N	Y	N	Y
27 Ortiz	Y	Y	Y	Y	N	N	Y
28 Rodriguez	Y	Y	Y	Y	N	Y	Y
29 Green	Y	Y	Y	Y	N	Y	Y
30 Johnson, E.B.	Y	Y	Y	Y	N	Y	Y
UTAH							
1 ***Hansen***	N	Y	N	N	Y	N	Y
2 ***Cook***	?	Y	N	N	Y	N	?
3 ***Cannon***	N	Y	N	N	Y	N	Y
VERMONT							
AL *Sanders*	Y	N	Y	Y	N	N	Y
VIRGINIA							
1 ***Bateman***	–	–	–	+	+	–	+
2 Pickett	N	Y	N	N	Y	Y	Y
3 Scott	Y	N	N	Y	N	Y	Y
4 Sisisky	N	Y	N	N	Y	Y	Y
5 Goode	N	Y	N	N	Y	N	?
6 ***Goodlatte***	N	Y	N	N	Y	N	Y
7 ***Bliley***	N	Y	N	N	Y	N	Y
8 Moran	Y	Y	N	Y	N	Y	Y
9 Boucher	Y	Y	Y	Y	N	Y	Y
10 ***Wolf***	N	Y	N	N	Y	N	Y
11 ***Davis***	N	Y	N	N	N	Y	Y
WASHINGTON							
1 ***White***	N	Y	N	N	N	N	?
2 ***Metcalf***	N	Y	N	N	Y	N	Y
3 ***Smith, Linda***	N	Y	N	N	Y	N	Y
4 ***Hastings***	N	Y	N	N	Y	N	Y
5 ***Nethercutt***	N	Y	N	N	Y	N	Y
6 Dicks	N	Y	N	Y	N	Y	Y
7 McDermott	Y	N	Y	Y	N	Y	Y
8 ***Dunn***	N	Y	N	N	Y	N	Y
9 Smith, Adam	Y	Y	N	Y	N	Y	Y
WEST VIRGINIA							
1 Mollohan	Y	Y	Y	Y	N	N	Y
2 Wise	Y	Y	N	Y	N	Y	Y
3 Rahall	Y	Y	Y	Y	N	N	Y
WISCONSIN							
1 ***Neumann***	N	Y	N	N	Y	N	Y
2 ***Klug***	N	Y	N	N	N	N	Y
3 Kind	Y	Y	Y	Y	N	Y	Y
4 Kleczka	Y	Y	N	Y	N	Y	Y
5 Barrett	Y	N	N	Y	N	Y	Y
6 ***Petri***	N	Y	N	N	N	N	Y
7 Obey	Y	?	Y	Y	N	Y	Y
8 Johnson	Y	Y	Y	Y	N	Y	Y
9 ***Sensenbrenner***	N	Y	N	N	Y	N	Y
WYOMING							
AL ***Cubin***	N	Y	N	N	Y	N	Y

Southern states - Ala., Ark., Fla., Ga., Ky., La., Miss., N.C., Okla., S.C., Tenn., Texas, Va.

Key

Y	Voted for (yea).
#	Paired for.
+	Announced for.
N	Voted against (nay).
X	Paired against.
–	Announced against.
P	Voted "present."
C	Voted "present" to avoid possible conflict of interest.
?	Did not vote or otherwise make a position known.

● Democrats ● *Republicans*
● Independent

118. S 1502. District of Columbia Student Scholarships/Commit. Norton, D-D.C., motion to commit the bill to the Government Reform and Oversight Committee with instructions to authorize $3.5 million for the District of Columbia control board to fund reading tutors in the District's 73 lowest performing schools, and authorize $3.5 million for the Education Department to fund reforms at the District's 70 lowest performing schools to be administered under the Comprehensive School Reform Demonstration education program. Motion rejected 198-224: R 2-219; D 195-5 (ND 148-0, SD 47-5); I 1-0. April 30, 1998.

119. S 1502. District of Columbia Student Scholarships/Passage. Passage of the bill to create a $7 million school scholarship program for low-income elementary and secondary students living in Washington, D.C. Passed 214-206: R 208-13; D 6-192 (ND 2-145, SD 4-47); I 0-1. April 30, 1998. Thus cleared for the president. A "nay" was a vote in support of the president's position.

120. H Res 414. Waiving Requirements for Considering a Rule/Adoption. Adoption of the resolution to waive the two-thirds majority required for considering a rule on the same day it is reported from the Rules Committee. Adopted 211-196: R 211-0; D 0-195 (ND 0-144, SD 0-51); I 0-1. April 30, 1998.

121. HR 3579. Fiscal 1998 Emergency Supplemental Appropriations/Conference Report. Adoption of the conference report on the bill to appropriate $6.1 billion in supplemental spending, including $2.6 billion for disaster relief to states, and $2.9 billion for operations in Bosnia and other overseas operations. Adopted 242-163: R 192-21; D 50-141 (ND 26-116, SD 24-25); I 0-1. April 30, 1998.

122. HR 6. Higher Education Act Reauthorization/Personal Identifier. Paul, R-Texas, amendment to prohibit the Education Department from using a student's Social Security number or any other identifier used in any federal program as the electronic personal identifier required under the bill. Rejected 112-286: R 93-122; D 19-163 (ND 15-115, SD 4-48); I 0-1. May 5, 1998.

123. HR 6. Higher Education Act Reauthorization/Information Technology. Owens, D-N.Y., amendment to establish a $100 million grant program for colleges and universities that will be used to establish and oversee information technology education recruitment projects. Rejected 172-234: R 4-213; D 167-21 (ND 127-9, SD 40-12); I 1-0. May 5, 1998.

124. HR 6. Higher Education Act Reauthorization/Achievement Awards. McGovern, D-Mass., amendment to authorize an achievement award to students eligible for Pell Grants who graduate in the top 10 percent of their high school class. Adopted 220-187: R 33-184; D 186-3 (ND 135-2, SD 51-1); I 1-0. May 5, 1998.

	118	119	120	121	122	123	124
ALABAMA							
1 *Callahan*	Y	Y	N	Y	N	Y	Y
2 *Everett*	Y	Y	N	Y	N	Y	Y
3 *Riley*	Y	Y	N	Y	N	Y	Y
4 *Aderholt*	Y	Y	N	Y	N	Y	Y
5 Cramer	Y	Y	N	Y	N	Y	N
6 *Bachus*	Y	Y	N	Y	N	Y	Y
7 Hilliard	Y	Y	Y	N	Y	Y	N
ALASKA							
AL *Young*	Y	Y	N	Y	N	Y	Y
ARIZONA							
1 *Salmon*	Y	Y	N	Y	N	Y	Y
2 Pastor	Y	Y	Y	N	Y	Y	N
3 *Stump*	Y	Y	N	Y	N	Y	Y
4 *Shadegg*	Y	Y	N	Y	N	Y	Y
5 *Kolbe*	Y	Y	N	Y	N	Y	Y
6 *Hayworth*	Y	Y	N	Y	N	Y	Y
ARKANSAS							
1 Berry	Y	Y	N	Y	Y	Y	N
2 Snyder	Y	Y	Y	N	Y	Y	N
3 *Hutchinson*	Y	Y	N	Y	N	Y	Y
4 *Dickey*	Y	Y	N	Y	N	Y	Y
CALIFORNIA							
1 *Riggs*	?	?	N	Y	N	Y	Y
2 *Herger*	Y	Y	N	Y	N	Y	Y
3 Fazio	Y	Y	Y	N	Y	Y	N
4 *Doolittle*	Y	Y	N	Y	N	Y	Y
5 Matsui	Y	Y	Y	N	Y	Y	N
6 Woolsey	Y	?	Y	N	Y	Y	N
7 Miller	Y	Y	Y	N	Y	Y	N
8 Pelosi	Y	Y	Y	N	Y	Y	N
9 Lee	Y	Y	Y	N	Y	Y	N
10 Tauscher	Y	Y	Y	N	Y	Y	N
11 *Pombo*	Y	Y	N	Y	N	Y	Y
12 Lantos	Y	Y	Y	N	Y	Y	N
13 Stark	Y	Y	Y	N	Y	Y	N
14 Eshoo	+	Y	Y	N	Y	Y	N
15 *Campbell*	Y	Y	N	N	Y	N	Y
16 Lofgren	+	Y	Y	N	Y	Y	N
17 Farr	Y	Y	Y	N	Y	Y	N
18 Condit	Y	Y	N	Y	N	Y	N
19 *Radanovich*	Y	?	N	Y	N	Y	Y
20 Dooley	Y	Y	Y	N	Y	Y	N
21 *Thomas*	Y	Y	N	Y	N	Y	Y
22 Capps, L.	Y	Y	Y	N	Y	Y	N
23 *Gallegly*	Y	Y	N	Y	N	Y	Y
24 Sherman	Y	Y	N	Y	N	Y	N
25 *McKeon*	Y	Y	N	Y	N	Y	Y
26 Berman	Y	Y	Y	N	Y	Y	N
27 *Rogan*	Y	Y	N	Y	N	Y	Y
28 *Dreier*	Y	Y	N	Y	N	Y	Y
29 Waxman	Y	Y	Y	N	Y	Y	N
30 Becerra	Y	Y	Y	N	Y	Y	N
31 Martinez	?	?	Y	N	Y	N	N
32 Dixon	?	?	?	?	?	?	?
33 Roybal-Allard	Y	Y	Y	N	Y	Y	N
34 Torres	Y	Y	Y	N	Y	Y	N
35 Waters	Y	Y	Y	N	Y	Y	N
36 Harman	+	Y	Y	N	Y	Y	N
37 Millender-McD.	+	+	Y	N	Y	Y	N

	118	119	120	121	122	123	124
38 *Horn*	Y	Y	N	Y	N	Y	Y
39 *Royce*	Y	Y	N	Y	N	Y	Y
40 *Lewis*	Y	Y	N	N	N	Y	Y
41 *Kim*	Y	Y	N	Y	N	Y	Y
42 Brown	Y	Y	Y	N	?	?	N
43 *Calvert*	Y	Y	N	Y	N	Y	Y
44 *Bono, M.*	Y	Y	N	Y	N	Y	Y
45 *Rohrabacher*	Y	Y	N	Y	N	Y	Y
46 Sanchez	Y	Y	Y	Y	Y	Y	N
47 *Cox*	Y	Y	N	Y	N	Y	Y
48 *Packard*	Y	Y	N	Y	N	Y	Y
49 *Bilbray*	?	?	N	Y	N	Y	Y
50 Filner	Y	Y	Y	N	Y	Y	N
51 *Cunningham*	Y	Y	N	Y	N	Y	Y
52 *Hunter*	Y	Y	N	Y	N	Y	Y
COLORADO							
1 DeGette	Y	Y	Y	N	Y	Y	N
2 Skaggs	Y	Y	Y	N	Y	Y	N
3 *McInnis*	Y	Y	N	Y	N	Y	Y
4 *Schaffer*	Y	Y	N	Y	N	Y	Y
5 *Hefley*	Y	Y	N	Y	N	Y	Y
6 *Schaefer*	Y	Y	N	Y	N	Y	Y
CONNECTICUT							
1 Kennelly	Y	Y	Y	N	Y	Y	?
2 Gejdenson	?	?	Y	N	Y	Y	N
3 DeLauro	Y	Y	N	?	Y	N	N
4 *Shays*	Y	Y	N	Y	N	Y	Y
5 Maloney	Y	Y	Y	N	Y	Y	N
6 *Johnson*	Y	Y	N	Y	N	Y	Y
DELAWARE							
AL *Castle*	Y	Y	N	Y	N	Y	Y
FLORIDA							
1 *Scarborough*	Y	Y	N	N	N	Y	Y
2 Boyd	Y	Y	Y	Y	Y	Y	N
3 Brown	Y	Y	Y	N	Y	Y	N
4 *Fowler*	Y	Y	N	Y	N	Y	Y
5 Thurman	Y	Y	Y	N	Y	Y	N
6 *Stearns*	Y	Y	N	Y	N	Y	Y
7 *Mica*	Y	Y	N	Y	N	Y	Y
8 *McCollum*	Y	Y	N	Y	N	Y	Y
9 *Bilirakis*	Y	Y	N	Y	N	Y	Y
10 *Young*	Y	Y	N	Y	N	Y	Y
11 Davis	Y	Y	Y	Y	N	Y	N
12 *Canady*	Y	Y	N	Y	N	Y	Y
13 *Miller*	Y	Y	N	Y	N	Y	Y
14 *Goss*	Y	Y	N	Y	N	Y	Y
15 *Weldon*	Y	Y	N	Y	N	Y	Y
16 *Foley*	?	?	N	N	N	Y	Y
17 Meek	Y	Y	Y	N	?	?	?
18 *Ros-Lehtinen*	Y	Y	Y	N	?	?	?
19 Wexler	Y	Y	N	Y	Y	Y	N
20 Deutsch	Y	Y	Y	N	Y	Y	N
21 *Diaz-Balart*	Y	Y	N	Y	N	Y	Y
22 *Shaw*	Y	Y	N	Y	N	Y	Y
23 Hastings	Y	Y	Y	N	Y	Y	N
GEORGIA							
1 *Kingston*	Y	Y	N	Y	N	Y	Y
2 Bishop	Y	Y	N	Y	N	Y	Y
3 *Collins*	Y	Y	N	Y	N	Y	Y
4 McKinney	Y	Y	Y	N	Y	Y	N
5 Lewis	Y	Y	Y	N	Y	Y	N
6 *Gingrich*			N	Y			
7 *Barr*	?	?	?	?	?	?	Y
8 *Chambliss*	Y	Y	N	Y	N	Y	Y
9 *Deal*	Y	Y	N	Y	N	Y	Y
10 *Norwood*	Y	Y	N	Y	N	Y	Y
11 *Linder*	Y	Y	N	Y	N	Y	Y
HAWAII							
1 Abercrombie	Y	Y	Y	N	Y	Y	N
2 Mink	Y	Y	Y	N	Y	Y	N
IDAHO							
1 *Chenoweth*	Y	Y	N	Y	N	Y	Y
2 *Crapo*	Y	Y	N	Y	N	Y	Y
ILLINOIS							
1 Rush	Y	Y	Y	N	Y	Y	N
2 Jackson	Y	Y	Y	N	Y	Y	N
3 Lipinski	Y	Y	N	Y	N	Y	Y
4 Gutierrez	Y	Y	Y	N	Y	Y	N
5 Blagojevich	Y	Y	Y	N	Y	Y	N
6 *Hyde*	?	?	N	Y	N	Y	Y
7 Davis	Y	Y	Y	N	Y	Y	N
8 *Crane*	Y	Y	N	Y	N	Y	Y
9 Yates	Y	Y	Y	N	Y	Y	N
10 *Porter*	Y	Y	N	Y	N	Y	Y
11 *Weller*	Y	Y	N	Y	N	Y	Y
12 Costello	Y	Y	N	Y	N	Y	N

ND Northern Democrats   SD Southern Democrats

	118	119	120	121	122	123	124
13 ***Fawell***	Y	Y	N	Y	N	Y	Y
14 ***Hastert***	Y	Y	N	Y	N	Y	Y
15 ***Ewing***	Y	Y	N	Y	N	Y	Y
16 ***Manzullo***	Y	Y	N	Y	N	Y	Y
17 Evans	Y	Y	Y	N	Y	Y	N
18 ***LaHood***	Y	Y	N	Y	N	Y	Y
19 Poshard	?	?	N	Y	Y	Y	N
20 ***Shimkus***	Y	Y	N	Y	N	Y	Y
INDIANA							
1 Visclosky	Y	Y	N	Y	Y	Y	N
2 ***McIntosh***	Y	Y	N	Y	N	Y	Y
3 Roemer	Y	Y	N	Y	Y	Y	N
4 ***Souder***	Y	Y	N	Y	N	Y	Y
5 ***Buyer***	Y	Y	N	Y	N	Y	Y
6 ***Burton***	Y	Y	N	Y	N	Y	Y
7 ***Pease***	Y	Y	N	Y	N	Y	Y
8 ***Hostettler***	Y	Y	N	Y	N	Y	Y
9 Hamilton	Y	Y	N	Y	Y	Y	N
10 Carson	Y	Y	Y	N	Y	Y	N
IOWA							
1 ***Leach***	Y	Y	N	Y	N	Y	Y
2 ***Nussle***	Y	Y	N	Y	N	Y	Y
3 Boswell	Y	Y	N	Y	Y	Y	N
4 ***Ganske***	Y	Y	N	N	N	Y	Y
5 ***Latham***	Y	Y	N	Y	N	Y	Y
KANSAS							
1 ***Moran***	Y	Y	N	Y	N	Y	Y
2 ***Ryun***	+	+	N	Y	N	Y	Y
3 ***Snowbarger***	Y	Y	N	Y	N	Y	Y
4 ***Tiahrt***	Y	Y	N	Y	N	Y	Y
KENTUCKY							
1 ***Whitfield***	Y	Y	N	Y	N	Y	Y
2 ***Lewis***	Y	Y	N	Y	N	Y	Y
3 ***Northup***	Y	Y	N	Y	N	Y	Y
4 ***Bunning***	Y	Y	N	Y	N	Y	Y
5 ***Rogers***	Y	Y	N	Y	N	Y	Y
6 Baesler	?	?	N	Y	Y	Y	N
LOUISIANA							
1 ***Livingston***	Y	Y	N	Y	N	Y	Y
2 Jefferson	?	?	Y	N	Y	Y	?
3 ***Tauzin***	Y	Y	N	Y	N	Y	Y
4 ***McCrery***	Y	Y	N	Y	N	Y	Y
5 ***Cooksey***	Y	Y	N	N	N	Y	Y
6 ***Baker***	Y	Y	N	Y	N	Y	Y
7 John	Y	Y	N	Y	Y	Y	N
MAINE							
1 Allen	Y	Y	Y	N	Y	Y	N
2 Baldacci	Y	Y	Y	Y	Y	Y	N
MARYLAND							
1 ***Gilchrest***	Y	Y	N	Y	N	Y	Y
2 ***Ehrlich***	Y	Y	N	Y	N	Y	Y
3 Cardin	Y	Y	Y	N	Y	Y	N
4 Wynn	Y	Y	Y	N	Y	Y	N
5 Hoyer	Y	Y	Y	N	Y	Y	N
6 ***Bartlett***	Y	Y	N	Y	N	Y	Y
7 Cummings	Y	Y	Y	N	Y	Y	N
8 ***Morella***	Y	Y	Y	N	N	Y	N
MASSACHUSETTS							
1 Olver	Y	Y	Y	N	Y	Y	N
2 Neal	Y	Y	Y	N	Y	Y	N
3 McGovern	Y	Y	Y	N	Y	Y	N
4 Frank	Y	Y	Y	N	Y	N	N
5 Meehan	Y	Y	Y	N	Y	Y	N
6 Tierney	Y	Y	Y	N	Y	Y	N
7 Markey	Y	Y	Y	N	Y	Y	N
8 Kennedy	Y	Y	Y	N	Y	Y	N
9 Moakley	Y	Y	Y	N	Y	Y	N
10 Delahunt	Y	Y	Y	N	Y	Y	N
MICHIGAN							
1 Stupak	Y	Y	Y	Y	Y	Y	N
2 ***Hoekstra***	Y	Y	N	Y	N	Y	Y
3 ***Ehlers***	Y	Y	N	Y	N	Y	Y
4 ***Camp***	Y	Y	N	Y	N	Y	Y
5 Barcia	Y	Y	N	Y	Y	Y	N
6 ***Upton***	Y	Y	N	Y	N	Y	Y
7 ***Smith***	Y	Y	N	Y	N	Y	Y
8 Stabenow	Y	Y	Y	N	Y	Y	N
9 Kildee	Y	Y	N	Y	Y	Y	N
10 Bonior	Y	Y	Y	N	Y	Y	N
11 ***Knollenberg***	Y	Y	N	Y	N	Y	Y
12 Levin	Y	Y	Y	N	Y	Y	N
13 Rivers	Y	Y	Y	N	Y	Y	N
14 Conyers	Y	Y	Y	N	Y	N	N
15 Kilpatrick	Y	Y	Y	N	Y	Y	N
16 Dingell	Y	Y	Y	N	Y	Y	N

	118	119	120	121	122	123	124
MINNESOTA							
1 ***Gutknecht***	Y	Y	N	Y	N	Y	Y
2 Minge	Y	Y	N	Y	Y	Y	N
3 ***Ramstad***	Y	Y	N	Y	N	Y	Y
4 Vento	Y	Y	Y	N	Y	Y	N
5 Sabo	Y	Y	Y	N	Y	Y	N
6 Luther	Y	Y	N	Y	Y	Y	N
7 Peterson	Y	Y	N	Y	Y	Y	N
8 Oberstar	Y	Y	Y	N	Y	N	N
MISSISSIPPI							
1 ***Wicker***	Y	Y	N	Y	N	Y	Y
2 Thompson	Y	Y	Y	N	Y	Y	N
3 ***Pickering***	Y	Y	N	Y	N	Y	Y
4 ***Parker***	Y	Y	N	Y	N	Y	Y
5 Taylor	Y	Y	N	Y	Y	Y	N
MISSOURI							
1 Clay	Y	Y	Y	N	Y	Y	N
2 ***Talent***	Y	Y	N	Y	N	Y	Y
3 Gephardt	Y	Y	Y	N	?	?	N
4 Skelton	Y	Y	N	Y	Y	Y	N
5 McCarthy	Y	Y	Y	Y	Y	Y	N
6 Danner	Y	Y	N	Y	Y	Y	N
7 ***Blunt***	?	?	N	Y	N	Y	Y
8 ***Emerson***	Y	Y	N	Y	N	Y	Y
9 ***Hulshof***	Y	Y	N	Y	N	Y	Y
MONTANA							
AL ***Hill***	Y	Y	N	Y	N	Y	Y
NEBRASKA							
1 ***Bereuter***	Y	Y	N	Y	N	Y	Y
2 ***Christensen***	?	?	N	Y	N	Y	Y
3 ***Barrett***	Y	Y	N	Y	N	Y	Y
NEVADA							
1 ***Ensign***	?	Y	N	Y	N	Y	Y
2 ***Gibbons***	Y	Y	N	Y	N	Y	Y
NEW HAMPSHIRE							
1 ***Sununu***	Y	Y	N	Y	N	Y	Y
2 ***Bass***	Y	Y	N	Y	N	Y	Y
NEW JERSEY							
1 Andrews	Y	Y	N	Y	Y	Y	N
2 ***LoBiondo***	Y	Y	N	Y	N	Y	Y
3 ***Saxton***	Y	Y	N	Y	N	Y	Y
4 ***Smith***	Y	Y	N	Y	N	Y	Y
5 ***Roukema***	Y	Y	N	Y	N	Y	Y
6 Pallone	Y	Y	Y	Y	Y	Y	N
7 ***Franks***	Y	Y	N	Y	N	Y	Y
8 Pascrell	Y	Y	N	Y	Y	Y	N
9 Rothman	Y	Y	Y	N	Y	Y	N
10 Payne	Y	Y	Y	N	Y	Y	N
11 ***Frelinghuysen***	Y	Y	N	Y	N	Y	Y
12 ***Pappas***	Y	Y	N	Y	N	Y	Y
13 Menendez	Y	Y	Y	N	Y	Y	N
NEW MEXICO							
1 Vacant							
2 ***Skeen***	Y	Y	N	Y	N	Y	Y
3 ***Redmond***	Y	Y	N	Y	N	Y	Y
NEW YORK							
1 ***Forbes***	Y	Y	N	Y	N	Y	Y
2 ***Lazio***	Y	Y	N	Y	N	Y	Y
3 ***King***	Y	Y	N	Y	N	Y	Y
4 McCarthy	Y	Y	Y	N	Y	Y	N
5 Ackerman	Y	Y	Y	N	Y	Y	N
6 Meeks	Y	Y	Y	N	Y	Y	N
7 Manton	Y	Y	Y	N	Y	Y	N
8 Nadler	Y	Y	Y	N	Y	N	N
9 Schumer	Y	Y	Y	N	?	?	N
10 Towns	?	?	Y	N	Y	Y	N
11 Owens	Y	Y	Y	N	Y	Y	N
12 Velázquez	Y	Y	Y	N	Y	Y	N
13 ***Fossella***	Y	Y	N	Y	N	Y	Y
14 Maloney	?	?	Y	N	Y	Y	N
15 Rangel	?	?	Y	N	Y	Y	N
16 Serrano	?	?	Y	N	Y	Y	N
17 Engel	+	+	Y	N	Y	Y	N
18 Lowey	Y	Y	Y	N	Y	Y	N
19 ***Kelly***	Y	Y	N	Y	N	Y	Y
20 ***Gilman***	Y	Y	N	Y	N	Y	Y
21 McNulty	Y	Y	N	Y	Y	Y	N
22 ***Solomon***	Y	Y	N	Y	N	Y	Y
23 ***Boehlert***	Y	Y	Y	N	N	Y	Y
24 ***McHugh***	Y	Y	N	Y	N	Y	Y
25 ***Walsh***	Y	Y	N	Y	N	Y	Y
26 Hinchey	Y	Y	Y	N	Y	Y	N
27 ***Paxon***	Y	Y	N	Y	N	Y	Y
28 Slaughter	Y	Y	Y	N	Y	Y	N
29 LaFalce	Y	Y	N	Y	Y	Y	N

	118	119	120	121	122	123	124
30 ***Quinn***	Y	Y	N	Y	N	Y	Y
31 ***Houghton***	Y	Y	N	Y	N	Y	Y
NORTH CAROLINA							
1 Clayton	Y	Y	Y	N	Y	Y	N
2 Etheridge	Y	Y	N	Y	Y	Y	N
3 ***Jones***	Y	Y	N	Y	N	Y	Y
4 Price	Y	Y	Y	Y	Y	Y	N
5 ***Burr***	Y	Y	N	Y	N	Y	Y
6 ***Coble***	Y	Y	N	Y	N	Y	Y
7 McIntyre	Y	Y	N	Y	Y	Y	N
8 Hefner	Y	Y	Y	Y	Y	Y	N
9 ***Myrick***	Y	Y	N	Y	N	Y	Y
10 ***Ballenger***	Y	Y	N	Y	N	Y	Y
11 ***Taylor***	+	+	N	Y	N	Y	Y
12 Watt	Y	Y	Y	N	Y	Y	N
NORTH DAKOTA							
AL Pomeroy	Y	Y	Y	Y	Y	Y	N
OHIO							
1 ***Chabot***	Y	Y	N	Y	N	Y	Y
2 ***Portman***	Y	Y	N	Y	N	Y	Y
3 Hall	Y	Y	N	Y	Y	Y	N
4 ***Oxley***	Y	Y	N	Y	N	Y	Y
5 ***Gillmor***	Y	Y	N	Y	N	Y	Y
6 Strickland	Y	Y	N	Y	Y	Y	N
7 ***Hobson***	Y	Y	N	Y	N	Y	Y
8 ***Boehner***	Y	Y	N	Y	N	Y	Y
9 Kaptur	Y	Y	N	Y	Y	Y	N
10 Kucinich	Y	Y	Y	N	Y	N	N
11 Stokes	Y	Y	Y	N	Y	Y	N
12 ***Kasich***	Y	Y	N	Y	N	Y	Y
13 Brown	Y	Y	Y	N	Y	Y	N
14 Sawyer	Y	Y	Y	N	Y	Y	N
15 ***Pryce***	Y	Y	N	Y	N	Y	Y
16 ***Regula***	Y	Y	N	Y	N	Y	Y
17 Traficant	Y	Y	N	Y	Y	Y	Y
18 ***Ney***	Y	Y	N	Y	N	Y	Y
19 ***LaTourette***	Y	Y	N	Y	N	Y	Y
OKLAHOMA							
1 ***Largent***	Y	Y	N	Y	N	Y	Y
2 ***Coburn***	Y	Y	N	Y	N	Y	Y
3 ***Watkins***	Y	Y	N	Y	N	Y	Y
4 ***Watts***	Y	Y	N	Y	N	Y	Y
5 ***Istook***	Y	Y	N	Y	N	Y	Y
6 ***Lucas***	Y	Y	N	Y	N	Y	Y
OREGON							
1 Furse	Y	Y	Y	N	Y	Y	N
2 ***Smith***	?	?	?	?	?	?	?
3 Blumenauer	Y	Y	Y	N	Y	Y	N
4 DeFazio	Y	Y	Y	N	Y	Y	N
5 Hooley	Y	Y	Y	N	Y	Y	N
PENNSYLVANIA							
1 Vacant							
2 Fattah	Y	Y	Y	N	Y	Y	N
3 Borski	Y	Y	Y	N	Y	Y	N
4 Klink	Y	Y	Y	Y	Y	Y	N
5 ***Peterson***	Y	Y	N	Y	N	Y	Y
6 Holden	Y	Y	N	Y	Y	Y	N
7 ***Weldon***	Y	Y	N	Y	N	Y	Y
8 ***Greenwood***	Y	Y	Y	N	N	Y	Y
9 ***Shuster***	Y	Y	N	Y	N	Y	Y
10 ***McDade***	Y	Y	N	Y	N	Y	Y
11 Kanjorski	Y	Y	Y	N	Y	Y	N
12 Murtha	Y	Y	N	Y	Y	Y	N
13 ***Fox***	Y	Y	N	Y	N	Y	Y
14 Coyne	Y	Y	Y	N	Y	Y	N
15 McHale	Y	Y	Y	N	Y	Y	N
16 ***Pitts***	Y	Y	N	Y	N	Y	Y
17 ***Gekas***	?	Y	N	Y	N	Y	Y
18 Doyle	Y	Y	N	Y	Y	Y	N
19 ***Goodling***	Y	Y	N	Y	N	Y	Y
20 Mascara	Y	Y	N	Y	Y	Y	N
21 ***English***	Y	Y	N	Y	N	Y	Y
RHODE ISLAND							
1 Kennedy	Y	Y	Y	N	Y	Y	N
2 Weygand	Y	Y	Y	N	Y	Y	N
SOUTH CAROLINA							
1 ***Sanford***	Y	Y	N	Y	N	Y	Y
2 ***Spence***	Y	Y	N	Y	N	Y	Y
3 ***Graham***	Y	Y	N	Y	N	Y	Y
4 ***Inglis***	?	?	N	Y	N	Y	Y
5 Spratt	Y	Y	N	Y	Y	Y	N
6 Clyburn	Y	Y	Y	N	Y	Y	N
SOUTH DAKOTA							
AL ***Thune***	Y	Y	N	Y	N	Y	Y

	118	119	120	121	122	123	124
TENNESSEE							
1 ***Jenkins***	Y	Y	N	Y	N	Y	Y
2 ***Duncan***	Y	Y	N	Y	N	Y	Y
3 ***Wamp***	Y	Y	N	Y	N	Y	Y
4 ***Hilleary***	Y	Y	N	Y	N	Y	Y
5 Clement	Y	Y	N	Y	Y	Y	N
6 Gordon	Y	Y	N	Y	Y	Y	N
7 ***Bryant***	Y	Y	N	Y	N	Y	Y
8 Tanner	?	Y	N	Y	Y	Y	N
9 Ford	Y	Y	N	Y	Y	Y	N
TEXAS							
1 Sandlin	?	?	?	?	?	?	?
2 Turner	Y	Y	N	Y	Y	Y	N
3 ***Johnson, Sam***	Y	Y	N	Y	N	Y	Y
4 Hall	Y	Y	N	Y	Y	Y	?
5 ***Sessions***	Y	Y	N	Y	N	Y	Y
6 ***Barton***	Y	Y	N	Y	N	Y	Y
7 ***Archer***	Y	Y	N	Y	N	Y	Y
8 ***Brady***	Y	Y	N	Y	N	Y	Y
9 Lampson	Y	Y	N	Y	Y	Y	N
10 Doggett	Y	Y	Y	N	Y	Y	N
11 Edwards	Y	Y	N	Y	Y	Y	N
12 ***Granger***	Y	Y	N	Y	N	Y	Y
13 ***Thornberry***	Y	Y	N	Y	N	Y	Y
14 ***Paul***	Y	Y	N	Y	N	N	Y
15 Hinojosa	Y	Y	Y	N	Y	Y	N
16 Reyes	Y	Y	Y	Y	Y	Y	N
17 Stenholm	Y	Y	N	Y	Y	Y	N
18 Jackson-Lee	Y	Y	Y	N	Y	Y	N
19 ***Combest***	Y	Y	N	Y	N	Y	Y
20 Gonzalez	?	?	?	?	?	?	?
21 ***Smith***	Y	Y	N	Y	N	Y	Y
22 ***DeLay***	Y	Y	N	Y	N	Y	Y
23 ***Bonilla***	Y	Y	N	Y	N	Y	Y
24 Frost	Y	Y	N	Y	Y	Y	N
25 Bentsen	Y	Y	N	Y	Y	Y	N
26 ***Armey***	Y	Y	N	Y	N	Y	Y
27 Ortiz	Y	Y	N	Y	Y	Y	N
28 Rodriguez	Y	Y	Y	Y	Y	Y	N
29 Green	Y	Y	N	Y	Y	Y	N
30 Johnson, E.B.	Y	Y	Y	N	Y	Y	N
UTAH							
1 ***Hansen***	Y	Y	N	Y	N	Y	Y
2 ***Cook***	?	?	?	Y	N	Y	Y
3 ***Cannon***	Y	Y	N	Y	N	Y	Y
VERMONT							
AL *Sanders*	Y	Y	Y	N	Y	N	N
VIRGINIA							
1 ***Bateman***	+	+	–	+	–	+	+
2 Pickett	Y	Y	N	Y	Y	Y	N
3 Scott	Y	Y	Y	N	Y	Y	N
4 Sisisky	Y	Y	N	Y	Y	Y	N
5 Goode	Y	Y	N	Y	Y	Y	N
6 ***Goodlatte***	Y	Y	N	Y	N	Y	Y
7 ***Bliley***	Y	Y	N	Y	N	Y	Y
8 Moran	Y	Y	Y	N	Y	Y	N
9 Boucher	Y	Y	N	Y	Y	Y	N
10 ***Wolf***	Y	Y	N	Y	N	Y	Y
11 ***Davis***	Y	Y	N	Y	N	Y	Y
WASHINGTON							
1 ***White***	?	?	N	Y	N	Y	Y
2 ***Metcalf***	Y	Y	N	Y	N	Y	Y
3 ***Smith, Linda***	Y	Y	N	Y	N	Y	Y
4 ***Hastings***	Y	Y	N	Y	N	Y	Y
5 ***Nethercutt***	Y	Y	N	Y	N	Y	Y
6 Dicks	Y	Y	Y	N	Y	Y	N
7 McDermott	Y	Y	Y	N	Y	Y	N
8 ***Dunn***	Y	Y	N	Y	N	Y	Y
9 Smith, Adam	Y	Y	Y	N	Y	Y	N
WEST VIRGINIA							
1 Mollohan	Y	Y	N	Y	Y	Y	N
2 Wise	Y	Y	N	Y	+	+	N
3 Rahall	Y	Y	N	Y	Y	Y	N
WISCONSIN							
1 ***Neumann***	Y	Y	N	Y	N	Y	Y
2 ***Klug***	Y	Y	N	Y	N	Y	Y
3 Kind	Y	Y	N	Y	Y	Y	N
4 Kleczka	Y	Y	N	Y	Y	Y	N
5 Barrett	Y	Y	Y	N	Y	Y	N
6 ***Petri***	Y	Y	N	Y	N	Y	Y
7 Obey	Y	Y	Y	N	Y	Y	N
8 Johnson	Y	Y	N	Y	Y	Y	N
9 ***Sensenbrenner***	Y	Y	N	Y	N	Y	Y
WYOMING							
AL ***Cubin***	Y	Y	N	Y	N	Y	Y

Southern states - Ala., Ark., Fla., Ga., Ky., La., Miss., N.C., Okla., S.C., Tenn., Texas, Va.

125. H Con Res 220. Extradite Palestinian Terrorists/Adoption. Gilman, R-N.Y., motion to suspend the rules and adopt the resolution to express the sense of Congress that the United States should demand that Yasir Arafat and the Palestinian Authority transfer to the United States for prosecution those residents of its territory who are suspected in the killings of American citizens. Motion agreed to 406-0: R 216-0; D 189-0 (ND 137-0, SD 52-0); I 1-0. May 5, 1998. A two-thirds majority of those present and voting (271 in this case) is required for adoption under suspension of the rules.

126. H Res 267. Drug-Free Schools/Adoption. Souder, R-Ind., motion to suspend the rules and adopt the resolution to express the sense of the House that all schools should be drug-free. Motion agreed to 408-1: R 218-1; D 189-0 (ND 137-0, SD 52-0); I 1-0. May 5, 1998. A two-thirds majority of those present and voting (273 in this case) is required for adoption under suspension of the rules.

127. HR 1872. Communications Satellite Privatization/Takings. Morella, R-Md., amendment to require that in implementing market access restrictions the FCC does not restrict Comsat in a manner that would create a liability under the takings clause of the Constitution. Rejected 111-304: R 50-167; D 61-136 (ND 47-97, SD 14-39); I 0-1. May 6, 1998.

128. HR 1872. Communications Satellite Privatization/Fresh Look. Tauzin, R-La., amendment to eliminate the "fresh look" provisions of the bill that permit a customer that is locked into a long-term business agreement with a telecommunications carrier to take a fresh look at more competitive alternatives. Rejected 80-339: R 41-179; D 39-159 (ND 29-116, SD 10-43); I 0-1. May 6, 1998.

129. HR 1872. Communications Satellite Privatization/Passage. Passage of the bill to establish a timeline and conditions for the privatization of Intelsat and Inmarsat, calling for Inmarsat to be privatized by 2001 and Intelsat by 2002. Passed 403-16: R 219-1; D 183-15 (ND 133-12, SD 50-3); I 1-0. May 6, 1998.

130. HR 6. Higher Education Act Reauthorization/College Sports. Roemer, D-Ind., amendment to eliminate the provision of the bill that requires colleges and universities to report planned elimination of college sport four years in advance of the reduction and to justify that decision. Adopted 292-129: R 98-124; D 193-5 (ND 141-5, SD 52-0); I 1-0. May 6, 1998.

131. HR 6. Higher Education Act Reauthorization/Labor Codes. Miller, D-Calif., amendment to state the sense of Congress that all American colleges and universities should adopt rigorous labor codes of conduct to assure that university and college licensed merchandise is not made by sweatshop and exploited adult or child labor either domestically or abroad. Adopted 393-28: R 195-27; D 197-1 (ND 146-0, SD 51-1); I 1-0. May 6, 1998.

Key

Y	Voted for (yea).
#	Paired for.
+	Announced for.
N	Voted against (nay).
X	Paired against.
-	Announced against.
P	Voted "present."
C	Voted "present" to avoid possible conflict of interest.
?	Did not vote or otherwise make a position known.

Democrats • ***Republicans***
Independent

	125	126	127	128	129	130	131
ALABAMA							
1 *Callahan*	N	Y	Y	Y	Y	N	N
2 *Everett*	N	Y	Y	N	Y	N	N
3 *Riley*	N	Y	Y	N	N	N	N
4 *Aderholt*	N	Y	Y	Y	Y	Y	N
5 Cramer	Y	N	Y	N	N	N	N
6 *Bachus*	N	Y	Y	Y	N	N	N
7 Hilliard	Y	N	N	N	N	Y	Y
ALASKA							
AL *Young*	X	N	Y	N	Y	N	N
ARIZONA							
1 *Salmon*	N	Y	Y	Y	N	N	N
2 Pastor	Y	N	N	N	Y	Y	Y
3 *Stump*	N	Y	Y	N	Y	N	N
4 *Shadegg*	N	Y	Y	N	Y	N	N
5 *Kolbe*	N	Y	Y	Y	N	N	N
6 *Hayworth*	N	Y	Y	Y	Y	N	N
ARKANSAS							
1 Berry	Y	N	N	N	Y	Y	Y
2 Snyder	Y	N	N	Y	Y	Y	Y
3 *Hutchinson*	N	N	Y	Y	N	N	N
4 *Dickey*	N	Y	Y	Y	N	N	N
CALIFORNIA							
1 *Riggs*	N	Y	Y	Y	N	N	N
2 *Herger*	N	Y	Y	Y	Y	N	N
3 Fazio	Y	N	N	N	N	Y	Y
4 *Doolittle*	N	Y	Y	Y	Y	N	N
5 Matsui	Y	N	N	N	N	Y	Y
6 Woolsey	Y	N	N	N	Y	Y	Y
7 Miller	Y	N	?	N	Y	Y	Y
8 Pelosi	Y	N	N	N	N	Y	Y
9 Lee	Y	N	N	N	N	Y	Y
10 Tauscher	Y	N	N	Y	Y	Y	Y
11 *Pombo*	N	Y	Y	Y	Y	N	N
12 Lantos	Y	N	N	?	?	?	
13 Stark	Y	N	N	N	N	Y	Y
14 Eshoo	Y	N	N	N	N	Y	Y
15 *Campbell*	N	Y	Y	N	Y	Y	Y
16 Lofgren	Y	N	N	N	Y	Y	Y
17 Farr	Y	N	N	N	N	Y	Y
18 Condit	Y	Y	N	Y	Y	N	Y
19 *Radanovich*	N	Y	?	N	N	N	N
20 Dooley	Y	N	N	Y	N	N	Y
21 *Thomas*	N	Y	Y	N	N	N	N
22 Capps, L.	Y	N	N	P	N	Y	Y
23 *Gallegly*	N	Y	Y	N	N	N	N
24 Sherman	Y	N	N	N	N	Y	Y
25 *McKeon*	N	Y	Y	Y	N	N	N
26 Berman	Y	N	N	?	N	Y	Y
27 *Rogan*	N	Y	Y	Y	N	N	Y
28 *Dreier*	N	Y	Y	Y	N	N	N
29 Waxman	Y	N	N	N	?	?	Y
30 Becerra	Y	N	N	N	?	?	Y
31 Martinez	Y	N	N	N	N	Y	Y
32 Dixon	?	?	?	?	N	Y	Y
33 Roybal-Allard	Y	N	N	N	N	Y	Y
34 Torres	Y	N	N	N	?	Y	Y
35 Waters	Y	N	N	N	?	Y	Y
36 Harman	Y	N	N	Y	?	?	?
37 Millender-McD.	Y	N	N	N	N	Y	Y

	125	126	127	128	129	130	131
38 *Horn*	N	Y	Y	Y	N	N	Y
39 *Royce*	N	Y	Y	N	N	N	N
40 *Lewis*	N	Y	Y	N	N	N	N
41 *Kim*	N	Y	Y	N	N	N	N
42 Brown	Y	?	N	N	N	N	Y
43 *Calvert*	N	Y	Y	N	N	N	N
44 *Bono, M.*	N	Y	Y	P	N	N	N
45 *Rohrabacher*	N	Y	Y	N	N	N	N
46 Sanchez	Y	N	N	Y	N	Y	Y
47 *Cox*	N	Y	Y	N	N	N	N
48 *Packard*	N	Y	Y	Y	N	N	N
49 *Bilbray*	N	Y	Y	N	N	N	Y
50 Filner	Y	N	N	N	N	Y	Y
51 *Cunningham*	N	Y	Y	Y	N	N	N
52 *Hunter*	N	Y	Y	Y	N	N	N
COLORADO							
1 DeGette	Y	N	N	N	N	Y	Y
2 Skaggs	Y	N	N	-	+	-	
3 *McInnis*	N	Y	Y	Y	N	N	N
4 *Schaffer*	N	Y	Y	Y	N	N	N
5 *Hefley*	N	Y	Y	Y	Y	N	N
6 *Schaefer*	N	Y	?	?	?	?	?
CONNECTICUT							
1 Kennelly	#	X	?	?	N	Y	Y
2 Gejdenson	Y	N	N	N	N	Y	Y
3 DeLauro	Y	N	N	N	N	Y	Y
4 *Shays*	N	Y	Y	N	N	Y	Y
5 Maloney	Y	N	N	N	N	Y	Y
6 *Johnson*	N	N	Y	N	N	Y	Y
DELAWARE							
AL *Castle*	N	Y	Y	N	N	N	N
FLORIDA							
1 *Scarborough*	N	Y	Y	Y	N	N	Y
2 Boyd	Y	Y	N	N	N	Y	Y
3 Brown	Y	N	N	N	N	Y	Y
4 *Fowler*	N	Y	Y	N	N	N	N
5 Thurman	Y	N	N	N	N	Y	Y
6 *Stearns*	Y	Y	Y	N	N	N	N
7 *Mica*	N	Y	Y	N	N	N	N
8 *McCollum*	N	Y	Y	N	N	N	N
9 *Bilirakis*	N	Y	Y	N	N	N	N
10 *Young*	N	Y	Y	N	N	N	N
11 Davis	Y	N	N	N	N	Y	Y
12 *Canady*	N	Y	Y	N	N	N	N
13 *Miller*	N	Y	Y	N	N	N	N
14 *Goss*	N	Y	Y	N	N	N	N
15 *Weldon*	N	Y	Y	N	N	N	N
16 *Foley*	N	Y	Y	Y	N	N	N
17 Meek	#	X	?	N	N	Y	Y
18 *Ros-Lehtinen*	N	Y	Y	N	N	N	N
19 Wexler	Y	N	N	N	N	Y	Y
20 Deutsch	Y	N	N	N	N	Y	Y
21 *Diaz-Balart*	N	Y	Y	N	N	N	N
22 *Shaw*	N	Y	Y	Y	N	N	N
23 Hastings	Y	N	N	N	?	?	?
GEORGIA							
1 *Kingston*	N	Y	Y	Y	N	N	N
2 Bishop	Y	N	N	Y	N	N	N
3 *Collins*	N	Y	Y	Y	N	N	N
4 McKinney	Y	N	N	Y	Y	Y	Y
5 Lewis	Y	N	N	N	N	Y	Y
6 *Gingrich*	N	Y					
7 *Barr*	N	Y	Y	Y	N	N	N
8 *Chambliss*	N	Y	Y	Y	N	N	N
9 *Deal*	N	Y	Y	Y	N	N	N
10 *Norwood*	N	Y	Y	Y	N	N	N
11 *Linder*	N	Y	Y	Y	N	N	N
HAWAII							
1 Abercrombie	Y	N	N	N	N	Y	Y
2 Mink	Y	N	N	N	N	Y	Y
IDAHO							
1 *Chenoweth*	N	Y	Y	Y	Y	N	Y
2 *Crapo*	N	N	?	N	Y	Y	Y
ILLINOIS							
1 Rush	Y	N	N	N	N	Y	Y
2 Jackson	Y	N	N	N	Y	Y	Y
3 Lipinski	Y	Y	N	N	N	N	N
4 Gutierrez	Y	N	N	N	N	Y	Y
5 Blagojevich	Y	N	N	N	Y	Y	Y
6 *Hyde*	N	Y	Y	Y	Y	N	N
7 Davis	Y	N	N	-	+	+	
8 *Crane*	N	Y	Y	Y	N	N	N
9 Yates	Y	N	N	N	N	Y	Y
10 *Porter*	Y	N	N	N	N	Y	N
11 *Weller*	N	Y	Y	Y	N	N	N
12 Costello	Y	N	N	N	N	Y	Y

ND Northern Democrats   SD Southern Democrats

	125	126	127	128	129	130	131
13 ***Fawell***	N	N	?	Y	N	N	N
14 ***Hastert***	N	Y	Y	Y	N	N	N
15 ***Ewing***	N	Y	Y	Y	N	N	N
16 ***Manzullo***	N	Y	Y	Y	Y	N	N
17 Evans	Y	N	N	Y	N	Y	Y
18 ***LaHood***	N	Y	Y	Y	N	N	N
19 Poshard	Y	N	N	N	N	Y	Y
20 ***Shimkus***	N	Y	Y	Y	Y	N	N
INDIANA							
1 Visclosky	Y	N	N	N	–	+	+
2 ***McIntosh***	N	Y	Y	Y	Y	N	N
3 Roemer	Y	N	N	N	N	Y	Y
4 ***Souder***	N	Y	Y	N	Y	N	N
5 ***Buyer***	N	Y	Y	Y	N	N	Y
6 ***Burton***	N	Y	Y	Y	N	N	N
7 ***Pease***	N	Y	Y	Y	Y	N	Y
8 ***Hostettler***	N	Y	Y	Y	Y	N	N
9 Hamilton	Y	N	N	N	N	Y	Y
10 Carson	Y	N	N	N	–	+	+
IOWA							
1 ***Leach***	N	N	Y	Y	N	N	Y
2 ***Nussle***	N	Y	Y	N	Y	N	Y
3 Boswell	Y	N	N	N	N	N	Y
4 ***Ganske***	N	Y	Y	Y	N	N	N
5 ***Latham***	N	Y	Y	Y	?	N	N
KANSAS							
1 ***Moran***	N	Y	Y	Y	Y	N	N
2 ***Ryun***	N	Y	Y	Y	Y	N	N
3 ***Snowbarger***	N	Y	Y	Y	Y	N	N
4 ***Tiahrt***	N	Y	Y	Y	Y	N	N
KENTUCKY							
1 ***Whitfield***	N	Y	Y	Y	N	N	N
2 ***Lewis***	N	Y	Y	Y	Y	N	N
3 ***Northup***	N	Y	Y	Y	Y	N	N
4 ***Bunning***	?	#	?	#	Y	N	N
5 ***Rogers***	N	Y	Y	Y	N	N	N
6 Baesler	Y	N	N	N	N	Y	Y
LOUISIANA							
1 ***Livingston***	N	Y	Y	Y	Y	N	N
2 Jefferson	Y	N	N	Y	N	Y	Y
3 ***Tauzin***	N	Y	Y	Y	?	?	?
4 ***McCrery***	N	Y	Y	Y	N	N	N
5 ***Cooksey***	N	Y	Y	Y	Y	N	N
6 ***Baker***	N	Y	Y	?	N	N	N
7 John	Y	N	N	Y	N	N	Y
MAINE							
1 Allen	Y	N	N	Y	N	Y	Y
2 Baldacci	Y	N	N	Y	N	Y	Y
MARYLAND							
1 ***Gilchrest***	N	Y	Y	Y	N	N	Y
2 ***Ehrlich***	N	Y	Y	Y	N	N	N
3 Cardin	Y	N	N	N	N	Y	Y
4 Wynn	Y	N	N	N	N	Y	Y
5 Hoyer	Y	N	N	N	N	Y	Y
6 ***Bartlett***	N	Y	Y	Y	Y	N	N
7 Cummings	Y	N	N	N	N	Y	Y
8 ***Morella***	Y	N	Y	N	N	Y	Y
MASSACHUSETTS							
1 Olver	Y	N	N	N	N	Y	Y
2 Neal	Y	N	N	N	N	Y	Y
3 McGovern	Y	N	N	N	N	Y	Y
4 Frank	Y	N	N	N	Y	Y	Y
5 Meehan	Y	N	?	?	N	Y	Y
6 Tierney	Y	N	N	N	N	Y	Y
7 Markey	Y	N	N	N	N	Y	Y
8 Kennedy	Y	N	N	N	N	Y	Y
9 Moakley	Y	N	N	N	N	Y	Y
10 Delahunt	Y	N	N	N	N	Y	Y
MICHIGAN							
1 Stupak	Y	N	N	N	N	Y	Y
2 ***Hoekstra***	N	Y	Y	N	Y	N	N
3 ***Ehlers***	N	Y	Y	N	Y	N	N
4 ***Camp***	N	Y	Y	N	Y	N	N
5 Barcia	Y	N	N	N	Y	Y	Y
6 ***Upton***	N	Y	Y	N	N	N	N
7 ***Smith***	X	#	?	?	Y	N	N
8 Stabenow	Y	N	N	N	N	Y	Y
9 Kildee	Y	N	N	N	N	Y	Y
10 Bonior	Y	N	N	N	Y	Y	Y
11 ***Knollenberg***	N	Y	Y	Y	N	N	N
12 Levin	Y	N	N	N	N	Y	Y
13 Rivers	Y	N	N	N	N	Y	Y
14 Conyers	Y	N	N	N	N	Y	Y
15 Kilpatrick	Y	N	N	N	N	Y	Y
16 Dingell	Y	N	N	N	N	Y	N

	125	126	127	128	129	130	131
MINNESOTA							
1 ***Gutknecht***	N	Y	Y	Y	N	N	N
2 Minge	Y	N	N	Y	N	Y	Y
3 ***Ramstad***	Y	N	Y	Y	N	N	Y
4 Vento	Y	N	N	N	N	Y	Y
5 Sabo	Y	N	N	N	N	N	Y
6 Luther	Y	N	N	N	N	Y	Y
7 Peterson	Y	N	N	Y	N	N	Y
8 Oberstar	Y	N	N	N	N	Y	Y
MISSISSIPPI							
1 ***Wicker***	N	Y	Y	Y	Y	N	N
2 Thompson	Y	N	N	?	N	Y	Y
3 ***Pickering***	N	Y	Y	Y	Y	N	N
4 ***Parker***	?	?	?	?	?	?	?
5 Taylor	N	Y	N	Y	N	N	Y
MISSOURI							
1 Clay	Y	N	N	N	N	Y	Y
2 ***Talent***	N	Y	Y	Y	N	N	N
3 Gephardt	Y	N	N	N	Y	Y	Y
4 Skelton	Y	N	N	N	N	N	Y
5 McCarthy	Y	N	N	N	N	Y	Y
6 Danner	Y	N	N	N	N	Y	Y
7 ***Blunt***	N	Y	Y	Y	N	N	N
8 ***Emerson***	N	Y	Y	Y	Y	N	Y
9 ***Hulshof***	N	Y	Y	Y	Y	N	N
MONTANA							
AL ***Hill***	N	Y	Y	Y	Y	N	N
NEBRASKA							
1 ***Bereuter***	N	Y	Y	Y	N	N	N
2 ***Christensen***	N	Y	Y	Y	?	?	?
3 ***Barrett***	N	Y	Y	Y	N	N	N
NEVADA							
1 ***Ensign***	N	Y	Y	Y	Y	N	N
2 ***Gibbons***	N	Y	Y	Y	Y	N	N
NEW HAMPSHIRE							
1 ***Sununu***	N	Y	Y	Y	Y	N	N
2 ***Bass***	N	Y	Y	Y	N	N	Y
NEW JERSEY							
1 Andrews	Y	N	N	N	N	Y	Y
2 ***LoBiondo***	N	N	Y	Y	N	N	Y
3 ***Saxton***	N	Y	Y	Y	N	N	N
4 ***Smith***	N	Y	Y	Y	N	N	Y
5 ***Roukema***	N	N	Y	Y	N	N	N
6 Pallone	Y	N	N	N	N	Y	Y
7 ***Franks***	N	Y	Y	Y	N	N	N
8 Pascrell	Y	N	N	N	N	Y	Y
9 Rothman	Y	N	N	N	N	Y	Y
10 Payne	Y	N	N	N	N	Y	Y
11 ***Frelinghuysen***	N	Y	Y	Y	N	N	N
12 ***Pappas***	N	Y	Y	Y	N	N	Y
13 Menendez	Y	N	N	N	?	Y	Y
NEW MEXICO							
1 Vacant							
2 ***Skeen***	N	Y	Y	Y	N	N	Y
3 ***Redmond***	N	Y	Y	Y	Y	N	Y
NEW YORK							
1 ***Forbes***	N	Y	Y	Y	–	–	–
2 ***Lazio***	N	Y	Y	Y	N	N	Y
3 ***King***	N	Y	Y	Y	N	N	Y
4 McCarthy	Y	N	N	Y	N	Y	Y
5 Ackerman	Y	N	N	N	N	Y	Y
6 Meeks	Y	N	N	N	?	?	?
7 Manton	Y	N	N	Y	N	Y	Y
8 Nadler	Y	N	N	N	N	Y	Y
9 Schumer	Y	N	N	N	N	Y	Y
10 Towns	Y	N	N	N	N	Y	Y
11 Owens	Y	N	N	N	N	Y	Y
12 Velázquez	Y	N	N	N	N	Y	Y
13 ***Fossella***	N	Y	Y	Y	?	?	?
14 Maloney	Y	N	N	?	N	Y	Y
15 Rangel	Y	N	N	N	N	Y	Y
16 Serrano	Y	N	N	N	N	Y	Y
17 Engel	Y	N	N	N	N	Y	Y
18 Lowey	Y	N	N	N	?	?	?
19 ***Kelly***	N	Y	Y	Y	Y	N	N
20 ***Gilman***	N	Y	Y	Y	N	N	N
21 McNulty	Y	N	N	N	?	?	?
22 ***Solomon***	N	Y	Y	Y	N	N	N
23 ***Boehlert***	N	N	Y	Y	N	N	N
24 ***McHugh***	?	N	Y	Y	N	N	N
25 ***Walsh***	N	Y	Y	Y	N	N	N
26 Hinchey	Y	N	N	N	Y	Y	Y
27 ***Paxon***	N	Y	Y	?	N	N	N
28 Slaughter	Y	N	N	N	N	Y	Y
29 LaFalce	Y	N	N	N	N	Y	Y

	125	126	127	128	129	130	131
30 ***Quinn***	N	Y	Y	Y	N	N	N
31 ***Houghton***	N	Y	Y	Y	N	N	N
NORTH CAROLINA							
1 Clayton	Y	N	N	N	N	Y	Y
2 Etheridge	Y	N	N	Y	N	Y	Y
3 ***Jones***	N	Y	Y	Y	N	N	N
4 Price	Y	N	N	N	N	Y	Y
5 ***Burr***	N	Y	Y	Y	N	N	N
6 ***Coble***	N	Y	Y	N	N	N	N
7 McIntyre	Y	N	N	Y	N	Y	Y
8 Hefner	Y	N	N	N	N	Y	Y
9 ***Myrick***	N	Y	Y	Y	N	N	N
10 ***Ballenger***	N	Y	Y	Y	N	N	N
11 ***Taylor***	N	Y	Y	Y	N	N	N
12 Watt	Y	N	N	N	N	Y	Y
NORTH DAKOTA							
AL Pomeroy	Y	N	N	Y	N	Y	Y
OHIO							
1 ***Chabot***	N	Y	Y	Y	Y	N	N
2 ***Portman***	N	Y	Y	Y	Y	N	N
3 Hall	Y	N	N	N	N	Y	Y
4 ***Oxley***	N	Y	Y	Y	N	N	N
5 ***Gillmor***	N	Y	Y	Y	Y	N	N
6 Strickland	Y	N	N	Y	N	Y	Y
7 ***Hobson***	N	Y	Y	Y	Y	N	N
8 ***Boehner***	N	+	Y	Y	Y	N	N
9 Kaptur	Y	N	?	N	?	?	?
10 Kucinich	Y	N	N	N	Y	Y	Y
11 Stokes	Y	N	N	N	?	?	?
12 ***Kasich***	N	Y	Y	Y	Y	N	N
13 Brown	Y	N	N	N	N	Y	Y
14 Sawyer	Y	N	N	N	N	Y	Y
15 ***Pryce***	N	Y	Y	Y	Y	N	N
16 ***Regula***	N	Y	Y	Y	Y	N	N
17 Traficant	Y	N	N	Y	N	N	Y
18 ***Ney***	N	Y	Y	Y	Y	N	N
19 ***LaTourette***	N	Y	Y	Y	N	N	N
OKLAHOMA							
1 ***Largent***	N	Y	Y	Y	Y	N	N
2 ***Coburn***	N	Y	Y	Y	Y	N	N
3 ***Watkins***	N	Y	Y	Y	Y	N	Y
4 ***Watts***	N	Y	Y	Y	Y	N	Y
5 ***Istook***	N	Y	Y	Y	N	N	N
6 ***Lucas***	N	Y	Y	Y	Y	N	N
OREGON							
1 Furse	Y	N	N	N	?	?	?
2 ***Smith***	N	Y	?	Y	N	N	N
3 Blumenauer	Y	N	N	N	N	Y	Y
4 DeFazio	Y	N	?	X	Y	Y	Y
5 Hooley	Y	N	N	N	N	Y	Y
PENNSYLVANIA							
1 Vacant							
2 Fattah	Y	N	N	N	N	Y	Y
3 Borski	Y	N	N	N	N	Y	Y
4 Klink	Y	N	N	N	N	Y	Y
5 ***Peterson***	N	Y	Y	Y	N	N	N
6 Holden	Y	N	N	Y	N	Y	Y
7 ***Weldon***	N	Y	?	Y	N	N	N
8 ***Greenwood***	N	Y	?	?	N	N	N
9 ***Shuster***	N	Y	Y	Y	N	N	N
10 ***McDade***	N	Y	Y	Y	N	N	N
11 Kanjorski	Y	N	N	N	Y	N	Y
12 Murtha	Y	N	N	N	N	Y	Y
13 ***Fox***	N	Y	Y	Y	N	N	Y
14 Coyne	Y	N	N	N	N	Y	Y
15 McHale	Y	N	N	Y	N	Y	Y
16 ***Pitts***	N	Y	Y	Y	N	N	N
17 ***Gekas***	N	Y	Y	Y	N	N	N
18 Doyle	Y	N	N	Y	N	Y	Y
19 ***Goodling***	N	Y	Y	Y	N	N	N
20 Mascara	Y	N	N	Y	N	Y	Y
21 ***English***	N	N	Y	Y	N	N	N
RHODE ISLAND							
1 Kennedy	Y	N	N	N	N	Y	Y
2 Weygand	Y	N	N	N	N	Y	Y
SOUTH CAROLINA							
1 ***Sanford***	N	Y	Y	N	Y	N	N
2 ***Spence***	N	Y	Y	Y	N	N	N
3 ***Graham***	N	Y	Y	Y	N	N	N
4 ***Inglis***	N	Y	Y	N	Y	N	N
5 Spratt	Y	N	N	N	N	Y	Y
6 Clyburn	Y	N	N	N	?	?	?
SOUTH DAKOTA							
AL ***Thune***	N	Y	Y	Y	Y	N	N

	125	126	127	128	129	130	131
TENNESSEE							
1 ***Jenkins***	N	Y	Y	Y	N	N	N
2 ***Duncan***	N	Y	Y	N	Y	N	N
3 ***Wamp***	N	Y	Y	Y	Y	N	N
4 ***Hilleary***	N	Y	Y	Y	N	N	N
5 Clement	Y	N	N	Y	N	Y	Y
6 Gordon	Y	N	N	Y	N	Y	Y
7 ***Bryant***	N	Y	Y	Y	N	N	N
8 Tanner	Y	N	N	Y	N	N	Y
9 Ford	Y	N	N	N	N	Y	Y
TEXAS							
1 Sandlin	?	?	?	?	N	Y	Y
2 Turner	Y	N	N	Y	N	N	Y
3 ***Johnson, Sam***	N	Y	?	Y	Y	N	N
4 Hall	N	?	?	?	Y	N	N
5 ***Sessions***	N	Y	Y	Y	Y	N	N
6 ***Barton***	N	Y	Y	Y	Y	N	N
7 ***Archer***	N	Y	Y	Y	Y	N	N
8 ***Brady***	N	Y	Y	Y	Y	N	N
9 Lampson	Y	N	N	N	N	Y	Y
10 Doggett	Y	N	N	N	N	Y	Y
11 Edwards	Y	N	N	Y	N	N	Y
12 ***Granger***	N	Y	Y	Y	N	N	N
13 ***Thornberry***	N	Y	Y	Y	Y	N	N
14 ***Paul***	N	P	Y	N	Y	N	N
15 Hinojosa	Y	N	N	N	N	Y	Y
16 Reyes	Y	N	N	Y	N	Y	Y
17 Stenholm	Y	N	N	Y	N	N	Y
18 Jackson-Lee	Y	N	N	N	N	Y	Y
19 ***Combest***	N	Y	Y	Y	N	N	N
20 Gonzalez	?	?	?	?	?	?	?
21 ***Smith***	N	Y	Y	Y	N	N	N
22 ***DeLay***	N	Y	Y	Y	Y	N	N
23 ***Bonilla***	N	Y	Y	Y	Y	N	N
24 Frost	Y	N	N	Y	N	Y	Y
25 Bentsen	Y	N	N	N	N	Y	Y
26 ***Armey***	N	Y	Y	Y	Y	N	N
27 Ortiz	Y	N	N	Y	N	Y	Y
28 Rodriguez	Y	N	N	Y	N	Y	Y
29 Green	Y	N	N	X	N	Y	Y
30 Johnson, E.B.	Y	N	N	N	N	Y	Y
UTAH							
1 ***Hansen***	N	Y	Y	Y	N	N	N
2 ***Cook***	N	Y	Y	Y	N	N	N
3 ***Cannon***	N	Y	Y	Y	Y	N	N
VERMONT							
AL *Sanders*	Y	N	N	N	N	Y	Y
VIRGINIA							
1 ***Bateman***	–	+	+	+	–	–	–
2 Pickett	N	N	N	Y	N	N	Y
3 Scott	Y	N	N	N	N	Y	Y
4 Sisisky	Y	N	N	Y	N	N	Y
5 Goode	N	Y	N	N	N	N	Y
6 ***Goodlatte***	N	Y	Y	Y	Y	N	Y
7 ***Bliley***	N	Y	?	#	N	N	Y
8 Moran	N	N	Y	N	Y	N	Y
9 Boucher	Y	N	N	N	N	Y	Y
10 ***Wolf***	N	Y	Y	Y	N	N	N
11 ***Davis***	N	Y	Y	Y	N	N	N
WASHINGTON							
1 ***White***	N	Y	Y	Y	Y	N	N
2 ***Metcalf***	N	Y	Y	?	Y	N	N
3 ***Smith, Linda***	N	Y	Y	Y	?	?	?
4 ***Hastings***	N	Y	Y	Y	Y	N	N
5 ***Nethercutt***	N	Y	Y	Y	Y	N	N
6 Dicks	Y	N	N	Y	N	Y	Y
7 McDermott	Y	N	N	N	Y	Y	Y
8 ***Dunn***	N	Y	?	?	N	N	N
9 Smith, Adam	Y	N	N	N	N	Y	Y
WEST VIRGINIA							
1 Mollohan	Y	N	N	Y	?	Y	Y
2 Wise	Y	N	N	N	N	Y	Y
3 Rahall	Y	N	N	N	?	?	?
WISCONSIN							
1 ***Neumann***	N	Y	Y	N	?	?	?
2 ***Klug***	N	Y	Y	N	N	N	N
3 Kind	Y	N	N	N	N	Y	Y
4 Kleczka	Y	N	N	N	Y	Y	Y
5 Barrett	Y	N	N	N	N	Y	Y
6 ***Petri***	N	Y	Y	Y	Y	N	N
7 Obey	Y	N	N	N	Y	Y	Y
8 Johnson	Y	N	N	N	N	Y	Y
9 ***Sensenbrenner***	N	Y	?	?	Y	N	N
WYOMING							
AL ***Cubin***	N	Y	Y	Y	?	N	N

Southern states - Ala., Ark., Fla., Ga., Ky., La., Miss., N.C., Okla., S.C., Tenn., Texas, Va.

Key

Y	Voted for (yea).
#	Paired for.
+	Announced for.
N	Voted against (nay).
X	Paired against.
−	Announced against.
P	Voted "present."
C	Voted "present" to avoid possible conflict of interest.
?	Did not vote or otherwise make a position known.

Democrats   Republicans
Independent

132. HR 6. Higher Education Act Reauthorization/Olympic Scholarships. Stupak, D-Mich., amendment to authorize $5 million for each of five fiscal years for the Olympic Scholarship program, which provides college scholarships for Olympic athletes while they train. Adopted 219-200: R 37-183; D 181-17 (ND 137-9, SD 44-8); I 1-0. May 6, 1998.

133. HR 6. Higher Education Act Reauthorization/Preferential Treatment. Riggs, R-Calif., amendment to prohibit any public institution of higher education that participates in any Higher Education Act program from discriminating against, or granting preferential treatment to any person or group in admissions based in whole or in part on race, sex, color, ethnicity or national origin. Rejected 171-249: R 166-55; D 5-193 (ND 2-143, SD 3-50); I 0-1. May 6, 1998. A "nay" was a vote in support of the president's position.

134. HR 6. Higher Education Act Reauthorization/Race. Campbell, R-Calif., amendment to provide that no person shall be excluded from, or have a diminished chance of acceptance to, the minority science and engineering improvement program of the Higher Education Act because of the applicant's race, color, religion or national origin. Rejected 189-227: R 184-34; D 5-192 (ND 1-144, SD 4-48); I 0-1. May 6, 1998.

135. HR 6. Higher Education Act Reauthorization/Passage. Passage of the bill to reauthorize federal student financial aid programs and other federal assistance to institutions of higher education through fiscal 2003. Passed 414-4: R 215-4; D 198-0 (ND 145-0, SD 53-0); I 1-0. May 6, 1998.

136. HR 2646. Education Savings Accounts/Motion to Instruct. Rangel, D-N.Y., motion to instruct the House conferees to agree to provisions relating to tax-favored financing for public school construction consistent, to the maximum extent possible, with the approach taken in HR 3320, the Public School Modernization Act of 1998. Motion rejected 192-222: R 5-214; D 186-8 (ND 139-5, SD 47-3); I 1-0. May 7, 1998.

137. HR 3694. Fiscal 1999 Intelligence Authorization/Authorization Reduction. Sanders, I-Vt., amendment to reduce the bill's authorization by 5 percent. The bill authorizes classified amounts in fiscal 1999 for U.S. intelligence agencies and intelligence-related activities of the U.S. government. Rejected 120-291: R 21-196; D 98-95 (ND 85-56, SD 13-39); I 1-0. May 7, 1998. (Subsequently, the bill passed by voice vote).

138. H Res 423. Drugs and Children/Adoption. Hastert, R-Ill., motion to suspend the rules and adopt the resolution to express the sense of the House that it is committed to working toward making America drug-free. Motion agreed to 412-2: R 217-2; D 194-0 (ND 141-0, SD 53-0); I 1-0. May 12, 1998. A two-thirds majority of those present and voting (276 in this case) is required for adoption under suspension of the rules.

	132	133	134	135	136	137	138
ALABAMA							
1 *Callahan*	Y	Y	N	N	Y	N	Y
2 *Everett*	Y	Y	N	Y	N	Y	Y
3 *Riley*	Y	Y	Y	N	Y	N	Y
4 *Aderholt*	Y	Y	N	N	Y	Y	Y
5 Cramer	Y	Y	N	Y	Y	Y	Y
6 *Bachus*	Y	Y	N	N	Y	Y	Y
7 Hilliard	Y	Y	Y	N	Y	Y	Y
ALASKA							
AL *Young*	Y	Y	Y	Y	Y	N	Y
ARIZONA							
1 *Salmon*	Y	Y	N	Y	N	Y	Y
2 Pastor	Y	Y	N	Y	Y	Y	Y
3 *Stump*	Y	Y	N	N	N	N	N
4 *Shadegg*	Y	Y	N	N	N	N	N
5 *Kolbe*	Y	Y	N	N	N	N	N
6 *Hayworth*	Y	Y	N	N	N	Y	Y
ARKANSAS							
1 Berry	Y	Y	Y	Y	N	Y	Y
2 Snyder	Y	Y	N	N	Y	Y	Y
3 *Hutchinson*	Y	Y	?	N	Y	N	Y
4 *Dickey*	Y	Y	N	N	Y	N	Y
CALIFORNIA							
1 *Riggs*	Y	Y	−	−	Y	Y	Y
2 *Herger*	Y	Y	N	N	N	N	N
3 Fazio	Y	Y	Y	N	Y	Y	Y
4 *Doolittle*	Y	Y	Y	N	N	N	N
5 Matsui	Y	Y	N	N	Y	Y	Y
6 Woolsey	Y	Y	N	N	Y	Y	Y
7 Miller	Y	Y	N	N	Y	Y	Y
8 Pelosi	Y	Y	?	N	Y	Y	Y
9 Lee	Y	Y	N	N	Y	Y	Y
10 Tauscher	Y	Y	N	N	Y	Y	Y
11 *Pombo*	Y	Y	Y	Y	N	Y	N
12 Lantos	?	?	N	N	Y	Y	Y
13 Stark	Y	Y	N	Y	Y	Y	Y
14 Eshoo	Y	Y	N	N	Y	Y	Y
15 *Campbell*	Y	Y	N	N	Y	Y	Y
16 Lofgren	Y	Y	N	N	Y	Y	Y
17 Farr	Y	Y	N	N	Y	Y	Y
18 Condit	Y	Y	Y	Y	N	Y	Y
19 *Radanovich*	Y	Y	?	?	?	?	?
20 Dooley	Y	Y	N	N	Y	Y	Y
21 *Thomas*	Y	Y	N	Y	N	Y	Y
22 Capps, L.	Y	Y	N	N	Y	Y	Y
23 *Gallegly*	Y	Y	N	N	N	Y	Y
24 Sherman	Y	Y	N	N	Y	Y	Y
25 *McKeon*	Y	Y	N	N	Y	N	Y
26 Berman	Y	Y	N	N	Y	Y	Y
27 *Rogan*	Y	Y	?	N	Y	N	Y
28 *Dreier*	Y	Y	N	N	N	Y	Y
29 Waxman	Y	Y	N	N	Y	Y	Y
30 Becerra	Y	Y	N	N	Y	Y	Y
31 Martinez	Y	Y	Y	N	Y	Y	Y
32 Dixon	Y	Y	N	N	Y	Y	Y
33 Roybal-Allard	Y	Y	N	N	Y	Y	Y
34 Torres	Y	Y	N	N	Y	Y	Y
35 Waters	Y	Y	N	N	Y	Y	Y
36 Harman	?	?	N	N	Y	Y	Y
37 Millender-McD.	Y	Y	N	N	Y	Y	Y

	132	133	134	135	136	137	138
38 *Horn*	Y	Y	N	Y	Y	Y	Y
39 *Royce*	Y	Y	N	N	Y	Y	Y
40 *Lewis*	Y	N	N	N	Y	N	Y
41 *Kim*	Y	Y	N	N	Y	N	Y
42 Brown	Y	Y	N	N	Y	Y	Y
43 *Calvert*	Y	Y	N	Y	Y	Y	Y
44 *Bono, M.*	Y	Y	N	Y	Y	Y	Y
45 *Rohrabacher*	Y	Y	N	N	Y	Y	N
46 Sanchez	Y	Y	N	Y	Y	Y	Y
47 *Cox*	Y	Y	N	Y	Y	Y	Y
48 *Packard*	Y	Y	N	N	N	N	N
49 *Bilbray*	Y	Y	N	N	Y	Y	Y
50 Filner	Y	Y	N	N	Y	Y	Y
51 *Cunningham*	Y	Y	N	Y	Y	Y	Y
52 *Hunter*	Y	N	N	N	Y	Y	Y
COLORADO							
1 DeGette	Y	Y	N	N	Y	Y	Y
2 Skaggs	+	+	−	+	−	+	+
3 *McInnis*	Y	Y	N	N	Y	Y	Y
4 *Schaffer*	Y	Y	N	N	N	Y	Y
5 *Hefley*	Y	N	N	N	Y	N	Y
6 *Schaefer*	?	?	Y	Y	Y	N	Y
CONNECTICUT							
1 Kennelly	Y	Y	N	N	Y	Y	Y
2 Gejdenson	Y	Y	N	N	Y	Y	Y
3 DeLauro	Y	Y	N	N	Y	Y	Y
4 *Shays*	Y	Y	N	N	Y	Y	Y
5 Maloney	Y	Y	N	N	Y	Y	Y
6 *Johnson*	Y	Y	N	N	Y	Y	Y
DELAWARE							
AL *Castle*	Y	Y	N	N	Y	Y	Y
FLORIDA							
1 *Scarborough*	Y	Y	N	N	Y	Y	Y
2 Boyd	Y	Y	N	N	Y	Y	Y
3 Brown	Y	Y	N	N	Y	Y	Y
4 *Fowler*	Y	Y	N	N	Y	N	Y
5 Thurman	Y	Y	N	N	Y	Y	Y
6 *Stearns*	Y	Y	N	N	Y	Y	Y
7 *Mica*	Y	N	N	Y	N	Y	Y
8 *McCollum*	Y	Y	?	N	Y	N	Y
9 *Bilirakis*	Y	Y	N	N	Y	N	Y
10 *Young*	Y	Y	N	N	Y	Y	Y
11 Davis	Y	Y	N	N	Y	Y	Y
12 *Canady*	Y	Y	N	Y	N	Y	Y
13 *Miller*	Y	Y	N	N	N	N	N
14 *Goss*	Y	Y	N	N	Y	N	Y
15 *Weldon*	Y	Y	N	N	Y	N	Y
16 *Foley*	Y	Y	N	N	Y	Y	Y
17 Meek	Y	Y	N	N	Y	Y	Y
18 *Ros-Lehtinen*	Y	Y	N	N	Y	N	Y
19 Wexler	Y	Y	N	N	Y	Y	Y
20 Deutsch	Y	Y	N	N	Y	Y	Y
21 *Diaz-Balart*	Y	Y	N	N	Y	N	Y
22 *Shaw*	Y	Y	N	N	Y	N	Y
23 Hastings	?	?	?	?	?	?	?
GEORGIA							
1 *Kingston*	Y	Y	N	N	Y	N	Y
2 Bishop	Y	Y	N	N	Y	Y	Y
3 *Collins*	Y	Y	N	Y	N	N	N
4 McKinney	Y	Y	N	Y	Y	Y	Y
5 Lewis	Y	Y	N	N	Y	Y	Y
6 *Gingrich*							
7 *Barr*	Y	Y	N	N	Y	N	N
8 *Chambliss*	Y	Y	N	Y	N	Y	Y
9 *Deal*	Y	Y	N	N	Y	N	Y
10 *Norwood*	Y	Y	N	N	Y	N	Y
11 *Linder*	Y	Y	N	N	Y	N	Y
HAWAII							
1 Abercrombie	Y	Y	N	N	Y	Y	Y
2 Mink	Y	Y	Y	Y	Y	Y	Y
IDAHO							
1 *Chenoweth*	Y	Y	Y	N	?	N	Y
2 *Crapo*	Y	Y	N	Y	N	Y	Y
ILLINOIS							
1 Rush	Y	Y	N	Y	Y	Y	Y
2 Jackson	Y	Y	N	N	Y	Y	Y
3 Lipinski	Y	Y	N	N	N	Y	Y
4 Gutierrez	Y	Y	N	N	Y	Y	Y
5 Blagojevich	Y	Y	N	N	Y	Y	Y
6 *Hyde*	Y	Y	N	N	N	Y	Y
7 Davis	+	+	Y	Y	Y	Y	Y
8 *Crane*	Y	Y	N	N	Y	N	Y
9 Yates	Y	Y	N	N	Y	Y	Y
10 *Porter*	Y	Y	N	N	Y	N	Y
11 *Weller*	Y	Y	N	N	Y	Y	Y
12 Costello	Y	Y	N	N	Y	Y	Y

ND Northern Democrats   SD Southern Democrats

	132	133	134	135	136	137	138
13 ***Fawell***	Y	Y	N	N	Y	N	Y
14 ***Hastert***	Y	Y	N	N	Y	N	Y
15 ***Ewing***	Y	Y	N	N	Y	Y	Y
16 ***Manzullo***	Y	Y	N	N	Y	N	Y
17 Evans	Y	Y	N	N	Y	Y	Y
18 ***LaHood***	Y	Y	N	N	Y	Y	Y
19 Poshard	Y	Y	N	N	Y	Y	Y
20 ***Shimkus***	Y	Y	N	N	Y	N	Y
INDIANA							
1 Visclosky	+	+	N	N	Y	Y	Y
2 ***McIntosh***	Y	Y	Y	N	Y	N	Y
3 Roemer	Y	Y	N	N	Y	Y	Y
4 ***Souder***	Y	Y	N	N	Y	N	Y
5 ***Buyer***	Y	Y	N	N	Y	Y	Y
6 ***Burton***	Y	Y	N	N	Y	N	Y
7 ***Pease***	Y	Y	N	N	Y	Y	Y
8 ***Hostettler***	Y	Y	N	N	Y	Y	Y
9 Hamilton	Y	Y	Y	Y	N	Y	Y
10 Carson	+	+	–	–	+	+	+
IOWA							
1 ***Leach***	Y	Y	N	N	Y	N	Y
2 ***Nussle***	Y	Y	Y	Y	Y	N	Y
3 Boswell	Y	Y	N	N	Y	Y	Y
4 ***Ganske***	Y	Y	N	N	Y	N	Y
5 ***Latham***	Y	Y	N	N	Y	N	Y
KANSAS							
1 ***Moran***	Y	Y	N	N	Y	Y	Y
2 ***Ryun***	Y	Y	N	N	Y	N	Y
3 ***Snowbarger***	Y	Y	N	Y	Y	N	Y
4 ***Tiahrt***	Y	Y	N	N	Y	N	N
KENTUCKY							
1 ***Whitfield***	Y	Y	N	N	Y	Y	Y
2 ***Lewis***	Y	Y	N	N	Y	N	Y
3 ***Northup***	Y	Y	Y	N	Y	N	Y
4 ***Bunning***	Y	Y	N	N	Y	N	Y
5 ***Rogers***	Y	Y	N	N	Y	Y	Y
6 Baesler	Y	Y	N	N	Y	Y	Y
LOUISIANA							
1 ***Livingston***	Y	Y	Y	Y	Y	N	Y
2 Jefferson	Y	Y	N	N	Y	Y	Y
3 ***Tauzin***	?	?	Y	Y	Y	Y	Y
4 ***McCrery***	Y	Y	N	Y	Y	Y	Y
5 ***Cooksey***	Y	Y	N	N	Y	N	Y
6 ***Baker***	Y	Y	Y	Y	Y	Y	Y
7 John	Y	Y	Y	Y	N	Y	Y
MAINE							
1 Allen	Y	Y	N	N	Y	Y	Y
2 Baldacci	Y	Y	N	N	Y	Y	Y
MARYLAND							
1 ***Gilchrest***	Y	Y	Y	Y	Y	N	Y
2 ***Ehrlich***	Y	Y	Y	N	Y	N	Y
3 Cardin	Y	Y	P	P	P	Y	Y
4 Wynn	Y	Y	Y	Y	N	Y	Y
5 Hoyer	Y	Y	Y	Y	N	Y	Y
6 ***Bartlett***	Y	Y	Y	Y	Y	Y	Y
7 Cummings	Y	Y	Y	Y	Y	Y	Y
8 ***Morella***	Y	Y	Y	Y	N	Y	Y
MASSACHUSETTS							
1 Olver	Y	Y	N	N	Y	Y	Y
2 Neal	Y	Y	N	N	Y	Y	Y
3 McGovern	Y	Y	N	N	Y	Y	Y
4 Frank	Y	Y	N	N	Y	Y	Y
5 Meehan	Y	Y	N	N	Y	Y	Y
6 Tierney	Y	Y	N	N	Y	Y	Y
7 Markey	Y	Y	N	N	Y	Y	Y
8 Kennedy	Y	Y	N	N	Y	Y	Y
9 Moakley	Y	Y	N	N	Y	Y	Y
10 Delahunt	Y	Y	N	N	Y	Y	Y
MICHIGAN							
1 Stupak	Y	Y	N	N	Y	Y	Y
2 ***Hoekstra***	Y	Y	N	N	Y	N	Y
3 ***Ehlers***	Y	Y	N	N	Y	Y	Y
4 ***Camp***	Y	Y	N	N	Y	Y	Y
5 Barcia	Y	Y	Y	Y	Y	Y	Y
6 ***Upton***	Y	Y	Y	Y	Y	Y	Y
7 ***Smith***	Y	Y	N	Y	Y	Y	N
8 Stabenow	Y	Y	N	N	Y	Y	Y
9 Kildee	Y	Y	N	N	Y	Y	Y
10 Bonior	Y	Y	Y	Y	Y	Y	Y
11 ***Knollenberg***	Y	Y	N	N	Y	N	Y
12 Levin	Y	Y	N	Y	Y	Y	Y
13 Rivers	Y	Y	Y	Y	Y	Y	Y
14 Conyers	Y	Y	Y	Y	N	Y	Y
15 Kilpatrick	Y	Y	Y	N	Y	Y	Y
16 Dingell	Y	Y	Y	Y	N	Y	Y

	132	133	134	135	136	137	138
MINNESOTA							
1 ***Gutknecht***	Y	Y	Y	N	Y	N	Y
2 Minge	Y	Y	Y	N	Y	Y	Y
3 ***Ramstad***	Y	Y	N	N	Y	Y	Y
4 Vento	Y	Y	N	N	Y	Y	Y
5 Sabo	Y	Y	Y	Y	Y	N	Y
6 Luther	Y	Y	N	N	Y	Y	Y
7 Peterson	Y	Y	Y	Y	N	Y	Y
8 Oberstar	Y	Y	Y	N	N	Y	Y
MISSISSIPPI							
1 ***Wicker***	Y	Y	N	N	Y	N	N
2 Thompson	Y	Y	Y	Y	Y	Y	Y
3 ***Pickering***	Y	Y	N	N	Y	N	Y
4 ***Parker***	?	?	N	N	Y	N	Y
5 Taylor	Y	Y	N	N	N	Y	Y
MISSOURI							
1 Clay	Y	Y	N	N	Y	Y	Y
2 ***Talent***	Y	Y	N	N	Y	Y	Y
3 Gephardt	Y	Y	N	N	Y	Y	Y
4 Skelton	Y	Y	Y	N	Y	Y	Y
5 McCarthy	Y	Y	Y	N	Y	Y	Y
6 Danner	Y	Y	N	N	Y	Y	Y
7 ***Blunt***	Y	Y	N	N	Y	Y	Y
8 ***Emerson***	Y	Y	N	Y	Y	Y	Y
9 ***Hulshof***	Y	Y	N	N	Y	Y	Y
MONTANA							
AL ***Hill***	Y	Y	N	N	Y	N	Y
NEBRASKA							
1 ***Bereuter***	Y	Y	N	N	Y	Y	Y
2 ***Christensen***	?	?	?	?	?	?	?
3 ***Barrett***	Y	Y	Y	Y	Y	Y	Y
NEVADA							
1 ***Ensign***	Y	Y	Y	N	Y	Y	Y
2 ***Gibbons***	Y	Y	N	N	Y	Y	Y
NEW HAMPSHIRE							
1 ***Sununu***	Y	Y	N	N	Y	N	Y
2 ***Bass***	Y	Y	N	N	Y	N	Y
NEW JERSEY							
1 Andrews	Y	Y	Y	N	Y	Y	Y
2 ***LoBiondo***	Y	Y	N	N	Y	N	Y
3 ***Saxton***	Y	Y	N	N	Y	Y	Y
4 ***Smith***	Y	Y	N	N	Y	Y	Y
5 ***Roukema***	Y	Y	N	N	Y	Y	Y
6 Pallone	Y	Y	N	N	Y	Y	Y
7 ***Franks***	Y	Y	N	N	Y	Y	Y
8 Pascrell	Y	Y	Y	Y	N	Y	Y
9 Rothman	Y	Y	N	N	Y	Y	Y
10 Payne	Y	Y	Y	N	Y	Y	Y
11 ***Frelinghuysen***	Y	Y	N	N	Y	Y	Y
12 ***Pappas***	Y	Y	N	N	Y	Y	Y
13 Menendez	Y	Y	Y	Y	N	Y	Y
NEW MEXICO							
1 Vacant							
2 ***Skeen***	Y	Y	N	N	Y	N	Y
3 ***Redmond***	Y	Y	Y	Y	Y	N	Y
NEW YORK							
1 ***Forbes***	+	Y	N	N	Y	N	Y
2 ***Lazio***	Y	Y	N	Y	Y	N	Y
3 ***King***	Y	Y	N	N	Y	Y	Y
4 McCarthy	Y	Y	Y	N	Y	Y	Y
5 Ackerman	Y	Y	N	N	Y	Y	Y
6 Meeks	?	?	Y	Y	Y	Y	Y
7 Manton	Y	Y	N	N	Y	Y	Y
8 Nadler	Y	Y	N	N	Y	Y	Y
9 Schumer	Y	Y	Y	N	Y	Y	Y
10 Towns	Y	Y	Y	Y	Y	Y	Y
11 Owens	Y	Y	Y	N	Y	Y	Y
12 Velázquez	Y	Y	N	N	Y	Y	Y
13 ***Fossella***	+	+	?	+	?	N	Y
14 Maloney	Y	Y	Y	N	Y	Y	Y
15 Rangel	Y	Y	Y	N	Y	Y	Y
16 Serrano	Y	Y	N	N	Y	Y	Y
17 Engel	Y	Y	N	N	Y	Y	Y
18 Lowey	?	?	N	N	Y	Y	Y
19 ***Kelly***	Y	Y	N	N	Y	N	Y
20 ***Gilman***	Y	Y	N	N	Y	N	Y
21 McNulty	?	?	?	?	?	?	?
22 ***Solomon***	Y	Y	N	N	Y	N	Y
23 ***Boehlert***	Y	Y	Y	N	Y	N	Y
24 ***McHugh***	Y	Y	N	N	Y	Y	Y
25 ***Walsh***	Y	Y	N	N	Y	Y	Y
26 Hinchey	Y	Y	N	N	Y	Y	Y
27 ***Paxon***	Y	Y	N	N	Y	Y	Y
28 Slaughter	Y	Y	N	N	Y	Y	Y
29 LaFalce	Y	Y	N	N	Y	Y	Y

	132	133	134	135	136	137	138
30 ***Quinn***	Y	Y	N	N	Y	Y	Y
31 ***Houghton***	Y	Y	N	N	Y	Y	Y
NORTH CAROLINA							
1 Clayton	Y	Y	Y	N	Y	Y	Y
2 Etheridge	Y	Y	N	N	Y	Y	Y
3 ***Jones***	Y	Y	N	Y	Y	Y	Y
4 Price	Y	Y	N	N	Y	Y	Y
5 ***Burr***	Y	Y	N	N	Y	N	Y
6 ***Coble***	Y	Y	N	N	Y	N	Y
7 McIntyre	Y	Y	N	N	Y	Y	Y
8 Hefner	Y	Y	N	N	Y	Y	Y
9 ***Myrick***	Y	Y	N	N	Y	Y	Y
10 ***Ballenger***	Y	Y	N	N	Y	N	Y
11 ***Taylor***	Y	Y	Y	N	Y	Y	N
12 Watt	Y	Y	Y	Y	Y	Y	Y
NORTH DAKOTA							
AL Pomeroy	Y	Y	N	N	Y	Y	Y
OHIO							
1 ***Chabot***	Y	Y	N	N	Y	Y	Y
2 ***Portman***	Y	Y	N	N	Y	Y	Y
3 Hall	Y	Y	Y	N	Y	Y	Y
4 ***Oxley***	Y	Y	Y	Y	Y	Y	Y
5 ***Gillmor***	Y	Y	N	N	Y	N	Y
6 Strickland	Y	Y	N	N	Y	Y	Y
7 ***Hobson***	Y	Y	N	N	Y	N	Y
8 ***Boehner***	Y	Y	Y	Y	Y	N	Y
9 Kaptur	?	?	Y	N	Y	Y	Y
10 Kucinich	Y	Y	Y	Y	N	Y	Y
11 Stokes	?	?	Y	N	Y	Y	Y
12 ***Kasich***	Y	Y	N	N	Y	N	Y
13 Brown	Y	Y	N	Y	Y	Y	Y
14 Sawyer	Y	Y	P	P	P	Y	Y
15 ***Pryce***	Y	Y	Y	N	Y	N	Y
16 ***Regula***	Y	Y	Y	N	Y	N	Y
17 Traficant	Y	Y	Y	Y	Y	N	Y
18 ***Ney***	Y	Y	N	N	Y	N	Y
19 ***LaTourette***	Y	Y	N	N	Y	N	Y
OKLAHOMA							
1 ***Largent***	Y	Y	N	N	Y	N	N
2 ***Coburn***	Y	Y	N	N	Y	N	N
3 ***Watkins***	Y	Y	N	N	Y	Y	Y
4 ***Watts***	Y	Y	N	N	Y	Y	Y
5 ***Istook***	Y	Y	N	N	Y	Y	Y
6 ***Lucas***	Y	Y	N	N	Y	N	Y
OREGON							
1 Furse	Y	Y	Y	Y	Y	Y	Y
2 ***Smith***	Y	Y	N	N	Y	Y	Y
3 Blumenauer	Y	Y	N	N	Y	Y	Y
4 DeFazio	Y	Y	N	N	Y	Y	Y
5 Hooley	Y	Y	N	N	Y	Y	Y
PENNSYLVANIA							
1 Vacant							
2 Fattah	?	?	N	N	Y	Y	Y
3 Borski	Y	Y	N	N	Y	Y	Y
4 Klink	Y	Y	Y	Y	N	Y	Y
5 ***Peterson***	Y	Y	N	N	Y	Y	Y
6 Holden	Y	Y	N	N	Y	Y	Y
7 ***Weldon***	Y	Y	N	N	Y	Y	Y
8 ***Greenwood***	Y	Y	N	N	Y	Y	Y
9 ***Shuster***	Y	Y	N	N	Y	N	Y
10 ***McDade***	Y	Y	N	N	Y	N	Y
11 Kanjorski	Y	Y	N	N	Y	Y	Y
12 Murtha	Y	Y	N	N	Y	Y	Y
13 ***Fox***	Y	Y	N	N	Y	N	Y
14 Coyne	Y	Y	N	N	Y	Y	Y
15 McHale	Y	Y	N	N	Y	Y	Y
16 ***Pitts***	Y	Y	N	N	Y	N	Y
17 ***Gekas***	Y	Y	Y	Y	Y	N	Y
18 Doyle	Y	Y	Y	Y	Y	?	?
19 ***Goodling***	?	Y	N	N	Y	N	Y
20 Mascara	Y	Y	Y	Y	Y	Y	Y
21 ***English***	Y	Y	N	N	Y	Y	Y
RHODE ISLAND							
1 Kennedy	Y	Y	N	N	Y	Y	Y
2 Weygand	Y	Y	N	N	Y	Y	Y
SOUTH CAROLINA							
1 ***Sanford***	Y	Y	N	N	Y	Y	N
2 ***Spence***	Y	Y	N	N	Y	Y	Y
3 ***Graham***	Y	Y	N	N	Y	Y	Y
4 ***Inglis***	Y	Y	N	N	Y	N	Y
5 Spratt	Y	Y	N	N	Y	?	?
6 Clyburn	?	?	Y	Y	Y	Y	Y
SOUTH DAKOTA							
AL ***Thune***	Y	Y	N	N	Y	Y	Y

	132	133	134	135	136	137	138
TENNESSEE							
1 ***Jenkins***	Y	Y	N	N	Y	Y	Y
2 ***Duncan***	Y	Y	N	N	Y	Y	Y
3 ***Wamp***	Y	Y	N	N	Y	Y	Y
4 ***Hilleary***	Y	Y	N	N	Y	Y	Y
5 Clement	Y	Y	N	N	Y	Y	Y
6 Gordon	Y	Y	N	N	Y	Y	Y
7 ***Bryant***	Y	Y	N	N	Y	Y	Y
8 Tanner	Y	Y	N	N	Y	Y	Y
9 Ford	Y	Y	N	Y	Y	Y	Y
TEXAS							
1 Sandlin	Y	Y	N	Y	Y	Y	Y
2 Turner	Y	Y	N	N	Y	Y	Y
3 ***Johnson, Sam***	Y	Y	Y	Y	Y	N	N
4 Hall	Y	Y	Y	Y	Y	Y	N
5 ***Sessions***	Y	Y	Y	Y	Y	N	N
6 ***Barton***	Y	Y	N	N	Y	Y	Y
7 ***Archer***	Y	Y	Y	N	Y	N	Y
8 ***Brady***	Y	Y	N	Y	Y	N	Y
9 Lampson	Y	Y	N	N	Y	Y	Y
10 Doggett	Y	Y	N	N	Y	Y	Y
11 Edwards	Y	Y	N	N	Y	Y	Y
12 ***Granger***	Y	Y	Y	N	Y	N	Y
13 ***Thornberry***	Y	Y	N	N	Y	N	N
14 ***Paul***	Y	N	Y	N	Y	Y	N
15 Hinojosa	Y	Y	N	N	Y	Y	Y
16 Reyes	Y	Y	N	N	Y	Y	Y
17 Stenholm	Y	Y	Y	N	Y	Y	Y
18 Jackson-Lee	Y	Y	N	N	Y	Y	Y
19 ***Combest***	Y	Y	N	N	Y	Y	Y
20 Gonzalez	?	?	?	?	?	?	?
21 ***Smith***	Y	Y	N	N	Y	Y	Y
22 ***DeLay***	Y	Y	Y	Y	Y	N	Y
23 ***Bonilla***	Y	Y	N	N	Y	Y	N
24 Frost	Y	Y	Y	N	Y	Y	Y
25 Bentsen	Y	Y	N	N	Y	Y	Y
26 ***Armey***	Y	Y	N	N	Y	N	Y
27 Ortiz	Y	Y	N	N	Y	Y	Y
28 Rodriguez	Y	Y	N	N	Y	Y	Y
29 Green	Y	Y	N	N	Y	Y	Y
30 Johnson, E.B.	Y	Y	Y	Y	Y	Y	Y
UTAH							
1 ***Hansen***	Y	Y	N	Y	Y	N	Y
2 ***Cook***	Y	Y	N	N	Y	N	Y
3 ***Cannon***	Y	Y	N	Y	Y	N	N
VERMONT							
AL *Sanders*	Y	Y	N	N	Y	Y	Y
VIRGINIA							
1 ***Bateman***	+	+	+	+	+	+	+
2 Pickett	Y	Y	N	N	Y	Y	Y
3 Scott	Y	Y	N	N	Y	Y	Y
4 Sisisky	Y	Y	N	N	Y	Y	Y
5 Goode	Y	Y	N	N	Y	Y	Y
6 ***Goodlatte***	Y	Y	N	N	Y	Y	Y
7 ***Bliley***	Y	Y	N	N	Y	N	Y
8 Moran	Y	Y	N	N	Y	Y	Y
9 Boucher	Y	Y	Y	Y	Y	Y	Y
10 ***Wolf***	Y	Y	N	N	Y	Y	Y
11 ***Davis***	Y	Y	N	N	Y	N	Y
WASHINGTON							
1 ***White***	Y	Y	N	N	Y	Y	Y
2 ***Metcalf***	Y	Y	N	N	Y	N	Y
3 ***Smith, Linda***	Y	Y	N	Y	Y	N	Y
4 ***Hastings***	Y	Y	N	N	Y	N	Y
5 ***Nethercutt***	Y	Y	Y	N	Y	Y	Y
6 Dicks	Y	Y	N	N	Y	Y	Y
7 McDermott	Y	Y	N	N	Y	Y	Y
8 ***Dunn***	?	Y	N	N	Y	N	Y
9 Smith, Adam	Y	Y	N	N	Y	Y	Y
WEST VIRGINIA							
1 Mollohan	Y	Y	N	N	Y	N	Y
2 Wise	Y	Y	N	N	Y	Y	Y
3 Rahall	?	?	N	N	Y	Y	Y
WISCONSIN							
1 ***Neumann***	?	?	?	?	?	?	?
2 ***Klug***	Y	Y	N	N	Y	Y	Y
3 Kind	Y	Y	N	N	Y	Y	Y
4 Kleczka	Y	Y	N	N	Y	Y	Y
5 Barrett	Y	Y	N	N	Y	Y	Y
6 ***Petri***	Y	Y	Y	Y	Y	N	Y
7 Obey	Y	Y	N	Y	Y	Y	Y
8 Johnson	Y	Y	N	N	Y	Y	Y
9 ***Sensenbrenner***	Y	Y	Y	Y	Y	Y	N
WYOMING							
AL ***Cubin***	Y	Y	N	Y	Y	N	N

Southern states - Ala., Ark., Fla., Ga., Ky., La., Miss., N.C., Okla., S.C., Tenn., Texas, Va.

Key

Y	Voted for (yea).
#	Paired for.
+	Announced for.
N	Voted against (nay).
X	Paired against.
–	Announced against.
P	Voted "present."
C	Voted "present" to avoid possible conflict of interest.
?	Did not vote or otherwise make a position known.

●
Democrats   **Republicans**
Independent

139. HR 3811. Deadbeat Parents Punishment/Passage. McCollum, R-Fla., motion to suspend the rules and pass the bill to increase penalties on parents who willfully fail to pay court-ordered child support for a child living in another state. Motion agreed to 402-16: R 213-8; D 188-8 (ND 136-7, SD 52-1); I 1-0. May 12, 1998. A two-thirds majority of those present and voting (279 in this case) is required for passage under suspension of the rules.

140. HR 2829. Bulletproof Vest Grants/Passage. McCollum, R-Fla., motion to suspend the rules and pass the bill to authorize a $25 million federal grant program to help local police departments purchase bulletproof vests. Motion agreed to 412-4: R 216-4; D 195-0 (ND 143-0, SD 52-0); I 1-0. May 12, 1998. A two-thirds majority of those present and voting (278 in this case) is required for passage under suspension of the rules.

141. H Res 422. Honoring Slain Law Enforcement Officers/Adoption. McCollum, R-Fla., motion to suspend the rules and adopt the resolution to express the sense of the House that law enforcement officers killed in the line of duty should be honored. Motion agreed to 416-0: R 220-0; D 195-0 (ND 143-0, SD 52-0); I 1-0. May 12, 1998. A two-thirds majority of those present and voting (278 in this case) is required for adoption under suspension of the rules.

142. HR 10. Financial Services Overhaul/Rule. Adoption of the rule (H Res 428) to provide for House floor consideration of the bill to eliminate barriers against affiliations between banking, securities, insurance and other firms. Adopted 311-105: R 201-18; D 109-87 (ND 75-69, SD 34-18); I 1-0. May 13, 1998.

143. HR 10. Financial Services Overhaul/Consumer Provisions. Bliley, R-Va., manager's amendment to add consumer protection provisions that allow federal banking regulators to preempt state bank insurance sales laws that conflict with federal rules, require federal banking and securities regulators to review existing consumer fee disclosure requirements, and require the General Accounting Office to report on concentration in the financial services industry and its impact on consumers. Adopted 407-11: R 210-10; D 196-1 (ND 145-0, SD 51-1); I 1-0. May 13, 1998.

144. HR 10. Financial Services Overhaul/National Bank Subsidiaries. LaFalce, D-N.Y., amendment to allow national bank subsidiaries to engage in any activity that is financial in nature, with the exception of underwriting insurance or engaging in real estate investment activities, even if it is not a permissible activity for the national bank itself. Rejected 115-306: R 15-207; D 99-99 (ND 76-70, SD 23-29); I 1-0. May 13, 1998.

145. HR 10. Financial Services Overhaul/Bank Holding Companies. Baker, R-La., amendment to expand the allowable activities of national bank subsidiaries, allowing subsidiaries to engage in activities that are generally allowable to bank holding companies, but which are not permissible for national banks. Rejected 140-281: R 133-89; D 7-191 (ND 1-147, SD 6-44); I 0-1. May 13, 1998.

	139	140	141	142	143	144	145
ALABAMA							
1 *Callahan*	Y	Y	Y	Y	Y	N	Y
2 *Everett*	Y	Y	Y	N	Y	N	Y
3 *Riley*	Y	Y	Y	N	N	Y	Y
4 *Aderholt*	Y	Y	Y	N	Y	N	Y
5 Cramer	Y	Y	Y	N	Y	N	Y
6 *Bachus*	Y	Y	Y	N	N	N	Y
7 Hilliard	Y	Y	Y	?	?	?	?
ALASKA							
AL *Young*	Y	Y	Y	Y	Y	N	N
ARIZONA							
1 *Salmon*	Y	Y	Y	Y	Y	N	Y
2 Pastor	Y	Y	Y	Y	Y	Y	N
3 *Stump*	Y	Y	Y	Y	Y	N	Y
4 *Shadegg*	Y	Y	Y	Y	Y	N	Y
5 *Kolbe*	Y	Y	Y	Y	Y	N	Y
6 *Hayworth*	Y	Y	Y	Y	N	Y	Y
ARKANSAS							
1 Berry	Y	Y	Y	Y	N	N	N
2 Snyder	Y	Y	Y	Y	Y	Y	N
3 *Hutchinson*	Y	Y	Y	Y	Y	N	Y
4 *Dickey*	Y	Y	Y	N	Y	N	Y
CALIFORNIA							
1 *Riggs*	Y	Y	Y	?	N	N	N
2 *Herger*	Y	Y	Y	Y	Y	N	N
3 Fazlo	Y	Y	Y	N	Y	N	N
4 *Doolittle*	Y	Y	Y	Y	Y	N	N
5 Matsui	Y	Y	Y	N	Y	N	N
6 Woolsey	Y	Y	Y	Y	Y	Y	N
7 Miller	Y	Y	Y	N	Y	N	N
8 Pelosi	Y	Y	Y	N	Y	N	N
9 Lee	N	Y	Y	N	Y	Y	N
10 Tauscher	Y	Y	Y	N	Y	N	N
11 *Pombo*	Y	Y	Y	Y	Y	N	Y
12 Lantos	Y	Y	Y	N	Y	Y	N
13 Stark	N	Y	Y	Y	Y	Y	N
14 Eshoo	Y	Y	Y	N	Y	Y	N
15 *Campbell*	Y	N	Y	Y	N	N	N
16 Lofgren	Y	Y	Y	N	Y	Y	N
17 Farr	Y	Y	Y	N	Y	Y	N
18 Condit	Y	Y	Y	Y	Y	N	N
19 *Radanovich*	Y	Y	Y	?	?	?	?
20 Dooley	Y	Y	Y	Y	Y	N	N
21 *Thomas*	Y	Y	Y	Y	Y	N	N
22 Capps, L.	Y	Y	Y	Y	Y	Y	N
23 *Gallegly*	Y	Y	Y	Y	Y	N	Y
24 Sherman	Y	Y	Y	N	Y	N	N
25 *McKeon*	Y	Y	Y	Y	Y	N	Y
26 Berman	Y	Y	Y	N	Y	Y	N
27 *Rogan*	Y	Y	Y	N	Y	N	N
28 *Dreier*	Y	Y	Y	Y	N	Y	Y
29 Waxman	Y	Y	Y	N	Y	N	N
30 Becerra	Y	Y	Y	N	Y	N	N
31 Martinez	Y	Y	Y	N	Y	Y	N
32 Dixon	Y	Y	Y	N	Y	Y	N
33 Roybal-Allard	Y	Y	Y	N	Y	Y	N
34 Torres	Y	Y	Y	N	Y	Y	N
35 Waters	Y	Y	Y	N	Y	Y	N
36 Harman	?	?	?	?	?	?	?
37 Millender-McD.	Y	Y	Y	N	Y	Y	N

	139	140	141	142	143	144	145
38 *Horn*	Y	Y	Y	Y	Y	N	Y
39 *Royce*	Y	Y	Y	Y	Y	N	N
40 *Lewis*	Y	Y	Y	Y	Y	N	N
41 *Kim*	Y	Y	Y	Y	Y	N	Y
42 Brown	Y	Y	Y	N	Y	Y	N
43 *Calvert*	Y	Y	Y	Y	Y	N	N
44 *Bono, M.*	Y	Y	Y	Y	Y	N	N
45 *Rohrabacher*	Y	Y	Y	Y	Y	N	Y
46 Sanchez	Y	Y	Y	Y	Y	N	N
47 *Cox*	Y	Y	Y	Y	Y	N	N
48 *Packard*	Y	Y	Y	Y	Y	N	N
49 *Bilbray*	Y	Y	Y	Y	Y	N	N
50 Filner	Y	Y	Y	N	Y	N	N
51 *Cunningham*	Y	Y	Y	Y	Y	N	N
52 *Hunter*	Y	Y	Y	Y	Y	N	Y
COLORADO							
1 DeGette	Y	Y	Y	Y	Y	N	N
2 Skaggs	+	+	+	+	+	–	–
3 *McInnis*	Y	Y	Y	Y	Y	Y	Y
4 *Schaffer*	Y	Y	Y	N	Y	N	N
5 *Hefley*	Y	Y	Y	N	Y	N	Y
6 *Schaefer*	Y	Y	Y	Y	Y	N	N
CONNECTICUT							
1 Kennelly	Y	Y	Y	Y	Y	N	N
2 Gejdenson	Y	Y	Y	Y	Y	N	N
3 DeLauro	Y	Y	Y	Y	Y	N	N
4 *Shays*	Y	Y	Y	Y	Y	N	N
5 Maloney	Y	Y	Y	N	Y	Y	N
6 *Johnson*	Y	Y	Y	Y	Y	N	N
DELAWARE							
AL *Castle*	Y	Y	Y	Y	Y	Y	Y
FLORIDA							
1 *Scarborough*	Y	Y	Y	N	N	N	N
2 Boyd	Y	Y	Y	Y	Y	N	N
3 Brown	Y	Y	Y	N	Y	N	N
4 *Fowler*	Y	Y	Y	Y	Y	N	N
5 Thurman	Y	Y	Y	Y	Y	N	N
6 *Stearns*	Y	Y	Y	N	Y	N	N
7 *Mica*	Y	Y	Y	N	Y	N	N
8 *McCollum*	Y	Y	Y	N	N	N	Y
9 *Bilirakis*	Y	Y	Y	N	Y	N	Y
10 *Young*	Y	Y	Y	Y	N	N	N
11 Davis	Y	Y	Y	Y	Y	N	N
12 *Canady*	Y	Y	Y	N	Y	N	Y
13 *Miller*	Y	Y	Y	Y	Y	N	N
14 *Goss*	Y	Y	Y	Y	Y	N	N
15 *Weldon*	Y	Y	Y	Y	Y	N	N
16 *Foley*	Y	Y	Y	Y	Y	N	Y
17 Meek	Y	Y	Y	N	Y	Y	N
18 *Ros-Lehtinen*	Y	Y	Y	Y	Y	N	N
19 Wexler	Y	?	?	Y	Y	N	N
20 Deutsch	Y	Y	Y	Y	Y	N	N
21 *Diaz-Balart*	Y	Y	Y	Y	Y	N	N
22 *Shaw*	Y	Y	Y	Y	Y	N	N
23 Hastings	N	Y	Y	N	Y	Y	N
GEORGIA							
1 *Kingston*	Y	Y	Y	Y	N	Y	N
2 Bishop	Y	Y	Y	Y	Y	N	Y
3 *Collins*	Y	Y	Y	Y	Y	N	N
4 McKinney	Y	Y	Y	N	Y	Y	N
5 Lewis	Y	Y	Y	N	Y	Y	N
6 *Gingrich*							
7 *Barr*	N	Y	Y	N	N	N	N
8 *Chambliss*	Y	Y	Y	N	Y	N	Y
9 *Deal*	Y	Y	Y	Y	Y	N	Y
10 *Norwood*	Y	Y	Y	N	Y	N	N
11 *Linder*	Y	?	Y	Y	Y	N	Y
HAWAII							
1 Abercrombie	Y	Y	Y	Y	Y	N	N
2 Mink	Y	Y	Y	?	Y	N	N
IDAHO							
1 *Chenoweth*	Y	Y	Y	Y	Y	N	Y
2 *Crapo*	Y	Y	Y	Y	Y	N	N
ILLINOIS							
1 Rush	Y	Y	Y	N	Y	Y	N
2 Jackson	N	Y	Y	N	Y	Y	N
3 Lipinski	Y	Y	Y	N	Y	N	N
4 Gutierrez	Y	Y	Y	N	Y	Y	N
5 Blagojevich	Y	Y	Y	Y	Y	N	N
6 *Hyde*	Y	Y	Y	N	Y	N	N
7 Davis	Y	Y	Y	N	Y	N	N
8 *Crane*	Y	Y	Y	Y	Y	N	N
9 Yates	Y	Y	Y	N	Y	N	N
10 *Porter*	Y	Y	Y	Y	Y	N	N
11 *Weller*	Y	Y	Y	Y	Y	N	N
12 Costello	Y	Y	Y	N	Y	N	N

ND Northern Democrats   SD Southern Democrats

	139	140	141	142	143	144	145
13 ***Fawell***	Y	Y	Y	Y	Y	N	Y
14 ***Hastert***	Y	Y	Y	Y	Y	N	N
15 ***Ewing***	Y	Y	Y	?	Y	N	Y
16 ***Manzullo***	N	Y	Y	Y	Y	N	N
17 Evans	Y	Y	Y	N	Y	Y	N
18 ***LaHood***	N	Y	Y	N	N	N	N
19 Poshard	Y	Y	Y	N	Y	N	N
20 ***Shimkus***	Y	Y	Y	Y	Y	N	N
INDIANA							
1 Visclosky	Y	Y	Y	Y	Y	Y	N
2 ***McIntosh***	Y	Y	Y	Y	Y	Y	Y
3 Roemer	Y	Y	Y	Y	Y	N	N
4 ***Souder***	Y	Y	Y	Y	Y	Y	Y
5 ***Buyer***	Y	Y	?	Y	Y	N	Y
6 ***Burton***	Y	Y	Y	Y	Y	N	N
7 ***Pease***	Y	Y	Y	Y	Y	N	Y
8 ***Hostettler***	Y	Y	Y	Y	Y	Y	Y
9 Hamilton	Y	Y	Y	Y	Y	N	N
10 Carson	Y	Y	Y	N	Y	Y	N
IOWA							
1 ***Leach***	Y	Y	Y	Y	Y	N	N
2 ***Nussle***	Y	Y	Y	Y	Y	N	Y
3 Boswell	Y	Y	Y	N	Y	Y	N
4 ***Ganske***	Y	Y	Y	Y	Y	N	N
5 ***Latham***	Y	Y	Y	Y	Y	N	Y
KANSAS							
1 ***Moran***	Y	Y	Y	Y	Y	N	Y
2 ***Ryun***	Y	Y	Y	Y	Y	N	Y
3 ***Snowbarger***	Y	Y	Y	Y	Y	N	Y
4 ***Tiahrt***	Y	Y	Y	N	N	N	Y
KENTUCKY							
1 ***Whitfield***	Y	Y	Y	Y	Y	N	N
2 ***Lewis***	Y	Y	Y	N	Y	N	N
3 ***Northup***	Y	Y	Y	Y	Y	N	N
4 ***Bunning***	Y	Y	Y	Y	Y	N	Y
5 ***Rogers***	Y	Y	Y	Y	Y	N	Y
6 Baesler	Y	Y	Y	N	Y	Y	N
LOUISIANA							
1 ***Livingston***	Y	Y	Y	Y	Y	N	N
2 Jefferson	Y	Y	Y	Y	Y	Y	N
3 ***Tauzin***	Y	Y	Y	Y	Y	N	Y
4 ***McCrery***	Y	Y	Y	Y	Y	N	Y
5 ***Cooksey***	Y	Y	Y	Y	Y	N	Y
6 ***Baker***	Y	Y	Y	Y	Y	N	Y
7 John	Y	Y	Y	Y	Y	N	N
MAINE							
1 Allen	Y	Y	Y	Y	Y	Y	N
2 Baldacci	Y	Y	Y	N	Y	N	N
MARYLAND							
1 ***Gilchrest***	?	?	?	?	?	?	Y
2 ***Ehrlich***	Y	Y	Y	Y	Y	N	Y
3 Cardin	Y	Y	Y	N	Y	Y	N
4 Wynn	Y	Y	Y	Y	Y	N	N
5 Hoyer	Y	Y	Y	N	Y	Y	N
6 ***Bartlett***	Y	Y	Y	Y	Y	N	Y
7 Cummings	Y	Y	Y	Y	Y	N	N
8 ***Morella***	Y	Y	Y	Y	Y	N	N
MASSACHUSETTS							
1 Olver	Y	Y	Y	N	Y	Y	N
2 Neal	Y	Y	Y	Y	Y	N	N
3 McGovern	Y	Y	Y	Y	Y	N	N
4 Frank	Y	Y	Y	N	Y	Y	N
5 Meehan	Y	Y	Y	N	Y	Y	N
6 Tierney	Y	Y	Y	N	Y	Y	N
7 Markey	Y	Y	Y	Y	Y	N	N
8 Kennedy	Y	Y	Y	N	Y	Y	N
9 Moakley	Y	Y	Y	Y	Y	Y	N
10 Delahunt	Y	Y	Y	N	Y	N	N
MICHIGAN							
1 Stupak	Y	Y	Y	Y	Y	N	N
2 ***Hoekstra***	Y	Y	Y	Y	Y	N	Y
3 ***Ehlers***	Y	Y	Y	Y	Y	N	N
4 ***Camp***	Y	Y	Y	Y	Y	N	Y
5 Barcia	Y	Y	Y	Y	Y	N	N
6 ***Upton***	Y	Y	Y	Y	Y	N	N
7 ***Smith***	Y	Y	Y	Y	Y	N	Y
8 Stabenow	Y	Y	Y	Y	Y	N	N
9 Kildee	Y	Y	Y	Y	Y	N	N
10 Bonior	Y	Y	Y	Y	Y	Y	N
11 ***Knollenberg***	Y	Y	Y	Y	Y	N	N
12 Levin	Y	Y	Y	Y	Y	N	N
13 Rivers	Y	Y	Y	Y	Y	N	N
14 Conyers	N	Y	Y	N	Y	Y	N
15 Kilpatrick	+	?	+	–	+	+	N
16 Dingell	Y	Y	Y	Y	Y	N	N

	139	140	141	142	143	144	145
MINNESOTA							
1 ***Gutknecht***	Y	Y	Y	Y	Y	N	Y
2 Minge	Y	Y	Y	Y	Y	N	N
3 ***Ramstad***	Y	Y	Y	Y	Y	Y	Y
4 Vento	Y	Y	Y	N	Y	Y	N
5 Sabo	N	Y	Y	Y	Y	Y	N
6 Luther	Y	Y	Y	N	Y	Y	N
7 Peterson	Y	Y	Y	Y	Y	N	Y
8 Oberstar	Y	Y	Y	Y	Y	Y	N
MISSISSIPPI							
1 ***Wicker***	Y	Y	Y	Y	Y	N	Y
2 Thompson	Y	Y	Y	N	Y	Y	N
3 ***Pickering***	Y	Y	Y	Y	Y	N	Y
4 ***Parker***	Y	Y	Y	Y	Y	N	N
5 Taylor	Y	Y	Y	N	Y	N	Y
MISSOURI							
1 Clay	Y	Y	Y	?	?	?	N
2 ***Talent***	Y	Y	Y	Y	Y	N	Y
3 Gephardt	Y	Y	Y	N	Y	N	N
4 Skelton	Y	Y	Y	N	Y	N	N
5 McCarthy	Y	Y	Y	N	Y	N	N
6 Danner	Y	Y	Y	N	Y	N	N
7 ***Blunt***	Y	N	Y	Y	Y	N	N
8 ***Emerson***	Y	Y	Y	Y	Y	N	Y
9 ***Hulshof***	Y	Y	Y	Y	Y	N	Y
MONTANA							
AL ***Hill***	Y	Y	Y	Y	Y	N	Y
NEBRASKA							
1 ***Bereuter***	Y	Y	Y	Y	Y	N	Y
2 ***Christensen***	?	?	?	?	?	?	?
3 ***Barrett***	Y	Y	Y	Y	Y	N	Y
NEVADA							
1 ***Ensign***	Y	Y	Y	Y	Y	N	Y
2 ***Gibbons***	Y	Y	Y	Y	?	Y	N
NEW HAMPSHIRE							
1 ***Sununu***	Y	Y	Y	Y	Y	N	Y
2 ***Bass***	Y	Y	Y	Y	Y	N	N
NEW JERSEY							
1 Andrews	Y	Y	Y	Y	Y	N	N
2 ***LoBiondo***	Y	Y	Y	Y	Y	N	N
3 ***Saxton***	Y	Y	Y	Y	Y	N	N
4 ***Smith***	Y	Y	Y	Y	Y	N	N
5 ***Roukema***	Y	Y	Y	Y	Y	N	N
6 Pallone	Y	Y	Y	Y	Y	N	N
7 ***Franks***	Y	Y	Y	Y	Y	N	N
8 Pascrell	Y	Y	Y	Y	Y	N	N
9 Rothman	Y	Y	Y	N	Y	N	N
10 Payne	Y	Y	Y	N	Y	Y	N
11 ***Frelinghuysen***	Y	Y	Y	Y	Y	N	N
12 ***Pappas***	Y	Y	Y	Y	Y	N	N
13 Menendez	?	?	?	N	Y	N	N
NEW MEXICO							
1 Vacant							
2 ***Skeen***	Y	Y	Y	Y	Y	N	N
3 ***Redmond***	Y	Y	Y	Y	Y	N	Y
NEW YORK							
1 ***Forbes***	Y	Y	Y	Y	Y	N	N
2 ***Lazio***	Y	Y	Y	Y	Y	N	Y
3 ***King***	Y	Y	Y	Y	Y	N	N
4 McCarthy	Y	Y	Y	Y	Y	N	N
5 Ackerman	Y	Y	Y	Y	Y	N	N
6 Meeks	Y	Y	Y	Y	Y	Y	N
7 Manton	Y	Y	Y	Y	Y	N	N
8 Nadler	Y	Y	Y	Y	Y	N	N
9 Schumer	?	?	?	N	Y	N	N
10 Towns	Y	Y	Y	N	Y	Y	N
11 Owens	Y	Y	Y	N	Y	Y	N
12 Velázquez	Y	Y	Y	Y	Y	Y	N
13 ***Fossella***	Y	Y	Y	Y	Y	N	N
14 Maloney	Y	Y	Y	Y	Y	N	N
15 Rangel	Y	Y	Y	Y	Y	N	N
16 Serrano	Y	Y	Y	N	Y	Y	N
17 Engel	Y	Y	Y	Y	Y	N	N
18 Lowey	Y	Y	Y	N	Y	N	N
19 ***Kelly***	Y	Y	Y	Y	Y	Y	Y
20 ***Gilman***	Y	Y	Y	Y	Y	N	N
21 McNulty	Y	Y	Y	Y	Y	N	N
22 ***Solomon***	Y	Y	Y	Y	Y	N	N
23 ***Boehlert***	Y	Y	Y	Y	Y	N	Y
24 ***McHugh***	Y	Y	Y	Y	Y	N	N
25 ***Walsh***	Y	Y	Y	Y	Y	N	N
26 Hinchey	Y	Y	Y	N	Y	Y	N
27 ***Paxon***	Y	Y	Y	Y	Y	N	?
28 Slaughter	Y	Y	Y	N	Y	Y	N
29 LaFalce	Y	Y	Y	N	Y	Y	N

	139	140	141	142	143	144	145
30 ***Quinn***	Y	Y	Y	Y	Y	N	N
31 ***Houghton***	Y	Y	Y	Y	Y	N	N
NORTH CAROLINA							
1 Clayton	Y	Y	Y	Y	Y	Y	N
2 Etheridge	Y	Y	Y	Y	Y	N	N
3 ***Jones***	Y	Y	Y	N	Y	N	Y
4 Price	Y	Y	Y	N	Y	Y	N
5 ***Burr***	Y	Y	Y	Y	Y	N	N
6 ***Coble***	Y	Y	Y	Y	Y	N	Y
7 McIntyre	Y	Y	Y	N	Y	N	N
8 Hefner	?	?	?	?	?	?	?
9 ***Myrick***	+	+	+	Y	Y	Y	Y
10 ***Ballenger***	Y	Y	Y	Y	Y	N	N
11 ***Taylor***	Y	Y	Y	Y	Y	N	Y
12 Watt	Y	Y	Y	N	Y	Y	N
NORTH DAKOTA							
AL Pomeroy	Y	Y	Y	Y	Y	N	N
OHIO							
1 ***Chabot***	Y	Y	Y	Y	Y	N	N
2 ***Portman***	Y	Y	Y	Y	Y	N	Y
3 Hall	Y	Y	Y	?	Y	Y	N
4 ***Oxley***	Y	Y	Y	Y	Y	N	N
5 ***Gillmor***	Y	Y	Y	Y	Y	N	N
6 Strickland	Y	Y	Y	Y	Y	N	N
7 ***Hobson***	Y	Y	Y	Y	Y	N	N
8 ***Boehner***	Y	Y	Y	Y	Y	N	Y
9 Kaptur	Y	Y	Y	Y	Y	Y	N
10 Kucinich	Y	Y	Y	N	Y	Y	N
11 Stokes	Y	Y	Y	N	Y	Y	N
12 ***Kasich***	Y	Y	Y	Y	Y	N	N
13 Brown	Y	Y	Y	Y	Y	N	N
14 Sawyer	Y	Y	Y	N	Y	N	N
15 ***Pryce***	Y	Y	Y	Y	Y	N	Y
16 ***Regula***	Y	Y	Y	Y	Y	N	Y
17 Traficant	Y	Y	Y	Y	Y	N	N
18 ***Ney***	Y	Y	Y	Y	Y	N	N
19 ***LaTourette***	Y	Y	Y	Y	Y	Y	Y
OKLAHOMA							
1 ***Largent***	Y	Y	Y	Y	Y	N	Y
2 ***Coburn***	Y	Y	Y	N	Y	N	Y
3 ***Watkins***	Y	Y	Y	Y	Y	N	Y
4 ***Watts***	N	Y	Y	Y	Y	N	Y
5 ***Istook***	Y	Y	Y	N	Y	N	Y
6 ***Lucas***	Y	Y	Y	Y	Y	N	Y
OREGON							
1 Furse	N	Y	Y	Y	Y	N	N
2 ***Smith***	Y	Y	Y	Y	Y	N	N
3 Blumenauer	Y	Y	Y	Y	Y	Y	N
4 DeFazio	Y	Y	Y	N	Y	Y	N
5 Hooley	Y	Y	Y	Y	Y	Y	N
PENNSYLVANIA							
1 Vacant							
2 Fattah	Y	Y	Y	N	?	Y	N
3 Borski	Y	Y	Y	N	Y	Y	N
4 Klink	Y	Y	Y	Y	Y	N	N
5 ***Peterson***	Y	Y	Y	Y	Y	N	Y
6 Holden	Y	Y	Y	Y	Y	N	N
7 ***Weldon***	Y	Y	Y	Y	Y	N	N
8 ***Greenwood***	?	?	?	Y	Y	N	N
9 ***Shuster***	Y	Y	Y	Y	Y	N	N
10 ***McDade***	Y	Y	Y	Y	Y	N	N
11 Kanjorski	Y	Y	Y	N	Y	Y	N
12 Murtha	Y	Y	Y	Y	Y	N	N
13 ***Fox***	Y	Y	Y	Y	Y	N	Y
14 Coyne	Y	Y	Y	Y	Y	Y	N
15 McHale	Y	Y	Y	N	Y	Y	N
16 ***Pitts***	Y	Y	Y	Y	Y	N	N
17 ***Gekas***	Y	Y	Y	?	Y	N	N
18 Doyle	Y	Y	Y	Y	Y	N	N
19 ***Goodling***	Y	Y	Y	Y	Y	N	N
20 Mascara	Y	Y	Y	Y	Y	N	N
21 ***English***	Y	Y	Y	Y	Y	N	Y
RHODE ISLAND							
1 Kennedy	Y	Y	Y	Y	Y	Y	N
2 Weygand	Y	Y	Y	Y	Y	Y	N
SOUTH CAROLINA							
1 ***Sanford***	Y	N	Y	Y	Y	N	N
2 ***Spence***	Y	Y	Y	Y	Y	N	N
3 ***Graham***	Y	Y	Y	Y	Y	N	Y
4 ***Inglis***	Y	Y	Y	Y	Y	N	Y
5 Spratt	Y	Y	Y	Y	Y	N	N
6 Clyburn	Y	Y	Y	N	Y	Y	N
SOUTH DAKOTA							
AL ***Thune***	Y	Y	Y	N	N	N	Y

	139	140	141	142	143	144	145
TENNESSEE							
1 ***Jenkins***	Y	Y	Y	Y	Y	N	Y
2 ***Duncan***	Y	Y	Y	N	Y	N	Y
3 ***Wamp***	Y	Y	Y	N	Y	N	Y
4 ***Hilleary***	Y	Y	Y	N	Y	N	Y
5 Clement	Y	Y	Y	Y	Y	N	N
6 Gordon	Y	Y	Y	Y	Y	N	Y
7 ***Bryant***	Y	Y	Y	Y	Y	N	Y
8 Tanner	Y	Y	Y	Y	Y	N	N
9 Ford	Y	Y	Y	Y	Y	N	N
TEXAS							
1 Sandlin	Y	Y	Y	N	Y	Y	N
2 Turner	Y	Y	Y	N	Y	N	N
3 ***Johnson, Sam***	Y	Y	Y	Y	N	N	Y
4 Hall	Y	Y	Y	Y	Y	N	P
5 ***Sessions***	N	Y	Y	Y	Y	N	Y
6 ***Barton***	Y	Y	Y	Y	Y	N	Y
7 ***Archer***	Y	Y	Y	Y	Y	N	Y
8 ***Brady***	Y	Y	Y	Y	Y	N	Y
9 Lampson	Y	Y	Y	N	Y	N	N
10 Doggett	Y	Y	Y	Y	Y	N	N
11 Edwards	Y	Y	Y	Y	Y	N	N
12 ***Granger***	Y	Y	Y	Y	Y	N	Y
13 ***Thornberry***	Y	Y	Y	Y	Y	N	Y
14 ***Paul***	N	N	Y	Y	Y	N	Y
15 Hinojosa	Y	Y	Y	Y	Y	N	N
16 Reyes	Y	Y	Y	Y	Y	N	N
17 Stenholm	Y	Y	Y	Y	Y	N	Y
18 Jackson-Lee	Y	Y	Y	Y	Y	N	N
19 ***Combest***	Y	Y	Y	Y	Y	N	Y
20 Gonzalez	?	?	?	?	?	?	?
21 ***Smith***	Y	Y	Y	Y	Y	N	Y
22 ***DeLay***	Y	Y	Y	Y	Y	N	Y
23 ***Bonilla***	Y	Y	Y	Y	Y	N	Y
24 Frost	Y	Y	Y	Y	Y	N	N
25 Bentsen	Y	Y	Y	N	Y	N	N
26 ***Armey***	Y	Y	Y	Y	Y	N	Y
27 Ortiz	Y	Y	Y	Y	Y	N	N
28 Rodriguez	Y	Y	Y	Y	Y	N	N
29 Green	Y	Y	Y	Y	Y	Y	–
30 Johnson, E.B.	Y	Y	Y	Y	Y	Y	N
UTAH							
1 ***Hansen***	Y	Y	Y	Y	Y	N	Y
2 ***Cook***	Y	Y	Y	Y	Y	N	Y
3 ***Cannon***	N	Y	Y	Y	Y	N	Y
VERMONT							
AL *Sanders*	Y	Y	Y	Y	Y	Y	N
VIRGINIA							
1 ***Bateman***	+	+	+	+	+	+	+
2 Pickett	Y	Y	Y	Y	Y	N	N
3 Scott	Y	Y	Y	N	Y	N	N
4 Sisisky	Y	Y	Y	Y	Y	N	N
5 Goode	Y	Y	Y	N	N	Y	Y
6 ***Goodlatte***	Y	Y	Y	Y	Y	Y	Y
7 ***Bliley***	Y	Y	Y	Y	Y	N	N
8 Moran	Y	Y	Y	Y	Y	Y	Y
9 Boucher	Y	Y	Y	Y	Y	N	Y
10 ***Wolf***	Y	Y	Y	Y	Y	N	Y
11 ***Davis***	Y	Y	Y	N	Y	Y	Y
WASHINGTON							
1 ***White***	Y	Y	Y	Y	?	N	N
2 ***Metcalf***	Y	Y	Y	Y	Y	N	N
3 ***Smith, Linda***	Y	Y	Y	Y	Y	N	Y
4 ***Hastings***	Y	Y	Y	Y	Y	N	N
5 ***Nethercutt***	Y	Y	Y	Y	Y	N	Y
6 Dicks	Y	Y	Y	N	Y	N	N
7 McDermott	Y	Y	Y	N	Y	Y	N
8 ***Dunn***	Y	Y	Y	Y	Y	N	N
9 Smith, Adam	Y	Y	Y	N	Y	Y	N
WEST VIRGINIA							
1 Mollohan	?	?	?	Y	Y	Y	N
2 Wise	Y	Y	Y	Y	Y	N	N
3 Rahall	?	?	?	Y	Y	N	N
WISCONSIN							
1 ***Neumann***	Y	Y	Y	Y	Y	N	Y
2 ***Klug***	Y	Y	Y	Y	Y	N	Y
3 Kind	Y	Y	Y	Y	Y	Y	N
4 Kleczka	Y	Y	Y	Y	Y	Y	N
5 Barrett	Y	Y	Y	N	Y	Y	N
6 ***Petri***	Y	Y	Y	Y	Y	Y	Y
7 Obey	Y	Y	Y	N	Y	Y	N
8 Johnson	Y	Y	Y	Y	Y	Y	N
9 ***Sensenbrenner***	N	Y	Y	Y	Y	N	Y
WYOMING							
AL ***Cubin***	Y	Y	Y	Y	Y	N	N

Southern states - Ala., Ark., Fla., Ga., Ky., La., Miss., N.C., Okla., S.C., Tenn., Texas, Va.

Key

Y	Voted for (yea).
#	Paired for.
+	Announced for.
N	Voted against (nay).
X	Paired against.
–	Announced against.
P	Voted "present."
C	Voted "present" to avoid possible conflict of interest.
?	Did not vote or otherwise make a position known.

•

Democrats **Republicans**
Independent

---

146. HR 10. Financial Services Overhaul/Financial Holding Company. Leach, R-Iowa, amendment to the Roukema amendment, to delete provisions of the bill that allow financial holding companies and wholesale financial holding companies to earn up to 5 percent of their revenues from commercial activities. The Roukema amendment would increase from 5 percent to 10 percent the amount of total financial holding company revenues that may be earned each year through commercial, non-financial activity. Adopted 229-193: R 138-83; D 90-110 (ND 72-75, SD 18-35); I 1-0. May 13, 1998.

147. HR 10. Financial Services Overhaul/Financial Holding Companies. Roukema, R-N.J., amendment, as amended, to delete provisions of the bill that allow financial holding companies and wholesale financial holding companies to earn up to 5 percent of their revenues from commercial activities. Adopted 218-204: R 131-91; D 86-113 (ND 67-79, SD 19-34); I 1-0. May 13, 1998.

148. HR 10. Financial Services Overhaul/Economic Impact. Kingston, R-Ga., amendment to require the General Accounting Office to conduct a study on the projected economic impact the bill will have on banks and other financial institutions that have total assets of $100 million or less. Adopted 404-18: R 221-2; D 182-16 (ND 129-16, SD 53-0); I 1-0. May 13, 1998.

149. HR 10. Financial Services Overhaul/Bank Insurance Fund. Roukema, R-N.J., amendment to require the FDIC to conduct a study on the Bank Insurance Fund and the Savings Association Insurance Fund to examine their safety and soundness in light of bank and thrift mergers and consolidations that have occurred since 1984. Adopted 406-13: R 212-7; D 193-6 (ND 141-5, SD 52-1); I 1-0. May 13, 1998.

150. HR 10. Financial Services Overhaul/Federal Savings Association. Metcalf, R-Wash., amendment to allow any federal savings association that converts to a national bank charter or state bank charter to retain the word "Federal" in its name, provided it remains an insured depository institution. Adopted 256-166: R 211-11; D 44-155 (ND 31-115, SD 13-40); I 1-0. May 13, 1998.

151. HR 10. Financial Services Overhaul/Passage. Passage of the bill to eliminate current Glass-Steagall Act and Bank Holding Company Act barriers against affiliations between banking, securities, insurance and other firms. Passed 214-213: R 153-73; D 61-139 (ND 47-100, SD 14-39); I 0-1. May 13, 1998.

152. Procedural Motion/Adjourn. Serrano, D-N.Y., motion to adjourn. Motion rejected 15-379: R 0-206; D 15-172 (ND 13-124, SD 2-48); I 0-1. May 14, 1998.

	146	147	148	149	150	151	152
ALABAMA							
1 *Callahan*	N	N	Y	Y	Y	N	N
2 *Everett*	N	N	Y	Y	Y	N	N
3 *Riley*	Y	Y	Y	Y	Y	N	N
4 *Aderholt*	Y	Y	Y	Y	Y	N	N
5 Cramer	Y	Y	Y	Y	N	Y	N
6 *Bachus*	Y	Y	Y	Y	Y	N	N
7 Hilliard	N	N	Y	Y	N	N	N
ALASKA							
AL *Young*	N	N	Y	Y	Y	N	?
ARIZONA							
1 *Salmon*	N	N	Y	Y	Y	Y	N
2 Pastor	N	N	Y	Y	N	Y	N
3 *Stump*	N	N	Y	N	Y	Y	N
4 *Shadegg*	Y	Y	Y	Y	Y	Y	N
5 *Kolbe*	Y	Y	Y	Y	N	Y	?
6 *Hayworth*	N	N	Y	Y	Y	N	N
ARKANSAS							
1 Berry	Y	Y	Y	Y	N	N	N
2 Snyder	Y	Y	Y	Y	N	N	N
3 *Hutchinson*	Y	Y	Y	Y	Y	N	N
4 *Dickey*	N	N	Y	N	Y	N	N
CALIFORNIA							
1 *Riggs*	N	N	Y	Y	Y	Y	?
2 *Herger*	Y	Y	Y	Y	Y	Y	N
3 Fazio	N	N	N	Y	N	Y	N
4 *Doolittle*	Y	Y	Y	Y	?	Y	N
5 Matsui	Y	Y	Y	N	N	N	N
6 Woolsey	Y	Y	Y	N	N	N	N
7 Miller	Y	Y	Y	Y	N	N	N
8 Pelosi	Y	Y	Y	N	N	N	N
9 Lee	N	N	Y	N	N	N	N
10 Tauscher	N	N	Y	Y	N	Y	N
11 *Pombo*	Y	N	Y	N	Y	N	?
12 Lantos	N	N	Y	Y	N	N	N
13 Stark	N	Y	N	Y	N	N	?
14 Eshoo	N	N	Y	N	N	Y	N
15 *Campbell*	Y	Y	Y	Y	Y	Y	N
16 Lofgren	Y	Y	Y	N	N	N	N
17 Farr	N	N	Y	N	N	N	N
18 Condit	Y	Y	Y	Y	N	Y	N
19 *Radanovich*	?	?	?	?	?	Y	?
20 Dooley	N	N	N	Y	N	Y	N
21 *Thomas*	Y	Y	Y	Y	Y	Y	N
22 Capps, L.	N	N	Y	Y	N	N	N
23 *Gallegly*	Y	Y	Y	Y	Y	Y	N
24 Sherman	N	N	Y	Y	N	N	N
25 *McKeon*	Y	Y	Y	Y	Y	Y	N
26 Berman	Y	Y	Y	Y	N	N	N
27 *Rogan*	N	N	Y	Y	Y	N	N
28 *Dreier*	N	N	Y	Y	N	N	N
29 Waxman	Y	Y	Y	N	N	N	N
30 Becerra	Y	Y	Y	Y	N	N	N
31 Martinez	Y	Y	Y	Y	N	N	Y
32 Dixon	Y	Y	Y	Y	N	N	?
33 Roybal-Allard	Y	Y	Y	Y	N	N	N
34 Torres	Y	Y	N	Y	N	N	?
35 Waters	N	N	Y	N	N	N	N
36 Harman	?	?	?	?	?	?	?
37 Millender-McD.	Y	N	Y	Y	N	N	N

	146	147	148	149	150	151	152
38 *Horn*	Y	Y	Y	Y	Y	Y	N
39 *Royce*	N	N	Y	N	Y	N	N
40 *Lewis*	Y	N	Y	?	Y	Y	N
41 *Kim*	Y	N	Y	Y	Y	Y	N
42 Brown	N	N	Y	Y	N	N	Y
43 *Calvert*	Y	Y	Y	Y	Y	Y	N
44 *Bono, M.*	N	Y	Y	Y	Y	Y	N
45 *Rohrabacher*	N	N	Y	Y	Y	N	N
46 Sanchez	N	N	N	N	N	N	N
47 *Cox*	Y	Y	Y	Y	?	Y	N
48 *Packard*	Y	Y	Y	Y	Y	Y	N
49 *Bilbray*	Y	Y	Y	Y	Y	Y	N
50 Filner	Y	Y	Y	N	Y	N	Y
51 *Cunningham*	N	N	Y	Y	Y	Y	N
52 *Hunter*	N	Y	Y	Y	Y	N	N
COLORADO							
1 DeGette	N	N	Y	Y	Y	Y	N
2 Skaggs	+	+	+	Y	–	–	–
3 *McInnis*	Y	Y	Y	Y	Y	N	N
4 *Schaffer*	N	N	Y	Y	Y	N	N
5 *Hefley*	N	N	Y	N	Y	N	N
6 *Schaefer*	Y	Y	Y	Y	Y	Y	N
CONNECTICUT							
1 Kennelly	N	N	Y	Y	N	Y	N
2 Gejdenson	Y	Y	Y	Y	N	Y	N
3 DeLauro	N	N	Y	Y	N	Y	N
4 *Shays*	N	N	Y	Y	N	Y	N
5 Maloney	N	N	Y	N	N	N	N
6 *Johnson*	Y	Y	Y	Y	N	Y	N
DELAWARE							
AL *Castle*	N	N	Y	Y	Y	Y	N
FLORIDA							
1 *Scarborough*	Y	Y	Y	Y	Y	Y	N
2 Boyd	Y	Y	Y	Y	N	Y	N
3 Brown	N	N	Y	N	N	N	N
4 *Fowler*	Y	Y	Y	Y	Y	N	?
5 Thurman	N	N	Y	Y	N	N	N
6 *Stearns*	N	N	Y	N	Y	?	?
7 *Mica*	Y	Y	Y	Y	Y	Y	N
8 *McCollum*	Y	Y	Y	Y	Y	Y	N
9 *Bilirakis*	Y	Y	Y	Y	Y	Y	N
10 *Young*	Y	Y	Y	Y	Y	Y	N
11 Davis	N	N	Y	N	N	N	?
12 *Canady*	Y	Y	Y	Y	Y	Y	N
13 *Miller*	Y	Y	Y	Y	Y	Y	N
14 *Goss*	Y	Y	Y	Y	Y	Y	N
15 *Weldon*	N	N	Y	Y	Y	Y	N
16 *Foley*	N	Y	Y	Y	Y	Y	N
17 Meek	Y	Y	Y	Y	N	N	N
18 *Ros-Lehtinen*	Y	Y	Y	Y	Y	Y	N
19 Wexler	N	N	Y	Y	N	N	N
20 Deutsch	N	N	Y	Y	N	Y	N
21 *Diaz-Balart*	Y	Y	Y	Y	Y	Y	N
22 *Shaw*	Y	Y	Y	Y	Y	Y	N
23 Hastings	N	N	Y	N	N	N	N
GEORGIA							
1 *Kingston*	Y	Y	Y	Y	N	Y	N
2 Bishop	Y	Y	Y	Y	N	N	N
3 *Collins*	Y	Y	Y	Y	N	Y	N
4 McKinney	N	N	Y	N	N	N	N
5 Lewis	N	N	Y	N	N	N	Y
6 *Gingrich*						Y	
7 *Barr*	Y	Y	Y	Y	Y	Y	N
8 *Chambliss*	Y	Y	Y	Y	Y	Y	N
9 *Deal*	Y	Y	Y	Y	Y	Y	N
10 *Norwood*	Y	Y	Y	Y	Y	Y	?
11 *Linder*	N	N	Y	Y	Y	Y	N
HAWAII							
1 Abercrombie	Y	Y	N	N	N	N	N
2 Mink	N	N	N	Y	N	N	N
IDAHO							
1 *Chenoweth*	Y	Y	Y	Y	Y	N	N
2 *Crapo*	Y	Y	Y	?	Y	Y	N
ILLINOIS							
1 Rush	Y	N	Y	Y	N	N	N
2 Jackson	Y	Y	Y	Y	N	N	N
3 Lipinski	Y	Y	Y	Y	N	N	N
4 Gutierrez	Y	Y	Y	Y	N	N	N
5 Blagojevich	Y	N	Y	Y	N	Y	N
6 *Hyde*	Y	N	Y	Y	Y	Y	N
7 Davis	N	N	Y	N	N	N	N
8 *Crane*	Y	Y	Y	Y	Y	Y	N
9 Yates	?	?	?	?	?	?	N
10 *Porter*	N	N	Y	Y	Y	Y	N
11 *Weller*	Y	Y	Y	Y	Y	Y	N
12 Costello	Y	Y	Y	Y	N	N	N

ND Northern Democrats SD Southern Democrats

	146	147	148	149	150	151	152
13 ***Fawell***	Y	Y	Y	Y	Y	Y	N
14 ***Hastert***	N	N	?	Y	Y	Y	N
15 ***Ewing***	Y	Y	Y	Y	Y	N	N
16 ***Manzullo***	Y	Y	Y	Y	Y	N	N
17 Evans	Y	Y	Y	Y	N	N	N
18 ***LaHood***	N	N	N	N	N	N	N
19 Poshard	Y	Y	Y	Y	N	N	N
20 ***Shimkus***	Y	N	Y	Y	N	Y	N
INDIANA							
1 Visclosky	N	N	Y	Y	Y	N	N
2 ***McIntosh***	Y	Y	Y	Y	Y	Y	N
3 Roemer	N	N	Y	Y	N	N	N
4 ***Souder***	Y	Y	Y	Y	Y	Y	N
5 ***Buyer***	N	Y	Y	Y	Y	Y	N
6 ***Burton***	N	Y	Y	Y	Y	Y	N
7 ***Pease***	Y	Y	Y	Y	Y	Y	N
8 ***Hostettler***	Y	Y	Y	N	Y	Y	N
9 Hamilton	Y	Y	Y	Y	N	N	N
10 Carson	N	N	Y	Y	N	N	N
IOWA							
1 ***Leach***	Y	Y	Y	Y	Y	Y	N
2 ***Nussle***	Y	Y	Y	Y	Y	Y	N
3 Boswell	Y	Y	Y	Y	Y	N	N
4 ***Ganske***	Y	Y	Y	Y	Y	Y	N
5 ***Latham***	Y	Y	Y	Y	Y	Y	N
KANSAS							
1 ***Moran***	Y	Y	Y	Y	Y	N	N
2 ***Ryun***	N	N	Y	Y	Y	N	N
3 ***Snowbarger***	N	N	Y	Y	Y	N	N
4 ***Tiahrt***	N	N	Y	Y	Y	N	N
KENTUCKY							
1 ***Whitfield***	Y	Y	Y	Y	Y	Y	N
2 ***Lewis***	N	N	Y	Y	Y	N	N
3 ***Northup***	Y	Y	Y	Y	Y	Y	N
4 ***Bunning***	N	N	Y	Y	Y	Y	N
5 ***Rogers***	Y	Y	Y	Y	Y	N	N
6 Baesler	Y	Y	Y	Y	N	N	N
LOUISIANA							
1 ***Livingston***	N	N	Y	Y	Y	Y	N
2 Jefferson	N	N	Y	Y	N	N	N
3 ***Tauzin***	N	N	Y	Y	Y	Y	N
4 ***McCrery***	Y	Y	Y	Y	Y	Y	N
5 ***Cooksey***	Y	Y	Y	Y	Y	Y	N
6 ***Baker***	N	N	Y	Y	Y	Y	N
7 John	Y	N	Y	Y	Y	Y	N
MAINE							
1 Allen	N	N	Y	Y	N	N	N
2 Baldacci	Y	Y	Y	Y	N	N	N
MARYLAND							
1 ***Gilchrest***	Y	Y	Y	Y	Y	Y	N
2 ***Ehrlich***	N	N	Y	Y	Y	Y	N
3 Cardin	Y	Y	Y	Y	N	N	N
4 Wynn	N	N	Y	Y	Y	N	N
5 Hoyer	Y	Y	Y	Y	N	N	Y
6 ***Bartlett***	N	N	Y	Y	Y	Y	N
7 Cummings	Y	N	Y	Y	N	N	N
8 ***Morella***	N	N	Y	Y	Y	Y	N
MASSACHUSETTS							
1 Olver	Y	Y	Y	Y	N	N	N
2 Neal	N	N	Y	Y	N	Y	N
3 McGovern	N	N	Y	Y	Y	Y	N
4 Frank	N	N	?	?	?	N	Y
5 Meehan	N	N	Y	Y	N	N	N
6 Tierney	Y	Y	Y	Y	N	N	N
7 Markey	Y	Y	Y	Y	N	Y	N
8 Kennedy	Y	Y	Y	Y	N	N	N
9 Moakley	N	N	Y	Y	N	N	N
10 Delahunt	Y	Y	Y	Y	N	Y	N
MICHIGAN							
1 Stupak	N	N	Y	Y	Y	Y	N
2 ***Hoekstra***	N	N	Y	Y	Y	Y	N
3 ***Ehlers***	Y	Y	Y	Y	Y	Y	N
4 ***Camp***	Y	Y	Y	Y	Y	N	N
5 Barcia	N	N	Y	Y	Y	Y	N
6 ***Upton***	Y	Y	Y	Y	Y	Y	N
7 ***Smith***	N	N	Y	Y	Y	Y	N
8 Stabenow	N	N	Y	Y	Y	Y	N
9 Kildee	Y	Y	Y	Y	N	N	N
10 Bonior	Y	Y	N	Y	N	N	N
11 ***Knollenberg***	N	N	Y	Y	Y	Y	N
12 Levin	N	N	Y	Y	N	Y	N
13 Rivers	Y	Y	Y	Y	Y	N	N
14 Conyers	Y	N	N	N	N	N	Y
15 Kilpatrick	N	N	Y	Y	Y	N	N
16 Dingell	N	N	Y	Y	Y	Y	N
MINNESOTA							
1 ***Gutknecht***	Y	Y	Y	Y	Y	N	N
2 Minge	Y	Y	Y	Y	N	N	N
3 ***Ramstad***	N	N	Y	Y	Y	N	N
4 Vento	N	N	N	Y	N	N	N
5 Sabo	Y	Y	N	N	N	N	Y
6 Luther	Y	Y	Y	Y	N	N	N
7 Peterson	Y	Y	Y	N	Y	N	N
8 Oberstar	Y	Y	N	N	N	N	N
MISSISSIPPI							
1 ***Wicker***	Y	Y	Y	Y	Y	N	N
2 Thompson	N	N	Y	Y	N	N	N
3 ***Pickering***	Y	Y	Y	Y	Y	N	N
4 ***Parker***	Y	Y	N	N	Y	Y	N
5 Taylor	N	Y	Y	Y	N	N	N
MISSOURI							
1 Clay	N	N	Y	Y	N	N	N
2 ***Talent***	N	N	Y	Y	Y	Y	?
3 Gephardt	Y	Y	Y	Y	N	N	N
4 Skelton	Y	Y	Y	Y	N	N	N
5 McCarthy	Y	Y	Y	Y	N	N	N
6 Danner	Y	Y	Y	Y	N	N	N
7 ***Blunt***	Y	Y	Y	Y	N	N	N
8 ***Emerson***	Y	Y	Y	Y	Y	Y	N
9 ***Hulshof***	Y	Y	Y	Y	Y	N	N
MONTANA							
AL ***Hill***	N	N	Y	Y	Y	Y	N
NEBRASKA							
1 ***Bereuter***	Y	Y	Y	Y	N	N	N
2 ***Christensen***	?	?	Y	Y	Y	N	?
3 ***Barrett***	Y	Y	Y	Y	Y	N	N
NEVADA							
1 ***Ensign***	Y	Y	Y	Y	Y	Y	N
2 ***Gibbons***	Y	Y	Y	Y	Y	Y	N
NEW HAMPSHIRE							
1 ***Sununu***	Y	Y	Y	Y	Y	Y	N
2 ***Bass***	Y	Y	Y	?	Y	Y	N
NEW JERSEY							
1 Andrews	Y	Y	Y	Y	N	Y	N
2 ***LoBiondo***	Y	N	Y	Y	Y	Y	N
3 ***Saxton***	Y	Y	Y	Y	Y	Y	N
4 ***Smith***	Y	Y	Y	Y	Y	Y	N
5 ***Roukema***	N	N	Y	Y	Y	Y	N
6 Pallone	Y	Y	Y	Y	Y	Y	N
7 ***Franks***	Y	Y	Y	Y	Y	Y	N
8 Pascrell	N	N	Y	Y	N	Y	N
9 Rothman	Y	Y	Y	Y	N	N	?
10 Payne	N	N	Y	Y	N	N	N
11 ***Frelinghuysen***	Y	Y	Y	Y	Y	Y	N
12 ***Pappas***	Y	N	Y	Y	Y	Y	N
13 Menendez	Y	Y	Y	Y	N	N	N
NEW MEXICO							
1 Vacant							
2 ***Skeen***	Y	Y	Y	Y	Y	N	N
3 ***Redmond***	Y	Y	Y	Y	Y	N	N
NEW YORK							
1 ***Forbes***	?	N	Y	Y	Y	Y	N
2 ***Lazio***	N	N	Y	Y	Y	Y	N
3 ***King***	N	N	Y	Y	Y	Y	N
4 McCarthy	N	N	Y	Y	Y	Y	N
5 Ackerman	N	N	Y	Y	N	Y	Y
7 Manton	N	N	Y	Y	Y	Y	N
6 Meeks	N	N	Y	Y	N	Y	?
8 Nadler	Y	N	Y	Y	N	Y	N
9 Schumer	N	N	Y	Y	N	Y	N
10 Towns	N	N	Y	Y	N	Y	N
11 Owens	N	N	Y	Y	N	N	N
12 Velázquez	N	N	N	Y	N	N	N
13 ***Fossella***	N	N	Y	Y	Y	Y	N
14 Maloney	Y	Y	Y	Y	N	Y	N
15 Rangel	N	N	Y	Y	Y	Y	N
16 Serrano	N	N	Y	Y	N	N	Y
17 Engel	N	N	Y	Y	N	Y	?
18 Lowey	N	N	Y	Y	N	Y	N
19 ***Kelly***	N	N	Y	Y	Y	Y	N
20 ***Gilman***	Y	Y	Y	Y	Y	Y	N
21 McNulty	N	N	Y	Y	N	Y	Y
22 ***Solomon***	N	N	Y	Y	Y	Y	N
23 ***Boehlert***	Y	Y	Y	Y	Y	Y	N
24 ***McHugh***	Y	Y	Y	Y	Y	N	N
25 ***Walsh***	N	N	Y	Y	Y	Y	N
26 Hinchey	Y	Y	Y	Y	N	N	N
27 ***Paxon***	N	N	Y	Y	Y	Y	N
28 Slaughter	Y	N	Y	Y	N	N	Y
29 LaFalce	N	N	Y	Y	N	N	N
30 ***Quinn***	Y	N	Y	Y	Y	Y	?
31 ***Houghton***	Y	Y	Y	Y	Y	Y	N
NORTH CAROLINA							
1 Clayton	N	N	Y	Y	N	N	N
2 Etheridge	N	N	Y	Y	Y	N	N
3 ***Jones***	N	Y	Y	Y	Y	N	?
4 Price	N	N	Y	Y	N	Y	N
5 ***Burr***	N	N	Y	Y	Y	N	N
6 ***Coble***	Y	Y	Y	Y	Y	Y	N
7 McIntyre	Y	Y	Y	Y	Y	N	N
8 Hefner	?	?	?	?	?	?	?
9 ***Myrick***	N	N	Y	Y	Y	Y	?
10 ***Ballenger***	Y	Y	Y	Y	Y	Y	N
11 ***Taylor***	Y	Y	Y	Y	Y	Y	N
12 Watt	N	N	Y	Y	N	N	N
NORTH DAKOTA							
AL Pomeroy	Y	Y	Y	Y	N	Y	N
OHIO							
1 ***Chabot***	Y	Y	Y	Y	Y	Y	N
2 ***Portman***	Y	Y	Y	Y	Y	Y	N
3 Hall	N	Y	Y	Y	Y	Y	N
4 ***Oxley***	Y	Y	Y	Y	Y	Y	N
5 ***Gillmor***	Y	Y	Y	Y	N	Y	N
6 Strickland	N	N	Y	Y	N	Y	N
7 ***Hobson***	Y	Y	Y	Y	Y	Y	N
8 ***Boehner***	N	N	Y	Y	Y	Y	N
9 Kaptur	Y	?	Y	Y	N	N	?
10 Kucinich	Y	Y	Y	Y	N	N	N
11 Stokes	N	N	Y	Y	N	N	N
12 ***Kasich***	Y	Y	Y	Y	Y	Y	N
13 Brown	N	N	Y	Y	Y	Y	N
14 Sawyer	N	N	Y	Y	Y	Y	N
15 ***Pryce***	Y	N	Y	Y	Y	Y	N
16 ***Regula***	Y	Y	Y	Y	Y	Y	N
17 Traficant	Y	Y	Y	Y	Y	N	?
18 ***Ney***	N	N	Y	Y	Y	Y	N
19 ***LaTourette***	N	N	Y	Y	Y	Y	N
OKLAHOMA							
1 ***Largent***	N	N	Y	Y	Y	N	N
2 ***Coburn***	Y	Y	Y	Y	Y	N	N
3 ***Watkins***	Y	Y	Y	Y	Y	N	N
4 ***Watts***	N	N	Y	Y	Y	N	N
5 ***Istook***	Y	Y	Y	Y	Y	N	N
6 ***Lucas***	Y	Y	Y	Y	Y	N	N
OREGON							
1 Furse	N	N	Y	Y	N	N	N
2 ***Smith***	Y	N	Y	Y	Y	N	N
3 Blumenauer	N	N	N	Y	N	N	N
4 DeFazio	Y	Y	P	Y	N	N	P
5 Hooley	N	N	Y	Y	Y	N	N
PENNSYLVANIA							
1 Vacant							
2 Fattah	N	N	Y	Y	N	N	?
3 Borski	Y	Y	Y	Y	N	N	N
4 Klink	N	N	Y	Y	N	N	N
5 ***Peterson***	Y	Y	Y	Y	Y	N	N
6 Holden	N	N	Y	Y	N	Y	N
7 ***Weldon***	N	N	Y	Y	Y	Y	?
8 ***Greenwood***	N	N	Y	Y	Y	Y	?
9 ***Shuster***	N	N	Y	Y	Y	N	N
10 ***McDade***	Y	Y	Y	Y	Y	Y	?
11 Kanjorski	Y	Y	N	N	N	N	N
12 Murtha	N	Y	Y	Y	N	Y	N
13 ***Fox***	Y	Y	Y	Y	Y	Y	N
14 Coyne	N	N	Y	Y	N	Y	N
15 McHale	N	N	Y	Y	N	N	N
16 ***Pitts***	N	N	Y	Y	Y	Y	N
17 ***Gekas***	N	Y	Y	Y	Y	Y	N
18 Doyle	N	N	Y	Y	N	Y	N
19 ***Goodling***	Y	Y	Y	Y	Y	Y	?
20 Mascara	N	N	Y	Y	N	N	N
21 ***English***	N	N	Y	Y	Y	Y	N
RHODE ISLAND							
1 Kennedy	Y	Y	Y	Y	N	N	N
2 Weygand	N	N	Y	Y	N	N	N
SOUTH CAROLINA							
1 ***Sanford***	Y	Y	Y	Y	Y	Y	N
2 ***Spence***	?	?	Y	Y	Y	Y	N
3 ***Graham***	Y	Y	Y	Y	Y	N	N
4 ***Inglis***	Y	Y	Y	Y	Y	Y	N
5 Spratt	N	N	Y	Y	N	Y	N
6 Clyburn	N	N	Y	Y	N	N	N
SOUTH DAKOTA							
AL ***Thune***	Y	Y	Y	Y	Y	N	N
TENNESSEE							
1 ***Jenkins***	Y	Y	Y	Y	Y	N	N
2 ***Duncan***	Y	Y	Y	Y	Y	N	N
3 ***Wamp***	Y	Y	Y	Y	Y	Y	N
4 ***Hilleary***	Y	Y	Y	Y	Y	N	N
5 Clement	Y	Y	Y	Y	N	N	N
6 Gordon	N	N	Y	Y	N	Y	N
7 ***Bryant***	N	N	Y	Y	Y	Y	?
8 Tanner	N	N	Y	Y	N	Y	N
9 Ford	N	N	Y	Y	N	Y	N
TEXAS							
1 Sandlin	Y	Y	Y	Y	N	N	N
2 Turner	N	N	Y	Y	Y	N	N
3 ***Johnson, Sam***	N	N	Y	Y	Y	N	N
4 Hall	N	N	Y	Y	Y	N	N
5 ***Sessions***	N	N	Y	Y	Y	N	N
6 ***Barton***	Y	Y	Y	Y	Y	N	?
7 ***Archer***	Y	Y	Y	Y	Y	Y	N
8 ***Brady***	Y	Y	Y	Y	Y	N	N
9 Lampson	N	Y	Y	Y	N	N	N
10 Doggett	N	N	Y	Y	N	N	N
11 Edwards	Y	N	Y	Y	N	N	N
12 ***Granger***	N	N	Y	Y	Y	N	N
13 ***Thornberry***	N	N	Y	Y	Y	N	N
14 ***Paul***	N	N	Y	Y	Y	N	N
15 Hinojosa	Y	Y	Y	Y	N	N	N
16 Reyes	Y	Y	Y	Y	N	N	?
17 Stenholm	N	N	Y	N	Y	N	?
18 Jackson-Lee	N	N	Y	Y	Y	N	N
19 ***Combest***	Y	Y	Y	Y	Y	N	N
20 Gonzalez	?	?	?	?	?	?	?
21 ***Smith***	Y	Y	Y	Y	Y	N	N
22 ***DeLay***	N	N	Y	Y	Y	Y	N
23 ***Bonilla***	Y	N	Y	Y	Y	N	N
24 Frost	N	N	Y	Y	Y	Y	N
25 Bentsen	N	Y	Y	Y	N	N	N
26 ***Armey***	N	N	Y	?	Y	Y	N
27 Ortiz	Y	Y	Y	Y	N	N	N
28 Rodriguez	Y	Y	Y	Y	N	N	N
29 Green	N	N	Y	Y	N	N	N
30 Johnson, E.B.	N	N	Y	Y	N	Y	Y
UTAH							
1 ***Hansen***	Y	Y	Y	Y	Y	Y	N
2 ***Cook***	N	N	Y	Y	N	Y	N
3 ***Cannon***	Y	N	Y	Y	Y	N	N
VERMONT							
AL *Sanders*	Y	Y	Y	Y	Y	N	N
VIRGINIA							
1 ***Bateman***	–	–	+	+	+	+	–
2 Pickett	Y	Y	Y	Y	N	N	N
3 Scott	N	N	Y	Y	Y	N	N
4 Sisisky	Y	Y	Y	Y	Y	N	N
5 Goode	Y	Y	Y	Y	Y	N	N
6 ***Goodlatte***	N	N	Y	Y	Y	Y	N
7 ***Bliley***	Y	Y	Y	Y	Y	Y	N
8 Moran	N	N	Y	Y	N	Y	N
9 Boucher	N	N	Y	Y	Y	N	N
10 ***Wolf***	Y	Y	Y	Y	Y	Y	N
11 ***Davis***	Y	N	Y	Y	Y	N	N
WASHINGTON							
1 ***White***	N	N	Y	Y	Y	Y	N
2 ***Metcalf***	Y	Y	Y	Y	Y	Y	N
3 ***Smith, Linda***	Y	Y	Y	Y	Y	Y	N
4 ***Hastings***	Y	Y	Y	Y	Y	Y	N
5 ***Nethercutt***	Y	Y	Y	?	Y	Y	N
6 Dicks	Y	Y	Y	Y	Y	Y	N
7 McDermott	Y	Y	Y	Y	Y	N	Y
8 ***Dunn***	N	Y	Y	Y	Y	Y	N
9 Smith, Adam	N	N	Y	Y	Y	Y	N
WEST VIRGINIA							
1 Mollohan	N	N	Y	Y	N	Y	N
2 Wise	N	N	Y	Y	N	Y	N
3 Rahall	N	N	Y	Y	Y	Y	N
WISCONSIN							
1 ***Neumann***	N	N	Y	Y	Y	Y	N
2 ***Klug***	Y	Y	Y	Y	Y	Y	N
3 Kind	N	N	N	Y	N	N	N
4 Kleczka	Y	Y	Y	Y	N	N	N
5 Barrett	Y	Y	Y	Y	N	N	N
6 ***Petri***	Y	Y	Y	Y	Y	N	N
7 Obey	Y	Y	Y	Y	N	N	N
8 Johnson	Y	Y	Y	Y	N	N	N
9 ***Sensenbrenner***	N	N	Y	Y	Y	Y	N
WYOMING							
AL ***Cubin***	Y	N	Y	Y	Y	Y	N

Southern states - Ala., Ark., Fla., Ga., Ky., La., Miss., N.C., Okla., S.C., Tenn., Texas, Va.

Key

Y	Voted for (yea).
#	Paired for.
+	Announced for.
N	Voted against (nay).
X	Paired against.
−	Announced against.
P	Voted "present."
C	Voted "present" to avoid possible conflict of interest.
?	Did not vote or otherwise make a position known.

Democrats   **Republicans**   *Independent*

153. Disapproval of Dan Burton/Motion to Table. Armey, R-Texas, motion to table (kill) the Gephardt, D-Mo., privileged resolution to disapprove of the way Dan Burton, R-Ind., has handled his role as chairman of the House Government Reform and Oversight Committee. Motion agreed to 223-196: R 220-0; D 3-195 (ND 0-146, SD 3-49); I 0-1. May 14, 1998.

154. HR 2431. Religious Persecution/Policy Recommendations. Hastings, D-Fla., amendment to allow the director of the Office of Religious Persecution Monitoring, in conjunction with the secretary of State, to make policy recommendations that emphasize the promotion and development of legal protections and respect for religious freedom in U.S. development programs. Adopted 415-3: R 216-2; D 198-1 (ND 145-1, SD 53-0); I 1-0. May 14, 1998.

155. HR 2431. Religious Persecution/Passage. Passage of the bill to establish a new office in the State Department to monitor religious persecution overseas, and to direct U.S. sanctions against countries and individuals determined to have engaged in religious persecution. Passed 375-41: R 206-14; D 169-27 (ND 123-20, SD 46-7); I 0-0. May 14, 1998.

156. HR 3534. Mandates Information/Tax Revenues. Moakley, D-Mass., amendment to strike provisions which exempt from points of order measures resulting in net decreases in tax revenue over five years. Rejected 176-233: R 1-212; D 174-21 (ND 132-10, SD 42-11); I 1-0. May 19, 1998.

157. HR 3534. Mandates Information/Public Health. Waxman, D-Calif., amendment to permit points of order against provisions in legislation which remove or make less stringent private sector mandates established to protect public health and the environment. Rejected 190-221: R 22-192; D 167-29 (ND 133-10, SD 34-19); I 1-0. May 19, 1998.

158. HR 3534. Mandates Information/Points of Order. Boehlert, R-N.Y., amendment to prohibit points of order to be raised against amendments offered on the floor. Rejected 189-223: R 27-188; D 161-35 (ND 130-13, SD 31-22); I 1-0. May 19, 1998.

159. HR 3534. Mandates Information/Civil Rights. Becerra, D-Calif., amendment to permit points of order against provisions which remove or make less stringent private sector mandates established to protect civil rights. Rejected 180-231: R 6-208; D 173-23 (ND 133-10, SD 40-13); I 1-0. May 19, 1998.

	153	154	155	156	157	158	159
ALABAMA							
1 *Callahan*	Y	Y	Y	N	N	N	N
2 *Everett*	Y	Y	Y	N	N	N	N
3 *Riley*	Y	Y	Y	N	N	N	N
4 *Aderholt*	Y	Y	Y	N	N	N	N
5 Cramer	N	Y	Y	N	N	N	N
6 *Bachus*	Y	Y	Y	N	N	N	N
7 Hilliard	N	Y	N	Y	Y	Y	Y
ALASKA							
AL *Young*	Y	Y	Y	N	N	N	N
ARIZONA							
1 *Salmon*	Y	Y	N	N	N	N	N
2 Pastor	N	Y	Y	Y	Y	Y	Y
3 *Stump*	Y	Y	N	N	N	N	N
4 *Shadegg*	Y	Y	N	N	N	N	N
5 *Kolbe*	Y	Y	N	N	N	N	N
6 *Hayworth*	Y	Y	Y	N	N	N	N
ARKANSAS							
1 Berry	N	Y	Y	Y	N	N	N
2 Snyder	N	Y	N	Y	N	N	N
3 *Hutchinson*	Y	Y	Y	N	N	N	N
4 *Dickey*	Y	Y	?	N	?	N	N
CALIFORNIA							
1 *Riggs*	?	?	?	N	N	N	N
2 *Herger*	Y	Y	Y	N	N	N	N
3 Fazio	N	Y	N	Y	Y	Y	Y
4 *Doolittle*	Y	Y	N	N	N	N	N
5 Matsui	N	Y	N	Y	Y	Y	Y
6 Woolsey	N	Y	Y	Y	Y	Y	Y
7 Miller	N	Y	Y	Y	Y	Y	Y
8 Pelosi	N	Y	Y	Y	Y	Y	Y
9 Lee	N	Y	Y	Y	Y	Y	Y
10 Tauscher	N	Y	Y	Y	N	Y	Y
11 *Pombo*	?	Y	N	N	N	N	N
12 Lantos	N	Y	Y	Y	Y	Y	Y
13 Stark	N	Y	Y	Y	Y	Y	Y
14 Eshoo	N	Y	Y	Y	Y	Y	Y
15 *Campbell*	Y	Y	N	N	N	N	N
16 Lofgren	N	Y	Y	Y	Y	Y	Y
17 Farr	N	Y	Y	Y	Y	Y	Y
18 Condit	N	Y	Y	Y	N	N	N
19 *Radanovich*	?	Y	Y	N	N	N	N
20 Dooley	N	Y	N	N	N	N	Y
21 *Thomas*	Y	Y	Y	N	N	N	N
22 Capps, L.	N	Y	Y	Y	Y	Y	Y
23 *Gallegly*	Y	Y	Y	N	N	N	N
24 Sherman	N	Y	Y	N	Y	N	N
25 *McKeon*	Y	Y	Y	N	N	N	N
26 Berman	N	Y	Y	Y	Y	Y	Y
27 *Rogan*	Y	Y	Y	−	−	−	Y
28 *Dreier*	Y	Y	Y	N	N	N	N
29 Waxman	N	Y	Y	Y	Y	Y	Y
30 Becerra	N	Y	Y	Y	Y	Y	Y
31 Martinez	N	Y	Y	Y	Y	Y	Y
32 Dixon	N	Y	Y	Y	Y	Y	Y
33 Roybal-Allard	N	Y	Y	Y	Y	Y	Y
34 Torres	?	?	?	Y	Y	Y	Y
35 Waters	N	Y	Y	Y	Y	Y	Y
36 Harman	?	?	?	?	?	?	?
37 Millender-McD.	N	Y	Y	Y	Y	Y	Y

	153	154	155	156	157	158	159
38 *Horn*	Y	Y	Y	N	Y	N	N
39 *Royce*	Y	Y	Y	N	N	N	N
40 *Lewis*	Y	?	?	N	N	N	N
41 *Kim*	Y	Y	Y	N	N	N	N
42 Brown	N	Y	N	Y	Y	Y	Y
43 *Calvert*	Y	Y	Y	N	N	N	N
44 *Bono, M.*	Y	Y	Y	N	N	N	N
45 *Rohrabacher*	Y	Y	Y	N	N	N	N
46 Sanchez	N	Y	Y	Y	Y	Y	Y
47 *Cox*	Y	Y	Y	N	N	N	N
48 *Packard*	Y	Y	Y	N	N	N	N
49 *Bilbray*	Y	Y	Y	N	Y	N	N
50 Filner	N	Y	Y	Y	Y	Y	Y
51 *Cunningham*	Y	Y	Y	N	N	N	N
52 *Hunter*	Y	Y	Y	N	N	N	N
COLORADO							
1 DeGette	N	Y	N	Y	Y	Y	Y
2 Skaggs	−	+	−	+	+	+	+
3 *McInnis*	Y	Y	Y	N	N	N	N
4 *Schaffer*	Y	Y	N	N	N	N	N
5 *Hefley*	Y	Y	Y	N	N	N	N
6 *Schaefer*	Y	Y	Y	N	N	N	N
CONNECTICUT							
1 Kennelly	N	Y	Y	Y	Y	Y	Y
2 Gejdenson	N	Y	Y	Y	Y	Y	Y
3 DeLauro	N	Y	Y	Y	Y	Y	Y
4 *Shays*	Y	Y	Y	Y	Y	Y	Y
5 Maloney	N	Y	N	Y	N	Y	Y
6 *Johnson*	Y	Y	Y	N	Y	N	N
DELAWARE							
AL *Castle*	Y	Y	Y	N	N	Y	N
FLORIDA							
1 *Scarborough*	Y	Y	Y	N	N	N	N
2 Boyd	N	Y	Y	N	N	N	N
3 Brown	N	Y	Y	Y	Y	Y	Y
4 *Fowler*	?	?	?	N	N	N	N
5 Thurman	N	Y	Y	Y	Y	Y	Y
6 *Stearns*	Y	Y	Y	N	N	N	N
7 *Mica*	Y	Y	N	N	N	N	N
8 *McCollum*	Y	Y	Y	N	N	N	N
9 *Bilirakis*	Y	Y	Y	N	N	N	N
10 *Young*	Y	Y	Y	N	N	N	N
11 Davis	N	Y	Y	N	N	N	Y
12 *Canady*	Y	Y	Y	N	N	N	N
13 *Miller*	Y	Y	N	N	N	N	?
14 *Goss*	Y	Y	Y	N	N	N	N
15 *Weldon*	Y	Y	N	N	N	N	N
16 *Foley*	Y	Y	Y	N	N	N	N
17 Meek	N	Y	Y	Y	Y	Y	Y
18 *Ros-Lehtinen*	Y	Y	Y	N	N	N	N
19 Wexler	N	Y	Y	Y	Y	Y	Y
20 Deutsch	N	Y	Y	Y	Y	Y	Y
21 *Diaz-Balart*	Y	Y	Y	N	N	N	N
22 *Shaw*	Y	Y	Y	N	N	N	N
23 Hastings	N	Y	Y	Y	Y	Y	Y
GEORGIA							
1 *Kingston*	Y	Y	Y	N	N	N	N
2 Bishop	N	Y	Y	Y	N	N	Y
3 *Collins*	Y	Y	Y	N	N	N	N
4 McKinney	N	Y	Y	Y	Y	Y	Y
5 Lewis	N	Y	Y	Y	Y	Y	Y
6 *Gingrich*							
7 *Barr*	Y	Y	N	N	N	N	N
8 *Chambliss*	Y	Y	Y	N	N	N	N
9 *Deal*	Y	Y	Y	N	N	N	N
10 *Norwood*	Y	Y	N	N	N	N	N
11 *Linder*	Y	Y	Y	N	N	N	N
HAWAII							
1 Abercrombie	N	Y	Y	Y	Y	Y	Y
2 Mink	N	Y	N	Y	Y	Y	Y
IDAHO							
1 *Chenoweth*	Y	N	N	N	N	N	Y
2 *Crapo*	Y	Y	N	N	N	N	N
ILLINOIS							
1 Rush	N	Y	Y	Y	Y	Y	Y
2 Jackson	N	Y	Y	Y	Y	Y	Y
3 Lipinski	N	Y	Y	Y	Y	Y	N
4 Gutierrez	N	Y	Y	Y	Y	Y	Y
5 Blagojevich	N	Y	Y	Y	Y	Y	Y
6 *Hyde*	Y	Y	Y	N	N	N	N
7 Davis	N	Y	Y	Y	Y	Y	Y
8 *Crane*	Y	Y	N	?	?	?	?
9 Yates	N	Y	Y	Y	Y	Y	Y
10 *Porter*	Y	Y	Y	N	N	N	N
11 *Weller*	Y	Y	Y	N	N	N	N
12 Costello	N	Y	Y	Y	Y	Y	Y

ND Northern Democrats   SD Southern Democrats

	153	154	155	156	157	158	159
13 ***Fawell***	Y	Y	Y	N	N	Y	N
14 ***Hastert***	Y	Y	Y	N	N	N	N
15 ***Ewing***	Y	Y	Y	–	–	–	–
16 ***Manzullo***	Y	Y	Y	N	N	N	N
17 Evans	N	Y	Y	Y	Y	Y	Y
18 ***LaHood***	Y	Y	Y	N	N	N	N
19 Poshard	N	Y	Y	Y	Y	Y	Y
20 ***Shimkus***	Y	Y	Y	N	N	N	N
INDIANA							
1 Visclosky	N	Y	Y	Y	Y	Y	Y
2 ***McIntosh***	Y	Y	Y	N	N	N	N
3 Roemer	N	Y	Y	N	N	N	N
4 ***Souder***	Y	?	Y	N	N	N	N
5 ***Buyer***	Y	Y	Y	N	N	N	N
6 ***Burton***	Y	Y	Y	N	N	N	N
7 ***Pease***	Y	Y	Y	N	N	N	N
8 ***Hostettler***	Y	Y	Y	N	N	N	N
9 Hamilton	N	Y	N	N	N	N	N
10 Carson	N	Y	Y	Y	Y	Y	Y
IOWA							
1 ***Leach***	Y	Y	Y	N	Y	Y	N
2 ***Nussle***	Y	Y	Y	N	N	N	N
3 Boswell	N	Y	Y	N	Y	Y	N
4 ***Ganske***	Y	Y	Y	?	?	?	?
5 ***Latham***	Y	Y	Y	N	N	N	N
KANSAS							
1 ***Moran***	Y	Y	Y	N	N	N	N
2 ***Ryun***	Y	Y	Y	–	–	–	–
3 ***Snowbarger***	Y	Y	Y	N	N	N	N
4 ***Tiahrt***	Y	Y	Y	N	N	N	N
KENTUCKY							
1 ***Whitfield***	Y	Y	Y	N	N	N	N
2 ***Lewis***	Y	Y	Y	N	N	N	N
3 ***Northup***	Y	Y	Y	N	N	N	N
4 ***Bunning***	Y	Y	Y	N	N	N	N
5 ***Rogers***	Y	Y	Y	N	N	N	N
6 Baesler	N	Y	Y	?	?	?	?
LOUISIANA							
1 ***Livingston***	Y	Y	Y	–	–	–	–
2 Jefferson	N	Y	N	Y	Y	Y	Y
3 ***Tauzin***	Y	Y	Y	N	N	N	N
4 ***McCrery***	Y	Y	Y	N	N	N	N
5 ***Cooksey***	Y	Y	Y	N	N	N	N
6 ***Baker***	Y	Y	Y	N	N	N	N
7 John	?	Y	Y	N	N	N	N
MAINE							
1 Allen	N	Y	Y	Y	Y	Y	Y
2 Baldacci	N	Y	Y	Y	Y	Y	Y
MARYLAND							
1 ***Gilchrest***	Y	Y	Y	N	Y	Y	N
2 ***Ehrlich***	Y	Y	Y	N	N	N	N
3 Cardin	N	Y	Y	Y	Y	Y	Y
4 Wynn	N	Y	Y	Y	Y	Y	Y
5 Hoyer	N	Y	Y	Y	Y	Y	Y
6 ***Bartlett***	Y	Y	Y	N	N	N	N
7 Cummings	N	Y	Y	Y	Y	Y	Y
8 ***Morella***	Y	Y	Y	Y	Y	Y	Y
MASSACHUSETTS							
1 Olver	N	Y	Y	Y	Y	Y	Y
2 Neal	N	Y	Y	Y	Y	Y	Y
3 McGovern	N	Y	Y	Y	Y	Y	Y
4 Frank	N	Y	Y	Y	Y	Y	Y
5 Meehan	N	Y	Y	Y	Y	Y	Y
6 Tierney	N	Y	Y	Y	Y	Y	Y
7 Markey	N	Y	Y	Y	Y	Y	Y
8 Kennedy	N	Y	Y	Y	Y	Y	Y
9 Moakley	N	Y	Y	Y	Y	Y	Y
10 Delahunt	N	Y	Y	Y	Y	Y	Y
MICHIGAN							
1 Stupak	N	Y	Y	Y	Y	Y	Y
2 ***Hoekstra***	Y	Y	Y	N	N	N	N
3 ***Ehlers***	Y	Y	Y	N	N	N	N
4 ***Camp***	Y	Y	Y	N	N	N	N
5 Barcia	N	Y	Y	Y	Y	N	Y
6 ***Upton***	Y	Y	Y	N	N	Y	N
7 ***Smith***	Y	Y	Y	N	N	N	N
8 Stabenow	N	Y	Y	Y	Y	Y	Y
9 Kildee	N	Y	Y	Y	Y	Y	Y
10 Bonior	N	Y	P	Y	Y	Y	Y
11 ***Knollenberg***	Y	Y	Y	N	N	N	N
12 Levin	N	Y	Y	Y	Y	Y	Y
13 Rivers	N	Y	Y	Y	Y	Y	Y
14 Conyers	N	Y	N	Y	Y	Y	Y
15 Kilpatrick	N	Y	Y	Y	Y	Y	Y
16 Dingell	N	Y	N	Y	Y	Y	Y

	153	154	155	156	157	158	159
MINNESOTA							
1 ***Gutknecht***	Y	Y	Y	N	N	N	N
2 Minge	N	Y	Y	Y	N	N	Y
3 ***Ramstad***	Y	Y	Y	N	Y	Y	N
4 Vento	N	Y	Y	Y	Y	Y	Y
5 Sabo	N	Y	N	Y	Y	Y	Y
6 Luther	N	Y	Y	Y	Y	Y	Y
7 Peterson	N	Y	Y	N	N	N	N
8 Oberstar	N	Y	N	Y	Y	Y	Y
MISSISSIPPI							
1 ***Wicker***	Y	Y	Y	N	N	N	N
2 Thompson	N	Y	Y	Y	Y	Y	Y
3 ***Pickering***	Y	Y	Y	N	N	N	N
4 ***Parker***	Y	Y	Y	N	N	N	N
5 Taylor	Y	Y	Y	Y	N	N	Y
MISSOURI							
1 Clay	N	Y	N	?	?	?	?
2 ***Talent***	Y	Y	Y	N	N	N	N
3 Gephardt	N	Y	Y	Y	Y	Y	Y
4 Skelton	N	Y	Y	Y	N	N	Y
5 McCarthy	N	Y	Y	Y	Y	Y	Y
6 Danner	N	Y	Y	N	N	N	N
7 ***Blunt***	Y	Y	Y	N	N	N	N
8 ***Emerson***	Y	Y	Y	N	N	N	N
9 ***Hulshof***	Y	Y	Y	N	N	N	N
MONTANA							
AL ***Hill***	Y	Y	Y	N	N	N	N
NEBRASKA							
1 ***Bereuter***	Y	Y	Y	N	N	N	N
2 ***Christensen***	Y	Y	Y	N	N	N	N
3 ***Barrett***	Y	Y	Y	N	N	N	N
NEVADA							
1 ***Ensign***	Y	Y	Y	N	N	N	N
2 ***Gibbons***	Y	Y	N	–	N	N	N
NEW HAMPSHIRE							
1 ***Sununu***	Y	Y	Y	N	N	N	N
2 ***Bass***	Y	Y	Y	N	N	N	N
NEW JERSEY							
1 Andrews	N	Y	Y	Y	Y	Y	Y
2 ***LoBiondo***	Y	Y	Y	N	Y	Y	N
3 ***Saxton***	Y	Y	Y	N	Y	Y	N
4 ***Smith***	Y	Y	Y	N	Y	Y	N
5 ***Roukema***	Y	Y	Y	N	Y	Y	N
6 Pallone	N	Y	Y	Y	Y	Y	Y
7 ***Franks***	Y	Y	Y	N	Y	Y	N
8 Pascrell	N	Y	Y	Y	Y	Y	Y
9 Rothman	N	Y	Y	Y	Y	Y	Y
10 Payne	N	Y	Y	Y	Y	Y	Y
11 ***Frelinghuysen***	Y	Y	Y	N	Y	Y	N
12 ***Pappas***	Y	Y	Y	N	N	N	N
13 Menendez	N	Y	Y	Y	Y	Y	Y
NEW MEXICO							
1 Vacant							
2 ***Skeen***	Y	Y	Y	N	N	N	N
3 ***Redmond***	Y	Y	Y	N	N	N	N
NEW YORK							
1 ***Forbes***	Y	Y	Y	N	Y	Y	Y
2 ***Lazio***	Y	Y	Y	N	Y	Y	N
3 ***King***	Y	Y	Y	N	N	N	N
4 McCarthy	Y	Y	Y	N	Y	Y	N
5 Ackerman	N	Y	Y	Y	Y	Y	Y
6 Meeks	N	Y	Y	?	?	?	?
7 Manton	N	Y	Y	Y	Y	Y	Y
8 Nadler	N	Y	Y	Y	Y	Y	Y
9 Schumer	N	Y	Y	?	?	?	?
10 Towns	N	Y	Y	Y	Y	Y	Y
11 Owens	N	Y	Y	Y	Y	Y	Y
12 Velázquez	N	Y	Y	Y	Y	Y	Y
13 ***Fossella***	Y	Y	Y	N	N	N	N
14 Maloney	N	Y	Y	Y	Y	Y	Y
15 Rangel	N	Y	N	Y	Y	Y	Y
16 Serrano	N	Y	Y	Y	Y	Y	Y
17 Engel	N	Y	Y	Y	Y	Y	Y
18 Lowey	N	Y	Y	Y	Y	Y	Y
19 ***Kelly***	Y	Y	Y	N	Y	Y	N
20 ***Gilman***	Y	Y	Y	N	Y	Y	N
21 McNulty	N	Y	Y	?	?	?	?
22 ***Solomon***	Y	Y	Y	N	N	N	N
23 ***Boehlert***	Y	Y	Y	N	Y	Y	N
24 ***McHugh***	Y	Y	Y	N	N	N	N
25 ***Walsh***	Y	Y	Y	N	Y	Y	N
26 Hinchey	N	Y	Y	Y	Y	Y	Y
27 ***Paxon***	Y	Y	Y	?	?	?	?
28 Slaughter	N	Y	Y	Y	Y	Y	Y
29 LaFalce	N	Y	Y	Y	Y	Y	Y

	153	154	155	156	157	158	159
30 ***Quinn***	?	?	?	N	N	Y	N
31 ***Houghton***	Y	Y	N	N	N	N	N
NORTH CAROLINA							
1 Clayton	N	Y	Y	Y	Y	Y	Y
2 Etheridge	N	Y	Y	Y	Y	Y	Y
3 ***Jones***	Y	Y	Y	N	N	N	N
4 Price	N	Y	Y	Y	Y	N	Y
5 ***Burr***	Y	Y	Y	N	N	N	N
6 ***Coble***	Y	Y	Y	N	N	N	N
7 McIntyre	N	Y	Y	N	N	N	N
8 Hefner	?	?	?	Y	Y	Y	Y
9 ***Myrick***	Y	Y	Y	N	N	N	N
10 ***Ballenger***	Y	Y	Y	N	N	N	N
11 ***Taylor***	Y	Y	Y	N	N	N	N
12 Watt	N	Y	N	Y	Y	Y	Y
NORTH DAKOTA							
AL Pomeroy	N	Y	Y	Y	N	Y	Y
OHIO							
1 ***Chabot***	Y	Y	Y	N	N	N	N
2 ***Portman***	Y	Y	Y	N	N	N	N
3 Hall	N	Y	Y	Y	Y	N	Y
4 ***Oxley***	Y	Y	Y	N	N	N	N
5 ***Gillmor***	Y	Y	Y	N	N	N	N
6 Strickland	N	Y	Y	Y	Y	Y	Y
7 ***Hobson***	Y	Y	Y	N	N	N	N
8 ***Boehner***	Y	Y	Y	N	N	N	N
9 Kaptur	N	Y	Y	Y	Y	Y	Y
10 Kucinich	N	Y	Y	Y	Y	Y	Y
11 Stokes	N	Y	N	Y	Y	Y	Y
12 ***Kasich***	Y	Y	Y	N	N	N	N
13 Brown	N	Y	Y	Y	Y	Y	Y
14 Sawyer	N	Y	Y	Y	Y	Y	Y
15 ***Pryce***	Y	Y	Y	N	N	N	N
16 ***Regula***	Y	Y	Y	N	N	N	N
17 Traficant	?	?	?	Y	N	N	N
18 ***Ney***	Y	Y	Y	N	N	N	N
19 ***LaTourette***	Y	Y	Y	N	N	Y	N
OKLAHOMA							
1 ***Largent***	Y	Y	Y	N	N	N	N
2 ***Coburn***	Y	Y	Y	N	N	N	N
3 ***Watkins***	Y	Y	Y	N	N	N	N
4 ***Watts***	Y	Y	Y	N	N	N	N
5 ***Istook***	Y	Y	Y	N	N	N	N
6 ***Lucas***	Y	Y	Y	N	N	N	N
OREGON							
1 Furse	N	Y	Y	Y	Y	Y	Y
2 ***Smith***	Y	Y	Y	N	N	N	N
3 Blumenauer	N	Y	N	Y	Y	Y	Y
4 DeFazio	N	Y	Y	Y	Y	Y	Y
5 Hooley	N	Y	Y	Y	Y	Y	Y
PENNSYLVANIA							
1 Vacant							
2 Fattah	N	Y	Y	?	?	?	?
3 Borski	N	Y	Y	Y	Y	Y	Y
4 Klink	N	Y	Y	Y	Y	Y	Y
5 ***Peterson***	Y	Y	Y	N	N	N	N
6 Holden	N	Y	Y	Y	Y	Y	Y
7 ***Weldon***	Y	?	Y	N	N	Y	N
8 ***Greenwood***	Y	Y	Y	?	?	?	?
9 ***Shuster***	Y	Y	Y	?	?	?	?
10 ***McDade***	Y	Y	Y	N	N	Y	N
11 Kanjorski	N	Y	Y	Y	Y	Y	Y
12 Murtha	N	Y	Y	Y	Y	Y	Y
13 ***Fox***	Y	Y	Y	N	Y	N	Y
14 Coyne	N	Y	Y	Y	Y	Y	Y
15 McHale	N	Y	Y	Y	Y	Y	Y
16 ***Pitts***	Y	Y	Y	N	N	N	N
17 ***Gekas***	Y	Y	Y	N	N	N	N
18 Doyle	N	Y	Y	Y	Y	Y	Y
19 ***Goodling***	Y	Y	Y	–	–	–	–
20 Mascara	N	Y	Y	Y	Y	Y	Y
21 ***English***	Y	Y	N	N	N	N	N
RHODE ISLAND							
1 Kennedy	N	Y	Y	Y	Y	Y	Y
2 Weygand	N	Y	Y	Y	Y	Y	Y
SOUTH CAROLINA							
1 ***Sanford***	Y	Y	N	N	N	N	N
2 ***Spence***	Y	Y	Y	N	N	N	N
3 ***Graham***	Y	Y	Y	N	N	N	N
4 ***Inglis***	Y	Y	Y	–	N	N	N
5 Spratt	N	Y	Y	Y	Y	Y	Y
6 Clyburn	N	Y	Y	Y	Y	Y	Y
SOUTH DAKOTA							
AL ***Thune***	Y	Y	Y	N	N	N	N

	153	154	155	156	157	158	159
TENNESSEE							
1 ***Jenkins***	Y	Y	Y	N	N	N	N
2 ***Duncan***	Y	Y	Y	N	N	N	N
3 ***Wamp***	Y	Y	Y	N	N	N	N
4 ***Hilleary***	Y	Y	Y	N	N	N	N
5 Clement	N	Y	Y	Y	Y	Y	Y
6 Gordon	N	Y	Y	Y	N	N	Y
7 ***Bryant***	Y	Y	Y	N	N	N	N
8 Tanner	N	Y	Y	N	N	N	N
9 Ford	N	Y	Y	Y	Y	Y	Y
TEXAS							
1 Sandlin	N	Y	Y	N	N	N	Y
2 Turner	N	Y	Y	N	N	N	N
3 ***Johnson, Sam***	Y	Y	Y	N	N	N	N
4 Hall	Y	Y	Y	Y	N	N	N
5 ***Sessions***	Y	Y	Y	N	N	N	N
6 ***Barton***	Y	Y	Y	N	N	N	N
7 ***Archer***	Y	Y	Y	N	N	N	N
8 ***Brady***	Y	Y	Y	N	N	N	N
9 Lampson	N	Y	Y	Y	Y	Y	Y
10 Doggett	N	Y	Y	Y	Y	Y	Y
11 Edwards	N	Y	Y	N	N	N	Y
12 ***Granger***	Y	Y	Y	N	N	N	N
13 ***Thornberry***	Y	Y	Y	N	N	N	N
14 ***Paul***	Y	N	N	N	N	N	N
15 Hinojosa	N	Y	Y	Y	Y	Y	Y
16 Reyes	N	Y	Y	Y	Y	N	Y
17 Stenholm	N	Y	Y	N	N	N	N
18 Jackson-Lee	N	Y	Y	Y	Y	Y	Y
19 ***Combest***	Y	Y	Y	N	N	N	N
20 Gonzalez	?	?	?	?	?	?	?
21 ***Smith***	Y	Y	Y	N	N	N	N
22 ***DeLay***	Y	Y	Y	N	N	N	N
23 ***Bonilla***	Y	Y	N	N	N	N	N
24 Frost	N	Y	Y	Y	Y	Y	Y
25 Bentsen	N	Y	Y	Y	Y	Y	Y
26 ***Armey***	Y	Y	Y	N	N	N	N
27 Ortiz	N	Y	Y	Y	Y	N	Y
28 Rodriguez	N	Y	Y	Y	Y	Y	Y
29 Green	N	Y	Y	Y	Y	Y	Y
30 Johnson, E.B.	N	Y	Y	Y	Y	Y	Y
UTAH							
1 ***Hansen***	Y	Y	Y	N	N	N	N
2 ***Cook***	Y	Y	Y	N	N	N	N
3 ***Cannon***	Y	?	Y	N	N	N	N
VERMONT							
AL *Sanders*	N	Y	+	Y	Y	Y	Y
VIRGINIA							
1 ***Bateman***	+	+	–	–	–	–	–
2 Pickett	N	Y	N	N	N	N	N
3 Scott	N	Y	Y	Y	Y	Y	Y
4 Sisisky	N	Y	Y	N	N	N	N
5 Goode	Y	Y	Y	N	N	N	N
6 ***Goodlatte***	Y	Y	Y	N	N	N	N
7 ***Bliley***	Y	Y	Y	N	N	N	N
8 Moran	N	Y	N	Y	Y	Y	Y
9 Boucher	N	Y	Y	Y	Y	Y	Y
10 ***Wolf***	Y	Y	Y	N	N	N	N
11 ***Davis***	Y	Y	Y	N	Y	N	N
WASHINGTON							
1 ***White***	Y	Y	Y	N	N	N	N
2 ***Metcalf***	Y	Y	Y	N	N	N	N
3 ***Smith, Linda***	Y	Y	Y	N	N	N	N
4 ***Hastings***	Y	Y	Y	N	N	N	N
5 ***Nethercutt***	Y	Y	Y	N	N	N	N
6 Dicks	N	Y	N	Y	Y	Y	Y
7 McDermott	N	Y	N	Y	Y	Y	Y
8 ***Dunn***	Y	Y	Y	N	N	N	N
9 Smith, Adam	N	Y	N	Y	Y	Y	Y
WEST VIRGINIA							
1 Mollohan	N	Y	?	Y	Y	Y	Y
2 Wise	N	Y	Y	Y	Y	Y	Y
3 Rahall	N	Y	Y	Y	Y	Y	Y
WISCONSIN							
1 ***Neumann***	Y	Y	Y	N	N	N	N
2 ***Klug***	Y	Y	Y	N	N	N	N
3 Kind	N	Y	Y	Y	Y	Y	Y
4 Kleczka	N	Y	Y	Y	Y	Y	Y
5 Barrett	N	Y	Y	Y	Y	Y	Y
6 ***Petri***	Y	Y	Y	N	N	Y	N
7 Obey	N	Y	?	Y	Y	Y	Y
8 Johnson	N	N	Y	?	Y	Y	Y
9 ***Sensenbrenner***	Y	Y	Y	N	N	N	N
WYOMING							
AL ***Cubin***	Y	Y	Y	N	N	N	N

Southern states - Ala., Ark., Fla., Ga., Ky., La., Miss., N.C., Okla., S.C., Tenn., Texas, Va.

Key

Y	Voted for (yea).
#	Paired for.
+	Announced for.
N	Voted against (nay).
X	Paired against.
–	Announced against.
P	Voted "present."
C	Voted "present" to avoid possible conflict of interest.
?	Did not vote or otherwise make a position known.

Democrats   **Republicans**
Independent

160. HR 3534. Mandates Information/Passage. Passage of the bill to require congressional committees to include in their reports on legislation detailed information on potential private sector mandates in excess of $100 million that result from the legislation. The bill also provides for points of order to be used to block consideration of legislation which contains such private sector mandates or whose committee reports lack the required information on the mandate. Passed 279-132: R 205-9; D 74-122 (ND 40-103, SD 34-19); I 0-1. May 19, 1998. A "nay" was a vote in support of the president's position.

161. H Res 440. Foreign Fundraising Resolution/Adoption. Adoption of the resolution to express the sense of the Congress that the Committee on Government Reform and Oversight should confer immunity from prosecution for information and testimony concerning illegal foreign fundraising activities. Adopted 402-0: R 210-0; D 191-0 (ND 139-0, SD 52-0); I 1-0. May 19, 1998.

162. HR 3039. Veterans Transitional Housing/Passage. Stump, R-Ariz., motion to suspend the rules and pass the bill to authorize the Veterans Affairs Department to guarantee loans for the development of transitional housing for homeless veterans. Motion agreed to 405-1: R 212-1; D 192-0 (ND 140-0, SD 52-0); I 1-0. May 19, 1998. A two-thirds majority of those present and voting (271 in this case) is required for passage under suspension of the rules.

163. HR 3718. Prison Release Orders/Passage. Coble, R-N.C., motion to suspend the rules and pass the bill to prohibit a federal court from carrying out any felony prisoner release order on the basis of prison conditions. Motion agreed to 352-53: R 211-2; D 141-50 (ND 99-40, SD 42-10); I 0-1. May 19, 1998. A two-thirds majority of those present and voting (270 in this case) is required for passage under suspension of the rules.

164. HR 3809. Drug Interdiction/Passage. Archer, R-Texas, motion to suspend the rules and pass the bill to authorize $2 billion in fiscal 1999 and $2.2 billion in fiscal 2000 for drug interdiction activities of the U.S. Customs Service. Motion agreed to 320-86: R 208-4; D 112-81 (ND 75-66, SD 37-15); I 0-1. May 19, 1998. A two-thirds majority of those present and voting (271 in this case) is required for passage under suspension of the rules.

165. HR 3616. Fiscal 1999 Defense Authorization/Previous Question. Frank, D-Mass., motion to order the previous question (thus ending debate and the possibility of amendment) on adoption of the rule (H Res 441) to provide for House floor consideration of the bill to authorize $270.4 billion for defense programs. Motion agreed to 281-134: R 216-1; D 65-132 (ND 38-105, SD 27-27); I 0-1. May 20, 1998.

166. HR 3616. Fiscal 1999 Defense Authorization/Rule. Adoption of the rule (H Res 441) to provide for House floor consideration of the bill to authorize $270.4 billion for defense programs. Adopted 304-108: R 213-3; D 91-104 (ND 0-141, SD 0-54); I 0-1. May 20, 1998.

	160	161	162	163	164	165	166
ALABAMA							
1 *Callahan*	Y	Y	Y	Y	Y	Y	Y
2 *Everett*	Y	Y	Y	Y	Y	Y	Y
3 *Riley*	Y	Y	Y	Y	Y	Y	+
4 *Aderholt*	Y	Y	Y	Y	Y	Y	Y
5 Cramer	Y	Y	Y	Y	Y	Y	Y
6 *Bachus*	Y	Y	Y	Y	Y	Y	Y
7 Hilliard	N	Y	Y	N	N	N	N
ALASKA							
AL *Young*	Y	Y	Y	Y	Y	Y	Y
ARIZONA							
1 *Salmon*	Y	Y	Y	Y	Y	Y	Y
2 Pastor	N	Y	Y	Y	N	N	Y
3 *Stump*	Y	Y	Y	Y	Y	Y	Y
4 *Shadegg*	Y	Y	Y	Y	Y	Y	Y
5 *Kolbe*	Y	Y	Y	Y	Y	Y	Y
6 *Hayworth*	Y	Y	Y	Y	Y	Y	Y
ARKANSAS							
1 Berry	Y	Y	Y	Y	Y	N	N
2 Snyder	Y	Y	Y	Y	Y	Y	Y
3 *Hutchinson*	Y	Y	Y	Y	Y	Y	Y
4 *Dickey*	Y	Y	Y	Y	Y	Y	Y
CALIFORNIA							
1 *Riggs*	Y	Y	Y	Y	Y	Y	Y
2 *Herger*	Y	Y	Y	Y	Y	Y	Y
3 Fazio	Y	Y	Y	Y	N	N	Y
4 *Doolittle*	Y	Y	Y	Y	Y	Y	Y
5 Matsui	N	Y	Y	Y	Y	N	N
6 Woolsey	N	Y	Y	?	Y	N	N
7 Miller	N	Y	Y	N	N	N	N
8 Pelosi	N	Y	Y	N	N	N	N
9 Lee	N	Y	Y	N	N	N	N
10 Tauscher	Y	Y	Y	Y	Y	N	Y
11 *Pombo*	Y	Y	Y	Y	Y	Y	Y
12 Lantos	N	Y	Y	Y	Y	Y	Y
13 Stark	N	Y	Y	N	N	N	N
14 Eshoo	N	Y	Y	Y	N	N	Y
15 *Campbell*	Y	Y	Y	Y	N	Y	N
16 Lofgren	N	Y	Y	Y	Y	N	N
17 Farr	N	Y	Y	Y	Y	N	Y
18 Condit	Y	Y	Y	Y	Y	N	Y
19 *Radanovich*	Y	Y	Y	Y	Y	Y	Y
20 Dooley	Y	Y	Y	Y	Y	N	Y
21 *Thomas*	Y	Y	Y	Y	Y	Y	?
22 Capps, L.	N	Y	Y	Y	Y	N	N
23 *Gallegly*	Y	Y	Y	Y	Y	Y	N
24 Sherman	Y	Y	Y	Y	Y	N	Y
25 *McKeon*	Y	Y	Y	Y	Y	Y	Y
26 Berman	N	Y	Y	Y	N	N	N
27 *Rogan*	Y	Y	Y	Y	Y	Y	Y
28 *Dreier*	Y	Y	Y	Y	Y	Y	Y
29 Waxman	N	Y	Y	Y	N	N	N
30 Becerra	N	Y	Y	Y	N	N	N
31 Martinez	N	Y	Y	Y	N	Y	Y
32 Dixon	N	Y	Y	N	Y	N	Y
33 Royal-Allard	N	Y	Y	Y	N	N	N
34 Torres	N	Y	Y	Y	N	N	N
35 Waters	N	?	Y	?	N	N	Y
36 Harman	?	?	?	?	?	?	?
37 Millender-McD.	N	Y	N	Y	N	Y	
38 *Horn*	Y	Y	Y	Y	Y	Y	Y
39 *Royce*	Y	Y	Y	Y	Y	Y	Y
40 *Lewis*	Y	Y	Y	Y	Y	Y	Y
41 *Kim*	Y	Y	Y	Y	Y	Y	Y
42 Brown	N	Y	Y	Y	Y	N	N
43 *Calvert*	Y	Y	Y	Y	Y	Y	Y
44 *Bono, M.*	Y	Y	Y	Y	Y	Y	Y
45 *Rohrabacher*	Y	Y	Y	Y	Y	Y	Y
46 Sanchez	Y	Y	Y	Y	Y	N	Y
47 *Cox*	Y	Y	Y	Y	Y	Y	Y
48 *Packard*	Y	Y	Y	Y	Y	Y	Y
49 *Bilbray*	N	+	Y	Y	N	N	Y
50 Filner	N	Y	Y	N	N	N	N
51 *Cunningham*	Y	Y	Y	Y	Y	Y	Y
52 *Hunter*	Y	Y	Y	Y	Y	Y	Y
COLORADO							
1 DeGette	N	Y	Y	N	N	N	N
2 Skaggs	–	+	+	–	?	N	N
3 *McInnis*	?	Y	Y	Y	Y	Y	Y
4 *Schaffer*	Y	Y	Y	Y	Y	Y	Y
5 *Hefley*	Y	Y	Y	Y	Y	Y	Y
6 *Schaefer*	Y	Y	Y	Y	Y	Y	Y
CONNECTICUT							
1 Kennelly	N	Y	Y	Y	Y	Y	Y
2 Gejdenson	N	Y	Y	Y	N	N	N
3 DeLauro	N	Y	Y	N	N	N	N
4 *Shays*	N	Y	Y	Y	Y	Y	N
5 Maloney	Y	Y	Y	Y	Y	Y	Y
6 *Johnson*	Y	Y	Y	Y	Y	Y	Y
DELAWARE							
AL *Castle*	Y	Y	Y	Y	Y	Y	Y
FLORIDA							
1 *Scarborough*	Y	Y	Y	Y	Y	Y	Y
2 Boyd	Y	Y	Y	Y	Y	N	N
3 Brown	N	Y	Y	N	Y	N	N
4 *Fowler*	Y	Y	Y	Y	Y	Y	Y
5 Thurman	Y	Y	Y	Y	Y	N	Y
6 *Stearns*	Y	Y	Y	Y	Y	Y	Y
7 *Mica*	Y	Y	Y	Y	Y	Y	Y
8 *McCollum*	Y	Y	Y	Y	Y	Y	Y
9 *Bilirakis*	Y	Y	Y	Y	Y	Y	Y
10 *Young*	Y	Y	Y	Y	Y	Y	Y
11 Davis	Y	Y	Y	Y	Y	N	N
12 *Canady*	Y	Y	Y	Y	Y	Y	Y
13 *Miller*	Y	Y	Y	Y	Y	Y	Y
14 *Goss*	Y	Y	Y	Y	Y	Y	Y
15 *Weldon*	Y	Y	Y	Y	Y	Y	Y
16 *Foley*	Y	Y	Y	Y	Y	Y	Y
17 Meek	N	?	?	?	?	N	Y
18 *Ros-Lehtinen*	N	Y	Y	Y	Y	Y	Y
19 Wexler	N	Y	Y	N	Y	N	N
20 Deutsch	N	Y	Y	N	N	N	N
21 *Diaz-Balart*	N	Y	Y	Y	Y	Y	Y
22 *Shaw*	Y	Y	Y	Y	Y	Y	Y
23 Hastings	N	Y	Y	N	N	N	N
GEORGIA							
1 *Kingston*	Y	Y	Y	Y	Y	Y	Y
2 Bishop	Y	Y	Y	Y	Y	Y	Y
3 *Collins*	Y	Y	Y	Y	Y	Y	Y
4 McKinney	N	Y	N	N	N	N	N
5 Lewis	N	Y	N	N	N	N	N
6 *Gingrich*							
7 *Barr*	Y	?	Y	Y	Y	Y	Y
8 *Chambliss*	Y	Y	Y	Y	Y	Y	Y
9 *Deal*	Y	Y	Y	Y	Y	Y	Y
10 *Norwood*	Y	Y	Y	Y	Y	Y	Y
11 *Linder*	Y	Y	Y	Y	Y	Y	Y
HAWAII							
1 Abercrombie	N	Y	Y	Y	Y	Y	Y
2 Mink	N	Y	Y	Y	Y	N	Y
IDAHO							
1 *Chenoweth*	Y	Y	Y	Y	Y	Y	Y
2 *Crapo*	Y	Y	Y	Y	Y	Y	Y
ILLINOIS							
1 Rush	N	Y	Y	N	N	N	N
2 Jackson	N	Y	Y	N	N	N	N
3 Lipinski	Y	Y	Y	Y	Y	Y	Y
4 Gutierrez	N	Y	Y	N	N	N	N
5 Blagojevich	N	Y	Y	Y	Y	Y	Y
6 *Hyde*	Y	Y	Y	Y	Y	Y	Y
7 Davis	N	Y	Y	N	N	N	N
8 *Crane*	?	?	?	?	?	?	?
9 Yates							
10 *Porter*	Y	Y	Y	Y	Y	Y	Y
11 *Weller*	Y	Y	Y	Y	Y	Y	Y
12 Costello	Y	Y	Y	Y	N	N	N

ND Northern Democrats   SD Southern Democrats

	160	161	162	163	164	165	166
13 ***Fawell***	Y	?	?	?	?	Y	Y
14 ***Hastert***	Y	Y	Y	Y	Y	Y	Y
15 ***Ewing***	+	+	+	+	+	+	+
16 ***Manzullo***	Y	Y	Y	Y	Y	Y	Y
17 Evans	N	Y	Y	N	N	N	N
18 ***LaHood***	Y	Y	Y	Y	Y	Y	Y
19 Poshard	Y	Y	Y	Y	N	N	N
20 ***Shimkus***	Y	Y	Y	Y	Y	Y	Y
INDIANA							
1 Visclosky	N	Y	Y	Y	N	Y	Y
2 ***McIntosh***	Y	?	?	?	?	Y	Y
3 Roemer	Y	Y	Y	Y	Y	Y	Y
4 ***Souder***	Y	Y	Y	Y	Y	Y	Y
5 ***Buyer***	?	Y	Y	Y	Y	Y	Y
6 ***Burton***	Y	Y	Y	Y	Y	Y	Y
7 ***Pease***	Y	Y	Y	Y	Y	Y	Y
8 ***Hostettler***	Y	Y	Y	Y	Y	Y	Y
9 Hamilton	Y	Y	Y	Y	Y	N	N
10 Carson	N	Y	Y	N	N	–	–
IOWA							
1 ***Leach***	Y	Y	Y	N	Y	Y	Y
2 ***Nussle***	Y	Y	Y	Y	Y	Y	Y
3 Boswell	Y	Y	Y	Y	Y	Y	Y
4 ***Ganske***	?	?	?	?	?	Y	Y
5 ***Latham***	Y	Y	Y	Y	Y	Y	Y
KANSAS							
1 ***Moran***	Y	Y	Y	Y	Y	Y	Y
2 ***Ryun***	+	Y	Y	Y	Y	Y	Y
3 ***Snowbarger***	Y	Y	Y	Y	Y	Y	Y
4 ***Tiahrt***	Y	Y	Y	Y	Y	Y	Y
KENTUCKY							
1 ***Whitfield***	Y	Y	Y	Y	Y	Y	Y
2 ***Lewis***	Y	Y	Y	Y	Y	Y	Y
3 ***Northup***	Y	Y	Y	Y	Y	?	Y
4 ***Bunning***	Y	Y	Y	Y	Y	Y	Y
5 ***Rogers***	Y	Y	Y	Y	Y	Y	Y
6 Baesler	?	?	?	?	?	N	N
LOUISIANA							
1 ***Livingston***	+	+	Y	Y	Y	Y	Y
2 Jefferson	N	Y	Y	Y	Y	N	Y
3 ***Tauzin***	Y	Y	Y	Y	Y	Y	Y
4 ***McCrery***	Y	Y	Y	Y	Y	Y	?
5 ***Cooksey***	Y	?	?	?	?	Y	Y
6 ***Baker***	Y	Y	Y	Y	Y	Y	Y
7 John	Y	Y	Y	Y	Y	Y	Y
MAINE							
1 Allen	N	Y	Y	Y	N	Y	Y
2 Baldacci	N	Y	Y	Y	N	Y	Y
MARYLAND							
1 ***Gilchrest***	N	Y	Y	Y	Y	Y	Y
2 ***Ehrlich***	Y	Y	Y	Y	Y	Y	Y
3 Cardin	N	Y	Y	Y	Y	N	N
4 Wynn	N	Y	Y	Y	Y	N	Y
5 Hoyer	N	Y	Y	Y	N	Y	Y
6 ***Bartlett***	Y	Y	Y	Y	Y	Y	Y
7 Cummings	N	?	Y	Y	Y	N	N
8 ***Morella***	N	Y	Y	Y	Y	Y	Y
MASSACHUSETTS							
1 Olver	N	Y	Y	N	N	N	N
2 Neal	N	Y	Y	Y	N	N	N
3 McGovern	N	Y	Y	Y	N	N	N
4 Frank	N	Y	Y	N	N	N	N
5 Meehan	N	Y	Y	N	Y	N	N
6 Tierney	N	Y	Y	N	N	N	N
7 Markey	N	Y	Y	Y	N	Y	Y
8 Kennedy	N	Y	?	Y	N	N	N
9 Moakley	N	Y	Y	Y	N	N	N
10 Delahunt	N	Y	Y	N	N	N	N
MICHIGAN							
1 Stupak	N	Y	Y	N	Y	N	N
2 ***Hoekstra***	Y	Y	Y	Y	Y	Y	Y
3 ***Ehlers***	Y	Y	Y	Y	Y	Y	Y
4 ***Camp***	Y	Y	Y	Y	Y	Y	Y
5 Barcia	Y	Y	Y	Y	Y	Y	Y
6 ***Upton***	Y	Y	Y	Y	Y	Y	Y
7 ***Smith***	Y	Y	Y	Y	Y	Y	Y
8 Stabenow	Y	Y	Y	Y	Y	–	–
9 Kildee	Y	Y	Y	Y	Y	N	Y
10 Bonior	N	Y	Y	N	N	N	N
11 ***Knollenberg***	Y	Y	Y	Y	Y	Y	Y
12 Levin	N	Y	Y	Y	Y	N	N
13 Rivers	Y	Y	Y	Y	Y	N	N
14 Conyers	N	Y	Y	N	N	N	N
15 Kilpatrick	N	Y	Y	N	N	N	Y
16 Dingell	N	Y	Y	N	N	N	N

	160	161	162	163	164	165	166
MINNESOTA							
1 ***Gutknecht***	Y	Y	Y	Y	Y	Y	Y
2 Minge	Y	Y	Y	Y	Y	Y	N
3 ***Ramstad***	Y	Y	Y	Y	Y	Y	Y
4 Vento	N	Y	Y	Y	N	N	N
5 Sabo	N	Y	Y	N	N	Y	Y
6 Luther	Y	Y	Y	Y	Y	N	N
7 Peterson	Y	Y	Y	Y	N	Y	Y
8 Oberstar	N	Y	Y	N	N	N	N
MISSISSIPPI							
1 ***Wicker***	Y	Y	Y	Y	Y	Y	Y
2 Thompson	N	Y	Y	N	N	Y	N
3 ***Pickering***	Y	Y	Y	Y	Y	Y	Y
4 ***Parker***	Y	Y	Y	Y	Y	Y	Y
5 Taylor	Y	Y	Y	Y	Y	Y	Y
MISSOURI							
1 Clay	?	?	?	?	?	?	?
2 ***Talent***	Y	Y	Y	Y	Y	Y	Y
3 Gephardt	N	Y	Y	Y	Y	N	N
4 Skelton	Y	Y	Y	Y	Y	Y	Y
5 McCarthy	Y	Y	Y	Y	Y	Y	Y
6 Danner	Y	Y	Y	Y	Y	Y	Y
7 ***Blunt***	Y	Y	Y	Y	Y	Y	Y
8 ***Emerson***	Y	Y	Y	Y	Y	Y	Y
9 ***Hulshof***	Y	Y	Y	Y	Y	Y	Y
MONTANA							
AL ***Hill***	Y	Y	Y	Y	Y	Y	Y
NEBRASKA							
1 ***Bereuter***	Y	Y	Y	Y	Y	Y	Y
2 ***Christensen***	Y	Y	Y	Y	Y	Y	Y
3 ***Barrett***	Y	Y	Y	Y	Y	Y	Y
NEVADA							
1 ***Ensign***	Y	Y	Y	Y	Y	Y	Y
2 ***Gibbons***	Y	Y	Y	Y	Y	Y	Y
NEW HAMPSHIRE							
1 ***Sununu***	Y	Y	Y	Y	Y	Y	Y
2 ***Bass***	Y	Y	Y	Y	Y	Y	Y
NEW JERSEY							
1 Andrews	N	Y	Y	Y	Y	?	?
2 ***LoBiondo***	Y	Y	Y	Y	Y	Y	Y
3 ***Saxton***	N	Y	Y	Y	Y	Y	Y
4 ***Smith***	Y	Y	Y	Y	Y	Y	Y
5 ***Roukema***	Y	Y	Y	Y	Y	Y	Y
6 Pallone	N	Y	Y	Y	Y	N	Y
7 ***Franks***	Y	Y	Y	Y	Y	Y	Y
8 Pascrell	N	Y	Y	Y	Y	Y	Y
9 Rothman	N	Y	Y	Y	Y	N	Y
10 Payne	N	Y	Y	N	N	N	?
11 ***Frelinghuysen***	Y	Y	Y	Y	Y	Y	Y
12 ***Pappas***	Y	Y	Y	Y	Y	Y	Y
13 Menendez	N	Y	Y	Y	Y	N	Y
NEW MEXICO							
1 Vacant							
2 ***Skeen***	Y	Y	Y	Y	Y	Y	Y
3 ***Redmond***	Y	Y	Y	Y	Y	Y	Y
NEW YORK							
1 ***Forbes***	N	Y	Y	Y	Y	Y	Y
2 ***Lazio***	Y	Y	Y	Y	Y	Y	Y
3 ***King***	Y	Y	Y	Y	Y	Y	Y
4 McCarthy	Y	Y	Y	Y	Y	Y	Y
5 Ackerman	N	Y	Y	Y	Y	N	N
6 Meeks	?	?	?	?	?	?	?
7 Manton	N	Y	Y	Y	N	N	?
8 Nadler	N	Y	Y	Y	N	N	N
9 Schumer	?	?	?	?	?	N	N
10 Towns	N	Y	Y	N	N	N	Y
11 Owens	N	Y	Y	N	N	N	N
12 Velázquez	N	Y	Y	N	N	N	N
13 ***Fossella***	Y	Y	Y	Y	Y	Y	Y
14 Maloney	N	Y	Y	Y	Y	N	N
15 Rangel	N	Y	Y	N	Y	N	N
16 Serrano	N	Y	Y	N	N	N	N
17 Engel	N	Y	Y	Y	N	N	N
18 Lowey	N	Y	Y	Y	Y	N	N
19 ***Kelly***	Y	Y	Y	Y	Y	Y	Y
20 ***Gilman***	Y	Y	Y	Y	Y	Y	Y
21 McNulty	?	?	?	?	?	N	N
22 ***Solomon***	Y	Y	Y	Y	Y	Y	Y
23 ***Boehlert***	N	Y	Y	Y	Y	Y	Y
24 ***McHugh***	Y	Y	Y	Y	Y	Y	Y
25 ***Walsh***	Y	Y	Y	Y	Y	Y	Y
26 Hinchey	N	?	?	?	?	?	?
27 ***Paxon***	?	?	?	?	?	?	?
28 Slaughter	N	Y	Y	Y	Y	N	Y
29 LaFalce	Y	Y	Y	Y	Y	N	N

	160	161	162	163	164	165	166
30 ***Quinn***	Y	Y	Y	Y	Y	Y	Y
31 ***Houghton***	Y	Y	Y	Y	Y	Y	Y
NORTH CAROLINA							
1 Clayton	Y	Y	Y	Y	Y	N	Y
2 Etheridge	Y	Y	Y	Y	Y	N	N
3 ***Jones***	Y	Y	Y	Y	Y	Y	Y
4 Price	Y	Y	Y	Y	Y	N	Y
5 ***Burr***	Y	Y	Y	Y	Y	Y	?
6 ***Coble***	Y	Y	Y	Y	Y	Y	Y
7 McIntyre	Y	Y	Y	Y	Y	Y	Y
8 Hefner	N	Y	Y	Y	Y	Y	Y
9 ***Myrick***	Y	Y	Y	Y	Y	Y	Y
10 ***Ballenger***	Y	Y	Y	Y	Y	Y	Y
11 ***Taylor***	Y	Y	Y	Y	Y	Y	Y
12 Watt	N	Y	Y	N	N	N	N
NORTH DAKOTA							
AL Pomeroy	Y	Y	Y	Y	Y	Y	Y
OHIO							
1 ***Chabot***	Y	Y	Y	Y	Y	Y	Y
2 ***Portman***	Y	Y	Y	Y	Y	Y	Y
3 Hall	Y	Y	Y	Y	Y	Y	Y
4 ***Oxley***	Y	Y	Y	Y	Y	Y	Y
5 ***Gillmor***	Y	Y	Y	Y	Y	Y	Y
6 Strickland	Y	Y	Y	Y	Y	N	N
7 ***Hobson***	Y	Y	Y	Y	Y	Y	Y
8 ***Boehner***	Y	Y	Y	Y	Y	Y	Y
9 Kaptur	N	Y	Y	Y	Y	N	N
10 Kucinich	N	Y	Y	Y	N	N	N
11 Stokes	N	Y	Y	N	N	N	N
12 ***Kasich***	Y	Y	Y	Y	Y	Y	Y
13 Brown	N	Y	Y	Y	N	N	N
14 Sawyer	N	Y	Y	Y	N	N	N
15 ***Pryce***	Y	Y	Y	Y	Y	Y	Y
16 ***Regula***	Y	Y	Y	Y	Y	Y	Y
17 Traficant	Y	Y	Y	Y	Y	Y	Y
18 ***Ney***	Y	Y	Y	Y	Y	?	Y
19 ***LaTourette***	Y	Y	Y	Y	Y	Y	Y
OKLAHOMA							
1 ***Largent***	Y	Y	Y	Y	Y	Y	Y
2 ***Coburn***	Y	Y	Y	Y	Y	Y	Y
3 ***Watkins***	Y	Y	Y	Y	Y	Y	Y
4 ***Watts***	Y	Y	Y	Y	Y	Y	Y
5 ***Istook***	Y	Y	Y	Y	Y	Y	Y
6 ***Lucas***	Y	Y	Y	Y	Y	Y	Y
OREGON							
1 Furse	N	Y	Y	N	N	N	N
2 ***Smith***	Y	Y	Y	Y	Y	Y	Y
3 Blumenauer	N	Y	Y	N	N	N	N
4 DeFazio	N	Y	Y	Y	N	N	N
5 Hooley	Y	Y	Y	Y	Y	N	N
PENNSYLVANIA							
1 Vacant							
2 Fattah	?	?	?	?	?	N	N
3 Borski	N	Y	Y	Y	Y	Y	Y
4 Klink	N	Y	Y	Y	Y	Y	Y
5 ***Peterson***	Y	Y	Y	Y	Y	Y	Y
6 Holden	Y	Y	Y	Y	Y	Y	Y
7 ***Weldon***	Y	Y	Y	Y	Y	Y	Y
8 ***Greenwood***	?	?	?	?	?	?	Y
9 ***Shuster***	?	?	?	?	?	Y	Y
10 ***McDade***	Y	?	?	?	?	Y	Y
11 Kanjorski	N	Y	Y	Y	Y	N	Y
12 Murtha	Y	Y	Y	Y	Y	Y	Y
13 ***Fox***	Y	Y	Y	Y	Y	Y	Y
14 Coyne	N	Y	Y	Y	Y	N	N
15 McHale	N	Y	Y	Y	Y	Y	Y
16 ***Pitts***	Y	Y	Y	Y	Y	Y	Y
17 ***Gekas***	Y	Y	Y	Y	Y	Y	Y
18 Doyle	Y	Y	Y	Y	Y	Y	Y
19 ***Goodling***	–	+	+	+	+	+	+
20 Mascara	N	Y	Y	Y	Y	Y	Y
21 ***English***	Y	Y	Y	Y	Y	Y	Y
RHODE ISLAND							
1 Kennedy	N	Y	Y	N	N	Y	Y
2 Weygand	Y	Y	Y	Y	Y	N	Y
SOUTH CAROLINA							
1 ***Sanford***	Y	Y	N	Y	N	Y	Y
2 ***Spence***	Y	Y	Y	Y	Y	Y	Y
3 ***Graham***	Y	Y	Y	Y	Y	Y	Y
4 ***Inglis***	Y	Y	Y	Y	Y	Y	Y
5 Spratt	Y	Y	Y	Y	Y	Y	Y
6 Clyburn	N	Y	Y	N	N	Y	Y
SOUTH DAKOTA							
AL ***Thune***	Y	Y	Y	Y	Y	Y	Y

	160	161	162	163	164	165	166
TENNESSEE							
1 ***Jenkins***	Y	Y	Y	Y	Y	Y	Y
2 ***Duncan***	Y	Y	Y	Y	Y	Y	Y
3 ***Wamp***	Y	Y	Y	Y	Y	Y	Y
4 ***Hilleary***	Y	Y	Y	Y	Y	Y	Y
5 Clement	Y	Y	Y	Y	Y	Y	Y
6 Gordon	Y	Y	Y	Y	Y	Y	Y
7 ***Bryant***	Y	Y	Y	Y	Y	Y	Y
8 Tanner	Y	Y	Y	Y	Y	Y	Y
9 Ford	Y	Y	Y	N	Y	N	Y
TEXAS							
1 Sandlin	Y	Y	Y	Y	Y	N	Y
2 Turner	Y	Y	Y	Y	Y	Y	Y
3 ***Johnson, Sam***	Y	Y	Y	Y	Y	Y	Y
4 Hall	Y	Y	Y	Y	Y	Y	Y
5 ***Sessions***	Y	Y	Y	Y	Y	Y	Y
6 ***Barton***	Y	Y	Y	Y	Y	Y	Y
7 ***Archer***	Y	?	?	?	?	Y	Y
8 ***Brady***	Y	Y	Y	Y	Y	Y	Y
9 Lampson	N	Y	Y	Y	Y	Y	Y
10 Doggett	N	Y	Y	Y	Y	N	N
11 Edwards	Y	Y	Y	Y	Y	Y	Y
12 ***Granger***	Y	Y	Y	Y	Y	Y	Y
13 ***Thornberry***	Y	Y	Y	Y	Y	Y	Y
14 ***Paul***	Y	Y	Y	Y	N	Y	Y
15 Hinojosa	Y	Y	Y	Y	Y	N	N
16 Reyes	Y	Y	Y	Y	N	Y	Y
17 Stenholm	Y	Y	Y	Y	Y	Y	Y
18 Jackson-Lee	N	Y	Y	Y	Y	N	N
19 ***Combest***	Y	Y	Y	Y	Y	Y	Y
20 Gonzalez	?	?	?	?	?	?	?
21 ***Smith***	Y	Y	Y	Y	Y	Y	Y
22 ***DeLay***	Y	Y	Y	Y	Y	Y	Y
23 ***Bonilla***	Y	Y	Y	Y	N	Y	Y
24 Frost	Y	Y	Y	Y	Y	Y	Y
25 Bentsen	Y	Y	Y	Y	Y	N	N
26 ***Armey***	Y	Y	Y	Y	+	?	?
27 Ortiz	Y	Y	Y	Y	N	Y	Y
28 Rodriguez	Y	Y	Y	Y	N	N	N
29 Green	Y	Y	Y	Y	N	N	N
30 Johnson, E.B.	N	Y	Y	N	N	N	N
UTAH							
1 ***Hansen***	Y	Y	Y	Y	Y	Y	Y
2 ***Cook***	Y	Y	Y	Y	Y	Y	Y
3 ***Cannon***	Y	Y	Y	Y	Y	Y	Y
VERMONT							
AL *Sanders*	N	Y	Y	N	N	N	N
VIRGINIA							
1 ***Bateman***	+	+	+	+	+	+	+
2 Pickett	Y	Y	Y	Y	Y	Y	Y
3 Scott	N	Y	Y	N	N	Y	Y
4 Sisisky	Y	Y	Y	Y	Y	Y	Y
5 Goode	Y	Y	Y	Y	Y	Y	Y
6 ***Goodlatte***	Y	Y	Y	Y	Y	Y	Y
7 ***Bliley***	Y	Y	Y	Y	Y	Y	Y
8 Moran	Y	Y	Y	Y	Y	Y	Y
9 Boucher	N	Y	Y	Y	Y	Y	Y
10 ***Wolf***	Y	Y	Y	Y	Y	Y	Y
11 ***Davis***	Y	Y	Y	Y	Y	Y	Y
WASHINGTON							
1 ***White***	Y	Y	Y	Y	Y	Y	Y
2 ***Metcalf***	Y	Y	Y	Y	Y	Y	Y
3 ***Smith, Linda***	Y	Y	Y	Y	Y	Y	Y
4 ***Hastings***	Y	Y	Y	Y	Y	Y	Y
5 ***Nethercutt***	Y	Y	Y	Y	Y	Y	Y
6 Dicks	N	?	?	?	?	Y	Y
7 McDermott	N	Y	Y	N	N	N	N
8 ***Dunn***	Y	Y	Y	Y	Y	Y	Y
9 Smith, Adam	Y	Y	Y	Y	N	Y	Y
WEST VIRGINIA							
1 Mollohan	N	Y	Y	Y	N	Y	Y
2 Wise	N	Y	Y	Y	Y	Y	Y
3 Rahall	N	Y	Y	Y	Y	N	N
WISCONSIN							
1 ***Neumann***	Y	Y	Y	Y	Y	Y	Y
2 ***Klug***	Y	Y	Y	Y	Y	Y	Y
3 Kind	Y	Y	Y	Y	Y	N	N
4 Kleczka	Y	Y	Y	N	Y	N	N
5 Barrett	N	Y	Y	N	N	N	N
6 ***Petri***	Y	Y	Y	Y	Y	Y	Y
7 Obey	N	Y	Y	N	N	N	N
8 Johnson	Y	Y	Y	Y	Y	N	N
9 ***Sensenbrenner***	Y	Y	Y	Y	Y	Y	Y
WYOMING							
AL ***Cubin***	Y	Y	Y	Y	Y	Y	Y

Southern states - Ala., Ark., Fla., Ga., Ky., La., Miss., N.C., Okla., S.C., Tenn., Texas, Va.

167. HR 3616. Fiscal 1999 Defense Authorization/Business Interests. Spence, R-S.C., amendment to express the sense of Congress that U.S. business interests should not be placed above U.S. national security interests and that during President Clinton's upcoming trip to China he should not conclude certain types of international agreements. Adopted 417-4: R 223-0; D 193-4 (ND 141-2, SD 52-2); I 1-0. May 20, 1998.

168. HR 3616. Fiscal 1999 Defense Authorization/Government Representative. Bereuter, R-Neb., amendment to prohibit the participation of U.S. citizens in the investigation of a failed launch of a U.S. satellite on a foreign launch vehicle. Adopted 414-7: R 220-1; D 193-6 (ND 142-3, SD 51-3); I 1-0. May 20, 1998. A "nay" was a vote in support of the president's position.

169. HR 3616. Fiscal 1999 Defense Authorization/Missile Equipment. Hefley, R-Colo., amendment to prevent the transfer of any U.S. missile equipment or technology that could be used by the People's Republic of China for strategic purposes. Adopted 412-6: R 217-1; D 194-5 (ND 143-2, SD 51-3); I 1-0. May 20, 1998. A "nay" was a vote in support of the president's position.

170. HR 3616. Fiscal 1999 Defense Authorization/U.S. Satellites. Hunter, R-Calif., amendment to prohibit the export or re-export of any U.S. satellites, including commercial satellites and their components, to the People's Republic of China. Adopted 364-54: R 210-10; D 153-44 (ND 110-34, SD 43-10); I 1-0. May 20, 1998. A "nay" was a vote in support of the president's position.

171. HR 3616. Fiscal 1999 Defense Authorization/Abortion. Lowey, D-N.Y., amendment to repeal provisions of current law that prohibit privately-funded abortions at overseas Defense Department medical facilities. Rejected 190-232: R 30-194; D 159-38 (ND 114-29, SD 45-9); I 1-0. May 20, 1998. A "yea" was a vote in support of the president's position.

172. HR 3616. Fiscal 1999 Defense Authorization/Kyoto Protocol. Gilman, R-N.Y., amendment to state that no provision of the Kyoto Protocol on global warming will restrict the procurement, training, operation or maintenance of U.S. armed forces. Adopted 420-0: R 223-0; D 196-0 (ND 142-0, SD 54-0); I 1-0. May 20, 1998.

173. HR 3616. Fiscal 1999 Defense Authorization/United Nations. Hefley, R-Colo., amendment to prohibit the assignment of any member of the U.S. armed services to duty with the United Nations Rapidly Deployable Mission Headquarters, or any other standing army under command of the U.N. Adopted 250-172: R 213-11; D 37-160 (ND 20-123, SD 17-37); I 0-1. May 20, 1998.

Key

Y	Voted for (yea).
#	Paired for.
+	Announced for.
N	Voted against (nay).
X	Paired against.
−	Announced against.
P	Voted "present."
C	Voted "present" to avoid possible conflict of interest.
?	Did not vote or otherwise make a position known.

Democrats   **Republicans**
Independent

	167	168	169	170	171	172	173
ALABAMA							
1 *Callahan*	Y	Y	Y	Y	N	Y	Y
2 *Everett*	Y	Y	Y	Y	N	Y	Y
3 *Riley*	Y	Y	Y	Y	N	Y	Y
4 *Aderholt*	Y	Y	Y	Y	N	Y	Y
5 Cramer	Y	Y	Y	Y	Y	Y	Y
6 *Bachus*	Y	Y	Y	N	Y	Y	Y
7 Hilliard	Y	Y	Y	Y	Y	Y	N
ALASKA							
AL *Young*	Y	Y	Y	Y	N	Y	Y
ARIZONA							
1 *Salmon*	Y	Y	Y	N	N	Y	Y
2 Pastor	Y	Y	Y	Y	Y	Y	N
3 *Stump*	Y	Y	Y	Y	N	Y	Y
4 *Shadegg*	Y	Y	Y	Y	N	Y	Y
5 *Kolbe*	Y	Y	Y	N	Y	N	Y
6 *Hayworth*	Y	Y	Y	Y	N	Y	Y
ARKANSAS							
1 Berry	Y	Y	Y	N	N	Y	Y
2 Snyder	Y	Y	Y	Y	Y	Y	Y
3 *Hutchinson*	Y	Y	Y	Y	N	Y	Y
4 *Dickey*	Y	Y	Y	N	Y	Y	Y
CALIFORNIA							
1 *Riggs*	Y	Y	Y	Y	N	Y	Y
2 *Herger*	Y	Y	Y	Y	N	Y	Y
3 Fazio	Y	Y	Y	N	Y	Y	N
4 *Doolittle*	Y	Y	Y	Y	N	Y	N
5 Matsui	Y	Y	Y	N	Y	Y	N
6 Woolsey	Y	Y	Y	Y	Y	Y	N
7 Miller	Y	Y	Y	Y	Y	Y	N
8 Pelosi	Y	Y	Y	Y	Y	Y	N
9 Lee	Y	Y	N	Y	Y	Y	N
10 Tauscher	Y	Y	N	Y	N	Y	N
11 *Pombo*	Y	Y	Y	Y	N	Y	Y
12 Lantos	Y	Y	Y	N	Y	Y	N
13 Stark	?	Y	Y	Y	Y	Y	N
14 Eshoo	Y	Y	N	Y	Y	Y	N
15 *Campbell*	Y	N	N	N	Y	N	N
16 Lofgren	Y	Y	N	Y	Y	Y	N
17 Farr	Y	Y	N	Y	Y	Y	N
18 Condit	Y	Y	Y	Y	Y	Y	Y
19 *Radanovich*	Y	Y	Y	Y	N	Y	Y
20 Dooley	Y	Y	N	Y	N	Y	N
21 *Thomas*	Y	Y	Y	Y	Y	Y	Y
22 Capps, L.	Y	Y	Y	Y	Y	Y	Y
23 *Gallegly*	Y	Y	Y	N	Y	Y	Y
24 Sherman	Y	Y	Y	N	Y	Y	N
25 *McKeon*	Y	Y	Y	N	Y	Y	Y
26 Berman	Y	Y	Y	Y	Y	Y	N
27 *Rogan*	Y	Y	Y	N	Y	Y	Y
28 *Dreier*	Y	Y	N	N	Y	Y	Y
29 Waxman	Y	Y	Y	Y	Y	Y	N
30 Becerra	Y	Y	Y	Y	Y	Y	N
31 Martinez	Y	Y	Y	Y	Y	Y	Y
32 Dixon	Y	Y	N	Y	Y	Y	N
33 Roybal-Allard	Y	Y	N	Y	Y	Y	N
34 Torres	Y	Y	Y	Y	Y	Y	N
35 Waters	Y	Y	N	Y	Y	Y	N
36 Harman	?	?	?	?	?	?	?
37 Millender-McD.	Y	Y	Y	Y	Y	Y	N

	167	168	169	170	171	172	173
38 *Horn*	Y	Y	Y	Y	Y	Y	Y
39 *Royce*	Y	Y	Y	Y	N	Y	Y
40 *Lewis*	Y	Y	Y	Y	N	Y	Y
41 *Kim*	Y	Y	Y	Y	N	Y	Y
42 Brown	Y	Y	Y	N	Y	N	Y
43 *Calvert*	Y	Y	Y	Y	N	Y	Y
44 *Bono, M.*	Y	Y	Y	Y	N	Y	Y
45 *Rohrabacher*	Y	Y	Y	Y	N	Y	Y
46 Sanchez	Y	Y	Y	N	Y	Y	N
47 *Cox*	Y	?	?	?	N	Y	Y
48 *Packard*	Y	Y	Y	Y	N	Y	Y
49 *Bilbray*	Y	Y	Y	Y	N	Y	Y
50 Filner	Y	Y	Y	Y	Y	Y	N
51 *Cunningham*	Y	Y	Y	Y	N	Y	Y
52 *Hunter*	Y	Y	Y	Y	N	Y	Y
COLORADO							
1 DeGette	Y	Y	Y	Y	Y	Y	N
2 Skaggs	Y	Y	Y	N	Y	Y	N
3 *McInnis*	Y	Y	Y	Y	N	Y	Y
4 *Schaffer*	Y	Y	Y	Y	N	Y	Y
5 *Hefley*	Y	Y	Y	Y	N	Y	Y
6 *Schaefer*	Y	Y	Y	Y	N	Y	Y
CONNECTICUT							
1 Kennelly	Y	Y	Y	Y	Y	Y	N
2 Gejdenson	Y	Y	Y	Y	Y	Y	N
3 DeLauro	Y	Y	Y	Y	Y	Y	N
4 *Shays*	Y	Y	Y	Y	Y	Y	Y
5 Maloney	Y	Y	Y	Y	Y	Y	N
6 *Johnson*	Y	Y	N	Y	Y	Y	N
DELAWARE							
AL *Castle*	Y	Y	Y	Y	Y	Y	Y
FLORIDA							
1 *Scarborough*	Y	Y	Y	Y	N	Y	Y
2 Boyd	Y	Y	Y	Y	N	Y	N
3 Brown	Y	Y	Y	Y	Y	Y	N
4 *Fowler*	Y	Y	Y	Y	Y	Y	Y
5 Thurman	Y	Y	Y	Y	Y	Y	N
6 *Stearns*	Y	Y	Y	Y	N	Y	Y
7 *Mica*	Y	Y	Y	Y	N	Y	Y
8 *McCollum*	Y	Y	Y	Y	N	Y	Y
9 *Bilirakis*	Y	Y	Y	Y	N	Y	Y
10 *Young*	Y	Y	Y	Y	N	Y	Y
11 Davis	Y	Y	Y	N	Y	Y	N
12 *Canady*	Y	Y	Y	Y	N	Y	Y
13 *Miller*	Y	Y	Y	Y	N	Y	Y
14 *Goss*	Y	Y	Y	Y	N	Y	Y
15 *Weldon*	Y	Y	+	Y	N	Y	Y
16 *Foley*	Y	Y	Y	Y	N	Y	Y
17 Meek	Y	Y	Y	Y	Y	Y	N
18 *Ros-Lehtinen*	Y	Y	N	Y	Y	Y	Y
19 Wexler	N	N	N	N	Y	N	N
20 Deutsch	Y	Y	Y	Y	Y	Y	N
21 *Diaz-Balart*	Y	+	Y	N	Y	Y	Y
22 *Shaw*	Y	Y	Y	Y	Y	Y	Y
23 Hastings	N	N	N	N	Y	N	N
GEORGIA							
1 *Kingston*	Y	Y	Y	Y	N	Y	Y
2 Bishop	Y	Y	Y	Y	N	Y	Y
3 *Collins*	Y	Y	Y	Y	N	Y	Y
4 McKinney	Y	Y	Y	Y	Y	Y	N
5 Lewis	Y	Y	Y	N	Y	Y	N
6 *Gingrich*							
7 *Barr*	Y	Y	Y	Y	N	Y	Y
8 *Chambliss*	Y	Y	Y	Y	N	Y	Y
9 *Deal*	Y	Y	Y	Y	N	Y	Y
10 *Norwood*	Y	?	Y	Y	N	Y	Y
11 *Linder*	Y	Y	Y	Y	N	Y	Y
HAWAII							
1 Abercrombie	Y	Y	Y	Y	Y	Y	N
2 Mink	Y	Y	Y	Y	Y	Y	N
IDAHO							
1 *Chenoweth*	Y	Y	Y	Y	N	Y	Y
2 *Crapo*	Y	Y	Y	Y	N	Y	Y
ILLINOIS							
1 Rush	Y	Y	Y	Y	Y	Y	N
2 Jackson	Y	Y	Y	Y	Y	Y	N
3 Lipinski	Y	Y	Y	Y	Y	Y	Y
4 Gutierrez	Y	Y	Y	Y	Y	Y	N
5 Blagojevich	Y	Y	Y	Y	Y	Y	N
6 *Hyde*	Y	Y	Y	Y	N	Y	Y
7 Davis	Y	Y	Y	Y	Y	Y	N
8 *Crane*	Y	Y	Y	N	N	Y	Y
9 Yates	Y	N	Y	N	Y	Y	N
10 *Porter*	Y	Y	N	Y	Y	Y	N
11 *Weller*	Y	Y	Y	Y	N	Y	Y
12 Costello	Y	Y	Y	Y	N	Y	N

ND Northern Democrats   SD Southern Democrats

	167	168	169	170	171	172	173
13 **Fawell**	Y	Y	?	Y	Y	Y	Y
14 **Hastert**	Y	Y	Y	Y	N	Y	Y
15 **Ewing**	+	+	+	+	X	+	+
16 **Manzullo**	Y	Y	Y	N	N	Y	Y
17 Evans	Y	Y	Y	Y	Y	Y	N
18 **LaHood**	Y	Y	Y	Y	N	Y	Y
19 Poshard	Y	Y	Y	Y	N	Y	Y
20 **Shimkus**	Y	Y	Y	Y	N	Y	Y
INDIANA							
1 Visclosky	Y	Y	Y	Y	Y	Y	N
2 **McIntosh**	Y	Y	?	Y	N	Y	Y
3 Roemer	Y	Y	Y	Y	N	Y	Y
4 **Souder**	Y	Y	Y	?	N	Y	Y
5 **Buyer**	Y	Y	Y	Y	N	Y	Y
6 **Burton**	Y	Y	Y	Y	N	Y	Y
7 **Pease**	Y	Y	Y	Y	N	Y	Y
8 **Hostettler**	Y	Y	Y	Y	N	Y	Y
9 Hamilton	N	N	N	N	N	Y	N
10 Carson	+	+	+	+	+	+	−
IOWA							
1 **Leach**	Y	Y	Y	Y	Y	Y	N
2 **Nussle**	Y	Y	Y	Y	N	Y	Y
3 Boswell	Y	Y	Y	Y	Y	Y	Y
4 **Ganske**	Y	Y	Y	Y	N	Y	Y
5 **Latham**	Y	Y	Y	Y	N	Y	Y
KANSAS							
1 **Moran**	Y	Y	Y	Y	N	Y	Y
2 **Ryun**	Y	Y	Y	Y	N	Y	Y
3 **Snowbarger**	Y	Y	Y	Y	N	Y	Y
4 **Tiahrt**	Y	Y	Y	Y	N	Y	Y
KENTUCKY							
1 **Whitfield**	Y	Y	Y	Y	N	Y	Y
2 **Lewis**	Y	Y	Y	Y	N	Y	Y
3 **Northup**	Y	Y	Y	Y	N	Y	Y
4 **Bunning**	Y	Y	Y	Y	N	Y	Y
5 **Rogers**	Y	Y	Y	Y	N	Y	Y
6 Baesler	Y	Y	Y	Y	Y	Y	N
LOUISIANA							
1 **Livingston**	Y	Y	Y	Y	N	Y	Y
2 Jefferson	Y	Y	Y	Y	Y	Y	N
3 **Tauzin**	Y	Y	Y	Y	N	Y	Y
4 **McCrery**	Y	Y	Y	Y	N	Y	Y
5 **Cooksey**	Y	Y	Y	Y	N	Y	Y
6 **Baker**	Y	Y	Y	Y	N	Y	Y
7 John	Y	Y	Y	Y	N	Y	N
MAINE							
1 Allen	Y	Y	Y	N	Y	Y	N
2 Baldacci	Y	Y	Y	Y	Y	Y	N
MARYLAND							
1 **Gilchrest**	Y	Y	Y	Y	Y	Y	Y
2 **Ehrlich**	Y	Y	Y	Y	Y	Y	Y
3 Cardin	Y	Y	Y	Y	Y	Y	N
4 Wynn	Y	Y	Y	Y	Y	Y	N
5 Hoyer	Y	Y	Y	Y	Y	Y	N
6 **Bartlett**	Y	Y	Y	Y	N	Y	Y
7 Cummings	Y	Y	Y	Y	Y	Y	N
8 **Morella**	Y	Y	Y	Y	Y	Y	N
MASSACHUSETTS							
1 Olver	Y	Y	Y	N	Y	Y	N
2 Neal	Y	Y	Y	Y	Y	Y	N
3 McGovern	Y	Y	Y	Y	Y	Y	N
4 Frank	Y	Y	Y	Y	Y	P	N
5 Meehan	Y	Y	Y	Y	Y	Y	N
6 Tierney	Y	Y	Y	Y	Y	Y	N
7 Markey	Y	Y	Y	Y	Y	Y	N
8 Kennedy	Y	Y	Y	Y	Y	Y	N
9 Moakley	Y	Y	Y	Y	N	Y	N
10 Delahunt	Y	Y	Y	Y	Y	Y	N
MICHIGAN							
1 Stupak	Y	Y	Y	Y	N	Y	N
2 **Hoekstra**	Y	Y	Y	Y	N	Y	Y
3 **Ehlers**	Y	Y	Y	N	N	Y	N
4 **Camp**	Y	Y	Y	Y	N	Y	Y
5 Barcia	Y	Y	Y	Y	N	Y	Y
6 **Upton**	Y	Y	Y	Y	N	Y	Y
7 **Smith**	Y	Y	Y	Y	N	Y	Y
8 Stabenow	+	+	+	−	#	+	+
9 Kildee	Y	Y	Y	Y	N	Y	N
10 Bonior	Y	Y	Y	Y	Y	Y	N
11 **Knollenberg**	Y	Y	Y	Y	N	Y	Y
12 Levin	Y	Y	Y	Y	Y	Y	N
13 Rivers	Y	Y	Y	Y	Y	Y	N
14 Conyers	Y	Y	Y	N	Y	Y	N
15 Kilpatrick	Y	Y	Y	N	Y	Y	N
16 Dingell	Y	Y	Y	Y	Y	Y	N

	167	168	169	170	171	172	173
MINNESOTA							
1 **Gutknecht**	Y	Y	Y	Y	N	Y	Y
2 Minge	Y	Y	Y	Y	Y	Y	N
3 **Ramstad**	Y	Y	Y	Y	Y	Y	Y
4 Vento	Y	Y	Y	Y	Y	Y	N
5 Sabo	Y	Y	Y	N	Y	Y	N
6 Luther	Y	Y	Y	Y	Y	Y	N
7 Peterson	Y	Y	Y	Y	N	Y	Y
8 Oberstar	Y	Y	Y	Y	N	Y	N
MISSISSIPPI							
1 **Wicker**	Y	Y	Y	Y	N	Y	Y
2 Thompson	Y	Y	Y	Y	Y	Y	N
3 **Pickering**	Y	Y	Y	Y	N	Y	Y
4 **Parker**	Y	Y	Y	Y	N	Y	Y
5 Taylor	Y	Y	Y	Y	N	Y	Y
MISSOURI							
1 Clay	?	?	?	?	?	?	?
2 **Talent**	Y	Y	Y	Y	N	Y	Y
3 Gephardt	Y	Y	Y	Y	Y	Y	N
4 Skelton	Y	Y	Y	Y	N	Y	N
5 McCarthy	Y	Y	Y	N	Y	Y	N
6 Danner	Y	Y	Y	Y	N	Y	Y
7 **Blunt**	Y	Y	Y	Y	N	Y	Y
8 **Emerson**	Y	Y	Y	Y	N	Y	Y
9 **Hulshof**	Y	Y	Y	Y	N	Y	Y
MONTANA							
AL **Hill**	Y	Y	?	Y	N	Y	Y
NEBRASKA							
1 **Bereuter**	Y	Y	Y	Y	N	Y	Y
2 **Christensen**	Y	Y	Y	Y	N	Y	Y
3 **Barrett**	Y	Y	Y	Y	N	Y	Y
NEVADA							
1 **Ensign**	Y	Y	Y	Y	N	Y	Y
2 **Gibbons**	Y	Y	Y	Y	N	Y	Y
NEW HAMPSHIRE							
1 **Sununu**	Y	Y	Y	Y	N	Y	Y
2 **Bass**	Y	Y	Y	+	Y	Y	Y
NEW JERSEY							
1 Andrews	Y	Y	Y	Y	Y	Y	Y
2 **LoBiondo**	Y	Y	Y	Y	N	Y	Y
3 **Saxton**	Y	Y	Y	Y	N	Y	Y
4 **Smith**	Y	Y	Y	Y	N	Y	Y
5 **Roukema**	Y	Y	Y	Y	Y	Y	Y
6 Pallone	Y	Y	Y	Y	Y	Y	N
7 **Franks**	Y	Y	Y	Y	Y	Y	Y
8 Pascrell	Y	Y	Y	Y	Y	Y	N
9 Rothman	Y	Y	Y	Y	Y	Y	N
10 Payne	Y	Y	Y	Y	Y	Y	N
11 **Frelinghuysen**	Y	Y	Y	Y	Y	Y	Y
12 **Pappas**	Y	Y	Y	Y	N	Y	Y
13 Menendez	Y	Y	Y	Y	Y	Y	N
NEW MEXICO							
1 Vacant							
2 **Skeen**	Y	Y	Y	Y	N	Y	Y
3 **Redmond**	Y	Y	Y	Y	N	Y	Y
NEW YORK							
1 **Forbes**	Y	Y	Y	Y	N	Y	Y
2 **Lazio**	Y	Y	Y	Y	N	Y	Y
3 **King**	Y	Y	Y	Y	N	Y	N
4 McCarthy	Y	Y	Y	Y	Y	Y	N
5 Ackerman	Y	Y	Y	N	Y	Y	N
6 Meeks	?	?	?	?	?	?	?
7 Manton	Y	Y	Y	Y	N	Y	N
8 Nadler	Y	Y	Y	Y	Y	Y	N
9 Schumer	Y	Y	Y	Y	Y	Y	N
10 Towns	Y	Y	Y	Y	Y	Y	N
11 Owens	Y	Y	Y	?	Y	Y	N
12 Velázquez	Y	Y	Y	Y	Y	Y	N
13 **Fossella**	Y	Y	Y	Y	N	Y	Y
14 Maloney	Y	Y	Y	Y	Y	Y	N
15 Rangel	Y	Y	Y	Y	Y	Y	N
16 Serrano	Y	Y	Y	N	Y	Y	N
17 Engel	Y	Y	Y	Y	Y	Y	N
18 Lowey	Y	Y	Y	Y	Y	Y	N
19 **Kelly**	Y	Y	Y	Y	Y	Y	N
20 **Gilman**	Y	Y	Y	Y	Y	Y	Y
21 McNulty	Y	Y	Y	Y	N	Y	Y
22 **Solomon**	Y	Y	Y	Y	N	Y	Y
23 **Boehlert**	Y	Y	Y	Y	Y	Y	Y
24 **McHugh**	Y	Y	Y	Y	N	Y	Y
25 **Walsh**	Y	Y	Y	Y	N	Y	Y
26 Hinchey	Y	Y	Y	Y	Y	Y	N
27 **Paxon**	Y	Y	Y	Y	N	Y	Y
28 Slaughter	Y	Y	Y	Y	Y	Y	N
29 LaFalce	Y	Y	Y	N	N	Y	N

	167	168	169	170	171	172	173
30 **Quinn**	Y	Y	Y	Y	N	Y	Y
31 **Houghton**	Y	Y	Y	N	Y	Y	N
NORTH CAROLINA							
1 Clayton	Y	Y	Y	N	Y	Y	N
2 Etheridge	Y	Y	Y	Y	Y	Y	Y
3 **Jones**	Y	Y	Y	Y	N	Y	Y
4 Price	Y	Y	Y	Y	Y	Y	N
5 **Burr**	Y	Y	Y	Y	N	Y	Y
6 **Coble**	Y	Y	Y	Y	N	Y	Y
7 McIntyre	Y	Y	Y	Y	N	Y	Y
8 Hefner	Y	Y	Y	Y	Y	Y	Y
9 **Myrick**	Y	Y	Y	Y	N	Y	Y
10 **Ballenger**	Y	Y	Y	Y	N	Y	Y
11 **Taylor**	Y	Y	Y	Y	N	Y	Y
12 Watt	Y	N	Y	N	Y	Y	N
NORTH DAKOTA							
AL Pomeroy	Y	Y	Y	Y	Y	Y	Y
OHIO							
1 **Chabot**	Y	Y	Y	Y	N	Y	Y
2 **Portman**	Y	Y	Y	Y	N	Y	Y
3 Hall	Y	Y	Y	Y	N	Y	N
4 **Oxley**	Y	Y	Y	Y	N	Y	Y
5 **Gillmor**	Y	Y	Y	Y	N	Y	Y
6 Strickland	Y	Y	Y	Y	Y	Y	Y
7 **Hobson**	Y	Y	Y	Y	N	Y	Y
8 **Boehner**	Y	Y	Y	Y	N	Y	Y
9 Kaptur	Y	Y	Y	Y	N	Y	Y
10 Kucinich	Y	Y	Y	Y	N	Y	N
11 Stokes	Y	Y	Y	Y	Y	Y	N
12 **Kasich**	Y	Y	Y	?	N	Y	Y
13 Brown	Y	Y	Y	Y	Y	Y	N
14 Sawyer	Y	Y	Y	N	Y	Y	N
15 **Pryce**	Y	Y	Y	Y	Y	Y	Y
16 **Regula**	Y	Y	Y	Y	N	Y	Y
17 Traficant	Y	Y	Y	Y	N	Y	Y
18 **Ney**	Y	Y	Y	Y	N	Y	Y
19 **LaTourette**	Y	Y	Y	Y	N	Y	Y
OKLAHOMA							
1 **Largent**	Y	Y	Y	Y	N	Y	Y
2 **Coburn**	Y	Y	Y	Y	N	Y	Y
3 **Watkins**	Y	Y	Y	Y	N	Y	Y
4 **Watts**	Y	Y	Y	Y	N	Y	Y
5 **Istook**	Y	Y	Y	Y	N	Y	Y
6 **Lucas**	Y	Y	Y	Y	N	Y	Y
OREGON							
1 Furse	Y	Y	Y	N	Y	Y	N
2 **Smith**	Y	Y	Y	Y	N	Y	Y
3 Blumenauer	Y	Y	Y	Y	Y	Y	N
4 DeFazio	Y	Y	Y	Y	Y	Y	Y
5 Hooley	Y	Y	Y	Y	Y	Y	N
PENNSYLVANIA							
1 Vacant							
2 Fattah	Y	Y	Y	N	Y	Y	N
3 Borski	Y	Y	Y	Y	N	Y	N
4 Klink	Y	Y	Y	Y	N	Y	N
5 **Peterson**	Y	Y	Y	Y	N	Y	Y
6 Holden	Y	Y	Y	Y	N	Y	N
7 **Weldon**	Y	Y	Y	Y	N	Y	Y
8 **Greenwood**	Y	Y	Y	Y	Y	Y	N
9 **Shuster**	Y	Y	Y	Y	N	Y	Y
10 **McDade**	Y	Y	Y	Y	N	?	Y
11 Kanjorski	Y	Y	Y	Y	N	Y	N
12 Murtha	Y	Y	Y	Y	?	?	?
13 **Fox**	Y	Y	Y	Y	N	Y	Y
14 Coyne	Y	Y	Y	Y	Y	Y	N
15 McHale	Y	Y	Y	Y	Y	Y	N
16 **Pitts**	Y	Y	Y	Y	N	Y	Y
17 **Gekas**	Y	Y	Y	Y	N	Y	Y
18 Doyle	Y	Y	Y	Y	N	Y	N
19 **Goodling**	Y	Y	Y	Y	N	Y	Y
20 Mascara	Y	Y	Y	Y	N	Y	N
21 **English**	Y	Y	Y	Y	N	Y	Y
RHODE ISLAND							
1 Kennedy	Y	Y	Y	Y	Y	Y	N
2 Weygand	Y	Y	Y	Y	N	Y	N
SOUTH CAROLINA							
1 **Sanford**	Y	Y	Y	Y	N	Y	Y
2 **Spence**	Y	Y	Y	Y	N	Y	Y
3 **Graham**	Y	Y	Y	Y	N	Y	Y
4 **Inglis**	Y	Y	Y	Y	N	Y	Y
5 Spratt	Y	Y	Y	?	?	Y	N
6 Clyburn	Y	Y	Y	Y	Y	Y	N
SOUTH DAKOTA							
AL **Thune**	Y	Y	Y	Y	N	Y	Y

	167	168	169	170	171	172	173
TENNESSEE							
1 **Jenkins**	Y	Y	Y	Y	N	Y	Y
2 **Duncan**	Y	Y	Y	Y	N	Y	Y
3 **Wamp**	Y	Y	Y	Y	N	Y	Y
4 **Hilleary**	Y	Y	Y	Y	N	Y	Y
5 Clement	Y	Y	Y	Y	Y	Y	Y
6 Gordon	Y	Y	Y	Y	Y	Y	Y
7 **Bryant**	Y	Y	Y	Y	N	Y	Y
8 Tanner	Y	Y	Y	Y	Y	Y	Y
9 Ford	Y	Y	Y	Y	Y	Y	N
TEXAS							
1 Sandlin	Y	Y	Y	Y	Y	Y	Y
2 Turner	Y	Y	Y	Y	Y	Y	Y
3 **Johnson, Sam**	Y	Y	Y	Y	N	Y	Y
4 Hall	Y	Y	Y	Y	N	Y	Y
5 **Sessions**	Y	Y	Y	Y	N	Y	Y
6 **Barton**	Y	Y	Y	Y	N	Y	Y
7 **Archer**	Y	Y	Y	Y	N	Y	Y
8 **Brady**	Y	Y	?	Y	N	Y	Y
9 Lampson	Y	Y	Y	Y	Y	Y	N
10 Doggett	Y	Y	Y	Y	Y	Y	N
11 Edwards	Y	Y	Y	Y	Y	Y	N
12 **Granger**	Y	Y	Y	Y	N	Y	Y
13 **Thornberry**	Y	Y	Y	Y	N	Y	Y
14 **Paul**	Y	Y	Y	Y	N	Y	Y
15 Hinojosa	Y	Y	Y	Y	Y	Y	N
16 Reyes	Y	Y	Y	N	Y	Y	N
17 Stenholm	Y	Y	Y	Y	N	Y	Y
18 Jackson-Lee	Y	Y	Y	Y	Y	Y	N
19 **Combest**	Y	Y	Y	Y	N	Y	Y
20 Gonzalez	?	?	?	?	?	?	?
21 **Smith**	Y	Y	Y	Y	N	Y	Y
22 **DeLay**	Y	Y	Y	Y	N	Y	Y
23 **Bonilla**	Y	Y	Y	Y	N	Y	Y
24 Frost	Y	Y	Y	Y	Y	Y	N
25 Bentsen	Y	Y	Y	Y	Y	Y	N
26 **Armey**	Y	Y	Y	Y	N	Y	Y
27 Ortiz	Y	Y	Y	N	N	Y	N
28 Rodriguez	Y	Y	Y	Y	Y	Y	N
29 Green	Y	Y	Y	Y	Y	Y	Y
30 Johnson, E.B.	Y	Y	Y	Y	Y	Y	N
UTAH							
1 **Hansen**	Y	Y	Y	Y	N	Y	Y
2 **Cook**	Y	Y	Y	Y	N	Y	Y
3 **Cannon**	?	Y	Y	Y	N	Y	Y
VERMONT							
AL *Sanders*	Y	Y	Y	Y	Y	Y	N
VIRGINIA							
1 **Bateman**	+	+	+	+	−	+	+
2 Pickett	Y	Y	Y	N	N	Y	N
3 Scott	Y	Y	Y	Y	Y	Y	N
4 Sisisky	Y	Y	Y	Y	Y	Y	N
5 Goode	Y	Y	Y	Y	N	Y	Y
6 **Goodlatte**	Y	Y	Y	Y	N	Y	Y
7 **Bliley**	Y	Y	Y	Y	N	Y	Y
8 Moran	Y	Y	N	N	Y	Y	N
9 Boucher	Y	Y	Y	Y	Y	Y	N
10 **Wolf**	Y	Y	Y	Y	N	Y	Y
11 **Davis**	Y	Y	Y	Y	N	Y	Y
WASHINGTON							
1 **White**	Y	Y	Y	Y	Y	Y	Y
2 **Metcalf**	Y	Y	Y	Y	N	Y	Y
3 **Smith, Linda**	Y	Y	Y	Y	N	Y	Y
4 **Hastings**	Y	Y	Y	Y	N	Y	Y
5 **Nethercutt**	Y	Y	Y	Y	N	Y	Y
6 Dicks	Y	Y	Y	Y	Y	Y	N
7 McDermott	N	N	N	N	Y	Y	N
8 **Dunn**	Y	Y	Y	Y	N	Y	Y
9 Smith, Adam	Y	Y	Y	N	Y	Y	N
WEST VIRGINIA							
1 Mollohan	?	Y	Y	Y	N	Y	N
2 Wise	Y	Y	Y	Y	?	?	?
3 Rahall	Y	Y	Y	Y	N	Y	N
WISCONSIN							
1 **Neumann**	Y	Y	Y	Y	N	Y	Y
2 **Klug**	Y	Y	Y	Y	N	Y	Y
3 Kind	Y	Y	Y	Y	Y	Y	N
4 Kleczka	Y	Y	Y	Y	Y	Y	N
5 Barrett	Y	Y	Y	Y	N	Y	N
6 **Petri**	Y	Y	Y	Y	N	Y	Y
7 Obey	Y	Y	Y	N	Y	Y	N
8 Johnson	Y	Y	Y	Y	Y	Y	Y
9 **Sensenbrenner**	Y	Y	Y	Y	N	Y	Y
WYOMING							
AL **Cubin**	Y	Y	Y	Y	N	Y	Y

Southern states - Ala., Ark., Fla., Ga., Ky., La., Miss., N.C., Okla., S.C., Tenn., Texas, Va.

174. HR 2400. Surface Transportation Reauthorization/Motion to Instruct. Obey, D-Wis., motion to instruct the House conferees to oppose provisions which prohibit or reduce service-connected disability compensation to veterans for smoking-related illnesses. Motion agreed to 422-0: R 224-0; D 197-0 (ND 143-0, SD 54-0); I 1-0. May 20, 1998.

175. Procedural Motion/Journal. Approval of the House Journal of Wednesday, May 20, 1998. Approved 339-58: R 188-17; D 150-41 (ND 108-30, SD 42-11); I 1-0. May 21, 1998.

176. H Res 432. President's Assertions of Executive Privilege/Adoption. Adoption of the resolution to express the sense of the House that all documents relating to any claims of executive privilege asserted by the president should be immediately made publicly available. Adopted 259-157: R 223-1; D 36-155 (ND 21-116, SD 15-39); I 0-1. May 21, 1998.

177. H Res 433. Presidential Cooperation with Investigation/Adoption. Adoption of the resolution to call on the president to immediately call upon his friends, former associates and appointees, and their associates, who have asserted their Fifth Amendment rights or left the country to avoid testifying in congressional investigations, to testify fully and truthfully before the relevant congressional committee. Adopted 342-69: R 221-0; D 120-69 (ND 86-52, SD 34-17); I 1-0. May 21, 1998.

178. HR 3616. Fiscal 1999 Defense Authorization/Military Retirees. Thornberry, R-Texas, amendment to authorize a demonstration program to offer enrollment in the Federal Employees Health Benefits Program to military Medicare-eligible retirees. Adopted 420-1: R 220-1; D 199-0 (ND 146-0, SD 53-0); I 1-0. May 21, 1998.

179. HR 3616. Fiscal 1999 Defense Authorization/U.S. Borders. Reyes, D-Texas, amendment to the Traficant, D-Ohio, amendment, to require the attorney general or the secretary of the Treasury to submit a formal request to the Defense Department asking for the deployment of troops along the border. The Traficant amendment would authorize the Defense Department to assign members of the armed forces to assist in patrolling U.S. borders. Rejected 179-243: R 9-210; D 169-33 (ND 126-22, SD 43-11); I 1-0. May 21, 1998.

180. HR 3616. Fiscal 1999 Defense Authorization/U.S. Border. Traficant, D-Ohio, amendment to authorize the Defense Department to assign members of the armed forces to assist the Immigration and Naturalization Service and the Customs Service in monitoring and patrolling U.S. borders. Adopted 288-132: R 203-14; D 85-117 (ND 57-91, SD 28-26); I 0-1. May 21, 1998.

[1] Robert A. Brady, D-Pa., was sworn in May 21, replacing Thomas M. Foglietta, D-Pa., who resigned Nov. 11, 1997.

Key

Y	Voted for (yea).
#	Paired for.
+	Announced for.
N	Voted against (nay).
X	Paired against.
–	Announced against.
P	Voted "present."
C	Voted "present" to avoid possible conflict of interest.
?	Did not vote or otherwise make a position known.

Democrats **Republicans** *Independent*

	174	175	176	177	178	179	180
ALABAMA							
1 *Callahan*	Y	Y	Y	Y	Y	N	Y
2 *Everett*	Y	Y	Y	Y	Y	N	Y
3 *Riley*	Y	Y	Y	Y	Y	N	Y
4 *Aderholt*	Y	N	Y	Y	Y	N	Y
5 Cramer	Y	Y	Y	Y	Y	N	Y
6 *Bachus*	Y	Y	Y	Y	Y	N	Y
7 Hilliard	Y	N	N	N	Y	Y	N
ALASKA							
AL *Young*	Y	?	Y	Y	Y	N	Y
ARIZONA							
1 *Salmon*	Y	Y	Y	Y	Y	N	Y
2 Pastor	Y	N	N	N	Y	Y	N
3 *Stump*	Y	Y	Y	Y	Y	N	N
4 *Shadegg*	Y	Y	Y	Y	Y	N	Y
5 *Kolbe*	Y	?	Y	Y	Y	Y	N
6 *Hayworth*	Y	Y	Y	Y	Y	N	Y
ARKANSAS							
1 Berry	Y	Y	Y	Y	Y	Y	N
2 Snyder	Y	Y	N	Y	Y	Y	N
3 *Hutchinson*	Y	Y	Y	Y	Y	N	Y
4 *Dickey*	Y	Y	Y	Y	Y	N	Y
CALIFORNIA							
1 *Riggs*	Y	Y	Y	Y	Y	N	Y
2 *Herger*	Y	Y	Y	Y	Y	N	Y
3 Fazio	Y	N	N	N	Y	Y	N
4 *Doolittle*	Y	Y	Y	Y	Y	N	Y
5 Matsui	Y	N	N	N	Y	Y	N
6 Woolsey	Y	N	P	Y	Y	Y	N
7 Miller	Y	N	N	N	Y	Y	N
8 Pelosi	?	Y	N	?	Y	Y	N
9 Lee	Y	N	N	N	Y	Y	N
10 Tauscher	Y	N	P	Y	Y	Y	N
11 *Pombo*	Y	Y	Y	Y	Y	N	Y
12 Lantos	Y	N	Y	Y	Y	Y	N
13 Stark	Y	N	N	N	Y	Y	N
14 Eshoo	Y	N	N	Y	Y	Y	N
15 *Campbell*	Y	Y	N	Y	Y	N	Y
16 Lofgren	Y	N	N	Y	Y	Y	N
17 Farr	Y	Y	?	Y	Y	Y	N
18 Condit	Y	Y	Y	Y	Y	Y	N
19 *Radanovich*	Y	Y	Y	Y	Y	N	Y
20 Dooley	Y	N	N	Y	Y	N	N
21 *Thomas*	Y	Y	N	N	Y	N	Y
22 Capps, L.	Y	N	N	Y	Y	Y	N
23 *Gallegly*	Y	Y	Y	Y	Y	N	Y
24 Sherman	Y	Y	N	Y	Y	N	Y
25 *McKeon*	Y	Y	Y	Y	Y	N	Y
26 Berman	Y	Y	P	P	Y	Y	N
27 *Rogan*	Y	Y	Y	Y	Y	N	Y
28 *Dreier*	Y	Y	Y	Y	Y	N	Y
29 Waxman	Y	N	Y	N	Y	Y	N
30 Becerra	Y	N	N	N	Y	Y	N
31 Martinez	Y	Y	N	Y	Y	Y	N
32 Dixon	Y	?	N	Y	Y	Y	N
33 Roybal-Allard	Y	N	N	Y	Y	Y	N
34 Torres	Y	?	?	?	?	?	?
35 Waters	Y	N	N	N	Y	N	N
36 Harman	?	?	?	?	?	?	?
37 Millender-McD.	Y	Y	N	N	Y	Y	N

	174	175	176	177	178	179	180
38 *Horn*	Y	Y	Y	Y	Y	N	Y
39 *Royce*	Y	Y	Y	Y	Y	N	Y
40 *Lewis*	Y	Y	Y	Y	Y	N	Y
41 *Kim*	Y	Y	Y	Y	Y	N	Y
42 Brown	Y	N	N	N	Y	Y	N
43 *Calvert*	Y	Y	Y	Y	Y	N	Y
44 *Bono, M.*	Y	?	Y	Y	Y	N	Y
45 *Rohrabacher*	Y	Y	Y	Y	Y	N	Y
46 Sanchez	Y	Y	N	P	Y	Y	Y
47 *Cox*	Y	?	Y	Y	Y	N	Y
48 *Packard*	Y	Y	Y	Y	Y	N	Y
49 *Bilbray*	Y	Y	Y	Y	Y	N	Y
50 Filner	Y	N	N	N	Y	Y	N
51 *Cunningham*	Y	Y	Y	Y	Y	N	Y
52 *Hunter*	Y	Y	Y	Y	Y	N	Y
COLORADO							
1 DeGette	Y	Y	N	N	Y	Y	N
2 Skaggs	Y	+	N	N	+	Y	N
3 *McInnis*	Y	Y	Y	Y	Y	N	Y
4 *Schaffer*	Y	N	Y	Y	Y	N	Y
5 *Hefley*	Y	N	Y	Y	Y	N	Y
6 *Schaefer*	Y	Y	Y	Y	Y	N	Y
CONNECTICUT							
1 Kennelly	Y	N	N	Y	Y	Y	N
2 Gejdenson	Y	Y	N	Y	Y	Y	N
3 DeLauro	Y	N	N	Y	Y	Y	N
4 *Shays*	Y	Y	Y	Y	Y	Y	N
5 Maloney	Y	Y	Y	Y	Y	Y	Y
6 *Johnson*	Y	Y	Y	Y	Y	N	Y
DELAWARE							
AL *Castle*	Y	Y	Y	Y	Y	Y	Y
FLORIDA							
1 *Scarborough*	Y	Y	Y	Y	Y	N	Y
2 Boyd	Y	Y	N	Y	Y	Y	N
3 Brown	Y	N	N	Y	Y	Y	N
4 *Fowler*	Y	Y	Y	Y	Y	N	Y
5 Thurman	Y	N	N	Y	Y	Y	N
6 *Stearns*	Y	Y	Y	Y	Y	N	Y
7 *Mica*	Y	Y	Y	Y	Y	N	Y
8 *McCollum*	Y	?	Y	Y	Y	N	Y
9 *Bilirakis*	Y	Y	Y	Y	Y	N	Y
10 *Young*	Y	Y	Y	Y	Y	N	Y
11 Davis	Y	N	N	Y	Y	N	Y
12 *Canady*	Y	Y	Y	Y	Y	N	Y
13 *Miller*	Y	Y	Y	Y	Y	N	Y
14 *Goss*	Y	Y	Y	Y	Y	N	Y
15 *Weldon*	Y	Y	Y	Y	Y	N	Y
16 *Foley*	Y	Y	Y	Y	Y	?	?
17 Meek	Y	N	N	N	Y	N	N
18 *Ros-Lehtinen*	Y	Y	Y	Y	Y	N	Y
19 Wexler	Y	N	N	N	Y	N	N
20 Deutsch	Y	N	N	Y	Y	N	N
21 *Diaz-Balart*	Y	Y	Y	Y	Y	N	Y
22 *Shaw*	Y	Y	Y	Y	Y	N	Y
23 Hastings	Y	N	N	N	Y	N	N
GEORGIA							
1 *Kingston*	Y	Y	Y	Y	Y	N	Y
2 Bishop	Y	Y	N	P	Y	Y	Y
3 *Collins*	Y	Y	Y	Y	Y	N	Y
4 McKinney	Y	Y	Y	Y	Y	Y	N
5 Lewis	Y	N	N	N	Y	N	N
6 *Gingrich*							
7 *Barr*	Y	?	Y	Y	Y	N	Y
8 *Chambliss*	Y	?	Y	Y	Y	N	Y
9 *Deal*	Y	Y	Y	Y	Y	N	Y
10 *Norwood*	Y	Y	Y	Y	Y	N	Y
11 *Linder*	Y	Y	Y	Y	Y	N	N
HAWAII							
1 Abercrombie	Y	Y	Y	Y	Y	N	Y
2 Mink	Y	Y	Y	Y	Y	Y	N
IDAHO							
1 *Chenoweth*	Y	Y	Y	Y	Y	N	Y
2 *Crapo*	Y	?	?	Y	Y	N	Y
ILLINOIS							
1 Rush	Y	Y	N	N	Y	N	N
2 Jackson	Y	Y	N	N	Y	Y	N
3 Lipinski	Y	Y	Y	Y	Y	N	Y
4 Gutierrez	Y	N	?	Y	Y	Y	N
5 Blagojevich	Y	Y	N	Y	Y	Y	N
6 *Hyde*	Y	?	Y	Y	Y	N	Y
7 Davis	Y	N	N	N	Y	Y	N
8 *Crane*	Y	?	Y	Y	Y	N	Y
9 Yates	Y	N	N	N	Y	N	N
10 *Porter*	Y	Y	Y	Y	Y	N	Y
11 *Weller*	Y	N	Y	Y	Y	N	Y
12 Costello	Y	N	N	Y	Y	N	Y

	174	175	176	177	178	179	180
13 **Fawell**	Y	Y	Y	Y	Y	N	Y
14 **Hastert**	Y	Y	Y	Y	Y	N	Y
15 **Ewing**	Y	Y	Y	Y	Y	N	Y
16 **Manzullo**	Y	Y	Y	Y	Y	N	Y
17 Evans	Y	Y	Y	Y	Y	Y	N
18 **LaHood**	Y	Y	Y	Y	Y	N	Y
19 Poshard	Y	N	N	Y	Y	Y	Y
20 **Shimkus**	Y	Y	Y	Y	Y	N	Y
INDIANA							
1 Visclosky	Y	N	N	N	Y	N	Y
2 **McIntosh**	Y	Y	Y	Y	Y	N	Y
3 Roemer	Y	Y	Y	Y	Y	N	Y
4 **Souder**	Y	Y	Y	Y	Y	N	Y
5 **Buyer**	Y	?	Y	Y	Y	N	N
6 **Burton**	Y	Y	Y	Y	Y	N	Y
7 **Pease**	Y	Y	Y	Y	Y	N	Y
8 **Hostettler**	Y	Y	Y	Y	Y	N	Y
9 Hamilton	Y	Y	Y	Y	Y	Y	N
10 Carson	+	P	N	N	Y	N	Y
IOWA							
1 **Leach**	Y	Y	Y	Y	Y	N	Y
2 **Nussle**	Y	N	Y	Y	Y	N	Y
3 Boswell	Y	Y	Y	Y	Y	N	Y
4 **Ganske**	Y	Y	Y	Y	P	N	Y
5 **Latham**	Y	Y	Y	Y	Y	N	Y
KANSAS							
1 **Moran**	Y	N	Y	Y	Y	N	Y
2 **Ryun**	Y	Y	Y	Y	Y	N	N
3 **Snowbarger**	Y	Y	Y	Y	Y	N	Y
4 **Tiahrt**	Y	Y	Y	Y	Y	N	Y
KENTUCKY							
1 **Whitfield**	Y	N	Y	Y	Y	Y	N
2 **Lewis**	Y	?	Y	Y	Y	N	Y
3 **Northup**	Y	Y	Y	Y	Y	N	Y
4 **Bunning**	Y	Y	Y	Y	Y	N	Y
5 **Rogers**	Y	Y	Y	Y	Y	N	Y
6 Baesler	Y	Y	Y	Y	Y	N	Y
LOUISIANA							
1 **Livingston**	Y	Y	Y	Y	Y	N	Y
2 Jefferson	Y	Y	N	N	Y	Y	Y
3 **Tauzin**	Y	Y	Y	Y	Y	N	Y
4 **McCrery**	Y	Y	Y	Y	Y	N	Y
5 **Cooksey**	Y	Y	Y	Y	Y	N	Y
6 **Baker**	Y	?	Y	Y	Y	N	Y
7 John	Y	Y	Y	Y	Y	Y	Y
MAINE							
1 Allen	Y	Y	N	Y	Y	Y	N
2 Baldacci	Y	N	N	Y	Y	Y	N
MARYLAND							
1 **Gilchrest**	Y	Y	Y	Y	Y	N	Y
2 **Ehrlich**	Y	Y	Y	Y	Y	N	N
3 Cardin	Y	Y	N	Y	Y	Y	N
4 Wynn	Y	Y	N	N	Y	Y	N
5 Hoyer	Y	Y	N	Y	Y	Y	N
6 **Bartlett**	Y	Y	Y	Y	Y	N	Y
7 Cummings	Y	Y	N	N	Y	Y	N
8 **Morella**	Y	Y	Y	Y	Y	Y	N
MASSACHUSETTS							
1 Olver	Y	Y	N	N	Y	Y	N
2 Neal	Y	Y	N	Y	Y	Y	N
3 McGovern	Y	Y	N	P	?	Y	N
4 Frank	Y	Y	N	P	Y	Y	N
5 Meehan	Y	Y	N	Y	Y	Y	Y
6 Tierney	Y	?	N	N	Y	Y	N
7 Markey	Y	N	N	N	Y	Y	N
8 Kennedy	Y	Y	N	N	Y	Y	N
9 Moakley	Y	Y	N	Y	Y	N	Y
10 Delahunt	Y	Y	N	N	Y	Y	N
MICHIGAN							
1 Stupak	Y	N	N	Y	Y	Y	N
2 **Hoekstra**	Y	Y	Y	Y	Y	N	Y
3 **Ehlers**	Y	Y	Y	Y	Y	Y	N
4 **Camp**	Y	Y	Y	Y	Y	N	Y
5 Barcia	Y	Y	Y	Y	Y	Y	Y
6 **Upton**	Y	Y	Y	Y	Y	N	Y
7 **Smith**	Y	Y	Y	Y	Y	N	Y
8 Stabenow	+	Y	Y	Y	Y	Y	Y
9 Kildee	Y	Y	Y	Y	Y	Y	Y
10 Bonior	Y	N	N	N	Y	Y	N
11 **Knollenberg**	Y	Y	Y	Y	Y	N	Y
12 Levin	Y	Y	N	N	Y	Y	Y
13 Rivers	Y	Y	P	Y	Y	N	Y
14 Conyers	Y	Y	N	N	Y	Y	N
15 Kilpatrick	Y	Y	N	Y	Y	Y	N
16 Dingell	Y	Y	N	Y	Y	Y	N

	174	175	176	177	178	179	180
MINNESOTA							
1 **Gutknecht**	Y	N	Y	Y	Y	N	Y
2 Minge	Y	Y	N	Y	Y	Y	N
3 **Ramstad**	Y	N	Y	Y	Y	N	Y
4 Vento	Y	N	N	N	Y	Y	N
5 Sabo	Y	N	N	Y	Y	Y	N
6 Luther	Y	Y	N	Y	Y	Y	Y
7 Peterson	Y	Y	Y	Y	Y	N	Y
8 Oberstar	Y	N	N	N	Y	Y	N
MISSISSIPPI							
1 **Wicker**	Y	N	Y	Y	?	?	?
2 Thompson	Y	N	N	N	Y	Y	N
3 **Pickering**	Y	Y	Y	Y	Y	N	Y
4 **Parker**	Y	Y	Y	?	?	?	?
5 Taylor	Y	N	Y	Y	Y	N	Y
MISSOURI							
1 Clay	?	N	N	N	Y	Y	N
2 **Talent**	Y	Y	Y	Y	Y	N	Y
3 Gephardt	Y	N	N	Y	Y	Y	Y
4 Skelton	Y	Y	N	Y	Y	Y	Y
5 McCarthy	Y	Y	N	Y	Y	Y	Y
6 Danner	Y	Y	Y	Y	Y	Y	Y
7 **Blunt**	Y	Y	Y	Y	Y	N	Y
8 **Emerson**	Y	Y	Y	Y	Y	N	Y
9 **Hulshof**	Y	Y	Y	Y	Y	N	Y
MONTANA							
AL **Hill**	Y	Y	Y	Y	Y	N	Y
NEBRASKA							
1 **Bereuter**	Y	Y	Y	Y	Y	N	Y
2 **Christensen**	Y	Y	Y	Y	Y	N	Y
3 **Barrett**	Y	Y	Y	Y	Y	N	?
NEVADA							
1 **Ensign**	Y	N	Y	Y	Y	N	Y
2 **Gibbons**	Y	N	Y	Y	Y	N	Y
NEW HAMPSHIRE							
1 **Sununu**	Y	Y	Y	Y	Y	N	Y
2 **Bass**	Y	?	Y	Y	Y	N	Y
NEW JERSEY							
1 Andrews	Y	Y	N	N	Y	N	Y
2 **LoBiondo**	Y	N	Y	Y	Y	N	Y
3 **Saxton**	Y	Y	Y	Y	Y	N	Y
4 **Smith**	Y	Y	Y	Y	Y	N	Y
5 **Roukema**	Y	Y	Y	Y	Y	N	Y
6 Pallone	Y	N	N	Y	Y	Y	Y
7 **Franks**	Y	Y	Y	?	Y	N	Y
8 Pascrell	Y	Y	Y	Y	Y	N	Y
9 Rothman	Y	Y	N	Y	Y	Y	N
10 Payne	Y	Y	N	N	Y	Y	N
11 **Frelinghuysen**	Y	?	Y	Y	Y	N	Y
12 **Pappas**	Y	Y	Y	Y	Y	N	Y
13 Menendez	Y	N	N	Y	Y	Y	N
NEW MEXICO							
1 Vacant							
2 **Skeen**	Y	Y	Y	Y	Y	N	Y
3 **Redmond**	Y	Y	Y	Y	Y	N	Y
NEW YORK							
1 **Forbes**	Y	Y	Y	Y	Y	N	Y
2 **Lazio**	Y	Y	Y	Y	Y	N	Y
3 **King**	Y	Y	Y	Y	Y	N	Y
4 McCarthy	Y	Y	Y	Y	Y	N	Y
5 Ackerman	Y	Y	N	N	Y	Y	N
6 Meeks	?	?	?	?	?	?	?
7 Manton	Y	Y	N	Y	Y	N	Y
8 Nadler	Y	Y	N	N	Y	Y	N
9 Schumer	?	?	?	Y	Y	Y	Y
10 Towns	Y	Y	N	N	Y	Y	N
11 Owens	Y	?	N	N	Y	N	Y
12 Velázquez	Y	N	N	N	Y	Y	N
13 **Fossella**	Y	Y	Y	Y	Y	N	Y
14 Maloney	Y	Y	N	P	Y	Y	Y
15 Rangel	Y	Y	N	N	Y	Y	N
16 Serrano	Y	Y	N	N	Y	Y	N
17 Engel	Y	Y	N	N	Y	Y	Y
18 Lowey	Y	N	N	Y	Y	Y	Y
19 **Kelly**	Y	Y	Y	Y	Y	N	Y
20 **Gilman**	Y	Y	Y	Y	Y	N	Y
21 McNulty	Y	Y	N	Y	Y	Y	Y
22 **Solomon**	Y	Y	Y	Y	Y	N	Y
23 **Boehlert**	Y	Y	Y	Y	Y	N	Y
24 **McHugh**	Y	Y	Y	Y	Y	N	Y
25 **Walsh**	Y	Y	Y	Y	Y	N	Y
26 Hinchey	Y	N	N	N	Y	Y	N
27 **Paxon**	Y	Y	Y	Y	Y	N	Y
28 Slaughter	Y	N	N	N	Y	Y	N
29 LaFalce	Y	Y	N	Y	Y	Y	Y

	174	175	176	177	178	179	180
30 **Quinn**	Y	Y	Y	Y	Y	?	?
31 **Houghton**	Y	Y	N	Y	Y	Y	N
NORTH CAROLINA							
1 Clayton	Y	Y	N	P	Y	Y	N
2 Etheridge	Y	Y	Y	Y	Y	Y	Y
3 **Jones**	Y	Y	Y	Y	Y	N	Y
4 Price	Y	Y	Y	Y	Y	Y	Y
5 **Burr**	Y	?	Y	Y	Y	N	Y
6 **Coble**	Y	Y	Y	Y	Y	N	Y
7 McIntyre	Y	Y	Y	Y	Y	N	Y
8 Hefner	Y	Y	N	Y	Y	Y	Y
9 **Myrick**	Y	Y	Y	Y	Y	N	Y
10 **Ballenger**	Y	Y	Y	Y	Y	N	Y
11 **Taylor**	Y	Y	Y	Y	Y	N	Y
12 Watt	Y	Y	N	P	Y	N	N
NORTH DAKOTA							
AL Pomeroy	Y	?	N	Y	Y	Y	Y
OHIO							
1 **Chabot**	Y	Y	Y	Y	Y	N	Y
2 **Portman**	Y	Y	Y	Y	Y	N	Y
3 Hall	Y	?	N	Y	Y	Y	Y
4 **Oxley**	Y	Y	Y	Y	Y	N	Y
5 **Gillmor**	Y	Y	Y	Y	Y	N	Y
6 Strickland	Y	Y	Y	Y	Y	Y	Y
7 **Hobson**	Y	Y	Y	Y	Y	N	Y
8 **Boehner**	Y	Y	Y	Y	Y	N	Y
9 Kaptur	Y	Y	?	Y	Y	Y	Y
10 Kucinich	Y	N	N	Y	Y	N	Y
11 Stokes	Y	Y	N	N	Y	Y	N
12 **Kasich**	Y	Y	Y	Y	Y	N	Y
13 Brown	Y	Y	N	N	Y	Y	N
14 Sawyer	Y	Y	N	Y	Y	Y	N
15 **Pryce**	?	Y	Y	Y	Y	N	Y
16 **Regula**	Y	Y	Y	Y	Y	N	Y
17 Traficant	Y	Y	Y	Y	Y	N	Y
18 **Ney**	Y	Y	Y	Y	Y	N	Y
19 **LaTourette**	Y	Y	Y	Y	Y	N	Y
OKLAHOMA							
1 **Largent**	Y	Y	Y	Y	Y	N	Y
2 **Coburn**	Y	Y	Y	Y	Y	N	Y
3 **Watkins**	Y	Y	Y	Y	Y	N	Y
4 **Watts**	Y	Y	Y	Y	Y	N	Y
5 **Istook**	Y	Y	Y	Y	Y	N	Y
6 **Lucas**	Y	Y	Y	Y	Y	N	Y
OREGON							
1 Furse	Y	Y	N	N	Y	Y	N
2 **Smith**	Y	Y	Y	Y	Y	N	Y
3 Blumenauer	Y	Y	N	Y	Y	Y	N
4 DeFazio	Y	N	N	P	Y	Y	N
5 Hooley	Y	Y	N	Y	Y	Y	N
PENNSYLVANIA							
1 Brady[1]			N	N	Y	Y	N
2 Fattah	Y	Y	N	N	Y	Y	N
3 Borski	Y	N	N	Y	Y	Y	N
4 Klink	Y	Y	N	Y	Y	N	Y
5 **Peterson**	Y	Y	Y	Y	Y	N	Y
6 Holden	Y	Y	Y	Y	Y	N	Y
7 **Weldon**	Y	Y	Y	Y	Y	N	Y
8 **Greenwood**	Y	Y	Y	Y	Y	N	Y
9 **Shuster**	Y	Y	Y	Y	Y	N	Y
10 **McDade**	Y	Y	Y	?	Y	?	?
11 Kanjorski	Y	Y	N	Y	Y	Y	N
12 Murtha	Y	Y	N	N	Y	Y	Y
13 **Fox**	Y	N	Y	Y	Y	N	Y
14 Coyne	Y	Y	N	Y	Y	Y	N
15 McHale	Y	Y	Y	Y	Y	Y	N
16 **Pitts**	Y	Y	Y	Y	Y	N	Y
17 **Gekas**	Y	Y	Y	Y	Y	N	Y
18 Doyle	Y	Y	N	Y	Y	Y	Y
19 **Goodling**	Y	P	Y	Y	Y	N	Y
20 Mascara	Y	Y	N	Y	Y	Y	Y
21 **English**	Y	N	Y	Y	Y	N	Y
RHODE ISLAND							
1 Kennedy	Y	Y	N	Y	Y	Y	N
2 Weygand	Y	Y	N	Y	Y	Y	N
SOUTH CAROLINA							
1 **Sanford**	Y	Y	Y	Y	Y	N	N
2 **Spence**	Y	Y	Y	Y	Y	N	Y
3 **Graham**	Y	Y	Y	Y	Y	N	Y
4 **Inglis**	Y	Y	Y	Y	Y	N	Y
5 Spratt	Y	Y	N	Y	Y	Y	Y
6 Clyburn	Y	Y	N	N	Y	Y	N
SOUTH DAKOTA							
AL **Thune**	Y	Y	Y	Y	Y	N	Y

	174	175	176	177	178	179	180
TENNESSEE							
1 **Jenkins**	Y	Y	Y	Y	Y	N	Y
2 **Duncan**	Y	Y	Y	Y	Y	N	Y
3 **Wamp**	Y	N	Y	Y	Y	N	Y
4 **Hilleary**	Y	N	Y	Y	Y	N	Y
5 Clement	Y	Y	N	Y	Y	Y	Y
6 Gordon	Y	Y	N	Y	Y	N	Y
7 **Bryant**	Y	Y	Y	Y	Y	N	Y
8 Tanner	Y	Y	N	Y	Y	Y	Y
9 Ford	Y	Y	N	Y	Y	Y	N
TEXAS							
1 Sandlin	Y	Y	N	Y	Y	Y	Y
2 Turner	Y	?	Y	Y	Y	N	Y
3 **Johnson, Sam**	Y	?	Y	?	?	?	?
4 Hall	Y	Y	Y	Y	Y	N	Y
5 **Sessions**	Y	Y	Y	Y	Y	N	Y
6 **Barton**	Y	?	Y	Y	Y	Y	Y
7 **Archer**	Y	Y	Y	Y	Y	N	Y
8 **Brady**	Y	Y	Y	Y	Y	N	Y
9 Lampson	Y	Y	N	Y	Y	Y	N
10 Doggett	Y	Y	N	Y	Y	Y	N
11 Edwards	Y	Y	N	Y	Y	Y	N
12 **Granger**	Y	?	Y	Y	Y	N	Y
13 **Thornberry**	Y	Y	Y	Y	Y	N	Y
14 **Paul**	Y	Y	Y	Y	Y	Y	N
15 Hinojosa	Y	Y	N	Y	Y	Y	N
16 Reyes	Y	Y	N	Y	Y	Y	N
17 Stenholm	Y	Y	Y	Y	Y	Y	Y
18 Jackson-Lee	Y	Y	N	N	Y	Y	N
19 **Combest**	Y	Y	Y	Y	Y	N	Y
20 Gonzalez	?	?	?	?	?	?	?
21 **Smith**	Y	Y	Y	Y	Y	N	Y
22 **DeLay**	Y	Y	Y	Y	Y	N	Y
23 **Bonilla**	Y	Y	Y	Y	Y	N	Y
24 Frost	Y	Y	N	Y	Y	Y	Y
25 Bentsen	Y	Y	N	Y	Y	Y	N
26 **Armey**	Y	Y	Y	Y	Y	N	?
27 Ortiz	Y	Y	N	Y	Y	Y	N
28 Rodriguez	Y	Y	N	N	Y	Y	N
29 Green	Y	N	Y	Y	Y	Y	N
30 Johnson, E.B.	Y	N	N	N	Y	Y	Y
UTAH							
1 **Hansen**	Y	Y	Y	Y	Y	N	Y
2 **Cook**	Y	Y	Y	Y	Y	N	Y
3 **Cannon**	Y	Y	Y	Y	Y	Y	Y
VERMONT							
AL *Sanders*	Y	Y	N	Y	Y	Y	N
VIRGINIA							
1 **Bateman**	+	+	+	+	+	+	−
2 Pickett	Y	N	N	N	?	Y	Y
3 Scott	Y	N	N	N	Y	Y	N
4 Sisisky	Y	Y	Y	Y	Y	Y	Y
5 Goode	Y	Y	Y	Y	Y	N	Y
6 **Goodlatte**	Y	Y	Y	Y	Y	N	Y
7 **Bliley**	Y	Y	Y	Y	Y	N	Y
8 Moran	Y	Y	N	N	Y	Y	Y
9 Boucher	Y	Y	N	Y	Y	Y	Y
10 **Wolf**	Y	Y	Y	Y	Y	N	Y
11 **Davis**	Y	Y	Y	Y	Y	N	Y
WASHINGTON							
1 **White**	Y	Y	Y	Y	Y	N	Y
2 **Metcalf**	Y	Y	Y	Y	Y	N	Y
3 **Smith, Linda**	Y	Y	Y	Y	Y	N	Y
4 **Hastings**	Y	Y	Y	Y	Y	N	Y
5 **Nethercutt**	Y	Y	Y	Y	Y	N	Y
6 Dicks	Y	Y	N	N	Y	Y	N
7 McDermott	Y	N	?	N	Y	Y	N
8 **Dunn**	Y	Y	Y	Y	Y	N	Y
9 Smith, Adam	Y	Y	N	Y	Y	Y	N
WEST VIRGINIA							
1 Mollohan	Y	Y	N	Y	Y	Y	N
2 Wise	Y	Y	N	Y	Y	Y	N
3 Rahall	Y	Y	N	Y	Y	N	Y
WISCONSIN							
1 **Neumann**	Y	Y	Y	Y	Y	N	Y
2 **Klug**	Y	Y	Y	Y	Y	N	Y
3 Kind	Y	Y	P	P	Y	Y	Y
4 Kleczka	Y	Y	N	Y	Y	Y	Y
5 Barrett	Y	Y	P	Y	Y	Y	N
6 **Petri**	Y	Y	Y	Y	Y	N	Y
7 Obey	Y	N	P	Y	Y	Y	Y
8 Johnson	Y	?	P	Y	Y	Y	N
9 **Sensenbrenner**	Y	Y	Y	Y	Y	N	Y
WYOMING							
AL **Cubin**	Y	Y	Y	Y	Y	N	Y

Southern states - Ala., Ark., Fla., Ga., Ky., La., Miss., N.C., Okla., S.C., Tenn., Texas, Va.

181. HR 3616. Fiscal 1999 Defense Authorization/Nuclear Exports. Gilman, R-N.Y., amendment to establish reporting requirements for nuclear exports comparable to those in existing law for conventional arms. Adopted 405-9: R 217-0; D 187-9 (ND 136-7, SD 51-2); I 1-0. May 21, 1998. A "nay" was a vote in support of the president's position.

182. HR 3616. Fiscal 1999 Defense Authorization/Motion to Recommit. Frank, D-Mass., motion to recommit the bill to the National Security Committee with instructions to report it back with an amendment that no funds appropriated for the Department of Defense for fiscal year 1999 may be used for the deployment of the U.S. armed forces in the Republic of Bosnia and Herzegovina after December 31, 1998, unless a law has been enacted that explicitly authorizes the deployment of such armed forces. Motion rejected 167-251: R 129-89; D 38-161 (ND 32-114, SD 6-47); I 0-1. May 21, 1998.

183. HR 3616. Fiscal 1999 Defense Authorization/Passage. Passage of the bill to authorize $270.4 billion for defense programs, including $49.1 billion for weapons procurement, $36.2 billion for research and development, $94.5 billion for operations and maintenance, $8.2 billion for military construction, and $11.9 billion for defense-related activities of the Department of Energy. Passed 357-60: R 207-10; D 150-49 (ND 100-46, SD 50-3); I 0-1. May 21, 1998.

184. HR 2400. Surface Transportation Reauthorization/Motion to Instruct. Obey, D-Wis., motion to instruct the House conferees to limit the aggregate number of earmarked demonstration projects to a number that does not exceed the aggregate number of projects earmarked during the 42 years since enactment of the Highway Trust Fund in 1956. Motion rejected 77-332: R 52-163; D 25-168 (ND 17-124, SD 8-44); I 0-1. May 21, 1998.

185. HR 2400. Surface Transportation Reauthorization/Motion to Instruct. Minge, D-Minn., motion to instruct the House conferees to ensure that spending in the conference agreement is fully paid for using Congressional Budget Office estimates. Motion rejected 156-251: R 92-122; D 64-128 (ND 41-99, SD 23-29); I 0-1. May 21, 1998.

186. HR 2183. Campaign Finance Revisions/Previous Question. Linder, R-Ga., motion to order the previous question (thus ending debate and the possibility of amendment) on adoption of the rule (H Res 442) to provide for House floor consideration of the bill to prohibit national political parties from accepting the largely unregulated "soft money" contributions, ban state parties from transferring soft money to parties in other states, double the aggregate annual limits that individuals can contribute to campaigns, index contribution limits to inflation and require third-parties to disclose their expenditures on issue-oriented advertisements once they reach a certain threshold. Motion agreed to 208-190: R 205-0; D 3-189 (ND 1-139, SD 2-50); I 0-1. May 21, 1998.

187. Procedural Motion/Adjourn. Stenholm, D-Texas, motion to adjourn. Motion rejected 59-304: R 3-191; D 56-113 (ND 37-84, SD 19-29); I 0-0. May 22, 1998.

Key

Y	Voted for (yea).
#	Paired for.
+	Announced for.
N	Voted against (nay).
X	Paired against.
−	Announced against.
P	Voted "present."
C	Voted "present" to avoid possible conflict of interest.
?	Did not vote or otherwise make a position known.

Democrats ***Republicans***
Independent

	181	182	183	184	185	186	187
ALABAMA							
1 *Callahan*	Y	N	Y	N	N	Y	?
2 *Everett*	Y	N	Y	N	Y	Y	N
3 *Riley*	Y	N	Y	N	N	Y	N
4 *Aderholt*	Y	N	Y	N	N	Y	N
5 Cramer	Y	N	N	N	N	N	N
6 *Bachus*	Y	Y	Y	N	N	Y	N
7 Hilliard	Y	N	Y	N	N	N	N
ALASKA							
AL *Young*	Y	Y	Y	N	N	Y	?
ARIZONA							
1 *Salmon*	Y	Y	Y	Y	Y	Y	N
2 Pastor	Y	N	Y	N	N	N	N
3 *Stump*	Y	Y	Y	Y	Y	Y	N
4 *Shadegg*	Y	N	Y	Y	Y	Y	N
5 *Kolbe*	Y	N	Y	N	N	Y	N
6 *Hayworth*	Y	Y	Y	Y	Y	Y	N
ARKANSAS							
1 Berry	Y	N	Y	N	N	N	Y
2 Snyder	Y	N	Y	N	N	N	N
3 *Hutchinson*	Y	Y	Y	N	Y	Y	N
4 *Dickey*	Y	N	Y	N	N	Y	?
CALIFORNIA							
1 *Riggs*	Y	N	Y	N	N	Y	?
2 *Herger*	Y	Y	Y	N	Y	?	?
3 Fazio	N	N	Y	N	Y	N	Y
4 *Doolittle*	Y	N	Y	N	N	Y	N
5 Matsui	Y	N	Y	N	N	N	N
6 Woolsey	Y	Y	N	N	N	N	N
7 Miller	Y	N	N	N	N	N	?
8 Pelosi	Y	N	N	N	N	N	?
9 Lee	Y	N	N	N	N	N	N
10 Tauscher	N	N	Y	N	N	N	Y
11 *Pombo*	Y	Y	Y	N	N	Y	N
12 Lantos	Y	N	Y	N	N	N	N
13 Stark	Y	Y	N	?	?	?	?
14 Eshoo	Y	N	Y	N	Y	N	N
15 *Campbell*	Y	Y	N	Y	Y	N	N
16 Lofgren	Y	Y	N	P	N	N	N
17 Farr	Y	Y	Y	N	Y	N	Y
18 Condit	Y	Y	Y	Y	Y	N	Y
19 *Radanovich*	Y	N	Y	N	Y	Y	N
20 Dooley	N	N	Y	N	N	N	Y
21 *Thomas*	Y	Y	Y	N	Y	Y	N
22 Capps, L.	Y	N	Y	N	N	N	Y
23 *Gallegly*	Y	N	Y	N	N	Y	N
24 Sherman	Y	N	Y	N	N	N	N
25 *McKeon*	Y	Y	Y	N	Y	Y	N
26 Berman	Y	N	?	?	?	?	?
27 *Rogan*	Y	N	Y	N	Y	Y	?
28 *Dreier*	Y	N	Y	N	Y	Y	N
29 Waxman	Y	N	?	?	?	?	?
30 Becerra	Y	N	N	N	N	N	N
31 Martinez	Y	N	N	N	N	?	?
32 Dixon	?	N	N	N	N	N	?
33 Roybal-Allard	Y	N	N	N	N	N	Y
34 Torres	?	?	?	?	?	?	?
35 Waters	Y	Y	Y	N	N	N	Y
36 Harman	?	?	?	?	?	?	?
37 Millender-McD.	Y	N	N	N	N	N	Y

	181	182	183	184	185	186	187
38 Horn	Y	N	Y	N	N	Y	N
39 *Royce*	Y	Y	N	N	N	Y	N
40 *Lewis*	Y	N	Y	N	N	Y	N
41 *Kim*	Y	N	Y	N	N	Y	N
42 Brown	N	Y	N	N	N	N	Y
43 *Calvert*	Y	N	Y	N	N	Y	N
44 *Bono, M.*	Y	N	Y	N	Y	Y	?
45 *Rohrabacher*	Y	Y	Y	Y	Y	Y	N
46 Sanchez	Y	N	Y	N	Y	N	N
47 *Cox*	Y	N	Y	Y	Y	Y	N
48 *Packard*	Y	N	Y	Y	Y	Y	N
49 *Bilbray*	Y	Y	Y	Y	Y	Y	N
50 Filner	Y	Y	N	N	N	N	?
51 *Cunningham*	Y	Y	Y	Y	Y	Y	N
52 *Hunter*	Y	N	Y	N	Y	Y	?
COLORADO							
1 DeGette	Y	N	N	N	Y	N	Y
2 Skaggs	+	−	+	+	+	−	−
3 *McInnis*	Y	Y	Y	N	N	Y	N
4 *Schaffer*	Y	Y	Y	Y	Y	Y	N
5 *Hefley*	Y	Y	Y	N	N	?	N
6 *Schaefer*	Y	Y	Y	N	Y	Y	N
CONNECTICUT							
1 Kennelly	Y	N	Y	N	N	N	Y
2 Gejdenson	Y	N	Y	N	N	N	N
3 DeLauro	Y	N	Y	N	N	N	Y
4 *Shays*	Y	Y	N	Y	Y	Y	N
5 Maloney	Y	N	Y	N	N	N	N
6 *Johnson*	Y	Y	Y	Y	Y	Y	N
DELAWARE							
AL *Castle*	Y	N	Y	Y	Y	Y	Y
FLORIDA							
1 *Scarborough*	Y	Y	Y	Y	Y	?	N
2 Boyd	Y	N	Y	N	Y	N	Y
3 Brown	Y	N	Y	N	N	N	Y
4 *Fowler*	Y	N	Y	N	N	Y	N
5 Thurman	Y	N	Y	N	Y	N	Y
6 *Stearns*	Y	N	Y	N	Y	Y	N
7 *Mica*	Y	Y	Y	N	Y	Y	N
8 *McCollum*	Y	Y	Y	Y	Y	Y	N
9 *Bilirakis*	Y	Y	Y	N	N	Y	?
10 *Young*	Y	N	Y	N	N	Y	N
11 Davis	Y	N	Y	N	N	N	N
12 *Canady*	Y	Y	Y	Y	Y	?	N
13 *Miller*	Y	N	Y	N	N	Y	N
14 *Goss*	Y	N	Y	N	N	Y	N
15 *Weldon*	Y	N	Y	N	N	N	N
16 *Foley*	?	?	?	?	?	?	?
17 Meek	Y	N	Y	N	N	N	N
18 *Ros-Lehtinen*	Y	N	Y	N	N	Y	N
19 Wexler	Y	N	Y	N	N	N	N
20 Deutsch	Y	N	?	?	?	?	?
21 *Diaz-Balart*	Y	N	Y	N	N	Y	N
22 *Shaw*	Y	N	Y	N	?	N	N
23 Hastings	Y	N	Y	N	N	N	Y
GEORGIA							
1 *Kingston*	Y	Y	Y	N	Y	Y	Y
2 Bishop	Y	N	Y	N	N	N	Y
3 *Collins*	Y	N	Y	N	Y	Y	N
4 McKinney	Y	Y	N	N	Y	N	N
5 Lewis	Y	N	Y	Y	N	N	Y
6 *Gingrich*							
7 *Barr*	Y	Y	Y	N	Y	Y	N
8 *Chambliss*	Y	N	Y	N	N	Y	N
9 *Deal*	Y	N	Y	N	Y	Y	N
10 *Norwood*	Y	Y	Y	N	Y	Y	N
11 *Linder*	Y	N	Y	N	Y	Y	N
HAWAII							
1 Abercrombie	Y	N	Y	N	N	N	Y
2 Mink	Y	Y	Y	N	N	N	Y
IDAHO							
1 *Chenoweth*	Y	Y	Y	Y	Y	Y	N
2 *Crapo*	Y	Y	Y	N	Y	Y	N
ILLINOIS							
1 Rush	Y	Y	N	N	N	N	N
2 Jackson	Y	Y	N	N	N	N	N
3 Lipinski	Y	Y	N	N	N	N	N
4 Gutierrez	Y	N	N	N	N	N	N
5 Blagojevich	Y	N	Y	N	N	N	N
6 *Hyde*	Y	N	Y	N	N	N	N
7 Davis	Y	N	N	N	N	N	?
8 *Crane*	Y	Y	Y	Y	Y	Y	N
9 Yates	?	?	X	?	?	?	N
10 *Porter*	Y	N	Y	N	N	Y	?
11 *Weller*	Y	Y	Y	N	N	Y	?
12 Costello	Y	Y	Y	N	N	Y	N

ND Northern Democrats   SD Southern Democrats

	181	182	183	184	185	186	187
13 ***Fawell***	Y	N	Y	N	N	Y	?
14 ***Hastert***	Y	Y	Y	N	N	Y	N
15 ***Ewing***	Y	Y	Y	N	N	Y	N
16 ***Manzullo***	Y	Y	Y	?	?	?	?
17 Evans	Y	N	Y	N	Y	N	N
18 ***LaHood***	Y	Y	Y	N	N	Y	N
19 Poshard	Y	Y	Y	N	Y	N	N
20 ***Shimkus***	Y	Y	Y	N	N	Y	N
INDIANA							
1 Visclosky	Y	N	Y	N	N	N	N
2 ***McIntosh***	Y	Y	Y	N	Y	Y	N
3 Roemer	Y	Y	Y	N	Y	N	N
4 ***Souder***	Y	Y	Y	Y	Y	Y	?
5 ***Buyer***	Y	N	Y	N	N	Y	N
6 ***Burton***	Y	Y	Y	N	N	?	N
7 ***Pease***	Y	Y	Y	N	N	Y	N
8 ***Hostettler***	Y	N	Y	N	N	Y	N
9 Hamilton	Y	N	Y	N	N	N	N
10 Carson	Y	N	Y	N	Y	N	N
IOWA							
1 ***Leach***	Y	N	Y	Y	Y	Y	N
2 ***Nussle***	Y	Y	Y	N	Y	Y	N
3 Boswell	Y	N	Y	N	N	N	N
4 ***Ganske***	Y	Y	Y	N	N	Y	N
5 ***Latham***	Y	Y	Y	N	N	Y	N
KANSAS							
1 ***Moran***	Y	Y	Y	N	N	Y	N
2 ***Ryun***	Y	Y	Y	N	N	Y	N
3 ***Snowbarger***	Y	Y	Y	N	N	Y	N
4 ***Tiahrt***	Y	Y	Y	N	N	Y	N
KENTUCKY							
1 ***Whitfield***	Y	Y	Y	N	?	Y	Y
2 ***Lewis***	Y	Y	Y	N	N	Y	N
3 ***Northup***	Y	N	Y	N	N	Y	N
4 ***Bunning***	Y	Y	Y	N	N	Y	N
5 ***Rogers***	Y	Y	Y	N	N	Y	N
6 Baesler	Y	N	Y	N	N	N	N
LOUISIANA							
1 ***Livingston***	Y	N	Y	N	N	Y	N
2 Jefferson	Y	N	Y	N	N	N	?
3 ***Tauzin***	Y	N	Y	N	N	Y	N
4 ***McCrery***	Y	N	Y	?	?	?	?
5 ***Cooksey***	Y	N	Y	N	N	Y	N
6 ***Baker***	Y	Y	Y	N	Y	Y	N
7 John	Y	N	Y	N	N	N	N
MAINE							
1 Allen	Y	N	Y	N	N	N	Y
2 Baldacci	Y	N	Y	N	N	N	N
MARYLAND							
1 ***Gilchrest***	Y	N	Y	N	N	Y	N
2 ***Ehrlich***	Y	N	Y	N	Y	Y	N
3 Cardin	Y	N	Y	N	Y	N	N
4 Wynn	Y	N	Y	N	N	N	N
5 Hoyer	Y	N	Y	N	Y	N	N
6 ***Bartlett***	Y	Y	Y	N	Y	Y	N
7 Cummings	Y	N	Y	N	N	N	N
8 ***Morella***	Y	N	N	Y	Y	Y	?
MASSACHUSETTS							
1 Olver	Y	N	Y	N	N	N	Y
2 Neal	Y	N	Y	N	N	N	N
3 McGovern	Y	N	N	N	N	N	Y
4 Frank	N	Y	N	N	N	N	N
5 Meehan	Y	N	Y	Y	Y	N	N
6 Tierney	Y	Y	Y	N	N	N	N
7 Markey	Y	N	N	N	N	N	?
8 Kennedy	Y	N	Y	N	N	N	N
9 Moakley	Y	N	Y	N	N	N	N
10 Delahunt	Y	N	N	N	N	N	Y
MICHIGAN							
1 Stupak	Y	N	Y	N	N	N	N
2 ***Hoekstra***	Y	N	N	Y	Y	Y	N
3 ***Ehlers***	Y	N	N	N	N	Y	N
4 ***Camp***	Y	Y	Y	N	N	Y	N
5 Barcia	Y	N	Y	N	N	N	N
6 ***Upton***	Y	Y	Y	N	N	Y	N
7 ***Smith***	Y	Y	Y	N	Y	Y	N
8 Stabenow	Y	N	Y	N	N	N	N
9 Kildee	Y	N	Y	N	N	N	N
10 Bonior	Y	N	N	N	N	N	Y
11 ***Knollenberg***	Y	N	Y	N	N	Y	N
12 Levin	Y	N	Y	N	Y	N	N
13 Rivers	Y	N	N	N	Y	N	N
14 Conyers	Y	Y	N	N	N	N	?
15 Kilpatrick	Y	N	Y	N	N	N	N
16 Dingell	Y	N	Y	N	N	N	N
MINNESOTA							
1 ***Gutknecht***	Y	N	Y	N	N	Y	?
2 Minge	Y	N	N	Y	Y	N	N
3 ***Ramstad***	Y	Y	Y	N	N	Y	N
4 Vento	Y	N	N	Y	N	N	N
5 Sabo	Y	N	Y	N	P	N	Y
6 Luther	Y	N	N	N	Y	N	N
7 Peterson	Y	Y	Y	N	P	N	N
8 Oberstar	Y	N	N	N	N	N	N
MISSISSIPPI							
1 ***Wicker***	?	?	?	?	?	?	?
2 Thompson	Y	N	Y	N	N	N	N
3 ***Pickering***	Y	Y	Y	N	N	Y	N
4 ***Parker***	?	?	?	?	?	?	?
5 Taylor	Y	N	Y	N	Y	N	N
MISSOURI							
1 Clay	Y	N	Y	N	N	N	Y
2 ***Talent***	Y	Y	Y	N	N	Y	N
3 Gephardt	Y	N	Y	N	Y	N	Y
4 Skelton	N	N	Y	N	N	N	N
5 McCarthy	Y	N	N	N	Y	N	–
6 Danner	Y	Y	Y	N	N	N	N
7 ***Blunt***	Y	Y	Y	N	N	Y	N
8 ***Emerson***	Y	Y	Y	N	Y	Y	N
9 ***Hulshof***	Y	Y	Y	N	Y	Y	N
MONTANA							
AL ***Hill***	Y	Y	Y	Y	Y	Y	N
NEBRASKA							
1 ***Bereuter***	Y	N	Y	N	N	Y	N
2 ***Christensen***	Y	Y	Y	Y	Y	Y	N
3 ***Barrett***	Y	Y	Y	N	Y	Y	N
NEVADA							
1 ***Ensign***	Y	Y	Y	N	Y	Y	N
2 ***Gibbons***	Y	Y	Y	Y	N	Y	N
NEW HAMPSHIRE							
1 ***Sununu***	Y	Y	Y	N	Y	Y	N
2 ***Bass***	Y	Y	Y	N	N	Y	N
NEW JERSEY							
1 Andrews	Y	N	Y	N	Y	N	N
2 ***LoBiondo***	Y	Y	Y	N	N	Y	N
3 ***Saxton***	Y	N	Y	N	N	Y	N
4 ***Smith***	Y	N	Y	N	N	Y	N
5 ***Roukema***	Y	Y	Y	N	N	Y	N
6 Pallone	Y	N	Y	N	N	N	Y
7 ***Franks***	Y	Y	N	N	N	Y	N
8 Pascrell	Y	N	Y	N	N	N	?
9 Rothman	Y	N	Y	N	N	N	N
10 Payne	Y	N	N	N	N	N	Y
11 ***Frelinghuysen***	Y	N	Y	N	N	Y	N
12 ***Pappas***	Y	N	Y	N	N	Y	N
13 Menendez	Y	N	Y	N	N	N	N
NEW MEXICO							
1 Vacant							
2 ***Skeen***	Y	N	Y	N	N	Y	N
3 ***Redmond***	Y	N	Y	N	N	Y	N
NEW YORK							
1 ***Forbes***	Y	Y	Y	N	N	Y	N
2 ***Lazio***	Y	N	Y	N	N	Y	N
3 ***King***	Y	N	Y	N	N	Y	N
4 McCarthy	Y	N	Y	N	N	N	N
5 Ackerman	Y	N	Y	N	N	N	?
6 Meeks	?	?	?	?	?	?	?
7 Manton	Y	N	Y	N	N	N	Y
8 Nadler	Y	N	N	N	N	N	?
9 Schumer	Y	N	Y	Y	Y	N	N
10 Towns	Y	Y	Y	?	?	?	?
11 Owens	Y	Y	N	N	N	N	?
12 Velázquez	Y	N	N	N	N	N	N
13 ***Fossella***	Y	N	Y	N	N	Y	N
14 Maloney	Y	N	Y	Y	Y	N	N
15 Rangel	Y	Y	Y	Y	N	N	?
16 Serrano	Y	Y	N	N	N	N	?
17 Engel	Y	N	N	N	N	N	N
18 Lowey	Y	N	N	N	N	N	N
19 ***Kelly***	Y	Y	Y	N	N	Y	N
20 ***Gilman***	Y	N	Y	N	N	Y	N
21 McNulty	Y	N	Y	N	N	N	N
22 ***Solomon***	Y	N	Y	N	N	Y	N
23 ***Boehlert***	Y	N	Y	N	N	Y	N
24 ***McHugh***	Y	N	Y	N	N	Y	N
25 ***Walsh***	Y	N	Y	N	N	Y	N
26 Hinchey	Y	N	N	N	N	N	?
27 ***Paxon***	Y	Y	Y	N	N	Y	N
28 Slaughter	Y	N	N	N	N	N	Y
29 LaFalce	Y	N	Y	N	Y	N	N
30 ***Quinn***	?	?	#	?	?	?	–
31 ***Houghton***	Y	N	Y	N	N	Y	N
NORTH CAROLINA							
1 Clayton	Y	N	Y	N	Y	N	Y
2 Etheridge	Y	N	Y	N	Y	N	N
3 ***Jones***	Y	N	Y	Y	Y	Y	N
4 Price	Y	N	Y	N	Y	N	N
5 ***Burr***	Y	N	Y	N	Y	?	N
6 ***Coble***	Y	Y	Y	N	Y	Y	N
7 McIntyre	N	N	Y	N	Y	N	Y
8 Hefner	Y	N	Y	N	Y	N	?
9 ***Myrick***	Y	Y	Y	Y	Y	Y	N
10 ***Ballenger***	Y	Y	Y	Y	Y	Y	N
11 ***Taylor***	?	?	?	?	?	?	?
12 Watt	Y	Y	Y	N	N	N	Y
NORTH DAKOTA							
AL Pomeroy	Y	N	Y	N	Y	N	Y
OHIO							
1 ***Chabot***	Y	Y	Y	Y	Y	Y	N
2 ***Portman***	Y	N	Y	Y	Y	Y	N
3 Hall	Y	N	Y	N	N	N	Y
4 ***Oxley***	?	N	Y	N	N	?	?
5 ***Gillmor***	Y	Y	Y	N	N	Y	N
6 Strickland	Y	N	Y	N	N	N	?
7 ***Hobson***	Y	N	Y	Y	Y	Y	N
8 ***Boehner***	Y	N	Y	N	N	?	N
9 Kaptur	Y	Y	Y	Y	N	N	?
10 Kucinich	Y	N	N	N	N	N	N
11 Stokes	Y	Y	Y	N	N	N	N
12 ***Kasich***	Y	Y	Y	Y	Y	Y	N
13 Brown	Y	N	N	Y	Y	N	Y
14 Sawyer	N	N	Y	Y	Y	N	Y
15 ***Pryce***	Y	Y	Y	N	Y	Y	N
16 ***Regula***	Y	Y	Y	N	N	Y	N
17 Traficant	Y	Y	Y	N	N	Y	N
18 ***Ney***	Y	Y	Y	?	?	Y	N
19 ***LaTourette***	Y	N	Y	N	Y	Y	N
OKLAHOMA							
1 ***Largent***	Y	Y	Y	Y	Y	Y	N
2 ***Coburn***	Y	Y	Y	Y	Y	?	N
3 ***Watkins***	Y	Y	Y	N	Y	Y	N
4 ***Watts***	Y	Y	Y	N	Y	Y	N
5 ***Istook***	Y	Y	Y	Y	N	Y	N
6 ***Lucas***	Y	Y	Y	N	Y	Y	N
OREGON							
1 Furse	Y	Y	N	N	N	N	?
2 ***Smith***	Y	N	Y	N	N	Y	N
3 Blumenauer	?	N	Y	N	N	N	N
4 DeFazio	Y	Y	N	N	N	?	?
5 Hooley	Y	Y	N	N	Y	N	N
PENNSYLVANIA							
1 Brady	Y	N	Y	N	N	N	?
2 Fattah	Y	N	Y	N	N	N	Y
3 Borski	Y	N	Y	N	N	N	N
4 Klink	Y	N	Y	N	N	N	N
5 ***Peterson***	Y	Y	Y	N	N	Y	N
6 Holden	Y	N	Y	N	N	N	N
7 ***Weldon***	Y	Y	Y	N	N	Y	N
8 ***Greenwood***	Y	Y	Y	N	N	Y	N
9 ***Shuster***	Y	N	Y	N	N	Y	N
10 ***McDade***	?	?	?	?	?	?	?
11 Kanjorski	Y	N	Y	N	N	N	N
12 Murtha	Y	N	Y	N	N	N	N
13 ***Fox***	Y	Y	Y	N	Y	Y	N
14 Coyne	?	N	Y	N	N	N	Y
15 McHale	Y	N	Y	N	N	N	N
16 ***Pitts***	Y	Y	Y	N	N	Y	N
17 ***Gekas***	Y	N	Y	N	N	Y	N
18 Doyle	Y	N	Y	N	N	N	N
19 ***Goodling***	Y	N	+	N	N	Y	N
20 Mascara	Y	N	Y	N	N	N	N
21 ***English***	Y	Y	Y	N	N	Y	N
RHODE ISLAND							
1 Kennedy	Y	N	Y	N	Y	N	N
2 Weygand	Y	N	Y	N	Y	N	?
SOUTH CAROLINA							
1 ***Sanford***	Y	Y	Y	Y	Y	Y	N
2 ***Spence***	Y	N	Y	N	N	Y	?
3 ***Graham***	Y	Y	Y	Y	Y	Y	?
4 ***Inglis***	Y	Y	Y	Y	Y	Y	?
5 Spratt	?	?	?	N	Y	N	N
6 Clyburn	Y	N	Y	N	N	N	N
SOUTH DAKOTA							
AL ***Thune***	Y	Y	Y	N	N	Y	N
TENNESSEE							
1 ***Jenkins***	Y	N	Y	N	N	Y	N
2 ***Duncan***	Y	Y	Y	N	N	Y	N
3 ***Wamp***	Y	Y	Y	N	Y	Y	N
4 ***Hilleary***	Y	Y	Y	Y	Y	Y	N
5 Clement	Y	N	Y	N	N	?	?
6 Gordon	Y	N	Y	N	N	N	N
7 ***Bryant***	Y	Y	Y	N	N	Y	N
8 Tanner	Y	N	Y	N	Y	N	Y
9 Ford	Y	N	Y	N	N	N	Y
TEXAS							
1 Sandlin	Y	N	Y	N	N	N	N
2 Turner	Y	N	Y	N	Y	N	N
3 ***Johnson, Sam***	?	?	?	?	?	?	?
4 Hall	Y	Y	Y	Y	Y	Y	N
5 ***Sessions***	Y	Y	Y	Y	Y	Y	?
6 ***Barton***	Y	N	Y	Y	Y	Y	N
7 ***Archer***	Y	Y	Y	Y	Y	Y	N
8 ***Brady***	Y	Y	Y	N	Y	Y	N
9 Lampson	Y	N	Y	N	N	N	N
10 Doggett	Y	Y	N	N	Y	N	N
11 Edwards	Y	N	Y	Y	Y	N	Y
12 ***Granger***	Y	Y	Y	N	N	Y	N
13 ***Thornberry***	Y	Y	Y	Y	Y	Y	N
14 ***Paul***	Y	Y	N	N	Y	?	N
15 Hinojosa	Y	N	Y	N	N	N	N
16 Reyes	Y	N	Y	N	N	N	?
17 Stenholm	Y	N	Y	Y	Y	N	Y
18 Jackson-Lee	Y	N	Y	N	N	N	N
19 ***Combest***	Y	Y	Y	N	Y	Y	N
20 Gonzalez	?	?	?	?	?	?	?
21 ***Smith***	Y	Y	Y	N	N	Y	N
22 ***DeLay***	Y	N	Y	N	N	Y	?
23 ***Bonilla***	Y	Y	Y	N	N	Y	N
24 Frost	Y	N	Y	N	N	N	N
25 Bentsen	Y	N	Y	N	Y	N	N
26 ***Armey***	Y	N	Y	N	N	Y	N
27 Ortiz	Y	N	Y	N	N	N	Y
28 Rodriguez	Y	N	Y	N	N	N	N
29 Green	Y	Y	Y	N	N	N	?
30 Johnson, E.B.	Y	N	Y	N	N	N	N
UTAH							
1 ***Hansen***	Y	N	Y	N	N	Y	N
2 ***Cook***	Y	Y	Y	N	N	Y	N
3 ***Cannon***	Y	Y	Y	N	Y	Y	N
VERMONT							
AL *Sanders*	Y	N	N	N	N	N	?
VIRGINIA							
1 ***Bateman***	+	–	+	–	–	+	–
2 Pickett	N	N	Y	N	Y	N	Y
3 Scott	Y	N	Y	N	Y	N	Y
4 Sisisky	Y	N	Y	Y	N	N	Y
5 Goode	Y	Y	Y	N	N	Y	N
6 ***Goodlatte***	Y	Y	Y	N	Y	Y	N
7 ***Bliley***	Y	N	Y	N	N	Y	N
8 Moran	Y	N	Y	?	?	N	N
9 Boucher	Y	N	Y	N	N	N	Y
10 ***Wolf***	Y	N	Y	Y	Y	Y	N
11 ***Davis***	Y	N	Y	N	Y	Y	N
WASHINGTON							
1 ***White***	Y	N	Y	N	N	Y	N
2 ***Metcalf***	Y	Y	Y	N	N	Y	N
3 ***Smith, Linda***	Y	N	Y	N	N	Y	N
4 ***Hastings***	Y	Y	Y	N	Y	Y	N
5 ***Nethercutt***	Y	Y	Y	Y	Y	Y	N
6 Dicks	Y	N	Y	N	N	N	N
7 McDermott	Y	N	N	N	Y	N	?
8 ***Dunn***	Y	N	Y	N	N	Y	N
9 Smith, Adam	Y	N	Y	N	Y	N	N
WEST VIRGINIA							
1 Mollohan	Y	N	Y	N	N	N	?
2 Wise	Y	N	Y	N	N	N	N
3 Rahall	Y	N	N	N	N	N	N
WISCONSIN							
1 ***Neumann***	Y	Y	Y	Y	Y	Y	N
2 ***Klug***	Y	Y	Y	Y	Y	Y	N
3 Kind	Y	N	N	Y	Y	N	N
4 Kleczka	Y	N	Y	Y	Y	N	N
5 Barrett	Y	N	N	Y	Y	N	N
6 ***Petri***	Y	Y	N	N	N	Y	N
7 Obey	Y	N	N	Y	Y	N	Y
8 Johnson	Y	N	Y	N	N	N	N
9 ***Sensenbrenner***	Y	Y	N	Y	Y	Y	N
WYOMING							
AL ***Cubin***	Y	Y	Y	Y	Y	Y	?

Southern states - Ala., Ark., Fla., Ga., Ky., La., Miss., N.C., Okla., S.C., Tenn., Texas, Va.

Key

Y	Voted for (yea).
#	Paired for.
+	Announced for.
N	Voted against (nay).
X	Paired against.
−	Announced against.
P	Voted "present."
C	Voted "present" to avoid possible conflict of interest.
?	Did not vote or otherwise make a position known.

Democrats   **Republicans**   *Independent*

---

188. S 1150. Agriculture Reauthorization Conference Report/Rule. Adoption of the rule (H Res 446) to dispose of the conference report on the bill to reauthorize agricultural research and education programs through fiscal 2002. The rule would have allowed a point of order to strike $818 million in funding in the conference report to restore food stamps to 250,000 legal immigrants. Rejected 120-289: R 118-98; D 2-190 (ND 1-140, SD 1-50); I 0-1. May 22, 1998.

189. HR 2676. Internal Revenue Service Overhaul/Motion to Instruct. Coyne, D-Pa., motion to instruct the House conferees to insist on the provisions in the House bill and thereby not further delay restructuring of the Internal Revenue Service. Motion agreed to 388-1: R 200-1; D 187-0 (ND 137-0, SD 50-0); I 1-0. May 22, 1998.

190. HR 2400. Surface Transportation Reauthorization Conference Report/Rule. Adoption of the rule (H Res 449) to waive points of order against the conference report on the bill to reauthorize federal highway and mass transit programs. Adopted 359-29: R 192-11; D 166-18 (ND 126-9, SD 40-9); I 1-0. May 22, 1998.

191. HR 2400. Surface Transportation Reauthorization/Motion to Recommit. Obey, D-Wis., motion to recommit the conference report to the Committee of Conference with instructions to strike those provisions of the conference report that prohibit or reduce service-connected disability compensation to veterans relating to use of tobacco products. Motion rejected 190-195: R 87-114; D 102-81 (ND 70-65, SD 32-16); I 1-0. May 22, 1998.

192. HR 2400. Surface Transportation Reauthorization/Conference Report. Adoption of the conference report on the bill to authorize $216 billion over six years for federal highway and mass transit programs. Adopted (thus cleared for the president) 297-86: R 143-56; D 153-30 (ND 116-19, SD 36-12); I 1-0. May 22, 1998.

193. Procedural Motion/Journal. Approval of the House Journal of Friday, May 22, 1998. Approved 354-35: R 188-14; D 165-21 (ND 121-14, SD 44-7); I 1-0. June 03, 1998.

194. HR 3808. Carl D. Pursell Post Office/Passage. McHugh, R-N.Y., motion to suspend the rules and pass the bill to designate a U.S. post office in Plymouth, Mich., as the "Carl D. Pursell Post Office." Motion agreed to 389-0: R 201-0; D 187-0 (ND 136-0, SD 51-0); I 1-0. June 03, 1998. A two-thirds majority of those present and voting (260 in this case) is required for passage under suspension of the rules.

	188	189	190	191	192	193	194
ALABAMA							
1 *Callahan*	N	Y	Y	?	?	Y	Y
2 *Everett*	N	Y	Y	N	Y	Y	Y
3 *Riley*	N	Y	Y	N	Y	Y	Y
4 *Aderholt*	N	Y	Y	Y	Y	Y	Y
5 Cramer	N	Y	Y	N	Y	Y	Y
6 *Bachus*	N	Y	Y	N	Y	Y	Y
7 Hilliard	N	Y	Y	N	Y	N	Y
ALASKA							
AL *Young*	N	Y	Y	Y	Y	Y	?
ARIZONA							
1 *Salmon*	Y	Y	Y	Y	N	?	?
2 Pastor	N	Y	Y	Y	Y	Y	Y
3 *Stump*	N	Y	Y	N	Y	Y	Y
4 *Shadegg*	Y	Y	N	Y	N	?	?
5 *Kolbe*	Y	Y	Y	N	N	?	?
6 *Hayworth*	N	Y	Y	Y	N	+	+
ARKANSAS							
1 Berry	N	Y	Y	N	Y	Y	Y
2 Snyder	N	Y	Y	N	Y	Y	Y
3 *Hutchinson*	N	?	Y	N	Y	Y	Y
4 *Dickey*	N	Y	Y	N	?	?	?
CALIFORNIA							
1 *Riggs*	?	?	?	?	?	Y	Y
2 *Herger*	Y	Y	Y	N	N	Y	Y
3 Fazio	N	Y	Y	?	?	N	Y
4 *Doolittle*	Y	Y	Y	N	?	?	?
5 Matsui	N	Y	Y	N	Y	Y	Y
6 Woolsey	N	Y	Y	Y	Y	Y	Y
7 Miller	?	?	?	?	?	Y	Y
8 Pelosi	N	Y	Y	Y	Y	Y	Y
9 Lee	N	Y	Y	N	Y	?	?
10 Tauscher	N	Y	Y	N	Y	Y	Y
11 *Pombo*	N	Y	Y	N	Y	Y	Y
12 Lantos	N	Y	Y	N	Y	Y	Y
13 Stark	?	Y	Y	Y	N	Y	Y
14 Eshoo	N	Y	Y	N	Y	Y	Y
15 *Campbell*	N	Y	Y	N	Y	Y	Y
16 Lofgren	N	?	?	?	Y	Y	Y
17 Farr	N	Y	Y	N	Y	Y	Y
18 Condit	N	Y	Y	N	Y	Y	Y
19 *Radanovich*	Y	Y	Y	N	Y	Y	Y
20 Dooley	N	Y	Y	Y	Y	Y	Y
21 *Thomas*	Y	Y	Y	N	Y	Y	Y
22 Capps, L.	N	Y	Y	Y	Y	Y	Y
23 *Gallegly*	Y	Y	Y	N	Y	Y	Y
24 Sherman	N	Y	Y	N	Y	Y	Y
25 *McKeon*	Y	Y	Y	N	Y	Y	Y
26 Berman	N	Y	Y	Y	N	Y	Y
27 *Rogan*	Y	Y	Y	Y	N	Y	N
28 *Dreier*	Y	Y	Y	N	Y	Y	Y
29 Waxman	N	Y	?	Y	N	Y	Y
30 Becerra	N	Y	N	Y	Y	Y	Y
31 Martinez	N	Y	Y	Y	?	Y	?
32 Dixon	N	Y	Y	N	+	Y	Y
33 Roybal-Allard	N	Y	Y	Y	Y	Y	Y
34 Torres	?	?	?	?	?	?	?
35 Waters	N	Y	Y	N	Y	Y	Y
36 Harman	?	?	?	?	?	?	?
37 Millender-McD.	N	Y	Y	N	Y	Y	Y

	188	189	190	191	192	193	194
38 *Horn*	N	Y	Y	N	Y	Y	Y
39 *Royce*	Y	Y	Y	?	?	Y	Y
40 *Lewis*	N	Y	Y	N	Y	Y	Y
41 *Kim*	N	Y	Y	N	Y	Y	Y
42 Brown	N	Y	N	Y	N	N	Y
43 *Calvert*	N	Y	Y	N	Y	Y	Y
44 *Bono, M.*	Y	Y	Y	N	Y	+	+
45 *Rohrabacher*	Y	Y	N	N	N	?	?
46 Sanchez	N	Y	Y	Y	Y	Y	Y
47 *Cox*	Y	Y	Y	N	N	?	?
48 *Packard*	Y	Y	Y	N	Y	Y	Y
49 *Bilbray*	N	Y	Y	N	Y	Y	Y
50 Filner	N	Y	Y	N	Y	N	Y
51 *Cunningham*	Y	Y	Y	Y	Y	Y	Y
52 *Hunter*	Y	Y	N	N	Y	Y	Y
COLORADO							
1 DeGette	N	Y	?	Y	Y	Y	Y
2 Skaggs	−	+	+	+	−	Y	Y
3 *McInnis*	Y	Y	Y	Y	N	?	?
4 *Schaffer*	Y	Y	Y	Y	N	N	Y
5 *Hefley*	Y	?	?	?	?	N	Y
6 *Schaefer*	Y	Y	Y	Y	Y	Y	Y
CONNECTICUT							
1 Kennelly	N	Y	Y	Y	Y	Y	Y
2 Gejdenson	N	Y	Y	Y	Y	Y	Y
3 DeLauro	N	Y	Y	Y	Y	Y	Y
4 *Shays*	N	Y	N	Y	N	Y	Y
5 Maloney	N	Y	Y	Y	Y	Y	Y
6 *Johnson*	N	Y	Y	N	Y	Y	Y
DELAWARE							
AL *Castle*	N	Y	Y	N	Y	Y	Y
FLORIDA							
1 *Scarborough*	Y	Y	Y	Y	N	Y	Y
2 Boyd	N	Y	N	Y	N	Y	Y
3 Brown	N	Y	Y	N	Y	Y	Y
4 *Fowler*	Y	Y	Y	N	Y	Y	Y
5 Thurman	N	Y	Y	N	Y	Y	Y
6 *Stearns*	Y	Y	Y	Y	Y	Y	Y
7 *Mica*	Y	Y	Y	N	Y	+	+
8 *McCollum*	Y	Y	Y	N	Y	Y	Y
9 *Bilirakis*	Y	Y	Y	N	Y	Y	Y
10 *Young*	Y	Y	Y	N	Y	Y	Y
11 Davis	N	Y	Y	N	Y	Y	Y
12 *Canady*	Y	N	Y	N	Y	Y	Y
13 *Miller*	Y	Y	Y	N	Y	Y	Y
14 *Goss*	Y	Y	Y	N	Y	Y	Y
15 *Weldon*	N	Y	N	Y	N	Y	Y
16 *Foley*	?	?	?	?	?	Y	Y
17 Meek	N	Y	Y	N	Y	Y	Y
18 *Ros-Lehtinen*	N	Y	N	Y	N	Y	Y
19 Wexler	N	Y	N	?	?	Y	Y
20 Deutsch	?	?	?	?	?	Y	Y
21 *Diaz-Balart*	N	Y	Y	N	Y	?	+
22 *Shaw*	Y	Y	N	N	Y	Y	Y
23 Hastings	N	Y	N	N	N	N	Y
GEORGIA							
1 *Kingston*	Y	?	?	?	X	Y	Y
2 Bishop	N	Y	Y	N	Y	Y	Y
3 *Collins*	Y	Y	N	Y	N	Y	Y
4 McKinney	N	Y	N	Y	Y	Y	Y
5 Lewis	N	Y	N	Y	N	Y	Y
6 *Gingrich*				N			
7 *Barr*	Y	Y	Y	Y	Y	Y	Y
8 *Chambliss*	Y	Y	Y	Y	Y	Y	Y
9 *Deal*	Y	Y	Y	N	Y	Y	Y
10 *Norwood*	Y	Y	Y	Y	Y	Y	Y
11 *Linder*	Y	Y	Y	Y	Y	Y	Y
HAWAII							
1 Abercrombie	N	Y	Y	N	Y	Y	Y
2 Mink	N	Y	Y	N	Y	Y	Y
IDAHO							
1 *Chenoweth*	N	Y	Y	Y	N	Y	Y
2 *Crapo*	N	Y	Y	Y	Y	Y	Y
ILLINOIS							
1 Rush	N	Y	Y	N	Y	Y	Y
2 Jackson	N	Y	Y	N	Y	Y	Y
3 Lipinski	N	Y	Y	N	Y	Y	Y
4 Gutierrez	N	Y	Y	Y	Y	Y	Y
5 Blagojevich	N	Y	Y	N	Y	?	?
6 *Hyde*	N	?	?	?	Y	Y	Y
7 Davis	N	Y	Y	N	Y	Y	Y
8 *Crane*	Y	Y	Y	N	Y	?	?
9 Yates	N	Y	N	Y	N	Y	Y
10 *Porter*	N	Y	Y	N	+	+	+
11 *Weller*	N	Y	Y	N	Y	N	Y
12 Costello	N	Y	Y	N	Y	Y	Y

ND Northern Democrats   SD Southern Democrats

	188	189	190	191	192	193	194
13 ***Fawell***	Y	?	?	?	?	Y	Y
14 ***Hastert***	Y	Y	Y	N	Y	Y	Y
15 ***Ewing***	N	Y	Y	N	Y	Y	Y
16 ***Manzullo***	Y	Y	Y	N	Y	N	Y
17 Evans	N	Y	Y	Y	Y	Y	Y
18 ***LaHood***	N	Y	Y	N	Y	Y	Y
19 Poshard	N	Y	Y	Y	Y	?	?
20 ***Shimkus***	N	Y	Y	N	Y	Y	Y
INDIANA							
1 Visclosky	N	Y	Y	N	Y	N	Y
2 ***McIntosh***	Y	Y	Y	Y	Y	Y	Y
3 Roemer	N	Y	Y	N	Y	Y	Y
4 ***Souder***	N	Y	N	Y	N	Y	Y
5 ***Buyer***	Y	Y	Y	N	Y	Y	?
6 ***Burton***	N	?	?	?	#	?	?
7 ***Pease***	N	Y	Y	N	Y	Y	Y
8 ***Hostettler***	Y	Y	Y	N	Y	Y	Y
9 Hamilton	N	Y	Y	N	Y	Y	Y
10 Carson	N	Y	Y	Y	Y	Y	Y
IOWA							
1 ***Leach***	N	Y	Y	Y	Y	Y	Y
2 ***Nussle***	N	Y	Y	N	Y	N	Y
3 Boswell	N	Y	Y	Y	Y	Y	Y
4 ***Ganske***	N	Y	Y	N	Y	Y	Y
5 ***Latham***	N	Y	Y	N	Y	Y	Y
KANSAS							
1 ***Moran***	N	Y	Y	N	Y	N	Y
2 ***Ryun***	N	Y	Y	N	Y	Y	Y
3 ***Snowbarger***	Y	Y	Y	N	Y	Y	Y
4 ***Tiahrt***	Y	Y	Y	Y	Y	Y	?
KENTUCKY							
1 ***Whitfield***	Y	Y	Y	Y	Y	Y	Y
2 ***Lewis***	Y	Y	Y	Y	Y	Y	Y
3 ***Northup***	N	Y	Y	N	Y	Y	Y
4 ***Bunning***	N	Y	Y	Y	Y	Y	Y
5 ***Rogers***	Y	Y	Y	N	+	Y	Y
6 Baesler	N	Y	Y	Y	Y	Y	?
LOUISIANA							
1 ***Livingston***	N	Y	Y	N	Y	Y	Y
2 Jefferson	N	Y	Y	Y	Y	Y	Y
3 ***Tauzin***	Y	Y	Y	N	Y	Y	Y
4 ***McCrery***	Y	?	?	?	?	Y	Y
5 ***Cooksey***	N	Y	Y	N	Y	Y	Y
6 ***Baker***	N	Y	Y	Y	Y	Y	Y
7 John	N	Y	Y	N	Y	Y	Y
MAINE							
1 Allen	N	Y	Y	N	Y	Y	Y
2 Baldacci	N	Y	Y	N	Y	Y	Y
MARYLAND							
1 ***Gilchrest***	N	Y	Y	N	Y	Y	Y
2 ***Ehrlich***	Y	Y	Y	N	Y	Y	Y
3 Cardin	N	Y	Y	Y	N	Y	Y
4 Wynn	N	Y	Y	Y	Y	Y	Y
5 Hoyer	N	Y	Y	Y	N	Y	Y
6 ***Bartlett***	Y	Y	Y	Y	N	Y	Y
7 Cummings	N	Y	Y	N	Y	Y	Y
8 ***Morella***	N	?	Y	Y	N	Y	Y
MASSACHUSETTS							
1 Olver	N	Y	Y	Y	Y	Y	Y
2 Neal	N	Y	Y	?	?	Y	Y
3 McGovern	N	Y	Y	Y	Y	Y	Y
4 Frank	N	Y	Y	N	Y	Y	Y
5 Meehan	N	Y	?	?	?	?	?
6 Tierney	N	Y	N	Y	N	Y	Y
7 Markey	N	Y	Y	N	Y	Y	Y
8 Kennedy	N	Y	Y	Y	Y	Y	Y
9 Moakley	N	Y	Y	Y	Y	?	?
10 Delahunt	N	Y	Y	Y	Y	Y	Y
MICHIGAN							
1 Stupak	N	Y	Y	Y	Y	Y	Y
2 ***Hoekstra***	Y	?	?	?	?	Y	Y
3 ***Ehlers***	N	Y	Y	N	Y	Y	Y
4 ***Camp***	Y	Y	Y	N	Y	Y	Y
5 Barcia	N	Y	Y	N	Y	?	Y
6 ***Upton***	N	Y	Y	N	Y	Y	Y
7 ***Smith***	N	Y	Y	Y	Y	Y	Y
8 Stabenow	N	Y	Y	Y	Y	Y	Y
9 Kildee	N	Y	Y	Y	Y	Y	Y
10 Bonior	N	Y	Y	N	Y	Y	Y
11 ***Knollenberg***	Y	Y	Y	N	Y	Y	Y
12 Levin	N	Y	Y	N	Y	Y	Y
13 Rivers	N	Y	Y	Y	Y	Y	Y
14 Conyers	?	?	?	?	?	Y	Y
15 Kilpatrick	N	Y	Y	N	Y	Y	Y
16 Dingell	N	Y	Y	N	Y	Y	Y

	188	189	190	191	192	193	194
MINNESOTA							
1 ***Gutknecht***	N	Y	Y	N	Y	Y	Y
2 Minge	N	Y	N	Y	N	Y	Y
3 ***Ramstad***	N	Y	Y	N	Y	Y	Y
4 Vento	N	Y	Y	N	Y	Y	Y
5 Sabo	N	Y	N	Y	N	N	Y
6 Luther	N	Y	Y	Y	Y	Y	Y
7 Peterson	N	Y	Y	Y	Y	Y	Y
8 Oberstar	N	Y	Y	N	Y	N	Y
MISSISSIPPI							
1 ***Wicker***	?	?	?	?	#	N	Y
2 Thompson	N	Y	Y	Y	Y	N	Y
3 ***Pickering***	Y	Y	Y	N	Y	Y	Y
4 ***Parker***	?	?	?	?	X	?	Y
5 Taylor	N	Y	Y	Y	N	N	Y
MISSOURI							
1 Clay	N	Y	Y	N	Y	N	Y
2 ***Talent***	N	Y	Y	Y	Y	Y	Y
3 Gephardt	N	?	?	?	Y	N	Y
4 Skelton	N	Y	Y	N	Y	Y	Y
5 McCarthy	N	Y	Y	Y	Y	Y	Y
6 Danner	N	Y	Y	N	Y	Y	Y
7 ***Blunt***	Y	?	Y	?	?	Y	Y
8 ***Emerson***	Y	Y	Y	Y	N	Y	Y
9 ***Hulshof***	Y	Y	Y	Y	Y	Y	Y
MONTANA							
AL ***Hill***	N	Y	Y	Y	Y	Y	Y
NEBRASKA							
1 ***Bereuter***	N	Y	Y	N	Y	Y	Y
2 ***Christensen***	N	Y	N	Y	N	Y	Y
3 ***Barrett***	N	Y	N	Y	N	Y	Y
NEVADA							
1 ***Ensign***	Y	Y	Y	Y	Y	N	Y
2 ***Gibbons***	Y	Y	Y	Y	Y	Y	Y
NEW HAMPSHIRE							
1 ***Sununu***	Y	Y	Y	N	Y	Y	Y
2 ***Bass***	Y	Y	Y	N	Y	Y	Y
NEW JERSEY							
1 Andrews	N	Y	Y	N	Y	Y	Y
2 ***LoBiondo***	N	Y	Y	N	Y	N	Y
3 ***Saxton***	Y	Y	Y	N	Y	Y	Y
4 ***Smith***	N	Y	Y	Y	Y	Y	Y
5 ***Roukema***	Y	Y	Y	Y	N	?	?
6 Pallone	N	Y	Y	N	Y	Y	Y
7 ***Franks***	N	Y	Y	N	Y	Y	Y
8 Pascrell	N	Y	Y	N	Y	Y	Y
9 Rothman	N	Y	Y	N	Y	+	+
10 Payne	N	Y	Y	N	Y	Y	Y
11 ***Frelinghuysen***	Y	Y	Y	N	N	Y	Y
12 ***Pappas***	N	Y	Y	Y	Y	Y	Y
13 Menendez	N	Y	Y	N	Y	N	Y
NEW MEXICO							
1 Vacant							
2 ***Skeen***	N	Y	Y	N	Y	Y	Y
3 ***Redmond***	N	Y	Y	N	Y	Y	Y
NEW YORK							
1 ***Forbes***	N	Y	Y	N	Y	?	?
2 ***Lazio***	N	Y	Y	N	Y	Y	Y
3 ***King***	?	?	?	?	?	Y	Y
4 McCarthy	N	Y	Y	N	Y	Y	Y
5 Ackerman	N	Y	Y	N	Y	Y	Y
6 Meeks	?	?	?	?	?	Y	Y
7 Manton	N	Y	Y	Y	Y	Y	Y
8 Nadler	N	Y	Y	N	Y	Y	Y
9 Schumer	N	Y	Y	Y	Y	Y	Y
10 Towns	?	?	?	?	?	Y	Y
11 Owens	N	Y	Y	N	Y	Y	Y
12 Velázquez	N	Y	Y	N	Y	N	Y
13 ***Fossella***	N	Y	Y	N	Y	Y	Y
14 Maloney	N	Y	N	Y	N	Y	Y
15 Rangel	N	?	?	?	?	Y	Y
16 Serrano	N	Y	Y	N	Y	Y	Y
17 Engel	N	Y	Y	Y	Y	Y	Y
18 Lowey	N	Y	Y	Y	Y	Y	Y
19 ***Kelly***	N	Y	Y	Y	Y	Y	Y
20 ***Gilman***	N	Y	Y	Y	N	Y	Y
21 McNulty	N	Y	Y	Y	N	Y	Y
22 ***Solomon***	Y	Y	Y	N	Y	Y	Y
23 ***Boehlert***	N	Y	Y	N	Y	Y	Y
24 ***McHugh***	N	Y	Y	N	Y	Y	Y
25 ***Walsh***	N	Y	Y	N	Y	Y	Y
26 Hinchey	N	Y	Y	Y	Y	Y	Y
27 ***Paxon***	Y	Y	Y	N	Y	Y	Y
28 Slaughter	N	Y	Y	Y	Y	Y	Y
29 LaFalce	N	Y	Y	Y	Y	?	?

	188	189	190	191	192	193	194
30 ***Quinn***	–	+	+	+	#	Y	Y
31 ***Houghton***	Y	Y	Y	N	Y	Y	Y
NORTH CAROLINA							
1 Clayton	N	Y	Y	Y	Y	Y	Y
2 Etheridge	N	Y	Y	Y	Y	N	Y
3 ***Jones***	Y	Y	Y	Y	N	Y	Y
4 Price	N	Y	Y	Y	N	Y	Y
5 ***Burr***	Y	?	?	?	X	Y	Y
6 ***Coble***	Y	Y	Y	N	Y	Y	Y
7 McIntyre	N	Y	Y	Y	Y	Y	Y
8 Hefner	N	Y	Y	Y	Y	Y	Y
9 ***Myrick***	Y	Y	Y	Y	N	Y	Y
10 ***Ballenger***	Y	Y	Y	Y	N	Y	Y
11 ***Taylor***	?	?	?	?	?	Y	Y
12 Watt	N	Y	Y	N	Y	Y	Y
NORTH DAKOTA							
AL Pomeroy	N	Y	Y	Y	Y	Y	Y
OHIO							
1 ***Chabot***	Y	Y	N	Y	N	Y	Y
2 ***Portman***	Y	Y	Y	N	N	Y	Y
3 Hall	N	Y	Y	N	Y	Y	Y
4 ***Oxley***	N	Y	Y	N	Y	Y	Y
5 ***Gillmor***	N	Y	Y	Y	Y	Y	Y
6 Strickland	N	Y	Y	Y	N	Y	Y
7 ***Hobson***	Y	Y	N	Y	N	Y	Y
8 ***Boehner***	Y	Y	N	N	N	Y	Y
9 Kaptur	N	Y	Y	Y	Y	Y	Y
10 Kucinich	N	Y	Y	Y	Y	N	Y
11 Stokes	N	Y	Y	N	Y	?	?
12 ***Kasich***	N	Y	Y	Y	N	Y	Y
13 Brown	N	Y	Y	Y	N	Y	Y
14 Sawyer	N	Y	Y	Y	Y	?	?
15 ***Pryce***	N	Y	Y	Y	Y	Y	Y
16 ***Regula***	N	Y	Y	Y	Y	Y	Y
17 Traficant	Y	Y	Y	N	Y	Y	Y
18 ***Ney***	N	Y	Y	N	Y	Y	Y
19 ***LaTourette***	N	Y	Y	N	Y	Y	Y
OKLAHOMA							
1 ***Largent***	Y	Y	N	Y	N	Y	Y
2 ***Coburn***	Y	Y	N	Y	N	Y	Y
3 ***Watkins***	N	Y	Y	Y	Y	Y	Y
4 ***Watts***	N	Y	Y	Y	Y	N	Y
5 ***Istook***	Y	Y	Y	N	Y	Y	Y
6 ***Lucas***	N	Y	Y	Y	Y	Y	Y
OREGON							
1 Furse	?	?	?	?	?	?	?
2 ***Smith***	P	?	?	?	?	?	Y
3 Blumenauer	N	Y	Y	N	Y	Y	Y
4 DeFazio	?	?	?	?	?	N	Y
5 Hooley	N	Y	Y	N	Y	?	?
PENNSYLVANIA							
1 Brady	N	Y	Y	N	Y	Y	Y
2 Fattah	N	Y	Y	N	Y	Y	Y
3 Borski	N	Y	Y	N	Y	Y	Y
4 Klink	N	Y	Y	N	Y	Y	Y
5 ***Peterson***	N	Y	Y	N	Y	Y	Y
6 Holden	N	Y	Y	N	Y	Y	Y
7 ***Weldon***	N	Y	Y	Y	Y	Y	Y
8 ***Greenwood***	Y	Y	Y	N	Y	Y	Y
9 ***Shuster***	Y	Y	Y	N	Y	Y	Y
10 ***McDade***	N	?	?	?	#	Y	Y
11 Kanjorski	N	Y	Y	N	Y	Y	Y
12 Murtha	N	Y	Y	N	Y	Y	Y
13 ***Fox***	N	Y	Y	Y	Y	N	Y
14 Coyne	N	Y	Y	N	Y	Y	Y
15 McHale	N	Y	Y	Y	Y	Y	Y
16 ***Pitts***	Y	Y	Y	N	Y	Y	Y
17 ***Gekas***	Y	Y	Y	N	Y	Y	Y
18 Doyle	N	Y	Y	N	Y	Y	Y
19 ***Goodling***	Y	Y	Y	N	Y	Y	Y
20 Mascara	N	Y	Y	N	Y	Y	Y
21 ***English***	Y	Y	Y	Y	Y	N	Y
RHODE ISLAND							
1 Kennedy	N	Y	N	Y	N	Y	Y
2 Weygand	N	Y	Y	Y	Y	Y	Y
SOUTH CAROLINA							
1 ***Sanford***	Y	?	?	?	X	Y	Y
2 ***Spence***	Y	Y	Y	N	N	Y	Y
3 ***Graham***	Y	Y	?	?	–	Y	Y
4 ***Inglis***	Y	Y	Y	Y	N	?	?
5 Spratt	N	Y	Y	Y	Y	Y	Y
6 Clyburn	N	Y	Y	N	Y	?	?
SOUTH DAKOTA							
AL ***Thune***	N	Y	Y	N	Y	+	+

	188	189	190	191	192	193	194
TENNESSEE							
1 ***Jenkins***	Y	Y	Y	N	Y	Y	Y
2 ***Duncan***	Y	Y	Y	N	Y	Y	Y
3 ***Wamp***	Y	?	?	?	#	?	?
4 ***Hilleary***	Y	Y	Y	Y	Y	Y	Y
5 Clement	N	Y	Y	N	Y	Y	Y
6 Gordon	N	Y	Y	Y	Y	Y	Y
7 ***Bryant***	N	Y	Y	N	Y	Y	Y
8 Tanner	N	Y	Y	Y	Y	Y	Y
9 Ford	N	Y	Y	N	Y	N	Y
TEXAS							
1 Sandlin	N	Y	Y	Y	Y	Y	Y
2 Turner	N	Y	Y	Y	Y	Y	Y
3 ***Johnson, Sam***	?	?	?	?	X	Y	Y
4 Hall	N	Y	N	Y	N	Y	Y
5 ***Sessions***	Y	Y	Y	Y	N	N	Y
6 ***Barton***	Y	Y	Y	Y	N	Y	Y
7 ***Archer***	Y	?	?	?	X	Y	Y
8 ***Brady***	Y	Y	Y	Y	Y	Y	Y
9 Lampson	N	Y	Y	Y	Y	?	Y
10 Doggett	N	Y	N	Y	Y	Y	Y
11 Edwards	N	Y	N	Y	N	Y	Y
12 ***Granger***	N	Y	Y	N	Y	Y	Y
13 ***Thornberry***	N	Y	Y	N	Y	Y	Y
14 ***Paul***	Y	Y	Y	N	N	Y	Y
15 Hinojosa	N	Y	Y	N	Y	Y	Y
16 Reyes	?	?	?	?	?	Y	Y
17 Stenholm	N	?	?	?	?	Y	Y
18 Jackson-Lee	N	Y	Y	Y	Y	Y	Y
19 ***Combest***	N	Y	Y	N	Y	Y	Y
20 Gonzalez	?	?	?	?	?	?	?
21 ***Smith***	Y	Y	Y	N	Y	Y	Y
22 ***DeLay***	Y	Y	Y	N	Y	?	?
23 ***Bonilla***	N	Y	Y	Y	N	Y	Y
24 Frost	N	Y	Y	N	Y	Y	Y
25 Bentsen	N	Y	N	Y	N	Y	Y
26 ***Armey***	Y	Y	Y	N	Y	Y	Y
27 Ortiz	N	Y	Y	N	Y	Y	Y
28 Rodriguez	N	Y	Y	Y	Y	Y	Y
29 Green	?	?	?	?	#	Y	Y
30 Johnson, E.B.	N	Y	Y	N	Y	Y	Y
UTAH							
1 ***Hansen***	N	Y	Y	N	Y	Y	Y
2 ***Cook***	N	Y	Y	N	Y	Y	Y
3 ***Cannon***	Y	Y	Y	Y	Y	Y	Y
VERMONT							
AL *Sanders*	N	Y	Y	Y	Y	Y	Y
VIRGINIA							
1 ***Bateman***	–	+	+	+	+	Y	Y
2 Pickett	N	Y	Y	Y	Y	N	Y
3 Scott	N	Y	Y	Y	Y	Y	Y
4 Sisisky	N	Y	Y	Y	Y	Y	Y
5 Goode	Y	Y	Y	Y	Y	Y	Y
6 ***Goodlatte***	Y	Y	Y	Y	Y	Y	Y
7 ***Bliley***	Y	Y	Y	N	Y	Y	Y
8 Moran	N	Y	Y	Y	N	Y	Y
9 Boucher	N	Y	?	?	?	?	?
10 ***Wolf***	N	Y	Y	Y	N	Y	Y
11 ***Davis***	N	Y	Y	N	Y	Y	Y
WASHINGTON							
1 ***White***	Y	Y	Y	N	N	Y	Y
2 ***Metcalf***	Y	Y	Y	Y	Y	Y	Y
3 ***Smith, Linda***	N	Y	Y	Y	N	?	?
4 ***Hastings***	Y	Y	Y	Y	N	Y	Y
5 ***Nethercutt***	N	Y	Y	Y	N	Y	Y
6 Dicks	N	?	Y	Y	N	Y	Y
7 McDermott	N	Y	Y	Y	Y	N	Y
8 ***Dunn***	Y	Y	Y	N	Y	Y	Y
9 Smith, Adam	N	Y	Y	Y	N	Y	Y
WEST VIRGINIA							
1 Mollohan	N	?	?	?	?	Y	Y
2 Wise	N	Y	Y	N	Y	Y	Y
3 Rahall	N	Y	Y	N	Y	Y	Y
WISCONSIN							
1 ***Neumann***	Y	Y	Y	Y	Y	Y	Y
2 ***Klug***	Y	Y	Y	N	Y	Y	Y
3 Kind	N	Y	Y	Y	Y	Y	Y
4 Kleczka	N	Y	Y	Y	Y	Y	Y
5 Barrett	N	Y	N	Y	N	Y	Y
6 ***Petri***	Y	Y	Y	N	Y	Y	Y
7 Obey	N	Y	N	Y	N	?	?
8 Johnson	N	Y	Y	Y	Y	Y	Y
9 ***Sensenbrenner***	Y	Y	Y	Y	N	Y	Y
WYOMING							
AL ***Cubin***	Y	Y	Y	N	Y	Y	Y

Southern states - Ala., Ark., Fla., Ga., Ky., La., Miss., N.C., Okla., S.C., Tenn., Texas, Va.

Key

Y	Voted for (yea).
#	Paired for.
+	Announced for.
N	Voted against (nay).
X	Paired against.
–	Announced against.
P	Voted "present."
C	Voted "present" to avoid possible conflict of interest.
?	Did not vote or otherwise make a position known.

Democrats **Republicans** *Independent*

---

195. HR 3630. Steven Schiff Post Office/Passage. McHugh, R-N.Y., motion to suspend the rules and pass the bill to designate a U.S. post office in Albuquerque, N.M., as the "Steven Schiff Post Office." Motion agreed to 391-0: R 202-0; D 188-0 (ND 136-0, SD 52-0); I 1-0. June 3, 1998. A two-thirds majority of those present and voting (261 in this case) is required for passage under suspension of the rules.

196. H J Res 78. Religious Freedom Constitutional Amendment/Rule. Adoption of the rule (H Res 453) to provide for House floor consideration of a constitutional amendment that would guarantee an individual's right to pray and recognize their religious beliefs on public property, including schools. Adopted 248-169: R 221-1; D 27-167 (ND 11-132, SD 16-35); I 0-1. June 4, 1998.

197. HR 3433. Vocational Rehabilitation Services/Passage. Passage of the bill to restructure the system under which individuals collecting disability benefits under the Social Security and Supplemental Security Income programs receive vocational rehabilitation services by providing a voucher that beneficiaries may use to obtain such services. Passed 410-1: R 218-0; D 191-1 (ND 138-1, SD 53-0); I 1-0. June 4, 1998. A "yea" was a vote in support of the president's position.

198. H J Res 78. Religious Freedom Constitutional Amendment/Reference to God. Bishop, D-Ga., amendment to delete the measure's reference to God, adding instead language stating that the measure's intent is "to secure the people's right to freedom of religion." Rejected 6-419: R 1-223; D 5-195 (ND 3-146, SD 2-49); I 0-1. June 4, 1998.

199. H J Res 78. Religious Freedom Constitutional Amendment/Equal Access to Benefits. Bishop, D-Ga., amendment to strike language at the end of the measure regarding equal access to benefits on account of religion. Rejected 23-399: R 5-217; D 18-181 (ND 5-142, SD 13-39); I 0-1. June 4, 1998.

200. H J Res 78. Religious Freedom Constitutional Amendment/Recommit. Scott, D-Va., motion to recommit the bill to the Judiciary Committee with instructions to report it back with a substitute amendment reaffirming the First Amendment to the Constitution. Motion rejected 203-223: R 23-201; D 179-22 (ND 141-8, SD 38-14); I 1-0. June 4, 1998.

201. H J Res 78. Religious Freedom Constitutional Amendment/Passage. Passage of the joint resolution to propose a constitutional amendment to guarantee an individual's right to pray and recognize their religious beliefs on public property, including schools. It also would bar governments from requiring anyone to participate in any religious activity or to deny benefits on the basis of religion. Rejected 224-203: R 197-28; D 27-174 (ND 9-140, SD 18-34); I 0-1. June 4, 1998. A two-thirds majority vote of those present and voting (285 in this case) is required to pass a joint resolution proposing an amendment to the Constitution.

	195	196	197	198	199	200	201
ALABAMA							
1 *Callahan*	Y	Y	Y	N	N	N	Y
2 *Everett*	Y	Y	Y	N	N	N	Y
3 *Riley*	Y	Y	Y	N	N	N	Y
4 *Aderholt*	Y	Y	Y	N	N	N	Y
5 Cramer	Y	Y	Y	N	N	N	Y
6 *Bachus*	Y	Y	Y	N	N	N	Y
7 Hilliard	Y	N	Y	N	N	Y	N
ALASKA							
AL *Young*	Y	Y	Y	N	N	N	Y
ARIZONA							
1 *Salmon*	?	Y	Y	N	N	N	Y
2 Pastor	Y	N	Y	N	N	Y	N
3 *Stump*	Y	Y	Y	N	N	N	Y
4 *Shadegg*	?	Y	Y	N	N	N	Y
5 *Kolbe*	?	Y	Y	N	N	N	Y
6 *Hayworth*	+	Y	Y	N	N	N	Y
ARKANSAS							
1 Berry	Y	Y	Y	N	Y	N	Y
2 Snyder	Y	N	Y	N	N	Y	N
3 *Hutchinson*	Y	Y	Y	N	N	N	Y
4 *Dickey*	?	Y	Y	N	N	N	Y
CALIFORNIA							
1 *Riggs*	Y	Y	Y	N	N	N	Y
2 *Herger*	Y	?	Y	N	N	N	Y
3 Fazio	Y	N	Y	N	N	Y	N
4 *Doolittle*	?	Y	Y	N	N	N	Y
5 Matsui	Y	N	Y	N	N	Y	N
6 Woolsey	Y	N	Y	N	N	Y	N
7 Miller	Y	N	Y	N	N	Y	N
8 Pelosi	Y	N	Y	N	N	Y	N
9 Lee	?	N	Y	N	N	Y	N
10 Tauscher	Y	N	Y	N	N	Y	N
11 *Pombo*	Y	Y	Y	N	N	N	Y
12 Lantos	Y	N	Y	Y	N	Y	N
13 Stark	Y	N	Y	N	N	Y	N
14 Eshoo	Y	N	Y	N	N	Y	N
15 *Campbell*	Y	N	Y	N	N	N	N
16 Lofgren	Y	N	Y	N	N	Y	N
17 Farr	Y	N	Y	N	N	Y	N
18 Condit	Y	Y	Y	N	N	N	Y
19 *Radanovich*	Y	Y	Y	N	N	N	Y
20 Dooley	Y	N	Y	N	N	Y	N
21 *Thomas*	Y	Y	Y	N	N	N	Y
22 Capps, L.	Y	N	Y	N	N	Y	N
23 *Gallegly*	Y	Y	Y	N	N	N	Y
24 Sherman	Y	N	Y	N	N	Y	N
25 *McKeon*	Y	Y	Y	N	N	N	Y
26 Berman	Y	N	Y	N	N	Y	N
27 *Rogan*	Y	Y	Y	N	N	N	Y
28 *Dreier*	Y	Y	Y	N	?	N	Y
29 Waxman	Y	N	Y	N	N	Y	N
30 Becerra	Y	N	Y	N	N	Y	N
31 Martinez	?	N	Y	N	N	Y	N
32 Dixon	Y	N	Y	N	N	Y	N
33 Roybal-Allard	?	N	Y	N	N	Y	N
34 Torres	?	N	Y	N	N	Y	N
35 Waters	Y	N	Y	N	N	Y	N
36 Harman	?	N	Y	N	N	Y	N
37 Millender-McD.	Y	N	Y	N	N	Y	N

	195	196	197	198	199	200	201
38 Horn	Y	Y	Y	N	N	Y	N
39 *Royce*	Y	Y	Y	N	N	N	Y
40 *Lewis*	Y	Y	Y	N	N	N	Y
41 *Kim*	Y	Y	Y	N	N	N	Y
42 Brown	Y	N	Y	N	N	Y	N
43 *Calvert*	Y	Y	Y	N	N	N	Y
44 *Bono, M.*	+	Y	Y	N	N	N	Y
45 *Rohrabacher*	?	Y	Y	N	N	N	Y
46 Sanchez	Y	N	Y	N	N	Y	N
47 *Cox*	Y	Y	Y	N	N	N	Y
48 *Packard*	Y	Y	Y	N	N	N	Y
49 *Bilbray*	Y	Y	Y	N	N	Y	Y
50 Filner	Y	N	Y	N	N	Y	N
51 *Cunningham*	Y	Y	Y	N	N	N	Y
52 *Hunter*	Y	Y	Y	?	N	Y	
COLORADO							
1 DeGette	Y	N	?	N	N	Y	N
2 Skaggs	Y	–	+	N	N	Y	N
3 *McInnis*	?	Y	Y	N	N	N	Y
4 *Schaffer*	Y	Y	Y	N	N	N	Y
5 *Hefley*	Y	Y	Y	N	N	N	Y
6 *Schaefer*	Y	Y	Y	N	N	N	Y
CONNECTICUT							
1 Kennelly	Y	N	Y	N	N	Y	N
2 Gejdenson	Y	N	Y	N	N	Y	N
3 DeLauro	Y	N	Y	N	N	Y	N
4 *Shays*	Y	Y	Y	N	N	Y	N
5 Maloney	Y	N	Y	N	N	Y	N
6 *Johnson*	Y	Y	Y	N	N	Y	N
DELAWARE							
AL *Castle*	Y	Y	Y	N	N	Y	N
FLORIDA							
1 *Scarborough*	Y	Y	Y	N	N	N	Y
2 Boyd	Y	N	Y	N	N	Y	N
3 Brown	Y	?	Y	N	N	Y	N
4 *Fowler*	Y	Y	Y	N	N	Y	Y
5 Thurman	Y	?	Y	N	N	Y	N
6 *Stearns*	Y	Y	Y	N	N	N	Y
7 *Mica*	+	Y	Y	N	N	N	Y
8 *McCollum*	Y	Y	Y	N	N	N	Y
9 *Bilirakis*	Y	Y	Y	N	N	N	Y
10 *Young*	Y	Y	Y	N	N	N	Y
11 Davis	Y	N	Y	N	N	Y	N
12 *Canady*	Y	Y	Y	N	N	N	Y
13 *Miller*	Y	Y	Y	N	N	N	Y
14 *Goss*	Y	Y	Y	N	N	N	Y
15 *Weldon*	Y	Y	Y	N	N	N	Y
16 *Foley*	Y	Y	Y	N	N	?	Y
17 Meek	Y	N	Y	N	N	Y	N
18 *Ros-Lehtinen*	Y	Y	Y	?	?	?	#
19 Wexler	Y	N	Y	N	N	Y	N
20 Deutsch	Y	N	Y	N	N	Y	N
21 *Diaz-Balart*	+	Y	Y	N	N	N	Y
22 *Shaw*	Y	Y	Y	N	N	N	Y
23 Hastings	Y	N	Y	N	N	Y	N
GEORGIA							
1 *Kingston*	Y	Y	Y	N	N	N	Y
2 Bishop	Y	Y	Y	Y	Y	N	Y
3 *Collins*	Y	Y	?	N	N	N	Y
4 McKinney	Y	N	Y	?	N	Y	N
5 Lewis	Y	N	Y	?	?	–	?
6 *Gingrich*							Y
7 *Barr*	Y	Y	Y	N	N	N	Y
8 *Chambliss*	Y	Y	Y	N	N	N	Y
9 *Deal*	Y	Y	Y	N	N	N	Y
10 *Norwood*	Y	Y	Y	N	N	N	Y
11 *Linder*	Y	Y	Y	N	N	N	Y
HAWAII							
1 Abercrombie	Y	N	Y	N	N	Y	N
2 Mink	Y	N	P	N	N	Y	N
IDAHO							
1 *Chenoweth*	Y	Y	Y	N	N	N	Y
2 *Crapo*	Y	Y	Y	N	N	N	Y
ILLINOIS							
1 Rush	Y	N	Y	N	N	Y	N
2 Jackson	Y	N	Y	N	N	Y	N
3 Lipinski	Y	N	Y	N	N	Y	N
4 Gutierrez	Y	N	Y	N	N	Y	N
5 Blagojevich	?	N	Y	N	N	Y	N
6 *Hyde*	Y	Y	Y	N	N	N	Y
7 Davis	Y	N	Y	N	N	Y	N
8 *Crane*	?	Y	Y	N	N	N	Y
9 Yates	Y	N	Y	N	N	Y	N
10 *Porter*	+	Y	Y	N	N	Y	N
11 *Weller*	Y	Y	Y	N	N	N	Y
12 Costello	Y	N	Y	N	N	Y	N

ND Northern Democrats   SD Southern Democrats

	195	196	197	198	199	200	201
13 ***Fawell***	Y	?	?	Y	Y	Y	N
14 ***Hastert***	Y	Y	Y	N	N	N	Y
15 ***Ewing***	Y	Y	Y	N	N	N	Y
16 ***Manzullo***	Y	Y	Y	N	N	N	Y
17 Evans	Y	N	Y	N	N	Y	N
18 ***LaHood***	Y	Y	Y	N	N	N	Y
19 Poshard	?	N	Y	N	N	Y	N
20 ***Shimkus***	Y	Y	Y	N	N	N	Y
INDIANA							
1 Visclosky	Y	N	Y	N	N	Y	N
2 ***McIntosh***	Y	Y	Y	N	N	N	Y
3 Roemer	Y	Y	Y	N	N	N	Y
4 ***Souder***	Y	Y	Y	N	N	N	Y
5 ***Buyer***	Y	Y	Y	N	N	N	Y
6 ***Burton***	?	Y	Y	N	N	N	Y
7 ***Pease***	Y	Y	Y	N	N	N	Y
8 ***Hostettler***	?	Y	Y	N	N	N	N
9 Hamilton	Y	Y	Y	N	N	Y	N
10 Carson	Y	N	Y	N	N	Y	N
IOWA							
1 ***Leach***	Y	Y	Y	N	N	Y	N
2 ***Nussle***	Y	Y	Y	N	N	N	Y
3 Boswell	Y	N	Y	N	N	Y	N
4 ***Ganske***	Y	Y	Y	N	N	N	Y
5 ***Latham***	Y	Y	Y	N	N	N	Y
KANSAS							
1 ***Moran***	Y	Y	Y	N	N	N	Y
2 ***Ryun***	Y	Y	Y	N	N	N	Y
3 ***Snowbarger***	Y	Y	Y	N	N	N	Y
4 ***Tiahrt***	Y	Y	Y	N	N	N	Y
KENTUCKY							
1 ***Whitfield***	Y	Y	Y	N	N	N	Y
2 ***Lewis***	Y	Y	Y	N	N	N	Y
3 ***Northup***	Y	Y	Y	N	N	Y	N
4 ***Bunning***	Y	Y	Y	N	N	N	Y
5 ***Rogers***	Y	Y	Y	N	N	N	Y
6 Baesler	Y	Y	Y	N	N	N	Y
LOUISIANA							
1 ***Livingston***	Y	Y	Y	N	N	N	Y
2 Jefferson	Y	N	Y	Y	Y	Y	N
3 ***Tauzin***	Y	Y	Y	N	N	N	Y
4 ***McCrery***	Y	Y	Y	N	N	N	Y
5 ***Cooksey***	Y	Y	Y	N	N	N	Y
6 ***Baker***	Y	Y	Y	N	N	N	Y
7 John	Y	Y	?	N	N	N	Y
MAINE							
1 Allen	Y	N	Y	N	N	Y	N
2 Baldacci	Y	N	Y	N	N	Y	N
MARYLAND							
1 ***Gilchrest***	Y	Y	Y	N	N	Y	N
2 ***Ehrlich***	Y	Y	Y	N	Y	N	N
3 Cardin	Y	N	Y	N	N	Y	N
4 Wynn	Y	N	Y	N	Y	Y	N
5 Hoyer	Y	N	Y	Y	N	Y	N
6 ***Bartlett***	Y	Y	Y	N	N	N	Y
7 Cummings	Y	N	Y	N	N	Y	N
8 ***Morella***	Y	Y	Y	N	N	Y	N
MASSACHUSETTS							
1 Olver	Y	N	Y	N	N	Y	N
2 Neal	?	N	Y	N	N	Y	N
3 McGovern	Y	?	?	N	N	Y	N
4 Frank	Y	N	N	N	N	Y	N
5 Meehan	?	?	?	N	N	Y	N
6 Tierney	Y	N	Y	N	N	Y	N
7 Markey	Y	N	Y	N	?	Y	N
8 Kennedy	Y	N	Y	N	N	Y	N
9 Moakley	?	N	Y	N	N	Y	N
10 Delahunt	Y	N	Y	N	N	Y	N
MICHIGAN							
1 Stupak	Y	N	Y	N	N	Y	N
2 ***Hoekstra***	Y	Y	Y	N	N	N	Y
3 ***Ehlers***	Y	Y	Y	N	N	N	Y
4 ***Camp***	Y	Y	Y	N	N	N	Y
5 Barcia	Y	Y	Y	N	N	N	Y
6 ***Upton***	Y	Y	Y	N	N	N	Y
7 ***Smith***	Y	Y	Y	N	N	N	Y
8 Stabenow	Y	N	Y	N	N	Y	N
9 Kildee	Y	N	Y	N	N	Y	N
10 Bonior	Y	N	Y	N	N	Y	N
11 ***Knollenberg***	Y	Y	Y	N	N	N	Y
12 Levin	Y	N	Y	N	N	Y	N
13 Rivers	Y	N	Y	N	N	Y	N
14 Conyers	Y	N	Y	N	N	Y	N
15 Kilpatrick	Y	N	Y	N	N	Y	N
16 Dingell	Y	N	Y	N	N	Y	N

	195	196	197	198	199	200	201
MINNESOTA							
1 ***Gutknecht***	Y	Y	Y	N	N	N	Y
2 Minge	Y	N	Y	N	N	Y	N
3 ***Ramstad***	Y	Y	Y	N	N	N	Y
4 Vento	Y	N	Y	N	N	Y	N
5 Sabo	Y	N	Y	N	N	Y	N
6 Luther	Y	N	Y	N	N	Y	N
7 Peterson	Y	Y	Y	N	N	N	Y
8 Oberstar	Y	N	Y	N	N	Y	N
MISSISSIPPI							
1 ***Wicker***	Y	Y	Y	N	N	N	Y
2 Thompson	Y	N	Y	N	N	Y	Y
3 ***Pickering***	Y	Y	Y	N	N	N	Y
4 ***Parker***	Y	Y	Y	N	N	N	Y
5 Taylor	Y	Y	Y	N	N	N	Y
MISSOURI							
1 Clay	Y	?	?	N	N	Y	N
2 ***Talent***	Y	?	Y	N	N	N	Y
3 Gephardt	Y	N	Y	N	N	Y	N
4 Skelton	Y	Y	?	N	N	N	Y
5 McCarthy	Y	N	Y	N	N	Y	N
6 Danner	Y	Y	Y	N	Y	Y	Y
7 ***Blunt***	Y	Y	Y	N	N	N	Y
8 ***Emerson***	Y	Y	Y	N	N	N	Y
9 ***Hulshof***	Y	Y	Y	N	N	N	Y
MONTANA							
AL ***Hill***	Y	Y	Y	N	N	N	Y
NEBRASKA							
1 ***Bereuter***	Y	Y	Y	N	N	N	Y
2 ***Christensen***	Y	Y	Y	N	N	N	Y
3 ***Barrett***	Y	Y	Y	N	N	N	Y
NEVADA							
1 ***Ensign***	Y	?	Y	N	N	Y	Y
2 ***Gibbons***	+	Y	Y	N	N	N	Y
NEW HAMPSHIRE							
1 ***Sununu***	Y	Y	Y	N	N	N	Y
2 ***Bass***	Y	Y	Y	N	N	N	Y
NEW JERSEY							
1 Andrews	Y	N	Y	N	N	Y	N
2 ***LoBiondo***	Y	Y	Y	N	N	N	Y
3 ***Saxton***	Y	Y	Y	N	N	Y	N
4 ***Smith***	Y	Y	Y	N	N	N	Y
5 ***Roukema***	?	Y	Y	N	N	N	Y
6 Pallone	Y	N	Y	N	N	Y	N
7 ***Franks***	Y	Y	Y	N	N	Y	N
8 Pascrell	Y	N	Y	N	N	Y	N
9 Rothman	+	N	Y	N	N	Y	N
10 Payne	Y	?	?	N	Y	Y	N
11 ***Frelinghuysen***	Y	Y	Y	N	N	Y	N
12 ***Pappas***	Y	Y	Y	N	N	N	Y
13 Menendez	Y	N	Y	N	N	Y	N
NEW MEXICO							
1 Vacant							
2 ***Skeen***	Y	Y	Y	N	N	N	Y
3 ***Redmond***	Y	Y	Y	N	N	N	Y
NEW YORK							
1 ***Forbes***	?	Y	Y	N	N	Y	Y
2 ***Lazio***	Y	Y	Y	N	Y	N	Y
3 ***King***	Y	Y	Y	N	N	N	Y
4 McCarthy	Y	N	Y	N	N	Y	N
5 Ackerman	Y	N	Y	N	N	Y	N
6 Meeks	Y	N	?	N	N	Y	N
7 Manton	Y	N	Y	N	N	Y	N
8 Nadler	Y	N	Y	N	N	Y	N
9 Schumer	Y	N	Y	N	N	Y	N
10 Towns	Y	N	Y	N	N	Y	N
11 Owens	Y	N	P	N	N	Y	N
12 Velázquez	Y	N	Y	N	N	Y	N
13 ***Fossella***	Y	Y	Y	N	N	N	Y
14 Maloney	Y	N	Y	N	N	Y	N
15 Rangel	Y	N	Y	N	N	Y	N
16 Serrano	Y	N	Y	N	N	Y	N
17 Engel	Y	N	Y	N	N	Y	N
18 Lowey	Y	N	Y	N	N	Y	N
19 ***Kelly***	Y	Y	Y	N	N	Y	N
20 ***Gilman***	Y	Y	Y	N	N	Y	N
21 McNulty	Y	N	Y	N	N	Y	N
22 ***Solomon***	Y	Y	Y	N	N	N	Y
23 ***Boehlert***	Y	Y	Y	N	N	Y	N
24 ***McHugh***	Y	Y	Y	N	N	N	Y
25 ***Walsh***	Y	Y	Y	N	N	N	Y
26 Hinchey	Y	N	Y	N	N	Y	N
27 ***Paxon***	Y	Y	Y	N	N	N	Y
28 Slaughter	Y	N	Y	N	N	Y	N
29 LaFalce	?	N	Y	N	N	Y	N

	195	196	197	198	199	200	201
30 ***Quinn***	Y	Y	Y	N	N	N	Y
31 ***Houghton***	Y	Y	?	N	N	N	N
NORTH CAROLINA							
1 Clayton	Y	N	Y	N	Y	Y	N
2 Etheridge	Y	N	Y	N	N	Y	N
3 ***Jones***	Y	Y	Y	N	N	N	Y
4 Price	Y	N	Y	N	N	Y	N
5 ***Burr***	Y	Y	Y	N	N	N	Y
6 ***Coble***	Y	Y	Y	N	N	N	Y
7 McIntyre	Y	Y	Y	N	N	N	Y
8 Hefner	Y	N	Y	N	N	Y	N
9 ***Myrick***	Y	Y	Y	N	N	N	Y
10 ***Ballenger***	Y	Y	Y	N	N	N	Y
11 ***Taylor***	Y	Y	Y	N	N	N	Y
12 Watt	Y	N	Y	N	Y	Y	N
NORTH DAKOTA							
AL Pomeroy	Y	N	Y	N	N	Y	N
OHIO							
1 ***Chabot***	Y	Y	Y	N	N	N	Y
2 ***Portman***	Y	Y	Y	N	N	N	Y
3 Hall	Y	Y	Y	N	N	Y	N
4 ***Oxley***	Y	Y	Y	N	N	N	Y
5 ***Gillmor***	Y	Y	Y	N	N	N	Y
6 Strickland	Y	N	Y	N	N	Y	N
7 ***Hobson***	Y	Y	Y	N	N	N	Y
8 ***Boehner***	Y	Y	Y	N	N	N	Y
9 Kaptur	Y	N	Y	N	N	Y	N
10 Kucinich	Y	N	Y	N	N	Y	N
11 Stokes	?	?	Y	N	N	Y	N
12 ***Kasich***	Y	Y	Y	N	N	N	Y
13 Brown	Y	N	Y	N	?	Y	N
14 Sawyer	?	N	Y	N	N	Y	N
15 ***Pryce***	Y	Y	Y	N	N	N	Y
16 ***Regula***	Y	Y	Y	N	N	N	Y
17 Traficant	Y	Y	Y	N	N	N	Y
18 ***Ney***	Y	Y	Y	N	N	N	Y
19 ***LaTourette***	Y	Y	Y	N	N	N	N
OKLAHOMA							
1 ***Largent***	Y	Y	?	N	N	N	Y
2 ***Coburn***	Y	Y	?	N	N	N	Y
3 ***Watkins***	Y	Y	Y	N	N	N	Y
4 ***Watts***	Y	Y	Y	N	N	N	Y
5 ***Istook***	Y	Y	Y	N	N	N	Y
6 ***Lucas***	Y	Y	Y	N	N	N	Y
OREGON							
1 Furse	?	?	?	?	?	?	X
2 ***Smith***	Y	Y	?	N	N	N	Y
3 Blumenauer	Y	N	Y	N	N	Y	N
4 DeFazio	Y	N	Y	N	N	Y	N
5 Hooley	Y	N	Y	N	N	Y	N
PENNSYLVANIA							
1 Brady	Y	N	Y	N	N	Y	N
2 Fattah	Y	N	Y	N	N	Y	N
3 Borski	Y	N	Y	N	N	Y	N
4 Klink	Y	N	Y	N	Y	Y	N
5 ***Peterson***	Y	Y	Y	N	N	N	Y
6 Holden	Y	N	Y	N	N	Y	N
7 ***Weldon***	Y	Y	Y	N	N	N	Y
8 ***Greenwood***	Y	Y	Y	N	N	Y	N
9 ***Shuster***	Y	Y	Y	N	N	N	Y
10 ***McDade***	Y	Y	?	?	?	?	?
11 Kanjorski	Y	N	Y	N	N	Y	N
12 Murtha	Y	Y	Y	N	N	Y	N
13 ***Fox***	Y	Y	Y	N	N	Y	N
14 Coyne	Y	N	Y	N	N	Y	N
15 McHale	Y	N	Y	N	N	Y	N
16 ***Pitts***	Y	Y	Y	N	N	N	Y
17 ***Gekas***	Y	Y	?	N	N	N	Y
18 Doyle	Y	N	Y	N	N	Y	N
19 ***Goodling***	Y	Y	Y	N	N	N	Y
20 Mascara	Y	N	Y	N	N	Y	N
21 ***English***	Y	N	Y	N	N	N	Y
RHODE ISLAND							
1 Kennedy	Y	N	Y	N	N	Y	N
2 Weygand	Y	N	Y	N	N	Y	N
SOUTH CAROLINA							
1 ***Sanford***	Y	Y	Y	N	N	N	Y
2 ***Spence***	Y	Y	Y	N	N	N	Y
3 ***Graham***	Y	Y	Y	N	N	N	Y
4 ***Inglis***	?	Y	Y	N	N	N	Y
5 Spratt	Y	?	Y	N	Y	Y	N
6 Clyburn	?	Y	Y	N	Y	Y	N
SOUTH DAKOTA							
AL ***Thune***	+	Y	Y	N	N	N	Y

	195	196	197	198	199	200	201
TENNESSEE							
1 ***Jenkins***	Y	Y	Y	N	N	N	Y
2 ***Duncan***	Y	Y	Y	N	N	N	Y
3 ***Wamp***	?	Y	Y	N	N	N	Y
4 ***Hilleary***	Y	Y	Y	N	N	N	Y
5 Clement	Y	Y	Y	N	N	N	Y
6 Gordon	Y	N	Y	N	N	N	Y
7 ***Bryant***	Y	Y	Y	N	N	N	Y
8 Tanner	Y	Y	Y	N	Y	Y	Y
9 Ford	Y	N	Y	N	N	Y	Y
TEXAS							
1 Sandlin	Y	Y	Y	N	N	N	Y
2 Turner	Y	Y	Y	N	N	N	Y
3 ***Johnson, Sam***	Y	Y	Y	N	N	N	Y
4 Hall	Y	Y	Y	N	N	N	Y
5 ***Sessions***	Y	Y	Y	N	N	N	Y
6 ***Barton***	Y	Y	Y	N	N	N	Y
7 ***Archer***	Y	Y	Y	N	N	N	Y
8 ***Brady***	Y	Y	Y	N	N	N	Y
9 Lampson	Y	N	Y	N	N	Y	N
10 Doggett	Y	N	Y	N	N	Y	N
11 Edwards	Y	N	Y	N	N	Y	N
12 ***Granger***	Y	Y	Y	N	N	N	Y
13 ***Thornberry***	Y	Y	Y	N	N	N	Y
14 ***Paul***	Y	Y	Y	N	Y	N	N
15 Hinojosa	Y	N	Y	N	N	Y	N
16 Reyes	Y	N	Y	?	?	?	?
17 Stenholm	Y	Y	Y	N	N	N	Y
18 Jackson-Lee	Y	N	Y	N	N	Y	N
19 ***Combest***	Y	Y	Y	N	N	N	Y
20 Gonzalez	?	?	?	?	?	?	?
21 ***Smith***	Y	Y	Y	N	N	N	Y
22 ***DeLay***	?	Y	Y	N	N	N	Y
23 ***Bonilla***	Y	Y	Y	N	N	N	Y
24 Frost	Y	N	Y	N	N	Y	N
25 Bentsen	Y	N	Y	N	N	Y	N
26 ***Armey***	?	Y	Y	N	N	N	Y
27 Ortiz	Y	Y	Y	N	Y	Y	Y
28 Rodriguez	Y	N	Y	N	N	Y	N
29 Green	Y	N	Y	N	Y	Y	N
30 Johnson, E.B.	Y	N	Y	N	Y	Y	N
UTAH							
1 ***Hansen***	Y	Y	Y	N	N	N	Y
2 ***Cook***	Y	Y	Y	N	N	N	Y
3 ***Cannon***	Y	Y	Y	N	N	N	Y
VERMONT							
AL *Sanders*	Y	N	Y	N	N	Y	N
VIRGINIA							
1 ***Bateman***	Y	Y	Y	N	N	N	Y
2 Pickett	Y	N	Y	N	N	Y	N
3 Scott	Y	N	Y	N	Y	Y	N
4 Sisisky	Y	N	Y	N	N	Y	N
5 Goode	Y	Y	Y	N	N	N	Y
6 ***Goodlatte***	Y	Y	Y	N	N	N	Y
7 ***Bliley***	Y	Y	Y	N	N	N	Y
8 Moran	Y	N	Y	N	N	Y	N
9 Boucher	?	N	Y	N	Y	Y	N
10 ***Wolf***	Y	Y	Y	N	N	N	Y
11 ***Davis***	Y	Y	Y	N	N	N	Y
WASHINGTON							
1 ***White***	Y	Y	Y	N	N	N	N
2 ***Metcalf***	Y	Y	Y	N	N	N	Y
3 ***Smith, Linda***	Y	Y	Y	N	N	N	Y
4 ***Hastings***	Y	Y	Y	N	N	N	Y
5 ***Nethercutt***	Y	Y	Y	N	N	N	Y
6 Dicks	Y	N	Y	N	N	Y	N
7 McDermott	Y	N	Y	N	N	Y	N
8 ***Dunn***	Y	Y	Y	N	N	N	Y
9 Smith, Adam	Y	N	Y	N	N	Y	N
WEST VIRGINIA							
1 Mollohan	Y	?	?	?	?	?	#
2 Wise	Y	N	Y	N	N	Y	N
3 Rahall	Y	Y	Y	N	N	N	Y
WISCONSIN							
1 ***Neumann***	Y	Y	Y	N	N	N	Y
2 ***Klug***	Y	Y	Y	N	N	N	Y
3 Kind	Y	N	Y	N	N	Y	N
4 Kleczka	Y	N	Y	N	N	Y	N
5 Barrett	Y	N	Y	N	N	Y	N
6 ***Petri***	Y	Y	Y	N	N	N	Y
7 Obey	?	N	Y	N	N	Y	N
8 Johnson	Y	N	Y	N	N	Y	N
9 ***Sensenbrenner***	Y	Y	Y	N	N	N	Y
WYOMING							
AL ***Cubin***	Y	Y	Y	N	N	N	Y

Southern states - Ala., Ark., Fla., Ga., Ky., La., Miss., N.C., Okla., S.C., Tenn., Texas, Va.

202. H Con Res 285. Tiananmen Square Resolution/Adoption. Adoption of the concurrent resolution to express the sense of the Congress that the president should reconsider his decision to be formally received in Tiananmen Square. Adopted 305-116: R 219-4; D 85-112 (ND 64-82, SD 21-30); I 1-0. June 4, 1998.

203. S 1150. Agriculture Reauthorization Conference Report/Consideration. Judgment of the House on proceeding to the consideration of the conference report on the bill to reauthorize agricultural research and education programs through fiscal 2002, despite the Solomon, R-N.Y., point of order regarding intergovernmental unfunded mandates. Agreed to consider the conference report 324-91: R 135-86; D 188-5 (ND 139-3, SD 49-2); I 1-0. June 4, 1998.

204. S 1150. Agricultural Reauthorization Conference Report/Adoption. Adoption of the conference report on the bill to reauthorize agricultural research and education programs through fiscal 2002. The conference report restores about $800 million over five years in funding for food stamp benefits for certain legal immigrants; directs about $500 million in mandatory funding for crop insurance programs; and directs about $600 million over five years to a new, mandatory agricultural research program. Adopted (thus cleared for the president) 364-50: R 170-48; D 193-2 (ND 144-0, SD 49-2); I 1-0. June 4, 1998.

205. H Con Res 284. Fiscal 1999 Budget Resolution/Rule. Adoption of the rule (H Res 455) to provide for House floor consideration of the concurrent resolution to adopt a five-year budget plan to reduce federal spending over 1999-2003 by $101 billion below levels provided under the Balanced Budget Act of 1997. Savings from the spending cuts would finance tax cuts, including an elimination of the so-called marriage penalty. Adopted 216-197: R 215-4; D 1-192 (ND 1-140, SD 0-52); I 0-1. June 4, 1998.

206. HR 3989. User Fee Authorization/Recommit. Moakley, D-Mass., motion to recommit the bill to the Ways and Means Committee with instructions to report it back with a substitute amendment to express the sense of the House that user fees in the Fiscal 1999 Budget Resolution (HConRes284) should be enacted as soon as possible. Motion rejected 0-416: R 0-221; D 0-194 (ND 0-143, SD 0-51); I 0-1. June 5, 1998.

207. HR 3989. User Fee Authorization/Passage. Passage of the bill to authorize the 36 user fee proposals contained in President Clinton's fiscal 1999 budget proposal. Rejected 0-421: R 0-223; D 0-197 (ND 0-145, SD 0-52); I 0-1. June 5, 1998.

208. H Con Res 284. Fiscal 1999 Budget Resolution/Conservative Action Team Substitute. Neumann, R-Wis., substitute amendment to adopt a five-year budget plan that would seek to limit the growth of government spending to the rate of inflation, while calling for $150 billion in tax reductions over five years, and increasing defense spending above current levels by $56 billion over five years. Rejected 158-262: R 155-67; D 3-194 (ND 0-146, SD 3-48); I 0-1. June 5, 1998.

Key

Y	Voted for (yea).
#	Paired for.
+	Announced for.
N	Voted against (nay).
X	Paired against.
−	Announced against.
P	Voted "present."
C	Voted "present" to avoid possible conflict of interest.
?	Did not vote or otherwise make a position known.

Democrats   **Republicans**
Independent

	202	203	204	205	206	207	208
ALABAMA							
1 *Callahan*	Y	Y	Y	Y	N	N	Y
2 *Everett*	Y	Y	Y	Y	N	N	Y
3 *Riley*	Y	Y	Y	Y	N	N	Y
4 *Aderholt*	Y	Y	Y	Y	N	N	Y
5 Cramer	N	Y	N	N	N	N	N
6 *Bachus*	Y	Y	Y	Y	N	N	Y
7 Hilliard	N	Y	Y	N	N	N	N
ALASKA							
AL *Young*	Y	Y	Y	?	N	N	Y
ARIZONA							
1 *Salmon*	Y	N	N	Y	N	N	Y
2 Pastor	N	Y	Y	N	N	N	N
3 *Stump*	Y	N	N	Y	N	N	Y
4 *Shadegg*	Y	N	N	Y	N	N	Y
5 *Kolbe*	Y	Y	Y	Y	N	N	N
6 *Hayworth*	Y	Y	Y	Y	N	N	Y
ARKANSAS							
1 Berry	N	Y	Y	N	N	N	N
2 Snyder	Y	Y	Y	N	N	N	N
3 *Hutchinson*	Y	Y	Y	Y	N	N	Y
4 *Dickey*	Y	Y	Y	Y	N	N	Y
CALIFORNIA							
1 *Riggs*	Y	Y	Y	Y	N	N	Y
2 *Herger*	Y	N	N	Y	N	N	Y
3 Fazio	N	Y	Y	N	N	N	N
4 *Doolittle*	Y	N	N	Y	N	N	Y
5 Matsui	N	Y	Y	N	N	N	N
6 Woolsey	Y	Y	Y	N	N	N	N
7 Miller	Y	Y	Y	N	N	N	N
8 Pelosi	Y	?	Y	N	?	N	N
9 Lee	Y	Y	Y	N	N	N	N
10 Tauscher	Y	Y	Y	N	N	N	N
11 *Pombo*	Y	N	Y	Y	N	N	Y
12 Lantos	Y	Y	Y	N	N	N	N
13 Stark	Y	Y	Y	?	N	N	N
14 Eshoo	N	Y	Y	N	N	N	N
15 *Campbell*	Y	Y	Y	Y	N	N	N
16 Lofgren	N	Y	Y	N	N	N	N
17 Farr	N	Y	Y	N	N	N	N
18 Condit	N	N	N	Y	N	N	N
19 *Radanovich*	Y	N	N	Y	N	N	Y
20 Dooley	N	Y	N	N	N	N	N
21 *Thomas*	Y	Y	Y	Y	N	N	Y
22 Capps, L.	Y	Y	Y	N	N	N	N
23 *Gallegly*	Y	N	Y	Y	N	N	Y
24 Sherman	N	Y	Y	N	N	N	N
25 *McKeon*	Y	Y	Y	Y	N	N	Y
26 Berman	N	Y	Y	N	N	N	N
27 *Rogan*	Y	Y	Y	Y	N	N	Y
28 *Dreier*	Y	N	Y	Y	N	N	Y
29 Waxman	N	Y	Y	N	N	N	N
30 Becerra	N	Y	Y	N	N	N	N
31 Martinez	N	Y	?	?	N	N	N
32 Dixon	N	Y	N	N	N	N	N
33 Roybal-Allard	N	Y	Y	N	N	N	N
34 Torres	N	Y	Y	N	N	N	N
35 Waters	N	Y	N	N	N	N	N
36 Harman	Y	+	+	?	?	N	N
37 Millender-McD.	N	Y	N	N	N	N	N

	202	203	204	205	206	207	208
38 *Horn*	Y	Y	Y	Y	N	N	N
39 *Royce*	Y	N	N	Y	N	N	Y
40 *Lewis*	Y	Y	Y	Y	N	N	Y
41 *Kim*	N	Y	Y	Y	N	N	N
42 Brown	N	Y	Y	N	N	N	N
43 *Calvert*	Y	Y	Y	Y	N	N	Y
44 *Bono, M.*	Y	Y	Y	Y	N	N	Y
45 *Rohrabacher*	Y	N	N	Y	N	N	Y
46 Sanchez	Y	Y	Y	N	N	N	N
47 *Cox*	Y	Y	Y	Y	N	N	Y
48 *Packard*	Y	Y	Y	Y	N	N	Y
49 *Bilbray*	Y	N	Y	Y	N	N	N
50 Filner	N	Y	Y	N	N	N	N
51 *Cunningham*	Y	N	Y	Y	N	N	Y
52 *Hunter*	Y	Y	N	Y	N	N	Y
COLORADO							
1 DeGette	N	Y	Y	N	N	N	N
2 Skaggs	N	Y	Y	N	N	N	N
3 *McInnis*	Y	Y	Y	Y	N	N	Y
4 *Schaffer*	Y	Y	Y	Y	N	N	Y
5 *Hefley*	Y	N	N	?	N	N	Y
6 *Schaefer*	Y	N	N	Y	N	N	Y
CONNECTICUT							
1 Kennelly	Y	Y	Y	N	N	N	N
2 Gejdenson	Y	Y	Y	N	?	?	?
3 DeLauro	Y	Y	Y	N	N	N	N
4 *Shays*	Y	Y	Y	Y	N	N	N
5 Maloney	Y	Y	Y	N	N	N	N
6 *Johnson*	Y	Y	Y	Y	N	N	N
DELAWARE							
AL *Castle*	Y	Y	Y	N	N	N	N
FLORIDA							
1 *Scarborough*	Y	N	N	Y	N	N	Y
2 Boyd	Y	Y	Y	N	N	N	N
3 Brown	N	Y	Y	N	N	N	N
4 *Fowler*	Y	N	Y	Y	N	N	Y
5 Thurman	Y	Y	Y	N	N	N	N
6 *Stearns*	Y	N	N	Y	N	N	Y
7 *Mica*	Y	N	Y	Y	N	N	Y
8 *McCollum*	Y	N	Y	Y	N	N	Y
9 *Bilirakis*	Y	N	Y	Y	N	N	N
10 *Young*	Y	N	Y	Y	N	N	N
11 Davis	N	Y	N	N	N	N	N
12 *Canady*	Y	Y	Y	Y	N	N	N
13 *Miller*	Y	N	N	Y	N	N	Y
14 *Goss*	Y	N	Y	Y	N	N	N
15 *Weldon*	Y	N	N	Y	N	N	Y
16 *Foley*	Y	Y	Y	Y	N	N	Y
17 Meek	N	Y	Y	N	N	N	N
18 *Ros-Lehtinen*	?	?	?	?	?	?	?
19 Wexler	N	Y	N	N	N	N	N
20 Deutsch	N	Y	N	N	N	N	N
21 *Diaz-Balart*	Y	Y	Y	N	N	N	N
22 *Shaw*	Y	N	Y	Y	N	N	N
23 Hastings	N	Y	Y	N	N	N	N
GEORGIA							
1 *Kingston*	Y	N	N	Y	N	N	Y
2 Bishop	N	Y	Y	N	N	N	N
3 *Collins*	Y	N	N	Y	N	N	Y
4 McKinney	N	Y	Y	N	N	N	N
5 Lewis	?	?	?	?	?	?	?
6 *Gingrich*	Y					N	N
7 *Barr*	Y	N	N	Y	N	N	Y
8 *Chambliss*	Y	Y	Y	Y	N	N	Y
9 *Deal*	Y	N	N	Y	N	N	Y
10 *Norwood*	Y	Y	Y	Y	N	N	Y
11 *Linder*	Y	Y	Y	Y	N	N	?
HAWAII							
1 Abercrombie	Y	Y	Y	N	N	N	N
2 Mink	N	Y	Y	N	N	N	N
IDAHO							
1 *Chenoweth*	Y	N	Y	Y	N	N	Y
2 *Crapo*	Y	N	Y	Y	N	N	N
ILLINOIS							
1 Rush	N	Y	Y	N	N	N	N
2 Jackson	Y	Y	Y	N	N	N	N
3 Lipinski	Y	Y	Y	N	N	N	N
4 Gutierrez	Y	Y	Y	N	N	N	N
5 Blagojevich	N	Y	Y	N	N	N	N
6 *Hyde*	Y	Y	Y	Y	N	N	Y
7 Davis	N	Y	Y	N	N	N	N
8 *Crane*	Y	N	N	Y	N	N	Y
9 Yates	N	?	?	?	N	N	N
10 *Porter*	Y	Y	Y	Y	N	N	N
11 *Weller*	Y	Y	Y	Y	N	N	Y
12 Costello	Y	Y	Y	N	N	N	N

	202	203	204	205	206	207	208
13 ***Fawell***	Y	N	Y	Y	N	N	N
14 ***Hastert***	Y	N	Y	Y	N	N	Y
15 ***Ewing***	Y	Y	Y	Y	N	N	Y
16 ***Manzullo***	Y	N	N	Y	N	N	Y
17 Evans	Y	Y	Y	N	N	N	N
18 ***LaHood***	Y	Y	Y	Y	N	N	Y
19 Poshard	Y	Y	Y	N	N	N	N
20 ***Shimkus***	Y	Y	Y	Y	N	N	Y
INDIANA							
1 Visclosky	Y	Y	Y	N	N	N	N
2 ***McIntosh***	Y	N	Y	Y	N	N	Y
3 Roemer	N	Y	Y	N	N	N	N
4 ***Souder***	Y	Y	Y	Y	N	N	N
5 ***Buyer***	Y	Y	Y	Y	?	N	N
6 ***Burton***	Y	Y	Y	Y	N	N	Y
7 ***Pease***	Y	Y	Y	Y	N	N	Y
8 ***Hostettler***	Y	N	N	Y	N	N	Y
9 Hamilton	N	Y	Y	N	N	N	N
10 Carson	N	Y	Y	N	N	N	N
IOWA							
1 ***Leach***	N	Y	Y	Y	N	N	N
2 ***Nussle***	Y	Y	Y	Y	N	N	N
3 Boswell	Y	Y	Y	N	N	N	N
4 ***Ganske***	Y	Y	Y	N	N	N	N
5 ***Latham***	Y	Y	Y	Y	N	N	N
KANSAS							
1 ***Moran***	Y	Y	Y	Y	N	N	Y
2 ***Ryun***	Y	Y	Y	Y	N	N	Y
3 ***Snowbarger***	Y	Y	Y	Y	N	N	Y
4 ***Tiahrt***	Y	N	N	Y	N	N	Y
KENTUCKY							
1 ***Whitfield***	Y	N	Y	?	N	N	N
2 ***Lewis***	Y	Y	Y	Y	N	N	Y
3 ***Northup***	Y	Y	Y	Y	N	N	N
4 ***Bunning***	Y	Y	Y	Y	N	N	N
5 ***Rogers***	Y	Y	Y	Y	N	N	N
6 Baesler	Y	Y	Y	N	N	N	N
LOUISIANA							
1 ***Livingston***	Y	N	Y	Y	N	N	Y
2 Jefferson	N	Y	Y	N	N	N	N
3 ***Tauzin***	Y	Y	Y	Y	N	N	N
4 ***McCrery***	Y	Y	Y	Y	N	N	Y
5 ***Cooksey***	Y	Y	Y	Y	?	N	Y
6 ***Baker***	Y	Y	Y	Y	N	N	Y
7 John	N	Y	Y	N	N	N	N
MAINE							
1 Allen	N	Y	Y	N	N	N	N
2 Baldacci	N	Y	Y	N	N	N	N
MARYLAND							
1 ***Gilchrest***	Y	Y	Y	Y	N	N	N
2 ***Ehrlich***	Y	N	Y	Y	N	N	Y
3 Cardin	Y	Y	Y	N	N	N	N
4 Wynn	N	Y	Y	N	N	N	N
5 Hoyer	N	?	Y	N	N	N	N
6 ***Bartlett***	Y	N	?	Y	N	N	Y
7 Cummings	N	Y	Y	N	N	N	N
8 ***Morella***	Y	Y	Y	N	N	N	N
MASSACHUSETTS							
1 Olver	N	Y	Y	N	N	N	N
2 Neal	N	Y	Y	N	N	N	N
3 McGovern	N	Y	Y	N	N	N	N
4 Frank	?	?	?	?	N	N	N
5 Meehan	N	Y	Y	N	N	N	N
6 Tierney	N	Y	Y	N	N	N	N
7 Markey	N	?	Y	N	N	N	N
8 Kennedy	N	Y	Y	N	?	?	?
9 Moakley	N	Y	Y	N	N	N	N
10 Delahunt	Y	Y	Y	N	N	N	N
MICHIGAN							
1 Stupak	N	Y	Y	N	N	N	N
2 ***Hoekstra***	Y	Y	Y	Y	N	N	Y
3 ***Ehlers***	Y	Y	Y	Y	N	N	N
4 ***Camp***	Y	Y	Y	Y	N	N	Y
5 Barcia	Y	Y	Y	N	N	N	N
6 ***Upton***	Y	Y	Y	Y	N	N	N
7 ***Smith***	Y	Y	Y	Y	N	N	Y
8 Stabenow	Y	Y	Y	N	N	N	N
9 Kildee	Y	Y	Y	N	N	N	N
10 Bonior	Y	Y	Y	N	N	N	N
11 ***Knollenberg***	Y	Y	Y	Y	N	N	Y
12 Levin	Y	Y	Y	N	N	N	N
13 Rivers	Y	Y	Y	N	N	N	N
14 Conyers	N	Y	Y	?	N	N	N
15 Kilpatrick	N	Y	Y	N	N	N	N
16 Dingell	N	Y	Y	N	N	N	N

	202	203	204	205	206	207	208
MINNESOTA							
1 ***Gutknecht***	Y	Y	Y	Y	N	N	N
2 Minge	Y	Y	Y	N	N	N	N
3 ***Ramstad***	Y	Y	Y	Y	N	N	N
4 Vento	N	Y	Y	N	N	N	N
5 Sabo	N	Y	Y	N	N	N	?
6 Luther	N	Y	Y	N	N	N	N
7 Peterson	Y	Y	Y	N	N	N	N
8 Oberstar	N	Y	Y	N	N	N	N
MISSISSIPPI							
1 ***Wicker***	Y	Y	Y	Y	N	N	Y
2 Thompson	Y	Y	Y	N	N	N	N
3 ***Pickering***	Y	Y	Y	Y	N	N	Y
4 ***Parker***	Y	Y	Y	Y	N	N	Y
5 Taylor	Y	N	N	N	N	N	Y
MISSOURI							
1 Clay	Y	Y	Y	N	N	N	N
2 ***Talent***	Y	Y	?	Y	N	N	Y
3 Gephardt	Y	Y	Y	N	N	N	N
4 Skelton	N	Y	Y	N	N	N	N
5 McCarthy	N	Y	Y	N	N	N	N
6 Danner	N	Y	Y	N	N	N	N
7 ***Blunt***	Y	Y	N	Y	N	N	Y
8 ***Emerson***	Y	Y	Y	N	N	N	Y
9 ***Hulshof***	Y	Y	Y	Y	N	N	Y
MONTANA							
AL ***Hill***	Y	Y	Y	Y	N	N	N
NEBRASKA							
1 ***Bereuter***	Y	Y	Y	Y	N	N	N
2 ***Christensen***	Y	Y	Y	Y	N	N	Y
3 ***Barrett***	Y	Y	Y	Y	N	N	N
NEVADA							
1 ***Ensign***	Y	N	N	Y	N	N	Y
2 ***Gibbons***	Y	N	Y	Y	N	N	Y
NEW HAMPSHIRE							
1 ***Sununu***	Y	N	N	Y	N	N	Y
2 ***Bass***	Y	N	N	Y	N	N	N
NEW JERSEY							
1 Andrews	N	Y	Y	N	N	N	N
2 ***LoBiondo***	Y	Y	Y	Y	N	N	N
3 ***Saxton***	Y	N	N	Y	N	N	Y
4 ***Smith***	Y	Y	Y	Y	N	N	N
5 ***Roukema***	Y	N	N	Y	N	N	N
6 Pallone	Y	Y	Y	N	N	N	N
7 ***Franks***	Y	Y	Y	Y	N	N	N
8 Pascrell	Y	Y	Y	N	N	N	N
9 Rothman	Y	Y	Y	N	N	N	N
10 Payne	Y	Y	Y	N	N	N	N
11 ***Frelinghuysen***	Y	Y	Y	Y	N	N	N
12 ***Pappas***	Y	N	N	Y	N	N	Y
13 Menendez	Y	Y	Y	N	N	N	N
NEW MEXICO							
1 Vacant							
2 ***Skeen***	Y	Y	Y	Y	N	N	N
3 ***Redmond***	Y	Y	Y	Y	N	N	Y
NEW YORK							
1 ***Forbes***	Y	Y	Y	Y	N	N	N
2 ***Lazio***	Y	Y	Y	Y	N	N	N
3 ***King***	Y	Y	Y	Y	N	N	N
4 McCarthy	Y	Y	Y	N	N	N	N
5 Ackerman	N	Y	Y	N	N	N	N
6 Meeks	Y	Y	Y	N	N	N	N
7 Manton	Y	Y	Y	N	N	N	N
8 Nadler	Y	Y	Y	N	N	N	N
9 Schumer	Y	Y	Y	?	?	?	N
10 Towns	N	Y	Y	N	N	N	N
11 Owens	N	Y	Y	N	N	N	N
12 Velázquez	N	Y	Y	N	N	N	N
13 ***Fossella***	Y	N	Y	Y	N	N	N
14 Maloney	Y	Y	Y	N	N	N	N
15 Rangel	N	Y	Y	N	N	N	N
16 Serrano	–	Y	Y	N	N	N	N
17 Engel	?	+	+	–	N	N	N
18 Lowey	Y	Y	Y	N	N	N	N
19 ***Kelly***	Y	Y	Y	Y	N	N	N
20 ***Gilman***	Y	N	Y	Y	N	N	N
21 McNulty	Y	Y	Y	N	N	N	N
22 ***Solomon***	Y	N	N	Y	N	N	Y
23 ***Boehlert***	Y	Y	Y	Y	N	N	N
24 ***McHugh***	Y	N	Y	Y	N	N	N
25 ***Walsh***	Y	Y	Y	Y	N	N	N
26 Hinchey	N	N	Y	N	N	N	N
27 ***Paxon***	Y	N	Y	Y	N	N	Y
28 Slaughter	Y	Y	Y	N	N	N	N
29 LaFalce	N	Y	Y	N	N	N	N

	202	203	204	205	206	207	208
30 ***Quinn***	Y	Y	Y	Y	N	N	N
31 ***Houghton***	N	Y	Y	Y	?	?	N
NORTH CAROLINA							
1 Clayton	N	Y	Y	N	N	N	N
2 Etheridge	Y	Y	Y	N	N	N	N
3 ***Jones***	Y	N	Y	Y	N	N	Y
4 Price	Y	Y	Y	N	N	N	N
5 ***Burr***	?	?	?	Y	N	N	Y
6 ***Coble***	Y	N	Y	Y	N	N	Y
7 McIntyre	Y	Y	Y	N	N	N	N
8 Hefner	N	Y	Y	N	N	N	N
9 ***Myrick***	+	–	–	Y	N	N	Y
10 ***Ballenger***	Y	Y	Y	Y	N	N	+
11 ***Taylor***	Y	N	Y	Y	N	N	Y
12 Watt	N	Y	Y	N	N	N	N
NORTH DAKOTA							
AL Pomeroy	Y	Y	Y	N	N	N	N
OHIO							
1 ***Chabot***	Y	N	N	Y	N	N	Y
2 ***Portman***	Y	Y	Y	Y	N	N	Y
3 Hall	Y	Y	Y	N	N	N	N
4 ***Oxley***	Y	Y	Y	Y	N	N	Y
5 ***Gillmor***	N	N	Y	Y	N	N	Y
6 Strickland	Y	Y	Y	N	N	N	N
7 ***Hobson***	Y	Y	Y	Y	N	N	N
8 ***Boehner***	Y	Y	Y	Y	N	N	Y
9 Kaptur	N	Y	Y	N	N	N	N
10 Kucinich	Y	Y	Y	N	N	N	N
11 Stokes	N	Y	Y	N	N	N	N
12 ***Kasich***	Y	Y	Y	Y	N	N	N
13 Brown	N	Y	Y	N	N	N	N
14 Sawyer	N	Y	Y	N	N	N	N
15 ***Pryce***	Y	Y	+	Y	N	N	N
16 ***Regula***	Y	Y	Y	Y	N	N	N
17 Traficant	Y	N	Y	Y	N	N	N
18 ***Ney***	Y	?	Y	Y	N	N	N
19 ***LaTourette***	Y	Y	Y	Y	N	N	N
OKLAHOMA							
1 ***Largent***	Y	N	N	Y	N	?	Y
2 ***Coburn***	Y	N	N	Y	N	N	Y
3 ***Watkins***	Y	Y	Y	Y	N	N	Y
4 ***Watts***	Y	Y	Y	Y	N	N	Y
5 ***Istook***	Y	N	N	Y	N	N	Y
6 ***Lucas***	Y	Y	Y	Y	N	N	Y
OREGON							
1 Furse	?	?	?	?	?	?	?
2 ***Smith***	Y	Y	Y	?	N	N	Y
3 Blumenauer	N	Y	Y	N	P	P	N
4 DeFazio	Y	Y	Y	N	N	N	N
5 Hooley	Y	Y	Y	N	N	N	N
PENNSYLVANIA							
1 Brady	N	Y	Y	N	N	N	N
2 Fattah	N	Y	Y	N	N	N	N
3 Borski	N	Y	Y	N	N	N	N
4 Klink	N	Y	Y	N	N	N	N
5 ***Peterson***	Y	Y	Y	Y	N	N	Y
6 Holden	Y	Y	Y	N	N	N	N
7 ***Weldon***	Y	Y	Y	Y	N	N	Y
8 ***Greenwood***	Y	N	N	Y	N	N	N
9 ***Shuster***	Y	N	Y	Y	N	N	Y
10 ***McDade***	?	?	?	?	?	?	?
11 Kanjorski	N	Y	Y	N	N	N	N
12 Murtha	N	Y	Y	N	N	N	N
13 ***Fox***	Y	Y	Y	Y	N	N	Y
14 Coyne	N	Y	Y	N	N	N	N
15 McHale	Y	Y	Y	N	N	N	N
16 ***Pitts***	Y	Y	Y	Y	N	N	Y
17 ***Gekas***	Y	Y	Y	Y	N	N	N
18 Doyle	Y	Y	Y	N	N	N	N
19 ***Goodling***	Y	Y	Y	Y	N	N	Y
20 Mascara	Y	Y	Y	N	N	N	N
21 ***English***	Y	N	Y	Y	N	N	N
RHODE ISLAND							
1 Kennedy	Y	Y	Y	N	N	N	N
2 Weygand	N	Y	Y	N	N	N	N
SOUTH CAROLINA							
1 ***Sanford***	Y	N	N	Y	N	N	Y
2 ***Spence***	Y	N	Y	Y	N	N	Y
3 ***Graham***	Y	Y	Y	Y	N	N	Y
4 ***Inglis***	Y	N	Y	Y	N	N	Y
5 Spratt	Y	Y	Y	N	N	N	N
6 Clyburn	N	Y	Y	N	N	N	N
SOUTH DAKOTA							
AL ***Thune***	Y	Y	Y	Y	N	N	Y

	202	203	204	205	206	207	208
TENNESSEE							
1 ***Jenkins***	Y	Y	Y	Y	N	N	Y
2 ***Duncan***	Y	N	Y	Y	N	N	Y
3 ***Wamp***	Y	N	Y	Y	N	N	Y
4 ***Hilleary***	Y	Y	Y	Y	N	N	Y
5 Clement	N	Y	Y	N	N	N	N
6 Gordon	N	Y	Y	N	N	N	N
7 ***Bryant***	Y	N	Y	Y	N	N	Y
8 Tanner	Y	Y	Y	N	N	N	?
9 Ford	N	Y	Y	N	N	N	N
TEXAS							
1 Sandlin	Y	Y	Y	N	N	N	N
2 Turner	Y	Y	Y	N	N	N	N
3 ***Johnson, Sam***	Y	N	N	Y	N	N	Y
4 Hall	Y	Y	Y	N	N	N	Y
5 ***Sessions***	Y	N	Y	Y	?	N	Y
6 ***Barton***	Y	N	N	Y	N	N	Y
7 ***Archer***	Y	N	N	Y	N	N	Y
8 ***Brady***	Y	Y	N	Y	N	N	Y
9 Lampson	Y	Y	Y	N	N	N	N
10 Doggett	Y	Y	Y	N	N	N	N
11 Edwards	N	Y	Y	N	N	N	N
12 ***Granger***	Y	Y	Y	Y	N	N	Y
13 ***Thornberry***	Y	Y	Y	Y	N	N	Y
14 ***Paul***	Y	N	N	Y	N	N	Y
15 Hinojosa	Y	Y	Y	N	N	N	N
16 Reyes	?	?	?	?	?	N	N
17 Stenholm	Y	Y	Y	N	N	N	N
18 Jackson-Lee	N	Y	Y	N	N	N	N
19 ***Combest***	Y	Y	Y	Y	N	N	Y
20 Gonzalez	?	?	?	?	?	?	?
21 ***Smith***	Y	N	Y	Y	N	N	Y
22 ***DeLay***	Y	N	N	Y	N	N	Y
23 ***Bonilla***	Y	Y	Y	Y	N	N	Y
24 Frost	N	Y	Y	N	N	N	N
25 Bentsen	N	Y	Y	N	N	N	N
26 ***Armey***	Y	N	Y	Y	N	N	Y
27 Ortiz	N	Y	Y	N	N	N	N
28 Rodriguez	N	Y	Y	N	N	N	N
29 Green	N	Y	Y	N	N	N	N
30 Johnson, E.B.	N	Y	Y	N	?	?	?
UTAH							
1 ***Hansen***	Y	Y	Y	Y	N	N	Y
2 ***Cook***	Y	Y	Y	Y	N	N	Y
3 ***Cannon***	Y	N	N	Y	N	N	Y
VERMONT							
AL *Sanders*	Y	Y	Y	N	N	N	N
VIRGINIA							
1 ***Bateman***	Y	Y	+	+	N	N	Y
2 Pickett	N	Y	Y	N	N	N	N
3 Scott	Y	Y	Y	N	N	N	N
4 Sisisky	Y	Y	Y	N	N	N	N
5 Goode	Y	N	N	N	N	N	Y
6 ***Goodlatte***	Y	N	N	Y	N	N	Y
7 ***Bliley***	Y	N	N	Y	N	N	N
8 Moran	?	?	?	N	N	N	N
9 Boucher	N	Y	Y	N	N	N	N
10 ***Wolf***	Y	Y	Y	Y	N	N	N
11 ***Davis***	Y	Y	Y	Y	N	N	N
WASHINGTON							
1 ***White***	Y	Y	Y	Y	N	N	Y
2 ***Metcalf***	Y	Y	Y	Y	N	N	Y
3 ***Smith, Linda***	Y	Y	Y	Y	N	N	Y
4 ***Hastings***	Y	N	Y	Y	N	N	Y
5 ***Nethercutt***	Y	Y	Y	Y	N	N	Y
6 Dicks	N	Y	Y	N	N	N	N
7 McDermott	N	Y	Y	N	N	N	N
8 ***Dunn***	Y	Y	Y	Y	N	N	Y
9 Smith, Adam	N	Y	Y	N	N	N	N
WEST VIRGINIA							
1 Mollohan	?	?	?	?	?	?	?
2 Wise	N	Y	Y	N	N	N	N
3 Rahall	N	Y	Y	N	N	N	N
WISCONSIN							
1 ***Neumann***	Y	N	N	Y	N	N	Y
2 ***Klug***	Y	Y	Y	Y	N	N	Y
3 Kind	N	Y	Y	N	N	N	N
4 Kleczka	N	Y	Y	N	N	N	N
5 Barrett	N	Y	Y	N	N	N	N
6 ***Petri***	Y	N	Y	Y	N	N	Y
7 Obey	Y	Y	Y	N	N	N	N
8 Johnson	Y	Y	Y	N	N	N	N
9 ***Sensenbrenner***	Y	N	N	Y	N	N	N
WYOMING							
AL ***Cubin***	Y	N	Y	Y	N	N	Y

Southern states - Ala., Ark., Fla., Ga., Ky., La., Miss., N.C., Okla., S.C., Tenn., Texas, Va.

209. H Con Res 284. Fiscal 1999 Budget Resolution/Democratic Substitute. Spratt, D-S.C., substitute amendment to adopt a five-year budget plan that would provide budget authority for discretionary spending at the levels agreed to in the 1997 Balanced Budget Act and provide for $30 billion in tax reductions over five years by closing so-called tax loopholes. The amendment would provide for $10 billion in new mandatory spending initiatives, including funds to reduce classroom sizes and child care. Rejected 164-257: R 0-223; D 164-33 (ND 128-19, SD 36-14); I 0-1. June 5, 1998.

210. H Con Res 284. Fiscal 1999 Budget Resolution/Adoption. Adoption of the concurrent resolution to adopt a five-year budget plan that would create a surplus of $63.4 billion by 2003, by cutting spending by $101 billion over five years and using the funds to finance tax reduction which would include the elimination of the so-called marriage penalty. The plan calls for an increase, by $5 billion, in defense spending, over the caps agreed to under the Balanced Budget Act of 1997. The resolution sets binding levels for the fiscal year ending Sept. 30, 1999: budget authority, $1,730.4 billion; outlays, $1,721.9 billion; revenues, $1,755.6 billion; and surplus, $33.7 billion. Adopted 216-204: R 213-9; D 3-194 (ND 1-145, SD 2-49); I 0-1. June 5, 1998.

211. HR 2709. Iran Missile Sanctions/Agreeing to Senate Amendment. Gilman, R-N.Y., motion to agree to the Senate amendment changing the effective date for sanctionable activities from Aug. 8, 1995, to Jan. 22, 1998. The bill would require economic sanctions against overseas companies and research institutes that have aided Iranian efforts to develop ballistic missiles that could reach Israel, U.S. forces in the Persian Gulf or Europe. It also contains provisions needed to implement a treaty banning chemical weapons that was approved by the Senate in 1997. Motion agreed to (thus clearing the bill for the president) 392-22: R 216-3; D 175-19 (ND 129-15, SD 46-4); I 1-0. June 9, 1998. A "nay" was a vote in support of the president's position.

212. H Res 417. Importance of Fathers/Adoption. McIntosh, R-Ind., motion to suspend the rules and adopt the resolution to express the sense of the House that a better America depends in large part on the active involvement of fathers in raising their children. The resolution encourages each father to accept this responsibility. Motion agreed to 415-0: R 217-0; D 197-0 (ND 146-0, SD 51-0); I 1-0. June 9, 1998. A two-thirds majority of those present and voting (277 in this case) is required for adoption under suspension of the rules.

213. H Res 447. Financial Management by Federal Agencies/Adoption. Horn, R-Calif., motion to suspend the rules and adopt the resolution to express the sense of the House that Congress must impose consequences on federal agencies that fail their annual financial audits and must conduct more vigorous oversight of these agencies. Motion agreed to 415-0: R 217-0; D 197-0 (ND 146-0, SD 51-0); I 1-0. June 9, 1998. A two-thirds majority of those present and voting (277 in this case) is required for adoption under suspension of the rules.

214. HR 1635. Underground Railroad Program/Passage. Hansen, R-Utah, motion to suspend the rules and pass the bill to direct the National Park Service to create a nationwide network of historic buildings, routes, projects and museums, which would be known as the "National Underground Railroad Network to Freedom Program." Motion agreed to 415-2: R 217-2; D 197-0 (ND 146-0, SD 51-0); I 1-0. June 9, 1998. A two-thirds majority of those present and voting (278 in this case) is required for passage under suspension of the rules.

215. H Con Res 270. U.S. Support for Taiwan/Adoption. Gilman, R-N.Y., motion to suspend the rules and adopt the concurrent resolution that would call on President Clinton, during his upcoming trip to China, to secure a commitment from the Chinese to stop threatening to use force against Taiwan and express the sense of the Congress that Taiwan should be commended for its recent economic success and democratic elections. Motion agreed to 411-0: R 216-0; D 194-0 (ND 143-0, SD 51-0); I 1-0. June 9, 1998. A two-thirds majority of those present and voting (274 in this case) is required for adoption under suspension of the rules.

Key

Y	Voted for (yea).
#	Paired for.
+	Announced for.
N	Voted against (nay).
X	Paired against.
–	Announced against.
P	Voted "present."
C	Voted "present" to avoid possible conflict of interest.
?	Did not vote or otherwise make a position known.

Democrats   **Republicans**   *Independent*

	209	210	211	212	213	214	215
ALABAMA							
1 *Callahan*	N	Y	Y	Y	Y	Y	Y
2 *Everett*	N	Y	Y	Y	Y	Y	Y
3 *Riley*	N	Y	Y	Y	Y	Y	?
4 *Aderholt*	N	Y	Y	Y	Y	Y	Y
5 Cramer	N	N	Y	Y	Y	Y	Y
6 *Bachus*	N	Y	Y	Y	Y	Y	Y
7 Hilliard	Y	N	Y	Y	Y	Y	Y
ALASKA							
AL *Young*	N	Y	Y	Y	Y	Y	Y
ARIZONA							
1 *Salmon*	N	Y	Y	Y	Y	Y	Y
2 Pastor	Y	N	Y	Y	Y	Y	Y
3 *Stump*	N	Y	Y	Y	Y	Y	Y
4 *Shadegg*	N	Y	Y	Y	Y	Y	Y
5 *Kolbe*	N	Y	Y	Y	Y	Y	Y
6 *Hayworth*	N	Y	Y	Y	Y	Y	Y
ARKANSAS							
1 Berry	N	N	Y	Y	Y	Y	Y
2 Snyder	Y	N	Y	Y	Y	Y	Y
3 *Hutchinson*	N	Y	Y	Y	Y	Y	Y
4 *Dickey*	N	Y	Y	Y	Y	Y	Y
CALIFORNIA							
1 *Riggs*	N	Y	Y	Y	Y	Y	Y
2 *Herger*	N	Y	Y	Y	Y	Y	Y
3 Fazio	Y	N	P	Y	Y	Y	Y
4 *Doolittle*	N	Y	Y	Y	Y	Y	Y
5 Matsui	Y	N	Y	Y	Y	Y	Y
6 Woolsey	Y	N	Y	Y	Y	Y	Y
7 Miller	Y	N	Y	Y	Y	Y	?
8 Pelosi	Y	N	Y	Y	Y	Y	Y
9 Lee	Y	N	Y	Y	Y	Y	Y
10 Tauscher	Y	N	Y	Y	Y	Y	Y
11 *Pombo*	N	Y	Y	Y	Y	Y	Y
12 Lantos	Y	N	Y	Y	Y	Y	Y
13 Stark	Y	N	Y	Y	Y	Y	Y
14 Eshoo	Y	N	Y	Y	Y	Y	Y
15 *Campbell*	N	N	Y	Y	Y	Y	Y
16 Lofgren	Y	N	Y	Y	Y	Y	Y
17 Farr	Y	N	+	+	+	+	+
18 Condit	N	Y	Y	Y	Y	Y	Y
19 *Radanovich*	N	Y	Y	Y	Y	Y	Y
20 Dooley	Y	N	Y	Y	Y	Y	Y
21 *Thomas*	N	Y	Y	Y	Y	Y	Y
22 Capps, L.	Y	N	Y	Y	Y	Y	Y
23 *Gallegly*	N	Y	Y	Y	Y	Y	Y
24 Sherman	Y	N	Y	Y	Y	Y	Y
25 *McKeon*	N	Y	Y	Y	Y	Y	Y
26 Berman	Y	N	Y	Y	Y	Y	Y
27 *Rogan*	N	Y	Y	Y	Y	Y	Y
28 *Dreier*	N	Y	Y	Y	Y	Y	Y
29 Waxman	Y	N	Y	?	?	?	?
30 Becerra	Y	N	Y	Y	Y	Y	Y
31 Martinez	Y	N	Y	Y	Y	Y	Y
32 Dixon	Y	N	Y	Y	Y	Y	Y
33 Roybal-Allard	Y	N	Y	Y	Y	Y	Y
34 Torres	Y	N	Y	Y	Y	Y	Y
35 Waters	Y	N	Y	Y	Y	Y	Y
36 Harman	Y	N	Y	Y	Y	Y	Y
37 Millender-McD.	Y	N	Y	Y	Y	Y	Y

	209	210	211	212	213	214	215
38 *Horn*	N	Y	Y	Y	Y	Y	Y
39 *Royce*	N	Y	Y	Y	Y	Y	Y
40 *Lewis*	N	Y	Y	Y	Y	Y	Y
41 *Kim*	N	Y	Y	Y	Y	Y	Y
42 Brown	Y	N	N	Y	Y	Y	Y
43 *Calvert*	N	Y	Y	Y	Y	Y	Y
44 *Bono, M.*	N	Y	Y	Y	Y	Y	Y
45 *Rohrabacher*	N	Y	Y	Y	Y	Y	Y
46 Sanchez	Y	N	Y	Y	Y	Y	?
47 *Cox*	N	Y	Y	Y	Y	Y	Y
48 *Packard*	N	Y	Y	Y	Y	Y	Y
49 *Bilbray*	?	N	Y	Y	Y	Y	Y
50 Filner	Y	N	Y	Y	Y	Y	Y
51 *Cunningham*	N	Y	Y	Y	Y	Y	Y
52 *Hunter*	N	Y	?	?	?	Y	Y
COLORADO							
1 DeGette	Y	N	Y	Y	Y	Y	Y
2 Skaggs	Y	N	Y	Y	Y	Y	Y
3 *McInnis*	N	Y	Y	Y	?	Y	Y
4 *Schaffer*	N	Y	Y	Y	Y	Y	Y
5 *Hefley*	N	N	Y	Y	Y	Y	Y
6 *Schaefer*	N	Y	Y	Y	Y	Y	Y
CONNECTICUT							
1 Kennelly	Y	N	Y	Y	Y	Y	Y
2 Gejdenson	Y	N	Y	Y	Y	Y	Y
3 DeLauro	Y	N	Y	Y	Y	Y	Y
4 *Shays*	N	Y	Y	Y	Y	Y	Y
5 Maloney	Y	N	Y	Y	Y	Y	Y
6 *Johnson*	N	N	Y	Y	Y	Y	Y
DELAWARE							
AL *Castle*	N	N	Y	Y	Y	Y	Y
FLORIDA							
1 *Scarborough*	N	Y	Y	Y	Y	Y	Y
2 Boyd	N	N	Y	Y	Y	Y	Y
3 Brown	Y	N	Y	Y	Y	Y	Y
4 *Fowler*	N	Y	Y	Y	Y	Y	Y
5 Thurman	Y	N	Y	Y	Y	Y	Y
6 *Stearns*	N	Y	Y	Y	Y	Y	Y
7 *Mica*	N	Y	Y	Y	Y	Y	Y
8 *McCollum*	N	Y	Y	Y	Y	Y	Y
9 *Bilirakis*	N	Y	Y	Y	Y	Y	Y
10 *Young*	N	Y	?	?	?	?	?
11 Davis	N	N	Y	Y	Y	Y	Y
12 *Canady*	N	Y	Y	Y	Y	Y	Y
13 *Miller*	N	Y	Y	Y	Y	Y	Y
14 *Goss*	N	Y	Y	Y	Y	Y	Y
15 *Weldon*	N	Y	Y	Y	Y	Y	Y
16 *Foley*	N	Y	Y	Y	Y	Y	Y
17 Meek	?	N	Y	Y	Y	Y	Y
18 *Ros-Lehtinen*	?	?	Y	Y	Y	Y	Y
19 Wexler	Y	N	+	+	+	+	+
20 Deutsch	Y	N	+	+	+	+	+
21 *Diaz-Balart*	N	Y	Y	Y	Y	Y	Y
22 *Shaw*	N	Y	Y	Y	Y	Y	Y
23 Hastings	Y	N	N	Y	Y	Y	Y
GEORGIA							
1 *Kingston*	N	Y	Y	Y	Y	Y	Y
2 Bishop	Y	N	?	Y	Y	Y	Y
3 *Collins*	N	Y	Y	Y	Y	Y	Y
4 McKinney	N	N	Y	Y	Y	Y	Y
5 Lewis	?	–	?	?	?	?	?
6 *Gingrich*	N	Y					
7 *Barr*	N	Y	Y	Y	Y	Y	Y
8 *Chambliss*	N	Y	Y	Y	Y	Y	Y
9 *Deal*	N	Y	Y	Y	Y	Y	Y
10 *Norwood*	N	Y	Y	Y	Y	Y	Y
11 *Linder*	N	Y	Y	Y	Y	Y	Y
HAWAII							
1 Abercrombie	Y	N	Y	Y	Y	Y	Y
2 Mink	Y	N	N	Y	Y	Y	Y
IDAHO							
1 *Chenoweth*	N	Y	Y	Y	Y	Y	Y
2 *Crapo*	N	Y	Y	Y	Y	Y	Y
ILLINOIS							
1 Rush	N	N	?	?	?	?	?
2 Jackson	N	N	Y	Y	Y	Y	Y
3 Lipinski	N	N	Y	Y	Y	Y	Y
4 Gutierrez	Y	N	Y	Y	Y	Y	Y
5 Blagojevich	Y	N	Y	Y	Y	Y	Y
6 *Hyde*	N	Y	Y	Y	Y	Y	?
7 Davis	Y	N	Y	Y	Y	Y	Y
8 *Crane*	N	Y	Y	Y	Y	Y	Y
9 Yates	Y	N	N	Y	Y	Y	Y
10 *Porter*	N	Y	Y	Y	Y	Y	Y
11 *Weller*	N	Y	Y	Y	Y	Y	Y
12 Costello	Y	N	Y	Y	Y	Y	Y

ND Northern Democrats   **SD** Southern Democrats

	209	210	211	212	213	214	215
13 ***Fawell***	N	Y	Y	?	Y	Y	Y
14 ***Hastert***	N	Y	Y	Y	Y	Y	Y
15 ***Ewing***	N	Y	Y	Y	Y	Y	Y
16 ***Manzullo***	N	Y	Y	Y	Y	Y	Y
17 Evans	Y	N	Y	Y	Y	Y	Y
18 ***LaHood***	N	Y	Y	Y	Y	Y	Y
19 Poshard	Y	N	Y	Y	Y	Y	Y
20 ***Shimkus***	N	Y	Y	Y	Y	Y	Y
INDIANA							
1 Visclosky	N	N	Y	Y	Y	Y	Y
2 ***McIntosh***	N	Y	Y	Y	Y	Y	Y
3 Roemer	N	N	Y	Y	Y	Y	Y
4 ***Souder***	N	P	Y	Y	Y	Y	Y
5 ***Buyer***	N	Y	Y	Y	Y	Y	Y
6 ***Burton***	N	Y	Y	Y	Y	Y	Y
7 ***Pease***	N	Y	Y	Y	Y	Y	Y
8 ***Hostettler***	N	Y	N	Y	Y	Y	Y
9 Hamilton	Y	N	N	Y	Y	Y	Y
10 Carson	Y	N	Y	Y	Y	Y	Y
IOWA							
1 ***Leach***	N	Y	?	Y	Y	Y	Y
2 ***Nussle***	N	Y	Y	Y	Y	Y	Y
3 Boswell	Y	N	Y	Y	Y	Y	Y
4 ***Ganske***	N	N	Y	Y	Y	Y	Y
5 ***Latham***	N	Y	Y	Y	Y	Y	Y
KANSAS							
1 ***Moran***	N	Y	N	Y	Y	Y	Y
2 ***Ryun***	N	Y	Y	Y	Y	Y	Y
3 ***Snowbarger***	N	Y	Y	?	Y	Y	Y
4 ***Tiahrt***	N	Y	Y	Y	Y	Y	Y
KENTUCKY							
1 ***Whitfield***	N	Y	Y	Y	Y	Y	Y
2 ***Lewis***	N	Y	Y	Y	Y	Y	Y
3 ***Northup***	N	Y	Y	Y	Y	Y	Y
4 ***Bunning***	N	Y	Y	Y	Y	Y	Y
5 ***Rogers***	N	Y	Y	Y	Y	Y	Y
6 Baesler	N	N	Y	Y	Y	Y	Y
LOUISIANA							
1 ***Livingston***	N	Y	Y	Y	Y	Y	Y
2 Jefferson	Y	N	N	Y	Y	Y	Y
3 ***Tauzin***	N	Y	Y	Y	Y	Y	Y
4 ***McCrery***	N	Y	Y	Y	Y	Y	Y
5 ***Cooksey***	N	Y	Y	Y	Y	Y	Y
6 ***Baker***	N	Y	Y	Y	Y	Y	Y
7 John	N	N	Y	Y	Y	Y	Y
MAINE							
1 Allen	Y	N	Y	Y	Y	Y	Y
2 Baldacci	Y	N	Y	Y	Y	Y	Y
MARYLAND							
1 ***Gilchrest***	N	Y	Y	Y	Y	Y	Y
2 ***Ehrlich***	N	Y	Y	Y	Y	Y	Y
3 Cardin	Y	N	Y	Y	Y	Y	Y
4 Wynn	Y	N	Y	Y	Y	Y	Y
5 Hoyer	Y	N	Y	Y	Y	Y	Y
6 ***Bartlett***	N	Y	Y	Y	Y	Y	Y
7 Cummings	Y	N	Y	Y	Y	Y	Y
8 ***Morella***	N	N	Y	Y	Y	Y	Y
MASSACHUSETTS							
1 Olver	Y	N	Y	Y	Y	Y	Y
2 Neal	Y	N	Y	Y	Y	Y	Y
3 McGovern	Y	N	Y	Y	Y	Y	Y
4 Frank	Y	N	Y	Y	Y	Y	Y
5 Meehan	N	N	Y	Y	Y	Y	Y
6 Tierney	Y	N	Y	Y	Y	Y	Y
7 Markey	Y	N	Y	Y	Y	Y	Y
8 Kennedy	?	?	N	Y	Y	Y	Y
9 Moakley	Y	N	Y	Y	Y	Y	Y
10 Delahunt	Y	N	Y	Y	Y	Y	Y
MICHIGAN							
1 Stupak	N	N	Y	Y	Y	Y	Y
2 ***Hoekstra***	N	Y	Y	Y	Y	Y	Y
3 ***Ehlers***	N	Y	Y	Y	Y	Y	Y
4 ***Camp***	N	Y	Y	Y	Y	Y	Y
5 Barcia	Y	N	Y	Y	Y	Y	Y
6 ***Upton***	N	Y	Y	Y	Y	Y	Y
7 ***Smith***	N	Y	Y	Y	Y	Y	Y
8 Stabenow	Y	N	Y	Y	Y	Y	Y
9 Kildee	Y	N	Y	Y	Y	Y	Y
10 Bonior	Y	N	P	Y	Y	Y	Y
11 ***Knollenberg***	N	Y	Y	Y	Y	Y	Y
12 Levin	Y	N	Y	Y	Y	Y	Y
13 Rivers	Y	N	Y	Y	Y	Y	Y
14 Conyers	Y	N	N	Y	Y	Y	Y
15 Kilpatrick	Y	N	Y	Y	Y	Y	Y
16 Dingell	Y	N	Y	Y	Y	Y	Y

	209	210	211	212	213	214	215
MINNESOTA							
1 ***Gutknecht***	N	Y	Y	Y	Y	Y	Y
2 Minge	N	N	Y	Y	Y	Y	Y
3 ***Ramstad***	N	Y	Y	Y	Y	Y	Y
4 Vento	Y	N	Y	Y	Y	Y	Y
5 Sabo	?	?	?	?	?	?	?
6 Luther	Y	N	Y	Y	Y	Y	Y
7 Peterson	N	N	Y	Y	Y	Y	Y
8 Oberstar	Y	N	Y	Y	Y	Y	Y
MISSISSIPPI							
1 ***Wicker***	N	Y	Y	Y	?	?	?
2 Thompson	Y	N	Y	Y	Y	Y	Y
3 ***Pickering***	N	Y	Y	Y	Y	Y	Y
4 ***Parker***	N	Y	Y	Y	Y	Y	Y
5 Taylor	N	N	Y	Y	Y	Y	Y
MISSOURI							
1 Clay	Y	N	Y	Y	Y	Y	Y
2 ***Talent***	N	Y	Y	Y	Y	Y	?
3 Gephardt	Y	N	P	Y	Y	Y	Y
4 Skelton	Y	N	Y	Y	Y	Y	Y
5 McCarthy	Y	N	Y	Y	Y	Y	Y
6 Danner	N	N	Y	Y	Y	Y	Y
7 ***Blunt***	N	Y	Y	Y	Y	Y	Y
8 ***Emerson***	N	Y	Y	Y	Y	Y	Y
9 ***Hulshof***	N	Y	Y	Y	Y	Y	Y
MONTANA							
AL ***Hill***	N	Y	Y	Y	Y	Y	Y
NEBRASKA							
1 ***Bereuter***	N	Y	Y	Y	Y	Y	Y
2 ***Christensen***	N	Y	Y	Y	Y	Y	Y
3 ***Barrett***	N	Y	Y	Y	Y	Y	Y
NEVADA							
1 ***Ensign***	N	Y	Y	Y	Y	Y	Y
2 ***Gibbons***	N	Y	Y	Y	Y	Y	Y
NEW HAMPSHIRE							
1 ***Sununu***	N	Y	Y	Y	Y	Y	Y
2 ***Bass***	N	Y	Y	Y	Y	Y	Y
NEW JERSEY							
1 Andrews	Y	N	Y	Y	Y	Y	Y
2 ***LoBiondo***	N	Y	Y	Y	Y	Y	Y
3 ***Saxton***	N	Y	Y	Y	Y	Y	Y
4 ***Smith***	N	Y	Y	Y	Y	Y	Y
5 ***Roukema***	N	Y	Y	Y	Y	?	?
6 Pallone	Y	N	Y	Y	Y	Y	Y
7 ***Franks***	N	Y	Y	Y	Y	Y	Y
8 Pascrell	Y	N	Y	Y	Y	Y	Y
9 Rothman	Y	N	Y	Y	Y	Y	Y
10 Payne	Y	N	Y	Y	Y	Y	Y
11 ***Frelinghuysen***	N	Y	Y	Y	Y	Y	Y
12 ***Pappas***	N	Y	Y	Y	Y	Y	Y
13 Menendez	Y	N	Y	Y	Y	Y	Y
NEW MEXICO							
1 Vacant							
2 ***Skeen***	N	Y	Y	Y	Y	Y	Y
3 ***Redmond***	N	Y	Y	Y	Y	Y	Y
NEW YORK							
1 ***Forbes***	N	Y	Y	Y	Y	Y	Y
2 ***Lazio***	N	Y	Y	Y	Y	Y	Y
3 ***King***	N	Y	Y	Y	Y	Y	Y
4 McCarthy	Y	N	Y	Y	Y	Y	Y
5 Ackerman	Y	N	Y	Y	Y	Y	Y
6 Meeks	N	N	Y	Y	Y	Y	Y
7 Manton	Y	N	Y	Y	Y	Y	Y
8 Nadler	Y	N	Y	Y	Y	Y	Y
9 Schumer	Y	N	?	?	?	?	?
10 Towns	Y	N	Y	Y	Y	Y	Y
11 Owens	Y	N	Y	Y	Y	Y	Y
12 Velázquez	Y	N	Y	Y	Y	Y	Y
13 ***Fossella***	N	Y	Y	Y	Y	Y	Y
14 Maloney	Y	N	Y	Y	Y	Y	Y
15 Rangel	Y	N	Y	Y	Y	Y	Y
16 Serrano	Y	N	Y	Y	Y	Y	Y
17 Engel	Y	N	Y	Y	Y	Y	Y
18 Lowey	Y	N	Y	Y	Y	Y	Y
19 ***Kelly***	N	Y	Y	Y	Y	Y	Y
20 ***Gilman***	N	Y	Y	Y	Y	Y	Y
21 McNulty	Y	N	Y	Y	Y	Y	Y
22 ***Solomon***	N	Y	Y	Y	Y	Y	Y
23 ***Boehlert***	N	Y	Y	Y	Y	Y	Y
24 ***McHugh***	N	Y	Y	Y	Y	Y	Y
25 ***Walsh***	N	Y	Y	Y	Y	Y	Y
26 Hinchey	Y	N	Y	Y	Y	Y	Y
27 ***Paxon***	N	Y	Y	Y	Y	Y	Y
28 Slaughter	Y	N	Y	Y	Y	Y	Y
29 LaFalce	Y	?	N	Y	Y	Y	Y

	209	210	211	212	213	214	215
30 ***Quinn***	N	N	Y	Y	Y	Y	Y
31 ***Houghton***	N	Y	?	?	?	?	?
NORTH CAROLINA							
1 Clayton	Y	N	Y	Y	Y	Y	Y
2 Etheridge	Y	N	Y	Y	Y	Y	Y
3 ***Jones***	N	Y	Y	Y	Y	Y	Y
4 Price	Y	N	Y	Y	Y	Y	Y
5 ***Burr***	N	Y	Y	Y	Y	Y	Y
6 ***Coble***	N	Y	Y	Y	Y	Y	Y
7 McIntyre	Y	N	Y	Y	Y	Y	Y
8 Hefner	Y	N	Y	Y	Y	Y	Y
9 ***Myrick***	N	Y	Y	Y	Y	Y	Y
10 ***Ballenger***	–	+	Y	+	+	+	+
11 ***Taylor***	N	Y	Y	Y	Y	Y	Y
12 Watt	Y	N	Y	Y	Y	Y	Y
NORTH DAKOTA							
AL Pomeroy	Y	N	Y	Y	Y	Y	Y
OHIO							
1 ***Chabot***	N	Y	Y	Y	Y	Y	Y
2 ***Portman***	N	Y	Y	Y	Y	Y	Y
3 Hall	Y	N	Y	Y	Y	Y	Y
4 ***Oxley***	N	Y	Y	Y	Y	Y	Y
5 ***Gillmor***	N	Y	Y	Y	Y	Y	Y
6 Strickland	Y	N	Y	Y	Y	Y	Y
7 ***Hobson***	N	Y	Y	Y	Y	Y	Y
8 ***Boehner***	N	Y	Y	Y	Y	Y	Y
9 Kaptur	Y	N	Y	Y	Y	Y	Y
10 Kucinich	N	N	Y	Y	Y	Y	Y
11 Stokes	Y	N	Y	Y	Y	Y	Y
12 ***Kasich***	N	Y	Y	Y	Y	Y	Y
13 Brown	Y	N	Y	Y	Y	Y	Y
14 Sawyer	Y	N	Y	Y	Y	Y	Y
15 ***Pryce***	N	Y	Y	Y	Y	Y	Y
16 ***Regula***	N	Y	Y	Y	Y	Y	Y
17 Traficant	N	N	Y	Y	Y	Y	Y
18 ***Ney***	N	Y	Y	Y	Y	Y	Y
19 ***LaTourette***	N	Y	Y	Y	Y	Y	Y
OKLAHOMA							
1 ***Largent***	N	Y	Y	Y	Y	Y	Y
2 ***Coburn***	N	Y	Y	Y	Y	Y	Y
3 ***Watkins***	N	Y	Y	Y	Y	Y	Y
4 ***Watts***	N	Y	Y	Y	Y	Y	Y
5 ***Istook***	N	Y	Y	Y	Y	Y	Y
6 ***Lucas***	N	Y	Y	Y	Y	Y	Y
OREGON							
1 Furse	?	?	N	Y	Y	Y	Y
2 ***Smith***	N	Y	Y	Y	Y	Y	Y
3 Blumenauer	Y	N	Y	Y	Y	Y	Y
4 DeFazio	N	N	Y	Y	Y	Y	Y
5 Hooley	Y	N	Y	Y	Y	Y	Y
PENNSYLVANIA							
1 Brady	Y	N	Y	Y	Y	Y	Y
2 Fattah	N	N	Y	Y	Y	Y	Y
3 Borski	Y	N	Y	Y	Y	Y	Y
4 Klink	Y	N	Y	Y	Y	Y	Y
5 ***Peterson***	N	Y	Y	Y	Y	Y	Y
6 Holden	Y	N	Y	Y	Y	Y	Y
7 ***Weldon***	N	Y	Y	Y	Y	Y	Y
8 ***Greenwood***	N	Y	Y	Y	Y	Y	Y
9 ***Shuster***	N	Y	Y	Y	Y	Y	Y
10 ***McDade***	?	?	Y	?	Y	Y	Y
11 Kanjorski	Y	N	N	Y	Y	Y	Y
12 Murtha	N	N	N	Y	Y	Y	?
13 ***Fox***	N	Y	Y	Y	Y	Y	Y
14 Coyne	Y	N	Y	Y	Y	Y	Y
15 McHale	Y	N	Y	Y	Y	Y	Y
16 ***Pitts***	N	Y	Y	Y	Y	Y	Y
17 ***Gekas***	N	Y	Y	Y	?	Y	Y
18 Doyle	Y	N	Y	Y	Y	Y	Y
19 ***Goodling***	N	Y	?	Y	Y	Y	Y
20 Mascara	N	N	Y	Y	Y	Y	Y
21 ***English***	N	Y	Y	Y	Y	Y	Y
RHODE ISLAND							
1 Kennedy	Y	N	Y	Y	Y	Y	Y
2 Weygand	Y	N	Y	Y	Y	Y	Y
SOUTH CAROLINA							
1 ***Sanford***	N	Y	Y	Y	Y	N	Y
2 ***Spence***	N	Y	Y	Y	Y	Y	Y
3 ***Graham***	N	Y	Y	Y	Y	Y	Y
4 ***Inglis***	N	Y	?	?	?	?	?
5 Spratt	Y	N	Y	Y	Y	Y	Y
6 Clyburn	Y	N	Y	Y	Y	Y	Y
SOUTH DAKOTA							
AL ***Thune***	N	Y	Y	Y	Y	Y	Y

	209	210	211	212	213	214	215
TENNESSEE							
1 ***Jenkins***	N	Y	Y	Y	Y	Y	Y
2 ***Duncan***	N	Y	Y	Y	Y	Y	Y
3 ***Wamp***	N	Y	Y	Y	Y	Y	Y
4 ***Hilleary***	N	Y	Y	Y	Y	Y	Y
5 Clement	Y	N	Y	Y	Y	Y	Y
6 Gordon	Y	N	Y	Y	Y	Y	Y
7 ***Bryant***	N	Y	Y	Y	Y	Y	Y
8 Tanner	?	?	Y	Y	Y	Y	Y
9 Ford	Y	N	Y	Y	Y	Y	Y
TEXAS							
1 Sandlin	N	N	Y	Y	Y	Y	Y
2 Turner	N	N	Y	Y	Y	Y	Y
3 ***Johnson, Sam***	N	Y	?	?	?	?	?
4 Hall	N	Y	Y	Y	Y	Y	Y
5 ***Sessions***	N	Y	Y	Y	Y	Y	Y
6 ***Barton***	N	Y	Y	Y	Y	Y	Y
7 ***Archer***	N	Y	Y	Y	Y	Y	Y
8 ***Brady***	N	Y	Y	Y	Y	Y	Y
9 Lampson	Y	N	Y	Y	Y	Y	Y
10 Doggett	Y	N	Y	Y	Y	Y	Y
11 Edwards	Y	N	Y	Y	Y	Y	Y
12 ***Granger***	N	Y	Y	Y	Y	Y	Y
13 ***Thornberry***	N	Y	Y	Y	Y	Y	Y
14 ***Paul***	N	?	N	Y	Y	N	Y
15 Hinojosa	Y	N	Y	Y	Y	Y	Y
16 Reyes	Y	N	Y	Y	Y	Y	Y
17 Stenholm	Y	N	Y	Y	Y	Y	Y
18 Jackson-Lee	Y	N	Y	Y	Y	Y	Y
19 ***Combest***	N	Y	Y	Y	Y	Y	Y
20 Gonzalez	?	?	?	?	?	?	?
21 ***Smith***	N	Y	Y	Y	Y	Y	Y
22 ***DeLay***	N	Y	Y	Y	Y	Y	Y
23 ***Bonilla***	N	Y	Y	Y	Y	Y	Y
24 Frost	Y	N	Y	Y	Y	Y	Y
25 Bentsen	Y	N	Y	Y	Y	Y	Y
26 ***Armey***	N	Y	Y	Y	Y	Y	Y
27 Ortiz	Y	N	Y	Y	Y	Y	Y
28 Rodriguez	Y	N	Y	Y	Y	Y	Y
29 Green	Y	N	Y	Y	Y	Y	Y
30 Johnson, E.B.	?	?	N	Y	Y	Y	Y
UTAH							
1 ***Hansen***	N	Y	Y	Y	Y	Y	Y
2 ***Cook***	N	Y	Y	Y	Y	Y	Y
3 ***Cannon***	N	Y	Y	Y	Y	Y	Y
VERMONT							
AL *Sanders*	N	N	Y	Y	Y	Y	Y
VIRGINIA							
1 ***Bateman***	N	Y	Y	Y	Y	Y	Y
2 Pickett	N	N	Y	Y	Y	Y	Y
3 Scott	Y	N	Y	Y	Y	Y	Y
4 Sisisky	Y	N	Y	Y	Y	Y	Y
5 Goode	N	Y	Y	Y	Y	Y	Y
6 ***Goodlatte***	N	Y	Y	Y	Y	Y	Y
7 ***Bliley***	N	Y	Y	Y	Y	Y	Y
8 Moran	Y	N	N	Y	Y	Y	Y
9 Boucher	N	N	Y	Y	Y	Y	Y
10 ***Wolf***	N	Y	Y	Y	Y	Y	Y
11 ***Davis***	N	Y	Y	Y	Y	Y	Y
WASHINGTON							
1 ***White***	N	Y	Y	Y	Y	Y	Y
2 ***Metcalf***	N	Y	Y	Y	Y	Y	Y
3 ***Smith, Linda***	N	N	Y	Y	Y	Y	Y
4 ***Hastings***	N	Y	Y	Y	Y	Y	Y
5 ***Nethercutt***	N	Y	Y	Y	Y	Y	Y
6 Dicks	Y	N	Y	Y	Y	Y	Y
7 McDermott	Y	N	N	Y	Y	Y	Y
8 ***Dunn***	N	Y	Y	Y	Y	Y	Y
9 Smith, Adam	Y	N	Y	Y	Y	Y	Y
WEST VIRGINIA							
1 Mollohan	?	?	Y	Y	Y	Y	Y
2 Wise	Y	N	Y	Y	Y	Y	Y
3 Rahall	N	N	N	Y	Y	Y	Y
WISCONSIN							
1 ***Neumann***	N	Y	Y	Y	Y	Y	Y
2 ***Klug***	N	Y	Y	Y	Y	Y	Y
3 Kind	Y	N	Y	Y	Y	Y	Y
4 Kleczka	Y	N	Y	Y	Y	Y	Y
5 Barrett	Y	N	Y	Y	Y	Y	Y
6 ***Petri***	N	Y	Y	Y	Y	Y	Y
7 Obey	Y	N	N	Y	Y	Y	Y
8 Johnson	Y	N	Y	Y	Y	Y	Y
9 ***Sensenbrenner***	N	Y	Y	Y	Y	Y	Y
WYOMING							
AL ***Cubin***	N	Y	Y	Y	Y	Y	Y

Southern states - Ala., Ark., Fla., Ga., Ky., La., Miss., N.C., Okla., S.C., Tenn., Texas, Va.

Key

- **Y** Voted for (yea).
- **#** Paired for.
- **+** Announced for.
- **N** Voted against (nay).
- **X** Paired against.
- **–** Announced against.
- **P** Voted "present."
- **C** Voted "present" to avoid possible conflict of interest.
- **?** Did not vote or otherwise make a position known.

Democrats   **Republicans**
Independent

216. HR 3150. Bankruptcy Overhaul/Consideration of Rule. Judgment of the House on proceeding to the consideration of the rule (H Res 462) to provide for House floor consideration of the bill to overhaul the nation's bankruptcy laws, despite the Nadler, D-N.Y., point of order regarding unfunded mandates. Agreed to consider the rule 248-166: R 215-1; D 33-164 (ND 19-125, SD 14-39); I 0-1. June 10, 1998.

217. HR 3150. Bankruptcy Overhaul/Previous Question. McInnis, R-Colo., motion to order the previous question (thus ending debate and the possibility of amendment) on adoption of the rule (H Res 462) to provide for House floor consideration of the bill to overhaul the nation's bankruptcy laws. Motion agreed to 236-183: R 217-0; D 19-182 (ND 12-135, SD 7-47); I 0-1. June 10, 1998.

218. HR 3150. Bankruptcy Overhaul/Rule. Adoption of the rule (H Res 462) to provide for House floor consideration of the bill to overhaul the nation's bankruptcy laws by barring individuals with average incomes or higher from filing for bankruptcy under Chapter 7 and thus walking away from most debts. Adopted 251-172: R 222-1; D 29-170 (ND 19-127, SD 10-43); I 0-1. June 10, 1998.

219. HR 3150. Bankruptcy Overhaul/Small Businesses. Nadler, D-N.Y., amendment to modify the bill's provisions related to small businesses, so as to eliminate added paperwork requirements and the definition that a small business is an entity with $5 million or less in debt. The amendment also would exclude from the calculation of a debtor's income that must be made available to repay unsecured creditors any expenditure necessary for the continuing operation of the debtor's business. Rejected 136-290: R 4-222; D 131-68 (ND 107-40, SD 24-28); I 1-0. June 10, 1998.

220. HR 3150. Bankruptcy Overhaul/Means-Testing Costs. Delahunt, D-Mass., amendment to authorize the U.S. Judicial Conference to reduce disbursements to unsecured non-priority creditors payable in Chapter 13 cases to cover the increased costs of implementing the bill's means-testing provisions. Rejected 149-278: R 2-224; D 146-54 (ND 118-29, SD 28-25); I 1-0. June 10, 1998.

221. HR 3150. Bankruptcy Overhaul/Homestead Property. Gekas, R-Pa., amendment to prohibit the conversion of non-exempt assets into exempt homestead property within one year of filing for bankruptcy. Adopted 222-204: R 181-44; D 41-159 (ND 9-139, SD 32-20); I 0-1. June 10, 1998.

222. HR 3150. Bankruptcy Overhaul/Recording Contracts. Scott, D-Va., amendment to strike provisions that prevent recording artists from discharging their obligations under contracts with recording companies when they file for bankruptcy. Rejected 111-316: R 4-222; D 106-94 (ND 84-63, SD 22-31); I 1-0. June 10, 1998.

	216	217	218	219	220	221	222
ALABAMA							
1 *Callahan*	Y	Y	Y	N	N	Y	N
2 *Everett*	Y	Y	Y	N	N	N	N
3 *Riley*	Y	Y	Y	N	N	N	N
4 *Aderholt*	Y	Y	Y	N	N	N	N
5 Cramer	Y	Y	Y	N	N	N	N
6 *Bachus*	Y	?	Y	N	N	N	N
7 Hilliard	N	N	N	Y	Y	N	N
ALASKA							
AL *Young*	Y	Y	Y	N	N	Y	N
ARIZONA							
1 *Salmon*	Y	Y	Y	N	N	Y	N
2 Pastor	N	N	N	Y	Y	N	N
3 *Stump*	Y	Y	Y	N	N	Y	N
4 *Shadegg*	Y	Y	Y	N	N	Y	N
5 *Kolbe*	Y	Y	Y	N	N	N	N
6 *Hayworth*	Y	Y	Y	N	N	Y	N
ARKANSAS							
1 Berry	N	Y	N	N	N	N	N
2 Snyder	Y	N	N	N	N	N	N
3 *Hutchinson*	Y	Y	Y	N	N	Y	N
4 *Dickey*	Y	Y	Y	N	N	Y	N
CALIFORNIA							
1 *Riggs*	Y	Y	Y	N	N	N	N
2 *Herger*	Y	Y	Y	N	N	Y	N
3 Fazio	N	N	N	Y	Y	N	N
4 *Doolittle*	Y	Y	Y	N	N	N	N
5 Matsui	N	N	N	Y	Y	N	N
6 Woolsey	N	N	N	Y	Y	N	Y
7 Miller	N	N	?	Y	Y	N	Y
8 Pelosi	N	N	N	Y	Y	N	Y
9 Lee	N	N	N	Y	Y	N	Y
10 Tauscher	Y	Y	Y	N	N	Y	N
11 *Pombo*	Y	Y	Y	N	N	Y	N
12 Lantos	N	N	N	Y	Y	N	N
13 Stark	N	N	N	Y	Y	N	Y
14 Eshoo	N	N	N	Y	Y	N	N
15 *Campbell*	Y	Y	Y	N	N	Y	N
16 Lofgren	?	N	N	Y	Y	N	N
17 Farr	–	–	–	+	+	–	–
18 Condit	Y	Y	Y	N	N	Y	N
19 *Radanovich*	Y	Y	Y	N	N	Y	N
20 Dooley	Y	Y	Y	N	N	Y	N
21 *Thomas*	Y	Y	Y	N	N	Y	N
22 Capps, L.	N	N	N	Y	N	N	Y
23 *Gallegly*	Y	Y	Y	N	N	Y	N
24 Sherman	Y	Y	N	N	N	Y	N
25 *McKeon*	Y	Y	Y	N	N	Y	N
26 Berman	N	?	?	?	?	?	?
27 *Rogan*	Y	Y	Y	N	N	Y	Y
28 *Dreier*	Y	Y	Y	N	N	Y	Y
29 Waxman	N	N	N	Y	Y	N	Y
30 Becerra	N	N	N	Y	Y	N	Y
31 Martinez	N	N	N	Y	Y	N	N
32 Dixon	N	N	N	Y	Y	N	N
33 Roybal-Allard	N	N	N	Y	Y	N	Y
34 Torres	N	?	N	Y	Y	N	Y
35 Waters	N	N	N	Y	Y	N	Y
36 Harman	?	N	Y	N	Y	N	Y
37 Millender-McD.	N	N	N	Y	Y	N	Y
38 *Horn*	Y	Y	Y	N	N	Y	N
39 *Royce*	Y	Y	Y	N	N	N	N
40 *Lewis*	Y	Y	Y	N	N	Y	N
41 *Kim*	Y	Y	Y	N	N	Y	N
42 Brown	N	?	?	Y	Y	N	Y
43 *Calvert*	Y	Y	Y	N	N	Y	N
44 *Bono, M.*	Y	Y	Y	N	N	Y	N
45 *Rohrabacher*	Y	Y	Y	N	N	N	N
46 Sanchez	N	N	N	Y	Y	N	N
47 *Cox*	Y	Y	Y	N	N	Y	N
48 *Packard*	Y	Y	Y	N	N	Y	N
49 *Bilbray*	Y	Y	Y	N	N	Y	N
50 Filner	N	N	N	Y	Y	N	Y
51 *Cunningham*	Y	Y	Y	N	N	Y	N
52 *Hunter*	Y	Y	Y	N	N	Y	N
COLORADO							
1 DeGette	N	N	N	Y	Y	N	Y
2 Skaggs	Y	N	N	Y	Y	N	N
3 *McInnis*	Y	Y	Y	N	N	Y	N
4 *Schaffer*	Y	Y	Y	N	N	Y	N
5 *Hefley*	Y	Y	Y	N	N	Y	N
6 *Schaefer*	Y	Y	Y	N	N	Y	N
CONNECTICUT							
1 Kennelly	N	N	N	Y	Y	N	N
2 Gejdenson	N	N	N	Y	Y	N	Y
3 DeLauro	N	N	N	Y	Y	N	Y
4 *Shays*	Y	Y	Y	N	N	Y	N
5 Maloney	Y	Y	Y	N	N	Y	N
6 *Johnson*	Y	Y	Y	N	N	Y	N
DELAWARE							
AL *Castle*	Y	Y	Y	N	N	N	N
FLORIDA							
1 *Scarborough*	Y	?	Y	N	N	N	N
2 Boyd	Y	Y	Y	N	N	Y	N
3 Brown	N	N	?	Y	Y	N	Y
4 *Fowler*	Y	Y	Y	N	N	Y	N
5 Thurman	N	N	N	Y	Y	N	Y
6 *Stearns*	Y	Y	Y	N	N	N	N
7 *Mica*	Y	Y	Y	N	N	N	N
8 *McCollum*	Y	Y	Y	N	N	Y	N
9 *Bilirakis*	Y	Y	Y	N	N	Y	N
10 *Young*	?	Y	Y	N	N	Y	N
11 Davis	Y	N	N	Y	N	Y	Y
12 *Canady*	Y	Y	Y	N	N	Y	N
13 *Miller*	Y	Y	Y	N	N	Y	N
14 *Goss*	Y	Y	Y	N	N	Y	N
15 *Weldon*	Y	Y	Y	N	N	Y	N
16 *Foley*	Y	Y	Y	N	N	Y	N
17 Meek	N	N	Y	Y	Y	N	Y
18 *Ros-Lehtinen*	Y	Y	Y	N	N	Y	N
19 Wexler	N	N	N	Y	Y	N	Y
20 Deutsch	Y	N	N	Y	Y	N	Y
21 *Diaz-Balart*	Y	Y	Y	N	N	Y	N
22 *Shaw*	Y	Y	Y	N	N	Y	N
23 Hastings	N	N	N	Y	Y	N	N
GEORGIA							
1 *Kingston*	Y	Y	N	N	N	N	N
2 Bishop	N	N	N	N	N	Y	Y
3 *Collins*	Y	Y	Y	N	N	N	N
4 McKinney	N	N	N	Y	Y	N	Y
5 Lewis	N	N	N	?	?	?	?
6 *Gingrich*							
7 *Barr*	Y	Y	Y	N	N	N	N
8 *Chambliss*	Y	Y	Y	N	N	N	N
9 *Deal*	Y	Y	Y	N	N	Y	N
10 *Norwood*	Y	Y	Y	N	N	Y	N
11 *Linder*	?	Y	Y	N	N	Y	N
HAWAII							
1 Abercrombie	N	N	N	Y	Y	N	Y
2 Mink	N	N	N	Y	Y	N	Y
IDAHO							
1 *Chenoweth*	Y	Y	Y	N	N	Y	N
2 *Crapo*	Y	Y	Y	N	N	Y	N
ILLINOIS							
1 Rush	N	N	N	Y	Y	N	Y
2 Jackson	N	N	N	Y	Y	N	Y
3 Lipinski	N	N	N	Y	Y	N	N
4 Gutierrez	N	N	N	Y	Y	N	Y
5 Blagojevich	N	N	N	N	N	N	N
6 *Hyde*	Y	Y	Y	N	N	Y	N
7 Davis	N	N	N	Y	Y	N	Y
8 *Crane*	Y	Y	Y	N	N	Y	N
9 Yates	N	N	N	Y	Y	N	Y
10 *Porter*	Y	Y	Y	N	N	Y	N
11 *Weller*	Y	Y	Y	N	N	Y	N
12 Costello	N	N	N	N	N	N	N

ND Northern Democrats   **SD** Southern Democrats

	216	217	218	219	220	221	222
13 ***Fawell***	Y	Y	Y	N	N	?	N
14 ***Hastert***	Y	Y	Y	N	N	Y	N
15 ***Ewing***	Y	Y	Y	N	N	Y	N
16 ***Manzullo***	Y	Y	Y	N	N	Y	N
17 Evans	N	N	N	Y	Y	N	N
18 ***LaHood***	Y	Y	Y	N	N	Y	N
19 Poshard	N	N	N	Y	Y	N	N
20 ***Shimkus***	Y	Y	Y	N	N	Y	N
INDIANA							
1 Visclosky	N	N	N	Y	Y	N	Y
2 ***McIntosh***	Y	Y	Y	N	N	N	N
3 Roemer	Y	Y	Y	N	N	N	N
4 ***Souder***	Y	Y	Y	Y	N	N	N
5 ***Buyer***	Y	Y	Y	N	N	N	N
6 ***Burton***	Y	Y	Y	N	N	Y	N
7 ***Pease***	Y	Y	Y	N	N	Y	N
8 ***Hostettler***	Y	Y	Y	N	N	Y	N
9 Hamilton	N	N	Y	N	N	N	Y
10 Carson	N	N	N	Y	Y	N	Y
IOWA							
1 ***Leach***	?	Y	Y	N	N	Y	N
2 ***Nussle***	Y	Y	Y	N	N	Y	N
3 Boswell	Y	Y	Y	N	N	Y	N
4 ***Ganske***	Y	Y	Y	N	N	Y	N
5 ***Latham***	Y	Y	Y	N	N	Y	N
KANSAS							
1 ***Moran***	Y	Y	Y	N	N	Y	N
2 ***Ryun***	Y	Y	Y	N	N	Y	N
3 ***Snowbarger***	Y	Y	Y	N	N	Y	N
4 ***Tiahrt***	Y	Y	Y	N	N	Y	N
KENTUCKY							
1 ***Whitfield***	Y	Y	Y	N	N	Y	N
2 ***Lewis***	Y	Y	Y	N	N	Y	N
3 ***Northup***	Y	Y	Y	N	N	Y	N
4 ***Bunning***	Y	Y	Y	N	N	Y	N
5 ***Rogers***	Y	Y	Y	N	N	Y	N
6 Baesler	Y	Y	Y	N	N	N	N
LOUISIANA							
1 ***Livingston***	Y	Y	Y	N	N	Y	N
2 Jefferson	N	N	N	N	Y	N	N
3 ***Tauzin***	Y	Y	Y	N	N	Y	N
4 ***McCrery***	Y	Y	Y	N	N	Y	N
5 ***Cooksey***	Y	Y	Y	N	N	Y	N
6 ***Baker***	Y	Y	Y	N	N	Y	N
7 John	N	N	N	N	Y	Y	N
MAINE							
1 Allen	N	N	N	Y	N	N	Y
2 Baldacci	N	N	N	Y	N	N	Y
MARYLAND							
1 ***Gilchrest***	Y	Y	Y	N	N	N	N
2 ***Ehrlich***	Y	Y	Y	N	N	Y	N
3 Cardin	Y	N	N	Y	N	N	N
4 Wynn	N	N	N	Y	Y	N	N
5 Hoyer	N	N	N	N	Y	N	N
6 ***Bartlett***	Y	Y	Y	N	N	Y	N
7 Cummings	N	N	N	Y	Y	N	N
8 ***Morella***	Y	Y	Y	N	N	N	N
MASSACHUSETTS							
1 Olver	N	?	N	Y	Y	N	Y
2 Neal	N	N	N	Y	Y	N	Y
3 McGovern	N	N	N	Y	Y	N	Y
4 Frank	Y	N	N	N	?	N	N
5 Meehan	N	N	N	Y	Y	N	N
6 Tierney	N	N	N	Y	Y	N	Y
7 Markey	N	N	N	N	Y	N	Y
8 Kennedy	N	N	N	Y	Y	N	N
9 Moakley	?	N	N	Y	Y	N	Y
10 Delahunt	N	N	N	Y	Y	N	Y
MICHIGAN							
1 Stupak	N	N	N	Y	Y	N	Y
2 ***Hoekstra***	Y	Y	Y	N	N	N	N
3 ***Ehlers***	Y	Y	Y	N	N	N	N
4 ***Camp***	Y	Y	Y	N	N	Y	N
5 Barcia	N	N	Y	Y	Y	Y	N
6 ***Upton***	Y	Y	Y	N	N	N	N
7 ***Smith***	Y	Y	Y	N	N	Y	N
8 Stabenow	N	N	N	N	N	N	N
9 Kildee	N	N	N	Y	Y	N	N
10 Bonior	N	N	N	Y	Y	N	Y
11 ***Knollenberg***	Y	Y	Y	N	N	Y	N
12 Levin	N	N	N	Y	Y	N	N
13 Rivers	N	N	N	Y	N	N	Y
14 Conyers	?	N	N	Y	Y	N	Y
15 Kilpatrick	N	N	N	Y	Y	N	Y
16 Dingell	Y	N	Y	Y	N	N	N
MINNESOTA							
1 ***Gutknecht***	Y	Y	Y	N	N	Y	N
2 Minge	N	N	Y	N	Y	N	N
3 ***Ramstad***	Y	Y	Y	N	N	Y	N
4 Vento	N	N	N	Y	Y	N	Y
5 Sabo	N	N	N	N	Y	N	Y
6 Luther	N	N	N	N	Y	N	Y
7 Peterson	Y	Y	Y	N	N	N	N
8 Oberstar	N	N	N	Y	Y	N	N
MISSISSIPPI							
1 ***Wicker***	Y	Y	Y	N	N	Y	N
2 Thompson	N	N	N	Y	Y	N	N
3 ***Pickering***	Y	Y	Y	N	N	Y	N
4 ***Parker***	Y	Y	Y	N	N	Y	N
5 Taylor	N	N	N	N	Y	N	N
MISSOURI							
1 Clay	N	N	N	Y	Y	N	Y
2 ***Talent***	Y	Y	Y	N	N	Y	N
3 Gephardt	N	N	N	Y	Y	N	Y
4 Skelton	N	N	N	N	Y	N	N
5 McCarthy	N	N	N	N	Y	N	Y
6 Danner	N	N	Y	N	Y	N	N
7 ***Blunt***	Y	Y	Y	N	N	Y	N
8 ***Emerson***	Y	Y	Y	N	N	N	N
9 ***Hulshof***	Y	Y	Y	N	N	Y	N
MONTANA							
AL ***Hill***	Y	Y	Y	N	N	Y	N
NEBRASKA							
1 ***Bereuter***	Y	Y	Y	N	N	N	N
2 ***Christensen***	Y	Y	Y	N	N	Y	N
3 ***Barrett***	Y	Y	Y	N	N	Y	N
NEVADA							
1 ***Ensign***	N	Y	Y	N	N	Y	N
2 ***Gibbons***	Y	Y	Y	N	N	Y	N
NEW HAMPSHIRE							
1 ***Sununu***	Y	Y	Y	N	N	Y	Y
2 ***Bass***	Y	Y	Y	N	N	Y	N
NEW JERSEY							
1 Andrews	N	N	N	N	N	Y	N
2 ***LoBiondo***	Y	Y	Y	N	N	N	N
3 ***Saxton***	Y	Y	Y	N	N	N	N
4 ***Smith***	Y	Y	Y	N	N	Y	N
5 ***Roukema***	Y	Y	Y	N	N	N	N
6 Pallone	N	N	N	Y	Y	N	Y
7 ***Franks***	Y	Y	Y	N	N	N	N
8 Pascrell	N	N	N	Y	Y	N	Y
9 Rothman	Y	Y	Y	N	N	N	Y
10 Payne	N	N	N	Y	Y	N	Y
11 ***Frelinghuysen***	Y	Y	Y	N	N	N	N
12 ***Pappas***	Y	Y	Y	N	N	Y	N
13 Menendez	N	N	N	N	N	N	Y
NEW MEXICO							
1 Vacant							
2 ***Skeen***	Y	Y	Y	N	N	Y	N
3 ***Redmond***	Y	Y	Y	N	N	Y	N
NEW YORK							
1 ***Forbes***	Y	Y	Y	N	N	Y	N
2 ***Lazio***	Y	Y	Y	N	N	Y	N
3 ***King***	Y	Y	Y	N	N	Y	N
4 McCarthy	N	N	N	Y	Y	N	Y
5 Ackerman	N	N	N	Y	Y	N	Y
6 Meeks	N	N	N	Y	Y	N	Y
7 Manton	N	N	N	Y	Y	N	Y
8 Nadler	N	N	N	Y	Y	N	N
9 Schumer	N	N	N	?	?	?	?
10 Towns	N	N	N	Y	Y	N	N
11 Owens	N	N	N	Y	Y	N	Y
12 Velázquez	N	N	N	Y	Y	N	Y
13 ***Fossella***	Y	Y	Y	N	N	Y	N
14 Maloney	N	N	N	Y	Y	N	N
15 Rangel	N	N	N	N	Y	N	N
16 Serrano	N	N	N	Y	Y	N	N
17 Engel	N	N	N	Y	Y	N	Y
18 Lowey	N	N	N	Y	Y	N	N
19 ***Kelly***	Y	Y	Y	N	N	Y	N
20 ***Gilman***	+	Y	Y	N	N	Y	N
21 McNulty	N	N	N	Y	Y	N	Y
22 ***Solomon***	Y	Y	Y	N	N	Y	N
23 ***Boehlert***	Y	Y	Y	N	N	N	N
24 ***McHugh***	Y	Y	Y	N	N	Y	N
25 ***Walsh***	Y	Y	Y	N	N	Y	N
26 Hinchey	N	N	N	Y	Y	N	Y
27 ***Paxon***	Y	Y	Y	N	N	Y	N
28 Slaughter	N	N	N	Y	Y	N	N
29 LaFalce	N	N	N	Y	Y	N	Y
30 ***Quinn***	Y	Y	Y	N	N	Y	N
31 ***Houghton***	?	?	?	N	N	N	N
NORTH CAROLINA							
1 Clayton	N	N	N	?	Y	N	Y
2 Etheridge	N	N	N	N	Y	N	N
3 ***Jones***	Y	Y	Y	N	N	Y	N
4 Price	N	N	N	Y	Y	N	N
5 ***Burr***	Y	Y	Y	N	N	Y	N
6 ***Coble***	Y	Y	Y	N	N	Y	N
7 McIntyre	N	N	Y	N	N	Y	N
8 Hefner	N	N	N	Y	Y	N	Y
9 ***Myrick***	Y	Y	Y	N	N	Y	N
10 ***Ballenger***	Y	Y	Y	N	N	Y	N
11 ***Taylor***	Y	Y	Y	N	N	Y	N
12 Watt	N	N	N	Y	Y	N	Y
NORTH DAKOTA							
AL Pomeroy	N	N	N	N	N	N	Y
OHIO							
1 ***Chabot***	Y	Y	Y	N	N	N	N
2 ***Portman***	Y	Y	Y	N	N	Y	N
3 Hall	N	N	N	Y	N	N	N
4 ***Oxley***	?	Y	Y	N	N	Y	N
5 ***Gillmor***	Y	Y	Y	N	N	Y	N
6 Strickland	N	N	N	Y	Y	N	Y
7 ***Hobson***	Y	Y	Y	N	N	N	N
8 ***Boehner***	Y	Y	Y	N	N	Y	N
9 Kaptur	N	N	N	Y	Y	N	Y
10 Kucinich	N	N	N	Y	Y	N	N
11 Stokes	N	N	N	Y	Y	N	Y
12 ***Kasich***	Y	Y	Y	N	N	N	N
13 Brown	N	N	N	Y	Y	N	N
14 Sawyer	Y	N	N	Y	Y	N	N
15 ***Pryce***	Y	Y	Y	N	N	N	N
16 ***Regula***	Y	Y	Y	N	N	N	N
17 Traficant	Y	Y	Y	N	N	Y	N
18 ***Ney***	Y	Y	Y	N	N	Y	N
19 ***LaTourette***	Y	Y	Y	N	N	N	N
OKLAHOMA							
1 ***Largent***	Y	Y	Y	N	N	N	N
2 ***Coburn***	Y	Y	Y	N	Y	Y	N
3 ***Watkins***	Y	Y	Y	N	N	Y	N
4 ***Watts***	Y	Y	Y	N	N	Y	N
5 ***Istook***	Y	Y	Y	N	N	N	N
6 ***Lucas***	Y	Y	Y	N	N	Y	N
OREGON							
1 Furse	N	N	N	Y	Y	N	Y
2 ***Smith***	Y	Y	Y	N	N	Y	N
3 Blumenauer	N	N	N	N	Y	N	?
4 DeFazio	N	N	N	Y	Y	N	Y
5 Hooley	N	N	N	Y	N	N	Y
PENNSYLVANIA							
1 Brady	N	N	N	Y	Y	N	Y
2 Fattah	N	N	N	Y	Y	N	Y
3 Borski	?	N	N	Y	Y	N	N
4 Klink	N	N	N	Y	Y	N	Y
5 ***Peterson***	Y	Y	Y	N	N	Y	N
6 Holden	Y	N	N	N	N	N	Y
7 ***Weldon***	Y	Y	Y	N	N	Y	N
8 ***Greenwood***	Y	Y	Y	N	N	Y	N
9 ***Shuster***	Y	Y	Y	N	N	Y	N
10 ***McDade***	Y	Y	Y	N	N	Y	N
11 Kanjorski	N	N	N	Y	Y	N	Y
12 Murtha	N	N	N	N	Y	N	Y
13 ***Fox***	Y	Y	Y	N	N	N	N
14 Coyne	N	N	N	Y	Y	N	Y
15 McHale	N	N	N	N	N	N	N
16 ***Pitts***	Y	Y	Y	N	N	Y	N
17 ***Gekas***	Y	Y	Y	N	N	Y	N
18 Doyle	N	N	N	Y	Y	N	N
19 ***Goodling***	Y	?	Y	N	N	Y	N
20 Mascara	N	N	N	Y	Y	N	Y
21 ***English***	Y	Y	Y	N	N	Y	N
RHODE ISLAND							
1 Kennedy	Y	N	Y	N	Y	N	N
2 Weygand	Y	N	N	N	Y	N	N
SOUTH CAROLINA							
1 ***Sanford***	Y	Y	Y	Y	N	Y	N
2 ***Spence***	Y	Y	Y	N	N	Y	N
3 ***Graham***	Y	Y	Y	N	N	Y	N
4 ***Inglis***	?	?	?	N	N	Y	N
5 Spratt	N	N	N	N	N	N	Y
6 Clyburn	N	N	N	Y	Y	N	N
SOUTH DAKOTA							
AL ***Thune***	Y	Y	Y	N	N	Y	N
TENNESSEE							
1 ***Jenkins***	Y	Y	Y	N	N	Y	N
2 ***Duncan***	Y	Y	Y	N	N	Y	N
3 ***Wamp***	Y	Y	Y	N	N	Y	N
4 ***Hilleary***	Y	Y	Y	N	N	Y	N
5 Clement	N	N	N	N	N	N	N
6 Gordon	Y	N	N	N	N	N	N
7 ***Bryant***	Y	Y	Y	N	N	Y	N
8 Tanner	N	N	N	N	N	N	N
9 Ford	N	N	N	N	Y	?	Y
TEXAS							
1 Sandlin	N	N	N	N	N	Y	Y
2 Turner	Y	N	N	N	N	Y	N
3 ***Johnson, Sam***	Y	Y	Y	N	N	Y	N
4 Hall	Y	N	N	N	N	Y	N
5 ***Sessions***	Y	Y	Y	N	N	Y	N
6 ***Barton***	Y	Y	Y	N	N	Y	N
7 ***Archer***	Y	Y	Y	N	N	Y	N
8 ***Brady***	Y	+	Y	N	N	Y	N
9 Lampson	N	N	N	Y	Y	Y	Y
10 Doggett	N	N	N	Y	N	Y	Y
11 Edwards	N	N	N	Y	Y	Y	N
12 ***Granger***	Y	Y	Y	N	N	Y	N
13 ***Thornberry***	Y	Y	Y	N	N	Y	N
14 ***Paul***	Y	Y	Y	N	N	Y	N
15 Hinojosa	N	N	N	Y	Y	Y	Y
16 Reyes	N	N	N	Y	Y	Y	Y
17 Stenholm	N	N	N	N	N	Y	N
18 Jackson-Lee	N	N	N	Y	Y	Y	Y
19 ***Combest***	Y	Y	Y	N	N	Y	N
20 Gonzalez	?	?	?	?	?	?	?
21 ***Smith***	Y	Y	Y	N	N	Y	N
22 ***DeLay***	Y	Y	Y	N	N	Y	N
23 ***Bonilla***	Y	Y	Y	N	N	Y	N
24 Frost	Y	N	Y	N	N	Y	N
25 Bentsen	N	N	N	N	N	Y	Y
26 ***Armey***	Y	Y	Y	N	N	Y	N
27 Ortiz	N	N	N	Y	Y	Y	Y
28 Rodriguez	N	N	N	Y	Y	Y	N
29 Green	N	N	N	Y	Y	Y	Y
30 Johnson, E.B.	N	N	N	Y	Y	Y	N
UTAH							
1 ***Hansen***	Y	Y	Y	N	N	Y	N
2 ***Cook***	?	Y	Y	N	N	Y	N
3 ***Cannon***	Y	Y	Y	N	N	Y	N
VERMONT							
AL *Sanders*	N	N	N	Y	Y	N	Y
VIRGINIA							
1 ***Bateman***	Y	Y	Y	N	N	Y	N
2 Pickett	?	N	N	N	N	Y	Y
3 Scott	N	N	N	Y	Y	N	Y
4 Sisisky	Y	N	Y	N	N	Y	Y
5 Goode	Y	Y	Y	N	N	Y	N
6 ***Goodlatte***	Y	Y	Y	N	N	Y	N
7 ***Bliley***	Y	Y	Y	N	N	Y	N
8 Moran	Y	Y	Y	N	N	N	N
9 Boucher	Y	Y	Y	N	N	Y	N
10 ***Wolf***	Y	Y	N	N	N	Y	N
11 ***Davis***	Y	Y	Y	N	N	Y	N
WASHINGTON							
1 ***White***	Y	Y	Y	N	N	Y	N
2 ***Metcalf***	Y	Y	Y	N	N	N	N
3 ***Smith, Linda***	Y	Y	Y	N	N	Y	N
4 ***Hastings***	Y	Y	Y	N	N	Y	N
5 ***Nethercutt***	Y	Y	Y	N	N	Y	N
6 Dicks	N	N	Y	Y	Y	N	N
7 McDermott	–	N	N	Y	Y	N	N
8 ***Dunn***	Y	?	Y	N	N	N	N
9 Smith, Adam	Y	Y	Y	N	N	N	Y
WEST VIRGINIA							
1 Mollohan	N	N	N	Y	Y	Y	Y
2 Wise	N	N	N	Y	Y	N	N
3 Rahall	N	N	N	Y	Y	Y	N
WISCONSIN							
1 ***Neumann***	Y	Y	Y	N	N	Y	N
2 ***Klug***	?	?	?	N	N	Y	N
3 Kind	N	Y	Y	N	N	N	Y
4 Kleczka	Y	Y	Y	N	N	N	Y
5 Barrett	N	N	N	N	Y	N	Y
6 ***Petri***	Y	Y	Y	N	N	N	N
7 Obey	N	N	N	N	Y	N	N
8 Johnson	N	N	N	N	Y	N	N
9 ***Sensenbrenner***	?	?	Y	N	N	N	Y
WYOMING							
AL ***Cubin***	Y	Y	Y	N	N	Y	N

Southern states - Ala., Ark., Fla., Ga., Ky., La., Miss., N.C., Okla., S.C., Tenn., Texas, Va.

223. HR 3150. Bankruptcy Overhaul/Democratic Substitute. Nadler, D-N.Y., substitute amendment to strike the bill's provisions regarding means-testing; requiring "adequate" income be committed to a repayment plan for unsecured creditors; and defining abuse of the bankruptcy system. Rejected 140-288: R 0-226; D 139-62 (ND 119-29, SD 20-33); I 1-0. June 10, 1998.

224. HR 3150. Bankruptcy Overhaul/Recommit. Conyers, D-Mich., motion to recommit the bill to the Judiciary Committee with instructions to report it back with an amendment to exclude child support and alimony payments from means-tests and to make accident victims priority creditors. Motion rejected 153-270: R 1-221; D 151-49 (ND 117-30, SD 34-19); I 1-0. June 10, 1998.

225. HR 3150. Bankruptcy Overhaul/Passage. Passage of the bill to overhaul the nation's bankruptcy laws by setting up a means-testing system to bar individuals with average incomes or higher from declaring bankruptcy under Chapter 7, and thus walking away from unsecured debts after the liquidation of certain assets. The bill also allows creditors, in addition to bankruptcy trustees, to challenge the validity of an individual's claim; and requires that debtors be informed of the various forms of bankruptcy relief before they file for bankruptcy. Passed 306-118: R 222-0; D 84-117 (ND 53-95, SD 31-22); I 0-1. June 10, 1998.

226. H J Res 119. Campaign Spending Constitutional Amendment/Passage. Passage of the joint resolution to propose a constitutional amendment to permit Congress and the states to go beyond court-set limits on the government's right to regulate campaign expenditures and contributions, as long as these regulations do not impair the public's right to a full and free discussion of all issues. Rejected 29-345: R 6-220; D 23-124 (ND 19-84, SD 4-40); I 0-1. June 11, 1998. A two-thirds majority vote of those present and voting (250 in this case) is required to pass a joint resolution proposing an amendment to the Constitution.

227. HR 2888. Compensation for Sales Employees/Requiring Overtime. Owens, D-N.Y., amendment to prohibit employers from requiring employees affected by the bill from working more than eight hours a day or 40 hours a week without the employee's consent. Rejected 181-246: R 1-225; D 179-21 (ND 138-11, SD 41-10); I 1-0. June 11, 1998.

228. HR 2888. Compensation for Sales Employees/Passage. Passage of the bill to provide an exemption from minimum wage and overtime laws for certain commission-earning sales employees who earn above a defined threshold per year. Passed 261-165: R 218-7; D 43-157 (ND 22-127, SD 21-30); I 0-1. June 11, 1998. A "nay" was a vote in support of the president's position.

229. HR 3494. Sexual Predator Punishment/National Hotline. Sherman, D-Calif., amendment to establish a national hotline for parents to access FBI databases and determine if an individual is registered as a convicted sexual predator. Adopted 247-175: R 124-98; D 123-76 (ND 94-53, SD 29-23); I 0-1. June 11, 1998.

Key

Y	Voted for (yea).
#	Paired for.
+	Announced for.
N	Voted against (nay).
X	Paired against.
–	Announced against.
P	Voted "present."
C	Voted "present" to avoid possible conflict of interest.
?	Did not vote or otherwise make a position known.

Democrats *Republicans* Independent

	223	224	225	226	227	228	229
ALABAMA							
1 *Callahan*	N	N	Y	N	N	Y	N
2 *Everett*	N	N	Y	N	N	Y	N
3 *Riley*	N	N	Y	N	N	Y	Y
4 *Aderholt*	N	N	Y	N	N	Y	N
5 Cramer	N	N	Y	?	N	Y	N
6 *Bachus*	N	N	Y	N	N	Y	N
7 Hilliard	Y	Y	N	N	Y	N	–
ALASKA							
AL *Young*	N	N	Y	N	N	Y	Y
ARIZONA							
1 *Salmon*	N	N	Y	N	N	Y	Y
2 Pastor	Y	Y	Y	N	Y	N	Y
3 *Stump*	N	N	Y	N	N	Y	N
4 *Shadegg*	N	N	Y	N	N	Y	N
5 *Kolbe*	N	N	Y	N	N	Y	N
6 *Hayworth*	N	N	Y	N	N	Y	N
ARKANSAS							
1 Berry	N	N	Y	N	Y	N	Y
2 Snyder	N	N	Y	N	Y	N	N
3 *Hutchinson*	N	N	Y	N	N	Y	N
4 *Dickey*	N	N	Y	N	N	Y	Y
CALIFORNIA							
1 *Riggs*	N	N	Y	N	N	Y	Y
2 *Herger*	N	N	Y	N	N	Y	Y
3 Fazio	Y	N	Y	N	Y	N	Y
4 *Doolittle*	N	N	Y	N	N	Y	N
5 Matsui	Y	Y	N	N	N	N	N
6 Woolsey	Y	Y	N	P	N	Y	N
7 Miller	Y	Y	N	P	Y	N	N
8 Pelosi	Y	Y	N	N	Y	N	N
9 Lee	Y	Y	N	N	Y	N	N
10 Tauscher	N	N	Y	P	N	Y	N
11 *Pombo*	Y	Y	N	N	N	Y	N
12 Lantos	Y	Y	N	N	Y	N	N
13 Stark	Y	Y	N	N	Y	N	N
14 Eshoo	Y	Y	N	P	Y	N	N
15 *Campbell*	N	N	Y	N	N	Y	Y
16 Lofgren	Y	Y	N	N	Y	N	N
17 Farr	+	+	–	–	–	–	–
18 Condit	N	N	Y	N	N	Y	Y
19 *Radanovich*	N	N	Y	N	N	Y	Y
20 Dooley	N	N	Y	N	N	Y	N
21 *Thomas*	N	N	Y	N	N	Y	Y
22 Capps, L.	Y	Y	Y	N	Y	Y	Y
23 *Gallegly*	N	N	Y	N	N	Y	Y
24 Sherman	N	N	Y	N	N	Y	Y
25 *McKeon*	N	N	Y	N	N	Y	Y
26 Berman	?	?	?	?	?	?	?
27 *Rogan*	N	N	Y	N	N	Y	Y
28 *Dreier*	N	N	Y	N	N	Y	Y
29 Waxman	Y	Y	N	P	N	Y	N
30 Becerra	Y	Y	N	P	Y	N	?
31 Martinez	Y	Y	N	N	Y	N	N
32 Dixon	Y	Y	N	N	Y	N	N
33 Roybal-Allard	Y	Y	N	N	Y	N	N
34 Torres	Y	Y	N	N	Y	N	N
35 Waters	Y	Y	N	N	Y	N	N
36 Harman	Y	Y	N	N	Y	N	N
37 Millender-McD.	Y	Y	N	N	Y	N	N

	223	224	225	226	227	228	229
38 *Horn*	N	N	Y	N	N	Y	Y
39 *Royce*	N	N	Y	N	N	Y	Y
40 *Lewis*	N	N	Y	N	?	Y	Y
41 *Kim*	N	N	Y	N	N	Y	N
42 Brown	Y	Y	N	N	Y	N	Y
43 *Calvert*	N	N	Y	N	N	Y	Y
44 *Bono, M.*	N	N	Y	N	N	N	Y
45 *Rohrabacher*	N	N	Y	N	N	Y	N
46 Sanchez	Y	Y	N	P	Y	N	Y
47 *Cox*	N	?	Y	N	N	Y	Y
48 *Packard*	N	N	Y	N	N	Y	Y
49 *Bilbray*	N	N	Y	N	N	Y	Y
50 Filner	Y	Y	N	N	Y	N	Y
51 *Cunningham*	N	N	Y	N	N	Y	Y
52 *Hunter*	N	N	Y	N	N	Y	N
COLORADO							
1 DeGette	Y	Y	N	N	Y	N	N
2 Skaggs	Y	Y	N	N	Y	N	N
3 *McInnis*	N	N	Y	N	N	Y	Y
4 *Schaffer*	N	N	Y	N	N	Y	N
5 *Hefley*	N	N	Y	N	N	Y	Y
6 *Schaefer*	N	N	Y	N	N	Y	Y
CONNECTICUT							
1 Kennelly	Y	Y	Y	N	Y	N	Y
2 Gejdenson	Y	Y	N	N	Y	N	Y
3 DeLauro	Y	Y	N	P	Y	N	Y
4 *Shays*	N	N	Y	N	N	Y	+
5 Maloney	N	N	Y	P	Y	N	Y
6 *Johnson*	N	N	Y	N	Y	Y	Y
DELAWARE							
AL *Castle*	N	N	Y	N	N	Y	N
FLORIDA							
1 *Scarborough*	N	N	Y	N	N	Y	Y
2 Boyd	N	N	Y	–	–	+	N
3 Brown	Y	Y	N	N	Y	N	Y
4 *Fowler*	N	N	Y	N	N	Y	Y
5 Thurman	N	Y	N	P	Y	N	Y
6 *Stearns*	N	N	Y	N	N	Y	Y
7 *Mica*	N	N	Y	N	N	Y	N
8 *McCollum*	N	N	Y	N	N	Y	Y
9 *Bilirakis*	N	N	Y	N	N	Y	Y
10 *Young*	N	N	Y	N	N	Y	N
11 Davis	N	N	Y	N	N	Y	N
12 *Canady*	N	N	Y	N	N	Y	N
13 *Miller*	N	N	Y	N	N	Y	N
14 *Goss*	N	N	Y	N	N	Y	N
15 *Weldon*	N	N	Y	N	N	Y	Y
16 *Foley*	N	N	Y	N	N	Y	N
17 Meek	Y	Y	N	N	Y	N	N
18 *Ros-Lehtinen*	N	N	Y	N	N	Y	N
19 Wexler	N	N	Y	P	Y	N	N
20 Deutsch	N	N	Y	P	Y	N	N
21 *Diaz-Balart*	N	N	Y	N	N	Y	N
22 *Shaw*	N	N	Y	N	N	Y	Y
23 Hastings	Y	Y	N	N	Y	N	N
GEORGIA							
1 *Kingston*	N	N	Y	N	N	Y	N
2 Bishop	Y	Y	Y	N	Y	N	Y
3 *Collins*	N	N	Y	N	N	Y	N
4 McKinney	Y	Y	N	N	Y	N	N
5 Lewis	?	?	?	?	?	?	?
6 *Gingrich*							
7 *Barr*	N	N	Y	N	N	Y	N
8 *Chambliss*	N	N	Y	N	N	Y	Y
9 *Deal*	N	N	Y	N	N	Y	N
10 *Norwood*	N	N	Y	N	N	Y	N
11 *Linder*	N	N	Y	N	N	Y	N
HAWAII							
1 Abercrombie	Y	Y	N	P	Y	N	Y
2 Mink	Y	Y	N	N	Y	N	N
IDAHO							
1 *Chenoweth*	N	N	Y	N	N	Y	Y
2 *Crapo*	N	N	Y	N	N	Y	Y
ILLINOIS							
1 Rush	Y	Y	N	N	Y	N	N
2 Jackson	Y	Y	N	N	Y	N	N
3 Lipinski	N	N	Y	Y	Y	Y	N
4 Gutierrez	Y	Y	N	P	Y	N	Y
5 Blagojevich	N	N	Y	P	Y	N	Y
6 *Hyde*	N	N	Y	N	N	Y	N
7 Davis	Y	Y	N	N	Y	N	N
8 *Crane*	N	N	Y	N	N	Y	N
9 Yates	Y	Y	N	N	Y	N	Y
10 *Porter*	N	N	Y	N	N	Y	N
11 *Weller*	N	N	Y	N	N	Y	N
12 Costello	N	Y	N	N	Y	N	Y

ND Northern Democrats   SD Southern Democrats

	223	224	225	226	227	228	229
13 **Fawell**	N	?	Y	N	N	Y	Y
14 **Hastert**	N	?	Y	N	N	Y	N
15 **Ewing**	N	N	Y	N	N	Y	N
16 **Manzullo**	N	N	Y	N	N	Y	Y
17 Evans	Y	Y	N	N	Y	N	Y
18 **LaHood**	N	N	Y	N	N	Y	N
19 Poshard	Y	Y	N	Y	Y	N	Y
20 **Shimkus**	N	N	Y	N	N	Y	Y
INDIANA							
1 Visclosky	Y	Y	N	N	Y	N	N
2 **McIntosh**	N	N	Y	N	N	Y	N
3 Roemer	N	N	Y	N	N	Y	Y
4 **Souder**	N	N	Y	N	N	Y	Y
5 **Buyer**	N	N	Y	N	N	Y	N
6 **Burton**	N	N	Y	N	N	Y	Y
7 **Pease**	N	N	Y	N	N	Y	Y
8 **Hostettler**	N	N	Y	N	N	Y	Y
9 Hamilton	N	N	Y	N	N	N	N
10 Carson	Y	Y	N	N	Y	N	Y
IOWA							
1 **Leach**	N	N	Y	Y	N	Y	Y
2 **Nussle**	N	N	Y	N	N	Y	Y
3 Boswell	N	N	Y	N	N	Y	Y
4 **Ganske**	N	N	Y	N	N	Y	Y
5 **Latham**	N	N	Y	N	N	Y	Y
KANSAS							
1 **Moran**	N	N	Y	N	N	Y	Y
2 **Ryun**	N	N	Y	N	N	Y	Y
3 **Snowbarger**	N	N	Y	N	N	Y	Y
4 **Tiahrt**	N	N	Y	N	N	Y	Y
KENTUCKY							
1 **Whitfield**	N	N	Y	N	N	Y	Y
2 **Lewis**	N	N	Y	N	N	Y	Y
3 **Northup**	N	N	Y	N	N	Y	N
4 **Bunning**	N	N	Y	N	N	Y	Y
5 **Rogers**	N	N	Y	N	N	Y	N
6 Baesler	N	N	Y	N	Y	N	Y
LOUISIANA							
1 **Livingston**	N	N	Y	N	N	Y	N
2 Jefferson	Y	Y	Y	N	Y	N	Y
3 **Tauzin**	N	N	Y	N	N	Y	N
4 **McCrery**	N	N	Y	N	N	Y	N
5 **Cooksey**	N	N	Y	N	N	Y	N
6 **Baker**	N	N	Y	N	N	Y	N
7 John	N	N	Y	N	N	Y	Y
MAINE							
1 Allen	Y	Y	N	N	Y	N	Y
2 Baldacci	Y	Y	Y	N	Y	N	Y
MARYLAND							
1 **Gilchrest**	N	N	Y	N	N	Y	N
2 **Ehrlich**	N	N	Y	N	N	Y	N
3 Cardin	N	Y	Y	P	Y	N	N
4 Wynn	Y	N	Y	N	Y	N	Y
5 Hoyer	N	N	Y	P	Y	N	Y
6 **Bartlett**	N	N	Y	N	N	Y	Y
7 Cummings	Y	Y	Y	N	Y	N	Y
8 **Morella**	N	N	Y	N	N	Y	Y
MASSACHUSETTS							
1 Olver	Y	Y	N	N	Y	N	Y
2 Neal	Y	Y	N	P	Y	N	Y
3 McGovern	Y	Y	N	P	Y	N	Y
4 Frank	N	N	Y	P	Y	N	N
5 Meehan	Y	Y	N	P	Y	N	Y
6 Tierney	Y	Y	N	P	Y	N	Y
7 Markey	Y	Y	N	N	Y	N	Y
8 Kennedy	Y	Y	N	Y	Y	N	Y
9 Moakley	Y	Y	N	P	Y	N	?
10 Delahunt	Y	Y	N	P	Y	N	N
MICHIGAN							
1 Stupak	Y	Y	N	Y	Y	N	N
2 **Hoekstra**	N	N	Y	N	N	Y	Y
3 **Ehlers**	N	N	Y	N	N	Y	N
4 **Camp**	N	N	Y	N	N	Y	Y
5 Barcia	N	Y	Y	N	Y	N	Y
6 **Upton**	N	N	Y	N	N	Y	Y
7 **Smith**	N	N	Y	N	N	Y	N
8 Stabenow	Y	Y	Y	P	Y	Y	N
9 Kildee	Y	Y	N	N	Y	N	Y
10 Bonior	Y	Y	N	P	Y	N	N
11 **Knollenberg**	N	N	Y	N	N	Y	N
12 Levin	Y	Y	N	P	Y	N	Y
13 Rivers	Y	Y	Y	N	Y	Y	Y
14 Conyers	Y	Y	N	N	Y	N	N
15 Kilpatrick	Y	Y	N	N	Y	N	N
16 Dingell	Y	Y	N	Y	Y	N	N

	223	224	225	226	227	228	229
MINNESOTA							
1 **Gutknecht**	N	N	Y	N	N	Y	N
2 Minge	Y	Y	Y	Y	Y	Y	Y
3 **Ramstad**	N	N	Y	N	N	Y	Y
4 Vento	Y	Y	N	Y	Y	N	N
5 Sabo	Y	Y	N	N	Y	N	N
6 Luther	Y	Y	Y	Y	Y	Y	Y
7 Peterson	N	N	Y	N	Y	Y	Y
8 Oberstar	Y	Y	N	N	Y	N	Y
MISSISSIPPI							
1 **Wicker**	N	N	Y	N	N	Y	Y
2 Thompson	Y	Y	N	N	Y	N	N
3 **Pickering**	N	N	Y	N	N	Y	Y
4 **Parker**	N	N	Y	N	N	Y	?
5 Taylor	N	N	Y	N	N	N	Y
MISSOURI							
1 Clay	Y	Y	N	N	Y	N	N
2 **Talent**	N	N	Y	N	N	Y	Y
3 Gephardt	Y	Y	N	P	Y	N	Y
4 Skelton	N	N	Y	N	Y	N	Y
5 McCarthy	Y	Y	Y	P	Y	Y	Y
6 Danner	N	N	Y	N	Y	Y	Y
7 **Blunt**	N	N	Y	N	N	Y	N
8 **Emerson**	N	N	Y	N	N	Y	Y
9 **Hulshof**	N	N	Y	N	N	Y	Y
MONTANA							
AL **Hill**	N	N	Y	N	N	Y	Y
NEBRASKA							
1 **Bereuter**	N	N	Y	Y	N	Y	Y
2 **Christensen**	N	N	Y	N	N	Y	Y
3 **Barrett**	N	N	Y	N	N	Y	Y
NEVADA							
1 **Ensign**	N	Y	Y	N	N	Y	Y
2 **Gibbons**	N	N	Y	N	N	Y	Y
NEW HAMPSHIRE							
1 **Sununu**	N	N	Y	N	N	Y	Y
2 **Bass**	N	N	Y	N	N	Y	N
NEW JERSEY							
1 Andrews	N	N	Y	N	N	Y	Y
2 **LoBiondo**	N	N	Y	N	N	Y	Y
3 **Saxton**	N	N	Y	N	N	Y	Y
4 **Smith**	N	N	Y	N	N	Y	Y
5 **Roukema**	N	N	Y	N	N	Y	Y
6 Pallone	Y	Y	N	P	Y	N	Y
7 **Franks**	N	N	Y	N	N	Y	Y
8 Pascrell	Y	Y	Y	N	Y	N	Y
9 Rothman	N	N	Y	P	Y	N	Y
10 Payne	Y	Y	N	N	Y	N	Y
11 **Frelinghuysen**	N	N	Y	N	N	Y	Y
12 **Pappas**	N	N	Y	N	N	Y	Y
13 Menendez	N	N	Y	P	Y	N	Y
NEW MEXICO							
1 Vacant							
2 **Skeen**	N	N	Y	N	N	Y	Y
3 **Redmond**	N	N	+	N	N	Y	Y
NEW YORK							
1 **Forbes**	N	N	Y	N	N	Y	Y
2 **Lazio**	N	N	Y	N	N	Y	Y
3 **King**	N	N	Y	N	N	Y	N
4 McCarthy	Y	Y	Y	N	N	Y	Y
5 Ackerman	Y	Y	N	N	Y	N	Y
6 Meeks	Y	Y	N	N	Y	N	N
7 Manton	Y	Y	N	N	Y	N	Y
8 Nadler	Y	Y	N	P	Y	N	Y
9 Schumer	?	?	?	?	Y	N	Y
10 Towns	Y	Y	Y	N	Y	N	Y
11 Owens	Y	Y	N	N	Y	N	N
12 Velázquez	Y	Y	Y	N	Y	N	Y
13 **Fossella**	N	N	Y	N	N	Y	Y
14 Maloney	Y	Y	N	P	Y	N	Y
15 Rangel	Y	Y	N	N	Y	N	N
16 Serrano	Y	Y	N	N	Y	N	Y
17 Engel	Y	Y	N	N	Y	N	Y
18 Lowey	Y	Y	N	P	Y	N	Y
19 **Kelly**	N	N	Y	N	N	Y	Y
20 **Gilman**	N	N	Y	N	N	N	Y
21 McNulty	Y	Y	N	N	Y	N	Y
22 **Solomon**	N	N	Y	N	N	Y	Y
23 **Boehlert**	N	N	Y	N	N	N	N
24 **McHugh**	N	N	Y	N	N	Y	Y
25 **Walsh**	N	N	Y	N	N	Y	Y
26 Hinchey	Y	Y	N	N	Y	N	Y
27 **Paxon**	N	N	Y	N	N	Y	?
28 Slaughter	Y	Y	N	P	Y	N	Y
29 LaFalce	Y	Y	N	Y	Y	N	Y

	223	224	225	226	227	228	229
30 **Quinn**	N	N	Y	N	N	Y	Y
31 **Houghton**	N	N	Y	N	N	Y	N
NORTH CAROLINA							
1 Clayton	Y	Y	N	N	Y	N	Y
2 Etheridge	Y	Y	Y	–	+	–	Y
3 **Jones**	N	N	Y	N	N	Y	Y
4 Price	Y	Y	Y	N	Y	Y	Y
5 **Burr**	N	N	Y	N	N	Y	N
6 **Coble**	N	N	Y	N	N	Y	N
7 McIntyre	N	Y	Y	N	Y	Y	Y
8 Hefner	Y	Y	N	N	Y	N	N
9 **Myrick**	N	N	Y	N	N	Y	N
10 **Ballenger**	N	N	Y	N	N	Y	N
11 **Taylor**	N	N	Y	N	N	Y	Y
12 Watt	Y	Y	N	N	Y	N	N
NORTH DAKOTA							
AL Pomeroy	Y	Y	Y	P	Y	N	Y
OHIO							
1 **Chabot**	N	N	Y	N	N	Y	Y
2 **Portman**	N	N	Y	N	N	Y	N
3 Hall	Y	Y	N	N	Y	N	N
4 **Oxley**	N	N	Y	N	N	Y	N
5 **Gillmor**	N	N	Y	Y	N	Y	N
6 Strickland	Y	Y	Y	N	Y	N	Y
7 **Hobson**	N	N	+	N	N	Y	N
8 **Boehner**	N	N	Y	N	N	Y	N
9 Kaptur	Y	Y	N	P	Y	N	Y
10 Kucinich	Y	Y	N	P	Y	N	Y
11 Stokes	Y	Y	N	N	Y	N	N
12 **Kasich**	N	N	Y	N	N	Y	N
13 Brown	Y	Y	N	P	Y	N	Y
14 Sawyer	Y	Y	N	P	Y	N	Y
15 **Pryce**	N	N	Y	N	N	Y	Y
16 **Regula**	N	N	Y	N	N	Y	N
17 Traficant	N	N	Y	N	N	Y	Y
18 **Ney**	N	N	Y	N	N	Y	Y
19 **LaTourette**	N	N	Y	N	N	Y	Y
OKLAHOMA							
1 **Largent**	N	?	?	N	N	Y	Y
2 **Coburn**	N	N	Y	N	N	Y	N
3 **Watkins**	N	N	Y	N	N	Y	Y
4 **Watts**	N	N	Y	N	N	Y	Y
5 **Istook**	N	N	Y	N	N	Y	Y
6 **Lucas**	N	N	Y	N	N	Y	Y
OREGON							
1 Furse	Y	Y	N	P	Y	N	Y
2 **Smith**	N	N	Y	N	N	Y	N
3 Blumenauer	Y	Y	Y	N	Y	N	N
4 DeFazio	Y	Y	N	Y	Y	N	Y
5 Hooley	Y	Y	Y	N	Y	N	Y
PENNSYLVANIA							
1 Brady	Y	Y	N	P	Y	N	N
2 Fattah	Y	Y	N	P	Y	N	N
3 Borski	Y	Y	N	P	Y	N	Y
4 Klink	Y	Y	N	N	Y	N	Y
5 **Peterson**	N	N	Y	N	N	Y	Y
6 Holden	Y	Y	Y	Y	Y	Y	Y
7 **Weldon**	N	N	Y	N	N	Y	Y
8 **Greenwood**	N	N	Y	N	N	Y	N
9 **Shuster**	N	N	Y	N	N	Y	N
10 **McDade**	N	N	Y	N	N	N	N
11 Kanjorski	Y	Y	N	P	Y	N	N
12 Murtha	Y	N	N	N	Y	N	N
13 **Fox**	N	N	Y	N	N	Y	Y
14 Coyne	Y	Y	N	P	Y	N	N
15 McHale	Y	Y	Y	N	Y	N	Y
16 **Pitts**	N	N	Y	N	N	Y	N
17 **Gekas**	N	N	Y	N	N	Y	N
18 Doyle	Y	Y	N	Y	Y	N	Y
19 **Goodling**	N	N	Y	N	N	Y	Y
20 Mascara	Y	Y	N	N	Y	N	Y
21 **English**	N	N	Y	N	Y	N	Y
RHODE ISLAND							
1 Kennedy	N	N	Y	Y	Y	N	Y
2 Weygand	N	N	Y	N	Y	N	Y
SOUTH CAROLINA							
1 **Sanford**	N	N	Y	N	N	Y	N
2 **Spence**	N	N	Y	N	N	Y	N
3 **Graham**	N	N	Y	N	N	Y	Y
4 **Inglis**	N	N	Y	N	N	Y	?
5 Spratt	N	Y	Y	N	Y	N	Y
6 Clyburn	Y	Y	Y	N	Y	N	Y
SOUTH DAKOTA							
AL **Thune**	N	N	Y	N	N	Y	Y

	223	224	225	226	227	228	229
TENNESSEE							
1 **Jenkins**	N	N	Y	N	N	Y	Y
2 **Duncan**	N	N	Y	N	N	Y	N
3 **Wamp**	N	N	Y	N	N	Y	Y
4 **Hilleary**	N	N	Y	N	N	Y	Y
5 Clement	N	N	Y	N	Y	Y	N
6 Gordon	N	N	Y	P	Y	Y	Y
7 **Bryant**	N	N	Y	N	N	Y	Y
8 Tanner	N	N	Y	N	N	Y	N
9 Ford	Y	Y	N	Y	Y	N	Y
TEXAS							
1 Sandlin	N	Y	Y	Y	Y	N	Y
2 Turner	N	N	Y	N	Y	Y	Y
3 **Johnson, Sam**	N	N	Y	N	N	Y	N
4 Hall	N	N	Y	N	N	Y	Y
5 **Sessions**	N	N	Y	N	N	Y	N
6 **Barton**	N	N	Y	N	N	Y	N
7 **Archer**	N	N	Y	N	N	Y	N
8 **Brady**	N	N	+	N	N	Y	Y
9 Lampson	N	Y	N	N	Y	N	N
10 Doggett	N	Y	Y	N	Y	Y	Y
11 Edwards	N	Y	N	N	Y	N	N
12 **Granger**	N	N	Y	N	N	Y	N
13 **Thornberry**	N	N	Y	N	N	Y	N
14 **Paul**	N	N	Y	N	N	Y	N
15 Hinojosa	Y	Y	N	N	Y	Y	Y
16 Reyes	Y	Y	N	N	Y	N	Y
17 Stenholm	N	N	Y	N	N	Y	Y
18 Jackson-Lee	N	Y	N	P	Y	N	Y
19 **Combest**	N	N	Y	N	N	Y	N
20 Gonzalez	?	?	?	?	?	?	?
21 **Smith**	N	N	Y	N	N	Y	N
22 **DeLay**	N	N	Y	N	N	Y	N
23 **Bonilla**	N	N	Y	N	N	Y	N
24 Frost	N	Y	Y	P	Y	N	Y
25 Bentsen	N	Y	Y	N	Y	Y	Y
26 **Armey**	N	N	Y	N	N	Y	N
27 Ortiz	Y	Y	N	N	Y	N	Y
28 Rodriguez	N	Y	N	N	Y	N	Y
29 Green	N	Y	N	Y	Y	N	Y
30 Johnson, E.B.	N	Y	N	N	Y	N	N
UTAH							
1 **Hansen**	N	N	Y	N	N	Y	Y
2 **Cook**	N	N	Y	N	N	Y	Y
3 **Cannon**	N	N	Y	N	N	Y	Y
VERMONT							
AL *Sanders*	Y	Y	N	N	Y	N	N
VIRGINIA							
1 **Bateman**	N	N	Y	N	N	Y	N
2 Pickett	N	N	Y	N	N	Y	N
3 Scott	Y	Y	N	N	Y	N	N
4 Sisisky	N	N	Y	N	N	Y	N
5 Goode	N	N	Y	N	N	Y	Y
6 **Goodlatte**	N	N	Y	N	N	Y	Y
7 **Bliley**	N	N	Y	N	N	Y	N
8 Moran	N	Y	Y	Y	Y	Y	N
9 Boucher	N	N	Y	N	Y	N	N
10 **Wolf**	N	N	Y	N	N	Y	N
11 **Davis**	N	N	Y	N	N	Y	N
WASHINGTON							
1 **White**	N	N	Y	N	N	Y	N
2 **Metcalf**	N	N	Y	N	N	Y	Y
3 **Smith, Linda**	N	N	Y	N	N	Y	N
4 **Hastings**	N	N	Y	N	N	Y	N
5 **Nethercutt**	N	N	Y	N	N	Y	N
6 Dicks	Y	?	Y	N	Y	N	N
7 McDermott	Y	Y	N	N	Y	N	N
8 **Dunn**	N	N	Y	N	N	Y	N
9 Smith, Adam	N	N	Y	Y	Y	N	Y
WEST VIRGINIA							
1 Mollohan	N	N	Y	N	Y	N	N
2 Wise	Y	Y	Y	P	Y	N	Y
3 Rahall	Y	Y	N	N	Y	N	N
WISCONSIN							
1 **Neumann**	N	N	Y	N	N	Y	Y
2 **Klug**	N	N	Y	N	N	Y	N
3 Kind	N	N	Y	N	N	Y	N
4 Kleczka	N	N	Y	N	Y	N	Y
5 Barrett	N	Y	N	Y	Y	N	N
6 **Petri**	N	N	Y	N	N	Y	Y
7 Obey	Y	Y	N	Y	Y	N	N
8 Johnson	Y	Y	Y	N	N	Y	Y
9 **Sensenbrenner**	N	N	Y	N	N	Y	N
WYOMING							
AL **Cubin**	N	N	Y	N	N	Y	Y

Southern states - Ala., Ark., Fla., Ga., Ky., La., Miss., N.C., Okla., S.C., Tenn., Texas, Va.

Key

Y	Voted for (yea).
#	Paired for.
+	Announced for.
N	Voted against (nay).
X	Paired against.
−	Announced against.
P	Voted "present."
C	Voted "present" to avoid possible conflict of interest.
?	Did not vote or otherwise make a position known.

● Democrats **Republicans** *Independent*

230. HR 3494. Sexual Predator Punishment/Passage. Passage of the bill to establish or increase penalties for Internet-based sex crimes against minors, as well as sentencing guidelines for crimes against children. Passed 416-0: R 218-0; D 197-0 (ND 145-0, SD 52-0); I 1-0. June 11, 1998.

231. James Byrd Resolution/Adoption. Adoption of the resolution to condemn the brutal killing of James Byrd Jr., in Jasper, Texas. Adopted 397-0: R 208-0; D 188-0 (ND 137-0, SD 51-0); I 1-0. June 11, 1998.

232. HR 1847. Telemarketing Fraud/Agreeing to Senate Amendment. Goodlatte, R-Va., motion to suspend the rules and agree to the Senate amendment changing specific sentencing requirements to a "substantial increase in penalties" for persons convicted of telemarketing fraud. The bill would increase penalties and require convicted persons to forfeit property used in telemarketing scams. Motion agreed to (thus clearing the bill for the president) 411-1: R 218-1; D 192-0 (ND 143-0, SD 49-0); I1-0. June 16, 1998. A two-thirds majority of those present and voting (275 in this case) is required for adoption under suspension of the rules.

233. H Res 401. Social Promotion/Adoption. Riggs, R-Calif., motion to suspend the rules and adopt the resolution to express the sense of the House that government officials, teachers and parents should encourage schools to promote students solely based on academic performance. Motion agreed to 405-1: R 217-0; D 187-1 (ND 140-1, SD 47-0); I 1-0. June 16, 1998. A two-thirds majority of those present and voting (271 in this case) is required for adoption under suspension of the rules.

234. HR 3097. Tax Code Termination/Previous Question. Hastings, R-Wash., motion to order the previous question (thus ending debate and the possibility of amendment) on the adoption of the rule (H Res 472) to provide for House floor consideration of the bill to terminate the tax code. Motion agreed to 229-194: R 220-0; D 9-193 (ND 4-146, SD 5-47); I 0-1. June 17, 1998. (Subsequently, the rule was adopted.)

235. HR 3097. Tax Code Termination/Rule. Adoption of the rule (H Res 472) to provide for House floor consideration of the bill that would terminate the tax code. Adopted 232-188: R 220-0; D 12-187 (ND 6-141, SD 6-46); I 0-1. June 17, 1998.

236. HR 2646. Education Savings Accounts Conference Report/Rule. Adoption of the rule (H Res 471) to provide for House floor consideration of the conference report to a bill that would allow individuals to set aside up to $2,000 a year in a tax-sheltered savings account that could be used to pay for educational expenses. Adopted 228-191: R 219-0; D 9-190 (ND 3-146, SD 6-44); I 0-1. June 17, 1998.

	230	231	232	233	234	235	236
ALABAMA							
1 *Callahan*	Y	?	Y	Y	Y	Y	Y
2 *Everett*	Y	+	Y	Y	Y	Y	Y
3 *Riley*	Y	Y	Y	Y	Y	Y	Y
4 *Aderholt*	Y	Y	Y	Y	Y	Y	Y
5 Cramer	Y	Y	Y	Y	N	Y	N
6 *Bachus*	Y	Y	Y	Y	Y	Y	Y
7 Hilliard	+	+	?	?	?	N	N
ALASKA							
AL *Young*	Y	Y	Y	Y	Y	Y	Y
ARIZONA							
1 *Salmon*	Y	Y	Y	Y	Y	Y	Y
2 Pastor	Y	Y	Y	Y	N	N	N
3 *Stump*	Y	Y	Y	Y	Y	Y	Y
4 *Shadegg*	Y	Y	Y	Y	Y	Y	Y
5 *Kolbe*	Y	Y	Y	Y	Y	Y	Y
6 *Hayworth*	Y	Y	Y	Y	Y	Y	Y
ARKANSAS							
1 Berry	Y	Y	Y	Y	N	N	N
2 Snyder	Y	Y	Y	Y	N	N	Y
3 *Hutchinson*	?	Y	Y	Y	Y	Y	Y
4 *Dickey*	Y	Y	Y	Y	Y	Y	Y
CALIFORNIA							
1 *Riggs*	Y	?	Y	Y	Y	Y	Y
2 *Herger*	Y	Y	Y	?	Y	Y	Y
3 Fazio	Y	Y	Y	Y	N	N	N
4 *Doolittle*	Y	Y	Y	Y	Y	Y	Y
5 Matsui	Y	Y	Y	Y	N	?	N
6 Woolsey	Y	Y	+	+	N	N	N
7 Miller	Y	Y	Y	Y	N	N	N
8 Pelosi	Y	Y	Y	Y	N	N	N
9 Lee	Y	Y	Y	Y	N	N	N
10 Tauscher	Y	Y	Y	Y	N	Y	N
11 *Pombo*	Y	Y	Y	Y	Y	Y	Y
12 Lantos	Y	Y	Y	Y	N	N	N
13 Stark	Y	Y	Y	Y	N	N	N
14 Eshoo	Y	Y	+	+	N	N	N
15 *Campbell*	Y	Y	Y	Y	Y	Y	Y
16 Lofgren	Y	Y	+	+	N	N	N
17 Farr	+	+	Y	Y	N	N	N
18 Condit	Y	Y	Y	Y	N	N	N
19 *Radanovich*	Y	Y	Y	Y	Y	Y	Y
20 Dooley	Y	Y	Y	Y	N	N	N
21 *Thomas*	Y	Y	Y	Y	Y	Y	Y
22 Capps, L.	Y	Y	Y	Y	N	N	Y
23 *Gallegly*	Y	Y	Y	Y	Y	Y	Y
24 Sherman	Y	Y	Y	Y	N	N	N
25 *McKeon*	Y	Y	Y	Y	Y	Y	Y
26 Berman	?	?	Y	Y	N	N	N
27 *Rogan*	Y	Y	Y	Y	Y	Y	Y
28 *Dreier*	Y	Y	Y	Y	Y	Y	Y
29 Waxman	Y	?	Y	Y	N	N	N
30 Becerra	?	?	Y	Y	N	N	N
31 Martinez	Y	Y	Y	Y	N	N	N
32 Dixon	Y	Y	Y	Y	N	N	N
33 Roybal-Allard	Y	Y	Y	Y	N	N	N
34 Torres	Y	Y	Y	Y	N	N	N
35 Waters	Y	Y	Y	?	N	?	N
36 Harman	Y	Y	Y	Y	N	N	N
37 Millender-McD.	Y	Y	Y	Y	N	N	N

	230	231	232	233	234	235	236
38 *Horn*	Y	Y	Y	Y	Y	Y	Y
39 *Royce*	Y	Y	Y	Y	Y	Y	Y
40 *Lewis*	Y	Y	?	?	?	?	?
41 *Kim*	Y	Y	Y	Y	Y	Y	Y
42 Brown	Y	Y	Y	?	N	N	N
43 *Calvert*	Y	Y	Y	Y	Y	Y	Y
44 *Bono, M.*	Y	Y	Y	Y	Y	Y	Y
45 *Rohrabacher*	Y	Y	Y	Y	Y	Y	Y
46 Sanchez	Y	Y	Y	Y	N	N	N
47 *Cox*	Y	Y	Y	Y	Y	Y	Y
48 *Packard*	Y	Y	Y	Y	Y	Y	Y
49 *Bilbray*	Y	Y	Y	Y	Y	Y	Y
50 Filner	Y	Y	Y	Y	N	N	N
51 *Cunningham*	Y	Y	Y	Y	Y	Y	Y
52 *Hunter*	Y	Y	Y	Y	Y	Y	Y
COLORADO							
1 DeGette	Y	Y	Y	?	N	N	N
2 Skaggs	Y	Y	Y	Y	N	N	N
3 *McInnis*	Y	Y	Y	Y	Y	Y	Y
4 *Schaffer*	Y	Y	Y	Y	Y	Y	Y
5 *Hefley*	Y	Y	Y	Y	Y	Y	Y
6 *Schaefer*	Y	Y	Y	Y	Y	Y	Y
CONNECTICUT							
1 Kennelly	Y	Y	Y	N	N	N	N
2 Gejdenson	Y	?	Y	Y	N	N	N
3 DeLauro	Y	Y	Y	N	N	N	N
4 *Shays*	+	+	Y	+	Y	Y	Y
5 Maloney	Y	Y	Y	Y	N	N	N
6 *Johnson*	Y	Y	Y	Y	Y	Y	Y
DELAWARE							
AL *Castle*	Y	Y	Y	Y	Y	Y	Y
FLORIDA							
1 *Scarborough*	Y	Y	Y	Y	Y	Y	Y
2 Boyd	Y	Y	Y	N	N	N	Y
3 Brown	Y	Y	?	?	N	N	N
4 *Fowler*	Y	Y	Y	Y	Y	Y	Y
5 Thurman	Y	Y	Y	N	N	N	N
6 *Stearns*	Y	Y	Y	Y	Y	Y	Y
7 *Mica*	Y	Y	Y	Y	Y	Y	Y
8 *McCollum*	Y	Y	Y	Y	Y	Y	Y
9 *Bilirakis*	Y	Y	Y	Y	Y	Y	Y
10 *Young*	Y	Y	Y	Y	Y	Y	Y
11 Davis	Y	Y	Y	Y	N	N	N
12 *Canady*	Y	Y	Y	Y	Y	Y	Y
13 *Miller*	Y	Y	Y	Y	Y	Y	Y
14 *Goss*	Y	Y	Y	Y	Y	Y	Y
15 *Weldon*	Y	Y	Y	Y	Y	Y	Y
16 *Foley*	Y	Y	Y	Y	Y	Y	Y
17 Meek	Y	Y	Y	N	?	N	N
18 *Ros-Lehtinen*	Y	Y	Y	Y	Y	Y	Y
19 Wexler	Y	Y	Y	Y	N	N	N
20 Deutsch	Y	Y	Y	Y	N	N	N
21 *Diaz-Balart*	Y	Y	Y	Y	Y	Y	Y
22 *Shaw*	Y	?	Y	Y	Y	Y	Y
23 Hastings	Y	Y	?	?	?	?	?
GEORGIA							
1 *Kingston*	Y	Y	Y	Y	Y	Y	Y
2 Bishop	Y	Y	Y	Y	Y	Y	Y
3 *Collins*	Y	Y	Y	Y	Y	Y	Y
4 McKinney	Y	Y	Y	N	N	Y	N
5 Lewis	?	?	?	N	N	N	N
6 *Gingrich*							
7 *Barr*	Y	?	Y	Y	Y	Y	Y
8 *Chambliss*	Y	Y	Y	Y	Y	Y	Y
9 *Deal*	Y	Y	Y	Y	Y	Y	Y
10 *Norwood*	Y	Y	Y	Y	Y	Y	Y
11 *Linder*	Y	Y	Y	Y	Y	Y	Y
HAWAII							
1 Abercrombie	Y	Y	Y	Y	N	?	N
2 Mink	Y	Y	Y	Y	N	N	N
IDAHO							
1 *Chenoweth*	Y	Y	Y	Y	Y	Y	Y
2 *Crapo*	Y	Y	Y	Y	Y	Y	Y
ILLINOIS							
1 Rush	Y	Y	?	?	N	N	N
2 Jackson	Y	Y	Y	Y	N	N	N
3 Lipinski	Y	Y	Y	Y	N	N	N
4 Gutierrez	Y	?	Y	Y	N	N	N
5 Blagojevich	Y	Y	Y	Y	N	N	N
6 *Hyde*	Y	Y	Y	Y	Y	Y	Y
7 Davis	Y	Y	Y	Y	N	N	N
8 *Crane*	Y	Y	Y	Y	Y	Y	Y
9 Yates	Y	Y	Y	Y	N	N	N
10 *Porter*	Y	Y	Y	Y	Y	Y	Y
11 *Weller*	Y	Y	Y	Y	Y	Y	Y
12 Costello	Y	Y	Y	Y	N	N	N

ND Northern Democrats   SD Southern Democrats

	230	231	232	233	234	235	236
13 ***Fawell***	Y	Y	Y	Y	Y	Y	Y
14 ***Hastert***	Y	Y	Y	Y	Y	Y	Y
15 ***Ewing***	Y	Y	Y	Y	Y	Y	Y
16 ***Manzullo***	Y	Y	Y	Y	Y	Y	Y
17 Evans	Y	Y	Y	Y	N	N	N
18 ***LaHood***	Y	Y	Y	Y	Y	Y	Y
19 Poshard	Y	Y	Y	Y	N	N	N
20 ***Shimkus***	Y	Y	Y	Y	Y	Y	Y
INDIANA							
1 Visclosky	Y	Y	Y	Y	N	N	N
2 ***McIntosh***	Y	Y	Y	Y	Y	Y	Y
3 Roemer	Y	Y	Y	Y	N	N	N
4 ***Souder***	Y	Y	Y	+	Y	Y	Y
5 ***Buyer***	Y	Y	?	?	Y	Y	Y
6 ***Burton***	Y	Y	Y	Y	Y	Y	Y
7 ***Pease***	Y	Y	Y	Y	Y	Y	Y
8 ***Hostettler***	Y	Y	Y	Y	Y	Y	Y
9 Hamilton	Y	Y	Y	Y	N	N	N
10 Carson	Y	Y	Y	Y	N	N	N
IOWA							
1 ***Leach***	Y	Y	Y	Y	Y	Y	Y
2 ***Nussle***	Y	Y	Y	Y	Y	Y	Y
3 Boswell	Y	Y	Y	Y	N	N	N
4 ***Ganske***	Y	Y	Y	Y	Y	Y	Y
5 ***Latham***	Y	Y	Y	Y	Y	Y	Y
KANSAS							
1 ***Moran***	Y	Y	Y	Y	Y	Y	Y
2 ***Ryun***	Y	Y	Y	Y	Y	Y	Y
3 ***Snowbarger***	Y	Y	Y	Y	Y	Y	Y
4 ***Tiahrt***	Y	Y	+	+	Y	Y	Y
KENTUCKY							
1 ***Whitfield***	Y	Y	Y	Y	Y	Y	Y
2 ***Lewis***	Y	Y	Y	Y	Y	Y	Y
3 ***Northup***	Y	Y	Y	Y	Y	Y	Y
4 ***Bunning***	Y	Y	Y	Y	Y	Y	Y
5 ***Rogers***	Y	Y	Y	Y	Y	Y	Y
6 Baesler	Y	Y	Y	Y	N	N	N
LOUISIANA							
1 ***Livingston***	Y	Y	Y	Y	Y	Y	Y
2 Jefferson	Y	Y	Y	Y	N	N	N
3 ***Tauzin***	Y	Y	Y	Y	Y	Y	Y
4 ***McCrery***	Y	Y	Y	Y	Y	Y	Y
5 ***Cooksey***	Y	?	Y	Y	Y	Y	Y
6 ***Baker***	Y	?	Y	Y	Y	Y	Y
7 John	Y	Y	Y	Y	N	N	Y
MAINE							
1 Allen	Y	Y	Y	Y	N	N	N
2 Baldacci	Y	Y	Y	Y	N	N	N
MARYLAND							
1 ***Gilchrest***	Y	Y	Y	Y	Y	Y	?
2 ***Ehrlich***	Y	Y	Y	Y	Y	Y	Y
3 Cardin	Y	Y	Y	Y	N	N	N
4 Wynn	Y	Y	Y	Y	N	N	N
5 Hoyer	Y	Y	Y	Y	N	N	N
6 ***Bartlett***	Y	Y	Y	Y	Y	Y	Y
7 Cummings	Y	Y	Y	Y	N	N	N
8 ***Morella***	Y	Y	Y	Y	Y	Y	Y
MASSACHUSETTS							
1 Olver	Y	Y	Y	Y	N	N	N
2 Neal	Y	Y	Y	Y	N	N	N
3 McGovern	Y	Y	Y	Y	N	N	N
4 Frank	Y	Y	Y	Y	N	N	N
5 Meehan	Y	?	Y	Y	N	N	N
6 Tierney	Y	Y	Y	Y	N	N	N
7 Markey	Y	Y	Y	Y	N	N	N
8 Kennedy	Y	?	?	?	N	N	N
9 Moakley	?	?	Y	Y	N	N	N
10 Delahunt	Y	Y	Y	Y	N	N	N
MICHIGAN							
1 Stupak	Y	Y	Y	Y	N	Y	N
2 ***Hoekstra***	Y	Y	Y	Y	Y	Y	Y
3 ***Ehlers***	Y	Y	Y	Y	Y	Y	Y
4 ***Camp***	Y	Y	Y	Y	Y	Y	Y
5 Barcia	Y	Y	Y	Y	N	N	N
6 ***Upton***	Y	Y	Y	Y	Y	Y	Y
7 ***Smith***	Y	Y	Y	Y	Y	Y	Y
8 Stabenow	Y	Y	Y	Y	N	N	N
9 Kildee	Y	Y	Y	Y	N	N	N
10 Bonior	Y	Y	Y	Y	N	N	N
11 ***Knollenberg***	Y	Y	Y	Y	Y	Y	Y
12 Levin	Y	Y	Y	Y	N	N	N
13 Rivers	Y	Y	Y	N	N	N	N
14 Conyers	Y	Y	Y	Y	N	N	N
15 Kilpatrick	Y	Y	Y	Y	N	N	N
16 Dingell	Y	Y	Y	Y	N	N	N
MINNESOTA							
1 ***Gutknecht***	Y	Y	Y	Y	Y	Y	Y
2 Minge	Y	Y	Y	Y	N	N	N
3 ***Ramstad***	Y	Y	Y	Y	Y	Y	Y
4 Vento	Y	Y	Y	Y	N	N	?
5 Sabo	Y	Y	Y	Y	N	N	N
6 Luther	Y	Y	Y	Y	N	N	N
7 Peterson	Y	Y	Y	Y	Y	Y	N
8 Oberstar	Y	Y	Y	Y	N	N	N
MISSISSIPPI							
1 ***Wicker***	Y	Y	Y	Y	Y	Y	Y
2 Thompson	Y	Y	Y	Y	N	N	N
3 ***Pickering***	Y	Y	Y	Y	Y	Y	Y
4 ***Parker***	?	?	Y	Y	Y	Y	Y
5 Taylor	Y	Y	Y	Y	N	N	Y
MISSOURI							
1 Clay	Y	Y	Y	Y	N	N	N
2 ***Talent***	Y	Y	Y	Y	Y	Y	Y
3 Gephardt	Y	Y	Y	Y	N	N	N
4 Skelton	Y	Y	Y	Y	N	N	N
5 McCarthy	Y	Y	Y	Y	N	N	N
6 Danner	Y	Y	Y	Y	Y	Y	N
7 ***Blunt***	Y	Y	Y	Y	Y	Y	Y
8 ***Emerson***	Y	Y	Y	Y	Y	Y	Y
9 ***Hulshof***	Y	Y	Y	Y	Y	Y	Y
MONTANA							
AL ***Hill***	Y	Y	Y	Y	Y	Y	Y
NEBRASKA							
1 ***Bereuter***	Y	Y	Y	Y	Y	Y	Y
2 ***Christensen***	Y	Y	Y	Y	Y	Y	Y
3 ***Barrett***	Y	Y	Y	Y	Y	Y	Y
NEVADA							
1 ***Ensign***	Y	Y	Y	Y	Y	Y	Y
2 ***Gibbons***	Y	Y	Y	Y	Y	Y	Y
NEW HAMPSHIRE							
1 ***Sununu***	Y	Y	Y	Y	Y	Y	Y
2 ***Bass***	Y	Y	Y	Y	Y	Y	Y
NEW JERSEY							
1 Andrews	Y	Y	Y	Y	N	N	N
2 ***LoBiondo***	Y	Y	Y	Y	Y	Y	Y
3 ***Saxton***	Y	Y	Y	Y	Y	Y	Y
4 ***Smith***	Y	Y	Y	Y	Y	Y	Y
5 ***Roukema***	Y	?	Y	Y	Y	Y	Y
6 Pallone	Y	Y	Y	Y	N	N	N
7 ***Franks***	Y	Y	Y	Y	Y	Y	Y
8 Pascrell	Y	Y	Y	Y	N	N	N
9 Rothman	Y	Y	Y	Y	N	N	N
10 Payne	Y	Y	Y	Y	N	N	N
11 ***Frelinghuysen***	Y	Y	Y	Y	Y	Y	Y
12 ***Pappas***	Y	Y	Y	Y	Y	Y	Y
13 Menendez	Y	Y	Y	Y	N	N	N
NEW MEXICO							
1 Vacant							
2 ***Skeen***	Y	Y	Y	Y	Y	Y	Y
3 ***Redmond***	Y	Y	Y	Y	Y	Y	Y
NEW YORK							
1 ***Forbes***	Y	Y	Y	Y	Y	Y	Y
2 ***Lazio***	Y	Y	Y	Y	Y	Y	Y
3 ***King***	Y	Y	Y	Y	Y	Y	Y
4 McCarthy	Y	Y	Y	Y	N	Y	N
6 Meeks	?	?	Y	Y	N	N	N
5 Ackerman	Y	Y	Y	Y	N	N	N
7 Manton	Y	Y	Y	Y	N	N	N
8 Nadler	Y	Y	Y	Y	N	N	N
9 Schumer	Y	?	?	?	N	N	N
10 Towns	Y	Y	Y	Y	N	N	N
11 Owens	Y	Y	Y	Y	N	N	N
12 Velázquez	Y	Y	Y	Y	N	N	N
13 ***Fossella***	Y	Y	Y	Y	Y	Y	Y
14 Maloney	Y	Y	Y	Y	N	N	N
15 Rangel	Y	Y	Y	Y	N	N	N
16 Serrano	Y	Y	Y	Y	N	N	N
17 Engel	Y	Y	Y	Y	N	N	N
18 Lowey	Y	Y	Y	Y	N	N	N
19 ***Kelly***	Y	Y	Y	Y	Y	Y	Y
20 ***Gilman***	Y	Y	Y	Y	Y	Y	Y
21 McNulty	Y	Y	?	?	?	?	?
22 ***Solomon***	Y	Y	Y	Y	Y	Y	Y
23 ***Boehlert***	Y	Y	Y	Y	Y	Y	Y
24 ***McHugh***	Y	Y	Y	Y	Y	Y	Y
25 ***Walsh***	Y	Y	Y	Y	Y	Y	Y
26 Hinchey	Y	Y	Y	Y	N	N	N
27 ***Paxon***	?	?	Y	Y	Y	Y	Y
28 Slaughter	Y	Y	Y	Y	N	N	N
29 LaFalce	Y	Y	Y	Y	N	N	N
30 ***Quinn***	Y	Y	Y	Y	Y	Y	Y
31 ***Houghton***	Y	?	Y	Y	Y	Y	Y
NORTH CAROLINA							
1 Clayton	Y	Y	Y	?	N	N	N
2 Etheridge	Y	Y	Y	Y	N	N	N
3 ***Jones***	Y	Y	Y	Y	Y	Y	Y
4 Price	Y	Y	Y	Y	N	N	N
5 ***Burr***	Y	Y	Y	Y	Y	Y	Y
6 ***Coble***	Y	Y	Y	Y	Y	Y	Y
7 McIntyre	Y	Y	Y	Y	Y	Y	N
8 Hefner	Y	?	Y	Y	N	N	?
9 ***Myrick***	Y	Y	Y	Y	Y	Y	Y
10 ***Ballenger***	Y	Y	+	+	Y	Y	Y
11 ***Taylor***	Y	Y	Y	Y	Y	Y	Y
12 Watt	Y	Y	Y	Y	N	N	N
NORTH DAKOTA							
AL Pomeroy	Y	Y	Y	Y	N	N	N
OHIO							
1 ***Chabot***	Y	Y	Y	Y	Y	Y	Y
2 ***Portman***	Y	Y	Y	Y	Y	Y	Y
3 Hall	Y	?	Y	Y	N	N	N
4 ***Oxley***	Y	Y	Y	Y	Y	Y	Y
5 ***Gillmor***	?	?	Y	Y	Y	Y	Y
6 Strickland	Y	Y	Y	Y	N	N	N
7 ***Hobson***	Y	Y	Y	Y	Y	Y	Y
8 ***Boehner***	Y	Y	Y	Y	Y	Y	Y
9 Kaptur	Y	Y	Y	Y	N	N	N
10 Kucinich	Y	Y	Y	Y	N	N	N
11 Stokes	Y	Y	Y	Y	N	N	N
12 ***Kasich***	Y	?	Y	Y	Y	Y	Y
13 Brown	Y	Y	Y	Y	N	N	N
14 Sawyer	Y	Y	Y	Y	N	N	N
15 ***Pryce***	Y	Y	Y	Y	Y	Y	Y
16 ***Regula***	Y	Y	Y	Y	Y	Y	Y
17 Traficant	Y	Y	Y	Y	Y	Y	Y
18 ***Ney***	Y	Y	Y	Y	?	?	?
19 ***LaTourette***	Y	Y	Y	Y	Y	Y	Y
OKLAHOMA							
1 ***Largent***	Y	?	Y	Y	Y	Y	Y
2 ***Coburn***	Y	Y	Y	Y	Y	Y	Y
3 ***Watkins***	Y	Y	Y	Y	Y	Y	Y
4 ***Watts***	Y	Y	Y	Y	Y	Y	Y
5 ***Istook***	Y	Y	Y	Y	Y	Y	Y
6 ***Lucas***	Y	Y	Y	Y	Y	Y	Y
OREGON							
1 Furse	Y	Y	Y	Y	N	N	N
2 ***Smith***	Y	Y	Y	Y	Y	Y	Y
3 Blumenauer	Y	Y	Y	Y	N	N	N
4 DeFazio	Y	Y	Y	Y	N	N	N
5 Hooley	Y	Y	Y	Y	N	N	N
PENNSYLVANIA							
1 Brady	Y	Y	Y	Y	N	N	N
2 Fattah	Y	Y	Y	Y	N	N	N
3 Borski	Y	Y	Y	Y	N	N	N
4 Klink	Y	Y	Y	Y	N	N	N
5 ***Peterson***	Y	Y	Y	Y	?	?	?
6 Holden	Y	Y	Y	Y	N	N	N
7 ***Weldon***	Y	Y	Y	Y	Y	Y	Y
8 ***Greenwood***	Y	Y	Y	Y	Y	Y	Y
9 ***Shuster***	Y	Y	Y	Y	Y	Y	Y
10 ***McDade***	Y	Y	Y	Y	Y	?	Y
11 Kanjorski	Y	Y	?	Y	N	N	N
12 Murtha	Y	?	Y	Y	N	N	N
13 ***Fox***	Y	Y	Y	Y	Y	Y	Y
14 Coyne	Y	Y	Y	Y	N	N	N
15 McHale	Y	Y	Y	Y	N	N	N
16 ***Pitts***	Y	Y	Y	Y	Y	Y	Y
17 ***Gekas***	Y	Y	Y	Y	Y	Y	Y
18 Doyle	Y	Y	Y	Y	N	N	N
19 ***Goodling***	Y	Y	Y	Y	Y	Y	Y
20 Mascara	Y	Y	Y	Y	N	N	N
21 ***English***	Y	Y	Y	Y	Y	Y	Y
RHODE ISLAND							
1 Kennedy	Y	Y	Y	Y	N	N	N
2 Weygand	Y	Y	Y	Y	N	N	N
SOUTH CAROLINA							
1 ***Sanford***	Y	Y	Y	Y	Y	Y	Y
2 ***Spence***	Y	Y	Y	Y	Y	Y	Y
3 ***Graham***	Y	Y	Y	Y	Y	Y	Y
4 ***Inglis***	?	?	?	?	Y	Y	Y
5 Spratt	Y	Y	Y	Y	N	N	N
6 Clyburn	Y	Y	Y	Y	N	N	N
SOUTH DAKOTA							
AL ***Thune***	Y	Y	Y	Y	Y	Y	Y
TENNESSEE							
1 ***Jenkins***	Y	Y	Y	Y	Y	Y	Y
2 ***Duncan***	Y	Y	Y	Y	Y	Y	Y
3 ***Wamp***	Y	Y	Y	Y	Y	Y	Y
4 ***Hilleary***	Y	Y	Y	Y	?	?	?
5 Clement	Y	Y	Y	Y	N	N	N
6 Gordon	Y	Y	Y	Y	N	N	N
7 ***Bryant***	Y	Y	Y	Y	Y	Y	Y
8 Tanner	Y	Y	Y	Y	N	N	N
9 Ford	Y	Y	+	+	–	N	N
TEXAS							
1 Sandlin	Y	Y	Y	Y	N	Y	N
2 Turner	Y	Y	Y	Y	N	N	N
3 ***Johnson, Sam***	?	?	Y	Y	?	?	?
4 Hall	Y	Y	Y	Y	Y	Y	Y
5 ***Sessions***	Y	Y	Y	Y	Y	Y	Y
6 ***Barton***	Y	?	Y	Y	Y	Y	Y
7 ***Archer***	Y	Y	Y	Y	Y	Y	Y
8 ***Brady***	Y	Y	Y	Y	Y	Y	Y
9 Lampson	Y	Y	Y	Y	N	N	N
10 Doggett	Y	Y	Y	Y	N	N	N
11 Edwards	Y	Y	Y	?	N	N	N
12 ***Granger***	Y	Y	Y	Y	Y	Y	Y
13 ***Thornberry***	Y	Y	Y	Y	Y	Y	Y
14 ***Paul***	P	Y	N	Y	Y	Y	Y
15 Hinojosa	Y	Y	Y	Y	N	N	N
16 Reyes	Y	Y	Y	Y	N	N	N
17 Stenholm	Y	Y	Y	Y	N	N	N
18 Jackson-Lee	Y	Y	Y	Y	N	N	N
19 ***Combest***	Y	Y	Y	Y	Y	Y	Y
20 Gonzalez	?	?	?	?	?	?	?
21 ***Smith***	Y	Y	Y	Y	Y	Y	Y
22 ***DeLay***	Y	Y	Y	Y	Y	Y	Y
23 ***Bonilla***	Y	Y	Y	Y	Y	Y	Y
24 Frost	Y	Y	Y	Y	N	N	N
25 Bentsen	Y	Y	Y	Y	N	N	N
26 ***Armey***	Y	Y	Y	Y	Y	Y	?
27 Ortiz	Y	Y	Y	Y	N	N	?
28 Rodriguez	Y	Y	Y	Y	N	N	N
29 Green	Y	Y	Y	Y	N	N	?
30 Johnson, E.B.	Y	Y	Y	Y	N	N	N
UTAH							
1 ***Hansen***	Y	Y	Y	Y	Y	Y	Y
2 ***Cook***	Y	Y	Y	Y	Y	Y	Y
3 ***Cannon***	Y	Y	Y	Y	Y	Y	Y
VERMONT							
AL *Sanders*	Y	Y	Y	Y	N	N	N
VIRGINIA							
1 ***Bateman***	Y	Y	Y	Y	Y	Y	Y
2 Pickett	Y	Y	Y	Y	N	N	N
3 Scott	Y	Y	Y	Y	N	N	N
4 Sisisky	Y	Y	Y	Y	N	N	N
5 Goode	Y	Y	Y	Y	Y	Y	N
6 ***Goodlatte***	Y	Y	Y	Y	Y	Y	Y
7 ***Bliley***	Y	Y	Y	Y	Y	Y	Y
8 Moran	Y	Y	Y	Y	N	N	N
9 Boucher	Y	Y	Y	Y	N	N	N
10 ***Wolf***	Y	Y	Y	Y	Y	Y	Y
11 ***Davis***	Y	Y	Y	Y	Y	Y	Y
WASHINGTON							
1 ***White***	Y	Y	Y	Y	Y	Y	Y
2 ***Metcalf***	Y	Y	Y	Y	Y	Y	Y
3 ***Smith, Linda***	Y	Y	?	?	Y	Y	Y
4 ***Hastings***	Y	Y	Y	Y	Y	Y	Y
5 ***Nethercutt***	Y	Y	Y	Y	Y	Y	Y
6 Dicks	Y	Y	Y	Y	N	N	N
7 McDermott	Y	Y	Y	Y	N	N	N
8 ***Dunn***	Y	Y	Y	Y	Y	Y	Y
9 Smith, Adam	+	+	Y	Y	N	N	N
WEST VIRGINIA							
1 Mollohan	Y	Y	Y	Y	N	N	N
2 Wise	Y	Y	Y	Y	N	N	N
3 Rahall	Y	Y	Y	Y	N	N	N
WISCONSIN							
1 ***Neumann***	Y	Y	Y	Y	Y	Y	Y
2 ***Klug***	Y	Y	Y	Y	Y	Y	Y
3 Kind	Y	Y	Y	Y	N	N	N
4 Kleczka	Y	Y	Y	Y	N	N	N
5 Barrett	Y	Y	Y	Y	N	N	N
6 ***Petri***	Y	Y	Y	Y	Y	Y	Y
7 Obey	Y	Y	Y	Y	N	N	N
8 Johnson	Y	Y	Y	Y	N	N	N
9 ***Sensenbrenner***	Y	Y	Y	Y	Y	Y	Y
WYOMING							
AL ***Cubin***	Y	Y	?	?	Y	Y	Y

Southern states - Ala., Ark., Fla., Ga., Ky., La., Miss., N.C., Okla., S.C., Tenn., Texas, Va.

237. Quorum Call. * 413 Responded. June 17, 1998.

238. HR 3097. Tax Code Termination/Recommit. Rangel, D-N.Y., motion to recommit the bill to the Ways and Means Committee with instructions to report it back with an amendment to replace the bill's language with a provision that would express the sense of Congress that tax reform should be enacted not later than April 15, 2001. Motion rejected 203-223: R 6-217; D 196-6 (ND 147-2, SD 49-4); I 1-0. June 17, 1998.

239. HR 3097. Tax Code Termination/Passage. Passage of the bill to abolish the tax code, except for the provisions that fund Social Security and Medicare, by Dec. 31, 2002. The bill would recommend that Congress enact a new tax code by July 4, 2002. Passed 219-209: R 204-20; D 15-188 (ND 6-144, SD 9-44); I 0-1. June 17, 1998. A "nay" vote was a vote in support of the president's position.

240. Quorum Call. * 392 Responded. June 17, 1998.

241. HR 2183. Campaign Finance Overhaul/White Substitute. White, R-Wash., substitute amendment to create a temporary 12-member commission to propose changes to the federal campaign finance system. Rejected 156-201: R 151-64; D 5-136 (ND 3-102, SD 2-34); I 0-1. June 17, 1998.

242. HR 2646. Education Savings Accounts/Recommit. Rangel, D-N.Y., motion to recommit the bill to the conference committee with instructions to report it back with instructions to the managers to agree to provisions regarding tax-favored financing for public school construction following the provisions of HR3320. Motion rejected 196-225: R 5-216; D 190-9 (ND 141-6, SD 49-3); I 1-0. June 18, 1998.

243. HR 2646. Education Savings Accounts/Conference Report. Adoption of the conference report on the bill to permit individuals to set aside up to $2,000 a year in a tax-sheltered savings account that could be used to pay for educational expenses. Adopted (thus sent to the Senate) 225-197: R 213-10; D 12-186 (ND 5-141, SD 7-45); I 0-1. June 18, 1998. A "nay" was a vote in support of the president's position.

244. H Res 463. Select Committee on National Security and China/Previous Question. Solomon, R-N.Y., motion to order the previous question (thus ending debate and the possibility of amendment) on adoption of the rule (H Res 476) to provide for House floor consideration of the bill to establish a Select Committee on U.S. National Security and Military/Commercial Concerns with the People's Republic of China. Motion agreed to 226-197: R 224-0; D 2-196 (ND 2-145, SD 0-51); I 0-1. June 18, 1998. (Subsequently, the rule was adopted.)

245. H Res 463. Select Committee on National Security and China/Adoption. Adoption of the resolution to establish a Select Committee on U.S. National Security and Military/Commercial Concerns with the People's Republic of China. The resolution authorizes the committee through the remainder of the 105th Congress and authorizes up to $2.5 million for committee expenses. Adopted 409-10: R 222-0; D 186-10 (ND 137-9, SD 49-1); I 1-0. June 18, 1998.

* CQ does not include quorum calls in its vote charts.

Key

Y	Voted for (yea).
#	Paired for.
+	Announced for.
N	Voted against (nay).
X	Paired against.
−	Announced against.
P	Voted "present."
C	Voted "present" to avoid possible conflict of interest.
?	Did not vote or otherwise make a position known.

Democrats   **Republicans**
Independent

	238	239	241	242	243	244	245
ALABAMA							
1 *Callahan*	N	Y	Y	N	Y	Y	Y
2 *Everett*	N	Y	Y	N	Y	Y	Y
3 *Riley*	N	Y	Y	N	Y	Y	Y
4 *Aderholt*	N	Y	Y	N	Y	Y	Y
5 Cramer	N	Y	P	Y	N	N	Y
6 *Bachus*	N	Y	Y	N	Y	Y	Y
7 Hilliard	Y	N	P	Y	N	N	Y
ALASKA							
AL *Young*	N	Y	Y	N	Y	Y	Y
ARIZONA							
1 *Salmon*	N	Y	Y	N	Y	Y	Y
2 Pastor	Y	N	N	Y	N	N	Y
3 *Stump*	N	Y	Y	N	Y	Y	Y
4 *Shadegg*	N	Y	Y	N	Y	Y	Y
5 *Kolbe*	N	Y	N	N	Y	Y	Y
6 *Hayworth*	N	Y	Y	N	Y	Y	Y
ARKANSAS							
1 Berry	Y	N	N	Y	N	N	Y
2 Snyder	Y	N	N	Y	N	N	Y
3 *Hutchinson*	N	Y	N	N	Y	Y	Y
4 *Dickey*	N	Y	Y	N	Y	Y	Y
CALIFORNIA							
1 *Riggs*	N	Y	Y	N	Y	Y	Y
2 *Herger*	N	Y	Y	N	Y	Y	Y
3 Fazio	Y	N	N	Y	N	N	Y
4 *Doolittle*	N	Y	Y	N	Y	Y	Y
5 Matsui	Y	N	N	Y	N	N	Y
6 Woolsey	Y	N	P	N	N	N	Y
7 Miller	Y	N	N	Y	N	N	Y
8 Pelosi	Y	N	N	Y	N	N	Y
9 Lee	Y	N	N	Y	N	N	Y
10 Tauscher	Y	N	P	N	N	Y	Y
11 *Pombo*	N	Y	Y	N	Y	Y	Y
12 Lantos	Y	N	P	Y	N	N	Y
13 Stark	Y	N	N	Y	N	N	Y
14 Eshoo	Y	N	P	N	N	N	Y
15 *Campbell*	N	Y	N	N	Y	Y	Y
16 Lofgren	Y	N	P	N	N	N	Y
17 Farr	Y	N	P	Y	N	N	Y
18 Condit	Y	Y	N	Y	N	N	Y
19 *Radanovich*	N	Y	Y	−	Y	Y	Y
20 Dooley	Y	N	P	Y	N	N	Y
21 *Thomas*	N	Y	N	N	Y	Y	Y
22 Capps, L.	Y	N	N	Y	N	N	Y
23 *Gallegly*	N	Y	Y	N	Y	Y	Y
24 Sherman	Y	N	?	Y	N	N	Y
25 *McKeon*	N	Y	Y	N	Y	Y	Y
26 Berman	Y	N	N	Y	N	N	Y
27 *Rogan*	N	Y	N	N	Y	Y	Y
28 *Dreier*	−	Y	Y	N	Y	Y	Y
29 Waxman	Y	N	N	Y	N	N	Y
30 Becerra	Y	N	N	Y	N	N	Y
31 Martinez	Y	N	Y	Y	N	?	?
32 Dixon	Y	N	N	Y	N	N	Y
33 Roybal-Allard	Y	N	N	Y	N	N	Y
34 Torres	Y	N	P	?	?	?	?
35 Waters	Y	N	N	Y	N	N	Y
36 Harman	Y	N	N	Y	N	N	Y
37 Millender-McD.	Y	N	N	Y	N	N	Y

	238	239	241	242	243	244	245
38 *Horn*	N	Y	N	Y	N	Y	Y
39 *Royce*	N	Y	Y	N	Y	Y	Y
40 *Lewis*	?	Y	N	N	Y	Y	Y
41 *Kim*	N	Y	Y	N	Y	Y	Y
42 Brown	Y	N	N	Y	N	N	Y
43 *Calvert*	N	Y	Y	N	Y	Y	Y
44 *Bono, M.*	N	Y	Y	N	Y	Y	Y
45 *Rohrabacher*	N	Y	Y	N	Y	Y	Y
46 Sanchez	Y	N	P	Y	N	N	Y
47 *Cox*	N	Y	Y	N	Y	Y	Y
48 *Packard*	N	Y	N	N	Y	Y	Y
49 *Bilbray*	N	Y	P	N	Y	Y	Y
50 Filner	Y	N	N	Y	N	N	Y
51 *Cunningham*	N	Y	?	N	Y	Y	Y
52 *Hunter*	N	Y	Y	N	Y	Y	Y
COLORADO							
1 DeGette	Y	N	P	Y	N	N	Y
2 Skaggs	Y	N	N	Y	N	N	Y
3 *McInnis*	N	Y	Y	N	Y	Y	Y
4 *Schaffer*	N	Y	N	N	Y	Y	Y
5 *Hefley*	N	Y	N	N	Y	Y	Y
6 *Schaefer*	N	Y	Y	N	Y	Y	Y
CONNECTICUT							
1 Kennelly	Y	N	N	Y	N	N	Y
2 Gejdenson	Y	N	N	Y	N	N	Y
3 DeLauro	Y	N	N	Y	N	N	Y
4 *Shays*	N	N	P	N	Y	Y	Y
5 Maloney	Y	Y	P	N	N	N	Y
6 *Johnson*	N	N	N	N	Y	Y	Y
DELAWARE							
AL *Castle*	Y	N	P	N	Y	Y	Y
FLORIDA							
1 *Scarborough*	N	Y	N	Y	N	Y	Y
2 Boyd	Y	N	N	Y	N	N	Y
3 Brown	Y	N	N	Y	N	N	Y
4 *Fowler*	N	Y	N	N	Y	Y	Y
5 Thurman	N	N	P	N	N	N	Y
6 *Stearns*	N	Y	Y	N	Y	Y	Y
7 *Mica*	N	Y	Y	N	Y	Y	Y
8 *McCollum*	N	Y	Y	N	Y	Y	Y
9 *Bilirakis*	N	Y	Y	N	Y	Y	Y
10 *Young*	N	Y	N	N	Y	Y	Y
11 Davis	Y	N	N	Y	N	N	Y
12 *Canady*	N	Y	N	N	Y	N	Y
13 *Miller*	N	Y	N	N	Y	Y	Y
14 *Goss*	N	Y	Y	N	Y	Y	Y
15 *Weldon*	N	Y	N	−	+	+	+
16 *Foley*	N	Y	N	N	Y	Y	Y
17 Meek	Y	N	N	Y	N	N	Y
18 *Ros-Lehtinen*	N	Y	N	Y	N	Y	Y
19 Wexler	Y	N	P	Y	N	N	Y
20 Deutsch	Y	N	P	Y	N	N	Y
21 *Diaz-Balart*	N	Y	N	Y	N	Y	Y
22 *Shaw*	N	N	N	N	Y	Y	Y
23 Hastings	?	?	?	?	?	?	?
GEORGIA							
1 *Kingston*	N	Y	N	N	Y	Y	Y
2 Bishop	Y	Y	P	Y	N	Y	N
3 *Collins*	N	Y	N	N	Y	Y	Y
4 McKinney	Y	N	N	Y	N	N	Y
5 Lewis	Y	N	N	Y	N	N	N
6 *Gingrich*		Y	Y		Y		
7 *Barr*	N	Y	N	N	Y	Y	Y
8 *Chambliss*	N	Y	N	N	Y	Y	Y
9 *Deal*	N	Y	Y	N	Y	Y	Y
10 *Norwood*	N	Y	Y	N	Y	Y	Y
11 Linder	N	Y	N	N	Y	Y	Y
HAWAII							
1 Abercrombie	Y	N	N	Y	N	N	Y
2 Mink	Y	N	N	Y	N	N	Y
IDAHO							
1 *Chenoweth*	N	Y	N	N	Y	Y	Y
2 *Crapo*	N	Y	N	N	Y	Y	Y
ILLINOIS							
1 Rush	Y	N	P	N	N	N	Y
2 Jackson	Y	N	N	Y	N	N	Y
3 Lipinski	Y	N	N	N	N	N	Y
4 Gutierrez	Y	N	N	Y	N	N	Y
5 Blagojevich	Y	N	N	Y	N	N	Y
6 *Hyde*	N	Y	Y	N	Y	Y	Y
7 Davis	Y	N	P	N	N	N	Y
8 *Crane*	N	Y	Y	N	Y	Y	Y
9 Yates	Y	N	N	Y	N	N	N
10 *Porter*	N	N	N	N	Y	Y	Y
11 *Weller*	N	Y	Y	N	Y	Y	Y
12 Costello	Y	N	N	Y	N	N	Y

ND Northern Democrats   SD Southern Democrats

	238	239	241	242	243	244	245
13 ***Fawell***	Y	N	Y	N	Y	Y	Y
14 ***Hastert***	N	Y	Y	N	Y	Y	Y
15 ***Ewing***	N	Y	Y	N	Y	Y	Y
16 ***Manzullo***	N	Y	Y	N	Y	Y	Y
17 Evans	Y	N	N	Y	N	N	Y
18 ***LaHood***	N	N	Y	N	Y	Y	Y
19 Poshard	Y	N	N	Y	N	N	Y
20 ***Shimkus***	N	Y	Y	N	Y	Y	Y
INDIANA							
1 Visclosky	Y	N	N	Y	N	N	Y
2 ***McIntosh***	N	+	Y	N	Y	Y	Y
3 Roemer	Y	N	N	Y	N	N	Y
4 ***Souder***	N	Y	Y	N	Y	Y	Y
5 ***Buyer***	N	Y	N	N	Y	Y	Y
6 ***Burton***	N	Y	N	N	Y	Y	Y
7 ***Pease***	N	Y	Y	N	Y	Y	Y
8 ***Hostettler***	N	Y	N	N	Y	Y	Y
9 Hamilton	Y	N	N	Y	N	N	Y
10 Carson	Y	N	N	Y	N	N	Y
IOWA							
1 ***Leach***	Y	N	P	+	+	Y	Y
2 ***Nussle***	N	Y	Y	N	Y	Y	Y
3 Boswell	Y	N	N	Y	N	N	Y
4 ***Ganske***	Y	N	N	N	Y	Y	Y
5 ***Latham***	N	Y	Y	N	Y	Y	Y
KANSAS							
1 ***Moran***	N	Y	N	N	Y	Y	Y
2 ***Ryun***	N	Y	Y	N	Y	Y	Y
3 ***Snowbarger***	N	Y	Y	N	Y	Y	Y
4 ***Tiahrt***	N	Y	Y	N	Y	Y	Y
KENTUCKY							
1 ***Whitfield***	N	Y	N	N	Y	Y	Y
2 ***Lewis***	N	Y	N	N	Y	Y	Y
3 ***Northup***	N	Y	N	N	Y	Y	Y
4 ***Bunning***	N	Y	N	N	Y	Y	Y
5 ***Rogers***	N	Y	N	N	Y	Y	Y
6 Baesler	Y	Y	N	Y	N	N	Y
LOUISIANA							
1 ***Livingston***	N	Y	Y	N	Y	Y	Y
2 Jefferson	Y	N	N	Y	N	N	Y
3 ***Tauzin***	N	Y	Y	N	Y	Y	Y
4 ***McCrery***	N	Y	Y	N	Y	Y	Y
5 ***Cooksey***	?	?	?	?	?	?	?
6 ***Baker***	N	Y	Y	N	Y	Y	Y
7 John	Y	N	N	Y	Y	N	Y
MAINE							
1 Allen	Y	N	N	Y	N	N	Y
2 Baldacci	Y	N	N	Y	–	N	Y
MARYLAND							
1 ***Gilchrest***	N	Y	N	N	Y	Y	Y
2 ***Ehrlich***	N	Y	Y	N	Y	Y	Y
3 Cardin	Y	N	P	Y	N	N	Y
4 Wynn	Y	N	N	Y	N	N	Y
5 Hoyer	Y	N	N	Y	N	N	Y
6 ***Bartlett***	N	Y	Y	N	Y	Y	Y
7 Cummings	Y	N	N	Y	N	N	Y
8 ***Morella***	Y	N	N	Y	N	Y	Y
MASSACHUSETTS							
1 Olver	Y	N	N	Y	N	N	Y
2 Neal	Y	N	N	Y	N	N	Y
3 McGovern	Y	N	N	Y	N	N	Y
4 Frank	Y	N	N	Y	N	N	Y
5 Meehan	Y	N	N	Y	N	N	Y
6 Tierney	Y	N	N	Y	N	N	Y
7 Markey	Y	N	N	Y	N	N	Y
8 Kennedy	Y	N	N	Y	N	N	Y
9 Moakley	Y	N	N	?	?	?	?
10 Delahunt	Y	N	P	Y	N	N	Y
MICHIGAN							
1 Stupak	Y	N	P	Y	N	N	Y
2 ***Hoekstra***	N	Y	Y	N	Y	Y	Y
3 ***Ehlers***	N	Y	Y	N	Y	Y	Y
4 ***Camp***	N	Y	Y	N	Y	Y	Y
5 Barcia	Y	N	P	Y	N	N	Y
6 ***Upton***	N	N	N	N	Y	Y	Y
7 ***Smith***	N	Y	Y	N	Y	Y	Y
8 Stabenow	Y	N	P	Y	N	N	Y
9 Kildee	Y	N	P	Y	N	N	Y
10 Bonior	Y	N	N	Y	N	N	Y
11 ***Knollenberg***	N	Y	Y	N	Y	Y	Y
12 Levin	Y	N	N	Y	N	N	Y
13 Rivers	Y	N	P	Y	N	N	Y
14 Conyers	Y	N	N	Y	N	N	N
15 Kilpatrick	Y	N	P	Y	N	N	Y
16 Dingell	Y	N	P	Y	N	N	Y
MINNESOTA							
1 ***Gutknecht***	N	Y	Y	N	Y	Y	+
2 Minge	Y	N	P	N	N	N	Y
3 ***Ramstad***	N	Y	N	N	Y	Y	Y
4 Vento	Y	N	N	Y	N	N	Y
5 Sabo	Y	N	N	N	N	N	Y
6 Luther	Y	N	N	Y	N	N	Y
7 Peterson	N	Y	Y	N	N	N	Y
8 Oberstar	Y	N	N	Y	N	N	N
MISSISSIPPI							
1 ***Wicker***	N	Y	Y	N	Y	Y	Y
2 Thompson	Y	N	N	Y	N	N	Y
3 ***Pickering***	N	Y	Y	N	Y	Y	Y
4 ***Parker***	N	Y	N	N	Y	Y	Y
5 Taylor	Y	Y	N	N	Y	N	Y
MISSOURI							
1 Clay	Y	N	N	Y	N	N	Y
2 ***Talent***	N	Y	Y	N	Y	Y	Y
3 Gephardt	Y	N	P	Y	N	N	Y
4 Skelton	Y	N	N	Y	N	N	Y
5 McCarthy	Y	N	N	Y	N	N	Y
6 Danner	Y	Y	N	Y	Y	N	Y
7 ***Blunt***	N	Y	Y	N	Y	Y	Y
8 ***Emerson***	N	Y	Y	N	Y	Y	Y
9 ***Hulshof***	N	Y	N	N	Y	Y	Y
MONTANA							
AL ***Hill***	N	Y	N	N	Y	Y	Y
NEBRASKA							
1 ***Bereuter***	Y	N	Y	N	Y	Y	Y
2 ***Christensen***	N	Y	Y	N	Y	Y	Y
3 ***Barrett***	N	Y	P	N	N	Y	Y
NEVADA							
1 ***Ensign***	N	Y	Y	N	Y	Y	Y
2 ***Gibbons***	N	Y	Y	N	Y	Y	Y
NEW HAMPSHIRE							
1 ***Sununu***	N	Y	Y	N	Y	Y	Y
2 ***Bass***	N	Y	N	N	Y	Y	Y
NEW JERSEY							
1 Andrews	Y	N	P	Y	N	N	Y
2 ***LoBiondo***	N	Y	P	Y	N	Y	Y
3 ***Saxton***	N	Y	Y	N	Y	Y	Y
4 ***Smith***	N	Y	Y	N	Y	Y	Y
5 ***Roukema***	N	N	N	N	Y	Y	Y
6 Pallone	Y	N	P	Y	N	N	Y
7 ***Franks***	N	Y	Y	N	Y	Y	Y
8 Pascrell	Y	N	P	Y	N	Y	Y
9 Rothman	Y	N	N	Y	N	N	Y
10 Payne	Y	N	N	Y	N	N	Y
11 ***Frelinghuysen***	N	N	Y	N	Y	Y	Y
12 ***Pappas***	N	Y	Y	N	Y	Y	Y
13 Menendez	Y	N	N	Y	N	N	Y
NEW MEXICO							
1 Vacant							
2 ***Skeen***	N	Y	N	N	Y	Y	Y
3 ***Redmond***	N	Y	Y	N	Y	Y	Y
NEW YORK							
1 ***Forbes***	N	Y	N	Y	Y	Y	Y
2 ***Lazio***	N	Y	N	N	Y	Y	Y
3 ***King***	N	Y	N	N	Y	Y	Y
4 McCarthy	Y	N	P	Y	N	N	Y
5 Ackerman	Y	N	N	Y	N	N	Y
6 Meeks	Y	N	N	Y	N	N	Y
7 Manton	Y	N	P	Y	N	N	Y
8 Nadler	Y	N	N	Y	N	N	N
9 Schumer	Y	N	?	Y	N	N	Y
10 Towns	Y	N	N	Y	N	N	?
11 Owens	Y	N	N	Y	N	N	Y
12 Velázquez	Y	N	N	Y	N	N	Y
13 ***Fossella***	N	Y	Y	N	Y	Y	Y
14 Maloney	Y	N	P	Y	N	N	Y
15 Rangel	Y	N	N	Y	N	N	Y
16 Serrano	Y	N	N	Y	N	N	Y
17 Engel	Y	N	P	Y	N	N	Y
18 Lowey	Y	N	N	Y	N	N	Y
19 ***Kelly***	N	Y	N	N	Y	Y	Y
20 ***Gilman***	N	Y	N	N	N	Y	Y
21 McNulty	?	?	?	?	?	?	?
22 ***Solomon***	N	Y	Y	N	Y	Y	Y
23 ***Boehlert***	N	N	N	N	N	Y	Y
24 ***McHugh***	N	Y	N	Y	N	Y	Y
25 ***Walsh***	N	N	N	N	Y	Y	Y
26 Hinchey	Y	N	N	Y	N	N	Y
27 ***Paxon***	N	Y	Y	N	Y	Y	Y
28 Slaughter	Y	N	P	Y	N	N	Y
29 LaFalce	Y	N	N	Y	N	N	Y
30 ***Quinn***	N	Y	P	N	Y	Y	Y
31 ***Houghton***	N	N	N	N	N	Y	?
NORTH CAROLINA							
1 Clayton	Y	N	N	Y	N	N	+
2 Etheridge	Y	N	P	Y	N	N	Y
3 ***Jones***	N	Y	Y	N	Y	Y	Y
4 Price	Y	N	P	Y	N	N	Y
5 ***Burr***	N	Y	Y	N	Y	Y	Y
6 ***Coble***	N	Y	Y	N	Y	Y	Y
7 McIntyre	Y	Y	N	Y	N	N	Y
8 Hefner	Y	N	N	Y	N	N	Y
9 ***Myrick***	N	Y	Y	N	Y	Y	Y
10 ***Ballenger***	N	Y	Y	N	Y	Y	Y
11 ***Taylor***	N	Y	Y	N	Y	Y	Y
12 Watt	Y	N	N	Y	N	N	Y
NORTH DAKOTA							
AL Pomeroy	Y	N	P	Y	N	N	Y
OHIO							
1 ***Chabot***	N	Y	Y	N	Y	Y	Y
2 ***Portman***	N	Y	Y	N	Y	Y	Y
3 Hall	Y	N	N	Y	Y	N	Y
4 ***Oxley***	N	Y	N	N	Y	Y	Y
5 ***Gillmor***	N	Y	Y	N	Y	Y	Y
6 Strickland	Y	Y	P	Y	N	N	Y
7 ***Hobson***	N	Y	Y	N	Y	Y	Y
8 ***Boehner***	N	Y	N	N	Y	Y	Y
9 Kaptur	Y	N	N	Y	N	N	Y
10 Kucinich	Y	N	P	Y	N	N	Y
11 Stokes	Y	N	N	Y	N	N	Y
12 ***Kasich***	N	Y	?	N	Y	Y	Y
13 Brown	Y	N	P	Y	N	N	Y
14 Sawyer	Y	N	N	Y	N	N	Y
15 ***Pryce***	N	Y	Y	N	Y	Y	Y
16 ***Regula***	N	Y	Y	N	Y	Y	Y
17 Traficant	N	Y	Y	Y	N	Y	Y
18 ***Ney***	N	Y	Y	N	Y	Y	Y
19 ***LaTourette***	N	Y	Y	N	Y	Y	Y
OKLAHOMA							
1 ***Largent***	N	Y	Y	N	Y	Y	Y
2 ***Coburn***	N	Y	Y	N	Y	Y	Y
3 ***Watkins***	N	Y	Y	N	Y	Y	Y
4 ***Watts***	N	Y	Y	N	Y	Y	Y
5 ***Istook***	N	Y	Y	N	Y	Y	Y
6 ***Lucas***	N	Y	Y	N	Y	Y	Y
OREGON							
1 Furse	Y	N	N	Y	N	N	N
2 ***Smith***	N	Y	Y	N	Y	Y	Y
3 Blumenauer	Y	N	N	Y	N	N	Y
4 DeFazio	Y	N	P	Y	N	N	Y
5 Hooley	Y	N	N	Y	N	N	Y
PENNSYLVANIA							
1 Brady	Y	N	N	Y	N	N	Y
2 Fattah	Y	N	N	Y	N	N	Y
3 Borski	Y	N	N	Y	N	N	Y
4 Klink	Y	N	N	Y	N	N	Y
5 ***Peterson***	N	Y	Y	N	Y	Y	Y
6 Holden	Y	N	N	Y	N	N	Y
7 ***Weldon***	N	Y	Y	N	Y	Y	Y
8 ***Greenwood***	N	Y	?	N	Y	Y	Y
9 ***Shuster***	N	Y	Y	N	Y	Y	Y
10 ***McDade***	N	Y	Y	N	Y	Y	Y
11 Kanjorski	Y	N	N	Y	N	N	N
12 Murtha	Y	N	N	Y	N	N	N
13 ***Fox***	N	Y	P	N	Y	Y	Y
14 Coyne	Y	N	N	Y	N	N	Y
15 McHale	Y	N	P	N	Y	N	Y
16 ***Pitts***	N	Y	Y	N	Y	Y	Y
17 ***Gekas***	N	Y	Y	N	Y	Y	Y
18 Doyle	Y	N	N	Y	N	N	Y
19 ***Goodling***	N	Y	Y	N	Y	Y	Y
20 Mascara	Y	N	N	Y	N	N	Y
21 ***English***	N	Y	Y	N	Y	Y	Y
RHODE ISLAND							
1 Kennedy	Y	N	N	Y	N	N	Y
2 Weygand	Y	N	N	Y	N	N	Y
SOUTH CAROLINA							
1 ***Sanford***	N	Y	N	N	Y	Y	Y
2 ***Spence***	N	Y	Y	N	Y	Y	Y
3 ***Graham***	N	Y	Y	N	Y	Y	Y
4 ***Inglis***	N	Y	Y	N	Y	Y	Y
5 Spratt	Y	N	P	Y	N	N	Y
6 Clyburn	Y	N	N	Y	N	N	Y
SOUTH DAKOTA							
AL ***Thune***	N	Y	Y	N	Y	?	Y
TENNESSEE							
1 ***Jenkins***	N	Y	Y	N	Y	Y	Y
2 ***Duncan***	N	Y	Y	N	Y	Y	Y
3 ***Wamp***	N	Y	P	N	Y	Y	Y
4 ***Hilleary***	N	Y	Y	N	Y	Y	Y
5 Clement	Y	N	P	Y	Y	N	?
6 Gordon	Y	N	P	Y	N	N	Y
7 ***Bryant***	N	Y	Y	N	Y	Y	Y
8 Tanner	Y	N	P	Y	N	N	Y
9 Ford	Y	N	N	Y	N	N	Y
TEXAS							
1 Sandlin	N	Y	P	Y	N	N	Y
2 Turner	Y	Y	P	Y	N	N	Y
3 ***Johnson, Sam***	N	Y	N	N	Y	Y	Y
4 Hall	N	Y	Y	N	Y	N	Y
5 ***Sessions***	N	Y	N	N	+	Y	Y
6 ***Barton***	N	Y	Y	N	Y	Y	Y
7 ***Archer***	N	Y	Y	N	Y	Y	Y
8 ***Brady***	N	Y	N	N	Y	Y	Y
9 Lampson	Y	N	N	Y	N	N	Y
10 Doggett	Y	N	N	Y	N	N	Y
11 Edwards	Y	N	N	Y	N	N	Y
12 ***Granger***	N	Y	N	N	Y	Y	Y
13 ***Thornberry***	N	Y	Y	N	Y	Y	Y
14 ***Paul***	N	Y	Y	N	N	Y	Y
15 Hinojosa	Y	N	N	Y	N	N	Y
16 Reyes	Y	N	N	Y	N	N	Y
17 Stenholm	Y	N	N	Y	N	N	Y
18 Jackson-Lee	Y	N	P	Y	N	N	Y
19 ***Combest***	N	Y	N	N	Y	Y	Y
20 Gonzalez	?	?	?	?	?	?	?
21 ***Smith***	N	Y	N	N	Y	Y	Y
22 ***DeLay***	N	Y	N	N	Y	Y	Y
23 ***Bonilla***	N	Y	Y	N	Y	Y	Y
24 Frost	Y	N	P	Y	N	N	Y
25 Bentsen	Y	N	N	Y	N	N	Y
26 ***Armey***	N	Y	N	N	Y	Y	Y
27 Ortiz	Y	N	N	Y	N	N	Y
28 Rodriguez	Y	N	N	Y	N	N	Y
29 Green	Y	N	N	+	–	–	+
30 Johnson, E.B.	Y	N	N	Y	N	N	Y
UTAH							
1 ***Hansen***	N	Y	Y	N	Y	Y	Y
2 ***Cook***	N	Y	N	N	Y	Y	Y
3 ***Cannon***	N	Y	N	N	Y	Y	Y
VERMONT							
AL *Sanders*	Y	N	N	Y	N	N	Y
VIRGINIA							
1 ***Bateman***	N	N	Y	N	N	Y	Y
2 Pickett	Y	N	N	Y	N	N	Y
3 Scott	Y	N	N	Y	N	N	Y
4 Sisisky	Y	N	P	Y	N	N	Y
5 Goode	N	Y	N	N	Y	N	Y
6 ***Goodlatte***	N	Y	Y	N	Y	Y	Y
7 ***Bliley***	N	Y	Y	N	Y	Y	Y
8 Moran	Y	N	N	Y	Y	?	Y
9 Boucher	Y	N	Y	Y	N	N	Y
10 ***Wolf***	N	N	Y	N	Y	Y	Y
11 ***Davis***	N	N	Y	N	Y	Y	Y
WASHINGTON							
1 ***White***	N	Y	Y	N	Y	Y	Y
2 ***Metcalf***	N	Y	Y	N	Y	Y	Y
3 ***Smith, Linda***	N	Y	N	N	Y	Y	Y
4 ***Hastings***	N	Y	Y	N	Y	Y	Y
5 ***Nethercutt***	N	Y	Y	N	Y	Y	Y
6 Dicks	Y	N	N	Y	N	N	Y
7 McDermott	Y	N	N	Y	N	N	N
8 ***Dunn***	N	Y	Y	N	Y	Y	Y
9 Smith, Adam	Y	N	N	Y	N	N	Y
WEST VIRGINIA							
1 Mollohan	Y	N	N	Y	N	N	N
2 Wise	?	N	N	?	?	N	Y
3 Rahall	Y	N	P	Y	N	N	Y
WISCONSIN							
1 ***Neumann***	N	Y	N	N	Y	Y	Y
2 ***Klug***	N	Y	Y	N	Y	Y	Y
3 Kind	Y	N	P	Y	N	N	Y
4 Kleczka	Y	N	N	Y	N	N	Y
5 Barrett	Y	N	N	Y	N	N	Y
6 ***Petri***	N	Y	Y	N	Y	Y	Y
7 Obey	Y	N	N	Y	N	N	Y
8 Johnson	Y	N	?	Y	N	N	Y
9 ***Sensenbrenner***	N	Y	Y	N	Y	Y	Y
WYOMING							
AL ***Cubin***	N	Y	Y	N	Y	Y	Y

Southern states - Ala., Ark., Fla., Ga., Ky., La., Miss., N.C., Okla., S.C., Tenn., Texas, Va.

Key

Y	Voted for (yea).
#	Paired for.
+	Announced for.
N	Voted against (nay).
X	Paired against.
−	Announced against.
P	Voted "present."
C	Voted "present" to avoid possible conflict of interest.
?	Did not vote or otherwise make a position known.

Democrats   ***Republicans***
Independent

246. HR 2183. Campaign Finance Overhaul/Previous Question. Linder, R-Ga., motion to order the previous question (thus ending debate and the possibility of amendment) on adoption of the rule (H Res 458) to provide for House floor consideration of the bill to amend the Federal Election Campaign Act to overhaul campaign finance laws. The rule waives points of order on 258 non-germane, secondary amendments to the 11 substitute amendments allowed by a previously adopted rule (H Res 442). Motion agreed to 221-194: R 219-0; D 2-193 (ND 1-144, SD 1-49); I 0-1. June 18, 1998. (Subsequently, the rule was adopted.)

247. HR 2183. Campaign Finance Overhaul/Rule. Adoption of the rule to provide for House floor consideration of the bill to amend the Federal Election Campaign Act to overhaul campaign finance laws. The rule waives points of order on 258 non-germane, secondary amendments to the 11 substitute amendments allowed by a previously adopted rule (H Res 442). Adopted 221-189: R 215-0; D 6-188 (ND 2-142, SD 4-46); I 0-1. June 18, 1998.

248. HR 4059. Fiscal 1999 Military Construction Appropriations/Rule. Adoption of the rule (H Res 477) to provide for House floor consideration of the bill to provide $8.2 billion in budget authority for military construction projects in fiscal 1999. The rule also deems House approval of an overall spending ceiling (302 (a) allocation) for the Appropriations Committee that is based on last year's balanced budget agreement. Adopted 231-178: R 214-0; D 17-177 (ND 12-133, SD 5-44); I 0-1. June 19, 1998.

249. HR 2183. Campaign Finance Overhaul Shays-Meehan Substitute/Thomas Substitute. Thomas, R-Calif., substitute amendment to the Shays-Meehan substitute amendment to the bill to overhaul campaign finance laws. The amendment would specify that if any provision of the act is found unconstitutional, then the entire act shall be treated as invalid. Rejected 155-254: R 149-65; D 6-188 (ND 4-140, SD 2-48); I 0-1. June 19, 1998.

250. HR 2183. Campaign Finance Overhaul Shays-Meehan Substitute/Commission. Maloney, D-N.Y., amendment to the Shays-Meehan substitute amendment to the bill to overhaul campaign finance laws. The amendment creates a 12-member commission to recommend changes to current campaign finance laws. Adopted 325-78: R 142-69; D 182-9 (ND 133-8, SD 49-1); I 1-0. June 19, 1998.

251. HR 2183. Campaign Finance Overhaul Shays-Meehan Substitute/Voter Participation Clarification. Gillmor, R-Ohio, amendment to the Shays-Meehan substitute amendment to the bill to overhaul campaign finance laws. The amendment clarifies the rights of registered voters to participate in campaigns and elections. Adopted 395-0: R 205-0; D 189-0 (ND 141-0, SD 48-0); I 1-0. June 19, 1998.

252. HR 4060. Fiscal 1999 Energy and Water Appropriations/Nuclear Energy Research Programs. Foley, R-Fla., amendment to remove a provision that would provide $5 million in funding for nuclear energy research and development programs. Rejected 147-261: R 58-162; D 88-99 (ND 80-54, SD 8-45); I 1-0. June 22, 1998.

	246	247	248	249	250	251	252
ALABAMA							
1 *Callahan*	Y	Y	Y	Y	N	?	N
2 *Everett*	Y	Y	Y	Y	N	?	N
3 *Riley*	Y	Y	Y	Y	N	Y	N
4 *Aderholt*	Y	Y	Y	N	Y	Y	N
5 Cramer	N	N	N	N	Y	Y	N
6 *Bachus*	Y	Y	Y	N	N	Y	N
7 Hilliard	N	N	N	N	Y	Y	Y
ALASKA							
AL *Young*	Y	Y	Y	Y	Y	Y	N
ARIZONA							
1 *Salmon*	Y	Y	Y	Y	N	?	Y
2 Pastor	N	N	Y	N	Y	N	N
3 *Stump*	Y	Y	Y	Y	N	Y	N
4 *Shadegg*	Y	Y	Y	Y	N	Y	N
5 *Kolbe*	Y	Y	Y	N	Y	Y	N
6 *Hayworth*	Y	Y	Y	Y	N	Y	N
ARKANSAS							
1 Berry	N	N	N	N	Y	Y	N
2 Snyder	N	N	N	N	Y	Y	N
3 *Hutchinson*	Y	Y	Y	N	Y	Y	N
4 *Dickey*	Y	Y	Y	Y	Y	Y	N
CALIFORNIA							
1 *Riggs*	Y	Y	Y	Y	Y	Y	N
2 *Herger*	Y	Y	Y	Y	N	Y	N
3 Fazio	N	N	N	N	Y	Y	N
4 *Doolittle*	Y	Y	Y	N	N	Y	N
5 Matsui	N	N	N	N	Y	Y	N
6 Woolsey	N	N	N	N	Y	Y	Y
7 Miller	N	N	N	N	Y	Y	?
8 Pelosi	N	N	N	N	Y	Y	Y
9 Lee	N	N	N	N	Y	Y	Y
10 Tauscher	N	N	N	N	Y	Y	N
11 *Pombo*	Y	Y	Y	Y	N	Y	N
12 Lantos	N	N	N	N	Y	Y	Y
13 Stark	N	N	N	N	Y	Y	Y
14 Eshoo	N	N	N	N	Y	Y	Y
15 *Campbell*	Y	Y	Y	N	Y	Y	Y
16 Lofgren	N	N	N	N	Y	Y	Y
17 Farr	N	N	N	N	Y	Y	Y
18 Condit	N	N	N	N	Y	Y	N
19 *Radanovich*	Y	Y	Y	Y	N	Y	N
20 Dooley	N	N	N	N	Y	Y	N
21 *Thomas*	Y	Y	Y	Y	N	Y	N
22 Capps, L.	N	N	N	N	Y	Y	N
23 *Gallegly*	Y	Y	Y	Y	N	Y	N
24 Sherman	N	N	N	N	Y	Y	N
25 *McKeon*	Y	Y	Y	Y	N	Y	N
26 Berman	N	N	N	N	Y	Y	N
27 *Rogan*	Y	Y	Y	Y	N	Y	N
28 *Dreier*	Y	Y	Y	Y	N	Y	N
29 Waxman	N	N	N	N	Y	Y	Y
30 Becerra	?	N	N	N	Y	Y	Y
31 Martinez	?	?	?	?	?	Y	N
32 Dixon	N	N	N	N	Y	Y	N
33 Roybal-Allard	N	N	N	N	Y	Y	N
34 Torres	?	?	?	?	?	?	?
35 Waters	N	N	N	N	Y	Y	Y
36 Harman	N	N	N	N	Y	Y	N
37 Millender-McD.	N	N	N	N	Y	Y	N

	246	247	248	249	250	251	252
38 *Horn*	Y	Y	Y	N	Y	Y	N
39 *Royce*	Y	Y	Y	Y	N	Y	N
40 *Lewis*	Y	Y	Y	Y	N	Y	N
41 *Kim*	Y	Y	Y	Y	N	Y	N
42 Brown	N	N	N	N	Y	Y	N
43 *Calvert*	Y	Y	Y	Y	N	Y	N
44 *Bono, M.*	Y	Y	Y	Y	N	Y	N
45 *Rohrabacher*	Y	Y	Y	Y	N	Y	N
46 Sanchez	N	N	N	N	Y	Y	N
47 *Cox*	Y	Y	Y	Y	Y	?	Y
48 *Packard*	Y	Y	Y	Y	N	Y	N
49 *Bilbray*	Y	Y	Y	N	Y	Y	N
50 Filner	N	N	N	N	Y	Y	N
51 *Cunningham*	Y	Y	Y	Y	N	Y	N
52 *Hunter*	Y	Y	Y	Y	Y	Y	N
COLORADO							
1 DeGette	N	N	N	N	Y	Y	N
2 Skaggs	N	N	N	?	Y	Y	N
3 *McInnis*	Y	Y	Y	N	Y	Y	N
4 *Schaffer*	Y	Y	Y	Y	N	Y	N
5 *Hefley*	Y	Y	Y	N	Y	Y	Y
6 *Schaefer*	Y	Y	Y	Y	N	Y	N
CONNECTICUT							
1 Kennelly	N	N	Y	N	+	Y	Y
2 Gejdenson	N	N	N	N	Y	Y	N
3 DeLauro	N	N	N	N	Y	Y	N
4 *Shays*	Y	Y	Y	N	Y	Y	Y
5 Maloney	N	N	Y	N	Y	Y	N
6 *Johnson*	Y	Y	Y	N	N	Y	N
DELAWARE							
AL *Castle*	Y	Y	Y	N	Y	Y	N
FLORIDA							
1 *Scarborough*	Y	Y	Y	Y	Y	Y	Y
2 Boyd	N	N	N	N	Y	Y	N
3 Brown	N	N	N	N	Y	Y	N
4 *Fowler*	Y	Y	Y	N	N	Y	N
5 Thurman	N	N	N	N	Y	Y	N
6 *Stearns*	Y	Y	Y	Y	Y	Y	N
7 *Mica*	Y	Y	Y	Y	Y	Y	N
8 *McCollum*	Y	Y	Y	Y	N	Y	N
9 *Bilirakis*	Y	Y	Y	Y	N	Y	N
10 *Young*	Y	Y	Y	Y	N	Y	N
11 Davis	N	N	N	N	Y	Y	N
12 *Canady*	Y	Y	Y	N	N	Y	N
13 *Miller*	Y	Y	Y	N	Y	Y	N
14 *Goss*	Y	Y	Y	Y	Y	Y	N
15 *Weldon*	+	+	+	?	?	+	?
16 *Foley*	Y	Y	Y	N	Y	Y	N
17 Meek	N	N	N	N	Y	Y	N
18 *Ros-Lehtinen*	Y	Y	Y	Y	Y	Y	N
19 Wexler	N	N	N	N	Y	Y	Y
20 Deutsch	N	N	N	N	Y	Y	N
21 *Diaz-Balart*	Y	Y	Y	Y	Y	Y	N
22 *Shaw*	Y	Y	?	?	Y	Y	Y
23 Hastings	?	?	?	?	?	?	Y
GEORGIA							
1 *Kingston*	Y	Y	Y	Y	Y	Y	Y
2 Bishop	N	N	N	N	Y	Y	N
3 *Collins*	Y	Y	Y	N	Y	N	Y
4 McKinney	N	N	N	N	Y	Y	Y
5 Lewis	?	?	?	?	?	?	Y
6 *Gingrich*							
7 *Barr*	Y	Y	?	?	?	?	N
8 *Chambliss*	Y	Y	Y	Y	N	Y	N
9 *Deal*	Y	Y	Y	Y	N	Y	N
10 *Norwood*	Y	Y	Y	Y	Y	Y	N
11 *Linder*	Y	Y	Y	Y	N	Y	N
HAWAII							
1 Abercrombie	N	N	N	N	Y	Y	Y
2 Mink	N	−	Y	N	Y	Y	Y
IDAHO							
1 *Chenoweth*	Y	Y	Y	Y	N	Y	N
2 *Crapo*	Y	Y	Y	Y	Y	Y	N
ILLINOIS							
1 Rush	N	N	N	N	Y	Y	?
2 Jackson	N	N	N	N	Y	Y	Y
3 Lipinski	N	N	N	N	Y	Y	N
4 Gutierrez	N	N	N	N	Y	Y	+
5 Blagojevich	N	N	N	N	Y	Y	N
6 *Hyde*	Y	Y	Y	Y	Y	Y	N
7 Davis	N	N	N	N	Y	Y	N
8 *Crane*	Y	Y	Y	Y	Y	Y	N
9 Yates	N	N	N	N	Y	Y	N
10 *Porter*	Y	Y	Y	N	Y	Y	N
11 *Weller*	Y	Y	Y	Y	N	Y	N
12 Costello	N	N	N	N	Y	Y	N

ND Northern Democrats   SD Southern Democrats

	246	247	248	249	250	251	252
13 ***Fawell***	Y	Y	Y	Y	Y	Y	N
14 ***Hastert***	Y	Y	+	Y	N	Y	N
15 ***Ewing***	Y	Y	Y	Y	Y	Y	N
16 ***Manzullo***	Y	Y	Y	Y	Y	Y	N
17 Evans	N	N	N	N	Y	Y	Y
18 ***LaHood***	Y	Y	Y	Y	Y	Y	Y
19 Poshard	N	N	N	N	Y	Y	?
20 ***Shimkus***	Y	Y	Y	Y	Y	Y	N
INDIANA							
1 Visclosky	N	N	N	N	Y	Y	N
2 ***McIntosh***	Y	Y	?	#	Y	Y	Y
3 Roemer	N	N	N	N	Y	Y	N
4 ***Souder***	Y	Y	Y	N	N	Y	N
5 ***Buyer***	Y	Y	Y	Y	N	Y	N
6 ***Burton***	Y	Y	Y	Y	N	Y	N
7 ***Pease***	Y	Y	Y	Y	Y	Y	N
8 ***Hostettler***	Y	Y	Y	Y	N	Y	N
9 Hamilton	N	N	N	N	Y	Y	N
10 Carson	N	N	N	N	Y	Y	–
IOWA							
1 ***Leach***	Y	Y	Y	N	Y	P	N
2 ***Nussle***	Y	Y	Y	N	Y	Y	N
3 Boswell	N	N	N	N	Y	Y	N
4 ***Ganske***	Y	Y	Y	N	Y	Y	N
5 ***Latham***	Y	Y	Y	Y	Y	Y	N
KANSAS							
1 ***Moran***	Y	Y	Y	N	N	Y	N
2 ***Ryun***	Y	Y	Y	Y	Y	Y	N
3 ***Snowbarger***	Y	Y	Y	Y	Y	Y	Y
4 ***Tiahrt***	Y	Y	Y	Y	N	Y	N
KENTUCKY							
1 ***Whitfield***	Y	Y	Y	Y	N	Y	Y
2 ***Lewis***	Y	?	Y	Y	N	Y	N
3 ***Northup***	Y	Y	Y	Y	N	Y	N
4 ***Bunning***	Y	Y	Y	Y	N	Y	N
5 ***Rogers***	Y	Y	Y	Y	Y	Y	N
6 Baesler	N	N	N	N	Y	Y	N
LOUISIANA							
1 ***Livingston***	Y	Y	Y	Y	Y	Y	?
2 Jefferson	N	N	?	N	Y	Y	N
3 ***Tauzin***	Y	Y	Y	Y	Y	Y	N
4 ***McCrery***	Y	Y	Y	Y	N	Y	N
5 ***Cooksey***	?	?	?	?	?	?	N
6 ***Baker***	Y	Y	Y	Y	N	?	?
7 John	N	N	N	N	Y	Y	N
MAINE							
1 Allen	N	N	N	N	Y	Y	Y
2 Baldacci	N	N	N	N	Y	Y	Y
MARYLAND							
1 ***Gilchrest***	Y	Y	Y	N	Y	Y	N
2 ***Ehrlich***	Y	Y	Y	N	Y	Y	N
3 Cardin	N	N	N	N	Y	Y	N
4 Wynn	N	N	N	N	Y	Y	N
5 Hoyer	N	N	N	N	Y	Y	N
6 ***Bartlett***	Y	Y	Y	Y	Y	Y	N
7 Cummings	N	N	N	N	Y	Y	N
8 ***Morella***	Y	Y	Y	X	+	+	Y
MASSACHUSETTS							
1 Olver	N	N	N	N	Y	Y	Y
2 Neal	N	N	N	N	Y	Y	Y
3 McGovern	N	N	N	N	Y	Y	Y
4 Frank	N	N	N	N	N	Y	Y
5 Meehan	N	N	N	N	Y	Y	?
6 Tierney	N	N	N	N	Y	Y	Y
7 Markey	N	N	N	N	Y	Y	Y
8 Kennedy	N	N	N	N	?	?	Y
9 Moakley	N	N	N	N	Y	Y	Y
10 Delahunt	N	N	N	N	Y	Y	Y
MICHIGAN							
1 Stupak	N	N	N	N	Y	Y	N
2 ***Hoekstra***	Y	Y	Y	Y	Y	Y	N
3 ***Ehlers***	Y	Y	Y	Y	Y	Y	N
4 ***Camp***	Y	Y	Y	Y	Y	Y	N
5 Barcia	N	N	N	N	Y	Y	N
6 ***Upton***	Y	Y	Y	N	Y	Y	N
7 ***Smith***	Y	Y	Y	N	Y	Y	N
8 Stabenow	N	N	N	N	Y	Y	Y
9 Kildee	N	N	N	N	Y	Y	Y
10 Bonior	N	N	N	N	N	Y	Y
11 ***Knollenberg***	Y	Y	Y	Y	Y	Y	N
12 Levin	N	N	N	N	Y	Y	Y
13 Rivers	N	N	N	N	Y	Y	Y
14 Conyers	N	N	N	N	Y	?	Y
15 Kilpatrick	N	N	N	N	Y	Y	Y
16 Dingell	N	Y	N	N	Y	Y	N
MINNESOTA							
1 ***Gutknecht***	+	+	+	+	+	+	N
2 Minge	N	N	N	N	Y	Y	Y
3 ***Ramstad***	Y	Y	Y	N	Y	Y	Y
4 Vento	N	N	N	N	Y	Y	Y
5 Sabo	N	N	N	Y	N	Y	Y
6 Luther	N	N	N	N	Y	Y	Y
7 Peterson	N	N	N	Y	Y	Y	Y
8 Oberstar	N	N	N	N	N	Y	Y
MISSISSIPPI							
1 ***Wicker***	Y	Y	Y	Y	N	Y	N
2 Thompson	N	N	N	N	Y	Y	N
3 ***Pickering***	Y	Y	Y	Y	N	Y	N
4 ***Parker***	?	?	?	?	?	?	N
5 Taylor	N	Y	Y	N	Y	Y	N
MISSOURI							
1 Clay	N	N	N	N	Y	Y	Y
2 ***Talent***	Y	Y	Y	Y	Y	Y	Y
3 Gephardt	N	N	N	N	?	?	Y
4 Skelton	N	N	Y	N	Y	Y	N
5 McCarthy	N	N	N	N	Y	Y	Y
6 Danner	N	?	N	N	Y	Y	Y
7 ***Blunt***	Y	Y	?	?	?	?	N
8 ***Emerson***	Y	Y	Y	Y	Y	Y	N
9 ***Hulshof***	Y	Y	Y	Y	N	Y	Y
MONTANA							
AL ***Hill***	Y	Y	Y	N	Y	Y	N
NEBRASKA							
1 ***Bereuter***	Y	Y	Y	N	Y	Y	N
2 ***Christensen***	Y	Y	Y	Y	Y	Y	Y
3 ***Barrett***	Y	Y	Y	N	Y	Y	N
NEVADA							
1 ***Ensign***	Y	Y	Y	Y	Y	Y	Y
2 ***Gibbons***	Y	Y	Y	Y	Y	Y	Y
NEW HAMPSHIRE							
1 ***Sununu***	?	?	?	?	?	?	Y
2 ***Bass***	Y	Y	Y	N	Y	Y	Y
NEW JERSEY							
1 Andrews	N	N	N	N	Y	Y	Y
2 ***LoBiondo***	Y	Y	Y	N	Y	Y	Y
3 ***Saxton***	Y	Y	Y	Y	Y	Y	N
4 ***Smith***	Y	Y	Y	Y	Y	?	Y
5 ***Roukema***	Y	Y	Y	N	Y	Y	Y
6 Pallone	N	N	N	N	Y	Y	Y
7 ***Franks***	Y	Y	Y	N	Y	Y	Y
8 Pascrell	N	N	N	N	Y	Y	?
9 Rothman	N	N	?	?	?	?	Y
10 Payne	N	N	N	N	Y	Y	Y
11 ***Frelinghuysen***	Y	Y	Y	N	Y	Y	N
12 ***Pappas***	Y	Y	Y	N	Y	Y	Y
13 Menendez	N	N	N	N	Y	Y	Y
NEW MEXICO							
1 Vacant							
2 ***Skeen***	Y	Y	Y	Y	N	Y	N
3 ***Redmond***	Y	Y	Y	Y	Y	Y	N
NEW YORK							
1 ***Forbes***	Y	Y	Y	N	Y	Y	N
2 ***Lazio***	Y	Y	Y	N	Y	Y	N
3 ***King***	Y	Y	Y	Y	N	Y	N
4 McCarthy	N	N	N	N	Y	Y	Y
5 Ackerman	N	N	N	N	Y	Y	?
6 Meeks	N	N	?	?	?	?	Y
7 Manton	N	N	N	N	Y	Y	N
8 Nadler	N	N	N	N	Y	Y	?
9 Schumer	N	?	?	?	Y	Y	?
10 Towns	?	?	N	N	Y	Y	?
11 Owens	N	N	N	N	Y	Y	–
12 Velázquez	N	N	N	N	Y	Y	Y
13 ***Fossella***	Y	Y	Y	Y	N	Y	N
14 Maloney	N	N	N	N	Y	Y	+
15 Rangel	N	N	N	N	Y	Y	?
16 Serrano	N	N	N	N	Y	Y	Y
17 Engel	N	N	N	N	Y	Y	Y
18 Lowey	N	N	N	N	Y	Y	Y
19 ***Kelly***	Y	Y	Y	N	Y	Y	N
20 ***Gilman***	Y	Y	Y	N	Y	Y	N
21 McNulty	?	?	?	?	?	?	?
22 ***Solomon***	Y	Y	Y	Y	Y	?	N
23 ***Boehlert***	Y	Y	Y	N	Y	Y	N
24 ***McHugh***	Y	Y	Y	N	Y	Y	N
25 ***Walsh***	Y	Y	Y	N	Y	Y	N
26 Hinchey	N	N	N	N	Y	Y	Y
27 ***Paxon***	Y	Y	Y	Y	N	Y	Y
28 Slaughter	N	N	N	N	Y	Y	N
29 LaFalce	N	N	N	N	Y	Y	N
30 ***Quinn***	Y	Y	Y	N	Y	Y	N
31 ***Houghton***	Y	Y	Y	N	Y	Y	N
NORTH CAROLINA							
1 Clayton	–	–	N	N	Y	Y	N
2 Etheridge	N	N	N	N	Y	Y	N
3 ***Jones***	Y	Y	Y	Y	Y	Y	N
4 Price	N	N	N	N	Y	Y	N
5 ***Burr***	Y	Y	Y	Y	Y	Y	N
6 ***Coble***	Y	Y	Y	N	Y	Y	Y
7 McIntyre	N	N	Y	N	Y	Y	N
8 Hefner	N	N	N	N	Y	Y	N
9 ***Myrick***	Y	Y	Y	Y	Y	Y	N
10 ***Ballenger***	Y	Y	Y	Y	N	Y	N
11 ***Taylor***	Y	Y	Y	Y	Y	Y	N
12 Watt	N	N	N	N	N	Y	N
NORTH DAKOTA							
AL Pomeroy	N	N	N	N	?	Y	N
OHIO							
1 ***Chabot***	Y	Y	Y	N	Y	Y	Y
2 ***Portman***	Y	?	Y	N	Y	Y	+
3 Hall	N	N	Y	N	Y	Y	N
4 ***Oxley***	Y	Y	?	Y	N	Y	–
5 ***Gillmor***	Y	Y	Y	Y	Y	Y	N
6 Strickland	?	N	N	N	Y	Y	N
7 ***Hobson***	Y	Y	Y	Y	Y	Y	N
8 ***Boehner***	Y	Y	Y	Y	N	Y	N
9 Kaptur	N	N	N	N	Y	P	N
10 Kucinich	N	N	N	N	Y	Y	Y
11 Stokes	N	N	N	N	Y	Y	Y
12 ***Kasich***	Y	Y	Y	?	?	?	Y
13 Brown	N	N	N	N	Y	Y	Y
14 Sawyer	N	N	N	N	Y	Y	N
15 ***Pryce***	Y	Y	Y	N	Y	Y	N
16 ***Regula***	Y	?	Y	N	Y	Y	N
17 Traficant	Y	Y	Y	Y	Y	Y	N
18 ***Ney***	Y	Y	Y	Y	Y	Y	Y
19 ***LaTourette***	Y	Y	Y	N	Y	Y	N
OKLAHOMA							
1 ***Largent***	Y	Y	Y	Y	Y	Y	Y
2 ***Coburn***	Y	Y	Y	Y	?	?	Y
3 ***Watkins***	Y	Y	Y	Y	Y	Y	N
4 ***Watts***	Y	Y	Y	Y	Y	Y	N
5 ***Istook***	Y	Y	Y	Y	Y	Y	N
6 ***Lucas***	Y	Y	Y	Y	Y	Y	N
OREGON							
1 Furse	N	N	N	N	Y	Y	Y
2 ***Smith***	Y	Y	Y	Y	N	Y	N
3 Blumenauer	N	N	N	N	Y	Y	Y
4 DeFazio	N	N	N	N	Y	Y	Y
5 Hooley	N	N	N	N	Y	Y	Y
PENNSYLVANIA							
1 Brady	N	N	N	N	Y	Y	N
2 Fattah	N	N	N	N	Y	Y	N
3 Borski	N	N	N	N	Y	Y	N
4 Klink	N	N	N	N	Y	Y	N
5 ***Peterson***	Y	Y	Y	Y	Y	Y	N
6 Holden	N	N	N	N	Y	?	N
7 ***Weldon***	Y	Y	Y	Y	Y	Y	N
8 ***Greenwood***	Y	Y	Y	N	Y	Y	N
9 ***Shuster***	Y	Y	Y	Y	Y	Y	N
10 ***McDade***	Y	Y	?	?	?	?	N
11 Kanjorski	N	N	Y	N	Y	Y	N
12 Murtha	N	N	Y	N	N	Y	N
13 ***Fox***	Y	Y	Y	N	Y	Y	N
14 Coyne	N	N	N	N	Y	Y	N
15 McHale	N	N	N	N	Y	Y	N
16 ***Pitts***	Y	Y	Y	Y	N	Y	Y
17 ***Gekas***	Y	?	Y	Y	N	Y	N
18 Doyle	N	N	N	N	Y	Y	N
19 ***Goodling***	Y	Y	Y	Y	+	+	N
20 Mascara	N	N	N	N	Y	Y	N
21 ***English***	Y	Y	Y	Y	P	Y	Y
RHODE ISLAND							
1 Kennedy	N	N	N	N	Y	Y	Y
2 Weygand	N	N	N	N	Y	Y	Y
SOUTH CAROLINA							
1 ***Sanford***	Y	Y	Y	N	Y	Y	Y
2 ***Spence***	Y	Y	Y	Y	Y	Y	N
3 ***Graham***	Y	Y	Y	N	Y	Y	N
4 ***Inglis***	Y	Y	Y	Y	Y	Y	Y
5 Spratt	N	N	N	N	Y	Y	N
6 Clyburn	N	N	N	N	Y	Y	N
SOUTH DAKOTA							
AL ***Thune***	Y	Y	Y	Y	Y	Y	Y
TENNESSEE							
1 ***Jenkins***	Y	?	Y	N	Y	Y	N
2 ***Duncan***	Y	Y	Y	N	Y	Y	Y
3 ***Wamp***	Y	Y	Y	N	Y	Y	N
4 ***Hilleary***	Y	Y	Y	N	Y	Y	N
5 Clement	N	N	N	N	Y	Y	N
6 Gordon	N	N	N	N	Y	Y	?
7 ***Bryant***	Y	Y	Y	N	Y	Y	N
8 Tanner	N	N	N	N	Y	Y	N
9 Ford	N	N	N	N	Y	Y	N
TEXAS							
1 Sandlin	N	N	N	N	Y	Y	N
2 Turner	N	N	N	N	Y	Y	N
3 ***Johnson, Sam***	Y	Y	Y	Y	?	?	N
4 Hall	Y	Y	N	Y	Y	Y	N
5 ***Sessions***	Y	Y	Y	Y	N	Y	N
6 ***Barton***	Y	Y	Y	Y	Y	Y	N
7 ***Archer***	?	Y	Y	Y	N	Y	N
8 ***Brady***	Y	Y	Y	N	N	Y	N
9 Lampson	N	N	N	N	Y	Y	Y
10 Doggett	N	N	N	N	Y	Y	Y
11 Edwards	N	N	N	N	Y	Y	N
12 ***Granger***	Y	Y	Y	Y	N	Y	N
13 ***Thornberry***	Y	Y	Y	Y	N	Y	N
14 ***Paul***	Y	Y	Y	Y	N	Y	Y
15 Hinojosa	N	N	N	N	Y	Y	N
16 Reyes	N	N	?	?	?	?	N
17 Stenholm	N	N	N	N	Y	Y	N
18 Jackson-Lee	N	N	N	N	Y	Y	N
19 ***Combest***	Y	Y	Y	Y	N	Y	N
20 Gonzalez	?	?	?	?	?	?	?
21 ***Smith***	Y	Y	Y	Y	N	Y	N
22 ***DeLay***	Y	Y	Y	Y	N	Y	N
23 ***Bonilla***	Y	Y	Y	Y	Y	Y	N
24 Frost	N	N	N	Y	Y	Y	N
25 Bentsen	N	N	N	N	Y	Y	N
26 ***Armey***	?	Y	Y	Y	N	Y	N
27 Ortiz	N	N	N	N	Y	?	N
28 Rodriguez	N	N	N	N	Y	Y	N
29 Green	–	–	–	–	+	+	N
30 Johnson, E.B.	N	N	N	N	Y	P	N
UTAH							
1 ***Hansen***	Y	Y	Y	Y	N	Y	N
2 ***Cook***	Y	Y	Y	N	Y	Y	N
3 ***Cannon***	Y	Y	Y	Y	N	Y	?
VERMONT							
AL *Sanders*	N	N	N	N	Y	Y	Y
VIRGINIA							
1 ***Bateman***	Y	Y	Y	Y	N	Y	N
2 Pickett	N	N	Y	N	Y	Y	N
3 Scott	N	N	N	N	Y	Y	N
4 Sisisky	N	N	Y	N	Y	Y	N
5 Goode	N	Y	Y	N	Y	Y	N
6 ***Goodlatte***	Y	Y	Y	Y	Y	Y	N
7 ***Bliley***	Y	Y	Y	Y	Y	Y	N
8 Moran	N	Y	N	N	Y	Y	N
9 Boucher	N	N	N	N	Y	Y	N
10 ***Wolf***	Y	Y	Y	N	Y	Y	N
11 ***Davis***	Y	Y	Y	N	Y	Y	N
WASHINGTON							
1 ***White***	Y	Y	Y	Y	Y	Y	N
2 ***Metcalf***	Y	Y	Y	N	Y	Y	Y
3 ***Smith, Linda***	Y	Y	Y	N	Y	Y	N
4 ***Hastings***	Y	Y	Y	Y	Y	Y	N
5 ***Nethercutt***	Y	Y	Y	Y	Y	Y	N
6 Dicks	N	N	N	N	Y	Y	N
7 McDermott	N	N	N	N	N	Y	Y
8 ***Dunn***	Y	?	Y	Y	Y	Y	N
9 Smith, Adam	N	N	N	N	Y	Y	Y
WEST VIRGINIA							
1 Mollohan	N	N	Y	N	N	Y	N
2 Wise	N	N	N	N	?	Y	N
3 Rahall	N	N	Y	N	Y	Y	N
WISCONSIN							
1 ***Neumann***	Y	Y	Y	N	N	Y	Y
2 ***Klug***	Y	Y	Y	N	?	Y	Y
3 Kind	N	N	N	N	Y	Y	Y
4 Kleczka	N	N	N	N	Y	Y	Y
5 Barrett	N	N	N	N	Y	Y	Y
6 ***Petri***	Y	Y	Y	Y	Y	Y	Y
7 Obey	N	N	N	Y	N	Y	N
8 Johnson	N	N	N	N	Y	Y	N
9 ***Sensenbrenner***	Y	Y	Y	Y	Y	Y	Y
WYOMING							
AL ***Cubin***	Y	Y	Y	Y	N	Y	N

Southern states - Ala., Ark., Fla., Ga., Ky., La., Miss., N.C., Okla., S.C., Tenn., Texas, Va.

253. HR 4060. Fiscal 1999 Energy and Water Appropriations/Passage. Passage of the bill to provide $21.1 billion in new budget authority for energy and water resources programs. The bill provides $184 million less than provided in fiscal 1998 and $648 million less than the president's request. Passed 405-4: R 217-4; D 187-0 (ND 134-0, SD 53-0); I 1-0. June 22, 1998.

254. HR 4059. Fiscal 1999 Military Construction Appropriations/Passage. Passage of the bill to provide $8.2 billion in new budget authority for military construction projects in fiscal 1999. The bill provides $450 million more than the president's request and $974 million less than the amount provided for fiscal 1998. Passed 396-10: R 216-3; D 179-7 (ND 127-6, SD 52-1); I 1-0. June 22, 1998.

255. H Con Res 288. Money Laundering/Passage. McCollum, R-Fla., motion to suspend the rules and pass the bill to express the sense of Congress that undercover law enforcement investigations are necessary to counter money-laundering schemes that involve financial institutions in the United States and other countries, including Mexico. Motion agreed to 404-3: R 217-3; D 186-0 (ND 133-0, SD 53-0); I 1-0. June 22, 1998. A two-thirds majority of those present and voting (272 in this case) is required for passage under suspension of the rules.

256. H Res 452. Postage Rate Increase/Passage. LaTourette, R-Ohio, motion to suspend the rules and pass the bill to express the sense of the House that the U.S. Postal Service's Board of Governors should reject the recommendation that postage rates be raised. Motion agreed to 393-12: R 212-6; D 180-6 (ND 127-6, SD 53-0); I 1-0. June 22, 1998. A two-thirds majority of those present and voting (270 in this case) is required for passage under suspension of the rules.

257. HR 3853. Small Business Drug-free Workplace Programs/Passage. Souder, R-Ind., motion to suspend the rules and pass the bill to authorize $10 million in fiscal 1999 to be used to stop illegal drug use by employees of small businesses. The bill would create a drug-free workplace demonstration program and authorize the Small Business Administration to make grants to nonprofit organizations to provide financial support and advice to small businesses seeking drug-free workplace programs. Motion agreed to 402-9: R 217-1; D 185-8 (ND 134-6, SD 51-2); I 0-0. June 23, 1998. A two-thirds majority of those present and voting (274 in this case) is required for passage under suspension of the rules.

258. HR 4101. Fiscal 1999 Agriculture Appropriations/Peanut Price Support Loans. Neumann, R-Wis., amendment to prohibit the use of funds in the bill to provide a peanut price-support loan greater than $550 per ton for the 1999 crop of quota peanuts. Rejected 181-244: R 101-123; D 80-120 (ND 76-73, SD 4-47); I 0-1. June 23, 1998.

259. HR 4101. Fiscal 1999 Agriculture Appropriations/Wildlife Service Livestock Protection Program. Bass, R-N.H., amendment to reduce the bill's funding by $10 million for the Agriculture Department's Wildlife Service livestock protection program, to try to reduce efforts by the agency to kill predators in Western states. Adopted 229-193: R 75-147; D 153-46 (ND 128-20, SD 25-26); I 1-0. June 23, 1998.

Key

Y	Voted for (yea).
#	Paired for.
+	Announced for.
N	Voted against (nay).
X	Paired against.
−	Announced against.
P	Voted "present."
C	Voted "present" to avoid possible conflict of interest.
?	Did not vote or otherwise make a position known.

Democrats   •   *Republicans*

Independent

	253	254	255	256	257	258	259
ALABAMA							
1 *Callahan*	Y	Y	Y	Y	Y	N	N
2 *Everett*	Y	Y	Y	Y	Y	N	N
3 *Riley*	Y	Y	Y	Y	Y	N	N
4 *Aderholt*	Y	Y	Y	Y	Y	N	N
5 Cramer	Y	Y	Y	Y	Y	N	N
6 *Bachus*	Y	Y	Y	Y	Y	N	N
7 Hilliard	Y	Y	Y	Y	Y	?	?
ALASKA							
AL *Young*	Y	Y	Y	Y	Y	N	N
ARIZONA							
1 *Salmon*	Y	Y	Y	Y	Y	Y	N
2 Pastor	Y	Y	Y	Y	Y	N	N
3 *Stump*	Y	Y	Y	Y	Y	N	N
4 *Shadegg*	Y	Y	Y	Y	Y	Y	N
5 *Kolbe*	Y	Y	N	N	Y	Y	N
6 *Hayworth*	Y	Y	Y	Y	Y	Y	N
ARKANSAS							
1 Berry	Y	Y	Y	Y	Y	N	Y
2 Snyder	Y	Y	Y	Y	Y	N	Y
3 *Hutchinson*	Y	Y	Y	Y	Y	Y	N
4 *Dickey*	Y	Y	Y	Y	Y	Y	N
CALIFORNIA							
1 *Riggs*	Y	Y	Y	Y	?	Y	N
2 *Herger*	Y	Y	?	Y	Y	N	N
3 Fazio	Y	Y	Y	Y	Y	N	N
4 *Doolittle*	Y	Y	Y	Y	Y	N	N
5 Matsui	Y	Y	Y	Y	Y	N	Y
6 Woolsey	Y	Y	Y	Y	Y	N	Y
7 Miller	?	?	?	?	?	Y	Y
8 Pelosi	Y	Y	Y	Y	Y	N	Y
9 Lee	Y	Y	Y	Y	Y	N	Y
10 Tauscher	Y	Y	Y	Y	Y	Y	Y
11 *Pombo*	Y	Y	Y	Y	Y	N	N
12 Lantos	Y	N	Y	Y	Y	Y	Y
13 Stark	Y	Y	Y	Y	Y	Y	Y
14 Eshoo	Y	Y	Y	Y	Y	N	Y
15 *Campbell*	Y	Y	Y	N	Y	Y	Y
16 Lofgren	Y	N	Y	Y	Y	Y	Y
17 Farr	Y	Y	Y	Y	Y	N	Y
18 Condit	Y	Y	Y	Y	Y	N	N
19 *Radanovich*	Y	Y	Y	Y	Y	Y	Y
20 Dooley	Y	Y	Y	Y	Y	N	N
21 *Thomas*	Y	Y	N	Y	N	N	N
22 Capps, L.	Y	Y	Y	Y	Y	Y	Y
23 *Gallegly*	Y	Y	Y	Y	Y	N	Y
24 Sherman	Y	Y	Y	Y	Y	Y	Y
25 *McKeon*	Y	Y	Y	Y	Y	N	N
26 Berman	Y	Y	Y	Y	Y	Y	Y
27 *Rogan*	Y	Y	Y	Y	Y	N	Y
28 *Dreier*	Y	Y	Y	Y	Y	N	N
29 Waxman	Y	Y	Y	Y	?	Y	Y
30 Becerra	?	?	?	?	Y	Y	Y
31 Martinez	Y	Y	Y	Y	Y	N	N
32 Dixon	Y	Y	Y	Y	Y	N	Y
33 Roybal-Allard	Y	Y	Y	Y	Y	N	Y
34 Torres	?	?	?	?	?	?	?
35 Waters	Y	Y	Y	Y	N	N	Y
36 Harman	Y	Y	Y	Y	Y	Y	Y
37 Millender-McD.	Y	Y	Y	Y	Y	N	Y

	253	254	255	256	257	258	259
38 *Horn*	Y	Y	Y	Y	Y	Y	Y
39 *Royce*	Y	N	Y	Y	Y	Y	Y
40 *Lewis*	Y	Y	Y	Y	?	N	N
41 *Kim*	Y	Y	Y	Y	Y	N	N
42 Brown	Y	Y	Y	Y	Y	Y	Y
43 *Calvert*	Y	Y	Y	Y	Y	N	N
44 *Bono, M.*	Y	Y	Y	Y	Y	Y	Y
45 *Rohrabacher*	Y	Y	Y	Y	Y	Y	N
46 Sanchez	Y	Y	Y	Y	Y	Y	Y
47 *Cox*	Y	Y	Y	?	Y	Y	Y
48 *Packard*	Y	Y	Y	Y	Y	N	N
49 *Bilbray*	Y	Y	Y	Y	Y	Y	N
50 Filner	Y	Y	Y	Y	Y	N	Y
51 *Cunningham*	Y	Y	Y	Y	Y	N	N
52 *Hunter*	Y	Y	Y	Y	?	N	N
COLORADO							
1 DeGette	Y	Y	Y	Y	Y	Y	Y
2 Skaggs	Y	Y	Y	Y	Y	Y	Y
3 *McInnis*	Y	Y	Y	Y	Y	Y	N
4 *Schaffer*	Y	Y	Y	Y	N	N	N
5 *Hefley*	Y	Y	Y	Y	N	N	N
6 *Schaefer*	Y	Y	Y	Y	?	?	?
CONNECTICUT							
1 Kennelly	Y	Y	Y	Y	Y	N	Y
2 Gejdenson	Y	Y	Y	Y	Y	N	Y
3 DeLauro	Y	Y	Y	Y	Y	N	Y
4 *Shays*	Y	Y	Y	Y	Y	Y	Y
5 Maloney	Y	Y	Y	Y	Y	Y	Y
6 *Johnson*	Y	Y	Y	Y	Y	Y	Y
DELAWARE							
AL *Castle*	Y	Y	Y	Y	Y	Y	Y
FLORIDA							
1 *Scarborough*	Y	Y	Y	Y	Y	N	N
2 Boyd	Y	Y	Y	Y	Y	N	N
3 Brown	Y	Y	Y	Y	Y	N	Y
4 *Fowler*	Y	Y	Y	Y	N	N	N
5 Thurman	Y	Y	Y	Y	Y	N	N
6 *Stearns*	Y	Y	Y	Y	Y	N	N
7 *Mica*	Y	Y	Y	Y	Y	N	N
8 *McCollum*	Y	Y	Y	Y	Y	N	N
9 *Bilirakis*	Y	Y	Y	Y	Y	N	N
10 *Young*	Y	Y	Y	Y	Y	N	N
11 Davis	Y	Y	Y	Y	Y	N	N
12 *Canady*	Y	Y	Y	Y	Y	N	N
13 *Miller*	Y	Y	Y	Y	Y	Y	Y
14 *Goss*	Y	Y	Y	Y	Y	Y	Y
15 *Weldon*	?	+	+	+	Y	N	Y
16 *Foley*	Y	Y	Y	Y	Y	N	N
17 Meek	Y	Y	Y	Y	Y	N	Y
18 *Ros-Lehtinen*	Y	Y	Y	Y	Y	Y	Y
19 Wexler	Y	Y	Y	Y	Y	N	Y
20 Deutsch	Y	Y	Y	Y	Y	N	Y
21 *Diaz-Balart*	Y	Y	Y	Y	Y	N	Y
22 *Shaw*	Y	Y	Y	Y	Y	Y	Y
23 Hastings	Y	Y	Y	Y	Y	N	Y
GEORGIA							
1 *Kingston*	Y	Y	Y	Y	Y	N	N
2 Bishop	Y	Y	Y	Y	Y	N	N
3 *Collins*	Y	Y	Y	Y	Y	N	N
4 McKinney	Y	N	Y	Y	Y	N	Y
5 Lewis	Y	Y	Y	Y	Y	N	Y
6 *Gingrich*							
7 *Barr*	Y	Y	Y	Y	Y	N	N
8 *Chambliss*	Y	Y	Y	Y	Y	N	N
9 *Deal*	Y	Y	Y	Y	Y	N	N
10 *Norwood*	Y	Y	Y	Y	Y	N	N
11 *Linder*	Y	Y	Y	Y	Y	N	N
HAWAII							
1 Abercrombie	Y	Y	Y	Y	Y	N	Y
2 Mink	Y	Y	Y	Y	Y	N	Y
IDAHO							
1 *Chenoweth*	Y	Y	Y	Y	Y	N	N
2 *Crapo*	Y	Y	Y	Y	Y	N	N
ILLINOIS							
1 Rush	?	?	?	?	Y	Y	Y
2 Jackson	Y	Y	Y	Y	Y	Y	Y
3 Lipinski	Y	Y	Y	Y	Y	Y	Y
4 Gutierrez	+	+	+	+	Y	Y	Y
5 Blagojevich	Y	Y	Y	Y	Y	Y	Y
6 *Hyde*	Y	Y	Y	Y	Y	Y	N
7 Davis	Y	Y	Y	Y	Y	Y	Y
8 *Crane*	Y	Y	Y	Y	Y	Y	Y
9 Yates	Y	N	Y	Y	+	Y	Y
10 *Porter*	Y	+	Y	Y	Y	Y	Y
11 *Weller*	Y	Y	Y	Y	Y	N	N
12 Costello	Y	Y	Y	Y	Y	N	Y

ND Northern Democrats   SD Southern Democrats

	253	254	255	256	257	258	259
13 ***Fawell***	Y	Y	Y	Y	Y	Y	Y
14 ***Hastert***	Y	Y	Y	Y	Y	N	N
15 ***Ewing***	Y	Y	Y	Y	Y	N	N
16 ***Manzullo***	Y	Y	Y	Y	Y	Y	Y
17 Evans	Y	Y	Y	Y	Y	N	Y
18 ***LaHood***	Y	Y	Y	N	Y	N	N
19 Poshard	?	?	?	?	?	N	Y
20 ***Shimkus***	Y	Y	Y	Y	Y	N	N
INDIANA							
1 Visclosky	Y	Y	Y	Y	Y	Y	Y
2 ***McIntosh***	Y	Y	Y	Y	Y	Y	N
3 Roemer	Y	Y	Y	Y	Y	Y	Y
4 ***Souder***	Y	Y	Y	Y	Y	Y	N
5 ***Buyer***	Y	Y	Y	Y	Y	N	Y
6 ***Burton***	Y	Y	Y	Y	Y	Y	N
7 ***Pease***	Y	Y	Y	Y	Y	N	Y
8 ***Hostettler***	Y	Y	Y	Y	Y	Y	N
9 Hamilton	Y	Y	Y	Y	Y	N	Y
10 Carson	+	+	+	+	Y	N	Y
IOWA							
1 ***Leach***	Y	Y	Y	Y	Y	N	N
2 ***Nussle***	Y	Y	Y	Y	Y	N	N
3 Boswell	Y	Y	Y	Y	Y	N	N
4 ***Ganske***	Y	Y	Y	Y	Y	Y	N
5 ***Latham***	Y	Y	Y	Y	Y	N	N
KANSAS							
1 ***Moran***	Y	Y	Y	Y	Y	N	N
2 ***Ryun***	Y	Y	Y	Y	Y	Y	N
3 ***Snowbarger***	Y	Y	Y	Y	Y	Y	N
4 ***Tiahrt***	Y	Y	Y	Y	Y	Y	N
KENTUCKY							
1 ***Whitfield***	Y	Y	Y	Y	?	N	Y
2 ***Lewis***	Y	Y	Y	Y	Y	N	N
3 ***Northup***	Y	Y	Y	Y	Y	Y	Y
4 ***Bunning***	Y	Y	Y	Y	Y	N	N
5 ***Rogers***	Y	Y	Y	Y	Y	N	N
6 Baesler	Y	Y	Y	Y	Y	N	N
LOUISIANA							
1 ***Livingston***	Y	Y	Y	Y	Y	N	N
2 Jefferson	Y	Y	Y	Y	Y	N	Y
3 ***Tauzin***	Y	Y	Y	Y	Y	N	?
4 ***McCrery***	Y	Y	Y	Y	Y	N	N
5 ***Cooksey***	Y	Y	Y	Y	Y	N	N
6 ***Baker***	?	?	?	?	?	N	N
7 John	Y	Y	Y	Y	Y	N	N
MAINE							
1 Allen	Y	Y	Y	Y	Y	Y	Y
2 Baldacci	Y	Y	Y	Y	Y	N	Y
MARYLAND							
1 ***Gilchrest***	Y	Y	Y	Y	Y	N	Y
2 ***Ehrlich***	Y	Y	Y	Y	Y	Y	Y
3 Cardin	Y	Y	Y	Y	Y	Y	Y
4 Wynn	Y	Y	Y	Y	Y	N	Y
5 Hoyer	Y	Y	Y	N	Y	N	Y
6 ***Bartlett***	Y	Y	Y	Y	Y	Y	N
7 Cummings	Y	Y	Y	Y	Y	N	Y
8 ***Morella***	Y	Y	Y	Y	Y	Y	Y
MASSACHUSETTS							
1 Olver	Y	Y	Y	Y	Y	Y	Y
2 Neal	Y	Y	Y	Y	Y	Y	Y
3 McGovern	Y	Y	Y	Y	Y	Y	Y
4 Frank	Y	N	Y	Y	N	Y	Y
5 Meehan	?	?	?	?	Y	Y	Y
6 Tierney	Y	Y	Y	Y	Y	Y	Y
7 Markey	Y	Y	Y	Y	Y	Y	Y
8 Kennedy	Y	Y	Y	Y	Y	Y	Y
9 Moakley	Y	Y	Y	Y	Y	N	Y
10 Delahunt	Y	Y	Y	Y	Y	N	Y
MICHIGAN							
1 Stupak	Y	Y	Y	Y	Y	N	N
2 ***Hoekstra***	Y	Y	Y	Y	Y	Y	N
3 ***Ehlers***	Y	Y	Y	N	Y	Y	Y
4 ***Camp***	Y	Y	Y	Y	Y	N	N
5 Barcia	Y	Y	Y	Y	Y	N	Y
6 ***Upton***	Y	Y	Y	Y	Y	Y	Y
7 ***Smith***	Y	Y	Y	Y	Y	N	N
8 Stabenow	Y	Y	Y	Y	Y	N	Y
9 Kildee	Y	Y	Y	Y	Y	N	Y
10 Bonior	Y	Y	Y	Y	Y	N	Y
11 ***Knollenberg***	Y	Y	Y	Y	Y	Y	N
12 Levin	Y	Y	Y	Y	Y	Y	Y
13 Rivers	Y	Y	Y	Y	Y	Y	Y
14 Conyers	Y	N	Y	Y	N	N	Y
15 Kilpatrick	Y	Y	Y	Y	Y	N	Y
16 Dingell	Y	Y	Y	Y	Y	N	N

	253	254	255	256	257	258	259
MINNESOTA							
1 ***Gutknecht***	Y	Y	Y	Y	Y	N	N
2 Minge	Y	Y	Y	Y	Y	N	Y
3 ***Ramstad***	Y	Y	Y	Y	Y	Y	Y
4 Vento	Y	Y	Y	Y	Y	Y	Y
5 Sabo	Y	Y	Y	Y	Y	N	Y
6 Luther	Y	Y	Y	Y	Y	Y	Y
7 Peterson	Y	Y	Y	Y	Y	N	N
8 Oberstar	Y	Y	Y	Y	?	N	N
MISSISSIPPI							
1 ***Wicker***	Y	Y	Y	Y	Y	N	N
2 Thompson	Y	Y	Y	Y	?	?	?
3 ***Pickering***	Y	Y	Y	Y	Y	N	N
4 ***Parker***	Y	Y	Y	Y	Y	N	N
5 Taylor	Y	Y	Y	Y	Y	N	Y
MISSOURI							
1 Clay	Y	Y	Y	Y	N	N	Y
2 ***Talent***	Y	Y	Y	Y	Y	N	N
3 Gephardt	Y	Y	Y	Y	?	N	Y
4 Skelton	Y	Y	Y	Y	Y	N	N
5 McCarthy	Y	Y	Y	Y	Y	Y	Y
6 Danner	Y	Y	Y	Y	Y	Y	N
7 ***Blunt***	Y	Y	Y	Y	Y	N	N
8 ***Emerson***	Y	Y	Y	Y	Y	N	N
9 ***Hulshof***	Y	Y	Y	Y	Y	Y	N
MONTANA							
AL ***Hill***	Y	Y	Y	Y	Y	N	N
NEBRASKA							
1 ***Bereuter***	Y	Y	Y	Y	Y	N	Y
2 ***Christensen***	Y	Y	Y	Y	Y	Y	N
3 ***Barrett***	Y	Y	Y	Y	Y	N	N
NEVADA							
1 ***Ensign***	N	Y	Y	Y	Y	Y	N
2 ***Gibbons***	N	Y	Y	Y	Y	Y	N
NEW HAMPSHIRE							
1 ***Sununu***	Y	Y	Y	Y	Y	Y	Y
2 ***Bass***	Y	Y	Y	Y	Y	Y	Y
NEW JERSEY							
1 Andrews	Y	Y	Y	Y	Y	Y	Y
2 ***LoBiondo***	Y	Y	Y	Y	Y	Y	Y
3 ***Saxton***	Y	Y	Y	Y	Y	N	Y
4 ***Smith***	Y	Y	Y	Y	Y	Y	Y
5 ***Roukema***	Y	Y	Y	Y	Y	Y	Y
6 Pallone	Y	Y	Y	Y	Y	Y	Y
7 ***Franks***	Y	Y	Y	Y	Y	Y	Y
8 Pascrell	?	?	?	?	Y	Y	Y
9 Rothman	Y	Y	Y	Y	?	Y	Y
10 Payne	Y	Y	Y	Y	Y	?	?
11 ***Frelinghuysen***	Y	Y	Y	Y	Y	Y	Y
12 ***Pappas***	Y	Y	Y	Y	Y	Y	Y
13 Menendez	Y	Y	Y	Y	Y	Y	Y
NEW MEXICO							
1 Vacant							
2 ***Skeen***	Y	Y	Y	Y	Y	N	N
3 ***Redmond***	Y	Y	Y	Y	Y	N	N
NEW YORK							
1 ***Forbes***	Y	Y	Y	Y	Y	Y	Y
2 ***Lazio***	Y	Y	Y	Y	Y	Y	N
3 ***King***	Y	Y	Y	Y	Y	N	Y
4 McCarthy	Y	Y	Y	Y	Y	Y	Y
5 Ackerman	?	?	?	?	?	N	Y
6 Meeks	Y	Y	Y	Y	Y	N	Y
7 Manton	Y	?	?	?	Y	N	Y
8 Nadler	?	?	?	?	N	Y	Y
9 Schumer	?	?	?	?	?	Y	Y
10 Towns	?	?	?	?	?	N	Y
11 Owens	+	+	+	+	Y	N	Y
12 Velázquez	Y	Y	Y	Y	Y	N	Y
13 ***Fossella***	Y	Y	Y	Y	Y	Y	Y
14 Maloney	+	+	+	+	Y	Y	Y
15 Rangel	?	?	?	?	Y	N	Y
16 Serrano	Y	Y	Y	Y	Y	N	Y
17 Engel	Y	Y	Y	Y	Y	Y	Y
18 Lowey	Y	Y	Y	Y	Y	Y	Y
19 ***Kelly***	Y	Y	Y	Y	Y	N	Y
20 ***Gilman***	Y	Y	Y	Y	Y	N	Y
21 McNulty	?	?	?	?	Y	Y	Y
22 ***Solomon***	Y	Y	Y	Y	Y	N	N
23 ***Boehlert***	Y	Y	Y	Y	Y	Y	Y
24 ***McHugh***	Y	Y	Y	Y	Y	Y	N
25 ***Walsh***	Y	Y	Y	Y	Y	N	N
26 Hinchey	Y	Y	Y	Y	Y	N	Y
27 ***Paxon***	Y	Y	Y	Y	Y	N	N
28 Slaughter	Y	Y	Y	Y	Y	N	+
29 LaFalce	Y	Y	Y	Y	Y	Y	N

	253	254	255	256	257	258	259
30 ***Quinn***	Y	Y	Y	Y	Y	Y	N
31 ***Houghton***	Y	Y	Y	Y	Y	N	Y
NORTH CAROLINA							
1 Clayton	Y	Y	Y	Y	Y	N	Y
2 Etheridge	Y	Y	Y	Y	Y	N	N
3 ***Jones***	Y	Y	Y	Y	Y	N	Y
4 Price	Y	Y	Y	Y	Y	N	Y
5 ***Burr***	Y	Y	Y	Y	Y	N	N
6 ***Coble***	Y	Y	Y	Y	Y	N	N
7 McIntyre	Y	Y	Y	Y	Y	N	N
8 Hefner	Y	Y	Y	Y	Y	N	N
9 ***Myrick***	Y	Y	Y	Y	Y	N	N
10 ***Ballenger***	Y	Y	Y	Y	Y	N	N
11 ***Taylor***	Y	Y	Y	Y	Y	N	N
12 Watt	Y	Y	Y	Y	N	N	Y
NORTH DAKOTA							
AL Pomeroy	Y	Y	Y	Y	Y	N	N
OHIO							
1 ***Chabot***	Y	Y	Y	Y	Y	Y	Y
2 ***Portman***	+	+	+	+	Y	Y	N
3 Hall	Y	Y	Y	Y	Y	Y	Y
4 ***Oxley***	+	+	+	+	Y	N	N
5 ***Gillmor***	Y	Y	Y	Y	Y	Y	N
6 Strickland	Y	Y	Y	Y	Y	Y	Y
7 ***Hobson***	Y	+	Y	Y	Y	Y	N
8 ***Boehner***	Y	Y	Y	Y	Y	N	N
9 Kaptur	Y	Y	Y	Y	Y	N	N
10 Kucinich	Y	Y	Y	Y	Y	Y	Y
11 Stokes	Y	Y	Y	Y	Y	N	Y
12 ***Kasich***	Y	Y	Y	?	Y	Y	N
13 Brown	Y	Y	Y	Y	Y	Y	Y
14 Sawyer	Y	Y	Y	Y	Y	Y	Y
15 ***Pryce***	Y	Y	Y	Y	Y	Y	N
16 ***Regula***	Y	Y	Y	Y	Y	Y	N
17 Traficant	Y	Y	Y	Y	Y	N	N
18 ***Ney***	Y	Y	Y	Y	Y	Y	N
19 ***LaTourette***	Y	Y	Y	Y	Y	Y	Y
OKLAHOMA							
1 ***Largent***	Y	Y	Y	Y	Y	N	N
2 ***Coburn***	Y	Y	Y	Y	Y	N	N
3 ***Watkins***	Y	Y	Y	Y	+	N	–
4 ***Watts***	Y	Y	Y	Y	Y	N	N
5 ***Istook***	Y	Y	Y	Y	Y	N	N
6 ***Lucas***	Y	Y	Y	Y	Y	N	N
OREGON							
1 Furse	Y	N	Y	Y	Y	N	Y
2 ***Smith***	Y	Y	Y	Y	Y	N	N
3 Blumenauer	Y	Y	Y	Y	Y	Y	Y
4 DeFazio	Y	Y	Y	Y	Y	N	Y
5 Hooley	Y	Y	Y	Y	Y	Y	Y
PENNSYLVANIA							
1 Brady	Y	Y	Y	N	Y	Y	Y
2 Fattah	Y	Y	Y	Y	N	Y	Y
3 Borski	Y	Y	Y	N	Y	Y	Y
4 Klink	Y	Y	Y	N	Y	N	Y
5 ***Peterson***	Y	Y	Y	Y	Y	Y	N
6 Holden	Y	Y	Y	Y	Y	N	Y
7 ***Weldon***	Y	Y	Y	Y	Y	Y	Y
8 ***Greenwood***	Y	Y	Y	Y	Y	Y	Y
9 ***Shuster***	Y	Y	Y	?	Y	N	N
10 ***McDade***	Y	Y	Y	Y	Y	N	N
11 Kanjorski	Y	Y	Y	Y	Y	Y	Y
12 Murtha	Y	Y	Y	Y	Y	N	N
13 ***Fox***	Y	Y	Y	Y	Y	Y	Y
14 Coyne	Y	Y	Y	Y	Y	Y	Y
15 McHale	Y	Y	Y	N	Y	Y	Y
16 ***Pitts***	Y	Y	Y	Y	Y	Y	N
17 ***Gekas***	Y	Y	Y	Y	Y	Y	N
18 Doyle	Y	Y	Y	Y	Y	Y	Y
19 ***Goodling***	Y	Y	Y	Y	Y	Y	Y
20 Mascara	Y	Y	Y	Y	Y	Y	Y
21 ***English***	Y	Y	Y	Y	Y	Y	Y
RHODE ISLAND							
1 Kennedy	Y	Y	Y	Y	Y	N	Y
2 Weygand	Y	Y	Y	Y	Y	Y	Y
SOUTH CAROLINA							
1 ***Sanford***	Y	Y	N	N	Y	Y	Y
2 ***Spence***	Y	Y	Y	Y	Y	N	N
3 ***Graham***	Y	Y	Y	Y	Y	N	N
4 ***Inglis***	Y	Y	Y	Y	Y	Y	Y
5 Spratt	Y	Y	Y	Y	Y	N	N
6 Clyburn	Y	Y	Y	Y	Y	?	?
SOUTH DAKOTA							
AL ***Thune***	Y	Y	Y	Y	Y	N	N

	253	254	255	256	257	258	259
TENNESSEE							
1 ***Jenkins***	Y	Y	Y	Y	Y	N	N
2 ***Duncan***	Y	Y	Y	Y	Y	Y	Y
3 ***Wamp***	Y	Y	Y	Y	Y	Y	Y
4 ***Hilleary***	Y	Y	Y	Y	Y	N	N
5 Clement	Y	Y	Y	Y	Y	N	N
6 Gordon	?	?	?	?	Y	Y	Y
7 ***Bryant***	Y	Y	Y	Y	Y	N	N
8 Tanner	Y	Y	Y	Y	Y	N	N
9 Ford	Y	Y	Y	Y	Y	N	Y
TEXAS							
1 Sandlin	Y	Y	Y	Y	Y	N	N
2 Turner	Y	Y	Y	Y	Y	N	N
3 ***Johnson, Sam***	Y	Y	Y	Y	Y	N	Y
4 Hall	Y	Y	Y	Y	Y	N	N
5 ***Sessions***	Y	Y	Y	Y	Y	N	N
6 ***Barton***	Y	Y	Y	Y	Y	N	Y
7 ***Archer***	Y	Y	Y	Y	Y	Y	N
8 ***Brady***	Y	Y	Y	Y	Y	N	N
9 Lampson	Y	Y	Y	Y	Y	N	Y
10 Doggett	Y	Y	Y	Y	Y	Y	Y
11 Edwards	Y	Y	Y	Y	Y	N	N
12 ***Granger***	Y	Y	Y	Y	Y	N	N
13 ***Thornberry***	Y	Y	Y	Y	Y	N	N
14 ***Paul***	N	N	N	Y	N	Y	Y
15 Hinojosa	Y	Y	Y	Y	Y	N	Y
16 Reyes	Y	Y	Y	Y	Y	N	Y
17 Stenholm	Y	Y	Y	Y	Y	N	N
18 Jackson-Lee	Y	Y	Y	Y	Y	N	Y
19 ***Combest***	Y	Y	Y	Y	Y	N	N
20 Gonzalez	?	?	?	?	?	?	?
21 ***Smith***	Y	Y	Y	Y	Y	N	N
22 ***DeLay***	Y	Y	Y	Y	Y	N	N
23 ***Bonilla***	Y	Y	Y	Y	Y	N	N
24 Frost	Y	Y	Y	Y	Y	N	N
25 Bentsen	Y	Y	Y	Y	Y	N	N
26 ***Armey***	Y	Y	Y	Y	Y	Y	N
27 Ortiz	Y	Y	Y	Y	Y	N	N
28 Rodriguez	Y	Y	Y	Y	Y	N	Y
29 Green	Y	Y	Y	Y	Y	N	N
30 Johnson, E.B.	Y	Y	Y	Y	Y	N	Y
UTAH							
1 ***Hansen***	Y	Y	Y	Y	Y	N	N
2 ***Cook***	Y	Y	Y	Y	Y	Y	N
3 ***Cannon***	?	?	?	?	?	?	?
VERMONT							
AL *Sanders*	Y	Y	Y	Y	?	N	Y
VIRGINIA							
1 ***Bateman***	Y	Y	Y	Y	Y	N	N
2 Pickett	Y	Y	Y	Y	Y	N	N
3 Scott	Y	Y	Y	Y	N	N	N
4 Sisisky	Y	Y	Y	Y	Y	N	N
5 Goode	Y	Y	Y	Y	Y	N	N
6 ***Goodlatte***	Y	Y	Y	Y	Y	N	N
7 ***Bliley***	Y	Y	Y	Y	Y	N	Y
8 Moran	Y	Y	Y	Y	Y	Y	Y
9 Boucher	Y	Y	Y	Y	Y	N	N
10 ***Wolf***	Y	Y	Y	Y	Y	Y	Y
11 ***Davis***	Y	Y	Y	Y	Y	N	Y
WASHINGTON							
1 ***White***	Y	Y	Y	Y	Y	Y	N
2 ***Metcalf***	Y	Y	Y	Y	Y	N	Y
3 ***Smith, Linda***	Y	Y	Y	Y	Y	Y	N
4 ***Hastings***	Y	Y	Y	Y	Y	N	N
5 ***Nethercutt***	Y	Y	Y	Y	Y	N	N
6 Dicks	Y	Y	Y	Y	Y	N	Y
7 McDermott	Y	Y	Y	Y	Y	N	Y
8 ***Dunn***	Y	Y	Y	Y	Y	Y	N
9 Smith, Adam	Y	Y	Y	N	Y	Y	Y
WEST VIRGINIA							
1 Mollohan	Y	Y	Y	Y	Y	N	N
2 Wise	Y	Y	Y	Y	Y	N	N
3 Rahall	Y	Y	Y	Y	Y	N	N
WISCONSIN							
1 ***Neumann***	Y	Y	Y	Y	Y	Y	Y
2 ***Klug***	Y	Y	Y	Y	Y	Y	N
3 Kind	Y	Y	Y	Y	Y	Y	Y
4 Kleczka	Y	Y	Y	Y	Y	N	Y
5 Barrett	Y	Y	Y	Y	Y	Y	Y
6 ***Petri***	Y	Y	Y	Y	Y	Y	Y
7 Obey	Y	Y	Y	Y	Y	Y	Y
8 Johnson	Y	Y	Y	Y	Y	Y	Y
9 ***Sensenbrenner***	N	N	Y	Y	Y	Y	Y
WYOMING							
AL ***Cubin***	Y	Y	Y	Y	Y	N	N

Southern states - Ala., Ark., Fla., Ga., Ky., La., Miss., N.C., Okla., S.C., Tenn., Texas, Va.

Key

Y	Voted for (yea).
#	Paired for.
+	Announced for.
N	Voted against (nay).
X	Paired against.
−	Announced against.
P	Voted "present."
C	Voted "present" to avoid possible conflict of interest.
?	Did not vote or otherwise make a position known.

Democrats **Republicans** *Independent*

---

260. HR 4101. Fiscal 1999 Agriculture Appropriations/FDA Testing and Approval of Abortion Pills. Coburn, R-Okla., amendment to prohibit the Food and Drug Administration from using funds appropriated in the bill to test, develop or approve any drug for chemically induced abortions. Adopted 223-202: R 188-37; D 35-164 (ND 26-120, SD 9-44); I 0-1. June 24, 1998.

261. HR 4101. Fiscal 1999 Agriculture Appropriations/Loan Rates for Sugar Processors. Miller, R-Fla., amendment to lower the loan rates the Agriculture Department provides to sugar cane and sugar beet processors by one cent. Rejected 167-258: R 109-116; D 58-141 (ND 53-93, SD 5-48); I 0-1. June 24, 1998.

262. HR 4101. Fiscal 1999 Agriculture Appropriations/Market Access Program. Royce, R-Calif., amendment to prohibit funds appropriated by the bill from being used to pay salaries or expenses of personnel in the Market Access Program, which promotes agriculture programs abroad. Rejected 118-307: R 75-150; D 42-157 (ND 38-107, SD 4-50); I 1-0. June 24, 1998.

263. HR 4101. Fiscal 1999 Agriculture Appropriations/Wildlife Service Livestock Protection Program. Bass, R-N.H., amendment to reduce the bill's funding for the Agriculture Department's Wildlife Service livestock protection program to try to reduce efforts by the agency to kill predators in Western states. Rejected 192-232: R 60-164; D 131-68 (ND 114-32, SD 17-36); I 1-0. June 24, 1998. (The amendment was initially debated and adopted on June 23 (vote 259) but a drafting error made it necessary to vote on the amendment again. Because it failed on the second vote, neither version is included in the bill text.)

264. HR 4101. Fiscal 1999 Agriculture Appropriations/Passage. Passage of the bill to provide $55.9 billion in fiscal 1999 for agriculture programs, $42.3 billion of which is mandatory spending for programs such as food stamps. The bill provides $6.1 billion more than appropriated in fiscal 1998 and $1.9 billion less than requested by President Clinton. Passed 373-48: R 199-23; D 173-25 (ND 125-20, SD 48-5); I 1-0. June 24, 1998.

265. HR 4103. Fiscal 1999 Defense Appropriations/Rule. Adoption of the rule (H Res 484) to provide for House floor consideration of the bill to provide $250.7 billion in defense spending for fiscal 1999. The rule struck $1.6 billion in "emergency" funding for the year 2000 computer problem at the Defense Department. Adopted 221-201: R 219-2; D 2-198 (ND 2-145, SD 0-53); I 0-1. June 24, 1998.

266. HR 4103. Fiscal 1999 Defense Appropriations/Passage. Passage of the bill to provide $250.7 billion in defense spending for fiscal 1999. The bill provides $510 million less than President Clinton's request and $3 billion more than the amount appropriated for fiscal 1998. Passed 358-61: R 209-13; D 149-47 (ND 101-42, SD 48-5); I 0-1. June 24, 1998.

	260	261	262	263	264	265	266
ALABAMA							
1 *Callahan*	Y	N	Y	N	Y	Y	Y
2 *Everett*	Y	N	N	N	Y	Y	Y
3 *Riley*	Y	N	N	N	Y	Y	Y
4 *Aderholt*	Y	N	N	N	Y	Y	Y
5 Cramer	Y	N	N	N	Y	N	Y
6 *Bachus*	Y	N	Y	N	Y	Y	Y
7 Hilliard	N	N	N	Y	N	Y	N
ALASKA							
AL *Young*	Y	N	N	N	Y	Y	Y
ARIZONA							
1 *Salmon*	Y	Y	Y	N	Y	Y	Y
2 Pastor	N	N	N	N	Y	N	Y
3 *Stump*	Y	N	N	N	Y	Y	Y
4 *Shadegg*	Y	Y	Y	N	Y	Y	Y
5 *Kolbe*	N	Y	Y	N	Y	Y	Y
6 *Hayworth*	Y	Y	Y	N	Y	Y	Y
ARKANSAS							
1 Berry	Y	N	N	N	N	N	N
2 Snyder	N	N	N	N	N	N	Y
3 *Hutchinson*	Y	Y	N	N	Y	+	Y
4 *Dickey*	Y	N	N	N	Y	Y	Y
CALIFORNIA							
1 *Riggs*	Y	Y	N	N	Y	Y	Y
2 *Herger*	Y	N	N	N	Y	Y	Y
3 Fazio	N	N	N	N	N	N	Y
4 *Doolittle*	Y	N	N	N	Y	Y	Y
5 Matsui	N	N	N	Y	N	N	Y
6 Woolsey	N	N	N	Y	N	N	N
7 Miller	N	Y	N	Y	?	N	N
8 Pelosi	N	N	N	Y	N	N	N
9 Lee	N	N	N	Y	N	N	N
10 Tauscher	N	Y	N	Y	N	Y	Y
11 *Pombo*	Y	N	N	N	Y	Y	Y
12 Lantos	N	N	N	Y	N	Y	Y
13 Stark	N	N	Y	Y	N	N	N
14 Eshoo	N	N	N	Y	N	Y	Y
15 *Campbell*	N	Y	Y	Y	N	Y	N
16 Lofgren	N	N	N	Y	N	Y	N
17 Farr	N	N	N	Y	N	Y	N
18 Condit	N	N	N	N	Y	N	Y
19 *Radanovich*	Y	Y	N	N	Y	Y	Y
20 Dooley	N	N	N	N	N	N	Y
21 *Thomas*	N	N	N	N	Y	Y	Y
22 Capps, L.	N	Y	N	Y	N	Y	N
23 *Gallegly*	Y	N	N	N	Y	Y	Y
24 Sherman	N	N	N	Y	N	Y	Y
25 *McKeon*	Y	N	N	N	Y	Y	Y
26 Berman	N	Y	N	Y	N	Y	N
27 *Rogan*	Y	Y	N	Y	Y	Y	Y
28 *Dreier*	Y	Y	N	N	Y	Y	Y
29 Waxman	N	Y	Y	Y	Y	Y	N
30 Becerra	N	N	N	Y	N	N	N
31 Martinez	N	N	N	N	Y	Y	N
32 Dixon	N	N	N	Y	N	Y	Y
33 Roybal-Allard	N	N	N	Y	N	Y	N
34 Torres	N	N	?	Y	Y	N	Y
35 Waters	N	N	N	Y	N	Y	N
36 Harman	N	N	N	Y	N	Y	Y
37 Millender-McD.	N	N	N	Y	N	Y	N
38 *Horn*	N	Y	N	Y	N	Y	N
39 *Royce*	Y	Y	Y	Y	N	Y	N
40 *Lewis*	Y	N	N	N	Y	Y	Y
41 *Kim*	Y	N	N	N	Y	Y	Y
42 Brown	N	N	N	Y	Y	N	N
43 *Calvert*	Y	N	N	N	Y	Y	Y
44 *Bono, M.*	Y	Y	N	N	Y	Y	Y
45 *Rohrabacher*	Y	Y	Y	N	Y	Y	Y
46 Sanchez	N	N	N	N	Y	N	Y
47 *Cox*	Y	Y	Y	N	Y	Y	Y
48 *Packard*	Y	N	N	N	Y	Y	Y
49 *Bilbray*	N	Y	Y	Y	Y	Y	Y
50 Filner	N	N	N	Y	N	Y	N
51 *Cunningham*	Y	N	N	N	Y	Y	Y
52 *Hunter*	Y	N	N	N	Y	Y	Y
COLORADO							
1 DeGette	N	N	N	Y	N	Y	N
2 Skaggs	N	Y	N	Y	N	Y	Y
3 *McInnis*	Y	Y	N	N	Y	Y	Y
4 *Schaffer*	Y	N	N	N	Y	Y	Y
5 *Hefley*	Y	Y	Y	N	Y	Y	Y
6 *Schaefer*	Y	N	N	N	Y	Y	Y
CONNECTICUT							
1 Kennelly	N	Y	Y	Y	Y	N	Y
2 Gejdenson	N	N	N	Y	N	Y	Y
3 DeLauro	N	N	N	Y	N	Y	Y
4 *Shays*	Y	Y	Y	Y	Y	Y	N
5 Maloney	N	Y	Y	Y	N	Y	Y
6 *Johnson*	N	Y	Y	Y	N	Y	Y
DELAWARE							
AL *Castle*	N	Y	Y	Y	N	Y	Y
FLORIDA							
1 *Scarborough*	Y	Y	Y	Y	N	Y	Y
2 Boyd	N	N	N	Y	N	Y	Y
3 Brown	N	N	N	Y	N	Y	Y
4 *Fowler*	N	N	Y	Y	Y	Y	Y
5 Thurman	N	N	N	Y	N	Y	Y
6 *Stearns*	Y	N	N	Y	Y	Y	Y
7 *Mica*	Y	N	Y	Y	Y	Y	Y
8 *McCollum*	Y	N	Y	N	Y	Y	Y
9 *Bilirakis*	Y	N	N	N	Y	Y	Y
10 *Young*	Y	N	N	N	Y	Y	Y
11 Davis	N	N	N	Y	N	Y	Y
12 *Canady*	Y	N	N	N	Y	Y	Y
13 *Miller*	N	Y	Y	Y	Y	Y	Y
14 *Goss*	Y	N	N	N	Y	Y	Y
15 *Weldon*	Y	N	N	N	Y	Y	Y
16 *Foley*	N	N	N	Y	N	Y	Y
17 Meek	N	N	N	Y	N	Y	N
18 *Ros-Lehtinen*	Y	Y	N	Y	Y	Y	Y
19 Wexler	N	N	N	Y	N	Y	Y
20 Deutsch	N	Y	Y	Y	N	Y	N
21 *Diaz-Balart*	Y	N	Y	N	Y	Y	Y
22 *Shaw*	Y	N	N	N	Y	Y	Y
23 Hastings	N	N	N	Y	N	Y	N
GEORGIA							
1 *Kingston*	Y	N	N	N	Y	Y	Y
2 Bishop	N	N	N	Y	N	Y	Y
3 *Collins*	Y	Y	N	N	Y	Y	Y
4 McKinney	N	Y	Y	Y	N	Y	Y
5 Lewis	N	N	N	Y	N	Y	Y
6 *Gingrich*							
7 *Barr*	Y	Y	N	N	Y	Y	Y
8 *Chambliss*	Y	N	N	N	Y	Y	Y
9 *Deal*	Y	Y	N	N	Y	Y	Y
10 *Norwood*	Y	N	N	N	Y	Y	Y
11 *Linder*	Y	Y	Y	Y	Y	Y	Y
HAWAII							
1 Abercrombie	N	N	N	N	Y	N	Y
2 Mink	N	N	N	N	Y	Y	Y
IDAHO							
1 *Chenoweth*	Y	N	N	N	N	Y	Y
2 *Crapo*	Y	N	N	N	Y	Y	Y
ILLINOIS							
1 Rush	N	Y	N	Y	N	N	N
2 Jackson	N	Y	N	Y	N	N	N
3 Lipinski	Y	Y	Y	Y	N	Y	?
4 Gutierrez	N	Y	N	Y	N	N	N
5 Blagojevich	N	Y	Y	Y	N	Y	N
6 *Hyde*	Y	Y	Y	N	Y	Y	Y
7 Davis	N	Y	N	Y	N	N	N
8 *Crane*	Y	Y	Y	N	Y	N	+
9 Yates	N	Y	N	Y	N	Y	?
10 *Porter*	N	Y	Y	Y	N	Y	Y
11 *Weller*	Y	N	Y	Y	Y	Y	Y
12 Costello	Y	N	N	Y	N	Y	Y

ND Northern Democrats   SD Southern Democrats

	260	261	262	263	264	265	266
13 ***Fawell***	N	Y	Y	Y	Y	?	Y
14 ***Hastert***	Y	N	Y	N	Y	Y	Y
15 ***Ewing***	Y	N	N	N	Y	Y	Y
16 ***Manzullo***	Y	Y	Y	N	Y	N	Y
17 Evans	N	N	N	Y	Y	N	Y
18 ***LaHood***	Y	N	N	N	Y	Y	Y
19 Poshard	Y	N	N	Y	Y	N	Y
20 ***Shimkus***	Y	N	N	N	Y	Y	Y
INDIANA							
1 Visclosky	N	Y	Y	N	Y	N	Y
2 ***McIntosh***	Y	Y	N	N	Y	Y	Y
3 Roemer	Y	N	N	Y	N	N	Y
4 ***Souder***	Y	Y	N	N	Y	Y	Y
5 ***Buyer***	Y	N	N	N	Y	Y	Y
6 ***Burton***	Y	N	N	N	Y	Y	Y
7 ***Pease***	Y	N	N	Y	Y	Y	Y
8 ***Hostettler***	Y	Y	Y	N	Y	Y	Y
9 Hamilton	?	?	?	?	?	?	?
10 Carson	N	N	N	Y	Y	N	Y
IOWA							
1 ***Leach***	N	N	N	N	Y	Y	Y
2 ***Nussle***	Y	N	N	N	Y	Y	Y
3 Boswell	N	N	N	N	Y	N	Y
4 ***Ganske***	N	N	N	N	Y	Y	Y
5 ***Latham***	Y	N	N	N	Y	Y	Y
KANSAS							
1 ***Moran***	Y	N	N	N	Y	Y	Y
2 ***Ryun***	Y	N	N	N	Y	Y	Y
3 ***Snowbarger***	Y	Y	N	N	Y	Y	Y
4 ***Tiahrt***	Y	N	N	N	Y	Y	Y
KENTUCKY							
1 ***Whitfield***	Y	N	N	N	Y	Y	Y
2 ***Lewis***	Y	N	N	N	Y	Y	Y
3 ***Northup***	Y	Y	N	N	+	Y	Y
4 ***Bunning***	Y	N	N	N	Y	Y	Y
5 ***Rogers***	Y	N	N	N	Y	Y	Y
6 Baesler	N	N	N	N	Y	?	?
LOUISIANA							
1 ***Livingston***	Y	N	N	N	Y	Y	Y
2 Jefferson	N	N	N	Y	Y	N	Y
3 ***Tauzin***	Y	N	N	N	Y	Y	Y
4 ***McCrery***	Y	N	N	N	Y	Y	Y
5 ***Cooksey***	N	N	N	N	Y	Y	Y
6 ***Baker***	Y	N	N	N	Y	Y	Y
7 John	Y	N	N	N	Y	N	Y
MAINE							
1 Allen	N	Y	N	Y	Y	N	Y
2 Baldacci	N	N	N	Y	Y	N	Y
MARYLAND							
1 ***Gilchrest***	N	Y	N	Y	Y	Y	Y
2 ***Ehrlich***	N	Y	Y	N	Y	Y	Y
3 Cardin	N	Y	N	Y	Y	N	Y
4 Wynn	N	N	N	Y	Y	N	Y
5 Hoyer	N	Y	N	N	Y	N	Y
6 ***Bartlett***	Y	Y	N	N	Y	Y	Y
7 Cummings	N	N	N	Y	Y	N	Y
8 ***Morella***	N	Y	Y	Y	Y	Y	N
MASSACHUSETTS							
1 Olver	N	Y	Y	Y	Y	N	N
2 Neal	N	N	N	Y	Y	N	Y
3 McGovern	N	N	N	Y	Y	N	N
4 Frank	N	Y	Y	Y	N	N	N
5 Meehan	N	Y	Y	Y	N	N	Y
6 Tierney	N	Y	Y	Y	N	N	Y
7 Markey	?	?	?	?	?	?	?
8 Kennedy	N	Y	Y	Y	Y	N	Y
9 Moakley	N	N	N	Y	Y	N	Y
10 Delahunt	N	N	N	Y	Y	N	N
MICHIGAN							
1 Stupak	Y	N	N	N	Y	N	Y
2 ***Hoekstra***	Y	Y	Y	N	Y	Y	N
3 ***Ehlers***	Y	N	Y	Y	Y	Y	N
4 ***Camp***	Y	N	N	N	Y	Y	Y
5 Barcia	Y	N	N	N	Y	N	Y
6 ***Upton***	N	Y	N	Y	Y	Y	N
7 ***Smith***	Y	N	N	N	Y	Y	Y
8 Stabenow	N	N	N	N	Y	N	Y
9 Kildee	Y	N	N	Y	Y	N	Y
10 Bonior	N	N	N	Y	Y	N	Y
11 ***Knollenberg***	Y	N	N	N	Y	Y	Y
12 Levin	N	N	N	Y	Y	N	Y
13 Rivers	N	N	Y	Y	Y	N	Y
14 Conyers	N	N	N	Y	Y	N	N
15 Kilpatrick	N	N	N	Y	Y	N	Y
16 Dingell	?	?	?	?	?	?	?

	260	261	262	263	264	265	266
MINNESOTA							
1 ***Gutknecht***	Y	N	N	N	Y	Y	Y
2 Minge	N	N	N	N	Y	N	N
3 ***Ramstad***	N	Y	Y	Y	N	Y	N
4 Vento	N	N	Y	Y	Y	N	N
5 Sabo	N	N	N	Y	N	N	Y
6 Luther	N	N	Y	Y	Y	N	N
7 Peterson	Y	N	N	N	Y	N	Y
8 Oberstar	Y	N	N	N	N	N	N
MISSISSIPPI							
1 ***Wicker***	Y	N	N	N	Y	Y	Y
2 Thompson	N	N	N	N	Y	N	Y
3 ***Pickering***	Y	N	N	N	Y	Y	Y
4 ***Parker***	Y	N	N	N	Y	Y	Y
5 Taylor	Y	N	Y	Y	N	N	Y
MISSOURI							
1 Clay	N	N	N	Y	Y	N	Y
2 ***Talent***	Y	N	N	N	Y	Y	Y
3 Gephardt	N	N	N	Y	Y	N	Y
4 Skelton	Y	N	N	N	Y	N	Y
5 McCarthy	N	Y	N	Y	Y	N	Y
6 Danner	N	N	N	N	Y	N	Y
7 ***Blunt***	Y	N	N	N	Y	Y	Y
8 ***Emerson***	Y	N	N	N	+	Y	Y
9 ***Hulshof***	Y	Y	N	N	Y	Y	Y
MONTANA							
AL ***Hill***	Y	N	N	N	Y	Y	Y
NEBRASKA							
1 ***Bereuter***	Y	N	N	N	Y	N	Y
2 ***Christensen***	Y	N	N	N	Y	Y	Y
3 ***Barrett***	Y	N	N	N	Y	Y	Y
NEVADA							
1 ***Ensign***	Y	Y	Y	N	N	Y	Y
2 ***Gibbons***	Y	Y	N	N	Y	Y	Y
NEW HAMPSHIRE							
1 ***Sununu***	Y	Y	Y	Y	N	Y	Y
2 ***Bass***	N	Y	Y	Y	Y	Y	Y
NEW JERSEY							
1 Andrews	N	Y	Y	Y	N	N	Y
2 ***LoBiondo***	Y	Y	Y	Y	Y	Y	Y
3 ***Saxton***	Y	N	Y	Y	Y	Y	Y
4 ***Smith***	Y	Y	N	Y	Y	Y	Y
5 ***Roukema***	N	Y	N	Y	Y	Y	Y
6 Pallone	N	Y	N	Y	Y	N	Y
7 ***Franks***	N	Y	Y	Y	N	Y	N
8 Pascrell	N	Y	Y	Y	Y	N	Y
9 Rothman	N	N	Y	Y	Y	N	Y
10 Payne	N	N	N	Y	Y	N	N
11 ***Frelinghuysen***	N	Y	N	Y	Y	Y	+
12 ***Pappas***	Y	Y	N	N	Y	Y	Y
13 Menendez	N	N	N	Y	N	N	Y
NEW MEXICO							
1 Vacant							
2 ***Skeen***	Y	N	N	N	Y	Y	Y
3 ***Redmond***	Y	N	N	N	Y	Y	Y
NEW YORK							
1 ***Forbes***	Y	Y	N	Y	Y	Y	Y
2 ***Lazio***	N	Y	N	Y	Y	Y	Y
3 ***King***	Y	N	N	N	Y	Y	Y
4 McCarthy	N	Y	Y	Y	Y	N	Y
5 Ackerman	N	N	N	Y	Y	N	Y
6 Meeks	N	N	N	Y	Y	N	N
7 Manton	Y	N	N	Y	Y	N	?
8 Nadler	N	Y	Y	Y	N	N	N
9 Schumer	N	Y	Y	Y	Y	N	Y
10 Towns	N	N	N	Y	Y	N	N
11 Owens	N	Y	N	Y	Y	N	N
12 Velázquez	N	Y	N	Y	Y	N	N
13 ***Fossella***	Y	Y	Y	N	Y	Y	Y
14 Maloney	N	Y	N	Y	Y	N	Y
15 Rangel	N	N	N	Y	Y	N	Y
16 Serrano	N	N	N	N	Y	N	Y
17 Engel	N	Y	N	Y	Y	N	Y
18 Lowey	N	Y	Y	Y	N	N	Y
19 ***Kelly***	N	Y	Y	Y	Y	Y	Y
20 ***Gilman***	N	N	N	Y	Y	Y	Y
21 McNulty	Y	Y	Y	Y	Y	N	Y
22 ***Solomon***	Y	N	N	N	Y	?	Y
23 ***Boehlert***	N	Y	Y	Y	Y	Y	Y
24 ***McHugh***	Y	Y	N	N	Y	Y	Y
25 ***Walsh***	Y	N	N	N	Y	Y	Y
26 Hinchey	N	Y	N	Y	Y	N	N
27 ***Paxon***	Y	N	N	N	Y	Y	Y
28 Slaughter	–	–	?	+	+	–	Y
29 LaFalce	Y	Y	N	N	Y	N	?

	260	261	262	263	264	265	266
30 ***Quinn***	Y	Y	N	N	Y	Y	Y
31 ***Houghton***	N	N	N	Y	Y	Y	Y
NORTH CAROLINA							
1 Clayton	N	N	N	N	Y	N	Y
2 Etheridge	N	N	N	N	Y	N	Y
3 ***Jones***	Y	N	N	Y	Y	Y	Y
4 Price	N	N	N	Y	Y	N	Y
5 ***Burr***	Y	N	N	N	Y	Y	Y
6 ***Coble***	Y	N	N	N	Y	Y	Y
7 McIntyre	Y	N	N	N	Y	N	Y
8 Hefner	N	N	N	N	Y	N	Y
9 ***Myrick***	Y	Y	Y	N	Y	Y	Y
10 ***Ballenger***	Y	N	N	N	Y	Y	Y
11 ***Taylor***	Y	N	N	N	Y	Y	Y
12 Watt	N	N	N	Y	Y	N	N
NORTH DAKOTA							
AL Pomeroy	N	N	N	N	Y	N	Y
OHIO							
1 ***Chabot***	Y	Y	Y	Y	N	Y	Y
2 ***Portman***	Y	Y	Y	N	N	Y	Y
3 Hall	Y	Y	N	Y	Y	N	Y
4 ***Oxley***	Y	N	N	N	Y	Y	Y
5 ***Gillmor***	Y	N	Y	N	Y	Y	Y
6 Strickland	N	N	N	N	Y	N	Y
7 ***Hobson***	Y	Y	Y	N	Y	Y	Y
8 ***Boehner***	Y	N	N	N	Y	Y	Y
9 Kaptur	N	N	N	N	Y	N	?
10 Kucinich	Y	Y	Y	Y	N	N	N
11 Stokes	N	N	N	Y	Y	N	Y
12 ***Kasich***	Y	Y	Y	N	Y	Y	Y
13 Brown	N	Y	Y	Y	Y	N	N
14 Sawyer	N	Y	N	Y	Y	N	Y
15 ***Pryce***	N	Y	Y	N	Y	Y	Y
16 ***Regula***	Y	Y	N	N	Y	Y	Y
17 Traficant	Y	N	N	N	Y	Y	Y
18 ***Ney***	Y	Y	Y	N	Y	Y	Y
19 ***LaTourette***	Y	Y	N	Y	Y	Y	Y
OKLAHOMA							
1 ***Largent***	Y	Y	Y	N	Y	Y	Y
2 ***Coburn***	Y	Y	Y	N	Y	Y	Y
3 ***Watkins***	Y	N	N	N	Y	Y	Y
4 ***Watts***	Y	N	N	N	Y	Y	Y
5 ***Istook***	Y	N	Y	N	Y	Y	Y
6 ***Lucas***	Y	N	N	N	Y	Y	Y
OREGON							
1 Furse	N	N	N	Y	Y	N	N
2 ***Smith***	Y	N	N	N	Y	Y	Y
3 Blumenauer	N	Y	N	Y	Y	N	Y
4 DeFazio	N	Y	Y	Y	Y	N	N
5 Hooley	N	N	N	N	Y	N	N
PENNSYLVANIA							
1 Brady	N	Y	Y	Y	Y	N	Y
2 Fattah	N	N	Y	Y	Y	N	N
3 Borski	Y	Y	Y	Y	Y	N	Y
4 Klink	Y	N	Y	Y	Y	N	Y
5 ***Peterson***	Y	Y	N	N	Y	Y	Y
6 Holden	Y	N	N	N	Y	N	Y
7 ***Weldon***	Y	Y	Y	Y	Y	Y	Y
8 ***Greenwood***	N	Y	N	Y	Y	Y	Y
9 ***Shuster***	Y	N	Y	N	Y	Y	Y
10 ***McDade***	Y	Y	Y	?	?	?	?
11 Kanjorski	Y	Y	N	N	Y	N	Y
12 Murtha	Y	N	N	N	Y	N	Y
13 ***Fox***	Y	Y	Y	Y	Y	Y	Y
14 Coyne	N	Y	Y	Y	Y	N	N
15 McHale	N	Y	N	Y	Y	N	Y
16 ***Pitts***	Y	Y	N	N	Y	Y	Y
17 ***Gekas***	Y	Y	N	N	Y	Y	Y
18 Doyle	+	+	+	+	+	N	Y
19 ***Goodling***	Y	Y	N	Y	Y	Y	Y
20 Mascara	Y	N	Y	N	Y	N	Y
21 ***English***	Y	Y	Y	Y	Y	Y	Y
RHODE ISLAND							
1 Kennedy	N	Y	Y	Y	Y	N	Y
2 Weygand	Y	N	N	Y	Y	N	Y
SOUTH CAROLINA							
1 ***Sanford***	Y	Y	Y	Y	N	Y	N
2 ***Spence***	Y	N	N	N	Y	Y	Y
3 ***Graham***	Y	N	N	N	Y	Y	Y
4 ***Inglis***	Y	Y	Y	Y	Y	Y	Y
5 Spratt	N	N	N	N	Y	N	Y
6 Clyburn	N	N	N	Y	Y	N	Y
SOUTH DAKOTA							
AL ***Thune***	Y	N	N	N	Y	Y	Y

	260	261	262	263	264	265	266
TENNESSEE							
1 ***Jenkins***	Y	N	N	N	Y	Y	Y
2 ***Duncan***	Y	Y	Y	Y	Y	Y	Y
3 ***Wamp***	Y	Y	Y	Y	Y	Y	Y
4 ***Hilleary***	Y	Y	N	N	Y	Y	Y
5 Clement	N	N	N	N	Y	N	Y
6 Gordon	?	Y	N	Y	Y	N	Y
7 ***Bryant***	Y	N	N	N	Y	Y	Y
8 Tanner	N	N	N	N	Y	N	Y
9 Ford	N	N	N	Y	+	N	Y
TEXAS							
1 Sandlin	N	N	N	N	Y	N	Y
2 Turner	N	N	N	N	Y	N	Y
3 ***Johnson, Sam***	Y	N	N	N	Y	Y	Y
4 Hall	Y	N	N	N	N	N	Y
5 ***Sessions***	Y	N	N	N	Y	Y	Y
6 ***Barton***	Y	N	N	N	Y	Y	Y
7 ***Archer***	Y	Y	Y	Y	Y	Y	Y
8 ***Brady***	Y	N	N	N	Y	Y	Y
9 Lampson	N	N	N	N	Y	N	Y
10 Doggett	N	Y	Y	Y	N	N	N
11 Edwards	N	N	N	N	Y	N	Y
12 ***Granger***	N	N	N	N	Y	Y	Y
13 ***Thornberry***	Y	N	N	N	Y	Y	Y
14 ***Paul***	Y	Y	Y	Y	N	Y	N
15 Hinojosa	N	N	N	N	Y	N	Y
16 Reyes	N	N	N	N	Y	N	Y
17 Stenholm	Y	N	N	N	Y	N	Y
18 Jackson-Lee	N	N	N	+	Y	N	Y
19 ***Combest***	Y	N	N	N	Y	Y	Y
20 Gonzalez	?	?	?	?	?	?	?
21 ***Smith***	Y	N	N	N	Y	Y	Y
22 ***DeLay***	Y	Y	Y	N	Y	Y	Y
23 ***Bonilla***	Y	N	N	N	Y	Y	Y
24 Frost	N	N	N	N	Y	N	Y
25 Bentsen	N	N	N	N	Y	N	Y
26 ***Armey***	Y	Y	Y	N	Y	Y	Y
27 Ortiz	Y	N	N	N	Y	N	Y
28 Rodriguez	N	N	N	N	Y	N	Y
29 Green	N	N	N	N	Y	N	Y
30 Johnson, E.B.	N	N	N	N	Y	N	Y
UTAH							
1 ***Hansen***	Y	Y	N	N	Y	Y	Y
2 ***Cook***	Y	Y	N	N	Y	Y	Y
3 ***Cannon***	?	?	?	?	?	?	Y
VERMONT							
AL *Sanders*	N	N	Y	Y	Y	N	N
VIRGINIA							
1 ***Bateman***	Y	N	N	N	Y	Y	Y
2 Pickett	N	N	N	N	Y	N	Y
3 Scott	N	N	N	N	Y	N	Y
4 Sisisky	N	P	N	N	N	N	Y
5 Goode	Y	N	N	N	Y	N	Y
6 ***Goodlatte***	Y	N	N	N	Y	Y	Y
7 ***Bliley***	Y	N	N	N	Y	Y	Y
8 Moran	N	Y	Y	Y	N	N	Y
9 Boucher	N	N	N	N	Y	N	Y
10 ***Wolf***	Y	Y	N	Y	Y	Y	+
11 ***Davis***	N	Y	Y	Y	Y	Y	Y
WASHINGTON							
1 ***White***	N	Y	N	N	Y	Y	Y
2 ***Metcalf***	Y	N	N	Y	Y	Y	Y
3 ***Smith, Linda***	Y	Y	N	N	Y	Y	Y
4 ***Hastings***	Y	N	N	N	Y	Y	Y
5 ***Nethercutt***	Y	N	N	N	Y	Y	Y
6 Dicks	N	N	N	Y	Y	N	Y
7 McDermott	N	N	N	Y	N	N	N
8 ***Dunn***	Y	Y	N	N	Y	Y	Y
9 Smith, Adam	N	N	N	Y	Y	N	Y
WEST VIRGINIA							
1 Mollohan	Y	N	N	N	Y	N	Y
2 Wise	N	N	N	N	Y	N	Y
3 Rahall	Y	N	N	N	Y	N	N
WISCONSIN							
1 ***Neumann***	Y	Y	Y	Y	Y	Y	Y
2 ***Klug***	N	Y	N	N	Y	Y	Y
3 Kind	N	Y	Y	Y	N	N	N
4 Kleczka	Y	N	Y	Y	N	N	N
5 Barrett	N	N	Y	Y	Y	N	N
6 ***Petri***	Y	Y	Y	Y	N	Y	N
7 Obey	N	N	N	Y	N	N	N
8 Johnson	N	N	N	Y	N	N	N
9 ***Sensenbrenner***	Y	Y	Y	Y	N	Y	N
WYOMING							
AL ***Cubin***	Y	N	N	N	Y	Y	Y

Southern states - Ala., Ark., Fla., Ga., Ky., La., Miss., N.C., Okla., S.C., Tenn., Texas, Va.

Key

Y	Voted for (yea).
#	Paired for.
+	Announced for.
N	Voted against (nay).
X	Paired against.
−	Announced against.
P	Voted "present."
C	Voted "present" to avoid possible conflict of interest.
?	Did not vote or otherwise make a position known.

Democrats **Republicans**
Independent

267. Adjournment Resolution/Rule. Adoption of the rule to provide for House floor consideration of the concurrent resolution to provide for adjournment. Adopted 225-188: R 218-0; D 7-187 (ND 7-138, SD 0-49); I 0-1. June 25, 1998.

268. HR 4104. Fiscal 1999 Treasury-Postal Appropriations/Rule. Adoption of the rule (H Res 485) to provide for House floor consideration of the bill to provide $29.2 billion in fiscal 1999 for the Treasury Department, Postal Service and other general government operations. Rejected 125-291: R 65-155; D 60-135 (ND 49-97, SD 11-38); I 0-1. June 25, 1998.

269. HR 4112. Fiscal 1999 Legislative Branch Appropriations/Previous Question. Pryce, R-Ohio, motion to order the previous question (thus ending debate and the possibility of amendment) on adoption of the rule (H Res 489) to provide for House floor consideration of the bill to provide $1.8 billion in funding for the House of Representatives and other legislative branch operations. Motion agreed to 222-194: R 220-0; D 2-193 (ND 1-145, SD 1-48); I 0-1. June 25, 1998. (Subsequently, the rule was adopted.)

270. HR 4112. Fiscal 1999 Legislative Branch Appropriations/Rule. Adoption of the rule (H Res 489) to provide for House floor consideration of the bill to provide $1.8 billion in funding for the House of Representatives and other legislative branch operations. Adopted 228-188: R 219-0; D 9-187 (ND 8-139, SD 1-48); I 0-1. June 25, 1998.

271. HR 4112. Fiscal 1999 Legislative Branch Appropriations/Recommit. Obey, D-Wis., motion to recommit the bill to the Appropriations Committee with instructions to report it back with an amendment to reduce the appropriation for the "Committee Employees Standing Committees, Special and Select" by about $8.3 million. Motion rejected 192-222: R 0-219; D 191-3 (ND 144-2, SD 47-1); I 1-0. June 25, 1998.

272. HR 4112. Fiscal 1999 Legislative Branch Appropriations/Passage. Passage of the bill to provide $1.8 billion for the House of Representatives and other legislative branch operations. Passed 235-179: R 199-20; D 36-158 (ND 28-118, SD 8-40); I 0-1. June 25, 1998.

273. HR 2676. Internal Revenue Service Overhaul/Recommit. McDermott, D-Wash., motion to recommit the bill to the conference committee with instructions to the managers on the part of the House to disagree with the section relating to lower capital gains rates to apply to property held more than one year. Motion rejected 116-292: R 0-218; D 115-74 (ND 94-46, SD 21-28); I 1-0. June 25, 1998.

[1] *Heather Wilson, R-N.M., was sworn in June 25, replacing Stephen H. Schiff, R-N.M., who died March 25.*

	267	268	269	270	271	272	273
ALABAMA							
1 *Callahan*	Y	N	Y	Y	N	Y	N
2 *Everett*	Y	N	Y	Y	N	Y	N
3 *Riley*	Y	N	Y	Y	N	Y	N
4 *Aderholt*	Y	N	Y	Y	N	Y	N
5 Cramer	N	N	N	N	Y	N	N
6 *Bachus*	Y	N	Y	Y	N	Y	N
7 Hilliard	N	N	N	N	Y	N	Y
ALASKA							
AL *Young*	Y	Y	Y	Y	N	Y	N
ARIZONA							
1 *Salmon*	Y	N	Y	Y	N	Y	N
2 Pastor	N	N	N	Y	Y	Y	N
3 *Stump*	Y	N	Y	Y	N	Y	N
4 *Shadegg*	Y	N	Y	Y	N	Y	N
5 *Kolbe*	Y	Y	Y	Y	N	Y	N
6 *Hayworth*	Y	N	Y	Y	N	Y	N
ARKANSAS							
1 Berry	N	N	N	N	Y	N	N
2 Snyder	N	N	N	N	Y	N	Y
3 *Hutchinson*	+	−	+	+	−	+	−
4 *Dickey*	Y	N	Y	Y	N	Y	N
CALIFORNIA							
1 *Riggs*	Y	N	Y	Y	N	Y	N
2 *Herger*	Y	N	Y	Y	N	Y	N
3 Fazio	N	N	N	Y	Y	Y	Y
4 *Doolittle*	Y	N	Y	Y	N	Y	N
5 Matsui	N	N	N	N	Y	N	Y
6 Woolsey	N	Y	N	N	Y	N	Y
7 Miller	N	N	N	N	Y	N	Y
8 Pelosi	N	Y	N	N	Y	N	Y
9 Lee	N	N	N	N	Y	N	Y
10 Tauscher	N	Y	N	N	Y	N	N
11 *Pombo*	Y	N	Y	Y	N	Y	N
12 Lantos	N	N	N	N	Y	N	Y
13 Stark	N	N	N	N	Y	N	Y
14 Eshoo	N	Y	N	N	Y	N	Y
15 *Campbell*	Y	Y	Y	Y	N	Y	N
16 Lofgren	N	N	N	N	Y	N	Y
17 Farr	N	N	N	N	Y	N	Y
18 Condit	N	Y	N	N	Y	N	N
19 *Radanovich*	Y	N	Y	Y	N	Y	N
20 Dooley	N	Y	N	N	Y	N	N
21 *Thomas*	?	N	Y	Y	N	Y	N
22 Capps, L.	N	N	N	N	Y	N	Y
23 *Gallegly*	Y	N	Y	Y	N	Y	N
24 Sherman	N	N	N	N	Y	N	N
25 *McKeon*	Y	N	Y	Y	N	Y	N
26 Berman	N	Y	N	N	Y	N	?
27 *Rogan*	Y	N	Y	Y	N	Y	N
28 *Dreier*	Y	Y	Y	Y	N	Y	N
29 Waxman	N	Y	N	N	Y	?	Y
30 Becerra	N	N	N	N	Y	N	Y
31 Martinez	N	N	N	N	Y	N	Y
32 Dixon	Y	Y	N	N	Y	Y	+
33 Roybal-Allard	N	N	N	N	Y	N	Y
34 Torres	N	N	N	N	Y	N	Y
35 Waters	Y	N	N	N	Y	N	Y
36 Harman	N	Y	N	N	Y	N	Y
37 Millender-McD.	−	Y	N	N	Y	N	Y

	267	268	269	270	271	272	273
38 *Horn*	Y	Y	Y	Y	N	N	N
39 *Royce*	Y	Y	Y	Y	N	N	N
40 *Lewis*	Y	N	Y	Y	N	Y	?
41 *Kim*	?	N	N	N	Y	N	N
42 Brown	?	N	N	N	Y	N	N
43 *Calvert*	Y	N	Y	Y	N	Y	N
44 *Bono, M.*	Y	N	Y	Y	N	Y	N
45 *Rohrabacher*	Y	N	Y	Y	N	Y	N
46 Sanchez	N	N	N	N	Y	N	N
47 *Cox*	Y	N	Y	Y	N	Y	?
48 *Packard*	Y	Y	Y	Y	N	Y	−
49 *Bilbray*	Y	Y	Y	Y	N	Y	N
50 Filner	N	N	N	N	Y	N	Y
51 *Cunningham*	Y	N	Y	Y	N	Y	N
52 *Hunter*	Y	N	Y	?	N	Y	N
COLORADO							
1 DeGette	N	Y	N	N	Y	N	Y
2 Skaggs	N	N	N	N	Y	Y	Y
3 *McInnis*	Y	Y	Y	Y	N	Y	N
4 *Schaffer*	Y	N	Y	Y	N	Y	N
5 *Hefley*	Y	N	Y	N	N	N	N
6 *Schaefer*	Y	Y	Y	Y	N	Y	N
CONNECTICUT							
1 Kennelly	N	N	N	N	Y	N	N
2 Gejdenson	N	Y	N	N	Y	N	Y
3 DeLauro	N	N	N	N	Y	N	Y
4 *Shays*	Y	Y	Y	Y	N	Y	N
5 Maloney	N	N	N	N	Y	N	N
6 *Johnson*	Y	Y	Y	Y	N	Y	N
DELAWARE							
AL *Castle*	Y	Y	Y	Y	N	Y	N
FLORIDA							
1 *Scarborough*	Y	N	Y	Y	?	Y	N
2 Boyd	N	N	N	N	Y	N	N
3 Brown	N	Y	N	N	Y	N	Y
4 *Fowler*	Y	Y	Y	Y	N	Y	N
5 Thurman	N	N	N	N	Y	N	N
6 *Stearns*	Y	N	Y	Y	N	Y	N
7 *Mica*	Y	N	Y	Y	N	Y	N
8 *McCollum*	Y	N	Y	Y	N	Y	N
9 *Bilirakis*	Y	Y	Y	Y	N	Y	N
10 *Young*	Y	N	Y	Y	N	Y	N
11 Davis	N	N	N	N	Y	N	N
12 *Canady*	Y	N	Y	Y	N	Y	N
13 *Miller*	Y	Y	Y	Y	N	Y	N
14 *Goss*	Y	Y	Y	Y	N	Y	N
15 *Weldon*	Y	N	Y	Y	N	Y	N
16 *Foley*	Y	Y	Y	Y	N	Y	N
17 Meek	N	N	N	N	Y	N	Y
18 *Ros-Lehtinen*	Y	Y	Y	Y	N	Y	N
19 Wexler	N	Y	N	N	Y	N	Y
20 Deutsch	N	N	N	N	Y	N	N
21 *Diaz-Balart*	Y	Y	Y	Y	N	Y	N
22 *Shaw*	Y	Y	Y	Y	N	Y	N
23 Hastings	N	Y	N	N	Y	N	Y
GEORGIA							
1 *Kingston*	Y	N	Y	Y	N	Y	N
2 Bishop	N	N	N	N	Y	N	N
3 *Collins*	Y	N	Y	Y	N	Y	N
4 McKinney	N	N	N	N	Y	N	N
5 Lewis	?	?	?	?	?	?	?
6 *Gingrich*							
7 *Barr*	Y	N	Y	Y	N	Y	N
8 *Chambliss*	Y	N	Y	Y	N	Y	N
9 *Deal*	Y	N	Y	Y	N	Y	N
10 *Norwood*	Y	N	Y	Y	N	Y	N
11 *Linder*	Y	Y	Y	Y	N	Y	N
HAWAII							
1 Abercrombie	N	N	N	N	Y	N	Y
2 Mink	N	N	N	N	Y	Y	Y
IDAHO							
1 *Chenoweth*	?	N	Y	Y	N	Y	N
2 *Crapo*	?	Y	Y	Y	N	Y	N
ILLINOIS							
1 Rush	N	N	N	N	Y	N	Y
2 Jackson	Y	N	N	N	Y	N	Y
3 Lipinski	Y	N	N	N	Y	N	Y
4 Gutierrez	N	N	N	N	Y	Y	Y
5 Blagojevich	N	Y	N	N	Y	N	Y
6 *Hyde*	Y	N	Y	Y	N	Y	N
7 Davis	N	N	N	N	Y	N	Y
8 *Crane*	Y	N	Y	Y	N	N	N
9 Yates	N	Y	N	N	Y	N	Y
10 *Porter*	Y	Y	Y	Y	N	Y	N
11 *Weller*	Y	N	Y	Y	N	Y	N
12 Costello	N	N	N	N	Y	N	Y

ND Northern Democrats   SD Southern Democrats

	267	268	269	270	271	272	273
13 ***Fawell***	Y	Y	Y	Y	N	Y	N
14 ***Hastert***	Y	Y	Y	Y	N	Y	N
15 ***Ewing***	Y	N	Y	Y	N	Y	N
16 ***Manzullo***	Y	N	Y	Y	N	Y	N
17 Evans	N	N	N	N	Y	N	Y
18 ***LaHood***	Y	N	Y	Y	N	Y	N
19 Poshard	N	N	N	N	Y	N	Y
20 ***Shimkus***	Y	N	Y	Y	N	Y	N
INDIANA							
1 Visclosky	N	N	N	N	Y	Y	Y
2 ***McIntosh***	Y	N	Y	Y	N	?	N
3 Roemer	N	N	N	N	Y	N	N
4 ***Souder***	Y	N	Y	Y	N	Y	?
5 ***Buyer***	Y	N	Y	Y	N	Y	N
6 ***Burton***	Y	N	Y	Y	N	Y	N
7 ***Pease***	Y	N	Y	Y	N	Y	N
8 ***Hostettler***	Y	N	Y	Y	N	N	N
9 Hamilton	?	?	?	?	?	?	?
10 Carson	N	Y	N	N	Y	Y	Y
IOWA							
1 ***Leach***	Y	Y	Y	Y	N	Y	N
2 ***Nussle***	Y	N	Y	Y	N	Y	N
3 Boswell	N	N	N	N	Y	N	N
4 ***Ganske***	Y	N	Y	Y	N	Y	N
5 ***Latham***	Y	N	Y	Y	N	Y	N
KANSAS							
1 ***Moran***	Y	N	Y	Y	N	N	N
2 ***Ryun***	Y	N	Y	Y	N	Y	N
3 ***Snowbarger***	Y	N	Y	Y	N	Y	N
4 ***Tiahrt***	Y	N	Y	Y	N	Y	N
KENTUCKY							
1 ***Whitfield***	Y	N	Y	Y	N	Y	N
2 ***Lewis***	Y	N	Y	Y	N	Y	N
3 ***Northup***	Y	Y	Y	Y	N	Y	N
4 ***Bunning***	Y	N	Y	Y	N	Y	N
5 ***Rogers***	Y	N	Y	Y	N	Y	N
6 Baesler	N	N	N	N	Y	Y	N
LOUISIANA							
1 ***Livingston***	Y	Y	Y	Y	N	Y	N
2 Jefferson	N	Y	N	N	Y	Y	Y
3 ***Tauzin***	Y	N	Y	Y	N	Y	N
4 ***McCrery***	Y	N	Y	Y	N	Y	N
5 ***Cooksey***	?	?	Y	Y	N	Y	N
6 ***Baker***	Y	N	Y	Y	N	N	N
7 John	N	N	N	N	Y	Y	N
MAINE							
1 Allen	N	N	N	N	Y	N	Y
2 Baldacci	N	Y	N	N	Y	N	Y
MARYLAND							
1 ***Gilchrest***	Y	Y	Y	Y	N	Y	N
2 ***Ehrlich***	Y	Y	Y	Y	N	Y	N
3 Cardin	N	Y	N	N	Y	N	Y
4 Wynn	N	N	N	N	Y	N	Y
5 Hoyer	N	N	N	N	Y	Y	Y
6 ***Bartlett***	Y	N	Y	Y	N	Y	N
7 Cummings	N	N	N	N	Y	N	Y
8 ***Morella***	Y	Y	Y	Y	N	Y	N
MASSACHUSETTS							
1 Olver	N	Y	N	N	Y	N	Y
2 Neal	N	Y	N	N	Y	N	?
3 McGovern	N	Y	N	N	Y	N	Y
4 Frank	N	N	N	N	Y	N	Y
5 Meehan	N	N	N	N	Y	N	?
6 Tierney	N	Y	N	N	Y	N	Y
7 Markey	?	?	?	?	?	?	?
8 Kennedy	N	N	N	N	Y	N	N
9 Moakley	?	?	?	?	?	?	?
10 Delahunt	N	Y	N	N	Y	N	Y
MICHIGAN							
1 Stupak	N	N	N	N	Y	N	Y
2 ***Hoekstra***	Y	N	Y	Y	N	Y	N
3 ***Ehlers***	Y	N	Y	Y	N	Y	N
4 ***Camp***	Y	N	Y	Y	N	Y	N
5 Barcia	N	N	N	N	Y	N	N
6 ***Upton***	Y	Y	Y	Y	N	Y	N
7 ***Smith***	Y	N	Y	Y	N	Y	N
8 Stabenow	N	Y	N	N	Y	N	N
9 Kildee	N	N	N	N	Y	N	Y
10 Bonior	N	?	N	N	Y	Y	Y
11 ***Knollenberg***	Y	Y	Y	Y	N	Y	N
12 Levin	N	Y	N	N	Y	N	Y
13 Rivers	N	Y	N	N	Y	N	Y
14 Conyers	N	Y	N	N	Y	N	Y
15 Kilpatrick	N	Y	N	N	Y	Y	Y
16 Dingell	?	?	?	?	?	?	?

	267	268	269	270	271	272	273
MINNESOTA							
1 ***Gutknecht***	Y	N	Y	Y	N	Y	N
2 Minge	N	Y	N	N	Y	N	Y
3 ***Ramstad***	Y	Y	Y	Y	N	Y	N
4 Vento	N	Y	N	N	Y	N	Y
5 Sabo	N	N	N	N	Y	Y	Y
6 Luther	N	Y	N	N	Y	N	Y
7 Peterson	N	N	N	N	Y	N	Y
8 Oberstar	N	N	N	N	Y	N	Y
MISSISSIPPI							
1 ***Wicker***	Y	Y	Y	Y	N	Y	N
2 Thompson	N	N	N	N	Y	N	Y
3 ***Pickering***	Y	N	Y	Y	N	Y	N
4 ***Parker***	Y	Y	Y	Y	N	Y	N
5 Taylor	N	N	N	N	Y	N	N
MISSOURI							
1 Clay	N	Y	N	N	Y	N	?
2 ***Talent***	Y	N	Y	Y	N	Y	N
3 Gephardt	N	N	N	N	Y	N	Y
4 Skelton	N	N	N	N	Y	Y	N
5 McCarthy	N	Y	N	N	Y	N	N
6 Danner	N	Y	N	Y	Y	Y	N
7 ***Blunt***	Y	N	Y	Y	N	Y	N
8 ***Emerson***	Y	N	Y	Y	N	Y	N
9 ***Hulshof***	+	–	+	+	–	–	–
MONTANA							
AL ***Hill***	Y	N	Y	Y	N	N	N
NEBRASKA							
1 ***Bereuter***	Y	N	Y	Y	N	Y	N
2 ***Christensen***	Y	N	Y	Y	N	Y	N
3 ***Barrett***	Y	N	Y	Y	N	Y	N
NEVADA							
1 ***Ensign***	Y	N	Y	Y	N	N	N
2 ***Gibbons***	Y	N	Y	Y	N	Y	N
NEW HAMPSHIRE							
1 ***Sununu***	Y	N	Y	Y	N	Y	N
2 ***Bass***	Y	Y	Y	Y	N	Y	N
NEW JERSEY							
1 Andrews	N	N	N	N	Y	N	Y
2 ***LoBiondo***	Y	N	Y	Y	N	Y	N
3 ***Saxton***	Y	N	Y	Y	N	Y	N
4 ***Smith***	Y	N	Y	Y	N	Y	N
5 ***Roukema***	Y	Y	Y	Y	N	Y	N
6 Pallone	N	N	N	N	+	N	Y
7 ***Franks***	Y	Y	Y	Y	N	Y	N
8 Pascrell	N	N	N	N	Y	Y	N
9 Rothman	N	N	N	N	Y	N	N
10 Payne	N	N	N	N	Y	N	Y
11 ***Frelinghuysen***	Y	Y	Y	Y	N	Y	N
12 ***Pappas***	Y	N	Y	Y	N	Y	N
13 Menendez	N	N	N	N	Y	N	Y
NEW MEXICO							
1 ***Wilson*** [1]							N
2 ***Skeen***	Y	N	Y	Y	N	Y	N
3 ***Redmond***	Y	N	Y	Y	N	Y	N
NEW YORK							
1 ***Forbes***	Y	N	Y	Y	N	Y	N
2 ***Lazio***	Y	Y	Y	Y	N	Y	N
3 ***King***	Y	N	Y	Y	N	Y	N
4 McCarthy	N	N	N	N	Y	Y	N
5 Ackerman	N	Y	N	N	Y	N	N
6 Meeks	N	N	N	N	Y	N	Y
7 Manton	N	N	N	N	Y	N	Y
8 Nadler	N	N	N	N	Y	N	Y
9 Schumer	N	Y	N	N	Y	N	N
10 Towns	N	N	N	N	Y	N	Y
11 Owens	N	N	N	N	Y	N	Y
12 Velázquez	N	Y	N	N	Y	N	?
13 ***Fossella***	Y	N	Y	Y	N	Y	N
14 Maloney	N	Y	N	N	Y	N	N
15 Rangel	N	N	N	N	Y	N	Y
16 Serrano	N	N	N	Y	Y	Y	?
17 Engel	N	Y	N	N	Y	N	Y
18 Lowey	N	Y	N	N	Y	N	N
19 ***Kelly***	Y	Y	Y	Y	N	Y	N
20 ***Gilman***	Y	Y	Y	Y	N	Y	N
21 McNulty	N	N	N	N	Y	N	N
22 ***Solomon***	Y	Y	Y	Y	N	Y	N
23 ***Boehlert***	Y	Y	Y	Y	N	Y	N
24 ***McHugh***	Y	N	Y	Y	N	Y	N
25 ***Walsh***	Y	N	Y	Y	N	Y	N
26 Hinchey	N	N	N	N	Y	N	Y
27 ***Paxon***	Y	Y	Y	Y	N	Y	N
28 Slaughter	N	Y	N	N	Y	N	N
29 LaFalce	N	N	N	N	Y	N	Y

	267	268	269	270	271	272	273
30 ***Quinn***	Y	N	Y	Y	N	Y	N
31 ***Houghton***	Y	Y	Y	Y	N	Y	N
NORTH CAROLINA							
1 Clayton	N	Y	N	N	Y	N	N
2 Etheridge	N	N	N	N	Y	N	Y
3 ***Jones***	Y	N	Y	Y	N	Y	N
4 Price	N	N	N	N	Y	Y	Y
5 ***Burr***	Y	N	Y	Y	N	Y	N
6 ***Coble***	Y	N	Y	Y	N	Y	N
7 McIntyre	N	N	N	N	Y	N	N
8 Hefner	N	Y	N	N	Y	N	Y
9 ***Myrick***	Y	N	Y	Y	N	Y	N
10 ***Ballenger***	Y	N	Y	Y	N	Y	N
11 ***Taylor***	Y	N	Y	Y	N	Y	N
12 Watt	N	N	N	N	Y	N	N
NORTH DAKOTA							
AL Pomeroy	N	N	N	N	Y	N	N
OHIO							
1 ***Chabot***	Y	N	Y	Y	N	Y	N
2 ***Portman***	Y	N	Y	Y	N	Y	N
3 Hall	Y	N	N	Y	Y	Y	N
4 ***Oxley***	Y	Y	Y	Y	N	Y	N
5 ***Gillmor***	Y	N	Y	Y	N	Y	N
6 Strickland	N	N	N	N	Y	N	Y
7 ***Hobson***	Y	Y	Y	Y	N	Y	N
8 ***Boehner***	Y	N	Y	Y	N	Y	N
9 Kaptur	N	N	?	N	Y	N	Y
10 Kucinich	N	N	N	N	Y	N	Y
11 Stokes	N	Y	N	N	Y	N	Y
12 ***Kasich***	Y	N	Y	Y	N	Y	N
13 Brown	N	Y	N	N	Y	N	Y
14 Sawyer	N	N	N	N	Y	N	Y
15 ***Pryce***	Y	Y	Y	Y	N	Y	N
16 ***Regula***	Y	N	Y	Y	N	Y	N
17 Traficant	Y	N	Y	Y	N	Y	N
18 ***Ney***	Y	N	Y	Y	N	Y	N
19 ***LaTourette***	Y	N	Y	Y	N	Y	N
OKLAHOMA							
1 ***Largent***	Y	N	Y	Y	N	Y	N
2 ***Coburn***	Y	Y	Y	Y	N	Y	N
3 ***Watkins***	Y	N	Y	Y	N	Y	N
4 ***Watts***	Y	N	Y	Y	N	Y	N
5 ***Istook***	Y	N	Y	Y	N	Y	N
6 ***Lucas***	Y	N	Y	Y	N	Y	N
OREGON							
1 Furse	N	Y	N	N	Y	N	Y
2 ***Smith***	Y	N	Y	Y	N	Y	N
3 Blumenauer	N	N	N	N	Y	N	Y
4 DeFazio	N	N	N	N	Y	N	Y
5 Hooley	N	Y	N	N	Y	N	N
PENNSYLVANIA							
1 Brady	N	N	N	N	Y	N	Y
2 Fattah	N	N	N	N	Y	Y	Y
3 Borski	N	N	N	N	Y	N	Y
4 Klink	N	N	N	N	Y	N	Y
5 ***Peterson***	Y	N	Y	Y	N	Y	N
6 Holden	N	N	N	N	Y	N	N
7 ***Weldon***	Y	N	Y	Y	?	?	N
8 ***Greenwood***	Y	Y	Y	Y	N	Y	N
9 ***Shuster***	Y	N	Y	Y	N	Y	N
10 ***McDade***	?	?	?	?	?	?	?
11 Kanjorski	N	N	N	N	Y	N	Y
12 Murtha	N	N	N	N	Y	N	N
13 ***Fox***	Y	Y	Y	Y	N	Y	N
14 Coyne	N	N	N	N	Y	N	Y
15 McHale	N	N	N	N	Y	N	Y
16 ***Pitts***	Y	N	Y	Y	N	Y	N
17 ***Gekas***	Y	N	Y	Y	N	Y	N
18 Doyle	N	N	N	N	Y	N	N
19 ***Goodling***	Y	N	Y	Y	N	Y	N
20 Mascara	N	N	N	N	Y	N	N
21 ***English***	Y	N	Y	Y	N	Y	N
RHODE ISLAND							
1 Kennedy	N	N	N	N	Y	N	Y
2 Weygand	N	N	N	N	Y	N	N
SOUTH CAROLINA							
1 ***Sanford***	Y	N	Y	Y	N	N	N
2 ***Spence***	Y	N	Y	Y	N	Y	N
3 ***Graham***	Y	?	Y	Y	N	Y	N
4 ***Inglis***	Y	N	Y	Y	N	Y	N
5 Spratt	N	N	N	N	Y	N	Y
6 Clyburn	N	N	N	N	Y	N	Y
SOUTH DAKOTA							
AL ***Thune***	Y	N	Y	Y	N	Y	N

	267	268	269	270	271	272	273
TENNESSEE							
1 ***Jenkins***	Y	N	Y	Y	N	Y	N
2 ***Duncan***	Y	N	Y	Y	N	Y	N
3 ***Wamp***	Y	N	Y	Y	N	Y	N
4 ***Hilleary***	Y	N	Y	?	N	N	N
5 Clement	N	N	N	N	Y	N	N
6 Gordon	N	N	N	N	?	?	N
7 ***Bryant***	Y	N	Y	Y	N	Y	N
8 Tanner	N	N	N	N	Y	N	N
9 Ford	N	N	N	N	Y	N	Y
TEXAS							
1 Sandlin	N	N	N	N	Y	N	N
2 Turner	?	?	?	?	?	?	?
3 ***Johnson, Sam***	Y	N	Y	Y	N	Y	N
4 Hall	N	N	Y	Y	Y	Y	N
5 ***Sessions***	Y	N	Y	Y	N	Y	N
6 ***Barton***	Y	Y	Y	Y	N	Y	N
7 ***Archer***	Y	Y	Y	Y	N	Y	N
8 ***Brady***	+	–	+	+	–	+	–
9 Lampson	?	?	?	?	?	?	?
10 Doggett	N	Y	N	N	Y	N	Y
11 Edwards	N	Y	N	N	Y	N	Y
12 ***Granger***	Y	Y	Y	Y	N	Y	N
13 ***Thornberry***	Y	N	Y	Y	N	Y	N
14 ***Paul***	Y	N	Y	Y	N	N	N
15 Hinojosa	–	–	–	–	+	+	+
16 Reyes	?	?	?	?	?	?	?
17 Stenholm	N	N	N	N	Y	N	Y
18 Jackson-Lee	N	Y	N	N	Y	N	Y
19 ***Combest***	Y	N	Y	Y	N	Y	N
20 Gonzalez	?	?	?	?	?	?	?
21 ***Smith***	Y	N	Y	Y	N	Y	N
22 ***DeLay***	Y	Y	Y	Y	N	Y	N
23 ***Bonilla***	Y	Y	Y	Y	N	Y	N
24 Frost	N	N	N	N	Y	N	N
25 Bentsen	N	N	N	N	Y	N	N
26 ***Armey***	Y	Y	Y	Y	N	Y	N
27 Ortiz	N	N	N	N	Y	N	Y
28 Rodriguez	N	N	N	N	Y	N	Y
29 Green	N	N	N	N	Y	N	N
30 Johnson, E.B.	N	N	N	N	Y	N	Y
UTAH							
1 ***Hansen***	Y	N	Y	Y	N	Y	N
2 ***Cook***	Y	N	Y	Y	N	Y	N
3 ***Cannon***	Y	N	Y	Y	N	Y	N
VERMONT							
AL *Sanders*	N	N	N	N	Y	N	Y
VIRGINIA							
1 ***Bateman***	Y	N	Y	Y	N	Y	N
2 Pickett	N	N	N	N	Y	Y	N
3 Scott	N	N	N	N	Y	N	Y
4 Sisisky	N	N	N	N	Y	Y	N
5 Goode	N	N	N	N	N	Y	N
6 ***Goodlatte***	Y	N	Y	Y	N	N	N
7 ***Bliley***	Y	Y	Y	Y	N	Y	N
8 Moran	N	N	N	N	Y	N	Y
9 Boucher	N	N	N	N	Y	N	N
10 ***Wolf***	Y	N	Y	Y	N	Y	N
11 ***Davis***	Y	Y	Y	Y	N	Y	N
WASHINGTON							
1 ***White***	Y	N	Y	Y	N	Y	N
2 ***Metcalf***	Y	N	Y	Y	N	Y	N
3 ***Smith, Linda***	Y	N	?	Y	N	N	N
4 ***Hastings***	Y	Y	Y	Y	N	Y	N
5 ***Nethercutt***	Y	Y	Y	Y	N	Y	N
6 Dicks	N	N	N	N	Y	Y	N
7 McDermott	N	Y	N	N	Y	N	Y
8 ***Dunn***	Y	Y	Y	Y	N	Y	N
9 Smith, Adam	N	N	N	N	Y	Y	Y
WEST VIRGINIA							
1 Mollohan	N	N	N	N	Y	Y	N
2 Wise	N	N	N	N	Y	N	Y
3 Rahall	N	N	N	N	Y	N	Y
WISCONSIN							
1 ***Neumann***	Y	N	Y	Y	N	Y	N
2 ***Klug***	Y	Y	?	?	?	?	?
3 Kind	N	N	N	N	Y	N	Y
4 Kleczka	N	N	N	N	Y	N	Y
5 Barrett	N	N	N	N	Y	N	Y
6 ***Petri***	Y	N	Y	Y	N	N	N
7 Obey	N	N	N	N	Y	N	Y
8 Johnson	N	N	N	N	Y	N	N
9 ***Sensenbrenner***	Y	N	Y	Y	N	N	N
WYOMING							
AL ***Cubin***	Y	N	Y	Y	N	Y	N

Southern states - Ala., Ark., Fla., Ga., Ky., La., Miss., N.C., Okla., S.C., Tenn., Texas, Va.

274. HR 2676. Internal Revenue Service Overhaul/Conference Report. Adoption of the conference report on the bill to restructure the management of the Internal Revenue Service by establishing an oversight board to oversee the agency's operations. Along with expanding certain taxpayer rights, the conference report also reduces from 18 months to 12 months the time a taxpayer must hold an investment before being eligible for the 20 percent tax rate on capital gains. The measure's $12.9 billion cost is offset by revenue-raising provisions, including one that permits wealthy elderly persons to convert traditional IRAs into the new Roth IRA and pay taxes on the converted money. Adopted (thus sent to the Senate) 402-8: R 220-1; D 181-7 (ND 132-7, SD 49-0); I 1-0. June 25, 1998.

275. HR 2183. Campaign Finance Overhaul/Shays-Meehan Substitute — Voter Guide Requirements. Doolittle, R-Calif., amendment to the Shays-Meehan substitute amendment to the bill to overhaul campaign finance laws. The Doolittle amendment would strike the section of the substitute that requires voter guides to list at least two candidates or federal officeholders and only include their voting record or position on certain issues, with no commentary. Rejected 201-219: R 183-40; D 18-178 (ND 11-133, SD 7-45); I 0-1. July 14, 1998.

276. HR 2183. Campaign Finance Overhaul/Shays-Meehan Substitute - Contributions. Fossella, R-N.Y., amendment to the Shays-Meehan substitute amendment to the bill to overhaul campaign finance laws. The Fossella amendment would prohibit non-citizens from making campaign contributions to federal elections. Adopted 282-126: R 200-17; D 81-109 (ND 57-84, SD 24-25); I 1-0. July 14, 1998.

277. HR 3682. Transporting Minors for an Abortion/Previous Question. Myrick, R-N.C., motion to order the previous question (thus ending debate and the possibility of amendment) on adoption of the rule (H Res 499) to provide for floor consideration of the bill to make it a federal crime for anyone other than the parent to transport a minor across state lines with the intent that she obtain an abortion. Motion agreed to 252-174: R 217-9; D 35-164 (ND 27-120, SD 8-44); I 0-1. July 15, 1998.

278. HR 3682. Transporting Minors for an Abortion/Rule. Adoption of the rule (H Res 499) to provide for House floor consideration of the bill that makes it a federal crime for anyone other than the parent to transport a minor across state lines with the intent that she obtain an abortion. The rule blocks all amendments and provides two hours of general debate. Adopted 247-173: R 209-14; D 38-158 (ND 29-117, SD 9-41); I 0-1. July 15, 1998.

279. HR 3682. Transporting Minors for an Abortion/Recommit. Scott, D-Va., motion to recommit the bill to the Judiciary Committee with instructions to report it back with an amendment to make it a federal offense only when force or a threat is used to transport a minor across state lines with the intent that she obtain an abortion. Motion rejected 158-269: R 10-216; D 147-53 (ND 110-37, SD 37-16); I 1-0. July 15, 1998.

280. HR 3682. Transporting Minors for an Abortion/Passage. Passage of the bill to make it a federal crime for anyone other than the parent to transport a minor across state lines with the intent that she obtain an abortion. Passed 276-150: R 209-14; D 67-135 (ND 43-105, SD 24-30); I 0-1. July 15, 1998. A "nay" was a vote in support of the president's position.

Key

Y	Voted for (yea).
#	Paired for.
+	Announced for.
N	Voted against (nay).
X	Paired against.
−	Announced against.
P	Voted "present."
C	Voted "present" to avoid possible conflict of interest.
?	Did not vote or otherwise make a position known.

Democrats   **Republicans**
Independent

	274	275	276	277	278	279	280
ALABAMA							
1 *Callahan*	Y	Y	Y	Y	Y	N	Y
2 *Everett*	Y	Y	Y	Y	Y	N	Y
3 *Riley*	Y	Y	Y	Y	Y	N	Y
4 *Aderholt*	Y	Y	Y	Y	?	N	Y
5 Cramer	Y	N	Y	N	N	N	Y
6 *Bachus*	Y	Y	Y	Y	Y	N	Y
7 Hilliard	Y	N	N	N	N	Y	Y
ALASKA							
AL *Young*	Y	?	?	Y	Y	N	Y
ARIZONA							
1 *Salmon*	Y	Y	Y	Y	Y	N	Y
2 Pastor	Y	N	N	N	N	Y	N
3 *Stump*	Y	Y	Y	Y	Y	N	Y
4 *Shadegg*	Y	Y	Y	Y	Y	N	Y
5 *Kolbe*	Y	Y	Y	Y	N	N	Y
6 *Hayworth*	Y	Y	Y	Y	Y	N	Y
ARKANSAS							
1 Berry	Y	N	Y	Y	Y	N	Y
2 Snyder	Y	N	Y	N	N	Y	N
3 *Hutchinson*	+	Y	Y	Y	Y	N	Y
4 *Dickey*	Y	Y	Y	?	N	Y	Y
CALIFORNIA							
1 *Riggs*	Y	Y	Y	Y	Y	N	Y
2 *Herger*	Y	Y	Y	Y	Y	N	Y
3 Fazio	N	N	N	N	N	Y	N
4 *Doolittle*	Y	Y	N	Y	Y	N	Y
5 Matsui	N	N	N	N	N	Y	N
6 Woolsey	N	N	N	N	N	Y	N
7 Miller	N	N	N	N	N	Y	N
8 Pelosi	Y	N	N	N	N	Y	N
9 Lee	N	N	N	N	N	Y	N
10 Tauscher	Y	N	N	N	N	Y	N
11 *Pombo*	Y	N	N	N	N	Y	Y
12 Lantos	Y	N	N	N	N	Y	N
13 Stark	Y	?	?	N	N	Y	N
14 Eshoo	Y	N	N	N	N	Y	N
15 *Campbell*	Y	N	Y	Y	N	Y	N
16 Lofgren	Y	N	N	N	N	Y	N
17 Farr	Y	N	N	N	N	Y	N
18 Condit	Y	N	Y	N	N	Y	Y
19 *Radanovich*	Y	N	Y	N	N	Y	Y
20 Dooley	Y	N	Y	N	N	Y	N
21 *Thomas*	Y	Y	Y	Y	Y	N	Y
22 Capps, L.	Y	N	N	−	N	Y	N
23 *Gallegly*	Y	N	Y	Y	Y	N	Y
24 Sherman	Y	N	N	N	N	Y	N
25 *McKeon*	Y	Y	Y	Y	Y	N	Y
26 Berman	?	N	N	N	N	Y	N
27 *Rogan*	Y	Y	Y	+	+	N	Y
28 *Dreier*	Y	Y	Y	Y	Y	N	Y
29 Waxman	Y	N	N	N	N	Y	N
30 Becerra	Y	N	N	N	N	Y	N
31 Martinez	N	N	?	N	N	Y	N
32 Dixon	+	N	N	N	N	Y	N
33 Roybal-Allard	Y	N	N	N	N	+	−
34 Torres	Y	N	N	N	N	Y	N
35 Waters	Y	N	N	N	N	Y	N
36 Harman	Y	N	N	N	N	Y	N
37 Millender-McD.	Y	N	N	N	N	Y	N

	274	275	276	277	278	279	280
38 *Horn*	Y	N	Y	Y	N	Y	N
39 *Royce*	Y	Y	Y	Y	Y	N	Y
40 *Lewis*	Y	Y	Y	Y	Y	N	Y
41 *Kim*	Y	Y	N	Y	Y	N	Y
42 Brown	Y	N	N	N	N	Y	N
43 *Calvert*	Y	Y	Y	Y	Y	N	Y
44 *Bono, M.*	Y	Y	Y	Y	Y	N	Y
45 *Rohrabacher*	Y	Y	N	Y	Y	N	Y
46 Sanchez	Y	N	Y	N	N	Y	N
47 *Cox*	Y	Y	Y	Y	Y	N	Y
48 *Packard*	+	Y	Y	Y	Y	N	Y
49 *Bilbray*	Y	N	Y	Y	N	Y	Y
50 Filner	Y	N	N	N	N	Y	N
51 *Cunningham*	Y	Y	Y	Y	Y	N	Y
52 *Hunter*	Y	Y	Y	Y	Y	N	Y
COLORADO							
1 DeGette	Y	N	N	N	N	Y	N
2 Skaggs	Y	N	N	N	N	Y	N
3 *McInnis*	Y	Y	Y	Y	Y	N	Y
4 *Schaffer*	Y	Y	Y	Y	Y	N	Y
5 *Hefley*	Y	Y	Y	Y	Y	N	Y
6 *Schaefer*	Y	Y	?	Y	Y	N	Y
CONNECTICUT							
1 Kennelly	Y	N	Y	N	N	Y	N
2 Gejdenson	Y	N	Y	N	N	Y	N
3 DeLauro	Y	N	Y	N	N	Y	N
4 *Shays*	Y	N	N	N	N	Y	N
5 Maloney	Y	N	Y	N	N	Y	N
6 *Johnson*	Y	N	N	N	N	Y	N
DELAWARE							
AL *Castle*	Y	N	Y	N	N	N	N
FLORIDA							
1 *Scarborough*	Y	Y	Y	Y	Y	N	Y
2 Boyd	Y	N	Y	N	N	Y	N
3 Brown	Y	N	N	N	N	Y	N
4 *Fowler*	Y	?	?	Y	Y	N	Y
5 Thurman	Y	N	Y	N	N	Y	N
6 *Stearns*	Y	Y	Y	Y	Y	N	Y
7 *Mica*	Y	Y	Y	Y	Y	N	Y
8 *McCollum*	Y	Y	Y	Y	Y	N	Y
9 *Bilirakis*	Y	Y	Y	Y	Y	N	Y
10 *Young*	Y	Y	Y	Y	Y	N	Y
11 Davis	Y	N	N	N	N	Y	N
12 *Canady*	Y	Y	Y	Y	Y	N	Y
13 *Miller*	Y	Y	Y	Y	Y	N	Y
14 *Goss*	Y	Y	Y	Y	Y	N	Y
15 *Weldon*	Y	Y	Y	Y	Y	N	Y
16 *Foley*	Y	N	Y	Y	Y	N	Y
17 Meek	Y	N	N	N	?	Y	N
18 *Ros-Lehtinen*	Y	Y	Y	Y	Y	N	Y
19 Wexler	Y	N	?	N	N	Y	N
20 Deutsch	Y	N	?	N	N	Y	N
21 *Diaz-Balart*	Y	Y	Y	Y	Y	N	Y
22 *Shaw*	Y	Y	Y	Y	Y	N	Y
23 Hastings	Y	N	N	N	N	Y	N
GEORGIA							
1 *Kingston*	Y	Y	Y	Y	N	Y	Y
2 Bishop	Y	Y	Y	Y	N	Y	Y
3 *Collins*	Y	Y	Y	Y	N	Y	Y
4 McKinney	Y	N	N	N	N	Y	N
5 Lewis	?	N	N	N	N	Y	N
6 *Gingrich*	Y	Y					
7 *Barr*	Y	Y	Y	Y	N	Y	Y
8 *Chambliss*	Y	Y	Y	Y	N	Y	Y
9 *Deal*	Y	?	?	Y	Y	N	Y
10 *Norwood*	Y	Y	Y	Y	N	Y	Y
11 *Linder*	Y	Y	Y	Y	N	Y	Y
HAWAII							
1 Abercrombie	Y	N	N	N	N	Y	N
2 Mink	Y	N	N	N	N	Y	N
IDAHO							
1 *Chenoweth*	Y	Y	Y	Y	Y	N	Y
2 *Crapo*	Y	Y	Y	Y	Y	N	Y
ILLINOIS							
1 Rush	Y	?	?	N	N	Y	N
2 Jackson	Y	N	N	N	N	Y	N
3 Lipinski	Y	N	Y	Y	Y	N	Y
4 Gutierrez	Y	N	N	N	N	Y	N
5 Blagojevich	Y	N	N	N	N	Y	N
6 *Hyde*	Y	Y	Y	Y	Y	N	Y
7 Davis	Y	N	N	N	N	Y	N
8 *Crane*	Y	Y	Y	Y	Y	N	Y
9 Yates	N	?	?	N	N	Y	N
10 *Porter*	Y	N	N	N	N	Y	−
11 *Weller*	Y	Y	Y	Y	Y	N	Y
12 Costello	Y	Y	Y	Y	Y	N	Y

ND Northern Democrats   SD Southern Democrats

	274	275	276	277	278	279	280
13 ***Fawell***	Y	N	Y	Y	Y	N	Y
14 ***Hastert***	Y	Y	Y	Y	Y	N	Y
15 ***Ewing***	Y	Y	Y	Y	Y	N	Y
16 ***Manzullo***	Y	Y	Y	Y	Y	N	Y
17 Evans	Y	N	Y	N	N	Y	N
18 ***LaHood***	Y	Y	Y	Y	Y	N	Y
19 Poshard	Y	Y	Y	Y	Y	N	Y
20 ***Shimkus***	Y	Y	Y	Y	Y	N	Y
INDIANA							
1 Visclosky	Y	N	N	N	N	Y	N
2 ***McIntosh***	Y	Y	N	Y	Y	N	Y
3 Roemer	Y	N	Y	Y	Y	N	Y
4 ***Souder***	?	Y	Y	Y	Y	N	Y
5 ***Buyer***	Y	Y	Y	Y	Y	N	Y
6 ***Burton***	Y	Y	?	Y	Y	N	Y
7 ***Pease***	Y	Y	Y	Y	Y	N	Y
8 ***Hostettler***	Y	Y	Y	Y	Y	N	Y
9 Hamilton	?	N	Y	Y	Y	N	Y
10 Carson	Y	N	N	N	N	Y	N
IOWA							
1 ***Leach***	Y	N	Y	Y	Y	N	Y
2 ***Nussle***	Y	Y	Y	Y	Y	N	Y
3 Boswell	Y	N	Y	N	N	Y	Y
4 ***Ganske***	Y	N	Y	Y	Y	N	Y
5 ***Latham***	Y	Y	Y	Y	Y	N	Y
KANSAS							
1 ***Moran***	Y	Y	Y	Y	Y	N	Y
2 ***Ryun***	Y	Y	Y	Y	Y	N	Y
3 ***Snowbarger***	Y	Y	Y	Y	Y	N	Y
4 ***Tiahrt***	Y	Y	Y	Y	Y	N	Y
KENTUCKY							
1 ***Whitfield***	Y	Y	Y	Y	Y	N	Y
2 ***Lewis***	Y	Y	Y	Y	Y	N	Y
3 ***Northup***	Y	Y	Y	Y	Y	N	Y
4 ***Bunning***	Y	Y	Y	Y	Y	N	Y
5 ***Rogers***	Y	Y	Y	Y	Y	N	Y
6 Baesler	Y	?	?	N	N	N	Y
LOUISIANA							
1 ***Livingston***	Y	Y	Y	Y	Y	N	Y
2 Jefferson	Y	N	N	N	N	Y	Y
3 ***Tauzin***	Y	Y	Y	Y	Y	N	+
4 ***McCrery***	Y	Y	Y	Y	Y	N	Y
5 ***Cooksey***	Y	Y	Y	Y	Y	N	Y
6 ***Baker***	Y	Y	Y	Y	Y	N	Y
7 John	Y	?	?	N	Y	N	Y
MAINE							
1 Allen	Y	N	N	N	N	Y	N
2 Baldacci	Y	N	Y	N	N	Y	N
MARYLAND							
1 ***Gilchrest***	Y	N	Y	Y	Y	N	N
2 ***Ehrlich***	Y	Y	Y	Y	Y	N	Y
3 Cardin	Y	N	N	N	N	Y	N
4 Wynn	Y	N	N	N	N	Y	N
5 Hoyer	Y	N	N	N	N	Y	N
6 ***Bartlett***	Y	Y	Y	Y	Y	N	Y
7 Cummings	Y	N	N	N	N	Y	N
8 ***Morella***	Y	N	N	N	N	Y	N
MASSACHUSETTS							
1 Olver	Y	?	?	N	N	Y	N
2 Neal	?	N	N	N	N	N	Y
3 McGovern	Y	N	N	N	N	Y	N
4 Frank	N	N	N	N	N	Y	N
5 Meehan	?	N	N	N	N	Y	N
6 Tierney	Y	N	N	N	N	Y	N
7 Markey	?	N	Y	N	N	Y	N
8 Kennedy	Y	N	Y	N	N	Y	N
9 Moakley	?	N	Y	?	?	N	Y
10 Delahunt	Y	N	N	N	N	Y	N
MICHIGAN							
1 Stupak	Y	Y	Y	Y	Y	N	Y
2 ***Hoekstra***	Y	Y	Y	Y	Y	N	Y
3 ***Ehlers***	Y	Y	N	Y	Y	N	Y
4 ***Camp***	Y	Y	Y	Y	Y	N	Y
5 Barcia	Y	Y	Y	Y	Y	N	Y
6 ***Upton***	Y	N	Y	Y	N	N	Y
7 ***Smith***	Y	Y	Y	Y	Y	N	Y
8 Stabenow	Y	N	Y	N	N	Y	N
9 Kildee	Y	N	Y	Y	Y	N	Y
10 Bonior	Y	N	N	N	N	N	Y
11 ***Knollenberg***	Y	Y	Y	Y	Y	N	Y
12 Levin	Y	N	Y	N	N	Y	N
13 Rivers	Y	N	Y	N	N	Y	N
14 Conyers	Y	N	N	N	N	Y	N
15 Kilpatrick	Y	N	N	N	N	Y	N
16 Dingell	?	N	N	?	?	?	?
MINNESOTA							
1 ***Gutknecht***	Y	Y	Y	Y	Y	N	Y
2 Minge	Y	N	N	N	N	Y	Y
3 ***Ramstad***	Y	N	Y	Y	Y	N	Y
4 Vento	Y	N	N	N	N	Y	Y
5 Sabo	N	N	N	N	N	Y	N
6 Luther	Y	N	Y	N	N	Y	N
7 Peterson	Y	Y	Y	Y	Y	N	Y
8 Oberstar	Y	Y	N	Y	Y	N	Y
MISSISSIPPI							
1 ***Wicker***	Y	Y	Y	Y	Y	N	Y
2 Thompson	Y	N	N	N	N	Y	N
3 ***Pickering***	Y	Y	Y	Y	Y	N	Y
4 ***Parker***	Y	N	Y	Y	Y	N	Y
5 Taylor	Y	N	Y	Y	Y	N	Y
MISSOURI							
1 Clay	?	N	N	N	N	Y	N
2 ***Talent***	Y	Y	N	Y	Y	N	Y
3 Gephardt	Y	N	?	N	N	Y	N
4 Skelton	Y	N	Y	Y	Y	N	Y
5 McCarthy	Y	N	Y	N	N	Y	N
6 Danner	Y	Y	Y	N	Y	N	Y
7 ***Blunt***	Y	Y	Y	Y	Y	N	Y
8 ***Emerson***	Y	Y	Y	Y	Y	N	Y
9 ***Hulshof***	+	Y	Y	Y	Y	N	Y
MONTANA							
AL ***Hill***	Y	Y	Y	Y	Y	?	?
NEBRASKA							
1 ***Bereuter***	Y	N	Y	Y	Y	N	Y
2 ***Christensen***	Y	Y	Y	Y	Y	N	Y
3 ***Barrett***	Y	N	Y	Y	Y	N	Y
NEVADA							
1 ***Ensign***	Y	Y	Y	Y	Y	N	Y
2 ***Gibbons***	Y	Y	Y	Y	Y	N	Y
NEW HAMPSHIRE							
1 ***Sununu***	Y	Y	Y	Y	Y	N	Y
2 ***Bass***	Y	N	Y	Y	N	Y	N
NEW JERSEY							
1 Andrews	Y	N	N	N	N	Y	N
2 ***LoBiondo***	Y	N	Y	Y	Y	N	Y
3 ***Saxton***	Y	N	Y	Y	Y	N	Y
4 ***Smith***	Y	Y	Y	Y	Y	N	Y
5 ***Roukema***	Y	N	Y	Y	Y	N	Y
6 Pallone	Y	N	N	N	N	Y	N
7 ***Franks***	Y	N	Y	Y	Y	N	Y
8 Pascrell	Y	N	N	N	Y	N	Y
9 Rothman	Y	N	Y	N	N	Y	N
10 Payne	Y	?	?	?	?	?	N
11 ***Frelinghuysen***	Y	N	Y	Y	Y	N	Y
12 ***Pappas***	Y	Y	Y	Y	Y	N	Y
13 Menendez	Y	N	N	N	N	Y	N
NEW MEXICO							
1 ***Wilson***	Y	Y	Y	Y	Y	N	Y
2 ***Skeen***	Y	Y	Y	Y	Y	N	Y
3 ***Redmond***	Y	Y	Y	Y	Y	N	Y
NEW YORK							
1 ***Forbes***	Y	N	Y	Y	Y	N	Y
2 ***Lazio***	Y	N	Y	Y	Y	N	Y
3 ***King***	Y	Y	N	Y	Y	N	Y
4 McCarthy	Y	N	N	Y	Y	N	Y
5 Ackerman	Y	N	N	N	N	Y	N
6 Meeks	Y	N	N	N	N	Y	N
7 Manton	Y	N	N	Y	Y	N	Y
8 Nadler	Y	N	N	N	N	Y	N
9 Schumer	Y	N	Y	N	N	Y	N
10 Towns	Y	N	N	N	N	Y	N
11 Owens	Y	N	N	N	N	Y	N
12 Velázquez	?	N	N	N	N	Y	N
13 ***Fossella***	Y	Y	Y	Y	Y	N	Y
14 Maloney	Y	N	N	N	N	Y	N
15 Rangel	Y	N	N	N	N	Y	N
16 Serrano	?	N	N	N	N	Y	N
17 Engel	Y	?	N	N	N	Y	N
18 Lowey	Y	N	N	N	N	Y	N
19 ***Kelly***	Y	N	Y	N	N	Y	Y
20 ***Gilman***	Y	N	Y	N	N	Y	N
21 McNulty	Y	?	?	?	?	?	?
22 ***Solomon***	Y	Y	Y	Y	Y	N	Y
23 ***Boehlert***	Y	N	N	N	N	N	N
24 ***McHugh***	Y	Y	Y	Y	Y	N	Y
25 ***Walsh***	Y	N	Y	Y	Y	N	Y
26 Hinchey	Y	N	Y	N	N	Y	N
27 ***Paxon***	Y	Y	Y	Y	Y	N	Y
28 Slaughter	Y	N	N	N	N	Y	N
29 LaFalce	Y	N	Y	Y	Y	N	Y
30 ***Quinn***	Y	Y	Y	Y	Y	N	Y
31 ***Houghton***	Y	N	Y	Y	N	N	N
NORTH CAROLINA							
1 Clayton	Y	N	N	N	N	Y	N
2 Etheridge	Y	N	Y	N	N	Y	Y
3 ***Jones***	Y	Y	Y	Y	Y	N	Y
4 Price	Y	N	Y	N	N	Y	N
5 ***Burr***	Y	Y	Y	Y	Y	N	Y
6 ***Coble***	Y	Y	Y	Y	Y	N	Y
7 McIntyre	Y	N	Y	Y	Y	N	Y
8 Hefner	Y	N	N	N	?	Y	N
9 ***Myrick***	Y	Y	Y	Y	Y	N	Y
10 ***Ballenger***	Y	Y	Y	Y	Y	N	Y
11 ***Taylor***	Y	Y	Y	Y	Y	N	Y
12 Watt	Y	Y	N	N	N	Y	N
NORTH DAKOTA							
AL Pomeroy	Y	N	Y	N	N	Y	Y
OHIO							
1 ***Chabot***	Y	Y	Y	Y	Y	N	Y
2 ***Portman***	Y	Y	Y	Y	Y	N	Y
3 Hall	Y	N	?	Y	Y	N	Y
4 ***Oxley***	Y	Y	Y	Y	Y	N	Y
5 ***Gillmor***	Y	N	Y	Y	Y	N	Y
6 Strickland	Y	N	Y	N	N	N	Y
7 ***Hobson***	Y	Y	Y	Y	Y	N	Y
8 ***Boehner***	Y	Y	Y	Y	Y	N	Y
9 Kaptur	Y	N	Y	N	N	Y	Y
10 Kucinich	Y	N	Y	Y	Y	N	Y
11 Stokes	Y	N	N	N	N	Y	N
12 ***Kasich***	Y	Y	Y	Y	Y	N	Y
13 Brown	Y	N	Y	N	N	Y	N
14 Sawyer	Y	N	Y	N	N	Y	N
15 ***Pryce***	Y	Y	Y	Y	Y	N	Y
16 ***Regula***	Y	Y	Y	Y	Y	N	Y
17 Traficant	Y	Y	Y	Y	Y	N	Y
18 ***Ney***	Y	Y	Y	Y	Y	N	Y
19 ***LaTourette***	Y	Y	Y	Y	Y	N	Y
OKLAHOMA							
1 ***Largent***	Y	Y	Y	Y	Y	N	Y
2 ***Coburn***	Y	Y	Y	Y	Y	N	Y
3 ***Watkins***	Y	Y	Y	Y	Y	N	Y
4 ***Watts***	Y	Y	Y	Y	Y	N	Y
5 ***Istook***	Y	Y	Y	Y	Y	N	Y
6 ***Lucas***	Y	Y	Y	Y	Y	N	Y
OREGON							
1 Furse	Y	N	N	N	N	Y	N
2 ***Smith***	Y	Y	?	Y	Y	N	Y
3 Blumenauer	Y	N	N	N	N	Y	N
4 DeFazio	Y	N	N	N	N	Y	N
5 Hooley	Y	N	Y	N	N	Y	N
PENNSYLVANIA							
1 Brady	Y	N	N	N	N	Y	N
2 Fattah	?	N	?	N	N	Y	N
3 Borski	Y	N	N	N	N	N	Y
4 Klink	Y	N	Y	Y	Y	N	Y
5 ***Peterson***	Y	Y	Y	Y	Y	N	Y
6 Holden	Y	N	Y	Y	Y	N	Y
7 ***Weldon***	Y	Y	Y	Y	Y	N	Y
8 ***Greenwood***	Y	N	Y	N	N	Y	N
9 ***Shuster***	Y	Y	?	Y	Y	N	Y
10 ***McDade***	?	?	?	Y	?	N	Y
11 Kanjorski	Y	N	N	Y	Y	N	Y
12 Murtha	Y	Y	N	Y	Y	N	Y
13 ***Fox***	Y	N	Y	Y	Y	N	Y
14 Coyne	Y	N	Y	N	N	Y	N
15 McHale	Y	N	N	N	N	N	Y
16 ***Pitts***	Y	Y	Y	Y	Y	N	Y
17 ***Gekas***	Y	Y	Y	Y	Y	N	Y
18 Doyle	Y	N	Y	Y	Y	N	Y
19 ***Goodling***	Y	Y	Y	Y	Y	N	Y
20 Mascara	Y	N	Y	Y	Y	N	Y
21 ***English***	Y	Y	Y	Y	Y	N	Y
RHODE ISLAND							
1 Kennedy	Y	N	N	N	N	Y	N
2 Weygand	Y	N	N	N	N	N	Y
SOUTH CAROLINA							
1 ***Sanford***	Y	N	N	Y	Y	N	Y
2 ***Spence***	Y	Y	Y	Y	Y	N	Y
3 ***Graham***	Y	Y	Y	Y	Y	N	Y
4 ***Inglis***	Y	Y	Y	Y	Y	N	Y
5 Spratt	Y	N	Y	N	N	Y	Y
6 Clyburn	Y	N	N	?	?	Y	N
SOUTH DAKOTA							
AL ***Thune***	Y	Y	Y	Y	Y	N	Y
TENNESSEE							
1 ***Jenkins***	Y	Y	Y	Y	Y	N	Y
2 ***Duncan***	Y	N	Y	Y	Y	N	Y
3 ***Wamp***	Y	N	Y	Y	Y	N	Y
4 ***Hilleary***	Y	+	+	Y	Y	N	Y
5 Clement	Y	N	Y	N	N	N	Y
6 Gordon	Y	Y	Y	N	N	N	Y
7 ***Bryant***	Y	Y	Y	Y	Y	N	Y
8 Tanner	Y	N	N	N	N	N	Y
9 Ford	Y	N	N	N	N	Y	N
TEXAS							
1 Sandlin	Y	N	Y	N	Y	Y	Y
2 Turner	?	N	Y	Y	Y	N	Y
3 ***Johnson, Sam***	Y	Y	Y	Y	Y	N	Y
4 Hall	Y	Y	Y	Y	Y	N	Y
5 ***Sessions***	Y	Y	Y	Y	Y	N	Y
6 ***Barton***	Y	Y	Y	Y	Y	N	Y
7 ***Archer***	Y	Y	Y	Y	Y	N	Y
8 ***Brady***	+	Y	Y	Y	Y	N	Y
9 Lampson	+	N	N	N	N	Y	N
10 Doggett	Y	N	?	N	N	Y	N
11 Edwards	Y	N	Y	N	N	Y	N
12 ***Granger***	Y	Y	Y	Y	Y	N	Y
13 ***Thornberry***	Y	Y	N	Y	Y	N	Y
14 ***Paul***	Y	Y	Y	Y	Y	N	N
15 Hinojosa	+	N	N	N	N	Y	N
16 Reyes	?	N	N	N	N	Y	Y
17 Stenholm	Y	N	Y	Y	N	N	Y
18 Jackson-Lee	Y	N	N	N	N	Y	N
19 ***Combest***	Y	Y	Y	Y	Y	N	Y
20 Gonzalez	?	?	?	?	?	?	?
21 ***Smith***	Y	Y	?	Y	Y	N	Y
22 ***DeLay***	Y	Y	Y	Y	Y	N	Y
23 ***Bonilla***	Y	Y	Y	Y	Y	N	Y
24 Frost	Y	N	N	N	N	Y	N
25 Bentsen	Y	N	Y	N	N	Y	N
26 ***Armey***	Y	Y	Y	Y	Y	N	Y
27 Ortiz	Y	Y	N	Y	Y	N	Y
28 Rodriguez	Y	N	N	N	N	Y	N
29 Green	Y	N	Y	N	N	Y	N
30 Johnson, E.B.	Y	N	N	N	N	Y	N
UTAH							
1 ***Hansen***	Y	Y	Y	Y	Y	N	Y
2 ***Cook***	Y	Y	Y	Y	Y	N	Y
3 ***Cannon***	Y	Y	Y	Y	Y	N	Y
VERMONT							
AL *Sanders*	Y	N	Y	N	N	Y	N
VIRGINIA							
1 ***Bateman***	Y	Y	Y	Y	Y	N	Y
2 Pickett	Y	N	Y	N	N	Y	N
3 Scott	Y	Y	N	N	N	Y	N
4 Sisisky	Y	N	Y	N	N	Y	N
5 Goode	Y	Y	Y	?	?	?	Y
6 ***Goodlatte***	Y	Y	Y	Y	Y	N	Y
7 ***Bliley***	Y	Y	Y	Y	Y	N	Y
8 Moran	Y	N	N	N	N	Y	N
9 Boucher	Y	N	Y	N	N	Y	N
10 ***Wolf***	Y	Y	Y	Y	Y	N	Y
11 ***Davis***	Y	Y	Y	Y	Y	N	Y
WASHINGTON							
1 ***White***	Y	Y	Y	Y	Y	N	Y
2 ***Metcalf***	Y	N	Y	Y	Y	N	Y
3 ***Smith, Linda***	N	Y	Y	Y	Y	N	Y
4 ***Hastings***	Y	Y	Y	Y	Y	N	Y
5 ***Nethercutt***	Y	Y	Y	Y	Y	N	Y
6 Dicks	Y	N	N	N	N	Y	N
7 McDermott	N	N	N	N	N	Y	N
8 ***Dunn***	Y	Y	Y	Y	Y	N	Y
9 Smith, Adam	Y	N	Y	N	N	Y	N
WEST VIRGINIA							
1 Mollohan	Y	Y	N	Y	Y	N	Y
2 Wise	Y	N	Y	N	N	Y	N
3 Rahall	Y	Y	Y	Y	Y	N	Y
WISCONSIN							
1 ***Neumann***	Y	Y	Y	Y	Y	N	Y
2 ***Klug***	?	N	Y	Y	Y	N	N
3 Kind	Y	N	N	N	N	Y	N
4 Kleczka	Y	N	Y	Y	Y	N	Y
5 Barrett	Y	N	N	N	N	Y	N
6 ***Petri***	Y	Y	Y	Y	Y	N	+
7 Obey	Y	N	Y	N	N	N	Y
8 Johnson	Y	N	Y	Y	Y	Y	Y
9 ***Sensenbrenner***	Y	Y	Y	Y	Y	N	Y
WYOMING							
AL ***Cubin***	Y	Y	Y	Y	Y	N	Y

Southern states - Ala., Ark., Fla., Ga., Ky., La., Miss., N.C., Okla., S.C., Tenn., Texas, Va.

281. HR 3267. Restore Salton Sea/Study Authorization. Miller, D-Calif., substitute amendment to authorize a study on alternatives for restoring the aquatic and environmental balance of the Salton Sea in California. The bill authorizes funds for both a study and a restoration project. Rejected 202-218: R 10-212; D 191-6 (ND 140-4, SD 51-2); I 1-0. July 15, 1998.

282. HR 3267. Restore Salton Sea/Passage. Passage of the bill to authorize a study and restoration project for the Salton Sea in Southern California and rename the area the "Sony Bono Salton Sea National Wildlife Refuge." Passed 221-200: R 195-28; D 26-171 (ND 17-127, SD 9-44); I 0-1. July 15, 1998. A "nay" was a vote in support of the president's position.

283. HR 4104. Fiscal 1999 Treasury, Postal Service Appropriations/Previous Question. Goss, R-Fla., motion to order the previous question (thus ending the possibility of amendment) on adoption of the rule (H Res 498) to provide for House floor consideration of the bill to provide $29.2 billion in fiscal 1999 for the Treasury Department, U.S. Postal Service, various offices of the Executive Office of the President and certain independent agencies. Motion agreed to 231-185: R 222-0; D 9-184 (ND 5-136, SD 4-48); I 0-1. July 15, 1998. (Subsequently, the rule was adopted.)

284. HR 4104. Fiscal 1999 Treasury, Postal Service Appropriations/Rule. Adoption of the rule (H Res 498) to provide for House floor consideration of the bill to provide $29.2 billion in fiscal 1999 for the Treasury Department, U.S. Postal Service, various offices of the Executive Office of the President and certain independent agencies. Adopted 218-201: R 198-23; D 20-177 (ND 14-130, SD 6-47); I 0-1. July 15, 1998.

285. HR 4194. Fiscal 1999 VA, HUD Appropriations/Rule. Adoption of the rule to provide for House floor consideration of the bill to provide $94.4 billion in fiscal 1999 for programs and activities of the Veterans Affairs and Housing and Urban Development departments and for independent agencies including the Environmental Protection Agency, National Science Foundation and the National Aeronautics and Space Administration. Adopted 227-195: R 222-1; D 5-193 (ND 4-141, SD 1-52); I 0-1. July 16, 1998.

286. HR 4104. Fiscal 1999 Treasury-Postal Appropriations/Funds for new Bureau of Alcohol, Tobacco and Firearms Agents. Schumer, D-N.Y., amendment to transfer to the Bureau of Alcohol, Tobacco and Firearms $2 million earmarked in the bill to compensate importers of certain assault-type weapons that were in transit when the administration extended the assault weapons ban. The amendment directs the agency to use the funds to hire additional agents. Rejected 122-301: R 3-221; D 119-79 (ND98-47, SD 21-32); I 0-1. July 16, 1998.

287. HR 4104. Fiscal 1999 Treasury-Postal Appropriations/Increase Federal Election Commission Funding. Maloney, D-N.Y., amendment to increase funding for the Federal Election Commission by $2.8 million. Adopted 214-210: R 27-196; D 186-14 (ND 139-8, SD 47-6); I 1-0. July 16, 1998.

Key

Y	Voted for (yea).
#	Paired for.
+	Announced for.
N	Voted against (nay).
X	Paired against.
–	Announced against.
P	Voted "present."
C	Voted "present" to avoid possible conflict of interest.
?	Did not vote or otherwise make a position known.

Democrats **Republicans** *Independent*

	281	282	283	284	285	286	287
ALABAMA							
1 *Callahan*	N	Y	Y	Y	Y	N	N
2 *Everett*	N	Y	Y	Y	Y	N	N
3 *Riley*	N	Y	Y	Y	Y	N	N
4 *Aderholt*	N	Y	Y	Y	Y	N	N
5 Cramer	Y	Y	N	N	N	N	Y
6 *Bachus*	N	Y	Y	N	N	N	N
7 Hilliard	Y	N	N	N	N	N	Y
ALASKA							
AL *Young*	N	Y	Y	Y	Y	N	N
ARIZONA							
1 *Salmon*	N	N	Y	Y	Y	N	N
2 Pastor	Y	N	N	N	N	Y	Y
3 *Stump*	N	N	Y	Y	Y	N	N
4 *Shadegg*	N	Y	Y	Y	Y	N	N
5 *Kolbe*	N	Y	Y	P	Y	N	N
6 *Hayworth*	N	Y	Y	Y	Y	N	N
ARKANSAS							
1 Berry	Y	N	N	N	N	Y	Y
2 Snyder	Y	N	N	N	N	Y	Y
3 *Hutchinson*	N	Y	Y	Y	Y	N	N
4 *Dickey*	N	Y	Y	Y	Y	N	N
CALIFORNIA							
1 *Riggs*	N	Y	Y	Y	Y	N	N
2 *Herger*	N	Y	Y	Y	Y	N	N
3 Fazio	Y	Y	N	N	N	N	Y
4 *Doolittle*	N	Y	Y	Y	Y	N	N
5 Matsui	Y	N	N	N	N	Y	Y
6 Woolsey	Y	N	N	N	N	Y	Y
7 Miller	Y	N	N	N	N	Y	Y
8 Pelosi	Y	N	N	N	N	Y	Y
9 Lee	Y	N	N	N	N	Y	Y
10 Tauscher	Y	N	N	N	N	Y	Y
11 *Pombo*	N	Y	Y	Y	Y	N	N
12 Lantos	Y	N	N	N	N	Y	Y
13 Stark	Y	N	N	N	N	Y	Y
14 Eshoo	Y	N	N	N	N	Y	Y
15 *Campbell*	N	N	Y	Y	Y	N	Y
16 Lofgren	Y	N	N	N	N	Y	Y
17 Farr	Y	N	N	N	N	Y	Y
18 Condit	Y	N	N	N	N	Y	Y
19 *Radanovich*	N	Y	Y	Y	Y	N	N
20 Dooley	Y	Y	N	N	N	Y	Y
21 *Thomas*	N	Y	Y	Y	Y	N	N
22 Capps, L.	Y	Y	N	N	N	Y	Y
23 *Gallegly*	N	Y	Y	Y	Y	N	N
24 Sherman	Y	N	N	N	N	Y	Y
25 *McKeon*	N	Y	Y	Y	Y	N	N
26 Berman	Y	N	N	N	N	Y	Y
27 *Rogan*	N	Y	Y	Y	Y	N	N
28 *Dreier*	N	Y	Y	Y	Y	N	N
29 Waxman	Y	N	N	N	N	Y	Y
30 Becerra	Y	–	N	N	N	Y	Y
31 Martinez	Y	N	N	N	N	Y	Y
32 Dixon	Y	N	N	N	N	Y	Y
33 Roybal-Allard	+	–	–	–	–	+	+
34 Torres	Y	N	N	N	N	Y	Y
35 Waters	Y	N	N	N	N	Y	Y
36 Harman	Y	N	N	N	N	Y	Y
37 Millender-McD.	Y	Y	N	N	N	Y	Y

	281	282	283	284	285	286	287
38 *Horn*	N	Y	Y	N	Y	N	Y
39 *Royce*	N	Y	Y	Y	Y	N	N
40 *Lewis*	N	Y	Y	Y	Y	N	N
41 *Kim*	N	Y	Y	Y	Y	N	N
42 Brown	Y	Y	N	N	N	N	Y
43 *Calvert*	N	Y	Y	Y	Y	N	N
44 *Bono, M.*	N	Y	Y	Y	Y	N	N
45 *Rohrabacher*	N	Y	Y	Y	Y	N	N
46 Sanchez	Y	N	N	N	N	Y	Y
47 *Cox*	N	Y	Y	Y	Y	N	N
48 *Packard*	N	Y	Y	Y	Y	N	N
49 *Bilbray*	N	Y	Y	Y	Y	N	N
50 Filner	Y	N	N	N	N	Y	Y
51 *Cunningham*	N	Y	Y	Y	Y	N	N
52 *Hunter*	N	Y	Y	Y	Y	N	N
COLORADO							
1 DeGette	Y	N	N	N	N	Y	Y
2 Skaggs	Y	N	N	N	N	Y	Y
3 *McInnis*	N	Y	Y	Y	Y	N	N
4 *Schaffer*	N	Y	Y	Y	Y	N	N
5 *Hefley*	N	N	Y	Y	Y	N	N
6 *Schaefer*	N	Y	Y	Y	Y	N	N
CONNECTICUT							
1 Kennelly	Y	N	?	?	?	?	?
2 Gejdenson	Y	N	N	N	N	Y	Y
3 DeLauro	Y	N	N	N	N	Y	Y
4 *Shays*	Y	N	Y	N	Y	N	Y
5 Maloney	Y	N	Y	N	Y	Y	Y
6 *Johnson*	N	Y	Y	N	Y	N	N
DELAWARE							
AL *Castle*	N	Y	Y	N	Y	N	Y
FLORIDA							
1 *Scarborough*	N	N	Y	Y	Y	N	N
2 Boyd	Y	N	N	N	N	Y	Y
3 Brown	Y	N	N	N	N	Y	Y
4 *Fowler*	N	Y	Y	Y	Y	N	N
5 Thurman	Y	N	N	N	N	Y	Y
6 *Stearns*	N	Y	Y	Y	Y	N	N
7 *Mica*	N	Y	Y	Y	Y	N	N
8 *McCollum*	N	Y	Y	Y	Y	N	N
9 *Bilirakis*	N	Y	Y	Y	Y	N	N
10 *Young*	N	Y	Y	Y	Y	N	N
11 Davis	Y	N	N	N	N	Y	Y
12 *Canady*	N	Y	Y	Y	Y	N	N
13 *Miller*	N	?	Y	Y	Y	N	N
14 *Goss*	N	Y	Y	Y	Y	N	N
15 *Weldon*	N	Y	Y	Y	Y	N	N
16 *Foley*	N	Y	Y	Y	Y	N	N
17 Meek	Y	N	N	N	N	Y	Y
18 *Ros-Lehtinen*	N	Y	Y	Y	Y	N	N
19 Wexler	Y	N	N	N	N	Y	Y
20 Deutsch	Y	N	N	N	N	Y	Y
21 *Diaz-Balart*	N	Y	Y	Y	Y	N	N
22 *Shaw*	N	Y	Y	Y	Y	N	N
23 Hastings	Y	N	N	N	N	Y	Y
GEORGIA							
1 *Kingston*	N	N	Y	Y	Y	N	N
2 Bishop	Y	N	N	N	N	Y	Y
3 *Collins*	N	Y	Y	Y	Y	N	N
4 McKinney	Y	N	N	N	N	Y	Y
5 Lewis	Y	N	N	N	N	Y	Y
6 *Gingrich*							
7 *Barr*	N	N	Y	Y	Y	N	N
8 *Chambliss*	N	Y	Y	Y	Y	N	N
9 *Deal*	N	Y	Y	Y	Y	N	N
10 *Norwood*	N	Y	Y	Y	?	N	N
11 *Linder*	?	?	Y	Y	Y	N	N
HAWAII							
1 Abercrombie	Y	N	N	N	Y	N	Y
2 Mink	Y	N	N	N	N	Y	Y
IDAHO							
1 *Chenoweth*	N	Y	Y	Y	Y	N	N
2 *Crapo*	N	Y	Y	Y	?	N	N
ILLINOIS							
1 Rush	Y	N	N	N	N	Y	Y
2 Jackson	Y	N	N	N	N	Y	Y
3 Lipinski	Y	N	Y	N	Y	Y	Y
4 Gutierrez	Y	N	N	N	N	Y	Y
5 Blagojevich	Y	N	N	N	N	N	Y
6 *Hyde*	N	Y	Y	Y	Y	N	N
7 Davis	Y	N	N	N	N	Y	Y
8 *Crane*	Y	Y	Y	Y	Y	N	N
9 Yates	?	?	?	?	N	N	Y
10 *Porter*	N	Y	Y	Y	N	N	Y
11 *Weller*	N	Y	Y	Y	Y	N	Y
12 Costello	Y	N	N	Y	N	Y	Y

ND Northern Democrats   SD Southern Democrats

	281	282	283	284	285	286	287
13 ***Fawell***	N	Y	Y	Y	Y	N	Y
14 ***Hastert***	N	Y	Y	Y	Y	N	N
15 ***Ewing***	N	Y	Y	Y	Y	N	N
16 ***Manzullo***	N	Y	Y	Y	Y	N	N
17 Evans	Y	N	N	N	N	Y	Y
18 ***LaHood***	N	Y	Y	Y	Y	N	N
19 Poshard	Y	N	N	N	N	Y	Y
20 ***Shimkus***	N	Y	Y	Y	Y	N	N
INDIANA							
1 Visclosky	Y	N	N	N	N	N	Y
2 ***McIntosh***	N	Y	Y	Y	Y	N	N
3 Roemer	Y	Y	N	N	N	N	Y
4 ***Souder***	N	Y	Y	Y	Y	N	N
5 ***Buyer***	N	Y	Y	Y	Y	N	N
6 ***Burton***	N	Y	Y	Y	Y	N	N
7 ***Pease***	N	Y	Y	Y	Y	N	N
8 ***Hostettler***	N	Y	Y	Y	Y	N	N
9 Hamilton	Y	N	N	N	N	N	Y
10 Carson	Y	N	N	N	N	Y	Y
IOWA							
1 ***Leach***	N	Y	Y	N	Y	N	Y
2 ***Nussle***	N	Y	Y	Y	Y	N	N
3 Boswell	Y	N	N	N	N	N	Y
4 ***Ganske***	N	Y	Y	N	Y	N	Y
5 ***Latham***	N	Y	Y	Y	Y	N	N
KANSAS							
1 ***Moran***	N	Y	Y	Y	Y	N	N
2 ***Ryun***	N	Y	Y	Y	Y	N	N
3 ***Snowbarger***	N	Y	Y	Y	Y	N	Y
4 ***Tiahrt***	N	Y	Y	Y	Y	N	N
KENTUCKY							
1 ***Whitfield***	N	Y	Y	?	Y	N	N
2 ***Lewis***	N	Y	Y	Y	Y	N	N
3 ***Northup***	N	Y	Y	Y	Y	N	N
4 ***Bunning***	N	Y	Y	Y	Y	N	N
5 ***Rogers***	?	Y	Y	Y	Y	N	N
6 Baesler	Y	N	N	N	N	N	Y
LOUISIANA							
1 ***Livingston***	N	Y	Y	Y	Y	N	N
2 Jefferson	Y	N	N	N	N	Y	Y
3 ***Tauzin***	N	Y	Y	Y	Y	N	N
4 ***McCrery***	N	Y	Y	Y	Y	N	N
5 ***Cooksey***	N	Y	Y	Y	Y	N	N
6 ***Baker***	N	Y	Y	Y	Y	N	N
7 John	Y	N	N	Y	N	N	N
MAINE							
1 Allen	Y	N	?	N	N	Y	Y
2 Baldacci	Y	N	N	N	N	Y	Y
MARYLAND							
1 ***Gilchrest***	N	Y	Y	N	Y	N	N
2 ***Ehrlich***	N	Y	Y	Y	Y	N	N
3 Cardin	Y	N	N	N	N	Y	Y
4 Wynn	Y	N	N	N	N	Y	N
5 Hoyer	Y	N	N	N	N	N	Y
6 ***Bartlett***	N	Y	Y	Y	Y	N	N
7 Cummings	Y	N	N	N	N	Y	Y
8 ***Morella***	N	Y	Y	N	Y	Y	Y
MASSACHUSETTS							
1 Olver	Y	N	N	N	N	Y	Y
2 Neal	Y	N	N	N	N	Y	Y
3 McGovern	Y	N	N	N	N	Y	Y
4 Frank	Y	Y	N	N	N	Y	Y
5 Meehan	Y	N	N	N	N	Y	Y
6 Tierney	Y	N	N	N	N	Y	Y
7 Markey	Y	N	N	N	N	Y	Y
8 Kennedy	N	Y	N	N	N	Y	Y
9 Moakley	Y	N	N	N	?	Y	Y
10 Delahunt	Y	N	N	N	N	Y	Y
MICHIGAN							
1 Stupak	Y	N	N	Y	N	N	Y
2 ***Hoekstra***	N	N	Y	Y	Y	N	N
3 ***Ehlers***	Y	N	Y	Y	Y	N	N
4 ***Camp***	N	N	Y	Y	Y	N	Y
5 Barcia	Y	N	Y	Y	N	N	Y
6 ***Upton***	N	N	Y	N	Y	N	Y
7 ***Smith***	N	Y	Y	Y	Y	N	Y
8 Stabenow	Y	N	N	N	N	Y	Y
9 Kildee	Y	N	Y	Y	N	Y	Y
10 Bonior	Y	N	N	N	N	Y	Y
11 ***Knollenberg***	N	Y	Y	Y	Y	N	N
12 Levin	Y	N	N	N	N	Y	Y
13 Rivers	Y	N	N	N	N	N	Y
14 Conyers	N	N	N	N	N	Y	Y
15 Kilpatrick	Y	N	N	N	N	Y	Y
16 Dingell	?	?	?	?	N	N	Y

	281	282	283	284	285	286	287
MINNESOTA							
1 ***Gutknecht***	N	Y	Y	Y	Y	N	N
2 Minge	Y	N	N	N	N	N	Y
3 ***Ramstad***	Y	N	Y	N	Y	N	Y
4 Vento	Y	N	N	N	N	Y	Y
5 Sabo	Y	N	N	N	N	Y	Y
6 Luther	Y	N	N	N	N	Y	Y
7 Peterson	Y	N	Y	Y	N	N	Y
8 Oberstar	Y	N	N	N	N	N	N
MISSISSIPPI							
1 ***Wicker***	N	Y	Y	Y	Y	N	N
2 Thompson	Y	N	N	N	N	Y	Y
3 ***Pickering***	N	Y	Y	Y	Y	–	N
4 ***Parker***	N	Y	Y	Y	Y	N	N
5 Taylor	N	Y	N	Y	N	N	Y
MISSOURI							
1 Clay	Y	N	N	N	N	Y	Y
2 ***Talent***	N	Y	Y	Y	Y	N	N
3 Gephardt	Y	N	N	N	N	N	Y
4 Skelton	N	Y	Y	Y	N	N	Y
5 McCarthy	Y	N	N	N	N	Y	Y
6 Danner	Y	N	N	Y	N	N	Y
7 ***Blunt***	N	Y	Y	Y	?	N	N
8 ***Emerson***	N	Y	Y	Y	Y	N	N
9 ***Hulshof***	N	Y	Y	Y	Y	N	Y
MONTANA							
AL ***Hill***	?	?	?	?	?	?	?
NEBRASKA							
1 ***Bereuter***	N	Y	Y	Y	Y	N	N
2 ***Christensen***	N	Y	Y	Y	Y	N	N
3 ***Barrett***	N	Y	Y	Y	Y	N	N
NEVADA							
1 ***Ensign***	N	Y	Y	Y	Y	N	N
2 ***Gibbons***	N	Y	Y	Y	Y	N	N
NEW HAMPSHIRE							
1 ***Sununu***	?	Y	?	Y	Y	N	N
2 ***Bass***	N	Y	Y	N	Y	N	N
NEW JERSEY							
1 Andrews	Y	N	N	N	N	Y	Y
2 ***LoBiondo***	N	N	Y	Y	Y	N	Y
3 ***Saxton***	N	Y	Y	Y	Y	N	N
4 ***Smith***	N	Y	Y	Y	Y	N	N
5 ***Roukema***	N	Y	Y	N	Y	N	Y
6 Pallone	Y	N	N	N	N	Y	Y
7 ***Franks***	N	Y	Y	N	Y	N	Y
8 Pascrell	Y	N	N	N	N	Y	Y
9 Rothman	Y	N	N	N	N	Y	Y
10 Payne	Y	N	N	N	N	Y	Y
11 ***Frelinghuysen***	N	Y	Y	N	Y	N	N
12 ***Pappas***	N	Y	Y	Y	Y	N	Y
13 Menendez	Y	N	N	N	N	Y	Y
NEW MEXICO							
1 ***Wilson***	N	Y	Y	Y	Y	N	N
2 ***Skeen***	N	Y	Y	Y	Y	N	N
3 ***Redmond***	N	Y	Y	Y	Y	N	N
NEW YORK							
1 ***Forbes***	Y	N	Y	Y	Y	N	N
2 ***Lazio***	N	Y	Y	Y	Y	N	Y
3 ***King***	N	Y	Y	Y	Y	N	N
4 McCarthy	Y	Y	N	N	Y	Y	Y
5 Ackerman	Y	N	N	N	N	Y	Y
6 Meeks	Y	N	?	N	N	?	Y
7 Manton	Y	N	N	N	N	Y	N
8 Nadler	Y	N	N	N	N	Y	Y
9 Schumer	?	?	?	?	N	Y	Y
10 Towns	Y	N	N	N	Y	Y	Y
11 Owens	Y	N	N	N	N	Y	Y
12 Velázquez	Y	N	N	N	N	Y	Y
13 ***Fossella***	N	Y	Y	Y	Y	N	N
14 Maloney	Y	N	N	N	N	Y	Y
15 Rangel	?	?	N	N	?	Y	Y
16 Serrano	Y	N	N	N	N	Y	Y
17 Engel	Y	N	N	N	N	Y	Y
18 Lowey	Y	N	N	N	N	Y	Y
19 ***Kelly***	N	Y	Y	N	Y	N	N
20 ***Gilman***	N	Y	Y	N	Y	N	Y
21 McNulty	?	?	?	?	?	?	?
22 ***Solomon***	N	Y	Y	Y	Y	N	N
23 ***Boehlert***	N	Y	Y	N	Y	N	Y
24 ***McHugh***	N	Y	Y	Y	Y	N	Y
25 ***Walsh***	N	Y	Y	Y	Y	N	N
26 Hinchey	Y	N	N	N	N	N	Y
27 ***Paxon***	N	Y	Y	Y	Y	N	N
28 Slaughter	Y	N	–	–	–	+	+
29 LaFalce	Y	N	N	N	N	Y	Y

	281	282	283	284	285	286	287
30 ***Quinn***	N	Y	Y	Y	Y	N	N
31 ***Houghton***	N	Y	Y	Y	Y	N	N
NORTH CAROLINA							
1 Clayton	Y	Y	N	N	N	Y	Y
2 Etheridge	Y	N	N	N	N	N	Y
3 ***Jones***	N	Y	Y	Y	Y	N	N
4 Price	Y	N	N	N	N	Y	Y
5 ***Burr***	N	Y	Y	Y	Y	N	N
6 ***Coble***	N	N	Y	Y	Y	N	N
7 McIntyre	Y	N	Y	Y	N	N	Y
8 Hefner	Y	N	N	N	N	?	Y
9 ***Myrick***	N	Y	Y	Y	Y	N	N
10 ***Ballenger***	N	Y	Y	Y	Y	N	N
11 ***Taylor***	N	Y	Y	Y	Y	N	N
12 Watt	Y	N	N	N	N	Y	Y
NORTH DAKOTA							
AL Pomeroy	Y	Y	N	N	N	N	Y
OHIO							
1 ***Chabot***	N	N	Y	Y	Y	N	N
2 ***Portman***	N	Y	Y	Y	Y	N	N
3 Hall	Y	N	N	N	N	Y	Y
4 ***Oxley***	N	?	Y	Y	Y	N	N
5 ***Gillmor***	N	Y	Y	Y	Y	N	N
6 Strickland	Y	N	N	N	N	N	Y
7 ***Hobson***	N	Y	Y	Y	Y	N	N
8 ***Boehner***	N	Y	Y	Y	Y	N	N
9 Kaptur	Y	Y	N	N	N	N	Y
10 Kucinich	Y	N	N	N	N	Y	Y
11 Stokes	Y	N	N	N	N	Y	Y
12 ***Kasich***	N	Y	Y	Y	Y	N	N
13 Brown	Y	N	N	N	N	Y	Y
14 Sawyer	Y	N	N	N	N	N	Y
15 ***Pryce***	N	Y	Y	Y	Y	N	N
16 ***Regula***	N	Y	Y	Y	Y	N	N
17 Traficant	N	Y	Y	Y	Y	N	N
18 ***Ney***	N	Y	Y	Y	Y	N	N
19 ***LaTourette***	N	Y	Y	Y	Y	Y	N
OKLAHOMA							
1 ***Largent***	N	Y	Y	Y	Y	N	N
2 ***Coburn***	N	Y	Y	Y	Y	N	N
3 ***Watkins***	N	N	Y	Y	Y	N	N
4 ***Watts***	N	Y	Y	Y	Y	N	N
5 ***Istook***	N	Y	Y	Y	Y	N	N
6 ***Lucas***	N	Y	Y	Y	Y	N	N
OREGON							
1 Furse	Y	N	N	N	N	Y	Y
2 ***Smith***	N	Y	?	?	Y	N	N
3 Blumenauer	Y	N	N	N	N	Y	Y
4 DeFazio	Y	N	N	N	N	N	N
5 Hooley	Y	N	N	N	N	Y	Y
PENNSYLVANIA							
1 Brady	Y	N	N	N	N	Y	Y
2 Fattah	Y	N	N	N	N	Y	Y
3 Borski	Y	N	N	N	N	Y	Y
4 Klink	Y	N	N	N	N	N	N
5 ***Peterson***	N	Y	Y	Y	Y	N	N
6 Holden	Y	N	N	Y	N	N	Y
7 ***Weldon***	N	Y	Y	Y	Y	N	N
8 ***Greenwood***	N	Y	Y	N	Y	N	Y
9 ***Shuster***	N	Y	?	?	Y	N	N
10 ***McDade***	N	Y	?	?	Y	?	?
11 Kanjorski	Y	N	N	N	N	N	Y
12 Murtha	Y	N	N	N	N	N	Y
13 ***Fox***	N	Y	Y	N	Y	N	N
14 Coyne	Y	N	N	N	N	Y	Y
15 McHale	Y	N	N	N	N	Y	Y
16 ***Pitts***	N	Y	Y	Y	Y	N	N
17 ***Gekas***	N	Y	Y	Y	Y	N	N
18 Doyle	Y	N	N	N	N	N	Y
19 ***Goodling***	N	Y	Y	Y	Y	N	N
20 Mascara	Y	N	N	N	N	N	Y
21 ***English***	N	Y	Y	Y	Y	N	N
RHODE ISLAND							
1 Kennedy	Y	N	N	N	N	+	Y
2 Weygand	+	N	N	N	N	Y	Y
SOUTH CAROLINA							
1 ***Sanford***	Y	N	Y	Y	Y	N	N
2 ***Spence***	N	Y	Y	Y	Y	N	N
3 ***Graham***	N	Y	Y	Y	Y	N	N
4 ***Inglis***	N	N	Y	Y	Y	N	N
5 Spratt	Y	N	N	N	N	N	Y
6 Clyburn	Y	N	N	N	N	Y	Y
SOUTH DAKOTA							
AL ***Thune***	N	Y	Y	Y	Y	N	N

	281	282	283	284	285	286	287
TENNESSEE							
1 ***Jenkins***	N	Y	Y	Y	Y	N	?
2 ***Duncan***	Y	N	Y	Y	Y	N	N
3 ***Wamp***	Y	N	Y	Y	Y	N	N
4 ***Hilleary***	N	Y	Y	Y	Y	N	N
5 Clement	Y	N	–	–	N	N	Y
6 Gordon	Y	N	N	N	N	N	Y
7 ***Bryant***	N	Y	Y	Y	Y	N	N
8 Tanner	Y	N	N	N	N	N	Y
9 Ford	Y	N	N	N	N	N	Y
TEXAS							
1 Sandlin	Y	N	N	N	N	N	N
2 Turner	Y	N	N	N	N	N	Y
3 ***Johnson, Sam***	N	Y	Y	Y	Y	N	N
4 Hall	N	Y	Y	Y	N	N	N
5 ***Sessions***	N	Y	Y	Y	Y	N	N
6 ***Barton***	N	Y	Y	Y	Y	N	?
7 ***Archer***	N	Y	Y	Y	Y	N	N
8 ***Brady***	N	Y	Y	Y	Y	N	N
9 Lampson	Y	N	N	N	N	N	Y
10 Doggett	Y	N	N	N	N	Y	Y
11 Edwards	Y	N	N	N	N	N	Y
12 ***Granger***	N	Y	Y	Y	Y	N	N
13 ***Thornberry***	N	Y	Y	Y	Y	N	N
14 ***Paul***	Y	N	Y	Y	Y	N	N
15 Hinojosa	Y	N	N	N	N	Y	Y
16 Reyes	?	?	N	N	N	Y	Y
17 Stenholm	Y	N	Y	Y	N	N	Y
18 Jackson-Lee	Y	N	N	N	N	Y	Y
19 ***Combest***	N	Y	Y	Y	Y	N	N
20 Gonzalez	?	?	?	?	?	?	?
21 ***Smith***	N	Y	Y	Y	Y	N	N
22 ***DeLay***	N	Y	Y	Y	Y	N	N
23 ***Bonilla***	N	Y	Y	Y	Y	N	N
24 Frost	Y	Y	N	N	N	N	Y
25 Bentsen	Y	N	N	N	N	N	Y
26 ***Armey***	N	Y	Y	Y	Y	N	N
27 Ortiz	Y	Y	N	N	N	N	Y
28 Rodriguez	Y	N	N	N	–	Y	Y
29 Green	Y	Y	N	N	N	N	Y
30 Johnson, E.B.	Y	N	N	N	N	N	Y
UTAH							
1 ***Hansen***	N	Y	Y	Y	Y	N	N
2 ***Cook***	N	Y	Y	Y	Y	N	N
3 ***Cannon***	N	Y	Y	Y	Y	N	N
VERMONT							
AL *Sanders*	Y	N	N	N	N	N	Y
VIRGINIA							
1 ***Bateman***	N	Y	Y	Y	Y	N	N
2 Pickett	Y	Y	N	N	N	N	N
3 Scott	Y	N	N	N	N	Y	Y
4 Sisisky	Y	Y	N	N	N	N	?
5 Goode	Y	N	Y	Y	Y	N	N
6 ***Goodlatte***	N	N	Y	Y	Y	N	N
7 ***Bliley***	N	Y	Y	Y	Y	N	N
8 Moran	Y	N	?	N	N	Y	Y
9 Boucher	Y	N	N	N	N	N	N
10 ***Wolf***	N	Y	Y	Y	Y	N	N
11 ***Davis***	N	Y	Y	Y	Y	N	N
WASHINGTON							
1 ***White***	N	Y	Y	Y	Y	N	N
2 ***Metcalf***	N	Y	Y	Y	Y	N	N
3 ***Smith, Linda***	N	Y	Y	Y	N	N	N
4 ***Hastings***	N	Y	Y	Y	Y	N	N
5 ***Nethercutt***	N	Y	Y	Y	Y	N	N
6 Dicks	Y	N	N	N	N	N	Y
7 McDermott	Y	N	N	N	N	Y	Y
8 ***Dunn***	N	Y	Y	Y	Y	N	N
9 Smith, Adam	Y	N	N	N	N	N	Y
WEST VIRGINIA							
1 Mollohan	Y	N	N	Y	N	N	Y
2 Wise	Y	N	N	N	N	N	Y
3 Rahall	Y	N	N	Y	N	N	N
WISCONSIN							
1 ***Neumann***	N	Y	Y	Y	Y	N	N
2 ***Klug***	N	N	Y	N	Y	N	N
3 Kind	Y	N	?	N	N	N	Y
4 Kleczka	Y	N	N	N	N	N	Y
5 Barrett	Y	N	N	N	N	Y	Y
6 ***Petri***	Y	N	Y	Y	Y	N	N
7 Obey	Y	N	N	N	N	N	Y
8 Johnson	Y	N	N	N	N	N	Y
9 ***Sensenbrenner***	?	N	Y	Y	Y	N	N
WYOMING							
AL ***Cubin***	N	Y	Y	Y	Y	N	N

Southern states - Ala., Ark., Fla., Ga., Ky., La., Miss., N.C., Okla., S.C., Tenn., Texas, Va.

Key

Y	Voted for (yea).
#	Paired for.
+	Announced for.
N	Voted against (nay).
X	Paired against.
−	Announced against.
P	Voted "present."
C	Voted "present" to avoid possible conflict of interest.
?	Did not vote or otherwise make a position known.

Democrats **Republicans**
Independent

288. HR 4104. Fiscal 1999 Treasury-Postal Appropriations/Federal Employee Health Plan Abortion Coverage. DeLauro, D-Conn., amendment to eliminate provisions banning the use of funds to pay for abortions under the Federal Employees Health Benefits Program. Rejected 183-239: R 29-196; D 153-43 (ND 114-33, SD 39-10); I 1-0. July 16, 1998.

289. HR 4104. Fiscal 1999 Treasury-Postal Appropriations/Annual Congressional Cost of Living Adjustment. Hefner, D-N.C., amendment to delete the provision that blocks members of Congress from receiving an annual cost of living adjustment. Rejected 79-342: R 29-195; D 50-146 (ND 41-106, SD 9-40); I 0-1. July 16, 1998.

290. HR 4104. Fiscal 1999 Treasury-Postal Appropriations/Insurance Coverage of Contraceptives. Lowey, D-N.Y. amendment to prohibit the Office of Personnel Management from accepting a contract that provides coverage for prescription drugs unless the plan also provides equivalent coverage for prescription contraception drugs. Adopted 224-198: R 48-177; D 175-21 (ND 130-17, SD 45-4); I 1-0. July 16, 1998.

291. HR 4104. Fiscal 1999 Treasury-Postal Appropriations/Exchange Stabilization Fund Restriction. Sanders, I-Vt. amendment to prohibit the use of funds in the bill to make any loan or credit in excess of $250 million to a foreign entity or government through the Exchange Stabilization Fund without congressional approval. Rejected 195-226: R 143-82; D 51-144 (ND 41-105, SD 10-39); I 1-0. July 16, 1998.

292. HR 4104. Fiscal 1999 Treasury-Postal Appropriations/Federal Employee Health Plan Abortion Coverage Ban. Smith, R-N.J. amendment to prohibit federal employee health plans from providing insurance coverage for drugs that induce abortion. Rejected 198-222: R 172-51; D 26-170 (ND 21-126, SD 5-44); I 0-1. July 16, 1998.

293. HR 4104. Fiscal 1999 Treasury-Postal Appropriations/Passage. Passage of the bill to provide funds for the Treasury Department, U.S. Postal Service, various offices of the Executive Office of the President and certain independent agencies. Passed 218-203: R 192-33; D 26-169 (ND 14-132, SD 12-37); I 0-1. July 16, 1998.

294. HR 3731. Steve Schiff Auditorium Designation/Passage. Passage of the bill to designate an auditorium within the Sandia Technology Transfer Center in Albuquerque, N.M., as the "Steve Schiff Auditorium." Passed 409-0: R 218-0; D 190-0 (ND 141-0, SD 49-0); I 1-0. July 16, 1998.

	288	289	290	291	292	293	294
ALABAMA							
1 *Callahan*	N	N	N	N	Y	Y	Y
2 *Everett*	N	N	N	Y	Y	Y	Y
3 *Riley*	N	N	N	Y	Y	Y	Y
4 *Aderholt*	N	N	N	Y	Y	N	Y
5 Cramer	Y	N	N	N	N	Y	Y
6 *Bachus*	N	N	N	Y	Y	Y	Y
7 Hilliard	Y	Y	Y	Y	N	N	Y
ALASKA							
AL *Young*	N	N	N	Y	Y	Y	Y
ARIZONA							
1 *Salmon*	N	N	N	Y	Y	Y	?
2 Pastor	Y	N	Y	N	N	Y	Y
3 *Stump*	N	N	N	N	Y	N	Y
4 *Shadegg*	N	N	N	Y	Y	Y	Y
5 *Kolbe*	Y	Y	Y	N	Y	Y	Y
6 *Hayworth*	N	N	N	Y	Y	N	Y
ARKANSAS							
1 Berry	N	N	Y	N	Y	N	Y
2 Snyder	Y	N	Y	N	N	N	Y
3 *Hutchinson*	N	N	N	Y	Y	Y	Y
4 *Dickey*	N	N	N	N	Y	Y	Y
CALIFORNIA							
1 *Riggs*	N	Y	N	Y	Y	Y	Y
2 *Herger*	N	N	N	Y	Y	Y	N
3 Fazio	Y	Y	Y	N	N	Y	Y
4 *Doolittle*	N	Y	N	Y	Y	Y	Y
5 Matsui	Y	N	Y	N	N	N	Y
6 Woolsey	Y	N	Y	N	N	N	Y
7 Miller	Y	Y	Y	N	N	N	Y
8 Pelosi	Y	Y	Y	N	N	N	Y
9 Lee	Y	Y	Y	N	N	N	Y
10 Tauscher	Y	N	Y	N	N	N	Y
11 *Pombo*	N	N	N	Y	Y	Y	Y
12 Lantos	Y	N	Y	N	N	N	Y
13 Stark	Y	Y	Y	Y	N	N	Y
14 Eshoo	Y	N	Y	N	N	N	Y
15 *Campbell*	Y	Y	Y	Y	N	N	Y
16 Lofgren	Y	N	Y	N	N	N	Y
17 Farr	Y	N	Y	N	N	N	Y
18 Condit	Y	N	Y	N	Y	Y	Y
19 *Radanovich*	N	N	N	Y	Y	Y	Y
20 Dooley	Y	N	Y	N	N	Y	?
21 *Thomas*	Y	Y	Y	N	N	N	Y
22 Capps, L.	Y	N	Y	N	N	N	Y
23 *Gallegly*	N	N	N	Y	Y	N	Y
24 Sherman	Y	N	Y	N	N	N	Y
25 *McKeon*	N	N	N	Y	Y	Y	Y
26 Berman	Y	Y	Y	N	N	N	?
27 *Rogan*	N	N	N	Y	Y	Y	Y
28 *Dreier*	N	N	N	Y	Y	Y	Y
29 Waxman	Y	Y	Y	N	N	N	Y
30 Becerra	Y	N	Y	N	N	N	Y
31 Martinez	Y	Y	Y	N	N	N	?
32 Dixon	Y	Y	Y	N	N	N	Y
33 Roybal-Allard	+	−	+	−	−	−	+
34 Torres	Y	N	Y	N	N	N	Y
35 Waters	Y	Y	Y	?	N	N	Y
36 Harman	Y	Y	Y	N	N	Y	?
37 Millender-McD.	Y	N	Y	N	N	N	Y

	288	289	290	291	292	293	294
38 *Horn*	Y	N	Y	N	N	Y	Y
39 *Royce*	N	N	N	Y	Y	Y	Y
40 *Lewis*	N	Y	N	Y	Y	N	Y
41 *Kim*	N	N	N	Y	N	N	Y
42 Brown	Y	N	Y	N	N	N	Y
43 *Calvert*	N	N	N	Y	Y	Y	Y
44 *Bono, M.*	N	N	N	Y	Y	Y	Y
45 *Rohrabacher*	N	N	N	Y	Y	Y	Y
46 Sanchez	Y	N	Y	N	N	N	Y
47 *Cox*	N	N	N	Y	Y	Y	Y
48 *Packard*	N	N	N	Y	Y	Y	Y
49 *Bilbray*	N	N	N	Y	Y	N	Y
50 Filner	#	−	#	−	X	X	+
51 *Cunningham*	N	N	N	Y	Y	Y	Y
52 *Hunter*	N	Y	N	Y	Y	Y	Y
COLORADO							
1 DeGette	Y	N	Y	N	N	N	Y
2 Skaggs	Y	Y	Y	N	N	N	Y
3 *McInnis*	N	N	N	N	N	N	Y
4 *Schaffer*	N	N	N	Y	Y	N	Y
5 *Hefley*	N	N	N	Y	N	N	Y
6 *Schaefer*	N	Y	N	Y	Y	Y	Y
CONNECTICUT							
1 Kennelly	#	?	?	?	?	?	?
2 Gejdenson	Y	N	Y	N	N	N	Y
3 DeLauro	Y	N	Y	N	N	N	Y
4 *Shays*	Y	N	Y	N	N	Y	Y
5 Maloney	Y	N	Y	N	N	Y	Y
6 *Johnson*	Y	N	Y	N	N	Y	?
DELAWARE							
AL *Castle*	Y	N	Y	N	N	Y	Y
FLORIDA							
1 *Scarborough*	N	N	N	Y	Y	N	Y
2 Boyd	N	N	Y	N	N	N	Y
3 Brown	Y	N	Y	N	N	N	Y
4 *Fowler*	N	Y	N	Y	Y	N	Y
5 Thurman	Y	N	Y	N	N	N	Y
6 *Stearns*	N	N	N	Y	Y	Y	Y
7 *Mica*	N	N	N	Y	Y	Y	Y
8 *McCollum*	N	Y	N	Y	Y	Y	Y
9 *Bilirakis*	N	N	N	Y	Y	Y	Y
10 *Young*	N	N	N	Y	Y	Y	Y
11 Davis	Y	N	Y	N	N	N	Y
12 *Canady*	N	N	N	Y	Y	Y	Y
13 *Miller*	Y	N	N	Y	N	N	Y
14 *Goss*	N	N	N	Y	Y	Y	Y
15 *Weldon*	N	N	N	Y	Y	Y	Y
16 *Foley*	Y	N	Y	N	Y	Y	Y
17 Meek	Y	Y	Y	N	N	N	Y
18 *Ros-Lehtinen*	N	Y	N	Y	Y	Y	Y
19 Wexler	Y	Y	Y	N	N	N	Y
20 Deutsch	Y	N	Y	N	N	N	Y
21 *Diaz-Balart*	N	N	N	Y	Y	Y	Y
22 *Shaw*	N	N	Y	N	Y	Y	Y
23 Hastings	Y	Y	Y	N	N	N	Y
GEORGIA							
1 *Kingston*	N	N	N	Y	Y	N	Y
2 Bishop	Y	N	Y	N	N	N	Y
3 *Collins*	N	N	N	Y	Y	N	Y
4 McKinney	N	Y	Y	N	N	N	Y
5 Lewis	?	?	?	?	?	?	?
6 *Gingrich*						Y	Y
7 *Barr*	N	N	N	Y	Y	N	Y
8 *Chambliss*	N	N	N	Y	Y	Y	Y
9 *Deal*	N	N	N	Y	Y	Y	Y
10 *Norwood*	N	N	N	Y	Y	N	Y
11 *Linder*	N	N	N	Y	Y	Y	Y
HAWAII							
1 Abercrombie	Y	N	Y	N	N	N	Y
2 Mink	Y	N	Y	N	N	N	Y
IDAHO							
1 *Chenoweth*	N	N	N	Y	Y	Y	Y
2 *Crapo*	N	N	N	Y	Y	Y	Y
ILLINOIS							
1 Rush	Y	N	Y	Y	N	N	Y
2 Jackson	Y	Y	Y	Y	N	N	Y
3 Lipinski	N	N	N	Y	Y	N	Y
4 Gutierrez	Y	N	Y	N	N	N	Y
5 Blagojevich	Y	N	Y	N	N	N	Y
6 *Hyde*	N	Y	N	Y	Y	Y	Y
7 Davis	Y	N	Y	N	N	N	Y
8 *Crane*	Y	Y	Y	N	N	?	?
9 Yates	Y	Y	Y	N	N	?	?
10 *Porter*	Y	Y	Y	N	N	Y	Y
11 *Weller*	N	N	N	Y	Y	Y	Y
12 Costello	N	N	N	Y	Y	N	Y

ND Northern Democrats   SD Southern Democrats

	288	289	290	291	292	293	294
13 ***Fawell***	Y	Y	Y	N	N	Y	Y
14 ***Hastert***	N	N	N	Y	Y	Y	Y
15 ***Ewing***	N	N	N	N	N	Y	Y
16 ***Manzullo***	N	N	N	Y	Y	Y	Y
17 Evans	Y	N	Y	Y	N	N	Y
18 ***LaHood***	N	N	N	Y	Y	Y	Y
19 Poshard	N	N	Y	Y	N	N	Y
20 ***Shimkus***	N	N	N	Y	Y	Y	Y
INDIANA							
1 Visclosky	Y	N	Y	Y	N	Y	Y
2 ***McIntosh***	N	N	N	Y	?	Y	Y
3 Roemer	N	N	Y	N	Y	N	Y
4 ***Souder***	N	N	N	Y	Y	Y	Y
5 ***Buyer***	N	N	N	N	Y	Y	Y
6 ***Burton***	N	Y	N	Y	Y	Y	Y
7 ***Pease***	N	N	N	Y	Y	Y	Y
8 ***Hostettler***	N	N	N	Y	Y	N	Y
9 Hamilton	N	N	Y	N	Y	N	Y
10 Carson	Y	N	Y	Y	N	N	Y
IOWA							
1 ***Leach***	N	N	Y	N	N	Y	Y
2 ***Nussle***	N	N	N	N	Y	Y	Y
3 Boswell	Y	N	Y	N	N	Y	Y
4 ***Ganske***	N	N	Y	Y	N	Y	Y
5 ***Latham***	N	N	N	N	Y	Y	Y
KANSAS							
1 ***Moran***	N	N	N	Y	Y	N	Y
2 ***Ryun***	N	N	N	Y	Y	Y	Y
3 ***Snowbarger***	N	N	N	Y	Y	Y	Y
4 ***Tiahrt***	N	N	N	Y	Y	N	Y
KENTUCKY							
1 ***Whitfield***	N	N	N	Y	Y	Y	Y
2 ***Lewis***	N	N	N	Y	Y	Y	Y
3 ***Northup***	N	N	N	N	Y	Y	Y
4 ***Bunning***	N	N	N	Y	Y	N	Y
5 ***Rogers***	N	N	N	Y	Y	Y	Y
6 Baesler	Y	N	Y	Y	N	Y	Y
LOUISIANA							
1 ***Livingston***	N	Y	N	Y	Y	Y	Y
2 Jefferson	Y	N	Y	N	N	N	Y
3 ***Tauzin***	N	N	N	Y	Y	Y	Y
4 ***McCrery***	N	Y	N	N	Y	Y	Y
5 ***Cooksey***	N	N	N	Y	N	Y	Y
6 ***Baker***	N	N	N	N	Y	N	Y
7 John	?	?	?	?	?	?	?
MAINE							
1 Allen	Y	N	Y	N	N	N	Y
2 Baldacci	Y	N	Y	N	N	N	Y
MARYLAND							
1 ***Gilchrest***	Y	N	Y	N	N	Y	Y
2 ***Ehrlich***	Y	N	Y	N	N	Y	Y
3 Cardin	Y	N	Y	N	N	N	Y
4 Wynn	Y	Y	Y	N	N	N	Y
5 Hoyer	Y	N	Y	N	N	Y	Y
6 ***Bartlett***	N	N	N	Y	Y	Y	Y
7 Cummings	Y	N	Y	Y	N	N	Y
8 ***Morella***	Y	N	Y	N	N	Y	Y
MASSACHUSETTS							
1 Olver	Y	N	Y	N	N	N	Y
2 Neal	N	N	Y	N	N	N	Y
3 McGovern	Y	N	Y	Y	N	N	Y
4 Frank	Y	Y	Y	N	N	N	Y
5 Meehan	Y	N	Y	N	N	N	Y
6 Tierney	Y	N	Y	N	N	N	Y
7 Markey	Y	N	Y	N	N	N	Y
8 Kennedy	Y	Y	Y	N	N	N	Y
9 Moakley	N	N	Y	N	N	N	Y
10 Delahunt	Y	Y	Y	Y	N	N	Y
MICHIGAN							
1 Stupak	N	N	N	Y	Y	N	Y
2 ***Hoekstra***	N	N	N	Y	Y	Y	Y
3 ***Ehlers***	N	N	N	N	Y	Y	Y
4 ***Camp***	N	N	N	N	Y	Y	Y
5 Barcia	N	N	N	Y	Y	N	Y
6 ***Upton***	N	N	Y	Y	N	Y	Y
7 ***Smith***	N	N	N	Y	Y	Y	Y
8 Stabenow	Y	N	Y	N	N	N	Y
9 Kildee	N	N	N	N	Y	N	Y
10 Bonior	N	N	Y	N	N	N	Y
11 ***Knollenberg***	N	Y	N	N	Y	Y	Y
12 Levin	Y	N	Y	N	N	N	Y
13 Rivers	Y	N	Y	N	N	N	Y
14 Conyers	Y	Y	Y	Y	N	N	Y
15 Kilpatrick	Y	N	Y	N	N	N	Y
16 Dingell	Y	Y	Y	N	N	N	Y
MINNESOTA							
1 ***Gutknecht***	N	N	N	Y	Y	N	Y
2 Minge	Y	N	Y	N	N	N	Y
3 ***Ramstad***	Y	N	Y	N	N	N	Y
4 Vento	Y	N	Y	N	N	N	Y
5 Sabo	Y	Y	Y	N	N	N	Y
6 Luther	Y	N	Y	N	N	N	Y
7 Peterson	N	N	N	N	Y	N	Y
8 Oberstar	N	N	Y	N	Y	N	Y
MISSISSIPPI							
1 ***Wicker***	N	N	N	N	Y	Y	Y
2 Thompson	Y	N	Y	N	N	N	Y
3 ***Pickering***	N	N	N	Y	Y	Y	Y
4 ***Parker***	?	?	?	?	?	?	?
5 Taylor	N	N	N	Y	Y	N	Y
MISSOURI							
1 Clay	Y	Y	Y	N	N	N	Y
2 ***Talent***	N	N	N	Y	Y	Y	Y
3 Gephardt	Y	N	Y	N	N	N	Y
4 Skelton	N	N	N	N	Y	N	Y
5 McCarthy	Y	N	Y	N	N	N	Y
6 Danner	N	N	Y	Y	Y	Y	Y
7 ***Blunt***	N	N	N	Y	Y	Y	Y
8 ***Emerson***	N	N	N	Y	Y	Y	Y
9 ***Hulshof***	N	N	N	Y	Y	Y	Y
MONTANA							
AL ***Hill***	X	?	?	?	?	?	?
NEBRASKA							
1 ***Bereuter***	N	N	Y	N	Y	Y	Y
2 ***Christensen***	N	N	N	Y	Y	Y	Y
3 ***Barrett***	N	N	N	N	Y	Y	Y
NEVADA							
1 ***Ensign***	N	N	Y	Y	Y	Y	Y
2 ***Gibbons***	N	N	Y	Y	N	Y	Y
NEW HAMPSHIRE							
1 ***Sununu***	N	N	N	Y	Y	Y	Y
2 ***Bass***	Y	N	Y	Y	N	Y	Y
NEW JERSEY							
1 Andrews	Y	N	Y	Y	N	N	Y
2 ***LoBiondo***	N	N	N	Y	Y	Y	Y
3 ***Saxton***	N	N	N	Y	Y	Y	Y
4 ***Smith***	N	N	N	Y	Y	N	?
5 ***Roukema***	Y	N	Y	N	N	Y	Y
6 Pallone	Y	N	Y	N	N	N	Y
7 ***Franks***	Y	N	Y	N	N	Y	Y
8 Pascrell	Y	N	Y	Y	N	N	Y
9 Rothman	Y	N	Y	N	N	N	Y
10 Payne	Y	Y	Y	N	N	N	Y
11 ***Frelinghuysen***	Y	N	Y	N	N	Y	Y
12 ***Pappas***	N	N	N	Y	Y	N	Y
13 Menendez	Y	N	Y	N	N	N	Y
NEW MEXICO							
1 ***Wilson***	N	N	Y	N	Y	Y	Y
2 ***Skeen***	N	N	N	N	Y	Y	Y
3 ***Redmond***	N	N	N	N	Y	Y	Y
NEW YORK							
1 ***Forbes***	N	N	N	Y	Y	Y	Y
2 ***Lazio***	Y	N	Y	N	N	Y	Y
3 ***King***	N	Y	N	N	Y	Y	Y
4 McCarthy	Y	N	Y	N	N	N	Y
6 Meeks	Y	Y	Y	N	N	N	Y
5 Ackerman	Y	Y	Y	N	N	N	Y
7 Manton	N	Y	Y	N	N	N	Y
8 Nadler	Y	Y	Y	Y	N	N	Y
9 Schumer	Y	N	Y	N	N	Y	Y
10 Towns	Y	Y	Y	N	N	N	Y
11 Owens	Y	Y	Y	Y	N	N	Y
12 Velázquez	Y	N	Y	Y	N	N	Y
13 ***Fossella***	N	N	N	Y	Y	Y	Y
14 Maloney	Y	N	Y	N	N	Y	Y
15 Rangel	Y	Y	Y	Y	N	N	Y
16 Serrano	Y	Y	Y	Y	N	N	Y
17 Engel	Y	Y	Y	N	N	N	Y
18 Lowey	Y	N	Y	N	N	Y	Y
19 ***Kelly***	Y	N	Y	N	N	Y	Y
20 ***Gilman***	Y	N	Y	N	N	Y	Y
21 McNulty	?	?	?	?	?	?	?
22 ***Solomon***	N	N	N	Y	Y	Y	Y
23 ***Boehlert***	Y	Y	Y	N	N	Y	Y
24 ***McHugh***	N	N	N	N	Y	Y	Y
25 ***Walsh***	N	N	N	N	Y	Y	Y
26 Hinchey	Y	N	Y	N	N	N	Y
27 ***Paxon***	N	Y	N	Y	Y	Y	Y
28 Slaughter	Y	N	Y	N	N	N	Y
29 LaFalce	N	N	N	N	Y	N	Y
30 ***Quinn***	N	N	N	Y	Y	Y	Y
31 ***Houghton***	Y	N	Y	N	N	Y	Y
NORTH CAROLINA							
1 Clayton	?	?	?	?	?	?	?
2 Etheridge	Y	N	Y	N	N	Y	Y
3 ***Jones***	N	N	N	Y	Y	N	Y
4 Price	Y	N	Y	N	N	Y	Y
5 ***Burr***	N	N	N	Y	Y	Y	Y
6 ***Coble***	N	N	N	Y	Y	Y	Y
7 McIntyre	N	N	Y	Y	N	N	Y
8 Hefner	Y	Y	Y	N	N	N	Y
9 ***Myrick***	N	–	N	Y	Y	Y	Y
10 ***Ballenger***	N	N	N	N	Y	Y	Y
11 ***Taylor***	N	N	N	N	Y	Y	Y
12 Watt	Y	Y	Y	N	N	N	Y
NORTH DAKOTA							
AL Pomeroy	Y	N	Y	N	N	N	Y
OHIO							
1 ***Chabot***	N	N	N	Y	Y	Y	Y
2 ***Portman***	N	N	N	Y	Y	Y	Y
3 Hall	N	N	N	N	Y	N	Y
4 ***Oxley***	N	N	Y	N	N	Y	Y
5 ***Gillmor***	N	N	N	Y	Y	Y	Y
6 Strickland	Y	N	Y	Y	N	N	Y
7 ***Hobson***	N	N	Y	Y	N	Y	Y
8 ***Boehner***	N	N	N	N	Y	Y	Y
9 Kaptur	N	N	Y	Y	N	N	Y
10 Kucinich	N	N	N	Y	Y	N	Y
11 Stokes	Y	Y	Y	N	N	N	Y
12 ***Kasich***	N	N	N	N	N	Y	Y
13 Brown	Y	N	Y	Y	N	N	Y
14 Sawyer	Y	N	Y	N	N	N	Y
15 ***Pryce***	Y	N	Y	N	N	Y	Y
16 ***Regula***	N	N	N	Y	N	Y	?
17 Traficant	N	N	N	Y	Y	N	Y
18 ***Ney***	N	N	N	Y	Y	N	Y
19 ***LaTourette***	N	N	N	N	Y	N	Y
OKLAHOMA							
1 ***Largent***	N	N	N	Y	Y	Y	Y
2 ***Coburn***	N	N	N	N	Y	Y	Y
3 ***Watkins***	N	N	N	Y	Y	Y	Y
4 ***Watts***	N	N	N	Y	Y	Y	Y
5 ***Istook***	N	N	N	Y	Y	Y	Y
6 ***Lucas***	N	N	N	Y	Y	Y	Y
OREGON							
1 Furse	Y	Y	Y	N	N	N	Y
2 ***Smith***	N	N	N	N	Y	Y	?
3 Blumenauer	Y	N	Y	N	N	N	Y
4 DeFazio	Y	N	Y	Y	N	N	Y
5 Hooley	Y	N	Y	N	N	Y	Y
PENNSYLVANIA							
1 Brady	Y	N	Y	N	N	N	Y
2 Fattah	Y	Y	Y	N	N	N	Y
3 Borski	N	N	Y	N	N	N	Y
4 Klink	N	N	N	Y	Y	N	?
5 ***Peterson***	N	N	N	Y	Y	Y	Y
6 Holden	N	N	N	Y	Y	N	Y
7 ***Weldon***	N	N	N	Y	Y	Y	Y
8 ***Greenwood***	Y	N	Y	N	N	Y	Y
9 ***Shuster***	N	N	N	Y	Y	Y	?
10 ***McDade***	N	Y	N	N	?	?	?
11 Kanjorski	N	Y	Y	N	N	N	Y
12 Murtha	N	Y	Y	N	N	N	Y
13 ***Fox***	N	N	Y	Y	N	Y	Y
14 Coyne	Y	N	Y	N	N	N	Y
15 McHale	N	Y	Y	N	Y	Y	Y
16 ***Pitts***	N	N	N	Y	Y	Y	Y
17 ***Gekas***	N	N	N	Y	Y	Y	Y
18 Doyle	N	N	N	Y	Y	N	Y
19 ***Goodling***	N	N	N	Y	Y	Y	Y
20 Mascara	N	N	N	Y	Y	N	Y
21 ***English***	N	N	N	Y	Y	Y	Y
RHODE ISLAND							
1 Kennedy	Y	N	Y	Y	N	N	Y
2 Weygand	N	N	Y	N	N	N	Y
SOUTH CAROLINA							
1 ***Sanford***	N	N	N	Y	Y	N	Y
2 ***Spence***	N	N	N	Y	Y	Y	Y
3 ***Graham***	N	N	N	Y	Y	Y	Y
4 ***Inglis***	N	N	N	Y	Y	N	Y
5 Spratt	Y	N	Y	N	N	N	Y
6 Clyburn	Y	N	Y	N	N	N	Y
SOUTH DAKOTA							
AL ***Thune***	N	N	N	N	Y	Y	Y
TENNESSEE							
1 ***Jenkins***	N	N	N	N	Y	Y	Y
2 ***Duncan***	N	N	N	Y	Y	N	Y
3 ***Wamp***	N	N	N	Y	Y	Y	Y
4 ***Hilleary***	N	N	N	Y	Y	N	Y
5 Clement	Y	N	Y	N	N	N	Y
6 Gordon	Y	N	Y	N	N	N	Y
7 ***Bryant***	N	N	N	Y	Y	Y	Y
8 Tanner	Y	N	Y	N	N	N	Y
9 Ford	+	–	+	–	–	–	+
TEXAS							
1 Sandlin	Y	N	Y	N	N	Y	Y
2 Turner	N	N	Y	Y	N	N	Y
3 ***Johnson, Sam***	N	Y	N	Y	Y	Y	Y
4 Hall	N	N	N	Y	Y	Y	Y
5 ***Sessions***	N	N	N	Y	Y	Y	Y
6 ***Barton***	N	N	N	N	Y	N	Y
7 ***Archer***	N	N	N	N	Y	Y	Y
8 ***Brady***	N	N	N	N	Y	Y	Y
9 Lampson	N	N	Y	N	N	Y	Y
10 Doggett	Y	N	Y	N	N	Y	Y
11 Edwards	N	N	Y	N	N	N	Y
12 ***Granger***	N	N	Y	N	N	Y	Y
13 ***Thornberry***	N	N	N	Y	Y	Y	Y
14 ***Paul***	N	N	N	Y	Y	N	Y
15 Hinojosa	Y	N	Y	N	N	N	Y
16 Reyes	Y	N	Y	N	N	N	Y
17 Stenholm	N	N	N	N	Y	N	Y
18 Jackson-Lee	Y	N	Y	N	N	N	Y
19 ***Combest***	N	N	N	N	Y	Y	Y
20 Gonzalez	?	?	?	?	?	?	?
21 ***Smith***	N	N	N	Y	Y	Y	Y
22 ***DeLay***	N	Y	N	N	Y	Y	Y
23 ***Bonilla***	Y	N	N	N	Y	Y	Y
24 Frost	Y	N	Y	N	N	N	Y
25 Bentsen	Y	N	Y	N	N	Y	Y
26 ***Armey***	N	N	N	Y	Y	Y	Y
27 Ortiz	X	–	X	–	#	#	+
28 Rodriguez	Y	N	Y	N	N	N	Y
29 Green	Y	N	Y	N	N	N	Y
30 Johnson, E.B.	Y	Y	Y	N	N	N	Y
UTAH							
1 ***Hansen***	N	N	N	N	Y	Y	Y
2 ***Cook***	N	N	Y	Y	N	Y	Y
3 ***Cannon***	N	Y	N	Y	Y	Y	Y
VERMONT							
AL *Sanders*	Y	N	Y	Y	N	N	Y
VIRGINIA							
1 ***Bateman***	N	N	N	N	Y	Y	?
2 Pickett	Y	N	Y	N	N	Y	Y
3 Scott	Y	Y	Y	N	N	N	Y
4 Sisisky	Y	N	Y	N	N	Y	Y
5 Goode	N	N	N	Y	Y	N	Y
6 ***Goodlatte***	N	N	N	Y	Y	N	Y
7 ***Bliley***	N	N	N	N	Y	Y	Y
8 Moran	Y	Y	Y	N	N	N	Y
9 Boucher	Y	N	Y	N	N	Y	Y
10 ***Wolf***	N	N	N	Y	Y	Y	Y
11 ***Davis***	Y	N	Y	N	N	Y	Y
WASHINGTON							
1 ***White***	Y	N	N	N	Y	Y	Y
2 ***Metcalf***	N	N	N	Y	Y	Y	Y
3 ***Smith, Linda***	N	N	N	Y	Y	N	Y
4 ***Hastings***	N	N	N	Y	Y	Y	Y
5 ***Nethercutt***	N	N	Y	Y	Y	Y	Y
6 Dicks	Y	N	Y	N	N	Y	Y
7 McDermott	Y	Y	Y	N	N	N	Y
8 ***Dunn***	N	N	Y	N	Y	Y	Y
9 Smith, Adam	Y	N	Y	N	N	N	Y
WEST VIRGINIA							
1 Mollohan	N	Y	N	Y	Y	N	Y
2 Wise	Y	N	Y	N	N	N	Y
3 Rahall	N	Y	N	N	Y	N	Y
WISCONSIN							
1 ***Neumann***	N	N	N	Y	Y	N	Y
2 ***Klug***	N	N	Y	Y	N	Y	Y
3 Kind	Y	N	Y	N	N	N	Y
4 Kleczka	N	N	Y	N	N	N	Y
5 Barrett	Y	N	Y	N	N	N	Y
6 ***Petri***	N	N	N	Y	Y	N	Y
7 Obey	Y	N	Y	N	N	N	Y
8 Johnson	Y	N	Y	N	N	N	Y
9 ***Sensenbrenner***	N	N	N	Y	Y	N	Y
WYOMING							
AL ***Cubin***	N	Y	N	Y	Y	Y	Y

Southern states - Ala., Ark., Fla., Ga., Ky., La., Miss., N.C., Okla., S.C., Tenn., Texas, Va.

295. HR 4194. Fiscal 1999 VA-HUD Appropriations/Housing Vouchers Funding Increase. Stokes, D-Ohio, en bloc amendment to increase by $97 million the funds provided for new Section 8 housing vouchers for families making the transition from welfare to work. Rejected 201-215: R 14-209; D 186-6 (ND 139-5, SD 47-1); I 1-0. July 17, 1998.

296. HR 4194. Fiscal 1999 VA-HUD Appropriations/Public Housing Overhaul. Lazio, R-N.Y. amendment to overhaul public housing management and allow increased local control over rents and occupancy standards. Adopted 230-181: R 215-4; D 15-176 (ND 8-136, SD 7-40); I 0-1. July 17, 1998.

297. HR 3874. Nutrition Programs Reauthorization/Passage. Goodling, R-Pa., motion to suspend the rules and pass the bill to reauthorize through 2003 the Women, Infants and Children nutrition program and a national summer food program for children of low-income families. Motion agreed to 383-1: R 210-1; D 172-0 (ND 129-0, SD 43-0); I 1-0. July 20, 1998. A two-thirds majority of those present and voting (256 in this case) is required for passage under the suspension of the rules.

298. H Con Res 208. Affordable Housing and Home Ownership Opportunities/Passage. Leach, R-Iowa, motion to suspend the rules and pass the bill to express the sense of Congress that the nation's priorities should include providing access to safe affordable housing and expanding home ownership activities. Motion agreed to 390-0: R 214-0; D 175-0 (ND 132-0, SD 43-0); I 1-0. July 20, 1998. A two-thirds majority of those present and voting (260 in this case) is required for passage under suspension of the rules.

299. H Res 392. Japanese Economic Reform/Passage. Bereuter, R-Neb. motion to suspend the rules and pass the bill to express the sense of the House that Japan should urgently undertake several economic reforms in order to enhance cooperation with its allies. Motion agreed to 391-2: R 213-2; D 177-0 (ND 133-0, SD 44-0); I 1-0. July 20, 1998. A two-thirds majority of those present and voting (262 in this case) is required for passage under suspension of the rules.

300. H Con Res 301. Commitment to Taiwan/Passage. Gilman, R-N.Y. motion to suspend the rules and pass the bill to express the sense of Congress affirming its longstanding commitment to Taiwan in accordance with the Taiwan Relations Act. Motion agreed to 390-1: R 213-1; D 176-0 (ND 132-0, SD 44-0); I 1-0. July 20, 1998. A two-thirds majority of those present and voting (261 in this case) is required for passage under suspension of the rules.

301. HR 2183. Campaign Finance Overhaul/Shays-Meehan Substitute — White House Facilities. Wicker, R-Miss., amendment to the Shays-Meehan substitute amendment to the bill to overhaul campaign finance laws. The amendment would prohibit the use of White House facilities in exchange for campaign donations. Adopted 391-4: R 218-0; D 172-4 (ND 130-2, SD 42-2); I 1-0. July 20, 1998.

Key

Y	Voted for (yea).
#	Paired for.
+	Announced for.
N	Voted against (nay).
X	Paired against.
−	Announced against.
P	Voted "present."
C	Voted "present" to avoid possible conflict of interest.
−	Did not vote or otherwise make a position known.

Democrats   ***Republicans***
Independent

	295	296	297	298	299	300	301
ALABAMA							
1 *Callahan*	N	?	Y	Y	Y	Y	Y
2 *Everett*	N	Y	Y	Y	Y	Y	Y
3 *Riley*	N	Y	Y	Y	Y	Y	Y
4 *Aderholt*	N	Y	Y	Y	Y	Y	Y
5 Cramer	Y	N	Y	Y	Y	Y	Y
6 *Bachus*	N	Y	Y	Y	Y	Y	Y
7 Hilliard	Y	N	?	?	?	?	?
ALASKA							
AL *Young*	N	Y	Y	Y	Y	Y	Y
ARIZONA							
1 *Salmon*	N	Y	Y	Y	Y	Y	Y
2 Pastor	Y	N	Y	Y	Y	Y	Y
3 *Stump*	N	Y	Y	Y	Y	Y	Y
4 *Shadegg*	N	Y	Y	Y	Y	Y	Y
5 *Kolbe*	N	Y	Y	Y	Y	Y	Y
6 *Hayworth*	N	Y	Y	Y	Y	Y	Y
ARKANSAS							
1 Berry	Y	N	Y	Y	Y	Y	Y
2 Snyder	?	?	Y	Y	Y	Y	Y
3 *Hutchinson*	N	Y	Y	Y	Y	Y	Y
4 *Dickey*	N	Y	Y	Y	Y	Y	Y
CALIFORNIA							
1 *Riggs*	N	Y	+	+	+	+	+
2 *Herger*	N	Y	Y	Y	Y	Y	Y
3 Fazio	Y	N	?	Y	Y	Y	Y
4 *Doolittle*	−	+	Y	Y	Y	Y	Y
5 Matsui	Y	N	Y	Y	Y	Y	Y
6 Woolsey	Y	N	Y	Y	Y	Y	Y
7 Miller	Y	N	Y	Y	Y	Y	Y
8 Pelosi	Y	N	Y	Y	Y	Y	Y
9 Lee	Y	N	Y	Y	Y	Y	Y
10 Tauscher	Y	N	Y	Y	Y	Y	Y
11 *Pombo*	N	Y	Y	Y	Y	Y	Y
12 Lantos	Y	N	Y	Y	Y	Y	Y
13 Stark	Y	N	Y	Y	Y	Y	Y
14 Eshoo	Y	N	Y	Y	Y	Y	Y
15 *Campbell*	Y	Y	N	Y	Y	Y	Y
16 Lofgren	Y	N	Y	Y	Y	Y	Y
17 Farr	Y	N	Y	Y	Y	Y	Y
18 Condit	Y	N	Y	Y	Y	Y	Y
19 *Radanovich*	N	Y	Y	Y	Y	Y	Y
20 Dooley	Y	N	Y	Y	Y	Y	Y
21 *Thomas*	N	Y	Y	Y	Y	Y	Y
22 Capps, L.	Y	N	Y	Y	Y	Y	Y
23 *Gallegly*	N	Y	Y	Y	Y	Y	Y
24 Sherman	Y	N	Y	Y	Y	Y	Y
25 *McKeon*	N	Y	Y	Y	Y	Y	Y
26 Berman	Y	N	Y	Y	Y	Y	Y
27 *Rogan*	N	Y	Y	Y	Y	Y	Y
28 *Dreier*	N	Y	Y	Y	Y	Y	Y
29 Waxman	Y	N	Y	Y	Y	Y	Y
30 Becerra	Y	N	Y	Y	Y	Y	Y
31 Martinez	Y	N	Y	Y	Y	Y	Y
32 Dixon	Y	N	?	?	?	?	?
33 Roybal-Allard	+	−	+	+	+	+	+
34 Torres	Y	N	Y	Y	Y	Y	Y
35 Waters	Y	N	Y	Y	Y	Y	Y
36 Harman	?	?	Y	Y	Y	Y	Y
37 Millender-McD.	+	−	+	+	+	+	+

	295	296	297	298	299	300	301
38 *Horn*	N	Y	+	Y	Y	Y	Y
39 *Royce*	N	Y	Y	Y	Y	Y	Y
40 *Lewis*	N	Y	Y	Y	Y	Y	Y
41 *Kim*	N	Y	Y	Y	Y	Y	Y
42 Brown	Y	N	Y	?	Y	Y	Y
43 *Calvert*	N	Y	Y	Y	Y	Y	Y
44 *Bono, M.*	N	Y	Y	Y	Y	Y	Y
45 *Rohrabacher*	N	Y	Y	Y	Y	Y	Y
46 Sanchez	Y	N	Y	Y	Y	Y	Y
47 *Cox*	N	Y	Y	Y	Y	Y	Y
48 *Packard*	N	Y	Y	Y	Y	Y	Y
49 *Bilbray*	N	Y	Y	Y	Y	Y	Y
50 Filner	+	−	Y	Y	Y	Y	Y
51 *Cunningham*	N	Y	Y	Y	Y	Y	Y
52 *Hunter*	N	Y	Y	Y	Y	Y	Y
COLORADO							
1 DeGette	Y	N	Y	Y	Y	Y	Y
2 Skaggs	Y	N	Y	Y	Y	Y	Y
3 *McInnis*	N	Y	Y	Y	Y	Y	Y
4 *Schaffer*	N	Y	Y	Y	Y	Y	Y
5 *Hefley*	N	Y	Y	Y	N	Y	Y
6 *Schaefer*	N	Y	Y	Y	Y	Y	Y
CONNECTICUT							
1 Kennelly	?	?	Y	Y	Y	Y	Y
2 Gejdenson	Y	N	Y	Y	Y	Y	Y
3 DeLauro	Y	N	Y	Y	Y	Y	Y
4 *Shays*	N	Y	Y	Y	Y	Y	Y
5 Maloney	Y	N	+	+	+	+	Y
6 *Johnson*	N	Y	Y	Y	Y	Y	Y
DELAWARE							
AL *Castle*	N	Y	Y	Y	Y	Y	Y
FLORIDA							
1 *Scarborough*	N	Y	Y	Y	Y	Y	Y
2 Boyd	Y	N	Y	Y	Y	Y	Y
3 Brown	Y	N	Y	Y	Y	Y	Y
4 *Fowler*	N	Y	Y	Y	Y	Y	Y
5 Thurman	Y	N	Y	Y	Y	Y	Y
6 *Stearns*	N	Y	Y	Y	Y	Y	Y
7 *Mica*	N	+	Y	Y	Y	Y	Y
8 *McCollum*	N	Y	Y	Y	Y	Y	Y
9 *Bilirakis*	N	Y	?	?	?	+	+
10 *Young*	N	Y	Y	Y	Y	Y	Y
11 Davis	Y	N	Y	Y	Y	Y	Y
12 *Canady*	N	Y	Y	Y	Y	Y	Y
13 *Miller*	N	Y	Y	Y	Y	Y	Y
14 *Goss*	N	Y	Y	Y	Y	Y	Y
15 *Weldon*	N	Y	Y	Y	Y	Y	Y
16 *Foley*	N	Y	Y	Y	Y	Y	Y
17 Meek	Y	N	Y	Y	Y	Y	Y
18 *Ros-Lehtinen*	Y	Y	+	+	+	+	Y
19 Wexler	Y	N	Y	Y	Y	Y	N
20 Deutsch	Y	N	Y	Y	Y	Y	Y
21 *Diaz-Balart*	Y	Y	+	+	+	+	Y
22 *Shaw*	N	Y	Y	Y	Y	Y	Y
23 Hastings	Y	N	Y	Y	Y	Y	N
GEORGIA							
1 *Kingston*	N	Y	Y	Y	Y	Y	Y
2 Bishop	Y	N	Y	Y	Y	Y	Y
3 *Collins*	N	Y	Y	Y	Y	Y	Y
4 McKinney	Y	N	Y	Y	Y	Y	Y
5 Lewis	?	?	?	?	?	?	?
6 *Gingrich*							
7 *Barr*	N	Y	Y	Y	Y	Y	Y
8 *Chambliss*	N	Y	Y	Y	Y	Y	Y
9 *Deal*	N	Y	Y	Y	Y	Y	Y
10 *Norwood*	N	Y	?	?	?	?	?
11 *Linder*	N	Y	Y	Y	Y	Y	Y
HAWAII							
1 Abercrombie	Y	N	Y	Y	Y	Y	Y
2 Mink	Y	N	Y	Y	Y	Y	Y
IDAHO							
1 *Chenoweth*	N	Y	Y	Y	Y	Y	Y
2 *Crapo*	N	Y	Y	Y	Y	Y	Y
ILLINOIS							
1 Rush	Y	N	Y	Y	Y	Y	Y
2 Jackson	Y	N	Y	Y	Y	Y	Y
3 Lipinski	Y	N	?	?	?	?	?
4 Gutierrez	Y	N	?	Y	?	Y	Y
5 Blagojevich	Y	N	?	?	?	?	?
6 *Hyde*	N	Y	Y	Y	Y	Y	Y
7 Davis	Y	N	Y	Y	Y	Y	Y
8 *Crane*	N	Y	Y	Y	Y	Y	Y
9 Yates	Y	N	Y	Y	Y	Y	Y
10 *Porter*	N	Y	Y	Y	Y	Y	Y
11 *Weller*	N	Y	Y	Y	Y	Y	Y
12 Costello	Y	N	Y	Y	Y	Y	Y

ND Northern Democrats   SD Southern Democrats

	295	296	297	298	299	300	301
13 ***Fawell***	N	Y	?	?	?	?	Y
14 ***Hastert***	N	Y	Y	Y	Y	Y	Y
15 ***Ewing***	N	Y	Y	Y	Y	Y	Y
16 ***Manzullo***	N	Y	Y	Y	Y	Y	Y
17 Evans	Y	N	Y	Y	Y	Y	Y
18 ***LaHood***	N	Y	Y	Y	Y	Y	Y
19 Poshard	Y	N	?	?	?	?	?
20 ***Shimkus***	N	Y	Y	Y	Y	Y	Y
INDIANA							
1 Visclosky	Y	N	Y	Y	Y	Y	Y
2 ***McIntosh***	N	Y	Y	Y	Y	Y	Y
3 Roemer	Y	N	Y	Y	Y	Y	Y
4 ***Souder***	N	Y	Y	Y	Y	Y	Y
5 ***Buyer***	N	Y	Y	Y	Y	Y	Y
6 ***Burton***	N	Y	Y	Y	Y	Y	Y
7 ***Pease***	N	Y	Y	Y	Y	Y	Y
8 ***Hostettler***	N	Y	Y	Y	Y	Y	Y
9 Hamilton	Y	N	Y	Y	Y	Y	Y
10 Carson	Y	N	Y	Y	Y	Y	Y
IOWA							
1 ***Leach***	N	Y	Y	Y	Y	Y	Y
2 ***Nussle***	N	Y	Y	Y	Y	Y	Y
3 Boswell	Y	N	Y	Y	Y	Y	Y
4 ***Ganske***	N	Y	Y	Y	Y	Y	Y
5 ***Latham***	N	Y	Y	Y	Y	Y	Y
KANSAS							
1 ***Moran***	N	Y	Y	Y	Y	Y	Y
2 ***Ryun***	N	Y	Y	Y	Y	Y	Y
3 ***Snowbarger***	N	Y	Y	Y	Y	Y	Y
4 ***Tiahrt***	N	Y	Y	Y	Y	Y	Y
KENTUCKY							
1 ***Whitfield***	N	Y	?	?	Y	Y	Y
2 ***Lewis***	N	Y	Y	Y	Y	Y	Y
3 ***Northup***	N	Y	Y	Y	Y	Y	Y
4 ***Bunning***	N	Y	Y	Y	Y	Y	Y
5 ***Rogers***	N	Y	Y	Y	Y	Y	Y
6 Baesler	Y	Y	Y	Y	Y	Y	Y
LOUISIANA							
1 ***Livingston***	N	?	Y	Y	Y	Y	Y
2 Jefferson	Y	?	?	?	?	?	?
3 ***Tauzin***	N	Y	Y	Y	Y	Y	Y
4 ***McCrery***	N	Y	Y	Y	Y	Y	Y
5 ***Cooksey***	N	Y	Y	Y	Y	Y	Y
6 ***Baker***	N	Y	?	?	?	?	?
7 John	?	?	?	?	?	?	?
MAINE							
1 Allen	Y	N	Y	Y	Y	Y	Y
2 Baldacci	Y	N	Y	Y	Y	Y	Y
MARYLAND							
1 ***Gilchrest***	N	Y	Y	Y	Y	Y	Y
2 ***Ehrlich***	N	Y	?	?	?	?	?
3 Cardin	Y	N	Y	Y	Y	Y	Y
4 Wynn	Y	N	Y	Y	Y	Y	Y
5 Hoyer	Y	N	Y	Y	Y	Y	Y
6 ***Bartlett***	N	Y	Y	Y	Y	Y	Y
7 Cummings	Y	N	Y	Y	Y	Y	Y
8 ***Morella***	Y	Y	Y	Y	Y	Y	Y
MASSACHUSETTS							
1 Olver	Y	N	Y	Y	Y	Y	Y
2 Neal	Y	N	Y	Y	Y	Y	Y
3 McGovern	Y	N	Y	Y	Y	Y	Y
4 Frank	Y	N	Y	Y	Y	Y	Y
5 Meehan	Y	N	Y	Y	Y	Y	Y
6 Tierney	Y	N	Y	Y	Y	Y	Y
7 Markey	Y	N	Y	Y	Y	Y	Y
8 Kennedy	Y	N	Y	Y	Y	Y	Y
9 Moakley	?	?	Y	Y	Y	Y	?
10 Delahunt	Y	N	Y	Y	Y	Y	Y
MICHIGAN							
1 Stupak	N	N	Y	Y	Y	Y	Y
2 ***Hoekstra***	N	Y	Y	Y	Y	Y	Y
3 ***Ehlers***	N	Y	Y	Y	Y	Y	Y
4 ***Camp***	N	Y	Y	Y	Y	Y	Y
5 Barcia	Y	N	Y	Y	Y	Y	Y
6 ***Upton***	N	Y	Y	Y	Y	Y	Y
7 ***Smith***	N	Y	Y	Y	Y	Y	Y
8 Stabenow	Y	N	Y	Y	Y	Y	Y
9 Kildee	Y	N	Y	Y	Y	Y	Y
10 Bonior	Y	N	Y	Y	Y	Y	Y
11 ***Knollenberg***	N	Y	Y	Y	Y	Y	Y
12 Levin	Y	N	Y	Y	Y	Y	Y
13 Rivers	Y	N	Y	Y	Y	Y	Y
14 Conyers	Y	N	Y	Y	Y	Y	Y
15 Kilpatrick	Y	N	+	+	+	+	Y
16 Dingell	Y	N	Y	Y	Y	Y	Y

	295	296	297	298	299	300	301
MINNESOTA							
1 ***Gutknecht***	N	Y	Y	Y	Y	Y	Y
2 Minge	Y	N	Y	Y	Y	Y	Y
3 ***Ramstad***	Y	Y	Y	Y	Y	Y	Y
4 Vento	Y	N	Y	Y	Y	Y	Y
5 Sabo	Y	N	Y	Y	Y	Y	Y
6 Luther	Y	Y	Y	Y	Y	Y	Y
7 Peterson	Y	N	Y	Y	Y	Y	Y
8 Oberstar	Y	N	Y	Y	Y	Y	Y
MISSISSIPPI							
1 ***Wicker***	N	Y	Y	Y	Y	Y	Y
2 Thompson	Y	N	?	?	?	?	?
3 ***Pickering***	N	Y	Y	Y	Y	Y	+
4 ***Parker***	?	?	Y	Y	Y	Y	Y
5 Taylor	Y	Y	Y	Y	Y	Y	Y
MISSOURI							
1 Clay	Y	N	Y	Y	Y	Y	Y
2 ***Talent***	N	Y	Y	Y	Y	Y	Y
3 Gephardt	Y	N	?	?	?	?	?
4 Skelton	Y	Y	Y	Y	Y	Y	Y
5 McCarthy	Y	N	Y	Y	Y	Y	Y
6 Danner	Y	Y	?	?	?	?	?
7 ***Blunt***	N	Y	Y	Y	Y	Y	Y
8 ***Emerson***	N	Y	Y	Y	Y	Y	Y
9 ***Hulshof***	N	Y	Y	Y	Y	Y	Y
MONTANA							
AL ***Hill***	?	?	Y	Y	Y	Y	Y
NEBRASKA							
1 ***Bereuter***	N	Y	Y	Y	Y	Y	Y
2 ***Christensen***	N	Y	Y	Y	Y	Y	Y
3 ***Barrett***	N	Y	Y	Y	Y	Y	Y
NEVADA							
1 ***Ensign***	Y	Y	Y	Y	Y	Y	Y
2 ***Gibbons***	N	Y	Y	Y	Y	Y	Y
NEW HAMPSHIRE							
1 ***Sununu***	N	Y	Y	Y	Y	Y	Y
2 ***Bass***	N	Y	Y	Y	Y	Y	Y
NEW JERSEY							
1 Andrews	Y	N	Y	Y	Y	Y	Y
2 ***LoBiondo***	Y	Y	Y	Y	Y	Y	Y
3 ***Saxton***	N	Y	Y	Y	Y	Y	Y
4 ***Smith***	Y	Y	Y	Y	Y	Y	Y
5 ***Roukema***	N	Y	Y	Y	Y	Y	Y
6 Pallone	Y	N	Y	Y	Y	Y	Y
7 ***Franks***	N	Y	Y	Y	Y	Y	Y
8 Pascrell	Y	N	Y	Y	Y	Y	Y
9 Rothman	Y	N	Y	Y	Y	Y	Y
10 Payne	Y	N	Y	Y	Y	Y	Y
11 ***Frelinghuysen***	N	Y	Y	Y	Y	Y	Y
12 ***Pappas***	N	Y	Y	Y	Y	Y	Y
13 Menendez	Y	N	+	Y	Y	Y	Y
NEW MEXICO							
1 ***Wilson***	N	Y	Y	Y	Y	Y	Y
2 ***Skeen***	N	Y	Y	Y	Y	Y	Y
3 ***Redmond***	N	Y	Y	Y	Y	Y	Y
NEW YORK							
1 ***Forbes***	N	Y	Y	Y	Y	Y	Y
2 ***Lazio***	N	Y	Y	Y	Y	Y	Y
3 ***King***	N	Y	Y	Y	Y	Y	Y
4 McCarthy	Y	N	Y	Y	Y	Y	Y
5 Ackerman	Y	N	?	?	?	?	?
6 Meeks	Y	N	Y	Y	Y	Y	Y
7 Manton	Y	N	Y	Y	Y	Y	Y
8 Nadler	Y	N	Y	Y	Y	Y	Y
9 Schumer	Y	N	Y	Y	Y	Y	Y
10 Towns	Y	N	?	?	?	?	?
11 Owens	Y	N	+	+	+	+	Y
12 Velázquez	Y	N	Y	Y	Y	Y	Y
13 ***Fossella***	N	Y	Y	Y	Y	Y	Y
14 Maloney	Y	N	+	+	+	+	+
15 Rangel	Y	N	Y	Y	Y	Y	Y
16 Serrano	Y	N	Y	Y	Y	Y	Y
17 Engel	Y	N	Y	Y	Y	Y	Y
18 Lowey	Y	N	Y	Y	Y	Y	Y
19 ***Kelly***	N	Y	Y	Y	Y	Y	Y
20 ***Gilman***	Y	Y	Y	Y	Y	Y	Y
21 McNulty	?	?	Y	Y	Y	Y	Y
22 ***Solomon***	N	Y	Y	Y	Y	Y	Y
23 ***Boehlert***	N	Y	Y	Y	Y	Y	Y
24 ***McHugh***	Y	N	Y	Y	Y	Y	Y
25 ***Walsh***	N	N	?	?	?	?	Y
26 Hinchey	Y	N	Y	Y	Y	Y	Y
27 ***Paxon***	N	Y	?	?	?	?	Y
28 Slaughter	Y	N	Y	Y	Y	Y	Y
29 LaFalce	Y	N	Y	Y	Y	Y	Y

	295	296	297	298	299	300	301
30 ***Quinn***	Y	Y	Y	Y	Y	Y	Y
31 ***Houghton***	N	Y	Y	Y	Y	Y	Y
NORTH CAROLINA							
1 Clayton	Y	N	Y	Y	Y	Y	Y
2 Etheridge	Y	N	Y	Y	Y	Y	Y
3 ***Jones***	N	Y	Y	Y	Y	Y	Y
4 Price	Y	N	Y	Y	Y	Y	Y
5 ***Burr***	N	Y	Y	Y	Y	Y	Y
6 ***Coble***	N	Y	+	+	+	+	+
7 McIntyre	Y	Y	Y	Y	Y	Y	Y
8 Hefner	Y	N	?	?	?	?	?
9 ***Myrick***	N	Y	Y	Y	Y	Y	Y
10 ***Ballenger***	N	Y	Y	Y	Y	Y	Y
11 ***Taylor***	N	Y	Y	Y	Y	Y	Y
12 Watt	Y	N	Y	Y	Y	Y	Y
NORTH DAKOTA							
AL Pomeroy	Y	N	?	?	Y	Y	Y
OHIO							
1 ***Chabot***	N	Y	Y	Y	Y	Y	Y
2 ***Portman***	N	Y	Y	Y	Y	Y	Y
3 Hall	Y	N	Y	Y	Y	Y	Y
4 ***Oxley***	N	Y	Y	Y	Y	Y	Y
5 ***Gillmor***	N	Y	Y	Y	Y	Y	Y
6 Strickland	Y	Y	Y	Y	Y	Y	Y
7 ***Hobson***	N	Y	Y	Y	Y	Y	Y
8 ***Boehner***	N	Y	Y	Y	Y	Y	Y
9 Kaptur	Y	N	Y	Y	Y	Y	Y
10 Kucinich	Y	N	Y	Y	Y	Y	Y
11 Stokes	Y	N	?	?	?	?	?
12 ***Kasich***	N	Y	Y	Y	Y	Y	Y
13 Brown	Y	N	Y	Y	Y	Y	Y
14 Sawyer	Y	N	Y	Y	Y	Y	Y
15 ***Pryce***	N	Y	Y	Y	Y	Y	Y
16 ***Regula***	N	Y	Y	Y	Y	Y	Y
17 Traficant	Y	Y	Y	Y	?	?	?
18 ***Ney***	N	Y	Y	Y	Y	Y	Y
19 ***LaTourette***	N	Y	Y	Y	Y	Y	Y
OKLAHOMA							
1 ***Largent***	N	Y	Y	Y	Y	Y	Y
2 ***Coburn***	N	Y	Y	Y	Y	Y	Y
3 ***Watkins***	N	Y	Y	Y	Y	Y	Y
4 ***Watts***	N	Y	Y	Y	Y	Y	Y
5 ***Istook***	N	Y	Y	Y	Y	Y	Y
6 ***Lucas***	N	Y	Y	Y	Y	Y	Y
OREGON							
1 Furse	Y	N	Y	Y	Y	Y	Y
2 ***Smith***	N	Y	Y	Y	Y	Y	Y
3 Blumenauer	Y	N	Y	Y	Y	Y	Y
4 DeFazio	Y	N	Y	Y	Y	Y	Y
5 Hooley	Y	N	Y	Y	Y	Y	Y
PENNSYLVANIA							
1 Brady	Y	N	Y	Y	Y	Y	Y
2 Fattah	Y	N	?	?	?	?	Y
3 Borski	N	Y	Y	Y	Y	Y	Y
4 Klink	N	Y	Y	Y	Y	Y	Y
5 ***Peterson***	N	Y	Y	Y	Y	Y	Y
6 Holden	N	N	Y	Y	Y	Y	Y
7 ***Weldon***	N	Y	Y	Y	Y	Y	Y
8 ***Greenwood***	N	Y	Y	Y	Y	Y	Y
9 ***Shuster***	N	Y	Y	Y	Y	Y	Y
10 ***McDade***	N	Y	?	?	?	?	?
11 Kanjorski	Y	N	Y	Y	Y	Y	N
12 Murtha	N	N	Y	Y	Y	Y	N
13 ***Fox***	Y	Y	Y	Y	Y	Y	Y
14 Coyne	Y	N	Y	Y	Y	Y	Y
15 McHale	Y	N	Y	Y	Y	Y	Y
16 ***Pitts***	N	Y	Y	Y	Y	Y	Y
17 ***Gekas***	N	Y	Y	Y	Y	Y	Y
18 Doyle	Y	N	Y	Y	Y	Y	Y
19 ***Goodling***	N	Y	Y	Y	Y	Y	Y
20 Mascara	Y	N	Y	Y	Y	Y	Y
21 ***English***	Y	Y	Y	Y	Y	Y	Y
RHODE ISLAND							
1 Kennedy	Y	N	Y	Y	Y	Y	Y
2 Weygand	Y	N	Y	Y	Y	Y	Y
SOUTH CAROLINA							
1 ***Sanford***	N	Y	Y	Y	Y	Y	Y
2 ***Spence***	N	Y	Y	Y	Y	?	Y
3 ***Graham***	N	Y	Y	Y	Y	Y	Y
4 ***Inglis***	N	Y	Y	Y	Y	Y	Y
5 Spratt	Y	N	Y	Y	Y	Y	Y
6 Clyburn	Y	N	Y	Y	Y	Y	Y
SOUTH DAKOTA							
AL ***Thune***	N	Y	Y	Y	Y	Y	Y

	295	296	297	298	299	300	301
TENNESSEE							
1 ***Jenkins***	N	Y	Y	Y	Y	Y	Y
2 ***Duncan***	N	Y	Y	Y	Y	Y	Y
3 ***Wamp***	N	Y	Y	Y	Y	Y	Y
4 ***Hilleary***	N	Y	?	Y	Y	Y	Y
5 Clement	Y	N	Y	Y	Y	Y	Y
6 Gordon	Y	N	Y	Y	Y	Y	Y
7 ***Bryant***	N	Y	Y	Y	Y	Y	Y
8 Tanner	?	?	Y	Y	Y	Y	Y
9 Ford	+	–	+	+	+	+	+
TEXAS							
1 Sandlin	Y	N	Y	Y	Y	Y	Y
2 Turner	Y	N	Y	Y	Y	Y	Y
3 ***Johnson, Sam***	N	Y	Y	Y	Y	Y	?
4 Hall	Y	Y	Y	Y	Y	Y	Y
5 ***Sessions***	N	Y	Y	Y	Y	Y	Y
6 ***Barton***	?	?	Y	Y	Y	Y	Y
7 ***Archer***	N	Y	Y	Y	Y	Y	Y
8 ***Brady***	N	Y	Y	Y	Y	Y	Y
9 Lampson	Y	N	Y	Y	Y	Y	Y
10 Doggett	Y	Y	Y	Y	Y	Y	Y
11 Edwards	Y	N	Y	Y	Y	Y	Y
12 ***Granger***	N	Y	Y	Y	Y	Y	Y
13 ***Thornberry***	N	Y	Y	Y	Y	Y	Y
14 ***Paul***	N	N	N	Y	N	N	Y
15 Hinojosa	Y	N	Y	Y	Y	Y	Y
16 Reyes	Y	N	?	?	Y	Y	Y
17 Stenholm	Y	Y	Y	Y	Y	Y	Y
18 Jackson-Lee	Y	N	Y	Y	Y	Y	Y
19 ***Combest***	N	Y	Y	Y	Y	Y	Y
20 Gonzalez	?	?	?	?	?	?	?
21 ***Smith***	N	Y	Y	Y	Y	Y	Y
22 ***DeLay***	N	Y	Y	Y	Y	Y	Y
23 ***Bonilla***	N	Y	Y	Y	Y	Y	Y
24 Frost	Y	N	?	?	?	?	?
25 Bentsen	Y	N	Y	Y	Y	Y	Y
26 ***Armey***	N	Y	Y	Y	Y	Y	Y
27 Ortiz	+	–	+	+	+	+	+
28 Rodriguez	Y	N	Y	Y	Y	Y	Y
29 Green	Y	N	Y	Y	Y	Y	Y
30 Johnson, E.B.	Y	N	Y	Y	Y	Y	+
UTAH							
1 ***Hansen***	N	Y	Y	Y	Y	Y	Y
2 ***Cook***	N	Y	+	Y	Y	Y	Y
3 ***Cannon***	N	Y	Y	Y	Y	Y	Y
VERMONT							
AL *Sanders*	Y	N	Y	Y	Y	Y	Y
VIRGINIA							
1 ***Bateman***	N	Y	Y	Y	Y	Y	Y
2 Pickett	Y	N	Y	Y	Y	Y	Y
3 Scott	Y	N	Y	Y	Y	Y	Y
4 Sisisky	Y	N	Y	Y	Y	Y	Y
5 Goode	Y	N	Y	Y	Y	Y	Y
6 ***Goodlatte***	N	Y	Y	Y	Y	Y	Y
7 ***Bliley***	N	Y	Y	Y	Y	Y	Y
8 Moran	Y	N	Y	Y	Y	Y	Y
9 Boucher	Y	N	?	?	?	?	Y
10 ***Wolf***	N	Y	Y	Y	Y	Y	Y
11 ***Davis***	Y	Y	Y	Y	Y	Y	Y
WASHINGTON							
1 ***White***	N	Y	Y	Y	Y	Y	Y
2 ***Metcalf***	N	Y	Y	Y	Y	Y	Y
3 ***Smith, Linda***	N	Y	Y	Y	Y	Y	Y
4 ***Hastings***	N	Y	Y	Y	Y	Y	Y
5 ***Nethercutt***	N	N	Y	Y	Y	Y	Y
6 Dicks	Y	N	Y	Y	Y	Y	Y
7 McDermott	Y	N	Y	Y	Y	Y	Y
8 ***Dunn***	N	?	Y	Y	Y	Y	Y
9 Smith, Adam	Y	N	Y	Y	Y	Y	Y
WEST VIRGINIA							
1 Mollohan	Y	N	Y	Y	Y	Y	Y
2 Wise	Y	N	Y	Y	Y	Y	Y
3 Rahall	Y	N	Y	Y	Y	Y	Y
WISCONSIN							
1 ***Neumann***	N	Y	Y	Y	Y	Y	Y
2 ***Klug***	N	Y	Y	Y	Y	Y	Y
3 Kind	Y	N	Y	Y	Y	Y	Y
4 Kleczka	Y	N	Y	Y	Y	Y	+
5 Barrett	Y	N	+	+	+	+	Y
6 ***Petri***	N	Y	Y	Y	Y	Y	Y
7 Obey	Y	N	Y	Y	Y	Y	Y
8 Johnson	Y	N	Y	Y	Y	Y	Y
9 ***Sensenbrenner***	N	Y	Y	Y	Y	Y	Y
WYOMING							
AL ***Cubin***	N	Y	Y	Y	Y	Y	Y

Southern states - Ala., Ark., Fla., Ga., Ky., La., Miss., N.C., Okla., S.C., Tenn., Texas, Va.

302. HR 2183. Campaign Finance Overhaul/Shays-Meehan Substitute — Non-Citizen Donations. Stearns, R-Fla., amendment to the Shays-Meehan substitute amendment to the bill to overhaul campaign finance laws. The amendment would prohibit donations from resident aliens and other non-citizens to state and local elections, as well as political parties. Adopted 267-131: R 195-23; D 71-108 (ND 50-84, SD 21-24); I 1-0. July 20, 1998.

303. HR 2183. Campaign Finance Overhaul/Shays-Meehan Substitute — "Willful Blindness" Defense. Pickering Jr., R-Miss., amendment to the Shays-Meehan substitute amendment to the bill to overhaul campaign finance laws. The amendment would prohibit "willful blindness" as a defense against a charge of violating the ban on accepting campaign contributions from foreign nationals. Adopted 344-56: R 203-17; D 140-39 (ND 104-30, SD 36-9); I 1-0. July 20, 1998.

304. HR 2183. Campaign Finance Overhaul/Shays-Meehan Substitute — Sense of Congress Regarding Federal Property. DeLay, R-Texas amendment to the Shays-Meehan substitute amendment to the bill to overhaul campaign finance laws. The amendment expresses the sense of Congress that federal law demonstrates that "controlling legal authority" prohibits the use of federal property to raise campaign funds. Adopted 360-36: R 219-0; D 140-36 (ND 103-28, SD 37-8); I 1-0. July 20, 1998.

305. HR 2183. Campaign Finance Overhaul/Shays-Meehan Substitute — Access in Exchange for Contributions. McInnis, R-Colo., amendment to the Shays-Meehan substitute amendment to the bill to overhaul campaign finance laws. The amendment prohibits anyone from soliciting or accepting campaign contributions in exchange for access to the White House, vice president's residence or the airplanes or helicopters on which the president or vice-president are traveling. Adopted 391-7: R 220-0; D 170-7(ND 127-5, SD 43-2); I 1-0. July 20, 1998.

306. HR 2183. Campaign Finance Overhaul/Shays-Meehan Substitute — Labor Union Reporting. Paxon, R-N.Y. amendment to the Shays-Meehan substitute amendment to the bill to overhaul campaign finance laws. The amendment would require labor unions to report all financial activities under current labor laws by category, such as political activities. Rejected 150-248: R 148-72; D 2-175 (ND 0-132, SD 2-43); I 0-1. July 20, 1998.

307. HR 2183. Campaign Finance Overhaul/Shays-Meehan Substitute — Air Force One Reimbursements. Hefley, R-Colo., amendment to the Shays-Meehan substitute amendment to the bill to overhaul campaign finance laws. The amendment would require political parties to reimburse the Air Force for the costs of using Air Force One if the president, vice president or any Cabinet secretary uses the aircraft for travel that includes a political fundraising event. Adopted 222-177: R 190-30; D 32-146 (ND 13-120, SD 19-26); I 0-1. July 20, 1998.

308. HR 2183. Campaign Finance Overhaul/Shays-Meehan Substitute — "Walking Around Money" Prohibition. Northup, R-Ky., amendment to the Shays-Meehan substitute amendment to the bill to overhaul campaign finance laws. The amendment prohibits so-called "walking around money" for candidates to be taken from campaign funds. Adopted 284-114: R 215-4; D 68-110 (ND 44-89, SD 24-21); I 1-0. July 20, 1998.

Key

Y	Voted for (yea).
#	Paired for.
+	Announced for.
N	Voted against (nay).
X	Paired against.
−	Announced against.
P	Voted "present."
C	Voted "present" to avoid possible conflict of interest.
?	Did not vote or otherwise make a position known.

Democrats   •   **Republicans**
Independent

	302	303	304	305	306	307	308
ALABAMA							
1 Callahan	Y	Y	Y	Y	Y	Y	Y
2 Everett	Y	Y	Y	Y	Y	Y	Y
3 Riley	Y	Y	Y	Y	Y	Y	Y
4 Aderholt	Y	Y	Y	Y	N	Y	Y
5 Cramer	Y	Y	Y	Y	N	Y	Y
6 Bachus	Y	Y	Y	Y	N	N	Y
7 Hilliard	?	?	?	?	?	?	?
ALASKA							
AL Young	Y	N	Y	Y	N	Y	Y
ARIZONA							
1 Salmon	N	Y	Y	Y	Y	Y	Y
2 Pastor	N	Y	Y	Y	N	N	N
3 Stump	Y	Y	Y	Y	Y	Y	Y
4 Shadegg	Y	Y	Y	Y	Y	Y	Y
5 Kolbe	Y	Y	Y	Y	Y	Y	Y
6 Hayworth	Y	Y	Y	Y	Y	Y	Y
ARKANSAS							
1 Berry	Y	Y	Y	Y	N	Y	Y
2 Snyder	Y	Y	Y	Y	N	N	N
3 Hutchinson	Y	Y	Y	Y	N	Y	Y
4 Dickey	Y	Y	Y	Y	Y	Y	Y
CALIFORNIA							
1 Riggs	+	+	+	+	+	+	+
2 Herger	Y	Y	Y	Y	Y	Y	Y
3 Fazio	N	N	N	Y	N	N	N
4 Doolittle	N	N	Y	Y	N	N	N
5 Matsui	N	Y	Y	Y	N	N	N
6 Woolsey	N	Y	Y	Y	N	N	N
7 Miller	N	N	N	Y	N	N	N
8 Pelosi	N	Y	Y	N	N	N	?
9 Lee	N	N	N	Y	N	N	N
10 Tauscher	Y	Y	Y	Y	N	N	N
11 Pombo	N	N	Y	Y	Y	Y	Y
12 Lantos	Y	Y	Y	Y	N	N	N
13 Stark	N	N	N	Y	N	N	N
14 Eshoo	N	Y	Y	Y	N	N	N
15 Campbell	N	Y	Y	Y	N	Y	N
16 Lofgren	N	Y	Y	Y	N	N	N
17 Farr	N	N	N	N	N	N	N
18 Condit	N	Y	Y	Y	N	N	Y
19 Radanovich	Y	Y	Y	Y	Y	Y	Y
20 Dooley	Y	Y	Y	Y	N	N	N
21 Thomas	Y	Y	Y	Y	N	Y	Y
22 Capps, L.	N	Y	Y	Y	N	N	N
23 Gallegly	Y	Y	Y	Y	N	Y	Y
24 Sherman	Y	Y	Y	Y	N	Y	N
25 McKeon	Y	Y	Y	Y	Y	Y	Y
26 Berman	N	Y	Y	Y	N	N	N
27 Rogan	Y	Y	Y	Y	Y	Y	Y
28 Dreier	Y	Y	Y	Y	Y	Y	Y
29 Waxman	N	Y	N	Y	N	N	N
30 Becerra	N	N	N	Y	N	N	N
31 Martinez	?	?	?	?	?	?	?
32 Dixon	?	?	?	?	?	?	?
33 Roybal-Allard	−	+	−	+	−	+	−
34 Torres	?	?	?	?	?	N	?
35 Waters	N	N	N	N	N	N	N
36 Harman	−	+	+	+	−	−	−
37 Millender-McD.	−	+	+	+	−	−	−
38 Horn	Y	Y	Y	Y	Y	Y	Y
39 Royce	Y	Y	Y	Y	Y	Y	Y
40 Lewis	N	Y	Y	Y	N	Y	Y
41 Kim	Y	Y	Y	N	N	N	Y
42 Brown	N	Y	Y	Y	N	N	N
43 Calvert	Y	Y	Y	Y	Y	Y	Y
44 Bono, M.	Y	Y	Y	Y	Y	Y	Y
45 Rohrabacher	Y	Y	Y	Y	Y	Y	Y
46 Sanchez	N	N	N	Y	N	N	N
47 Cox	Y	Y	Y	Y	Y	Y	Y
48 Packard	Y	Y	Y	Y	Y	Y	Y
49 Bilbray	N	Y	Y	Y	N	Y	Y
50 Filner	N	Y	Y	Y	N	N	N
51 Cunningham	Y	Y	Y	Y	N	Y	Y
52 Hunter	Y	Y	Y	Y	N	Y	Y
COLORADO							
1 DeGette	N	Y	Y	Y	N	N	Y
2 Skaggs	N	N	Y	Y	N	N	Y
3 McInnis	Y	Y	Y	Y	Y	Y	Y
4 Schaffer	Y	Y	Y	Y	Y	Y	Y
5 Hefley	Y	Y	Y	Y	Y	Y	Y
6 Schaefer	Y	Y	Y	Y	Y	Y	Y
CONNECTICUT							
1 Kennelly	Y	Y	Y	?	?	?	?
2 Gejdenson	Y	Y	Y	Y	N	Y	Y
3 DeLauro	Y	Y	Y	Y	N	N	Y
4 Shays	N	Y	Y	N	N	N	N
5 Maloney	Y	Y	Y	Y	N	N	Y
6 Johnson	Y	Y	Y	Y	N	Y	Y
DELAWARE							
AL Castle	Y	Y	Y	Y	N	N	Y
FLORIDA							
1 Scarborough	Y	Y	?	Y	Y	Y	Y
2 Boyd	Y	Y	Y	Y	N	N	N
3 Brown	N	N	Y	Y	N	N	N
4 Fowler	Y	Y	Y	Y	Y	Y	Y
5 Thurman	Y	Y	Y	Y	N	Y	Y
6 Stearns	Y	Y	Y	Y	Y	Y	Y
7 Mica	Y	Y	Y	Y	Y	Y	Y
8 McCollum	Y	Y	Y	Y	Y	Y	Y
9 Bilirakis	+	?	+	+	?	+	+
10 Young	Y	Y	Y	Y	Y	Y	Y
11 Davis	Y	Y	Y	Y	N	N	N
12 Canady	Y	Y	Y	Y	Y	Y	Y
13 Miller	Y	Y	Y	Y	Y	Y	Y
14 Goss	Y	Y	Y	Y	N	Y	Y
15 Weldon	Y	N	Y	Y	N	Y	Y
16 Foley	Y	Y	Y	Y	N	Y	Y
17 Meek	N	N	N	N	N	N	N
18 Ros-Lehtinen	N	N	N	Y	N	Y	Y
19 Wexler	N	N	N	N	N	N	N
20 Deutsch	Y	Y	Y	Y	N	Y	Y
21 Diaz-Balart	N	N	Y	N	N	Y	Y
22 Shaw	Y	Y	Y	Y	N	Y	Y
23 Hastings	N	N	N	Y	N	N	N
GEORGIA							
1 Kingston	Y	Y	Y	Y	Y	Y	Y
2 Bishop	N	Y	Y	Y	Y	Y	Y
3 Collins	Y	Y	Y	Y	Y	Y	Y
4 McKinney	N	Y	Y	Y	N	N	Y
5 Lewis	?	?	?	?	?	?	?
6 Gingrich							
7 Barr	Y	Y	Y	Y	Y	Y	Y
8 Chambliss	Y	Y	Y	Y	Y	Y	Y
9 Deal	Y	Y	Y	Y	Y	Y	Y
10 Norwood	?	?	?	?	?	?	?
11 Linder	Y	Y	Y	Y	Y	Y	Y
HAWAII							
1 Abercrombie	N	Y	Y	Y	N	N	N
2 Mink	N	N	N	Y	N	N	N
IDAHO							
1 Chenoweth	N	Y	Y	Y	Y	Y	Y
2 Crapo	N	Y	Y	Y	Y	Y	Y
ILLINOIS							
1 Rush	Y	Y	Y	N	N	N	N
2 Jackson	N	N	Y	N	N	N	N
3 Lipinski	?	?	?	?	?	?	?
4 Gutierrez	N	N	Y	N	N	N	N
5 Blagojevich	?	?	?	?	?	?	?
6 Hyde	Y	Y	Y	Y	Y	Y	Y
7 Davis	N	Y	Y	N	N	N	N
8 Crane	Y	Y	Y	Y	Y	Y	Y
9 Yates	?	?	?	?	?	?	?
10 Porter	Y	Y	Y	Y	N	N	Y
11 Weller	Y	Y	Y	Y	N	Y	Y
12 Costello	Y	Y	Y	Y	N	Y	Y

	302	303	304	305	306	307	308
13 ***Fawell***	Y	Y	Y	Y	Y	Y	Y
14 ***Hastert***	Y	Y	Y	Y	Y	Y	Y
15 ***Ewing***	Y	Y	Y	Y	Y	Y	Y
16 ***Manzullo***	Y	Y	Y	Y	Y	Y	Y
17 Evans	Y	Y	Y	Y	N	N	N
18 ***LaHood***	Y	Y	Y	Y	N	Y	Y
19 Poshard	?	?	?	?	?	?	?
20 ***Shimkus***	Y	Y	Y	Y	N	Y	Y
INDIANA							
1 Visclosky	N	Y	Y	Y	N	N	N
2 ***McIntosh***	Y	Y	Y	Y	Y	N	Y
3 Roemer	Y	Y	Y	Y	N	N	Y
4 ***Souder***	Y	Y	Y	Y	Y	Y	Y
5 ***Buyer***	Y	N	Y	Y	Y	Y	Y
6 ***Burton***	Y	Y	Y	Y	Y	Y	Y
7 ***Pease***	Y	Y	Y	Y	N	Y	Y
8 ***Hostettler***	Y	Y	Y	Y	Y	Y	Y
9 Hamilton	Y	Y	Y	Y	N	N	Y
10 Carson	N	N	Y	Y	N	N	N
IOWA							
1 ***Leach***	Y	Y	Y	Y	N	N	Y
2 ***Nussle***	Y	Y	Y	Y	Y	Y	Y
3 Boswell	Y	Y	Y	Y	N	N	Y
4 ***Ganske***	Y	Y	Y	Y	N	N	Y
5 ***Latham***	Y	N	Y	Y	Y	N	Y
KANSAS							
1 ***Moran***	Y	Y	Y	Y	N	Y	Y
2 ***Ryun***	Y	Y	Y	Y	Y	Y	Y
3 ***Snowbarger***	Y	Y	Y	Y	Y	Y	Y
4 ***Tiahrt***	Y	Y	Y	Y	Y	Y	Y
KENTUCKY							
1 ***Whitfield***	Y	Y	Y	Y	Y	Y	Y
2 ***Lewis***	Y	Y	Y	Y	Y	Y	Y
3 ***Northup***	Y	Y	Y	Y	Y	Y	Y
4 ***Bunning***	Y	Y	Y	Y	Y	Y	Y
5 ***Rogers***	Y	Y	Y	Y	Y	Y	Y
6 Baesler	Y	Y	Y	Y	N	N	Y
LOUISIANA							
1 ***Livingston***	Y	Y	Y	Y	Y	Y	Y
2 Jefferson	?	?	?	?	?	?	?
3 ***Tauzin***	Y	Y	Y	Y	Y	Y	Y
4 ***McCrery***	Y	Y	Y	Y	N	Y	Y
5 ***Cooksey***	Y	Y	Y	Y	Y	Y	Y
6 ***Baker***	?	?	?	?	?	?	?
7 John	?	?	?	?	?	?	?
MAINE							
1 Allen	N	Y	N	Y	N	N	N
2 Baldacci	Y	Y	Y	Y	N	N	Y
MARYLAND							
1 ***Gilchrest***	Y	Y	Y	Y	Y	Y	Y
2 ***Ehrlich***	?	?	?	?	?	?	?
3 Cardin	N	Y	Y	Y	N	N	N
4 Wynn	N	N	Y	Y	N	N	N
5 Hoyer	N	Y	Y	Y	N	N	N
6 ***Bartlett***	Y	Y	Y	Y	Y	Y	Y
7 Cummings	N	Y	Y	Y	N	N	N
8 ***Morella***	N	Y	Y	Y	N	Y	Y
MASSACHUSETTS							
1 Olver	N	Y	Y	Y	N	N	N
2 Neal	N	N	Y	Y	N	N	N
3 McGovern	N	Y	Y	Y	N	N	N
4 Frank	N	N	Y	Y	N	N	N
5 Meehan	N	Y	?	Y	N	N	N
6 Tierney	N	Y	Y	Y	N	N	N
7 Markey	Y	Y	?	?	?	?	?
8 Kennedy	Y	Y	Y	Y	N	N	N
9 Moakley	?	?	?	?	?	?	?
10 Delahunt	N	Y	Y	Y	N	N	N
MICHIGAN							
1 Stupak	Y	Y	Y	Y	N	N	Y
2 ***Hoekstra***	Y	Y	Y	Y	Y	Y	Y
3 ***Ehlers***	Y	Y	Y	Y	N	Y	Y
4 ***Camp***	Y	Y	Y	Y	Y	Y	Y
5 Barcia	Y	Y	Y	Y	N	N	Y
6 ***Upton***	Y	Y	Y	Y	Y	Y	Y
7 ***Smith***	N	Y	Y	Y	N	Y	Y
8 Stabenow	Y	Y	Y	Y	N	Y	Y
9 Kildee	Y	Y	Y	Y	N	Y	Y
10 Bonior	N	Y	Y	Y	N	N	N
11 ***Knollenberg***	Y	Y	Y	Y	Y	Y	Y
12 Levin	Y	Y	Y	Y	N	N	N
13 Rivers	N	Y	Y	Y	N	N	N
14 Conyers	N	N	N	N	N	N	N
15 Kilpatrick	N	N	Y	Y	N	N	N
16 Dingell	N	Y	Y	Y	N	N	N

	302	303	304	305	306	307	308
MINNESOTA							
1 ***Gutknecht***	Y	Y	Y	Y	N	Y	Y
2 Minge	N	Y	Y	Y	N	N	Y
3 ***Ramstad***	Y	Y	Y	Y	N	Y	Y
4 Vento	N	Y	Y	Y	N	N	N
5 Sabo	N	N	N	Y	N	N	Y
6 Luther	Y	Y	Y	Y	N	N	Y
7 Peterson	Y	Y	Y	Y	N	N	Y
8 Oberstar	N	Y	Y	Y	N	N	N
MISSISSIPPI							
1 ***Wicker***	Y	Y	Y	Y	Y	Y	Y
2 Thompson	?	?	?	?	?	?	?
3 ***Pickering***	+	Y	Y	Y	Y	Y	Y
4 ***Parker***	Y	Y	Y	Y	Y	Y	Y
5 Taylor	Y	Y	Y	Y	Y	Y	Y
MISSOURI							
1 Clay	N	Y	N	Y	N	N	N
2 ***Talent***	N	Y	Y	Y	Y	N	Y
3 Gephardt	?	?	?	?	?	?	?
4 Skelton	Y	Y	?	Y	N	N	Y
5 McCarthy	N	Y	Y	Y	N	N	N
6 Danner	?	?	?	?	?	?	?
7 ***Blunt***	Y	N	Y	Y	N	Y	Y
8 ***Emerson***	Y	Y	Y	Y	Y	Y	Y
9 ***Hulshof***	Y	Y	Y	Y	Y	Y	Y
MONTANA							
AL ***Hill***	Y	Y	Y	Y	Y	Y	Y
NEBRASKA							
1 ***Bereuter***	Y	Y	Y	Y	N	Y	Y
2 ***Christensen***	Y	Y	Y	Y	Y	Y	Y
3 ***Barrett***	Y	Y	Y	Y	N	Y	Y
NEVADA							
1 ***Ensign***	N	N	Y	Y	N	N	Y
2 ***Gibbons***	Y	Y	Y	Y	Y	Y	Y
NEW HAMPSHIRE							
1 ***Sununu***	Y	Y	Y	Y	Y	Y	Y
2 ***Bass***	Y	Y	Y	Y	N	Y	Y
NEW JERSEY							
1 Andrews	N	Y	Y	Y	N	N	N
2 ***LoBiondo***	Y	Y	Y	Y	N	Y	Y
3 ***Saxton***	?	Y	Y	Y	N	Y	Y
4 ***Smith***	Y	Y	Y	Y	N	Y	Y
5 ***Roukema***	Y	Y	Y	Y	N	Y	Y
6 Pallone	N	Y	Y	Y	N	N	Y
7 ***Franks***	Y	Y	Y	Y	N	Y	Y
8 Pascrell	N	Y	Y	Y	N	N	Y
9 Rothman	Y	Y	Y	Y	N	Y	N
10 Payne	N	N	N	Y	N	N	N
11 ***Frelinghuysen***	Y	Y	Y	Y	N	Y	Y
12 ***Pappas***	Y	Y	Y	Y	N	Y	Y
13 Menendez	N	Y	Y	Y	N	N	N
NEW MEXICO							
1 ***Wilson***	Y	N	Y	Y	N	Y	Y
2 ***Skeen***	Y	Y	Y	Y	Y	Y	Y
3 ***Redmond***	Y	Y	Y	Y	N	Y	Y
NEW YORK							
1 ***Forbes***	Y	Y	Y	Y	N	N	Y
2 ***Lazio***	Y	N	Y	Y	N	Y	Y
3 ***King***	N	N	Y	Y	N	N	N
4 McCarthy	N	Y	Y	Y	N	N	N
5 Ackerman	?	?	?	?	?	?	?
6 Meeks	N	N	Y	Y	N	N	N
7 Manton	N	Y	Y	Y	N	N	N
8 Nadler	N	N	N	Y	N	N	N
9 Schumer	Y	Y	Y	Y	N	Y	Y
10 Towns	?	?	?	?	?	?	?
11 Owens	N	Y	Y	Y	N	N	N
12 Velázquez	N	Y	Y	Y	N	N	N
13 ***Fossella***	Y	Y	Y	Y	Y	Y	Y
14 Maloney	–	+	+	+	–	N	Y
15 Rangel	N	Y	Y	Y	N	N	N
16 Serrano	N	Y	Y	Y	N	N	N
17 Engel	N	N	N	Y	N	N	N
18 Lowey	N	Y	Y	Y	N	N	N
19 ***Kelly***	Y	Y	Y	Y	N	Y	Y
20 ***Gilman***	Y	Y	Y	Y	N	N	Y
21 McNulty	N	Y	Y	Y	N	N	N
22 ***Solomon***	Y	Y	Y	Y	Y	Y	Y
23 ***Boehlert***	N	Y	Y	Y	N	N	N
24 ***McHugh***	Y	Y	Y	Y	N	Y	Y
25 ***Walsh***	Y	Y	Y	Y	N	Y	Y
26 Hinchey	Y	Y	Y	Y	N	Y	N
27 ***Paxon***	Y	Y	Y	Y	Y	Y	Y
28 Slaughter	Y	Y	Y	Y	N	N	N
29 LaFalce	N	Y	Y	Y	N	N	N

	302	303	304	305	306	307	308
30 ***Quinn***	Y	Y	Y	Y	N	Y	Y
31 ***Houghton***	N	Y	Y	Y	N	N	Y
NORTH CAROLINA							
1 Clayton	N	Y	Y	Y	N	N	N
2 Etheridge	Y	Y	Y	Y	N	Y	Y
3 ***Jones***	Y	Y	Y	Y	Y	Y	Y
4 Price	Y	Y	Y	Y	N	Y	Y
5 ***Burr***	Y	Y	Y	Y	Y	Y	Y
6 ***Coble***	+	+	+	+	+	+	+
7 McIntyre	Y	Y	Y	Y	N	Y	Y
8 Hefner	?	?	?	?	?	?	?
9 ***Myrick***	Y	Y	Y	Y	Y	Y	Y
10 ***Ballenger***	Y	Y	Y	Y	Y	Y	Y
11 ***Taylor***	Y	Y	Y	Y	Y	Y	Y
12 Watt	N	Y	N	Y	N	N	N
NORTH DAKOTA							
AL Pomeroy	Y	Y	Y	Y	N	N	Y
OHIO							
1 ***Chabot***	Y	Y	Y	Y	Y	Y	Y
2 ***Portman***	Y	Y	Y	Y	Y	N	Y
3 Hall	N	Y	Y	Y	N	Y	N
4 ***Oxley***	Y	Y	Y	Y	Y	Y	Y
5 ***Gillmor***	Y	Y	Y	Y	N	N	Y
6 Strickland	Y	Y	Y	Y	N	Y	Y
7 ***Hobson***	Y	Y	Y	Y	N	Y	Y
8 ***Boehner***	Y	Y	Y	Y	Y	Y	Y
9 Kaptur	Y	Y	Y	Y	N	Y	N
10 Kucinich	Y	N	N	N	N	N	N
11 Stokes	?	?	?	?	?	?	?
12 ***Kasich***	Y	Y	Y	Y	Y	Y	Y
13 Brown	Y	Y	Y	Y	N	N	N
14 Sawyer	Y	Y	Y	Y	N	N	N
15 ***Pryce***	Y	Y	Y	Y	Y	Y	Y
16 ***Regula***	Y	Y	Y	Y	N	N	Y
17 Traficant	?	?	?	?	?	?	?
18 ***Ney***	Y	Y	Y	Y	N	Y	Y
19 ***LaTourette***	Y	N	Y	Y	N	Y	Y
OKLAHOMA							
1 ***Largent***	Y	Y	Y	Y	Y	Y	Y
2 ***Coburn***	Y	Y	Y	Y	N	Y	?
3 ***Watkins***	Y	Y	Y	Y	Y	Y	Y
4 ***Watts***	Y	Y	Y	Y	Y	N	Y
5 ***Istook***	Y	Y	Y	Y	Y	Y	Y
6 ***Lucas***	Y	Y	Y	Y	Y	Y	Y
OREGON							
1 Furse	N	Y	N	Y	N	N	N
2 ***Smith***	Y	Y	Y	Y	Y	Y	Y
3 Blumenauer	N	Y	Y	Y	N	N	Y
4 DeFazio	Y	Y	Y	Y	N	N	Y
5 Hooley	Y	Y	Y	Y	N	N	Y
PENNSYLVANIA							
1 Brady	N	Y	N	Y	N	N	N
2 Fattah	N	Y	N	Y	N	N	N
3 Borski	N	Y	N	Y	N	N	N
4 Klink	Y	Y	Y	Y	N	N	N
5 ***Peterson***	Y	Y	Y	Y	Y	Y	Y
6 Holden	Y	Y	Y	Y	N	N	N
7 ***Weldon***	Y	Y	Y	Y	N	Y	Y
8 ***Greenwood***	Y	Y	Y	Y	N	Y	Y
9 ***Shuster***	Y	Y	Y	Y	Y	Y	Y
10 ***McDade***	?	?	?	?	?	?	?
11 Kanjorski	N	N	N	Y	N	N	N
12 Murtha	N	N	N	Y	N	N	N
13 ***Fox***	Y	Y	Y	Y	N	Y	Y
14 Coyne	Y	Y	Y	Y	N	Y	Y
15 McHale	N	Y	Y	Y	N	N	N
16 ***Pitts***	Y	Y	Y	Y	Y	Y	Y
17 ***Gekas***	Y	Y	Y	Y	Y	Y	Y
18 Doyle	Y	Y	Y	Y	N	N	N
19 ***Goodling***	Y	Y	Y	Y	Y	Y	Y
20 Mascara	Y	Y	Y	Y	N	Y	Y
21 ***English***	Y	Y	Y	Y	N	Y	Y
RHODE ISLAND							
1 Kennedy	N	N	Y	Y	N	N	N
2 Weygand	N	Y	Y	Y	N	N	Y
SOUTH CAROLINA							
1 ***Sanford***	Y	Y	Y	Y	N	Y	Y
2 ***Spence***	Y	Y	Y	Y	Y	Y	Y
3 ***Graham***	Y	Y	Y	Y	Y	Y	Y
4 ***Inglis***	Y	Y	Y	Y	Y	Y	Y
5 Spratt	Y	Y	Y	Y	N	N	Y
6 Clyburn	N	N	Y	N	N	N	N
SOUTH DAKOTA							
AL ***Thune***	Y	Y	Y	Y	Y	Y	Y

	302	303	304	305	306	307	308
TENNESSEE							
1 ***Jenkins***	Y	Y	Y	Y	Y	Y	Y
2 ***Duncan***	Y	Y	Y	Y	Y	Y	Y
3 ***Wamp***	Y	Y	Y	Y	N	Y	Y
4 ***Hilleary***	Y	Y	Y	Y	Y	Y	Y
5 Clement	Y	Y	Y	Y	N	Y	N
6 Gordon	Y	Y	Y	Y	N	N	Y
7 ***Bryant***	Y	Y	Y	Y	Y	Y	Y
8 Tanner	Y	Y	N	Y	N	Y	N
9 Ford	–	+	–	+	–	–	–
TEXAS							
1 Sandlin	Y	Y	Y	Y	N	N	N
2 Turner	Y	Y	Y	Y	N	Y	Y
3 ***Johnson, Sam***	Y	Y	Y	Y	Y	N	Y
4 Hall	N	Y	Y	Y	N	Y	Y
5 ***Sessions***	Y	Y	Y	Y	Y	Y	Y
6 ***Barton***	Y	Y	Y	Y	Y	N	Y
7 ***Archer***	Y	Y	Y	Y	Y	Y	Y
8 ***Brady***	Y	Y	Y	Y	Y	Y	Y
9 Lampson	N	Y	Y	Y	N	Y	Y
10 Doggett	N	Y	Y	Y	N	N	N
11 Edwards	N	Y	Y	Y	N	N	N
12 ***Granger***	Y	Y	Y	Y	Y	N	Y
13 ***Thornberry***	N	Y	Y	Y	Y	N	Y
14 ***Paul***	N	N	Y	Y	N	Y	Y
15 Hinojosa	N	Y	Y	Y	N	N	N
16 Reyes	N	Y	Y	Y	N	N	N
17 Stenholm	N	Y	Y	Y	N	Y	Y
18 Jackson-Lee	N	N	N	Y	N	N	N
19 ***Combest***	Y	Y	Y	Y	Y	Y	Y
20 Gonzalez	?	?	?	?	?	?	?
21 ***Smith***	Y	Y	Y	Y	Y	Y	Y
22 ***DeLay***	N	Y	Y	Y	Y	Y	Y
23 ***Bonilla***	Y	Y	Y	Y	Y	N	Y
24 Frost	?	?	?	?	?	?	?
25 Bentsen	N	Y	Y	Y	N	N	N
26 ***Armey***	Y	Y	Y	Y	Y	Y	Y
27 Ortiz	+	+	+	+	–	–	+
28 Rodriguez	N	Y	Y	Y	N	N	Y
29 Green	N	Y	Y	Y	N	Y	Y
30 Johnson, E.B.	N	N	Y	Y	N	N	N
UTAH							
1 ***Hansen***	Y	Y	Y	Y	Y	Y	Y
2 ***Cook***	Y	Y	Y	Y	Y	Y	Y
3 ***Cannon***	Y	Y	Y	Y	Y	Y	Y
VERMONT							
AL *Sanders*	Y	Y	Y	Y	N	N	Y
VIRGINIA							
1 ***Bateman***	Y	Y	Y	Y	Y	Y	Y
2 Pickett	Y	Y	Y	Y	N	Y	Y
3 Scott	N	N	N	Y	N	N	N
4 Sisisky	Y	Y	Y	Y	N	Y	Y
5 Goode	Y	Y	Y	Y	Y	Y	Y
6 ***Goodlatte***	Y	Y	Y	Y	Y	Y	Y
7 ***Bliley***	Y	Y	Y	Y	Y	N	Y
8 Moran	N	N	N	Y	N	N	Y
9 Boucher	Y	Y	Y	Y	N	N	Y
10 ***Wolf***	Y	Y	Y	Y	Y	Y	Y
11 ***Davis***	Y	N	Y	Y	Y	Y	Y
WASHINGTON							
1 ***White***	Y	Y	Y	Y	N	Y	Y
2 ***Metcalf***	Y	Y	Y	Y	N	Y	N
3 ***Smith, Linda***	Y	Y	Y	Y	Y	Y	Y
4 ***Hastings***	Y	Y	Y	Y	Y	Y	Y
5 ***Nethercutt***	Y	Y	Y	Y	Y	Y	Y
6 Dicks	N	Y	Y	Y	N	N	Y
7 McDermott	N	N	N	Y	N	N	N
8 ***Dunn***	Y	Y	Y	Y	Y	Y	Y
9 Smith, Adam	Y	Y	N	Y	N	N	Y
WEST VIRGINIA							
1 Mollohan	N	N	N	Y	N	N	Y
2 Wise	Y	Y	Y	Y	N	N	Y
3 Rahall	Y	Y	N	Y	N	N	N
WISCONSIN							
1 ***Neumann***	Y	Y	Y	Y	N	Y	Y
2 ***Klug***	Y	Y	Y	Y	Y	Y	Y
3 Kind	N	Y	Y	Y	N	N	Y
4 Kleczka	Y	Y	Y	Y	N	Y	Y
5 Barrett	N	Y	Y	Y	N	N	Y
6 ***Petri***	Y	Y	Y	Y	N	Y	Y
7 Obey	Y	Y	N	Y	N	N	Y
8 Johnson	Y	Y	Y	Y	N	N	Y
9 ***Sensenbrenner***	Y	Y	Y	Y	Y	Y	Y
WYOMING							
AL ***Cubin***	Y	Y	Y	Y	Y	Y	Y

Southern states - Ala., Ark., Fla., Ga., Ky., La., Miss., N.C., Okla., S.C., Tenn., Texas, Va.

309. Procedural Motion/Adjourn. Yates, D-Ill. motion to adjourn. Motion rejected 7-382: R 0-207; D 7-175 (ND 7-128, SD 0-47); I 0-0. July 21, 1998.

310. HR 4193. Fiscal 1999 Interior Appropriations/Previous Question. Hastings, R-Wash., motion to order the previous question (thus ending debate and the possibility of amendment) on adoption of the rule (H Res 504) to provide for House floor consideration of the bill to provide $13.4 billion in funding for the Department of Interior and related agencies for fiscal 1999. Motion agreed to 223-196: R 220-0; D 3-195 (ND 1-147, SD 2-48); I 0-1. July 21, 1998. (Subsequently, the rule was adopted.)

311. HR 4193. Fiscal 1999 Interior Appropriations/Rule. Adoption of the rule (H Res 504) to provide for House floor consideration of the bill to provide $13.4 billion in funding for the Department of Interior and related agencies in fiscal 1999. Adopted 224-191: R 219-1; D 5-189 (ND 3-144, SD 2-45); I 0-1. July 21, 1998.

312. HR 4193. Fiscal 1999 Interior Appropriations/NEA Funding. Johnson, R-Conn., amendment to reinstate $98 million in funding for the National Endowment of the Arts in fiscal 1999, which was struck from the bill by a point of order. The amendment was made in order by the rule (H Res 405) that provided for House floor consideration of HR4193. Adopted 253-173: R 58-166; D 194-7 (ND 147-2, SD 47-5); I 1-0. July 21, 1998.

313. HR 4193. Fiscal 1999 Interior Appropriations/Energy Efficiency and Conservation Programs Funding. Skaggs, D-Colo., amendment to increase funding for certain energy efficiency and conservation programs. Rejected 212-213: R 59-166; D 152-47 (ND 117-30, SD 35-17); I 1-0. July 21, 1998.

314. HR 4193. Fiscal 1999 Interior Appropriations/Payments in Lieu of Taxes Fund Increase. Sanders, I-Vt. amendment to increase by $20 million funds in the bill earmarked for payments in lieu of taxes, which are federal payments intended to make up for taxes localities might otherwise collect if federal lands were not federally owned. Adopted 241-185: R 117-109; D 123-76 (ND 94-53, SD 29-23); I 1-0. July 21, 1998.

315. HR 4193. Fiscal 1999 Interior Appropriations/Land and Water Conservation Fund Increase. McGovern, D-Mass., amendment to increase funding by $30 million for the state-side program of the Land and Water Conservation Fund. Rejected 203-221: R 51-174; D 151-47 (ND 114-32, SD 37-15); I 1-0. July 21, 1998.

Key

Y	Voted for (yea).
#	Paired for.
+	Announced for.
N	Voted against (nay).
X	Paired against.
−	Announced against.
P	Voted "present."
C	Voted "present" to avoid possible conflict of interest.
?	Did not vote or otherwise make a position known.

● Democrats **Republicans** *Independent*

	309	310	311	312	313	314	315
ALABAMA							
1 *Callahan*	N	Y	Y	N	N	N	N
2 *Everett*	N	Y	Y	N	N	N	N
3 *Riley*	N	Y	Y	N	N	N	N
4 *Aderholt*	N	Y	Y	N	N	N	N
5 Cramer	N	N	N	Y	N	Y	N
6 *Bachus*	N	Y	Y	N	N	N	N
7 Hilliard	N	N	?	Y	Y	Y	Y
ALASKA							
AL *Young*	?	Y	Y	N	N	Y	N
ARIZONA							
1 *Salmon*	N	Y	Y	N	Y	N	Y
2 Pastor	N	N	N	Y	Y	Y	Y
3 *Stump*	N	Y	Y	N	N	N	N
4 *Shadegg*	N	Y	Y	N	N	Y	N
5 *Kolbe*	Y	Y	Y	Y	Y	Y	N
6 *Hayworth*	N	Y	Y	N	Y	Y	Y
ARKANSAS							
1 Berry	N	N	N	Y	Y	Y	Y
2 Snyder	N	N	N	Y	Y	Y	Y
3 *Hutchinson*	N	Y	Y	N	N	Y	N
4 *Dickey*	N	Y	Y	N	N	N	N
CALIFORNIA							
1 *Riggs*	N	Y	Y	N	N	Y	N
2 *Herger*	N	Y	Y	N	N	N	N
3 Fazio	N	N	N	Y	Y	Y	Y
4 *Doolittle*	?	Y	Y	N	N	Y	N
5 Matsui	N	N	N	Y	Y	Y	Y
6 Woolsey	N	N	N	Y	Y	N	Y
7 Miller	Y	N	N	Y	Y	N	Y
8 Pelosi	?	N	N	Y	Y	N	Y
9 Lee	N	N	N	Y	Y	N	Y
10 Tauscher	N	N	N	Y	Y	N	Y
11 *Pombo*	N	Y	Y	N	N	Y	N
12 Lantos	N	N	N	Y	Y	N	Y
13 Stark	N	N	N	Y	Y	N	Y
14 Eshoo	N	N	N	Y	Y	N	Y
15 *Campbell*	N	Y	Y	Y	Y	Y	Y
16 Lofgren	N	N	N	Y	Y	Y	Y
17 Farr	N	N	N	Y	Y	N	Y
18 Condit	N	N	N	N	N	N	Y
19 *Radanovich*	N	Y	Y	N	N	Y	−
20 Dooley	N	N	N	Y	N	N	Y
21 *Thomas*	N	Y	Y	N	N	N	N
22 Capps, L.	N	N	N	Y	Y	Y	Y
23 *Gallegly*	N	Y	Y	N	N	N	N
24 Sherman	N	N	N	Y	Y	Y	Y
25 *McKeon*	N	Y	Y	N	N	N	N
26 Berman	N	N	N	Y	Y	N	Y
27 *Rogan*	N	Y	Y	N	N	N	N
28 *Dreier*	N	Y	Y	N	N	N	N
29 Waxman	N	N	N	Y	Y	Y	Y
30 Becerra	N	N	N	Y	Y	Y	Y
31 Martinez	N	N	N	Y	Y	Y	Y
32 Dixon	?	?	?	?	?	?	?
33 Roybal-Allard	N	N	N	Y	Y	Y	Y
34 Torres	N	N	N	Y	Y	Y	Y
35 Waters	N	N	N	Y	Y	Y	Y
36 Harman	?	N	N	Y	?	?	?
37 Millender-McD.	N	N	N	Y	Y	Y	Y

	309	310	311	312	313	314	315
38 *Horn*	N	Y	Y	N	N	Y	N
39 *Royce*	N	Y	Y	N	N	N	Y
40 *Lewis*	N	Y	Y	N	N	N	Y
41 *Kim*	N	Y	Y	N	N	N	N
42 Brown	N	N	Y	N	N	N	N
43 *Calvert*	N	Y	Y	N	N	Y	N
44 *Bono, M.*	N	Y	Y	N	N	Y	N
45 *Rohrabacher*	N	Y	Y	N	N	N	N
46 Sanchez	N	N	N	Y	Y	N	Y
47 *Cox*	N	Y	Y	N	N	N	N
48 *Packard*	N	Y	Y	N	N	N	N
49 *Bilbray*	N	Y	Y	Y	Y	Y	Y
50 Filner	Y	N	N	Y	Y	Y	Y
51 *Cunningham*	N	Y	Y	N	N	N	N
52 *Hunter*	N	Y	Y	N	N	Y	N
COLORADO							
1 DeGette	N	N	N	Y	Y	Y	Y
2 Skaggs	N	N	Y	Y	N	N	Y
3 *McInnis*	N	Y	Y	Y	N	Y	N
4 *Schaffer*	Y	Y	Y	N	N	Y	N
5 *Hefley*	N	Y	Y	N	N	N	N
6 *Schaefer*	N	Y	Y	N	N	N	N
CONNECTICUT							
1 Kennelly	?	?	?	Y	Y	N	Y
2 Gejdenson	N	N	N	Y	N	N	N
3 DeLauro	N	N	N	Y	Y	Y	Y
4 *Shays*	N	Y	Y	Y	Y	Y	Y
5 Maloney	N	N	N	Y	N	N	Y
6 *Johnson*	N	Y	Y	Y	Y	Y	Y
DELAWARE							
AL *Castle*	N	Y	Y	Y	Y	N	N
FLORIDA							
1 *Scarborough*	N	Y	N	N	Y	N	Y
2 Boyd	N	N	Y	Y	Y	Y	Y
3 Brown	N	N	N	Y	Y	Y	Y
4 *Fowler*	N	Y	Y	N	Y	N	Y
5 Thurman	N	N	N	Y	Y	Y	Y
6 *Stearns*	N	Y	Y	N	N	N	N
7 *Mica*	N	Y	Y	N	N	N	Y
8 *McCollum*	N	Y	Y	N	N	N	N
9 *Bilirakis*	?	?	?	N	Y	N	Y
10 *Young*	?	Y	Y	?	?	?	?
11 Davis	N	N	N	Y	Y	Y	Y
12 *Canady*	N	?	Y	N	N	N	N
13 *Miller*	N	Y	Y	N	N	N	N
14 *Goss*	N	Y	Y	N	N	N	N
15 *Weldon*	N	Y	Y	N	N	N	N
16 *Foley*	N	Y	Y	Y	Y	Y	N
17 Meek	N	N	N	Y	Y	Y	Y
18 *Ros-Lehtinen*	N	Y	Y	N	N	N	N
19 Wexler	N	N	N	Y	Y	Y	Y
20 Deutsch	N	N	N	Y	Y	Y	Y
21 *Diaz-Balart*	N	Y	Y	N	N	N	N
22 *Shaw*	N	Y	Y	N	N	N	N
23 Hastings	N	N	?	Y	Y	Y	Y
GEORGIA							
1 *Kingston*	N	Y	Y	N	N	N	N
2 Bishop	N	N	N	Y	Y	Y	Y
3 *Collins*	N	Y	Y	N	Y	Y	Y
4 McKinney	N	N	N	Y	Y	Y	Y
5 Lewis	N	N	N	Y	Y	Y	Y
6 *Gingrich*							
7 *Barr*	N	Y	Y	N	N	Y	N
8 *Chambliss*	N	Y	Y	N	N	N	N
9 *Deal*	N	Y	Y	N	N	Y	N
10 *Norwood*	?	?	?	−	N	Y	N
11 *Linder*	N	Y	Y	N	N	N	N
HAWAII							
1 Abercrombie	N	N	N	Y	N	Y	Y
2 Mink	N	N	N	Y	Y	Y	Y
IDAHO							
1 *Chenoweth*	N	Y	Y	N	N	Y	N
2 *Crapo*	?	Y	Y	N	N	Y	N
ILLINOIS							
1 Rush	N	N	N	Y	Y	Y	Y
2 Jackson	N	N	N	Y	Y	Y	Y
3 Lipinski	N	N	N	Y	Y	Y	Y
4 Gutierrez	N	N	N	Y	Y	Y	Y
5 Blagojevich	N	N	N	Y	Y	Y	Y
6 *Hyde*	N	Y	Y	N	N	N	N
7 Davis	N	N	N	Y	Y	Y	Y
8 *Crane*	N	Y	Y	N	N	Y	N
9 Yates	N	N	N	Y	Y	Y	Y
10 *Porter*	?	Y	Y	Y	N	N	N
11 *Weller*	Y	Y	Y	N	N	Y	Y
12 Costello	N	N	N	Y	Y	Y	Y

ND Northern Democrats   SD Southern Democrats

	309	310	311	312	313	314	315
13 **Fawell**	N	Y	Y	Y	Y	N	Y
14 **Hastert**	N	Y	Y	N	Y	N	N
15 **Ewing**	?	Y	Y	N	N	N	N
16 **Manzullo**	N	Y	Y	N	Y	Y	N
17 Evans	?	N	N	Y	Y	Y	Y
18 **LaHood**	N	Y	Y	Y	Y	N	N
19 Poshard	?	N	N	Y	N	N	Y
20 **Shimkus**	N	Y	Y	N	N	N	N
INDIANA							
1 Visclosky	N	N	N	Y	N	N	N
2 **McIntosh**	N	Y	Y	N	N	Y	N
3 Roemer	N	N	N	Y	Y	N	N
4 **Souder**	N	Y	Y	N	N	N	N
5 **Buyer**	N	Y	Y	N	N	Y	N
6 **Burton**	?	Y	Y	N	N	N	Y
7 **Pease**	N	Y	Y	N	N	N	Y
8 **Hostettler**	N	Y	Y	N	N	Y	N
9 Hamilton	N	N	Y	Y	N	N	N
10 Carson	N	N	N	Y	Y	Y	Y
IOWA							
1 **Leach**	N	Y	Y	Y	Y	Y	Y
2 **Nussle**	N	Y	Y	N	Y	Y	N
3 Boswell	N	N	N	Y	N	Y	N
4 **Ganske**	N	Y	Y	Y	Y	Y	N
5 **Latham**	N	Y	Y	N	N	Y	N
KANSAS							
1 **Moran**	N	Y	Y	N	N	Y	N
2 **Ryun**	N	Y	Y	N	N	N	N
3 **Snowbarger**	N	Y	Y	N	N	N	Y
4 **Tiahrt**	N	Y	Y	N	N	N	N
KENTUCKY							
1 **Whitfield**	N	Y	Y	N	Y	Y	N
2 **Lewis**	N	Y	Y	N	N	Y	N
3 **Northup**	?	Y	Y	N	N	Y	N
4 **Bunning**	N	Y	Y	N	N	Y	N
5 **Rogers**	N	Y	Y	N	Y	Y	N
6 Baesler	N	N	N	Y	Y	Y	Y
LOUISIANA							
1 **Livingston**	N	Y	?	N	N	N	N
2 Jefferson	N	N	N	Y	Y	Y	Y
3 **Tauzin**	N	Y	Y	N	N	N	N
4 **McCrery**	?	Y	Y	N	N	N	N
5 **Cooksey**	N	Y	Y	N	N	N	N
6 **Baker**	?	?	?	N	N	N	N
7 John	?	?	?	?	?	?	?
MAINE							
1 Allen	N	N	N	Y	Y	Y	Y
2 Baldacci	N	N	N	Y	Y	Y	Y
MARYLAND							
1 **Gilchrest**	N	Y	Y	Y	N	N	N
2 **Ehrlich**	N	Y	Y	N	N	Y	Y
3 Cardin	?	N	N	Y	Y	N	Y
4 Wynn	N	N	N	Y	Y	Y	Y
5 Hoyer	N	N	N	Y	Y	N	N
6 **Bartlett**	N	Y	Y	Y	N	N	N
7 Cummings	N	N	N	Y	Y	Y	Y
8 **Morella**	N	Y	Y	Y	Y	Y	Y
MASSACHUSETTS							
1 Olver	N	N	N	Y	Y	N	Y
2 Neal	N	N	N	Y	Y	Y	Y
3 McGovern	N	N	N	Y	Y	Y	Y
4 Frank	N	N	N	Y	Y	N	Y
5 Meehan	N	N	N	Y	Y	Y	Y
6 Tierney	N	N	N	Y	Y	N	Y
7 Markey	?	N	N	Y	Y	Y	Y
8 Kennedy	N	N	N	Y	Y	Y	Y
9 Moakley	N	N	N	Y	N	?	?
10 Delahunt	N	N	N	Y	Y	Y	Y
MICHIGAN							
1 Stupak	N	N	N	Y	Y	Y	Y
2 **Hoekstra**	N	Y	Y	N	N	Y	N
3 **Ehlers**	N	Y	Y	Y	Y	N	N
4 **Camp**	N	Y	Y	N	Y	Y	Y
5 Barcia	N	N	N	Y	Y	Y	Y
6 **Upton**	N	Y	Y	Y	Y	N	Y
7 **Smith**	N	Y	Y	Y	N	Y	Y
8 Stabenow	N	N	N	Y	Y	Y	Y
9 Kildee	N	N	N	Y	Y	Y	Y
10 Bonior	N	N	N	Y	Y	Y	Y
11 **Knollenberg**	N	Y	Y	N	N	N	N
12 Levin	N	N	N	Y	Y	Y	Y
13 Rivers	N	N	N	Y	Y	Y	Y
14 Conyers	Y	N	N	Y	Y	Y	Y
15 Kilpatrick	N	N	N	Y	Y	Y	Y
16 Dingell	N	N	N	Y	Y	N	Y
MINNESOTA							
1 **Gutknecht**	N	Y	Y	N	N	N	N
2 Minge	N	N	N	Y	Y	Y	N
3 **Ramstad**	N	Y	Y	Y	Y	Y	N
4 Vento	N	N	N	Y	Y	Y	Y
5 Sabo	N	N	N	Y	Y	N	N
6 Luther	N	N	N	Y	Y	Y	Y
7 Peterson	?	N	N	Y	Y	Y	N
8 Oberstar	N	N	N	Y	Y	Y	Y
MISSISSIPPI							
1 **Wicker**	N	Y	Y	N	N	Y	N
2 Thompson	N	N	N	Y	Y	Y	Y
3 **Pickering**	?	Y	Y	N	N	Y	N
4 **Parker**	N	Y	Y	N	Y	Y	N
5 Taylor	N	N	N	N	N	Y	N
MISSOURI							
1 Clay	N	N	N	Y	Y	Y	N
2 **Talent**	N	Y	Y	N	N	N	N
3 Gephardt	Y	N	N	Y	Y	N	Y
4 Skelton	N	N	N	N	Y	Y	Y
5 McCarthy	N	N	N	Y	Y	Y	Y
6 Danner	?	N	N	Y	Y	Y	Y
7 **Blunt**	N	Y	Y	N	N	N	N
8 **Emerson**	N	Y	Y	N	Y	Y	N
9 **Hulshof**	N	Y	Y	N	Y	Y	Y
MONTANA							
AL **Hill**	?	Y	Y	N	N	Y	N
NEBRASKA							
1 **Bereuter**	N	Y	Y	Y	N	N	Y
2 **Christensen**	N	Y	Y	N	N	N	N
3 **Barrett**	N	Y	Y	N	N	N	N
NEVADA							
1 **Ensign**	N	Y	Y	N	Y	Y	Y
2 **Gibbons**	N	Y	Y	N	N	Y	N
NEW HAMPSHIRE							
1 **Sununu**	N	Y	Y	Y	Y	Y	Y
2 **Bass**	N	Y	Y	Y	Y	Y	Y
NEW JERSEY							
1 Andrews	N	N	N	Y	Y	Y	Y
2 **LoBiondo**	N	Y	Y	Y	Y	Y	N
3 **Saxton**	N	Y	Y	Y	N	N	N
4 **Smith**	N	Y	Y	N	Y	Y	Y
5 **Roukema**	?	Y	Y	Y	N	Y	N
6 Pallone	N	N	N	Y	Y	Y	Y
7 **Franks**	N	Y	Y	Y	Y	Y	N
8 Pascrell	N	N	N	Y	Y	Y	Y
9 Rothman	N	N	N	Y	Y	Y	Y
10 Payne	N	N	N	Y	Y	Y	N
11 **Frelinghuysen**	N	Y	Y	Y	N	N	N
12 **Pappas**	N	Y	Y	N	Y	Y	Y
13 Menendez	N	N	N	Y	Y	Y	Y
NEW MEXICO							
1 **Wilson**	N	Y	Y	N	N	N	N
2 **Skeen**	N	Y	Y	Y	N	N	N
3 **Redmond**	N	Y	Y	N	N	N	N
NEW YORK							
1 **Forbes**	N	Y	Y	Y	Y	N	Y
2 **Lazio**	N	Y	Y	Y	Y	N	Y
3 **King**	N	Y	Y	N	Y	N	Y
4 McCarthy	N	N	N	Y	Y	Y	Y
5 Ackerman	N	N	N	Y	Y	Y	Y
6 Meeks	N	N	N	Y	Y	N	Y
7 Manton	N	N	N	Y	Y	Y	Y
8 Nadler	Y	N	N	Y	Y	Y	Y
9 Schumer	?	N	N	Y	Y	Y	Y
10 Towns	N	N	N	Y	Y	Y	Y
11 Owens	?	N	N	Y	Y	Y	Y
12 Velázquez	N	N	N	Y	Y	Y	Y
13 **Fossella**	N	Y	Y	N	Y	N	N
14 Maloney	N	N	N	Y	Y	Y	Y
15 Rangel	N	N	N	Y	Y	N	Y
16 Serrano	N	N	N	Y	Y	Y	Y
17 Engel	?	N	N	Y	Y	N	Y
18 Lowey	N	N	N	Y	Y	N	Y
19 **Kelly**	N	Y	Y	Y	Y	Y	Y
20 **Gilman**	N	Y	Y	Y	Y	N	Y
21 McNulty	?	?	?	?	?	?	?
22 **Solomon**	N	Y	Y	N	?	Y	N
23 **Boehlert**	N	Y	Y	Y	Y	Y	Y
24 **McHugh**	N	Y	Y	Y	Y	Y	N
25 **Walsh**	N	Y	Y	Y	Y	Y	N
26 Hinchey	N	N	?	Y	Y	Y	Y
27 **Paxon**	N	Y	Y	N	N	N	N
28 Slaughter	N	N	N	Y	Y	Y	Y
29 LaFalce	N	N	N	Y	Y	Y	Y
30 **Quinn**	N	Y	Y	Y	Y	Y	Y
31 **Houghton**	N	Y	Y	Y	N	Y	Y
NORTH CAROLINA							
1 Clayton	N	N	N	Y	Y	Y	Y
2 Etheridge	N	N	N	Y	Y	Y	Y
3 **Jones**	N	Y	Y	N	N	Y	N
4 Price	N	N	N	Y	Y	N	Y
5 **Burr**	N	Y	Y	N	N	N	N
6 **Coble**	N	Y	Y	N	N	Y	N
7 McIntyre	N	N	N	Y	Y	Y	Y
8 Hefner	?	N	N	Y	N	Y	Y
9 **Myrick**	N	Y	Y	N	N	Y	Y
10 **Ballenger**	N	Y	Y	Y	N	N	N
11 **Taylor**	N	Y	Y	N	N	Y	N
12 Watt	N	N	N	Y	Y	Y	Y
NORTH DAKOTA							
AL Pomeroy	N	N	N	Y	N	N	N
OHIO							
1 **Chabot**	N	Y	Y	N	N	Y	N
2 **Portman**	N	Y	Y	N	N	Y	N
3 Hall	N	N	N	Y	N	N	N
4 **Oxley**	N	Y	Y	N	N	N	N
5 **Gillmor**	N	Y	Y	Y	N	N	N
6 Strickland	N	N	N	Y	Y	Y	Y
7 **Hobson**	N	Y	Y	N	N	N	N
8 **Boehner**	N	Y	Y	N	N	N	N
9 Kaptur	?	N	N	Y	N	Y	Y
10 Kucinich	N	N	N	Y	N	N	N
11 Stokes	N	N	N	Y	?	Y	N
12 **Kasich**	N	Y	Y	N	Y	Y	N
13 Brown	N	N	N	Y	Y	Y	Y
14 Sawyer	N	N	N	Y	Y	N	N
15 **Pryce**	N	Y	Y	N	N	N	N
16 **Regula**	N	Y	Y	Y	N	N	N
17 Traficant	N	Y	Y	Y	N	N	N
18 **Ney**	N	Y	Y	N	N	N	N
19 **LaTourette**	N	Y	Y	Y	N	Y	N
OKLAHOMA							
1 **Largent**	N	Y	Y	N	N	N	N
2 **Coburn**	N	Y	Y	N	N	N	N
3 **Watkins**	N	Y	Y	N	N	N	N
4 **Watts**	N	Y	Y	N	N	N	N
5 **Istook**	N	Y	Y	N	N	N	N
6 **Lucas**	N	Y	Y	N	N	N	N
OREGON							
1 Furse	N	N	N	Y	Y	Y	Y
2 **Smith**	N	Y	Y	N	N	Y	N
3 Blumenauer	N	N	N	Y	Y	Y	Y
4 DeFazio	Y	N	N	Y	Y	Y	Y
5 Hooley	N	N	N	Y	Y	Y	Y
PENNSYLVANIA							
1 Brady	N	N	N	Y	N	N	N
2 Fattah	N	N	N	Y	N	N	N
3 Borski	N	N	N	Y	N	N	N
4 Klink	N	N	N	Y	N	N	Y
5 **Peterson**	N	?	Y	N	N	Y	N
6 Holden	N	N	N	Y	N	N	N
7 **Weldon**	?	Y	Y	Y	Y	N	Y
8 **Greenwood**	N	Y	Y	Y	Y	N	Y
9 **Shuster**	N	Y	Y	N	N	N	N
10 **McDade**	?	?	?	?	N	N	N
11 Kanjorski	N	N	N	Y	N	N	?
12 Murtha	N	N	N	Y	N	N	N
13 **Fox**	N	Y	Y	Y	Y	N	Y
14 Coyne	N	N	N	Y	N	N	Y
15 McHale	?	N	N	Y	Y	N	Y
16 **Pitts**	N	Y	Y	N	Y	N	Y
17 **Gekas**	N	?	?	N	Y	Y	Y
18 Doyle	N	N	N	Y	N	N	N
19 **Goodling**	N	Y	Y	N	N	Y	N
20 Mascara	N	N	N	Y	N	N	N
21 **English**	N	Y	Y	Y	Y	N	N
RHODE ISLAND							
1 Kennedy	N	N	N	Y	Y	Y	Y
2 Weygand	N	N	N	Y	Y	Y	Y
SOUTH CAROLINA							
1 **Sanford**	N	Y	Y	N	N	N	N
2 **Spence**	N	Y	Y	N	N	N	N
3 **Graham**	N	Y	?	N	N	Y	Y
4 **Inglis**	N	Y	Y	N	N	N	Y
5 Spratt	N	N	N	Y	Y	Y	Y
6 Clyburn	N	N	N	Y	Y	Y	Y
SOUTH DAKOTA							
AL **Thune**	N	Y	Y	N	Y	Y	Y
TENNESSEE							
1 **Jenkins**	N	Y	Y	N	N	Y	N
2 **Duncan**	N	Y	Y	N	Y	Y	N
3 **Wamp**	N	Y	Y	N	N	N	N
4 **Hilleary**	N	Y	Y	N	N	N	N
5 Clement	N	N	N	Y	Y	N	Y
6 Gordon	N	N	N	Y	Y	N	N
7 **Bryant**	N	Y	Y	N	N	Y	N
8 Tanner	N	N	N	N	Y	Y	N
9 Ford	–	–	–	+	+	+	+
TEXAS							
1 Sandlin	N	N	N	Y	N	N	N
2 Turner	?	N	N	N	N	N	Y
3 **Johnson, Sam**	N	Y	Y	N	N	N	N
4 Hall	N	Y	Y	N	N	N	N
5 **Sessions**	N	Y	Y	N	N	N	N
6 **Barton**	N	Y	Y	N	N	N	N
7 **Archer**	N	Y	Y	N	N	Y	N
8 **Brady**	N	Y	Y	N	N	N	N
9 Lampson	N	N	N	Y	N	N	Y
10 Doggett	N	N	N	Y	Y	N	Y
11 Edwards	N	N	N	Y	N	N	N
12 **Granger**	N	Y	Y	Y	N	N	N
13 **Thornberry**	N	Y	Y	N	N	N	N
14 **Paul**	N	Y	Y	N	Y	Y	N
15 Hinojosa	N	–	–	Y	Y	Y	Y
16 Reyes	N	N	N	Y	N	N	Y
17 Stenholm	?	Y	Y	N	N	N	N
18 Jackson-Lee	N	N	N	Y	N	N	Y
19 **Combest**	N	Y	Y	N	N	N	N
20 Gonzalez	?	?	?	?	?	?	?
21 **Smith**	N	Y	Y	N	N	N	N
22 **DeLay**	?	Y	Y	N	N	N	N
23 **Bonilla**	N	Y	Y	N	N	N	N
24 Frost	N	N	N	Y	N	N	N
25 Bentsen	N	N	N	Y	N	N	N
26 **Armey**	?	Y	Y	N	N	Y	N
27 Ortiz	–	–	–	Y	N	N	N
28 Rodriguez	N	N	?	Y	Y	N	Y
29 Green	N	N	N	Y	N	N	N
30 Johnson, E.B.	N	N	N	Y	Y	N	N
UTAH							
1 **Hansen**	N	Y	Y	N	N	Y	N
2 **Cook**	N	Y	Y	Y	N	N	N
3 **Cannon**	N	Y	Y	N	N	Y	N
VERMONT							
AL *Sanders*	?	N	N	Y	Y	Y	Y
VIRGINIA							
1 **Bateman**	N	Y	Y	N	N	N	N
2 Pickett	?	N	N	Y	N	N	N
3 Scott	N	N	N	Y	Y	N	Y
4 Sisisky	N	N	N	Y	N	N	N
5 Goode	N	N	N	Y	Y	Y	Y
6 **Goodlatte**	N	Y	Y	N	N	Y	N
7 **Bliley**	N	Y	Y	N	N	N	N
8 Moran	N	N	N	Y	Y	N	Y
9 Boucher	N	N	N	Y	Y	Y	N
10 **Wolf**	N	Y	Y	N	N	N	N
11 **Davis**	N	Y	Y	Y	N	N	Y
WASHINGTON							
1 **White**	N	Y	Y	N	N	Y	N
2 **Metcalf**	N	Y	Y	N	Y	Y	N
3 **Smith, Linda**	N	Y	Y	N	N	Y	N
4 **Hastings**	N	Y	Y	N	N	Y	N
5 **Nethercutt**	N	Y	Y	N	N	Y	Y
6 Dicks	N	N	N	Y	N	Y	Y
7 McDermott	Y	N	N	Y	Y	N	Y
8 **Dunn**	?	Y	Y	N	N	Y	N
9 Smith, Adam	N	N	N	Y	Y	Y	Y
WEST VIRGINIA							
1 Mollohan	N	N	N	Y	N	N	N
2 Wise	N	N	N	Y	Y	N	N
3 Rahall	N	N	N	Y	Y	Y	N
WISCONSIN							
1 **Neumann**	N	Y	Y	N	Y	Y	Y
2 **Klug**	N	Y	Y	Y	N	Y	Y
3 Kind	N	N	N	Y	Y	Y	Y
4 Kleczka	N	N	N	Y	Y	Y	Y
5 Barrett	N	N	N	Y	Y	Y	Y
6 **Petri**	N	Y	Y	N	Y	Y	Y
7 Obey	N	N	N	Y	Y	Y	Y
8 Johnson	N	N	N	Y	Y	Y	Y
9 **Sensenbrenner**	N	Y	Y	N	N	Y	N
WYOMING							
AL **Cubin**	N	Y	Y	N	N	Y	N

Southern states - Ala., Ark., Fla., Ga., Ky., La., Miss., N.C., Okla., S.C., Tenn., Texas, Va.

316. Quorum Call.* 408 Responded. July 22, 1998.

317. H J Res 121. "Normal Trade Relations" Status for China Disapproval/Passage. Passage of the bill to deny the president's request to provide "normal trade relations" (formerly known as "most-favored-nation" or MFN trade status) for items produced in China for the period July 1998 through July 1999. Rejected 166-264: R 78-149; D 87-115 (ND 73-76, SD 14-39); I 1-0. July 22, 1998.

318. HR 1689. Securities Litigation Federal Filing Requirement/Passage. Bliley, R-Va., motion to suspend the rules and pass the bill to require class action lawsuits alleging securities fraud to be filed in federal rather than state courts. Motion agreed to 340-83: R 221-2; D 119-80 (ND 82-65, SD 37-15); I 0-1. July 22, 1998. A two-thirds majority of those present and voting (283 in this case) is required for passage under suspension of the rules.

319. HR 4193. Fiscal 1999 Interior Appropriations/Indian Health Service Support Costs Allocation. Parker, R-Miss., amendment to strike a provision in the bill that directs the Indian Health Service to allocate contract support costs funding on a pro rata basis to all tribal contractors. Rejected 135-289: R 46-178; D 89-110 (ND 67-80, SD 22-30); I 0-1. July 22, 1998.

320. HR 4193. Fiscal 1999 Interior Appropriations/Trust Fund Use Restrictions. Miller, D-Calif., amendment to prohibit the use of certain trust funds (the Knuston-Vandenberg restoration fund and the timber salvage fund) from being used for administrative overhead expenses. Adopted 236-182: R 58-163; D 177-19 (ND 137-9, SD 40-10); I 1-0. July 22, 1998.

321. HR 1122. Abortion Procedure Ban/Discharge Motion. Canady, R-Fla., motion to discharge from the Judiciary Committee and bring to the House floor the bill that would ban certain late-term abortion procedures. Motion agreed to 295-131: R 219-6; D 76-124 (ND 49-99, SD 27-25); I 0-1. July 23, 1998.

322. HR 3616. Fiscal 1999 Defense Authorization/Motion to Instruct. Skelton, D-Mo., motion to instruct the House conferees to insist upon the House bill's authorization levels for Theater Missile Defense programs and space-based lasers. Motion agreed to 424-0: R 225-0; D 198-0 (ND 147-0, SD 51-0); I 1-0. July 23, 1998.

323. HR 3616. Fiscal 1999 Defense Authorization/Closed Conference. Spence, R-S.C., motion to close portions of the conference to the public during consideration of national security issues. Motion agreed to 412-5: R 217-0; D 194-5 (ND 142-5, SD 52-0); I 1-0. July 23, 1998.

* CQ does not include quorum calls in its vote charts.

Key

Y	Voted for (yea).
#	Paired for.
+	Announced for.
N	Voted against (nay).
X	Paired against.
–	Announced against.
P	Voted "present."
C	Voted "present" to avoid possible conflict of interest.
?	Did not vote or otherwise make a position known.

Democrats **Republicans** *Independent*

	317	318	319	320	321	322	323
ALABAMA							
1 *Callahan*	N	Y	N	N	Y	Y	Y
2 *Everett*	Y	Y	N	N	Y	Y	Y
3 *Riley*	Y	Y	Y	N	Y	Y	Y
4 *Aderholt*	Y	Y	Y	N	Y	Y	Y
5 Cramer	N	Y	N	Y	Y	Y	Y
6 *Bachus*	N	Y	N	N	Y	Y	Y
7 Hilliard	N	N	Y	Y	N	Y	Y
ALASKA							
AL *Young*	Y	Y	N	N	Y	Y	Y
ARIZONA							
1 *Salmon*	N	Y	Y	Y	Y	Y	Y
2 Pastor	N	N	Y	N	N	Y	Y
3 *Stump*	N	Y	N	N	Y	Y	?
4 *Shadegg*	N	Y	N	N	Y	Y	Y
5 *Kolbe*	N	Y	N	Y	Y	Y	Y
6 *Hayworth*	N	Y	N	N	Y	Y	Y
ARKANSAS							
1 Berry	N	Y	N	Y	Y	Y	Y
2 Snyder	N	Y	N	Y	N	Y	Y
3 *Hutchinson*	N	Y	N	N	Y	Y	Y
4 *Dickey*	Y	Y	N	N	Y	Y	Y
CALIFORNIA							
1 *Riggs*	N	Y	N	N	Y	Y	Y
2 *Herger*	N	?	N	N	Y	Y	Y
3 Fazio	N	Y	N	Y	N	Y	Y
4 *Doolittle*	Y	Y	Y	N	Y	Y	Y
5 Matsui	N	Y	N	Y	N	Y	Y
6 Woolsey	Y	N	N	Y	N	N	N
7 Miller	Y	Y	N	Y	N	Y	Y
8 Pelosi	Y	Y	N	Y	N	Y	?
9 Lee	Y	N	Y	Y	N	Y	Y
10 Tauscher	N	Y	N	Y	N	Y	Y
11 *Pombo*	Y	Y	Y	N	Y	Y	Y
12 Lantos	Y	Y	N	Y	N	Y	Y
13 Stark	Y	N	N	Y	N	Y	N
14 Eshoo	N	Y	N	Y	N	Y	Y
15 *Campbell*	N	Y	N	N	Y	N	Y
16 Lofgren	N	Y	N	Y	N	Y	Y
17 Farr	N	Y	N	Y	N	Y	Y
18 Condit	Y	Y	Y	?	Y	Y	Y
19 *Radanovich*	N	Y	+	–	Y	Y	Y
20 Dooley	N	Y	N	Y	N	Y	Y
21 *Thomas*	N	Y	N	N	Y	Y	Y
22 Capps, L.	N	Y	Y	Y	N	Y	Y
23 *Gallegly*	Y	Y	N	N	Y	Y	Y
24 Sherman	N	Y	N	Y	N	Y	Y
25 *McKeon*	N	Y	N	N	Y	Y	Y
26 Berman	N	N	N	Y	N	Y	Y
27 *Rogan*	N	Y	N	N	Y	Y	Y
28 *Dreier*	N	Y	N	N	Y	Y	Y
29 Waxman	Y	N	Y	Y	N	Y	Y
30 Becerra	N	N	N	Y	N	Y	Y
31 Martinez	N	Y	N	Y	N	Y	Y
32 Dixon	N	N	N	Y	N	Y	Y
33 Roybal-Allard	N	N	Y	Y	N	Y	Y
34 Torres	Y	N	Y	Y	N	Y	Y
35 Waters	Y	Y	Y	Y	N	Y	Y
36 Harman	N	Y	N	Y	N	Y	Y
37 Millender-McD.	N	N	Y	Y	N	Y	Y

	317	318	319	320	321	322	323
38 *Horn*	Y	Y	N	Y	N	Y	Y
39 *Royce*	Y	Y	N	N	Y	Y	Y
40 *Lewis*	N	Y	N	N	Y	Y	Y
41 *Kim*	N	Y	N	N	Y	Y	Y
42 Brown	N	N	Y	N	Y	N	Y
43 *Calvert*	N	Y	N	N	Y	Y	Y
44 *Bono, M.*	N	Y	N	N	Y	Y	Y
45 *Rohrabacher*	Y	Y	Y	Y	Y	Y	Y
46 Sanchez	Y	Y	N	Y	N	Y	Y
47 *Cox*	Y	Y	N	Y	N	Y	Y
48 *Packard*	N	Y	N	N	Y	Y	Y
49 *Bilbray*	N	Y	Y	Y	Y	Y	Y
50 Filner	N	N	Y	Y	N	Y	Y
51 *Cunningham*	N	Y	N	N	Y	Y	Y
52 *Hunter*	Y	Y	?	?	Y	Y	?
COLORADO							
1 DeGette	N	N	N	Y	N	Y	Y
2 Skaggs	N	N	N	Y	N	Y	Y
3 *McInnis*	N	Y	N	N	Y	Y	Y
4 *Schaffer*	Y	Y	N	N	Y	Y	Y
5 *Hefley*	Y	Y	N	N	Y	Y	Y
6 *Schaefer*	Y	Y	Y	Y	Y	Y	Y
CONNECTICUT							
1 Kennelly	N	Y	N	Y	N	Y	Y
2 Gejdenson	Y	Y	N	Y	N	Y	Y
3 DeLauro	Y	Y	Y	Y	N	Y	Y
4 *Shays*	N	Y	N	Y	N	Y	Y
5 Maloney	Y	Y	N	Y	N	Y	Y
6 *Johnson*	N	N	N	Y	N	Y	Y
DELAWARE							
AL *Castle*	N	N	N	Y	N	Y	Y
FLORIDA							
1 *Scarborough*	Y	Y	Y	Y	Y	Y	Y
2 Boyd	N	N	N	Y	N	Y	Y
3 Brown	N	N	N	Y	N	Y	Y
4 *Fowler*	Y	Y	N	N	Y	Y	Y
5 Thurman	N	N	Y	Y	N	Y	Y
6 *Stearns*	Y	Y	?	Y	Y	Y	Y
7 *Mica*	N	Y	N	N	Y	Y	Y
8 *McCollum*	N	Y	N	N	Y	Y	Y
9 *Bilirakis*	N	Y	N	N	Y	Y	Y
10 *Young*	?	?	?	?	?	?	?
11 Davis	N	Y	Y	Y	N	Y	Y
12 *Canady*	N	Y	N	N	Y	Y	Y
13 *Miller*	N	Y	N	N	Y	Y	Y
14 *Goss*	N	Y	N	N	Y	Y	Y
15 *Weldon*	Y	Y	N	N	Y	Y	Y
16 *Foley*	N	Y	N	N	Y	Y	Y
17 Meek	N	N	Y	N	Y	Y	Y
18 *Ros-Lehtinen*	Y	Y	N	Y	N	Y	Y
19 Wexler	Y	Y	Y	N	Y	Y	Y
20 Deutsch	N	Y	Y	N	Y	Y	Y
21 *Diaz-Balart*	Y	Y	N	Y	N	Y	Y
22 *Shaw*	N	Y	N	N	Y	Y	Y
23 Hastings	Y	Y	Y	Y	N	Y	Y
GEORGIA							
1 *Kingston*	Y	Y	N	N	Y	Y	Y
2 Bishop	Y	Y	Y	N	Y	Y	Y
3 *Collins*	Y	Y	N	N	Y	Y	Y
4 McKinney	Y	N	Y	N	P	Y	Y
5 Lewis	Y	N	N	?	N	Y	Y
6 *Gingrich*	N	Y					
7 *Barr*	Y	Y	N	N	Y	Y	Y
8 *Chambliss*	Y	Y	N	N	Y	Y	Y
9 *Deal*	Y	Y	N	N	Y	Y	Y
10 *Norwood*	Y	Y	N	N	Y	Y	Y
11 *Linder*	N	Y	N	N	Y	Y	Y
HAWAII							
1 Abercrombie	Y	N	N	Y	N	?	Y
2 Mink	Y	N	N	Y	N	Y	Y
IDAHO							
1 *Chenoweth*	Y	Y	N	N	Y	Y	Y
2 *Crapo*	N	Y	N	N	Y	Y	Y
ILLINOIS							
1 Rush	N	Y	Y	Y	N	Y	Y
2 Jackson	Y	N	Y	Y	N	Y	Y
3 Lipinski	Y	N	N	Y	N	Y	Y
4 Gutierrez	Y	N	N	Y	N	Y	Y
5 Blagojevich	N	N	Y	N	Y	Y	Y
6 *Hyde*	Y	Y	N	N	Y	Y	Y
7 Davis	N	N	Y	Y	N	Y	Y
8 *Crane*	N	Y	N	N	Y	Y	Y
9 Yates	Y	N	N	Y	N	Y	Y
10 *Porter*	N	Y	N	Y	N	Y	Y
11 *Weller*	Y	Y	N	N	Y	Y	Y
12 Costello	Y	N	N	Y	Y	Y	Y

ND Northern Democrats   SD Southern Democrats

	317	318	319	320	321	322	323
13 ***Fawell***	N	?	N	Y	Y	Y	?
14 ***Hastert***	N	Y	Y	N	Y	Y	Y
15 ***Ewing***	N	Y	N	N	Y	Y	Y
16 ***Manzullo***	N	Y	N	N	Y	Y	Y
17 Evans	Y	N	N	Y	N	Y	Y
18 ***LaHood***	N	Y	N	Y	Y	Y	Y
19 Poshard	N	Y	?	?	Y	Y	Y
20 ***Shimkus***	N	Y	N	N	Y	Y	Y
INDIANA							
1 Visclosky	Y	Y	N	N	Y	Y	Y
2 ***McIntosh***	N	Y	Y	N	Y	Y	Y
3 Roemer	N	Y	N	Y	Y	Y	Y
4 ***Souder***	Y	Y	N	N	Y	Y	Y
5 ***Buyer***	N	Y	N	N	Y	Y	?
6 ***Burton***	Y	Y	N	N	Y	Y	Y
7 ***Pease***	N	Y	N	N	Y	Y	Y
8 ***Hostettler***	Y	Y	N	N	Y	Y	Y
9 Hamilton	N	Y	N	Y	Y	Y	Y
10 Carson	Y	N	N	Y	N	Y	Y
IOWA							
1 ***Leach***	N	Y	N	Y	Y	?	Y
2 ***Nussle***	N	Y	Y	N	Y	Y	Y
3 Boswell	N	Y	Y	Y	Y	Y	Y
4 ***Ganske***	Y	Y	N	Y	Y	Y	Y
5 ***Latham***	N	Y	Y	N	Y	Y	Y
KANSAS							
1 ***Moran***	N	Y	Y	N	Y	Y	Y
2 ***Ryun***	N	Y	N	N	Y	Y	Y
3 ***Snowbarger***	N	Y	N	N	Y	Y	Y
4 ***Tiahrt***	Y	Y	N	N	Y	Y	Y
KENTUCKY							
1 ***Whitfield***	N	Y	N	N	Y	Y	Y
2 ***Lewis***	N	Y	N	N	Y	Y	Y
3 ***Northup***	N	Y	N	N	Y	Y	Y
4 ***Bunning***	Y	Y	N	N	Y	Y	Y
5 ***Rogers***	Y	Y	N	N	Y	Y	Y
6 Baesler	N	Y	N	Y	Y	Y	Y
LOUISIANA							
1 ***Livingston***	N	Y	N	N	Y	Y	Y
2 Jefferson	N	Y	Y	Y	Y	Y	Y
3 ***Tauzin***	N	Y	N	N	Y	Y	Y
4 ***McCrery***	N	Y	N	N	Y	Y	Y
5 ***Cooksey***	N	Y	N	N	Y	Y	?
6 ***Baker***	N	Y	N	N	Y	Y	Y
7 John	N	Y	N	+	Y	Y	Y
MAINE							
1 Allen	N	Y	N	Y	N	Y	Y
2 Baldacci	N	N	N	Y	N	Y	Y
MARYLAND							
1 ***Gilchrest***	N	Y	N	N	Y	Y	Y
2 ***Ehrlich***	Y	Y	N	N	Y	Y	Y
3 Cardin	Y	Y	Y	Y	N	Y	Y
4 Wynn	Y	Y	N	Y	N	Y	Y
5 Hoyer	Y	Y	N	N	N	Y	Y
6 ***Bartlett***	Y	Y	Y	Y	Y	Y	Y
7 Cummings	Y	N	N	Y	N	Y	Y
8 ***Morella***	N	Y	N	Y	N	Y	Y
MASSACHUSETTS							
1 Olver	Y	N	N	Y	N	Y	Y
2 Neal	N	Y	N	Y	Y	Y	Y
3 McGovern	N	Y	Y	Y	N	Y	Y
4 Frank	Y	Y	N	Y	N	Y	Y
5 Meehan	N	Y	N	Y	N	Y	Y
6 Tierney	Y	N	N	Y	N	Y	Y
7 Markey	Y	N	?	?	?	?	?
8 Kennedy	Y	Y	Y	Y	N	Y	Y
9 Moakley	N	Y	?	?	Y	Y	Y
10 Delahunt	Y	N	Y	Y	N	Y	Y
MICHIGAN							
1 Stupak	Y	N	Y	Y	Y	Y	Y
2 ***Hoekstra***	N	Y	N	N	Y	Y	Y
3 ***Ehlers***	N	Y	N	N	Y	Y	Y
4 ***Camp***	N	Y	Y	N	Y	Y	Y
5 Barcia	Y	Y	Y	Y	Y	Y	Y
6 ***Upton***	N	Y	N	Y	Y	Y	Y
7 ***Smith***	N	Y	N	N	Y	Y	Y
8 Stabenow	N	Y	Y	Y	N	Y	Y
9 Kildee	Y	Y	Y	Y	Y	Y	Y
10 Bonior	Y	N	Y	Y	Y	Y	Y
11 ***Knollenberg***	N	Y	N	N	Y	Y	Y
12 Levin	N	N	Y	Y	N	Y	Y
13 Rivers	Y	N	Y	Y	N	Y	Y
14 Conyers	N	N	N	Y	N	Y	N
15 Kilpatrick	Y	Y	Y	Y	N	Y	Y
16 Dingell	N	N	N	Y	Y	Y	Y

	317	318	319	320	321	322	323
MINNESOTA							
1 ***Gutknecht***	N	Y	N	N	Y	Y	Y
2 Minge	N	Y	Y	Y	Y	Y	Y
3 ***Ramstad***	N	Y	Y	Y	Y	Y	Y
4 Vento	Y	Y	Y	Y	N	Y	Y
5 Sabo	Y	Y	Y	N	N	Y	Y
6 Luther	N	Y	N	Y	N	Y	Y
7 Peterson	N	Y	Y	N	Y	Y	Y
8 Oberstar	N	N	Y	Y	Y	Y	Y
MISSISSIPPI							
1 ***Wicker***	N	Y	Y	N	Y	Y	Y
2 Thompson	Y	N	Y	Y	N	Y	Y
3 ***Pickering***	Y	Y	Y	N	Y	Y	Y
4 ***Parker***	N	Y	Y	N	Y	Y	Y
5 Taylor	Y	N	Y	N	Y	Y	Y
MISSOURI							
1 Clay	Y	N	Y	?	N	Y	Y
2 ***Talent***	N	Y	N	N	Y	Y	Y
3 Gephardt	Y	N	N	Y	Y	Y	Y
4 Skelton	N	Y	N	Y	Y	Y	Y
5 McCarthy	N	Y	N	Y	N	Y	Y
6 Danner	Y	Y	N	Y	Y	Y	Y
7 ***Blunt***	Y	N	N	Y	Y	Y	?
8 ***Emerson***	N	Y	N	N	Y	Y	Y
9 ***Hulshof***	N	Y	Y	Y	Y	Y	Y
MONTANA							
AL ***Hill***	N	Y	N	N	Y	Y	Y
NEBRASKA							
1 ***Bereuter***	N	Y	N	N	Y	Y	Y
2 ***Christensen***	Y	Y	N	N	Y	Y	Y
3 ***Barrett***	N	Y	N	N	Y	Y	Y
NEVADA							
1 ***Ensign***	Y	Y	N	Y	Y	Y	Y
2 ***Gibbons***	Y	Y	N	Y	Y	Y	Y
NEW HAMPSHIRE							
1 ***Sununu***	Y	Y	Y	N	Y	Y	Y
2 ***Bass***	N	Y	N	N	Y	Y	Y
NEW JERSEY							
1 Andrews	N	Y	N	Y	N	Y	Y
2 ***LoBiondo***	Y	Y	Y	Y	Y	Y	Y
3 ***Saxton***	Y	Y	Y	Y	Y	Y	Y
4 ***Smith***	Y	Y	N	Y	Y	Y	Y
5 ***Roukema***	N	Y	N	Y	Y	Y	Y
6 Pallone	Y	Y	Y	Y	N	Y	Y
7 ***Franks***	N	Y	N	Y	Y	Y	Y
8 Pascrell	Y	Y	N	Y	Y	Y	Y
9 Rothman	Y	Y	Y	Y	N	Y	Y
10 Payne	Y	N	Y	Y	N	Y	Y
11 ***Frelinghuysen***	N	Y	N	N	Y	Y	Y
12 ***Pappas***	Y	Y	N	Y	Y	Y	Y
13 Menendez	Y	N	Y	Y	N	Y	Y
NEW MEXICO							
1 ***Wilson***	N	Y	N	N	Y	Y	Y
2 ***Skeen***	N	Y	N	N	Y	Y	Y
3 ***Redmond***	N	Y	Y	N	Y	Y	Y
NEW YORK							
1 ***Forbes***	Y	Y	N	Y	Y	Y	Y
2 ***Lazio***	N	Y	Y	Y	Y	Y	?
3 ***King***	Y	Y	N	Y	Y	Y	Y
4 McCarthy	Y	Y	N	Y	N	Y	Y
5 Ackerman	N	Y	N	Y	N	Y	Y
6 Meeks	N	Y	Y	Y	N	Y	Y
7 Manton	N	Y	Y	Y	Y	Y	Y
8 Nadler	Y	N	N	Y	N	Y	Y
9 Schumer	N	N	N	Y	N	Y	Y
10 Towns	N	Y	N	Y	N	Y	Y
11 Owens	Y	N	N	Y	N	Y	Y
12 Velázquez	Y	Y	N	Y	N	Y	Y
13 ***Fossella***	N	Y	Y	Y	Y	Y	Y
14 Maloney	N	Y	N	Y	N	Y	Y
15 Rangel	N	Y	Y	Y	N	Y	Y
16 Serrano	–	–	–	+	–	+	+
17 Engel	Y	N	Y	Y	N	Y	Y
18 Lowey	N	P	N	Y	N	Y	Y
19 ***Kelly***	N	Y	N	?	Y	Y	Y
20 ***Gilman***	Y	Y	N	Y	N	Y	Y
21 McNulty	?	?	Y	Y	Y	Y	Y
22 ***Solomon***	Y	Y	N	N	Y	Y	Y
23 ***Boehlert***	N	Y	N	Y	Y	Y	Y
24 ***McHugh***	N	Y	N	N	Y	Y	Y
25 ***Walsh***	N	Y	N	Y	Y	Y	Y
26 Hinchey	Y	N	N	Y	Y	Y	Y
27 ***Paxon***	N	Y	N	N	Y	Y	Y
28 Slaughter	N	Y	N	Y	N	Y	Y
29 LaFalce	N	Y	N	Y	Y	Y	Y

	317	318	319	320	321	322	323
30 ***Quinn***	N	Y	N	Y	Y	Y	Y
31 ***Houghton***	N	Y	N	Y	Y	Y	Y
NORTH CAROLINA							
1 Clayton	Y	N	N	Y	N	Y	Y
2 Etheridge	N	Y	N	Y	Y	Y	Y
3 ***Jones***	Y	Y	N	N	Y	Y	Y
4 Price	N	Y	N	Y	N	Y	Y
5 ***Burr***	Y	Y	Y	N	Y	Y	Y
6 ***Coble***	N	Y	N	N	Y	Y	Y
7 McIntyre	Y	Y	Y	Y	Y	Y	Y
8 Hefner	Y	Y	Y	Y	Y	Y	Y
9 ***Myrick***	Y	Y	N	N	Y	Y	Y
10 ***Ballenger***	N	Y	N	Y	Y	Y	Y
11 ***Taylor***	Y	Y	N	N	Y	Y	Y
12 Watt	N	N	N	Y	N	Y	Y
NORTH DAKOTA							
AL Pomeroy	N	Y	Y	Y	Y	Y	Y
OHIO							
1 ***Chabot***	N	Y	N	Y	Y	Y	Y
2 ***Portman***	N	Y	N	Y	Y	Y	Y
3 Hall	Y	N	N	Y	Y	Y	Y
4 ***Oxley***	N	Y	N	N	Y	Y	Y
5 ***Gillmor***	N	Y	N	N	Y	Y	Y
6 Strickland	Y	Y	N	Y	Y	Y	Y
7 ***Hobson***	Y	Y	N	N	Y	Y	Y
8 ***Boehner***	N	Y	Y	N	Y	Y	Y
9 Kaptur	Y	N	N	Y	Y	Y	Y
10 Kucinich	Y	N	Y	Y	Y	Y	Y
11 Stokes	Y	N	Y	Y	N	Y	Y
12 ***Kasich***	Y	Y	N	N	Y	Y	Y
13 Brown	Y	Y	N	Y	N	Y	Y
14 Sawyer	N	Y	N	Y	N	Y	Y
15 ***Pryce***	N	Y	N	N	Y	Y	Y
16 ***Regula***	N	Y	N	N	Y	Y	Y
17 Traficant	Y	Y	Y	Y	Y	Y	Y
18 ***Ney***	Y	Y	N	Y	Y	Y	Y
19 ***LaTourette***	N	Y	N	Y	Y	Y	Y
OKLAHOMA							
1 ***Largent***	N	Y	N	N	Y	Y	Y
2 ***Coburn***	Y	Y	N	N	Y	Y	Y
3 ***Watkins***	N	Y	N	N	Y	Y	Y
4 ***Watts***	N	Y	N	N	Y	Y	Y
5 ***Istook***	N	Y	N	N	Y	Y	Y
6 ***Lucas***	N	Y	N	N	Y	Y	Y
OREGON							
1 Furse	N	Y	Y	Y	N	Y	N
2 ***Smith***	N	Y	N	N	Y	Y	Y
3 Blumenauer	N	Y	N	Y	N	Y	Y
4 DeFazio	Y	N	Y	Y	N	Y	N
5 Hooley	N	+	Y	Y	N	Y	Y
PENNSYLVANIA							
1 Brady	Y	N	N	Y	N	Y	Y
2 Fattah	N	N	Y	Y	N	Y	Y
3 Borski	Y	N	N	Y	Y	Y	Y
4 Klink	Y	N	Y	N	Y	Y	Y
5 ***Peterson***	N	Y	N	N	Y	Y	Y
6 Holden	N	Y	Y	Y	Y	Y	Y
7 ***Weldon***	N	Y	N	Y	Y	Y	Y
8 ***Greenwood***	N	Y	Y	Y	N	Y	Y
9 ***Shuster***	N	Y	N	N	Y	Y	Y
10 ***McDade***	Y	Y	N	N	Y	Y	Y
11 Kanjorski	N	N	N	Y	Y	Y	Y
12 Murtha	N	Y	N	N	Y	?	?
13 ***Fox***	N	Y	N	Y	Y	Y	Y
14 Coyne	Y	N	Y	Y	N	Y	Y
15 McHale	N	Y	Y	Y	Y	Y	Y
16 ***Pitts***	N	Y	Y	N	Y	Y	Y
17 ***Gekas***	N	Y	N	N	Y	Y	Y
18 Doyle	N	Y	N	Y	Y	Y	Y
19 ***Goodling***	Y	Y	N	N	Y	Y	Y
20 Mascara	Y	Y	N	Y	Y	Y	Y
21 ***English***	N	Y	Y	Y	Y	Y	Y
RHODE ISLAND							
1 Kennedy	Y	Y	Y	Y	Y	Y	Y
2 Weygand	Y	Y	Y	Y	Y	Y	Y
SOUTH CAROLINA							
1 ***Sanford***	Y	Y	N	N	Y	Y	?
2 ***Spence***	Y	Y	N	N	Y	Y	Y
3 ***Graham***	Y	Y	N	N	Y	Y	Y
4 ***Inglis***	Y	Y	N	N	Y	Y	Y
5 Spratt	Y	Y	Y	Y	Y	Y	Y
6 Clyburn	Y	N	Y	Y	N	Y	Y
SOUTH DAKOTA							
AL ***Thune***	N	Y	N	N	Y	Y	Y

	317	318	319	320	321	322	323
TENNESSEE							
1 ***Jenkins***	Y	Y	Y	N	Y	Y	Y
2 ***Duncan***	Y	Y	N	N	Y	Y	Y
3 ***Wamp***	Y	Y	N	N	Y	Y	Y
4 ***Hilleary***	Y	Y	Y	N	Y	Y	Y
5 Clement	N	Y	N	Y	Y	Y	Y
6 Gordon	N	Y	N	Y	Y	Y	Y
7 ***Bryant***	N	Y	Y	N	Y	Y	Y
8 Tanner	N	Y	N	Y	Y	Y	Y
9 Ford	–	+	–	+	–	+	+
TEXAS							
1 Sandlin	N	Y	Y	N	Y	Y	Y
2 Turner	N	Y	Y	N	Y	Y	Y
3 ***Johnson, Sam***	N	Y	N	N	Y	Y	Y
4 Hall	N	?	Y	N	Y	Y	Y
5 ***Sessions***	N	Y	N	N	Y	Y	Y
6 ***Barton***	Y	Y	N	N	Y	Y	Y
7 ***Archer***	N	Y	N	N	Y	Y	Y
8 ***Brady***	N	Y	N	N	Y	Y	Y
9 Lampson	N	Y	Y	Y	Y	Y	Y
10 Doggett	N	N	N	Y	N	Y	Y
11 Edwards	N	Y	N	N	N	Y	Y
12 ***Granger***	N	Y	N	N	Y	Y	Y
13 ***Thornberry***	N	Y	N	N	Y	Y	Y
14 ***Paul***	N	N	N	Y	Y	Y	Y
15 Hinojosa	N	Y	N	Y	Y	Y	Y
16 Reyes	N	Y	Y	Y	Y	Y	Y
17 Stenholm	N	Y	N	N	Y	Y	Y
18 Jackson-Lee	N	Y	N	Y	N	Y	Y
19 ***Combest***	N	Y	Y	N	Y	Y	Y
20 Gonzalez	?	?	?	?	?	?	?
21 ***Smith***	N	Y	N	N	?	Y	Y
22 ***DeLay***	N	Y	Y	N	Y	Y	Y
23 ***Bonilla***	N	Y	N	N	Y	Y	Y
24 Frost	N	N	N	Y	N	Y	Y
25 Bentsen	N	Y	N	Y	N	Y	Y
26 ***Armey***	N	Y	Y	N	Y	Y	Y
27 Ortiz	N	Y	N	Y	Y	Y	Y
28 Rodriguez	N	Y	N	Y	N	Y	Y
29 Green	N	Y	–	+	–	+	?
30 Johnson, E.B.	N	N	N	Y	N	Y	Y
UTAH							
1 ***Hansen***	N	Y	N	N	Y	Y	?
2 ***Cook***	Y	Y	N	Y	Y	Y	Y
3 ***Cannon***	N	Y	N	N	Y	Y	Y
VERMONT							
AL *Sanders*	Y	N	N	Y	N	Y	Y
VIRGINIA							
1 ***Bateman***	N	Y	Y	N	Y	Y	Y
2 Pickett	N	Y	N	N	N	Y	Y
3 Scott	N	N	Y	Y	N	Y	Y
4 Sisisky	Y	Y	N	N	Y	Y	Y
5 Goode	Y	Y	N	Y	Y	Y	Y
6 ***Goodlatte***	N	+	N	N	Y	Y	Y
7 ***Bliley***	N	Y	Y	N	Y	Y	Y
8 Moran	N	Y	N	N	Y	Y	Y
9 Boucher	N	Y	N	Y	N	Y	Y
10 ***Wolf***	Y	Y	N	N	Y	Y	Y
11 ***Davis***	N	Y	N	N	Y	Y	Y
WASHINGTON							
1 ***White***	N	Y	N	N	Y	Y	Y
2 ***Metcalf***	N	Y	N	Y	Y	Y	Y
3 ***Smith, Linda***	Y	Y	N	?	Y	Y	Y
4 ***Hastings***	N	Y	N	N	Y	Y	Y
5 ***Nethercutt***	N	Y	N	N	Y	Y	Y
6 Dicks	N	N	Y	N	N	Y	Y
7 McDermott	N	N	Y	Y	N	Y	Y
8 ***Dunn***	N	Y	N	N	Y	Y	Y
9 Smith, Adam	N	Y	Y	Y	N	Y	Y
WEST VIRGINIA							
1 Mollohan	Y	N	N	N	Y	Y	Y
2 Wise	N	N	N	Y	N	Y	Y
3 Rahall	N	N	N	Y	Y	Y	Y
WISCONSIN							
1 ***Neumann***	Y	Y	N	Y	Y	Y	Y
2 ***Klug***	Y	Y	N	Y	Y	Y	Y
3 Kind	N	Y	Y	Y	Y	Y	Y
4 Kleczka	N	Y	Y	Y	Y	Y	Y
5 Barrett	N	Y	Y	Y	Y	Y	Y
6 ***Petri***	N	Y	N	Y	Y	Y	Y
7 Obey	Y	N	Y	Y	Y	Y	Y
8 Johnson	N	Y	Y	Y	Y	Y	Y
9 ***Sensenbrenner***	Y	Y	N	Y	Y	Y	Y
WYOMING							
AL ***Cubin***	N	?	N	N	Y	Y	Y

Southern states - Ala., Ark., Fla., Ga., Ky., La., Miss., N.C., Okla., S.C., Tenn., Texas, Va.

Key

Y	Voted for (yea).
#	Paired for.
+	Announced for.
N	Voted against (nay).
X	Paired against.
–	Announced against.
P	Voted "present."
C	Voted "present" to avoid possible conflict of interest.
?	Did not vote or otherwise make a position known.

Democrats   **Republicans**
Independent

324. Quorum Call.* 400 responded. July 23, 1998.

325. HR 1122. Abortion Procedure Ban/Veto Override. Passage, over President Clinton's Oct. 10, 1997 veto of the bill to ban certain late-term abortion procedures. Passed 296-132: R 219-8; D 77-123 (ND 50-98, SD 27-25); I 0-1. July 23, 1998. A two-thirds majority of those present and voting (286 in this case) of both houses is required to override a veto. A "nay" was a vote in support of the president's position.

326. HR 4193. Fiscal 1999 Interior Appropriations/National Parks Fee-Collection Programs. DeFazio, D-Ore., amendment to strike the bill's provision that extends for two years the fee-collection demonstration program in effect at various sites of the National Park Service, Forest Service, Bureau of Land Management and Fish and Wildlife Service. Rejected 81-341: R 33-190; D 47-151 (ND 40-107, SD 7-43); I 1-0. July 23, 1998.

327. HR 4193. Fiscal 1999 Interior Appropriations/Columbia River Watershed Management. McDermott, D-Wash., amendment to strike the bill's provisions that place certain limitations on the use of funds for implementation of the proposed regional strategy to manage the Columbia River watershed. Rejected 202-221: R 15-208; D 186-13 (ND 141-6, SD 45-7); I 1-0. July 23, 1998. A "yea" was a vote in support of the president's position.

328. HR 4193. Fiscal 1999 Interior Appropriations/Chugach National Forest Road Construction. Hinchey, D-N.Y., amendment to strike the bill's provisions providing for a road construction easement in the Chugach National Forest in Alaska. Rejected 176-249: R 35-191; D 140-58 (ND 118-28, SD 22-30); I 1-0. July 23, 1998.

329. HR 4193. Fiscal 1999 Interior Appropriations/Tongass National Forest Road Construction Prohibition. Miller, D-Calif., amendment to prohibit the use of funds in the bill for new road construction in the Tongass National Forest in Alaska. Rejected 186-237: R 16-206; D 169-31 (ND 135-13, SD 34-18); I 1-0. July 23, 1998.

330. HR 4193. Fiscal 1999 Interior Appropriations/National Park Service Funding Increase. Pappas, R-N.J., amendment to increase funding for National Park Service land acquisition and state assistance by $50 million. The amendment offsets the increase by reducing funding for the National Endowment for the Arts. Rejected 139-285: R 134-90; D 5-194 (ND 1-146, SD 4-48); I 0-1. July 23, 1998.

331. HR 4193. Fiscal 1999 Interior Appropriations/Passage. Passage of the bill to provide $13.4 billion in funding for the Interior Department and related agencies. The bill provides $695 million less than requested by the president. Passed 245-181: R 207-18; D 38-162 (ND 24-124, SD 14-38); I 0-1. July 23, 1998.

* CQ does not include quorum calls in its vote charts.

	325	326	327	328	329	330	331
ALABAMA							
1 *Callahan*	Y	N	N	N	N	Y	Y
2 *Everett*	Y	N	N	N	N	Y	N
3 *Riley*	Y	N	N	N	N	Y	Y
4 *Aderholt*	Y	N	N	N	N	Y	Y
5 Cramer	Y	N	Y	N	Y	N	N
6 *Bachus*	Y	N	N	N	N	Y	Y
7 Hilliard	N	N	Y	N	Y	N	N
ALASKA							
AL *Young*	Y	N	N	N	N	Y	Y
ARIZONA							
1 *Salmon*	Y	Y	N	N	N	Y	Y
2 Pastor	N	N	Y	Y	Y	N	N
3 *Stump*	Y	N	N	N	N	N	N
4 *Shadegg*	Y	Y	N	N	N	Y	Y
5 *Kolbe*	N	N	N	N	N	N	Y
6 *Hayworth*	Y	Y	N	N	N	Y	Y
ARKANSAS							
1 Berry	Y	N	Y	N	Y	N	N
2 Snyder	N	Y	Y	Y	Y	N	N
3 *Hutchinson*	Y	N	N	N	N	Y	Y
4 *Dickey*	Y	N	N	N	N	N	Y
CALIFORNIA							
1 *Riggs*	Y	N	N	N	N	Y	Y
2 *Herger*	Y	Y	N	N	N	Y	Y
3 Fazio	N	N	Y	Y	Y	N	N
4 *Doolittle*	Y	N	N	N	–	Y	Y
5 Matsui	N	N	Y	Y	Y	N	N
6 Woolsey	N	N	Y	Y	Y	N	N
7 Miller	N	N	Y	Y	Y	N	N
8 Pelosi	N	N	Y	Y	Y	N	N
9 Lee	N	N	Y	Y	Y	N	N
10 Tauscher	N	N	Y	Y	Y	N	N
11 *Pombo*	Y	N	N	N	N	Y	Y
12 Lantos	N	N	Y	Y	Y	N	N
13 Stark	N	N	Y	Y	Y	N	N
14 Eshoo	N	N	Y	Y	Y	N	N
15 *Campbell*	N	N	N	N	N	N	N
16 Lofgren	N	N	Y	Y	Y	N	N
17 Farr	N	N	Y	Y	Y	N	Y
18 Condit	Y	N	N	N	N	Y	N
19 *Radanovich*	Y	N	N	N	N	N	Y
20 Dooley	N	N	Y	Y	Y	N	N
21 *Thomas*	Y	N	N	N	N	Y	Y
22 Capps, L.	N	Y	Y	Y	Y	N	N
23 *Gallegly*	Y	N	N	N	N	N	Y
24 Sherman	N	N	Y	Y	Y	N	Y
25 *McKeon*	Y	N	N	N	N	N	Y
26 Berman	N	N	Y	Y	Y	N	N
27 *Rogan*	Y	Y	N	N	N	Y	Y
28 *Dreier*	Y	N	N	N	N	Y	Y
29 Waxman	N	N	Y	Y	Y	N	N
30 Becerra	N	N	Y	Y	Y	N	N
31 Martinez	N	N	N	N	N	Y	N
32 Dixon	N	N	Y	Y	Y	N	Y
33 Roybal-Allard	N	N	Y	Y	Y	N	N
34 Torres	N	N	Y	Y	Y	N	N
35 Waters	N	N	Y	Y	Y	N	N
36 Harman	N	Y	Y	Y	Y	N	Y
37 Millender-McD.	N	N	Y	Y	Y	N	N
38 *Horn*	N	Y	Y	N	N	N	Y
39 *Royce*	Y	Y	N	N	N	Y	N
40 *Lewis*	Y	N	N	N	N	N	Y
41 *Kim*	Y	N	N	N	N	N	Y
42 Brown	N	Y	Y	Y	Y	N	N
43 *Calvert*	Y	N	N	N	N	Y	Y
44 *Bono, M.*	Y	Y	N	N	N	Y	Y
45 *Rohrabacher*	Y	N	N	N	N	N	Y
46 Sanchez	N	N	Y	Y	Y	N	N
47 *Cox*	Y	N	N	N	N	N	Y
48 *Packard*	Y	N	N	N	N	N	Y
49 *Bilbray*	Y	N	N	N	N	Y	Y
50 Filner	N	Y	Y	Y	Y	N	N
51 *Cunningham*	Y	N	N	N	N	Y	Y
52 *Hunter*	Y	?	N	N	N	N	Y
COLORADO							
1 DeGette	N	N	Y	Y	Y	N	N
2 Skaggs	N	N	Y	Y	Y	N	N
3 *McInnis*	Y	N	N	N	N	N	Y
4 *Schaffer*	Y	N	N	N	N	N	Y
5 *Hefley*	Y	N	N	N	N	Y	N
6 *Schaefer*	Y	N	N	N	N	Y	Y
CONNECTICUT							
1 Kennelly	N	N	Y	Y	Y	N	N
2 Gejdenson	N	N	Y	Y	Y	N	N
3 DeLauro	N	N	Y	Y	Y	N	N
4 *Shays*	Y	N	Y	Y	Y	N	Y
5 Maloney	Y	N	Y	Y	Y	N	N
6 *Johnson*	N	N	N	Y	Y	N	Y
DELAWARE							
AL *Castle*	Y	N	Y	Y	N	N	Y
FLORIDA							
1 *Scarborough*	Y	Y	?	N	N	Y	Y
2 Boyd	Y	N	Y	N	N	N	N
3 Brown	N	N	Y	Y	Y	N	N
4 *Fowler*	Y	N	N	N	N	N	Y
5 Thurman	N	N	Y	N	N	N	N
6 *Stearns*	Y	Y	N	N	N	Y	Y
7 *Mica*	Y	N	N	N	N	N	Y
8 *McCollum*	Y	N	N	N	N	Y	Y
9 *Bilirakis*	Y	N	N	N	N	Y	Y
10 *Young*	?	?	?	?	?	?	?
11 Davis	Y	N	Y	Y	Y	N	N
12 *Canady*	Y	N	N	N	N	Y	Y
13 *Miller*	Y	N	N	N	N	Y	Y
14 *Goss*	Y	N	N	N	N	Y	Y
15 *Weldon*	Y	N	N	N	N	Y	Y
16 *Foley*	Y	N	N	N	N	N	Y
17 Meek	N	N	Y	Y	Y	N	N
18 *Ros-Lehtinen*	Y	N	N	N	N	Y	N
19 Wexler	N	Y	Y	Y	Y	N	N
20 Deutsch	N	Y	Y	Y	Y	N	N
21 *Diaz-Balart*	Y	N	N	N	N	N	N
22 *Shaw*	Y	N	N	N	N	N	Y
23 Hastings	N	N	Y	N	Y	N	N
GEORGIA							
1 *Kingston*	Y	N	N	N	N	Y	Y
2 Bishop	Y	N	N	N	N	N	N
3 *Collins*	Y	N	N	N	N	Y	Y
4 McKinney	N	Y	Y	Y	N	N	N
5 Lewis	?	?	?	?	?	?	?
6 *Gingrich*	Y	N	N	N	N	Y	Y
7 *Barr*	Y	N	N	N	N	Y	N
8 *Chambliss*	Y	N	N	N	N	N	Y
9 *Deal*	Y	N	N	N	N	Y	Y
10 *Norwood*	Y	N	?	N	N	Y	Y
11 *Linder*	Y	N	N	N	N	Y	Y
HAWAII							
1 Abercrombie	N	Y	Y	N	Y	N	N
2 Mink	N	Y	Y	Y	Y	N	N
IDAHO							
1 *Chenoweth*	Y	Y	N	N	N	Y	Y
2 *Crapo*	Y	Y	N	N	N	Y	Y
ILLINOIS							
1 Rush	N	Y	Y	N	Y	N	N
2 Jackson	Y	Y	Y	Y	Y	N	N
3 Lipinski	Y	Y	Y	Y	Y	N	N
4 Gutierrez	N	Y	Y	Y	Y	N	N
5 Blagojevich	Y	Y	?	Y	N	N	N
6 *Hyde*	Y	N	N	N	N	Y	Y
7 Davis	N	N	Y	N	Y	N	N
8 *Crane*	Y	N	N	N	N	N	N
9 Yates	N	N	Y	Y	Y	N	N
10 *Porter*	Y	N	Y	N	N	Y	Y
11 *Weller*	Y	N	?	N	N	Y	Y
12 Costello	Y	N	Y	N	Y	N	N

	325	326	327	328	329	330	331
13 ***Fawell***	Y	N	N	Y	N	N	Y
14 ***Hastert***	Y	N	N	N	N	N	Y
15 ***Ewing***	Y	N	N	N	N	N	Y
16 ***Manzullo***	Y	Y	N	N	N	Y	Y
17 Evans	N	Y	Y	Y	Y	N	N
18 ***LaHood***	Y	N	N	Y	N	N	Y
19 Poshard	Y	N	Y	Y	Y	N	N
20 ***Shimkus***	Y	N	N	N	N	Y	Y
INDIANA							
1 Visclosky	Y	N	Y	N	Y	N	Y
2 ***McIntosh***	Y	Y	N	N	?	Y	Y
3 Roemer	Y	N	Y	Y	Y	N	N
4 ***Souder***	Y	N	N	N	N	Y	Y
5 ***Buyer***	Y	N	N	N	N	Y	Y
6 ***Burton***	Y	N	N	N	N	Y	Y
7 ***Pease***	Y	N	N	N	Y	N	Y
8 ***Hostettler***	Y	Y	N	N	N	N	N
9 Hamilton	Y	N	Y	Y	Y	N	Y
10 Carson	N	Y	Y	Y	Y	N	N
IOWA							
1 ***Leach***	Y	N	Y	Y	Y	N	Y
2 ***Nussle***	Y	N	N	N	N	Y	Y
3 Boswell	Y	Y	N	N	N	N	Y
4 ***Ganske***	Y	N	N	N	N	N	Y
5 ***Latham***	Y	N	N	N	N	Y	Y
KANSAS							
1 ***Moran***	Y	Y	N	N	Y	Y	Y
2 ***Ryun***	Y	N	N	N	N	Y	Y
3 ***Snowbarger***	Y	N	N	N	N	Y	Y
4 ***Tiahrt***	Y	N	N	N	N	Y	N
KENTUCKY							
1 ***Whitfield***	Y	N	N	N	N	N	Y
2 ***Lewis***	Y	N	N	N	N	N	Y
3 ***Northup***	Y	N	N	N	N	Y	Y
4 ***Bunning***	Y	N	N	N	N	N	Y
5 ***Rogers***	Y	N	N	N	N	Y	Y
6 Baesler	Y	N	Y	Y	N	N	Y
LOUISIANA							
1 ***Livingston***	Y	N	N	N	N	Y	Y
2 Jefferson	Y	N	Y	N	Y	N	N
3 ***Tauzin***	Y	N	N	N	N	N	Y
4 ***McCrery***	Y	N	N	N	N	N	Y
5 ***Cooksey***	Y	N	N	N	N	Y	Y
6 ***Baker***	Y	N	N	N	N	N	Y
7 John	Y	N	N	N	N	N	Y
MAINE							
1 Allen	N	N	Y	Y	Y	N	N
2 Baldacci	N	N	Y	Y	Y	N	N
MARYLAND							
1 ***Gilchrest***	Y	N	N	N	N	N	Y
2 ***Ehrlich***	Y	N	N	N	N	Y	Y
3 Cardin	N	N	Y	Y	Y	N	N
4 Wynn	N	N	Y	Y	Y	N	N
5 Hoyer	N	N	Y	Y	Y	N	Y
6 ***Bartlett***	Y	N	N	N	N	Y	Y
7 Cummings	N	Y	Y	Y	Y	N	N
8 ***Morella***	N	N	Y	Y	Y	N	Y
MASSACHUSETTS							
1 Olver	N	N	Y	Y	Y	N	N
2 Neal	Y	N	Y	Y	Y	N	N
3 McGovern	N	N	Y	Y	Y	N	N
4 Frank	N	N	Y	N	Y	N	N
5 Meehan	N	N	Y	Y	Y	N	Y
6 Tierney	N	N	Y	Y	Y	N	N
7 Markey	?	?	?	?	?	?	?
8 Kennedy	N	N	Y	Y	Y	N	N
9 Moakley	Y	N	Y	Y	Y	N	N
10 Delahunt	N	N	Y	Y	Y	N	N
MICHIGAN							
1 Stupak	Y	N	Y	N	Y	N	N
2 ***Hoekstra***	Y	Y	N	N	N	Y	Y
3 ***Ehlers***	Y	N	N	Y	N	N	Y
4 ***Camp***	Y	Y	N	N	N	N	Y
5 Barcia	Y	Y	Y	N	N	N	N
6 ***Upton***	Y	N	N	Y	N	N	Y
7 ***Smith***	Y	N	N	N	N	Y	Y
8 Stabenow	N	N	Y	Y	Y	N	N
9 Kildee	Y	N	Y	Y	Y	N	N
10 Bonior	Y	N	Y	Y	Y	N	N
11 ***Knollenberg***	Y	N	N	N	N	Y	Y
12 Levin	N	N	Y	Y	Y	N	N
13 Rivers	N	N	Y	Y	Y	N	N
14 Conyers	N	Y	Y	Y	Y	–	N
15 Kilpatrick	N	N	Y	N	Y	N	N
16 Dingell	Y	N	Y	N	N	N	N

	325	326	327	328	329	330	331
MINNESOTA							
1 ***Gutknecht***	Y	N	N	N	N	Y	Y
2 Minge	Y	N	Y	Y	Y	N	N
3 ***Ramstad***	Y	N	Y	Y	Y	N	Y
4 Vento	N	N	Y	Y	Y	N	N
5 Sabo	N	N	Y	Y	Y	N	N
6 Luther	N	N	Y	Y	Y	N	N
7 Peterson	Y	Y	N	N	N	N	N
8 Oberstar	Y	N	Y	N	N	N	Y
MISSISSIPPI							
1 ***Wicker***	Y	N	N	N	N	Y	Y
2 Thompson	N	N	Y	N	Y	N	N
3 ***Pickering***	Y	N	N	N	N	Y	Y
4 ***Parker***	Y	N	N	N	?	?	Y
5 Taylor	Y	N	Y	N	N	Y	Y
MISSOURI							
1 Clay	N	N	Y	N	Y	N	N
2 ***Talent***	Y	N	N	N	N	Y	Y
3 Gephardt	Y	N	Y	Y	Y	N	N
4 Skelton	Y	N	Y	N	N	Y	Y
5 McCarthy	N	N	Y	Y	Y	N	N
6 Danner	Y	N	Y	N	N	N	Y
7 ***Blunt***	Y	N	N	N	N	Y	Y
8 ***Emerson***	Y	Y	N	N	N	Y	Y
9 ***Hulshof***	Y	Y	N	Y	N	Y	Y
MONTANA							
AL ***Hill***	Y	Y	N	N	N	Y	Y
NEBRASKA							
1 ***Bereuter***	Y	N	N	N	N	N	Y
2 ***Christensen***	Y	N	N	N	N	Y	N
3 ***Barrett***	Y	N	N	N	N	Y	Y
NEVADA							
1 ***Ensign***	Y	N	N	N	N	Y	Y
2 ***Gibbons***	Y	N	N	N	N	N	Y
NEW HAMPSHIRE							
1 ***Sununu***	Y	Y	N	N	N	Y	Y
2 ***Bass***	Y	Y	N	Y	N	N	Y
NEW JERSEY							
1 Andrews	N	N	Y	Y	Y	N	N
2 ***LoBiondo***	Y	N	Y	Y	N	N	Y
3 ***Saxton***	Y	N	Y	N	N	N	Y
4 ***Smith***	Y	N	N	Y	N	Y	Y
5 ***Roukema***	Y	N	N	Y	N	N	Y
6 Pallone	N	Y	Y	Y	Y	N	N
7 ***Franks***	Y	N	N	Y	P	N	Y
8 Pascrell	Y	Y	Y	Y	Y	N	N
9 Rothman	N	Y	Y	?	Y	N	N
10 Payne	N	N	Y	N	Y	N	N
11 ***Frelinghuysen***	Y	N	N	N	N	N	Y
12 ***Pappas***	Y	N	Y	Y	N	Y	Y
13 Menendez	N	Y	Y	Y	Y	N	N
NEW MEXICO							
1 ***Wilson***	Y	N	N	N	N	N	Y
2 ***Skeen***	Y	N	N	N	N	N	Y
3 ***Redmond***	Y	N	N	N	N	N	Y
NEW YORK							
1 ***Forbes***	Y	N	Y	Y	Y	N	Y
2 ***Lazio***	Y	N	Y	Y	N	N	Y
3 ***King***	Y	N	N	N	N	Y	Y
4 McCarthy	N	N	Y	Y	Y	N	N
5 Ackerman	N	N	Y	Y	Y	N	N
6 Meeks	N	N	Y	N	Y	N	N
7 Manton	Y	N	Y	Y	Y	N	N
8 Nadler	N	Y	Y	Y	Y	N	N
9 Schumer	N	Y	Y	Y	Y	N	N
10 Towns	N	?	Y	Y	Y	N	N
11 Owens	N	Y	Y	Y	Y	N	N
12 Velázquez	N	Y	Y	Y	Y	N	N
13 ***Fossella***	Y	N	N	Y	N	Y	Y
14 Maloney	N	Y	Y	Y	Y	N	N
15 Rangel	N	N	Y	Y	Y	N	N
16 Serrano	–	–	+	+	+	–	–
17 Engel	N	Y	Y	Y	Y	N	N
18 Lowey	N	N	Y	Y	Y	N	N
19 ***Kelly***	Y	N	Y	Y	Y	N	Y
20 ***Gilman***	N	N	N	Y	N	N	Y
21 McNulty	Y	N	Y	Y	Y	N	N
22 ***Solomon***	Y	?	N	N	N	Y	Y
23 ***Boehlert***	N	N	Y	Y	N	N	Y
24 ***McHugh***	Y	N	N	N	N	N	Y
25 ***Walsh***	Y	N	Y	N	N	N	Y
26 Hinchey	N	N	Y	Y	Y	N	N
27 ***Paxon***	Y	N	N	N	N	Y	Y
28 Slaughter	N	Y	Y	Y	Y	N	N
29 LaFalce	Y	N	Y	Y	Y	N	N

	325	326	327	328	329	330	331
30 ***Quinn***	Y	N	N	Y	N	N	Y
31 ***Houghton***	Y	N	N	N	N	N	Y
NORTH CAROLINA							
1 Clayton	N	N	Y	Y	Y	N	N
2 Etheridge	Y	Y	Y	Y	Y	N	Y
3 ***Jones***	Y	N	N	N	N	Y	Y
4 Price	N	N	Y	Y	Y	N	N
5 ***Burr***	Y	N	N	N	N	Y	Y
6 ***Coble***	Y	N	N	N	N	Y	Y
7 McIntyre	Y	Y	Y	N	Y	N	Y
8 Hefner	Y	Y	Y	Y	N	N	Y
9 ***Myrick***	Y	N	N	N	N	Y	Y
10 ***Ballenger***	Y	N	N	N	N	N	Y
11 ***Taylor***	Y	N	N	N	N	?	Y
12 Watt	N	?	Y	Y	Y	N	N
NORTH DAKOTA							
AL Pomeroy	Y	N	Y	Y	Y	N	N
OHIO							
1 ***Chabot***	Y	Y	N	Y	Y	Y	Y
2 ***Portman***	Y	N	N	N	N	N	Y
3 Hall	Y	N	Y	Y	Y	N	N
4 ***Oxley***	Y	N	N	N	N	N	Y
5 ***Gillmor***	Y	N	N	N	N	N	Y
6 Strickland	Y	Y	Y	Y	Y	N	Y
7 ***Hobson***	Y	N	N	Y	N	Y	Y
8 ***Boehner***	Y	N	N	N	N	Y	Y
9 Kaptur	Y	N	?	Y	Y	N	Y
10 Kucinich	Y	Y	Y	Y	Y	N	N
11 Stokes	N	N	Y	N	Y	N	N
12 ***Kasich***	Y	N	N	N	N	Y	Y
13 Brown	N	N	Y	Y	Y	N	N
14 Sawyer	N	N	Y	Y	Y	N	N
15 ***Pryce***	Y	N	N	N	N	N	Y
16 ***Regula***	Y	N	N	N	N	N	Y
17 Traficant	Y	N	N	N	N	N	Y
18 ***Ney***	Y	N	N	N	N	Y	Y
19 ***LaTourette***	Y	N	N	N	N	N	Y
OKLAHOMA							
1 ***Largent***	Y	N	N	N	N	N	Y
2 ***Coburn***	Y	N	N	N	N	Y	Y
3 ***Watkins***	Y	N	N	N	N	N	Y
4 ***Watts***	Y	N	N	N	N	N	Y
5 ***Istook***	Y	N	N	N	N	Y	Y
6 ***Lucas***	Y	N	N	N	N	N	Y
OREGON							
1 Furse	N	Y	Y	Y	Y	N	N
2 ***Smith***	Y	N	N	N	N	N	Y
3 Blumenauer	N	N	Y	Y	Y	N	N
4 DeFazio	N	Y	Y	Y	Y	N	N
5 Hooley	N	Y	Y	Y	Y	N	N
PENNSYLVANIA							
1 Brady	?	?	?	?	?	?	?
2 Fattah	N	N	Y	N	Y	N	N
3 Borski	Y	N	Y	Y	Y	N	N
4 Klink	Y	N	Y	Y	Y	N	N
5 ***Peterson***	Y	N	N	N	N	Y	Y
6 Holden	Y	N	Y	Y	Y	N	N
7 ***Weldon***	Y	N	N	Y	N	Y	Y
8 ***Greenwood***	N	N	N	N	Y	N	Y
9 ***Shuster***	Y	N	N	N	N	Y	Y
10 ***McDade***	Y	N	N	N	N	N	Y
11 Kanjorski	Y	N	Y	Y	Y	N	N
12 Murtha	Y	N	N	N	N	N	N
13 ***Fox***	Y	N	N	N	N	N	Y
14 Coyne	N	N	Y	Y	Y	N	N
15 McHale	Y	Y	Y	Y	Y	N	N
16 ***Pitts***	Y	Y	N	N	N	Y	Y
17 ***Gekas***	Y	N	N	N	N	Y	Y
18 Doyle	Y	N	Y	Y	Y	N	N
19 ***Goodling***	Y	N	N	N	N	Y	Y
20 Mascara	Y	N	Y	Y	Y	N	N
21 ***English***	Y	N	N	N	N	N	Y
RHODE ISLAND							
1 Kennedy	Y	N	Y	Y	Y	N	Y
2 Weygand	Y	N	Y	Y	Y	N	N
SOUTH CAROLINA							
1 ***Sanford***	Y	N	N	N	N	Y	Y
2 ***Spence***	Y	N	N	N	N	N	Y
3 ***Graham***	Y	N	N	N	N	Y	Y
4 ***Inglis***	Y	N	N	N	N	Y	Y
5 Spratt	Y	N	Y	Y	Y	N	N
6 Clyburn	N	N	Y	N	Y	N	N
SOUTH DAKOTA							
AL ***Thune***	Y	Y	N	N	N	N	Y

	325	326	327	328	329	330	331
TENNESSEE							
1 ***Jenkins***	Y	Y	N	N	N	Y	Y
2 ***Duncan***	Y	N	N	N	N	Y	Y
3 ***Wamp***	Y	N	N	N	N	Y	Y
4 ***Hilleary***	Y	N	N	N	N	Y	Y
5 Clement	Y	N	Y	N	Y	N	N
6 Gordon	Y	N	Y	Y	Y	N	Y
7 ***Bryant***	Y	N	N	N	N	Y	Y
8 Tanner	Y	N	N	N	N	Y	N
9 Ford	–	–	+	+	–	–	–
TEXAS							
1 Sandlin	Y	N	Y	N	N	N	N
2 Turner	Y	N	N	N	N	Y	N
3 ***Johnson, Sam***	Y	N	N	N	N	Y	Y
4 Hall	Y	N	N	N	N	Y	N
5 ***Sessions***	Y	N	N	N	N	Y	Y
6 ***Barton***	Y	N	N	N	N	Y	Y
7 ***Archer***	Y	N	N	N	N	Y	Y
8 ***Brady***	Y	N	N	N	N	Y	+
9 Lampson	Y	N	Y	Y	Y	N	N
10 Doggett	N	N	Y	Y	Y	N	N
11 Edwards	N	N	Y	N	N	N	N
12 ***Granger***	Y	N	N	N	N	N	Y
13 ***Thornberry***	Y	N	N	N	N	N	Y
14 ***Paul***	Y	Y	N	N	Y	Y	N
15 Hinojosa	Y	N	Y	Y	Y	N	N
16 Reyes	Y	N	Y	N	N	N	N
17 Stenholm	Y	N	N	N	N	N	N
18 Jackson-Lee	N	N	Y	N	Y	N	N
19 ***Combest***	Y	N	N	N	N	Y	Y
20 Gonzalez	?	?	?	?	?	?	?
21 ***Smith***	Y	N	N	N	N	Y	Y
22 ***DeLay***	Y	N	N	N	N	Y	Y
23 ***Bonilla***	Y	N	N	N	N	N	Y
24 Frost	N	N	Y	Y	Y	N	N
25 Bentsen	N	N	Y	Y	Y	N	N
26 ***Armey***	Y	N	N	N	N	Y	Y
27 Ortiz	Y	N	Y	N	N	N	N
28 Rodriguez	N	N	Y	Y	Y	N	N
29 Green	N	N	Y	Y	Y	N	N
30 Johnson, E.B.	N	N	Y	N	Y	N	N
UTAH							
1 ***Hansen***	Y	N	N	N	N	N	Y
2 ***Cook***	Y	N	N	N	N	N	Y
3 ***Cannon***	Y	N	N	N	N	Y	Y
VERMONT							
AL *Sanders*	N	Y	Y	Y	Y	N	N
VIRGINIA							
1 ***Bateman***	Y	N	N	N	N	N	Y
2 Pickett	N	N	N	N	N	N	Y
3 Scott	N	N	Y	N	Y	N	N
4 Sisisky	Y	N	Y	N	N	N	Y
5 Goode	Y	N	N	N	N	N	Y
6 ***Goodlatte***	Y	N	N	N	N	N	Y
7 ***Bliley***	Y	N	N	N	N	N	Y
8 Moran	Y	N	Y	N	Y	N	Y
9 Boucher	N	N	Y	Y	Y	N	Y
10 ***Wolf***	Y	N	N	N	N	Y	Y
11 ***Davis***	Y	?	N	N	N	N	Y
WASHINGTON							
1 ***White***	Y	Y	N	N	N	Y	Y
2 ***Metcalf***	Y	Y	N	N	Y	Y	Y
3 ***Smith, Linda***	Y	Y	N	N	N	Y	N
4 ***Hastings***	Y	N	N	N	N	Y	Y
5 ***Nethercutt***	Y	N	N	N	N	Y	Y
6 Dicks	N	N	Y	N	Y	Y	Y
7 McDermott	N	N	Y	Y	Y	N	N
8 ***Dunn***	Y	N	N	N	N	N	Y
9 Smith, Adam	N	N	Y	Y	Y	N	N
WEST VIRGINIA							
1 Mollohan	Y	Y	Y	N	N	N	Y
2 Wise	N	Y	Y	Y	Y	N	Y
3 Rahall	Y	Y	Y	Y	Y	N	Y
WISCONSIN							
1 ***Neumann***	Y	N	N	Y	N	Y	Y
2 ***Klug***	Y	Y	N	N	N	Y	Y
3 Kind	Y	N	Y	Y	Y	N	N
4 Kleczka	Y	N	Y	Y	Y	N	N
5 Barrett	Y	N	Y	Y	Y	N	N
6 ***Petri***	Y	N	N	Y	N	Y	Y
7 Obey	Y	N	Y	Y	Y	N	N
8 Johnson	Y	N	Y	Y	Y	N	N
9 ***Sensenbrenner***	Y	N	N	Y	Y	Y	N
WYOMING							
AL ***Cubin***	Y	N	N	N	N	N	Y

Southern states - Ala., Ark., Fla., Ga., Ky., La., Miss., N.C., Okla., S.C., Tenn., Texas, Va.

332. HR 4194. Fiscal 1999 VA-HUD Appropriations/EPA Educational Outreach Programs Clarification. Obey, D-Wis., amendment to clarify that no limitation of funds in the bill can apply to funds to be used by the Environmental Protection Agency or the Council on Environmental Quality for conducting educational outreach or informational seminars. Adopted 226-198: R 50-175; D 175-23 (ND 138-8, SD 37-15); I 1-0. July 23, 1998.

333. Quorum Call.* 352 Responded. July 23, 1998.

334. HR 4194. Fiscal 1999 VA-HUD Appropriations/EPA Fund Limitation Clarification. Waxman, D-Calif., amendment to clarify that certain bill provisions and committee report language restricting various EPA and Council on Environmental Quality actions do not apply "where such activities are authorized by law." Rejected 176-243: R 27-196; D 148-47 (ND 117-26, SD 31-21); I 1-0. July 23, 1998.

335. HR 4250. Revamp Medical Insurance Regulations/Rule. Adoption of the rule (H Res 509) to provide for House floor consideration of the bill to revamp medical insurance regulations. Adopted 279-143: R 219-3; D 60-139 (ND 42-105, SD 18-34); I 0-1. July 24, 1998.

336. HR 4250. Revamp Medical Insurance Regulations/Dingell-Ganske Substitute. Dingell, D-Mich., substitute amendment to revamp medical insurance regulations. The substitute would remove provisions allowing Medical Savings Accounts and nonprofit health organizations (HealthMarts) and would permit individuals to sue their health plans under state law for personal injury or wrongful death. Rejected 212-217: R 10-217; D 201-0 (ND 149-0, SD 52-0); I 1-0. July 24, 1998.

337. HR 4250. Revamp Medical Insurance Regulations/Motion to Table. Armey, R-Texas, motion to table (kill) the appeal of the chair's ruling that the Berry, D-Ark., motion to recommit is out of order. Motion agreed to 222-204: R 222-1; D 0-202 (ND 0-149, SD 0-53); I 0-1. July 24, 1998.

338. HR 4250. Revamp Medical Insurance Regulations/Recommit. Berry, D-Ark., motion to recommit the bill to the House Education and the Workforce Committee with instructions to report it back with an amendment to allow doctors, not health plans, to determine what can be considered medically necessary. Motion rejected 205-221: R 5-220; D 199-1 (ND 147-1, SD 52-0); I 1-0. July 24, 1998.

339. HR 4250. Revamp Medical Insurance Regulations/Passage. Passage of the bill to revise managed care and medical insurance regulations. The bill would provide a range of patient protections, create a two-step appeals process for challenging a health plan administrator's decisions and expand the availability of medical savings accounts. Passed 216-210: R 213-12; D 3-197 (ND 2-147, SD 1-50); I 0-1. July 24, 1998. A "nay" was a vote in support of the president's position.

* CQ does not include quorum calls in its vote charts.

Key

Y	Voted for (yea).
#	Paired for.
+	Announced for.
N	Voted against (nay).
X	Paired against.
–	Announced against.
P	Voted "present."
C	Voted "present" to avoid possible conflict of interest.
?	Did not vote or otherwise make a position known.

Democrats **Republicans**
Independent

	332	334	335	336	337	338	339
ALABAMA							
1 *Callahan*	N	N	Y	N	Y	N	Y
2 *Everett*	N	N	Y	N	Y	N	Y
3 *Riley*	N	N	Y	N	Y	N	Y
4 *Aderholt*	N	N	Y	N	Y	N	Y
5 Cramer	N	N	Y	Y	N	Y	N
6 *Bachus*	N	N	Y	N	Y	N	Y
7 Hilliard	Y	Y	N	Y	N	Y	N
ALASKA							
AL *Young*	N	?	?	N	Y	N	Y
ARIZONA							
1 *Salmon*	N	N	Y	N	Y	N	Y
2 Pastor	Y	Y	Y	Y	N	Y	N
3 *Stump*	N	N	Y	N	Y	N	Y
4 *Shadegg*	N	N	Y	N	Y	N	Y
5 *Kolbe*	Y	N	Y	N	Y	N	Y
6 *Hayworth*	N	N	Y	N	Y	N	Y
ARKANSAS							
1 Berry	N	N	N	Y	N	Y	N
2 Snyder	Y	Y	Y	Y	N	Y	N
3 *Hutchinson*	N	N	Y	N	Y	N	Y
4 *Dickey*	N	N	Y	N	Y	N	Y
CALIFORNIA							
1 *Riggs*	N	N	Y	N	Y	N	Y
2 *Herger*	N	N	?	N	Y	N	Y
3 Fazio	Y	Y	N	Y	N	Y	N
4 *Doolittle*	N	N	?	N	Y	N	Y
5 Matsui	Y	Y	N	Y	N	Y	N
6 Woolsey	Y	Y	N	Y	N	Y	N
7 Miller	Y	Y	N	Y	N	Y	N
8 Pelosi	Y	Y	N	Y	N	Y	N
9 Lee	Y	Y	N	Y	N	Y	N
10 Tauscher	Y	Y	N	Y	N	Y	N
11 *Pombo*	N	N	Y	N	Y	N	Y
12 Lantos	Y	Y	N	Y	N	Y	N
13 Stark	Y	?	N	Y	N	Y	N
14 Eshoo	Y	Y	N	Y	N	Y	N
15 *Campbell*	Y	Y	N	N	Y	N	N
16 Lofgren	Y	Y	N	Y	N	Y	N
17 Farr	Y	Y	N	Y	N	Y	N
18 Condit	N	N	N	Y	N	Y	N
19 *Radanovich*	N	N	Y	N	Y	N	Y
20 Dooley	Y	N	N	Y	N	Y	N
21 *Thomas*	N	N	Y	N	Y	N	Y
22 Capps, L.	Y	Y	N	Y	N	Y	N
23 *Gallegly*	Y	N	Y	N	Y	N	Y
24 Sherman	Y	Y	N	Y	N	Y	N
25 *McKeon*	N	N	Y	N	Y	N	Y
26 Berman	Y	Y	N	Y	N	Y	N
27 *Rogan*	N	N	Y	N	Y	N	Y
28 *Dreier*	N	N	Y	N	Y	N	Y
29 Waxman	Y	Y	N	Y	N	Y	N
30 Becerra	Y	Y	N	Y	N	Y	N
31 Martinez	Y	Y	N	Y	N	Y	N
32 Dixon	Y	Y	N	Y	N	Y	N
33 Roybal-Allard	Y	Y	N	Y	N	Y	N
34 Torres	Y	Y	?	Y	N	Y	N
35 Waters	Y	Y	N	Y	N	Y	N
36 Harman	Y	Y	N	Y	N	Y	N
37 Millender-McD.	Y	Y	Y	Y	N	Y	N

	332	334	335	336	337	338	339
38 *Horn*	Y	Y	Y	N	Y	N	Y
39 *Royce*	N	N	Y	N	Y	N	Y
40 *Lewis*	Y	N	Y	N	Y	N	Y
41 *Kim*	N	N	Y	N	Y	N	Y
42 Brown	Y	Y	N	Y	N	Y	N
43 *Calvert*	N	N	Y	N	Y	N	Y
44 *Bono, M.*	N	N	Y	N	Y	N	Y
45 *Rohrabacher*	N	N	Y	N	Y	N	Y
46 Sanchez	Y	Y	N	Y	N	Y	N
47 *Cox*	N	N	Y	N	Y	N	Y
48 *Packard*	N	N	Y	N	Y	N	Y
49 *Bilbray*	Y	Y	Y	N	Y	N	Y
50 Filner	Y	Y	N	Y	N	Y	N
51 *Cunningham*	N	N	Y	N	Y	N	Y
52 *Hunter*	N	N	Y	N	Y	N	Y
COLORADO							
1 DeGette	Y	Y	N	Y	N	Y	N
2 Skaggs	Y	Y	N	Y	N	Y	N
3 *McInnis*	N	N	Y	N	Y	N	Y
4 *Schaffer*	N	N	Y	N	Y	N	Y
5 *Hefley*	N	N	Y	N	Y	N	Y
6 *Schaefer*	N	N	Y	N	Y	N	Y
CONNECTICUT							
1 Kennelly	Y	Y	Y	Y	N	Y	N
2 Gejdenson	Y	Y	N	Y	N	Y	N
3 DeLauro	Y	Y	N	Y	N	Y	N
4 *Shays*	Y	Y	Y	Y	N	Y	N
5 Maloney	Y	Y	N	Y	N	Y	N
6 *Johnson*	Y	Y	N	?	N	Y	N
DELAWARE							
AL *Castle*	Y	Y	N	N	Y	N	Y
FLORIDA							
1 *Scarborough*	N	N	Y	N	Y	N	Y
2 Boyd	N	N	Y	Y	N	Y	N
3 Brown	Y	Y	N	Y	N	Y	N
4 *Fowler*	N	N	Y	N	Y	N	Y
5 Thurman	Y	Y	N	Y	N	Y	N
6 *Stearns*	N	N	Y	N	Y	N	Y
7 *Mica*	N	N	Y	N	Y	N	Y
8 *McCollum*	N	N	Y	N	Y	N	Y
9 *Bilirakis*	Y	N	Y	N	Y	N	Y
10 *Young*	?	?	?	?	?	?	?
11 Davis	Y	Y	N	Y	N	Y	N
12 *Canady*	Y	N	Y	N	Y	N	Y
13 *Miller*	Y	N	Y	N	Y	N	Y
14 *Goss*	Y	N	Y	N	Y	N	Y
15 *Weldon*	N	N	Y	N	Y	N	Y
16 *Foley*	N	N	Y	N	Y	N	Y
17 Meek	Y	Y	N	Y	N	Y	N
18 *Ros-Lehtinen*	Y	N	Y	N	Y	N	Y
19 Wexler	Y	Y	N	Y	N	Y	N
20 Deutsch	Y	Y	N	Y	N	Y	N
21 *Diaz-Balart*	Y	N	Y	N	Y	N	Y
22 *Shaw*	Y	N	Y	N	Y	N	Y
23 Hastings	Y	Y	N	Y	N	Y	N
GEORGIA							
1 *Kingston*	N	N	Y	N	Y	N	Y
2 Bishop	N	N	Y	Y	N	Y	N
3 *Collins*	N	N	Y	N	Y	N	Y
4 McKinney	Y	Y	N	Y	N	Y	N
5 Lewis	?	?	N	Y	N	Y	N
6 *Gingrich*				N	Y	N	Y
7 *Barr*	N	N	Y	N	Y	N	Y
8 *Chambliss*	N	N	Y	N	Y	N	Y
9 *Deal*	N	N	Y	N	Y	N	Y
10 *Norwood*	N	N	Y	N	Y	N	Y
11 *Linder*	N	N	Y	?	?	?	
HAWAII							
1 Abercrombie	Y	Y	N	Y	N	Y	N
2 Mink	Y	Y	N	Y	N	Y	N
IDAHO							
1 *Chenoweth*	N	N	?	N	Y	N	N
2 *Crapo*	N	N	Y	N	Y	N	N
ILLINOIS							
1 Rush	Y	Y	N	Y	N	Y	N
2 Jackson	Y	Y	N	Y	N	Y	N
3 Lipinski	Y	N	Y	Y	N	Y	N
4 Gutierrez	Y	N	?	Y	N	Y	N
5 Blagojevich	Y	Y	N	Y	N	Y	N
6 *Hyde*	?	N	Y	N	Y	N	Y
7 Davis	Y	Y	N	Y	N	Y	N
8 *Crane*	N	N	Y	N	Y	N	Y
9 Yates	?	?	?	?	?	?	?
10 *Porter*	Y	N	Y	N	Y	N	Y
11 *Weller*	N	N	Y	N	Y	N	Y
12 Costello	Y	Y	N	Y	N	Y	N

ND Northern Democrats   SD Southern Democrats

Member	332	334	335	336	337	338	339
13 ***Fawell***	N	N	Y	N	Y	N	Y
14 ***Hastert***	N	N	Y	N	Y	N	Y
15 ***Ewing***	Y	N	Y	N	Y	N	Y
16 ***Manzullo***	N	N	Y	N	Y	N	Y
17 Evans	Y	Y	N	Y	N	Y	N
18 ***LaHood***	N	N	Y	N	Y	N	Y
19 Poshard	Y	Y	N	Y	N	Y	N
20 ***Shimkus***	N	N	Y	N	Y	N	Y
INDIANA							
1 Visclosky	Y	N	N	Y	N	Y	N
2 ***McIntosh***	N	N	Y	N	Y	N	Y
3 Roemer	Y	N	Y	Y	N	Y	N
4 ***Souder***	N	N	Y	N	Y	N	Y
5 ***Buyer***	N	N	Y	N	Y	N	Y
6 ***Burton***	N	N	Y	N	Y	N	Y
7 ***Pease***	Y	N	Y	N	Y	N	Y
8 ***Hostettler***	N	N	Y	N	Y	N	Y
9 Hamilton	Y	N	Y	Y	N	Y	N
10 Carson	Y	Y	N	Y	N	Y	N
IOWA							
1 ***Leach***	Y	Y	Y	Y	Y	N	Y
2 ***Nussle***	N	N	Y	N	Y	N	Y
3 Boswell	N	N	Y	Y	N	Y	N
4 ***Ganske***	Y	N	Y	Y	Y	Y	N
5 ***Latham***	N	N	Y	N	Y	N	Y
KANSAS							
1 ***Moran***	N	N	Y	N	Y	N	Y
2 ***Ryun***	N	N	Y	N	Y	N	Y
3 ***Snowbarger***	N	N	Y	N	Y	N	Y
4 ***Tiahrt***	N	N	Y	N	Y	N	Y
KENTUCKY							
1 ***Whitfield***	N	?	Y	N	Y	N	Y
2 ***Lewis***	N	N	Y	N	Y	N	Y
3 ***Northup***	N	N	Y	N	Y	N	Y
4 ***Bunning***	N	N	Y	N	Y	N	Y
5 ***Rogers***	N	N	Y	N	Y	N	Y
6 Baesler	N	N	Y	Y	N	Y	N
LOUISIANA							
1 ***Livingston***	N	N	Y	N	Y	N	Y
2 Jefferson	Y	Y	?	Y	N	Y	N
3 ***Tauzin***	N	N	Y	N	Y	N	Y
4 ***McCrery***	N	N	Y	N	Y	N	Y
5 ***Cooksey***	N	N	Y	N	Y	N	Y
6 ***Baker***	N	N	Y	N	Y	N	Y
7 John	N	N	N	Y	N	?	?
MAINE							
1 Allen	Y	Y	N	Y	N	Y	N
2 Baldacci	Y	Y	N	Y	N	Y	N
MARYLAND							
1 ***Gilchrest***	Y	Y	Y	N	Y	N	Y
2 ***Ehrlich***	N	N	Y	N	Y	N	Y
3 Cardin	Y	Y	N	Y	N	Y	N
4 Wynn	Y	Y	N	Y	N	Y	N
5 Hoyer	Y	Y	N	Y	N	Y	N
6 ***Bartlett***	N	N	Y	N	Y	N	Y
7 Cummings	Y	Y	Y	Y	N	Y	N
8 ***Morella***	Y	Y	Y	Y	Y	Y	N
MASSACHUSETTS							
1 Olver	Y	Y	N	Y	N	Y	N
2 Neal	Y	Y	N	Y	N	Y	N
3 McGovern	Y	Y	N	Y	N	Y	N
4 Frank	Y	Y	N	Y	N	Y	N
5 Meehan	Y	Y	N	Y	N	?	N
6 Tierney	Y	Y	N	Y	N	Y	N
7 Markey	?	?	?	?	?	?	?
8 Kennedy	Y	Y	Y	Y	N	Y	N
9 Moakley	Y	?	N	Y	N	Y	N
10 Delahunt	Y	Y	Y	Y	N	Y	N
MICHIGAN							
1 Stupak	Y	Y	N	Y	N	Y	N
2 ***Hoekstra***	N	N	Y	N	Y	N	Y
3 ***Ehlers***	Y	Y	Y	N	Y	N	Y
4 ***Camp***	N	N	Y	N	Y	N	Y
5 Barcia	Y	N	N	Y	N	Y	N
6 ***Upton***	Y	N	Y	N	Y	N	Y
7 ***Smith***	Y	N	Y	N	Y	N	Y
8 Stabenow	Y	Y	N	Y	N	Y	N
9 Kildee	Y	Y	Y	Y	N	Y	N
10 Bonior	Y	Y	N	Y	N	Y	N
11 ***Knollenberg***	N	N	Y	N	Y	N	Y
12 Levin	Y	Y	N	Y	N	Y	N
13 Rivers	Y	Y	Y	Y	N	Y	N
14 Conyers	Y	+	N	Y	N	Y	N
15 Kilpatrick	Y	Y	Y	Y	N	Y	N
16 Dingell	Y	N	Y	Y	N	Y	N
MINNESOTA							
1 ***Gutknecht***	N	N	Y	N	Y	N	Y
2 Minge	Y	Y	N	Y	N	Y	N
3 ***Ramstad***	Y	Y	Y	N	Y	N	Y
4 Vento	Y	Y	N	Y	N	Y	N
5 Sabo	Y	Y	N	Y	N	Y	N
6 Luther	Y	Y	N	Y	N	Y	N
7 Peterson	N	N	N	Y	N	Y	N
8 Oberstar	Y	Y	N	Y	N	Y	N
MISSISSIPPI							
1 ***Wicker***	N	N	Y	N	Y	N	Y
2 Thompson	Y	Y	N	Y	N	Y	N
3 ***Pickering***	N	N	Y	N	Y	N	Y
4 ***Parker***	N	N	Y	N	Y	N	Y
5 Taylor	Y	N	Y	Y	N	Y	N
MISSOURI							
1 Clay	Y	Y	N	Y	N	Y	N
2 ***Talent***	N	N	Y	N	Y	N	Y
3 Gephardt	Y	Y	N	Y	N	Y	N
4 Skelton	N	N	Y	Y	N	Y	N
5 McCarthy	Y	Y	Y	Y	N	Y	N
6 Danner	N	N	Y	Y	N	Y	Y
7 ***Blunt***	N	N	Y	N	Y	N	Y
8 ***Emerson***	N	N	Y	N	Y	N	Y
9 ***Hulshof***	N	N	Y	N	Y	N	Y
MONTANA							
AL ***Hill***	N	N	Y	N	Y	N	Y
NEBRASKA							
1 ***Bereuter***	N	N	Y	N	Y	N	Y
2 ***Christensen***	N	N	Y	N	Y	N	Y
3 ***Barrett***	N	N	Y	N	Y	N	Y
NEVADA							
1 ***Ensign***	N	Y	Y	N	Y	N	Y
2 ***Gibbons***	N	N	Y	N	Y	N	Y
NEW HAMPSHIRE							
1 ***Sununu***	N	N	Y	N	Y	N	Y
2 ***Bass***	N	N	Y	N	Y	N	Y
NEW JERSEY							
1 Andrews	Y	Y	N	Y	N	Y	N
2 ***LoBiondo***	N	Y	Y	N	Y	N	Y
3 ***Saxton***	Y	Y	Y	N	Y	N	Y
4 ***Smith***	Y	Y	Y	N	Y	N	Y
5 ***Roukema***	Y	Y	Y	Y	Y	Y	N
6 Pallone	Y	Y	Y	Y	N	Y	N
7 ***Franks***	Y	Y	Y	N	Y	N	Y
8 Pascrell	Y	Y	Y	Y	N	Y	N
9 Rothman	Y	Y	Y	Y	N	Y	N
10 Payne	Y	Y	N	Y	N	Y	N
11 ***Frelinghuysen***	Y	N	Y	N	Y	N	Y
12 ***Pappas***	N	N	Y	N	Y	N	Y
13 Menendez	Y	Y	N	Y	N	Y	N
NEW MEXICO							
1 ***Wilson***	N	N	Y	N	Y	N	Y
2 ***Skeen***	N	N	Y	N	Y	N	Y
3 ***Redmond***	N	N	Y	N	Y	N	Y
NEW YORK							
1 ***Forbes***	Y	Y	N	Y	N	Y	N
2 ***Lazio***	Y	Y	Y	N	Y	N	Y
3 ***King***	N	N	Y	N	Y	N	Y
4 McCarthy	Y	Y	Y	Y	N	Y	N
5 Ackerman	Y	Y	N	Y	N	Y	N
6 Meeks	Y	Y	N	Y	N	Y	N
7 Manton	Y	Y	Y	Y	N	Y	N
8 Nadler	Y	Y	N	Y	N	Y	N
9 Schumer	Y	Y	N	Y	N	Y	N
10 Towns	Y	Y	N	Y	N	Y	N
11 Owens	Y	Y	N	Y	N	Y	N
12 Velázquez	?	Y	N	Y	N	Y	N
13 ***Fossella***	Y	N	Y	N	Y	N	Y
14 Maloney	Y	Y	N	Y	N	Y	N
15 Rangel	Y	Y	N	Y	N	Y	N
16 Serrano	+	+	N	Y	N	Y	N
17 Engel	Y	Y	N	Y	N	Y	N
18 Lowey	Y	Y	N	Y	N	Y	N
19 ***Kelly***	Y	Y	Y	N	Y	N	Y
20 ***Gilman***	Y	Y	Y	N	Y	N	Y
21 McNulty	Y	Y	N	Y	N	Y	N
22 ***Solomon***	Y	N	Y	N	Y	N	Y
23 ***Boehlert***	Y	Y	Y	Y	Y	N	Y
24 ***McHugh***	Y	N	Y	N	Y	N	Y
25 ***Walsh***	Y	N	Y	N	Y	N	Y
26 Hinchey	Y	Y	N	Y	N	Y	N
27 ***Paxon***	N	N	Y	N	Y	N	Y
28 Slaughter	Y	Y	N	Y	N	Y	N
29 LaFalce	Y	Y	N	Y	N	Y	N
30 ***Quinn***	Y	N	Y	N	Y	N	Y
31 ***Houghton***	N	N	Y	N	Y	N	Y
NORTH CAROLINA							
1 Clayton	Y	Y	Y	Y	N	Y	N
2 Etheridge	Y	N	Y	Y	N	Y	N
3 ***Jones***	N	N	Y	N	Y	N	Y
4 Price	Y	Y	N	Y	N	Y	N
5 ***Burr***	N	N	Y	N	Y	N	Y
6 ***Coble***	N	N	Y	N	Y	N	Y
7 McIntyre	N	N	Y	Y	N	Y	N
8 Hefner	Y	Y	Y	Y	N	Y	N
9 ***Myrick***	N	N	Y	N	Y	N	Y
10 ***Ballenger***	N	N	Y	N	Y	N	Y
11 ***Taylor***	N	N	Y	N	Y	N	Y
12 Watt	Y	Y	N	Y	N	Y	N
NORTH DAKOTA							
AL Pomeroy	N	N	N	Y	N	Y	N
OHIO							
1 ***Chabot***	N	N	Y	N	Y	N	Y
2 ***Portman***	N	N	Y	N	Y	N	Y
3 Hall	Y	?	N	Y	N	Y	N
4 ***Oxley***	N	N	Y	N	Y	N	Y
5 ***Gillmor***	N	N	Y	N	?	N	Y
6 Strickland	Y	N	N	Y	N	Y	N
7 ***Hobson***	N	N	Y	N	Y	N	Y
8 ***Boehner***	N	N	Y	N	Y	N	Y
9 Kaptur	Y	Y	N	Y	N	Y	N
10 Kucinich	Y	Y	N	Y	N	Y	N
11 Stokes	Y	Y	N	Y	N	Y	N
12 ***Kasich***	N	N	Y	N	Y	N	Y
13 Brown	Y	Y	N	Y	N	Y	N
14 Sawyer	Y	Y	Y	Y	N	Y	N
15 ***Pryce***	N	N	Y	N	Y	N	Y
16 ***Regula***	Y	N	Y	N	Y	N	Y
17 Traficant	N	N	Y	Y	N	Y	Y
18 ***Ney***	N	N	Y	N	Y	N	Y
19 ***LaTourette***	Y	Y	Y	Y	Y	N	Y
OKLAHOMA							
1 ***Largent***	N	N	Y	N	Y	N	Y
2 ***Coburn***	N	N	Y	N	Y	N	Y
3 ***Watkins***	N	N	Y	N	Y	N	Y
4 ***Watts***	N	N	Y	N	Y	N	Y
5 ***Istook***	N	N	N	N	Y	N	Y
6 ***Lucas***	N	N	Y	N	Y	N	Y
OREGON							
1 Furse	Y	Y	N	Y	N	Y	N
2 ***Smith***	N	?	Y	N	Y	N	Y
3 Blumenauer	Y	Y	Y	Y	N	Y	N
4 DeFazio	Y	Y	N	Y	N	Y	N
5 Hooley	Y	Y	Y	Y	N	Y	N
PENNSYLVANIA							
1 Brady	?	?	N	Y	N	Y	N
2 Fattah	Y	Y	N	Y	N	Y	N
3 Borski	Y	Y	N	Y	N	Y	N
4 Klink	Y	N	N	Y	N	Y	N
5 ***Peterson***	N	N	Y	N	Y	N	Y
6 Holden	Y	N	Y	Y	N	Y	N
7 ***Weldon***	Y	Y	Y	N	?	N	Y
8 ***Greenwood***	Y	Y	Y	N	Y	N	Y
9 ***Shuster***	N	?	Y	N	Y	N	Y
10 ***McDade***	N	N	Y	N	Y	N	Y
11 Kanjorski	Y	N	Y	Y	N	Y	N
12 Murtha	Y	N	Y	Y	N	Y	N
13 ***Fox***	Y	Y	Y	Y	Y	Y	Y
14 Coyne	Y	Y	N	Y	N	Y	N
15 McHale	Y	Y	N	Y	N	Y	N
16 ***Pitts***	N	N	Y	N	Y	N	Y
17 ***Gekas***	N	N	Y	N	Y	N	Y
18 Doyle	Y	N	Y	Y	N	Y	N
19 ***Goodling***	N	N	Y	N	Y	N	Y
20 Mascara	Y	N	Y	Y	N	Y	N
21 ***English***	N	N	Y	N	Y	N	Y
RHODE ISLAND							
1 Kennedy	Y	Y	N	Y	N	Y	N
2 Weygand	Y	Y	Y	Y	N	Y	N
SOUTH CAROLINA							
1 ***Sanford***	Y	N	Y	N	Y	N	N
2 ***Spence***	N	N	Y	N	Y	N	Y
3 ***Graham***	N	N	Y	N	Y	N	Y
4 ***Inglis***	N	N	Y	N	Y	N	Y
5 Spratt	Y	Y	N	Y	N	Y	N
6 Clyburn	Y	Y	N	Y	N	Y	N
SOUTH DAKOTA							
AL ***Thune***	N	N	Y	N	Y	N	Y
TENNESSEE							
1 ***Jenkins***	N	N	Y	N	Y	N	Y
2 ***Duncan***	N	N	Y	N	Y	N	Y
3 ***Wamp***	N	N	Y	N	Y	N	Y
4 ***Hilleary***	N	N	Y	N	Y	N	Y
5 Clement	N	Y	Y	Y	N	Y	N
6 Gordon	Y	N	Y	Y	N	Y	N
7 ***Bryant***	N	N	Y	N	Y	N	Y
8 Tanner	Y	N	N	Y	N	Y	N
9 Ford	+	+	−	+	−	+	−
TEXAS							
1 Sandlin	Y	N	N	Y	N	Y	N
2 Turner	Y	N	N	Y	N	Y	N
3 ***Johnson, Sam***	N	N	Y	N	Y	N	Y
4 Hall	N	N	Y	Y	N	Y	N
5 ***Sessions***	N	N	Y	N	Y	N	Y
6 ***Barton***	N	N	Y	N	Y	N	Y
7 ***Archer***	N	N	Y	N	Y	N	Y
8 ***Brady***	N	N	Y	N	Y	N	N
9 Lampson	Y	Y	N	Y	N	Y	N
10 Doggett	Y	Y	N	Y	N	Y	N
11 Edwards	Y	Y	N	Y	N	Y	N
12 ***Granger***	N	N	Y	N	Y	N	Y
13 ***Thornberry***	N	N	Y	N	Y	N	Y
14 ***Paul***	N	N	Y	N	Y	N	N
15 Hinojosa	Y	Y	N	+	N	Y	N
16 Reyes	Y	N	N	Y	N	Y	N
17 Stenholm	N	N	N	Y	N	Y	N
18 Jackson-Lee	Y	Y	Y	Y	N	Y	N
19 ***Combest***	N	N	Y	N	Y	N	Y
20 Gonzalez	?	?	?	?	?	?	?
21 ***Smith***	N	N	Y	N	Y	N	Y
22 ***DeLay***	N	N	Y	N	Y	N	Y
23 ***Bonilla***	N	N	Y	N	Y	N	N
24 Frost	Y	Y	Y	Y	N	Y	N
25 Bentsen	Y	Y	N	Y	N	Y	N
26 ***Armey***	N	N	Y	N	Y	N	Y
27 Ortiz	N	N	Y	Y	N	Y	N
28 Rodriguez	N	Y	N	Y	N	Y	?
29 Green	Y	Y	N	Y	N	Y	N
30 Johnson, E.B.	Y	Y	N	Y	N	Y	N
UTAH							
1 ***Hansen***	N	N	Y	N	Y	N	Y
2 ***Cook***	N	N	Y	N	Y	N	Y
3 ***Cannon***	N	N	Y	N	Y	N	Y
VERMONT							
AL *Sanders*	Y	Y	N	Y	N	Y	N
VIRGINIA							
1 ***Bateman***	N	N	Y	N	Y	N	Y
2 Pickett	N	N	N	Y	N	Y	N
3 Scott	Y	Y	N	Y	N	Y	N
4 Sisisky	N	N	N	Y	N	Y	N
5 Goode	N	N	Y	Y	N	Y	Y
6 ***Goodlatte***	N	N	Y	N	Y	N	Y
7 ***Bliley***	N	N	Y	N	Y	N	Y
8 Moran	Y	Y	Y	Y	N	Y	N
9 Boucher	Y	N	N	Y	N	Y	N
10 ***Wolf***	N	N	Y	N	Y	N	Y
11 ***Davis***	Y	N	Y	N	Y	N	Y
WASHINGTON							
1 ***White***	N	N	Y	N	Y	N	Y
2 ***Metcalf***	N	N	Y	N	Y	N	Y
3 ***Smith, Linda***	N	N	Y	N	Y	N	Y
4 ***Hastings***	N	N	Y	N	Y	N	Y
5 ***Nethercutt***	N	N	Y	N	Y	N	Y
6 Dicks	Y	Y	N	Y	N	Y	N
7 McDermott	Y	Y	N	Y	N	Y	N
8 ***Dunn***	N	N	Y	N	Y	N	Y
9 Smith, Adam	Y	Y	Y	Y	N	Y	N
WEST VIRGINIA							
1 Mollohan	N	N	Y	Y	N	Y	N
2 Wise	Y	N	Y	Y	N	Y	N
3 Rahall	Y	N	Y	Y	N	Y	N
WISCONSIN							
1 ***Neumann***	N	N	Y	N	Y	N	Y
2 ***Klug***	Y	N	Y	N	Y	?	?
3 Kind	Y	Y	Y	Y	N	Y	N
4 Kleczka	Y	Y	N	Y	N	Y	N
5 Barrett	Y	Y	N	Y	N	Y	N
6 ***Petri***	N	N	Y	N	Y	N	Y
7 Obey	Y	Y	Y	Y	N	Y	N
8 Johnson	Y	Y	N	Y	N	Y	N
9 ***Sensenbrenner***	N	N	Y	N	Y	N	Y
WYOMING							
AL ***Cubin***	N	N	Y	N	Y	N	Y

Southern states - Ala., Ark., Fla., Ga., Ky., La., Miss., N.C., Okla., S.C., Tenn., Texas, Va.

Key

Y	Voted for (yea).
#	Paired for.
+	Announced for.
N	Voted against (nay).
X	Paired against.
−	Announced against.
P	Voted "present."
C	Voted "present" to avoid possible conflict of interest.
?	Did not vote or otherwise make a position known.

Democrats **Republicans** *Independent*

340. H Con Res 311. Honoring the Memory of U.S. Capitol Policemen Gibson and Chestnut/Adoption. Adoption of the resolution to honor Det. John Michael Gibson and Pfc. Jacob Joseph Chestnut of the U.S. Capitol Police, who were killed in the line of duty July 24, 1998. Adopted 392-0: R 210-0; D 181-0 (ND 133-0, SD 48-0); I 1-0. July 27, 1998.

341. Quorum Call.* 378 Responded. July 28, 1998.

342. Procedural Motion/Adjourn. Gutknecht, R-Minn., motion to adjourn. Motion agreed to 392-0: R 211-0; D 180-0 (ND 133-0, SD 47-0); I 1-0. July 28, 1998.

343. HR 629. Texas, Maine and Vermont Low-Level Radioactive Waste Compact/Rule. Adoption of the rule (H Res 511) to provide for House floor consideration of the conference report on the bill that would allow Maine and Vermont to export low-level radioactive waste to a facility in Texas. Adopted 313-108: R 219-4; D 93-104 (ND 60-87, SD 33-17); I 1-0. July 29, 1998.

344. HR 629. Texas, Maine and Vermont Low-Level Radioactive Waste Compact/Conference Report. Adoption of the conference report on the bill that would allow Maine and Vermont to export low-level radioactive waste to a facility in Texas. Adopted (thus sent to the Senate) 305-117: R 197-26; D 107-91 (ND 71-77, SD 36-14); I 1-0. July 29, 1998.

345. HR 4194. Fiscal 1999 VA-HUD Appropriations/International Space Station Termination. Roemer, D-Ind., amendment to cut NASA funding by $1.6 billion and terminate the international space station. Rejected 109-323: R 47-179; D 61-144 (ND 59-92, SD 2-52); I 1-0. July 29, 1998.

346. HR 4194. Fiscal 1999 VA-HUD Appropriations/VA Health Care Network Funding Distribution. Hinchey, D-N.Y., amendment to prohibit the use of funds by the Department of Veterans Affairs to administer its Veterans Equitable Resource Allocation (VERA) System, which distributes funding for regional VA health care networks in a way that accounts for shifting populations of veterans. Rejected 146-285: R 62-164; D 83-121 (ND 82-68, SD 1-53); I 1-0. July 29, 1998.

347. HR 4194. Fiscal 1999 VA-HUD Appropriations/AIDS Patient Housing Program Funding Redistribution. Hilleary, R-Tenn. amendment to cut by $21 million the bill's appropriation for Housing Opportunities for Persons with AIDS. The amendment would redistribute the funds for VA grants to construct state extended care facilities. Adopted 231-200: R 184-42; D 47-157 (ND 21-129, SD 26-28); I 0-1. July 29, 1998.

* CQ does not include quorum calls in its vote charts.

	340	342	343	344	345	346	347
ALABAMA							
1 *Callahan*	Y	Y	Y	Y	N	N	Y
2 *Everett*	Y	Y	Y	Y	N	N	Y
3 *Riley*	Y	Y	Y	Y	N	N	Y
4 *Aderholt*	Y	Y	Y	Y	N	N	Y
5 Cramer	Y	?	Y	Y	N	N	Y
6 *Bachus*	Y	Y	Y	N	N	N	Y
7 Hilliard	Y	Y	N	Y	N	N	N
ALASKA							
AL *Young*	Y	?	Y	Y	N	N	Y
ARIZONA							
1 *Salmon*	Y	Y	Y	Y	N	N	Y
2 Pastor	Y	Y	N	N	N	N	Y
3 *Stump*	Y	Y	Y	Y	N	N	Y
4 *Shadegg*	Y	Y	Y	Y	N	N	Y
5 *Kolbe*	?	Y	Y	Y	N	N	N
6 *Hayworth*	Y	Y	Y	Y	N	N	Y
ARKANSAS							
1 Berry	Y	Y	Y	Y	N	N	N
2 Snyder	Y	Y	Y	Y	N	N	N
3 *Hutchinson*	Y	Y	Y	Y	N	N	Y
4 *Dickey*	Y	Y	Y	Y	N	N	Y
CALIFORNIA							
1 *Riggs*	?	?	Y	Y	N	N	N
2 *Herger*	Y	Y	Y	Y	N	N	Y
3 Fazio	Y	Y	Y	N	N	N	N
4 *Doolittle*	Y	Y	Y	Y	N	N	Y
5 Matsui	Y	Y	N	N	N	N	N
6 Woolsey	Y	Y	N	N	Y	N	N
7 Miller	Y	Y	N	N	N	N	N
8 Pelosi	Y	Y	N	N	N	N	N
9 Lee	Y	Y	N	N	Y	N	N
10 Tauscher	Y	Y	Y	Y	N	N	N
11 *Pombo*	Y	Y	Y	N	N	N	Y
12 Lantos	Y	Y	N	N	N	N	N
13 Stark	?	?	N	N	Y	N	N
14 Eshoo	Y	Y	N	N	N	N	N
15 *Campbell*	Y	Y	Y	Y	N	N	N
16 Lofgren	Y	N	N	N	N	N	N
17 Farr	Y	Y	N	N	N	N	N
18 Condit	Y	?	Y	Y	N	N	N
19 *Radanovich*	Y	Y	Y	Y	N	N	Y
20 Dooley	Y	Y	Y	Y	N	N	N
21 *Thomas*	Y	Y	Y	Y	N	N	N
22 Capps, L.	Y	Y	N	N	N	N	N
23 *Gallegly*	Y	Y	Y	Y	N	N	N
24 Sherman	Y	N	N	N	N	N	N
25 *McKeon*	Y	Y	Y	Y	N	N	N
26 Berman	Y	Y	N	N	N	N	N
27 *Rogan*	Y	Y	Y	N	N	N	N
28 *Dreier*	Y	Y	Y	Y	N	N	N
29 Waxman	?	?	N	N	N	N	N
30 Becerra	+	Y	N	N	N	N	N
31 Martinez	Y	?	Y	N	N	N	N
32 Dixon	Y	N	N	N	N	N	N
33 Roybal-Allard	+	Y	N	N	N	N	N
34 Torres	?	Y	N	N	N	N	N
35 Waters	?	Y	N	N	N	N	N
36 Harman	Y	Y	N	N	N	N	N
37 Millender-McD.	Y	N	+	N	N	N	

	340	342	343	344	345	346	347
38 *Horn*	Y	Y	Y	Y	N	N	N
39 *Royce*	Y	Y	Y	Y	N	N	N
40 *Lewis*	?	Y	Y	Y	N	N	N
41 *Kim*	Y	Y	Y	Y	N	N	N
42 Brown	Y	Y	N	N	N	N	N
43 *Calvert*	Y	Y	Y	Y	N	N	N
44 *Bono, M.*	Y	Y	Y	Y	N	N	N
45 *Rohrabacher*	Y	Y	Y	Y	N	N	N
46 Sanchez	Y	Y	Y	N	N	N	N
47 *Cox*	?	Y	Y	Y	N	N	N
48 *Packard*	Y	Y	Y	Y	N	N	N
49 *Bilbray*	Y	Y	Y	Y	N	N	N
50 Filner	Y	Y	N	N	Y	N	N
51 *Cunningham*	Y	Y	Y	Y	N	N	N
52 *Hunter*	Y	Y	?	Y	N	N	Y
COLORADO							
1 DeGette	Y	Y	Y	Y	N	N	N
2 Skaggs	Y	Y	Y	N	N	N	N
3 *McInnis*	Y	Y	Y	Y	N	Y	N
4 *Schaffer*	Y	Y	Y	Y	N	Y	Y
5 *Hefley*	Y	Y	Y	Y	N	N	Y
6 *Schaefer*	?	Y	Y	Y	N	N	Y
CONNECTICUT							
1 Kennelly	Y	Y	Y	N	N	Y	N
2 Gejdenson	Y	Y	N	Y	N	Y	N
3 DeLauro	Y	Y	N	N	N	Y	N
4 *Shays*	Y	Y	Y	Y	Y	Y	N
5 Maloney	Y	Y	Y	Y	N	Y	N
6 *Johnson*	Y	Y	Y	Y	N	Y	N
DELAWARE							
AL *Castle*	Y	Y	Y	N	N	Y	N
FLORIDA							
1 *Scarborough*	Y	?	Y	Y	N	N	Y
2 Boyd	Y	Y	Y	Y	N	N	N
3 Brown	Y	Y	Y	N	N	N	N
4 *Fowler*	Y	Y	Y	Y	N	N	Y
5 Thurman	Y	Y	Y	Y	N	N	N
6 *Stearns*	Y	Y	Y	Y	N	N	Y
7 *Mica*	Y	Y	Y	Y	N	N	Y
8 *McCollum*	Y	Y	Y	Y	N	N	Y
9 *Bilirakis*	Y	Y	Y	Y	N	N	Y
10 *Young*	?	?	?	?	?	?	?
11 Davis	Y	Y	Y	N	N	N	N
12 *Canady*	Y	Y	Y	Y	N	N	Y
13 *Miller*	Y	Y	Y	Y	N	N	Y
14 *Goss*	Y	Y	Y	Y	N	N	Y
15 *Weldon*	Y	Y	Y	Y	N	N	N
16 *Foley*	Y	Y	Y	Y	N	N	N
17 Meek	Y	Y	Y	N	N	N	N
18 *Ros-Lehtinen*	?	Y	Y	N	N	N	N
19 Wexler	?	Y	N	N	N	N	N
20 Deutsch	Y	Y	N	N	N	N	N
21 *Diaz-Balart*	Y	Y	Y	N	N	N	N
22 *Shaw*	Y	Y	Y	Y	N	Y	N
23 Hastings	?	?	N	N	N	N	N
GEORGIA							
1 *Kingston*	?	Y	Y	Y	Y	Y	Y
2 Bishop	Y	Y	Y	N	N	N	Y
3 *Collins*	Y	Y	Y	N	N	N	Y
4 McKinney	Y	?	N	N	N	N	N
5 Lewis	Y	Y	N	N	N	N	N
6 *Gingrich*	Y						
7 *Barr*	Y	Y	Y	Y	N	N	Y
8 *Chambliss*	Y	Y	Y	N	N	N	Y
9 *Deal*	Y	Y	Y	Y	N	N	Y
10 *Norwood*	Y	Y	Y	N	N	N	Y
11 *Linder*	Y	?	Y	Y	N	N	Y
HAWAII							
1 Abercrombie	Y	N	N	N	Y	N	N
2 Mink	Y	Y	N	N	Y	N	N
IDAHO							
1 *Chenoweth*	Y	Y	Y	Y	N	N	Y
2 *Crapo*	Y	Y	Y	Y	N	N	Y
ILLINOIS							
1 Rush	Y	N	N	N	N	Y	N
2 Jackson	Y	N	N	N	N	Y	N
3 Lipinski	?	Y	Y	Y	N	Y	Y
4 Gutierrez	Y	Y	N	Y	N	Y	Y
5 Blagojevich	Y	N	N	N	N	N	N
6 *Hyde*	Y	Y	Y	Y	N	Y	Y
7 Davis	Y	N	N	N	N	Y	N
8 *Crane*	Y	Y	Y	Y	N	Y	Y
9 Yates	?	Y	Y	Y	Y	N	N
10 *Porter*	Y	Y	Y	Y	N	N	N
11 *Weller*	Y	Y	Y	Y	Y	N	Y
12 Costello	Y	Y	Y	Y	N	N	Y

	340	342	343	344	345	346	347
13 ***Fawell***	Y	Y	Y	Y	N	Y	N
14 ***Hastert***	Y	Y	Y	Y	N	Y	Y
15 ***Ewing***	Y	Y	Y	Y	N	Y	Y
16 ***Manzullo***	Y	Y	Y	Y	Y	Y	Y
17 Evans	Y	?	N	N	Y	N	N
18 ***LaHood***	Y	Y	Y	N	N	Y	Y
19 Poshard	?	?	N	Y	Y	Y	N
20 ***Shimkus***	Y	Y	Y	Y	N	Y	Y
INDIANA							
1 Visclosky	Y	Y	Y	N	Y	Y	N
2 ***McIntosh***	Y	Y	Y	Y	N	Y	Y
3 Roemer	Y	Y	Y	Y	Y	Y	Y
4 ***Souder***	Y	Y	Y	Y	N	Y	Y
5 ***Buyer***	Y	?	Y	Y	N	N	N
6 ***Burton***	Y	P	Y	Y	N	N	Y
7 ***Pease***	Y	Y	Y	Y	N	N	Y
8 ***Hostettler***	Y	Y	Y	Y	N	N	Y
9 Hamilton	Y	Y	Y	Y	Y	N	N
10 Carson	Y	Y	Y	Y	Y	N	N
IOWA							
1 ***Leach***	Y	Y	Y	Y	Y	Y	N
2 ***Nussle***	Y	Y	Y	Y	Y	Y	Y
3 Boswell	Y	Y	Y	Y	N	Y	Y
4 ***Ganske***	Y	Y	Y	Y	Y	Y	N
5 ***Latham***	Y	Y	Y	Y	Y	Y	Y
KANSAS							
1 ***Moran***	Y	Y	Y	Y	N	N	Y
2 ***Ryun***	Y	Y	Y	Y	N	N	Y
3 ***Snowbarger***	Y	Y	Y	Y	N	N	Y
4 ***Tiahrt***	+	Y	Y	Y	N	N	Y
KENTUCKY							
1 ***Whitfield***	?	Y	Y	Y	N	N	Y
2 ***Lewis***	Y	Y	Y	Y	N	N	Y
3 ***Northup***	Y	Y	Y	Y	N	N	Y
4 ***Bunning***	Y	Y	Y	Y	N	N	Y
5 ***Rogers***	Y	Y	Y	Y	N	N	Y
6 Baesler	Y	Y	Y	N	N	N	Y
LOUISIANA							
1 ***Livingston***	Y	Y	Y	Y	N	N	Y
2 Jefferson	Y	Y	N	N	N	N	N
3 ***Tauzin***	?	Y	Y	Y	N	N	Y
4 ***McCrery***	Y	Y	Y	Y	N	N	Y
5 ***Cooksey***	Y	Y	Y	Y	N	N	Y
6 ***Baker***	Y	Y	Y	Y	N	N	Y
7 John	Y	Y	Y	Y	N	N	N
MAINE							
1 Allen	Y	Y	Y	Y	N	Y	N
2 Baldacci	Y	Y	Y	Y	N	Y	N
MARYLAND							
1 ***Gilchrest***	Y	Y	Y	Y	N	N	N
2 ***Ehrlich***	Y	Y	Y	Y	N	N	Y
3 Cardin	Y	Y	N	Y	N	N	N
4 Wynn	Y	Y	N	Y	N	N	N
5 Hoyer	Y	Y	Y	Y	N	N	N
6 ***Bartlett***	Y	Y	Y	Y	N	N	Y
7 Cummings	Y	Y	N	N	N	N	N
8 ***Morella***	Y	Y	Y	N	N	N	N
MASSACHUSETTS							
1 Olver	Y	Y	N	Y	N	Y	N
2 Neal	Y	Y	N	Y	N	Y	N
3 McGovern	Y	Y	N	N	N	Y	N
4 Frank	Y	Y	Y	Y	Y	Y	N
5 Meehan	Y	Y	N	N	Y	Y	N
6 Tierney	Y	Y	N	N	Y	Y	N
7 Markey	?	Y	N	N	Y	Y	N
8 Kennedy	Y	Y	N	N	Y	Y	N
9 Moakley	?	?	?	?	Y	Y	N
10 Delahunt	Y	Y	N	N	Y	Y	N
MICHIGAN							
1 Stupak	Y	Y	Y	Y	Y	Y	Y
2 ***Hoekstra***	Y	Y	Y	Y	Y	Y	Y
3 ***Ehlers***	Y	Y	Y	Y	N	Y	Y
4 ***Camp***	Y	Y	Y	Y	Y	Y	Y
5 Barcia	Y	Y	Y	Y	N	Y	Y
6 ***Upton***	Y	Y	Y	Y	Y	Y	Y
7 ***Smith***	Y	?	Y	Y	Y	Y	Y
8 Stabenow	Y	Y	N	N	N	Y	N
9 Kildee	Y	Y	Y	N	Y	Y	N
10 Bonior	Y	Y	N	N	N	Y	N
11 ***Knollenberg***	Y	Y	Y	Y	N	N	N
12 Levin	Y	Y	Y	Y	Y	Y	N
13 Rivers	Y	Y	Y	Y	Y	Y	N
14 Conyers	?	?	N	N	Y	Y	N
15 Kilpatrick	Y	Y	N	N	N	Y	N
16 Dingell	Y	Y	Y	Y	Y	N	N
MINNESOTA							
1 ***Gutknecht***	Y	Y	Y	Y	N	N	Y
2 Minge	Y	Y	Y	Y	Y	N	Y
3 ***Ramstad***	Y	Y	Y	Y	Y	N	Y
4 Vento	Y	Y	Y	Y	Y	N	N
5 Sabo	Y	Y	Y	Y	N	N	N
6 Luther	Y	Y	N	Y	Y	N	N
7 Peterson	Y	Y	Y	Y	Y	N	Y
8 Oberstar	Y	Y	Y	Y	Y	Y	N
MISSISSIPPI							
1 ***Wicker***	Y	Y	Y	Y	N	N	Y
2 Thompson	?	Y	N	N	N	N	N
3 ***Pickering***	Y	Y	Y	Y	N	N	Y
4 ***Parker***	Y	Y	Y	Y	N	N	Y
5 Taylor	Y	Y	Y	Y	N	N	Y
MISSOURI							
1 Clay	Y	Y	N	Y	N	N	N
2 ***Talent***	Y	Y	Y	?	N	N	Y
3 Gephardt	Y	Y	Y	Y	N	N	N
4 Skelton	Y	Y	Y	Y	N	N	Y
5 McCarthy	+	Y	Y	Y	N	Y	N
6 Danner	Y	Y	Y	Y	Y	N	Y
7 ***Blunt***	Y	Y	Y	Y	N	N	Y
8 ***Emerson***	Y	Y	Y	Y	N	N	Y
9 ***Hulshof***	Y	Y	Y	Y	N	Y	Y
MONTANA							
AL ***Hill***	Y	Y	Y	Y	N	N	Y
NEBRASKA							
1 ***Bereuter***	Y	Y	Y	Y	Y	Y	Y
2 ***Christensen***	Y	Y	Y	Y	Y	N	Y
3 ***Barrett***	Y	Y	Y	Y	N	N	Y
NEVADA							
1 ***Ensign***	Y	Y	N	N	Y	N	Y
2 ***Gibbons***	Y	Y	N	N	N	N	Y
NEW HAMPSHIRE							
1 ***Sununu***	Y	Y	Y	Y	N	Y	N
2 ***Bass***	Y	Y	Y	Y	Y	Y	Y
NEW JERSEY							
1 Andrews	Y	Y	N	N	N	Y	N
2 ***LoBiondo***	Y	Y	Y	N	Y	Y	Y
3 ***Saxton***	Y	Y	Y	Y	N	Y	Y
4 ***Smith***	Y	Y	Y	N	N	Y	Y
5 ***Roukema***	Y	Y	Y	Y	Y	Y	Y
6 Pallone	Y	Y	Y	N	Y	Y	N
7 ***Franks***	Y	Y	Y	N	Y	Y	Y
8 Pascrell	Y	Y	N	N	N	Y	N
9 Rothman	Y	Y	N	N	N	Y	N
10 Payne	Y	Y	N	N	Y	Y	N
11 ***Frelinghuysen***	Y	Y	Y	Y	N	Y	N
12 ***Pappas***	Y	Y	Y	N	N	Y	Y
13 Menendez	Y	Y	N	N	N	Y	N
NEW MEXICO							
1 ***Wilson***	Y	Y	Y	Y	N	N	Y
2 ***Skeen***	Y	Y	N	N	N	N	Y
3 ***Redmond***	Y	Y	Y	Y	N	N	Y
NEW YORK							
1 ***Forbes***	Y	Y	Y	N	N	Y	N
2 ***Lazio***	Y	Y	Y	Y	Y	Y	N
3 ***King***	Y	Y	Y	Y	N	Y	Y
4 McCarthy	Y	Y	Y	Y	N	Y	N
5 Ackerman	?	Y	N	N	N	Y	N
6 Meeks	Y	Y	N	N	N	Y	N
7 Manton	Y	?	Y	Y	N	Y	N
8 Nadler	?	?	N	N	Y	Y	N
9 Schumer	Y	?	N	N	Y	Y	N
10 Towns	Y	?	?	N	N	Y	N
11 Owens	Y	Y	N	N	Y	Y	N
12 Velázquez	Y	Y	N	N	Y	?	?
13 ***Fossella***	Y	Y	Y	Y	Y	Y	Y
14 Maloney	Y	Y	N	N	Y	Y	N
15 Rangel	Y	?	N	N	N	Y	N
16 Serrano	Y	Y	N	Y	N	Y	N
17 Engel	Y	Y	?	N	N	Y	N
18 Lowey	Y	Y	N	Y	Y	Y	N
19 ***Kelly***	Y	Y	Y	N	Y	Y	N
20 ***Gilman***	Y	Y	Y	Y	N	Y	N
21 McNulty	Y	Y	N	N	N	Y	N
22 ***Solomon***	Y	Y	Y	Y	N	Y	Y
23 ***Boehlert***	Y	Y	Y	Y	N	Y	N
24 ***McHugh***	Y	Y	Y	Y	Y	Y	Y
25 ***Walsh***	?	Y	Y	Y	N	Y	Y
26 Hinchey	Y	Y	N	N	N	Y	N
27 ***Paxon***	Y	Y	Y	Y	Y	Y	Y
28 Slaughter	Y	?	N	N	Y	Y	N
29 LaFalce	Y	Y	N	Y	Y	Y	N
30 ***Quinn***	Y	Y	Y	Y	N	Y	Y
31 ***Houghton***	Y	Y	Y	Y	N	Y	N
NORTH CAROLINA							
1 Clayton	Y	Y	+	+	N	N	Y
2 Etheridge	Y	Y	+	+	N	N	Y
3 ***Jones***	Y	Y	Y	Y	N	N	Y
4 Price	?	?	?	?	N	N	N
5 ***Burr***	Y	Y	Y	Y	N	N	N
6 ***Coble***	Y	Y	Y	Y	Y	N	Y
7 McIntyre	Y	?	Y	Y	N	N	Y
8 Hefner	Y	?	Y	Y	N	N	N
9 ***Myrick***	Y	Y	Y	Y	Y	N	Y
10 ***Ballenger***	Y	Y	Y	Y	N	N	Y
11 ***Taylor***	Y	Y	Y	Y	N	N	Y
12 Watt	Y	Y	N	N	N	N	N
NORTH DAKOTA							
AL Pomeroy	?	Y	Y	Y	Y	N	Y
OHIO							
1 ***Chabot***	Y	Y	Y	Y	Y	N	Y
2 ***Portman***	Y	Y	Y	Y	Y	N	Y
3 Hall	Y	Y	Y	Y	N	N	N
4 ***Oxley***	Y	Y	Y	Y	N	N	Y
5 ***Gillmor***	Y	Y	Y	Y	N	N	Y
6 Strickland	Y	Y	N	N	Y	N	N
7 ***Hobson***	Y	Y	Y	Y	N	N	N
8 ***Boehner***	Y	Y	Y	Y	N	N	Y
9 Kaptur	Y	Y	?	Y	Y	N	N
10 Kucinich	Y	Y	N	N	N	N	N
11 Stokes	Y	Y	N	Y	N	N	N
12 ***Kasich***	Y	Y	Y	N	N	N	Y
13 Brown	Y	Y	Y	Y	Y	Y	N
14 Sawyer	Y	Y	N	Y	N	N	N
15 ***Pryce***	Y	Y	Y	Y	N	N	Y
16 ***Regula***	Y	Y	Y	Y	N	N	Y
17 Traficant	Y	Y	Y	Y	N	N	Y
18 ***Ney***	Y	Y	Y	Y	N	N	Y
19 ***LaTourette***	Y	Y	Y	Y	N	N	Y
OKLAHOMA							
1 ***Largent***	?	Y	Y	Y	Y	N	Y
2 ***Coburn***	Y	Y	Y	Y	Y	N	Y
3 ***Watkins***	Y	?	Y	Y	N	N	Y
4 ***Watts***	Y	Y	Y	Y	N	N	Y
5 ***Istook***	Y	Y	Y	Y	N	N	Y
6 ***Lucas***	Y	Y	Y	Y	N	N	Y
OREGON							
1 Furse	Y	?	N	N	N	N	N
2 ***Smith***	Y	?	Y	Y	N	N	Y
3 Blumenauer	Y	Y	Y	Y	Y	N	N
4 DeFazio	?	Y	N	N	Y	N	N
5 Hooley	Y	Y	N	N	N	N	N
PENNSYLVANIA							
1 Brady	Y	Y	N	N	N	Y	N
2 Fattah	Y	Y	N	N	N	Y	N
3 Borski	Y	Y	N	Y	N	Y	N
4 Klink	Y	?	Y	Y	N	Y	Y
5 ***Peterson***	Y	Y	Y	Y	N	Y	Y
6 Holden	Y	Y	N	N	Y	Y	Y
7 ***Weldon***	Y	Y	Y	Y	N	Y	Y
8 ***Greenwood***	Y	?	Y	Y	N	Y	N
9 ***Shuster***	?	?	Y	Y	Y	Y	Y
10 ***McDade***	?	Y	?	Y	N	Y	N
11 Kanjorski	Y	Y	N	N	Y	Y	Y
12 Murtha	?	?	Y	Y	N	Y	N
13 ***Fox***	Y	Y	Y	Y	N	Y	Y
14 Coyne	Y	Y	N	Y	Y	Y	N
15 McHale	Y	Y	Y	?	N	Y	N
16 ***Pitts***	Y	Y	Y	Y	N	Y	Y
17 ***Gekas***	Y	Y	Y	Y	N	Y	Y
18 Doyle	Y	Y	N	N	Y	Y	Y
19 ***Goodling***	Y	?	Y	Y	Y	Y	Y
20 Mascara	Y	Y	Y	Y	N	Y	Y
21 ***English***	Y	Y	Y	N	N	Y	Y
RHODE ISLAND							
1 Kennedy	Y	Y	Y	N	N	Y	N
2 Weygand	Y	Y	N	N	N	Y	N
SOUTH CAROLINA							
1 ***Sanford***	?	Y	Y	Y	Y	N	Y
2 ***Spence***	Y	Y	Y	Y	N	N	Y
3 ***Graham***	Y	Y	Y	Y	N	N	Y
4 ***Inglis***	Y	Y	Y	Y	Y	N	Y
5 Spratt	Y	Y	Y	Y	N	N	Y
6 Clyburn	Y	Y	N	Y	N	N	N
SOUTH DAKOTA							
AL ***Thune***	Y	Y	Y	Y	N	N	Y
TENNESSEE							
1 ***Jenkins***	Y	Y	Y	?	N	N	Y
2 ***Duncan***	Y	Y	Y	Y	Y	N	Y
3 ***Wamp***	Y	Y	Y	Y	Y	N	Y
4 ***Hilleary***	Y	Y	Y	Y	Y	N	Y
5 Clement	Y	Y	Y	Y	N	N	N
6 Gordon	Y	Y	Y	Y	N	N	Y
7 ***Bryant***	Y	Y	Y	Y	N	N	Y
8 Tanner	Y	Y	Y	Y	N	N	Y
9 Ford	Y	Y	N	N	N	Y	N
TEXAS							
1 Sandlin	Y	Y	Y	Y	N	N	Y
2 Turner	Y	Y	Y	Y	N	N	Y
3 ***Johnson, Sam***	Y	Y	Y	Y	N	N	Y
4 Hall	Y	Y	Y	Y	N	N	Y
5 ***Sessions***	Y	Y	Y	Y	N	N	Y
6 ***Barton***	Y	Y	Y	Y	N	N	Y
7 ***Archer***	Y	?	Y	Y	N	N	Y
8 ***Brady***	Y	Y	Y	Y	N	N	Y
9 Lampson	Y	Y	Y	Y	N	N	N
10 Doggett	Y	Y	N	N	N	N	N
11 Edwards	Y	Y	Y	Y	N	N	Y
12 ***Granger***	Y	?	Y	+	N	N	N
13 ***Thornberry***	Y	Y	Y	Y	N	N	Y
14 ***Paul***	Y	Y	Y	N	Y	N	Y
15 Hinojosa	Y	?	–	–	N	N	Y
16 Reyes	Y	Y	N	N	N	N	Y
17 Stenholm	Y	Y	Y	Y	N	N	Y
18 Jackson-Lee	Y	Y	Y	Y	N	N	N
19 ***Combest***	Y	Y	Y	Y	N	N	Y
20 Gonzalez	?	?	?	?	?	?	?
21 ***Smith***	Y	Y	Y	Y	N	N	Y
22 ***DeLay***	Y	Y	Y	Y	N	N	Y
23 ***Bonilla***	?	Y	N	N	N	N	Y
24 Frost	Y	Y	Y	Y	N	N	N
25 Bentsen	Y	Y	Y	Y	N	N	N
26 ***Armey***	Y	Y	Y	Y	N	N	Y
27 Ortiz	Y	Y	N	N	N	N	Y
28 Rodriguez	Y	Y	N	N	N	N	Y
29 Green	Y	Y	Y	Y	N	N	Y
30 Johnson, E.B.	Y	Y	Y	Y	N	N	N
UTAH							
1 ***Hansen***	Y	Y	Y	Y	N	N	Y
2 ***Cook***	Y	Y	Y	Y	N	N	Y
3 ***Cannon***	?	?	Y	Y	N	N	Y
VERMONT							
AL *Sanders*	Y	Y	Y	Y	Y	Y	N
VIRGINIA							
1 ***Bateman***	Y	Y	Y	Y	Y	N	Y
2 Pickett	?	Y	Y	Y	N	N	Y
3 Scott	Y	Y	N	Y	N	N	N
4 Sisisky	Y	Y	Y	Y	N	N	Y
5 Goode	Y	Y	Y	Y	Y	N	Y
6 ***Goodlatte***	Y	Y	Y	Y	Y	N	Y
7 ***Bliley***	Y	Y	Y	Y	N	N	Y
8 Moran	Y	Y	Y	Y	N	N	N
9 Boucher	Y	Y	Y	Y	N	N	Y
10 ***Wolf***	Y	Y	Y	Y	N	N	Y
11 ***Davis***	Y	Y	Y	Y	N	N	N
WASHINGTON							
1 ***White***	Y	Y	Y	Y	N	N	Y
2 ***Metcalf***	Y	Y	Y	Y	N	N	Y
3 ***Smith, Linda***	Y	Y	Y	Y	N	N	Y
4 ***Hastings***	Y	Y	Y	Y	N	N	Y
5 ***Nethercutt***	Y	Y	Y	N	N	N	Y
6 Dicks	Y	?	Y	Y	N	N	N
7 McDermott	Y	Y	N	N	N	N	N
8 ***Dunn***	Y	Y	Y	Y	N	N	Y
9 Smith, Adam	Y	Y	Y	Y	N	N	N
WEST VIRGINIA							
1 Mollohan	Y	Y	Y	Y	N	Y	N
2 Wise	Y	Y	Y	Y	N	Y	N
3 Rahall	Y	Y	Y	N	N	N	Y
WISCONSIN							
1 ***Neumann***	Y	Y	Y	Y	Y	Y	Y
2 ***Klug***	Y	Y	Y	Y	Y	N	Y
3 Kind	Y	Y	Y	Y	Y	Y	N
4 Kleczka	Y	Y	Y	Y	Y	Y	N
5 Barrett	Y	Y	Y	Y	Y	Y	N
6 ***Petri***	Y	Y	Y	N	N	Y	Y
7 Obey	Y	Y	Y	Y	Y	Y	N
8 Johnson	Y	Y	Y	Y	N	Y	Y
9 ***Sensenbrenner***	Y	Y	Y	N	N	Y	Y
WYOMING							
AL ***Cubin***	Y	Y	?	Y	N	N	Y

Southern states - Ala., Ark., Fla., Ga., Ky., La., Miss., N.C., Okla., S.C., Tenn., Texas, Va.

348. Quorum Call.* 414 Responded. July 29, 1998.

349. HR 4194. Fiscal 1999 VA-HUD Appropriations/San Francisco's Unmarried Domestic Partner Ordinance. Riggs, R-Calif., amendment to prohibit any funds in the bill from being used to implement the San Francisco ordinance that requires private companies and organizations contracting with or receiving grants from the city to provide health care benefits to unmarried domestic partners of their workers. Adopted 214-212: R 189-33; D 25-178 (ND 10-139, SD 15-39); I 0-1. July 29, 1998.

350. HR 4194. Fiscal 1999 VA-HUD Appropriations/VA Medical Care Funding Increase. Coburn, R-Okla., amendment to increase the bill's funding for VA medical care by $304 million. The amendment would offset the increase by cutting the funding for non-overhead administrative expenses of the Federal Housing Administration. Adopted 351-73: R 215-9; D 135-64 (ND 91-54, SD 44-10); I 1-0. July 29, 1998.

351. HR 4194. Fiscal 1999 VA-HUD Appropriations/Recommit. Obey, D-Wis., motion to recommit the bill to the Appropriations Committee with instructions to report it back with an amendment to delete provisions that prohibit funding to promulgate certain rules dealing with chemical treatment of upholstery fabrics under the Flammable Fabrics Act. Motion rejected 164-261: R 4-221; D 159-40 (ND 133-12, SD 26-28); I 1-0. July 29, 1998.

352. HR 4194. Fiscal 1999 VA-HUD Appropriations/Passage. Passage of the bill to provide $71.3 billion in discretionary spending to the Veterans Affairs and Housing and Urban Development departments and 17 independent agencies. Passed 259-164: R 205-18; D 54-145 (ND 22-124, SD 32-21); I 0-1. July 29, 1998.

353. HR 4059. Fiscal 1999 Military Construction Appropriations/Conference Report. Adoption of the conference report on the bill to provide $8.45 billion in funding for military construction projects. Adopted (thus sent to the Senate) 417-1: R 219-1; D 197-0 (ND 143-0, SD 54-0); I 1-0. July 29, 1998.

354. Quorum Call.* 403 Responded. July 29, 1998.

355. HR 4328. Fiscal 1999 Transportation Appropriations/Passage. Passage of the bill to provide $46.9 billion in funding for highways and infrastructure and other transportation related projects in fiscal 1999. Passed 391-25: R 197-23; D 193-2 (ND 140-1, SD 53-1); I 1-0. July 30, 1998.

356. H J Res 120. Disapproval of Presidential Waiver for Vietnam/Passage. Passage of the joint resolution to disapprove President Clinton's waiver that allows Vietnam to participate in certain U.S. trade support and investment promotion programs. Rejected 163-260: R 127-93; D 35-167 (ND 29-119, SD 6-48); I 1-0. July 30, 1998.

* CQ does not include quorum calls in its vote charts.

Key

Y	Voted for (yea).
#	Paired for.
+	Announced for.
N	Voted against (nay).
X	Paired against.
−	Announced against.
P	Voted "present."
C	Voted "present" to avoid possible conflict of interest.
?	Did not vote or otherwise make a position known.

Democrats **Republicans** *Independent*

	349	350	351	352	353	355	356
ALABAMA							
1 *Callahan*	Y	Y	N	Y	Y	Y	N
2 *Everett*	Y	Y	N	Y	Y	Y	Y
3 *Riley*	Y	Y	N	Y	Y	Y	Y
4 *Aderholt*	Y	Y	N	Y	Y	Y	Y
5 Cramer	Y	Y	Y	Y	Y	Y	Y
6 *Bachus*	Y	Y	N	Y	Y	Y	Y
7 Hilliard	N	Y	Y	N	Y	Y	N
ALASKA							
AL *Young*	Y	Y	N	Y	Y	Y	N
ARIZONA							
1 *Salmon*	Y	Y	N	N	Y	N	N
2 Pastor	N	Y	Y	N	Y	Y	N
3 *Stump*	Y	Y	N	Y	Y	N	Y
4 *Shadegg*	Y	Y	N	Y	Y	N	Y
5 *Kolbe*	N	N	Y	Y	Y	Y	N
6 *Hayworth*	Y	Y	N	Y	Y	Y	N
ARKANSAS							
1 Berry	Y	Y	N	N	Y	Y	N
2 Snyder	N	Y	Y	N	Y	Y	N
3 *Hutchinson*	Y	Y	N	Y	Y	Y	Y
4 *Dickey*	Y	Y	N	Y	Y	Y	Y
CALIFORNIA							
1 *Riggs*	Y	Y	N	Y	Y	Y	−
2 *Herger*	Y	Y	N	N	Y	N	N
3 Fazio	N	N	Y	N	Y	?	N
4 *Doolittle*	Y	Y	N	Y	Y	Y	Y
5 Matsui	N	Y	Y	N	Y	?	N
6 Woolsey	N	N	Y	N	Y	Y	N
7 Miller	N	N	Y	N	Y	Y	N
8 Pelosi	N	N	Y	N	Y	Y	N
9 Lee	N	N	Y	N	Y	Y	N
10 Tauscher	N	Y	Y	N	Y	Y	N
11 *Pombo*	Y	Y	N	Y	Y	N	Y
12 Lantos	N	Y	Y	N	Y	Y	N
13 Stark	N	N	Y	N	Y	?	N
14 Eshoo	N	N	Y	N	Y	Y	N
15 *Campbell*	N	Y	N	Y	Y	N	N
16 Lofgren	N	N	Y	N	Y	Y	N
17 Farr	N	Y	Y	N	Y	Y	N
18 Condit	N	N	Y	N	Y	Y	N
19 *Radanovich*	Y	Y	N	Y	Y	Y	N
20 Dooley	N	N	Y	N	Y	Y	N
21 *Thomas*	Y	Y	N	Y	Y	Y	N
22 Capps, L.	N	Y	Y	N	Y	Y	N
23 *Gallegly*	Y	Y	N	Y	Y	Y	Y
24 Sherman	N	N	Y	N	Y	Y	N
25 *McKeon*	Y	Y	N	Y	Y	Y	N
26 Berman	N	N	Y	N	Y	Y	N
27 *Rogan*	Y	Y	N	Y	Y	Y	N
28 *Dreier*	Y	Y	N	Y	Y	Y	N
29 Waxman	N	N	Y	N	Y	Y	N
30 Becerra	N	N	Y	N	Y	+	N
31 Martinez	N	N	Y	N	Y	Y	N
32 Dixon	N	N	Y	N	Y	Y	N
33 Royal-Allard	N	N	Y	N	Y	Y	N
34 Torres	N	N	?	N	?	Y	Y
35 Waters	N	N	Y	N	Y	Y	Y
36 Harman	N	?	?	?	?	N	N
37 Millender-McD.	N	Y	Y	N	Y	Y	N

	349	350	351	352	353	355	356
38 *Horn*	N	Y	N	Y	Y	N	Y
39 *Royce*	Y	Y	N	N	Y	N	Y
40 *Lewis*	N	N	N	Y	Y	Y	N
41 *Kim*	Y	Y	N	Y	Y	Y	N
42 Brown	N	N	Y	Y	Y	Y	N
43 *Calvert*	Y	Y	N	Y	Y	Y	Y
44 *Bono, M.*	Y	Y	N	Y	Y	Y	Y
45 *Rohrabacher*	Y	Y	N	Y	Y	Y	Y
46 Sanchez	N	Y	N	Y	Y	Y	N
47 *Cox*	Y	Y	N	N	Y	?	Y
48 *Packard*	Y	Y	N	Y	Y	Y	Y
49 *Bilbray*	N	Y	N	Y	Y	Y	N
50 Filner	N	N	Y	N	Y	Y	N
51 *Cunningham*	Y	Y	N	Y	Y	Y	N
52 *Hunter*	Y	Y	N	Y	Y	Y	Y
COLORADO							
1 DeGette	N	N	Y	N	Y	Y	N
2 Skaggs	N	N	Y	N	Y	Y	N
3 *McInnis*	Y	Y	N	Y	Y	Y	N
4 *Schaffer*	Y	Y	N	Y	N	Y	Y
5 *Hefley*	Y	Y	N	Y	Y	Y	Y
6 *Schaefer*	Y	Y	N	Y	Y	Y	Y
CONNECTICUT							
1 Kennelly	N	Y	N	Y	N	Y	N
2 Gejdenson	N	Y	Y	N	Y	Y	N
3 DeLauro	N	Y	Y	N	Y	Y	N
4 *Shays*	N	N	Y	N	Y	Y	N
5 Maloney	N	Y	Y	N	Y	Y	N
6 *Johnson*	N	N	Y	N	Y	Y	N
DELAWARE							
AL *Castle*	N	N	Y	N	Y	Y	N
FLORIDA							
1 *Scarborough*	Y	Y	N	Y	Y	Y	Y
2 Boyd	N	Y	Y	N	Y	Y	N
3 Brown	N	Y	Y	Y	Y	Y	N
4 *Fowler*	N	N	Y	Y	Y	Y	N
5 Thurman	N	Y	Y	Y	Y	Y	N
6 *Stearns*	Y	Y	N	Y	Y	Y	Y
7 *Mica*	Y	Y	N	Y	Y	Y	Y
8 *McCollum*	Y	Y	N	Y	?	Y	Y
9 *Bilirakis*	Y	Y	N	Y	Y	Y	Y
10 *Young*	?	?	?	?	?	?	?
11 Davis	N	Y	N	Y	Y	Y	N
12 *Canady*	Y	Y	N	Y	Y	Y	Y
13 *Miller*	N	Y	N	Y	Y	Y	N
14 *Goss*	N	Y	Y	N	Y	Y	N
15 *Weldon*	Y	Y	N	Y	Y	Y	Y
16 *Foley*	N	Y	N	Y	Y	Y	N
17 Meek	N	N	Y	Y	Y	Y	N
18 *Ros-Lehtinen*	Y	Y	N	Y	Y	Y	N
19 Wexler	N	Y	N	Y	N	N	N
20 Deutsch	N	Y	Y	N	Y	Y	N
21 *Diaz-Balart*	Y	N	N	Y	Y	Y	N
22 *Shaw*	N	Y	N	Y	Y	Y	N
23 Hastings	N	N	Y	N	Y	Y	N
GEORGIA							
1 *Kingston*	Y	Y	N	Y	Y	Y	Y
2 Bishop	Y	Y	N	Y	Y	Y	N
3 *Collins*	Y	Y	N	Y	Y	Y	N
4 McKinney	N	Y	Y	N	Y	Y	N
5 Lewis	N	Y	Y	N	Y	Y	N
6 *Gingrich*							
7 *Barr*	Y	Y	N	Y	Y	Y	Y
8 *Chambliss*	Y	Y	N	?	Y	Y	N
9 *Deal*	Y	Y	N	Y	Y	Y	Y
10 *Norwood*	Y	Y	N	Y	?	Y	Y
11 *Linder*	Y	Y	N	Y	?	Y	Y
HAWAII							
1 Abercrombie	N	Y	Y	N	Y	Y	N
2 Mink	N	Y	Y	N	Y	Y	N
IDAHO							
1 *Chenoweth*	Y	Y	N	N	Y	N	Y
2 *Crapo*	Y	Y	N	Y	Y	Y	Y
ILLINOIS							
1 Rush	N	N	Y	N	Y	Y	N
2 Jackson	N	N	Y	N	Y	Y	Y
3 Lipinski	Y	Y	Y	Y	Y	Y	Y
4 Gutierrez	N	N	Y	N	Y	Y	N
5 Blagojevich	N	N	Y	N	Y	Y	N
6 *Hyde*	Y	Y	N	Y	Y	Y	N
7 Davis	N	Y	Y	N	Y	Y	N
8 *Crane*	Y	Y	N	Y	Y	Y	N
9 Yates	?	?	?	?	?	?	N
10 *Porter*	−	Y	N	Y	Y	Y	Y
11 *Weller*	Y	Y	N	Y	Y	Y	N
12 Costello	Y	Y	Y	Y	Y	Y	Y

ND Northern Democrats   SD Southern Democrats

	349	350	351	352	353	355	356
13 ***Fawell***	Y	N	N	Y	Y	Y	N
14 ***Hastert***	Y	Y	N	Y	Y	Y	Y
15 ***Ewing***	Y	Y	N	Y	Y	?	N
16 ***Manzullo***	Y	Y	N	Y	Y	Y	N
17 Evans	N	Y	Y	N	Y	Y	N
18 ***LaHood***	Y	Y	N	Y	Y	Y	Y
19 Poshard	N	Y	Y	N	Y	Y	N
20 ***Shimkus***	Y	Y	N	Y	Y	Y	N
INDIANA							
1 Visclosky	N	Y	Y	N	Y	Y	N
2 ***McIntosh***	Y	Y	N	Y	Y	Y	N
3 Roemer	Y	Y	Y	N	Y	Y	N
4 ***Souder***	Y	Y	N	Y	Y	N	Y
5 ***Buyer***	Y	Y	N	Y	Y	Y	Y
6 ***Burton***	?	?	N	Y	Y	Y	Y
7 ***Pease***	Y	Y	N	Y	Y	Y	N
8 ***Hostettler***	Y	Y	N	N	Y	Y	N
9 Hamilton	Y	Y	Y	N	Y	Y	N
10 Carson	N	Y	Y	N	Y	Y	N
IOWA							
1 ***Leach***	N	Y	N	Y	Y	Y	N
2 ***Nussle***	Y	Y	N	Y	Y	Y	N
3 Boswell	N	Y	N	Y	Y	Y	N
4 ***Ganske***	Y	Y	N	Y	Y	Y	N
5 ***Latham***	Y	Y	N	Y	Y	Y	N
KANSAS							
1 ***Moran***	Y	Y	N	Y	Y	N	N
2 ***Ryun***	Y	Y	N	Y	Y	Y	Y
3 ***Snowbarger***	Y	Y	N	Y	Y	Y	Y
4 ***Tiahrt***	Y	Y	N	Y	Y	Y	Y
KENTUCKY							
1 ***Whitfield***	Y	Y	N	Y	?	Y	Y
2 ***Lewis***	Y	Y	N	Y	Y	Y	Y
3 ***Northup***	Y	Y	N	Y	Y	Y	Y
4 ***Bunning***	Y	Y	N	Y	Y	Y	Y
5 ***Rogers***	Y	Y	N	Y	?	Y	Y
6 Baesler	Y	Y	N	Y	Y	Y	N
LOUISIANA							
1 ***Livingston***	Y	N	N	Y	Y	Y	N
2 Jefferson	N	Y	Y	N	Y	Y	N
3 ***Tauzin***	Y	Y	N	Y	Y	Y	Y
4 ***McCrery***	N	Y	N	Y	Y	Y	N
5 ***Cooksey***	Y	Y	N	Y	Y	Y	Y
6 ***Baker***	Y	Y	N	Y	Y	Y	Y
7 John	Y	Y	N	Y	Y	Y	N
MAINE							
1 Allen	N	Y	Y	N	Y	Y	N
2 Baldacci	N	Y	Y	N	Y	Y	N
MARYLAND							
1 ***Gilchrest***	N	N	N	Y	Y	Y	N
2 ***Ehrlich***	Y	Y	N	Y	Y	Y	Y
3 Cardin	N	Y	Y	N	Y	Y	N
4 Wynn	N	Y	Y	N	Y	Y	N
5 Hoyer	N	N	Y	N	Y	Y	N
6 ***Bartlett***	Y	Y	N	Y	Y	Y	Y
7 Cummings	N	N	Y	N	Y	Y	N
8 ***Morella***	N	Y	Y	N	Y	Y	N
MASSACHUSETTS							
1 Olver	N	N	Y	N	Y	Y	N
2 Neal	N	N	?	?	?	Y	?
3 McGovern	N	Y	Y	N	Y	Y	Y
4 Frank	N	N	?	?	?	?	N
5 Meehan	N	?	Y	N	Y	Y	N
6 Tierney	N	N	Y	N	Y	Y	N
7 Markey	N	N	Y	N	Y	Y	N
8 Kennedy	N	N	Y	N	Y	Y	N
9 Moakley	?	?	?	?	?	?	N
10 Delahunt	N	N	Y	N	Y	Y	N
MICHIGAN							
1 Stupak	N	Y	Y	N	Y	Y	Y
2 ***Hoekstra***	Y	Y	N	N	Y	N	Y
3 ***Ehlers***	Y	Y	N	Y	Y	Y	N
4 ***Camp***	Y	Y	N	Y	Y	Y	N
5 Barcia	N	Y	Y	N	Y	Y	N
6 ***Upton***	Y	Y	N	Y	Y	Y	Y
7 ***Smith***	Y	Y	N	Y	Y	Y	Y
8 Stabenow	N	Y	Y	N	Y	Y	N
9 Kildee	N	Y	Y	N	Y	Y	Y
10 Bonior	N	N	Y	N	Y	Y	Y
11 ***Knollenberg***	Y	N	N	Y	Y	Y	N
12 Levin	N	Y	Y	N	Y	Y	N
13 Rivers	N	Y	Y	N	Y	Y	Y
14 Conyers	N	N	Y	N	Y	Y	N
15 Kilpatrick	N	N	Y	N	Y	Y	N
16 Dingell	N	Y	N	N	Y	?	N

	349	350	351	352	353	355	356
MINNESOTA							
1 ***Gutknecht***	Y	Y	N	Y	Y	Y	Y
2 Minge	N	Y	N	N	Y	Y	N
3 ***Ramstad***	Y	Y	N	Y	Y	Y	N
4 Vento	N	N	Y	N	Y	Y	Y
5 Sabo	N	N	Y	Y	Y	Y	N
6 Luther	N	N	Y	N	Y	Y	N
7 Peterson	Y	Y	N	N	Y	Y	N
8 Oberstar	N	N	Y	N	Y	Y	N
MISSISSIPPI							
1 ***Wicker***	Y	Y	N	Y	Y	Y	N
2 Thompson	N	Y	N	Y	Y	Y	N
3 ***Pickering***	Y	Y	N	Y	Y	Y	N
4 ***Parker***	Y	Y	N	Y	Y	Y	N
5 Taylor	Y	Y	N	Y	Y	Y	N
MISSOURI							
1 Clay	N	?	Y	N	Y	Y	N
2 ***Talent***	Y	Y	N	Y	Y	Y	Y
3 Gephardt	N	Y	Y	N	Y	Y	N
4 Skelton	Y	Y	Y	N	Y	Y	N
5 McCarthy	N	Y	Y	N	Y	Y	N
6 Danner	Y	Y	N	Y	Y	Y	N
7 ***Blunt***	Y	Y	N	Y	Y	Y	Y
8 ***Emerson***	Y	Y	N	Y	Y	Y	Y
9 ***Hulshof***	Y	Y	N	Y	Y	Y	N
MONTANA							
AL ***Hill***	Y	Y	N	Y	Y	N	Y
NEBRASKA							
1 ***Bereuter***	Y	Y	N	Y	Y	Y	N
2 ***Christensen***	Y	Y	N	Y	Y	Y	Y
3 ***Barrett***	Y	Y	N	Y	Y	Y	N
NEVADA							
1 ***Ensign***	N	Y	N	Y	Y	Y	Y
2 ***Gibbons***	Y	Y	N	Y	Y	Y	Y
NEW HAMPSHIRE							
1 ***Sununu***	Y	Y	N	Y	Y	Y	N
2 ***Bass***	N	Y	N	Y	Y	Y	N
NEW JERSEY							
1 Andrews	N	Y	Y	N	Y	Y	Y
2 ***LoBiondo***	Y	Y	N	Y	Y	Y	Y
3 ***Saxton***	N	Y	N	Y	Y	Y	Y
4 ***Smith***	Y	Y	N	Y	Y	Y	Y
5 ***Roukema***	Y	Y	N	Y	Y	Y	N
6 Pallone	N	Y	Y	N	Y	Y	N
7 ***Franks***	N	Y	N	Y	Y	Y	N
8 Pascrell	N	Y	Y	N	Y	Y	Y
9 Rothman	N	Y	Y	N	Y	Y	N
10 Payne	N	N	Y	N	Y	Y	N
11 ***Frelinghuysen***	N	Y	N	Y	Y	Y	Y
12 ***Pappas***	Y	Y	N	Y	Y	Y	Y
13 Menendez	N	Y	Y	N	Y	Y	Y
NEW MEXICO							
1 ***Wilson***	Y	Y	N	Y	Y	Y	N
2 ***Skeen***	Y	Y	N	Y	Y	Y	N
3 ***Redmond***	Y	Y	N	Y	Y	Y	N
NEW YORK							
1 ***Forbes***	N	Y	N	Y	Y	Y	Y
2 ***Lazio***	N	N	N	Y	Y	Y	Y
3 ***King***	Y	Y	N	Y	Y	Y	Y
4 McCarthy	N	Y	Y	N	Y	Y	Y
5 Ackerman	N	Y	Y	N	Y	Y	N
6 Meeks	N	N	Y	N	Y	Y	Y
7 Manton	N	Y	Y	N	Y	Y	Y
8 Nadler	N	N	Y	N	Y	Y	Y
9 Schumer	N	Y	Y	N	Y	Y	N
10 Towns	N	Y	Y	N	?	Y	?
11 Owens	N	N	Y	N	Y	Y	N
12 Velázquez	N	N	Y	N	Y	Y	N
13 ***Fossella***	Y	Y	N	Y	Y	Y	Y
14 Maloney	N	Y	Y	N	Y	Y	N
15 Rangel	N	N	Y	N	?	Y	N
16 Serrano	N	Y	Y	N	Y	Y	N
17 Engel	N	Y	Y	N	Y	Y	N
18 Lowey	N	Y	Y	N	Y	Y	N
19 ***Kelly***	N	Y	N	Y	Y	Y	Y
20 ***Gilman***	N	Y	N	Y	Y	Y	N
21 McNulty	N	Y	Y	N	Y	Y	Y
22 ***Solomon***	Y	Y	N	Y	Y	Y	Y
23 ***Boehlert***	N	Y	N	Y	Y	Y	N
24 ***McHugh***	Y	Y	N	Y	Y	Y	N
25 ***Walsh***	Y	Y	N	Y	Y	Y	N
26 Hinchey	N	Y	Y	N	Y	Y	Y
27 ***Paxon***	Y	Y	N	Y	Y	Y	N
28 Slaughter	N	Y	Y	N	Y	Y	N
29 LaFalce	N	N	Y	N	Y	Y	N

	349	350	351	352	353	355	356
30 ***Quinn***	Y	Y	N	Y	Y	Y	Y
31 ***Houghton***	N	Y	N	Y	Y	Y	N
NORTH CAROLINA							
1 Clayton	N	N	N	Y	Y	Y	N
2 Etheridge	N	Y	N	Y	Y	Y	N
3 ***Jones***	Y	Y	N	Y	Y	N	Y
4 Price	N	Y	N	Y	Y	Y	N
5 ***Burr***	Y	Y	N	Y	Y	N	–
6 ***Coble***	Y	Y	N	Y	Y	Y	Y
7 McIntyre	Y	Y	N	Y	Y	Y	Y
8 Hefner	N	Y	N	Y	Y	Y	N
9 ***Myrick***	Y	Y	N	Y	Y	Y	Y
10 ***Ballenger***	Y	Y	N	Y	Y	Y	N
11 ***Taylor***	Y	Y	N	Y	Y	Y	N
12 Watt	N	N	N	N	Y	Y	N
NORTH DAKOTA							
AL Pomeroy	N	Y	Y	N	Y	Y	N
OHIO							
1 ***Chabot***	Y	Y	N	Y	Y	N	Y
2 ***Portman***	Y	Y	N	Y	Y	Y	N
3 Hall	Y	Y	Y	Y	Y	?	N
4 ***Oxley***	Y	Y	N	Y	Y	Y	N
5 ***Gillmor***	Y	Y	N	Y	Y	Y	N
6 Strickland	N	Y	Y	N	Y	Y	Y
7 ***Hobson***	Y	Y	N	Y	Y	Y	Y
8 ***Boehner***	Y	?	N	Y	Y	Y	N
9 Kaptur	N	N	Y	Y	Y	Y	N
10 Kucinich	N	N	Y	N	Y	N	Y
11 Stokes	N	N	Y	Y	Y	Y	N
12 ***Kasich***	Y	Y	N	Y	Y	N	N
13 Brown	N	Y	Y	N	Y	Y	Y
14 Sawyer	N	Y	Y	N	Y	Y	N
15 ***Pryce***	Y	Y	N	Y	Y	Y	N
16 ***Regula***	Y	Y	N	Y	Y	Y	Y
17 Traficant	Y	Y	N	Y	Y	Y	Y
18 ***Ney***	Y	Y	N	Y	Y	Y	Y
19 ***LaTourette***	?	Y	N	Y	Y	?	N
OKLAHOMA							
1 ***Largent***	Y	Y	N	Y	Y	Y	N
2 ***Coburn***	Y	Y	N	Y	Y	Y	Y
3 ***Watkins***	Y	Y	N	Y	Y	Y	N
4 ***Watts***	Y	Y	N	Y	Y	Y	Y
5 ***Istook***	Y	Y	N	Y	Y	Y	?
6 ***Lucas***	Y	Y	N	Y	Y	Y	N
OREGON							
1 Furse	N	N	Y	N	Y	Y	N
2 ***Smith***	Y	Y	N	Y	Y	?	N
3 Blumenauer	N	N	Y	N	Y	Y	N
4 DeFazio	N	Y	Y	N	Y	Y	Y
5 Hooley	N	Y	Y	N	Y	Y	N
PENNSYLVANIA							
1 Brady	N	Y	Y	N	Y	Y	N
2 Fattah	N	Y	Y	N	Y	Y	N
3 Borski	N	Y	Y	N	Y	Y	N
4 Klink	N	Y	Y	N	Y	Y	N
5 ***Peterson***	Y	Y	N	Y	Y	Y	Y
6 Holden	Y	Y	N	Y	Y	Y	Y
7 ***Weldon***	Y	Y	Y	?	Y	Y	N
8 ***Greenwood***	Y	Y	N	Y	Y	Y	N
9 ***Shuster***	Y	Y	?	Y	Y	Y	Y
10 ***McDade***	?	N	N	?	Y	?	?
11 Kanjorski	N	Y	Y	N	Y	Y	N
12 Murtha	N	Y	Y	Y	Y	?	N
13 ***Fox***	Y	Y	N	Y	Y	Y	Y
14 Coyne	N	Y	Y	N	Y	Y	Y
15 McHale	N	Y	Y	N	Y	Y	N
16 ***Pitts***	Y	Y	N	Y	Y	Y	Y
17 ***Gekas***	Y	Y	N	Y	Y	Y	Y
18 Doyle	N	Y	Y	Y	Y	Y	N
19 ***Goodling***	Y	Y	N	Y	Y	Y	Y
20 Mascara	N	Y	Y	Y	Y	Y	N
21 ***English***	N	Y	N	N	Y	Y	Y
RHODE ISLAND							
1 Kennedy	N	N	Y	N	Y	Y	Y
2 Weygand	N	Y	Y	N	Y	Y	N
SOUTH CAROLINA							
1 ***Sanford***	N	Y	N	N	Y	N	N
2 ***Spence***	Y	Y	N	Y	Y	Y	Y
3 ***Graham***	Y	Y	N	Y	Y	N	Y
4 ***Inglis***	Y	Y	N	Y	Y	Y	Y
5 Spratt	N	Y	N	Y	Y	Y	N
6 Clyburn	N	Y	N	N	Y	Y	N
SOUTH DAKOTA							
AL ***Thune***	Y	Y	N	Y	Y	Y	Y

	349	350	351	352	353	355	356
TENNESSEE							
1 ***Jenkins***	Y	Y	N	Y	Y	Y	Y
2 ***Duncan***	Y	Y	N	N	?	Y	Y
3 ***Wamp***	Y	Y	N	Y	Y	Y	Y
4 ***Hilleary***	Y	Y	N	Y	Y	Y	Y
5 Clement	N	Y	Y	Y	Y	Y	N
6 Gordon	N	Y	Y	?	Y	Y	N
7 ***Bryant***	Y	Y	N	Y	Y	Y	Y
8 Tanner	Y	Y	N	Y	Y	Y	N
9 Ford	N	Y	Y	Y	Y	Y	N
TEXAS							
1 Sandlin	Y	Y	N	Y	Y	Y	N
2 Turner	Y	Y	N	Y	Y	Y	Y
3 ***Johnson, Sam***	Y	Y	N	Y	Y	?	Y
4 Hall	Y	Y	N	Y	Y	Y	Y
5 ***Sessions***	Y	Y	N	Y	Y	N	Y
6 ***Barton***	Y	Y	N	Y	Y	Y	Y
7 ***Archer***	Y	Y	N	Y	Y	Y	N
8 ***Brady***	Y	Y	N	Y	Y	Y	N
9 Lampson	N	Y	Y	Y	Y	Y	N
10 Doggett	N	N	Y	N	Y	Y	N
11 Edwards	N	Y	Y	N	Y	Y	N
12 ***Granger***	Y	Y	N	Y	Y	Y	N
13 ***Thornberry***	Y	Y	N	Y	Y	Y	Y
14 ***Paul***	Y	Y	N	N	N	N	Y
15 Hinojosa	N	Y	N	Y	Y	Y	N
16 Reyes	N	Y	N	Y	Y	Y	N
17 Stenholm	Y	Y	N	Y	Y	Y	N
18 Jackson-Lee	N	Y	Y	N	Y	Y	Y
19 ***Combest***	Y	Y	N	Y	Y	Y	N
20 Gonzalez	?	?	?	?	?	?	?
21 ***Smith***	Y	Y	N	Y	Y	Y	Y
22 ***DeLay***	Y	Y	N	Y	Y	Y	Y
23 ***Bonilla***	Y	Y	N	Y	Y	Y	Y
24 Frost	N	Y	N	Y	Y	Y	N
25 Bentsen	N	N	Y	N	Y	Y	N
26 ***Armey***	Y	Y	N	Y	Y	Y	Y
27 Ortiz	Y	Y	N	Y	Y	Y	N
28 Rodriguez	N	Y	Y	N	Y	Y	N
29 Green	N	N	Y	N	Y	Y	Y
30 Johnson, E.B.	N	Y	Y	N	Y	Y	N
UTAH							
1 ***Hansen***	Y	Y	N	Y	Y	Y	Y
2 ***Cook***	Y	Y	N	Y	Y	Y	Y
3 ***Cannon***	Y	Y	N	Y	Y	Y	N
VERMONT							
AL *Sanders*	N	Y	Y	N	Y	Y	Y
VIRGINIA							
1 ***Bateman***	Y	Y	N	Y	Y	Y	N
2 Pickett	Y	Y	N	Y	Y	Y	N
3 Scott	N	N	Y	Y	Y	Y	N
4 Sisisky	N	Y	N	N	Y	Y	N
5 Goode	Y	Y	N	Y	Y	Y	Y
6 ***Goodlatte***	Y	Y	N	Y	Y	Y	N
7 ***Bliley***	Y	Y	N	Y	Y	Y	N
8 Moran	N	N	Y	Y	Y	Y	N
9 Boucher	N	Y	N	Y	Y	Y	N
10 ***Wolf***	Y	Y	Y	Y	Y	Y	Y
11 ***Davis***	N	Y	N	Y	Y	Y	Y
WASHINGTON							
1 ***White***	N	Y	N	Y	Y	Y	N
2 ***Metcalf***	Y	Y	N	Y	Y	Y	Y
3 ***Smith, Linda***	Y	Y	N	N	Y	Y	?
4 ***Hastings***	Y	Y	N	Y	Y	Y	N
5 ***Nethercutt***	Y	Y	N	Y	Y	Y	N
6 Dicks	N	Y	Y	Y	Y	Y	N
7 McDermott	N	N	Y	N	Y	Y	N
8 ***Dunn***	Y	Y	N	Y	Y	Y	N
9 Smith, Adam	N	Y	Y	N	Y	Y	N
WEST VIRGINIA							
1 Mollohan	N	N	N	Y	Y	Y	N
2 Wise	N	Y	Y	Y	Y	Y	N
3 Rahall	N	Y	N	Y	Y	Y	?
WISCONSIN							
1 ***Neumann***	Y	Y	Y	Y	Y	Y	Y
2 ***Klug***	Y	Y	N	N	Y	Y	Y
3 Kind	N	Y	N	N	Y	Y	N
4 Kleczka	N	Y	Y	N	Y	Y	N
5 Barrett	N	Y	Y	N	Y	Y	N
6 ***Petri***	Y	Y	N	N	Y	Y	N
7 Obey	N	?	Y	N	Y	Y	N
8 Johnson	N	Y	Y	N	Y	Y	N
9 ***Sensenbrenner***	Y	Y	N	N	Y	Y	N
WYOMING							
AL ***Cubin***	N	Y	N	Y	Y	Y	Y

Southern states - Ala., Ark., Fla., Ga., Ky., La., Miss., N.C., Okla., S.C., Tenn., Texas, Va.

Key

Y	Voted for (yea).
#	Paired for.
+	Announced for.
N	Voted against (nay).
X	Paired against.
–	Announced against.
P	Voted "present."
C	Voted "present" to avoid possible conflict of interest.
?	Did not vote or otherwise make a position known.

Democrats   **Republicans**
Independent

357. H Res 507. Special Investigative Authority In Teamsters Union Probe/Adoption. Adoption of the resolution to authorize the staff of the Education and the Workforce Committee to take depositions, under oath, in a closed session, as a part of the committee's investigation of the Teamsters Union. Adopted 222-200: R 219-2; D 3-197 (ND 0-146, SD 3-51); I 0-1. July 30, 1998.

358. HR 2183. Campaign Finance Overhaul/Shays-Meehan Substitute — Motor Voter Modification. Goodlatte, R-Va., amendment to the Shays-Meehan substitute amendment to the bill to overhaul campaign finance laws. The amendment would modify the "motor voter" voter registration law by requiring voters to provide proof of citizenship when registering to vote. Rejected 165-260: R 163-59; D 2-200 (ND 2-146, SD 0-54); I 0-1. July 30, 1998.

359. HR 2183. Campaign Finance Overhaul/Shays-Meehan Substitute — Photo ID requirement. Wicker, R-Miss., amendment to the Shays-Meehan substitute amendment to the bill to overhaul campaign finance laws. The amendment would allow states to require voters to produce valid photo identification at their ballot stations in order to vote. Rejected 192-231: R 185-36; D 7-194 (ND 4-143, SD 3-51); I 0-1. July 30, 1998.

360. HR 2183. Campaign Finance Overhaul/Shays-Meehan Substitute — Contributions Limitations. Calvert, R-Calif., amendment to the Shays-Meehan substitute amendment to the bill to overhaul campaign finance laws. The amendment would limit the amount of campaign contributions a candidate may accept from individuals outside his or her district to the level of contributions received from district residents. Rejected 147-278: R 137-84; D 10-193 (ND 7-142, SD 3-51); I 0-1. July 30, 1998.

361. HR 2183. Campaign Finance Overhaul/Shays-Meehan Substitute — Voter Guide Clarification. Smith, R-Wash., amendment to the Shays-Meehan substitute amendment to the bill to overhaul campaign finance laws. The amendment would clarify that only voter guides clearly advocating the election or defeat of a candidate are required to be disclosed to the Federal Election Commission. Adopted 343-84: R 152-71; D 190-13 (ND 140-9, SD 50-4); I 1-0. July 30, 1998.

362. HR 2183. Campaign Finance Overhaul/Shays-Meehan Substitute — Matching Opponent's Personal Funds. Rohrabacher, R-Calif., amendment to the Shays-Meehan substitute amendment to the bill to overhaul campaign finance laws. The amendment would allow a candidate whose opponent spends more than $1,000 in personal funds to accept contributions from any legal source up to the same amount of personal funds spent in the campaign. Rejected 155-272: R 139-84; D 16-187 (ND 12-137, SD 4-50); I 0-1. July 30, 1998.

363. HR 2183. Campaign Finance Overhaul/Shays-Meehan Substitute — Ballot Petition Signature Requirements. Paul, R-Texas, amendment to the Shays-Meehan substitute amendment to the bill to overhaul campaign finance laws. The amendment would alter certain ballot petition signature requirements to try to widen participation by third parties in national elections. Rejected 62-363: R 45-176; D 16-187 (ND 14-135, SD 2-52); I 1-0. July 30, 1998.

	357	358	359	360	361	362	363
ALABAMA							
1 *Callahan*	Y	Y	Y	Y	N	Y	N
2 *Everett*	Y	Y	Y	Y	N	Y	N
3 *Riley*	Y	Y	Y	N	N	Y	N
4 *Aderholt*	Y	Y	Y	N	N	Y	N
5 Cramer	N	N	N	N	Y	N	N
6 *Bachus*	Y	Y	Y	Y	Y	Y	N
7 Hilliard	N	N	N	N	N	N	N
ALASKA							
AL *Young*	Y	Y	Y	Y	Y	Y	Y
ARIZONA							
1 *Salmon*	Y	Y	Y	Y	Y	Y	N
2 Pastor	N	N	N	N	Y	N	N
3 *Stump*	Y	Y	Y	Y	N	Y	N
4 *Shadegg*	Y	Y	Y	Y	Y	Y	N
5 *Kolbe*	Y	Y	Y	Y	Y	Y	N
6 *Hayworth*	Y	Y	Y	Y	Y	Y	N
ARKANSAS							
1 Berry	N	N	N	N	Y	N	N
2 Snyder	N	N	N	N	Y	N	N
3 *Hutchinson*	Y	N	N	N	N	N	N
4 *Dickey*	Y	Y	Y	Y	Y	Y	N
CALIFORNIA							
1 *Riggs*	+	+	+	+	+	–	–
2 *Herger*	Y	Y	Y	Y	N	Y	?
3 Fazio	N	N	N	N	Y	N	N
4 *Doolittle*	Y	Y	Y	N	N	Y	N
5 Matsui	N	N	N	N	Y	N	N
6 Woolsey	N	N	N	N	Y	N	N
7 Miller	N	N	N	N	Y	N	N
8 Pelosi	N	N	N	N	Y	N	N
9 Lee	N	N	N	N	Y	N	N
10 Tauscher	N	N	N	N	Y	N	N
11 *Pombo*	Y	Y	Y	Y	N	Y	Y
12 Lantos	N	N	N	N	Y	N	N
13 Stark	N	N	N	N	Y	N	N
14 Eshoo	N	N	N	N	Y	N	N
15 *Campbell*	N	N	N	N	Y	N	N
16 Lofgren	N	N	N	N	Y	N	N
17 Farr	N	N	N	N	Y	N	N
18 Condit	N	N	Y	Y	Y	N	N
19 *Radanovich*	Y	Y	Y	Y	N	Y	N
20 Dooley	N	N	N	N	Y	N	N
21 *Thomas*	Y	Y	Y	Y	Y	Y	N
22 Capps, L.	N	N	N	N	Y	N	N
23 *Gallegly*	Y	Y	Y	Y	N	Y	N
24 Sherman	N	N	N	N	Y	N	N
25 *McKeon*	Y	Y	Y	Y	Y	Y	N
26 Berman	N	N	N	N	Y	N	N
27 *Rogan*	Y	Y	Y	N	Y	N	Y
28 *Dreier*	Y	Y	Y	N	Y	N	N
29 Waxman	N	N	N	N	Y	N	N
30 Becerra	N	N	N	N	Y	N	N
31 Martinez	N	N	Y	N	Y	N	N
32 Dixon	N	N	N	N	Y	N	N
33 Roybal-Allard	N	N	N	N	Y	N	N
34 Torres	?	N	N	N	Y	N	Y
35 Waters	?	N	N	N	Y	N	N
36 Harman	N	N	N	N	Y	N	N
37 Millender-McD.	N	N	N	N	Y	N	N
38 *Horn*	Y	Y	Y	Y	N	Y	N

	357	358	359	360	361	362	363
39 *Royce*	Y	Y	Y	Y	N	Y	Y
40 *Lewis*	Y	Y	Y	Y	Y	N	Y
41 *Kim*	Y	N	Y	N	Y	N	N
42 Brown	N	N	N	N	Y	N	N
43 *Calvert*	Y	Y	Y	Y	Y	Y	N
44 *Bono, M.*	Y	Y	Y	N	Y	N	N
45 *Rohrabacher*	Y	Y	Y	N	Y	Y	N
46 Sanchez	N	N	N	N	Y	N	N
47 *Cox*	?	Y	Y	N	Y	N	Y
48 *Packard*	Y	Y	Y	Y	N	Y	N
49 *Bilbray*	Y	N	N	N	Y	N	N
50 Filner	N	N	N	N	Y	N	N
51 *Cunningham*	Y	Y	N	Y	N	Y	N
52 *Hunter*	Y	Y	Y	Y	Y	N	N
COLORADO							
1 DeGette	N	N	N	N	Y	N	N
2 Skaggs	N	N	N	N	Y	N	N
3 *McInnis*	Y	Y	Y	N	Y	N	N
4 *Schaffer*	Y	N	Y	N	Y	N	N
5 *Hefley*	Y	Y	Y	N	N	Y	N
6 *Schaefer*	Y	Y	Y	N	N	Y	N
CONNECTICUT							
1 Kennelly	N	N	N	N	Y	N	N
2 Gejdenson	N	N	N	N	Y	N	N
3 DeLauro	N	N	N	N	Y	N	N
4 *Shays*	Y	N	N	N	Y	N	N
5 Maloney	N	N	N	N	Y	N	N
6 *Johnson*	Y	N	N	N	Y	N	N
DELAWARE							
AL *Castle*	Y	N	N	N	Y	N	N
FLORIDA							
1 *Scarborough*	Y	Y	?	Y	N	Y	N
2 Boyd	N	N	N	N	Y	N	N
3 Brown	N	N	N	N	Y	N	N
4 *Fowler*	Y	Y	Y	N	N	Y	N
5 Thurman	N	N	N	N	Y	N	N
6 *Stearns*	Y	Y	Y	N	N	Y	N
7 *Mica*	Y	Y	Y	Y	Y	Y	Y
8 *McCollum*	Y	Y	Y	Y	N	Y	N
9 *Bilirakis*	Y	Y	Y	N	N	N	N
10 *Young*	?	?	?	?	?	?	?
11 Davis	N	N	N	N	Y	N	N
12 *Canady*	Y	Y	Y	Y	N	Y	N
13 *Miller*	Y	Y	Y	Y	N	Y	N
14 *Goss*	Y	Y	Y	N	N	Y	N
15 *Weldon*	Y	Y	Y	Y	Y	N	N
16 *Foley*	Y	Y	Y	N	N	Y	N
17 Meek	N	N	N	N	N	N	N
18 *Ros-Lehtinen*	Y	N	N	N	Y	N	N
19 Wexler	N	N	N	N	Y	N	N
20 Deutsch	N	N	N	N	Y	N	N
21 *Diaz-Balart*	Y	N	N	N	Y	N	N
22 *Shaw*	Y	Y	Y	Y	Y	Y	N
23 Hastings	N	N	N	N	N	N	N
GEORGIA							
1 *Kingston*	Y	Y	Y	Y	N	N	N
2 Bishop	N	N	N	N	Y	N	N
3 *Collins*	Y	Y	Y	Y	N	Y	N
4 McKinney	N	N	N	N	Y	N	N
5 Lewis	N	N	N	N	Y	N	N
6 *Gingrich*	Y						
7 *Barr*	Y	Y	Y	Y	N	N	N
8 *Chambliss*	Y	Y	Y	Y	N	Y	N
9 *Deal*	Y	Y	Y	N	Y	N	N
10 *Norwood*	Y	Y	Y	N	Y	Y	Y
11 *Linder*	?	?	Y	Y	Y	N	N
HAWAII							
1 Abercrombie	N	N	N	Y	N	Y	Y
2 Mink	N	N	N	N	Y	Y	Y
IDAHO							
1 *Chenoweth*	Y	N	Y	N	Y	Y	N
2 *Crapo*	Y	N	Y	Y	N	Y	N
ILLINOIS							
1 Rush	N	N	N	N	Y	N	N
2 Jackson	N	N	N	N	Y	N	N
3 Lipinski	N	Y	N	Y	Y	N	N
4 Gutierrez	N	N	N	N	Y	N	N
5 Blagojevich	N	N	N	N	Y	N	N
6 *Hyde*	Y	Y	Y	N	Y	N	N
7 Davis	N	N	N	N	Y	N	N
8 *Crane*	Y	Y	Y	Y	Y	Y	Y
9 Yates	N	N	N	N	Y	N	N
10 *Porter*	Y	Y	Y	N	Y	N	N
11 *Weller*	Y	Y	Y	N	Y	N	N
12 Costello	N	N	N	N	Y	N	N
13 *Fawell*	Y	Y	Y	Y	Y	Y	N

ND Northern Democrats   SD Southern Democrats

	357	358	359	360	361	362	363
14 ***Hastert***	Y	Y	Y	Y	N	N	N
15 ***Ewing***	Y	Y	Y	Y	Y	N	N
16 ***Manzullo***	Y	N	Y	Y	N	Y	N
17 Evans	N	N	N	N	Y	N	N
18 ***LaHood***	Y	Y	Y	Y	Y	N	N
19 Poshard	N	N	N	N	Y	N	N
20 ***Shimkus***	Y	Y	Y	N	Y	Y	Y
INDIANA							
1 Visclosky	N	N	N	N	Y	N	N
2 ***McIntosh***	Y	Y	Y	N	Y	Y	Y
3 Roemer	N	N	N	N	Y	N	Y
4 ***Souder***	Y	N	N	Y	Y	Y	N
5 ***Buyer***	Y	Y	Y	?	Y	N	N
6 ***Burton***	Y	Y	Y	Y	N	Y	N
7 ***Pease***	Y	Y	Y	Y	Y	Y	N
8 ***Hostettler***	Y	Y	Y	N	Y	Y	Y
9 Hamilton	N	N	N	N	Y	N	N
10 Carson	N	N	N	N	Y	N	N
IOWA							
1 ***Leach***	Y	N	N	N	Y	N	Y
2 ***Nussle***	Y	Y	Y	Y	Y	N	N
3 Boswell	N	N	Y	N	Y	N	Y
4 ***Ganske***	Y	N	N	Y	Y	N	N
5 ***Latham***	Y	Y	Y	N	Y	N	N
KANSAS							
1 ***Moran***	Y	Y	Y	Y	N	Y	Y
2 ***Ryun***	Y	Y	Y	N	N	Y	N
3 ***Snowbarger***	Y	Y	Y	Y	Y	Y	N
4 ***Tiahrt***	Y	Y	Y	Y	Y	Y	Y
KENTUCKY							
1 ***Whitfield***	Y	Y	Y	N	N	N	N
2 ***Lewis***	Y	Y	Y	N	Y	Y	N
3 ***Northup***	Y	N	Y	N	N	N	N
4 ***Bunning***	Y	Y	Y	N	Y	Y	N
5 ***Rogers***	Y	Y	Y	N	N	Y	N
6 Baesler	N	N	N	N	Y	N	N
LOUISIANA							
1 ***Livingston***	Y	Y	Y	Y	Y	Y	N
2 Jefferson	N	N	N	N	Y	N	N
3 ***Tauzin***	Y	Y	Y	Y	Y	N	N
4 ***McCrery***	Y	Y	Y	Y	Y	Y	N
5 ***Cooksey***	Y	Y	Y	N	Y	Y	Y
6 ***Baker***	Y	Y	Y	Y	N	Y	N
7 John	N	N	N	N	Y	N	N
MAINE							
1 Allen	N	N	N	N	Y	N	N
2 Baldacci	N	N	N	N	Y	N	N
MARYLAND							
1 ***Gilchrest***	Y	N	N	N	Y	N	N
2 ***Ehrlich***	Y	Y	Y	Y	N	Y	N
3 Cardin	N	N	N	N	Y	N	N
4 Wynn	N	N	N	N	Y	N	N
5 Hoyer	N	N	N	N	Y	N	N
6 ***Bartlett***	Y	Y	Y	Y	N	Y	Y
7 Cummings	N	N	N	N	Y	N	N
8 ***Morella***	Y	N	N	N	Y	N	N
MASSACHUSETTS							
1 Olver	N	N	N	N	Y	N	N
2 Neal	?	N	N	N	Y	N	N
3 McGovern	N	N	N	N	Y	N	N
4 Frank	N	N	N	N	Y	N	N
5 Meehan	N	N	N	N	Y	N	N
6 Tierney	N	N	N	N	Y	N	N
7 Markey	N	N	N	N	Y	N	N
8 Kennedy	N	N	?	N	Y	N	N
9 Moakley	N	?	?	?	?	?	?
10 Delahunt	N	N	N	N	Y	N	N
MICHIGAN							
1 Stupak	N	N	N	Y	Y	N	N
2 ***Hoekstra***	Y	Y	Y	Y	N	N	Y
3 ***Ehlers***	Y	Y	Y	Y	Y	N	Y
4 ***Camp***	Y	Y	Y	Y	N	N	N
5 Barcia	N	N	N	Y	Y	N	N
6 ***Upton***	Y	Y	Y	Y	Y	N	N
7 ***Smith***	Y	Y	Y	Y	N	N	N
8 Stabenow	N	N	N	N	Y	N	N
9 Kildee	N	N	N	N	Y	N	N
10 Bonior	N	N	N	N	Y	N	N
11 ***Knollenberg***	Y	Y	Y	Y	N	N	N
12 Levin	N	N	N	N	Y	N	N
13 Rivers	N	N	N	N	Y	N	N
14 Conyers	N	N	N	N	Y	Y	N
15 Kilpatrick	N	N	N	N	Y	N	N
16 Dingell	N	N	N	N	Y	N	N
MINNESOTA							
1 ***Gutknecht***	Y	Y	Y	Y	Y	Y	N
2 Minge	N	N	N	N	Y	N	N
3 ***Ramstad***	Y	N	N	N	Y	N	N
4 Vento	N	N	N	N	Y	N	N
5 Sabo	N	N	N	N	Y	Y	N
6 Luther	N	N	N	Y	Y	N	N
7 Peterson	N	N	N	N	N	N	N
8 Oberstar	N	N	N	N	Y	N	N
MISSISSIPPI							
1 ***Wicker***	Y	Y	Y	N	N	Y	N
2 Thompson	N	N	N	N	Y	N	N
3 ***Pickering***	Y	Y	Y	N	N	Y	N
4 ***Parker***	Y	N	N	N	Y	N	N
5 Taylor	Y	N	Y	Y	Y	N	N
MISSOURI							
1 Clay	N	N	N	N	Y	Y	N
2 ***Talent***	Y	Y	Y	Y	Y	Y	N
3 Gephardt	N	N	N	N	N	N	N
4 Skelton	N	N	N	N	Y	N	N
5 McCarthy	N	N	N	N	Y	N	N
6 Danner	N	N	N	N	Y	N	N
7 ***Blunt***	Y	Y	Y	Y	Y	Y	N
8 ***Emerson***	Y	Y	Y	N	Y	N	N
9 ***Hulshof***	Y	Y	Y	Y	N	N	Y
MONTANA							
AL ***Hill***	Y	N	Y	Y	Y	N	Y
NEBRASKA							
1 ***Bereuter***	Y	Y	Y	Y	Y	N	N
2 ***Christensen***	Y	Y	Y	N	Y	Y	N
3 ***Barrett***	Y	N	N	Y	Y	N	N
NEVADA							
1 ***Ensign***	Y	Y	Y	N	Y	Y	N
2 ***Gibbons***	Y	Y	Y	Y	Y	Y	N
NEW HAMPSHIRE							
1 ***Sununu***	Y	N	Y	N	N	Y	Y
2 ***Bass***	Y	N	N	N	Y	N	N
NEW JERSEY							
1 Andrews	N	N	N	N	Y	N	N
2 ***LoBiondo***	Y	N	N	N	Y	N	N
3 ***Saxton***	Y	N	Y	Y	Y	Y	N
4 ***Smith***	Y	N	Y	N	N	N	N
5 ***Roukema***	Y	N	N	N	Y	N	N
6 Pallone	N	N	N	N	Y	N	N
7 ***Franks***	Y	N	N	N	Y	N	N
8 Pascrell	N	N	N	N	Y	N	N
9 Rothman	N	N	N	N	Y	N	N
10 Payne	N	N	N	N	Y	N	N
11 ***Frelinghuysen***	Y	N	N	N	Y	N	N
12 ***Pappas***	Y	N	Y	N	N	N	N
13 Menendez	N	N	N	N	Y	N	N
NEW MEXICO							
1 ***Wilson***	Y	Y	Y	N	Y	Y	N
2 ***Skeen***	Y	Y	Y	N	N	Y	N
3 ***Redmond***	Y	Y	Y	N	Y	Y	Y
NEW YORK							
1 ***Forbes***	N	N	N	N	Y	N	N
2 ***Lazio***	Y	N	Y	N	Y	N	N
3 ***King***	Y	N	Y	N	N	Y	N
4 McCarthy	N	N	N	N	Y	N	N
5 Ackerman	N	N	N	N	Y	N	N
6 Meeks	N	N	N	N	Y	N	N
7 Manton	N	N	N	N	Y	N	N
8 Nadler	N	N	N	N	Y	N	Y
9 Schumer	N	N	N	N	Y	N	N
10 Towns	?	?	?	?	?	?	?
11 Owens	N	N	N	N	Y	N	N
12 Velázquez	N	N	N	N	Y	N	N
13 ***Fossella***	Y	Y	Y	N	Y	Y	N
14 Maloney	N	N	N	N	Y	N	N
15 Rangel	N	?	?	N	Y	N	N
16 Serrano	N	N	N	N	Y	N	N
17 Engel	N	N	N	N	Y	N	N
18 Lowey	N	N	N	N	Y	N	N
19 ***Kelly***	Y	N	N	N	Y	N	N
20 ***Gilman***	Y	N	N	N	Y	N	N
21 McNulty	N	N	N	N	Y	N	N
22 ***Solomon***	Y	Y	Y	N	N	Y	N
23 ***Boehlert***	Y	N	N	N	Y	N	N
24 ***McHugh***	Y	Y	Y	Y	Y	N	N
25 ***Walsh***	Y	N	N	Y	Y	N	N
26 Hinchey	N	N	N	N	Y	N	N
27 ***Paxon***	Y	Y	Y	Y	N	Y	N
28 Slaughter	N	N	N	N	N	N	N
29 LaFalce	N	N	N	N	Y	N	N
30 ***Quinn***	Y	N	N	Y	Y	N	N
31 ***Houghton***	Y	N	N	N	Y	N	N
NORTH CAROLINA							
1 Clayton	N	N	N	N	Y	N	N
2 Etheridge	N	N	N	N	Y	N	N
3 ***Jones***	Y	Y	Y	Y	N	Y	N
4 Price	N	N	N	N	Y	N	N
5 ***Burr***	+	Y	Y	Y	N	N	N
6 ***Coble***	Y	Y	Y	Y	Y	Y	Y
7 McIntyre	N	N	N	N	Y	N	N
8 Hefner	N	N	N	N	Y	N	N
9 ***Myrick***	Y	Y	Y	Y	Y	Y	N
10 ***Ballenger***	Y	Y	Y	Y	Y	N	N
11 ***Taylor***	Y	Y	Y	Y	Y	Y	Y
12 Watt	N	N	N	N	Y	N	N
NORTH DAKOTA							
AL Pomeroy	N	N	N	N	Y	N	N
OHIO							
1 ***Chabot***	Y	N	Y	Y	Y	Y	N
2 ***Portman***	Y	N	Y	Y	Y	N	N
3 Hall	N	N	N	N	Y	N	N
4 ***Oxley***	Y	Y	Y	Y	N	N	N
5 ***Gillmor***	Y	N	Y	Y	Y	Y	N
6 Strickland	N	N	N	N	Y	N	N
7 ***Hobson***	Y	Y	Y	N	Y	Y	N
8 ***Boehner***	Y	Y	Y	Y	Y	Y	N
9 Kaptur	N	N	N	N	Y	N	N
10 Kucinich	N	N	N	N	Y	Y	N
11 Stokes	N	N	N	N	Y	N	N
12 ***Kasich***	Y	Y	Y	N	Y	Y	N
13 Brown	N	N	N	N	Y	N	N
14 Sawyer	N	N	N	N	Y	N	N
15 ***Pryce***	Y	Y	Y	Y	Y	Y	N
16 ***Regula***	Y	N	Y	Y	Y	Y	N
17 Traficant	N	Y	Y	N	Y	Y	Y
18 ***Ney***	Y	Y	Y	Y	Y	N	N
19 ***LaTourette***	Y	N	N	Y	Y	Y	Y
OKLAHOMA							
1 ***Largent***	Y	Y	Y	N	Y	Y	Y
2 ***Coburn***	Y	Y	Y	Y	Y	Y	N
3 ***Watkins***	Y	Y	Y	Y	Y	Y	N
4 ***Watts***	Y	Y	Y	N	Y	Y	Y
5 ***Istook***	?	?	?	?	?	?	?
6 ***Lucas***	Y	Y	Y	Y	Y	Y	N
OREGON							
1 Furse	N	N	N	N	Y	N	N
2 ***Smith***	Y	Y	Y	N	Y	N	N
3 Blumenauer	N	N	N	N	Y	N	N
4 DeFazio	N	N	N	N	Y	N	N
5 Hooley	N	N	N	N	Y	N	N
PENNSYLVANIA							
1 Brady	N	N	N	N	Y	N	N
2 Fattah	N	N	N	N	Y	N	N
3 Borski	N	N	N	N	Y	N	N
4 Klink	N	N	N	N	Y	Y	N
5 ***Peterson***	Y	Y	Y	Y	Y	Y	N
6 Holden	N	N	N	N	Y	Y	N
7 ***Weldon***	Y	Y	Y	Y	Y	Y	N
8 ***Greenwood***	Y	N	N	N	Y	N	N
9 ***Shuster***	Y	Y	Y	Y	Y	Y	N
10 ***McDade***	?	?	?	?	?	?	?
11 Kanjorski	N	N	N	N	Y	N	N
12 Murtha	N	N	N	N	N	Y	Y
13 ***Fox***	Y	N	N	–	Y	N	Y
14 Coyne	N	N	N	N	Y	N	N
15 McHale	N	N	N	N	Y	N	N
16 ***Pitts***	Y	Y	Y	N	N	N	N
17 ***Gekas***	Y	Y	Y	Y	Y	Y	N
18 Doyle	N	N	N	N	Y	N	Y
19 ***Goodling***	Y	Y	Y	Y	N	Y	Y
20 Mascara	N	N	N	N	Y	N	N
21 ***English***	Y	N	Y	Y	Y	N	N
RHODE ISLAND							
1 Kennedy	N	N	N	N	Y	N	N
2 Weygand	N	N	N	N	Y	N	N
SOUTH CAROLINA							
1 ***Sanford***	Y	N	N	N	Y	N	Y
2 ***Spence***	Y	Y	Y	Y	Y	Y	N
3 ***Graham***	Y	Y	Y	Y	Y	N	N
4 ***Inglis***	Y	Y	Y	Y	Y	Y	N
5 Spratt	N	N	N	N	Y	N	N
6 Clyburn	N	N	N	N	Y	N	N
SOUTH DAKOTA							
AL ***Thune***	Y	Y	Y	Y	Y	Y	N
TENNESSEE							
1 ***Jenkins***	Y	Y	Y	Y	Y	Y	N
2 ***Duncan***	Y	Y	Y	Y	Y	Y	N
3 ***Wamp***	Y	Y	Y	Y	Y	N	N
4 ***Hilleary***	Y	Y	Y	Y	Y	Y	Y
5 Clement	N	N	N	N	Y	N	N
6 Gordon	N	N	N	N	Y	N	N
7 ***Bryant***	Y	Y	Y	N	N	Y	N
8 Tanner	N	N	N	N	Y	N	N
9 Ford	N	N	N	N	Y	N	N
TEXAS							
1 Sandlin	N	N	N	N	Y	N	N
2 Turner	N	N	N	N	Y	N	N
3 ***Johnson, Sam***	Y	Y	Y	N	N	Y	N
4 Hall	Y	N	Y	N	Y	Y	N
5 ***Sessions***	Y	Y	Y	Y	N	Y	Y
6 ***Barton***	Y	Y	Y	Y	N	N	N
7 ***Archer***	Y	Y	Y	Y	Y	Y	N
8 ***Brady***	Y	N	Y	Y	Y	Y	N
9 Lampson	N	N	N	N	Y	N	N
10 Doggett	N	N	N	N	Y	N	Y
11 Edwards	N	N	N	N	Y	N	N
12 ***Granger***	Y	Y	Y	N	Y	Y	N
13 ***Thornberry***	Y	Y	Y	N	Y	Y	N
14 ***Paul***	N	N	Y	N	Y	Y	Y
15 Hinojosa	N	N	N	N	Y	N	N
16 Reyes	N	N	N	N	Y	N	N
17 Stenholm	N	N	N	N	Y	N	N
18 Jackson-Lee	N	N	N	N	Y	N	N
19 ***Combest***	Y	Y	Y	Y	Y	Y	N
20 Gonzalez	?	?	?	?	?	?	?
21 ***Smith***	Y	Y	Y	Y	Y	N	N
22 ***DeLay***	Y	Y	Y	Y	N	Y	N
23 ***Bonilla***	Y	Y	Y	N	Y	Y	N
24 Frost	N	N	N	N	Y	N	N
25 Bentsen	N	N	N	N	Y	N	N
26 ***Armey***	Y	Y	Y	Y	N	Y	Y
27 Ortiz	N	N	N	N	Y	N	N
28 Rodriguez	N	N	N	N	Y	N	N
29 Green	N	N	N	N	Y	N	N
30 Johnson, E.B.	N	N	N	N	Y	N	N
UTAH							
1 ***Hansen***	Y	Y	Y	Y	N	Y	N
2 ***Cook***	Y	N	N	Y	Y	N	Y
3 ***Cannon***	Y	Y	Y	Y	N	Y	N
VERMONT							
AL *Sanders*	N	N	N	N	Y	N	Y
VIRGINIA							
1 ***Bateman***	Y	Y	?	N	N	Y	?
2 Pickett	N	N	N	N	Y	N	N
3 Scott	N	N	N	N	Y	N	N
4 Sisisky	N	N	N	N	Y	N	N
5 Goode	Y	N	Y	Y	N	Y	N
6 ***Goodlatte***	Y	Y	Y	Y	Y	Y	N
7 ***Bliley***	Y	Y	Y	N	Y	Y	N
8 Moran	N	N	N	Y	Y	Y	Y
9 Boucher	N	N	N	N	Y	Y	N
10 ***Wolf***	Y	Y	Y	Y	Y	N	N
11 ***Davis***	Y	Y	Y	Y	Y	Y	N
WASHINGTON							
1 ***White***	Y	N	Y	Y	Y	Y	N
2 ***Metcalf***	Y	N	N	N	Y	N	Y
3 ***Smith, Linda***	Y	N	N	N	Y	N	Y
4 ***Hastings***	Y	Y	Y	Y	N	Y	N
5 ***Nethercutt***	Y	Y	Y	Y	Y	Y	Y
6 Dicks	N	N	N	N	Y	N	N
7 McDermott	N	N	N	N	Y	N	N
8 ***Dunn***	Y	Y	Y	Y	Y	Y	N
9 Smith, Adam	N	N	N	N	Y	N	N
WEST VIRGINIA							
1 Mollohan	N	N	N	N	N	N	N
2 Wise	N	N	N	N	Y	N	N
3 Rahall	?	N	N	N	Y	N	Y
WISCONSIN							
1 ***Neumann***	Y	Y	Y	Y	Y	N	N
2 ***Klug***	Y	N	Y	Y	Y	N	N
3 Kind	N	N	N	N	Y	N	N
4 Kleczka	N	N	N	N	Y	N	N
5 Barrett	N	N	N	N	Y	N	N
6 ***Petri***	Y	N	Y	Y	Y	Y	N
7 Obey	N	N	N	N	N	N	N
8 Johnson	N	N	N	N	Y	N	N
9 ***Sensenbrenner***	Y	Y	Y	Y	N	Y	N
WYOMING							
AL ***Cubin***	Y	Y	Y	N	Y	Y	N

Southern states - Ala., Ark., Fla., Ga., Ky., La., Miss., N.C., Okla., S.C., Tenn., Texas, Va.

364. HR 2183. Campaign Finance Overhaul/Shays-Meehan Substitute — Open Debate Requirement. Paul, R-Texas, amendment to the Shays-Meehan substitute amendment to the bill to overhaul campaign finance laws. The amendment would require recipients of federal matching campaign funds to agree not to participate in debates to which every other candidate for that office who either qualifies for federal funds or is on the ballot in a minimum of 40 states, is not invited. Rejected 88-337: R 67-156; D 20-181 (ND 19-129, SD 1-52); I 1-0. July 30, 1998.

365. HR 2183. Campaign Finance Overhaul/Shays-Meehan Substitute — Issue Ad Restrictions. DeLay, R-Texas, amendment to the Shays-Meehan substitute amendment to the bill to overhaul campaign finance laws. The amendment would remove certain restrictions on issue ads by creating an exemption for any communication dealing with any issue that may be the subject of a vote. Rejected 185-241: R 175-48; D 10-192 (ND 7-141, SD 3-51); I 0-1. July 30, 1998.

366. HR 2183. Campaign Finance Overhaul/Shays-Meehan Substitute — Citizenship Tests. Peterson, R-Pa., amendment to the Shays-Meehan substitute amendment to the bill to overhaul campaign finance laws. The amendment would require the establishment of a voluntary pilot program to help state and local officials determine voter eligibility by testing citizenship. Rejected 165-260: R 163-59; D 2-200 (ND 1-147, SD 1-53); I 0-1. July 30, 1998.

367. HR 2183. Campaign Finance Overhaul/Shays-Meehan Substitute — Bilingual Voting Material. Barr, R-Ga., amendment to the Shays-Meehan substitute amendment to the bill to overhaul campaign finance laws. The amendment would prohibit states from providing voters with voting materials in any language other than English. Rejected 142-261: R 137-74; D 5-186 (ND 2-140, SD 3-46); I 0-1. July 31, 1998.

368. HR 2183. Campaign Finance Overhaul/Shays-Meehan Substitute — Campaign Contribution Clarification. McIntosh, R-Ind., amendment to the Shays-Meehan substitute amendment to the bill to overhaul campaign finance laws. The amendment would clarify that contact between federal office-holders and interest groups regarding pending legislation or the office-holder's position on legislation is not considered a coordinated campaign contribution. Rejected 195-218: R 184-31; D 11-186 (ND 7-139, SD 4-47); I 0-1. July 31, 1998.

369. HR 2183. Campaign Finance Overhaul/Shays-Meehan Substitute — Lower Postage Rate for Candidate Mailings. Horn, R-Calif., amendment to the Shays-Meehan Substitute amendment to the bill to overhaul campaign finance laws. The amendment would allow candidates to use the lowest available postage rate of seven cents for up to two campaign mailings per household within the district they seek to represent. Current law allows a 14 cent rate for candidates. Rejected 117-294: R 91-123; D 25-171(ND 19-126, SD 7-44); I 1-0. July 31, 1998.

370. HR 2183. Campaign Finance Overhaul/Shays-Meehan Substitute — Contributions Raised Within State. Shaw, R-Fla., amendment to the Shays-Meehan substitute amendment to the bill to overhaul campaign finance laws. The amendment would require candidates to raise 50 percent of contributions from inside their own state. Rejected 160-253: R 152-62; D 8-190 (ND 4-143, SD 4-47); I 0-1. July 31, 1998.

Key

Y	Voted for (yea).
#	Paired for.
+	Announced for.
N	Voted against (nay).
X	Paired against.
−	Announced against.
P	Voted "present."
C	Voted "present" to avoid possible conflict of interest.
?	Did not vote or otherwise make a position known.

Democrats **Republicans**
Independent

	364	365	366	367	368	369	370
ALABAMA							
1 *Callahan*	N	Y	Y	Y	Y	N	Y
2 *Everett*	N	Y	Y	?	Y	N	Y
3 *Riley*	N	Y	Y	Y	Y	Y	N
4 *Aderholt*	N	Y	Y	Y	Y	Y	N
5 Cramer	N	N	N	N	N	N	N
6 *Bachus*	N	N	N	Y	N	Y	N
7 Hilliard	N	N	N	N	N	N	N
ALASKA							
AL *Young*	Y	Y	Y	Y	Y	Y	Y
ARIZONA							
1 *Salmon*	Y	Y	Y	+	+	−	+
2 Pastor	Y	N	N	N	N	Y	N
3 *Stump*	N	Y	Y	Y	N	Y	N
4 *Shadegg*	Y	Y	Y	Y	N	Y	Y
5 *Kolbe*	N	Y	N	N	Y	N	N
6 *Hayworth*	Y	Y	Y	N	Y	N	Y
ARKANSAS							
1 Berry	N	N	N	N	N	N	N
2 Snyder	N	N	N	N	N	N	N
3 *Hutchinson*	N	N	N	Y	N	Y	N
4 *Dickey*	N	Y	Y	Y	Y	Y	Y
CALIFORNIA							
1 *Riggs*	−	+	+	+	+	−	+
2 *Herger*	N	Y	Y	Y	N	Y	N
3 Fazio	N	N	N	N	N	N	N
4 *Doolittle*	Y	Y	Y	Y	Y	Y	Y
5 Matsui	N	N	N	N	N	N	N
6 Woolsey	N	N	N	N	N	N	N
7 Miller	N	N	N	N	N	N	N
8 Pelosi	N	N	N	N	N	N	N
9 Lee	N	N	N	N	N	N	N
10 Tauscher	N	N	N	N	N	N	N
11 *Pombo*	Y	Y	Y	Y	Y	Y	Y
12 Lantos	N	N	N	N	N	N	N
13 Stark	N	N	N	N	N	N	N
14 Eshoo	N	N	N	N	N	N	N
15 *Campbell*	Y	N	N	Y	N	Y	N
16 Lofgren	N	N	N	N	N	N	N
17 Farr	N	N	N	N	N	N	N
18 Condit	N	Y	N	Y	N	Y	N
19 *Radanovich*	N	Y	Y	Y	N	Y	N
20 Dooley	N	N	N	N	N	N	N
21 *Thomas*	N	Y	Y	N	Y	Y	Y
22 Capps, L.	N	N	N	N	N	N	N
23 *Gallegly*	N	Y	Y	Y	Y	Y	N
24 Sherman	Y	N	N	N	N	Y	N
25 *McKeon*	N	Y	Y	Y	Y	Y	N
26 Berman	N	N	N	N	N	Y	N
27 *Rogan*	N	Y	Y	?	?	?	Y
28 *Dreier*	N	Y	Y	Y	Y	Y	N
29 Waxman	N	N	N	?	N	Y	N
30 Becerra	N	N	N	N	N	N	N
31 Martinez	N	N	N	Y	N	Y	N
32 Dixon	N	N	N	N	N	N	N
33 Roybal-Allard	N	N	N	N	N	N	N
34 Torres	Y	N	N	N	N	N	N
35 Waters	N	N	N	N	N	N	N
36 Harman	N	N	N	N	N	N	N
37 Millender-McD.	N	N	N	N	N	N	N
38 *Horn*	N	N	Y	N	Y	Y	N

	364	365	366	367	368	369	370
39 *Royce*	Y	Y	Y	Y	Y	N	Y
40 *Lewis*	N	Y	Y	N	Y	Y	N
41 *Kim*	N	Y	Y	Y	Y	Y	N
42 Brown	N	N	N	N	N	N	N
43 *Calvert*	N	Y	Y	Y	Y	Y	Y
44 *Bono, M.*	N	Y	Y	Y	Y	Y	Y
45 *Rohrabacher*	N	Y	Y	Y	Y	Y	Y
46 Sanchez	N	N	N	N	N	N	N
47 *Cox*	N	Y	Y	?	Y	Y	N
48 *Packard*	N	Y	Y	Y	Y	Y	N
49 *Bilbray*	N	Y	?	N	N	N	N
50 Filner	Y	N	N	N	N	N	N
51 *Cunningham*	Y	Y	Y	Y	Y	Y	N
52 *Hunter*	Y	Y	Y	Y	Y	Y	Y
COLORADO							
1 DeGette	Y	N	N	N	N	N	N
2 Skaggs	N	N	N	N	N	N	N
3 *McInnis*	N	Y	N	Y	N	Y	N
4 *Schaffer*	N	Y	N	Y	N	Y	N
5 *Hefley*	N	Y	N	Y	Y	N	N
6 *Schaefer*	Y	Y	Y	Y	N	Y	N
CONNECTICUT							
1 Kennelly	N	N	N	N	N	N	N
2 Gejdenson	N	N	N	N	N	N	N
3 DeLauro	N	N	N	N	N	N	N
4 *Shays*	N	N	N	N	N	N	N
5 Maloney	Y	N	N	N	N	N	N
6 *Johnson*	N	N	N	N	Y	N	N
DELAWARE							
AL *Castle*	N	N	N	N	N	N	N
FLORIDA							
1 *Scarborough*	Y	Y	Y	Y	Y	N	Y
2 Boyd	N	N	N	N	N	N	N
3 Brown	N	N	N	N	N	N	N
4 *Fowler*	N	Y	Y	Y	Y	Y	N
5 Thurman	N	N	N	N	N	N	N
6 *Stearns*	N	Y	Y	Y	Y	Y	N
7 *Mica*	N	Y	Y	N	Y	Y	N
8 *McCollum*	N	Y	Y	Y	Y	Y	N
9 *Bilirakis*	Y	Y	Y	Y	Y	Y	N
10 *Young*	?	?	?	?	?	?	?
11 Davis	N	N	N	N	N	N	N
12 *Canady*	N	Y	Y	Y	N	Y	N
13 *Miller*	N	Y	Y	Y	N	Y	N
14 *Goss*	N	Y	Y	Y	N	Y	N
15 *Weldon*	N	Y	Y	Y	Y	Y	Y
16 *Foley*	Y	N	N	Y	Y	Y	N
17 Meek	N	N	N	N	N	N	N
18 *Ros-Lehtinen*	N	Y	N	Y	Y	Y	N
19 Wexler	?	N	N	N	N	N	N
20 Deutsch	N	N	N	N	N	N	N
21 *Diaz-Balart*	N	Y	N	Y	Y	Y	N
22 *Shaw*	N	Y	N	Y	Y	Y	Y
23 Hastings	N	N	N	N	N	N	N
GEORGIA							
1 *Kingston*	N	Y	Y	Y	Y	N	Y
2 Bishop	N	N	N	?	N	N	N
3 *Collins*	Y	Y	Y	Y	Y	Y	Y
4 McKinney	N	N	N	N	N	N	N
5 Lewis	N	N	N	N	N	N	N
6 *Gingrich*							
7 *Barr*	N	Y	Y	Y	Y	N	Y
8 *Chambliss*	Y	Y	Y	Y	Y	Y	Y
9 *Deal*	Y	Y	Y	Y	Y	Y	Y
10 *Norwood*	Y	Y	Y	Y	Y	Y	Y
11 *Linder*	N	Y	Y	Y	Y	N	Y
HAWAII							
1 Abercrombie	Y	N	N	N	N	N	N
2 Mink	Y	N	N	N	N	N	N
IDAHO							
1 *Chenoweth*	Y	Y	N	Y	Y	N	Y
2 *Crapo*	N	Y	N	N	Y	N	Y
ILLINOIS							
1 Rush	N	N	N	N	N	N	N
2 Jackson	N	N	N	N	N	N	N
3 Lipinski	N	N	N	Y	N	N	N
4 Gutierrez	N	N	N	N	N	N	N
5 Blagojevich	N	N	N	N	N	N	N
6 *Hyde*	N	Y	Y	Y	Y	Y	N
7 Davis	Y	N	N	N	N	Y	N
8 *Crane*	Y	Y	Y	Y	Y	Y	Y
9 Yates	?	?	?	N	N	N	N
10 *Porter*	N	N	N	N	N	Y	N
11 *Weller*	N	Y	Y	Y	Y	Y	Y
12 Costello	N	N	N	N	N	N	N
13 *Fawell*	N	Y	Y	Y	N	Y	N

ND Northern Democrats   SD Southern Democrats

	364	365	366	367	368	369	370
14 ***Hastert***	N	Y	Y	Y	Y	N	Y
15 ***Ewing***	N	Y	N	Y	N	Y	Y
16 ***Manzullo***	N	Y	Y	Y	Y	N	Y
17 Evans	N	N	N	N	N	N	N
18 ***LaHood***	N	Y	N	Y	Y	Y	Y
19 Poshard	N	N	N	N	N	N	N
20 ***Shimkus***	Y	Y	Y	Y	Y	Y	Y
INDIANA							
1 Visclosky	Y	N	N	N	N	Y	N
2 ***McIntosh***	Y	Y	Y	Y	Y	Y	Y
3 Roemer	N	N	N	N	N	N	N
4 ***Souder***	N	N	Y	Y	Y	N	Y
5 ***Buyer***	N	Y	Y	?	?	?	?
6 ***Burton***	N	Y	Y	Y	Y	Y	N
7 ***Pease***	Y	Y	Y	Y	Y	N	Y
8 ***Hostettler***	N	Y	Y	Y	Y	N	Y
9 Hamilton	N	N	N	N	N	N	N
10 Carson	N	N	N	N	N	Y	N
IOWA							
1 ***Leach***	Y	N	N	N	N	Y	N
2 ***Nussle***	N	N	N	Y	Y	Y	Y
3 Boswell	N	N	N	N	N	N	N
4 ***Ganske***	N	N	N	N	N	N	Y
5 ***Latham***	N	Y	N	Y	Y	N	Y
KANSAS							
1 ***Moran***	Y	Y	Y	N	Y	N	Y
2 ***Ryun***	N	Y	Y	Y	Y	N	N
3 ***Snowbarger***	Y	Y	Y	Y	Y	N	N
4 ***Tiahrt***	Y	Y	Y	Y	Y	N	Y
KENTUCKY							
1 ***Whitfield***	Y	Y	Y	Y	Y	N	Y
2 ***Lewis***	N	Y	N	Y	Y	N	N
3 ***Northup***	N	Y	Y	Y	Y	Y	Y
4 ***Bunning***	N	Y	N	Y	Y	N	N
5 ***Rogers***	N	Y	Y	Y	Y	N	N
6 Baesler	N	N	N	N	N	N	N
LOUISIANA							
1 ***Livingston***	N	Y	Y	Y	Y	Y	Y
2 Jefferson	N	N	N	N	N	Y	N
3 ***Tauzin***	N	Y	Y	N	Y	N	Y
4 ***McCrery***	N	Y	Y	?	?	?	?
5 ***Cooksey***	Y	Y	Y	Y	Y	N	Y
6 ***Baker***	N	Y	Y	Y	Y	N	Y
7 John	N	N	N	?	?	?	?
MAINE							
1 Allen	N	N	N	N	N	N	N
2 Baldacci	N	N	N	N	N	Y	N
MARYLAND							
1 ***Gilchrest***	N	N	N	N	N	N	N
2 ***Ehrlich***	N	Y	Y	Y	Y	Y	Y
3 Cardin	N	N	N	?	?	?	N
4 Wynn	N	N	N	–	–	+	–
5 Hoyer	N	N	N	N	N	N	N
6 ***Bartlett***	Y	Y	Y	Y	Y	Y	Y
7 Cummings	N	N	N	N	N	N	N
8 ***Morella***	N	N	N	N	N	N	N
MASSACHUSETTS							
1 Olver	N	N	N	N	N	N	N
2 Neal	N	N	N	N	N	N	N
3 McGovern	N	N	N	N	N	N	N
4 Frank	N	N	N	N	N	N	N
5 Meehan	N	N	N	N	N	N	N
6 Tierney	N	N	N	N	N	N	N
7 Markey	N	N	N	N	N	N	N
8 Kennedy	N	N	N	N	N	N	N
9 Moakley	?	?	?	?	?	?	?
10 Delahunt	N	N	N	N	N	N	N
MICHIGAN							
1 Stupak	N	N	N	N	Y	N	N
2 ***Hoekstra***	Y	Y	Y	N	Y	N	Y
3 ***Ehlers***	N	Y	Y	N	N	Y	Y
4 ***Camp***	Y	Y	Y	N	Y	Y	Y
5 Barcia	Y	Y	N	N	Y	N	N
6 ***Upton***	N	N	Y	Y	Y	N	Y
7 ***Smith***	N	N	Y	Y	Y	Y	Y
8 Stabenow	N	N	N	N	N	N	N
9 Kildee	N	N	N	N	N	N	N
10 Bonior	N	N	N	N	N	N	N
11 ***Knollenberg***	N	N	Y	Y	Y	Y	Y
12 Levin	N	N	N	N	N	N	N
13 Rivers	Y	N	N	N	N	N	N
14 Conyers	Y	N	N	?	N	N	N
15 Kilpatrick	N	N	N	N	N	N	N
16 Dingell	N	N	N	N	N	N	N
MINNESOTA							
1 ***Gutknecht***	N	Y	Y	Y	Y	Y	Y
2 Minge	N	N	N	N	N	N	N
3 ***Ramstad***	N	N	N	N	N	N	N
4 Vento	N	N	N	N	N	Y	N
5 Sabo	N	N	N	N	N	Y	N
6 Luther	Y	N	N	N	N	N	Y
7 Peterson	N	Y	N	N	N	N	Y
8 Oberstar	N	N	N	N	N	N	N
MISSISSIPPI							
1 ***Wicker***	N	Y	Y	Y	Y	Y	N
2 Thompson	N	N	N	N	N	N	N
3 ***Pickering***	N	Y	Y	Y	Y	N	N
4 ***Parker***	N	N	N	?	?	?	?
5 Taylor	N	N	N	N	N	N	Y
MISSOURI							
1 Clay	N	N	N	N	N	N	N
2 ***Talent***	N	Y	Y	N	Y	N	Y
3 Gephardt	N	N	N	N	N	N	N
4 Skelton	N	N	N	N	N	N	N
5 McCarthy	Y	N	N	N	N	N	N
6 Danner	N	N	N	N	N	N	N
7 ***Blunt***	N	Y	Y	N	Y	N	Y
8 ***Emerson***	N	Y	Y	Y	Y	N	Y
9 ***Hulshof***	Y	Y	Y	Y	Y	N	Y
MONTANA							
AL ***Hill***	Y	Y	Y	Y	Y	N	Y
NEBRASKA							
1 ***Bereuter***	N	Y	Y	N	Y	N	Y
2 ***Christensen***	N	Y	Y	?	?	?	?
3 ***Barrett***	N	N	N	N	N	N	Y
NEVADA							
1 ***Ensign***	Y	Y	Y	?	Y	N	Y
2 ***Gibbons***	Y	Y	Y	Y	Y	N	Y
NEW HAMPSHIRE							
1 ***Sununu***	Y	Y	N	Y	Y	N	N
2 ***Bass***	N	N	N	N	Y	N	N
NEW JERSEY							
1 Andrews	N	N	N	N	N	N	N
2 ***LoBiondo***	N	N	N	N	N	N	N
3 ***Saxton***	N	Y	Y	N	N	Y	Y
4 ***Smith***	N	Y	N	N	Y	Y	Y
5 ***Roukema***	N	N	N	Y	N	N	N
6 Pallone	N	N	N	N	N	N	N
7 ***Franks***	N	N	N	N	N	N	N
8 Pascrell	N	N	N	N	N	N	N
9 Rothman	N	N	N	N	N	N	N
10 Payne	N	N	N	N	N	N	N
11 ***Frelinghuysen***	N	N	N	N	N	N	N
12 ***Pappas***	Y	Y	Y	Y	Y	Y	Y
13 Menendez	N	N	N	N	N	N	N
NEW MEXICO							
1 ***Wilson***	N	Y	Y	N	Y	N	N
2 ***Skeen***	N	Y	Y	N	Y	Y	N
3 ***Redmond***	Y	Y	Y	N	Y	Y	N
NEW YORK							
1 ***Forbes***	N	N	N	–	–	–	–
2 ***Lazio***	N	N	Y	N	N	N	Y
3 ***King***	N	Y	N	Y	Y	Y	N
4 McCarthy	N	N	N	N	N	N	N
5 Ackerman	N	N	N	N	N	N	N
6 Meeks	N	N	N	N	N	N	N
7 Manton	N	N	N	N	N	N	N
8 Nadler	N	N	N	N	N	Y	N
9 Schumer	N	N	N	N	N	N	N
10 Towns	?	?	?	N	N	N	N
11 Owens	N	N	N	N	N	N	N
12 Velázquez	N	N	N	?	?	?	?
13 ***Fossella***	N	Y	Y	Y	Y	Y	N
14 Maloney	N	N	N	N	N	N	N
15 Rangel	N	N	N	N	N	N	N
16 Serrano	N	N	N	N	N	N	N
17 Engel	N	N	N	–	N	N	N
18 Lowey	N	N	N	N	N	N	N
19 ***Kelly***	N	N	N	N	N	N	N
20 ***Gilman***	N	N	N	N	N	Y	N
21 McNulty	N	N	N	N	N	N	N
22 ***Solomon***	N	Y	Y	Y	Y	N	Y
23 ***Boehlert***	N	N	N	N	N	Y	N
24 ***McHugh***	Y	Y	Y	N	Y	Y	Y
25 ***Walsh***	Y	N	N	N	N	N	N
26 Hinchey	N	N	N	?	N	N	N
27 ***Paxon***	N	Y	Y	Y	Y	Y	Y
28 Slaughter	N	N	N	N	N	Y	N
29 LaFalce	N	N	N	N	N	Y	N
30 ***Quinn***	N	N	N	N	N	Y	Y
31 ***Houghton***	N	N	N	N	N	N	N
NORTH CAROLINA							
1 Clayton	N	N	N	N	N	N	N
2 Etheridge	N	N	N	N	N	N	N
3 ***Jones***	N	Y	Y	Y	Y	N	Y
4 Price	N	N	N	N	N	N	N
5 ***Burr***	N	Y	Y	Y	Y	N	Y
6 ***Coble***	Y	N	Y	Y	Y	N	Y
7 McIntyre	N	N	N	N	Y	N	N
8 Hefner	N	N	N	?	?	?	?
9 ***Myrick***	N	Y	Y	Y	Y	N	N
10 ***Ballenger***	N	Y	Y	Y	Y	Y	Y
11 ***Taylor***	Y	Y	Y	Y	Y	N	Y
12 Watt	N	N	N	N	N	N	N
NORTH DAKOTA							
AL Pomeroy	N	N	N	N	N	N	N
OHIO							
1 ***Chabot***	N	Y	N	Y	Y	N	Y
2 ***Portman***	N	Y	N	N	Y	Y	Y
3 Hall	N	N	N	N	N	N	N
4 ***Oxley***	N	Y	Y	Y	Y	Y	Y
5 ***Gillmor***	N	N	Y	N	Y	N	Y
6 Strickland	N	N	N	N	N	N	N
7 ***Hobson***	Y	Y	Y	Y	Y	Y	Y
8 ***Boehner***	N	Y	Y	Y	Y	N	Y
9 Kaptur	N	N	N	N	N	N	N
10 Kucinich	N	N	N	N	N	N	N
11 Stokes	N	N	N	N	N	N	N
12 ***Kasich***	Y	Y	Y	Y	Y	N	N
13 Brown	N	N	N	?	?	?	?
14 Sawyer	N	N	N	N	N	N	N
15 ***Pryce***	Y	Y	Y	N	Y	Y	Y
16 ***Regula***	Y	Y	Y	Y	Y	Y	Y
17 Traficant	Y	Y	Y	Y	Y	Y	N
18 ***Ney***	Y	Y	Y	Y	+	–	+
19 ***LaTourette***	Y	Y	N	Y	N	Y	Y
OKLAHOMA							
1 ***Largent***	N	Y	N	Y	Y	Y	Y
2 ***Coburn***	Y	Y	Y	Y	Y	N	Y
3 ***Watkins***	Y	Y	Y	Y	Y	N	Y
4 ***Watts***	Y	Y	Y	N	Y	Y	N
5 ***Istook***	?	?	?	?	?	?	?
6 ***Lucas***	N	Y	Y	Y	Y	N	Y
OREGON							
1 Furse	N	N	N	N	N	N	N
2 ***Smith***	N	Y	N	N	Y	N	?
3 Blumenauer	N	N	N	N	N	N	N
4 DeFazio	Y	N	N	N	N	N	N
5 Hooley	Y	N	N	N	N	N	N
PENNSYLVANIA							
1 Brady	N	N	N	N	N	Y	N
2 Fattah	N	N	N	N	N	Y	N
3 Borski	N	N	N	N	N	Y	N
4 Klink	N	Y	N	N	N	N	N
5 ***Peterson***	N	Y	Y	Y	Y	Y	Y
6 Holden	N	N	N	N	N	N	N
7 ***Weldon***	N	N	N	Y	Y	N	Y
8 ***Greenwood***	N	N	N	N	N	Y	N
9 ***Shuster***	Y	Y	Y	Y	Y	Y	Y
10 ***McDade***	?	?	?	N	Y	Y	N
11 Kanjorski	N	N	N	N	N	N	N
12 Murtha	N	Y	N	N	Y	N	N
13 ***Fox***	N	N	–	N	N	N	N
14 Coyne	N	N	N	N	N	N	N
15 McHale	N	N	N	N	N	N	N
16 ***Pitts***	N	Y	Y	Y	Y	N	N
17 ***Gekas***	N	Y	Y	Y	Y	Y	Y
18 Doyle	N	N	N	N	N	Y	N
19 ***Goodling***	N	Y	Y	Y	Y	Y	Y
20 Mascara	N	N	N	N	N	N	N
21 ***English***	N	Y	Y	N	Y	Y	Y
RHODE ISLAND							
1 Kennedy	N	N	N	N	N	N	N
2 Weygand	N	N	N	N	N	N	N
SOUTH CAROLINA							
1 ***Sanford***	Y	N	N	N	Y	Y	N
2 ***Spence***	N	Y	Y	Y	Y	N	N
3 ***Graham***	N	Y	N	Y	N	N	Y
4 ***Inglis***	N	Y	N	Y	Y	N	Y
5 Spratt	N	N	N	N	N	N	?
6 Clyburn	N	N	N	N	N	Y	N
SOUTH DAKOTA							
AL ***Thune***	Y	Y	Y	Y	Y	N	Y
TENNESSEE							
1 ***Jenkins***	N	Y	Y	Y	Y	N	Y
2 ***Duncan***	Y	Y	Y	Y	Y	N	Y
3 ***Wamp***	Y	N	Y	N	Y	N	Y
4 ***Hilleary***	Y	Y	Y	Y	Y	N	Y
5 Clement	N	N	N	N	N	Y	N
6 Gordon	N	N	N	N	N	Y	N
7 ***Bryant***	N	Y	Y	Y	Y	N	N
8 Tanner	N	N	N	N	N	N	N
9 Ford	N	N	N	N	N	N	N
TEXAS							
1 Sandlin	N	N	N	N	N	N	N
2 Turner	N	N	N	N	N	N	N
3 ***Johnson, Sam***	N	Y	Y	Y	Y	N	Y
4 Hall	N	Y	N	Y	Y	N	Y
5 ***Sessions***	Y	Y	Y	Y	Y	?	Y
6 ***Barton***	N	Y	Y	?	Y	N	Y
7 ***Archer***	N	Y	Y	Y	Y	Y	Y
8 ***Brady***	N	Y	Y	N	Y	Y	Y
9 Lampson	N	N	N	N	N	N	N
10 Doggett	N	N	N	N	N	Y	N
11 Edwards	N	N	N	N	N	N	N
12 ***Granger***	N	Y	Y	N	Y	N	Y
13 ***Thornberry***	N	Y	Y	N	Y	N	Y
14 ***Paul***	Y	Y	Y	N	Y	N	N
15 Hinojosa	N	N	N	N	N	N	N
16 Reyes	N	N	N	N	N	N	N
17 Stenholm	N	N	N	N	N	N	N
18 Jackson-Lee	Y	N	N	N	N	N	N
19 ***Combest***	N	Y	Y	Y	Y	Y	Y
20 Gonzalez	?	?	?	?	?	?	?
21 ***Smith***	N	Y	Y	Y	Y	Y	Y
22 ***DeLay***	N	Y	Y	?	?	?	?
23 ***Bonilla***	N	Y	Y	N	Y	N	N
24 Frost	N	N	N	N	N	N	N
25 Bentsen	N	N	N	N	N	N	N
26 ***Armey***	N	Y	N	Y	Y	Y	Y
27 Ortiz	N	N	N	N	N	N	N
28 Rodriguez	N	N	N	N	N	N	N
29 Green	N	N	N	N	N	N	N
30 Johnson, E.B.	N	N	N	?	?	?	N
UTAH							
1 ***Hansen***	N	Y	Y	Y	Y	N	Y
2 ***Cook***	Y	Y	N	Y	Y	Y	Y
3 ***Cannon***	N	Y	Y	Y	Y	Y	Y
VERMONT							
AL *Sanders*	Y	N	N	N	N	Y	N
VIRGINIA							
1 ***Bateman***	N	Y	Y	Y	Y	Y	N
2 Pickett	N	N	N	Y	N	N	N
3 Scott	N	Y	N	N	Y	Y	N
4 Sisisky	N	N	N	N	N	N	N
5 Goode	N	Y	Y	Y	Y	N	Y
6 ***Goodlatte***	N	Y	Y	Y	Y	N	Y
7 ***Bliley***	N	Y	Y	Y	Y	Y	N
8 Moran	N	N	N	?	N	N	Y
9 Boucher	N	N	N	N	N	N	N
10 ***Wolf***	N	N	Y	Y	Y	N	Y
11 ***Davis***	N	Y	Y	N	Y	N	Y
WASHINGTON							
1 ***White***	N	N	N	N	Y	N	Y
2 ***Metcalf***	Y	N	N	N	N	N	N
3 ***Smith, Linda***	Y	N	N	N	N	N	N
4 ***Hastings***	N	Y	Y	Y	Y	N	Y
5 ***Nethercutt***	Y	Y	Y	Y	Y	N	Y
6 Dicks	N	N	N	N	N	N	N
7 McDermott	N	N	N	N	N	N	N
8 ***Dunn***	N	Y	Y	Y	Y	N	Y
9 Smith, Adam	N	N	N	N	N	N	N
WEST VIRGINIA							
1 Mollohan	N	Y	N	N	N	?	N
2 Wise	N	N	N	N	N	N	N
3 Rahall	Y	N	N	N	Y	N	N
WISCONSIN							
1 ***Neumann***	Y	Y	Y	Y	Y	Y	Y
2 ***Klug***	N	N	Y	N	Y	N	Y
3 Kind	N	N	N	N	N	N	N
4 Kleczka	N	N	N	N	N	N	N
5 Barrett	N	N	N	N	N	N	N
6 ***Petri***	N	N	Y	Y	Y	Y	Y
7 Obey	N	N	N	N	N	N	N
8 Johnson	N	N	N	N	N	N	N
9 ***Sensenbrenner***	N	Y	Y	Y	Y	N	Y
WYOMING							
AL ***Cubin***	Y	Y	Y	Y	Y	N	Y

Southern states - Ala., Ark., Fla., Ga., Ky., La., Miss., N.C., Okla., S.C., Tenn., Texas, Va.

Key

Y	Voted for (yea).
#	Paired for.
+	Announced for.
N	Voted against (nay).
X	Paired against.
–	Announced against.
P	Voted "present."
C	Voted "present" to avoid possible conflict of interest.
?	Did not vote or otherwise make a position known.

•

Democrats **Republicans**
Independent

371. HR 2183. Campaign Finance Overhaul/Shays-Meehan Substitute — FEC Clearinghouse. Kaptur, D-Ohio, amendment to the Shays-Meehan amendment to the bill to overhaul campaign finance laws. The amendment would establish a clearinghouse of political activities within the Federal Election Commission. Adopted 341-74: R 149-66; D 191-8 (ND 143-4, SD 48-4); I 1-0. July 31, 1998.

372. HR 2183. Campaign Finance Overhaul/Shays-Meehan Substitute — Political Donations From Certain Legal Residents. Stearns, R-Fla., amendment to the Shays-Meehan substitute amendment to the bill to overhaul campaign finance laws. The amendment would allow permenant legal residents who serve in the military to make political contributions. Adopted 385-29: R 190-24; D 194-5 (ND 145-2, SD 49-3); I 1-0. July 31, 1998.

373. HR 2183. Campaign Finance Overhaul/Shays-Meehan Substitute — Soft Money Solicitation. Stearns, R-Fla., amendment to the Shays-Meehan substitute amendment to the bill to overhaul campaign finance laws. The amendment would prohibit presidential and vice-presidential candidates from receiving public funding from the federal Presidential Election Campaign Fund unless the candidate certifies that they will not solicit soft money donations. Adopted 368-44: R 192-21; D 175-23 (ND 129-17, SD 46-6); I 1-0. July 31, 1998.

374. HR 2183. Campaign Finance Overhaul/Shays-Meehan Substitute — Raise Individual Contribution Limit. Whitfield, R-Ky., amendment to the Shays-Meehan substitute amendment to the bill to overhaul campaign finance laws. The amendment would raise the individual contribution limit to candidates from $1,000 to $3,000. Rejected 102-315: R 99-118; D 3-196 (ND 3-144, SD 0-52); I 0-1. July 31, 1998.

375. HR 2183. Campaign Finance Overhaul/Shays-Meehan Substitute — Express Advocacy Definition. Whitfield, R-Ky., amendment to the Shays-Meehan substitute amendment to the bill to overhaul campaign finance laws. The amendment would remove the bill's expanded version of the definition of express advocacy and maintain current law. Rejected 173-238: R 164-50; D 9-187 (ND 4-140, SD 5-47); I 0-1. July 31, 1998.

376. HR 2183. Campaign Finance Overhaul/Shays-Meehan Substitute — Contribution Bundling Ban. English, R-Pa., amendment to the Shays-Meehan Substitute amendment to the bill to overhaul campaign finance laws. The amendment would prohibit bundling of campaign contributions for distribution to candidates or political parties. Rejected 134-276: R 124-91; D 10-184 (ND 9-133, SD 1-51); I 0-1. July 31, 1998.

377. HR 3743. Withhold Contributions to Iranian Energy Program/Passage. Gilman, R-N.Y. motion to suspend the rules and pass the bill to withhold U.S. proportional voluntary contributions to the International Atomic Energy Agency (IAEA) for its programs in Iran. Motion agreed to 405-13: R 224-0; D 180-13 (ND 130-12, SD 50-1); I 1-0. Aug. 3, 1998. A two-thirds majority of those present and voting (279 in this case) is required for passage under suspension of the rules.

	371	372	373	374	375	376	377
ALABAMA							
1 *Callahan*	Y	Y	Y	Y	Y	Y	Y
2 *Everett*	Y	Y	Y	Y	Y	N	Y
3 *Riley*	Y	Y	Y	Y	Y	N	Y
4 *Aderholt*	N	Y	Y	N	Y	N	Y
5 Cramer	Y	Y	Y	N	N	N	Y
6 *Bachus*	Y	Y	Y	N	N	N	Y
7 Hilliard	N	Y	Y	N	N	N	?
ALASKA							
AL *Young*	Y	Y	Y	Y	Y	Y	Y
ARIZONA							
1 *Salmon*	+	+	+	N	Y	Y	Y
2 Pastor	Y	Y	N	N	N	N	Y
3 *Stump*	Y	Y	Y	Y	Y	N	Y
4 *Shadegg*	N	Y	Y	Y	Y	N	Y
5 *Kolbe*	Y	Y	Y	N	Y	N	Y
6 *Hayworth*	Y	Y	Y	N	Y	Y	Y
ARKANSAS							
1 Berry	Y	Y	Y	N	N	N	Y
2 Snyder	Y	Y	Y	N	N	N	Y
3 *Hutchinson*	N	Y	N	N	Y	N	Y
4 *Dickey*	Y	Y	Y	Y	Y	N	Y
CALIFORNIA							
1 *Riggs*	+	+	+	+	–	+	Y
2 *Herger*	Y	Y	Y	Y	Y	Y	Y
3 Fazio	Y	Y	N	N	N	N	Y
4 *Doolittle*	N	N	Y	Y	Y	N	Y
5 Matsul	Y	Y	Y	N	N	N	Y
6 Woolsey	Y	Y	Y	N	N	N	Y
7 Miller	Y	Y	Y	N	N	N	Y
8 Pelosi	Y	Y	Y	N	N	N	Y
9 Lee	Y	Y	Y	N	N	N	Y
10 Tauscher	Y	Y	Y	N	N	N	Y
11 *Pombo*	N	Y	N	Y	Y	N	Y
12 Lantos	Y	Y	Y	N	N	N	Y
13 Stark	Y	Y	Y	N	N	N	Y
14 Eshoo	Y	Y	Y	N	N	N	Y
15 *Campbell*	Y	Y	N	N	N	N	Y
16 Lofgren	Y	Y	Y	N	N	N	Y
17 Farr	Y	Y	N	N	N	N	Y
18 Condit	Y	Y	N	N	N	N	Y
19 *Radanovich*	N	Y	N	Y	Y	Y	Y
20 Dooley	Y	Y	Y	N	N	N	N
21 *Thomas*	Y	Y	Y	Y	Y	Y	Y
22 Capps, L.	Y	Y	Y	N	N	N	Y
23 *Gallegly*	Y	Y	Y	N	N	N	Y
24 Sherman	Y	Y	Y	N	N	N	Y
25 *McKeon*	N	Y	Y	Y	Y	Y	Y
26 Berman	Y	Y	Y	N	N	N	Y
27 *Rogan*	?	?	?	?	?	?	Y
28 *Dreier*	N	Y	N	Y	Y	N	Y
29 Waxman	Y	Y	Y	N	N	N	Y
30 Becerra	Y	Y	Y	N	N	N	Y
31 Martinez	N	Y	Y	Y	Y	N	?
32 Dixon	Y	Y	Y	N	N	N	Y
33 Roybal-Allard	Y	Y	Y	N	N	N	Y
34 Torres	Y	Y	Y	N	N	N	N
35 Waters	Y	Y	?	N	N	N	Y
36 Harman	Y	Y	Y	N	N	N	Y
37 Millender-McD.	Y	Y	Y	N	N	N	Y
38 *Horn*	Y	Y	Y	N	N	N	Y

	371	372	373	374	375	376	377
39 *Royce*	Y	Y	Y	N	Y	N	Y
40 *Lewis*	Y	N	N	Y	N	Y	Y
41 *Kim*	Y	Y	Y	N	Y	N	Y
42 Brown	Y	Y	Y	N	N	N	Y
43 *Calvert*	Y	Y	Y	Y	Y	Y	Y
44 *Bono, M.*	Y	Y	Y	Y	Y	Y	Y
45 *Rohrabacher*	Y	Y	Y	N	Y	N	Y
46 Sanchez	Y	Y	N	N	N	N	Y
47 *Cox*	Y	Y	Y	Y	Y	Y	Y
48 *Packard*	N	N	N	N	N	Y	Y
49 *Bilbray*	Y	Y	Y	N	N	N	Y
50 Filner	Y	Y	N	N	N	N	Y
51 *Cunningham*	Y	Y	Y	Y	Y	Y	Y
52 *Hunter*	Y	Y	Y	N	Y	Y	Y
COLORADO							
1 DeGette	Y	Y	Y	N	N	N	Y
2 Skaggs	Y	Y	Y	N	N	N	N
3 *McInnis*	Y	Y	Y	Y	Y	N	Y
4 *Schaffer*	Y	Y	Y	Y	Y	N	Y
5 *Hefley*	Y	Y	Y	Y	Y	Y	Y
6 *Schaefer*	Y	Y	Y	Y	Y	Y	Y
CONNECTICUT							
1 Kennelly	Y	Y	Y	N	N	N	Y
2 Gejdenson	Y	Y	Y	N	–	–	N
3 DeLauro	Y	Y	Y	N	N	N	Y
4 *Shays*	Y	Y	Y	N	N	N	Y
5 Maloney	Y	Y	Y	N	N	N	Y
6 *Johnson*	Y	Y	Y	N	N	N	Y
DELAWARE							
AL *Castle*	Y	Y	Y	N	N	N	Y
FLORIDA							
1 *Scarborough*	Y	Y	Y	N	Y	N	Y
2 Boyd	Y	Y	Y	N	N	N	Y
3 Brown	Y	Y	Y	N	N	N	Y
4 *Fowler*	Y	Y	Y	Y	Y	Y	Y
5 Thurman	Y	Y	Y	N	N	N	Y
6 *Stearns*	Y	Y	Y	N	Y	N	Y
7 *Mica*	N	Y	Y	N	Y	Y	Y
8 *McCollum*	N	N	Y	Y	Y	Y	Y
9 *Bilirakis*	N	Y	Y	N	Y	N	Y
10 *Young*	?	?	?	?	?	?	Y
11 Davis	Y	Y	N	N	N	N	Y
12 *Canady*	Y	Y	Y	N	Y	N	Y
13 *Miller*	Y	Y	Y	Y	Y	N	Y
14 Goss	N	Y	Y	N	Y	N	Y
15 *Weldon*	Y	Y	+	Y	Y	N	Y
16 *Foley*	Y	Y	Y	N	N	N	Y
17 Meek	Y	Y	N	N	N	N	Y
18 *Ros-Lehtinen*	Y	Y	Y	N	N	N	Y
19 Wexler	Y	Y	Y	N	N	N	Y
20 Deutsch	Y	Y	Y	N	N	N	Y
21 *Diaz-Balart*	Y	Y	Y	N	Y	N	Y
22 *Shaw*	Y	Y	Y	Y	Y	Y	Y
23 Hastings	Y	N	Y	N	N	N	Y
GEORGIA							
1 *Kingston*	Y	Y	Y	Y	Y	Y	Y
2 Bishop	Y	Y	N	Y	N	N	Y
3 *Collins*	N	Y	Y	N	Y	N	Y
4 McKinney	Y	Y	N	N	N	N	Y
5 Lewis	Y	N	N	N	N	N	Y
6 *Gingrich*							
7 *Barr*	Y	N	Y	Y	Y	N	Y
8 *Chambliss*	N	Y	Y	Y	Y	N	Y
9 *Deal*	Y	Y	Y	Y	Y	N	Y
10 *Norwood*	N	Y	Y	Y	Y	N	Y
11 *Linder*	N	N	Y	Y	Y	Y	Y
HAWAII							
1 Abercrombie	Y	Y	Y	N	N	N	Y
2 Mink	Y	Y	Y	N	N	N	Y
IDAHO							
1 *Chenoweth*	Y	Y	Y	Y	N	Y	N
2 *Crapo*	Y	Y	Y	N	Y	Y	Y
ILLINOIS							
1 Rush	Y	Y	Y	N	N	N	Y
2 Jackson	N	Y	Y	N	N	N	Y
3 Lipinski	Y	Y	Y	N	N	N	Y
4 Gutierrez	Y	Y	Y	N	N	N	Y
5 Blagojevich	Y	Y	Y	N	N	N	Y
6 *Hyde*	Y	N	N	N	Y	N	Y
7 Davis	Y	Y	Y	N	N	N	Y
8 *Crane*	N	Y	Y	Y	Y	Y	Y
9 Yates	Y	Y	Y	N	N	N	Y
10 *Porter*	Y	Y	Y	N	N	N	Y
11 *Weller*	Y	Y	Y	N	Y	N	Y
12 Costello	Y	Y	Y	N	Y	?	?
13 *Fawell*	Y	N	Y	N	Y	N	Y

ND Northern Democrats   SD Southern Democrats

	371	372	373	374	375	376	377
14 ***Hastert***	N	Y	Y	Y	Y	Y	Y
15 ***Ewing***	N	Y	Y	N	Y	Y	Y
16 ***Manzullo***	Y	Y	Y	N	Y	Y	Y
17 Evans	Y	Y	Y	N	N	N	Y
18 ***LaHood***	N	Y	Y	N	N	Y	Y
19 Poshard	Y	Y	Y	N	N	N	?
20 ***Shimkus***	N	Y	Y	Y	Y	N	Y
INDIANA							
1 Visclosky	Y	Y	N	N	N	N	Y
2 ***McIntosh***	N	Y	Y	Y	Y	Y	Y
3 Roemer	Y	Y	Y	N	N	N	Y
4 ***Souder***	Y	Y	Y	N	Y	Y	Y
5 ***Buyer***	?	?	?	?	?	?	Y
6 ***Burton***	N	Y	Y	Y	Y	Y	Y
7 ***Pease***	Y	N	Y	N	Y	N	Y
8 ***Hostettler***	N	Y	Y	Y	Y	N	Y
9 Hamilton	Y	Y	Y	N	N	N	N
10 Carson	Y	Y	N	N	N	N	Y
IOWA							
1 ***Leach***	Y	Y	Y	N	N	N	Y
2 ***Nussle***	Y	Y	Y	N	N	Y	Y
3 Boswell	Y	Y	Y	N	N	N	Y
4 ***Ganske***	Y	Y	Y	N	N	N	Y
5 ***Latham***	Y	Y	Y	N	Y	Y	Y
KANSAS							
1 ***Moran***	N	N	N	N	Y	Y	Y
2 ***Ryun***	N	Y	Y	Y	Y	N	Y
3 ***Snowbarger***	Y	Y	Y	Y	Y	Y	Y
4 ***Tiahrt***	N	N	Y	Y	Y	Y	Y
KENTUCKY							
1 ***Whitfield***	Y	Y	Y	Y	Y	Y	Y
2 ***Lewis***	Y	Y	Y	Y	Y	Y	Y
3 ***Northup***	Y	Y	Y	N	Y	Y	Y
4 ***Bunning***	Y	Y	Y	N	Y	Y	Y
5 ***Rogers***	Y	Y	Y	N	Y	Y	Y
6 Baesler	Y	Y	Y	N	N	N	Y
LOUISIANA							
1 ***Livingston***	N	Y	Y	Y	Y	Y	Y
2 Jefferson	Y	Y	N	N	N	N	Y
3 ***Tauzin***	Y	Y	Y	Y	Y	Y	Y
4 ***McCrery***	?	?	?	N	Y	Y	Y
5 ***Cooksey***	N	Y	Y	Y	Y	Y	Y
6 ***Baker***	Y	Y	Y	Y	Y	Y	Y
7 John	?	?	?	?	?	?	Y
MAINE							
1 Allen	Y	Y	Y	N	N	N	Y
2 Baldacci	Y	Y	Y	N	N	N	Y
MARYLAND							
1 ***Gilchrest***	Y	?	Y	N	N	N	Y
2 ***Ehrlich***	Y	Y	Y	N	Y	Y	Y
3 Cardin	Y	Y	Y	N	N	N	Y
4 Wynn	+	+	–	–	–	–	Y
5 Hoyer	N	Y	Y	N	N	N	Y
6 ***Bartlett***	Y	Y	Y	N	Y	Y	Y
7 Cummings	Y	Y	Y	N	N	N	Y
8 ***Morella***	Y	Y	Y	N	N	N	Y
MASSACHUSETTS							
1 Olver	Y	Y	Y	N	N	N	?
2 Neal	Y	Y	Y	N	N	N	Y
3 McGovern	Y	Y	Y	N	N	N	Y
4 Frank	Y	N	Y	N	N	N	Y
5 Meehan	Y	Y	Y	N	N	N	Y
6 Tierney	Y	Y	Y	N	N	N	Y
7 Markey	Y	Y	Y	N	N	N	Y
8 Kennedy	Y	Y	Y	N	N	Y	Y
9 Moakley	?	?	?	?	?	?	Y
10 Delahunt	Y	Y	Y	N	N	?	Y
MICHIGAN							
1 Stupak	Y	Y	Y	N	N	N	Y
2 ***Hoekstra***	Y	Y	Y	N	Y	Y	Y
3 ***Ehlers***	N	Y	Y	N	Y	Y	Y
4 ***Camp***	Y	Y	Y	N	Y	Y	Y
5 Barcia	Y	Y	Y	N	N	Y	Y
6 ***Upton***	Y	Y	Y	N	N	Y	Y
7 ***Smith***	Y	Y	Y	N	N	Y	Y
8 Stabenow	Y	Y	Y	N	N	N	Y
9 Kildee	Y	Y	Y	N	N	N	Y
10 Bonior	Y	Y	N	N	N	N	Y
11 ***Knollenberg***	N	N	N	Y	Y	Y	Y
12 Levin	Y	Y	Y	N	N	N	Y
13 Rivers	Y	Y	Y	N	N	N	Y
14 Conyers	Y	Y	Y	N	N	N	?
15 Kilpatrick	Y	Y	Y	N	N	N	+
16 Dingell	Y	Y	Y	N	N	N	Y

	371	372	373	374	375	376	377
MINNESOTA							
1 ***Gutknecht***	Y	N	Y	N	Y	Y	Y
2 Minge	Y	Y	Y	N	N	N	Y
3 ***Ramstad***	N	Y	Y	N	N	N	Y
4 Vento	Y	Y	Y	N	N	N	Y
5 Sabo	Y	Y	N	N	N	N	Y
6 Luther	Y	Y	Y	N	N	Y	Y
7 Peterson	N	Y	Y	N	Y	Y	Y
8 Oberstar	Y	Y	Y	N	N	N	–
MISSISSIPPI							
1 ***Wicker***	Y	Y	Y	Y	Y	N	Y
2 Thompson	Y	Y	Y	N	N	N	Y
3 ***Pickering***	Y	Y	Y	N	Y	Y	Y
4 ***Parker***	?	?	?	?	?	?	Y
5 Taylor	Y	Y	Y	N	N	N	Y
MISSOURI							
1 Clay	Y	Y	Y	N	N	N	Y
2 ***Talent***	Y	Y	Y	N	Y	Y	Y
3 Gephardt	Y	Y	N	N	N	N	Y
4 Skelton	Y	Y	Y	N	N	N	Y
5 McCarthy	Y	Y	Y	N	N	N	Y
6 Danner	Y	Y	Y	N	N	N	Y
7 ***Blunt***	Y	Y	Y	Y	Y	N	Y
8 ***Emerson***	Y	Y	Y	N	Y	Y	Y
9 ***Hulshof***	Y	Y	Y	N	Y	Y	Y
MONTANA							
AL ***Hill***	N	Y	Y	Y	Y	Y	Y
NEBRASKA							
1 ***Bereuter***	Y	Y	N	Y	N	Y	Y
2 ***Christensen***	?	?	?	?	?	?	?
3 ***Barrett***	N	Y	Y	N	N	N	Y
NEVADA							
1 ***Ensign***	Y	Y	Y	Y	N	N	Y
2 ***Gibbons***	N	Y	Y	Y	Y	Y	Y
NEW HAMPSHIRE							
1 ***Sununu***	N	N	N	N	Y	N	Y
2 ***Bass***	Y	Y	Y	N	N	N	Y
NEW JERSEY							
1 Andrews	Y	Y	Y	N	N	N	Y
2 ***LoBiondo***	Y	Y	Y	N	N	N	Y
3 ***Saxton***	Y	Y	Y	N	Y	Y	Y
4 ***Smith***	Y	Y	Y	N	Y	Y	Y
5 ***Roukema***	Y	Y	Y	N	N	N	Y
6 Pallone	Y	Y	Y	N	N	N	Y
7 ***Franks***	Y	Y	Y	N	N	?	Y
8 Pascrell	Y	Y	Y	N	N	N	Y
9 Rothman	Y	Y	Y	N	N	N	Y
10 Payne	Y	Y	N	N	N	N	Y
11 ***Frelinghuysen***	Y	Y	Y	N	N	N	Y
12 ***Pappas***	Y	Y	Y	N	Y	Y	Y
13 Menendez	Y	Y	Y	N	N	N	Y
NEW MEXICO							
1 ***Wilson***	N	Y	Y	N	Y	N	Y
2 ***Skeen***	N	Y	Y	Y	Y	Y	Y
3 ***Redmond***	N	Y	Y	N	Y	N	Y
NEW YORK							
1 ***Forbes***	–	+	+	–	–	–	Y
2 ***Lazio***	Y	Y	Y	N	Y	N	Y
3 ***King***	Y	Y	N	Y	Y	N	Y
4 McCarthy	Y	Y	Y	N	N	N	Y
5 Ackerman	Y	Y	Y	N	N	N	Y
6 Meeks	Y	Y	Y	N	N	N	Y
7 Manton	Y	Y	Y	N	N	N	Y
8 Nadler	Y	Y	Y	N	N	N	Y
9 Schumer	Y	Y	Y	N	N	N	Y
10 Towns	Y	Y	N	N	N	N	?
11 Owens	Y	Y	N	N	N	N	Y
12 Velázquez	?	?	?	?	?	?	Y
13 ***Fossella***	N	Y	N	Y	Y	N	Y
14 Maloney	Y	Y	Y	N	N	N	Y
15 Rangel	Y	Y	Y	N	N	N	Y
16 Serrano	Y	Y	Y	N	N	N	Y
17 Engel	Y	Y	Y	N	N	N	Y
18 Lowey	Y	Y	Y	N	N	N	Y
19 ***Kelly***	N	Y	Y	N	N	N	Y
20 ***Gilman***	N	Y	Y	N	N	N	Y
21 McNulty	Y	Y	Y	N	?	?	Y
22 ***Solomon***	N	Y	N	Y	?	?	Y
23 ***Boehlert***	Y	Y	Y	N	N	N	Y
24 ***McHugh***	Y	Y	Y	N	Y	Y	Y
25 ***Walsh***	N	Y	Y	N	N	N	Y
26 Hinchey	Y	Y	Y	N	N	N	Y
27 ***Paxon***	N	Y	Y	Y	Y	Y	Y
28 Slaughter	Y	Y	Y	N	N	N	Y
29 LaFalce	Y	Y	Y	N	N	N	N
30 ***Quinn***	Y	Y	Y	N	N	N	Y

	371	372	373	374	375	376	377
31 ***Houghton***	Y	Y	Y	N	N	N	Y
NORTH CAROLINA							
1 Clayton	Y	Y	Y	N	N	N	?
2 Etheridge	Y	Y	Y	N	N	N	Y
3 ***Jones***	Y	N	Y	Y	Y	Y	Y
4 Price	Y	Y	Y	N	N	N	Y
5 ***Burr***	N	Y	N	N	Y	Y	Y
6 ***Coble***	Y	N	Y	N	N	N	Y
7 McIntyre	Y	Y	Y	N	N	N	Y
8 Hefner	?	?	?	?	?	?	Y
9 ***Myrick***	Y	Y	Y	Y	N	N	Y
10 ***Ballenger***	N	Y	+	+	+	+	Y
11 ***Taylor***	Y	Y	Y	N	Y	Y	Y
12 Watt	Y	Y	N	N	Y	N	Y
NORTH DAKOTA							
AL Pomeroy	Y	Y	Y	N	N	N	?
OHIO							
1 ***Chabot***	Y	Y	Y	N	Y	Y	Y
2 ***Portman***	Y	Y	Y	N	Y	Y	Y
3 Hall	Y	Y	Y	N	N	N	Y
4 ***Oxley***	N	Y	Y	Y	Y	N	Y
5 ***Gillmor***	Y	Y	Y	N	N	N	Y
6 Strickland	Y	Y	Y	N	N	N	Y
7 ***Hobson***	Y	Y	Y	N	Y	Y	Y
8 ***Boehner***	Y	Y	Y	Y	Y	Y	Y
9 Kaptur	Y	Y	Y	N	N	Y	Y
10 Kucinich	Y	Y	Y	N	N	N	Y
11 Stokes	Y	Y	Y	N	N	N	?
12 ***Kasich***	Y	Y	Y	Y	?	N	Y
13 Brown	?	?	?	?	?	?	Y
14 Sawyer	Y	Y	Y	N	N	N	N
15 ***Pryce***	N	Y	Y	N	Y	Y	Y
16 ***Regula***	Y	Y	Y	N	Y	Y	Y
17 Traficant	Y	Y	Y	Y	Y	Y	Y
18 ***Ney***	–	–	+	N	Y	Y	Y
19 ***LaTourette***	N	Y	Y	N	Y	Y	Y
OKLAHOMA							
1 ***Largent***	N	N	Y	N	Y	N	Y
2 ***Coburn***	N	N	Y	Y	Y	Y	Y
3 ***Watkins***	Y	Y	Y	N	Y	N	Y
4 ***Watts***	N	Y	N	N	Y	N	Y
5 ***Istook***	?	?	?	?	?	?	?
6 ***Lucas***	N	Y	Y	N	Y	Y	Y
OREGON							
1 Furse	Y	Y	Y	N	N	N	N
2 ***Smith***	N	Y	Y	Y	Y	Y	Y
3 Blumenauer	Y	Y	Y	N	N	N	Y
4 DeFazio	Y	Y	Y	N	N	N	Y
5 Hooley	Y	Y	Y	N	N	N	Y
PENNSYLVANIA							
1 Brady	Y	Y	N	N	N	N	Y
2 Fattah	Y	Y	N	N	N	N	Y
3 Borski	Y	Y	N	N	N	N	Y
4 Klink	Y	Y	N	N	N	Y	N
5 ***Peterson***	Y	Y	Y	Y	Y	Y	Y
6 Holden	Y	Y	Y	N	N	N	Y
7 ***Weldon***	Y	Y	Y	N	N	N	Y
8 ***Greenwood***	Y	Y	Y	N	N	N	Y
9 ***Shuster***	Y	Y	Y	Y	Y	Y	Y
10 ***McDade***	Y	Y	Y	Y	?	Y	?
11 Kanjorski	Y	Y	Y	N	N	N	Y
12 Murtha	Y	Y	N	Y	N	N	Y
13 ***Fox***	Y	Y	Y	N	N	N	Y
14 Coyne	Y	Y	Y	N	N	N	Y
15 McHale	Y	Y	Y	N	N	N	Y
16 ***Pitts***	N	N	Y	Y	Y	Y	Y
17 ***Gekas***	Y	Y	Y	N	Y	Y	Y
18 Doyle	Y	Y	Y	N	N	N	Y
19 ***Goodling***	Y	Y	Y	N	Y	Y	Y
20 Mascara	Y	Y	Y	N	N	N	Y
21 ***English***	Y	Y	Y	N	Y	Y	Y
RHODE ISLAND							
1 Kennedy	Y	Y	Y	N	N	N	Y
2 Weygand	Y	Y	Y	N	N	N	Y
SOUTH CAROLINA							
1 ***Sanford***	N	Y	Y	N	N	N	Y
2 ***Spence***	Y	Y	Y	N	Y	Y	Y
3 ***Graham***	Y	Y	Y	N	Y	N	Y
4 ***Inglis***	Y	Y	Y	N	Y	N	Y
5 Spratt	Y	Y	Y	N	N	N	Y
6 Clyburn	Y	Y	N	N	N	N	Y
SOUTH DAKOTA							
AL ***Thune***	Y	Y	Y	N	Y	Y	Y

	371	372	373	374	375	376	377
TENNESSEE							
1 ***Jenkins***	Y	Y	Y	Y	Y	N	Y
2 ***Duncan***	Y	Y	Y	Y	N	N	Y
3 ***Wamp***	Y	Y	Y	N	N	N	Y
4 ***Hilleary***	Y	Y	Y	N	Y	Y	Y
5 Clement	Y	Y	Y	N	N	N	Y
6 Gordon	Y	Y	Y	N	N	N	Y
7 ***Bryant***	N	N	Y	Y	Y	Y	Y
8 Tanner	Y	Y	Y	N	N	N	Y
9 Ford	Y	Y	Y	N	N	N	Y
TEXAS							
1 Sandlin	Y	Y	Y	N	N	N	Y
2 Turner	Y	Y	Y	N	N	N	Y
3 ***Johnson, Sam***	N	Y	Y	Y	Y	Y	Y
4 Hall	N	Y	Y	N	Y	N	Y
5 ***Sessions***	N	Y	Y	Y	Y	Y	Y
6 ***Barton***	Y	N	Y	Y	Y	Y	Y
7 ***Archer***	Y	Y	Y	Y	Y	Y	Y
8 ***Brady***	Y	Y	Y	Y	Y	Y	Y
9 Lampson	Y	Y	Y	N	N	N	Y
10 Doggett	Y	Y	Y	N	N	N	Y
11 Edwards	Y	Y	Y	N	N	N	Y
12 ***Granger***	Y	Y	Y	N	Y	N	Y
13 ***Thornberry***	Y	Y	N	Y	Y	N	Y
14 ***Paul***	N	Y	Y	Y	Y	N	Y
15 Hinojosa	Y	Y	Y	N	N	N	Y
16 Reyes	Y	Y	Y	N	N	N	Y
17 Stenholm	N	Y	Y	N	N	N	Y
18 Jackson-Lee	Y	Y	Y	N	N	N	Y
19 ***Combest***	Y	Y	Y	N	Y	Y	Y
20 Gonzalez	?	?	?	?	?	?	?
21 ***Smith***	Y	Y	Y	Y	Y	Y	Y
22 ***DeLay***	?	?	?	?	?	?	Y
23 ***Bonilla***	N	N	N	Y	Y	N	Y
24 Frost	Y	Y	Y	N	N	N	Y
25 Bentsen	Y	N	N	N	N	N	Y
26 ***Armey***	Y	Y	Y	Y	Y	Y	Y
27 Ortiz	Y	Y	Y	N	N	N	+
28 Rodriguez	Y	Y	Y	N	N	N	Y
29 Green	Y	Y	Y	N	N	N	Y
30 Johnson, E.B.	Y	Y	N	N	N	N	Y
UTAH							
1 ***Hansen***	N	Y	Y	Y	Y	Y	Y
2 ***Cook***	Y	Y	Y	N	Y	Y	Y
3 ***Cannon***	Y	Y	Y	Y	Y	Y	Y
VERMONT							
AL *Sanders*	Y	Y	Y	N	N	N	Y
VIRGINIA							
1 ***Bateman***	Y	Y	Y	N	Y	N	Y
2 Pickett	N	Y	Y	N	N	N	Y
3 Scott	Y	Y	Y	N	Y	N	Y
4 Sisisky	Y	Y	Y	N	N	N	Y
5 Goode	Y	N	Y	N	Y	Y	Y
6 ***Goodlatte***	Y	N	Y	N	Y	Y	Y
7 ***Bliley***	Y	Y	Y	Y	Y	Y	Y
8 Moran	Y	Y	Y	N	N	N	N
9 Boucher	Y	Y	Y	N	N	N	Y
10 ***Wolf***	Y	Y	Y	N	Y	Y	Y
11 ***Davis***	N	Y	Y	Y	Y	N	Y
WASHINGTON							
1 ***White***	Y	Y	Y	N	N	N	Y
2 ***Metcalf***	Y	Y	Y	N	N	N	Y
3 ***Smith, Linda***	Y	Y	Y	N	N	N	Y
4 ***Hastings***	Y	Y	Y	N	Y	N	Y
5 ***Nethercutt***	Y	Y	Y	N	Y	Y	Y
6 Dicks	Y	Y	Y	N	N	N	Y
7 McDermott	Y	Y	Y	N	N	N	N
8 ***Dunn***	Y	N	N	N	Y	Y	Y
9 Smith, Adam	Y	N	Y	N	N	N	Y
WEST VIRGINIA							
1 Mollohan	Y	Y	N	N	Y	?	Y
2 Wise	Y	Y	Y	N	N	N	Y
3 Rahall	Y	Y	Y	N	N	Y	N
WISCONSIN							
1 ***Neumann***	Y	Y	Y	N	Y	N	Y
2 ***Klug***	Y	Y	Y	N	N	Y	Y
3 Kind	Y	Y	Y	N	N	N	Y
4 Kleczka	Y	Y	Y	N	N	N	Y
5 Barrett	Y	Y	Y	N	N	N	Y
6 ***Petri***	Y	Y	Y	N	Y	N	Y
7 Obey	Y	Y	Y	N	N	N	N
8 Johnson	Y	Y	Y	N	N	N	Y
9 ***Sensenbrenner***	Y	N	Y	N	Y	N	Y
WYOMING							
AL ***Cubin***	Y	Y	Y	Y	Y	Y	Y

Southern states - Ala., Ark., Fla., Ga., Ky., La., Miss., N.C., Okla., S.C., Tenn., Texas, Va.

Key

Y	Voted for (yea).
#	Paired for.
+	Announced for.
N	Voted against (nay).
X	Paired against.
–	Announced against.
P	Voted "present."
C	Voted "present" to avoid possible conflict of interest.
?	Did not vote or otherwise make a position known.

Democrats *Republicans*
Independent

378. S J Res 54. Condemn Iraq for Breach of International Obligations/Passage. Gilman, R-N.Y., motion to suspend the rules and pass the bill that finds the government of Iraq in an "unacceptable" breach of its international obligations because of its repeated efforts to hamper the United Nations in finding and destroying Iraq's weapons of mass destruction. Motion agreed to 407-6: R 219-1; D 187-5 (ND 137-4, SD 50-1); I 1-0. Aug. 3, 1998. A two-thirds majority of those present and voting (276 in this case) is required for passage under suspension of the rules.

379. HR 2183. Campaign Finance Overhaul/Shays-Meehan Substitute. Shays, R-Conn., substitute amendment to the bill to overhaul campaign finance laws. The amendment would ban soft money contributions for federal elections, expand regulations on advertising that advocates a candidate and tighten the definition of what constitutes coordination with a federal candidate. Adopted 237-186: R 51-175; D 185-11 (ND 138-6, SD 47-5); I 1-0. Aug. 3, 1998. Final adoption is contingent upon the outcome of votes on other substitute amendments. Whichever gets the most votes and at least a majority prevails.

380. H Con Res 213. Sense of Congress Regarding European Union Imports/Passage. Crane, R-Ill., motion to suspend the rules and pass the bill to express the sense of Congress that the European Union is unfairly restricting U.S. agricultural imports and that eliminating restrictions should be a top priority in trade negotiations. Motion agreed to 420-4: R 222-2; D 197-2 (ND 144-2, SD 53-0); I 1-0. Aug. 4, 1998. A two-thirds majority of those present and voting (283 in this case) is required for passage under suspension of the rules.

381. HR 4276. Fiscal 1999 Commerce, Justice, State Appropriations/Legal Services Corporation Funding Increase. Mollohan, D-W.Va., amendment to increase funding for Legal Services Corporation from $141 million to $250 million. Adopted 255-170: R 57-168; D 197-2 (ND 146-0, SD 51-2); I 1-0. Aug. 4, 1998.

382. HR 4276. Fiscal 1999 Commerce, Justice, State Appropriations/Eliminate TV Marti Funding. Skaggs, D-Colo., amendment to eliminate the bill's appropriation for TV Marti, a federal government television broadcast to Cuba. Rejected 172-251: R 29-195; D 142-56 (ND 109-35, SD 33-21); I 1-0. Aug. 4, 1998.

383. HR 4276. Fiscal 1999 Commerce, Justice, State Appropriations/Decrease Economic Development Administration Funding. Souder, R-Ind., amendment to decrease funding for the Economic Development Administration, and transfer the funds to "drug court" programs for juvenile drug offenders. Rejected 91-327: R 88-133; D 3-193 (ND 0-142, SD 3-51); I 0-1. Aug. 4, 1998.

384. HR 4276. Fiscal 1999 Commerce, Justice, State Appropriations/Decrease Advanced Technology Program Funding. Bass, R-N.H., amendment to decrease the bill's appropriation for the Advanced Technology Program by $43 million, in an effort to prohibit the program from awarding new grants. Rejected 155-267: R 135-88; D 20-178 (ND 12-132, SD 8-46); I 0-1. Aug. 4, 1998.

	378	379	380	381	382	383	384
ALABAMA							
1 *Callahan*	Y	N	Y	N	N	N	N
2 *Everett*	Y	N	Y	N	N	N	N
3 *Riley*	Y	N	Y	N	N	N	N
4 *Aderholt*	Y	N	Y	N	N	N	N
5 Cramer	Y	Y	Y	Y	N	N	N
6 *Bachus*	Y	Y	Y	N	N	Y	Y
7 Hilliard	?	?	Y	Y	Y	N	N
ALASKA							
AL *Young*	Y	N	Y	N	N	N	N
ARIZONA							
1 *Salmon*	Y	N	Y	N	N	Y	Y
2 Pastor	Y	Y	Y	Y	N	N	Y
3 *Stump*	Y	N	Y	N	N	N	Y
4 *Shadegg*	Y	N	Y	N	N	Y	Y
5 *Kolbe*	Y	N	Y	N	Y	N	Y
6 *Hayworth*	Y	N	Y	N	N	Y	Y
ARKANSAS							
1 Berry	Y	Y	Y	Y	Y	N	Y
2 Snyder	Y	Y	Y	Y	Y	N	N
3 *Hutchinson*	?	N	Y	N	N	N	N
4 *Dickey*	Y	N	Y	N	N	N	N
CALIFORNIA							
1 *Riggs*	Y	N	Y	N	N	Y	Y
2 *Herger*	Y	N	Y	N	N	N	Y
3 Fazio	Y	Y	Y	Y	Y	N	N
4 *Doolittle*	Y	N	Y	N	N	N	Y
5 Matsui	Y	Y	Y	Y	Y	N	N
6 Woolsey	Y	Y	Y	Y	Y	N	N
7 Miller	Y	Y	Y	Y	Y	N	N
8 Pelosi	Y	Y	Y	Y	Y	N	N
9 Lee	N	Y	Y	Y	Y	N	N
10 Tauscher	Y	Y	Y	Y	N	N	N
11 *Pombo*	Y	N	Y	N	N	N	N
12 Lantos	Y	Y	Y	Y	N	N	N
13 Stark	Y	Y	Y	Y	Y	?	N
14 Eshoo	Y	Y	Y	Y	Y	N	N
15 *Campbell*	Y	Y	Y	N	N	Y	Y
16 Lofgren	Y	Y	Y	Y	Y	N	N
17 Farr	Y	Y	Y	Y	Y	N	N
18 Condit	Y	Y	Y	Y	N	N	N
19 *Radanovich*	Y	N	Y	N	N	N	N
20 Dooley	Y	Y	Y	Y	N	N	N
21 *Thomas*	Y	Y	Y	N	N	N	N
22 Capps, L.	Y	Y	Y	Y	Y	N	N
23 *Gallegly*	Y	Y	Y	N	N	N	N
24 Sherman	Y	Y	Y	Y	N	N	N
25 *McKeon*	Y	N	Y	N	N	Y	Y
26 Berman	Y	Y	Y	Y	Y	N	N
27 *Rogan*	Y	N	Y	N	N	N	N
28 *Dreier*	Y	N	Y	N	N	N	N
29 Waxman	Y	Y	Y	Y	Y	N	N
30 Becerra	Y	Y	Y	Y	Y	N	N
31 Martinez	?	?	Y	Y	Y	N	N
32 Dixon	Y	Y	Y	Y	Y	N	N
33 Roybal-Allard	Y	Y	Y	Y	Y	N	N
34 Torres	Y	Y	Y	Y	Y	N	N
35 Waters	N	Y	N	Y	Y	N	N
36 Harman	Y	Y	Y	Y	N	N	N
37 Millender-McD.	Y	Y	Y	Y	–	N	N
38 *Horn*	Y	Y	Y	Y	N	N	N

	378	379	380	381	382	383	384
39 *Royce*	Y	N	Y	N	N	Y	Y
40 *Lewis*	Y	N	Y	N	N	N	N
41 *Kim*	Y	N	Y	N	N	N	N
42 Brown	Y	Y	Y	Y	N	N	N
43 *Calvert*	Y	N	Y	N	N	N	N
44 *Bono, M.*	Y	N	Y	N	N	N	N
45 *Rohrabacher*	Y	N	Y	N	N	N	N
46 Sanchez	Y	Y	Y	Y	Y	N	N
47 *Cox*	Y	N	Y	N	N	Y	Y
48 *Packard*	Y	N	Y	N	N	N	N
49 *Bilbray*	Y	N	Y	N	N	N	N
50 Filner	Y	Y	Y	Y	Y	N	N
51 *Cunningham*	Y	N	?	?	?	?	?
52 *Hunter*	Y	N	Y	N	N	Y	N
COLORADO							
1 DeGette	Y	Y	Y	Y	Y	N	N
2 Skaggs	Y	Y	Y	Y	Y	N	N
3 *McInnis*	Y	N	?	?	?	?	?
4 *Schaffer*	Y	N	Y	N	N	Y	Y
5 *Hefley*	Y	N	Y	N	N	Y	Y
6 *Schaefer*	Y	N	Y	N	N	Y	Y
CONNECTICUT							
1 Kennelly	Y	Y	Y	Y	N	N	N
2 Gejdenson	Y	Y	Y	Y	Y	N	N
3 DeLauro	Y	Y	Y	Y	N	N	N
4 *Shays*	Y	Y	Y	Y	Y	N	N
5 Maloney	Y	Y	Y	Y	N	N	N
6 *Johnson*	Y	Y	Y	Y	N	N	N
DELAWARE							
AL *Castle*	Y	Y	Y	Y	N	N	N
FLORIDA							
1 *Scarborough*	Y	N	Y	N	N	Y	Y
2 Boyd	Y	Y	Y	Y	N	N	Y
3 Brown	Y	Y	Y	Y	N	N	N
4 *Fowler*	Y	N	Y	N	N	Y	Y
5 Thurman	Y	Y	Y	Y	N	N	N
6 *Stearns*	Y	N	Y	N	N	N	N
7 *Mica*	Y	N	Y	N	N	N	N
8 *McCollum*	Y	N	Y	N	N	N	N
9 *Bilirakis*	Y	N	Y	N	N	N	N
10 *Young*	Y	N	Y	N	N	N	N
11 Davis	Y	Y	Y	Y	N	N	Y
12 *Canady*	Y	N	Y	N	N	Y	Y
13 *Miller*	Y	N	Y	N	N	N	N
14 *Goss*	Y	N	Y	N	N	Y	Y
15 *Weldon*	Y	N	Y	N	N	Y	Y
16 *Foley*	Y	N	Y	N	N	Y	Y
17 Meek	Y	Y	Y	Y	N	N	N
18 *Ros-Lehtinen*	Y	N	Y	N	N	N	N
19 Wexler	Y	Y	Y	Y	N	N	N
20 Deutsch	Y	Y	Y	Y	N	N	N
21 *Diaz-Balart*	Y	N	Y	N	N	N	N
22 *Shaw*	Y	N	Y	N	N	Y	Y
23 Hastings	Y	Y	Y	Y	N	N	N
GEORGIA							
1 *Kingston*	Y	N	Y	N	N	N	Y
2 Bishop	Y	N	Y	N	N	N	N
3 *Collins*	Y	N	Y	N	N	N	N
4 McKinney	N	Y	Y	Y	Y	N	Y
5 Lewis	Y	Y	Y	Y	Y	N	N
6 *Gingrich*	N						
7 *Barr*	Y	N	Y	N	N	Y	Y
8 *Chambliss*	Y	N	Y	N	N	Y	Y
9 *Deal*	Y	N	Y	N	N	N	N
10 *Norwood*	Y	N	Y	N	N	Y	Y
11 *Linder*	Y	N	Y	N	N	N	Y
HAWAII							
1 Abercrombie	Y	Y	Y	Y	Y	N	N
2 Mink	Y	Y	Y	Y	Y	N	Y
IDAHO							
1 *Chenoweth*	Y	N	N	N	N	N	N
2 *Crapo*	Y	N	Y	N	N	N	N
ILLINOIS							
1 Rush	Y	Y	Y	Y	Y	N	N
2 Jackson	N	Y	Y	Y	Y	N	N
3 Lipinski	Y	Y	Y	Y	N	N	N
4 Gutierrez	?	Y	Y	Y	Y	N	N
5 Blagojevich	Y	Y	Y	Y	N	N	N
6 *Hyde*	Y	N	Y	N	N	N	N
7 Davis	Y	Y	Y	Y	Y	N	N
8 *Crane*	Y	N	Y	N	N	Y	Y
9 Yates	Y	Y	Y	Y	Y	?	?
10 *Porter*	Y	Y	Y	Y	N	N	N
11 *Weller*	Y	N	Y	N	N	N	N
12 Costello	Y	Y	Y	Y	N	N	N
13 *Fawell*	Y	N	Y	Y	N	Y	N

ND Northern Democrats   SD Southern Democrats

	378	379	380	381	382	383	384
14 ***Hastert***	Y	N	Y	N	N	Y	Y
15 ***Ewing***	Y	N	Y	N	N	N	N
16 ***Manzullo***	Y	N	Y	N	N	Y	Y
17 Evans	Y	Y	Y	Y	Y	N	N
18 ***LaHood***	Y	N	Y	Y	N	N	N
19 Poshard	?	?	?	Y	Y	N	N
20 ***Shimkus***	Y	Y	Y	N	N	N	Y
INDIANA							
1 Visclosky	Y	Y	Y	Y	Y	N	Y
2 ***McIntosh***	Y	N	Y	N	N	Y	N
3 Roemer	Y	Y	Y	Y	Y	N	N
4 ***Souder***	Y	N	Y	N	N	Y	Y
5 ***Buyer***	Y	N	Y	N	N	N	Y
6 ***Burton***	Y	N	?	N	N	Y	Y
7 ***Pease***	Y	N	Y	N	N	Y	Y
8 ***Hostettler***	Y	N	Y	N	N	Y	Y
9 Hamilton	Y	Y	Y	Y	Y	N	N
10 Carson	Y	Y	Y	Y	Y	N	Y
IOWA							
1 ***Leach***	Y	Y	Y	Y	N	Y	Y
2 ***Nussle***	Y	N	Y	N	N	N	N
3 Boswell	Y	Y	Y	Y	N	N	N
4 ***Ganske***	Y	Y	Y	Y	Y	N	Y
5 ***Latham***	Y	N	Y	N	N	N	N
KANSAS							
1 ***Moran***	Y	N	Y	N	N	N	Y
2 ***Ryun***	Y	N	Y	N	N	Y	Y
3 ***Snowbarger***	Y	N	Y	N	N	Y	Y
4 ***Tiahrt***	Y	N	Y	N	N	Y	Y
KENTUCKY							
1 ***Whitfield***	Y	N	Y	N	N	N	Y
2 ***Lewis***	Y	N	Y	N	N	N	Y
3 ***Northup***	?	N	Y	N	N	N	N
4 ***Bunning***	Y	N	Y	N	N	N	Y
5 ***Rogers***	?	N	Y	N	N	N	N
6 Baesler	Y	Y	Y	Y	Y	N	Y
LOUISIANA							
1 ***Livingston***	Y	N	Y	N	N	N	Y
2 Jefferson	Y	Y	Y	Y	Y	N	N
3 ***Tauzin***	Y	N	Y	Y	N	Y	N
4 ***McCrery***	Y	N	Y	Y	N	N	Y
5 ***Cooksey***	Y	N	Y	N	N	N	N
6 ***Baker***	Y	N	Y	N	N	N	Y
7 John	Y	N	Y	Y	N	N	N
MAINE							
1 Allen	Y	Y	Y	Y	Y	N	N
2 Baldacci	Y	Y	Y	Y	N	N	N
MARYLAND							
1 ***Gilchrest***	Y	Y	Y	Y	Y	N	N
2 ***Ehrlich***	Y	N	Y	Y	N	Y	Y
3 Cardin	Y	Y	Y	Y	N	N	N
4 Wynn	Y	Y	Y	Y	Y	N	N
5 Hoyer	Y	Y	Y	Y	Y	N	N
6 ***Bartlett***	Y	N	Y	N	N	N	N
7 Cummings	Y	Y	Y	Y	Y	N	N
8 ***Morella***	Y	Y	Y	Y	Y	N	N
MASSACHUSETTS							
1 Olver	?	Y	Y	Y	Y	N	N
2 Neal	Y	Y	Y	Y	Y	N	N
3 McGovern	Y	Y	Y	Y	Y	N	N
4 Frank	Y	Y	Y	Y	Y	N	N
5 Meehan	Y	Y	Y	Y	Y	N	N
6 Tierney	Y	Y	Y	Y	Y	N	N
7 Markey	Y	Y	Y	Y	Y	N	N
8 Kennedy	Y	Y	Y	Y	N	N	N
9 Moakley	Y	Y	Y	Y	Y	?	?
10 Delahunt	Y	Y	Y	Y	Y	N	N
MICHIGAN							
1 Stupak	Y	N	Y	Y	Y	N	N
2 ***Hoekstra***	Y	N	Y	N	Y	Y	Y
3 ***Ehlers***	Y	N	Y	Y	Y	N	N
4 ***Camp***	Y	N	Y	Y	Y	Y	Y
5 Barcia	Y	Y	Y	Y	N	N	N
6 ***Upton***	Y	Y	Y	Y	Y	Y	Y
7 ***Smith***	Y	Y	Y	N	N	Y	Y
8 Stabenow	Y	Y	Y	Y	Y	N	N
9 Kildee	Y	Y	Y	Y	Y	N	N
10 Bonior	N	Y	Y	Y	Y	N	N
11 ***Knollenberg***	Y	N	Y	N	N	N	Y
12 Levin	Y	Y	Y	Y	Y	N	N
13 Rivers	Y	Y	Y	Y	Y	N	N
14 Conyers	?	?	?	?	?	?	?
15 Kilpatrick	+	+	?	?	?	?	?
16 Dingell	Y	Y	Y	Y	Y	N	N
MINNESOTA							
1 ***Gutknecht***	Y	N	Y	N	N	Y	Y
2 Minge	Y	Y	Y	Y	Y	N	N
3 ***Ramstad***	Y	Y	Y	Y	Y	Y	Y
4 Vento	Y	Y	Y	Y	Y	N	N
5 Sabo	Y	Y	Y	Y	Y	N	N
6 Luther	Y	Y	Y	Y	Y	N	Y
7 Peterson	Y	N	Y	Y	Y	N	Y
8 Oberstar	+	+	Y	Y	Y	N	N
MISSISSIPPI							
1 ***Wicker***	Y	N	Y	N	N	N	N
2 Thompson	Y	Y	Y	Y	Y	N	N
3 ***Pickering***	Y	N	Y	N	N	–	+
4 ***Parker***	Y	Y	Y	N	Y	N	N
5 Taylor	Y	Y	Y	N	Y	N	Y
MISSOURI							
1 Clay	Y	Y	Y	Y	?	?	?
2 ***Talent***	Y	N	Y	N	N	Y	Y
3 Gephardt	Y	Y	Y	Y	N	N	N
4 Skelton	Y	Y	Y	Y	N	N	Y
5 McCarthy	Y	Y	+	+	+	–	–
6 Danner	Y	Y	Y	Y	Y	N	N
7 ***Blunt***	Y	N	Y	N	N	Y	Y
8 ***Emerson***	Y	N	Y	N	N	N	N
9 ***Hulshof***	Y	N	Y	Y	N	N	Y
MONTANA							
AL ***Hill***	Y	N	Y	N	N	N	Y
NEBRASKA							
1 ***Bereuter***	Y	Y	Y	N	N	N	N
2 ***Christensen***	?	–	Y	N	Y	Y	Y
3 ***Barrett***	Y	Y	Y	N	Y	Y	N
NEVADA							
1 ***Ensign***	Y	N	Y	N	N	N	Y
2 ***Gibbons***	Y	N	Y	N	Y	N	Y
NEW HAMPSHIRE							
1 ***Sununu***	Y	N	Y	N	Y	Y	Y
2 ***Bass***	Y	Y	Y	N	N	N	Y
NEW JERSEY							
1 Andrews	Y	Y	Y	Y	N	N	Y
2 ***LoBiondo***	Y	Y	Y	N	N	N	Y
3 ***Saxton***	Y	Y	Y	N	N	N	N
4 ***Smith***	Y	N	Y	Y	N	N	N
5 ***Roukema***	Y	Y	Y	N	Y	Y	Y
6 Pallone	Y	Y	Y	Y	N	N	N
7 ***Franks***	Y	Y	Y	Y	N	N	Y
8 Pascrell	Y	Y	Y	Y	N	N	N
9 Rothman	Y	Y	Y	Y	N	N	N
10 Payne	Y	Y	Y	Y	Y	N	N
11 ***Frelinghuysen***	Y	Y	Y	Y	N	N	Y
12 ***Pappas***	Y	N	Y	N	N	N	Y
13 Menendez	Y	Y	Y	Y	N	N	N
NEW MEXICO							
1 ***Wilson***	Y	N	Y	Y	N	N	N
2 ***Skeen***	Y	N	Y	N	N	N	N
3 ***Redmond***	Y	N	Y	N	N	N	Y
NEW YORK							
1 ***Forbes***	Y	Y	Y	Y	N	N	N
2 ***Lazio***	Y	Y	Y	Y	N	N	Y
3 ***King***	Y	N	Y	N	N	N	N
4 McCarthy	?	Y	Y	Y	Y	N	N
5 Ackerman	Y	Y	Y	Y	N	N	N
6 Meeks	Y	Y	Y	Y	Y	N	N
7 Manton	Y	Y	Y	Y	N	N	N
8 Nadler	Y	Y	Y	Y	Y	N	N
9 Schumer	Y	Y	Y	?	Y	N	Y
10 Towns	?	?	?	?	?	?	?
11 Owens	Y	Y	Y	Y	Y	N	N
12 Velázquez	Y	Y	Y	Y	Y	N	N
13 ***Fossella***	Y	N	Y	N	N	N	Y
14 Maloney	Y	Y	Y	Y	Y	N	N
15 Rangel	Y	Y	Y	Y	Y	N	N
16 Serrano	Y	Y	Y	Y	Y	N	N
17 Engel	Y	Y	Y	Y	N	N	N
18 Lowey	Y	Y	Y	Y	Y	N	N
19 ***Kelly***	Y	Y	Y	N	Y	N	N
20 ***Gilman***	Y	Y	Y	Y	N	Y	Y
21 McNulty	Y	Y	Y	Y	N	N	N
22 ***Solomon***	Y	N	Y	N	N	Y	Y
23 ***Boehlert***	Y	Y	Y	Y	Y	N	N
24 ***McHugh***	Y	N	Y	Y	N	N	Y
25 ***Walsh***	Y	Y	Y	Y	Y	N	N
26 Hinchey	Y	Y	Y	Y	Y	N	N
27 ***Paxon***	Y	N	Y	N	N	Y	Y
28 Slaughter	Y	Y	Y	Y	Y	N	N
29 LaFalce	Y	Y	Y	Y	Y	N	N
30 ***Quinn***	Y	Y	Y	Y	Y	N	N
31 ***Houghton***	Y	Y	Y	Y	Y	N	N
NORTH CAROLINA							
1 Clayton	Y	Y	Y	Y	Y	N	N
2 Etheridge	Y	Y	Y	Y	Y	N	N
3 ***Jones***	Y	N	Y	N	N	N	N
4 Price	Y	Y	Y	Y	Y	N	N
5 ***Burr***	Y	N	Y	N	N	N	N
6 ***Coble***	Y	N	Y	N	Y	Y	Y
7 McIntyre	Y	Y	Y	Y	Y	N	Y
8 Hefner	Y	Y	Y	Y	Y	N	N
9 ***Myrick***	Y	N	Y	N	N	Y	Y
10 ***Ballenger***	Y	N	Y	N	N	Y	Y
11 ***Taylor***	Y	N	Y	N	N	N	N
12 Watt	Y	Y	Y	Y	Y	N	N
NORTH DAKOTA							
AL Pomeroy	?	?	Y	Y	Y	N	N
OHIO							
1 ***Chabot***	Y	N	Y	N	N	Y	Y
2 ***Portman***	Y	N	Y	N	N	Y	Y
3 Hall	Y	Y	Y	Y	?	N	N
4 ***Oxley***	Y	N	Y	N	N	?	?
5 ***Gillmor***	Y	Y	Y	N	N	N	N
6 Strickland	Y	Y	Y	Y	Y	N	N
7 ***Hobson***	Y	N	Y	N	N	Y	Y
8 ***Boehner***	Y	N	Y	N	N	Y	Y
9 Kaptur	Y	Y	Y	Y	N	N	N
10 Kucinich	Y	Y	Y	Y	N	N	N
11 Stokes	Y	Y	Y	Y	Y	N	N
12 ***Kasich***	Y	N	Y	N	N	Y	Y
13 Brown	Y	Y	Y	Y	Y	N	N
14 Sawyer	Y	Y	Y	Y	Y	N	N
15 ***Pryce***	Y	N	Y	Y	N	Y	Y
16 ***Regula***	Y	Y	Y	Y	Y	N	N
17 Traficant	Y	N	Y	Y	N	N	N
18 ***Ney***	Y	N	Y	Y	N	N	Y
19 ***LaTourette***	Y	Y	Y	Y	N	N	N
OKLAHOMA							
1 ***Largent***	Y	N	Y	Y	N	Y	Y
2 ***Coburn***	Y	N	Y	N	N	Y	Y
3 ***Watkins***	Y	N	Y	N	N	N	Y
4 ***Watts***	Y	N	Y	Y	N	N	Y
5 ***Istook***	?	?	Y	N	N	Y	Y
6 ***Lucas***	Y	N	Y	N	N	N	N
OREGON							
1 Furse	Y	Y	Y	Y	?	N	N
2 ***Smith***	Y	N	Y	N	N	N	N
3 Blumenauer	Y	Y	Y	Y	Y	N	N
4 DeFazio	Y	Y	N	Y	Y	N	Y
5 Hooley	Y	Y	Y	Y	Y	N	N
PENNSYLVANIA							
1 Brady	Y	Y	Y	Y	Y	N	N
2 Fattah	Y	Y	Y	Y	Y	N	N
3 Borski	Y	Y	Y	Y	Y	N	N
4 Klink	Y	Y	Y	Y	Y	N	N
5 ***Peterson***	Y	N	Y	N	N	N	N
6 Holden	Y	Y	Y	Y	Y	N	N
7 ***Weldon***	Y	Y	Y	Y	N	N	N
8 ***Greenwood***	Y	Y	Y	Y	N	N	Y
9 ***Shuster***	Y	N	Y	N	Y	N	Y
10 ***McDade***	?	Y	Y	Y	N	?	N
11 Kanjorski	Y	Y	Y	Y	Y	N	N
12 Murtha	Y	N	Y	Y	N	N	N
13 ***Fox***	Y	Y	Y	Y	N	Y	Y
14 Coyne	Y	Y	Y	Y	N	N	N
15 McHale	Y	Y	Y	Y	N	N	N
16 ***Pitts***	Y	N	Y	N	N	Y	Y
17 ***Gekas***	Y	N	Y	Y	N	N	N
18 Doyle	Y	Y	Y	Y	Y	N	N
19 ***Goodling***	Y	N	Y	Y	N	N	Y
20 Mascara	Y	Y	Y	Y	Y	N	N
21 ***English***	Y	N	Y	N	N	N	N
RHODE ISLAND							
1 Kennedy	Y	Y	Y	Y	N	N	N
2 Weygand	Y	Y	Y	Y	Y	N	N
SOUTH CAROLINA							
1 ***Sanford***	Y	Y	Y	N	N	Y	Y
2 ***Spence***	Y	N	Y	N	N	N	N
3 ***Graham***	Y	Y	Y	N	N	N	N
4 ***Inglis***	Y	N	Y	N	N	Y	N
5 Spratt	Y	Y	Y	Y	N	N	N
6 Clyburn	Y	Y	Y	Y	Y	N	N
SOUTH DAKOTA							
AL ***Thune***	Y	N	Y	N	N	N	Y
TENNESSEE							
1 ***Jenkins***	Y	N	Y	N	N	N	N
2 ***Duncan***	Y	Y	Y	N	N	N	Y
3 ***Wamp***	?	Y	Y	N	N	N	Y
4 ***Hilleary***	Y	N	Y	N	N	N	Y
5 Clement	Y	Y	Y	Y	Y	N	N
6 Gordon	Y	Y	Y	Y	N	N	N
7 ***Bryant***	Y	N	Y	N	N	N	Y
8 Tanner	Y	Y	Y	Y	Y	N	N
9 Ford	Y	Y	Y	Y	Y	N	N
TEXAS							
1 Sandlin	Y	Y	Y	Y	Y	N	N
2 Turner	Y	Y	Y	Y	Y	N	Y
3 ***Johnson, Sam***	Y	N	Y	N	N	Y	Y
4 Hall	Y	N	Y	N	N	Y	Y
5 ***Sessions***	Y	N	Y	N	N	Y	N
6 ***Barton***	Y	N	Y	N	N	Y	Y
7 ***Archer***	Y	N	Y	N	N	?	N
8 ***Brady***	Y	N	Y	N	N	N	N
9 Lampson	Y	Y	Y	Y	N	N	N
10 Doggett	Y	Y	Y	Y	Y	Y	N
11 Edwards	Y	Y	Y	Y	Y	N	N
12 ***Granger***	Y	N	Y	N	N	N	Y
13 ***Thornberry***	Y	N	Y	N	N	Y	Y
14 ***Paul***	N	N	N	N	Y	Y	Y
15 Hinojosa	Y	Y	Y	Y	Y	N	N
16 Reyes	Y	Y	Y	Y	N	N	N
17 Stenholm	Y	Y	Y	Y	N	N	N
18 Jackson-Lee	Y	Y	Y	Y	N	N	N
19 ***Combest***	Y	N	Y	N	N	N	N
20 Gonzalez	?	?	?	?	?	?	?
21 ***Smith***	Y	N	Y	N	N	N	N
22 ***DeLay***	Y	N	Y	N	N	Y	Y
23 ***Bonilla***	Y	N	Y	N	N	N	N
24 Frost	Y	Y	Y	Y	Y	N	N
25 Bentsen	Y	Y	Y	Y	Y	N	N
26 ***Armey***	Y	N	Y	N	N	Y	Y
27 Ortiz	+	+	Y	Y	N	N	N
28 Rodriguez	Y	Y	Y	Y	Y	N	N
29 Green	Y	Y	Y	Y	N	N	N
30 Johnson, E.B.	Y	Y	Y	Y	Y	N	N
UTAH							
1 ***Hansen***	Y	N	Y	N	N	N	Y
2 ***Cook***	Y	Y	Y	N	N	N	N
3 ***Cannon***	Y	N	Y	N	N	Y	Y
VERMONT							
AL *Sanders*	Y	Y	Y	Y	Y	N	N
VIRGINIA							
1 ***Bateman***	Y	N	Y	N	N	Y	N
2 Pickett	Y	Y	Y	Y	Y	N	N
3 Scott	Y	N	Y	Y	Y	N	N
4 Sisisky	Y	Y	Y	Y	N	N	N
5 Goode	Y	N	?	?	N	N	N
6 ***Goodlatte***	Y	N	Y	N	N	N	N
7 ***Bliley***	Y	N	Y	N	N	N	N
8 Moran	?	Y	Y	Y	Y	N	N
9 Boucher	Y	Y	Y	Y	Y	N	N
10 ***Wolf***	Y	N	Y	N	?	Y	N
11 ***Davis***	Y	N	Y	Y	N	N	N
WASHINGTON							
1 ***White***	Y	N	Y	Y	N	N	Y
2 ***Metcalf***	Y	Y	Y	N	N	N	Y
3 ***Smith, Linda***	Y	Y	Y	N	N	Y	Y
4 ***Hastings***	Y	N	Y	N	N	N	Y
5 ***Nethercutt***	Y	N	Y	Y	Y	N	Y
6 Dicks	Y	Y	Y	Y	Y	N	N
7 McDermott	Y	Y	Y	Y	Y	N	N
8 ***Dunn***	Y	N	Y	N	N	N	Y
9 Smith, Adam	Y	Y	Y	Y	Y	N	N
WEST VIRGINIA							
1 Mollohan	Y	N	Y	Y	Y	N	N
2 Wise	Y	Y	Y	Y	N	N	N
3 Rahall	Y	N	Y	Y	Y	N	N
WISCONSIN							
1 ***Neumann***	Y	N	Y	N	Y	Y	Y
2 ***Klug***	Y	Y	Y	Y	N	N	N
3 Kind	Y	Y	Y	Y	Y	N	N
4 Kleczka	Y	Y	Y	Y	Y	N	N
5 Barrett	Y	Y	Y	Y	Y	N	Y
6 ***Petri***	Y	N	Y	N	N	N	Y
7 Obey	Y	Y	Y	Y	Y	N	N
8 Johnson	Y	Y	Y	Y	Y	N	N
9 ***Sensenbrenner***	Y	N	Y	N	Y	Y	Y
WYOMING							
AL ***Cubin***	Y	N	Y	N	N	Y	Y

Southern states - Ala., Ark., Fla., Ga., Ky., La., Miss., N.C., Okla., S.C., Tenn., Texas, Va.

Key

Y	Voted for (yea).
#	Paired for.
+	Announced for.
N	Voted against (nay).
X	Paired against.
–	Announced against.
P	Voted "present."
C	Voted "present" to avoid possible conflict of interest.
?	Did not vote or otherwise make a position known.

Democrats **Republicans** *Independent*

385. HR 4276. Fiscal 1999 Commerce, Justice, State Appropriations/Transfer Funds From "Truth-In-Sentencing" Programs to Prevention Programs. Scott, D-Va., amendment to transfer $105 million from prison "truth-in-sentencing" incentive grants to drug treatment and crime prevention programs. Rejected 149-271: R 12-210; D 136-61 (ND 102-41, SD 34-20); I 1-0. Aug. 4, 1998.

386. HR 4276. Fiscal 1999 Commerce, Justice, State Appropriations/Decrease Public Broadcasting Funding. Gutknecht, R-Minn., amendment to cut funding for public broadcasting by $6 million. Rejected 136-286: R 124-99; D 12-186 (ND 5-139, SD 7-47); I 0-1. Aug. 4, 1998.

387. HR 4276. Fiscal 1999 Commerce, Justice, State Appropriations/Fund Abortion Services for Women in Prison. DeGette, D-Ill., amendment to strike language in the bill that prohibits federal funds from being used for abortions for women in prison. Rejected 148-271: R 13-209; D 134-62 (ND 103-39, SD 31-23); I 1-0. Aug. 4, 1998.

388. HR 4276. Fiscal 1999 Commerce, Justice, State Appropriations/Allow Census Bureau to Develop Statistical Sampling. Mollohan, D-W.Va., amendment to strike the bill's restrictions on funding for the year 2000 census which would allow the Census Bureau to continue to plan, test and prepare to implement statistical sampling methods along with statistical sampling. Rejected 201-227: R 2-222; D 198-5 (ND 147-2, SD 51-3); I 1-0. Aug. 5, 1998.

389. HR 4276. Fiscal 1999 Commerce, Justice, State Appropriations/Increase Clean Water Initiative Funding. Pallone, D-N.J., amendment to fully fund the Clean Water Initiative by providing $8 million for states to develop and implement plans to control non-point course pollution. Rejected 158-267: R 44-179; D 114-87 (ND 101-47, SD 13-40); I 0-1. Aug. 5, 1998.

390. HR 4276. Fiscal 1999 Commerce, Justice, State Appropriations/Increase Public Telecommunication Facilities Program Funding. Engel, D-N.Y., amendment to provide an additional $5 million to the Public Telecommunication Facilities Planning Program. Rejected 168-259: R 26-196; D 141-63 (ND 108-42, SD 33-21); I 1-0. Aug. 5, 1998.

391. HR 4276. Fiscal 1999 Commerce, Justice, State Appropriations/Eliminate Funding for Advanced Technology Program. Royce, R-Calif., amendment to eliminate funding for the Advanced Technology Program and direct it to close out all operations. Rejected 137-291: R 127-98; D 10-192 (ND 7-141, SD 3-51); I 0-1. Aug. 5, 1998.

	385	386	387	388	389	390	391
ALABAMA							
1 *Callahan*	N	N	N	N	N	N	N
2 *Everett*	N	N	N	N	N	N	N
3 *Riley*	N	Y	N	N	N	Y	N
4 *Aderholt*	N	N	N	N	N	N	N
5 Cramer	N	N	Y	N	N	Y	N
6 *Bachus*	N	Y	N	N	N	N	Y
7 Hilliard	Y	N	Y	Y	N	Y	N
ALASKA							
AL *Young*	N	N	N	N	N	N	N
ARIZONA							
1 *Salmon*	N	N	N	N	N	N	Y
2 Pastor	Y	Y	Y	Y	N	Y	N
3 *Stump*	N	Y	N	N	N	N	Y
4 *Shadegg*	N	Y	N	N	N	N	Y
5 *Kolbe*	N	N	N	N	N	N	Y
6 *Hayworth*	N	Y	N	N	N	N	Y
ARKANSAS							
1 Berry	N	Y	N	Y	N	Y	Y
2 Snyder	Y	N	N	Y	Y	N	N
3 *Hutchinson*	N	N	N	N	N	N	N
4 *Dickey*	N	N	N	N	N	N	Y
CALIFORNIA							
1 *Riggs*	N	Y	N	N	N	N	Y
2 *Herger*	N	Y	N	N	N	N	Y
3 Fazio	Y	N	Y	Y	?	N	N
4 *Doolittle*	Y	Y	N	N	N	N	Y
5 Matsui	Y	N	Y	Y	Y	Y	N
6 Woolsey	Y	N	Y	Y	N	Y	N
7 Miller	Y	N	Y	Y	Y	Y	N
8 Pelosi	Y	N	Y	Y	Y	Y	N
9 Lee	Y	N	Y	Y	Y	Y	N
10 Tauscher	N	N	Y	Y	Y	Y	N
11 *Pombo*	N	Y	N	N	N	N	Y
12 Lantos	N	Y	Y	Y	N	N	N
13 Stark	Y	N	Y	Y	Y	Y	N
14 Eshoo	Y	N	Y	Y	Y	Y	N
15 *Campbell*	Y	Y	N	Y	N	Y	N
16 Lofgren	Y	N	Y	Y	N	Y	N
17 Farr	Y	N	Y	Y	Y	Y	N
18 Condit	Y	N	N	Y	N	N	N
19 *Radanovich*	N	Y	N	N	N	N	Y
20 Dooley	Y	N	Y	Y	N	Y	N
21 *Thomas*	N	N	Y	N	N	N	N
22 Capps, L.	Y	N	Y	Y	Y	Y	N
23 *Gallegly*	N	Y	N	N	N	N	Y
24 Sherman	Y	N	Y	Y	Y	Y	N
25 *McKeon*	N	N	N	N	N	N	Y
26 Berman	Y	N	Y	Y	Y	Y	N
27 *Rogan*	N	Y	N	N	N	N	Y
28 *Dreier*	N	N	N	N	N	N	Y
29 Waxman	Y	N	Y	Y	Y	Y	N
30 Becerra	Y	N	Y	Y	Y	Y	N
31 Martinez	N	N	Y	Y	N	N	N
32 Dixon	Y	N	Y	Y	N	Y	N
33 Roybal-Allard	Y	N	Y	Y	Y	Y	N
34 Torres	Y	N	Y	Y	N	N	N
35 Waters	Y	N	Y	?	N	Y	N
36 Harman	N	N	Y	Y	Y	Y	N
37 Millender-McD.	+	Y	N	Y	N	Y	N
38 *Horn*	N	N	Y	N	N	N	N

	385	386	387	388	389	390	391
39 *Royce*	N	Y	N	N	N	Y	N
40 *Lewis*	N	N	N	N	N	N	N
41 *Kim*	N	N	N	N	N	N	N
42 Brown	Y	N	Y	Y	N	Y	N
43 *Calvert*	N	N	N	N	N	N	N
44 *Bono, M.*	N	N	N	N	N	N	N
45 *Rohrabacher*	N	Y	N	N	N	N	Y
46 Sanchez	Y	Y	Y	Y	Y	Y	N
47 *Cox*	N	Y	N	?	N	Y	N
48 *Packard*	N	N	N	N	N	N	N
49 *Bilbray*	N	N	N	Y	N	Y	N
50 Filner	Y	N	Y	Y	N	Y	N
51 *Cunningham*	?	?	?	?	?	?	?
52 *Hunter*	N	Y	N	N	N	N	N
COLORADO							
1 DeGette	Y	N	Y	Y	Y	Y	N
2 Skaggs	Y	N	Y	N	Y	N	?
3 *McInnis*	?	?	?	?	N	?	Y
4 *Schaffer*	N	Y	N	N	N	N	Y
5 *Hefley*	N	N	N	N	N	Y	N
6 *Schaefer*	N	N	N	N	N	N	Y
CONNECTICUT							
1 Kennelly	N	N	Y	Y	Y	Y	N
2 Gejdenson	N	N	Y	Y	Y	Y	N
3 DeLauro	N	N	Y	Y	Y	Y	N
4 *Shays*	N	Y	Y	Y	Y	N	Y
5 Maloney	N	N	Y	Y	Y	Y	N
6 *Johnson*	N	Y	Y	N	Y	N	N
DELAWARE							
AL *Castle*	N	N	N	Y	Y	N	N
FLORIDA							
1 *Scarborough*	N	N	N	N	N	N	Y
2 Boyd	N	N	Y	Y	N	Y	N
3 Brown	Y	N	Y	Y	N	N	N
4 *Fowler*	N	Y	Y	N	N	N	N
5 Thurman	N	N	Y	Y	N	Y	N
6 *Stearns*	N	Y	N	N	N	N	N
7 *Mica*	N	N	N	N	N	N	N
8 *McCollum*	N	Y	N	N	N	N	N
9 *Bilirakis*	N	N	N	N	N	N	N
10 *Young*	N	N	N	N	N	N	N
11 Davis	Y	N	Y	Y	N	N	N
12 *Canady*	N	Y	N	N	N	N	N
13 *Miller*	N	Y	N	N	N	N	N
14 *Goss*	N	Y	N	N	N	N	N
15 *Weldon*	N	Y	N	N	N	N	N
16 *Foley*	N	Y	N	N	Y	N	N
17 Meek	N	N	Y	Y	N	N	N
18 *Ros-Lehtinen*	N	N	N	N	N	N	N
19 Wexler	N	N	Y	N	Y	N	N
20 Deutsch	N	N	Y	Y	N	N	N
21 *Diaz-Balart*	N	Y	N	N	N	N	N
22 *Shaw*	N	N	N	N	N	N	N
23 Hastings	N	N	Y	Y	N	N	N
GEORGIA							
1 *Kingston*	N	Y	N	N	N	?	N
2 Bishop	Y	N	Y	Y	Y	Y	N
3 *Collins*	N	Y	N	N	N	N	Y
4 McKinney	Y	N	Y	Y	Y	Y	Y
5 Lewis	Y	N	Y	Y	Y	Y	N
6 *Gingrich*				N			
7 *Barr*	N	Y	N	N	N	N	N
8 *Chambliss*	N	Y	N	N	N	N	N
9 *Deal*	N	Y	N	N	N	N	N
10 *Norwood*	N	Y	N	N	N	N	Y
11 *Linder*	N	Y	N	N	N	N	Y
HAWAII							
1 Abercrombie	Y	N	Y	Y	N	N	N
2 Mink	Y	N	Y	Y	Y	Y	N
IDAHO							
1 *Chenoweth*	N	Y	N	N	N	N	Y
2 *Crapo*	N	Y	N	N	N	N	Y
ILLINOIS							
1 Rush	Y	N	Y	Y	Y	Y	N
2 Jackson	Y	N	Y	Y	Y	Y	N
3 Lipinski	N	N	N	Y	N	Y	N
4 Gutierrez	Y	N	Y	Y	Y	Y	N
5 Blagojevich	N	N	Y	Y	Y	Y	N
6 *Hyde*	N	N	N	N	N	N	N
7 Davis	Y	N	Y	Y	Y	Y	N
8 *Crane*	N	Y	N	N	N	N	Y
9 Yates	?	?	?	Y	Y	Y	N
10 *Porter*	N	N	Y	Y	N	N	N
11 *Weller*	N	Y	?	N	Y	N	N
12 Costello	N	N	N	Y	N	Y	N
13 *Fawell*	N	N	Y	Y	N	N	N

ND Northern Democrats   SD Southern Democrats

	385	386	387	388	389	390	391
14 ***Hastert***	N	Y	N	N	N	N	Y
15 ***Ewing***	N	N	N	N	Y	N	N
16 ***Manzullo***	N	Y	N	N	N	N	Y
17 Evans	N	N	Y	Y	N	N	N
18 ***LaHood***	N	N	N	N	N	Y	N
19 Poshard	N	N	N	Y	Y	N	N
20 ***Shimkus***	N	N	N	N	N	N	Y
INDIANA							
1 Visclosky	Y	N	N	Y	Y	Y	Y
2 ***McIntosh***	N	Y	N	N	N	N	Y
3 Roemer	N	N	N	Y	Y	Y	N
4 ***Souder***	N	Y	N	N	N	N	N
5 ***Buyer***	N	Y	N	N	N	N	N
6 ***Burton***	N	Y	N	N	N	N	N
7 ***Pease***	Y	Y	N	N	N	Y	Y
8 ***Hostettler***	N	Y	N	N	N	N	Y
9 Hamilton	Y	N	N	Y	Y	Y	N
10 Carson	Y	N	Y	Y	Y	Y	N
IOWA							
1 ***Leach***	Y	N	N	N	Y	Y	Y
2 ***Nussle***	N	N	N	N	N	N	Y
3 Boswell	N	N	Y	N	N	Y	N
4 ***Ganske***	N	N	N	N	N	Y	Y
5 ***Latham***	N	N	N	N	N	N	Y
KANSAS							
1 ***Moran***	N	N	N	N	N	Y	Y
2 ***Ryun***	N	Y	N	N	N	N	Y
3 ***Snowbarger***	N	Y	N	N	N	Y	Y
4 ***Tiahrt***	N	Y	N	N	N	Y	Y
KENTUCKY							
1 ***Whitfield***	N	N	N	N	N	N	Y
2 ***Lewis***	N	N	N	N	N	N	N
3 ***Northup***	N	N	N	N	N	N	N
4 ***Bunning***	N	N	N	N	N	N	N
5 ***Rogers***	N	N	N	N	N	N	N
6 Baesler	N	N	Y	Y	N	Y	N
LOUISIANA							
1 ***Livingston***	N	N	N	N	N	N	Y
2 Jefferson	Y	N	Y	Y	N	N	N
3 ***Tauzin***	N	N	N	N	N	N	N
4 ***McCrery***	N	N	N	N	N	N	N
5 ***Cooksey***	N	N	N	N	N	N	Y
6 ***Baker***	N	N	N	N	N	N	N
7 John	N	N	N	Y	N	N	N
MAINE							
1 Allen	Y	N	Y	Y	Y	N	N
2 Baldacci	Y	N	Y	Y	Y	N	N
MARYLAND							
1 ***Gilchrest***	N	N	N	N	Y	N	N
2 ***Ehrlich***	N	Y	N	N	N	N	Y
3 Cardin	Y	N	Y	Y	Y	Y	N
4 Wynn	Y	N	Y	Y	Y	Y	N
5 Hoyer	Y	N	Y	Y	Y	Y	N
6 ***Bartlett***	N	Y	N	N	N	N	N
7 Cummings	Y	N	Y	Y	Y	Y	N
8 ***Morella***	Y	N	Y	Y	Y	Y	N
MASSACHUSETTS							
1 Olver	Y	N	Y	Y	Y	Y	N
2 Neal	Y	N	N	Y	Y	N	N
3 McGovern	Y	N	Y	Y	Y	Y	N
4 Frank	Y	N	Y	Y	Y	Y	N
5 Meehan	Y	Y	Y	Y	Y	Y	N
6 Tierney	Y	N	Y	Y	Y	Y	N
7 Markey	Y	N	Y	Y	Y	Y	N
8 Kennedy	Y	N	Y	Y	Y	N	N
9 Moakley	?	?	?	Y	Y	N	N
10 Delahunt	Y	N	Y	Y	Y	N	N
MICHIGAN							
1 Stupak	N	N	N	Y	N	N	N
2 ***Hoekstra***	N	Y	N	N	Y	N	Y
3 ***Ehlers***	N	N	N	N	Y	N	N
4 ***Camp***	N	Y	N	N	N	N	Y
5 Barcia	N	N	N	Y	Y	Y	N
6 ***Upton***	N	Y	N	N	Y	N	Y
7 ***Smith***	N	Y	N	N	N	N	Y
8 Stabenow	Y	N	Y	Y	Y	Y	N
9 Kildee	Y	N	N	Y	Y	Y	N
10 Bonior	Y	N	N	Y	Y	Y	N
11 ***Knollenberg***	N	N	N	N	N	N	Y
12 Levin	N	N	Y	Y	N	Y	N
13 Rivers	N	N	Y	Y	Y	Y	N
14 Conyers	?	?	?	Y	N	N	N
15 Kilpatrick	?	?	?	Y	Y	Y	N
16 Dingell	N	N	N	Y	Y	Y	N

	385	386	387	388	389	390	391
MINNESOTA							
1 ***Gutknecht***	N	Y	N	N	N	N	Y
2 Minge	Y	N	Y	Y	N	Y	N
3 ***Ramstad***	Y	N	N	N	Y	Y	Y
4 Vento	Y	N	Y	Y	Y	Y	N
5 Sabo	Y	N	Y	Y	N	Y	N
6 Luther	Y	N	Y	Y	Y	Y	Y
7 Peterson	Y	N	N	Y	N	N	Y
8 Oberstar	Y	N	N	Y	Y	Y	N
MISSISSIPPI							
1 ***Wicker***	Y	Y	N	N	N	N	N
2 Thompson	Y	N	Y	Y	N	Y	N
3 ***Pickering***	–	+	–	–	–	–	–
4 ***Parker***	N	N	N	N	N	N	N
5 Taylor	N	N	N	N	N	N	N
MISSOURI							
1 Clay	?	?	?	?	?	?	?
2 ***Talent***	N	Y	N	N	N	N	Y
3 Gephardt	N	N	Y	Y	Y	Y	N
4 Skelton	Y	N	N	Y	N	N	N
5 McCarthy	–	–	+	Y	Y	Y	N
6 Danner	N	N	N	Y	N	Y	N
7 ***Blunt***	N	Y	N	N	N	N	N
8 ***Emerson***	N	Y	N	N	N	N	Y
9 ***Hulshof***	N	N	N	N	Y	Y	Y
MONTANA							
AL ***Hill***	N	Y	N	N	N	Y	Y
NEBRASKA							
1 ***Bereuter***	N	N	N	N	N	Y	N
2 ***Christensen***	N	Y	N	N	N	N	N
3 ***Barrett***	N	N	N	N	N	N	N
NEVADA							
1 ***Ensign***	Y	Y	N	N	Y	Y	Y
2 ***Gibbons***	N	Y	N	N	N	N	Y
NEW HAMPSHIRE							
1 ***Sununu***	N	Y	N	N	Y	N	Y
2 ***Bass***	N	N	N	N	Y	Y	Y
NEW JERSEY							
1 Andrews	N	Y	Y	Y	Y	N	Y
2 ***LoBiondo***	N	Y	N	N	Y	N	Y
3 ***Saxton***	N	N	N	N	Y	N	N
4 ***Smith***	N	Y	N	N	Y	N	Y
5 ***Roukema***	N	N	N	N	Y	Y	N
6 Pallone	Y	N	Y	Y	Y	Y	N
7 ***Franks***	N	N	N	N	Y	N	N
8 Pascrell	N	N	Y	Y	Y	Y	N
9 Rothman	N	N	Y	Y	Y	N	N
10 Payne	Y	N	Y	Y	Y	Y	N
11 ***Frelinghuysen***	N	N	Y	N	Y	N	Y
12 ***Pappas***	N	Y	N	N	Y	N	Y
13 Menendez	N	N	Y	Y	Y	N	N
NEW MEXICO							
1 ***Wilson***	N	N	N	N	N	N	N
2 ***Skeen***	N	N	N	N	N	N	N
3 ***Redmond***	N	Y	N	N	N	N	N
NEW YORK							
1 ***Forbes***	N	N	N	N	Y	Y	N
2 ***Lazio***	N	Y	N	N	Y	Y	N
3 ***King***	N	N	N	N	N	N	N
4 McCarthy	N	N	Y	Y	Y	Y	N
5 Ackerman	Y	N	Y	Y	Y	N	N
6 Meeks	Y	Y	Y	Y	Y	Y	N
7 Manton	Y	N	N	Y	N	Y	N
8 Nadler	Y	N	Y	Y	Y	Y	N
9 Schumer	N	N	Y	Y	Y	Y	N
10 Towns	?	?	?	Y	Y	Y	N
11 Owens	Y	N	Y	Y	Y	Y	N
12 Velázquez	Y	N	Y	Y	N	Y	N
13 ***Fossella***	N	Y	N	N	Y	N	Y
14 Maloney	Y	N	Y	Y	+	Y	N
15 Rangel	Y	Y	Y	Y	Y	Y	N
16 Serrano	Y	N	Y	Y	Y	Y	N
17 Engel	Y	N	Y	Y	Y	Y	N
18 Lowey	N	N	Y	Y	Y	Y	N
19 ***Kelly***	N	N	Y	N	Y	Y	N
20 ***Gilman***	Y	Y	Y	N	Y	N	N
21 McNulty	Y	N	N	Y	Y	Y	N
22 ***Solomon***	N	Y	N	N	N	N	N
23 ***Boehlert***	N	N	Y	N	Y	N	N
24 ***McHugh***	N	N	N	N	Y	N	N
25 ***Walsh***	N	N	N	N	Y	N	N
26 Hinchey	Y	N	Y	Y	Y	Y	N
27 ***Paxon***	N	Y	N	N	N	N	Y
28 Slaughter	Y	N	Y	Y	Y	Y	?
29 LaFalce	Y	N	N	Y	Y	Y	N
30 ***Quinn***	N	N	N	N	N	N	N

	385	386	387	388	389	390	391
31 ***Houghton***	N	N	Y	N	N	N	N
NORTH CAROLINA							
1 Clayton	Y	N	Y	Y	N	N	N
2 Etheridge	N	N	N	Y	N	Y	N
3 ***Jones***	N	Y	N	N	Y	N	N
4 Price	N	N	Y	Y	N	Y	N
5 ***Burr***	N	N	N	N	Y	N	N
6 ***Coble***	N	Y	N	N	N	N	Y
7 McIntyre	N	N	N	Y	Y	N	Y
8 Hefner	Y	N	N	Y	N	Y	N
9 ***Myrick***	N	Y	N	N	N	N	Y
10 ***Ballenger***	N	Y	N	N	Y	N	Y
11 ***Taylor***	N	N	N	N	N	N	N
12 Watt	Y	N	Y	Y	N	Y	N
NORTH DAKOTA							
AL Pomeroy	N	N	N	Y	N	Y	N
OHIO							
1 ***Chabot***	N	Y	N	N	N	N	Y
2 ***Portman***	N	Y	N	N	N	N	Y
3 Hall	Y	N	N	Y	Y	Y	N
4 ***Oxley***	?	?	?	N	N	N	N
5 ***Gillmor***	N	Y	N	N	N	N	N
6 Strickland	N	N	?	Y	Y	Y	Y
7 ***Hobson***	N	Y	N	N	N	N	Y
8 ***Boehner***	N	Y	N	N	N	N	Y
9 Kaptur	Y	N	N	Y	Y	N	N
10 Kucinich	N	N	N	Y	N	Y	N
11 Stokes	Y	N	Y	Y	N	Y	N
12 ***Kasich***	N	Y	N	N	N	N	Y
13 Brown	Y	N	Y	Y	Y	Y	N
14 Sawyer	Y	N	Y	Y	Y	Y	N
15 ***Pryce***	N	Y	N	N	N	N	Y
16 ***Regula***	N	N	N	N	N	N	N
17 Traficant	N	N	N	N	N	N	N
18 ***Ney***	N	N	N	N	N	N	Y
19 ***LaTourette***	Y	N	N	N	Y	N	N
OKLAHOMA							
1 ***Largent***	N	Y	N	N	N	Y	Y
2 ***Coburn***	N	Y	N	N	N	N	Y
3 ***Watkins***	N	Y	N	N	N	N	Y
4 ***Watts***	N	Y	N	N	N	N	Y
5 ***Istook***	N	N	N	N	N	N	Y
6 ***Lucas***	N	N	N	N	N	N	Y
OREGON							
1 Furse	Y	N	Y	Y	Y	Y	N
2 ***Smith***	N	N	N	N	N	N	N
3 Blumenauer	Y	N	Y	Y	Y	Y	N
4 DeFazio	Y	N	Y	Y	N	Y	N
5 Hooley	N	N	Y	Y	Y	N	N
PENNSYLVANIA							
1 Brady	Y	N	Y	Y	Y	N	N
2 Fattah	Y	N	Y	Y	Y	N	N
3 Borski	N	N	N	Y	Y	N	N
4 Klink	Y	N	N	Y	Y	N	N
5 ***Peterson***	N	N	N	N	N	N	N
6 Holden	N	N	N	Y	N	Y	N
7 ***Weldon***	N	N	N	?	?	?	N
8 ***Greenwood***	Y	Y	Y	N	N	N	Y
9 ***Shuster***	N	Y	N	N	N	N	N
10 ***McDade***	?	N	N	N	N	N	N
11 Kanjorski	N	N	N	Y	N	Y	N
12 Murtha	Y	N	N	Y	Y	N	N
13 ***Fox***	N	Y	N	N	Y	N	Y
14 Coyne	Y	N	Y	Y	N	Y	N
15 McHale	N	N	N	Y	Y	Y	N
16 ***Pitts***	N	Y	N	N	N	N	Y
17 ***Gekas***	N	N	N	N	N	N	N
18 Doyle	N	N	N	Y	N	Y	N
19 ***Goodling***	N	N	N	N	N	N	Y
20 Mascara	N	N	N	Y	N	Y	N
21 ***English***	N	N	N	N	N	N	N
RHODE ISLAND							
1 Kennedy	Y	N	Y	Y	Y	N	N
2 Weygand	Y	N	N	Y	Y	Y	N
SOUTH CAROLINA							
1 ***Sanford***	N	Y	N	N	N	N	Y
2 ***Spence***	N	N	N	N	N	N	N
3 ***Graham***	N	Y	N	N	Y	N	N
4 ***Inglis***	N	Y	N	N	N	N	Y
5 Spratt	N	N	N	Y	N	Y	N
6 Clyburn	Y	N	Y	Y	N	Y	N
SOUTH DAKOTA							
AL ***Thune***	N	Y	N	N	N	N	Y

	385	386	387	388	389	390	391
TENNESSEE							
1 ***Jenkins***	N	Y	N	N	N	N	Y
2 ***Duncan***	Y	Y	N	N	N	N	Y
3 ***Wamp***	N	Y	N	N	N	Y	Y
4 ***Hilleary***	N	N	N	N	N	N	Y
5 Clement	Y	N	N	Y	Y	Y	N
6 Gordon	N	N	N	Y	N	Y	N
7 ***Bryant***	N	N	N	N	N	N	N
8 Tanner	N	Y	N	Y	N	Y	N
9 Ford	Y	N	Y	Y	?	Y	N
TEXAS							
1 Sandlin	Y	N	Y	Y	N	Y	N
2 Turner	Y	Y	N	Y	Y	N	N
3 ***Johnson, Sam***	N	Y	N	N	N	N	Y
4 Hall	Y	Y	N	N	N	N	N
5 ***Sessions***	N	Y	N	N	N	N	Y
6 ***Barton***	N	Y	N	N	N	N	N
7 ***Archer***	N	Y	N	N	N	N	Y
8 ***Brady***	N	Y	N	N	N	N	N
9 Lampson	Y	N	N	Y	Y	N	N
10 Doggett	Y	N	Y	Y	Y	Y	N
11 Edwards	Y	N	N	Y	N	Y	N
12 ***Granger***	N	Y	N	N	N	N	Y
13 ***Thornberry***	N	Y	N	N	N	N	Y
14 ***Paul***	N	Y	N	N	N	N	Y
15 Hinojosa	Y	N	Y	Y	Y	Y	N
16 Reyes	Y	N	N	Y	Y	Y	N
17 Stenholm	Y	Y	N	Y	N	N	N
18 Jackson-Lee	Y	N	Y	Y	N	Y	N
19 ***Combest***	N	Y	N	N	N	N	N
20 Gonzalez	?	?	?	?	?	?	?
21 ***Smith***	N	Y	N	N	N	N	N
22 ***DeLay***	N	Y	N	N	N	N	Y
23 ***Bonilla***	N	N	N	N	N	N	N
24 Frost	Y	N	Y	Y	N	Y	N
25 Bentsen	N	N	Y	Y	N	N	N
26 ***Armey***	N	Y	N	N	N	N	Y
27 Ortiz	Y	Y	N	Y	Y	Y	N
28 Rodriguez	Y	N	Y	Y	N	Y	N
29 Green	Y	N	Y	Y	N	N	N
30 Johnson, E.B.	Y	N	Y	Y	N	Y	N
UTAH							
1 ***Hansen***	N	N	N	N	N	N	Y
2 ***Cook***	N	Y	N	N	N	N	N
3 ***Cannon***	N	Y	N	N	N	N	Y
VERMONT							
AL *Sanders*	Y	N	Y	Y	N	Y	N
VIRGINIA							
1 ***Bateman***	N	N	N	N	N	N	N
2 Pickett	Y	N	Y	Y	N	N	N
3 Scott	Y	N	Y	Y	N	N	N
4 Sisisky	Y	N	N	Y	N	N	N
5 Goode	N	N	N	N	N	N	N
6 ***Goodlatte***	N	N	N	N	N	N	Y
7 ***Bliley***	N	Y	N	N	N	N	N
8 Moran	Y	N	Y	Y	Y	Y	N
9 Boucher	N	N	Y	Y	N	Y	N
10 ***Wolf***	N	N	N	N	N	N	N
11 ***Davis***	Y	N	N	N	N	N	N
WASHINGTON							
1 ***White***	N	N	N	N	Y	N	Y
2 ***Metcalf***	N	N	N	N	N	N	Y
3 ***Smith, Linda***	N	Y	N	N	N	N	Y
4 ***Hastings***	N	Y	N	N	N	N	N
5 ***Nethercutt***	N	N	N	N	N	N	Y
6 Dicks	Y	N	N	Y	N	Y	N
7 McDermott	Y	N	Y	Y	Y	N	N
8 ***Dunn***	N	N	N	N	N	N	Y
9 Smith, Adam	N	N	Y	Y	Y	N	N
WEST VIRGINIA							
1 Mollohan	Y	N	N	Y	N	Y	N
2 Wise	N	N	Y	Y	N	Y	N
3 Rahall	Y	N	N	Y	Y	Y	N
WISCONSIN							
1 ***Neumann***	N	Y	N	N	N	N	Y
2 ***Klug***	N	Y	N	N	N	N	Y
3 Kind	Y	N	Y	Y	N	Y	N
4 Kleczka	Y	N	N	Y	N	N	N
5 Barrett	Y	N	Y	Y	N	Y	Y
6 ***Petri***	N	Y	N	N	N	N	Y
7 Obey	Y	N	?	Y	N	Y	N
8 Johnson	Y	N	N	Y	Y	N	Y
9 ***Sensenbrenner***	N	Y	N	N	N	N	Y
WYOMING							
AL ***Cubin***	N	Y	N	N	N	N	Y

Southern states - Ala., Ark., Fla., Ga., Ky., La., Miss., N.C., Okla., S.C., Tenn., Texas, Va.

Key

Y	Voted for (yea).
#	Paired for.
+	Announced for.
N	Voted against (nay).
X	Paired against.
–	Announced against.
P	Voted "present."
C	Voted "present" to avoid possible conflict of interest.
?	Did not vote or otherwise make a position known.

Democrats **Republicans** *Independent*

392. HR 4276. Fiscal 1999 Commerce, Justice, State Appropriations/Eliminate U.N. Debt Payment Funding. Bartlett, R-Md., amendment to eliminate the $475 million allocated in the bill for debt payments to the United Nations. Rejected 151-279: R 141-84; D 10-194 (ND 6-144, SD 4-50); I 0-1. Aug. 5, 1998.

393. HR 4276. Fiscal 1999 Commerce, Justice, State Appropriations/Increase Funding for Small Business Loan Program. Talent, R-Mo., amendment to increase the Small Business Administration's business loans program account by $7.09 million to $236 million. The increase is offset by reducing funding by $7.1 million for administrative expenses. Adopted 312-114: R 219-4; D 93-109 (ND 67-83, SD 26-26); I 0-1. Aug. 5, 1998.

394. HR 4276. Fiscal 1999 Commerce, Justice, State Appropriations/Decrease U.N. Debt Payment Funding. Stearns, R-Fla., amendment to reduce appropriations for U.S. debt payments to the United Nations by $109 million. Rejected 165-261: R 155-69; D 10-191 (ND 6-141, SD 4-50); I 0-1. Aug. 5, 1998.

395. HR 4276. Fiscal 1999 Commerce, Justice, State Appropriations/Jurisdictional Parity for Fisheries Enforcement. Callahan, R-Ala., amendment to provide jurisdictional parity for fisheries enforcement in the Gulf of Mexico for the states of Alabama, Louisiana and Mississippi with the states of Florida and Texas. Rejected 141-283: R 121-101; D 20-181 (ND 8-139, SD 12-42); I 0-1. Aug. 5, 1998.

396. HR 4276. Fiscal 1999 Commerce, Justice, State Appropriations/Special Prosecutors and State Ethical Standards. Conyers Jr., D-Mich., amendment to add special prosecutors (such as an independent counsel) to the bill's list of prosecutors who would be required by the bill to follow each state's ethical standards for the states in which aspects of a case are pending. Adopted 249-182: R 48-178; D 200-4 (ND 147-3, SD 53-1); I 1-0. Aug. 5, 1998.

397. HR 4276. Fiscal 1999 Commerce, Justice, State Appropriations/Strike State Ethical Standards for Prosecutors. Hutchinson, R-Ark., amendment to strike the provision of the bill establishing a new category of punishable conduct for federal prosecutors and requiring that all federal prosecutors abide by each state's standards for the states in which aspects of a case are pending. Rejected 82-345: R 55-169; D 27-175 (ND 15-134, SD 12-41); I 0-1. Aug. 5, 1998.

398. HR 4276. Fiscal 1999 Commerce, Justice, State Appropriations/Prohibit Funding to Enforce Executive Orders. Hefley, R-Colo., amendment to prohibit funds in this bill or any other act from being used to implement or enforce two presidential executive orders. The first prohibits federal agencies from discriminating against individuals in hiring or awarding grants because of sexual orientation. The second order establishes a new set of "federalism" criteria for federal agencies to follow when formulating or implementing related policies. Rejected 176-252: R 161-63; D 15-188 (ND 3-146, SD 12-42); I 0-1. Aug. 5, 1998.

	392	393	394	395	396	397	398
ALABAMA							
1 Callahan	N	N	Y	N	Y	N	Y
2 Everett	Y	Y	Y	N	N	N	Y
3 Riley	Y	Y	Y	Y	N	N	Y
4 Aderholt	Y	Y	Y	Y	N	N	Y
5 Cramer	N	N	Y	N	Y	Y	Y
6 Bachus	Y	Y	Y	Y	Y	N	Y
7 Hilliard	N	N	N	N	Y	N	N
ALASKA							
AL Young	Y	Y	N	Y	N	N	Y
ARIZONA							
1 Salmon	Y	Y	Y	N	Y	Y	Y
2 Pastor	N	N	N	N	Y	N	N
3 Stump	Y	Y	Y	N	N	N	N
4 Shadegg	Y	Y	Y	Y	N	Y	Y
5 Kolbe	N	Y	N	N	N	N	N
6 Hayworth	Y	Y	Y	N	N	N	Y
ARKANSAS							
1 Berry	N	N	Y	N	Y	N	Y
2 Snyder	N	Y	N	N	N	N	N
3 Hutchinson	Y	Y	Y	Y	N	N	Y
4 Dickey	Y	Y	Y	Y	N	N	Y
CALIFORNIA							
1 Riggs	N	N	Y	N	Y	Y	Y
2 Herger	Y	Y	Y	Y	N	N	Y
3 Fazio	N	N	N	N	Y	N	N
4 Doolittle	Y	Y	Y	Y	N	Y	Y
5 Matsui	N	N	N	N	Y	N	N
6 Woolsey	N	N	N	N	Y	N	N
7 Miller	N	N	N	N	Y	N	N
8 Pelosi	N	N	N	N	Y	N	N
9 Lee	N	N	N	N	Y	N	N
10 Tauscher	N	Y	N	N	Y	N	N
11 Pombo	Y	Y	Y	Y	N	N	Y
12 Lantos	N	N	N	N	Y	N	N
13 Stark	N	N	N	N	Y	N	N
14 Eshoo	N	N	N	N	Y	N	N
15 Campbell	Y	Y	Y	Y	Y	N	Y
16 Lofgren	N	N	N	N	Y	N	N
17 Farr	N	N	N	N	Y	N	N
18 Condit	N	Y	Y	N	Y	N	Y
19 Radanovich	Y	Y	Y	N	Y	N	Y
20 Dooley	N	N	N	N	Y	N	N
21 Thomas	N	Y	N	Y	N	N	N
22 Capps, L.	N	Y	Y	Y	N	N	Y
23 Gallegly	Y	Y	Y	Y	Y	N	N
24 Sherman	N	N	N	N	Y	N	N
25 McKeon	Y	Y	Y	N	Y	N	Y
26 Berman	N	N	N	N	Y	N	N
27 Rogan	Y	Y	Y	Y	Y	Y	Y
28 Dreier	Y	Y	Y	N	N	N	Y
29 Waxman	N	N	N	N	Y	N	N
30 Becerra	N	N	N	N	Y	N	N
31 Martinez	N	N	N	N	Y	N	N
32 Dixon	N	N	N	N	Y	N	N
33 Roybal-Allard	N	N	N	N	Y	N	N
34 Torres	N	Y	N	Y	N	Y	N
35 Waters	N	N	N	N	Y	N	N
36 Harman	N	N	N	N	Y	N	N
37 Millender-McD.	N	N	N	N	Y	N	N
38 Horn	N	Y	N	N	Y	N	N

	392	393	394	395	396	397	398
39 Royce	Y	Y	Y	N	Y	N	Y
40 Lewis	N	Y	N	Y	N	N	N
41 Kim	N	Y	N	Y	N	N	N
42 Brown	N	N	N	N	Y	N	N
43 Calvert	N	Y	Y	Y	N	N	Y
44 Bono, M.	Y	Y	Y	Y	N	N	Y
45 Rohrabacher	Y	Y	Y	Y	N	N	Y
46 Sanchez	N	N	N	N	Y	N	N
47 Cox	Y	Y	Y	N	Y	N	N
48 Packard	Y	Y	Y	N	Y	N	Y
49 Bilbray	N	Y	N	N	Y	N	Y
50 Filner	N	N	N	N	Y	N	N
51 Cunningham	?	?	?	?	?	?	?
52 Hunter	Y	Y	N	N	Y	N	N
COLORADO							
1 DeGette	N	N	N	N	Y	N	N
2 Skaggs	N	N	N	N	Y	N	N
3 McInnis	Y	Y	Y	Y	N	N	Y
4 Schaffer	Y	Y	Y	N	N	Y	Y
5 Hefley	Y	Y	Y	N	N	Y	Y
6 Schaefer	Y	Y	Y	N	N	Y	Y
CONNECTICUT							
1 Kennelly	N	N	N	N	Y	N	N
2 Gejdenson	N	N	N	N	Y	N	N
3 DeLauro	N	N	N	Y	Y	N	N
4 Shays	N	Y	N	N	Y	N	N
5 Maloney	N	Y	N	N	Y	N	Y
6 Johnson	N	Y	N	N	N	N	N
DELAWARE							
AL Castle	N	Y	N	N	N	N	N
FLORIDA							
1 Scarborough	Y	Y	Y	N	N	N	N
2 Boyd	N	N	N	N	Y	Y	N
3 Brown	N	Y	N	N	Y	N	N
4 Fowler	N	Y	N	N	Y	N	N
5 Thurman	N	N	N	N	Y	N	N
6 Stearns	Y	Y	Y	N	N	N	Y
7 Mica	Y	Y	Y	N	N	N	Y
8 McCollum	Y	Y	Y	Y	N	N	Y
9 Bilirakis	Y	Y	Y	N	N	N	Y
10 Young	N	Y	N	N	Y	N	N
11 Davis	N	N	N	N	Y	N	N
12 Canady	Y	Y	Y	N	Y	N	Y
13 Miller	N	Y	Y	N	N	N	Y
14 Goss	Y	Y	Y	N	N	N	Y
15 Weldon	Y	Y	Y	N	Y	N	Y
16 Foley	Y	Y	Y	N	N	N	Y
17 Meek	N	N	N	N	Y	N	N
18 Ros-Lehtinen	Y	Y	Y	N	Y	N	N
19 Wexler	N	Y	N	N	Y	N	N
20 Deutsch	N	N	N	N	Y	N	N
21 Diaz-Balart	Y	Y	Y	N	N	N	N
22 Shaw	N	Y	N	N	Y	N	N
23 Hastings	N	N	N	N	Y	N	N
GEORGIA							
1 Kingston	Y	Y	Y	Y	N	N	Y
2 Bishop	N	Y	N	Y	Y	N	Y
3 Collins	Y	Y	Y	N	Y	N	Y
4 McKinney	N	N	N	N	Y	N	N
5 Lewis	N	?	N	N	Y	N	N
6 Gingrich	Y	Y	Y	Y	N	Y	?
7 Barr	Y	Y	Y	Y	N	Y	?
8 Chambliss	Y	Y	Y	Y	N	N	Y
9 Deal	Y	Y	Y	Y	N	N	Y
10 Norwood	Y	Y	Y	Y	N	N	Y
11 Linder	Y	Y	Y	Y	N	N	Y
HAWAII							
1 Abercrombie	N	N	N	N	Y	N	N
2 Mink	N	Y	N	N	Y	N	N
IDAHO							
1 Chenoweth	Y	Y	Y	Y	N	N	Y
2 Crapo	Y	?	Y	Y	N	N	Y
ILLINOIS							
1 Rush	N	N	N	N	Y	N	N
2 Jackson	N	Y	N	N	Y	N	N
3 Lipinski	N	Y	N	N	Y	N	Y
4 Gutierrez	N	N	N	N	Y	N	N
5 Blagojevich	N	Y	?	N	Y	N	N
6 Hyde	N	Y	N	N	Y	N	N
7 Davis	N	Y	N	N	Y	N	N
8 Crane	Y	Y	Y	N	N	N	Y
9 Yates	N	N	N	N	Y	?	?
10 Porter	N	Y	N	N	Y	N	N
11 Weller	Y	Y	Y	N	N	N	Y
12 Costello	N	Y	N	N	Y	N	N
13 Fawell	N	Y	N	N	N	N	Y

ND Northern Democrats   SD Southern Democrats

	392	393	394	395	396	397	398
14 ***Hastert***	Y	Y	Y	N	N	N	Y
15 ***Ewing***	N	Y	Y	N	N	N	Y
16 ***Manzullo***	Y	Y	Y	N	N	N	Y
17 Evans	N	N	N	N	Y	N	N
18 ***LaHood***	N	Y	N	N	Y	N	Y
19 Poshard	N	Y	N	N	Y	N	N
20 ***Shimkus***	Y	Y	Y	Y	N	N	N
INDIANA							
1 Visclosky	N	N	N	N	Y	N	N
2 ***McIntosh***	Y	Y	Y	Y	N	N	Y
3 Roemer	Y	Y	Y	N	N	N	N
4 ***Souder***	Y	Y	Y	Y	N	Y	Y
5 ***Buyer***	Y	Y	Y	?	N	N	Y
6 ***Burton***	Y	Y	Y	Y	N	N	Y
7 ***Pease***	Y	Y	Y	N	N	N	Y
8 ***Hostettler***	Y	Y	Y	Y	N	N	Y
9 Hamilton	N	Y	N	N	N	N	N
10 Carson	N	N	N	N	Y	N	N
IOWA							
1 ***Leach***	N	Y	N	N	Y	N	N
2 ***Nussle***	Y	Y	Y	N	Y	Y	Y
3 Boswell	N	Y	N	N	Y	Y	N
4 ***Ganske***	N	Y	N	N	N	N	N
5 ***Latham***	N	Y	N	N	N	Y	Y
KANSAS							
1 ***Moran***	Y	Y	Y	Y	N	N	Y
2 ***Ryun***	Y	Y	Y	Y	N	Y	Y
3 ***Snowbarger***	Y	Y	Y	Y	N	Y	Y
4 ***Tiahrt***	Y	Y	Y	Y	N	N	Y
KENTUCKY							
1 ***Whitfield***	Y	Y	Y	N	N	Y	Y
2 ***Lewis***	Y	Y	Y	Y	N	Y	Y
3 ***Northup***	N	Y	Y	Y	N	N	Y
4 ***Bunning***	Y	Y	Y	Y	N	Y	Y
5 ***Rogers***	N	Y	N	Y	N	Y	Y
6 Baesler	N	Y	N	N	Y	N	Y
LOUISIANA							
1 ***Livingston***	N	Y	N	Y	N	N	Y
2 Jefferson	N	N	N	Y	Y	Y	N
3 ***Tauzin***	Y	Y	Y	Y	N	N	Y
4 ***McCrery***	Y	Y	Y	Y	N	N	N
5 ***Cooksey***	Y	Y	Y	Y	N	Y	N
6 ***Baker***	Y	Y	Y	Y	N	Y	Y
7 John	N	Y	N	Y	Y	Y	Y
MAINE							
1 Allen	N	Y	N	N	Y	N	N
2 Baldacci	N	Y	N	N	Y	N	N
MARYLAND							
1 ***Gilchrest***	N	Y	N	N	N	N	N
2 ***Ehrlich***	Y	Y	Y	N	N	Y	N
3 Cardin	N	N	N	N	Y	N	N
4 Wynn	N	N	N	N	Y	N	N
5 Hoyer	N	N	N	N	Y	N	N
6 ***Bartlett***	Y	Y	Y	Y	N	N	Y
7 Cummings	N	N	N	N	Y	N	N
8 ***Morella***	N	Y	N	N	N	Y	N
MASSACHUSETTS							
1 Olver	N	N	N	N	Y	N	N
2 Neal	N	N	N	N	Y	N	N
3 McGovern	N	Y	N	N	Y	N	N
4 Frank	N	N	N	N	Y	N	N
5 Meehan	N	Y	N	N	Y	Y	N
6 Tierney	N	Y	N	N	Y	N	N
7 Markey	N	N	N	N	Y	N	N
8 Kennedy	N	Y	N	N	Y	N	N
9 Moakley	N	N	N	N	Y	?	?
10 Delahunt	N	N	N	N	Y	N	N
MICHIGAN							
1 Stupak	N	N	N	?	Y	N	N
2 ***Hoekstra***	Y	Y	Y	N	N	N	Y
3 ***Ehlers***	N	Y	N	N	N	N	N
4 ***Camp***	Y	Y	Y	N	N	N	Y
5 Barcia	Y	Y	Y	N	Y	N	N
6 ***Upton***	N	Y	Y	N	Y	N	N
7 ***Smith***	Y	Y	Y	N	N	Y	N
8 Stabenow	N	Y	N	N	Y	N	N
9 Kildee	N	N	N	N	Y	N	N
10 Bonior	N	Y	N	N	Y	N	N
11 ***Knollenberg***	N	Y	N	Y	N	N	N
12 Levin	N	Y	N	N	Y	Y	N
13 Rivers	N	N	N	N	Y	N	N
14 Conyers	N	Y	N	N	Y	Y	N
15 Kilpatrick	N	N	N	N	Y	N	N
16 Dingell	N	N	N	Y	Y	N	N
MINNESOTA							
1 ***Gutknecht***	Y	Y	Y	Y	Y	N	Y
2 Minge	N	N	N	N	Y	N	N
3 ***Ramstad***	N	Y	N	N	Y	N	Y
4 Vento	N	N	N	N	Y	N	N
5 Sabo	N	N	N	N	Y	N	N
6 Luther	N	Y	N	N	Y	N	N
7 Peterson	N	N	Y	Y	Y	N	Y
8 Oberstar	N	N	N	N	Y	N	N
MISSISSIPPI							
1 ***Wicker***	N	Y	N	Y	Y	N	Y
2 Thompson	N	N	N	Y	Y	N	N
3 ***Pickering***	+	+	+	+	N	N	Y
4 ***Parker***	N	Y	N	Y	N	N	Y
5 Taylor	Y	Y	Y	Y	Y	N	Y
MISSOURI							
1 Clay	?	?	?	?	?	N	N
2 ***Talent***	Y	Y	Y	N	N	N	Y
3 Gephardt	N	Y	N	N	Y	N	N
4 Skelton	N	Y	N	Y	Y	N	N
5 McCarthy	N	Y	N	N	Y	N	N
6 Danner	Y	Y	Y	N	Y	N	N
7 ***Blunt***	Y	Y	Y	Y	N	N	Y
8 ***Emerson***	Y	Y	Y	Y	N	N	Y
9 ***Hulshof***	Y	Y	Y	N	N	Y	Y
MONTANA							
AL ***Hill***	Y	Y	Y	Y	Y	N	Y
NEBRASKA							
1 ***Bereuter***	N	Y	N	N	N	N	Y
2 ***Christensen***	Y	Y	Y	N	N	Y	Y
3 ***Barrett***	Y	Y	Y	Y	N	Y	Y
NEVADA							
1 ***Ensign***	Y	Y	Y	N	N	N	Y
2 ***Gibbons***	Y	Y	Y	Y	N	N	Y
NEW HAMPSHIRE							
1 ***Sununu***	N	Y	Y	N	N	Y	Y
2 ***Bass***	N	Y	N	N	N	N	Y
NEW JERSEY							
1 Andrews	N	N	N	N	Y	N	N
2 ***LoBiondo***	Y	Y	Y	N	Y	N	N
3 ***Saxton***	N	N	N	N	N	N	N
4 ***Smith***	N	Y	N	N	Y	N	Y
5 ***Roukema***	N	Y	N	N	N	N	N
6 Pallone	N	N	N	N	Y	N	N
7 ***Franks***	N	Y	N	N	Y	N	N
8 Pascrell	N	N	N	N	Y	N	N
9 Rothman	N	Y	N	N	Y	Y	N
10 Payne	N	N	N	N	Y	N	N
11 ***Frelinghuysen***	N	Y	N	N	N	N	N
12 ***Pappas***	Y	Y	Y	N	Y	N	Y
13 Menendez	N	N	N	N	Y	N	N
NEW MEXICO							
1 ***Wilson***	N	Y	Y	N	N	Y	N
2 ***Skeen***	Y	Y	Y	N	N	N	Y
3 ***Redmond***	Y	Y	Y	Y	N	Y	Y
NEW YORK							
1 ***Forbes***	N	Y	N	N	Y	N	N
2 ***Lazio***	N	Y	N	N	N	N	N
3 ***King***	N	Y	N	Y	Y	N	Y
4 McCarthy	N	Y	N	N	Y	N	N
5 Ackerman	N	Y	?	?	Y	N	N
6 Meeks	N	N	N	N	Y	N	N
7 Manton	N	Y	N	Y	Y	N	N
8 Nadler	N	N	N	N	Y	N	N
9 Schumer	N	Y	N	N	Y	N	N
10 Towns	N	N	N	N	Y	N	N
11 Owens	N	N	N	N	Y	N	N
12 Velázquez	N	Y	N	N	Y	N	N
13 ***Fossella***	Y	Y	Y	N	N	N	Y
14 Maloney	N	Y	N	N	Y	Y	N
15 Rangel	Y	N	N	N	Y	N	N
16 Serrano	N	N	N	N	Y	N	N
17 Engel	N	N	N	N	Y	N	N
18 Lowey	N	N	N	N	Y	N	N
19 ***Kelly***	N	Y	N	N	Y	N	N
20 ***Gilman***	N	Y	–	N	Y	N	N
21 McNulty	N	Y	N	N	Y	N	N
22 ***Solomon***	Y	Y	Y	Y	N	N	Y
23 ***Boehlert***	N	Y	N	N	Y	N	N
24 ***McHugh***	N	Y	N	N	Y	N	Y
25 ***Walsh***	N	Y	N	N	Y	N	Y
26 Hinchey	N	N	N	N	Y	N	N
27 ***Paxon***	Y	Y	Y	Y	N	?	Y
28 Slaughter	N	N	N	N	Y	N	N
29 LaFalce	N	N	N	N	Y	Y	N
30 ***Quinn***	N	Y	N	N	N	N	Y
31 ***Houghton***	N	N	N	N	Y	N	N
NORTH CAROLINA							
1 Clayton	N	N	N	N	Y	Y	N
2 Etheridge	N	N	N	N	Y	Y	N
3 ***Jones***	Y	Y	Y	N	N	Y	Y
4 Price	N	N	N	N	Y	Y	N
5 ***Burr***	Y	Y	Y	Y	N	Y	Y
6 ***Coble***	Y	Y	Y	Y	N	N	Y
7 McIntyre	Y	Y	Y	N	Y	N	Y
8 Hefner	N	N	N	N	Y	N	N
9 ***Myrick***	Y	?	Y	Y	N	Y	Y
10 ***Ballenger***	N	Y	N	Y	N	Y	Y
11 ***Taylor***	N	Y	N	Y	N	N	Y
12 Watt	N	N	N	N	Y	Y	N
NORTH DAKOTA							
AL Pomeroy	N	Y	N	N	Y	N	N
OHIO							
1 ***Chabot***	Y	Y	Y	Y	N	Y	Y
2 ***Portman***	N	Y	Y	N	N	Y	Y
3 Hall	N	N	N	N	Y	N	Y
4 ***Oxley***	N	Y	N	Y	N	N	N
5 ***Gillmor***	N	Y	N	Y	Y	N	Y
6 Strickland	N	N	N	N	Y	N	N
7 ***Hobson***	N	Y	Y	N	N	N	N
8 ***Boehner***	N	Y	N	Y	N	N	Y
9 Kaptur	Y	Y	N	N	Y	N	N
10 Kucinich	N	N	N	N	Y	N	N
11 Stokes	N	N	N	N	Y	N	N
12 ***Kasich***	N	Y	Y	N	Y	N	Y
13 Brown	N	N	N	N	Y	N	N
14 Sawyer	N	N	N	N	Y	N	N
15 ***Pryce***	N	Y	N	N	Y	N	N
16 ***Regula***	N	Y	N	Y	N	N	N
17 Traficant	Y	Y	Y	N	Y	N	N
18 ***Ney***	Y	Y	Y	N	N	N	Y
19 ***LaTourette***	N	Y	N	N	N	N	N
OKLAHOMA							
1 ***Largent***	Y	Y	Y	N	N	N	Y
2 ***Coburn***	Y	Y	Y	?	N	Y	Y
3 ***Watkins***	Y	Y	Y	N	N	N	Y
4 ***Watts***	Y	Y	Y	Y	N	Y	Y
5 ***Istook***	Y	Y	Y	Y	N	N	Y
6 ***Lucas***	Y	Y	Y	Y	N	N	Y
OREGON							
1 Furse	N	Y	N	N	Y	N	N
2 ***Smith***	N	Y	N	Y	N	N	Y
3 Blumenauer	N	Y	N	N	Y	N	N
4 DeFazio	N	Y	N	N	Y	N	N
5 Hooley	N	Y	N	N	Y	N	N
PENNSYLVANIA							
1 Brady	N	N	N	N	Y	N	N
2 Fattah	N	N	N	N	Y	N	N
3 Borski	N	N	N	N	Y	N	N
4 Klink	N	Y	N	N	Y	N	N
5 ***Peterson***	Y	Y	Y	Y	Y	N	Y
6 Holden	N	Y	N	N	Y	N	N
7 ***Weldon***	N	Y	N	N	N	N	Y
8 ***Greenwood***	N	Y	N	N	N	N	N
9 ***Shuster***	Y	Y	Y	Y	Y	N	Y
10 ***McDade***	Y	Y	Y	?	N	N	N
11 Kanjorski	N	Y	N	N	Y	N	N
12 Murtha	N	N	N	N	Y	N	N
13 ***Fox***	N	Y	N	N	Y	N	N
14 Coyne	N	N	N	N	Y	N	N
15 McHale	N	Y	?	?	Y	N	N
16 ***Pitts***	Y	Y	Y	Y	N	N	Y
17 ***Gekas***	Y	N	N	Y	N	N	Y
18 Doyle	N	N	N	N	Y	N	N
19 ***Goodling***	Y	Y	Y	Y	N	?	?
20 Mascara	N	N	N	N	Y	N	N
21 ***English***	N	Y	N	N	Y	N	N
RHODE ISLAND							
1 Kennedy	N	N	N	N	Y	N	N
2 Weygand	N	Y	N	N	Y	N	N
SOUTH CAROLINA							
1 ***Sanford***	Y	Y	Y	N	N	N	Y
2 ***Spence***	Y	Y	Y	Y	N	N	Y
3 ***Graham***	Y	Y	Y	Y	N	N	Y
4 ***Inglis***	Y	Y	Y	N	N	Y	Y
5 Spratt	N	Y	N	N	Y	N	N
6 Clyburn	N	N	N	N	Y	N	N
SOUTH DAKOTA							
AL ***Thune***	Y	Y	Y	N	N	Y	Y
TENNESSEE							
1 ***Jenkins***	Y	Y	Y	Y	N	Y	Y
2 ***Duncan***	Y	Y	Y	Y	Y	N	Y
3 ***Wamp***	Y	Y	Y	Y	N	N	Y
4 ***Hilleary***	Y	Y	Y	Y	N	N	Y
5 Clement	N	?	N	N	Y	N	N
6 Gordon	N	Y	N	N	Y	N	N
7 ***Bryant***	Y	Y	Y	Y	N	Y	Y
8 Tanner	N	Y	N	N	Y	N	Y
9 Ford	N	N	N	N	Y	N	N
TEXAS							
1 Sandlin	N	Y	N	N	Y	Y	Y
2 Turner	N	Y	N	N	Y	N	Y
3 ***Johnson, Sam***	Y	N	Y	Y	N	N	Y
4 Hall	Y	N	Y	N	Y	N	Y
5 ***Sessions***	Y	Y	Y	Y	N	Y	Y
6 ***Barton***	Y	Y	Y	Y	N	Y	Y
7 ***Archer***	N	Y	N	N	N	N	Y
8 ***Brady***	N	Y	N	Y	N	Y	Y
9 Lampson	N	Y	N	N	Y	N	N
10 Doggett	N	Y	N	N	Y	N	N
11 Edwards	N	Y	N	N	Y	N	N
12 ***Granger***	N	Y	Y	Y	N	Y	N
13 ***Thornberry***	Y	Y	Y	Y	N	Y	Y
14 ***Paul***	Y	Y	Y	Y	Y	N	Y
15 Hinojosa	N	N	N	N	Y	N	N
16 Reyes	N	N	N	N	Y	Y	N
17 Stenholm	N	Y	N	N	Y	N	Y
18 Jackson-Lee	N	Y	N	N	Y	N	N
19 ***Combest***	Y	Y	Y	Y	N	Y	Y
20 Gonzalez	?	?	?	?	?	?	?
21 ***Smith***	N	Y	Y	Y	N	N	Y
22 ***DeLay***	Y	Y	Y	Y	N	N	Y
23 ***Bonilla***	Y	Y	Y	Y	N	N	Y
24 Frost	N	N	N	N	Y	N	N
25 Bentsen	N	Y	N	N	Y	N	N
26 ***Armey***	Y	Y	Y	Y	N	Y	Y
27 Ortiz	N	Y	N	Y	Y	N	N
28 Rodriguez	N	N	N	N	Y	N	N
29 Green	N	N	N	N	Y	N	N
30 Johnson, E.B.	N	N	N	N	Y	N	N
UTAH							
1 ***Hansen***	Y	Y	Y	Y	N	N	Y
2 ***Cook***	Y	Y	Y	Y	N	N	Y
3 ***Cannon***	Y	Y	Y	N	N	N	Y
VERMONT							
AL *Sanders*	N	N	N	N	Y	N	N
VIRGINIA							
1 ***Bateman***	N	Y	N	N	N	N	N
2 Pickett	N	N	N	Y	Y	N	N
3 Scott	N	N	N	N	Y	N	N
4 Sisisky	N	Y	N	Y	Y	N	N
5 Goode	Y	Y	Y	Y	Y	Y	Y
6 ***Goodlatte***	Y	Y	Y	Y	Y	N	Y
7 ***Bliley***	Y	Y	Y	Y	N	N	N
8 Moran	N	N	N	N	Y	?	N
9 Boucher	N	N	N	N	Y	N	N
10 ***Wolf***	N	Y	N	N	N	Y	Y
11 ***Davis***	N	Y	N	Y	N	Y	N
WASHINGTON							
1 ***White***	N	Y	N	Y	N	N	Y
2 ***Metcalf***	Y	Y	Y	Y	N	N	Y
3 ***Smith, Linda***	Y	Y	Y	Y	N	N	Y
4 ***Hastings***	Y	Y	Y	Y	N	Y	Y
5 ***Nethercutt***	Y	Y	Y	Y	N	Y	Y
6 Dicks	N	N	N	N	Y	N	N
7 McDermott	N	Y	N	N	Y	N	N
8 ***Dunn***	N	Y	Y	Y	N	Y	Y
9 Smith, Adam	N	Y	N	N	Y	N	N
WEST VIRGINIA							
1 Mollohan	N	N	N	N	Y	N	N
2 Wise	N	N	N	N	Y	N	N
3 Rahall	N	Y	N	N	Y	N	N
WISCONSIN							
1 ***Neumann***	Y	Y	Y	N	N	N	Y
2 ***Klug***	N	Y	Y	N	Y	N	N
3 Kind	N	Y	N	N	Y	Y	N
4 Kleczka	N	N	N	N	Y	N	N
5 Barrett	N	Y	N	N	Y	Y	N
6 ***Petri***	Y	Y	Y	N	N	N	Y
7 Obey	N	Y	N	N	Y	N	N
8 Johnson	N	Y	N	N	Y	N	N
9 ***Sensenbrenner***	Y	Y	Y	N	N	N	Y
WYOMING							
AL ***Cubin***	Y	Y	Y	Y	N	Y	Y

Southern states - Ala., Ark., Fla., Ga., Ky., La., Miss., N.C., Okla., S.C., Tenn., Texas, Va.

399. HR 4276. Fiscal 1999 Commerce, Justice, State Appropriations/Prohibit Funds for Enforcing Executive Order on Federalism. Kolbe, R-Ariz., amendment to prohibit any funds from the bill or any other act from being used to implement or enforce a presidential order that established new "federalism" criteria that federal agencies must follow when formulating and implementing policies that have federalism implications. Adopted 417-2: R 220-0; D 196-2 (ND 145-2, SD 51-0); I 1-0. Aug. 5, 1998.

400. HR 4276. Fiscal 1999 Commerce, Justice, State Appropriations/Funding to Implement Congressional Action Regarding International Agreement. McIntosh, R-Ind., amendment to prohibit funding for a committee to implement a 1997 agreement between the U.S., Russia, Kazakhstan, the Ukraine and Belarus on the Anti-Ballistic Missile Defense Treaty in an effort to allow congressional debate on the issue. Adopted 240-188: R 220-4; D 20-183 (ND 10-139, SD 10-44); I 0-1. Aug. 5, 1998.

401. HR 4276. Fiscal 1999 Commerce, Justice, State Appropriations/Prohibit Funds for Certain Legal Challenges. Kucinich, D-Ohio, amendment to prohibit any of the bill's funds from being used for any federal legal challenge to state, local or tribal law. Rejected 200-228: R 71-153; D 128-75 (ND 103-46, SD 25-29); I 1-0. Aug. 5, 1998.

402. HR 4276. Fiscal 1999 Commerce, Justice, State Appropriations/Passage. Passage of the bill to provide $33.5 billion in funding for the Departments of Commerce, Justice and State, related agencies and the federal judiciary in fiscal 1999. Passed 225-203: R 197-27; D 28-175 (ND 25-124, SD 3-51); I 0-1. Aug. 6, 1998. Aug. 6, 1998, in the session that began Aug. 5 and is recorded in the Aug. 5 Congressional Record.

403. HR 2183. Overhaul Campaign Finance Laws/Doolittle Substitute. Doolittle, R-Calif., substitute amendment to the bill to overhaul campaign finance laws. The amendment would eliminate all federal contribution limits and end public financing of presidential campaigns. Rejected 131-299: R 127-97; D 4-201 (ND 3-148, SD 1-53); I 0-1. Aug. 6, 1998. Aug. 6, 1998, in the session that began Aug. 5 and is recorded in the Aug. 5 Congressional Record.

404. HR 2183. Campaign Finance Overhaul/Hutchinson Substitute. Hutchinson, R-Ark., substitute amendment to the bill to overhaul campaign finance laws. The amendment would prohibit national parties from accepting soft money, double the aggregate annual limit individuals may contribute to campaigns and generally require organizations to disclose their expenditures on issue-oriented advertisements that mention congressional candidates. Rejected 147-222: R 121-102; D 26-119 (ND 13-93, SD 13-26); I 0-1. Aug. 6, 1998.

405. HR 2183. Campaign Finance Overhaul/Passage. Passage of the bill to ban soft money contributions for federal elections, expand regulations on advertising that advocates a candidate and tighten the definition of what constitutes coordination with a federal candidate. The text of the bill is the Shays-Meehan substitute adopted by the House on Aug. 3. Passed 252-179: R 61-164; D 190-15 (ND 142-9, SD 48-6); I 1-0. Aug. 6, 1998.

ND Northern Democrats   SD Southern Democrats

Key

Y	Voted for (yea).
#	Paired for.
+	Announced for.
N	Voted against (nay).
X	Paired against.
–	Announced against.
P	Voted "present."
C	Voted "present" to avoid possible conflict of interest.
?	Did not vote or otherwise make a position known.

Democrats   **Republicans**
Independent

	399	400	401	402	403	404	405
ALABAMA							
1 *Callahan*	Y	Y	N	Y	Y	N	N
2 *Everett*	Y	N	Y	Y	Y	Y	N
3 *Riley*	Y	Y	Y	Y	Y	Y	N
4 *Aderholt*	Y	Y	Y	Y	Y	Y	N
5 Cramer	Y	Y	Y	N	N	Y	N
6 *Bachus*	Y	Y	Y	Y	N	Y	Y
7 Hilliard	Y	N	Y	N	N	N	Y
ALASKA							
AL *Young*	Y	Y	N	Y	Y	Y	N
ARIZONA							
1 *Salmon*	Y	Y	N	Y	Y	Y	N
2 Pastor	Y	N	Y	N	N	Y	Y
3 *Stump*	Y	Y	N	Y	N	N	N
4 *Shadegg*	Y	Y	Y	Y	Y	Y	N
5 *Kolbe*	Y	Y	Y	Y	Y	Y	N
6 *Hayworth*	Y	Y	Y	Y	Y	N	N
ARKANSAS							
1 Berry	Y	N	N	N	N	Y	Y
2 Snyder	Y	N	N	N	N	N	Y
3 *Hutchinson*	?	Y	N	Y	N	N	N
4 *Dickey*	Y	Y	N	Y	Y	Y	N
CALIFORNIA							
1 *Riggs*	Y	Y	N	Y	Y	Y	Y
2 *Herger*	Y	Y	N	Y	N	N	N
3 Fazio	Y	N	N	N	N	N	Y
4 *Doolittle*	Y	Y	Y	Y	Y	Y	N
5 Matsui	Y	N	N	N	N	N	Y
6 Woolsey	Y	N	N	N	N	N	Y
7 Miller	Y	N	Y	N	N	N	Y
8 Pelosi	Y	N	Y	N	N	N	Y
9 Lee	Y	N	Y	N	N	P	Y
10 Tauscher	Y	N	N	N	N	N	Y
11 *Pombo*	Y	Y	Y	Y	Y	N	N
12 Lantos	Y	N	Y	N	N	N	Y
13 Stark	Y	N	Y	N	N	N	Y
14 Eshoo	Y	N	Y	N	N	N	Y
15 *Campbell*	Y	N	Y	Y	N	N	Y
16 Lofgren	Y	N	N	N	N	P	Y
17 Farr	Y	N	Y	N	N	N	Y
18 Condit	?	Y	Y	Y	N	N	Y
19 *Radanovich*	Y	Y	Y	Y	Y	Y	N
20 Dooley	Y	N	N	N	N	P	Y
21 *Thomas*	Y	N	Y	Y	Y	Y	Y
22 Capps, L.	Y	N	Y	N	N	P	Y
23 *Gallegly*	Y	Y	Y	N	N	N	N
24 Sherman	Y	N	Y	N	N	P	Y
25 *McKeon*	Y	Y	N	Y	Y	Y	N
26 Berman	Y	N	Y	N	N	N	Y
27 *Rogan*	Y	Y	N	Y	Y	N	N
28 *Dreier*	Y	Y	N	Y	Y	N	N
29 Waxman	Y	N	Y	N	N	P	Y
30 Becerra	Y	N	Y	N	N	N	Y
31 Martinez	Y	N	N	N	N	N	Y
32 Dixon	Y	N	Y	N	N	N	Y
33 Roybal-Allard	Y	N	Y	N	N	N	Y
34 Torres	Y	N	Y	N	N	P	Y
35 Waters	Y	N	N	N	N	P	Y
36 Harman	Y	N	N	N	N	N	Y
37 Millender-McD.	Y	N	Y	N	N	P	Y
38 *Horn*	Y	N	Y	N	Y	N	Y

	399	400	401	402	403	404	405
39 *Royce*	Y	Y	N	Y	Y	Y	N
40 *Lewis*	Y	Y	N	Y	Y	Y	N
41 *Kim*	Y	Y	Y	Y	Y	N	Y
42 Brown	Y	N	N	Y	N	P	Y
43 *Calvert*	Y	Y	N	Y	Y	Y	N
44 *Bono, M.*	Y	Y	Y	Y	Y	Y	N
45 *Rohrabacher*	Y	Y	N	Y	Y	Y	N
46 Sanchez	Y	N	N	N	N	N	Y
47 *Cox*	+	Y	N	Y	Y	Y	N
48 *Packard*	Y	Y	Y	Y	Y	Y	N
49 *Bilbray*	Y	N	N	N	N	N	Y
50 Filner	Y	N	Y	N	N	P	Y
51 *Cunningham*	?	?	?	?	?	?	?
52 *Hunter*	Y	Y	Y	Y	Y	Y	N
COLORADO							
1 DeGette	Y	N	Y	N	N	Y	Y
2 Skaggs	Y	N	Y	N	P	Y	Y
3 *McInnis*	Y	Y	N	N	Y	N	N
4 *Schaffer*	Y	Y	Y	N	Y	N	N
5 *Hefley*	Y	Y	Y	N	Y	N	N
6 *Schaefer*	Y	Y	Y	Y	Y	Y	N
CONNECTICUT							
1 Kennelly	Y	N	Y	N	N	N	N
2 Gejdenson	Y	N	N	N	N	N	Y
3 DeLauro	Y	N	Y	N	N	P	Y
4 *Shays*	Y	Y	N	Y	N	Y	Y
5 Maloney	Y	N	N	N	N	P	Y
6 *Johnson*	Y	Y	N	Y	N	N	Y
DELAWARE							
AL *Castle*	Y	Y	N	Y	–	N	Y
FLORIDA							
1 *Scarborough*	Y	Y	Y	Y	Y	Y	N
2 Boyd	Y	N	Y	N	N	Y	Y
3 Brown	Y	N	Y	N	N	N	Y
4 *Fowler*	Y	Y	Y	Y	Y	Y	N
5 Thurman	Y	N	Y	N	N	N	Y
6 *Stearns*	Y	Y	Y	N	Y	N	N
7 *Mica*	Y	Y	Y	Y	Y	Y	N
8 *McCollum*	Y	Y	Y	Y	Y	Y	N
9 *Bilirakis*	Y	Y	Y	Y	Y	Y	N
10 *Young*	Y	?	?	?	N	N	N
11 Davis	Y	N	N	N	N	N	Y
12 *Canady*	Y	Y	Y	Y	Y	N	N
13 *Miller*	Y	Y	Y	Y	Y	Y	N
14 *Goss*	Y	Y	Y	Y	Y	Y	N
15 *Weldon*	Y	Y	N	Y	Y	N	N
16 *Foley*	Y	Y	N	Y	N	N	Y
17 Meek	Y	N	Y	N	N	N	N
18 *Ros-Lehtinen*	Y	Y	Y	Y	Y	Y	Y
19 Wexler	Y	N	Y	N	N	P	Y
20 Deutsch	Y	N	Y	N	N	P	Y
21 *Diaz-Balart*	Y	Y	Y	Y	Y	Y	Y
22 *Shaw*	Y	Y	Y	Y	Y	Y	N
23 Hastings	Y	N	Y	N	N	N	Y
GEORGIA							
1 *Kingston*	Y	Y	Y	Y	Y	Y	N
2 Bishop	Y	N	Y	N	N	N	N
3 *Collins*	Y	N	Y	N	Y	N	N
4 McKinney	Y	N	N	N	N	N	Y
5 Lewis	Y	N	Y	N	N	P	Y
6 *Gingrich*	Y	N	Y				
7 *Barr*	Y	Y	Y	Y	Y	N	N
8 *Chambliss*	Y	Y	N	Y	Y	Y	N
9 *Deal*	Y	Y	N	Y	Y	N	Y
10 *Norwood*	Y	Y	N	Y	Y	N	N
11 *Linder*	Y	Y	N	Y	Y	Y	N
HAWAII							
1 Abercrombie	Y	N	Y	N	N	N	N
2 Mink	Y	N	Y	N	N	N	N
IDAHO							
1 *Chenoweth*	Y	Y	Y	Y	N	Y	N
2 *Crapo*	Y	Y	Y	Y	N	Y	N
ILLINOIS							
1 Rush	Y	N	N	N	N	N	Y
2 Jackson	Y	N	Y	N	N	N	Y
3 Lipinski	Y	N	N	N	N	N	Y
4 Gutierrez	Y	N	Y	N	N	P	Y
5 Blagojevich	Y	N	N	Y	N	P	Y
6 *Hyde*	Y	Y	N	Y	Y	Y	Y
7 Davis	Y	N	N	N	N	N	Y
8 *Crane*	?	Y	N	Y	Y	Y	N
9 Yates	?	?	?	?	N	N	Y
10 *Porter*	Y	N	N	Y	N	N	Y
11 *Weller*	Y	Y	N	Y	Y	N	N
12 Costello	Y	N	N	N	N	N	Y
13 *Fawell*	Y	Y	N	Y	Y	N	N

	399	400	401	402	403	404	405
14 **Hastert**	Y	Y	N	Y	Y	Y	N
15 **Ewing**	Y	Y	N	Y	N	Y	N
16 **Manzullo**	Y	Y	N	Y	N	N	N
17 Evans	Y	N	Y	N	N	N	Y
18 **LaHood**	Y	Y	N	Y	N	Y	N
19 Poshard	Y	N	Y	N	N	N	Y
20 **Shimkus**	Y	Y	N	Y	Y	Y	Y
INDIANA							
1 Visclosky	Y	Y	Y	Y	N	N	Y
2 **McIntosh**	Y	Y	Y	Y	Y	N	N
3 Roemer	Y	N	N	N	N	N	Y
4 **Souder**	Y	Y	N	Y	N	N	N
5 **Buyer**	Y	Y	N	Y	Y	Y	N
6 **Burton**	Y	Y	Y	Y	Y	N	N
7 **Pease**	Y	Y	N	Y	N	N	N
8 **Hostettler**	Y	Y	N	N	Y	N	N
9 Hamilton	Y	N	N	N	N	N	Y
10 Carson	N	N	Y	N	N	P	Y
IOWA							
1 **Leach**	Y	N	N	Y	N	N	Y
2 **Nussle**	Y	Y	N	Y	N	Y	N
3 Boswell	Y	N	N	Y	N	Y	Y
4 **Ganske**	Y	Y	N	Y	N	N	Y
5 **Latham**	Y	Y	N	Y	Y	N	N
KANSAS							
1 **Moran**	Y	Y	N	N	N	Y	N
2 **Ryun**	Y	Y	N	Y	Y	Y	N
3 **Snowbarger**	Y	Y	N	Y	Y	Y	N
4 **Tiahrt**	Y	Y	N	N	Y	Y	N
KENTUCKY							
1 **Whitfield**	Y	Y	N	Y	Y	Y	N
2 **Lewis**	Y	Y	N	Y	Y	N	N
3 **Northup**	Y	Y	N	Y	Y	Y	N
4 **Bunning**	Y	Y	Y	Y	N	N	N
5 **Rogers**	Y	Y	N	Y	Y	N	N
6 Baesler	Y	Y	Y	Y	N	N	Y
LOUISIANA							
1 **Livingston**	Y	Y	N	Y	Y	Y	N
2 Jefferson	Y	N	N	N	N	N	Y
3 **Tauzin**	Y	Y	N	Y	Y	Y	N
4 **McCrery**	Y	Y	N	Y	Y	Y	N
5 **Cooksey**	Y	Y	N	Y	Y	Y	N
6 **Baker**	Y	Y	N	Y	Y	Y	N
7 John	Y	N	N	N	N	Y	N
MAINE							
1 Allen	Y	N	N	N	N	Y	Y
2 Baldacci	Y	N	Y	Y	N	P	Y
MARYLAND							
1 **Gilchrest**	Y	Y	Y	Y	N	N	Y
2 **Ehrlich**	Y	Y	N	Y	Y	N	N
3 Cardin	Y	N	N	N	N	N	Y
4 Wynn	Y	N	N	N	N	P	Y
5 Hoyer	Y	N	N	N	N	P	Y
6 **Bartlett**	Y	Y	Y	N	Y	N	N
7 Cummings	Y	N	Y	N	N	N	Y
8 **Morella**	Y	N	N	Y	N	N	Y
MASSACHUSETTS							
1 Olver	Y	N	N	N	N	P	Y
2 Neal	Y	N	N	N	N	N	Y
3 McGovern	Y	N	Y	N	N	P	Y
4 Frank	Y	N	Y	N	N	N	Y
5 Meehan	Y	N	Y	N	N	N	Y
6 Tierney	Y	N	Y	N	N	N	Y
7 Markey	Y	N	Y	N	N	N	Y
8 Kennedy	Y	N	Y	N	N	N	Y
9 Moakley	?	?	?	?	N	N	Y
10 Delahunt	Y	N	Y	N	N	P	Y
MICHIGAN							
1 Stupak	Y	N	Y	N	N	N	N
2 **Hoekstra**	Y	Y	N	Y	Y	Y	N
3 **Ehlers**	Y	Y	N	Y	N	Y	N
4 **Camp**	Y	Y	N	Y	Y	N	N
5 Barcia	Y	N	Y	Y	N	P	Y
6 **Upton**	Y	Y	N	Y	N	Y	Y
7 **Smith**	Y	Y	Y	Y	N	Y	Y
8 Stabenow	Y	N	Y	Y	N	Y	Y
9 Kildee	Y	N	Y	N	N	N	Y
10 Bonior	Y	N	Y	N	N	P	Y
11 **Knollenberg**	Y	Y	N	Y	Y	N	N
12 Levin	Y	N	N	N	N	N	Y
13 Rivers	Y	N	Y	N	N	P	Y
14 Conyers	Y	N	Y	N	N	P	Y
15 Kilpatrick	Y	N	Y	N	N	P	Y
16 Dingell	Y	N	N	N	N	N	Y

	399	400	401	402	403	404	405
MINNESOTA							
1 **Gutknecht**	Y	Y	Y	Y	Y	N	N
2 Minge	Y	N	N	N	N	P	Y
3 **Ramstad**	Y	Y	N	Y	N	N	Y
4 Vento	Y	N	N	N	N	N	Y
5 Sabo	Y	N	N	N	N	P	Y
6 Luther	Y	N	N	N	N	N	Y
7 Peterson	Y	Y	Y	N	N	N	N
8 Oberstar	Y	N	Y	N	N	N	Y
MISSISSIPPI							
1 **Wicker**	Y	Y	N	Y	Y	Y	N
2 Thompson	Y	N	N	N	N	N	Y
3 **Pickering**	Y	Y	N	N	Y	Y	N
4 **Parker**	Y	Y	N	Y	N	N	N
5 Taylor	Y	Y	Y	N	N	N	Y
MISSOURI							
1 Clay	?	N	Y	N	N	N	Y
2 **Talent**	Y	Y	N	Y	N	Y	N
3 Gephardt	Y	N	Y	N	N	P	Y
4 Skelton	Y	Y	N	N	N	P	Y
5 McCarthy	Y	N	N	N	N	N	Y
6 Danner	Y	Y	Y	N	N	N	Y
7 **Blunt**	Y	Y	N	Y	Y	Y	N
8 **Emerson**	Y	Y	Y	Y	N	Y	N
9 **Hulshof**	Y	Y	N	Y	N	Y	Y
MONTANA							
AL **Hill**	Y	Y	N	Y	N	Y	Y
NEBRASKA							
1 **Bereuter**	Y	Y	N	Y	N	N	Y
2 **Christensen**	Y	Y	N	Y	Y	N	N
3 **Barrett**	Y	Y	N	Y	N	N	Y
NEVADA							
1 **Ensign**	Y	Y	Y	N	N	Y	N
2 **Gibbons**	Y	Y	Y	N	Y	Y	N
NEW HAMPSHIRE							
1 **Sununu**	Y	Y	N	Y	Y	Y	N
2 **Bass**	Y	Y	N	Y	N	N	Y
NEW JERSEY							
1 Andrews	Y	Y	Y	N	N	N	Y
2 **LoBiondo**	Y	Y	Y	Y	N	N	Y
3 **Saxton**	Y	Y	Y	Y	N	Y	Y
4 **Smith**	Y	Y	Y	Y	N	Y	N
5 **Roukema**	Y	Y	N	Y	N	N	Y
6 Pallone	Y	N	Y	N	N	P	Y
7 **Franks**	Y	Y	Y	Y	N	N	Y
8 Pascrell	Y	N	Y	Y	N	N	Y
9 Rothman	Y	N	Y	N	N	N	Y
10 Payne	Y	N	Y	N	N	N	Y
11 **Frelinghuysen**	Y	Y	N	Y	N	N	Y
12 **Pappas**	Y	Y	Y	Y	N	Y	N
13 Menendez	Y	N	Y	N	N	P	Y
NEW MEXICO							
1 **Wilson**	Y	Y	N	Y	Y	Y	N
2 **Skeen**	Y	Y	N	Y	Y	N	N
3 **Redmond**	Y	Y	N	Y	Y	N	N
NEW YORK							
1 **Forbes**	Y	Y	Y	Y	N	N	Y
2 **Lazio**	Y	Y	N	Y	N	N	Y
3 **King**	Y	Y	Y	Y	Y	Y	N
4 McCarthy	Y	N	Y	N	N	N	Y
5 Ackerman	Y	N	Y	N	N	N	Y
6 Meeks	Y	N	Y	N	N	P	Y
7 Manton	Y	N	Y	N	N	N	Y
8 Nadler	Y	N	Y	N	N	N	Y
9 Schumer	Y	N	Y	N	N	N	Y
10 Towns	Y	N	Y	N	N	N	Y
11 Owens	Y	N	Y	N	N	N	Y
12 Velázquez	Y	N	Y	N	N	P	Y
13 **Fossella**	Y	Y	N	Y	Y	N	N
14 Maloney	Y	N	Y	N	N	N	Y
15 Rangel	Y	N	Y	N	N	P	Y
16 Serrano	Y	N	Y	N	N	N	Y
17 Engel	Y	N	Y	N	N	P	Y
18 Lowey	Y	N	N	N	N	N	Y
19 **Kelly**	Y	Y	Y	Y	N	N	Y
20 **Gilman**	Y	Y	Y	Y	N	N	Y
21 McNulty	Y	N	Y	N	N	N	Y
22 **Solomon**	Y	Y	N	Y	Y	Y	N
23 **Boehlert**	Y	Y	N	Y	N	N	Y
24 **McHugh**	Y	Y	Y	Y	N	Y	Y
25 **Walsh**	Y	Y	Y	Y	N	N	Y
26 Hinchey	Y	N	Y	N	N	N	Y
27 **Paxon**	Y	Y	N	Y	Y	N	N
28 Slaughter	Y	N	N	N	N	P	Y
29 LaFalce	Y	N	N	N	N	N	Y
30 **Quinn**	Y	Y	Y	Y	N	N	Y

	399	400	401	402	403	404	405
31 **Houghton**	Y	Y	N	Y	N	N	Y
NORTH CAROLINA							
1 Clayton	Y	N	Y	N	N	P	Y
2 Etheridge	Y	N	N	N	N	P	Y
3 **Jones**	Y	Y	Y	Y	Y	Y	N
4 Price	Y	N	N	N	N	P	Y
5 **Burr**	Y	Y	N	Y	N	N	Y
6 **Coble**	Y	Y	N	Y	Y	N	N
7 McIntyre	Y	Y	Y	N	N	Y	Y
8 Hefner	Y	N	Y	N	N	N	Y
9 **Myrick**	Y	Y	N	Y	N	Y	N
10 **Ballenger**	Y	Y	N	Y	Y	Y	N
11 **Taylor**	Y	Y	N	Y	Y	Y	N
12 Watt	Y	N	N	N	N	Y	Y
NORTH DAKOTA							
AL Pomeroy	Y	N	Y	N	N	P	Y
OHIO							
1 **Chabot**	Y	Y	Y	N	N	Y	N
2 **Portman**	Y	Y	N	Y	N	N	N
3 Hall	Y	N	N	N	N	N	Y
4 **Oxley**	Y	Y	N	Y	Y	N	N
5 **Gillmor**	Y	Y	Y	Y	N	Y	Y
6 Strickland	Y	N	Y	Y	N	N	Y
7 **Hobson**	Y	Y	N	Y	Y	Y	N
8 **Boehner**	Y	Y	N	Y	Y	N	N
9 Kaptur	Y	Y	Y	N	N	N	Y
10 Kucinich	Y	N	Y	N	N	P	Y
11 Stokes	Y	N	Y	N	N	N	Y
12 **Kasich**	Y	Y	N	Y	Y	N	N
13 Brown	Y	N	Y	N	N	N	Y
14 Sawyer	Y	N	N	N	N	P	Y
15 **Pryce**	Y	Y	N	Y	Y	Y	N
16 **Regula**	Y	Y	N	Y	N	N	Y
17 Traficant	Y	Y	Y	Y	Y	N	N
18 **Ney**	Y	Y	Y	Y	N	Y	N
19 **LaTourette**	Y	N	Y	Y	N	P	Y
OKLAHOMA							
1 **Largent**	Y	Y	N	N	Y	Y	N
2 **Coburn**	?	Y	N	Y	Y	Y	N
3 **Watkins**	Y	Y	Y	Y	Y	N	N
4 **Watts**	Y	Y	Y	Y	N	N	N
5 **Istook**	Y	Y	Y	Y	N	N	N
6 **Lucas**	Y	Y	Y	Y	Y	Y	N
OREGON							
1 Furse	Y	N	Y	N	N	P	Y
2 **Smith**	Y	?	?	?	Y	Y	N
3 Blumenauer	Y	N	N	N	N	Y	Y
4 DeFazio	Y	N	Y	N	N	P	Y
5 Hooley	Y	N	N	Y	N	Y	Y
PENNSYLVANIA							
1 Brady	Y	N	Y	N	N	N	Y
2 Fattah	Y	N	Y	N	N	N	Y
3 Borski	Y	N	Y	N	N	N	Y
4 Klink	Y	N	Y	N	N	N	Y
5 **Peterson**	Y	Y	N	Y	Y	N	N
6 Holden	Y	N	Y	Y	N	N	Y
7 **Weldon**	?	Y	N	Y	N	Y	Y
8 **Greenwood**	Y	Y	N	Y	N	N	Y
9 **Shuster**	Y	?	?	?	Y	Y	N
10 **McDade**	Y	Y	Y	Y	Y	?	Y
11 Kanjorski	Y	N	N	Y	N	N	Y
12 Murtha	Y	Y	Y	Y	N	N	N
13 **Fox**	Y	Y	Y	Y	N	N	Y
14 Coyne	Y	N	Y	N	N	N	Y
15 McHale	Y	Y	N	N	N	N	Y
16 **Pitts**	Y	Y	N	Y	Y	Y	N
17 **Gekas**	Y	Y	N	Y	Y	Y	Y
18 Doyle	Y	N	Y	Y	N	N	Y
19 **Goodling**	?	Y	Y	Y	Y	N	N
20 Mascara	Y	N	Y	Y	N	N	Y
21 **English**	Y	Y	N	Y	N	Y	N
RHODE ISLAND							
1 Kennedy	Y	N	Y	N	N	Y	Y
2 Weygand	Y	N	N	N	N	Y	Y
SOUTH CAROLINA							
1 **Sanford**	Y	Y	N	N	N	N	Y
2 **Spence**	Y	Y	Y	Y	Y	Y	N
3 **Graham**	Y	Y	Y	Y	N	Y	Y
4 **Inglis**	Y	Y	Y	Y	?	?	?
5 Spratt	Y	N	N	N	N	N	Y
6 Clyburn	Y	N	Y	N	N	N	Y
SOUTH DAKOTA							
AL **Thune**	Y	Y	N	Y	N	Y	Y

	399	400	401	402	403	404	405
TENNESSEE							
1 **Jenkins**	Y	Y	Y	Y	Y	Y	N
2 **Duncan**	Y	Y	Y	N	N	Y	Y
3 **Wamp**	Y	Y	Y	N	N	Y	Y
4 **Hilleary**	Y	Y	Y	N	N	Y	N
5 Clement	Y	N	N	N	N	N	Y
6 Gordon	Y	N	Y	N	N	P	Y
7 **Bryant**	Y	Y	N	Y	Y	Y	N
8 Tanner	Y	N	N	N	N	P	Y
9 Ford	Y	N	N	N	N	P	Y
TEXAS							
1 Sandlin	Y	N	N	N	N	P	Y
2 Turner	Y	N	N	N	N	Y	Y
3 **Johnson, Sam**	Y	Y	N	Y	Y	N	N
4 Hall	Y	Y	Y	Y	Y	Y	N
5 **Sessions**	Y	Y	N	Y	Y	N	N
6 **Barton**	Y	Y	N	Y	Y	Y	N
7 **Archer**	Y	Y	N	Y	N	Y	N
8 **Brady**	Y	Y	N	Y	Y	Y	N
9 Lampson	?	N	N	N	N	Y	Y
10 Doggett	Y	N	Y	N	N	N	Y
11 Edwards	Y	N	N	N	N	N	Y
12 **Granger**	Y	Y	N	Y	N	Y	N
13 **Thornberry**	Y	Y	N	Y	Y	Y	N
14 **Paul**	Y	Y	Y	N	Y	Y	N
15 Hinojosa	?	N	N	N	N	P	Y
16 Reyes	?	Y	N	N	N	P	Y
17 Stenholm	Y	Y	N	N	N	P	Y
18 Jackson-Lee	N	N	N	N	N	N	Y
19 **Combest**	Y	Y	N	Y	Y	Y	N
20 Gonzalez	?	?	?	?	?	?	?
21 **Smith**	Y	Y	N	Y	N	N	N
22 **DeLay**	Y	Y	N	Y	Y	N	N
23 **Bonilla**	Y	Y	N	Y	Y	N	N
24 Frost	Y	N	N	N	N	P	Y
25 Bentsen	Y	N	N	N	N	N	Y
26 **Armey**	Y	Y	N	Y	Y	N	N
27 Ortiz	Y	N	N	N	N	N	Y
28 Rodriguez	Y	N	Y	N	N	P	Y
29 Green	Y	N	Y	N	N	N	Y
30 Johnson, E.B.	Y	N	N	N	N	N	Y
UTAH							
1 **Hansen**	Y	Y	N	Y	Y	Y	N
2 **Cook**	Y	Y	N	Y	N	Y	Y
3 **Cannon**	Y	Y	N	Y	Y	N	N
VERMONT							
AL *Sanders*	Y	N	Y	N	N	N	Y
VIRGINIA							
1 **Bateman**	Y	Y	N	Y	N	Y	N
2 Pickett	Y	Y	N	N	N	N	Y
3 Scott	Y	N	N	N	N	Y	N
4 Sisisky	Y	Y	N	N	N	Y	Y
5 Goode	Y	Y	Y	N	N	Y	N
6 **Goodlatte**	Y	Y	N	N	Y	Y	N
7 **Bliley**	Y	Y	N	Y	Y	Y	N
8 Moran	Y	N	N	N	N	N	Y
9 Boucher	Y	N	Y	Y	N	N	Y
10 **Wolf**	Y	Y	Y	Y	N	Y	N
11 **Davis**	Y	Y	N	Y	N	Y	N
WASHINGTON							
1 **White**	Y	Y	N	Y	Y	Y	Y
2 **Metcalf**	Y	Y	Y	Y	N	N	Y
3 **Smith, Linda**	Y	Y	Y	Y	N	N	Y
4 **Hastings**	Y	Y	N	Y	Y	N	N
5 **Nethercutt**	Y	Y	Y	Y	Y	N	N
6 Dicks	Y	N	N	Y	N	N	Y
7 McDermott	Y	N	N	N	N	P	Y
8 **Dunn**	Y	Y	Y	Y	Y	N	N
9 Smith, Adam	Y	N	N	N	N	N	Y
WEST VIRGINIA							
1 Mollohan	Y	N	Y	Y	N	N	N
2 Wise	Y	N	Y	Y	N	N	Y
3 Rahall	Y	N	Y	Y	N	N	N
WISCONSIN							
1 **Neumann**	Y	Y	Y	N	N	N	N
2 **Klug**	Y	Y	N	N	Y	N	Y
3 Kind	Y	N	N	N	N	Y	Y
4 Kleczka	Y	N	Y	N	N	N	Y
5 Barrett	Y	N	Y	N	N	N	Y
6 **Petri**	Y	Y	N	N	N	Y	Y
7 Obey	Y	N	Y	N	N	N	Y
8 Johnson	Y	N	Y	N	N	Y	Y
9 **Sensenbrenner**	Y	Y	N	N	N	Y	N
WYOMING							
AL **Cubin**	Y	Y	N	Y	Y	N	N

Southern states - Ala., Ark., Fla., Ga., Ky., La., Miss., N.C., Okla., S.C., Tenn., Texas, Va.

Key

Y	Voted for (yea).
#	Paired for.
+	Announced for.
N	Voted against (nay).
X	Paired against.
−	Announced against.
P	Voted "present."
C	Voted "present" to avoid possible conflict of interest.
?	Did not vote or otherwise make a position known.

Democrats **Republicans**
Independent

406. HR 4380. Fiscal 1999 District of Columbia Appropriations/Rule. Adoption of the rule (H Res 517) to provide for House floor consideration of the bill to appropriate $491 million in federal funds and $6.8 billion from the D.C. Treasury for government operations and activities of the District of Columbia in fiscal 1999. Adopted 220-204: R 218-3; D 2-200 (ND 1-147, SD 1-53); I 0-1. Aug. 6, 1998.

407. HR 4380. Fiscal 1999 District of Columbia Appropriations/Fund Advisory Neighborhood Commissions. Norton, D-D.C., amendment to fund the Advisory Neighborhood Commissions at the requested level of $573,000 in fiscal 1999. Rejected 187-237: R 8-215; D 178-22 (ND 139-8, SD 39-14); I 1-0. Aug. 6, 1998.

408. HR 4380. Fiscal 1999 District of Columbia Appropriations/Allow Use of Local Funds for Abortions. Norton, D-D.C. amendment to allow use of local funds for abortions. Rejected 180-243: R 27-196; D 152-47 (ND 115-31, SD 37-16); I 1-0. Aug. 6, 1998.

409. HR 4380. Fiscal 1999 District of Columbia Appropriations/Allow Use of Local Funds to Sue for Voting Rights. Norton, D-D.C., amendment to strike the prohibition against the use of local funds to sue Congress for voting rights in the House and Senate. Rejected 181-243: R 9-214; D 171-29 (ND 136-11, SD 35-18); I 1-0. Aug. 6, 1998.

410. HR 4380. Fiscal 1999 District of Columbia Appropriations/Residence Requirement for D.C. Government Employees. Norton, D-D.C., amendment to strike the provision in the bill that repeals the D.C. law requiring new D.C. government employees reside in the District of Columbia. Rejected 109-313: R 17-205; D 91-108 (ND 68-78, SD 23-30); I 1-0. Aug. 6, 1998.

411. HR 4380. Fiscal 1999 District of Columbia Appropriations/Education "Vouchers" for D.C. Students. Armey, R-Texas, amendment to establish a new program to provide education scholarships ("vouchers") to an estimated 2,000 poor D.C. public school students. Adopted 214-208: R 207-15; D 7-192 (ND 3-143, SD 4-49); I 0-1. Aug. 6, 1998.

412. HR 4380. Fiscal 1999 District of Columbia Appropriations/Needle Exchange Federal and Local Funds Prohibition. Tiahrt, R-Kan., amendment to prohibit federal and local funds from being spent on needle exchange programs in the District of Columbia. Adopted 250-169: R 205-15; D 45-153 (ND 26-120, SD 19-33); I 0-1. Aug. 7, 1998. Aug. 7, 1998, in the session that began Aug. 6 and is recorded in the Aug. 6 Congressional Record.

	406	407	408	409	410	411	412
ALABAMA							
1 *Callahan*	Y	N	N	N	N	Y	Y
2 *Everett*	Y	N	N	N	N	Y	Y
3 *Riley*	Y	N	N	N	N	Y	Y
4 *Aderholt*	Y	N	N	N	Y	Y	Y
5 Cramer	N	N	N	N	Y	N	?
6 *Bachus*	Y	N	N	N	N	Y	Y
7 Hilliard	N	Y	Y	Y	Y	N	N
ALASKA							
AL *Young*	Y	N	N	N	N	Y	Y
ARIZONA							
1 *Salmon*	Y	N	N	N	N	Y	Y
2 Pastor	N	Y	Y	Y	Y	N	N
3 *Stump*	Y	N	N	N	N	Y	Y
4 *Shadegg*	Y	N	N	N	N	Y	Y
5 *Kolbe*	Y	Y	Y	N	N	Y	Y
6 *Hayworth*	Y	N	N	N	N	Y	Y
ARKANSAS							
1 Berry	N	Y	N	Y	Y	N	N
2 Snyder	N	Y	Y	Y	N	N	N
3 *Hutchinson*	Y	N	N	N	N	Y	Y
4 *Dickey*	Y	N	N	N	N	Y	Y
CALIFORNIA							
1 *Riggs*	Y	N	N	N	N	Y	Y
2 *Herger*	Y	N	N	N	N	Y	Y
3 Fazio	N	Y	Y	Y	Y	N	N
4 *Doolittle*	Y	N	N	N	N	Y	Y
5 Matsui	N	Y	Y	Y	Y	N	N
6 Woolsey	N	Y	Y	Y	N	N	N
7 Miller	N	Y	Y	Y	Y	N	N
8 Pelosi	N	Y	Y	Y	Y	N	N
9 Lee	N	Y	Y	Y	Y	N	N
10 Tauscher	N	Y	Y	Y	Y	N	N
11 *Pombo*	Y	N	N	N	N	Y	Y
12 Lantos	N	Y	Y	Y	Y	N	N
13 Stark	N	Y	Y	Y	Y	?	?
14 Eshoo	N	Y	Y	Y	N	N	N
15 *Campbell*	Y	Y	Y	Y	Y	N	Y
16 Lofgren	N	Y	P	N	N	N	N
17 Farr	N	Y	Y	Y	Y	N	N
18 Condit	N	Y	N	Y	N	Y	N
19 *Radanovich*	Y	N	N	N	N	Y	Y
20 Dooley	N	Y	Y	Y	Y	N	N
21 *Thomas*	Y	N	N	N	N	Y	Y
22 Capps, L.	N	Y	Y	Y	Y	N	N
23 *Gallegly*	Y	N	N	N	N	Y	Y
24 Sherman	N	Y	Y	Y	N	N	N
25 *McKeon*	Y	N	N	N	N	Y	Y
26 Berman	N	Y	Y	Y	Y	N	N
27 *Rogan*	Y	N	N	N	N	Y	Y
28 *Dreier*	Y	N	N	N	N	Y	Y
29 Waxman	N	Y	Y	Y	Y	N	N
30 Becerra	N	Y	Y	Y	Y	N	N
31 Martinez	N	Y	Y	Y	Y	N	N
32 Dixon	N	Y	Y	Y	P	N	N
33 Roybal-Allard	N	Y	Y	Y	Y	N	N
34 Torres	N	Y	Y	Y	Y	N	N
35 Waters	N	Y	Y	Y	Y	N	N
36 Harman	N	?	?	?	?	N	N
37 Millender-McD.	N	Y	Y	Y	Y	N	N
38 *Horn*	Y	Y	Y	Y	Y	Y	Y

	406	407	408	409	410	411	412
39 *Royce*	?	N	N	N	N	Y	Y
40 *Lewis*	Y	N	N	N	N	Y	Y
41 *Kim*	Y	Y	N	N	N	Y	Y
42 Brown	N	Y	Y	Y	Y	N	N
43 *Calvert*	Y	N	N	N	N	Y	Y
44 *Bono, M.*	Y	N	N	N	N	Y	Y
45 *Rohrabacher*	Y	N	N	N	N	Y	Y
46 Sanchez	N	Y	Y	Y	Y	N	N
47 *Cox*	Y	N	N	N	N	Y	Y
48 *Packard*	+	−	−	−	−	+	+
49 *Bilbray*	Y	N	N	N	N	Y	Y
50 Filner	N	Y	Y	Y	Y	N	N
51 *Cunningham*	?	?	?	?	?	?	?
52 *Hunter*	?	N	N	N	N	Y	Y
COLORADO							
1 DeGette	N	Y	Y	Y	N	N	N
2 Skaggs	N	Y	Y	Y	N	N	N
3 *McInnis*	Y	N	N	N	N	Y	Y
4 *Schaffer*	Y	N	N	N	Y	Y	Y
5 *Hefley*	Y	N	N	N	N	Y	Y
6 *Schaefer*	Y	N	N	N	N	Y	Y
CONNECTICUT							
1 Kennelly	N	Y	Y	Y	N	N	N
2 Gejdenson	N	Y	Y	Y	N	N	N
3 DeLauro	N	Y	Y	Y	N	N	N
4 *Shays*	Y	N	Y	N	N	Y	Y
5 Maloney	N	Y	Y	Y	N	N	N
6 *Johnson*	N	N	Y	N	N	N	N
DELAWARE							
AL *Castle*	Y	Y	Y	N	N	Y	N
FLORIDA							
1 *Scarborough*	Y	Y	N	N	N	Y	Y
2 Boyd	N	N	N	N	N	Y	Y
3 Brown	N	Y	Y	Y	Y	N	N
4 *Fowler*	Y	N	N	N	N	Y	Y
5 Thurman	N	Y	Y	Y	N	N	N
6 *Stearns*	?	N	N	N	?	N	N
7 *Mica*	Y	N	N	N	N	Y	Y
8 *McCollum*	Y	N	N	N	N	Y	Y
9 *Bilirakis*	Y	N	N	N	N	Y	Y
10 *Young*	Y	N	N	N	N	?	?
11 Davis	N	Y	Y	Y	N	N	N
12 *Canady*	Y	N	N	N	N	Y	Y
13 *Miller*	Y	N	N	N	N	Y	Y
14 *Goss*	Y	N	N	N	N	Y	Y
15 *Weldon*	Y	N	N	N	N	Y	Y
16 *Foley*	Y	N	N	N	N	Y	N
17 Meek	N	Y	Y	Y	N	N	N
18 *Ros-Lehtinen*	Y	N	N	N	N	Y	Y
19 Wexler	N	Y	Y	Y	N	N	N
20 Deutsch	N	Y	Y	Y	N	N	N
21 *Diaz-Balart*	Y	N	N	N	N	Y	Y
22 *Shaw*	Y	N	N	N	N	Y	Y
23 Hastings	N	Y	Y	Y	N	N	N
GEORGIA							
1 *Kingston*	Y	N	N	N	N	Y	Y
2 Bishop	N	Y	Y	Y	N	N	N
3 *Collins*	Y	N	N	N	N	Y	Y
4 McKinney	N	Y	Y	Y	N	N	N
5 Lewis	N	Y	Y	Y	Y	N	N
6 *Gingrich*							
7 *Barr*	Y	N	N	N	N	Y	Y
8 *Chambliss*	Y	N	N	N	N	Y	Y
9 *Deal*	Y	N	N	N	N	Y	Y
10 *Norwood*	Y	N	N	N	N	Y	Y
11 *Linder*	Y	N	N	N	N	Y	Y
HAWAII							
1 Abercrombie	N	Y	Y	Y	Y	N	N
2 Mink	N	Y	Y	Y	Y	N	N
IDAHO							
1 *Chenoweth*	Y	N	N	N	N	N	Y
2 *Crapo*	?	N	N	N	N	N	Y
ILLINOIS							
1 Rush	N	Y	Y	Y	Y	N	N
2 Jackson	N	Y	Y	Y	Y	N	N
3 Lipinski	N	N	N	N	Y	Y	Y
4 Gutierrez	N	Y	Y	Y	Y	N	N
5 Blagojevich	N	Y	Y	Y	N	Y	N
6 *Hyde*	Y	N	N	N	Y	Y	Y
7 Davis	N	Y	Y	Y	Y	N	N
8 *Crane*	Y	N	N	N	N	Y	Y
9 Yates	N	?	?	?	?	?	?
10 *Porter*	Y	N	N	N	N	Y	Y
11 *Weller*	Y	N	N	N	N	Y	Y
12 Costello	N	N	N	N	Y	Y	Y
13 *Fawell*	Y	N	N	N	N	N	Y

ND Northern Democrats   SD Southern Democrats

Member	406	407	408	409	410	411	412
14 ***Hastert***	Y	N	N	N	N	Y	Y
15 ***Ewing***	Y	N	N	N	N	Y	Y
16 ***Manzullo***	Y	N	N	N	N	Y	Y
17 Evans	N	Y	Y	Y	N	N	N
18 ***LaHood***	Y	N	N	N	N	Y	Y
19 Poshard	N	Y	N	Y	Y	N	Y
20 ***Shimkus***	Y	N	N	N	N	Y	Y
INDIANA							
1 Visclosky	N	Y	Y	Y	Y	N	Y
2 ***McIntosh***	Y	N	N	N	N	Y	Y
3 Roemer	N	Y	N	N	N	N	Y
4 ***Souder***	Y	N	N	N	N	Y	Y
5 ***Buyer***	Y	N	N	N	N	Y	?
6 ***Burton***	Y	N	?	N	N	Y	Y
7 ***Pease***	Y	N	N	N	N	Y	Y
8 ***Hostettler***	Y	N	N	N	N	Y	Y
9 Hamilton	N	Y	N	Y	N	N	Y
10 Carson	N	Y	Y	Y	Y	N	N
IOWA							
1 ***Leach***	Y	N	N	N	N	N	Y
2 ***Nussle***	Y	N	N	N	N	Y	Y
3 Boswell	N	Y	Y	N	N	N	Y
4 ***Ganske***	Y	N	N	N	N	Y	N
5 ***Latham***	Y	N	N	N	N	Y	Y
KANSAS							
1 ***Moran***	Y	N	N	N	N	Y	Y
2 ***Ryun***	Y	N	N	N	N	Y	Y
3 ***Snowbarger***	Y	N	N	N	N	Y	Y
4 ***Tiahrt***	Y	N	N	N	N	Y	Y
KENTUCKY							
1 ***Whitfield***	Y	N	N	N	N	Y	Y
2 ***Lewis***	Y	N	N	N	N	Y	Y
3 ***Northup***	Y	N	N	N	N	Y	Y
4 ***Bunning***	Y	N	N	N	N	Y	Y
5 ***Rogers***	Y	N	N	N	N	Y	Y
6 Baesler	N	N	N	N	N	N	Y
LOUISIANA							
1 ***Livingston***	Y	N	N	N	N	Y	Y
2 Jefferson	N	Y	Y	Y	Y	N	N
3 ***Tauzin***	Y	N	N	N	N	Y	Y
4 ***McCrery***	Y	N	N	N	N	Y	Y
5 ***Cooksey***	Y	N	N	N	N	Y	Y
6 ***Baker***	Y	N	N	N	N	Y	Y
7 John	N	N	N	N	N	N	Y
MAINE							
1 Allen	N	Y	Y	Y	N	N	N
2 Baldacci	N	Y	Y	Y	N	N	N
MARYLAND							
1 ***Gilchrest***	Y	N	Y	N	N	Y	Y
2 ***Ehrlich***	Y	N	N	N	N	Y	Y
3 Cardin	N	Y	Y	Y	N	N	N
4 Wynn	N	Y	Y	Y	N	N	N
5 Hoyer	N	Y	Y	Y	N	N	N
6 ***Bartlett***	Y	N	N	N	N	Y	Y
7 Cummings	N	Y	Y	Y	Y	N	N
8 ***Morella***	N	Y	Y	Y	N	N	N
MASSACHUSETTS							
1 Olver	N	Y	Y	Y	N	N	N
2 Neal	N	Y	N	Y	N	N	N
3 McGovern	N	Y	Y	Y	Y	N	N
4 Frank	N	Y	Y	Y	Y	N	N
5 Meehan	N	Y	Y	Y	N	N	N
6 Tierney	N	Y	Y	Y	Y	N	N
7 Markey	N	Y	Y	Y	Y	N	N
8 Kennedy	N	Y	Y	Y	Y	Y	N
9 Moakley	N	?	?	?	?	?	?
10 Delahunt	N	Y	Y	Y	N	N	N
MICHIGAN							
1 Stupak	N	Y	N	Y	N	N	N
2 ***Hoekstra***	Y	N	N	N	N	Y	Y
3 ***Ehlers***	Y	N	N	N	Y	Y	Y
4 ***Camp***	Y	N	N	N	N	Y	Y
5 Barcia	N	Y	N	Y	N	N	Y
6 ***Upton***	Y	N	N	N	N	Y	Y
7 ***Smith***	Y	N	N	N	Y	Y	Y
8 Stabenow	N	Y	Y	Y	N	N	N
9 Kildee	N	Y	N	Y	Y	N	N
10 Bonior	N	Y	N	Y	Y	N	N
11 ***Knollenberg***	Y	N	N	N	N	Y	Y
12 Levin	N	Y	Y	Y	Y	N	N
13 Rivers	N	Y	Y	Y	Y	N	N
14 Conyers	N	Y	Y	Y	Y	?	?
15 Kilpatrick	N	Y	Y	Y	Y	N	N
16 Dingell	?	Y	Y	Y	N	N	N
MINNESOTA							
1 ***Gutknecht***	Y	N	N	N	N	Y	Y
2 Minge	N	Y	Y	Y	N	N	Y
3 ***Ramstad***	Y	N	Y	N	N	N	Y
4 Vento	N	Y	Y	Y	Y	N	N
5 Sabo	N	Y	Y	Y	N	N	N
6 Luther	N	Y	Y	Y	Y	N	Y
7 Peterson	N	N	N	Y	N	N	Y
8 Oberstar	N	Y	N	Y	N	N	N
MISSISSIPPI							
1 ***Wicker***	Y	N	N	N	N	Y	Y
2 Thompson	N	?	?	?	?	?	?
3 ***Pickering***	Y	N	N	N	N	Y	Y
4 ***Parker***	Y	N	N	N	N	Y	Y
5 Taylor	Y	N	N	N	N	Y	Y
MISSOURI							
1 Clay	?	N	Y	Y	Y	N	N
2 ***Talent***	Y	N	N	N	N	Y	Y
3 Gephardt	N	Y	Y	Y	Y	N	N
4 Skelton	N	Y	N	N	N	N	Y
5 McCarthy	N	Y	Y	Y	N	N	N
6 Danner	N	N	N	N	N	N	Y
7 ***Blunt***	Y	N	N	N	N	Y	Y
8 ***Emerson***	Y	N	N	N	N	Y	Y
9 ***Hulshof***	Y	N	N	N	N	Y	Y
MONTANA							
AL ***Hill***	Y	N	N	N	N	Y	Y
NEBRASKA							
1 ***Bereuter***	Y	N	N	Y	N	Y	Y
2 ***Christensen***	Y	N	N	N	N	Y	Y
3 ***Barrett***	Y	N	N	N	N	Y	Y
NEVADA							
1 ***Ensign***	Y	N	N	N	N	Y	N
2 ***Gibbons***	Y	N	N	N	N	Y	Y
NEW HAMPSHIRE							
1 ***Sununu***	Y	N	N	N	N	Y	Y
2 ***Bass***	Y	N	Y	N	N	Y	Y
NEW JERSEY							
1 Andrews	N	Y	Y	Y	N	N	N
2 ***LoBiondo***	Y	N	N	N	N	N	Y
3 ***Saxton***	Y	N	N	N	N	Y	Y
4 ***Smith***	Y	N	N	N	N	Y	Y
5 ***Roukema***	Y	N	Y	N	N	N	Y
6 Pallone	N	Y	Y	Y	Y	N	N
7 ***Franks***	Y	N	Y	Y	N	Y	Y
8 Pascrell	N	Y	Y	Y	N	N	Y
9 Rothman	N	Y	Y	Y	Y	N	N
10 Payne	N	Y	Y	Y	Y	N	N
11 ***Frelinghuysen***	Y	N	Y	N	N	Y	N
12 ***Pappas***	Y	N	N	N	N	Y	Y
13 Menendez	N	Y	Y	Y	Y	N	N
NEW MEXICO							
1 ***Wilson***	Y	N	N	N	N	Y	Y
2 ***Skeen***	Y	N	N	N	N	Y	Y
3 ***Redmond***	Y	N	N	N	N	Y	Y
NEW YORK							
1 ***Forbes***	Y	N	N	N	N	Y	Y
2 ***Lazio***	Y	N	Y	N	Y	Y	Y
3 ***King***	Y	N	N	N	N	Y	Y
4 McCarthy	N	Y	Y	Y	N	N	N
5 Ackerman	N	Y	Y	Y	N	N	N
6 Meeks	N	Y	Y	Y	Y	N	N
7 Manton	?	?	?	?	?	?	?
8 Nadler	N	Y	Y	Y	N	N	N
9 Schumer	N	Y	Y	Y	N	N	N
10 Towns	N	Y	Y	Y	Y	N	N
11 Owens	N	Y	Y	Y	Y	N	N
12 Velázquez	N	Y	Y	Y	Y	N	N
13 ***Fossella***	Y	N	N	N	N	Y	Y
14 Maloney	N	Y	Y	Y	N	N	N
15 Rangel	N	Y	Y	Y	N	N	N
16 Serrano	N	Y	Y	Y	Y	N	N
17 Engel	N	Y	Y	Y	N	N	N
18 Lowey	N	Y	Y	Y	N	N	N
19 ***Kelly***	Y	N	Y	N	N	Y	Y
20 ***Gilman***	Y	N	Y	Y	N	Y	Y
21 McNulty	N	Y	N	Y	N	N	Y
22 ***Solomon***	Y	N	N	N	N	Y	Y
23 ***Boehlert***	Y	N	Y	N	N	N	N
24 ***McHugh***	Y	N	N	N	N	N	Y
25 ***Walsh***	Y	N	N	N	N	Y	Y
26 Hinchey	N	Y	Y	Y	N	N	N
27 ***Paxon***	Y	N	N	N	N	Y	Y
28 Slaughter	N	Y	Y	N	N	N	N
29 LaFalce	N	Y	N	Y	N	N	N
30 ***Quinn***	Y	N	N	N	N	Y	Y
31 ***Houghton***	N	N	Y	N	N	Y	N
NORTH CAROLINA							
1 Clayton	N	Y	Y	Y	Y	N	N
2 Etheridge	N	Y	N	N	N	N	Y
3 ***Jones***	Y	N	N	N	N	Y	Y
4 Price	N	Y	Y	N	N	N	N
5 ***Burr***	Y	N	N	N	N	Y	Y
6 ***Coble***	Y	N	N	N	Y	Y	Y
7 McIntyre	N	N	N	N	N	N	Y
8 Hefner	N	Y	Y	N	N	N	N
9 ***Myrick***	Y	N	N	N	N	Y	Y
10 ***Ballenger***	Y	N	N	N	N	Y	Y
11 ***Taylor***	Y	N	N	N	Y	Y	Y
12 Watt	N	Y	Y	Y	Y	N	N
NORTH DAKOTA							
AL Pomeroy	N	Y	Y	N	N	N	Y
OHIO							
1 ***Chabot***	Y	N	N	N	N	Y	Y
2 ***Portman***	Y	N	N	N	N	Y	Y
3 Hall	N	Y	N	Y	N	N	Y
4 ***Oxley***	Y	N	N	N	N	Y	Y
5 ***Gillmor***	Y	N	N	N	N	Y	Y
6 Strickland	N	Y	Y	Y	N	N	Y
7 ***Hobson***	Y	N	Y	N	Y	Y	Y
8 ***Boehner***	Y	N	N	N	N	Y	Y
9 Kaptur	N	Y	N	Y	Y	N	N
10 Kucinich	N	Y	N	Y	Y	N	N
11 Stokes	N	Y	Y	Y	Y	N	N
12 ***Kasich***	Y	N	N	N	N	Y	Y
13 Brown	N	Y	Y	Y	Y	N	N
14 Sawyer	N	Y	Y	Y	Y	N	N
15 ***Pryce***	Y	N	Y	N	N	Y	Y
16 ***Regula***	Y	N	N	N	N	Y	Y
17 Traficant	Y	Y	N	N	N	N	Y
18 ***Ney***	Y	N	N	N	N	N	Y
19 ***LaTourette***	Y	N	N	N	N	Y	Y
OKLAHOMA							
1 ***Largent***	Y	N	N	N	N	Y	Y
2 ***Coburn***	Y	N	N	N	N	Y	Y
3 ***Watkins***	Y	N	N	N	Y	Y	Y
4 ***Watts***	Y	N	N	N	N	Y	Y
5 ***Istook***	Y	N	N	N	N	Y	Y
6 ***Lucas***	Y	N	N	N	Y	Y	Y
OREGON							
1 Furse	N	Y	Y	Y	N	N	N
2 ***Smith***	Y	N	N	N	N	?	?
3 Blumenauer	N	Y	Y	Y	Y	N	N
4 DeFazio	N	Y	Y	N	N	N	N
5 Hooley	N	Y	Y	Y	Y	N	N
PENNSYLVANIA							
1 Brady	N	Y	Y	Y	Y	N	N
2 Fattah	N	Y	Y	Y	Y	N	N
3 Borski	N	Y	N	Y	Y	N	N
4 Klink	N	N	N	Y	N	N	N
5 ***Peterson***	Y	N	N	N	N	Y	Y
6 Holden	N	Y	N	Y	Y	N	Y
7 ***Weldon***	Y	N	N	N	N	Y	Y
8 ***Greenwood***	Y	N	Y	N	N	Y	N
9 ***Shuster***	Y	N	N	N	N	Y	Y
10 ***McDade***	Y	?	?	?	?	?	?
11 Kanjorski	N	Y	N	Y	N	N	N
12 Murtha	N	Y	N	Y	N	N	Y
13 ***Fox***	Y	N	N	N	N	Y	Y
14 Coyne	N	Y	Y	Y	Y	N	N
15 McHale	N	Y	Y	Y	N	N	N
16 ***Pitts***	Y	N	N	N	N	Y	Y
17 ***Gekas***	Y	N	N	?	N	Y	Y
18 Doyle	N	N	N	Y	N	N	N
19 ***Goodling***	Y	N	N	N	Y	Y	Y
20 Mascara	N	Y	N	Y	N	N	Y
21 ***English***	Y	N	N	N	N	N	Y
RHODE ISLAND							
1 Kennedy	N	Y	Y	Y	Y	N	N
2 Weygand	N	Y	N	Y	N	N	N
SOUTH CAROLINA							
1 ***Sanford***	Y	N	N	N	N	Y	Y
2 ***Spence***	Y	N	N	N	N	Y	Y
3 ***Graham***	Y	N	N	N	N	Y	Y
4 ***Inglis***	?	N	N	N	N	Y	Y
5 Spratt	N	N	Y	Y	N	N	Y
6 Clyburn	N	Y	Y	Y	Y	N	N
SOUTH DAKOTA							
AL ***Thune***	Y	N	N	N	N	Y	Y
TENNESSEE							
1 ***Jenkins***	Y	N	N	N	N	Y	Y
2 ***Duncan***	Y	N	N	N	Y	Y	Y
3 ***Wamp***	Y	N	N	N	N	Y	Y
4 ***Hilleary***	Y	N	N	N	N	Y	Y
5 Clement	N	N	N	Y	Y	N	Y
6 Gordon	N	Y	Y	N	N	N	Y
7 ***Bryant***	Y	N	N	N	N	Y	Y
8 Tanner	N	Y	Y	N	N	N	Y
9 Ford	N	Y	Y	Y	Y	N	N
TEXAS							
1 Sandlin	N	Y	Y	Y	Y	N	Y
2 Turner	N	Y	N	N	N	N	Y
3 ***Johnson, Sam***	Y	N	N	N	N	Y	Y
4 Hall	N	N	N	Y	N	Y	Y
5 ***Sessions***	Y	N	N	N	N	Y	Y
6 ***Barton***	Y	N	N	N	N	Y	Y
7 ***Archer***	Y	N	N	N	N	Y	Y
8 ***Brady***	Y	N	N	N	Y	Y	Y
9 Lampson	N	Y	N	Y	Y	N	N
10 Doggett	N	Y	Y	Y	Y	N	N
11 Edwards	N	Y	Y	Y	N	N	N
12 ***Granger***	Y	N	N	N	N	Y	Y
13 ***Thornberry***	Y	N	N	N	N	Y	Y
14 ***Paul***	Y	?	N	N	Y	N	Y
15 Hinojosa	N	Y	Y	N	N	N	N
16 Reyes	N	Y	Y	Y	N	N	Y
17 Stenholm	N	N	N	N	N	N	Y
18 Jackson-Lee	N	Y	Y	Y	Y	N	N
19 ***Combest***	Y	N	N	N	N	Y	Y
20 Gonzalez	?	?	?	?	?	?	?
21 ***Smith***	Y	N	N	N	N	Y	Y
22 ***DeLay***	Y	N	N	N	N	Y	Y
23 ***Bonilla***	Y	N	Y	N	N	Y	N
24 Frost	N	Y	Y	Y	N	N	N
25 Bentsen	N	Y	Y	Y	Y	N	N
26 ***Armey***	Y	N	N	N	N	Y	Y
27 Ortiz	N	Y	N	N	N	N	Y
28 Rodriguez	N	Y	Y	Y	Y	N	N
29 Green	N	Y	Y	Y	N	N	Y
30 Johnson, E.B.	N	Y	Y	Y	Y	N	N
UTAH							
1 ***Hansen***	Y	N	N	N	N	?	?
2 ***Cook***	Y	N	N	N	N	Y	Y
3 ***Cannon***	Y	N	N	N	N	Y	Y
VERMONT							
AL *Sanders*	N	Y	Y	Y	Y	N	N
VIRGINIA							
1 ***Bateman***	Y	N	N	N	N	Y	Y
2 Pickett	N	N	Y	N	N	N	Y
3 Scott	N	Y	Y	Y	Y	N	N
4 Sisisky	N	N	Y	Y	N	N	N
5 Goode	N	N	N	N	N	Y	Y
6 ***Goodlatte***	Y	N	N	N	N	Y	Y
7 ***Bliley***	Y	N	N	Y	N	Y	Y
8 Moran	N	Y	Y	Y	N	N	N
9 Boucher	N	N	N	N	N	N	N
10 ***Wolf***	Y	N	N	Y	N	Y	Y
11 ***Davis***	Y	N	N	Y	N	Y	Y
WASHINGTON							
1 ***White***	Y	N	Y	N	N	Y	Y
2 ***Metcalf***	Y	N	N	N	N	Y	Y
3 ***Smith, Linda***	Y	N	N	N	N	Y	Y
4 ***Hastings***	Y	N	N	N	N	Y	Y
5 ***Nethercutt***	Y	N	N	N	N	Y	Y
6 Dicks	N	Y	Y	Y	N	N	N
7 McDermott	N	Y	Y	Y	Y	N	N
8 ***Dunn***	Y	Y	Y	N	N	Y	Y
9 Smith, Adam	N	Y	Y	N	Y	N	N
WEST VIRGINIA							
1 Mollohan	N	Y	N	Y	N	N	Y
2 Wise	N	Y	Y	Y	N	N	Y
3 Rahall	N	Y	N	Y	N	N	N
WISCONSIN							
1 ***Neumann***	Y	N	N	N	N	Y	Y
2 ***Klug***	Y	N	Y	N	N	Y	Y
3 Kind	N	Y	Y	Y	N	N	N
4 Kleczka	N	N	Y	Y	N	N	N
5 Barrett	N	Y	Y	Y	Y	N	N
6 ***Petri***	Y	N	N	N	N	Y	Y
7 Obey	N	Y	Y	Y	Y	N	N
8 Johnson	N	Y	Y	N	Y	N	Y
9 ***Sensenbrenner***	Y	N	N	N	N	Y	Y
WYOMING							
AL ***Cubin***	Y	N	N	N	?	Y	Y

Southern states - Ala., Ark., Fla., Ga., Ky., La., Miss., N.C., Okla., S.C., Tenn., Texas, Va.

Key

Y	Voted for (yea).
#	Paired for.
+	Announced for.
N	Voted against (nay).
X	Paired against.
−	Announced against.
P	Voted "present."
C	Voted "present" to avoid possible conflict of interest.
?	Did not vote or otherwise make a position known.

Democrats **Republicans** *Independent*

413. HR 4380. Fiscal 1999 District of Columbia Appropriations/Needle Exchange Federal Funds Prohibition. Moran, D-Va., amendment to prohibit federal funds from being spent on needle exchange programs in the District of Columbia. Rejected 173-247: R 21-200; D 151-47 (ND 115-31, SD 36-16); I 1-0. Aug. 7, 1998. Aug. 7, 1998, in the session that began Aug. 6 and is recorded in the Aug. 6 Congressional Record.

414. HR 4380. Fiscal 1999 District of Columbia Appropriations/Prohibit Certain Joint Adoptions. Largent, R-Okla., amendment to prohibit joint adoptions in the District of Columbia by people who are not related by marriage or blood. Adopted 227-192: R 190-30; D 37-161 (ND 16-130, SD 21-31); I 0-1. Aug. 7, 1998. Aug. 7, 1998, in the session that began Aug. 6 and is recorded in the Aug. 6 Congressional Record.

415. HR 4380. Fiscal 1999 District of Columbia Appropriations/Penalty for Minors' Tobacco Possession. Bilbray, R-Calif., amendment to make it illegal for anyone under 18 years of age to possess any cigarette or tobacco product in the District of Columbia. A first violation would carry a penalty of up to $50. Adopted 283-138: R 207-14; D 76-123 (ND 48-99, SD 28-24); I 0-1. Aug. 7, 1998. Aug. 7, 1998, in the session that began Aug. 6 and is recorded in the Aug. 6 Congressional Record.

416. HR 4380. Fiscal 1999 District of Columbia Appropriations/Passage. Passage of the bill to appropriate $491 million in federal funds and $6.8 billion from the D.C. treasury for government operations and related activities in the District of Columbia in fiscal 1999. Passed 214-206: R 211-11; D 3-194 (ND 1-144, SD 2-50); I 0-1. Aug. 7, 1998. Aug. 7, 1998, in the session that began Aug. 6 and is recorded in the Aug. 6 Congressional Record. A "nay" was a vote in support of the president's position.

417. HR 678. Thomas Edison Commemorative Coin/Passage. Castle, R-Del., motion to suspend the rules and pass the bill to require the Treasury Department to issue up to 500,000 silver dollar coins that commemorate the 125th anniversary of the invention of the light bulb in 1879 by Thomas A. Edison. Motion agreed to 397-1: R 215-1; D 181-0 (ND 134-0, SD 47-0); I 1-0. Sept. 9, 1998. A two-thirds majority of those present and voting (266 in this case) is required for passage under suspension of the rules.

418. HR 1560. Lewis and Clark Expedition Commemorative Coin/Passage. Castle, R-Del., motion to suspend the rules and pass the bill to require the Treasury Department to issue silver dollar and half-dollar coins that commemorate the bicentennial of the 28-month expedition led by Meriwether Lewis and William Clark. Motion agreed to 398-2: R 214-2; D 183-0 (ND 136-0, SD 47-0); I 1-0. Sept. 9, 1998. A two-thirds majority of those present and voting (267 in this case) is required for passage under suspension of the rules.

419. H Res 459. Anniversary of U.S.-Korea Relations/Passage. Gilman, R-N.Y., motion to suspend the rules and pass the bill to express the sense of the House congratulating the Republic of Korea (South Korea) on the 50th anniversary of its founding. Motion agreed to 400-0: R 214-0; D 185-0 (ND 137-0, SD 48-0); I 1-0. Sept. 9, 1998. A two-thirds majority of those present and voting (267 in this case) is required for passage under suspension of the rules.

	413	414	415	416	417	418	419
ALABAMA							
1 *Callahan*	N	Y	Y	Y	Y	Y	Y
2 *Everett*	N	Y	Y	Y	Y	Y	Y
3 *Riley*	N	Y	Y	Y	Y	Y	Y
4 *Aderholt*	N	Y	Y	Y	Y	Y	Y
5 Cramer	?	?	?	?	Y	Y	Y
6 *Bachus*	N	Y	Y	Y	Y	Y	Y
7 Hilliard	Y	N	N	N	Y	Y	Y
ALASKA							
AL *Young*	N	Y	N	Y	?	?	?
ARIZONA							
1 *Salmon*	N	Y	Y	Y	Y	Y	Y
2 Pastor	Y	N	Y	N	Y	Y	Y
3 *Stump*	N	Y	Y	Y	Y	Y	Y
4 *Shadegg*	N	Y	Y	Y	Y	Y	Y
5 *Kolbe*	N	N	Y	Y	?	?	?
6 *Hayworth*	N	Y	Y	Y	Y	Y	Y
ARKANSAS							
1 Berry	Y	Y	Y	N	Y	Y	Y
2 Snyder	Y	N	N	N	Y	Y	Y
3 *Hutchinson*	N	Y	Y	Y	Y	Y	Y
4 *Dickey*	N	Y	Y	Y	Y	Y	Y
CALIFORNIA							
1 *Riggs*	N	Y	Y	Y	?	?	?
2 *Herger*	N	Y	Y	Y	Y	Y	Y
3 Fazio	Y	N	N	N	Y	Y	Y
4 *Doolittle*	N	Y	Y	Y	Y	Y	Y
5 Matsui	Y	N	N	N	Y	Y	Y
6 Woolsey	Y	N	N	N	Y	Y	Y
7 Miller	Y	N	N	N	Y	Y	Y
8 Pelosi	Y	N	N	N	Y	Y	Y
9 Lee	Y	N	N	N	Y	Y	Y
10 Tauscher	Y	N	Y	N	Y	Y	Y
11 *Pombo*	N	Y	Y	Y	Y	Y	Y
12 Lantos	Y	N	N	N	Y	Y	Y
13 Stark	?	?	?	?	Y	Y	Y
14 Eshoo	Y	N	N	N	Y	Y	Y
15 *Campbell*	N	N	N	N	Y	Y	Y
16 Lofgren	Y	N	N	N	Y	Y	Y
17 Farr	Y	N	N	N	Y	Y	Y
18 Condit	Y	N	N	N	Y	Y	Y
19 *Radanovich*	N	Y	Y	Y	Y	Y	Y
20 Dooley	Y	N	N	N	Y	Y	Y
21 *Thomas*	N	Y	Y	Y	Y	Y	Y
22 Capps, L.	Y	N	Y	N	Y	Y	Y
23 *Gallegly*	Y	Y	Y	Y	Y	Y	Y
24 Sherman	N	N	Y	N	Y	Y	Y
25 *McKeon*	N	Y	Y	Y	Y	Y	Y
26 Berman	Y	N	N	N	?	Y	Y
27 *Rogan*	N	Y	Y	Y	Y	Y	Y
28 *Dreier*	N	Y	Y	Y	Y	Y	Y
29 Waxman	Y	N	N	N	Y	Y	Y
30 Becerra	Y	N	N	N	Y	Y	Y
31 Martinez	Y	N	N	N	Y	Y	Y
32 Dixon	Y	N	N	N	?	?	Y
33 Roybal-Allard	Y	N	N	N	Y	Y	Y
34 Torres	Y	N	N	N	Y	Y	Y
35 Waters	N	N	N	?	Y	Y	Y
36 Harman	Y	N	Y	N	Y	Y	Y
37 Millender-McD.	Y	N	N	N	Y	Y	Y
38 *Horn*	N	Y	Y	Y	Y	Y	Y

	413	414	415	416	417	418	419
39 *Royce*	N	Y	Y	Y	Y	Y	Y
40 *Lewis*	N	Y	Y	Y	?	?	Y
41 *Kim*	N	Y	Y	Y	Y	Y	Y
42 Brown	Y	N	N	N	Y	Y	Y
43 *Calvert*	N	Y	Y	Y	Y	Y	Y
44 *Bono, M.*	N	Y	Y	Y	Y	Y	Y
45 *Rohrabacher*	N	Y	Y	Y	Y	Y	Y
46 Sanchez	Y	N	N	N	Y	Y	Y
47 *Cox*	N	Y	Y	Y	Y	Y	Y
48 *Packard*	−	+	+	+	Y	Y	Y
49 *Bilbray*	N	?	Y	Y	Y	Y	Y
50 Filner	N	N	N	N	Y	Y	Y
51 *Cunningham*	?	?	?	?	Y	Y	Y
52 *Hunter*	N	Y	Y	Y	Y	Y	Y
COLORADO							
1 DeGette	N	N	N	N	Y	Y	Y
2 Skaggs	Y	N	N	N	Y	Y	Y
3 *McInnis*	N	Y	Y	Y	Y	Y	Y
4 *Schaffer*	N	Y	Y	Y	Y	Y	Y
5 *Hefley*	N	Y	Y	Y	Y	Y	Y
6 *Schaefer*	N	Y	Y	Y	?	?	Y
CONNECTICUT							
1 Kennelly	Y	N	Y	N	?	?	?
2 Gejdenson	Y	N	N	N	Y	Y	Y
3 DeLauro	Y	N	N	N	Y	Y	Y
4 *Shays*	Y	N	Y	Y	Y	Y	Y
5 Maloney	Y	N	Y	N	Y	Y	Y
6 *Johnson*	Y	N	Y	N	Y	Y	Y
DELAWARE							
AL *Castle*	Y	Y	Y	N	Y	Y	Y
FLORIDA							
1 *Scarborough*	N	Y	Y	Y	Y	Y	Y
2 Boyd	Y	N	N	N	Y	Y	Y
3 Brown	Y	N	N	N	?	?	?
4 *Fowler*	N	Y	Y	Y	Y	Y	Y
5 Thurman	Y	N	N	N	Y	Y	Y
6 *Stearns*	N	Y	Y	Y	Y	Y	Y
7 *Mica*	N	Y	Y	Y	Y	Y	Y
8 *McCollum*	N	Y	Y	Y	Y	Y	Y
9 *Bilirakis*	N	Y	Y	Y	Y	Y	Y
10 *Young*	?	?	?	?	Y	Y	Y
11 Davis	Y	N	N	N	Y	Y	Y
12 *Canady*	N	Y	Y	Y	Y	Y	Y
13 *Miller*	Y	N	N	Y	Y	Y	Y
14 *Goss*	N	Y	Y	Y	Y	Y	Y
15 *Weldon*	N	Y	Y	Y	Y	Y	Y
16 *Foley*	Y	N	N	Y	Y	Y	Y
17 Meek	Y	N	N	N	?	?	Y
18 *Ros-Lehtinen*	N	Y	Y	Y	Y	Y	Y
19 Wexler	Y	N	Y	N	?	?	?
20 Deutsch	Y	N	Y	N	+	+	+
21 *Diaz-Balart*	N	Y	Y	Y	Y	Y	Y
22 *Shaw*	N	Y	Y	Y	Y	Y	Y
23 Hastings	Y	N	N	N	Y	Y	Y
GEORGIA							
1 *Kingston*	N	Y	Y	Y	Y	Y	Y
2 Bishop	Y	Y	Y	N	Y	Y	Y
3 *Collins*	N	Y	Y	Y	Y	Y	Y
4 McKinney	N	N	N	N	Y	Y	Y
5 Lewis	Y	N	N	N	Y	Y	Y
6 *Gingrich*							
7 *Barr*	N	Y	Y	Y	Y	Y	Y
8 *Chambliss*	N	Y	Y	Y	Y	Y	Y
9 *Deal*	N	Y	Y	Y	Y	Y	Y
10 *Norwood*	N	Y	Y	Y	Y	Y	Y
11 *Linder*	N	Y	Y	Y	Y	Y	Y
HAWAII							
1 Abercrombie	Y	N	N	N	Y	Y	Y
2 Mink	Y	N	N	N	Y	Y	Y
IDAHO							
1 *Chenoweth*	N	Y	Y	N	Y	Y	Y
2 *Crapo*	N	Y	Y	N	Y	Y	Y
ILLINOIS							
1 Rush	Y	N	N	N	?	?	?
2 Jackson	Y	N	N	N	Y	Y	Y
3 Lipinski	N	Y	Y	N	Y	Y	Y
4 Gutierrez	Y	N	N	N	Y	Y	Y
5 Blagojevich	Y	N	N	N	Y	Y	Y
6 *Hyde*	N	Y	Y	Y	Y	Y	Y
7 Davis	Y	N	N	N	Y	Y	Y
8 *Crane*	N	Y	Y	Y	Y	Y	Y
9 Yates	?	?	?	?	Y	Y	Y
10 *Porter*	Y	N	Y	N	Y	Y	Y
11 *Weller*	N	Y	Y	Y	Y	Y	Y
12 Costello	N	Y	Y	N	Y	Y	Y
13 *Fawell*	N	Y	Y	N	Y	Y	Y

ND Northern Democrats   SD Southern Democrats

	413	414	415	416	417	418	419
14 **Hastert**	N	Y	Y	Y	Y	Y	Y
15 **Ewing**	N	Y	Y	Y	Y	Y	Y
16 **Manzullo**	Y	Y	Y	Y	Y	Y	Y
17 Evans	Y	N	Y	N	Y	Y	Y
18 **LaHood**	Y	Y	Y	Y	Y	Y	Y
19 Poshard	N	Y	Y	N	?	?	?
20 **Shimkus**	N	Y	Y	Y	Y	Y	Y
INDIANA							
1 Visclosky	N	N	Y	N	Y	Y	Y
2 **McIntosh**	N	Y	Y	Y	Y	Y	Y
3 Roemer	N	Y	Y	N	Y	Y	Y
4 **Souder**	N	Y	Y	Y	Y	Y	Y
5 **Buyer**	N	Y	Y	Y	?	?	?
6 **Burton**	N	Y	Y	Y	Y	Y	Y
7 **Pease**	N	Y	Y	Y	Y	Y	Y
8 **Hostettler**	N	Y	Y	Y	Y	Y	Y
9 Hamilton	N	Y	Y	N	Y	Y	Y
10 Carson	N	N	N	N	Y	Y	Y
IOWA							
1 **Leach**	N	N	Y	Y	Y	Y	Y
2 **Nussle**	N	Y	Y	Y	Y	Y	Y
3 Boswell	N	N	Y	N	Y	Y	Y
4 **Ganske**	N	Y	N	Y	Y	Y	Y
5 **Latham**	N	Y	Y	Y	Y	Y	Y
KANSAS							
1 **Moran**	N	Y	Y	Y	Y	Y	Y
2 **Ryun**	N	Y	Y	Y	Y	Y	Y
3 **Snowbarger**	N	Y	Y	Y	Y	Y	Y
4 **Tiahrt**	N	Y	Y	Y	Y	Y	Y
KENTUCKY							
1 **Whitfield**	N	N	Y	Y	Y	Y	Y
2 **Lewis**	N	Y	Y	Y	Y	Y	Y
3 **Northup**	N	Y	N	Y	Y	Y	Y
4 **Bunning**	N	Y	Y	Y	Y	Y	Y
5 **Rogers**	N	Y	Y	Y	Y	Y	Y
6 Baesler	N	Y	Y	N	Y	Y	Y
LOUISIANA							
1 **Livingston**	N	Y	Y	Y	Y	Y	Y
2 Jefferson	Y	N	N	N	Y	Y	Y
3 **Tauzin**	N	Y	Y	Y	Y	Y	Y
4 **McCrery**	N	Y	Y	Y	Y	Y	Y
5 **Cooksey**	N	Y	Y	Y	Y	Y	Y
6 **Baker**	N	Y	Y	Y	Y	Y	Y
7 John	N	Y	Y	N	?	?	?
MAINE							
1 Allen	N	N	N	N	Y	Y	Y
2 Baldacci	Y	N	N	N	Y	Y	Y
MARYLAND							
1 **Gilchrest**	Y	Y	Y	Y	Y	Y	Y
2 **Ehrlich**	N	Y	Y	Y	?	?	?
3 Cardin	Y	N	Y	N	Y	Y	Y
4 Wynn	Y	N	N	N	Y	Y	Y
5 Hoyer	Y	N	Y	N	Y	Y	Y
6 **Bartlett**	N	Y	Y	Y	Y	Y	Y
7 Cummings	Y	N	N	N	Y	Y	Y
8 **Morella**	Y	N	N	N	Y	Y	Y
MASSACHUSETTS							
1 Olver	Y	N	N	N	Y	Y	Y
2 Neal	Y	N	N	N	Y	Y	Y
3 McGovern	Y	N	Y	N	Y	Y	Y
4 Frank	Y	N	N	N	Y	Y	Y
5 Meehan	Y	N	N	N	Y	Y	Y
6 Tierney	Y	N	N	N	Y	Y	Y
7 Markey	N	N	N	N	Y	Y	Y
8 Kennedy	Y	N	N	N	?	?	?
9 Moakley	?	?	?	?	?	?	?
10 Delahunt	Y	N	N	N	Y	Y	Y
MICHIGAN							
1 Stupak	Y	Y	N	N	Y	Y	Y
2 **Hoekstra**	N	Y	Y	Y	?	?	?
3 **Ehlers**	N	Y	Y	Y	Y	Y	Y
4 **Camp**	N	N	Y	Y	Y	Y	Y
5 Barcia	Y	Y	Y	N	?	?	?
6 **Upton**	Y	Y	Y	Y	Y	Y	Y
7 **Smith**	N	Y	Y	Y	Y	Y	Y
8 Stabenow	N	N	Y	N	Y	Y	Y
9 Kildee	Y	N	N	N	Y	Y	Y
10 Bonior	N	N	N	N	Y	Y	Y
11 **Knollenberg**	N	Y	Y	Y	Y	Y	Y
12 Levin	Y	N	N	N	Y	Y	Y
13 Rivers	N	N	N	N	Y	Y	Y
14 Conyers	?	?	N	N	Y	Y	Y
15 Kilpatrick	Y	N	N	N	Y	Y	Y
16 Dingell	Y	N	N	N	Y	Y	Y

	413	414	415	416	417	418	419
MINNESOTA							
1 **Gutknecht**	N	Y	Y	Y	Y	Y	Y
2 Minge	Y	Y	Y	N	Y	Y	Y
3 **Ramstad**	N	Y	Y	N	Y	Y	Y
4 Vento	Y	N	N	N	Y	Y	Y
5 Sabo	Y	N	Y	N	Y	Y	Y
6 Luther	Y	N	Y	N	Y	Y	Y
7 Peterson	Y	Y	Y	N	Y	Y	Y
8 Oberstar	Y	N	N	N	Y	Y	Y
MISSISSIPPI							
1 **Wicker**	N	Y	Y	Y	Y	Y	Y
2 Thompson	?	?	?	?	Y	Y	Y
3 **Pickering**	N	Y	Y	Y	Y	Y	Y
4 **Parker**	N	Y	Y	Y	Y	Y	Y
5 Taylor	N	Y	Y	N	Y	Y	Y
MISSOURI							
1 Clay	Y	N	N	N	Y	Y	Y
2 **Talent**	N	Y	Y	Y	Y	Y	Y
3 Gephardt	Y	N	Y	N	Y	Y	Y
4 Skelton	N	Y	Y	N	Y	Y	Y
5 McCarthy	Y	N	N	N	Y	Y	Y
6 Danner	N	N	Y	N	Y	Y	Y
7 **Blunt**	N	Y	Y	Y	Y	Y	Y
8 **Emerson**	N	Y	Y	Y	Y	Y	Y
9 **Hulshof**	N	Y	Y	Y	Y	Y	Y
MONTANA							
AL **Hill**	N	Y	Y	Y	Y	Y	Y
NEBRASKA							
1 **Bereuter**	N	Y	Y	Y	Y	Y	Y
2 **Christensen**	N	Y	Y	Y	Y	Y	Y
3 **Barrett**	N	Y	Y	Y	Y	Y	Y
NEVADA							
1 **Ensign**	Y	Y	N	Y	Y	Y	Y
2 **Gibbons**	N	Y	Y	Y	Y	Y	Y
NEW HAMPSHIRE							
1 **Sununu**	N	Y	Y	Y	Y	Y	Y
2 **Bass**	N	N	Y	Y	Y	Y	Y
NEW JERSEY							
1 Andrews	Y	N	Y	N	Y	Y	Y
2 **LoBiondo**	N	Y	Y	N	Y	Y	Y
3 **Saxton**	N	Y	Y	Y	Y	Y	Y
4 **Smith**	N	Y	Y	Y	Y	Y	Y
5 **Roukema**	N	Y	Y	Y	?	?	?
6 Pallone	Y	N	N	N	Y	Y	Y
7 **Franks**	N	N	Y	Y	Y	Y	Y
8 Pascrell	N	N	Y	?	Y	Y	Y
9 Rothman	N	N	Y	N	Y	Y	Y
10 Payne	Y	N	N	N	Y	Y	Y
11 **Frelinghuysen**	Y	N	Y	Y	Y	Y	Y
12 **Pappas**	N	Y	Y	Y	Y	Y	Y
13 Menendez	Y	N	Y	N	Y	Y	Y
NEW MEXICO							
1 **Wilson**	N	N	Y	Y	Y	Y	Y
2 **Skeen**	N	Y	N	Y	Y	Y	Y
3 **Redmond**	N	Y	Y	Y	Y	Y	Y
NEW YORK							
1 **Forbes**	N	N	Y	Y	Y	Y	Y
2 **Lazio**	N	Y	Y	Y	Y	Y	Y
3 **King**	N	Y	Y	Y	Y	Y	Y
4 McCarthy	Y	N	Y	N	Y	Y	Y
5 Ackerman	Y	N	N	N	?	?	?
6 Meeks	Y	N	N	N	Y	Y	Y
7 Manton	?	?	?	?	Y	Y	Y
8 Nadler	Y	N	N	N	Y	Y	Y
9 Schumer	Y	N	Y	N	?	?	?
10 Towns	Y	N	N	N	?	?	?
11 Owens	Y	N	N	N	Y	Y	Y
12 Velázquez	Y	N	N	N	Y	Y	Y
13 **Fossella**	N	Y	Y	Y	Y	Y	Y
14 Maloney	Y	N	Y	N	Y	Y	Y
15 Rangel	Y	N	N	N	Y	Y	Y
16 Serrano	Y	N	N	N	Y	Y	Y
17 Engel	Y	N	N	N	Y	Y	Y
18 Lowey	Y	N	Y	N	Y	Y	Y
19 **Kelly**	N	N	Y	Y	Y	Y	Y
20 **Gilman**	N	Y	Y	Y	Y	Y	Y
21 McNulty	Y	N	N	N	Y	Y	Y
22 **Solomon**	N	Y	Y	Y	Y	Y	Y
23 **Boehlert**	Y	N	Y	Y	Y	Y	Y
24 **McHugh**	N	Y	Y	N	Y	Y	Y
25 **Walsh**	N	Y	Y	Y	Y	Y	Y
26 Hinchey	N	N	N	N	Y	Y	Y
27 **Paxon**	N	Y	Y	Y	Y	Y	Y
28 Slaughter	Y	N	N	N	Y	Y	Y
29 LaFalce	Y	N	N	N	Y	Y	Y
30 **Quinn**	N	Y	Y	Y	Y	Y	Y

	413	414	415	416	417	418	419
31 **Houghton**	N	N	Y	Y	Y	Y	Y
NORTH CAROLINA							
1 Clayton	Y	N	N	N	Y	Y	Y
2 Etheridge	N	Y	N	N	Y	Y	Y
3 **Jones**	N	Y	Y	Y	Y	Y	Y
4 Price	Y	N	Y	N	Y	Y	Y
5 **Burr**	N	Y	Y	Y	Y	Y	?
6 **Coble**	N	Y	Y	Y	Y	Y	Y
7 McIntyre	N	Y	Y	Y	Y	Y	Y
8 Hefner	Y	N	N	N	Y	Y	Y
9 **Myrick**	N	Y	Y	Y	Y	Y	Y
10 **Ballenger**	N	Y	Y	Y	Y	Y	Y
11 **Taylor**	N	Y	Y	Y	Y	Y	Y
12 Watt	Y	N	N	N	Y	Y	Y
NORTH DAKOTA							
AL Pomeroy	Y	Y	N	N	Y	Y	Y
OHIO							
1 **Chabot**	N	Y	Y	Y	Y	Y	Y
2 **Portman**	N	Y	Y	Y	Y	Y	Y
3 Hall	N	Y	Y	N	Y	Y	Y
4 **Oxley**	N	Y	Y	Y	Y	Y	Y
5 **Gillmor**	N	Y	Y	Y	Y	Y	Y
6 Strickland	Y	N	N	N	Y	Y	Y
7 **Hobson**	N	N	Y	Y	Y	Y	Y
8 **Boehner**	N	Y	Y	Y	Y	N	Y
9 Kaptur	Y	N	N	N	?	Y	Y
10 Kucinich	Y	N	Y	N	Y	Y	Y
11 Stokes	N	N	N	N	Y	Y	Y
12 **Kasich**	N	Y	Y	Y	Y	Y	Y
13 Brown	Y	N	N	N	Y	Y	Y
14 Sawyer	Y	N	N	N	Y	Y	Y
15 **Pryce**	N	N	Y	Y	+	+	+
16 **Regula**	N	Y	Y	Y	Y	Y	Y
17 Traficant	N	Y	Y	Y	Y	Y	Y
18 **Ney**	N	Y	Y	Y	Y	Y	Y
19 **LaTourette**	N	N	Y	Y	Y	Y	Y
OKLAHOMA							
1 **Largent**	N	Y	Y	Y	Y	Y	Y
2 **Coburn**	N	Y	Y	Y	Y	Y	Y
3 **Watkins**	N	Y	Y	Y	Y	Y	Y
4 **Watts**	N	Y	Y	Y	Y	Y	Y
5 **Istook**	N	Y	Y	Y	Y	Y	Y
6 **Lucas**	N	Y	Y	Y	Y	Y	Y
OREGON							
1 Furse	Y	N	N	N	?	?	?
2 **Smith**	?	?	?	?	Y	Y	Y
3 Blumenauer	N	N	N	N	?	?	Y
4 DeFazio	Y	N	N	N	Y	Y	Y
5 Hooley	Y	N	Y	N	?	?	?
PENNSYLVANIA							
1 Brady	Y	N	N	N	Y	Y	Y
2 Fattah	Y	N	N	N	Y	Y	Y
3 Borski	Y	N	N	N	?	?	?
4 Klink	Y	N	N	N	Y	Y	Y
5 **Peterson**	N	Y	Y	Y	Y	Y	Y
6 Holden	Y	Y	Y	N	Y	Y	Y
7 **Weldon**	N	Y	Y	Y	Y	Y	Y
8 **Greenwood**	Y	N	N	Y	Y	Y	Y
9 **Shuster**	N	Y	Y	Y	Y	Y	Y
10 **McDade**	?	?	?	?	Y	Y	Y
11 Kanjorski	Y	N	N	N	Y	Y	Y
12 Murtha	Y	Y	N	N	Y	Y	Y
13 **Fox**	N	N	Y	Y	Y	Y	Y
14 Coyne	Y	N	N	N	Y	Y	Y
15 McHale	Y	N	N	N	Y	Y	Y
16 **Pitts**	N	Y	Y	Y	Y	Y	Y
17 **Gekas**	N	N	Y	Y	Y	Y	Y
18 Doyle	Y	N	Y	N	Y	Y	Y
19 **Goodling**	N	Y	Y	Y	Y	Y	Y
20 Mascara	Y	Y	Y	N	Y	Y	Y
21 **English**	N	Y	Y	Y	Y	Y	Y
RHODE ISLAND							
1 Kennedy	N	N	N	N	Y	Y	?
2 Weygand	N	N	N	N	Y	Y	Y
SOUTH CAROLINA							
1 **Sanford**	N	Y	Y	Y	Y	Y	Y
2 **Spence**	N	Y	Y	Y	Y	Y	Y
3 **Graham**	N	Y	Y	Y	Y	Y	?
4 **Inglis**	N	Y	Y	Y	Y	Y	Y
5 Spratt	N	Y	N	N	Y	Y	Y
6 Clyburn	Y	N	N	N	Y	Y	Y
SOUTH DAKOTA							
AL **Thune**	N	Y	Y	Y	Y	Y	Y

	413	414	415	416	417	418	419
TENNESSEE							
1 **Jenkins**	N	Y	Y	Y	Y	Y	Y
2 **Duncan**	N	Y	Y	N	Y	Y	Y
3 **Wamp**	N	Y	Y	Y	Y	Y	Y
4 **Hilleary**	N	Y	Y	Y	Y	Y	Y
5 Clement	N	Y	Y	N	Y	Y	Y
6 Gordon	N	Y	Y	N	Y	Y	Y
7 **Bryant**	N	Y	Y	Y	Y	Y	Y
8 Tanner	Y	Y	Y	N	Y	Y	Y
9 Ford	Y	Y	N	N	+	+	+
TEXAS							
1 Sandlin	Y	Y	Y	N	Y	Y	Y
2 Turner	N	Y	Y	N	Y	Y	Y
3 **Johnson, Sam**	N	Y	Y	Y	Y	Y	Y
4 Hall	N	Y	Y	N	Y	Y	Y
5 **Sessions**	N	Y	Y	Y	Y	Y	Y
6 **Barton**	N	Y	N	Y	Y	Y	Y
7 **Archer**	N	Y	Y	Y	Y	Y	Y
8 **Brady**	N	Y	Y	Y	Y	Y	Y
9 Lampson	Y	N	Y	N	?	?	?
10 Doggett	N	N	Y	N	Y	Y	Y
11 Edwards	Y	N	Y	N	Y	Y	Y
12 **Granger**	N	Y	Y	Y	Y	Y	Y
13 **Thornberry**	N	Y	Y	Y	Y	Y	Y
14 **Paul**	N	Y	N	N	N	N	Y
15 Hinojosa	Y	N	Y	N	Y	Y	Y
16 Reyes	Y	N	Y	N	Y	Y	Y
17 Stenholm	N	Y	Y	N	Y	Y	Y
18 Jackson-Lee	Y	N	N	N	Y	Y	Y
19 **Combest**	N	Y	Y	Y	Y	Y	Y
20 Gonzalez	?	?	?	?	?	?	?
21 **Smith**	N	Y	Y	Y	Y	Y	Y
22 **DeLay**	N	Y	Y	Y	Y	Y	Y
23 **Bonilla**	Y	N	N	Y	Y	Y	Y
24 Frost	Y	N	Y	N	Y	Y	Y
25 Bentsen	Y	N	N	N	Y	Y	Y
26 **Armey**	N	Y	Y	Y	Y	Y	Y
27 Ortiz	Y	Y	Y	N	Y	Y	Y
28 Rodriguez	Y	N	Y	N	Y	Y	Y
29 Green	N	N	Y	N	Y	Y	Y
30 Johnson, E.B.	Y	N	N	N	Y	Y	Y
UTAH							
1 **Hansen**	?	?	?	?	Y	Y	Y
2 **Cook**	N	Y	Y	Y	Y	Y	Y
3 **Cannon**	N	Y	Y	Y	Y	Y	Y
VERMONT							
AL *Sanders*	Y	N	N	N	Y	Y	Y
VIRGINIA							
1 **Bateman**	N	Y	Y	Y	Y	Y	Y
2 Pickett	N	Y	Y	N	Y	Y	Y
3 Scott	Y	N	N	N	Y	Y	Y
4 Sisisky	Y	Y	N	N	Y	Y	Y
5 Goode	N	Y	Y	Y	Y	Y	Y
6 **Goodlatte**	N	Y	Y	Y	Y	Y	Y
7 **Bliley**	N	Y	Y	Y	Y	Y	Y
8 Moran	Y	N	Y	N	?	Y	Y
9 Boucher	Y	N	N	N	Y	Y	Y
10 **Wolf**	N	Y	Y	Y	Y	Y	?
11 **Davis**	Y	Y	Y	Y	?	Y	Y
WASHINGTON							
1 **White**	N	Y	Y	Y	Y	Y	Y
2 **Metcalf**	N	Y	Y	Y	Y	Y	Y
3 **Smith, Linda**	N	Y	Y	Y	?	?	?
4 **Hastings**	N	Y	Y	Y	Y	Y	Y
5 **Nethercutt**	N	Y	Y	Y	Y	Y	Y
6 Dicks	Y	N	Y	N	Y	Y	Y
7 McDermott	Y	N	N	N	Y	Y	Y
8 **Dunn**	N	Y	Y	Y	Y	Y	Y
9 Smith, Adam	Y	N	Y	N	+	+	+
WEST VIRGINIA							
1 Mollohan	Y	N	N	N	Y	Y	Y
2 Wise	N	N	N	N	Y	Y	Y
3 Rahall	Y	N	N	N	Y	Y	Y
WISCONSIN							
1 **Neumann**	N	Y	Y	Y	Y	Y	Y
2 **Klug**	Y	Y	Y	Y	Y	Y	Y
3 Kind	Y	N	Y	N	Y	Y	Y
4 Kleczka	Y	N	Y	N	Y	Y	Y
5 Barrett	Y	N	N	N	Y	Y	Y
6 **Petri**	N	Y	Y	Y	Y	Y	Y
7 Obey	Y	N	N	N	Y	Y	Y
8 Johnson	N	N	Y	N	Y	Y	Y
9 **Sensenbrenner**	N	Y	Y	Y	Y	Y	Y
WYOMING							
AL **Cubin**	N	Y	Y	Y	Y	Y	Y

Southern states - Ala., Ark., Fla., Ga., Ky., La., Miss., N.C., Okla., S.C., Tenn., Texas, Va.

420. HR 2863. Migratory Bird Hunting Regulations/Passage. Passage of the bill to eliminate the current strict liability for hunters who shoot migratory birds over fields that have been baited to attract birds, and instead make it illegal to shoot such fowl if the hunter knew or should have known that the area had been baited. Passed 322-90: R 216-3; D 105-87 (ND 66-74, SD 39-13); I 1-0. Sept. 10, 1998.

421. HR 2538. Guadalupe-Hidalgo Treaty Land Claims/Passage. Passage of the bill to establish a presidential commission to make recommendations to resolve land claims in New Mexico by descendants of Mexican citizens when the treaty ending the Mexican-American War was signed in 1848. Passed 223-187: R 211-10; D 12-176 (ND 11-126, SD 1-50); I 0-1. Sept. 10, 1998.

422. HR 3892. Bilingual Education Block Grants/Federal Law Compliance. Martinez, D-Calif., amendment to the Riggs, R-Calif., amendmen that would allow school systems to receive subgrants only if they were not in violation of any state law or state constitutional provision regarding education of English language learners. The Martinez amendment would add, "except if necessary for the eligible entity to comply with Federal law (including a Federal court order)." Rejected 205-208: R 14-204; D 190-4 (ND 141-1, SD 49-3); I 1-0. Sept. 10, 1998. (Subsequently, the Riggs amendment was adopted.)

423. HR 3892. Bilingual Education Block Grants/State Law Compliance. Riggs, R-Calif., amendment to allow school systems to receive subgrants only if they were not in violation of any state law or state constitutional provision regarding education of English language learners. Adopted 230-184: R 215-5; D 15-178 (ND 4-138, SD 11-40); I 0-1. Sept. 10, 1998.

424. HR 3892. Bilingual Education Block Grants/Passage. Passage of the bill to turn existing bilingual and immigrant education programs into a block grant program and provide states and local school districts with broader discretion to determine a method of teaching for students learning English as a second language. Passed 221-189: R 207-10; D 14-178 (ND 5-136, SD 9-42); I 0-1. Sept. 10, 1998. A "nay" vote was a vote in support of the president's position.

425. H Res 525. Distribution of Starr Report/Adoption. Adoption of the resolution to provide for the release and distribution of the report from Independent Counsel Kenneth W. Starr regarding allegations of criminal offenses and other misconduct by President Clinton. Under the resolution, the Judiciary Committee will review the materials to determine whether they contain grounds for impeachment. It also requires the committee to immediately release the initial 445-page report, and release other documents to the public on Sept. 28 unless the committee votes not to release certain materials. Adopted 363-63: R 224-0; D 138-63 (ND 102-46, SD 36-17); I 1-0. Sept. 11, 1998.

426. S 2206. Federal Programs Reauthorizations/Passage. Goodling, R-Pa., motion to suspend the rules and pass the bill to reauthorize several programs, including Head Start, the Community Development Block Grant and the Low Income Home Energy Assistance Program. Motion agreed to 346-20: R 185-20; D 160-0 (ND 115-0, SD 45-0); I 1-0. Sept. 14, 1998. A two-thirds majority of those present and voting (244 in this case) is required for passage under suspension of the rules.

Key

Y	Voted for (yea).
#	Paired for.
+	Announced for.
N	Voted against (nay).
X	Paired against.
−	Announced against.
P	Voted "present."
C	Voted "present" to avoid possible conflict of interest.
?	Did not vote or otherwise make a position known.

Democrats   **Republicans**   *Independent*

	420	421	422	423	424	425	426
ALABAMA							
1 *Callahan*	Y	Y	N	Y	Y	Y	Y
2 *Everett*	Y	Y	N	Y	Y	Y	Y
3 *Riley*	Y	Y	N	Y	Y	Y	Y
4 *Aderholt*	Y	Y	N	Y	Y	Y	Y
5 Cramer	Y	N	Y	Y	Y	Y	Y
6 *Bachus*	Y	Y	N	Y	Y	Y	?
7 Hilliard	Y	N	Y	N	N	N	Y
ALASKA							
AL *Young*	?	#	?	?	?	?	Y
ARIZONA							
1 *Salmon*	Y	N	N	Y	Y	Y	Y
2 Pastor	Y	N	Y	N	N	Y	Y
3 *Stump*	Y	Y	N	Y	Y	Y	N
4 *Shadegg*	?	N	N	Y	Y	Y	Y
5 *Kolbe*	Y	Y	N	Y	Y	Y	Y
6 *Hayworth*	Y	Y	N	Y	Y	Y	Y
ARKANSAS							
1 Berry	+	X	#	X	X	Y	Y
2 Snyder	Y	N	Y	N	N	Y	Y
3 *Hutchinson*	Y	Y	N	Y	Y	Y	Y
4 *Dickey*	Y	Y	N	Y	Y	Y	Y
CALIFORNIA							
1 *Riggs*	Y	Y	N	Y	Y	Y	?
2 *Herger*	Y	Y	N	Y	Y	Y	Y
3 Fazio	Y	N	Y	N	N	Y	Y
4 *Doolittle*	Y	Y	N	Y	Y	Y	N
5 Matsui	N	N	Y	N	N	Y	Y
6 Woolsey	N	N	Y	N	N	N	Y
7 Miller	N	N	Y	N	N	N	Y
8 Pelosi	N	N	Y	N	N	N	?
9 Lee	N	N	Y	N	N	N	Y
10 Tauscher	N	N	Y	N	N	Y	Y
11 *Pombo*	Y	Y	N	Y	Y	Y	N
12 Lantos	N	N	Y	N	N	Y	Y
13 Stark	N	N	Y	N	N	N	Y
14 Eshoo	N	N	Y	N	N	Y	Y
15 *Campbell*	N	N	Y	N	N	N	Y
16 Lofgren	N	N	Y	N	N	N	Y
17 Farr	N	N	Y	N	N	N	Y
18 Condit	Y	Y	N	Y	Y	Y	Y
19 *Radanovich*	Y	Y	N	Y	Y	Y	N
20 Dooley	Y	?	Y	N	Y	Y	Y
21 *Thomas*	Y	Y	N	Y	Y	Y	Y
22 Capps, L.	Y	N	Y	N	N	N	Y
23 *Gallegly*	Y	Y	N	Y	Y	Y	Y
24 Sherman	N	N	Y	N	N	Y	Y
25 *McKeon*	Y	Y	N	Y	Y	Y	Y
26 Berman	N	N	Y	N	N	Y	Y
27 *Rogan*	Y	Y	N	Y	Y	Y	?
28 *Dreier*	Y	Y	N	Y	Y	Y	?
29 Waxman	N	N	Y	N	N	Y	Y
30 Becerra	N	N	Y	N	N	N	Y
31 Martinez	N	N	Y	N	N	N	Y
32 Dixon	N	Y	Y	N	N	N	Y
33 Roybal-Allard	N	N	Y	N	N	N	Y
34 Torres	N	N	Y	N	N	N	Y
35 Waters	N	N	Y	N	N	N	Y
36 Harman	Y	N	Y	N	N	Y	?
37 Millender-McD.	N	N	Y	N	N	N	Y
38 *Horn*							
39 *Royce*	Y	N	N	Y	Y	Y	N
40 *Lewis*	Y	N	Y	Y	Y	Y	Y
41 *Kim*	Y	Y	N	Y	Y	Y	Y
42 Brown	Y	?	Y	Y	N	N	Y
43 *Calvert*	Y	Y	N	Y	Y	Y	Y
44 *Bono, M.*	Y	Y	N	Y	Y	Y	Y
45 *Rohrabacher*	Y	N	Y	N	Y	Y	Y
46 Sanchez	Y	N	Y	N	N	Y	Y
47 *Cox*	Y	Y	N	Y	Y	Y	Y
48 *Packard*	Y	Y	N	Y	Y	Y	Y
49 *Bilbray*	Y	Y	N	Y	Y	Y	Y
50 Filner	N	N	Y	N	N	N	Y
51 *Cunningham*	Y	Y	N	Y	Y	Y	Y
52 *Hunter*	Y	Y	?	Y	Y	Y	Y
COLORADO							
1 DeGette	N	N	Y	N	N	N	Y
2 Skaggs	Y	N	Y	N	N	N	Y
3 *McInnis*	Y	Y	N	Y	Y	Y	Y
4 *Schaffer*	Y	Y	N	Y	Y	Y	Y
5 *Hefley*	Y	Y	N	Y	Y	Y	Y
6 *Schaefer*	Y	Y	N	Y	Y	Y	Y
CONNECTICUT							
1 Kennelly	?	?	?	?	?	Y	Y
2 Gejdenson	Y	N	Y	N	N	Y	Y
3 DeLauro	N	N	Y	N	N	Y	Y
4 *Shays*	N	Y	Y	N	Y	Y	Y
5 Maloney	N	N	Y	N	N	Y	+
6 *Johnson*	N	Y	Y	Y	N	Y	Y
DELAWARE							
AL *Castle*	Y	Y	N	Y	Y	Y	Y
FLORIDA							
1 *Scarborough*	Y	Y	X	#	#	?	N
2 Boyd	Y	N	Y	N	Y	N	Y
3 Brown	N	N	Y	N	N	N	?
4 *Fowler*	Y	Y	N	Y	Y	Y	Y
5 Thurman	Y	N	Y	N	Y	N	Y
6 *Stearns*	Y	Y	N	Y	Y	Y	N
7 *Mica*	Y	Y	N	Y	Y	Y	Y
8 *McCollum*	Y	Y	N	Y	Y	Y	Y
9 *Bilirakis*	Y	Y	N	Y	Y	Y	Y
10 *Young*	Y	Y	N	Y	Y	Y	?
11 Davis	Y	Y	N	Y	Y	Y	Y
12 *Canady*	Y	Y	N	Y	Y	Y	Y
13 *Miller*	Y	Y	N	Y	Y	Y	N
14 *Goss*	Y	Y	N	Y	Y	Y	−
15 *Weldon*	Y	Y	N	Y	Y	Y	Y
16 *Foley*	Y	Y	N	Y	Y	Y	Y
17 Meek	N	N	Y	N	N	N	Y
18 *Ros-Lehtinen*	Y	Y	N	Y	Y	Y	+
19 Wexler	N	N	Y	N	N	Y	Y
20 Deutsch	Y	N	Y	N	N	N	Y
21 *Diaz-Balart*	Y	Y	N	Y	Y	Y	Y
22 *Shaw*	Y	Y	N	Y	Y	Y	Y
23 Hastings	N	N	Y	N	N	N	?
GEORGIA							
1 *Kingston*	Y	Y	N	Y	Y	Y	Y
2 Bishop	Y	N	Y	N	N	Y	Y
3 *Collins*	Y	Y	N	Y	Y	Y	N
4 McKinney	N	N	Y	N	N	N	Y
5 Lewis	N	N	Y	N	N	N	?
6 *Gingrich*	Y						
7 *Barr*	Y	N	N	Y	Y	Y	?
8 *Chambliss*	Y	Y	N	Y	Y	Y	Y
9 *Deal*	Y	Y	N	Y	Y	Y	N
10 *Norwood*	Y	Y	N	Y	Y	Y	Y
11 *Linder*	Y	Y	N	Y	Y	Y	Y
HAWAII							
1 Abercrombie	N	N	Y	N	N	Y	Y
2 Mink	N	Y	Y	N	N	Y	Y
IDAHO							
1 *Chenoweth*	Y	Y	N	Y	Y	Y	Y
2 *Crapo*	Y	Y	N	Y	N	Y	+
ILLINOIS							
1 Rush	?	?	Y	N	N	N	?
2 Jackson	N	N	Y	N	N	N	Y
3 Lipinski	Y	N	Y	N	Y	Y	Y
4 Gutierrez	N	N	Y	N	N	N	Y
5 Blagojevich	N	N	Y	N	N	Y	Y
6 *Hyde*	Y	Y	N	Y	Y	Y	Y
7 Davis	N	N	Y	N	N	N	Y
8 *Crane*	Y	N	Y	Y	Y	Y	N
9 Yates	N	N	Y	N	N	N	?
10 *Porter*	Y	Y	N	Y	N	N	Y
11 *Weller*	Y	Y	N	Y	Y	Y	Y
12 Costello	Y	N	Y	N	Y	Y	Y
13 *Fawell*	Y	Y	N	Y	Y	Y	Y

ND Northern Democrats   SD Southern Democrats

	420	421	422	423	424	425	426
14 ***Hastert***	Y	Y	N	Y	Y	Y	Y
15 ***Ewing***	Y	Y	N	Y	Y	Y	Y
16 ***Manzullo***	Y	Y	N	Y	Y	Y	?
17 Evans	N	N	Y	N	N	Y	?
18 ***LaHood***	Y	?	N	Y	Y	Y	?
19 Poshard	?	?	?	?	?	?	?
20 ***Shimkus***	Y	Y	N	Y	Y	Y	Y
INDIANA							
1 Visclosky	N	Y	Y	N	N	Y	Y
2 ***McIntosh***	Y	Y	N	Y	Y	Y	N
3 Roemer	Y	N	Y	N	N	Y	Y
4 ***Souder***	Y	Y	N	Y	Y	Y	Y
5 ***Buyer***	Y	Y	N	Y	Y	Y	Y
6 ***Burton***	Y	Y	N	Y	Y	Y	Y
7 ***Pease***	Y	Y	N	Y	Y	Y	Y
8 ***Hostettler***	Y	Y	N	Y	Y	Y	Y
9 Hamilton	Y	N	Y	N	N	Y	Y
10 Carson	Y	N	Y	N	N	N	+
IOWA							
1 ***Leach***	Y	Y	Y	Y	Y	Y	Y
2 ***Nussle***	Y	Y	N	Y	?	Y	Y
3 Boswell	Y	N	Y	N	N	Y	Y
4 ***Ganske***	Y	N	N	Y	Y	Y	Y
5 ***Latham***	Y	Y	N	Y	Y	Y	Y
KANSAS							
1 ***Moran***	Y	Y	N	Y	Y	Y	Y
2 ***Ryun***	Y	Y	N	Y	Y	Y	+
3 ***Snowbarger***	Y	Y	N	Y	Y	Y	Y
4 ***Tiahrt***	Y	Y	N	Y	Y	Y	+
KENTUCKY							
1 ***Whitfield***	Y	Y	N	Y	Y	Y	Y
2 ***Lewis***	Y	Y	N	Y	Y	Y	Y
3 ***Northup***	Y	Y	N	Y	Y	Y	Y
4 ***Bunning***	Y	Y	N	Y	Y	Y	Y
5 ***Rogers***	Y	Y	N	Y	Y	Y	Y
6 Baesler	Y	N	Y	Y	Y	Y	Y
LOUISIANA							
1 ***Livingston***	Y	Y	N	Y	Y	Y	Y
2 Jefferson	Y	N	Y	N	N	N	?
3 ***Tauzin***	?	?	?	?	?	Y	?
4 ***McCrery***	Y	Y	N	Y	?	Y	Y
5 ***Cooksey***	Y	Y	N	Y	Y	Y	Y
6 ***Baker***	Y	Y	N	Y	Y	Y	Y
7 John	Y	N	Y	Y	Y	Y	Y
MAINE							
1 Allen	Y	N	Y	N	N	Y	Y
2 Baldacci	Y	N	Y	N	N	Y	Y
MARYLAND							
1 ***Gilchrest***	Y	Y	N	Y	Y	Y	Y
2 ***Ehrlich***	Y	Y	?	?	#	Y	Y
3 Cardin	N	N	Y	N	N	Y	Y
4 Wynn	N	N	Y	N	N	Y	Y
5 Hoyer	Y	N	Y	N	N	Y	Y
6 ***Bartlett***	Y	Y	N	Y	Y	Y	Y
7 Cummings	Y	N	Y	N	N	N	Y
8 ***Morella***	?	Y	Y	N	N	Y	Y
MASSACHUSETTS							
1 Olver	N	N	Y	N	N	Y	Y
2 Neal	N	N	Y	N	N	N	?
3 McGovern	N	N	?	?	X	Y	Y
4 Frank	N	N	Y	N	N	N	Y
5 Meehan	N	N	Y	N	N	N	Y
6 Tierney	N	N	Y	N	N	Y	Y
7 Markey	N	N	Y	N	N	N	Y
8 Kennedy	?	?	Y	N	N	N	?
9 Moakley	?	?	Y	N	N	Y	?
10 Delahunt	N	N	Y	N	N	N	Y
MICHIGAN							
1 Stupak	Y	N	Y	N	N	Y	Y
2 ***Hoekstra***	Y	Y	N	Y	Y	Y	Y
3 ***Ehlers***	Y	Y	N	Y	Y	Y	Y
4 ***Camp***	Y	Y	N	Y	Y	Y	Y
5 Barcia	?	?	?	?	?	?	Y
6 ***Upton***	Y	N	N	Y	Y	Y	Y
7 ***Smith***	Y	Y	N	Y	Y	Y	Y
8 Stabenow	Y	N	Y	N	N	Y	+
9 Kildee	N	N	Y	N	N	Y	Y
10 Bonior	N	N	Y	N	N	Y	Y
11 ***Knollenberg***	Y	Y	N	Y	Y	Y	Y
12 Levin	Y	N	Y	N	N	Y	Y
13 Rivers	N	N	Y	N	N	Y	Y
14 Conyers	Y	Y	Y	N	N	N	Y
15 Kilpatrick	Y	N	Y	N	N	N	+
16 Dingell	Y	?	Y	N	N	Y	?
MINNESOTA							
1 ***Gutknecht***	Y	Y	N	Y	Y	Y	Y
2 Minge	Y	N	Y	N	N	Y	+
3 ***Ramstad***	Y	N	Y	Y	N	Y	Y
4 Vento	N	N	Y	N	N	Y	Y
5 Sabo	N	N	Y	N	N	N	Y
6 Luther	Y	N	Y	N	N	Y	Y
7 Peterson	Y	N	Y	Y	Y	Y	Y
8 Oberstar	N	N	Y	N	N	Y	+
MISSISSIPPI							
1 ***Wicker***	Y	Y	N	Y	Y	Y	Y
2 Thompson	Y	N	Y	N	N	N	Y
3 ***Pickering***	Y	Y	N	Y	Y	Y	+
4 ***Parker***	Y	Y	N	Y	Y	Y	Y
5 Taylor	Y	N	Y	Y	Y	Y	Y
MISSOURI							
1 Clay	N	N	Y	N	N	N	Y
2 ***Talent***	Y	Y	N	Y	Y	Y	Y
3 Gephardt	Y	?	?	?	?	Y	Y
4 Skelton	Y	N	Y	N	N	Y	Y
5 McCarthy	Y	N	Y	N	N	Y	+
6 Danner	Y	N	Y	Y	Y	Y	?
7 ***Blunt***	Y	Y	N	Y	Y	Y	Y
8 ***Emerson***	Y	Y	N	Y	Y	Y	Y
9 ***Hulshof***	Y	Y	N	Y	Y	Y	Y
MONTANA							
AL ***Hill***	Y	Y	N	Y	Y	Y	Y
NEBRASKA							
1 ***Bereuter***	Y	Y	N	Y	Y	Y	Y
2 ***Christensen***	Y	Y	N	Y	Y	Y	Y
3 ***Barrett***	Y	Y	N	Y	Y	Y	Y
NEVADA							
1 ***Ensign***	Y	Y	N	Y	Y	Y	Y
2 ***Gibbons***	Y	Y	N	Y	Y	Y	Y
NEW HAMPSHIRE							
1 ***Sununu***	Y	Y	N	Y	Y	Y	Y
2 ***Bass***	Y	Y	N	Y	Y	Y	Y
NEW JERSEY							
1 Andrews	N	N	Y	N	N	Y	Y
2 ***LoBiondo***	Y	Y	N	Y	Y	Y	Y
3 ***Saxton***	Y	Y	N	Y	Y	Y	?
4 ***Smith***	Y	Y	N	Y	Y	Y	Y
5 ***Roukema***	Y	Y	N	Y	Y	Y	Y
6 Pallone	N	N	Y	N	N	Y	Y
7 ***Franks***	Y	Y	N	Y	Y	Y	Y
8 Pascrell	N	N	Y	N	N	Y	Y
9 Rothman	N	N	Y	N	N	Y	?
10 Payne	N	N	Y	N	N	N	Y
11 ***Frelinghuysen***	Y	Y	N	Y	Y	Y	Y
12 ***Pappas***	Y	Y	N	Y	Y	Y	Y
13 Menendez	Y	N	Y	N	N	Y	Y
NEW MEXICO							
1 ***Wilson***	Y	Y	N	Y	Y	Y	Y
2 ***Skeen***	Y	Y	Y	Y	Y	Y	Y
3 ***Redmond***	Y	Y	Y	Y	N	Y	Y
NEW YORK							
1 ***Forbes***	Y	Y	N	Y	Y	Y	Y
2 ***Lazio***	Y	Y	N	Y	Y	Y	Y
3 ***King***	Y	Y	N	Y	Y	Y	Y
4 McCarthy	Y	N	Y	N	N	Y	Y
5 Ackerman	Y	N	Y	N	N	N	?
6 Meeks	N	N	Y	N	N	N	?
7 Manton	Y	N	Y	N	N	Y	Y
8 Nadler	N	N	Y	N	N	N	?
9 Schumer	?	?	?	?	?	Y	?
10 Towns	?	?	?	?	?	N	?
11 Owens	N	N	Y	N	N	N	?
12 Velázquez	N	N	Y	N	N	N	?
13 ***Fossella***	Y	Y	N	Y	Y	Y	Y
14 Maloney	N	N	Y	N	N	Y	+
15 Rangel	Y	Y	Y	N	N	Y	?
16 Serrano	N	Y	Y	N	N	N	Y
17 Engel	?	N	Y	N	N	N	?
18 Lowey	N	N	Y	N	N	Y	?
19 ***Kelly***	Y	Y	N	Y	Y	Y	Y
20 ***Gilman***	Y	Y	N	Y	N	Y	Y
21 McNulty	N	N	Y	N	N	Y	Y
22 ***Solomon***	Y	Y	N	Y	Y	Y	Y
23 ***Boehlert***	Y	Y	N	Y	Y	Y	Y
24 ***McHugh***	Y	Y	N	Y	Y	Y	Y
25 ***Walsh***	Y	Y	N	Y	Y	Y	Y
26 Hinchey	N	N	Y	N	N	N	Y
27 ***Paxon***	?	Y	N	Y	Y	Y	Y
28 Slaughter	N	N	Y	N	N	Y	Y
29 LaFalce	N	N	Y	N	N	Y	Y
30 ***Quinn***	Y	Y	N	Y	Y	Y	Y
31 ***Houghton***	Y	Y	Y	Y	Y	Y	Y
NORTH CAROLINA							
1 Clayton	N	N	Y	N	N	N	?
2 Etheridge	Y	N	Y	–	–	Y	Y
3 ***Jones***	Y	Y	N	Y	Y	Y	Y
4 Price	Y	N	Y	N	N	Y	Y
5 ***Burr***	Y	Y	?	?	?	Y	Y
6 ***Coble***	Y	Y	N	Y	Y	Y	N
7 McIntyre	Y	N	Y	Y	Y	Y	?
8 Hefner	?	?	Y	N	N	N	Y
9 ***Myrick***	Y	Y	N	Y	Y	Y	Y
10 ***Ballenger***	Y	Y	N	Y	Y	Y	Y
11 ***Taylor***	Y	Y	N	Y	Y	Y	?
12 Watt	N	N	Y	N	N	N	?
NORTH DAKOTA							
AL Pomeroy	Y	N	Y	N	N	Y	Y
OHIO							
1 ***Chabot***	Y	Y	N	Y	Y	Y	Y
2 ***Portman***	Y	Y	N	Y	Y	Y	Y
3 Hall	Y	N	Y	N	N	Y	Y
4 ***Oxley***	Y	Y	N	N	Y	Y	Y
5 ***Gillmor***	Y	Y	N	Y	Y	Y	Y
6 Strickland	Y	N	Y	N	N	Y	Y
7 ***Hobson***	Y	Y	N	Y	Y	Y	Y
8 ***Boehner***	Y	Y	N	Y	Y	Y	Y
9 Kaptur	Y	N	Y	N	?	Y	Y
10 Kucinich	N	N	Y	N	N	Y	Y
11 Stokes	?	N	Y	N	N	N	Y
12 ***Kasich***	Y	?	N	Y	Y	Y	Y
13 Brown	N	N	Y	N	N	Y	Y
14 Sawyer	Y	N	Y	N	N	Y	Y
15 ***Pryce***	+	+	–	+	+	+	+
16 ***Regula***	Y	Y	N	Y	Y	Y	Y
17 Traficant	Y	Y	Y	Y	Y	Y	Y
18 ***Ney***	Y	Y	Y	N	N	Y	Y
19 ***LaTourette***	Y	Y	N	Y	Y	Y	Y
OKLAHOMA							
1 ***Largent***	Y	N	?	?	Y	Y	Y
2 ***Coburn***	Y	Y	N	Y	Y	Y	N
3 ***Watkins***	Y	Y	N	Y	Y	Y	Y
4 ***Watts***	Y	Y	N	Y	Y	Y	Y
5 ***Istook***	Y	Y	N	Y	Y	Y	N
6 ***Lucas***	Y	Y	N	Y	Y	Y	Y
OREGON							
1 Furse	?	?	?	?	?	?	?
2 ***Smith***	Y	Y	N	Y	Y	Y	Y
3 Blumenauer	N	N	Y	N	N	Y	?
4 DeFazio	Y	N	Y	N	N	Y	Y
5 Hooley	Y	N	Y	N	N	Y	?
PENNSYLVANIA							
1 Brady	N	N	Y	N	N	N	Y
2 Fattah	N	N	Y	N	N	N	Y
3 Borski	Y	N	Y	N	N	Y	Y
4 Klink	Y	N	Y	N	N	Y	?
5 ***Peterson***	Y	Y	N	Y	Y	Y	Y
6 Holden	Y	N	Y	N	N	Y	Y
7 ***Weldon***	Y	Y	N	Y	Y	Y	Y
8 ***Greenwood***	Y	Y	N	Y	Y	Y	Y
9 ***Shuster***	Y	Y	N	Y	Y	Y	Y
10 ***McDade***	?	?	N	Y	Y	Y	?
11 Kanjorski	Y	N	Y	N	N	Y	Y
12 Murtha	Y	N	Y	N	N	Y	Y
13 ***Fox***	Y	Y	N	Y	Y	Y	Y
14 Coyne	Y	N	Y	N	N	Y	Y
15 McHale	Y	N	Y	N	N	Y	Y
16 ***Pitts***	Y	Y	N	Y	Y	Y	Y
17 ***Gekas***	Y	Y	N	Y	Y	Y	Y
18 Doyle	Y	N	Y	N	N	Y	Y
19 ***Goodling***	Y	Y	N	Y	Y	Y	Y
20 Mascara	Y	N	Y	N	N	Y	Y
21 ***English***	Y	Y	N	Y	Y	Y	?
RHODE ISLAND							
1 Kennedy	N	N	Y	N	N	N	Y
2 Weygand	N	N	Y	N	N	Y	Y
SOUTH CAROLINA							
1 ***Sanford***	Y	N	N	Y	Y	Y	N
2 ***Spence***	Y	Y	N	Y	Y	Y	Y
3 ***Graham***	Y	Y	N	Y	Y	Y	Y
4 ***Inglis***	Y	Y	N	Y	Y	Y	Y
5 Spratt	Y	N	Y	N	N	Y	Y
6 Clyburn	N	N	Y	N	N	N	Y
SOUTH DAKOTA							
AL ***Thune***	Y	Y	N	Y	Y	Y	Y
TENNESSEE							
1 ***Jenkins***	Y	Y	N	Y	Y	+	Y
2 ***Duncan***	Y	Y	N	Y	Y	Y	N
3 ***Wamp***	Y	Y	N	Y	Y	Y	Y
4 ***Hilleary***	Y	Y	N	Y	Y	Y	Y
5 Clement	Y	N	Y	N	N	Y	Y
6 Gordon	Y	N	Y	N	Y	Y	Y
7 ***Bryant***	Y	Y	N	Y	Y	Y	Y
8 Tanner	Y	N	Y	N	N	Y	Y
9 Ford	N	N	Y	N	N	N	Y
TEXAS							
1 Sandlin	Y	N	Y	N	N	Y	Y
2 Turner	Y	N	Y	N	N	Y	Y
3 ***Johnson, Sam***	Y	Y	N	Y	Y	Y	Y
4 Hall	Y	N	N	Y	Y	Y	Y
5 ***Sessions***	Y	Y	N	Y	Y	Y	?
6 ***Barton***	Y	Y	N	Y	Y	Y	Y
7 ***Archer***	Y	Y	?	Y	Y	Y	Y
8 ***Brady***	Y	Y	N	Y	Y	Y	Y
9 Lampson	Y	N	Y	N	N	Y	Y
10 Doggett	Y	N	Y	N	N	Y	?
11 Edwards	Y	N	Y	N	N	Y	Y
12 ***Granger***	Y	Y	N	Y	Y	Y	Y
13 ***Thornberry***	Y	Y	N	Y	Y	Y	Y
14 ***Paul***	Y	Y	N	Y	N	Y	N
15 Hinojosa	Y	N	Y	N	N	Y	Y
16 Reyes	Y	N	Y	N	N	Y	Y
17 Stenholm	Y	N	Y	Y	N	Y	Y
18 Jackson-Lee	N	N	Y	N	N	N	Y
19 ***Combest***	Y	Y	N	Y	Y	Y	Y
20 Gonzalez	?	?	?	?	?	?	?
21 ***Smith***	Y	Y	N	Y	?	Y	Y
22 ***DeLay***	Y	Y	N	Y	Y	Y	N
23 ***Bonilla***	Y	Y	N	Y	Y	Y	Y
24 Frost	Y	N	Y	N	N	Y	Y
25 Bentsen	Y	N	Y	N	N	Y	Y
26 ***Armey***	Y	Y	N	Y	Y	Y	Y
27 Ortiz	Y	N	Y	N	N	Y	Y
28 Rodriguez	Y	N	Y	N	N	Y	Y
29 Green	Y	N	Y	N	N	Y	+
30 Johnson, E.B.	N	N	–	–	–	–	Y
UTAH							
1 ***Hansen***	Y	Y	N	Y	Y	Y	?
2 ***Cook***	Y	Y	N	Y	Y	Y	?
3 ***Cannon***	Y	?	N	Y	Y	Y	Y
VERMONT							
AL *Sanders*	Y	N	Y	N	N	Y	Y
VIRGINIA							
1 ***Bateman***	Y	Y	N	Y	Y	Y	Y
2 Pickett	Y	Y	N	Y	Y	Y	Y
3 Scott	Y	N	Y	N	N	N	Y
4 Sisisky	Y	?	Y	Y	N	Y	Y
5 Goode	Y	N	N	Y	Y	Y	Y
6 ***Goodlatte***	Y	N	N	Y	Y	Y	Y
7 ***Bliley***	Y	Y	N	Y	Y	Y	Y
8 Moran	N	N	Y	N	N	N	Y
9 Boucher	Y	N	Y	N	N	Y	Y
10 ***Wolf***	Y	Y	N	Y	Y	Y	Y
11 ***Davis***	Y	Y	N	Y	?	Y	Y
WASHINGTON							
1 ***White***	Y	Y	N	Y	Y	Y	Y
2 ***Metcalf***	Y	Y	N	Y	Y	Y	Y
3 ***Smith, Linda***	Y	Y	N	Y	Y	Y	Y
4 ***Hastings***	Y	Y	N	Y	Y	Y	Y
5 ***Nethercutt***	Y	Y	N	Y	Y	Y	Y
6 Dicks	Y	N	Y	N	N	Y	Y
7 McDermott	Y	N	Y	N	N	N	Y
8 ***Dunn***	?	Y	N	Y	Y	Y	Y
9 Smith, Adam	Y	N	Y	N	N	Y	Y
WEST VIRGINIA							
1 Mollohan	Y	N	Y	N	N	N	Y
2 Wise	Y	?	?	?	?	Y	Y
3 Rahall	Y	N	Y	N	N	Y	Y
WISCONSIN							
1 ***Neumann***	Y	Y	N	Y	Y	Y	Y
2 ***Klug***	Y	Y	N	Y	Y	Y	Y
3 Kind	Y	N	Y	N	N	Y	Y
4 Kleczka	Y	N	Y	N	N	Y	Y
5 Barrett	N	N	Y	N	N	Y	Y
6 ***Petri***	Y	Y	N	Y	Y	Y	Y
7 Obey	Y	N	Y	N	N	Y	Y
8 Johnson	Y	N	Y	N	N	Y	Y
9 ***Sensenbrenner***	Y	Y	N	Y	Y	Y	N
WYOMING							
AL ***Cubin***	Y	Y	N	Y	Y	Y	Y

Southern states - Ala., Ark., Fla., Ga., Ky., La., Miss., N.C., Okla., S.C., Tenn., Texas, Va.

Key

Y	Voted for (yea).
#	Paired for.
+	Announced for.
N	Voted against (nay).
X	Paired against.
−	Announced against.
P	Voted "present."
C	Voted "present" to avoid possible conflict of interest.
?	Did not vote or otherwise make a position known.

Democrats **Republicans**
Independent

427. H Con Res 304. War Crimes in Yugoslavia/Passage. Bereuter, R-Neb., motion to suspend the rules and pass the bill to express the sense of Congress that the United States should publicly declare that it considers there to be probable cause that Slobodan Milosevic, president of the Federal Republic of Yugoslavia, has committed war crimes, crimes against humanity and genocide. Motion agreed to 369-1: R 204-1; D 164-0 (ND 118-0, SD 46-0); I 1-0. Sept. 14, 1998. A two-thirds majority of those present and voting (247 in this case) is required for passage under suspension of the rules.

428. H Con Res 254. Extradition of Criminals Living in Cuba/Passage. Bereuter, R-Neb., motion to suspend the rules and pass the bill to express the sense of Congress that the government of Cuba should extradite to the United States convicted murderer Joanne Chesimard and all other individuals living in Cuba who have fled the United States to avoid prosecution or confinement for criminal offenses. Motion agreed to 371-0: R 205-0; D 165-0 (ND 119-0, SD 46-0); I 1-0. Sept. 14, 1998. A two-thirds majority of those present and voting (248 in this case) is required for passage under suspension of the rules.

429. H Con Res 185. Universal Declaration of Human Rights/Passage. Gilman, R-N.Y., motion to suspend the rules and pass the bill to express the sense of Congress, on the 50th anniversary of the signing of the Universal Declaration of Human Rights, recommitting the United States to the document's principles. Motion agreed to 370-2: R 204-2; D 165-0 (ND 119-0, SD 46-0); I 1-0. Sept. 14, 1998. A two-thirds majority of those present and voting (248 in this case) is required for passage under suspension of the rules.

430. HR 4101. Fiscal 1999 Agriculture Appropriations/Motion to Instruct/Previous Question. Coburn, R-Okla., motion to order the previous question (thus ending debate) on adoption of the Kaptur, D-Ohio, motion to instruct conferees on the fiscal 1999 Agriculture Appropriations to agree to Senate provisions providing emergency funding (with no off-setting deductions) for agricultural disaster assistance. Motion agreed to 331-66: R 154-65; D 176-1 (ND 129-0, SD 47-1); I 1-0. Sept. 15, 1998. (Subsequently, the motion to instruct was adopted by voice vote.)

431. HR 4103. Fiscal 1999 Defense Appropriations/Motion to Instruct. Obey, D-Wis., motion to instruct the House conferees to redirect funds designated for low-priority congressionally-directed projects not requested in the Defense Department budget request to high-priority military readiness projects. Motion agreed to 348-61: R 180-38; D 167-23 (ND 125-14, SD 42-9); I 1-0. Sept. 15, 1998.

432. HR 4103. Fiscal 1999 Defense Appropriations/Closed Conference. Young, R-Fla., motion to close portions of the conference to the public during consideration of national security issues. Motion agreed to 405-2: R 219-0; D 185-2 (ND 135-2, SD 50-0); I 1-0. Sept. 15, 1998.

433. HR 4328. Fiscal 1999 Transportation Appropriations/Motion to Instruct. Sabo, D-Minn., motion to instruct House conferees to disagree with a provision in the Senate bill that would allow helicopters unrestricted access to wilderness areas and national parks in Alaska. Motion agreed to 249-161: R 69-149; D 179-12 (ND 134-6, SD 45-6); I 1-0. Sept. 15, 1998.

	427	428	429	430	431	432	433
ALABAMA							
1 *Callahan*	Y	Y	Y	Y	Y	N	N
2 *Everett*	Y	Y	Y	Y	Y	Y	N
3 *Riley*	Y	Y	Y	−	Y	N	N
4 *Aderholt*	Y	Y	Y	Y	Y	N	N
5 Cramer	Y	Y	Y	Y	Y	Y	Y
6 *Bachus*	?	?	?	Y	N	N	N
7 Hilliard	Y	Y	Y	Y	Y	Y	N
ALASKA							
AL *Young*	Y	Y	Y	?	N	Y	N
ARIZONA							
1 *Salmon*	Y	Y	Y	N	Y	N	N
2 Pastor	Y	Y	Y	Y	Y	Y	Y
3 *Stump*	Y	Y	Y	N	N	N	N
4 *Shadegg*	Y	Y	Y	N	Y	N	N
5 *Kolbe*	Y	Y	Y	Y	Y	Y	Y
6 *Hayworth*	Y	Y	Y	N	Y	Y	N
ARKANSAS							
1 Berry	Y	Y	Y	Y	Y	Y	Y
2 Snyder	Y	Y	Y	Y	Y	Y	Y
3 *Hutchinson*	Y	Y	Y	Y	N	N	N
4 *Dickey*	Y	Y	Y	N	Y	Y	?
CALIFORNIA							
1 *Riggs*	?	?	?	?	?	?	?
2 *Herger*	Y	Y	Y	N	Y	N	N
3 Fazio	Y	Y	Y	Y	Y	Y	Y
4 *Doolittle*	Y	Y	Y	N	Y	N	N
5 Matsui	Y	Y	Y	Y	Y	Y	Y
6 Woolsey	Y	Y	Y	Y	Y	Y	Y
7 Miller	Y	Y	Y	Y	Y	Y	Y
8 Pelosi	?	?	?	Y	Y	Y	Y
9 Lee	Y	Y	Y	Y	Y	Y	Y
10 Tauscher	Y	Y	Y	Y	Y	Y	Y
11 *Pombo*	Y	Y	Y	N	Y	N	N
12 Lantos	Y	Y	Y	Y	Y	Y	Y
13 Stark	Y	Y	Y	Y	Y	Y	Y
14 Eshoo	Y	Y	Y	?	Y	Y	Y
15 *Campbell*	Y	Y	Y	N	Y	N	Y
16 Lofgren	Y	Y	Y	Y	Y	Y	Y
17 Farr	Y	Y	Y	Y	Y	Y	Y
18 Condit	Y	Y	Y	Y	Y	Y	Y
19 *Radanovich*	Y	Y	Y	N	Y	N	N
20 Dooley	Y	Y	Y	Y	Y	Y	Y
21 *Thomas*	Y	Y	Y	Y	Y	N	Y
22 Capps, L.	Y	Y	Y	Y	Y	Y	Y
23 *Gallegly*	Y	Y	Y	Y	Y	Y	N
24 Sherman	Y	Y	Y	Y	Y	Y	Y
25 *McKeon*	Y	Y	Y	Y	Y	N	N
26 Berman	Y	?	Y	Y	Y	Y	Y
27 *Rogan*	Y	Y	Y	Y	Y	N	N
28 *Dreier*	Y	Y	Y	Y	Y	Y	N
29 Waxman	?	?	?	Y	Y	Y	Y
30 Becerra	Y	Y	Y	Y	Y	Y	Y
31 Martinez	Y	Y	Y	Y	Y	Y	Y
32 Dixon	Y	Y	Y	Y	Y	Y	Y
33 Roybal-Allard	Y	Y	Y	Y	Y	Y	Y
34 Torres	Y	Y	Y	?	?	?	?
35 Waters	Y	Y	Y	Y	Y	N	Y
36 Harman	?	?	?	?	?	?	?
37 Millender-McD.	Y	Y	Y	Y	Y	Y	Y
38 *Horn*	Y	Y	Y	Y	Y	Y	Y

	427	428	429	430	431	432	433
39 *Royce*	Y	Y	Y	N	Y	Y	N
40 *Lewis*	Y	Y	Y	Y	Y	Y	N
41 *Kim*	Y	Y	Y	Y	Y	Y	N
42 Brown	Y	Y	Y	Y	Y	Y	Y
43 *Calvert*	Y	Y	Y	Y	Y	N	N
44 *Bono, M.*	Y	Y	Y	Y	Y	N	N
45 *Rohrabacher*	Y	Y	Y	?	Y	N	Y
46 Sanchez	Y	Y	Y	Y	Y	Y	Y
47 *Cox*	Y	Y	Y	N	Y	N	N
48 *Packard*	Y	Y	Y	Y	Y	N	N
49 *Bilbray*	Y	Y	Y	Y	Y	Y	Y
50 Filner	Y	Y	Y	Y	Y	Y	Y
51 *Cunningham*	?	Y	Y	Y	Y	N	N
52 *Hunter*	Y	Y	Y	Y	N	Y	N
COLORADO							
1 DeGette	Y	Y	Y	Y	Y	Y	Y
2 Skaggs	Y	Y	Y	Y	Y	Y	Y
3 *McInnis*	Y	Y	Y	Y	Y	Y	Y
4 *Schaffer*	Y	Y	Y	N	Y	N	Y
5 *Hefley*	Y	Y	Y	N	Y	N	N
6 *Schaefer*	Y	Y	Y	Y	Y	Y	Y
CONNECTICUT							
1 Kennelly	?	?	?	Y	Y	Y	Y
2 Gejdenson	Y	Y	Y	Y	Y	Y	Y
3 DeLauro	Y	Y	Y	Y	Y	Y	Y
4 *Shays*	Y	Y	N	Y	Y	Y	Y
5 Maloney	+	+	+	Y	Y	Y	Y
6 *Johnson*	Y	Y	Y	Y	Y	Y	Y
DELAWARE							
AL *Castle*	Y	Y	Y	Y	Y	Y	Y
FLORIDA							
1 *Scarborough*	Y	Y	N	Y	N	N	N
2 Boyd	Y	Y	Y	Y	Y	Y	Y
3 Brown	?	?	?	Y	Y	Y	Y
4 *Fowler*	Y	Y	Y	Y	Y	Y	N
5 Thurman	Y	Y	Y	Y	Y	Y	Y
6 *Stearns*	Y	Y	N	Y	Y	N	N
7 *Mica*	Y	Y	Y	Y	Y	Y	N
8 *McCollum*	Y	Y	Y	Y	Y	N	N
9 *Bilirakis*	Y	Y	Y	Y	Y	N	N
10 *Young*	?	?	?	Y	Y	Y	N
11 Davis	Y	Y	Y	Y	Y	Y	Y
12 *Canady*	Y	Y	Y	Y	Y	N	N
13 *Miller*	Y	Y	Y	Y	Y	Y	Y
14 *Goss*	+	+	+	+	−	+	−
15 *Weldon*	Y	Y	Y	N	N	Y	N
16 *Foley*	Y	Y	Y	Y	Y	Y	N
17 Meek	Y	Y	Y	Y	Y	Y	Y
18 *Ros-Lehtinen*	+	+	+	Y	Y	Y	Y
19 Wexler	Y	Y	Y	Y	Y	Y	Y
20 Deutsch	Y	Y	Y	Y	Y	Y	Y
21 *Diaz-Balart*	Y	Y	Y	Y	Y	Y	Y
22 *Shaw*	Y	Y	Y	Y	Y	Y	N
23 Hastings	?	?	?	?	Y	Y	Y
GEORGIA							
1 *Kingston*	Y	Y	Y	Y	Y	N	N
2 Bishop	Y	Y	Y	Y	Y	Y	Y
3 *Collins*	Y	Y	Y	Y	N	Y	N
4 McKinney	Y	Y	Y	Y	Y	Y	Y
5 Lewis	?	?	?	?	?	?	?
6 *Gingrich*							
7 *Barr*	?	?	?	N	N	Y	N
8 *Chambliss*	Y	Y	Y	N	Y	Y	N
9 *Deal*	Y	Y	Y	N	Y	N	N
10 *Norwood*	Y	Y	Y	N	Y	N	N
11 *Linder*	Y	Y	Y	N	Y	Y	N
HAWAII							
1 Abercrombie	Y	Y	Y	Y	Y	Y	Y
2 Mink	Y	Y	Y	?	N	Y	Y
IDAHO							
1 *Chenoweth*	Y	Y	N	Y	Y	Y	N
2 *Crapo*	+	+	+	Y	Y	Y	N
ILLINOIS							
1 Rush	?	?	?	Y	Y	Y	Y
2 Jackson	Y	Y	Y	Y	Y	Y	Y
3 Lipinski	Y	Y	Y	Y	Y	Y	Y
4 Gutierrez	Y	Y	Y	Y	Y	Y	Y
5 Blagojevich	Y	Y	Y	Y	Y	Y	Y
6 *Hyde*	Y	Y	Y	N	Y	N	N
7 Davis	Y	Y	Y	Y	Y	Y	Y
8 *Crane*	Y	Y	Y	Y	N	N	N
9 Yates	?	?	?	Y	Y	Y	Y
10 *Porter*	Y	Y	Y	Y	Y	Y	Y
11 *Weller*	Y	Y	Y	Y	Y	Y	N
12 Costello	Y	Y	Y	Y	Y	Y	Y
13 *Fawell*	Y	Y	Y	Y	Y	Y	Y

ND Northern Democrats   SD Southern Democrats

	427	428	429	430	431	432	433
14 ***Hastert***	Y	Y	Y	Y	N	Y	N
15 ***Ewing***	Y	Y	Y	N	Y	Y	Y
16 ***Manzullo***	?	?	?	N	Y	Y	N
17 Evans	Y	Y	Y	Y	Y	Y	Y
18 ***LaHood***	?	?	?	Y	N	Y	Y
19 Poshard	?	?	?	?	?	?	?
20 ***Shimkus***	Y	Y	Y	Y	Y	Y	Y
INDIANA							
1 Visclosky	Y	Y	Y	Y	N	Y	Y
2 ***McIntosh***	Y	Y	Y	N	Y	Y	N
3 Roemer	Y	Y	Y	Y	Y	Y	Y
4 ***Souder***	Y	Y	Y	Y	Y	Y	N
5 ***Buyer***	?	Y	Y	Y	N	Y	N
6 ***Burton***	Y	Y	Y	Y	Y	Y	N
7 ***Pease***	Y	Y	Y	Y	N	Y	Y
8 ***Hostettler***	Y	Y	Y	N	N	Y	N
9 Hamilton	?	Y	Y	Y	Y	Y	Y
10 Carson	+	Y	Y	Y	Y	Y	Y
IOWA							
1 ***Leach***	Y	Y	Y	N	Y	Y	Y
2 ***Nussle***	Y	Y	Y	N	Y	Y	N
3 Boswell	Y	Y	Y	Y	Y	Y	Y
4 ***Ganske***	Y	Y	Y	Y	Y	Y	N
5 ***Latham***	Y	Y	Y	N	Y	Y	N
KANSAS							
1 ***Moran***	Y	Y	Y	Y	Y	Y	N
2 ***Ryun***	Y	Y	Y	N	N	Y	N
3 ***Snowbarger***	Y	Y	Y	N	Y	Y	N
4 ***Tiahrt***	+	+	+	N	Y	Y	N
KENTUCKY							
1 ***Whitfield***	Y	Y	Y	Y	Y	Y	Y
2 ***Lewis***	Y	Y	Y	Y	Y	Y	N
3 ***Northup***	Y	Y	Y	Y	Y	Y	Y
4 ***Bunning***	Y	Y	Y	Y	Y	Y	N
5 ***Rogers***	Y	Y	Y	Y	N	Y	N
6 Baesler	Y	Y	Y	Y	Y	Y	Y
LOUISIANA							
1 ***Livingston***	Y	Y	Y	Y	Y	Y	N
2 Jefferson	?	?	?	?	Y	Y	Y
3 ***Tauzin***	?	?	?	Y	?	?	?
4 ***McCrery***	Y	Y	Y	Y	Y	Y	N
5 ***Cooksey***	Y	Y	Y	Y	Y	Y	N
6 ***Baker***	Y	Y	Y	Y	Y	Y	N
7 John	Y	Y	Y	Y	Y	Y	Y
MAINE							
1 Allen	Y	Y	Y	Y	Y	+	Y
2 Baldacci	Y	Y	Y	Y	Y	Y	Y
MARYLAND							
1 ***Gilchrest***	Y	Y	Y	Y	Y	Y	Y
2 ***Ehrlich***	Y	Y	Y	Y	Y	Y	?
3 Cardin	Y	Y	Y	Y	Y	Y	Y
4 Wynn	Y	Y	Y	?	?	?	?
5 Hoyer	Y	Y	Y	Y	Y	Y	Y
6 ***Bartlett***	Y	Y	Y	N	N	Y	N
7 Cummings	Y	Y	Y	Y	Y	Y	Y
8 ***Morella***	Y	Y	Y	?	Y	Y	Y
MASSACHUSETTS							
1 Olver	Y	Y	Y	Y	Y	Y	Y
2 Neal	?	?	?	Y	Y	Y	Y
3 McGovern	Y	Y	Y	?	Y	Y	Y
4 Frank	Y	Y	Y	Y	Y	Y	Y
5 Meehan	Y	Y	Y	Y	Y	Y	Y
6 Tierney	Y	Y	Y	?	Y	Y	Y
7 Markey	Y	Y	Y	Y	Y	Y	Y
8 Kennedy	?	?	?	?	Y	Y	Y
9 Moakley	?	?	?	Y	Y	Y	Y
10 Delahunt	Y	Y	Y	Y	Y	Y	Y
MICHIGAN							
1 Stupak	Y	Y	Y	Y	Y	Y	Y
2 ***Hoekstra***	Y	Y	Y	N	Y	Y	Y
3 ***Ehlers***	Y	Y	Y	Y	Y	Y	Y
4 ***Camp***	Y	Y	Y	Y	Y	Y	Y
5 Barcia	Y	Y	Y	Y	Y	Y	Y
6 ***Upton***	Y	Y	Y	Y	Y	Y	Y
7 ***Smith***	Y	Y	Y	N	Y	Y	Y
8 Stabenow	+	+	+	+	Y	Y	Y
9 Kildee	Y	Y	Y	Y	Y	Y	Y
10 Bonior	Y	Y	Y	Y	Y	Y	Y
11 ***Knollenberg***	Y	Y	Y	Y	Y	Y	N
12 Levin	Y	Y	Y	Y	Y	Y	Y
13 Rivers	Y	Y	Y	Y	Y	Y	Y
14 Conyers	Y	Y	Y	Y	Y	Y	Y
15 Kilpatrick	+	+	+	Y	Y	Y	Y
16 Dingell	Y	Y	Y	Y	Y	Y	Y

	427	428	429	430	431	432	433
MINNESOTA							
1 ***Gutknecht***	Y	Y	Y	Y	Y	Y	Y
2 Minge	+	+	+	Y	Y	Y	Y
3 ***Ramstad***	Y	Y	Y	Y	Y	Y	Y
4 Vento	Y	Y	Y	Y	Y	Y	Y
5 Sabo	Y	Y	Y	Y	Y	Y	Y
6 Luther	Y	Y	Y	Y	Y	Y	Y
7 Peterson	Y	Y	Y	Y	Y	Y	N
8 Oberstar	+	+	+	+	N	Y	Y
MISSISSIPPI							
1 ***Wicker***	Y	Y	Y	Y	N	Y	N
2 Thompson	Y	Y	Y	Y	Y	Y	Y
3 ***Pickering***	+	+	+	Y	Y	?	N
4 ***Parker***	Y	Y	Y	Y	Y	Y	N
5 Taylor	Y	Y	Y	Y	N	Y	Y
MISSOURI							
1 Clay	Y	Y	Y	Y	Y	Y	Y
2 ***Talent***	Y	Y	Y	Y	Y	Y	Y
3 Gephardt	Y	Y	Y	Y	Y	Y	Y
4 Skelton	Y	Y	Y	Y	N	Y	Y
5 McCarthy	Y	Y	Y	Y	Y	Y	Y
6 Danner	Y	Y	Y	Y	Y	Y	Y
7 ***Blunt***	Y	Y	Y	Y	Y	Y	N
8 ***Emerson***	Y	Y	Y	Y	Y	Y	N
9 ***Hulshof***	Y	Y	Y	Y	Y	Y	Y
MONTANA							
AL ***Hill***	Y	Y	Y	Y	Y	Y	N
NEBRASKA							
1 ***Bereuter***	Y	Y	Y	Y	Y	Y	N
2 ***Christensen***	Y	Y	Y	N	Y	Y	N
3 ***Barrett***	Y	Y	Y	Y	Y	Y	N
NEVADA							
1 ***Ensign***	Y	Y	Y	N	Y	Y	Y
2 ***Gibbons***	Y	Y	Y	Y	N	Y	N
NEW HAMPSHIRE							
1 ***Sununu***	Y	Y	Y	N	Y	Y	N
2 ***Bass***	Y	Y	Y	Y	Y	Y	Y
NEW JERSEY							
1 Andrews	Y	Y	Y	Y	Y	Y	Y
2 ***LoBiondo***	Y	Y	Y	N	Y	Y	Y
3 ***Saxton***	Y	Y	Y	Y	Y	Y	N
4 ***Smith***	Y	Y	Y	Y	Y	Y	Y
5 ***Roukema***	Y	Y	Y	N	Y	Y	Y
6 Pallone	Y	Y	Y	Y	Y	Y	Y
7 ***Franks***	Y	Y	Y	Y	Y	Y	Y
8 Pascrell	Y	Y	Y	Y	Y	Y	Y
9 Rothman	?	?	?	Y	Y	Y	Y
10 Payne	Y	Y	Y	Y	Y	Y	Y
11 ***Frelinghuysen***	Y	Y	Y	N	Y	Y	Y
12 ***Pappas***	Y	Y	Y	N	Y	Y	Y
13 Menendez	Y	Y	Y	Y	Y	Y	Y
NEW MEXICO							
1 ***Wilson***	Y	Y	Y	Y	Y	Y	Y
2 ***Skeen***	Y	Y	Y	Y	Y	Y	N
3 ***Redmond***	Y	Y	Y	Y	Y	Y	Y
NEW YORK							
1 ***Forbes***	Y	Y	Y	Y	Y	Y	Y
2 ***Lazio***	Y	Y	?	Y	Y	Y	Y
3 ***King***	Y	Y	Y	Y	N	Y	N
4 McCarthy	Y	Y	Y	Y	Y	Y	Y
5 Ackerman	?	?	?	Y	Y	Y	Y
6 Meeks	?	?	?	?	?	?	?
7 Manton	Y	Y	Y	?	?	?	?
8 Nadler	?	?	?	?	?	?	?
9 Schumer	?	?	?	?	?	?	?
10 Towns	?	?	?	?	?	?	?
11 Owens	?	?	?	?	?	?	?
12 Velázquez	?	?	?	?	?	?	?
13 ***Fossella***	Y	Y	Y	Y	N	Y	N
14 Maloney	+	+	+	Y	Y	Y	Y
15 Rangel	?	?	?	Y	Y	Y	Y
16 Serrano	Y	Y	Y	Y	Y	Y	Y
17 Engel	?	?	?	?	?	?	?
18 Lowey	?	?	?	Y	Y	?	Y
19 ***Kelly***	Y	Y	Y	Y	Y	Y	Y
20 ***Gilman***	Y	Y	Y	Y	Y	Y	Y
21 McNulty	Y	Y	Y	Y	Y	Y	Y
22 ***Solomon***	Y	Y	Y	Y	Y	Y	N
23 ***Boehlert***	Y	Y	Y	Y	Y	Y	Y
24 ***McHugh***	Y	Y	Y	Y	N	Y	Y
25 ***Walsh***	Y	Y	Y	Y	Y	Y	Y
26 Hinchey	Y	Y	Y	Y	Y	Y	Y
27 ***Paxon***	Y	Y	Y	N	Y	Y	N
28 Slaughter	Y	Y	Y	Y	N	Y	Y
29 LaFalce	Y	Y	Y	Y	Y	Y	Y
30 ***Quinn***	Y	Y	Y	Y	Y	Y	Y

	427	428	429	430	431	432	433
31 ***Houghton***	Y	Y	Y	Y	Y	Y	N
NORTH CAROLINA							
1 Clayton	?	?	?	?	?	?	?
2 Etheridge	Y	Y	Y	Y	Y	Y	Y
3 ***Jones***	Y	Y	Y	N	Y	Y	N
4 Price	Y	Y	Y	Y	Y	Y	Y
5 ***Burr***	Y	Y	Y	N	Y	Y	N
6 ***Coble***	Y	Y	Y	N	N	Y	N
7 McIntyre	?	?	?	?	?	?	?
8 Hefner	Y	Y	Y	Y	Y	Y	Y
9 ***Myrick***	Y	Y	Y	N	Y	Y	N
10 ***Ballenger***	Y	Y	Y	Y	Y	Y	N
11 ***Taylor***	?	?	?	N	N	Y	N
12 Watt	?	?	?	Y	Y	Y	Y
NORTH DAKOTA							
AL Pomeroy	Y	Y	Y	Y	Y	Y	N
OHIO							
1 ***Chabot***	Y	Y	Y	Y	Y	Y	Y
2 ***Portman***	Y	Y	Y	Y	Y	Y	N
3 Hall	Y	Y	Y	Y	Y	Y	Y
4 ***Oxley***	Y	Y	Y	Y	Y	Y	N
5 ***Gillmor***	Y	Y	Y	Y	Y	Y	Y
6 Strickland	Y	Y	Y	Y	Y	Y	Y
7 ***Hobson***	Y	Y	Y	Y	Y	Y	Y
8 ***Boehner***	Y	?	Y	Y	Y	Y	N
9 Kaptur	Y	Y	Y	Y	Y	Y	Y
10 Kucinich	P	Y	Y	Y	Y	Y	Y
11 Stokes	Y	Y	Y	Y	Y	Y	Y
12 ***Kasich***	Y	Y	Y	Y	Y	Y	N
13 Brown	Y	Y	Y	Y	Y	Y	Y
14 Sawyer	Y	Y	Y	Y	Y	Y	Y
15 ***Pryce***	+	+	+	+	+	+	+
16 ***Regula***	Y	Y	Y	Y	Y	Y	Y
17 Traficant	Y	Y	Y	Y	Y	Y	N
18 ***Ney***	Y	Y	Y	Y	Y	Y	Y
19 ***LaTourette***	Y	Y	Y	Y	Y	Y	N
OKLAHOMA							
1 ***Largent***	Y	Y	Y	N	Y	Y	N
2 ***Coburn***	Y	Y	Y	N	Y	Y	N
3 ***Watkins***	Y	Y	Y	Y	Y	Y	N
4 ***Watts***	Y	Y	Y	Y	Y	Y	N
5 ***Istook***	Y	Y	Y	N	Y	Y	N
6 ***Lucas***	Y	Y	Y	Y	Y	Y	N
OREGON							
1 Furse	Y	Y	Y	Y	Y	Y	Y
2 ***Smith***	Y	Y	Y	N	Y	Y	N
3 Blumenauer	?	?	?	Y	Y	Y	Y
4 DeFazio	Y	Y	Y	Y	Y	N	Y
5 Hooley	?	?	?	Y	Y	Y	Y
PENNSYLVANIA							
1 Brady	Y	Y	Y	Y	N	Y	Y
2 Fattah	Y	Y	Y	?	N	Y	Y
3 Borski	Y	Y	Y	Y	N	Y	Y
4 Klink	?	?	?	Y	N	Y	Y
5 ***Peterson***	Y	Y	Y	Y	Y	Y	N
6 Holden	Y	Y	Y	Y	N	Y	Y
7 ***Weldon***	Y	Y	Y	Y	Y	Y	N
8 ***Greenwood***	Y	Y	Y	N	Y	Y	Y
9 ***Shuster***	Y	Y	Y	Y	Y	Y	N
10 ***McDade***	?	?	?	Y	?	?	?
11 Kanjorski	Y	Y	Y	Y	N	Y	N
12 Murtha	Y	Y	Y	Y	N	Y	N
13 ***Fox***	Y	Y	Y	N	Y	Y	Y
14 Coyne	Y	Y	?	Y	Y	Y	Y
15 McHale	Y	Y	Y	Y	Y	Y	Y
16 ***Pitts***	Y	Y	Y	N	Y	Y	N
17 ***Gekas***	?	Y	Y	Y	N	Y	N
18 Doyle	Y	Y	Y	Y	Y	Y	Y
19 ***Goodling***	Y	Y	Y	N	N	Y	N
20 Mascara	Y	Y	Y	Y	Y	Y	Y
21 ***English***	?	?	?	Y	Y	Y	N
RHODE ISLAND							
1 Kennedy	Y	Y	Y	Y	Y	Y	Y
2 Weygand	Y	Y	Y	?	Y	Y	Y
SOUTH CAROLINA							
1 ***Sanford***	Y	Y	Y	N	Y	Y	Y
2 ***Spence***	Y	Y	Y	Y	Y	Y	N
3 ***Graham***	Y	?	Y	?	Y	Y	N
4 ***Inglis***	Y	Y	Y	Y	Y	Y	N
5 Spratt	Y	Y	Y	Y	Y	Y	Y
6 Clyburn	Y	Y	Y	Y	Y	Y	Y
SOUTH DAKOTA							
AL ***Thune***	Y	Y	Y	Y	N	Y	N

	427	428	429	430	431	432	433
TENNESSEE							
1 ***Jenkins***	Y	Y	Y	Y	Y	Y	N
2 ***Duncan***	Y	Y	Y	N	Y	Y	N
3 ***Wamp***	Y	Y	Y	N	Y	Y	N
4 ***Hilleary***	Y	Y	Y	Y	Y	Y	N
5 Clement	Y	Y	Y	Y	N	Y	Y
6 Gordon	Y	Y	Y	Y	N	Y	Y
7 ***Bryant***	Y	Y	Y	Y	Y	Y	N
8 Tanner	Y	Y	Y	Y	Y	Y	Y
9 Ford	Y	Y	Y	Y	Y	Y	Y
TEXAS							
1 Sandlin	Y	Y	Y	Y	Y	Y	Y
2 Turner	Y	Y	Y	Y	Y	+	N
3 ***Johnson, Sam***	Y	Y	Y	N	N	Y	N
4 Hall	Y	Y	Y	Y	Y	Y	N
5 ***Sessions***	?	?	?	Y	Y	Y	N
6 ***Barton***	Y	Y	Y	Y	Y	Y	N
7 ***Archer***	Y	?	Y	N	Y	Y	N
8 ***Brady***	Y	Y	Y	N	N	Y	N
9 Lampson	Y	Y	Y	Y	Y	Y	Y
10 Doggett	Y	Y	Y	Y	Y	Y	Y
11 Edwards	Y	Y	Y	Y	Y	Y	Y
12 ***Granger***	Y	Y	?	Y	Y	Y	N
13 ***Thornberry***	Y	Y	Y	Y	N	Y	N
14 ***Paul***	N	Y	N	N	Y	Y	N
15 Hinojosa	Y	Y	Y	Y	N	Y	Y
16 Reyes	Y	Y	Y	Y	N	Y	Y
17 Stenholm	Y	Y	Y	Y	Y	Y	N
18 Jackson-Lee	Y	Y	Y	Y	Y	Y	Y
19 ***Combest***	Y	Y	Y	Y	Y	Y	N
20 Gonzalez	?	?	?	?	?	?	?
21 ***Smith***	Y	Y	Y	Y	Y	Y	Y
22 ***DeLay***	Y	Y	Y	Y	?	?	?
23 ***Bonilla***	Y	Y	Y	Y	Y	Y	N
24 Frost	Y	Y	Y	Y	N	Y	Y
25 Bentsen	Y	Y	Y	Y	Y	Y	Y
26 ***Armey***	Y	Y	Y	Y	Y	Y	N
27 Ortiz	Y	Y	Y	Y	Y	Y	Y
28 Rodriguez	Y	Y	Y	Y	N	Y	N
29 Green	+	+	+	+	Y	Y	N
30 Johnson, E.B.	Y	Y	Y	Y	Y	Y	Y
UTAH							
1 ***Hansen***	?	?	?	Y	Y	Y	N
2 ***Cook***	?	?	?	Y	Y	Y	N
3 ***Cannon***	Y	Y	Y	N	Y	Y	N
VERMONT							
AL *Sanders*	Y	Y	Y	Y	Y	Y	Y
VIRGINIA							
1 ***Bateman***	Y	Y	Y	Y	N	Y	N
2 Pickett	Y	Y	Y	Y	Y	Y	Y
3 Scott	Y	Y	Y	Y	Y	Y	Y
4 Sisisky	Y	Y	Y	Y	N	Y	Y
5 Goode	Y	Y	Y	Y	N	Y	Y
6 ***Goodlatte***	Y	Y	Y	N	Y	Y	Y
7 ***Bliley***	Y	Y	Y	Y	Y	Y	N
8 Moran	Y	Y	Y	N	Y	Y	Y
9 Boucher	Y	Y	Y	Y	Y	Y	Y
10 ***Wolf***	Y	Y	Y	Y	Y	Y	Y
11 ***Davis***	Y	Y	Y	Y	?	Y	Y
WASHINGTON							
1 ***White***	Y	Y	Y	Y	Y	Y	Y
2 ***Metcalf***	Y	Y	Y	Y	Y	Y	Y
3 ***Smith, Linda***	Y	Y	Y	?	?	?	?
4 ***Hastings***	Y	Y	Y	Y	Y	Y	N
5 ***Nethercutt***	Y	Y	Y	Y	Y	Y	N
6 Dicks	Y	Y	Y	Y	Y	Y	Y
7 McDermott	Y	Y	Y	Y	Y	Y	Y
8 ***Dunn***	Y	Y	Y	Y	Y	Y	Y
9 Smith, Adam	Y	Y	Y	Y	Y	Y	Y
WEST VIRGINIA							
1 Mollohan	Y	Y	Y	Y	N	Y	Y
2 Wise	Y	?	Y	Y	Y	Y	Y
3 Rahall	Y	Y	Y	Y	Y	Y	Y
WISCONSIN							
1 ***Neumann***	Y	Y	Y	N	Y	Y	Y
2 ***Klug***	Y	Y	Y	N	Y	Y	Y
3 Kind	Y	Y	Y	Y	Y	Y	Y
4 Kleczka	Y	Y	Y	Y	Y	Y	Y
5 Barrett	Y	Y	Y	Y	Y	Y	Y
6 ***Petri***	Y	Y	Y	N	Y	Y	Y
7 Obey	Y	Y	Y	Y	Y	Y	Y
8 Johnson	Y	Y	Y	Y	Y	Y	Y
9 ***Sensenbrenner***	Y	Y	Y	N	Y	Y	Y
WYOMING							
AL ***Cubin***	Y	Y	Y	N	N	Y	N

Southern states - Ala., Ark., Fla., Ga., Ky., La., Miss., N.C., Okla., S.C., Tenn., Texas, Va.

Key

Y	Voted for (yea).
#	Paired for.
+	Announced for.
N	Voted against (nay).
X	Paired against.
–	Announced against.
P	Voted "present."
C	Voted "present" to avoid possible conflict of interest.
?	Did not vote or otherwise make a position known.

Democrats **Republicans** *Independent*

---

434. HR 4194. Fiscal 1999 VA-HUD Appropriations/Motion to Instruct. Obey, D-Wis., motion to instruct House conferees to insist on the House position providing funds for the Department of Veterans Affairs medical care account. Motion agreed to 405-1: R 216-1; D 188-0 (ND 139-0, SD 49-0); I 1-0. Sept. 15, 1998.

435. H J Res 117. Medicinal Marijuana/Passage. McCollum, R-Fla., motion to suspend the rules and pass the joint resolution that expresses the sense of Congress to oppose efforts to circumvent existing federal processes for determining the safety of Schedule I drugs, including marijuana, for medicinal use without valid scientific evidence. Motion agreed to 310-93: R 207-6; D 103-86 (ND 67-73, SD 36-13); I 0-1. Sept. 15, 1998. A two-thirds majority of those present and voting (269 in this case) is required for passage under suspension of the rules.

436. S 2073. Juvenile Crime and Missing Children Laws Amendments/Passage. Goodling, R-Pa., motion to suspend the rules and pass the bill to authorize annual grants to the National Center for Missing and Exploited Children and to make it easier for federal authorities to prosecute and try as adults juveniles ages 14 and older who commit federal violent crimes or federal drug-trafficking offenses. Motion agreed to 280-126: R 209-6; D 71-119 (ND 42-98, SD 29-21); I 0-1. Sept. 15, 1998. A two-thirds majority of those present and voting (271 in this case) is required for passage under suspension of the rules.

437. HR 4382. Mammography Standards/Passage. Bilirakis, R-Fla., motion to suspend the rules and pass the bill to reauthorize through fiscal 2002 the Mammography Quality Standards Act, which established uniform national standards for breast cancer diagnosis tests. Motion agreed to 401-1: R 212-0; D 188-1 (ND 139-1, SD 49-0); I 1-0. Sept. 15, 1998. A two-thirds majority of those present and voting (268 in this case) is required for passage under suspension of the rules.

438. HR 4300. International Drug Interdiction and Eradication/Defense Department Counter-Drug Mission. McCollum, R-Fla., amendment to express the sense of Congress that the administrative priorities for assets of the Defense Department should be revised so that the counter-drug mission of the department be second only to its war-fighting mission. Adopted 362-61: R 215-7; D 147-53 (ND 98-48, SD 49-5); I 0-1. Sept. 16, 1998.

439. HR 4300. International Drug Interdiction and Eradication/Drug Interdiction by U.S. Armed Forces. Reyes, D-Texas amendment to the Traficant, D-Ohio amendment to ban members of the armed forces from directly patrolling U.S. borders as a part of the efforts to keep illegal drugs outside of the United States. Rejected 167-256: R 21-201; D 145-55 (ND 112-34, SD 33-21); I 1-0. Sept. 16, 1998.

440. HR 4300. International Drug Interdiction and Eradication/Drug Interdiction by U.S. Armed Forces. Traficant, D-Ohio, amendment to direct the U.S. armed forces to assist in the efforts to keep illegal drugs out of the United States. The assistance could include patrolling U.S. borders. Adopted 291-133: R 202-20; D 89-112 (ND 57-90, SD 32-22); I 0-1. Sept. 16, 1998.

	434	435	436	437	438	439	440
ALABAMA							
1 *Callahan*	N	Y	Y	Y	Y	Y	N
2 *Everett*	N	Y	Y	Y	Y	Y	N
3 *Riley*	N	Y	Y	Y	Y	Y	N
4 *Aderholt*	N	Y	Y	Y	Y	Y	N
5 Cramer	N	Y	N	Y	N	N	N
6 *Bachus*	N	Y	Y	Y	Y	Y	N
7 Hilliard	Y	Y	N	Y	Y	?	?
ALASKA							
AL *Young*	N	Y	N	Y	Y	Y	Y
ARIZONA							
1 *Salmon*	N	Y	Y	Y	Y	Y	N
2 Pastor	Y	Y	N	Y	N	Y	N
3 *Stump*	N	Y	Y	Y	Y	Y	N
4 *Shadegg*	N	Y	Y	Y	Y	Y	N
5 *Kolbe*	N	Y	N	Y	N	N	N
6 *Hayworth*	N	Y	Y	Y	Y	Y	N
ARKANSAS							
1 Berry	N	Y	N	Y	Y	N	?
2 Snyder	N	Y	N	Y	N	N	N
3 *Hutchinson*	N	Y	N	Y	Y	Y	N
4 *Dickey*	N	Y	Y	Y	Y	Y	N
CALIFORNIA							
1 *Riggs*	?	?	?	?	?	?	?
2 *Herger*	N	Y	Y	Y	Y	Y	N
3 Fazio	Y	Y	?	?	N	Y	Y
4 *Doolittle*	N	Y	N	Y	Y	Y	N
5 Matsui	N	Y	N	Y	N	Y	N
6 Woolsey	Y	N	N	Y	N	Y	N
7 Miller	Y	N	N	Y	N	Y	N
8 Pelosi	Y	N	N	Y	N	Y	N
9 Lee	Y	N	N	Y	N	Y	N
10 Tauscher	N	Y	N	Y	N	Y	N
11 *Pombo*	N	Y	N	Y	Y	Y	N
12 Lantos	N	Y	?	?	N	Y	N
13 Stark	Y	N	N	Y	N	Y	N
14 Eshoo	N	Y	N	Y	N	Y	N
15 *Campbell*	Y	N	N	Y	N	Y	N
16 Lofgren	Y	N	N	Y	N	Y	N
17 Farr	Y	Y	N	Y	N	Y	N
18 Condit	N	Y	N	Y	Y	Y	Y
19 *Radanovich*	?	Y	Y	Y	Y	Y	Y
20 Dooley	N	Y	N	Y	N	Y	N
21 *Thomas*	N	Y	N	Y	Y	Y	N
22 Capps, L.	N	Y	N	Y	?	Y	N
23 *Gallegly*	N	Y	Y	Y	Y	Y	N
24 Sherman	N	Y	N	Y	Y	Y	N
25 *McKeon*	N	Y	N	Y	Y	Y	N
26 Berman	N	Y	N	Y	N	Y	N
27 *Rogan*	N	Y	N	Y	Y	Y	N
28 *Dreier*	N	Y	Y	Y	Y	Y	N
29 Waxman	N	Y	N	N	N	Y	N
30 Becerra	N	Y	N	Y	–	Y	N
31 Martinez	N	?	N	Y	N	Y	N
32 Dixon	N	Y	N	Y	N	Y	N
33 Roybal-Allard	Y	N	N	Y	N	Y	N
34 Torres	Y	N	N	Y	N	Y	N
35 Waters	Y	Y	?	?	Y	Y	N
36 Harman	N	Y	?	Y	Y	N	N
37 Millender-McD.	Y	Y	N	Y	N	Y	N
38 *Horn*	N	?	?	Y	Y	Y	Y

	434	435	436	437	438	439	440
39 *Royce*	N	Y	N	Y	?	Y	Y
40 *Lewis*	N	Y	N	Y	Y	Y	N
41 *Kim*	N	Y	N	Y	Y	Y	N
42 Brown	Y	Y	N	Y	Y	?	Y
43 *Calvert*	N	Y	Y	Y	Y	Y	N
44 *Bono, M.*	N	Y	N	Y	Y	Y	N
45 *Rohrabacher*	N	Y	Y	Y	Y	Y	N
46 Sanchez	N	Y	N	Y	N	Y	+
47 *Cox*	N	Y	N	Y	Y	Y	N
48 *Packard*	N	Y	N	Y	Y	Y	N
49 *Bilbray*	N	Y	N	Y	Y	Y	N
50 Filner	Y	N	N	Y	N	Y	N
51 *Cunningham*	N	Y	Y	Y	Y	?	Y
52 *Hunter*	N	Y	Y	Y	Y	Y	N
COLORADO							
1 DeGette	N	Y	N	Y	N	Y	N
2 Skaggs	N	N	N	Y	N	Y	N
3 *McInnis*	N	Y	Y	Y	Y	Y	N
4 *Schaffer*	N	Y	Y	Y	Y	Y	N
5 *Hefley*	N	Y	Y	Y	Y	Y	N
6 *Schaefer*	N	Y	Y	Y	Y	Y	N
CONNECTICUT							
1 Kennelly	N	Y	N	Y	Y	Y	?
2 Gejdenson	N	Y	?	?	Y	N	Y
3 DeLauro	N	Y	N	Y	N	Y	N
4 *Shays*	N	Y	Y	Y	Y	Y	Y
5 Maloney	N	Y	Y	Y	N	N	N
6 *Johnson*	N	Y	N	Y	Y	Y	Y
DELAWARE							
AL *Castle*	N	Y	N	Y	Y	N	Y
FLORIDA							
1 *Scarborough*	N	Y	Y	Y	Y	?	N
2 Boyd	N	Y	N	Y	N	N	N
3 Brown	Y	Y	N	Y	N	Y	N
4 *Fowler*	N	Y	Y	Y	Y	Y	N
5 Thurman	N	Y	N	Y	N	N	N
6 *Stearns*	N	Y	Y	Y	Y	Y	N
7 *Mica*	N	Y	Y	Y	Y	Y	N
8 *McCollum*	N	Y	Y	Y	Y	Y	N
9 *Bilirakis*	N	Y	Y	Y	Y	Y	N
10 *Young*	N	Y	N	Y	Y	Y	N
11 Davis	N	Y	N	N	N	N	N
12 *Canady*	N	Y	Y	Y	Y	Y	N
13 *Miller*	N	Y	Y	Y	Y	Y	N
14 Goss	–	+	+	+	+	+	–
15 *Weldon*	N	Y	Y	Y	Y	Y	N
16 *Foley*	N	Y	Y	Y	Y	Y	N
17 Meek	Y	Y	N	Y	Y	N	?
18 *Ros-Lehtinen*	N	Y	N	Y	Y	Y	Y
19 Wexler	N	Y	?	Y	N	N	N
20 Deutsch	N	Y	N	Y	N	N	N
21 *Diaz-Balart*	N	Y	N	Y	Y	Y	Y
22 *Shaw*	N	Y	Y	Y	Y	Y	N
23 Hastings	N	Y	N	Y	N	N	N
GEORGIA							
1 *Kingston*	N	Y	N	Y	Y	Y	N
2 Bishop	N	Y	Y	Y	Y	Y	Y
3 *Collins*	N	Y	N	Y	Y	Y	N
4 McKinney	Y	Y	N	Y	N	Y	N
5 Lewis	N	N	N	Y	N	Y	?
6 *Gingrich*	Y						
7 *Barr*	N	Y	N	Y	Y	Y	N
8 *Chambliss*	N	Y	N	Y	Y	Y	N
9 *Deal*	N	Y	Y	Y	Y	Y	N
10 *Norwood*	N	Y	N	Y	Y	Y	Y
11 *Linder*	N	Y	N	Y	Y	Y	N
HAWAII							
1 Abercrombie	Y	Y	N	Y	N	Y	N
2 Mink	Y	Y	N	Y	N	?	Y
IDAHO							
1 *Chenoweth*	N	N	N	Y	Y	Y	Y
2 *Crapo*	N	Y	N	Y	Y	Y	Y
ILLINOIS							
1 Rush	Y	N	N	Y	N	Y	N
2 Jackson	Y	N	N	Y	N	Y	N
3 Lipinski	N	Y	N	Y	Y	Y	Y
4 Gutierrez	N	Y	N	Y	?	Y	N
5 Blagojevich	N	Y	N	Y	N	Y	N
6 *Hyde*	N	Y	Y	Y	Y	Y	Y
7 Davis	Y	N	N	Y	N	Y	N
8 *Crane*	N	Y	N	Y	Y	Y	N
9 Yates	N	N	?	N	Y	N	Y
10 *Porter*	N	Y	N	Y	Y	Y	Y
11 *Weller*	N	Y	Y	Y	Y	Y	N
12 Costello	N	Y	Y	Y	Y	Y	Y
13 *Fawell*	N	Y	Y	Y	Y	Y	Y

ND Northern Democrats   **SD** Southern Democrats

	434	435	436	437	438	439	440
14 ***Hastert***	N	Y	N	Y	Y	Y	N
15 ***Ewing***	N	Y	N	Y	Y	Y	N
16 ***Manzullo***	N	Y	N	Y	Y	Y	N
17 Evans	N	Y	N	Y	Y	N	Y
18 ***LaHood***	N	Y	Y	Y	Y	Y	N
19 Poshard	?	?	?	?	?	?	?
20 ***Shimkus***	N	Y	Y	Y	Y	Y	N
INDIANA							
1 Visclosky	N	N	N	Y	Y	N	Y
2 ***McIntosh***	N	Y	Y	Y	Y	Y	N
3 Roemer	N	Y	N	Y	Y	N	N
4 ***Souder***	N	Y	Y	Y	Y	Y	Y
5 ***Buyer***	N	Y	Y	?	Y	Y	N
6 ***Burton***	N	Y	Y	Y	Y	Y	N
7 ***Pease***	N	Y	Y	Y	Y	Y	N
8 ***Hostettler***	N	Y	Y	Y	Y	Y	Y
9 Hamilton	Y	N	N	Y	Y	N	N
10 Carson	Y	N	N	Y	Y	N	Y
IOWA							
1 ***Leach***	N	Y	N	Y	Y	Y	Y
2 ***Nussle***	N	Y	Y	Y	Y	Y	N
3 Boswell	N	Y	?	Y	Y	N	N
4 ***Ganske***	N	Y	N	Y	Y	Y	Y
5 ***Latham***	N	Y	Y	Y	Y	Y	N
KANSAS							
1 ***Moran***	N	Y	N	Y	Y	Y	N
2 ***Ryun***	N	Y	Y	Y	Y	Y	N
3 ***Snowbarger***	N	Y	Y	Y	Y	Y	N
4 ***Tiahrt***	N	Y	Y	Y	Y	Y	N
KENTUCKY							
1 ***Whitfield***	N	Y	N	Y	Y	?	?
2 ***Lewis***	N	Y	N	Y	Y	Y	N
3 ***Northup***	N	Y	N	Y	Y	Y	N
4 ***Bunning***	N	Y	N	Y	Y	Y	N
5 ***Rogers***	N	Y	N	Y	Y	Y	N
6 Baesler	N	Y	N	Y	Y	N	Y
LOUISIANA							
1 ***Livingston***	N	Y	N	Y	Y	Y	N
2 Jefferson	N	Y	N	Y	Y	N	N
3 ***Tauzin***	N	Y	?	?	Y	Y	N
4 ***McCrery***	N	Y	N	Y	Y	Y	N
5 ***Cooksey***	N	Y	Y	Y	Y	Y	N
6 ***Baker***	N	Y	N	Y	Y	Y	N
7 John	N	Y	?	?	?	N	N
MAINE							
1 Allen	N	Y	N	Y	Y	N	N
2 Baldacci	N	Y	N	Y	Y	N	N
MARYLAND							
1 ***Gilchrest***	N	Y	N	Y	Y	Y	Y
2 ***Ehrlich***	N	Y	N	Y	Y	Y	Y
3 Cardin	N	Y	N	Y	Y	N	Y
4 Wynn	Y	Y	N	Y	Y	N	Y
5 Hoyer	N	Y	N	Y	Y	N	Y
6 ***Bartlett***	N	Y	Y	Y	Y	Y	?
7 Cummings	N	Y	N	Y	Y	N	Y
8 ***Morella***	N	Y	N	Y	Y	N	Y
MASSACHUSETTS							
1 Olver	Y	N	N	Y	Y	N	Y
2 Neal	N	Y	N	Y	Y	N	Y
3 McGovern	N	Y	N	Y	Y	N	Y
4 Frank	N	N	N	N	Y	N	Y
5 Meehan	N	Y	N	Y	Y	N	Y
6 Tierney	Y	Y	N	Y	Y	N	Y
7 Markey	N	Y	N	Y	Y	N	Y
8 Kennedy	N	Y	N	Y	Y	N	Y
9 Moakley	Y	Y	N	Y	Y	N	Y
10 Delahunt	N	Y	N	Y	Y	N	Y
MICHIGAN							
1 Stupak	N	Y	N	Y	Y	Y	Y
2 ***Hoekstra***	N	Y	N	Y	Y	Y	Y
3 ***Ehlers***	N	Y	Y	Y	Y	Y	Y
4 ***Camp***	N	Y	Y	Y	Y	Y	Y
5 Barcia	N	Y	N	Y	Y	Y	Y
6 ***Upton***	N	Y	Y	Y	Y	Y	Y
7 ***Smith***	N	Y	Y	Y	Y	Y	Y
8 Stabenow	Y	Y	N	Y	Y	N	Y
9 Kildee	N	Y	N	Y	Y	Y	Y
10 Bonior	Y	N	N	Y	Y	N	Y
11 ***Knollenberg***	N	Y	N	Y	Y	Y	Y
12 Levin	N	Y	N	Y	Y	N	Y
13 Rivers	Y	Y	N	Y	Y	N	Y
14 Conyers	+	N	N	N	Y	N	Y
15 Kilpatrick	Y	Y	N	Y	Y	N	Y
16 Dingell	N	Y	N	N	Y	N	Y
MINNESOTA							
1 ***Gutknecht***	N	Y	Y	Y	Y	Y	Y
2 Minge	Y	Y	N	Y	Y	N	N
3 ***Ramstad***	N	Y	N	Y	Y	N	Y
4 Vento	Y	N	N	Y	Y	N	Y
5 Sabo	Y	N	N	Y	Y	N	N
6 Luther	Y	Y	N	Y	Y	N	N
7 Peterson	N	Y	N	Y	Y	Y	Y
8 Oberstar	Y	N	N	Y	Y	Y	Y
MISSISSIPPI							
1 ***Wicker***	N	Y	N	Y	Y	Y	N
2 Thompson	Y	Y	N	Y	Y	N	Y
3 ***Pickering***	N	Y	Y	Y	Y	Y	N
4 ***Parker***	N	Y	Y	Y	Y	Y	N
5 Taylor	N	Y	Y	Y	Y	Y	N
MISSOURI							
1 Clay	Y	Y	?	?	Y	N	?
2 ***Talent***	N	Y	Y	Y	Y	Y	Y
3 Gephardt	Y	Y	N	Y	Y	N	?
4 Skelton	N	Y	N	Y	Y	N	N
5 McCarthy	Y	Y	N	Y	Y	N	Y
6 Danner	N	Y	?	?	Y	N	N
7 ***Blunt***	N	Y	?	+	Y	Y	N
8 ***Emerson***	N	Y	Y	Y	Y	Y	N
9 ***Hulshof***	N	Y	N	Y	Y	Y	N
MONTANA							
AL ***Hill***	N	Y	N	Y	Y	Y	N
NEBRASKA							
1 ***Bereuter***	N	Y	N	?	Y	N	N
2 ***Christensen***	N	Y	N	Y	Y	Y	Y
3 ***Barrett***	N	Y	N	Y	Y	Y	Y
NEVADA							
1 ***Ensign***	N	Y	N	Y	Y	Y	Y
2 ***Gibbons***	N	Y	Y	Y	Y	Y	N
NEW HAMPSHIRE							
1 ***Sununu***	N	Y	N	Y	Y	Y	Y
2 ***Bass***	N	Y	N	Y	Y	Y	Y
NEW JERSEY							
1 Andrews	N	Y	N	Y	Y	N	Y
2 ***LoBiondo***	N	Y	Y	Y	Y	Y	Y
3 ***Saxton***	N	Y	N	Y	Y	Y	N
4 ***Smith***	N	Y	N	Y	Y	Y	Y
5 ***Roukema***	N	Y	Y	Y	Y	N	Y
6 Pallone	N	Y	N	Y	Y	N	Y
7 ***Franks***	N	Y	Y	Y	Y	Y	Y
8 Pascrell	N	Y	N	Y	Y	N	Y
9 Rothman	N	Y	N	Y	Y	N	Y
10 Payne	Y	N	N	Y	Y	N	Y
11 ***Frelinghuysen***	N	Y	N	Y	Y	Y	Y
12 ***Pappas***	N	Y	Y	Y	Y	Y	Y
13 Menendez	N	Y	N	Y	Y	N	Y
NEW MEXICO							
1 ***Wilson***	N	Y	N	Y	Y	Y	N
2 ***Skeen***	N	Y	N	Y	Y	Y	N
3 ***Redmond***	N	Y	N	Y	Y	Y	N
NEW YORK							
1 ***Forbes***	N	Y	N	Y	?	Y	N
2 ***Lazio***	N	Y	N	Y	Y	Y	Y
3 ***King***	N	Y	N	Y	Y	Y	–
4 McCarthy	N	Y	N	Y	Y	N	Y
5 Ackerman	N	Y	N	Y	Y	N	Y
6 Meeks	?	?	?	?	Y	N	Y
7 Manton	N	Y	N	Y	Y	Y	Y
8 Nadler	Y	N	N	N	Y	N	N
9 Schumer	?	?	?	?	?	?	?
10 Towns	?	?	?	?	Y	N	Y
11 Owens	Y	N	N	Y	Y	N	Y
12 Velázquez	Y	N	N	Y	Y	N	Y
13 ***Fossella***	N	Y	Y	Y	Y	Y	Y
14 Maloney	N	Y	N	Y	Y	N	Y
15 Rangel	N	Y	N	Y	Y	N	Y
16 Serrano	N	Y	N	Y	Y	N	Y
17 Engel	N	Y	N	Y	Y	N	Y
18 Lowey	Y	Y	N	Y	Y	N	Y
19 ***Kelly***	N	Y	N	Y	Y	Y	Y
20 ***Gilman***	N	Y	Y	Y	Y	Y	Y
21 McNulty	N	Y	N	Y	Y	N	Y
22 ***Solomon***	N	Y	Y	Y	Y	Y	N
23 ***Boehlert***	N	Y	N	Y	Y	Y	Y
24 ***McHugh***	?	?	Y	Y	Y	Y	Y
25 ***Walsh***	N	Y	Y	Y	Y	Y	Y
26 Hinchey	Y	Y	N	Y	Y	N	Y
27 ***Paxon***	N	Y	Y	Y	Y	Y	N
28 Slaughter	N	Y	N	Y	Y	N	Y
29 LaFalce	N	Y	N	Y	Y	N	Y
30 ***Quinn***	N	Y	Y	Y	Y	Y	N
31 ***Houghton***	N	Y	N	Y	Y	Y	Y
NORTH CAROLINA							
1 Clayton	Y	Y	?	Y	Y	N	Y
2 Etheridge	N	Y	N	Y	Y	N	Y
3 ***Jones***	N	Y	Y	Y	Y	Y	Y
4 Price	N	Y	N	Y	Y	N	Y
5 ***Burr***	N	Y	Y	Y	Y	Y	Y
6 ***Coble***	N	Y	Y	Y	Y	Y	Y
7 McIntyre	N	Y	Y	Y	Y	Y	Y
8 Hefner	N	Y	?	?	?	N	Y
9 ***Myrick***	N	Y	Y	Y	Y	Y	+
10 ***Ballenger***	N	Y	Y	Y	Y	Y	N
11 ***Taylor***	N	Y	Y	Y	Y	Y	N
12 Watt	Y	N	N	Y	Y	N	Y
NORTH DAKOTA							
AL Pomeroy	N	Y	N	Y	Y	N	N
OHIO							
1 ***Chabot***	N	Y	Y	Y	Y	Y	N
2 ***Portman***	N	Y	N	Y	Y	Y	N
3 Hall	N	Y	N	Y	Y	N	Y
4 ***Oxley***	N	Y	N	Y	Y	Y	N
5 ***Gillmor***	N	Y	N	Y	Y	Y	N
6 Strickland	N	Y	N	Y	Y	N	Y
7 ***Hobson***	N	Y	N	Y	Y	Y	N
8 ***Boehner***	N	Y	N	Y	Y	Y	N
9 Kaptur	?	Y	N	Y	Y	N	N
10 Kucinich	N	Y	N	Y	Y	Y	Y
11 Stokes	Y	Y	?	?	?	N	Y
12 ***Kasich***	N	Y	N	Y	Y	Y	N
13 Brown	N	Y	N	Y	Y	N	Y
14 Sawyer	N	Y	N	Y	Y	N	Y
15 ***Pryce***	–	+	–	+	+	+	+
16 ***Regula***	N	Y	N	Y	Y	Y	N
17 Traficant	N	Y	Y	Y	Y	Y	N
18 ***Ney***	N	Y	N	Y	Y	Y	Y
19 ***LaTourette***	N	Y	N	Y	Y	Y	N
OKLAHOMA							
1 ***Largent***	N	Y	Y	Y	Y	Y	N
2 ***Coburn***	N	Y	Y	Y	Y	Y	N
3 ***Watkins***	N	Y	Y	Y	Y	Y	N
4 ***Watts***	N	Y	N	Y	Y	Y	N
5 ***Istook***	N	Y	Y	Y	Y	Y	N
6 ***Lucas***	N	Y	N	Y	Y	Y	N
OREGON							
1 Furse	Y	Y	N	Y	Y	N	Y
2 ***Smith***	N	Y	N	Y	Y	Y	N
3 Blumenauer	N	Y	N	Y	Y	N	Y
4 DeFazio	Y	N	N	Y	Y	N	Y
5 Hooley	N	Y	N	Y	Y	N	Y
PENNSYLVANIA							
1 Brady	Y	Y	N	Y	Y	N	N
2 Fattah	Y	Y	N	Y	Y	N	Y
3 Borski	N	Y	N	Y	Y	N	Y
4 Klink	N	Y	N	Y	Y	N	Y
5 ***Peterson***	N	Y	?	Y	Y	Y	N
6 Holden	N	Y	N	Y	Y	Y	Y
7 ***Weldon***	N	Y	N	Y	Y	Y	Y
8 ***Greenwood***	N	Y	N	Y	Y	Y	N
9 ***Shuster***	N	Y	N	Y	Y	Y	N
10 ***McDade***	N	Y	N	Y	Y	Y	Y
11 Kanjorski	N	Y	N	Y	Y	N	N
12 Murtha	N	Y	N	Y	Y	N	N
13 ***Fox***	N	Y	Y	Y	Y	Y	Y
14 Coyne	N	Y	N	Y	Y	N	Y
15 McHale	N	Y	N	Y	Y	N	Y
16 ***Pitts***	N	Y	N	Y	Y	Y	Y
17 ***Gekas***	N	Y	N	Y	Y	Y	N
18 Doyle	N	Y	N	Y	Y	Y	Y
19 ***Goodling***	N	Y	Y	Y	Y	Y	N
20 Mascara	N	Y	N	Y	Y	Y	Y
21 ***English***	N	Y	N	Y	Y	Y	Y
RHODE ISLAND							
1 Kennedy	N	Y	N	Y	Y	N	Y
2 Weygand	N	Y	N	Y	Y	N	Y
SOUTH CAROLINA							
1 ***Sanford***	N	N	Y	Y	Y	Y	N
2 ***Spence***	N	Y	Y	Y	Y	Y	N
3 ***Graham***	N	Y	Y	Y	Y	Y	N
4 ***Inglis***	N	Y	Y	Y	Y	Y	N
5 Spratt	N	Y	N	Y	Y	N	N
6 Clyburn	Y	Y	?	?	Y	N	Y
SOUTH DAKOTA							
AL ***Thune***	N	Y	Y	Y	Y	Y	N
TENNESSEE							
1 ***Jenkins***	N	Y	Y	Y	Y	Y	N
2 ***Duncan***	N	Y	Y	Y	Y	Y	Y
3 ***Wamp***	N	Y	Y	Y	Y	Y	N
4 ***Hilleary***	N	Y	Y	Y	Y	Y	Y
5 Clement	N	Y	N	Y	Y	N	N
6 Gordon	N	Y	N	Y	Y	N	N
7 ***Bryant***	N	Y	Y	Y	Y	Y	N
8 Tanner	N	Y	N	Y	Y	N	N
9 Ford	Y	Y	N	Y	Y	N	Y
TEXAS							
1 Sandlin	N	Y	N	Y	Y	N	N
2 Turner	N	Y	Y	Y	Y	N	N
3 ***Johnson, Sam***	N	Y	N	Y	Y	Y	N
4 Hall	N	Y	Y	Y	Y	Y	Y
5 ***Sessions***	N	Y	Y	Y	Y	Y	N
6 ***Barton***	N	Y	Y	Y	Y	Y	N
7 ***Archer***	N	Y	N	Y	Y	Y	N
8 ***Brady***	N	Y	?	?	Y	+	N
9 Lampson	N	Y	N	Y	Y	N	N
10 Doggett	Y	Y	N	Y	Y	N	Y
11 Edwards	N	Y	N	Y	Y	N	N
12 ***Granger***	N	Y	Y	Y	Y	Y	N
13 ***Thornberry***	N	Y	N	Y	Y	Y	N
14 ***Paul***	Y	N	N	N	Y	?	Y
15 Hinojosa	Y	Y	N	Y	Y	N	Y
16 Reyes	N	N	N	Y	Y	N	N
17 Stenholm	N	Y	Y	Y	Y	N	N
18 Jackson-Lee	Y	N	N	Y	Y	N	N
19 ***Combest***	N	Y	Y	Y	Y	Y	N
20 Gonzalez	?	?	?	?	?	?	?
21 ***Smith***	N	Y	Y	Y	Y	Y	N
22 ***DeLay***	N	Y	N	Y	Y	Y	N
23 ***Bonilla***	N	Y	N	Y	Y	Y	N
24 Frost	N	Y	N	Y	Y	N	N
25 Bentsen	N	Y	N	Y	Y	N	N
26 ***Armey***	N	Y	N	Y	Y	Y	N
27 Ortiz	N	Y	N	Y	Y	N	N
28 Rodriguez	N	Y	N	Y	Y	N	N
29 Green	N	Y	N	Y	Y	N	N
30 Johnson, E.B.	N	Y	N	Y	Y	N	?
UTAH							
1 ***Hansen***	N	Y	Y	Y	Y	Y	N
2 ***Cook***	N	Y	Y	Y	Y	Y	Y
3 ***Cannon***	N	Y	Y	Y	Y	Y	N
VERMONT							
AL *Sanders*	Y	N	N	Y	Y	N	Y
VIRGINIA							
1 ***Bateman***	N	Y	?	?	Y	Y	N
2 Pickett	N	Y	N	Y	Y	N	N
3 Scott	Y	N	N	N	Y	N	Y
4 Sisisky	N	Y	N	Y	Y	N	Y
5 Goode	N	Y	Y	Y	Y	Y	Y
6 ***Goodlatte***	N	Y	N	Y	Y	Y	N
7 ***Bliley***	N	Y	N	Y	Y	Y	Y
8 Moran	Y	N	N	Y	Y	N	Y
9 Boucher	N	Y	N	Y	Y	N	Y
10 ***Wolf***	N	Y	N	Y	Y	Y	Y
11 ***Davis***	N	Y	N	Y	Y	Y	Y
WASHINGTON							
1 ***White***	N	Y	Y	Y	Y	Y	N
2 ***Metcalf***	N	Y	Y	Y	?	Y	N
3 ***Smith, Linda***	?	?	Y	Y	Y	Y	Y
4 ***Hastings***	N	Y	N	Y	Y	Y	N
5 ***Nethercutt***	N	Y	Y	Y	Y	Y	N
6 Dicks	N	Y	?	?	Y	N	Y
7 McDermott	Y	N	N	Y	Y	N	Y
8 ***Dunn***	N	Y	Y	Y	Y	Y	N
9 Smith, Adam	N	Y	N	Y	Y	N	Y
WEST VIRGINIA							
1 Mollohan	N	Y	N	Y	Y	Y	Y
2 Wise	N	Y	N	Y	Y	N	N
3 Rahall	N	Y	N	Y	Y	Y	Y
WISCONSIN							
1 ***Neumann***	N	Y	Y	Y	Y	Y	Y
2 ***Klug***	N	Y	N	Y	Y	N	N
3 Kind	N	Y	N	Y	Y	N	Y
4 Kleczka	Y	Y	N	Y	Y	N	Y
5 Barrett	Y	Y	N	Y	Y	N	Y
6 ***Petri***	N	Y	N	Y	Y	Y	N
7 Obey	Y	N	N	N	Y	N	Y
8 Johnson	N	Y	N	Y	Y	N	Y
9 ***Sensenbrenner***	N	Y	N	Y	Y	Y	Y
WYOMING							
AL ***Cubin***	N	Y	N	Y	Y	Y	Y

Southern states - Ala., Ark., Fla., Ga., Ky., La., Miss., N.C., Okla., S.C., Tenn., Texas, Va.

Key

Y	Voted for (yea).
#	Paired for.
+	Announced for.
N	Voted against (nay).
X	Paired against.
–	Announced against.
P	Voted "present."
C	Voted "present" to avoid possible conflict of interest.
?	Did not vote or otherwise make a position known.

Democrats   *Republicans*
Independent

441. HR 4300. International Drug Interdiction and Eradication/Military Assistance. Waters, D-Calif., amendment to strike the bill's authorization for funding for direct military assistance for Colombia and Mexico. Rejected 67-354: R 1-220; D 65-134 (ND 51-94, SD 14-40); I 1-0. Sept. 16, 1998.

442. HR 4300. International Drug Interdiction and Eradication/Passage. Passage of the bill to authorize $2.3 billion through fiscal 2001 for a variety of programs to strengthen narcotics interdiction and eradication programs in Central and South America. Passed 384-39: R 219-3; D 165-35 (ND 117-29, SD 48-6); I 0-1. Sept. 16, 1998.

443. HR 4550. Drug Abuse Prevention and Treatment Programs/Drug Testing for Federal Employees. Taylor, D-Miss., amendment to require all federal employees to submit to random, unannounced drug tests. Rejected 123-281: R 113-105; D 10-175 (ND 3-133, SD 7-42); I 0-1. Sept. 16, 1998.

444. HR 4550. Drug Abuse Prevention and Treatment Programs/Passage. Passage of the bill to establish numerous new programs to help reduce the demand for illegal drugs in the United States, and to improve drug prevention and treatment programs. Passed 396-9: R 216-1; D 179-8 (ND 130-7, SD 49-1); I 1-0. Sept. 16, 1998.

445. H J Res 128. Fiscal 1999 Continuing Appropriations/Passage. Passage of the joint resolution to provide continuing appropriations through Oct. 9 for fiscal 1999 spending bills not yet enacted. The continuing resolution sets spending levels at fiscal 1998 spending levels and prohibits new initiatives and projects. Passed 421-0: R 221-0; D 199-0 (ND 147-0, SD 52-0); I 1-0. Sept. 17, 1998.

446. HR 4569. Fiscal 1999 Foreign Operations Appropriations/Rule. Adoption of the rule (H Res 542) to provide for floor consideration of the bill to provide $12.5 billion for foreign aid and export assistance. Adopted 229-188: R 211-8; D 18-179 (ND 13-131, SD 5-48); I 0-1. Sept. 17, 1998.

447. HR 4569. Fiscal 1999 Foreign Operations Appropriations/U.S. Assistance to Azerbaijan. Porter, R-Ill., amendment to eliminate a provision in the bill that repeals the Freedom Support Act, which prohibits U.S. assistance to Azerbaijan. Adopted 231-182: R 88-131; D 142-51 (ND 121-23, SD 21-28); I 1-0. Sept. 17, 1998.

	441	442	443	444	445	446	447
ALABAMA							
1 *Callahan*	N	Y	Y	Y	Y	Y	N
2 *Everett*	N	Y	Y	Y	Y	Y	N
3 *Riley*	N	Y	Y	Y	Y	Y	N
4 *Aderholt*	N	Y	Y	Y	Y	Y	N
5 Cramer	N	Y	N	Y	Y	N	N
6 *Bachus*	N	Y	Y	Y	Y	Y	N
7 Hilliard	Y	Y	N	Y	Y	?	?
ALASKA							
AL *Young*	N	Y	N	Y	Y	Y	Y
ARIZONA							
1 *Salmon*	N	Y	Y	Y	Y	Y	N
2 Pastor	Y	Y	N	Y	Y	N	Y
3 *Stump*	N	Y	Y	Y	Y	Y	N
4 *Shadegg*	N	Y	Y	Y	Y	Y	N
5 *Kolbe*	N	Y	N	Y	Y	Y	N
6 *Hayworth*	N	Y	Y	Y	Y	Y	Y
ARKANSAS							
1 Berry	N	Y	N	Y	Y	N	?
2 Snyder	N	Y	N	Y	Y	N	N
3 *Hutchinson*	N	Y	Y	Y	Y	Y	N
4 *Dickey*	N	Y	Y	Y	Y	Y	N
CALIFORNIA							
1 *Riggs*	?	?	?	?	?	?	?
2 *Herger*	N	Y	Y	Y	Y	Y	N
3 Fazio	Y	Y	?	?	?	N	Y
4 *Doolittle*	N	Y	N	Y	Y	Y	Y
5 Matsui	N	Y	N	Y	Y	N	Y
6 Woolsey	Y	N	N	Y	Y	N	Y
7 Miller	Y	N	N	Y	Y	N	Y
8 Pelosi	Y	N	N	Y	Y	N	Y
9 Lee	Y	N	N	Y	Y	N	Y
10 Tauscher	N	Y	N	Y	Y	N	N
11 *Pombo*	N	Y	N	Y	Y	Y	N
12 Lantos	N	Y	?	?	Y	N	Y
13 Stark	Y	N	N	Y	Y	N	Y
14 Eshoo	N	Y	N	Y	Y	N	Y
15 *Campbell*	N	Y	N	Y	Y	N	N
16 Lofgren	N	Y	N	Y	Y	N	Y
17 Farr	Y	Y	N	Y	Y	N	Y
18 Condit	N	Y	Y	Y	Y	N	Y
19 *Radanovich*	?	Y	Y	Y	Y	Y	N
20 Dooley	N	Y	N	Y	Y	N	Y
21 *Thomas*	N	Y	N	Y	Y	Y	N
22 Capps, L.	N	Y	N	Y	Y	?	Y
23 *Gallegly*	N	Y	Y	Y	Y	Y	N
24 Sherman	N	Y	N	Y	Y	N	Y
25 *McKeon*	N	Y	N	Y	Y	Y	Y
26 Berman	N	Y	N	Y	Y	N	Y
27 *Rogan*	N	Y	N	Y	Y	Y	Y
28 *Dreier*	N	Y	N	Y	Y	Y	Y
29 Waxman	N	Y	N	Y	N	Y	N
30 Becerra	N	Y	N	Y	Y	–	Y
31 Martinez	N	Y	N	Y	N	N	N
32 Dixon	N	Y	N	Y	Y	N	Y
33 Roybal-Allard	N	Y	N	Y	Y	N	Y
34 Torres	Y	N	N	Y	Y	N	Y
35 Waters	Y	Y	?	?	Y	N	Y
36 Harman	N	Y	?	?	Y	N	N
37 Millender-McD.	Y	Y	N	Y	Y	N	Y
38 *Horn*	N	?	?	?	Y	N	Y

	441	442	443	444	445	446	447
39 *Royce*	N	Y	N	Y	?	Y	Y
40 *Lewis*	N	Y	N	Y	Y	Y	N
41 *Kim*	N	Y	N	Y	Y	Y	Y
42 Brown	N	Y	N	Y	Y	?	Y
43 *Calvert*	N	Y	N	Y	Y	Y	N
44 *Bono, M.*	N	Y	N	Y	Y	Y	Y
45 *Rohrabacher*	N	Y	N	Y	Y	Y	N
46 Sanchez	N	Y	N	Y	Y	N	+
47 *Cox*	N	Y	N	Y	Y	Y	Y
48 *Packard*	N	Y	N	Y	Y	Y	N
49 *Bilbray*	N	Y	Y	Y	Y	Y	N
50 Filner	Y	N	N	Y	Y	N	Y
51 *Cunningham*	N	Y	N	Y	Y	?	Y
52 *Hunter*	N	Y	Y	Y	Y	Y	Y
COLORADO							
1 DeGette	N	Y	N	Y	Y	N	Y
2 Skaggs	N	N	N	Y	Y	N	Y
3 *McInnis*	N	Y	N	Y	Y	Y	N
4 *Schaffer*	N	Y	Y	Y	Y	Y	N
5 *Hefley*	N	Y	Y	Y	Y	Y	N
6 *Schaefer*	N	Y	Y	Y	Y	Y	N
CONNECTICUT							
1 Kennelly	N	Y	N	Y	Y	N	?
2 Gejdenson	N	Y	?	?	Y	N	Y
3 DeLauro	N	Y	N	Y	N	N	Y
4 *Shays*	N	Y	Y	Y	Y	Y	Y
5 Maloney	N	Y	N	Y	Y	N	N
6 *Johnson*	N	Y	N	Y	Y	Y	Y
DELAWARE							
AL *Castle*	N	Y	N	Y	N	N	Y
FLORIDA							
1 *Scarborough*	N	Y	Y	Y	Y	?	N
2 Boyd	N	Y	N	Y	N	N	N
3 Brown	Y	Y	N	Y	N	N	Y
4 *Fowler*	N	Y	N	Y	Y	Y	N
5 Thurman	N	Y	N	Y	N	N	N
6 *Stearns*	N	Y	Y	Y	Y	Y	N
7 *Mica*	N	Y	Y	Y	Y	Y	Y
8 *McCollum*	N	Y	Y	Y	Y	Y	Y
9 *Bilirakis*	N	Y	Y	Y	Y	Y	Y
10 *Young*	N	Y	N	Y	Y	Y	N
11 Davis	N	Y	N	Y	N	N	N
12 *Canady*	N	Y	Y	Y	Y	Y	Y
13 *Miller*	N	Y	Y	Y	Y	Y	N
14 *Goss*	–	+	+	+	+	+	–
15 *Weldon*	N	Y	Y	Y	Y	Y	N
16 *Foley*	N	Y	Y	Y	Y	Y	N
17 Meek	Y	Y	N	Y	N	?	?
18 *Ros-Lehtinen*	N	Y	N	Y	Y	Y	Y
19 Wexler	N	Y	?	?	N	N	N
20 Deutsch	N	Y	N	Y	N	N	N
21 *Diaz-Balart*	N	Y	N	Y	Y	Y	Y
22 *Shaw*	N	Y	Y	Y	Y	Y	N
23 Hastings	N	Y	N	Y	N	N	N
GEORGIA							
1 *Kingston*	N	Y	N	Y	Y	Y	N
2 Bishop	N	Y	Y	Y	Y	Y	Y
3 *Collins*	N	Y	N	Y	Y	Y	N
4 McKinney	Y	Y	N	Y	N	Y	Y
5 Lewis	N	N	N	Y	N	?	Y
6 *Gingrich*			Y				
7 *Barr*	N	Y	N	Y	Y	Y	N
8 *Chambliss*	N	Y	Y	Y	Y	Y	N
9 *Deal*	N	Y	Y	Y	Y	Y	N
10 *Norwood*	N	Y	N	Y	Y	Y	N
11 *Linder*	N	Y	N	Y	Y	Y	N
HAWAII							
1 Abercrombie	Y	Y	N	Y	Y	N	Y
2 Mink	Y	Y	N	Y	Y	?	Y
IDAHO							
1 *Chenoweth*	N	N	Y	Y	Y	Y	Y
2 *Crapo*	N	Y	N	Y	Y	Y	Y
ILLINOIS							
1 Rush	N	Y	N	Y	Y	N	?
2 Jackson	Y	N	N	Y	Y	N	Y
3 Lipinski	N	Y	N	Y	N	Y	N
4 Gutierrez	N	Y	N	Y	Y	?	Y
5 Blagojevich	N	Y	N	Y	N	N	Y
6 *Hyde*	N	Y	N	Y	Y	Y	Y
7 Davis	N	N	N	Y	N	N	Y
8 *Crane*	N	Y	N	Y	Y	Y	N
9 Yates	N	N	?	?	N	Y	N
10 *Porter*	N	Y	N	Y	Y	Y	Y
11 *Weller*	N	Y	N	Y	Y	Y	N
12 Costello	N	Y	Y	Y	Y	Y	N
13 *Fawell*	N	Y	Y	Y	Y	Y	Y

ND Northern Democrats   SD Southern Democrats

Southern states - Ala., Ark., Fla., Ga., Ky., La., Miss., N.C., Okla., S.C., Tenn., Texas, Va.

Key

Y	Voted for (yea).
#	Paired for.
+	Announced for.
N	Voted against (nay).
X	Paired against.
−	Announced against.
P	Voted "present."
C	Voted "present" to avoid possible conflict of interest.
?	Did not vote or otherwise make a position known.

Democrats   **Republicans**   *Independent*

---

448. HR 4569. Fiscal 1999 Foreign Operations Appropriations/School of the Americas Funding. Kennedy, D-Mass., amendment to bar any funds from being made available for programs at the U.S. Army School of the Americas located at Fort Benning, Ga. Rejected 201-212: R 49-171; D 151-41 (ND 122-18, SD 29-23); I 1-0. Sept. 17, 1998.

449. HR 4569. Fiscal 1999 Foreign Operations Appropriations/Passage. Passage of the bill to provide $12.5 billion for foreign aid and export assistance. The measure also provides $3.4 billion in credits for the International Monetary Fund (IMF). Passed 255-161: R 186-34; D 69-126 (ND 49-94, SD 20-32); I 0-1. Sept. 17, 1998.

450. HR 3248. Education Block Grants/Native Hawaiian Education Act. Mink, D-Hawaii, amendment to eliminate the bill's repeal of the Native Hawaiian Education Act. Rejected 200-207: R 8-207; D 191-0 (ND 139-0, SD 52-0); I 1-0. Sept. 18, 1998.

451. HR 3248. Education Block Grants/Class Size Reduction Substitute. Martinez, D-Calif., substitute amendment to strike the bill's text and substitute provisions that establish a program intended to reduce class size in grades 1 through 3 to an average of 18 students per class. Rejected 190-215: R 5-211; D 184-4 (ND 135-0, SD 49-4); I 1-0. Sept. 18, 1998.

452. HR 3248. Education Block Grants/Passage. Passage of the bill to repeal 31 elementary and secondary education programs and establish a block grant program in their place. Programs affected would include Goals 2000, School to Work, and Eisenhower Professional Development State Grants. Passed 212-198: R 207-11; D 5-186 (ND 1-137, SD 4-49); I 0-1. Sept. 18, 1998.

453. H Res 545. Impeachment of Kenneth W. Starr/Motion to Table. LaHood, R-Ill., motion to table (kill) the Hastings, D-Fla., privileged resolution to impeach Independent Counsel Kenneth W. Starr for "high crimes and misdemeanors." Motion agreed to 340-71: R 215-0; D 125-71 (ND 92-50, SD 33-21); I 0-0. Sept. 23, 1998.

454. H Res 144. National Lewis and Clark Bicentennial Council/Passage. Chenoweth, R-Idaho, motion to suspend the rules and pass the bill to express its support of the National Lewis and Clark Bicentennial Council and the commemorative activities that it is planning for the bicentennial. Motion agreed to 416-0: R 218-0; D 198-0 (ND 144-0, SD 54-0); I 0-0. Sept. 23, 1998. A two-thirds majority of those present and voting (278 in this case) is required for passage under suspension of the rules.

	448	449	450	451	452	453	454
ALABAMA							
1 *Callahan*	N	Y	N	N	Y	Y	Y
2 *Everett*	N	Y	N	N	Y	Y	Y
3 *Riley*	N	Y	N	N	Y	Y	Y
4 *Aderholt*	N	Y	N	N	Y	Y	Y
5 Cramer	?	Y	N	Y	N	Y	Y
6 *Bachus*	N	Y	N	N	Y	Y	Y
7 Hilliard	Y	N	?	Y	N	N	Y
ALASKA							
AL *Young*	N	Y	Y	N	N	Y	Y
ARIZONA							
1 *Salmon*	Y	Y	N	N	Y	Y	Y
2 Pastor	Y	N	Y	Y	N	N	Y
3 *Stump*	N	N	N	N	Y	Y	Y
4 *Shadegg*	N	Y	N	N	Y	Y	Y
5 *Kolbe*	N	Y	N	N	Y	Y	Y
6 *Hayworth*	N	Y	N	N	Y	Y	Y
ARKANSAS							
1 Berry	N	N	Y	Y	N	Y	Y
2 Snyder	N	N	Y	Y	N	Y	Y
3 *Hutchinson*	N	Y	−	N	Y	Y	Y
4 *Dickey*	N	Y	N	N	Y	Y	Y
CALIFORNIA							
1 *Riggs*	?	?	?	?	?	?	?
2 *Herger*	N	N	N	N	Y	Y	Y
3 Fazio	Y	N	Y	Y	N	Y	Y
4 *Doolittle*	N	N	N	N	Y	Y	Y
5 Matsui	Y	N	Y	Y	N	Y	Y
6 Woolsey	Y	N	Y	Y	N	Y	Y
7 Miller	Y	N	?	?	?	Y	Y
8 Pelosi	Y	N	Y	Y	N	N	Y
9 Lee	Y	N	Y	Y	N	N	Y
10 Tauscher	+	N	Y	Y	N	Y	Y
11 *Pombo*	N	N	N	N	Y	Y	Y
12 Lantos	Y	Y	Y	Y	N	Y	Y
13 Stark	Y	N	Y	Y	N	Y	Y
14 Eshoo	Y	N	Y	Y	N	Y	Y
15 *Campbell*	N	N	N	N	Y	N	Y
16 Lofgren	Y	N	Y	Y	N	+	Y
17 Farr	Y	N	Y	Y	N	N	Y
18 Condit	N	N	Y	?	N	Y	Y
19 *Radanovich*	N	Y	N	N	Y	Y	?
20 Dooley	Y	Y	Y	Y	N	Y	Y
21 *Thomas*	N	Y	N	N	Y	Y	Y
22 Capps, L.	Y	N	Y	Y	N	Y	Y
23 *Gallegly*	N	Y	N	Y	Y	Y	Y
24 Sherman	Y	Y	Y	Y	N	Y	Y
25 *McKeon*	N	Y	N	N	Y	Y	Y
26 Berman	Y	Y	Y	Y	N	Y	Y
27 *Rogan*	N	N	N	N	Y	Y	Y
28 *Dreier*	N	Y	N	N	Y	Y	Y
29 Waxman	Y	Y	Y	Y	N	Y	Y
30 Becerra	Y	N	Y	?	N	Y	Y
31 Martinez	N	N	Y	Y	N	Y	Y
32 Dixon	Y	Y	Y	Y	N	Y	Y
33 Roybal-Allard	Y	N	Y	Y	N	Y	Y
34 Torres	Y	N	?	?	?	?	?
35 Waters	Y	N	Y	Y	N	Y	Y
36 Harman	Y	Y	Y	Y	N	Y	Y
37 Millender-McD.	Y	N	Y	Y	N	Y	?
38 *Horn*	N	Y	N	Y	Y	Y	Y

	448	449	450	451	452	453	454
39 *Royce*	N	N	N	Y	Y	Y	Y
40 *Lewis*	N	Y	N	N	Y	Y	Y
41 *Kim*	N	Y	N	Y	Y	Y	Y
42 Brown	N	Y	Y	Y	?	N	Y
43 *Calvert*	N	Y	N	N	Y	Y	Y
44 *Bono, M.*	N	Y	N	N	Y	Y	Y
45 *Rohrabacher*	N	N	N	N	Y	Y	Y
46 Sanchez	+	−	+	+	−	Y	Y
47 *Cox*	N	Y	?	?	Y	Y	Y
48 *Packard*	N	Y	N	N	Y	Y	Y
49 *Bilbray*	N	Y	N	N	N	Y	Y
50 Filner	Y	N	Y	Y	N	N	Y
51 *Cunningham*	N	N	N	N	Y	Y	Y
52 *Hunter*	N	Y	N	?	Y	?	Y
COLORADO							
1 DeGette	Y	N	Y	Y	N	Y	Y
2 Skaggs	Y	N	Y	Y	N	Y	Y
3 *McInnis*	N	Y	N	N	Y	Y	Y
4 *Schaffer*	Y	N	N	N	Y	Y	Y
5 *Hefley*	N	N	N	N	Y	Y	Y
6 *Schaefer*	N	Y	N	N	Y	Y	Y
CONNECTICUT							
1 Kennelly	?	?	?	#	X	?	?
2 Gejdenson	Y	N	Y	N	Y	Y	Y
3 DeLauro	Y	N	Y	Y	N	Y	Y
4 *Shays*	Y	Y	N	Y	Y	Y	Y
5 Maloney	Y	N	Y	Y	N	Y	Y
6 *Johnson*	Y	Y	N	N	N	Y	Y
DELAWARE							
AL *Castle*	N	N	N	N	Y	Y	Y
FLORIDA							
1 *Scarborough*	Y	?	N	N	Y	Y	Y
2 Boyd	N	Y	N	N	Y	Y	Y
3 Brown	Y	N	Y	N	N	Y	Y
4 *Fowler*	N	Y	N	N	Y	Y	Y
5 Thurman	Y	Y	Y	Y	N	Y	Y
6 *Stearns*	N	N	N	N	Y	Y	Y
7 *Mica*	N	Y	X	X	#	Y	Y
8 *McCollum*	N	Y	?	N	Y	Y	Y
9 *Bilirakis*	N	Y	N	N	Y	Y	Y
10 *Young*	N	N	N	N	Y	Y	Y
11 Davis	N	?	Y	Y	N	Y	Y
12 *Canady*	N	Y	N	N	Y	Y	Y
13 *Miller*	Y	Y	N	N	Y	Y	Y
14 *Goss*	−	+	−	−	+	+	+
15 *Weldon*	N	Y	N	N	Y	Y	Y
16 *Foley*	Y	Y	N	N	Y	Y	Y
17 Meek	?	?	?	?	?	N	Y
18 *Ros-Lehtinen*	N	Y	N	N	Y	Y	Y
19 Wexler	Y	N	Y	Y	N	Y	Y
20 Deutsch	N	Y	Y	Y	N	N	Y
21 *Diaz-Balart*	N	Y	N	N	Y	+	+
22 *Shaw*	N	Y	N	N	Y	?	?
23 Hastings	N	Y	Y	Y	N	N	Y
GEORGIA							
1 *Kingston*	N	Y	N	N	Y	Y	Y
2 Bishop	N	Y	Y	Y	N	Y	Y
3 *Collins*	N	Y	N	N	Y	Y	Y
4 McKinney	Y	Y	Y	Y	N	N	Y
5 Lewis	Y	Y	Y	Y	N	N	Y
6 *Gingrich*			N		Y		
7 *Barr*	N	N	N	N	Y	Y	Y
8 *Chambliss*	N	Y	N	N	Y	Y	Y
9 *Deal*	N	Y	N	Y	Y	Y	Y
10 *Norwood*	N	Y	N	N	Y	Y	Y
11 *Linder*	N	Y	N	N	Y	Y	Y
HAWAII							
1 Abercrombie	Y	Y	Y	Y	N	Y	Y
2 Mink	Y	N	Y	Y	N	N	Y
IDAHO							
1 *Chenoweth*	N	N	N	N	Y	Y	Y
2 *Crapo*	N	Y	N	N	Y	Y	Y
ILLINOIS							
1 Rush	?	?	Y	N	N	N	Y
2 Jackson	Y	N	Y	Y	N	N	Y
3 Lipinski	Y	Y	Y	N	Y	Y	Y
4 Gutierrez	Y	Y	Y	Y	N	Y	Y
5 Blagojevich	Y	N	?	?	?	Y	Y
6 *Hyde*	N	Y	N	N	Y	Y	Y
7 Davis	+	Y	Y	Y	N	N	Y
8 *Crane*	N	N	N	N	Y	Y	Y
9 Yates	Y	N	Y	Y	N	N	Y
10 *Porter*	Y	Y	N	Y	Y	Y	Y
11 *Weller*	Y	Y	N	N	Y	Y	Y
12 Costello	Y	Y	Y	N	Y	Y	Y
13 *Fawell*	?	?	?	?	?	Y	Y

ND Northern Democrats   SD Southern Democrats

	448	449	450	451	452	453	454
14 **Hastert**	N	Y	N	N	Y	Y	Y
15 **Ewing**	N	Y	N	N	Y	Y	Y
16 **Manzullo**	N	Y	N	N	Y	Y	Y
17 Evans	Y	N	Y	Y	N	Y	Y
18 **LaHood**	Y	Y	N	N	Y	Y	Y
19 Poshard	?	?	?	?	?	?	?
20 **Shimkus**	N	Y	N	N	Y	Y	Y
INDIANA							
1 Visclosky	N	Y	Y	Y	N	Y	Y
2 **McIntosh**	?	Y	N	N	Y	Y	Y
3 Roemer	Y	N	Y	Y	N	Y	Y
4 **Souder**	N	Y	N	N	Y	Y	Y
5 **Buyer**	N	Y	N	N	Y	Y	Y
6 **Burton**	N	Y	–	–	+	+	+
7 **Pease**	N	Y	?	?	?	Y	Y
8 **Hostettler**	N	N	N	N	Y	Y	Y
9 Hamilton	N	N	Y	Y	N	Y	Y
10 Carson	Y	N	Y	Y	N	N	Y
IOWA							
1 **Leach**	Y	Y	N	Y	N	Y	Y
2 **Nussle**	Y	Y	N	N	Y	Y	Y
3 Boswell	N	Y	Y	Y	N	Y	Y
4 **Ganske**	N	Y	N	N	Y	Y	Y
5 **Latham**	N	Y	N	N	Y	Y	Y
KANSAS							
1 **Moran**	Y	N	N	N	Y	Y	Y
2 **Ryun**	N	Y	N	N	Y	Y	Y
3 **Snowbarger**	N	Y	N	N	Y	Y	Y
4 **Tiahrt**	N	Y	N	N	Y	Y	Y
KENTUCKY							
1 **Whitfield**	N	Y	Y	N	Y	Y	Y
2 **Lewis**	N	Y	N	N	Y	Y	Y
3 **Northup**	N	Y	N	N	Y	Y	Y
4 **Bunning**	N	Y	N	N	Y	Y	Y
5 **Rogers**	N	N	N	N	Y	Y	Y
6 Baesler	Y	Y	Y	Y	N	Y	Y
LOUISIANA							
1 **Livingston**	N	Y	N	N	Y	Y	Y
2 Jefferson	Y	N	Y	Y	N	N	Y
3 **Tauzin**	N	Y	N	N	Y	Y	Y
4 **McCrery**	N	Y	N	N	Y	Y	Y
5 **Cooksey**	N	Y	N	N	Y	Y	Y
6 **Baker**	N	Y	N	N	Y	Y	Y
7 John	N	Y	Y	Y	N	Y	Y
MAINE							
1 Allen	Y	Y	Y	Y	N	Y	Y
2 Baldacci	Y	N	Y	Y	N	Y	Y
MARYLAND							
1 **Gilchrest**	Y	Y	N	N	Y	Y	Y
2 **Ehrlich**	N	Y	N	N	Y	Y	Y
3 Cardin	Y	Y	Y	Y	N	Y	Y
4 Wynn	Y	N	Y	Y	N	N	Y
5 Hoyer	N	N	Y	?	N	Y	Y
6 **Bartlett**	N	Y	N	N	Y	Y	Y
7 Cummings	Y	N	Y	Y	N	N	Y
8 **Morella**	Y	Y	Y	Y	N	Y	Y
MASSACHUSETTS							
1 Olver	Y	N	Y	Y	N	N	Y
2 Neal	Y	N	Y	Y	N	Y	Y
3 McGovern	Y	Y	Y	Y	N	Y	Y
4 Frank	Y	N	Y	Y	N	Y	Y
5 Meehan	Y	N	Y	Y	N	Y	Y
6 Tierney	Y	Y	Y	Y	N	Y	Y
7 Markey	Y	N	Y	Y	N	Y	Y
8 Kennedy	Y	N	Y	Y	N	Y	Y
9 Moakley	Y	N	Y	Y	N	Y	Y
10 Delahunt	Y	N	Y	Y	N	Y	Y
MICHIGAN							
1 Stupak	Y	N	Y	Y	N	Y	Y
2 **Hoekstra**	N	N	N	N	Y	Y	Y
3 **Ehlers**	Y	Y	N	N	Y	Y	Y
4 **Camp**	Y	Y	N	N	Y	Y	Y
5 Barcia	Y	Y	Y	Y	N	Y	Y
6 **Upton**	Y	Y	N	N	Y	Y	Y
7 **Smith**	N	Y	N	N	Y	Y	Y
8 Stabenow	Y	Y	Y	Y	N	Y	Y
9 Kildee	Y	Y	Y	Y	N	Y	Y
10 Bonior	Y	N	Y	Y	N	N	Y
11 **Knollenberg**	N	Y	N	N	Y	Y	Y
12 Levin	Y	Y	Y	Y	N	Y	Y
13 Rivers	Y	Y	Y	Y	N	Y	Y
14 Conyers	Y	N	Y	?	N	N	Y
15 Kilpatrick	Y	N	Y	Y	N	N	Y
16 Dingell	?	N	Y	Y	N	Y	Y

	448	449	450	451	452	453	454
MINNESOTA							
1 **Gutknecht**	Y	Y	N	N	Y	Y	Y
2 Minge	Y	N	Y	Y	N	Y	Y
3 **Ramstad**	Y	Y	Y	N	N	Y	Y
4 Vento	Y	N	Y	Y	N	N	Y
5 Sabo	Y	N	Y	Y	N	N	Y
6 Luther	Y	N	Y	Y	N	Y	Y
7 Peterson	Y	Y	Y	Y	N	Y	Y
8 Oberstar	Y	N	Y	Y	N	N	Y
MISSISSIPPI							
1 **Wicker**	N	Y	N	N	Y	Y	Y
2 Thompson	Y	N	Y	Y	N	N	Y
3 **Pickering**	N	Y	N	N	Y	Y	Y
4 **Parker**	N	Y	?	?	?	Y	Y
5 Taylor	N	N	Y	Y	Y	Y	Y
MISSOURI							
1 Clay	?	?	?	?	?	N	Y
2 **Talent**	Y	Y	N	N	Y	Y	Y
3 Gephardt	?	?	Y	Y	N	N	Y
4 Skelton	N	Y	Y	Y	N	Y	Y
5 McCarthy	Y	N	Y	Y	N	Y	Y
6 Danner	Y	N	Y	Y	N	Y	Y
7 **Blunt**	N	Y	N	N	Y	Y	Y
8 **Emerson**	N	Y	N	N	Y	Y	Y
9 **Hulshof**	Y	Y	N	N	Y	Y	Y
MONTANA							
AL **Hill**	N	Y	N	N	Y	Y	Y
NEBRASKA							
1 **Bereuter**	N	Y	N	N	Y	Y	Y
2 **Christensen**	N	Y	N	N	Y	Y	Y
3 **Barrett**	N	Y	N	N	Y	Y	Y
NEVADA							
1 **Ensign**	N	Y	N	N	Y	+	+
2 **Gibbons**	N	Y	N	N	Y	Y	Y
NEW HAMPSHIRE							
1 **Sununu**	N	N	N	N	Y	Y	Y
2 **Bass**	N	Y	N	N	Y	Y	Y
NEW JERSEY							
1 Andrews	Y	Y	Y	Y	N	N	Y
2 **LoBiondo**	Y	Y	N	N	Y	Y	Y
3 **Saxton**	N	Y	N	N	Y	Y	Y
4 **Smith**	Y	Y	Y	N	Y	Y	Y
5 **Roukema**	Y	Y	N	N	Y	Y	Y
6 Pallone	Y	Y	Y	Y	N	Y	Y
7 **Franks**	Y	Y	N	N	Y	Y	Y
8 Pascrell	Y	Y	Y	Y	N	Y	Y
9 Rothman	Y	Y	Y	Y	N	Y	Y
10 Payne	Y	N	Y	Y	N	N	Y
11 **Frelinghuysen**	N	Y	N	N	Y	Y	Y
12 **Pappas**	N	Y	N	N	Y	Y	Y
13 Menendez	Y	Y	Y	Y	N	N	Y
NEW MEXICO							
1 **Wilson**	N	Y	N	N	Y	Y	Y
2 **Skeen**	N	Y	N	N	Y	Y	Y
3 **Redmond**	N	Y	N	N	Y	Y	Y
NEW YORK							
1 **Forbes**	Y	Y	N	Y	Y	Y	Y
2 **Lazio**	Y	Y	N	N	Y	Y	Y
3 **King**	–	+	N	N	Y	Y	Y
4 McCarthy	Y	Y	Y	Y	N	Y	Y
5 Ackerman	Y	N	Y	Y	N	N	Y
6 Meeks	Y	N	Y	Y	N	N	Y
7 Manton	?	?	#	?	?	Y	Y
8 Nadler	Y	Y	Y	Y	N	N	Y
9 Schumer	?	?	?	?	?	?	?
10 Towns	Y	N	Y	Y	N	?	Y
11 Owens	Y	Y	Y	Y	N	N	Y
12 Velázquez	Y	N	Y	Y	N	?	?
13 **Fossella**	N	Y	N	N	Y	Y	Y
14 Maloney	Y	Y	Y	Y	N	?	Y
15 Rangel	Y	N	Y	Y	N	N	Y
16 Serrano	Y	Y	Y	Y	N	N	Y
17 Engel	Y	Y	Y	Y	N	N	Y
18 Lowey	Y	Y	Y	Y	N	Y	Y
19 **Kelly**	Y	Y	N	N	N	Y	Y
20 **Gilman**	N	Y	N	N	N	Y	Y
21 McNulty	Y	N	Y	Y	N	Y	Y
22 **Solomon**	N	Y	N	N	Y	Y	Y
23 **Boehlert**	Y	Y	N	N	N	Y	Y
24 **McHugh**	N	Y	N	N	Y	Y	Y
25 **Walsh**	Y	Y	N	N	Y	Y	Y
26 Hinchey	Y	Y	Y	Y	N	N	Y
27 **Paxon**	N	Y	N	N	Y	Y	Y
28 Slaughter	Y	Y	Y	Y	N	N	Y
29 LaFalce	N	N	Y	Y	N	Y	Y
30 **Quinn**	Y	Y	N	N	N	Y	Y

	448	449	450	451	452	453	454
31 **Houghton**	N	Y	N	N	Y	Y	Y
NORTH CAROLINA							
1 Clayton	Y	N	Y	Y	N	N	Y
2 Etheridge	Y	N	Y	Y	N	Y	Y
3 **Jones**	N	N	N	N	Y	Y	Y
4 Price	Y	N	Y	Y	N	Y	Y
5 **Burr**	N	Y	N	N	Y	Y	Y
6 **Coble**	Y	Y	N	N	Y	Y	Y
7 McIntyre	N	Y	Y	Y	Y	Y	Y
8 Hefner	Y	N	Y	Y	N	N	Y
9 **Myrick**	–	+	N	N	Y	Y	Y
10 **Ballenger**	N	Y	N	N	Y	Y	Y
11 **Taylor**	N	Y	N	N	Y	Y	Y
12 Watt	Y	N	Y	Y	N	N	Y
NORTH DAKOTA							
AL Pomeroy	Y	N	Y	Y	N	Y	Y
OHIO							
1 **Chabot**	N	Y	N	N	Y	Y	Y
2 **Portman**	N	Y	N	N	Y	Y	Y
3 Hall	Y	N	Y	Y	N	Y	Y
4 **Oxley**	N	Y	N	N	Y	Y	Y
5 **Gillmor**	N	Y	N	N	Y	Y	?
6 Strickland	Y	Y	Y	Y	N	Y	Y
7 **Hobson**	N	Y	N	N	Y	Y	Y
8 **Boehner**	N	Y	N	N	Y	Y	Y
9 Kaptur	N	Y	?	?	?	?	?
10 Kucinich	Y	Y	Y	Y	N	Y	Y
11 Stokes	Y	N	?	?	?	N	Y
12 **Kasich**	N	Y	N	N	Y	Y	Y
13 Brown	Y	N	Y	Y	N	N	Y
14 Sawyer	Y	N	Y	Y	N	Y	Y
15 **Pryce**	–	+	–	–	+	+	+
16 **Regula**	Y	Y	N	N	Y	Y	Y
17 Traficant	N	N	Y	Y	N	Y	Y
18 **Ney**	N	Y	N	Y	N	Y	Y
19 **LaTourette**	Y	Y	N	Y	Y	Y	Y
OKLAHOMA							
1 **Largent**	Y	Y	N	N	Y	Y	Y
2 **Coburn**	N	N	N	N	Y	?	Y
3 **Watkins**	N	N	N	N	Y	Y	Y
4 **Watts**	N	Y	?	N	Y	?	Y
5 **Istook**	N	N	N	N	Y	Y	Y
6 **Lucas**	N	N	N	N	Y	Y	Y
OREGON							
1 Furse	Y	N	Y	Y	N	N	Y
2 **Smith**	N	N	N	N	Y	Y	Y
3 Blumenauer	Y	Y	Y	Y	N	N	Y
4 DeFazio	Y	N	?	?	?	N	Y
5 Hooley	Y	Y	Y	Y	N	N	Y
PENNSYLVANIA							
1 Brady	N	N	Y	Y	N	N	Y
2 Fattah	Y	N	Y	Y	N	N	Y
3 Borski	Y	N	Y	Y	N	Y	Y
4 Klink	N	N	Y	Y	N	Y	Y
5 **Peterson**	N	N	N	N	Y	Y	Y
6 Holden	N	Y	Y	Y	N	Y	Y
7 **Weldon**	N	Y	N	N	Y	Y	Y
8 **Greenwood**	Y	N	N	N	Y	Y	Y
9 **Shuster**	N	N	N	N	Y	Y	Y
10 **McDade**	N	Y	?	?	?	?	Y
11 Kanjorski	N	N	Y	Y	N	N	Y
12 Murtha	N	N	Y	Y	N	Y	Y
13 **Fox**	Y	Y	Y	N	Y	Y	Y
14 Coyne	Y	N	Y	Y	N	N	Y
15 McHale	Y	N	Y	Y	N	Y	Y
16 **Pitts**	N	Y	N	N	Y	Y	Y
17 **Gekas**	N	Y	N	N	Y	Y	Y
18 Doyle	Y	Y	Y	Y	N	Y	Y
19 **Goodling**	N	Y	N	N	Y	Y	Y
20 Mascara	N	N	Y	Y	N	Y	Y
21 **English**	Y	Y	N	N	Y	Y	Y
RHODE ISLAND							
1 Kennedy	Y	Y	Y	Y	N	N	Y
2 Weygand	Y	Y	Y	Y	N	Y	Y
SOUTH CAROLINA							
1 **Sanford**	Y	N	N	N	Y	Y	Y
2 **Spence**	N	Y	N	N	Y	Y	Y
3 **Graham**	Y	Y	N	N	Y	+	Y
4 **Inglis**	N	Y	N	N	Y	Y	Y
5 Spratt	N	N	Y	Y	N	Y	Y
6 Clyburn	N	N	Y	Y	N	N	Y
SOUTH DAKOTA							
AL **Thune**	N	Y	N	N	Y	Y	Y

	448	449	450	451	452	453	454
TENNESSEE							
1 **Jenkins**	N	Y	N	N	Y	Y	Y
2 **Duncan**	Y	N	N	N	Y	Y	Y
3 **Wamp**	Y	Y	N	N	Y	Y	Y
4 **Hilleary**	N	N	N	N	Y	Y	Y
5 Clement	Y	N	Y	Y	N	Y	Y
6 Gordon	Y	N	Y	Y	N	N	Y
7 **Bryant**	N	Y	N	N	Y	Y	Y
8 Tanner	N	N	Y	Y	N	Y	Y
9 Ford	Y	N	Y	Y	N	N	Y
TEXAS							
1 Sandlin	N	N	Y	Y	N	Y	Y
2 Turner	N	Y	Y	Y	N	Y	Y
3 **Johnson, Sam**	N	Y	N	N	Y	Y	Y
4 Hall	N	N	Y	N	Y	Y	Y
5 **Sessions**	N	Y	N	N	Y	Y	Y
6 **Barton**	N	Y	N	N	Y	Y	Y
7 **Archer**	N	Y	N	N	Y	Y	Y
8 **Brady**	N	Y	N	N	Y	Y	Y
9 Lampson	Y	Y	Y	Y	N	Y	Y
10 Doggett	Y	N	Y	Y	N	Y	Y
11 Edwards	N	N	Y	Y	N	Y	Y
12 **Granger**	N	Y	N	N	Y	Y	Y
13 **Thornberry**	N	Y	N	N	Y	Y	Y
14 **Paul**	Y	N	N	N	P	Y	Y
15 Hinojosa	Y	N	Y	Y	N	N	Y
16 Reyes	N	N	Y	Y	N	Y	Y
17 Stenholm	N	N	Y	N	N	Y	Y
18 Jackson-Lee	Y	Y	Y	Y	N	Y	Y
19 **Combest**	N	N	N	N	Y	Y	Y
20 Gonzalez	?	?	?	?	?	?	?
21 **Smith**	N	Y	N	N	Y	Y	Y
22 **DeLay**	N	Y	N	N	Y	Y	Y
23 **Bonilla**	N	Y	N	N	Y	Y	Y
24 Frost	N	Y	Y	Y	N	N	Y
25 Bentsen	Y	Y	Y	Y	N	Y	Y
26 **Armey**	N	Y	N	N	Y	Y	Y
27 Ortiz	N	Y	Y	Y	N	Y	Y
28 Rodriguez	Y	Y	Y	Y	N	Y	Y
29 Green	Y	Y	Y	Y	N	N	Y
30 Johnson, E.B.	Y	N	Y	Y	N	N	Y
UTAH							
1 **Hansen**	N	N	N	N	Y	Y	Y
2 **Cook**	N	Y	N	N	Y	Y	Y
3 **Cannon**	N	Y	Y	N	Y	Y	Y
VERMONT							
AL *Sanders*	Y	N	Y	Y	N	?	?
VIRGINIA							
1 **Bateman**	N	Y	N	N	Y	Y	Y
2 Pickett	N	Y	Y	Y	N	Y	Y
3 Scott	Y	N	Y	Y	N	N	Y
4 Sisisky	N	Y	Y	Y	N	Y	Y
5 Goode	Y	N	N	Y	Y	Y	Y
6 **Goodlatte**	N	Y	N	N	Y	Y	Y
7 **Bliley**	N	Y	N	N	Y	Y	Y
8 Moran	Y	N	Y	Y	N	Y	Y
9 Boucher	Y	N	Y	Y	N	Y	Y
10 **Wolf**	N	Y	N	N	Y	Y	Y
11 **Davis**	N	Y	Y	N	Y	Y	Y
WASHINGTON							
1 **White**	N	Y	N	N	Y	Y	Y
2 **Metcalf**	N	Y	N	N	Y	Y	Y
3 **Smith, Linda**	N	Y	N	N	Y	Y	Y
4 **Hastings**	N	Y	N	N	Y	Y	Y
5 **Nethercutt**	N	Y	N	N	Y	Y	Y
6 Dicks	Y	Y	Y	Y	N	Y	Y
7 McDermott	Y	N	Y	Y	N	Y	Y
8 **Dunn**	N	Y	N	N	Y	Y	Y
9 Smith, Adam	Y	N	Y	Y	Y	Y	Y
WEST VIRGINIA							
1 Mollohan	N	N	Y	Y	N	Y	Y
2 Wise	N	N	Y	Y	N	Y	Y
3 Rahall	Y	N	Y	Y	N	N	Y
WISCONSIN							
1 **Neumann**	Y	Y	N	N	Y	Y	Y
2 **Klug**	Y	Y	N	N	Y	Y	Y
3 Kind	Y	N	Y	Y	N	Y	Y
4 Kleczka	Y	N	Y	Y	N	Y	Y
5 Barrett	Y	N	Y	Y	N	Y	Y
6 **Petri**	Y	N	N	N	Y	Y	Y
7 Obey	Y	N	Y	Y	N	Y	Y
8 Johnson	Y	N	Y	Y	N	Y	Y
9 **Sensenbrenner**	Y	N	N	N	Y	Y	Y
WYOMING							
AL **Cubin**	N	Y	N	N	Y	Y	Y

Southern states - Ala., Ark., Fla., Ga., Ky., La., Miss., N.C., Okla., S.C., Tenn., Texas, Va.

455. H Res 505. Diplomatic Relations with Pacific Island Nations/Passage. Gilman, R-N.Y., motion to suspend the rules and pass the bill to encourage the United States to actively engage the governments of the South Pacific region in order to support U.S. commercial and strategic interests and promote democratic values. Motion agreed to 414-1: R 218-1; D 196-0 (ND 142-0, SD 54-0); I 0-0. Sept. 23, 1998. A two-thirds majority of those present and voting (277 in this case) is required for passage under suspension of the rules.

456. H Con Res 315. Condemn Serbian Atrocities in Kosovo/Passage. Gilman, R-N.Y., motion to suspend the rules and pass the bill to express the sense of Congress that it deeply deplores and strongly condemns the loss of life and the extensive destruction of property in Kosovo that is the consequence of the brutal actions of Serbian police and military forces against the ethnic Albanian population of the province. Motion agreed to 410-0: R 216-0; D 194-0 (ND 141-0, SD 53-0); I 0-0. Sept. 23, 1998. A two-thirds majority of those present and voting (274 in this case) is required for passage under suspension of the rules

457. HR 4112. Fiscal 1999 Legislative Branch Appropriations/Conference Report. Adoption of the conference report on the bill to provide about $2.35 billion for the House, Senate and various congressional agencies and offices, such as the Library of Congress, General Accounting Office and Congressional Budget Office. Adopted (thus sent to the Senate) 356-65: R 187-31; D 168-34 (ND 124-23, SD 44-11); I 1-0. Sept. 24, 1998.

458. HR 3616. Fiscal 1999 Defense Authorization/Conference Report. Adoption of the conference report on the bill to authorize $270.5 billion in defense spending for fiscal 1999. Adopted (thus sent to the Senate) 373-50: R 207-11; D 166-38 (ND 113-36, SD 53-2); I 0-1. Sept. 24, 1998.

459. HR 3736. High-Tech Workers Visa/Democratic Substitute. Watt, D-N.C., substitute amendment to increase the number of six-year H-1B skill and profession-based visas for foreign workers. The total increase over the next five years would be lower than the overall number allowed by the bill. The substitute amendment also would require all employers using H-1B workers attest they have tried to recruit qualified U.S. workers and have not laid off U.S. workers. Rejected 177-242: R 21-201; D 156-40 (ND 119-23, SD 37-17); I 0-1. Sept. 24, 1998.

460. HR 3736. High-Tech Worker Visas/Passage. Passage of the bill to increase the number of six-year H-1B skill and profession-based visas for foreign workers from 65,000 to 115,000 in fiscal 1999 and 2000 and 107,500 in fiscal 2001. The bill also would require some employers using H-1B workers to prove they have tried to recruit qualified U.S. workers and have not laid off U.S. workers. Passed 288-133: R 189-34; D 99-98 (ND 66-76, SD 33-22); I 0-1. Sept. 24, 1998. A "nay" was a vote in support of the president's position.

461. H Res 552. Tax Cut and Social Security Savings/Previous Question. Solomon, R-N.Y., motion to order the previous question (thus ending debate and the possibility of amendment) on adoption of the rule to provide for House floor consideration of the bills to cut taxes by $80 billion over five years (HR 4579) and to set aside 90 percent of any budget surplus in a special Treasury account until Congress enacts legislation to ensure the long-term solvency of the Social Security program (HR 4578). Motion agreed to 219-202: R 217-1; D 2-200 (ND 2-145, SD 0-55); I 0-1. Sept. 25, 1998.

Key

Y	Voted for (yea).
#	Paired for.
+	Announced for.
N	Voted against (nay).
X	Paired against.
–	Announced against.
P	Voted "present."
C	Voted "present" to avoid possible conflict of interest.
?	Did not vote or otherwise make a position known.

Democrats **Republicans**
Independent

	455	456	457	458	459	460	461
ALABAMA							
1 *Callahan*	Y	Y	Y	Y	N	Y	Y
2 *Everett*	Y	Y	Y	+	N	Y	Y
3 *Riley*	Y	Y	Y	+	N	Y	Y
4 *Aderholt*	Y	Y	Y	+	N	Y	Y
5 Cramer	Y	Y	Y	Y	N	Y	N
6 *Bachus*	Y	Y	Y	Y	N	N	Y
7 Hilliard	Y	Y	Y	Y	Y	N	N
ALASKA							
AL *Young*	Y	Y	Y	Y	N	N	Y
ARIZONA							
1 *Salmon*	Y	Y	N	Y	N	Y	Y
2 Pastor	Y	Y	Y	Y	Y	Y	N
3 *Stump*	Y	Y	N	Y	N	N	Y
4 *Shadegg*	Y	Y	N	Y	N	Y	Y
5 *Kolbe*	Y	Y	Y	Y	N	Y	Y
6 *Hayworth*	Y	Y	Y	Y	N	Y	Y
ARKANSAS							
1 Berry	Y	Y	Y	Y	N	N	N
2 Snyder	Y	Y	Y	Y	N	N	N
3 *Hutchinson*	Y	Y	Y	Y	N	Y	Y
4 *Dickey*	Y	Y	Y	Y	N	Y	Y
CALIFORNIA							
1 *Riggs*	?	?	Y	Y	N	N	Y
2 *Herger*	Y	Y	N	Y	N	Y	Y
3 Fazio	Y	Y	Y	Y	N	Y	N
4 *Doolittle*	Y	Y	Y	Y	N	Y	Y
5 Matsui	Y	Y	Y	Y	N	Y	N
6 Woolsey	Y	Y	N	Y	Y	N	N
7 Miller	Y	Y	N	Y	Y	N	N
8 Pelosi	Y	Y	N	Y	Y	N	N
9 Lee	Y	Y	N	N	Y	N	N
10 Tauscher	Y	Y	Y	Y	N	Y	N
11 *Pombo*	Y	Y	Y	Y	N	Y	Y
12 Lantos	Y	Y	Y	Y	N	Y	N
13 Stark	Y	Y	Y	Y	N	N	N
14 Eshoo	Y	Y	Y	Y	N	Y	N
15 *Campbell*	Y	Y	Y	N	Y	Y	Y
16 Lofgren	Y	N	N	N	Y	N	N
17 Farr	Y	Y	N	Y	Y	N	N
18 Condit	Y	Y	N	N	N	N	N
19 *Radanovich*	Y	Y	Y	Y	N	Y	Y
20 Dooley	Y	Y	Y	Y	N	Y	N
21 *Thomas*	Y	Y	Y	N	N	Y	Y
22 Capps, L.	Y	Y	Y	Y	N	N	N
23 *Gallegly*	Y	Y	Y	Y	N	N	Y
24 Sherman	Y	Y	Y	Y	N	N	N
25 *McKeon*	Y	Y	Y	Y	N	Y	Y
26 Berman	Y	Y	Y	Y	N	Y	N
27 *Rogan*	Y	Y	Y	Y	N	Y	Y
28 *Dreier*	Y	Y	Y	Y	N	Y	Y
29 Waxman	Y	Y	Y	Y	N	Y	N
30 Becerra	+	+	Y	Y	Y	Y	N
31 Martinez	?	?	Y	Y	N	N	N
32 Dixon	Y	Y	Y	Y	N	N	N
33 Roybal-Allard	Y	Y	Y	Y	N	N	N
34 Torres	?	?	Y	Y	?	?	N
35 Waters	?	N	Y	Y	N	?	N
36 Harman	Y	Y	Y	Y	N	N	N
37 Millender-McD.	Y	Y	Y	Y	N	N	N
38 *Horn*	Y	Y	Y	Y	N	Y	Y

	455	456	457	458	459	460	461
39 *Royce*	Y	Y	N	Y	N	Y	Y
40 *Lewis*	Y	Y	Y	Y	N	Y	Y
41 *Kim*	Y	Y	Y	Y	N	Y	Y
42 Brown	Y	Y	Y	Y	N	Y	N
43 *Calvert*	Y	Y	Y	Y	N	Y	Y
44 *Bono, M.*	Y	Y	Y	Y	N	Y	Y
45 *Rohrabacher*	Y	Y	Y	Y	N	Y	Y
46 Sanchez	+	+	Y	Y	–	+	N
47 *Cox*	Y	Y	N	Y	N	Y	Y
48 *Packard*	Y	Y	Y	Y	N	Y	Y
49 *Bilbray*	Y	Y	Y	Y	N	Y	Y
50 Filner	Y	Y	N	Y	N	N	N
51 *Cunningham*	Y	Y	Y	Y	N	Y	Y
52 *Hunter*	Y	Y	Y	Y	N	N	Y
COLORADO							
1 DeGette	Y	Y	Y	Y	N	N	N
2 Skaggs	Y	Y	Y	Y	Y	N	N
3 *McInnis*	Y	Y	Y	Y	N	Y	Y
4 *Schaffer*	Y	Y	N	Y	N	Y	Y
5 *Hefley*	Y	Y	N	Y	N	N	Y
6 *Schaefer*	Y	Y	Y	?	?	?	Y
CONNECTICUT							
1 Kennelly	?	?	?	?	?	?	?
2 Gejdenson	Y	Y	N	Y	Y	N	N
3 DeLauro	Y	Y	Y	Y	N	N	N
4 *Shays*	Y	Y	N	N	N	Y	Y
5 Maloney	Y	Y	Y	Y	Y	N	N
6 *Johnson*	Y	Y	Y	Y	N	Y	Y
DELAWARE							
AL *Castle*	Y	Y	Y	Y	N	Y	Y
FLORIDA							
1 *Scarborough*	Y	Y	N	Y	N	Y	Y
2 Boyd	Y	Y	N	Y	N	Y	N
3 Brown	Y	Y	Y	Y	N	N	N
4 *Fowler*	Y	Y	Y	Y	N	N	Y
5 Thurman	Y	Y	Y	Y	N	N	N
6 *Stearns*	Y	Y	N	Y	N	Y	Y
7 *Mica*	Y	Y	Y	Y	N	Y	Y
8 *McCollum*	Y	Y	Y	Y	N	Y	Y
9 *Bilirakis*	Y	Y	Y	Y	N	Y	Y
10 *Young*	Y	Y	Y	Y	N	Y	Y
11 Davis	Y	Y	Y	Y	N	Y	N
12 *Canady*	Y	Y	Y	Y	N	Y	Y
13 *Miller*	Y	Y	Y	Y	N	Y	Y
14 *Goss*	+	+	+	+	–	+	+
15 *Weldon*	Y	Y	Y	Y	N	Y	Y
16 *Foley*	Y	Y	Y	Y	N	Y	Y
17 Meek	Y	Y	Y	Y	N	N	N
18 *Ros-Lehtinen*	Y	Y	+	Y	Y	N	Y
19 Wexler	Y	Y	Y	Y	?	N	N
20 Deutsch	Y	N	Y	Y	N	N	N
21 *Diaz-Balart*	+	+	+	Y	Y	Y	Y
22 *Shaw*	?	?	?	?	N	Y	Y
23 Hastings	Y	Y	Y	Y	Y	Y	N
GEORGIA							
1 *Kingston*	Y	Y	Y	Y	N	Y	Y
2 Bishop	Y	Y	Y	Y	Y	Y	N
3 *Collins*	Y	Y	Y	Y	N	N	Y
4 McKinney	Y	N	N	N	Y	N	N
5 Lewis	Y	Y	Y	Y	N	N	N
6 *Gingrich*							Y
7 *Barr*	Y	N	Y	Y	N	N	Y
8 *Chambliss*	Y	Y	Y	Y	Y	Y	Y
9 *Deal*	Y	Y	Y	Y	N	N	Y
10 *Norwood*	Y	Y	Y	Y	N	N	?
11 *Linder*	Y	Y	?	Y	N	Y	Y
HAWAII							
1 Abercrombie	Y	Y	Y	Y	Y	N	N
2 Mink	Y	Y	Y	Y	Y	N	N
IDAHO							
1 *Chenoweth*	Y	Y	N	Y	N	N	Y
2 *Crapo*	Y	Y	N	Y	N	Y	Y
ILLINOIS							
1 Rush	Y	Y	N	N	N	N	N
2 Jackson	Y	Y	N	N	N	N	N
3 Lipinski	Y	Y	Y	Y	N	N	N
4 Gutierrez	Y	Y	N	N	Y	N	N
5 Blagojevich	Y	Y	Y	Y	N	N	N
6 *Hyde*	?	?	Y	Y	N	Y	Y
7 Davis	Y	Y	N	N	Y	N	N
8 *Crane*	Y	N	Y	N	Y	N	Y
9 Yates	?	?	Y	N	?	?	N
10 *Porter*	Y	Y	N	Y	N	N	Y
11 *Weller*	Y	Y	Y	Y	N	Y	Y
12 Costello	Y	Y	Y	Y	N	N	N
13 *Fawell*	Y	Y	Y	N	N	Y	Y

ND Northern Democrats   SD Southern Democrats

	455	456	457	458	459	460	461
14 ***Hastert***	Y	Y	Y	Y	N	Y	Y
15 ***Ewing***	Y	Y	Y	Y	N	Y	Y
16 ***Manzullo***	Y	Y	Y	Y	N	Y	Y
17 Evans	Y	Y	Y	Y	Y	N	N
18 ***LaHood***	Y	Y	Y	Y	N	Y	Y
19 Poshard	?	?	?	?	?	?	N
20 ***Shimkus***	Y	Y	Y	Y	N	Y	Y
INDIANA							
1 Visclosky	Y	Y	Y	Y	Y	N	N
2 ***McIntosh***	Y	Y	Y	Y	N	Y	Y
3 Roemer	Y	Y	N	Y	Y	Y	N
4 ***Souder***	Y	?	Y	Y	N	Y	Y
5 ***Buyer***	Y	Y	Y	Y	N	Y	Y
6 ***Burton***	+	+	+	+	−	+	#
7 ***Pease***	Y	Y	Y	Y	N	Y	Y
8 ***Hostettler***	Y	Y	N	Y	N	N	Y
9 Hamilton	Y	Y	Y	Y	Y	Y	N
10 Carson	Y	Y	Y	Y	Y	N	N
IOWA							
1 ***Leach***	Y	Y	Y	Y	N	Y	Y
2 ***Nussle***	Y	Y	N	Y	N	Y	Y
3 Boswell	Y	Y	Y	Y	Y	Y	N
4 ***Ganske***	Y	Y	Y	Y	N	Y	Y
5 ***Latham***	Y	Y	Y	Y	N	Y	Y
KANSAS							
1 ***Moran***	Y	Y	N	Y	N	Y	Y
2 ***Ryun***	Y	Y	Y	Y	N	Y	Y
3 ***Snowbarger***	Y	Y	Y	Y	N	Y	Y
4 ***Tiahrt***	Y	Y	Y	Y	N	Y	Y
KENTUCKY							
1 ***Whitfield***	Y	Y	Y	Y	N	N	Y
2 ***Lewis***	Y	Y	Y	Y	N	Y	Y
3 ***Northup***	Y	Y	Y	Y	N	Y	Y
4 ***Bunning***	Y	Y	Y	Y	N	Y	Y
5 ***Rogers***	Y	Y	Y	Y	N	Y	?
6 Baesler	Y	Y	Y	Y	Y	N	N
LOUISIANA							
1 ***Livingston***	Y	Y	Y	Y	N	Y	?
2 Jefferson	Y	Y	Y	Y	Y	N	N
3 ***Tauzin***	Y	Y	Y	Y	N	Y	Y
4 ***McCrery***	Y	Y	Y	Y	N	Y	Y
5 ***Cooksey***	Y	Y	Y	Y	N	Y	Y
6 ***Baker***	Y	Y	Y	Y	N	Y	Y
7 John	Y	Y	Y	Y	N	Y	N
MAINE							
1 Allen	Y	Y	Y	Y	Y	Y	N
2 Baldacci	Y	Y	Y	Y	Y	Y	N
MARYLAND							
1 ***Gilchrest***	Y	Y	Y	Y	N	Y	Y
2 ***Ehrlich***	Y	Y	?	?	N	Y	Y
3 Cardin	Y	Y	?	Y	Y	Y	N
4 Wynn	Y	Y	Y	Y	Y	N	N
5 Hoyer	Y	Y	Y	Y	Y	Y	N
6 ***Bartlett***	Y	Y	Y	N	N	Y	Y
7 Cummings	Y	Y	Y	Y	Y	N	N
8 ***Morella***	Y	Y	Y	N	N	Y	Y
MASSACHUSETTS							
1 Olver	Y	Y	N	Y	Y	N	N
2 Neal	Y	Y	Y	Y	Y	Y	N
3 McGovern	Y	Y	N	Y	Y	Y	N
4 Frank	Y	Y	N	Y	Y	Y	N
5 Meehan	Y	Y	N	Y	Y	Y	N
6 Tierney	Y	Y	N	Y	Y	Y	N
7 Markey	Y	Y	Y	Y	Y	Y	N
8 Kennedy	Y	Y	Y	Y	Y	Y	N
9 Moakley	Y	Y	Y	Y	Y	N	X
10 Delahunt	Y	Y	Y	N	Y	Y	N
MICHIGAN							
1 Stupak	Y	Y	Y	Y	N	N	N
2 ***Hoekstra***	Y	Y	Y	N	N	Y	Y
3 ***Ehlers***	Y	Y	Y	Y	Y	Y	Y
4 ***Camp***	Y	Y	Y	Y	N	Y	Y
5 Barcia	Y	Y	Y	Y	Y	N	N
6 ***Upton***	Y	Y	Y	Y	N	Y	Y
7 ***Smith***	Y	Y	Y	Y	Y	N	Y
8 Stabenow	Y	Y	Y	Y	Y	Y	N
9 Kildee	Y	Y	Y	Y	Y	N	N
10 Bonior	Y	Y	Y	Y	N	N	N
11 ***Knollenberg***	Y	Y	Y	Y	N	Y	Y
12 Levin	Y	Y	Y	Y	Y	Y	N
13 Rivers	Y	Y	Y	N	Y	N	N
14 Conyers	Y	Y	N	N	Y	N	N
15 Kilpatrick	Y	Y	Y	Y	Y	N	N
16 Dingell	Y	Y	Y	Y	Y	N	N

	455	456	457	458	459	460	461
MINNESOTA							
1 ***Gutknecht***	Y	Y	Y	Y	N	Y	Y
2 Minge	Y	Y	N	N	Y	Y	N
3 ***Ramstad***	Y	Y	Y	Y	N	Y	Y
4 Vento	Y	Y	N	N	Y	Y	N
5 Sabo	Y	Y	Y	Y	Y	Y	N
6 Luther	Y	Y	N	N	Y	Y	N
7 Peterson	Y	Y	Y	Y	N	N	N
8 Oberstar	Y	Y	Y	N	Y	N	N
MISSISSIPPI							
1 ***Wicker***	Y	Y	Y	Y	N	Y	Y
2 Thompson	Y	Y	Y	Y	Y	N	N
3 ***Pickering***	Y	Y	Y	Y	N	Y	Y
4 ***Parker***	Y	Y	Y	Y	N	Y	Y
5 Taylor	Y	Y	N	Y	N	N	N
MISSOURI							
1 Clay	Y	Y	Y	Y	Y	N	N
2 ***Talent***	Y	Y	Y	Y	N	Y	Y
3 Gephardt	Y	Y	Y	Y	Y	Y	N
4 Skelton	Y	Y	Y	Y	?	?	N
5 McCarthy	Y	Y	Y	Y	Y	Y	N
6 Danner	Y	Y	Y	Y	Y	N	N
7 ***Blunt***	Y	Y	N	Y	N	N	Y
8 ***Emerson***	Y	Y	Y	Y	N	N	Y
9 ***Hulshof***	Y	Y	N	Y	N	Y	Y
MONTANA							
AL ***Hill***	Y	Y	Y	Y	N	Y	Y
NEBRASKA							
1 ***Bereuter***	Y	Y	Y	Y	Y	Y	Y
2 ***Christensen***	Y	Y	N	Y	N	Y	Y
3 ***Barrett***	Y	Y	Y	Y	N	Y	Y
NEVADA							
1 ***Ensign***	+	Y	N	Y	N	Y	Y
2 ***Gibbons***	Y	Y	Y	Y	N	Y	Y
NEW HAMPSHIRE							
1 ***Sununu***	Y	Y	Y	Y	N	Y	Y
2 ***Bass***	Y	Y	Y	Y	N	Y	Y
NEW JERSEY							
1 Andrews	Y	Y	Y	Y	Y	N	N
2 ***LoBiondo***	Y	Y	Y	Y	N	N	Y
3 ***Saxton***	Y	Y	Y	Y	N	Y	Y
4 ***Smith***	Y	Y	Y	Y	N	N	Y
5 ***Roukema***	Y	Y	Y	Y	N	Y	Y
6 Pallone	Y	Y	Y	Y	Y	N	N
7 ***Franks***	Y	Y	Y	N	N	N	Y
8 Pascrell	Y	Y	Y	Y	Y	Y	N
9 Rothman	Y	Y	N	Y	?	N	N
10 Payne	Y	Y	N	N	Y	N	N
11 ***Frelinghuysen***	Y	Y	Y	Y	N	Y	Y
12 ***Pappas***	Y	Y	Y	Y	N	Y	Y
13 Menendez	Y	Y	Y	Y	Y	Y	N
NEW MEXICO							
1 ***Wilson***	Y	Y	Y	Y	N	Y	Y
2 ***Skeen***	Y	Y	Y	Y	N	Y	Y
3 ***Redmond***	Y	Y	Y	Y	N	Y	Y
NEW YORK							
1 ***Forbes***	Y	Y	Y	Y	Y	Y	Y
2 ***Lazio***	Y	Y	Y	Y	N	Y	Y
3 ***King***	Y	Y	Y	Y	N	Y	Y
4 McCarthy	Y	Y	Y	Y	N	Y	Y
5 Ackerman	Y	Y	Y	Y	Y	Y	N
6 Meeks	Y	Y	Y	N	Y	N	?
7 Manton	Y	Y	Y	Y	?	?	N
8 Nadler	Y	Y	Y	N	Y	Y	N
9 Schumer	Y	Y	Y	Y	Y	Y	N
10 Towns	Y	Y	Y	Y	Y	N	N
11 Owens	Y	Y	Y	N	Y	N	N
12 Velázquez	?	?	N	N	Y	N	N
13 ***Fossella***	Y	Y	Y	Y	N	Y	Y
14 Maloney	Y	Y	Y	Y	Y	Y	N
15 Rangel	Y	Y	?	N	Y	N	N
16 Serrano	Y	Y	Y	N	Y	N	N
17 Engel	Y	Y	Y	Y	Y	N	?
18 Lowey	Y	Y	Y	N	Y	Y	N
19 ***Kelly***	Y	Y	Y	Y	N	Y	Y
20 ***Gilman***	Y	Y	Y	Y	Y	Y	Y
21 McNulty	Y	Y	Y	Y	Y	N	N
22 ***Solomon***	Y	Y	Y	Y	N	N	Y
23 ***Boehlert***	Y	Y	Y	Y	Y	Y	Y
24 ***McHugh***	Y	Y	Y	Y	N	Y	Y
25 ***Walsh***	Y	Y	Y	Y	N	Y	Y
26 Hinchey	Y	?	Y	Y	Y	N	N
27 ***Paxon***	Y	Y	Y	Y	N	Y	Y
28 Slaughter	Y	Y	Y	Y	Y	Y	N
29 LaFalce	Y	Y	Y	Y	Y	Y	N
30 ***Quinn***	Y	Y	Y	Y	N	Y	Y

	455	456	457	458	459	460	461
31 ***Houghton***	Y	Y	Y	Y	N	Y	Y
NORTH CAROLINA							
1 Clayton	Y	Y	Y	Y	Y	Y	N
2 Etheridge	Y	Y	Y	Y	Y	Y	N
3 ***Jones***	Y	Y	Y	Y	N	Y	Y
4 Price	Y	Y	Y	Y	Y	Y	N
5 ***Burr***	Y	Y	Y	Y	N	Y	Y
6 ***Coble***	Y	Y	Y	Y	N	Y	Y
7 McIntyre	Y	Y	Y	Y	Y	Y	N
8 Hefner	Y	Y	Y	Y	Y	Y	N
9 ***Myrick***	Y	Y	Y	Y	N	Y	Y
10 ***Ballenger***	Y	Y	Y	Y	N	Y	Y
11 ***Taylor***	Y	Y	Y	Y	N	Y	Y
12 Watt	Y	Y	Y	Y	Y	Y	N
NORTH DAKOTA							
AL Pomeroy	Y	Y	Y	Y	Y	Y	N
OHIO							
1 ***Chabot***	Y	Y	Y	Y	N	Y	Y
2 ***Portman***	Y	Y	Y	Y	N	Y	Y
3 Hall	Y	Y	Y	Y	N	Y	N
4 ***Oxley***	Y	Y	Y	Y	N	Y	Y
5 ***Gillmor***	Y	Y	Y	Y	N	Y	Y
6 Strickland	Y	Y	Y	Y	Y	N	N
7 ***Hobson***	Y	Y	Y	Y	N	Y	Y
8 ***Boehner***	Y	Y	Y	Y	N	Y	Y
9 Kaptur	Y	Y	Y	Y	Y	N	N
10 Kucinich	Y	Y	Y	N	Y	N	N
11 Stokes	Y	Y	Y	Y	Y	N	N
12 ***Kasich***	Y	Y	Y	Y	N	Y	Y
13 Brown	Y	Y	Y	Y	Y	N	N
14 Sawyer	Y	Y	Y	Y	Y	Y	N
15 ***Pryce***	+	+	+	+	−	+	+
16 ***Regula***	Y	Y	Y	Y	Y	Y	Y
17 Traficant	Y	Y	Y	Y	N	N	Y
18 ***Ney***	Y	Y	Y	Y	N	Y	Y
19 ***LaTourette***	Y	Y	Y	Y	N	Y	Y
OKLAHOMA							
1 ***Largent***	Y	Y	Y	Y	N	Y	Y
2 ***Coburn***	Y	Y	Y	Y	Y	Y	Y
3 ***Watkins***	Y	Y	Y	Y	N	Y	Y
4 ***Watts***	Y	Y	Y	Y	N	N	Y
5 ***Istook***	Y	Y	Y	Y	N	Y	Y
6 ***Lucas***	Y	Y	Y	Y	N	Y	Y
OREGON							
1 Furse	Y	Y	Y	N	Y	Y	N
2 ***Smith***	Y	Y	Y	Y	N	Y	Y
3 Blumenauer	Y	Y	Y	N	N	Y	N
4 DeFazio	Y	Y	Y	N	N	N	N
5 Hooley	Y	Y	Y	N	N	Y	N
PENNSYLVANIA							
1 Brady	Y	Y	Y	Y	Y	N	N
2 Fattah	Y	Y	Y	Y	Y	N	N
3 Borski	Y	Y	Y	Y	Y	N	N
4 Klink	Y	Y	N	Y	Y	N	N
5 ***Peterson***	Y	Y	Y	Y	N	Y	Y
6 Holden	Y	Y	Y	Y	Y	N	N
7 ***Weldon***	Y	Y	Y	Y	N	Y	Y
8 ***Greenwood***	Y	Y	Y	Y	N	Y	Y
9 ***Shuster***	Y	Y	Y	Y	N	Y	Y
10 ***McDade***	Y	Y	Y	Y	Y	Y	?
11 Kanjorski	Y	Y	Y	Y	Y	N	N
12 Murtha	Y	Y	Y	Y	?	?	N
13 ***Fox***	Y	Y	Y	Y	N	Y	Y
14 Coyne	Y	Y	Y	Y	Y	N	N
15 McHale	Y	Y	Y	Y	Y	Y	N
16 ***Pitts***	Y	Y	Y	Y	N	Y	Y
17 ***Gekas***	Y	?	Y	Y	N	Y	Y
18 Doyle	Y	Y	Y	Y	Y	N	N
19 ***Goodling***	Y	Y	Y	Y	N	Y	Y
20 Mascara	Y	Y	Y	Y	Y	N	N
21 ***English***	Y	Y	Y	Y	N	Y	Y
RHODE ISLAND							
1 Kennedy	Y	Y	Y	Y	Y	Y	N
2 Weygand	Y	Y	Y	Y	Y	Y	N
SOUTH CAROLINA							
1 ***Sanford***	Y	Y	N	Y	N	Y	N
2 ***Spence***	Y	Y	Y	Y	N	Y	Y
3 ***Graham***	Y	Y	Y	Y	N	Y	Y
4 ***Inglis***	Y	Y	N	Y	N	Y	Y
5 Spratt	Y	Y	Y	Y	Y	Y	N
6 Clyburn	Y	Y	Y	Y	Y	N	N
SOUTH DAKOTA							
AL ***Thune***	Y	Y	Y	Y	N	Y	Y

	455	456	457	458	459	460	461
TENNESSEE							
1 ***Jenkins***	Y	Y	Y	Y	N	Y	Y
2 ***Duncan***	Y	Y	Y	Y	N	N	Y
3 ***Wamp***	Y	Y	Y	Y	N	N	Y
4 ***Hilleary***	Y	Y	N	Y	N	N	Y
5 Clement	Y	Y	Y	Y	N	Y	N
6 Gordon	Y	Y	Y	Y	Y	Y	N
7 ***Bryant***	Y	Y	Y	Y	N	Y	Y
8 Tanner	Y	Y	N	Y	N	Y	N
9 Ford	Y	Y	Y	Y	Y	Y	N
TEXAS							
1 Sandlin	Y	Y	Y	Y	N	N	N
2 Turner	Y	Y	Y	Y	N	N	N
3 ***Johnson, Sam***	Y	Y	Y	+	N	Y	Y
4 Hall	Y	Y	N	Y	N	Y	N
5 ***Sessions***	Y	Y	Y	Y	N	Y	Y
6 ***Barton***	Y	Y	Y	Y	N	Y	Y
7 ***Archer***	Y	Y	Y	Y	N	Y	Y
8 ***Brady***	Y	Y	+	+	−	+	Y
9 Lampson	Y	Y	Y	Y	Y	N	N
10 Doggett	Y	Y	N	Y	Y	Y	N
11 Edwards	Y	Y	Y	Y	N	Y	N
12 ***Granger***	Y	Y	Y	Y	N	Y	Y
13 ***Thornberry***	Y	Y	Y	Y	N	Y	Y
14 ***Paul***	N	P	N	N	N	Y	?
15 Hinojosa	Y	?	Y	Y	Y	Y	N
16 Reyes	Y	Y	Y	Y	Y	Y	N
17 Stenholm	Y	Y	N	Y	N	Y	N
18 Jackson-Lee	Y	Y	Y	Y	Y	Y	N
19 ***Combest***	Y	Y	Y	Y	N	N	Y
20 Gonzalez	?	?	Y	Y	Y	N	N
21 ***Smith***	Y	Y	Y	Y	N	Y	Y
22 ***DeLay***	Y	Y	Y	Y	N	Y	Y
23 ***Bonilla***	Y	Y	Y	Y	N	Y	Y
24 Frost	Y	Y	Y	Y	Y	Y	N
25 Bentsen	Y	Y	Y	Y	N	Y	N
26 ***Armey***	Y	Y	Y	Y	N	Y	Y
27 Ortiz	Y	Y	Y	Y	Y	Y	N
28 Rodriguez	Y	Y	Y	Y	Y	N	N
29 Green	Y	Y	N	Y	Y	N	N
30 Johnson, E.B.	Y	Y	Y	Y	Y	Y	N
UTAH							
1 ***Hansen***	Y	Y	Y	Y	N	Y	Y
2 ***Cook***	Y	Y	Y	Y	N	Y	Y
3 ***Cannon***	Y	?	Y	Y	N	Y	Y
VERMONT							
AL *Sanders*	?	?	Y	N	N	N	N
VIRGINIA							
1 ***Bateman***	Y	Y	Y	Y	N	Y	Y
2 Pickett	Y	Y	Y	Y	N	Y	N
3 Scott	Y	Y	Y	Y	Y	Y	N
4 Sisisky	Y	Y	Y	Y	Y	Y	N
5 Goode	Y	Y	N	N	N	N	N
6 ***Goodlatte***	Y	Y	N	Y	N	Y	Y
7 ***Bliley***	Y	Y	Y	Y	N	Y	Y
8 Moran	Y	Y	Y	Y	Y	Y	N
9 Boucher	Y	Y	Y	Y	Y	N	N
10 ***Wolf***	Y	Y	Y	Y	N	Y	Y
11 ***Davis***	Y	Y	Y	Y	N	Y	Y
WASHINGTON							
1 ***White***	Y	Y	Y	Y	N	Y	Y
2 ***Metcalf***	Y	Y	Y	Y	N	N	Y
3 ***Smith, Linda***	Y	Y	N	Y	N	Y	Y
4 ***Hastings***	Y	Y	Y	Y	N	Y	Y
5 ***Nethercutt***	Y	Y	Y	Y	N	Y	Y
6 Dicks	Y	Y	Y	Y	Y	N	N
7 McDermott	Y	Y	Y	N	Y	Y	N
8 ***Dunn***	Y	Y	Y	Y	N	Y	Y
9 Smith, Adam	Y	Y	Y	Y	Y	Y	N
WEST VIRGINIA							
1 Mollohan	Y	Y	Y	Y	Y	N	N
2 Wise	Y	Y	Y	Y	Y	N	N
3 Rahall	Y	Y	Y	Y	Y	N	N
WISCONSIN							
1 ***Neumann***	Y	Y	N	Y	N	Y	Y
2 ***Klug***	Y	Y	Y	N	N	Y	Y
3 Kind	Y	Y	N	N	Y	Y	N
4 Kleczka	Y	?	Y	Y	Y	N	N
5 Barrett	Y	Y	N	N	Y	Y	N
6 ***Petri***	Y	Y	N	N	N	Y	Y
7 Obey	Y	Y	Y	Y	N	Y	N
8 Johnson	Y	Y	Y	Y	Y	N	N
9 ***Sensenbrenner***	Y	Y	N	N	Y	Y	Y
WYOMING							
AL ***Cubin***	Y	Y	Y	Y	N	Y	?

Southern states - Ala., Ark., Fla., Ga., Ky., La., Miss., N.C., Okla., S.C., Tenn., Texas, Va.

Key

Y	Voted for (yea).
#	Paired for.
+	Announced for.
N	Voted against (nay).
X	Paired against.
–	Announced against.
P	Voted "present."
C	Voted "present" to avoid possible conflict of interest.
?	Did not vote or otherwise make a position known.

Democrats **Republicans** *Independent*

462. H Res 552. Tax Cut and Social Security Savings/Rule. Adoption of the rule to provide for House floor consideration of the bills to cut taxes by $80 billion over five years (HR 4579) and to set aside 90 percent of any budget surplus in a special Treasury account until Congress enacts legislation to ensure the long-term solvency of the Social Security program (HR 4578). Adopted 215-208: R 212-7; D 3-200 (ND 3-145, SD 0-55); I 0-1. Sept. 25, 1998.

463. HR 4578. Surplus to Social Security/Social Security Trust Fund. Rangel, D-N.C., substitute amendment to transfer 100 percent of any Social Security Trust Fund surpluses to the Federal Reserve Bank of New York to be held in trust for the Social Security system. Rejected 210-216: R 8-215; D 201-1 (ND 146-1, SD 55-0); I 1-0. Sept. 25, 1998.

464. HR 4578. Surplus to Social Security/Passage. Passage of the bill to set aside 90 percent of any budget surplus in a special Treasury account until Congress enacts legislation to ensure the long-term solvency of the Social Security system. Passed 240-188: R 220-5; D 20-182 (ND 12-135, SD 8-47); I 0-1. Sept. 25, 1998. A "nay" was a vote in support of the president's position.

465. HR 2621. Fast-Track Trade Authority/Previous Question. Dreier, R-Calif., motion to order the previous question (thus ending debate and the possibility of amendment) on adoption of the rule (H Res 553) to provide for House floor consideration of the bill to allow expedited negotiation and implementation of trade agreements between the executive branch and foreign countries. Motion agreed to 230-193: R 223-0; D 7-192 (ND 3-142, SD 4-50); I 0-1. Sept. 25, 1998. (Subsequently, the rule was adopted by voice vote.)

466. HR 2621. Fast-Track Trade Authority/Passage. Passage of the bill to allow expedited negotiation and implementation of trade agreements between the executive branch and foreign countries. Rejected 180-243: R 151-71; D 29-171 (ND 13-133, SD 16-38); I 0-1. Sept. 25, 1998.

467. Procedural Motion/Journal. Approval of the House Journal of Friday, Sept. 25, 1998. Approved 334-50: R 181-18; D 152-32 (ND 110-25, SD 42-7); I 1-0. Sept. 26, 1998.

468. HR 4579. Tax Cuts/Democratic Substitute. Rangel, D-N.Y., substitute amendment that includes all of the tax cuts in the underlying bill but would prohibit most from taking effect until Congress enacts legislation to ensure the long-term solvency of the Social Security system. Rejected 197-227: R 0-221; D 196-6 (ND 143-5, SD 53-1); I 1-0. Sept. 26, 1998.

	462	463	464	465	466	467	468
ALABAMA							
1 *Callahan*	Y	N	Y	Y	Y	?	X
2 *Everett*	Y	N	Y	Y	Y	N	N
3 *Riley*	Y	N	Y	Y	N	Y	N
4 *Aderholt*	Y	Y	Y	Y	N	N	N
5 Cramer	N	Y	N	N	Y	Y	Y
6 *Bachus*	Y	N	Y	Y	Y	Y	N
7 Hilliard	N	Y	N	N	N	N	Y
ALASKA							
AL *Young*	Y	N	Y	Y	N	?	N
ARIZONA							
1 *Salmon*	Y	N	Y	Y	Y	Y	N
2 Pastor	N	Y	N	N	N	Y	Y
3 *Stump*	Y	N	Y	Y	N	Y	N
4 *Shadegg*	Y	Y	Y	Y	Y	Y	N
5 *Kolbe*	Y	N	Y	Y	Y	N	N
6 *Hayworth*	Y	N	Y	Y	Y	Y	N
ARKANSAS							
1 Berry	N	Y	N	N	Y	Y	Y
2 Snyder	N	Y	N	N	Y	Y	Y
3 *Hutchinson*	Y	N	Y	+	Y	N	Y
4 *Dickey*	Y	N	Y	Y	Y	Y	N
CALIFORNIA							
1 *Riggs*	Y	N	Y	Y	Y	?	N
2 *Herger*	Y	N	Y	Y	Y	Y	N
3 Fazio	N	Y	N	N	N	?	Y
4 *Doolittle*	Y	N	Y	Y	Y	N	N
5 Matsui	N	N	N	N	N	Y	Y
6 Woolsey	N	Y	N	N	N	Y	Y
7 Miller	N	Y	N	N	N	Y	Y
8 Pelosi	N	Y	N	N	N	?	Y
9 Lee	N	Y	N	N	N	Y	Y
10 Tauscher	N	Y	N	Y	N	Y	Y
11 *Pombo*	Y	N	Y	Y	N	Y	N
12 Lantos	N	Y	N	N	N	Y	Y
13 Stark	N	Y	N	N	N	Y	Y
14 Eshoo	N	Y	N	N	Y	Y	Y
15 *Campbell*	N	Y	N	Y	Y	Y	N
16 Lofgren	N	Y	N	N	N	Y	Y
17 Farr	N	Y	N	N	N	Y	Y
18 Condit	N	Y	Y	N	N	Y	Y
19 *Radanovich*	Y	N	Y	Y	Y	Y	N
20 Dooley	N	Y	N	Y	Y	Y	Y
21 *Thomas*	Y	N	Y	Y	Y	Y	N
22 Capps, L.	N	Y	N	N	Y	Y	Y
23 *Gallegly*	Y	N	Y	Y	N	Y	N
24 Sherman	N	Y	N	N	Y	Y	Y
25 *McKeon*	Y	N	Y	Y	Y	Y	N
26 Berman	N	Y	N	Y	N	?	#
27 *Rogan*	Y	N	Y	Y	Y	Y	N
28 *Dreier*	Y	N	Y	Y	Y	Y	N
29 Waxman	N	Y	N	N	N	?	Y
30 Becerra	N	Y	N	N	N	N	Y
31 Martinez	N	Y	N	N	P	?	Y
32 Dixon	N	Y	N	N	N	Y	Y
33 Roybal-Allard	N	Y	N	N	N	Y	Y
34 Torres	N	Y	N	N	N	Y	Y
35 Waters	N	?	N	N	N	N	Y
36 Harman	N	Y	N	Y	N	?	Y
37 Millender-McD.	N	Y	N	N	N	Y	Y
38 *Horn*	Y	N	Y	Y	Y	Y	N

	462	463	464	465	466	467	468
39 *Royce*	Y	N	Y	Y	N	Y	N
40 *Lewis*	Y	N	Y	Y	Y	Y	N
41 *Kim*	Y	N	Y	Y	Y	Y	N
42 Brown	N	Y	N	N	N	N	Y
43 *Calvert*	Y	N	Y	Y	Y	Y	N
44 *Bono, M.*	Y	N	Y	Y	Y	Y	N
45 *Rohrabacher*	Y	N	Y	Y	N	Y	N
46 Sanchez	N	Y	N	N	Y	Y	Y
47 *Cox*	Y	?	Y	Y	Y	?	N
48 *Packard*	Y	N	Y	Y	Y	Y	N
49 *Bilbray*	Y	N	Y	Y	Y	?	N
50 Filner	N	Y	N	N	N	N	Y
51 *Cunningham*	Y	N	Y	Y	Y	Y	N
52 *Hunter*	Y	N	Y	Y	N	Y	N
COLORADO							
1 DeGette	N	Y	N	N	N	Y	Y
2 Skaggs	N	Y	N	N	P	Y	Y
3 *McInnis*	Y	N	Y	Y	Y	Y	N
4 *Schaffer*	Y	N	Y	Y	Y	N	N
5 *Hefley*	Y	N	Y	Y	Y	N	N
6 *Schaefer*	Y	N	Y	Y	Y	?	N
CONNECTICUT							
1 Kennelly	?	?	?	?	N	?	Y
2 Gejdenson	N	Y	N	N	N	Y	Y
3 DeLauro	N	Y	N	N	N	Y	Y
4 *Shays*	Y	N	Y	Y	Y	Y	N
5 Maloney	N	Y	N	N	N	N	Y
6 *Johnson*	Y	N	Y	Y	Y	Y	N
DELAWARE							
AL *Castle*	Y	N	N	Y	Y	Y	N
FLORIDA							
1 *Scarborough*	Y	N	Y	Y	N	Y	N
2 Boyd	N	Y	N	N	N	Y	Y
3 Brown	N	Y	N	N	N	?	Y
4 *Fowler*	Y	N	Y	Y	?	?	X
5 Thurman	N	Y	N	N	N	Y	Y
6 *Stearns*	Y	N	Y	Y	N	Y	N
7 *Mica*	Y	N	Y	Y	Y	Y	N
8 *McCollum*	Y	N	Y	Y	Y	Y	N
9 *Bilirakis*	Y	N	Y	Y	N	Y	N
10 *Young*	Y	N	Y	Y	Y	?	N
11 Davis	N	Y	N	N	N	Y	Y
12 *Canady*	Y	N	Y	Y	N	Y	N
13 *Miller*	Y	N	Y	Y	N	Y	N
14 *Goss*	+	–	+	+	+	+	–
15 *Weldon*	Y	N	Y	Y	Y	N	N
16 *Foley*	Y	N	Y	Y	Y	Y	N
17 Meek	N	Y	N	N	N	Y	Y
18 *Ros-Lehtinen*	Y	N	Y	Y	N	Y	N
19 Wexler	N	Y	N	N	N	Y	Y
20 Deutsch	N	Y	N	N	N	Y	Y
21 *Diaz-Balart*	Y	N	Y	Y	N	?	N
22 *Shaw*	Y	N	Y	Y	Y	Y	N
23 Hastings	N	Y	N	N	N	Y	Y
GEORGIA							
1 *Kingston*	Y	N	Y	Y	Y	Y	N
2 Bishop	N	Y	N	N	Y	Y	Y
3 *Collins*	Y	N	Y	Y	Y	Y	N
4 McKinney	N	Y	N	N	N	N	Y
5 Lewis	N	Y	N	N	N	N	Y
6 *Gingrich*		N	Y		Y		N
7 *Barr*	Y	N	Y	Y	Y	Y	N
8 *Chambliss*	Y	N	Y	Y	Y	Y	N
9 *Deal*	Y	N	Y	Y	N	Y	N
10 *Norwood*	?	N	Y	Y	N	Y	N
11 *Linder*	Y	?	Y	Y	Y	Y	N
HAWAII							
1 Abercrombie	N	Y	N	N	N	Y	Y
2 Mink	N	Y	N	N	N	Y	Y
IDAHO							
1 *Chenoweth*	Y	Y	Y	Y	Y	Y	N
2 *Crapo*	Y	N	Y	Y	N	?	N
ILLINOIS							
1 Rush	N	Y	N	?	N	Y	Y
2 Jackson	N	Y	N	N	N	N	Y
3 Lipinski	N	Y	N	N	N	N	Y
4 Gutierrez	N	Y	N	N	N	Y	Y
5 Blagojevich	N	Y	N	N	N	Y	Y
6 *Hyde*	Y	N	Y	Y	Y	Y	N
7 Davis	N	Y	N	N	N	Y	Y
8 *Crane*	Y	N	Y	Y	Y	N	N
9 Yates	N	?	?	?	?	?	Y
10 *Porter*	Y	N	Y	Y	Y	Y	N
11 *Weller*	Y	N	Y	Y	N	Y	N
12 Costello	N	Y	N	N	N	Y	Y
13 *Fawell*	Y	N	Y	Y	N	Y	N

ND Northern Democrats   SD Southern Democrats

	462	463	464	465	466	467	468
14 ***Hastert***	Y	N	Y	Y	Y	Y	N
15 ***Ewing***	Y	N	Y	Y	Y	Y	N
16 ***Manzullo***	Y	N	Y	Y	Y	Y	N
17 Evans	N	Y	N	N	N	Y	Y
18 ***LaHood***	Y	N	N	Y	Y	Y	N
19 Poshard	N	Y	N	N	N	N	Y
20 ***Shimkus***	Y	N	Y	Y	Y	Y	N
INDIANA							
1 Visclosky	N	Y	N	N	N	?	Y
2 ***McIntosh***	N	N	Y	Y	Y	Y	N
3 Roemer	Y	Y	Y	N	N	Y	N
4 ***Souder***	Y	N	Y	Y	N	Y	N
5 ***Buyer***	Y	N	Y	Y	N	Y	N
6 ***Burton***	?	X	#	?	?	?	X
7 ***Pease***	Y	N	Y	Y	Y	Y	N
8 ***Hostettler***	Y	N	Y	Y	N	Y	N
9 Hamilton	N	Y	N	Y	Y	Y	N
10 Carson	N	Y	N	N	N	Y	Y
IOWA							
1 ***Leach***	Y	N	Y	Y	Y	Y	N
2 ***Nussle***	Y	N	Y	Y	Y	Y	N
3 Boswell	N	Y	Y	Y	Y	Y	Y
4 ***Ganske***	Y	N	Y	Y	Y	Y	N
5 ***Latham***	Y	N	Y	Y	Y	Y	N
KANSAS							
1 ***Moran***	Y	N	Y	Y	Y	N	N
2 ***Ryun***	Y	N	Y	Y	Y	Y	N
3 ***Snowbarger***	Y	N	Y	Y	Y	Y	N
4 ***Tiahrt***	Y	N	Y	Y	Y	?	N
KENTUCKY							
1 ***Whitfield***	Y	N	Y	Y	N	N	N
2 ***Lewis***	Y	N	Y	Y	Y	Y	N
3 ***Northup***	Y	N	Y	Y	Y	Y	N
4 ***Bunning***	Y	N	Y	Y	Y	Y	N
5 ***Rogers***	Y	N	Y	Y	N	?	N
6 Baesler	N	Y	N	N	N	Y	Y
LOUISIANA							
1 ***Livingston***	Y	N	Y	Y	Y	Y	N
2 Jefferson	N	Y	N	?	?	Y	Y
3 ***Tauzin***	Y	N	Y	Y	Y	?	N
4 ***McCrery***	Y	N	Y	Y	Y	?	N
5 ***Cooksey***	Y	N	Y	Y	Y	Y	N
6 ***Baker***	Y	N	Y	Y	Y	Y	N
7 John	N	Y	N	N	N	Y	Y
MAINE							
1 Allen	N	Y	N	N	N	Y	Y
2 Baldacci	N	Y	N	N	N	Y	Y
MARYLAND							
1 ***Gilchrest***	Y	N	Y	Y	Y	Y	N
2 ***Ehrlich***	Y	N	Y	Y	Y	Y	N
3 Cardin	N	Y	N	N	N	Y	Y
4 Wynn	N	Y	N	N	N	Y	Y
5 Hoyer	N	Y	N	N	N	Y	Y
6 ***Bartlett***	Y	N	Y	Y	N	Y	N
7 Cummings	N	Y	N	N	N	Y	Y
8 ***Morella***	N	N	N	Y	Y	?	N
MASSACHUSETTS							
1 Olver	N	Y	N	N	N	?	#
2 Neal	N	Y	N	N	N	Y	Y
3 McGovern	N	Y	N	N	N	Y	Y
4 Frank	N	Y	N	N	N	Y	Y
5 Meehan	N	Y	N	N	N	Y	Y
6 Tierney	N	Y	N	N	N	Y	Y
7 Markey	N	Y	N	N	N	Y	Y
8 Kennedy	N	Y	N	N	N	Y	Y
9 Moakley	?	#	X	?	N	Y	Y
10 Delahunt	N	Y	N	N	N	Y	Y
MICHIGAN							
1 Stupak	N	Y	N	N	N	N	Y
2 ***Hoekstra***	Y	N	Y	Y	N	N	N
3 ***Ehlers***	Y	N	Y	Y	Y	Y	N
4 ***Camp***	Y	N	Y	Y	Y	Y	N
5 Barcia	N	Y	Y	N	N	N	Y
6 ***Upton***	Y	N	Y	Y	Y	Y	N
7 ***Smith***	Y	Y	Y	Y	N	P	N
8 Stabenow	N	Y	N	N	N	Y	Y
9 Kildee	N	Y	N	N	N	Y	Y
10 Bonior	N	Y	N	N	N	N	Y
11 ***Knollenberg***	Y	N	Y	Y	Y	Y	N
12 Levin	N	Y	N	N	N	Y	Y
13 Rivers	N	Y	N	N	N	Y	Y
14 Conyers	N	Y	N	N	N	Y	Y
15 Kilpatrick	N	Y	N	N	N	Y	Y
16 Dingell	N	Y	N	N	N	Y	Y
MINNESOTA							
1 ***Gutknecht***	N	N	Y	Y	Y	N	N
2 Minge	N	Y	N	N	Y	Y	Y
3 ***Ramstad***	Y	N	Y	Y	Y	N	N
4 Vento	N	Y	N	N	N	Y	Y
5 Sabo	N	N	N	N	N	N	N
6 Luther	N	Y	N	N	N	Y	Y
7 Peterson	N	Y	N	N	N	Y	Y
8 Oberstar	N	Y	N	N	N	N	Y
MISSISSIPPI							
1 ***Wicker***	Y	N	Y	Y	Y	N	N
2 Thompson	N	Y	N	N	N	N	Y
3 ***Pickering***	Y	N	Y	Y	Y	?	N
4 ***Parker***	Y	N	Y	Y	Y	Y	N
5 Taylor	N	Y	Y	N	N	?	#
MISSOURI							
1 Clay	N	Y	N	N	N	N	Y
2 ***Talent***	Y	N	Y	Y	Y	Y	N
3 Gephardt	N	Y	N	N	N	?	Y
4 Skelton	N	Y	N	N	Y	Y	Y
5 McCarthy	N	Y	N	N	N	Y	Y
6 Danner	N	Y	Y	N	N	Y	Y
7 ***Blunt***	Y	N	Y	Y	Y	Y	N
8 ***Emerson***	Y	Y	Y	Y	Y	Y	N
9 ***Hulshof***	Y	N	Y	Y	Y	N	N
MONTANA							
AL ***Hill***	Y	N	N	Y	N	Y	N
NEBRASKA							
1 ***Bereuter***	Y	N	Y	Y	Y	Y	N
2 ***Christensen***	Y	N	Y	Y	Y	Y	N
3 ***Barrett***	Y	N	Y	Y	Y	Y	N
NEVADA							
1 ***Ensign***	Y	N	Y	Y	N	N	N
2 ***Gibbons***	Y	N	Y	Y	N	N	N
NEW HAMPSHIRE							
1 ***Sununu***	Y	N	Y	Y	Y	Y	N
2 ***Bass***	Y	N	Y	Y	Y	Y	N
NEW JERSEY							
1 Andrews	N	Y	N	N	N	Y	Y
2 ***LoBiondo***	Y	N	Y	Y	N	N	N
3 ***Saxton***	Y	N	Y	Y	+	+	–
4 ***Smith***	Y	N	Y	Y	N	Y	N
5 ***Roukema***	Y	N	Y	Y	Y	Y	N
6 Pallone	N	Y	N	N	N	Y	Y
7 ***Franks***	Y	N	Y	Y	Y	Y	N
8 Pascrell	N	Y	N	N	N	Y	Y
9 Rothman	N	Y	N	N	N	Y	Y
10 Payne	N	Y	N	?	N	?	Y
11 ***Frelinghuysen***	Y	N	Y	Y	Y	Y	N
12 ***Pappas***	Y	N	Y	Y	N	Y	N
13 Menendez	N	Y	N	N	N	Y	Y
NEW MEXICO							
1 ***Wilson***	Y	N	Y	Y	Y	Y	N
2 ***Skeen***	Y	N	Y	Y	Y	Y	N
3 ***Redmond***	Y	N	Y	Y	Y	Y	N
NEW YORK							
1 ***Forbes***	Y	Y	Y	Y	N	Y	N
2 ***Lazio***	Y	N	Y	Y	Y	Y	N
3 ***King***	Y	N	Y	Y	Y	Y	N
4 McCarthy	Y	Y	Y	N	N	Y	Y
5 Ackerman	N	Y	N	N	N	Y	Y
6 Meeks	?	Y	N	N	N	Y	Y
7 Manton	N	Y	N	N	N	Y	Y
8 Nadler	N	Y	N	N	N	Y	Y
9 Schumer	N	Y	N	N	N	Y	Y
10 Towns	N	Y	N	N	N	?	Y
11 Owens	N	Y	N	N	N	Y	Y
12 Velázquez	N	Y	N	N	N	N	Y
13 ***Fossella***	Y	N	Y	Y	Y	Y	N
14 Maloney	N	Y	N	N	N	Y	Y
15 Rangel	N	Y	N	N	N	Y	Y
16 Serrano	N	Y	N	N	N	Y	Y
17 Engel	N	Y	N	N	N	Y	Y
18 Lowey	N	Y	N	N	N	Y	Y
19 ***Kelly***	Y	N	Y	Y	Y	N	N
20 ***Gilman***	Y	N	Y	Y	N	Y	N
21 McNulty	N	Y	N	N	N	N	Y
22 ***Solomon***	Y	N	Y	Y	Y	Y	N
23 ***Boehlert***	Y	N	Y	Y	N	Y	N
24 ***McHugh***	Y	N	Y	Y	Y	Y	N
25 ***Walsh***	Y	N	Y	Y	N	Y	N
26 Hinchey	N	Y	N	N	N	N	Y
27 ***Paxon***	Y	N	Y	Y	Y	Y	N
28 Slaughter	N	Y	N	N	N	Y	Y
29 LaFalce	N	Y	N	N	N	N	Y
30 ***Quinn***	Y	N	Y	Y	N	Y	N
31 ***Houghton***	Y	N	Y	Y	Y	Y	N
NORTH CAROLINA							
1 Clayton	N	Y	N	N	N	Y	Y
2 Etheridge	N	Y	N	N	Y	Y	Y
3 ***Jones***	Y	N	Y	Y	N	N	N
4 Price	N	Y	N	N	Y	Y	Y
5 ***Burr***	Y	N	Y	Y	Y	Y	N
6 ***Coble***	Y	N	Y	Y	N	Y	N
7 McIntyre	N	Y	N	N	N	Y	Y
8 Hefner	N	Y	N	N	N	Y	Y
9 ***Myrick***	Y	N	Y	Y	Y	Y	N
10 ***Ballenger***	Y	N	Y	Y	Y	Y	N
11 ***Taylor***	Y	N	Y	Y	N	Y	N
12 Watt	N	Y	N	N	N	Y	Y
NORTH DAKOTA							
AL Pomeroy	N	Y	N	N	N	Y	Y
OHIO							
1 ***Chabot***	Y	N	Y	Y	Y	Y	N
2 ***Portman***	Y	N	Y	Y	Y	Y	N
3 Hall	N	Y	N	N	N	Y	Y
4 ***Oxley***	Y	N	Y	Y	Y	Y	N
5 ***Gillmor***	Y	N	Y	Y	Y	Y	N
6 Strickland	N	Y	N	N	N	Y	Y
7 ***Hobson***	Y	N	Y	Y	Y	Y	N
8 ***Boehner***	Y	N	Y	Y	Y	Y	N
9 Kaptur	N	Y	N	N	N	?	Y
10 Kucinich	N	Y	N	N	N	N	Y
11 Stokes	N	Y	N	N	N	N	Y
12 ***Kasich***	Y	N	Y	Y	Y	?	N
13 Brown	N	Y	?	N	N	Y	Y
14 Sawyer	N	Y	N	N	Y	Y	Y
15 ***Pryce***	+	–	+	+	+	+	–
16 ***Regula***	Y	N	Y	Y	N	Y	N
17 Traficant	Y	Y	N	N	N	Y	Y
18 ***Ney***	Y	N	Y	Y	N	Y	N
19 ***LaTourette***	Y	N	Y	Y	N	Y	N
OKLAHOMA							
1 ***Largent***	Y	N	Y	Y	Y	Y	N
2 ***Coburn***	N	N	Y	Y	N	?	?
3 ***Watkins***	Y	N	Y	Y	Y	Y	N
4 ***Watts***	Y	N	Y	Y	Y	Y	N
5 ***Istook***	Y	N	Y	Y	Y	Y	N
6 ***Lucas***	Y	N	Y	Y	Y	Y	N
OREGON							
1 Furse	N	Y	N	?	?	?	?
2 ***Smith***	Y	N	Y	Y	Y	Y	N
3 Blumenauer	N	Y	N	N	P	Y	Y
4 DeFazio	N	Y	N	N	N	N	Y
5 Hooley	N	Y	Y	N	Y	Y	Y
PENNSYLVANIA							
1 Brady	N	Y	N	N	N	N	Y
2 Fattah	N	Y	N	N	N	N	Y
3 Borski	N	Y	N	N	N	N	Y
4 Klink	N	Y	N	N	N	N	Y
5 ***Peterson***	Y	N	Y	Y	Y	Y	N
6 Holden	N	Y	N	N	N	Y	Y
7 ***Weldon***	Y	N	Y	Y	N	Y	N
8 ***Greenwood***	Y	N	Y	Y	Y	Y	N
9 ***Shuster***	Y	N	Y	Y	N	Y	N
10 ***McDade***	?	N	Y	Y	N	?	N
11 Kanjorski	N	Y	N	N	N	Y	Y
12 Murtha	N	Y	N	N	N	N	Y
13 ***Fox***	Y	N	Y	Y	N	N	N
14 Coyne	N	Y	N	N	N	Y	Y
15 McHale	N	Y	N	N	N	Y	Y
16 ***Pitts***	Y	N	Y	Y	Y	Y	N
17 ***Gekas***	Y	N	Y	Y	Y	Y	N
18 Doyle	N	Y	N	N	N	?	Y
19 ***Goodling***	Y	N	Y	Y	N	Y	N
20 Mascara	N	Y	N	N	N	Y	Y
21 ***English***	Y	N	Y	?	N	N	N
RHODE ISLAND							
1 Kennedy	N	Y	N	N	N	Y	Y
2 Weygand	N	Y	N	N	N	Y	Y
SOUTH CAROLINA							
1 ***Sanford***	N	N	N	Y	Y	Y	N
2 ***Spence***	Y	N	Y	Y	N	Y	N
3 ***Graham***	Y	N	Y	Y	N	Y	N
4 ***Inglis***	Y	N	Y	Y	Y	Y	N
5 Spratt	N	Y	N	N	N	Y	Y
6 Clyburn	N	Y	N	N	N	N	Y
SOUTH DAKOTA							
AL ***Thune***	Y	N	Y	Y	Y	Y	N
TENNESSEE							
1 ***Jenkins***	Y	N	Y	Y	N	Y	N
2 ***Duncan***	Y	N	Y	Y	N	Y	N
3 ***Wamp***	Y	N	Y	Y	N	Y	N
4 ***Hilleary***	Y	N	Y	Y	N	Y	N
5 Clement	N	Y	N	N	Y	?	Y
6 Gordon	N	Y	Y	N	N	Y	Y
7 ***Bryant***	Y	N	Y	Y	Y	Y	N
8 Tanner	N	Y	N	Y	Y	Y	Y
9 Ford	N	Y	N	N	Y	Y	Y
TEXAS							
1 Sandlin	N	Y	Y	N	N	Y	Y
2 Turner	N	Y	Y	N	N	Y	Y
3 ***Johnson, Sam***	Y	N	Y	Y	Y	Y	N
4 Hall	N	Y	Y	Y	Y	Y	Y
5 ***Sessions***	Y	N	Y	Y	Y	Y	N
6 ***Barton***	Y	N	Y	Y	Y	?	N
7 ***Archer***	Y	N	Y	Y	Y	Y	N
8 ***Brady***	Y	N	Y	Y	Y	Y	N
9 Lampson	N	Y	N	N	N	Y	Y
10 Doggett	N	Y	N	N	N	Y	Y
11 Edwards	N	Y	N	N	Y	Y	Y
12 ***Granger***	Y	N	Y	Y	Y	Y	N
13 ***Thornberry***	?	N	Y	Y	Y	Y	N
14 ***Paul***	?	N	Y	Y	N	Y	N
15 Hinojosa	N	Y	N	N	N	Y	Y
16 Reyes	N	Y	N	N	N	P	Y
17 Stenholm	N	Y	N	Y	Y	Y	Y
18 Jackson-Lee	N	Y	N	N	N	Y	Y
19 ***Combest***	Y	N	Y	Y	Y	Y	N
20 Gonzalez	N	Y	N	N	N	?	Y
21 ***Smith***	Y	N	Y	Y	Y	Y	N
22 ***DeLay***	Y	N	Y	Y	Y	Y	N
23 ***Bonilla***	Y	N	Y	Y	Y	Y	N
24 Frost	N	Y	N	N	N	Y	Y
25 Bentsen	N	Y	N	N	Y	?	Y
26 ***Armey***	Y	N	Y	Y	Y	Y	N
27 Ortiz	N	Y	N	N	Y	Y	Y
28 Rodriguez	N	Y	N	N	N	Y	Y
29 Green	N	Y	N	N	N	N	Y
30 Johnson, E.B.	N	Y	N	N	Y	N	Y
UTAH							
1 ***Hansen***	Y	N	Y	Y	Y	Y	N
2 ***Cook***	Y	N	Y	Y	N	Y	N
3 ***Cannon***	Y	N	Y	Y	Y	Y	N
VERMONT							
AL *Sanders*	N	Y	N	N	N	Y	Y
VIRGINIA							
1 ***Bateman***	Y	N	Y	Y	Y	?	N
2 Pickett	N	Y	N	N	Y	N	Y
3 Scott	N	Y	N	N	N	Y	Y
4 Sisisky	N	Y	N	N	N	Y	Y
5 Goode	N	Y	Y	N	Y	Y	N
6 ***Goodlatte***	Y	N	Y	Y	Y	Y	N
7 ***Bliley***	Y	N	Y	Y	Y	Y	N
8 Moran	N	Y	N	N	Y	Y	Y
9 Boucher	N	Y	N	N	N	Y	Y
10 ***Wolf***	Y	N	Y	Y	Y	Y	N
11 ***Davis***	Y	N	Y	Y	Y	Y	N
WASHINGTON							
1 ***White***	Y	N	Y	Y	Y	Y	N
2 ***Metcalf***	Y	N	Y	Y	N	Y	N
3 ***Smith, Linda***	N	Y	Y	Y	N	Y	N
4 ***Hastings***	Y	N	Y	Y	Y	Y	N
5 ***Nethercutt***	Y	N	Y	Y	Y	Y	N
6 Dicks	N	Y	N	N	N	Y	Y
7 McDermott	N	Y	N	N	N	Y	Y
8 ***Dunn***	Y	N	Y	Y	Y	Y	N
9 Smith, Adam	N	Y	N	N	N	Y	Y
WEST VIRGINIA							
1 Mollohan	N	Y	N	N	N	Y	Y
2 Wise	N	Y	N	N	N	Y	Y
3 Rahall	N	Y	N	N	N	Y	Y
WISCONSIN							
1 ***Neumann***	N	Y	Y	Y	N	Y	N
2 ***Klug***	Y	N	Y	Y	Y	Y	N
3 Kind	N	Y	N	N	N	Y	Y
4 Kleczka	N	Y	N	N	N	Y	Y
5 Barrett	N	Y	N	N	N	Y	Y
6 ***Petri***	Y	N	Y	Y	Y	Y	N
7 Obey	N	Y	N	N	N	Y	Y
8 Johnson	N	Y	N	N	N	Y	Y
9 ***Sensenbrenner***	Y	N	Y	Y	Y	Y	N
WYOMING							
AL ***Cubin***	?	N	Y	Y	Y	Y	N

Southern states - Ala., Ark., Fla., Ga., Ky., La., Miss., N.C., Okla., S.C., Tenn., Texas, Va.

Key

Y Voted for (yea).
\# Paired for.
\+ Announced for.
N Voted against (nay).
X Paired against.
– Announced against.
P Voted "present."
C Voted "present" to avoid possible conflict of interest.
? Did not vote or otherwise make a position known.

Democrats **Republicans**
Independent

---

469. HR 4579. Tax Cuts/Passage. Passage of the bill to cut taxes by $80.1 billion over five years, including $6.6 billion in cuts in fiscal 1999, by extending expired provisions such as the research tax credit, reducing taxes for farmers and married couples and making health insurance premiums 100 percent deductible for the self-employed. Passed 229-195: R 210-11; D 19-183 (ND 13-135, SD 6-48); I 0-1. Sept. 26, 1998. A "nay" was a vote in support of the president's position.

470. HR 3891. Product Identification Codes/Passage. Goodlatte, R-Va., motion to suspend the rules and pass the bill to establish fines and prison sentences for individuals who are convicted of tampering with or counterfeiting any product identification codes. Motion rejected 245-167: R 177-37; D 68-129 (ND 49-96, SD 19-33); I 0-1. Sept. 28, 1998. A two-thirds majority of those present and voting (275 in this case) is required for passage under suspension of the rules.

471. HR 4103. Fiscal 1999 Defense Appropriations/Conference Report. Adoption of the conference report on the bill to provide $250.5 billion in defense spending for fiscal 1999. Adopted (thus sent to the Senate) 369-43: R 204-10; D 165-32 (ND 115-30, SD 50-2); I 0-1. Sept. 28, 1998.

472. HR 4060. Fiscal 1999 Energy and Water Appropriations/Conference Report. Adoption of the conference report on the bill to provide $20.9 billion for fiscal 1999 spending on water, energy and defense-related projects. The conference report also calls for eliminating certain subsidies for the publicly funded Tennessee Valley Authority (TVA). Adopted (thus sent to the Senate) 389-25: R 199-16; D 189-9 (ND 143-3, SD 46-6); I 1-0. Sept. 28, 1998.

473. HR 3150. Consumer Bankruptcy Revisions/Motion to Instruct. Nadler, D-N.Y., motion to instruct House conferees to accept Senate provisions that would prevent credit card companies from either dropping customers who pay off all their debts each month, or charging them fees. Motion agreed to 295-119: R 100-115; D 194-4 (ND 143-3, SD 51-1); I 1-0. Sept. 28, 1998.

474. S 2073. Juvenile Crime Block Grants/Procedural Motion. Goodling, R-Pa., motion to go to conference on the bill to consolidate juvenile crime prevention funding, including boot camps, gang prevention and mentoring programs, into block grants to the states. The bill would also reauthorize programs to serve runaway and homeless youth and the National Missing Children Center. Motion agreed to 376-36: R 212-0; D 164-35 (ND 116-29, SD 48-6); I 0-1. Oct. 1, 1998.

475. HR 4104. Fiscal 1999 Treasury Postal Appropriations Conference Report/Rule. Adoption of the rule (H Res 563) to provide for House floor consideration of the conference report on the bill to provide about $27 billion in fiscal 1999 funding for the Treasury Department, U.S. Postal Service subsidies, the Executive Office of the President and several independent agencies. Rejected 106-294: R 89-117; D 17-176 (ND 13-127, SD 4-49); I 0-1. Oct. 1, 1998.

	469	470	471	472	473	474	475
ALABAMA							
1 *Callahan*	#	?	?	?	?	?	?
2 *Everett*	Y	Y	Y	Y	N	Y	N
3 *Riley*	Y	Y	Y	Y	N	Y	N
4 *Aderholt*	N	Y	Y	N	Y	Y	Y
5 Cramer	Y	Y	Y	N	Y	Y	N
6 *Bachus*	Y	N	Y	N	Y	Y	N
7 Hilliard	N	N	Y	Y	Y	N	N
ALASKA							
AL *Young*	Y	Y	Y	Y	N	Y	Y
ARIZONA							
1 *Salmon*	Y	Y	Y	Y	Y	Y	Y
2 Pastor	N	N	Y	Y	Y	Y	Y
3 *Stump*	Y	Y	Y	Y	N	Y	N
4 *Shadegg*	Y	Y	Y	Y	Y	Y	Y
5 *Kolbe*	Y	N	Y	Y	Y	Y	N
6 *Hayworth*	Y	Y	Y	Y	Y	Y	N
ARKANSAS							
1 Berry	N	N	Y	Y	Y	Y	N
2 Snyder	N	N	Y	Y	Y	Y	N
3 *Hutchinson*	Y	Y	Y	Y	Y	Y	N
4 *Dickey*	Y	N	Y	Y	N	Y	N
CALIFORNIA							
1 *Riggs*	Y	Y	Y	Y	N	Y	N
2 *Herger*	Y	Y	Y	Y	N	Y	N
3 Fazio	N	Y	Y	Y	Y	N	N
4 *Doolittle*	Y	Y	Y	Y	N	Y	N
5 Matsui	N	Y	Y	Y	Y	Y	N
6 Woolsey	N	N	Y	Y	Y	Y	N
7 Miller	N	?	?	?	?	Y	N
8 Pelosi	N	N	Y	Y	Y	Y	N
9 Lee	N	N	N	Y	Y	N	N
10 Tauscher	Y	Y	Y	Y	N	Y	N
11 *Pombo*	Y	Y	Y	Y	N	Y	N
12 Lantos	N	N	Y	Y	Y	Y	N
13 Stark	N	N	N	Y	Y	N	?
14 Eshoo	N	N	Y	Y	Y	Y	N
15 *Campbell*	Y	N	Y	N	Y	N	Y
16 Lofgren	N	Y	Y	Y	Y	Y	N
17 Farr	N	Y	Y	Y	Y	N	N
18 Condit	Y	Y	Y	Y	Y	Y	N
19 *Radanovich*	Y	Y	Y	Y	N	Y	N
20 Dooley	N	N	Y	Y	Y	Y	N
21 *Thomas*	Y	Y	Y	Y	N	Y	?
22 Capps, L.	Y	Y	Y	Y	Y	Y	N
23 *Gallegly*	Y	Y	Y	Y	N	Y	N
24 Sherman	N	N	Y	Y	Y	Y	N
25 *McKeon*	Y	Y	Y	Y	N	Y	N
26 Berman	X	N	Y	Y	Y	Y	N
27 *Rogan*	Y	Y	Y	Y	N	Y	N
28 *Dreier*	Y	N	Y	Y	N	Y	N
29 Waxman	N	N	Y	Y	Y	Y	N
30 Becerra	N	N	Y	Y	Y	Y	N
31 Martinez	N	?	?	?	?	?	?
32 Dixon	N	N	Y	Y	Y	Y	N
33 Roybal-Allard	N	N	Y	Y	Y	Y	N
34 Torres	N	N	Y	Y	Y	Y	N
35 Waters	N	N	?	Y	Y	N	N
36 Harman	N	N	Y	Y	Y	Y	N
37 Millender-McD.	N	N	Y	Y	Y	Y	N
38 *Horn*	Y	Y	Y	Y	Y	Y	N

	469	470	471	472	473	474	475
39 *Royce*	Y	Y	Y	N	Y	N	Y
40 *Lewis*	Y	Y	+	Y	N	Y	Y
41 *Kim*	Y	Y	Y	Y	N	Y	Y
42 Brown	N	Y	Y	Y	N	Y	N
43 *Calvert*	Y	N	Y	Y	N	Y	N
44 *Bono, M.*	Y	Y	Y	Y	N	Y	N
45 *Rohrabacher*	Y	Y	Y	Y	N	Y	N
46 Sanchez	N	Y	Y	Y	Y	Y	N
47 *Cox*	Y	N	Y	Y	Y	Y	N
48 *Packard*	Y	Y	Y	Y	N	+	+
49 *Bilbray*	Y	Y	Y	Y	Y	Y	N
50 Filner	N	N	N	Y	Y	N	N
51 *Cunningham*	Y	Y	Y	Y	N	Y	N
52 *Hunter*	Y	Y	Y	Y	N	Y	N
COLORADO							
1 DeGette	N	N	Y	Y	Y	Y	N
2 Skaggs	N	N	Y	Y	Y	Y	N
3 *McInnis*	Y	Y	Y	Y	Y	?	N
4 *Schaffer*	Y	Y	Y	Y	N	Y	N
5 *Hefley*	Y	Y	N	Y	N	Y	N
6 *Schaefer*	Y	Y	Y	Y	N	Y	N
CONNECTICUT							
1 Kennelly	Y	?	?	?	?	?	?
2 Gejdenson	N	N	Y	N	Y	N	N
3 DeLauro	N	N	Y	Y	Y	Y	N
4 *Shays*	Y	N	Y	N	Y	Y	N
5 Maloney	N	N	Y	Y	Y	Y	N
6 *Johnson*	Y	Y	Y	Y	N	Y	N
DELAWARE							
AL *Castle*	N	Y	Y	Y	Y	Y	Y
FLORIDA							
1 *Scarborough*	Y	Y	Y	Y	Y	Y	Y
2 Boyd	Y	Y	Y	Y	Y	Y	N
3 Brown	N	?	?	?	?	Y	N
4 *Fowler*	#	?	?	?	?	?	?
5 Thurman	N	N	Y	Y	Y	Y	N
6 *Stearns*	Y	Y	Y	N	N	Y	N
7 *Mica*	Y	N	Y	Y	Y	Y	N
8 *McCollum*	Y	Y	Y	Y	N	Y	N
9 *Bilirakis*	Y	Y	Y	Y	N	Y	N
10 *Young*	Y	Y	Y	Y	N	Y	?
11 Davis	N	Y	Y	Y	Y	Y	N
12 *Canady*	Y	Y	Y	Y	N	Y	N
13 *Miller*	Y	N	Y	N	Y	N	Y
14 Goss	+	+	+	+	–	+	+
15 *Weldon*	Y	N	Y	Y	Y	Y	Y
16 *Foley*	Y	Y	Y	Y	Y	Y	Y
17 Meek	N	N	Y	Y	Y	Y	N
18 *Ros-Lehtinen*	Y	–	?	?	?	Y	N
19 Wexler	N	N	Y	Y	Y	Y	N
20 Deutsch	N	N	Y	Y	Y	Y	N
21 *Diaz-Balart*	Y	N	Y	Y	Y	Y	N
22 *Shaw*	Y	N	Y	N	Y	N	N
23 Hastings	N	N	Y	Y	Y	Y	N
GEORGIA							
1 *Kingston*	Y	Y	Y	Y	Y	Y	Y
2 Bishop	Y	N	Y	Y	Y	Y	N
3 *Collins*	Y	Y	Y	Y	N	Y	N
4 McKinney	N	N	N	N	Y	N	N
5 Lewis	N	N	Y	Y	Y	Y	N
6 *Gingrich*	Y						
7 *Barr*	Y	Y	Y	Y	N	Y	N
8 *Chambliss*	Y	Y	Y	Y	N	Y	N
9 *Deal*	Y	Y	Y	Y	N	?	?
10 *Norwood*	Y	Y	Y	Y	N	Y	N
11 *Linder*	Y	Y	Y	Y	N	Y	Y
HAWAII							
1 Abercrombie	N	Y	Y	Y	Y	Y	N
2 Mink	N	Y	Y	Y	Y	N	N
IDAHO							
1 *Chenoweth*	N	Y	Y	N	N	Y	N
2 *Crapo*	Y	Y	Y	Y	N	Y	N
ILLINOIS							
1 Rush	N	N	N	Y	Y	Y	N
2 Jackson	N	N	N	Y	Y	Y	N
3 Lipinski	N	N	Y	Y	Y	Y	N
4 Gutierrez	N	N	N	Y	Y	Y	Y
5 Blagojevich	N	N	N	Y	Y	Y	N
6 *Hyde*	Y	Y	Y	Y	N	Y	N
7 Davis	N	N	N	Y	Y	Y	N
8 *Crane*	Y	Y	Y	N	N	?	N
9 Yates	N	N	N	Y	Y	N	?
10 *Porter*	Y	Y	Y	Y	N	Y	N
11 *Weller*	Y	Y	Y	Y	N	Y	Y
12 Costello	N	N	Y	Y	Y	Y	N
13 *Fawell*	Y	Y	Y	Y	Y	?	?

ND Northern Democrats   SD Southern Democrats

	469	470	471	472	473	474	475
14 ***Hastert***	Y	N	Y	Y	Y	Y	Y
15 ***Ewing***	Y	Y	Y	Y	Y	Y	N
16 ***Manzullo***	Y	N	Y	Y	N	Y	N
17 Evans	N	Y	Y	Y	Y	Y	N
18 ***LaHood***	N	Y	Y	Y	Y	Y	N
19 Poshard	N	?	?	?	?	?	?
20 ***Shimkus***	Y	Y	Y	Y	Y	Y	N
INDIANA							
1 Visclosky	N	N	Y	Y	Y	Y	N
2 ***McIntosh***	Y	Y	Y	Y	N	Y	N
3 Roemer	Y	Y	Y	N	Y	Y	N
4 ***Souder***	Y	Y	Y	Y	Y	Y	N
5 ***Buyer***	Y	Y	Y	Y	Y	Y	N
6 ***Burton***	#	Y	Y	Y	N	Y	Y
7 ***Pease***	Y	Y	Y	Y	N	Y	N
8 ***Hostettler***	Y	Y	Y	Y	N	Y	N
9 Hamilton	N	Y	Y	Y	Y	Y	N
10 Carson	N	Y	Y	Y	Y	Y	N
IOWA							
1 ***Leach***	Y	N	Y	Y	N	Y	N
2 ***Nussle***	Y	Y	Y	Y	N	Y	N
3 Boswell	Y	Y	Y	Y	Y	Y	Y
4 ***Ganske***	Y	Y	Y	Y	Y	Y	Y
5 ***Latham***	Y	Y	Y	Y	N	Y	N
KANSAS							
1 ***Moran***	Y	Y	Y	Y	Y	Y	Y
2 ***Ryun***	Y	Y	Y	Y	N	Y	N
3 ***Snowbarger***	Y	N	Y	Y	N	Y	N
4 ***Tiahrt***	Y	Y	Y	Y	N	Y	N
KENTUCKY							
1 ***Whitfield***	Y	Y	Y	Y	Y	Y	N
2 ***Lewis***	Y	Y	Y	Y	Y	Y	N
3 ***Northup***	Y	Y	Y	Y	Y	Y	Y
4 ***Bunning***	Y	Y	Y	Y	Y	Y	N
5 ***Rogers***	Y	Y	Y	Y	Y	Y	N
6 Baesler	N	Y	Y	Y	Y	Y	N
LOUISIANA							
1 ***Livingston***	Y	N	Y	Y	Y	Y	?
2 Jefferson	N	Y	Y	Y	Y	Y	N
3 ***Tauzin***	Y	Y	Y	Y	Y	Y	?
4 ***McCrery***	Y	Y	Y	Y	N	?	Y
5 ***Cooksey***	Y	Y	Y	Y	N	Y	N
6 ***Baker***	Y	?	?	?	?	Y	N
7 John	N	?	?	?	?	Y	N
MAINE							
1 Allen	N	N	Y	Y	Y	Y	N
2 Baldacci	N	N	Y	Y	Y	Y	N
MARYLAND							
1 ***Gilchrest***	Y	Y	Y	Y	N	Y	Y
2 ***Ehrlich***	Y	Y	Y	Y	Y	Y	Y
3 Cardin	N	Y	Y	Y	Y	Y	N
4 Wynn	N	N	Y	Y	Y	N	N
5 Hoyer	N	Y	Y	Y	Y	Y	N
6 ***Bartlett***	Y	Y	Y	Y	N	Y	N
7 Cummings	N	Y	Y	Y	Y	Y	N
8 ***Morella***	N	Y	Y	Y	Y	Y	Y
MASSACHUSETTS							
1 Olver	X	N	Y	Y	Y	N	Y
2 Neal	N	?	Y	Y	Y	Y	Y
3 McGovern	N	Y	Y	Y	Y	Y	N
4 Frank	N	Y	N	Y	Y	Y	N
5 Meehan	N	N	Y	Y	Y	Y	N
6 Tierney	N	N	Y	Y	Y	Y	N
7 Markey	N	N	Y	Y	Y	Y	N
8 Kennedy	N	N	Y	Y	Y	Y	N
9 Moakley	N	N	Y	Y	Y	Y	N
10 Delahunt	N	Y	N	Y	Y	N	N
MICHIGAN							
1 Stupak	N	N	Y	Y	Y	Y	N
2 ***Hoekstra***	Y	N	N	Y	Y	Y	N
3 ***Ehlers***	Y	Y	Y	Y	Y	Y	N
4 ***Camp***	Y	Y	Y	Y	N	Y	Y
5 Barcia	Y	N	Y	Y	Y	Y	N
6 ***Upton***	Y	Y	N	Y	Y	Y	Y
7 ***Smith***	Y	N	Y	Y	Y	Y	N
8 Stabenow	N	Y	Y	Y	Y	Y	N
9 Kildee	N	N	Y	Y	Y	Y	N
10 Bonior	N	N	Y	Y	Y	N	N
11 ***Knollenberg***	Y	Y	Y	Y	N	Y	Y
12 Levin	N	N	Y	Y	Y	Y	N
13 Rivers	N	N	N	Y	Y	Y	N
14 Conyers	N	N	N	Y	Y	N	Y
15 Kilpatrick	N	N	Y	Y	Y	Y	N
16 Dingell	N	N	Y	Y	Y	Y	N
MINNESOTA							
1 ***Gutknecht***	N	Y	Y	Y	Y	Y	Y
2 Minge	N	N	N	Y	Y	Y	N
3 ***Ramstad***	Y	Y	Y	Y	Y	Y	Y
4 Vento	N	N	N	Y	Y	Y	N
5 Sabo	N	N	Y	Y	Y	N	N
6 Luther	N	N	N	Y	Y	Y	N
7 Peterson	N	Y	Y	Y	Y	Y	N
8 Oberstar	N	N	N	Y	Y	N	N
MISSISSIPPI							
1 ***Wicker***	Y	Y	Y	Y	Y	Y	Y
2 Thompson	N	N	Y	Y	Y	?	N
3 ***Pickering***	Y	Y	Y	N	Y	Y	N
4 ***Parker***	Y	Y	Y	Y	N	Y	Y
5 Taylor	X	–	+	+	+	Y	N
MISSOURI							
1 Clay	N	N	Y	Y	Y	Y	?
2 ***Talent***	Y	Y	Y	Y	Y	Y	N
3 Gephardt	N	N	Y	Y	Y	Y	N
4 Skelton	N	N	Y	Y	Y	Y	N
5 McCarthy	N	N	Y	Y	Y	Y	N
6 Danner	Y	N	Y	Y	Y	Y	N
7 ***Blunt***	Y	Y	Y	N	Y	Y	Y
8 ***Emerson***	N	Y	Y	Y	Y	Y	N
9 ***Hulshof***	Y	Y	Y	Y	Y	?	Y
MONTANA							
AL ***Hill***	N	Y	Y	Y	N	Y	N
NEBRASKA							
1 ***Bereuter***	Y	Y	Y	Y	Y	Y	N
2 ***Christensen***	Y	?	?	?	?	Y	N
3 ***Barrett***	Y	Y	Y	Y	Y	Y	N
NEVADA							
1 ***Ensign***	Y	N	Y	N	Y	Y	Y
2 ***Gibbons***	Y	Y	Y	N	N	Y	Y
NEW HAMPSHIRE							
1 ***Sununu***	Y	Y	Y	Y	N	Y	N
2 ***Bass***	Y	Y	Y	Y	Y	Y	Y
NEW JERSEY							
1 Andrews	N	N	Y	Y	Y	Y	N
2 ***LoBiondo***	Y	Y	Y	Y	Y	Y	N
3 ***Saxton***	+	Y	Y	Y	Y	Y	N
4 ***Smith***	Y	Y	Y	Y	N	Y	N
5 ***Roukema***	Y	Y	Y	Y	N	Y	?
6 Pallone	N	N	Y	Y	Y	Y	N
7 ***Franks***	Y	Y	N	Y	Y	Y	N
8 Pascrell	N	N	Y	Y	Y	Y	N
9 Rothman	N	Y	Y	Y	Y	?	N
10 Payne	N	N	N	Y	Y	N	N
11 ***Frelinghuysen***	Y	Y	Y	Y	N	Y	Y
12 ***Pappas***	Y	Y	Y	Y	Y	Y	N
13 Menendez	N	Y	Y	Y	Y	Y	N
NEW MEXICO							
1 ***Wilson***	Y	Y	Y	Y	Y	Y	Y
2 ***Skeen***	Y	Y	Y	Y	N	Y	N
3 ***Redmond***	Y	Y	Y	Y	Y	Y	N
NEW YORK							
1 ***Forbes***	Y	N	Y	Y	Y	Y	Y
2 ***Lazio***	Y	N	Y	Y	Y	Y	Y
3 ***King***	Y	N	Y	Y	N	?	?
4 McCarthy	Y	N	Y	Y	Y	Y	Y
5 Ackerman	N	N	Y	Y	Y	Y	N
6 Meeks	N	N	Y	Y	Y	Y	N
7 Manton	N	N	Y	Y	Y	Y	N
8 Nadler	N	N	N	Y	Y	N	N
9 Schumer	N	?	?	?	?	Y	Y
10 Towns	N	N	Y	Y	Y	Y	?
11 Owens	N	N	N	Y	Y	N	Y
12 Velázquez	N	N	N	Y	Y	Y	N
13 ***Fossella***	Y	N	Y	Y	N	+	N
14 Maloney	N	Y	Y	Y	Y	Y	N
15 Rangel	N	N	Y	Y	Y	Y	Y
16 Serrano	N	N	Y	Y	Y	Y	N
17 Engel	N	N	Y	Y	Y	Y	N
18 Lowey	N	N	Y	Y	Y	Y	Y
19 ***Kelly***	Y	N	Y	Y	N	Y	Y
20 ***Gilman***	Y	N	Y	Y	Y	Y	Y
21 McNulty	N	Y	Y	Y	Y	Y	N
22 ***Solomon***	Y	N	Y	Y	N	Y	Y
23 ***Boehlert***	Y	Y	Y	Y	Y	Y	Y
24 ***McHugh***	Y	N	Y	Y	Y	Y	N
25 ***Walsh***	Y	Y	Y	Y	Y	Y	?
26 Hinchey	N	Y	Y	Y	Y	N	N
27 ***Paxon***	Y	?	?	?	?	Y	Y
28 Slaughter	N	N	Y	Y	Y	N	N
29 LaFalce	N	N	Y	Y	Y	Y	N
30 ***Quinn***	Y	Y	Y	Y	Y	?	N
31 ***Houghton***	Y	Y	Y	Y	N	Y	Y
NORTH CAROLINA							
1 Clayton	N	N	Y	Y	Y	Y	N
2 Etheridge	N	Y	Y	Y	Y	Y	N
3 ***Jones***	Y	Y	Y	Y	N	Y	N
4 Price	N	N	Y	Y	Y	Y	Y
5 ***Burr***	Y	Y	Y	Y	N	Y	Y
6 ***Coble***	Y	Y	Y	Y	N	Y	Y
7 McIntyre	N	Y	Y	Y	Y	Y	N
8 Hefner	N	N	Y	Y	Y	Y	N
9 ***Myrick***	Y	Y	Y	Y	N	Y	Y
10 ***Ballenger***	Y	Y	Y	Y	N	Y	N
11 ***Taylor***	Y	Y	Y	Y	N	Y	Y
12 Watt	N	N	Y	Y	Y	Y	N
NORTH DAKOTA							
AL Pomeroy	N	N	Y	Y	Y	Y	N
OHIO							
1 ***Chabot***	Y	N	Y	Y	N	Y	N
2 ***Portman***	Y	Y	Y	Y	Y	Y	N
3 Hall	N	N	Y	Y	Y	Y	?
4 ***Oxley***	Y	Y	Y	Y	N	Y	?
5 ***Gillmor***	Y	Y	Y	Y	N	Y	Y
6 Strickland	N	Y	Y	Y	Y	Y	N
7 ***Hobson***	Y	Y	Y	Y	Y	Y	Y
8 ***Boehner***	Y	Y	Y	Y	N	Y	Y
9 Kaptur	N	Y	Y	Y	Y	Y	N
10 Kucinich	N	Y	N	Y	Y	Y	N
11 Stokes	N	N	Y	Y	Y	Y	N
12 ***Kasich***	Y	Y	Y	Y	N	Y	N
13 Brown	N	N	Y	Y	Y	Y	N
14 Sawyer	N	N	Y	Y	Y	Y	N
15 ***Pryce***	+	+	+	+	+	+	+
16 ***Regula***	Y	Y	Y	Y	Y	Y	Y
17 Traficant	N	N	Y	Y	Y	Y	N
18 ***Ney***	Y	Y	Y	Y	Y	Y	N
19 ***LaTourette***	Y	Y	Y	Y	Y	Y	Y
OKLAHOMA							
1 ***Largent***	Y	?	?	?	Y	Y	?
2 ***Coburn***	?	?	Y	Y	Y	Y	N
3 ***Watkins***	Y	Y	Y	Y	Y	Y	N
4 ***Watts***	Y	Y	Y	Y	N	Y	N
5 ***Istook***	Y	Y	Y	Y	N	Y	Y
6 ***Lucas***	Y	Y	Y	Y	N	Y	N
OREGON							
1 Furse	?	Y	N	Y	Y	N	N
2 ***Smith***	Y	Y	Y	Y	N	Y	?
3 Blumenauer	N	N	N	Y	Y	Y	N
4 DeFazio	N	N	N	Y	Y	N	?
5 Hooley	Y	Y	N	Y	Y	Y	N
PENNSYLVANIA							
1 Brady	N	Y	Y	Y	Y	Y	N
2 Fattah	N	Y	Y	Y	Y	Y	N
3 Borski	N	N	Y	Y	Y	Y	N
4 Klink	N	N	Y	Y	Y	Y	N
5 ***Peterson***	Y	Y	Y	Y	Y	Y	N
6 Holden	N	Y	Y	Y	Y	Y	N
7 ***Weldon***	Y	Y	Y	Y	Y	Y	N
8 ***Greenwood***	Y	Y	Y	Y	Y	Y	Y
9 ***Shuster***	Y	Y	Y	Y	N	Y	?
10 ***McDade***	Y	Y	Y	Y	Y	Y	?
11 Kanjorski	N	N	Y	Y	Y	Y	N
12 Murtha	N	N	Y	Y	Y	Y	?
13 ***Fox***	Y	Y	Y	Y	Y	Y	Y
14 Coyne	N	N	Y	Y	Y	Y	N
15 McHale	N	N	Y	Y	Y	Y	N
16 ***Pitts***	Y	Y	Y	Y	N	Y	N
17 ***Gekas***	Y	Y	Y	Y	N	Y	Y
18 Doyle	N	N	Y	Y	Y	Y	N
19 ***Goodling***	Y	Y	Y	Y	N	Y	N
20 Mascara	N	N	Y	Y	Y	Y	N
21 ***English***	Y	Y	Y	Y	Y	Y	Y
RHODE ISLAND							
1 Kennedy	N	Y	Y	Y	Y	N	N
2 Weygand	N	N	Y	Y	Y	Y	N
SOUTH CAROLINA							
1 ***Sanford***	N	N	N	N	N	Y	N
2 ***Spence***	Y	Y	Y	Y	N	Y	Y
3 ***Graham***	Y	Y	Y	Y	Y	Y	N
4 ***Inglis***	Y	Y	Y	Y	Y	?	N
5 Spratt	N	Y	Y	Y	Y	Y	N
6 Clyburn	N	N	Y	Y	Y	N	N
SOUTH DAKOTA							
AL ***Thune***	Y	Y	Y	Y	Y	Y	N
TENNESSEE							
1 ***Jenkins***	Y	+	+	–	+	Y	Y
2 ***Duncan***	Y	Y	Y	Y	Y	Y	N
3 ***Wamp***	Y	Y	Y	Y	Y	Y	N
4 ***Hilleary***	Y	Y	Y	N	Y	Y	N
5 Clement	N	N	Y	N	Y	Y	?
6 Gordon	Y	Y	Y	N	Y	Y	N
7 ***Bryant***	Y	Y	Y	Y	N	Y	N
8 Tanner	N	Y	Y	N	Y	Y	N
9 Ford	N	N	Y	N	Y	Y	N
TEXAS							
1 Sandlin	Y	N	Y	Y	Y	Y	N
2 Turner	Y	Y	Y	Y	Y	Y	N
3 ***Johnson, Sam***	Y	Y	Y	Y	?	Y	N
4 Hall	N	Y	Y	Y	Y	Y	N
5 ***Sessions***	Y	Y	Y	Y	N	Y	N
6 ***Barton***	Y	Y	Y	Y	N	Y	N
7 ***Archer***	Y	Y	Y	Y	N	Y	Y
8 ***Brady***	Y	N	Y	Y	N	Y	N
9 Lampson	N	N	Y	Y	Y	Y	N
10 Doggett	N	N	N	Y	Y	Y	Y
11 Edwards	N	N	Y	Y	Y	Y	N
12 ***Granger***	Y	Y	Y	Y	N	Y	N
13 ***Thornberry***	Y	Y	Y	Y	N	Y	N
14 ***Paul***	Y	N	N	N	N	Y	Y
15 Hinojosa	N	N	Y	Y	Y	Y	N
16 Reyes	N	N	Y	Y	Y	Y	N
17 Stenholm	N	Y	Y	Y	Y	Y	N
18 Jackson-Lee	N	N	Y	Y	Y	N	N
19 ***Combest***	Y	?	?	?	?	Y	N
20 Gonzalez	N	Y	Y	Y	Y	Y	N
21 ***Smith***	Y	Y	Y	Y	Y	Y	N
22 ***DeLay***	Y	N	Y	Y	N	Y	Y
23 ***Bonilla***	Y	Y	Y	Y	N	Y	Y
24 Frost	N	N	Y	Y	Y	Y	N
25 Bentsen	N	N	Y	Y	Y	Y	N
26 ***Armey***	Y	?	?	?	?	Y	Y
27 Ortiz	N	Y	Y	Y	Y	Y	N
28 Rodriguez	N	N	Y	Y	Y	Y	N
29 Green	N	N	Y	Y	Y	Y	N
30 Johnson, E.B.	N	N	Y	Y	Y	Y	N
UTAH							
1 ***Hansen***	Y	Y	Y	Y	Y	Y	?
2 ***Cook***	Y	Y	Y	Y	Y	Y	N
3 ***Cannon***	Y	Y	Y	Y	N	Y	N
VERMONT							
AL *Sanders*	N	N	N	Y	Y	N	N
VIRGINIA							
1 ***Bateman***	Y	Y	Y	Y	N	Y	Y
2 Pickett	N	N	Y	Y	Y	Y	N
3 Scott	N	N	Y	Y	Y	N	N
4 Sisisky	N	N	Y	Y	Y	Y	N
5 Goode	Y	Y	Y	Y	Y	Y	N
6 ***Goodlatte***	Y	Y	Y	Y	N	Y	N
7 ***Bliley***	Y	Y	Y	Y	Y	Y	Y
8 Moran	N	Y	Y	Y	N	Y	–
9 Boucher	N	Y	Y	Y	Y	Y	N
10 ***Wolf***	Y	Y	Y	Y	Y	Y	Y
11 ***Davis***	Y	Y	Y	Y	N	Y	Y
WASHINGTON							
1 ***White***	Y	Y	Y	Y	N	Y	Y
2 ***Metcalf***	Y	Y	Y	Y	N	Y	N
3 ***Smith, Linda***	N	Y	Y	Y	N	Y	N
4 ***Hastings***	Y	Y	Y	Y	N	Y	Y
5 ***Nethercutt***	Y	Y	Y	Y	N	Y	Y
6 Dicks	N	N	Y	Y	Y	?	Y
7 McDermott	N	N	N	Y	Y	N	N
8 ***Dunn***	Y	Y	Y	Y	N	Y	Y
9 Smith, Adam	N	Y	Y	Y	Y	Y	N
WEST VIRGINIA							
1 Mollohan	N	N	Y	Y	Y	Y	N
2 Wise	N	N	Y	Y	Y	Y	N
3 Rahall	N	N	Y	Y	Y	N	N
WISCONSIN							
1 ***Neumann***	N	Y	Y	N	N	Y	N
2 ***Klug***	Y	N	Y	Y	N	Y	?
3 Kind	N	Y	Y	Y	Y	Y	N
4 Kleczka	N	Y	N	N	Y	Y	N
5 Barrett	N	Y	N	Y	Y	Y	N
6 ***Petri***	Y	Y	N	N	N	Y	N
7 Obey	N	Y	N	Y	Y	Y	N
8 Johnson	N	N	Y	Y	Y	Y	N
9 ***Sensenbrenner***	Y	Y	N	N	Y	Y	N
WYOMING							
AL ***Cubin***	Y	Y	Y	Y	Y	Y	N

Southern states - Ala., Ark., Fla., Ga., Ky., La., Miss., N.C., Okla., S.C., Tenn., Texas, Va.

Key

Y	Voted for (yea).
#	Paired for.
+	Announced for.
N	Voted against (nay).
X	Paired against.
–	Announced against.
P	Voted "present."
C	Voted "present" to avoid possible conflict of interest.
?	Did not vote or otherwise make a position known.

Democrats **Republicans**
Independent

476. HR 4274. Fiscal 1999 Labor, Health and Human Services Appropriations/Rule. Adoption of the rule (H Res 564) to provide for House floor consideration of the bill to appropriate $290.8 billion for the Labor, Health and Human Services (HHS), and Education Departments and related agencies for fiscal 1999. Adopted 216-200: R 211-6; D 5-193 (ND 0-143, SD 5-50); I 0-1. Oct. 2, 1998.

477. Procedural Motion/Journal. Approval of the House Journal of Thursday Oct. 1, 1998. Approved 346-60: R 195-16; D 150-44 (ND 106-35, SD 44-9); I 1-0. Oct. 2, 1998.

478. HR 4101. Fiscal 1999 Agriculture Appropriations/Recommit. Pomeroy, D-N.D., motion to recommit the conference report to the conference committee with instructions to report it back with an amendment to increase emergency funding for farmers. Motion rejected 156-236: R 8-200; D 147-36 (ND 110-21, SD 37-15); I 1-0. Oct. 2, 1998.

479. HR 4101. Fiscal 1999 Agriculture Appropriations/Conference Report. Adoption of the conference report on the bill to provide about $55.9 billion in funding for agriculture spending in fiscal 1999. The conference report also provides $4.2 billion in emergency funding for aid to farmers dealing with problems including natural disasters and loss of markets. Adopted (thus sent to the Senate) 333-53: R 179-25; D 153-28 (ND 104-25, SD 49-3); I 1-0. Oct. 2, 1998. A "nay" was a vote in support of the president's position.

480. HR 4614. New Hampshire Land Transfer/Passage. Horn, R-Calif., motion to suspend the rules and pass the bill to transfer two acres of U.S. Coast Guard land to the town of New Castle, N.H. Motion rejected 230-168: R 210-0; D 20-167 (ND 10-126, SD 10-41); I 0-1. Oct. 5, 1998. A two-thirds majority of those present and voting (266 in this case) is required for passage under suspension of the rules.

481. HR 1154. Indian Tribe Federal Recognition/Passage. Young, R-Alaska, motion to suspend the rules and pass the bill to create a new process for granting federal recognition to Indian tribes. Motion rejected 190-208: R 40-171; D 149-37 (ND 109-26, SD 40-11); I 1-0. Oct. 5, 1998. A two-thirds majority of those present and voting (266 in this case) is required for passage under suspension of the rules.

482. HR 4655. Assistance for Iraqi Opposition Groups/Passage. Gilman, R-N.Y., motion to suspend the rules and pass the bill to authorize U.S. assistance to certain Iraqi opposition groups engaged in the fight against the regime of Saddam Hussein. Motion agreed to 360-38: R 202-9; D 157-29 (ND 113-22, SD 44-7); I 1-0. Oct. 5, 1998. A two-thirds majority of those present and voting (266 in this case) is required for passage under suspension of the rules.

	476	477	478	479	480	481	482
ALABAMA							
1 *Callahan*	?	?	?	?	Y	N	Y
2 *Everett*	Y	Y	N	Y	Y	N	N
3 *Riley*	Y	Y	N	Y	Y	N	Y
4 *Aderholt*	Y	N	N	Y	Y	N	Y
5 Cramer	N	Y	Y	Y	N	N	Y
6 *Bachus*	Y	Y	N	Y	Y	N	Y
7 Hilliard	N	N	Y	N	Y	N	N
ALASKA							
AL *Young*	Y	Y	N	Y	Y	Y	Y
ARIZONA							
1 *Salmon*	Y	Y	?	?	Y	Y	Y
2 Pastor	N	Y	Y	Y	N	Y	Y
3 *Stump*	Y	Y	N	Y	Y	N	Y
4 *Shadegg*	Y	Y	N	Y	Y	N	Y
5 *Kolbe*	Y	Y	N	Y	Y	N	Y
6 *Hayworth*	Y	Y	N	Y	Y	Y	Y
ARKANSAS							
1 Berry	N	N	Y	N	Y	Y	Y
2 Snyder	N	N	Y	N	Y	N	Y
3 *Hutchinson*	Y	Y	N	Y	N	Y	Y
4 *Dickey*	Y	N	N	Y	N	Y	Y
CALIFORNIA							
1 *Riggs*	Y	Y	N	+	–	N	+
2 *Herger*	Y	Y	N	Y	Y	N	Y
3 Fazio	N	N	Y	N	Y	N	Y
4 *Doolittle*	Y	Y	N	Y	Y	N	Y
5 Matsui	N	Y	Y	Y	N	Y	Y
6 Woolsey	N	Y	Y	Y	N	Y	Y
7 Miller	N	N	Y	N	N	N	Y
8 Pelosi	N	Y	Y	?	?	?	?
9 Lee	N	N	Y	N	N	N	Y
10 Tauscher	N	N	Y	N	N	N	Y
11 *Pombo*	Y	Y	N	Y	Y	N	Y
12 Lantos	N	Y	Y	N	Y	N	Y
13 Stark	N	Y	Y	N	N	N	Y
14 Eshoo	N	Y	N	Y	N	N	Y
15 *Campbell*	Y	Y	N	N	Y	N	Y
16 Lofgren	N	Y	Y	N	N	N	Y
17 Farr	N	Y	Y	N	N	N	Y
18 Condit	N	Y	Y	N	Y	N	Y
19 *Radanovich*	Y	Y	N	Y	Y	N	Y
20 Dooley	N	N	Y	N	Y	N	Y
21 *Thomas*	Y	N	N	Y	Y	N	Y
22 Capps, L.	N	Y	Y	N	Y	N	Y
23 *Gallegly*	Y	Y	N	Y	Y	N	Y
24 Sherman	N	N	Y	N	Y	N	Y
25 *McKeon*	Y	Y	N	Y	Y	N	Y
26 Berman	N	Y	Y	N	N	N	Y
27 *Rogan*	Y	N	N	Y	Y	N	Y
28 *Dreier*	Y	Y	N	Y	Y	N	Y
29 Waxman	N	?	Y	N	Y	N	Y
30 Becerra	N	N	Y	–	+	+	+
31 Martinez	?	?	?	N	Y	Y	Y
32 Dixon	N	Y	Y	?	?	?	?
33 Roybal-Allard	N	Y	Y	–	+	+	+
34 Torres	N	Y	?	N	Y	Y	Y
35 Waters	N	N	Y	N	N	Y	N
36 Harman	?	?	?	?	?	?	?
37 Millender-McD.	N	Y	Y	?	?	?	?
38 *Horn*	Y	Y	N	Y	Y	N	Y

	476	477	478	479	480	481	482
39 *Royce*	Y	Y	N	N	Y	N	Y
40 *Lewis*	Y	Y	N	Y	Y	Y	Y
41 *Kim*	Y	Y	N	Y	Y	N	Y
42 Brown	N	N	Y	N	Y	N	N
43 *Calvert*	Y	Y	N	Y	?	?	#
44 *Bono, M.*	Y	Y	N	Y	Y	N	Y
45 *Rohrabacher*	Y	N	N	Y	Y	N	Y
46 Sanchez	Y	N	Y	N	Y	N	Y
47 *Cox*	Y	Y	N	N	Y	N	Y
48 *Packard*	Y	Y	N	Y	Y	N	Y
49 *Bilbray*	Y	Y	N	Y	Y	N	Y
50 Filner	N	N	Y	N	N	Y	Y
51 *Cunningham*	Y	Y	?	?	Y	N	Y
52 *Hunter*	Y	Y	N	Y	Y	Y	Y
COLORADO							
1 DeGette	N	Y	Y	Y	N	Y	Y
2 Skaggs	N	Y	Y	N	Y	N	Y
3 *McInnis*	Y	Y	N	Y	Y	N	Y
4 *Schaffer*	Y	N	N	Y	Y	Y	Y
5 *Hefley*	?	?	?	?	Y	N	Y
6 *Schaefer*	Y	Y	N	Y	?	?	?
CONNECTICUT							
1 Kennelly	?	?	?	?	?	?	?
2 Gejdenson	N	Y	Y	N	N	N	Y
3 DeLauro	N	Y	Y	N	N	N	Y
4 *Shays*	Y	Y	N	N	Y	N	Y
5 Maloney	N	N	Y	N	N	N	Y
6 *Johnson*	Y	Y	N	Y	Y	N	Y
DELAWARE							
AL *Castle*	Y	Y	N	N	Y	N	Y
FLORIDA							
1 *Scarborough*	Y	Y	N	N	?	N	Y
2 Boyd	N	Y	N	Y	N	Y	Y
3 Brown	N	Y	Y	N	Y	N	Y
4 *Fowler*	?	?	?	?	Y	N	Y
5 Thurman	N	Y	Y	N	Y	N	Y
6 *Stearns*	Y	N	N	Y	Y	Y	Y
7 *Mica*	Y	Y	N	Y	Y	N	Y
8 *McCollum*	Y	Y	N	Y	Y	N	Y
9 *Bilirakis*	Y	Y	N	Y	Y	N	Y
10 *Young*	Y	Y	N	Y	?	?	?
11 Davis	N	Y	Y	N	Y	N	Y
12 *Canady*	Y	Y	N	Y	Y	N	Y
13 *Miller*	Y	Y	N	N	Y	N	Y
14 *Goss*	+	+	–	–	Y	N	Y
15 *Weldon*	Y	Y	N	Y	Y	N	Y
16 *Foley*	Y	Y	N	Y	Y	N	Y
17 Meek	N	Y	?	N	N	N	Y
18 *Ros-Lehtinen*	Y	Y	N	Y	?	?	?
19 Wexler	N	Y	Y	N	Y	N	Y
20 Deutsch	N	Y	?	N	Y	N	Y
21 *Diaz-Balart*	Y	Y	N	Y	Y	N	Y
22 *Shaw*	Y	Y	N	Y	Y	N	Y
23 Hastings	N	N	Y	N	Y	N	Y
GEORGIA							
1 *Kingston*	Y	Y	N	Y	Y	N	Y
2 Bishop	N	Y	Y	–	+	+	Y
3 *Collins*	Y	Y	N	Y	Y	N	Y
4 McKinney	N	Y	Y	N	N	N	N
5 Lewis	N	N	Y	N	Y	N	N
6 *Gingrich*							
7 *Barr*	Y	Y	N	N	Y	N	Y
8 *Chambliss*	Y	Y	N	Y	Y	N	Y
9 *Deal*	Y	Y	N	Y	Y	N	Y
10 *Norwood*	Y	Y	N	Y	?	?	?
11 *Linder*	Y	Y	N	Y	Y	N	Y
HAWAII							
1 Abercrombie	N	Y	Y	Y	N	Y	N
2 Mink	N	Y	Y	Y	N	Y	Y
IDAHO							
1 *Chenoweth*	Y	N	N	Y	N	N	N
2 *Crapo*	Y	Y	N	Y	Y	N	Y
ILLINOIS							
1 Rush	N	Y	N	Y	N	Y	N
2 Jackson	N	Y	N	Y	N	Y	N
3 Lipinski	?	?	?	?	N	N	Y
4 Gutierrez	N	N	Y	Y	N	Y	Y
5 Blagojevich	N	Y	Y	N	N	Y	Y
6 *Hyde*	Y	Y	?	?	Y	N	Y
7 Davis	N	Y	N	Y	N	Y	N
8 *Crane*	Y	N	N	N	Y	N	Y
9 Yates	N	Y	N	?	?	X	Y
10 *Porter*	Y	Y	N	Y	Y	N	Y
11 *Weller*	N	N	N	Y	Y	N	Y
12 Costello	N	N	?	N	Y	N	Y
13 *Fawell*	Y	Y	N	Y	Y	N	Y

H-136

	476	477	478	479	480	481	482
14 ***Hastert***	Y	Y	N	Y	Y	N	Y
15 ***Ewing***	Y	Y	N	Y	Y	N	N
16 ***Manzullo***	Y	Y	N	Y	Y	N	Y
17 Evans	?	Y	Y	Y	N	Y	Y
18 ***LaHood***	Y	Y	N	Y	Y	N	N
19 Poshard	?	?	?	?	?	?	?
20 ***Shimkus***	Y	Y	N	Y	Y	N	Y
INDIANA							
1 Visclosky	N	N	N	Y	N	N	Y
2 ***McIntosh***	Y	Y	N	N	Y	N	Y
3 Roemer	N	Y	Y	Y	N	N	Y
4 ***Souder***	Y	Y	N	Y	Y	N	Y
5 ***Buyer***	Y	Y	N	Y	Y	N	Y
6 ***Burton***	Y	Y	N	Y	Y	N	Y
7 ***Pease***	Y	Y	N	Y	Y	N	Y
8 ***Hostettler***	Y	Y	N	N	Y	N	N
9 Hamilton	N	Y	N	Y	N	Y	Y
10 Carson	N	P	Y	Y	N	Y	N
IOWA							
1 ***Leach***	N	Y	Y	Y	Y	N	Y
2 ***Nussle***	Y	Y	Y	Y	Y	N	Y
3 Boswell	N	Y	Y	Y	N	N	Y
4 ***Ganske***	Y	Y	N	Y	Y	N	Y
5 ***Latham***	Y	Y	N	Y	Y	N	Y
KANSAS							
1 ***Moran***	Y	N	N	Y	Y	N	Y
2 ***Ryun***	Y	Y	N	Y	Y	N	Y
3 ***Snowbarger***	Y	+	–	+	Y	N	Y
4 ***Tiahrt***	Y	Y	N	Y	Y	N	Y
KENTUCKY							
1 ***Whitfield***	Y	Y	N	?	Y	N	Y
2 ***Lewis***	Y	Y	N	Y	Y	N	Y
3 ***Northup***	Y	Y	N	Y	Y	N	Y
4 ***Bunning***	Y	Y	N	Y	Y	N	Y
5 ***Rogers***	Y	Y	N	Y	?	?	?
6 Baesler	N	Y	N	Y	Y	N	Y
LOUISIANA							
1 ***Livingston***	?	?	N	Y	Y	N	Y
2 Jefferson	N	Y	Y	Y	Y	Y	N
3 ***Tauzin***	?	?	?	?	?	?	?
4 ***McCrery***	Y	Y	N	Y	Y	N	Y
5 ***Cooksey***	Y	Y	N	Y	Y	N	Y
6 ***Baker***	Y	Y	N	Y	Y	N	Y
7 John	Y	Y	N	Y	N	Y	Y
MAINE							
1 Allen	N	Y	Y	Y	N	Y	Y
2 Baldacci	N	Y	N	Y	N	Y	Y
MARYLAND							
1 ***Gilchrest***	Y	Y	N	Y	Y	Y	Y
2 ***Ehrlich***	Y	Y	N	Y	Y	Y	Y
3 Cardin	N	Y	Y	Y	Y	N	Y
4 Wynn	N	N	Y	Y	N	Y	Y
5 Hoyer	N	Y	Y	Y	N	Y	Y
6 ***Bartlett***	Y	Y	N	Y	Y	N	N
7 Cummings	N	Y	Y	Y	N	Y	Y
8 ***Morella***	N	Y	N	Y	Y	N	Y
MASSACHUSETTS							
1 Olver	N	N	Y	Y	N	Y	Y
2 Neal	N	Y	Y	Y	?	?	?
3 McGovern	N	Y	Y	Y	?	?	?
4 Frank	N	Y	Y	N	N	Y	Y
5 Meehan	N	Y	?	?	N	Y	Y
6 Tierney	N	Y	Y	Y	N	Y	Y
7 Markey	N	Y	Y	Y	N	Y	Y
8 Kennedy	N	Y	Y	Y	N	Y	Y
9 Moakley	N	Y	?	?	?	?	?
10 Delahunt	N	Y	Y	Y	Y	Y	Y
MICHIGAN							
1 Stupak	N	?	?	?	?	?	?
2 ***Hoekstra***	Y	Y	N	N	Y	N	Y
3 ***Ehlers***	Y	Y	N	Y	Y	N	Y
4 ***Camp***	Y	Y	N	Y	Y	N	Y
5 Barcia	N	Y	Y	Y	N	Y	Y
6 ***Upton***	Y	Y	N	Y	Y	N	Y
7 ***Smith***	Y	Y	N	Y	Y	N	Y
8 Stabenow	N	Y	Y	Y	N	Y	Y
9 Kildee	N	Y	Y	Y	N	Y	Y
10 Bonior	N	N	Y	Y	N	Y	Y
11 ***Knollenberg***	Y	Y	N	Y	Y	Y	Y
12 Levin	N	Y	Y	Y	N	Y	Y
13 Rivers	N	Y	N	N	N	Y	N
14 Conyers	N	Y	Y	Y	N	Y	N
15 Kilpatrick	N	Y	?	?	N	Y	Y
16 Dingell	N	Y	Y	Y	N	N	Y

	476	477	478	479	480	481	482
MINNESOTA							
1 ***Gutknecht***	Y	Y	N	Y	Y	Y	Y
2 Minge	N	Y	Y	Y	Y	Y	Y
3 ***Ramstad***	Y	N	N	Y	Y	N	Y
4 Vento	N	N	Y	N	N	Y	N
5 Sabo	N	N	Y	Y	Y	Y	N
6 Luther	N	Y	Y	Y	N	Y	Y
7 Peterson	N	Y	Y	Y	Y	Y	Y
8 Oberstar	N	N	Y	N	N	Y	Y
MISSISSIPPI							
1 ***Wicker***	Y	N	N	Y	Y	N	Y
2 Thompson	N	N	Y	Y	N	Y	Y
3 ***Pickering***	Y	?	N	Y	Y	Y	Y
4 ***Parker***	?	?	?	?	Y	Y	Y
5 Taylor	Y	N	Y	N	Y	N	Y
MISSOURI							
1 Clay	?	?	?	?	N	Y	N
2 ***Talent***	Y	Y	N	Y	Y	N	Y
3 Gephardt	N	N	?	?	Y	Y	Y
4 Skelton	N	Y	N	Y	N	N	N
5 McCarthy	N	Y	N	Y	N	Y	Y
6 Danner	N	Y	Y	Y	N	Y	Y
7 ***Blunt***	Y	Y	N	Y	Y	N	Y
8 ***Emerson***	Y	Y	Y	Y	Y	Y	Y
9 ***Hulshof***	Y	N	N	Y	Y	Y	Y
MONTANA							
AL ***Hill***	Y	Y	Y	Y	Y	N	Y
NEBRASKA							
1 ***Bereuter***	Y	Y	Y	Y	Y	N	Y
2 ***Christensen***	Y	Y	N	Y	Y	N	Y
3 ***Barrett***	Y	Y	N	Y	Y	N	Y
NEVADA							
1 ***Ensign***	Y	Y	N	N	Y	N	Y
2 ***Gibbons***	Y	N	N	Y	Y	N	Y
NEW HAMPSHIRE							
1 ***Sununu***	Y	Y	?	?	Y	N	Y
2 ***Bass***	Y	Y	N	Y	Y	N	Y
NEW JERSEY							
1 Andrews	N	Y	N	N	N	N	Y
2 ***LoBiondo***	Y	N	N	Y	Y	N	Y
3 ***Saxton***	Y	Y	N	Y	Y	N	Y
4 ***Smith***	Y	Y	N	Y	Y	N	Y
5 ***Roukema***	Y	Y	N	Y	Y	N	Y
6 Pallone	N	N	Y	N	Y	Y	Y
7 ***Franks***	Y	Y	N	N	Y	N	Y
8 Pascrell	N	Y	N	Y	N	Y	Y
9 Rothman	N	Y	N	N	N	Y	Y
10 Payne	N	Y	Y	N	N	Y	N
11 ***Frelinghuysen***	Y	Y	N	N	Y	N	Y
12 ***Pappas***	Y	Y	N	N	Y	N	Y
13 Menendez	N	N	?	?	N	N	Y
NEW MEXICO							
1 ***Wilson***	Y	Y	N	Y	Y	N	Y
2 ***Skeen***	Y	Y	N	Y	Y	N	Y
3 ***Redmond***	Y	Y	N	Y	Y	Y	Y
NEW YORK							
1 ***Forbes***	Y	Y	N	Y	Y	N	Y
2 ***Lazio***	Y	Y	N	Y	Y	N	Y
3 ***King***	?	?	?	?	Y	N	Y
4 McCarthy	N	Y	N	Y	N	N	Y
5 Ackerman	N	Y	Y	Y	N	Y	Y
6 Meeks	N	Y	Y	Y	N	Y	Y
7 Manton	N	Y	Y	Y	Y	Y	Y
8 Nadler	N	Y	Y	Y	N	Y	Y
9 Schumer	N	Y	Y	Y	N	Y	Y
10 Towns	N	N	Y	Y	N	Y	N
11 Owens	N	Y	Y	?	?	?	?
12 Velázquez	N	N	Y	Y	N	Y	Y
13 ***Fossella***	Y	Y	N	Y	Y	N	Y
14 Maloney	N	Y	Y	Y	N	N	Y
15 Rangel	N	N	Y	Y	N	Y	Y
16 Serrano	N	Y	N	Y	N	Y	N
17 Engel	N	Y	Y	Y	N	Y	Y
18 Lowey	N	Y	Y	Y	N	N	Y
19 ***Kelly***	Y	Y	N	Y	Y	N	Y
20 ***Gilman***	Y	Y	N	Y	Y	Y	Y
21 McNulty	N	N	Y	Y	Y	Y	Y
22 ***Solomon***	Y	Y	N	Y	Y	N	Y
23 ***Boehlert***	Y	Y	N	Y	?	?	?
24 ***McHugh***	N	Y	N	Y	Y	N	Y
25 ***Walsh***	Y	Y	N	Y	Y	Y	N
26 Hinchey	N	N	Y	Y	N	Y	Y
27 ***Paxon***	Y	Y	N	Y	Y	N	Y
28 Slaughter	N	N	Y	Y	N	N	Y
29 LaFalce	N	N	N	Y	N	N	Y
30 ***Quinn***	Y	Y	N	Y	Y	Y	Y

	476	477	478	479	480	481	482
31 ***Houghton***	Y	Y	?	?	Y	Y	Y
NORTH CAROLINA							
1 Clayton	N	Y	Y	Y	N	Y	Y
2 Etheridge	N	Y	N	Y	N	Y	Y
3 ***Jones***	Y	Y	N	Y	Y	N	Y
4 Price	N	Y	Y	Y	N	Y	Y
5 ***Burr***	Y	Y	N	Y	Y	N	Y
6 ***Coble***	Y	Y	N	Y	Y	N	Y
7 McIntyre	N	Y	Y	Y	N	Y	Y
8 Hefner	N	N	N	Y	N	Y	Y
9 ***Myrick***	Y	Y	N	Y	Y	N	Y
10 ***Ballenger***	Y	?	N	Y	Y	N	Y
11 ***Taylor***	Y	Y	N	Y	Y	N	Y
12 Watt	N	Y	Y	Y	N	Y	Y
NORTH DAKOTA							
AL Pomeroy	N	Y	Y	N	N	N	Y
OHIO							
1 ***Chabot***	Y	Y	N	N	Y	N	Y
2 ***Portman***	Y	Y	N	Y	Y	N	Y
3 Hall	N	Y	N	Y	N	N	Y
4 ***Oxley***	Y	Y	N	Y	Y	N	Y
5 ***Gillmor***	Y	Y	N	?	Y	N	Y
6 Strickland	N	N	Y	Y	N	Y	Y
7 ***Hobson***	Y	Y	N	Y	Y	N	Y
8 ***Boehner***	Y	Y	N	Y	Y	N	Y
9 Kaptur	N	Y	Y	Y	Y	Y	Y
10 Kucinich	N	N	Y	N	N	N	Y
11 Stokes	N	Y	?	?	?	?	?
12 ***Kasich***	Y	Y	N	Y	Y	N	Y
13 Brown	N	Y	Y	Y	N	Y	Y
14 Sawyer	N	Y	Y	Y	N	Y	Y
15 ***Pryce***	+	+	–	+	+	–	+
16 ***Regula***	Y	Y	N	Y	Y	N	Y
17 Traficant	N	Y	N	Y	Y	Y	Y
18 ***Ney***	N	Y	N	Y	Y	N	Y
19 ***LaTourette***	Y	Y	N	Y	Y	N	Y
OKLAHOMA							
1 ***Largent***	Y	Y	N	Y	Y	N	Y
2 ***Coburn***	Y	Y	N	Y	Y	N	Y
3 ***Watkins***	Y	Y	Y	Y	Y	N	Y
4 ***Watts***	Y	Y	N	Y	Y	N	Y
5 ***Istook***	Y	Y	N	Y	Y	N	Y
6 ***Lucas***	Y	Y	N	Y	Y	N	Y
OREGON							
1 Furse	N	Y	Y	Y	N	Y	N
2 ***Smith***	Y	Y	N	Y	Y	N	Y
3 Blumenauer	N	Y	Y	N	N	Y	Y
4 DeFazio	?	?	?	?	N	Y	Y
5 Hooley	N	Y	Y	Y	N	Y	Y
PENNSYLVANIA							
1 Brady	N	Y	?	?	N	Y	Y
2 Fattah	N	Y	?	?	N	Y	Y
3 Borski	N	N	Y	?	N	Y	Y
4 Klink	N	N	Y	Y	N	N	Y
5 ***Peterson***	Y	Y	N	Y	Y	N	Y
6 Holden	N	Y	Y	Y	N	N	Y
7 ***Weldon***	Y	Y	N	Y	Y	Y	Y
8 ***Greenwood***	Y	Y	N	Y	?	?	?
9 ***Shuster***	Y	Y	N	?	?	?	?
10 ***McDade***	Y	Y	N	Y	?	?	#
11 Kanjorski	N	Y	Y	Y	N	N	Y
12 Murtha	N	Y	N	Y	N	?	?
13 ***Fox***	N	N	N	Y	Y	N	Y
14 Coyne	N	Y	Y	Y	N	Y	Y
15 McHale	N	Y	Y	Y	N	Y	Y
16 ***Pitts***	?	?	?	?	Y	N	Y
17 ***Gekas***	Y	Y	N	Y	Y	Y	Y
18 Doyle	N	Y	Y	Y	N	N	Y
19 ***Goodling***	Y	Y	N	Y	Y	Y	Y
20 Mascara	N	Y	Y	Y	N	N	Y
21 ***English***	Y	N	N	Y	Y	N	Y
RHODE ISLAND							
1 Kennedy	N	Y	Y	Y	N	Y	Y
2 Weygand	N	Y	Y	Y	N	N	Y
SOUTH CAROLINA							
1 ***Sanford***	Y	Y	N	N	?	?	?
2 ***Spence***	Y	Y	N	Y	Y	N	Y
3 ***Graham***	Y	Y	N	Y	Y	N	Y
4 ***Inglis***	Y	Y	N	Y	Y	N	Y
5 Spratt	N	Y	Y	Y	?	?	?
6 Clyburn	N	?	Y	Y	N	Y	Y
SOUTH DAKOTA							
AL ***Thune***	Y	Y	Y	Y	Y	N	Y

	476	477	478	479	480	481	482
TENNESSEE							
1 ***Jenkins***	Y	Y	N	Y	Y	N	Y
2 ***Duncan***	Y	Y	N	Y	Y	N	Y
3 ***Wamp***	Y	Y	N	Y	Y	N	Y
4 ***Hilleary***	Y	N	N	Y	Y	N	Y
5 Clement	N	Y	Y	Y	Y	Y	Y
6 Gordon	N	Y	Y	Y	N	Y	Y
7 ***Bryant***	Y	?	N	Y	Y	N	Y
8 Tanner	N	Y	N	Y	N	Y	Y
9 Ford	N	Y	N	Y	N	Y	N
TEXAS							
1 Sandlin	N	Y	N	Y	N	Y	Y
2 Turner	N	Y	Y	Y	N	N	Y
3 ***Johnson, Sam***	Y	Y	N	N	Y	Y	Y
4 Hall	Y	Y	N	Y	Y	Y	Y
5 ***Sessions***	Y	Y	N	Y	Y	N	Y
6 ***Barton***	Y	Y	?	?	Y	N	Y
7 ***Archer***	Y	?	N	Y	Y	N	Y
8 ***Brady***	Y	Y	N	Y	Y	N	Y
9 Lampson	N	Y	Y	Y	N	Y	Y
10 Doggett	N	Y	N	N	N	Y	N
11 Edwards	N	Y	N	Y	N	Y	Y
12 ***Granger***	Y	Y	N	Y	?	?	?
13 ***Thornberry***	Y	Y	N	Y	Y	N	Y
14 ***Paul***	Y	Y	Y	N	Y	N	N
15 Hinojosa	N	Y	Y	Y	–	+	+
16 Reyes	N	Y	Y	Y	N	Y	Y
17 Stenholm	Y	N	N	Y	Y	Y	Y
18 Jackson-Lee	N	Y	Y	Y	N	Y	Y
19 ***Combest***	Y	Y	N	Y	Y	Y	Y
20 Gonzalez	N	Y	Y	Y	N	Y	Y
21 ***Smith***	Y	Y	N	Y	Y	N	Y
22 ***DeLay***	Y	?	?	?	Y	N	Y
23 ***Bonilla***	Y	Y	N	Y	Y	N	Y
24 Frost	N	Y	Y	Y	?	?	?
25 Bentsen	N	Y	N	Y	N	N	Y
26 ***Armey***	Y	Y	?	Y	Y	Y	Y
27 Ortiz	N	Y	Y	Y	N	Y	Y
28 Rodriguez	N	Y	Y	Y	N	Y	Y
29 Green	N	N	Y	Y	N	Y	Y
30 Johnson, E.B.	N	Y	Y	Y	N	Y	Y
UTAH							
1 ***Hansen***	Y	Y	N	?	?	?	?
2 ***Cook***	Y	Y	N	Y	Y	N	Y
3 ***Cannon***	Y	Y	N	Y	Y	Y	Y
VERMONT							
AL *Sanders*	N	Y	Y	Y	N	Y	Y
VIRGINIA							
1 ***Bateman***	Y	Y	N	Y	Y	N	Y
2 Pickett	N	N	?	?	Y	N	Y
3 Scott	N	Y	Y	Y	N	Y	Y
4 Sisisky	N	Y	Y	Y	Y	Y	Y
5 Goode	Y	Y	Y	Y	Y	N	Y
6 ***Goodlatte***	Y	Y	N	Y	Y	N	Y
7 ***Bliley***	Y	Y	N	Y	Y	N	Y
8 Moran	N	?	Y	Y	N	Y	Y
9 Boucher	N	Y	?	Y	N	N	Y
10 ***Wolf***	Y	Y	N	Y	Y	N	Y
11 ***Davis***	Y	Y	N	Y	Y	N	Y
WASHINGTON							
1 ***White***	Y	Y	N	Y	Y	N	Y
2 ***Metcalf***	Y	Y	N	Y	Y	N	Y
3 ***Smith, Linda***	Y	Y	N	Y	Y	N	Y
4 ***Hastings***	Y	Y	N	?	Y	N	Y
5 ***Nethercutt***	Y	Y	N	Y	Y	N	Y
6 Dicks	N	Y	Y	Y	N	Y	Y
7 McDermott	N	N	Y	N	N	Y	Y
8 ***Dunn***	Y	Y	N	Y	Y	N	Y
9 Smith, Adam	N	Y	?	?	N	Y	Y
WEST VIRGINIA							
1 Mollohan	N	Y	Y	Y	N	Y	Y
2 Wise	N	Y	?	?	N	Y	Y
3 Rahall	N	Y	Y	Y	N	Y	Y
WISCONSIN							
1 ***Neumann***	Y	Y	N	N	Y	N	Y
2 ***Klug***	Y	Y	?	?	Y	N	Y
3 Kind	N	Y	Y	N	N	Y	Y
4 Kleczka	N	Y	Y	N	N	Y	Y
5 Barrett	N	Y	Y	N	N	Y	Y
6 ***Petri***	Y	Y	N	N	Y	N	Y
7 Obey	N	N	Y	N	N	Y	Y
8 Johnson	N	N	Y	N	N	Y	Y
9 ***Sensenbrenner***	Y	Y	N	N	Y	N	Y
WYOMING							
AL ***Cubin***	Y	Y	N	Y	Y	N	Y

Southern states - Ala., Ark., Fla., Ga., Ky., La., Miss., N.C., Okla., S.C., Tenn., Texas, Va.

Key

Y	Voted for (yea).
#	Paired for.
+	Announced for.
N	Voted against (nay).
X	Paired against.
−	Announced against.
P	Voted "present."
C	Voted "present" to avoid possible conflict of interest.
?	Did not vote or otherwise make a position known.

Democrats **Republicans**
Independent

483. HR 4194. Fiscal 1999 VA-HUD Appropriations/Conference Report. Adoption of the conference report on the bill to provide $93.4 billion in funding for veterans, housing, space and science programs in fiscal 1999. Adopted (thus sent to the Senate) 409-14: R 213-9; D 195-5 (ND 141-5, SD 54-0); I 1-0. Oct. 6, 1998.

484. H Res 575. Expedited Consideration of Legislative Business/Adoption. Adoption of the resolution to allow for expedited consideration of appropriations bills, appropriations conference reports and any continuing resolutions between Oct. 6 and Oct. 11, 1998. The measure, called a "martial law resolution," also allows the Speaker to schedule suspension bills on any day between Oct. 6 and Oct. 11, 1998. Adopted 218-206: R 218-3; D 0-202 (ND 0-148, SD 0-54); I 0-1. Oct. 6, 1998.

485. HR 4259. Indian Higher Education Demonstration Project/Civil Service Requirements Substitute. Cummings, D-Md., substitute amendment to require current federal civil service procedures to remain in effect for temporary alternative personnel management demonstration projects to be carried out at Haskell Indian Nations University and Southwestern Indian Polytechnic Institute. Rejected 181-244: R 0-224; D 180-20 (ND 137-9, SD 43-11); I 1-0. Oct. 6, 1998. (Subsequently, the bill was passed by voice vote.)

486. HR 3694. Fiscal 1999 Intelligence Authorization/Recommit. Barr, R-Ga., motion to recommit the bill to the conference committee with instructions to report it back with an amendment deleting the section of the bill that expands the government's power to place wiretaps on telephones. Motion rejected 148-267: R 90-127; D 57-140 (ND 44-98, SD 13-42); I 1-0. Oct. 7, 1998.

487. HR 3694. Fiscal 1999 Intelligence Authorization/Conference Report. Adoption of the conference report on the bill to authorize classified amounts in fiscal 1999 for U.S. intelligence agencies and intelligence-related activities of the U.S. government, including the Central Intelligence Agency, the National Security Agency, and the foreign intelligence activities of the Defense Department, FBI, State Department and other agencies. The total funding level is classified, but this year's authorization is reportedly slightly higher than fiscal 1998 levels. Adopted (thus sent to the Senate) 337-83: R 174-47; D 163-35 (ND 117-27, SD 46-8); I 0-1. Oct. 7, 1998.

488. HR 4570. National Parks and Public Lands Revisions/Rule. Adoption of the rule (H Res 573) to provide for House floor consideration of the bill composed of the provisions of numerous (roughly 100) independently introduced bills dealing with National Parks and other public lands. Adopted 225-198: R 222-0; D 3-197 (ND 3-142, SD 0-55); I 0-1. Oct. 7, 1998.

489. HR 4570. National Parks and Public Lands Revisions/Passage. Passage of the bill composed of the provisions of numerous (roughly 100) independently introduced bills dealing with National Parks and other public lands. Defeated 123-302: R 117-107; D 6-194 (ND 3-143, SD 3-51); I 0-1. Oct. 7, 1998. A "nay" was a vote in support of the president's position.

	483	484	485	486	487	488	489
ALABAMA							
1 *Callahan*	Y	Y	N	N	Y	Y	Y
2 *Everett*	Y	Y	N	Y	Y	Y	N
3 *Riley*	Y	Y	N	Y	Y	Y	Y
4 *Aderholt*	Y	Y	N	Y	Y	Y	N
5 Cramer	Y	N	N	N	N	N	N
6 *Bachus*	Y	Y	N	Y	N	Y	N
7 Hilliard	Y	N	Y	N	N	N	N
ALASKA							
AL *Young*	Y	Y	N	N	Y	Y	Y
ARIZONA							
1 *Salmon*	Y	Y	N	Y	Y	Y	Y
2 Pastor	Y	N	Y	Y	Y	N	N
3 *Stump*	Y	Y	N	Y	Y	Y	N
4 *Shadegg*	Y	Y	N	N	Y	Y	Y
5 *Kolbe*	Y	Y	N	N	Y	Y	Y
6 *Hayworth*	Y	Y	N	Y	N	Y	Y
ARKANSAS							
1 Berry	Y	N	Y	N	Y	N	N
2 Snyder	Y	N	Y	N	N	N	N
3 *Hutchinson*	Y	Y	N	N	?	Y	N
4 *Dickey*	Y	Y	N	N	Y	Y	Y
CALIFORNIA							
1 *Riggs*	+	+	?	N	Y	Y	N
2 *Herger*	Y	Y	N	Y	Y	Y	Y
3 Fazio	Y	N	Y	N	Y	N	?
4 *Doolittle*	Y	Y	N	Y	N	Y	Y
5 Matsui	Y	N	?	Y	Y	N	N
6 Woolsey	Y	N	Y	N	N	N	N
7 Miller	Y	N	Y	N	N	N	N
8 Pelosi	Y	N	Y	N	N	N	N
9 Lee	Y	N	Y	N	N	N	N
10 Tauscher	Y	N	Y	N	Y	N	N
11 *Pombo*	Y	Y	N	Y	N	Y	Y
12 Lantos	Y	N	Y	N	Y	N	N
13 Stark	Y	N	?	N	N	N	N
14 Eshoo	Y	N	Y	N	Y	N	N
15 *Campbell*	Y	N	Y	Y	Y	Y	Y
16 Lofgren	Y	N	Y	N	N	N	N
17 Farr	Y	N	Y	N	Y	N	N
18 Condit	Y	N	N	N	Y	N	N
19 *Radanovich*	Y	Y	N	Y	Y	Y	Y
20 Dooley	Y	N	Y	N	Y	N	N
21 *Thomas*	Y	Y	N	N	Y	Y	N
22 Capps, L.	Y	N	Y	N	N	N	N
23 *Gallegly*	Y	Y	N	Y	N	Y	N
24 Sherman	Y	N	Y	N	Y	N	N
25 *McKeon*	Y	Y	N	−	+	Y	Y
26 Berman	Y	N	Y	N	Y	N	N
27 *Rogan*	Y	Y	N	Y	Y	Y	Y
28 *Dreier*	Y	Y	N	Y	Y	Y	Y
29 Waxman	Y	N	Y	N	Y	N	N
30 Becerra	Y	N	Y	N	Y	N	N
31 Martinez	Y	N	Y	?	N	N	N
32 Dixon	Y	N	Y	N	N	N	N
33 Roybal-Allard	Y	N	Y	N	N	N	N
34 Torres	?	N	Y	Y	Y	N	N
35 Waters	Y	N	Y	N	N	N	N
36 Harman	Y	N	Y	N	Y	N	N
37 Millender-McD.	Y	N	Y	N	N	N	N
38 *Horn*	Y	Y	N	N	Y	Y	Y

	483	484	485	486	487	488	489
39 *Royce*	Y	Y	N	Y	Y	Y	Y
40 *Lewis*	Y	Y	N	Y	Y	Y	Y
41 *Kim*	Y	Y	N	Y	N	Y	Y
42 Brown	+	N	Y	N	N	Y	N
43 *Calvert*	Y	?	N	N	Y	Y	Y
44 *Bono, M.*	Y	Y	N	N	Y	Y	Y
45 *Rohrabacher*	Y	Y	N	Y	N	Y	N
46 Sanchez	Y	N	Y	N	Y	N	N
47 *Cox*	Y	Y	N	Y	Y	Y	Y
48 *Packard*	Y	Y	N	N	Y	Y	Y
49 *Bilbray*	Y	Y	N	N	Y	Y	Y
50 Filner	Y	N	Y	N	N	N	N
51 *Cunningham*	Y	Y	N	Y	N	Y	Y
52 *Hunter*	Y	Y	N	Y	Y	Y	Y
COLORADO							
1 DeGette	Y	N	Y	N	Y	N	N
2 Skaggs	Y	N	Y	N	Y	N	N
3 *McInnis*	Y	Y	N	Y	Y	Y	Y
4 *Schaffer*	N	Y	N	Y	N	Y	Y
5 *Hefley*	Y	Y	N	Y	Y	Y	Y
6 *Schaefer*	Y	Y	N	N	Y	Y	Y
CONNECTICUT							
1 Kennelly	?	?	?	?	?	?	?
2 Gejdenson	Y	N	Y	N	Y	N	N
3 DeLauro	Y	N	Y	N	N	N	N
4 *Shays*	Y	Y	N	N	Y	Y	Y
5 Maloney	Y	N	Y	+	N	Y	N
6 *Johnson*	Y	Y	N	N	Y	Y	N
DELAWARE							
AL *Castle*	Y	Y	N	N	Y	Y	N
FLORIDA							
1 *Scarborough*	N	Y	N	Y	N	Y	N
2 Boyd	Y	N	N	N	Y	N	N
3 Brown	Y	N	Y	N	N	N	N
4 *Fowler*	Y	Y	N	N	Y	Y	N
5 Thurman	Y	N	Y	N	Y	N	N
6 *Stearns*	Y	?	N	Y	N	Y	N
7 *Mica*	Y	Y	N	Y	Y	Y	Y
8 *McCollum*	Y	Y	N	N	Y	Y	Y
9 *Bilirakis*	Y	Y	N	N	Y	Y	Y
10 *Young*	Y	Y	N	N	Y	Y	Y
11 Davis	Y	N	Y	N	Y	N	N
12 *Canady*	Y	Y	N	N	Y	Y	Y
13 *Miller*	Y	Y	N	Y	Y	Y	Y
14 *Goss*	Y	Y	N	N	Y	Y	Y
15 *Weldon*	Y	Y	N	N	Y	Y	Y
16 *Foley*	Y	Y	N	N	Y	Y	Y
17 Meek	Y	N	Y	N	N	N	N
18 *Ros-Lehtinen*	Y	N	N	N	Y	Y	Y
19 Wexler	Y	N	Y	N	N	N	N
20 Deutsch	Y	N	Y	N	Y	N	N
21 *Diaz-Balart*	Y	N	N	N	Y	Y	Y
22 *Shaw*	Y	Y	N	Y	Y	Y	Y
23 Hastings	Y	N	Y	N	N	N	N
GEORGIA							
1 *Kingston*	Y	Y	N	Y	N	Y	Y
2 Bishop	Y	N	Y	N	N	N	N
3 *Collins*	Y	Y	N	Y	Y	Y	Y
4 McKinney	Y	N	Y	N	N	N	N
5 Lewis	Y	N	Y	Y	?	N	N
6 *Gingrich*							
7 *Barr*	Y	Y	N	Y	N	Y	Y
8 *Chambliss*	Y	Y	N	N	Y	Y	Y
9 *Deal*	Y	Y	N	Y	N	Y	Y
10 *Norwood*	Y	Y	N	Y	N	Y	Y
11 *Linder*	?	?	N	N	Y	Y	Y
HAWAII							
1 Abercrombie	Y	N	Y	Y	Y	N	N
2 Mink	Y	N	Y	Y	Y	N	N
IDAHO							
1 *Chenoweth*	Y	Y	N	Y	N	Y	N
2 *Crapo*	Y	Y	N	Y	N	Y	N
ILLINOIS							
1 Rush	Y	N	?	N	Y	N	N
2 Jackson	Y	N	Y	Y	N	N	N
3 Lipinski	N	N	Y	N	Y	N	Y
4 Gutierrez	Y	N	Y	N	N	N	N
5 Blagojevich	Y	N	Y	N	N	N	N
6 *Hyde*	Y	Y	N	N	Y	Y	N
7 Davis	Y	N	Y	N	Y	N	N
8 *Crane*	N	Y	N	N	N	Y	Y
9 Yates	Y	N	N	N	N	N	N
10 *Porter*	Y	Y	N	N	Y	Y	Y
11 *Weller*	Y	Y	N	Y	Y	Y	Y
12 Costello	Y	N	Y	N	Y	N	N
13 *Fawell*	?	?	N	N	Y	Y	Y

ND Northern Democrats   SD Southern Democrats

Member	483	484	485	486	487	488	489
14 ***Hastert***	Y	Y	N	N	Y	Y	Y
15 ***Ewing***	Y	Y	N	N	Y	Y	N
16 ***Manzullo***	Y	Y	N	Y	N	Y	N
17 Evans	Y	N	Y	N	Y	N	N
18 ***LaHood***	Y	Y	N	N	Y	Y	N
19 Poshard	?	?	?	?	?	?	?
20 ***Shimkus***	Y	Y	N	N	Y	Y	N
INDIANA							
1 Visclosky	Y	N	Y	N	Y	N	N
2 ***McIntosh***	Y	Y	N	Y	N	Y	N
3 Roemer	N	N	Y	N	N	N	N
4 ***Souder***	Y	Y	N	?	Y	Y	Y
5 ***Buyer***	Y	Y	N	N	Y	Y	Y
6 ***Burton***	Y	Y	N	Y	N	Y	Y
7 ***Pease***	Y	Y	N	N	Y	Y	N
8 ***Hostettler***	N	Y	N	Y	N	Y	N
9 Hamilton	Y	N	N	N	Y	N	N
10 Carson	Y	N	Y	Y	Y	N	N
IOWA							
1 ***Leach***	Y	Y	N	N	Y	Y	N
2 ***Nussle***	Y	Y	N	N	Y	Y	N
3 Boswell	Y	N	Y	N	Y	N	N
4 ***Ganske***	Y	Y	N	N	Y	Y	N
5 ***Latham***	Y	Y	N	N	Y	Y	N
KANSAS							
1 ***Moran***	Y	Y	N	Y	Y	Y	N
2 ***Ryun***	Y	Y	N	Y	N	Y	N
3 ***Snowbarger***	Y	Y	N	Y	Y	Y	Y
4 ***Tiahrt***	Y	N	N	Y	N	Y	N
KENTUCKY							
1 ***Whitfield***	Y	Y	N	Y	Y	Y	N
2 ***Lewis***	Y	Y	N	Y	N	Y	Y
3 ***Northup***	Y	Y	N	N	Y	Y	N
4 ***Bunning***	Y	Y	N	N	Y	Y	Y
5 ***Rogers***	Y	Y	N	N	Y	Y	Y
6 Baesler	Y	N	N	N	Y	N	N
LOUISIANA							
1 ***Livingston***	Y	Y	N	N	Y	Y	Y
2 Jefferson	Y	N	Y	N	Y	N	N
3 ***Tauzin***	Y	Y	N	N	Y	Y	Y
4 ***McCrery***	Y	Y	N	?	?	?	?
5 ***Cooksey***	Y	Y	N	Y	Y	Y	Y
6 ***Baker***	Y	Y	N	N	Y	Y	Y
7 John	Y	N	N	N	Y	N	N
MAINE							
1 Allen	Y	N	Y	N	Y	N	N
2 Baldacci	Y	N	Y	N	Y	N	N
MARYLAND							
1 ***Gilchrest***	Y	Y	N	N	Y	Y	N
2 ***Ehrlich***	Y	Y	N	Y	Y	Y	N
3 Cardin	Y	N	Y	Y	Y	N	N
4 Wynn	Y	N	Y	N	Y	N	N
5 Hoyer	Y	N	Y	N	Y	N	N
6 ***Bartlett***	Y	Y	N	Y	Y	Y	N
7 Cummings	Y	N	Y	Y	Y	N	N
8 ***Morella***	Y	Y	N	N	Y	Y	N
MASSACHUSETTS							
1 Olver	Y	N	Y	N	Y	N	N
2 Neal	Y	N	Y	Y	Y	N	N
3 McGovern	Y	N	Y	Y	Y	N	N
4 Frank	Y	N	Y	N	Y	N	N
5 Meehan	Y	N	Y	N	Y	N	N
6 Tierney	Y	N	Y	N	N	N	N
7 Markey	Y	N	Y	N	Y	N	N
8 Kennedy	Y	N	Y	?	?	?	?
9 Moakley	Y	N	Y	N	Y	N	N
10 Delahunt	Y	N	Y	Y	Y	N	N
MICHIGAN							
1 Stupak	Y	N	Y	N	Y	Y	N
2 ***Hoekstra***	Y	Y	N	N	Y	Y	N
3 ***Ehlers***	Y	Y	N	N	Y	Y	N
4 ***Camp***	Y	Y	N	Y	?	Y	N
5 Barcia	Y	N	Y	Y	Y	Y	N
6 ***Upton***	Y	Y	N	N	Y	Y	N
7 ***Smith***	Y	Y	N	Y	Y	Y	N
8 Stabenow	Y	N	Y	N	Y	N	N
9 Kildee	Y	N	Y	N	Y	N	N
10 Bonior	Y	N	Y	Y	N	N	N
11 ***Knollenberg***	Y	Y	N	N	Y	Y	Y
12 Levin	Y	N	Y	N	Y	N	N
13 Rivers	Y	N	Y	Y	Y	N	N
14 Conyers	N	N	Y	Y	N	N	N
15 Kilpatrick	Y	?	Y	Y	N	N	N
16 Dingell	Y	N	Y	N	Y	Y	Y
MINNESOTA							
1 ***Gutknecht***	Y	Y	N	Y	Y	Y	N
2 Minge	Y	N	Y	N	Y	N	N
3 ***Ramstad***	Y	Y	N	N	Y	Y	N
4 Vento	Y	N	Y	N	Y	N	N
5 Sabo	Y	N	Y	N	Y	N	N
6 Luther	Y	N	Y	N	Y	N	N
7 Peterson	Y	N	N	N	Y	N	N
8 Oberstar	Y	N	Y	N	Y	N	N
MISSISSIPPI							
1 ***Wicker***	Y	Y	N	N	Y	Y	Y
2 Thompson	Y	N	Y	Y	Y	N	N
3 ***Pickering***	Y	Y	N	Y	Y	Y	Y
4 ***Parker***	Y	Y	?	Y	Y	Y	Y
5 Taylor	Y	N	N	N	Y	N	N
MISSOURI							
1 Clay	Y	N	Y	?	N	N	N
2 ***Talent***	Y	Y	N	Y	N	Y	N
3 Gephardt	Y	N	Y	N	?	N	N
4 Skelton	Y	N	N	N	Y	N	N
5 McCarthy	Y	N	Y	N	Y	N	N
6 Danner	Y	N	Y	N	Y	N	N
7 ***Blunt***	Y	Y	N	N	Y	Y	Y
8 ***Emerson***	Y	Y	N	Y	Y	Y	N
9 ***Hulshof***	Y	Y	N	N	Y	Y	N
MONTANA							
AL ***Hill***	Y	Y	N	Y	N	Y	Y
NEBRASKA							
1 ***Bereuter***	Y	Y	N	N	Y	Y	Y
2 ***Christensen***	Y	Y	N	Y	N	Y	Y
3 ***Barrett***	Y	Y	N	N	Y	Y	Y
NEVADA							
1 ***Ensign***	Y	Y	N	Y	N	Y	N
2 ***Gibbons***	Y	Y	N	N	Y	Y	Y
NEW HAMPSHIRE							
1 ***Sununu***	Y	Y	N	Y	Y	Y	N
2 ***Bass***	Y	Y	N	N	Y	Y	N
NEW JERSEY							
1 Andrews	Y	N	Y	?	Y	N	N
2 ***LoBiondo***	Y	Y	N	N	Y	Y	N
3 ***Saxton***	Y	Y	N	N	Y	Y	N
4 ***Smith***	Y	Y	N	N	Y	Y	N
5 ***Roukema***	Y	Y	N	?	Y	Y	Y
6 Pallone	Y	N	Y	N	Y	N	N
7 ***Franks***	Y	Y	N	N	Y	Y	N
8 Pascrell	Y	N	Y	N	Y	N	N
9 Rothman	Y	N	Y	N	Y	N	N
10 Payne	Y	N	Y	Y	N	N	N
11 ***Frelinghuysen***	Y	Y	N	N	Y	Y	Y
12 ***Pappas***	Y	Y	N	Y	Y	Y	N
13 Menendez	Y	N	Y	N	Y	N	N
NEW MEXICO							
1 ***Wilson***	+	Y	N	Y	Y	Y	Y
2 ***Skeen***	Y	Y	N	N	Y	Y	Y
3 ***Redmond***	Y	Y	N	Y	N	Y	Y
NEW YORK							
1 ***Forbes***	Y	Y	N	N	Y	Y	N
2 ***Lazio***	Y	Y	N	N	Y	Y	N
3 ***King***	Y	Y	N	N	Y	Y	N
4 McCarthy	Y	N	Y	N	Y	N	N
5 Ackerman	Y	N	Y	N	Y	N	N
6 Meeks	Y	N	Y	Y	N	N	N
7 Manton	Y	N	Y	N	Y	N	N
8 Nadler	Y	N	Y	N	Y	N	N
9 Schumer	Y	N	Y	N	Y	N	N
10 Towns	Y	N	Y	Y	N	N	N
11 Owens	Y	N	Y	Y	N	N	N
12 Velázquez	N	N	Y	Y	N	N	N
13 ***Fossella***	Y	Y	N	Y	Y	Y	N
14 Maloney	Y	N	Y	N	Y	N	N
15 Rangel	Y	N	Y	Y	Y	N	N
16 Serrano	Y	N	Y	Y	Y	?	N
17 Engel	Y	N	Y	N	Y	N	N
18 Lowey	Y	N	Y	N	Y	N	N
19 ***Kelly***	Y	Y	N	N	Y	Y	N
20 ***Gilman***	Y	Y	N	N	Y	?	N
21 McNulty	Y	N	Y	N	Y	N	N
22 ***Solomon***	Y	Y	N	?	Y	Y	Y
23 ***Boehlert***	Y	Y	N	N	Y	Y	N
24 ***McHugh***	Y	Y	N	N	Y	Y	Y
25 ***Walsh***	Y	Y	N	N	Y	Y	N
26 Hinchey	Y	N	Y	Y	N	N	N
27 ***Paxon***	Y	Y	N	N	Y	Y	Y
28 Slaughter	Y	N	Y	N	Y	N	N
29 LaFalce	Y	N	Y	?	?	?	?
30 ***Quinn***	Y	Y	N	N	Y	Y	N
31 ***Houghton***	Y	Y	N	N	Y	Y	N
NORTH CAROLINA							
1 Clayton	Y	N	Y	Y	N	N	N
2 Etheridge	Y	N	Y	N	Y	N	N
3 ***Jones***	Y	Y	N	Y	N	Y	N
4 Price	Y	N	Y	N	Y	N	N
5 ***Burr***	Y	Y	N	N	Y	Y	N
6 ***Coble***	Y	Y	N	N	Y	Y	Y
7 McIntyre	Y	N	Y	N	Y	N	N
8 Hefner	Y	N	Y	N	Y	N	?
9 ***Myrick***	Y	Y	N	Y	N	Y	N
10 ***Ballenger***	Y	Y	N	Y	Y	Y	Y
11 ***Taylor***	Y	Y	N	N	Y	Y	Y
12 Watt	Y	N	Y	Y	N	N	N
NORTH DAKOTA							
AL Pomeroy	Y	N	Y	N	Y	N	N
OHIO							
1 ***Chabot***	Y	Y	N	Y	Y	Y	N
2 ***Portman***	Y	Y	N	N	Y	Y	N
3 Hall	Y	N	Y	N	Y	N	N
4 ***Oxley***	Y	Y	N	N	Y	Y	Y
5 ***Gillmor***	Y	Y	N	Y	Y	Y	Y
6 Strickland	Y	N	Y	N	Y	N	N
7 ***Hobson***	Y	Y	N	N	Y	Y	N
8 ***Boehner***	Y	Y	N	N	Y	Y	Y
9 Kaptur	Y	N	Y	N	Y	N	N
10 Kucinich	Y	N	Y	N	N	N	N
11 Stokes	Y	N	Y	Y	Y	N	N
12 ***Kasich***	Y	Y	N	N	Y	Y	N
13 Brown	Y	N	Y	N	N	N	N
14 Sawyer	Y	N	Y	N	Y	N	N
15 ***Pryce***	+	+	–	–	+	+	–
16 ***Regula***	Y	Y	N	N	Y	Y	Y
17 Traficant	Y	N	N	Y	Y	N	N
18 ***Ney***	Y	Y	N	Y	Y	Y	N
19 ***LaTourette***	Y	Y	N	N	Y	Y	N
OKLAHOMA							
1 ***Largent***	Y	Y	N	Y	Y	Y	N
2 ***Coburn***	Y	Y	N	Y	N	Y	N
3 ***Watkins***	Y	Y	N	Y	Y	Y	Y
4 ***Watts***	Y	Y	N	Y	N	Y	Y
5 ***Istook***	Y	N	N	Y	N	Y	Y
6 ***Lucas***	Y	Y	N	Y	N	Y	Y
OREGON							
1 Furse	Y	N	Y	Y	N	?	N
2 ***Smith***	Y	Y	N	N	Y	Y	Y
3 Blumenauer	Y	N	N	N	Y	N	N
4 DeFazio	N	N	Y	Y	N	N	N
5 Hooley	Y	N	Y	N	N	N	N
PENNSYLVANIA							
1 Brady	Y	N	Y	N	Y	N	N
2 Fattah	Y	N	Y	?	?	N	N
3 Borski	Y	N	Y	N	Y	N	N
4 Klink	Y	N	Y	Y	Y	N	N
5 ***Peterson***	Y	Y	N	?	Y	Y	N
6 Holden	Y	N	Y	N	Y	N	N
7 ***Weldon***	Y	Y	N	N	Y	?	Y
8 ***Greenwood***	Y	Y	N	N	Y	Y	N
9 ***Shuster***	Y	Y	N	N	Y	Y	Y
10 ***McDade***	Y	Y	N	Y	Y	Y	Y
11 Kanjorski	Y	N	Y	Y	Y	N	N
12 Murtha	Y	N	N	N	Y	N	N
13 ***Fox***	Y	Y	N	N	Y	Y	N
14 Coyne	Y	N	Y	Y	Y	N	N
15 McHale	?	N	Y	N	Y	N	N
16 ***Pitts***	Y	Y	N	Y	Y	Y	Y
17 ***Gekas***	Y	Y	N	N	Y	Y	+
18 Doyle	Y	N	Y	N	Y	N	N
19 ***Goodling***	Y	Y	N	?	Y	Y	Y
20 Mascara	Y	N	Y	N	Y	N	N
21 ***English***	N	Y	N	Y	Y	Y	N
RHODE ISLAND							
1 Kennedy	Y	N	Y	N	Y	N	N
2 Weygand	Y	N	Y	N	Y	N	N
SOUTH CAROLINA							
1 ***Sanford***	N	Y	N	Y	N	Y	N
2 ***Spence***	Y	Y	N	N	Y	Y	Y
3 ***Graham***	Y	Y	N	?	N	Y	N
4 ***Inglis***	Y	Y	N	Y	Y	Y	N
5 Spratt	Y	N	N	N	Y	N	N
6 Clyburn	Y	N	Y	Y	Y	N	N
SOUTH DAKOTA							
AL ***Thune***	Y	Y	N	N	Y	Y	Y
TENNESSEE							
1 ***Jenkins***	Y	Y	N	Y	Y	Y	Y
2 ***Duncan***	Y	Y	N	Y	N	Y	Y
3 ***Wamp***	Y	Y	N	Y	N	Y	Y
4 ***Hilleary***	Y	Y	N	Y	N	Y	Y
5 Clement	Y	?	Y	N	Y	N	N
6 Gordon	Y	N	N	N	N	N	N
7 ***Bryant***	Y	Y	N	Y	Y	Y	Y
8 Tanner	Y	N	Y	N	Y	N	N
9 Ford	Y	N	Y	Y	Y	N	N
TEXAS							
1 Sandlin	Y	N	Y	N	Y	N	N
2 Turner	Y	N	Y	N	Y	N	N
3 ***Johnson, Sam***	Y	Y	N	N	Y	Y	Y
4 Hall	Y	N	N	N	Y	N	Y
5 ***Sessions***	Y	Y	N	N	Y	Y	Y
6 ***Barton***	Y	Y	N	N	Y	Y	Y
7 ***Archer***	Y	Y	N	N	Y	Y	Y
8 ***Brady***	Y	Y	N	N	Y	Y	Y
9 Lampson	Y	N	Y	N	Y	N	N
10 Doggett	Y	N	Y	Y	Y	N	N
11 Edwards	Y	N	Y	N	Y	N	N
12 ***Granger***	Y	Y	N	N	Y	Y	Y
13 ***Thornberry***	Y	Y	N	Y	Y	Y	Y
14 ***Paul***	N	Y	N	Y	N	Y	N
15 Hinojosa	Y	N	Y	N	Y	N	N
16 Reyes	Y	N	Y	N	Y	N	N
17 Stenholm	Y	N	N	N	Y	N	Y
18 Jackson-Lee	Y	N	Y	Y	Y	N	N
19 ***Combest***	Y	Y	N	N	Y	Y	Y
20 Gonzalez	Y	N	Y	N	Y	N	N
21 ***Smith***	Y	Y	N	N	Y	Y	Y
22 ***DeLay***	Y	Y	N	Y	Y	Y	Y
23 ***Bonilla***	Y	Y	N	Y	N	Y	Y
24 Frost	Y	N	Y	N	Y	N	N
25 Bentsen	Y	N	Y	N	Y	N	N
26 ***Armey***	Y	Y	N	N	Y	Y	Y
27 Ortiz	Y	N	Y	N	Y	N	Y
28 Rodriguez	Y	N	Y	N	Y	N	N
29 Green	Y	N	Y	N	N	N	N
30 Johnson, E.B.	Y	N	Y	N	Y	N	N
UTAH							
1 ***Hansen***	Y	Y	N	N	Y	Y	Y
2 ***Cook***	Y	Y	N	N	Y	Y	Y
3 ***Cannon***	Y	Y	N	Y	Y	Y	Y
VERMONT							
AL *Sanders*	Y	N	Y	Y	N	N	N
VIRGINIA							
1 ***Bateman***	Y	Y	N	N	Y	Y	Y
2 Pickett	Y	N	N	N	Y	N	N
3 Scott	Y	N	Y	Y	Y	N	N
4 Sisisky	Y	N	Y	N	Y	N	N
5 Goode	Y	N	N	Y	N	N	N
6 ***Goodlatte***	Y	Y	N	Y	Y	Y	N
7 ***Bliley***	Y	Y	N	N	Y	Y	Y
8 Moran	+	N	Y	N	Y	N	N
9 Boucher	Y	N	?	N	Y	N	N
10 ***Wolf***	Y	Y	N	N	Y	Y	N
11 ***Davis***	Y	?	N	N	Y	?	N
WASHINGTON							
1 ***White***	Y	Y	N	–	Y	Y	N
2 ***Metcalf***	Y	Y	N	Y	N	Y	Y
3 ***Smith, Linda***	Y	Y	N	Y	N	Y	N
4 ***Hastings***	Y	Y	N	N	Y	Y	Y
5 ***Nethercutt***	Y	Y	N	N	Y	Y	N
6 Dicks	Y	N	N	N	Y	N	N
7 McDermott	Y	N	Y	N	N	N	N
8 ***Dunn***	Y	Y	N	N	+	Y	Y
9 Smith, Adam	Y	N	Y	N	Y	N	N
WEST VIRGINIA							
1 Mollohan	Y	N	Y	Y	Y	N	N
2 Wise	Y	N	Y	N	Y	N	N
3 Rahall	Y	N	Y	N	Y	N	N
WISCONSIN							
1 ***Neumann***	Y	N	N	Y	N	Y	N
2 ***Klug***	Y	Y	N	N	Y	Y	N
3 Kind	Y	N	Y	?	Y	N	N
4 Kleczka	Y	N	Y	N	Y	N	N
5 Barrett	Y	N	Y	Y	Y	N	N
6 ***Petri***	N	Y	N	Y	N	Y	N
7 Obey	Y	N	Y	N	Y	N	N
8 Johnson	Y	N	Y	Y	Y	N	N
9 ***Sensenbrenner***	N	Y	N	Y	N	Y	N
WYOMING							
AL ***Cubin***	Y	Y	N	Y	N	Y	Y

Southern states - Ala., Ark., Fla., Ga., Ky., La., Miss., N.C., Okla., S.C., Tenn., Texas, Va.

Key

Y	Voted for (yea).
#	Paired for.
+	Announced for.
N	Voted against (nay).
X	Paired against.
–	Announced against.
P	Voted "present."
C	Voted "present" to avoid possible conflict of interest.
?	Did not vote or otherwise make a position known.

Democrats **Republicans**
Independent

490. HR 4104. Fiscal 1999 Treasury Postal Appropriations/Rule. Adoption of the rule (H Res 579) to provide for House floor consideration of the bill to provide $13.44 billion in fiscal 1999 funding for the Treasury Department, U.S. Postal Service subsidies, the Executive Office of the President and several independent agencies. Adopted 231-194: R 217-6; D 14-187 (ND 8-139, SD 6-48); I 0-1. Oct. 7, 1998.

491. HR 4616. Corporal Harold Gomez Post Office/Passage. McHugh, R-N.Y., motion to suspend the rules and pass the bill to designate a U.S. post office in East Chicago, Indiana as the "Corporal Harold Gomez Post Office." Motion agreed to 425-0: R 222-0; D 202-0 (ND 147-0, SD 55-0); I 1-0. Oct. 7, 1998. A two-thirds majority of those present and voting (284 in this case) is required for passage under suspension of the rules.

492. HR 2348. Mervyn Dymally Post Office/Passage. McHugh, R-N.Y., motion to suspend the rules and pass the bill to designate a U.S. post office in Compton, Calif. as the "Mervyn Dymally Post Office Building." Motion agreed to 421-1: R 221-1; D 199-0 (ND 144-0, SD 55-0); I 1-0. Oct. 7, 1998. A two-thirds majority of those present and voting (282 in this case) is required for passage under suspension of the rules.

493. HR 4104. Fiscal 1999 Treasury Postal Appropriations/Recommit. Hoyer, D-Md., motion to recommit the bill to the conference committee with instructions to report it back with an amendment requiring federal health plans that cover other prescription drugs to also cover prescription contraceptives. Motion rejected 202-226: R 21-203; D 180-23 (ND 132-16, SD 48-7); I 1-0. Oct. 7, 1998.

494. HR 4104. Fiscal 1999 Treasury Postal Appropriations/Conference Report. Adoption of the conference report on the bill to provide $13.44 billion in fiscal 1999 funding for the Treasury Department, U.S. Postal Service subsidies, the Executive Office of the President and several independent agencies. Adopted (thus sent to the Senate) 290-137: R 209-15; D 81-121 (ND 51-96, SD 30-25); I 0-1. Oct. 7, 1998.

495. Procedural Motion/Journal. Approval of the House Journal of Wednesday, Oct. 7, 1998. Approved 325-72: R 190-19; D 134-53 (ND 98-40, SD 36-13); I 1-0. Oct. 8, 1998.

496. Quorum Call.* 423 Responded. Oct. 8, 1998.

497. H Res 581. Open Impeachment Inquiry/Recommit. Boucher, D-Va., motion to recommit the bill to the Judiciary Committee with instructions to report it back with an amendment that would authorize the committee to conduct an impeachment inquiry against the president after first determining whether the allegations against the president by Independent Counsel Kenneth W. Starr, if true, constituted grounds for impeachment. If the allegations did not meet this standard, then the committee could consider alternative sanctions. The committee would have to conclude its work in time for the House to consider its recommendations by Dec. 31, unless the committee requested an extension. Rejected 198-236: R 1-226; D 196-10 (ND 145-6, SD 51-4); I 1-0. Oct. 8, 1998.

CQ does not include quorum calls in its vote charts.

	490	491	492	493	494	495	497
ALABAMA							
1 *Callahan*	Y	Y	Y	N	Y	Y	N
2 *Everett*	Y	Y	Y	N	Y	Y	N
3 *Riley*	Y	Y	Y	N	Y	Y	N
4 *Aderholt*	Y	Y	Y	N	Y	N	N
5 Cramer	N	Y	Y	N	Y	Y	Y
6 *Bachus*	Y	Y	Y	N	Y	Y	N
7 Hilliard	N	Y	Y	Y	N	N	Y
ALASKA							
AL *Young*	Y	Y	Y	N	Y	Y	N
ARIZONA							
1 *Salmon*	Y	Y	Y	N	Y	Y	N
2 Pastor	N	Y	?	Y	Y	Y	Y
3 *Stump*	Y	Y	Y	N	Y	Y	N
4 *Shadegg*	Y	Y	Y	N	Y	P	N
5 *Kolbe*	Y	Y	Y	N	Y	Y	N
6 *Hayworth*	Y	Y	Y	N	Y	Y	N
ARKANSAS							
1 Berry	N	Y	Y	N	Y	N	Y
2 Snyder	N	Y	Y	Y	Y	Y	Y
3 *Hutchinson*	Y	Y	Y	N	Y	Y	N
4 *Dickey*	Y	Y	Y	N	Y	Y	Y
CALIFORNIA							
1 *Riggs*	Y	Y	Y	N	Y	?	N
2 *Herger*	Y	Y	Y	N	Y	?	N
3 Fazio	N	Y	Y	Y	N	Y	Y
4 *Doolittle*	Y	Y	N	N	N	Y	N
5 Matsui	N	Y	Y	Y	N	Y	Y
6 Woolsey	N	Y	Y	Y	N	Y	Y
7 Miller	N	?	?	Y	N	?	Y
8 Pelosi	N	Y	Y	Y	N	Y	Y
9 Lee	N	Y	Y	N	N	N	Y
10 Tauscher	N	Y	Y	Y	N	Y	Y
11 *Pombo*	Y	Y	Y	N	Y	Y	N
12 Lantos	N	Y	Y	Y	N	Y	Y
13 Stark	N	Y	Y	N	N	N	Y
14 Eshoo	N	Y	Y	Y	N	Y	Y
15 *Campbell*	N	Y	Y	Y	Y	Y	Y
16 Lofgren	N	Y	Y	Y	N	Y	Y
17 Farr	N	Y	Y	Y	N	Y	Y
18 Condit	N	Y	Y	Y	N	Y	Y
19 *Radanovich*	Y	Y	Y	N	Y	N	N
20 Dooley	N	Y	Y	Y	Y	Y	Y
21 *Thomas*	Y	Y	Y	N	Y	N	N
22 Capps, L.	N	Y	Y	Y	N	Y	Y
23 *Gallegly*	Y	Y	Y	N	Y	N	N
24 Sherman	N	Y	?	Y	N	Y	Y
25 *McKeon*	Y	Y	Y	N	Y	N	N
26 Berman	N	Y	Y	Y	N	Y	Y
27 *Rogan*	Y	Y	Y	N	N	N	N
28 *Dreier*	Y	Y	Y	N	Y	N	N
29 Waxman	?	Y	Y	Y	N	Y	Y
30 Becerra	N	Y	Y	N	N	N	Y
31 Martinez	N	Y	Y	Y	Y	P	Y
32 Dixon	N	Y	Y	Y	N	?	Y
33 Roybal-Allard	N	Y	Y	Y	N	Y	Y
34 Torres	N	Y	Y	Y	Y	Y	Y
35 Waters	N	Y	Y	Y	N	N	Y
36 Harman	N	Y	Y	Y	N	Y	Y
37 Millender-McD.	N	Y	Y	Y	N	Y	Y
38 *Horn*	Y	Y	Y	N	Y	Y	N

	490	491	492	493	494	495	497
39 *Royce*	Y	Y	Y	N	Y	Y	N
40 *Lewis*	Y	Y	Y	N	Y	Y	N
41 *Kim*	Y	Y	Y	N	Y	Y	N
42 Brown	N	Y	Y	N	N	N	Y
43 *Calvert*	Y	Y	Y	N	Y	Y	N
44 *Bono, M.*	Y	Y	Y	N	Y	Y	N
45 *Rohrabacher*	Y	Y	Y	N	Y	Y	N
46 Sanchez	N	Y	Y	Y	N	Y	Y
47 *Cox*	Y	Y	Y	N	Y	Y	N
48 *Packard*	Y	Y	Y	N	Y	Y	N
49 *Bilbray*	N	Y	Y	Y	Y	Y	N
50 Filner	N	Y	Y	N	N	N	Y
51 *Cunningham*	Y	Y	Y	N	Y	P	N
52 *Hunter*	Y	Y	Y	N	Y	Y	N
COLORADO							
1 DeGette	N	Y	Y	Y	N	Y	Y
2 Skaggs	N	Y	Y	N	Y	Y	Y
3 *McInnis*	Y	Y	Y	N	Y	Y	N
4 *Schaffer*	Y	Y	Y	N	N	N	N
5 *Hefley*	Y	Y	Y	N	Y	N	N
6 *Schaefer*	Y	Y	Y	N	Y	?	N
CONNECTICUT							
1 Kennelly	?	?	?	?	?	Y	Y
2 Gejdenson	N	Y	Y	Y	N	Y	Y
3 DeLauro	N	Y	Y	Y	N	Y	Y
4 *Shays*	N	Y	Y	Y	Y	Y	N
5 Maloney	N	Y	Y	Y	N	?	Y
6 *Johnson*	Y	Y	Y	Y	Y	Y	N
DELAWARE							
AL *Castle*	Y	Y	Y	Y	Y	Y	N
FLORIDA							
1 *Scarborough*	Y	Y	Y	N	Y	?	N
2 Boyd	N	Y	Y	Y	Y	Y	Y
3 Brown	N	Y	Y	Y	N	Y	Y
4 *Fowler*	Y	Y	Y	N	Y	Y	N
5 Thurman	N	Y	Y	Y	N	Y	Y
6 *Stearns*	Y	Y	Y	N	Y	Y	N
7 *Mica*	Y	Y	Y	N	Y	Y	N
8 *McCollum*	Y	Y	Y	N	Y	Y	N
9 *Bilirakis*	Y	Y	Y	N	Y	Y	N
10 *Young*	Y	Y	Y	N	Y	Y	N
11 Davis	N	Y	Y	Y	Y	?	Y
12 *Canady*	Y	Y	Y	N	Y	Y	N
13 *Miller*	Y	Y	Y	N	Y	Y	N
14 *Goss*	Y	Y	Y	N	Y	Y	N
15 *Weldon*	Y	Y	Y	N	Y	Y	N
16 *Foley*	Y	Y	Y	N	Y	Y	N
17 Meek	N	Y	Y	Y	Y	?	Y
18 *Ros-Lehtinen*	Y	Y	Y	N	N	N	N
19 Wexler	N	Y	Y	Y	N	Y	Y
20 Deutsch	N	Y	Y	Y	N	Y	Y
21 *Diaz-Balart*	N	Y	N	N	N	Y	N
22 *Shaw*	Y	Y	Y	N	Y	Y	N
23 Hastings	N	Y	Y	Y	N	N	Y
GEORGIA							
1 *Kingston*	Y	Y	Y	N	Y	Y	N
2 Bishop	N	Y	Y	Y	Y	Y	Y
3 *Collins*	Y	Y	Y	N	Y	N	N
4 McKinney	N	Y	Y	N	Y	N	Y
5 Lewis	N	Y	Y	N	N	N	Y
6 *Gingrich*							N
7 *Barr*	Y	Y	Y	N	N	Y	N
8 *Chambliss*	Y	Y	Y	N	Y	Y	N
9 *Deal*	Y	Y	Y	N	Y	N	N
10 *Norwood*	Y	Y	Y	N	Y	N	N
11 *Linder*	Y	Y	Y	N	Y	Y	N
HAWAII							
1 Abercrombie	N	Y	Y	N	Y	Y	Y
2 Mink	N	Y	Y	N	Y	Y	Y
IDAHO							
1 *Chenoweth*	Y	Y	Y	N	N	Y	N
2 *Crapo*	Y	Y	Y	N	Y	Y	N
ILLINOIS							
1 Rush	N	Y	Y	N	Y	Y	Y
2 Jackson	N	Y	Y	N	Y	Y	Y
3 Lipinski	Y	Y	Y	N	Y	N	Y
4 Gutierrez	N	Y	Y	N	N	N	Y
5 Blagojevich	N	Y	Y	N	Y	Y	Y
6 *Hyde*	Y	Y	Y	N	Y	?	N
7 Davis	N	Y	Y	N	Y	N	Y
8 *Crane*	Y	Y	Y	N	N	?	N
9 Yates	?	?	?	?	?	?	Y
10 *Porter*	Y	Y	Y	N	Y	Y	Y
11 *Weller*	?	Y	Y	N	Y	Y	N
12 Costello	Y	Y	Y	N	Y	N	Y
13 *Fawell*	Y	Y	Y	N	Y	Y	N

ND Northern Democrats   SD Southern Democrats

	490	491	492	493	494	495	497
14 ***Hastert***	Y	Y	Y	N	Y	Y	N
15 ***Ewing***	Y	Y	Y	N	Y	Y	N
16 ***Manzullo***	Y	Y	Y	N	Y	N	N
17 Evans	N	Y	Y	Y	N	Y	N
18 ***LaHood***	Y	Y	Y	N	Y	Y	N
19 Poshard	?	?	?	?	?	N	Y
20 ***Shimkus***	Y	Y	Y	N	Y	Y	N
INDIANA							
1 Visclosky	N	Y	Y	Y	Y	N	Y
2 ***McIntosh***	Y	Y	Y	N	Y	Y	N
3 Roemer	N	Y	Y	Y	N	Y	Y
4 ***Souder***	Y	Y	Y	N	Y	Y	N
5 ***Buyer***	Y	Y	Y	N	Y	Y	N
6 ***Burton***	Y	Y	Y	N	Y	Y	N
7 ***Pease***	Y	Y	Y	N	Y	Y	N
8 ***Hostettler***	Y	Y	Y	N	Y	Y	N
9 Hamilton	N	Y	Y	Y	Y	Y	Y
10 Carson	N	Y	Y	Y	N	P	Y
IOWA							
1 ***Leach***	Y	Y	Y	Y	Y	Y	N
2 ***Nussle***	Y	Y	Y	N	Y	Y	N
3 Boswell	N	Y	Y	Y	Y	Y	Y
4 ***Ganske***	Y	Y	Y	N	Y	Y	N
5 ***Latham***	Y	Y	Y	N	Y	Y	N
KANSAS							
1 ***Moran***	Y	Y	Y	N	N	N	N
2 ***Ryun***	Y	Y	Y	N	Y	Y	N
3 ***Snowbarger***	Y	Y	Y	N	Y	Y	N
4 ***Tiahrt***	Y	Y	Y	N	Y	Y	N
KENTUCKY							
1 ***Whitfield***	Y	Y	Y	N	Y	Y	N
2 ***Lewis***	Y	Y	Y	N	Y	Y	N
3 ***Northup***	Y	Y	Y	N	Y	Y	N
4 ***Bunning***	Y	Y	Y	N	Y	Y	N
5 ***Rogers***	Y	?	Y	N	Y	Y	N
6 Baesler	N	Y	Y	Y	Y	Y	Y
LOUISIANA							
1 ***Livingston***	Y	Y	Y	N	Y	Y	N
2 Jefferson	N	Y	Y	Y	N	?	Y
3 ***Tauzin***	Y	Y	Y	N	Y	Y	N
4 ***McCrery***	?	?	?	?	?	?	N
5 ***Cooksey***	Y	?	Y	N	Y	Y	N
6 ***Baker***	Y	Y	Y	N	Y	Y	N
7 John	Y	Y	Y	N	Y	Y	Y
MAINE							
1 Allen	N	Y	Y	Y	Y	Y	Y
2 Baldacci	N	Y	Y	Y	N	Y	Y
MARYLAND							
1 ***Gilchrest***	Y	Y	Y	N	Y	Y	N
2 ***Ehrlich***	Y	Y	Y	N	Y	Y	N
3 Cardin	N	Y	Y	Y	Y	Y	Y
4 Wynn	N	Y	Y	Y	Y	N	Y
5 Hoyer	N	Y	Y	Y	Y	Y	Y
6 ***Bartlett***	Y	Y	Y	N	Y	Y	N
7 Cummings	N	Y	Y	Y	N	Y	Y
8 ***Morella***	N	Y	Y	Y	Y	Y	N
MASSACHUSETTS							
1 Olver	N	Y	Y	Y	Y	N	Y
2 Neal	Y	Y	Y	Y	Y	Y	Y
3 McGovern	N	Y	Y	Y	N	N	Y
4 Frank	N	Y	Y	Y	N	N	Y
5 Meehan	N	Y	Y	Y	N	Y	Y
6 Tierney	N	Y	Y	Y	N	Y	Y
7 Markey	N	Y	Y	Y	?	Y	Y
8 Kennedy	N	Y	Y	Y	N	Y	Y
9 Moakley	N	Y	Y	Y	Y	Y	Y
10 Delahunt	N	Y	Y	Y	N	Y	Y
MICHIGAN							
1 Stupak	N	Y	Y	N	Y	N	Y
2 ***Hoekstra***	Y	Y	Y	N	Y	Y	N
3 ***Ehlers***	Y	Y	Y	N	Y	Y	N
4 ***Camp***	Y	Y	Y	N	Y	Y	N
5 Barcia	Y	Y	Y	N	Y	Y	Y
6 ***Upton***	Y	Y	Y	Y	Y	Y	N
7 ***Smith***	Y	Y	Y	N	Y	N	N
8 Stabenow	N	Y	Y	Y	N	Y	Y
9 Kildee	Y	Y	Y	N	Y	Y	Y
10 Bonior	N	Y	Y	Y	N	N	Y
11 ***Knollenberg***	Y	Y	Y	N	Y	Y	N
12 Levin	N	Y	Y	Y	N	Y	Y
13 Rivers	N	Y	Y	Y	N	Y	Y
14 Conyers	N	Y	?	Y	N	?	Y
15 Kilpatrick	N	Y	Y	Y	N	Y	Y
16 Dingell	N	Y	Y	Y	N	Y	Y
MINNESOTA							
1 ***Gutknecht***	Y	Y	Y	N	Y	N	N
2 Minge	N	Y	Y	Y	N	Y	Y
3 ***Ramstad***	Y	Y	Y	Y	Y	N	N
4 Vento	N	Y	Y	Y	Y	N	Y
5 Sabo	N	Y	Y	Y	Y	N	Y
6 Luther	N	Y	Y	Y	N	Y	Y
7 Peterson	N	Y	Y	N	N	Y	Y
8 Oberstar	N	Y	Y	Y	Y	N	Y
MISSISSIPPI							
1 ***Wicker***	Y	Y	Y	N	Y	N	N
2 Thompson	N	Y	Y	Y	N	N	Y
3 ***Pickering***	Y	Y	Y	N	Y	Y	N
4 ***Parker***	Y	Y	Y	N	Y	Y	N
5 Taylor	Y	Y	Y	N	N	N	N
MISSOURI							
1 Clay	N	Y	Y	Y	N	N	Y
2 ***Talent***	Y	Y	Y	N	Y	Y	N
3 Gephardt	N	Y	Y	Y	N	N	Y
4 Skelton	N	Y	Y	N	Y	N	Y
5 McCarthy	N	Y	Y	Y	N	Y	Y
6 Danner	N	Y	Y	N	Y	Y	Y
7 ***Blunt***	Y	Y	Y	N	Y	Y	N
8 ***Emerson***	Y	Y	Y	N	Y	Y	N
9 ***Hulshof***	Y	Y	Y	N	Y	N	N
MONTANA							
AL ***Hill***	Y	Y	Y	N	Y	N	N
NEBRASKA							
1 ***Bereuter***	Y	Y	N	N	Y	Y	N
2 ***Christensen***	Y	Y	Y	N	Y	Y	N
3 ***Barrett***	Y	Y	Y	N	Y	Y	N
NEVADA							
1 ***Ensign***	Y	Y	Y	Y	Y	N	N
2 ***Gibbons***	Y	Y	Y	N	Y	N	N
NEW HAMPSHIRE							
1 ***Sununu***	Y	Y	Y	N	Y	Y	N
2 ***Bass***	Y	Y	Y	Y	Y	Y	N
NEW JERSEY							
1 Andrews	N	Y	Y	Y	N	Y	Y
2 ***LoBiondo***	Y	Y	Y	N	Y	N	N
3 ***Saxton***	?	Y	Y	N	Y	Y	N
4 ***Smith***	Y	Y	?	N	Y	Y	N
5 ***Roukema***	Y	Y	Y	Y	Y	Y	N
6 Pallone	N	Y	Y	Y	N	N	Y
7 ***Franks***	Y	Y	Y	N	Y	Y	N
8 Pascrell	N	Y	Y	Y	Y	Y	Y
9 Rothman	N	Y	Y	Y	N	Y	Y
10 Payne	N	Y	Y	Y	N	Y	Y
11 ***Frelinghuysen***	Y	Y	Y	Y	Y	Y	N
12 ***Pappas***	Y	Y	Y	N	Y	Y	N
13 Menendez	N	Y	Y	Y	N	N	Y
NEW MEXICO							
1 ***Wilson***	Y	Y	Y	N	Y	Y	N
2 ***Skeen***	Y	Y	Y	N	Y	?	N
3 ***Redmond***	Y	Y	Y	N	Y	Y	N
NEW YORK							
1 ***Forbes***	Y	Y	Y	N	Y	Y	N
2 ***Lazio***	Y	Y	Y	Y	Y	Y	N
3 ***King***	Y	Y	Y	N	Y	Y	N
4 McCarthy	N	Y	Y	Y	N	Y	Y
5 Ackerman	N	Y	Y	Y	N	N	Y
6 Meeks	N	Y	Y	Y	N	N	Y
7 Manton	N	Y	Y	Y	Y	P	Y
8 Nadler	N	Y	Y	Y	N	Y	Y
9 Schumer	N	Y	Y	Y	N	Y	Y
10 Towns	N	Y	Y	Y	N	N	Y
11 Owens	N	Y	Y	Y	N	Y	Y
12 Velázquez	N	Y	Y	Y	N	N	Y
13 ***Fossella***	Y	Y	Y	N	Y	Y	N
14 Maloney	N	Y	Y	Y	N	Y	Y
15 Rangel	N	Y	Y	Y	N	Y	Y
16 Serrano	N	Y	Y	Y	N	Y	N
17 Engel	N	Y	Y	Y	N	?	Y
18 Lowey	N	Y	Y	Y	N	Y	Y
19 ***Kelly***	N	Y	Y	Y	Y	Y	N
20 ***Gilman***	Y	Y	Y	Y	Y	Y	N
21 McNulty	N	Y	Y	Y	N	N	Y
22 ***Solomon***	Y	Y	?	N	Y	Y	N
23 ***Boehlert***	Y	Y	Y	Y	Y	Y	N
24 ***McHugh***	Y	Y	Y	N	Y	Y	N
25 ***Walsh***	Y	Y	Y	N	Y	Y	N
26 Hinchey	N	Y	Y	Y	N	N	Y
27 ***Paxon***	Y	Y	Y	N	Y	Y	N
28 Slaughter	N	Y	Y	Y	Y	?	Y
29 LaFalce	N	Y	Y	N	Y	N	Y
30 ***Quinn***	Y	Y	Y	N	Y	Y	N
31 ***Houghton***	Y	Y	Y	N	Y	?	N
NORTH CAROLINA							
1 Clayton	N	Y	Y	Y	Y	Y	Y
2 Etheridge	N	Y	Y	Y	N	Y	Y
3 ***Jones***	Y	Y	Y	N	Y	Y	N
4 Price	N	Y	Y	Y	Y	Y	Y
5 ***Burr***	Y	Y	Y	N	Y	Y	N
6 ***Coble***	Y	Y	Y	N	Y	Y	N
7 McIntyre	N	Y	Y	Y	Y	Y	Y
8 Hefner	N	Y	Y	Y	N	?	Y
9 ***Myrick***	Y	Y	Y	N	Y	Y	N
10 ***Ballenger***	Y	Y	Y	N	Y	Y	N
11 ***Taylor***	Y	Y	Y	N	Y	Y	N
12 Watt	N	Y	Y	Y	N	Y	Y
NORTH DAKOTA							
AL Pomeroy	N	Y	Y	Y	Y	Y	Y
OHIO							
1 ***Chabot***	Y	Y	Y	N	Y	Y	N
2 ***Portman***	Y	Y	Y	N	Y	Y	N
3 Hall	N	Y	Y	N	Y	Y	Y
4 ***Oxley***	Y	Y	Y	N	Y	Y	N
5 ***Gillmor***	Y	Y	Y	N	Y	Y	N
6 Strickland	N	Y	Y	Y	Y	?	Y
7 ***Hobson***	Y	Y	Y	N	Y	Y	N
8 ***Boehner***	Y	Y	Y	N	Y	Y	N
9 Kaptur	N	Y	Y	Y	Y	Y	Y
10 Kucinich	Y	Y	Y	Y	Y	N	Y
11 Stokes	N	Y	Y	Y	N	Y	Y
12 ***Kasich***	Y	Y	Y	N	Y	?	N
13 Brown	N	Y	Y	Y	N	N	Y
14 Sawyer	N	Y	Y	Y	Y	Y	Y
15 ***Pryce***	+	+	+	–	+	+	–
16 ***Regula***	Y	Y	Y	N	Y	Y	N
17 Traficant	N	Y	Y	Y	Y	Y	Y
18 ***Ney***	Y	Y	Y	N	Y	Y	N
19 ***LaTourette***	Y	Y	Y	N	Y	Y	N
OKLAHOMA							
1 ***Largent***	Y	Y	Y	N	Y	Y	N
2 ***Coburn***	Y	Y	Y	N	Y	Y	N
3 ***Watkins***	Y	Y	Y	N	Y	Y	N
4 ***Watts***	Y	Y	Y	N	Y	Y	N
5 ***Istook***	Y	Y	Y	N	Y	Y	N
6 ***Lucas***	Y	Y	Y	N	Y	Y	N
OREGON							
1 Furse	N	Y	Y	Y	N	N	Y
2 ***Smith***	Y	Y	Y	?	?	Y	N
3 Blumenauer	N	Y	Y	Y	N	Y	Y
4 DeFazio	N	Y	Y	Y	N	N	Y
5 Hooley	N	Y	Y	Y	N	Y	Y
PENNSYLVANIA							
1 Brady	N	Y	Y	Y	N	N	Y
2 Fattah	N	Y	Y	Y	N	N	Y
3 Borski	N	Y	Y	Y	Y	N	Y
4 Klink	N	Y	Y	N	Y	Y	Y
5 ***Peterson***	Y	Y	Y	N	Y	Y	N
6 Holden	N	Y	Y	N	Y	Y	Y
7 ***Weldon***	Y	Y	Y	N	Y	Y	N
8 ***Greenwood***	Y	?	Y	N	Y	Y	N
9 ***Shuster***	Y	Y	Y	N	Y	Y	N
10 ***McDade***	Y	Y	Y	N	Y	?	N
11 Kanjorski	N	Y	Y	Y	Y	Y	N
12 Murtha	N	Y	Y	Y	Y	Y	Y
13 ***Fox***	Y	Y	Y	Y	Y	N	N
14 Coyne	N	Y	Y	Y	N	Y	Y
15 McHale	N	Y	Y	Y	Y	Y	N
16 ***Pitts***	Y	Y	Y	N	Y	Y	N
17 ***Gekas***	Y	Y	Y	N	Y	Y	N
18 Doyle	N	Y	Y	N	Y	Y	Y
19 ***Goodling***	Y	Y	Y	N	Y	Y	N
20 Mascara	N	Y	Y	N	Y	Y	Y
21 ***English***	Y	Y	Y	N	Y	N	N
RHODE ISLAND							
1 Kennedy	N	Y	Y	Y	N	N	Y
2 Weygand	N	Y	Y	Y	Y	Y	Y
SOUTH CAROLINA							
1 ***Sanford***	Y	Y	Y	N	N	P	N
2 ***Spence***	Y	Y	Y	N	Y	Y	N
3 ***Graham***	Y	Y	Y	N	Y	Y	N
4 ***Inglis***	Y	Y	Y	N	Y	Y	N
5 Spratt	N	Y	Y	Y	Y	Y	Y
6 Clyburn	N	Y	Y	Y	N	N	Y
SOUTH DAKOTA							
AL ***Thune***	Y	Y	Y	N	Y	Y	N
TENNESSEE							
1 ***Jenkins***	Y	Y	Y	N	Y	Y	N
2 ***Duncan***	Y	Y	Y	N	N	Y	N
3 ***Wamp***	Y	Y	Y	N	Y	Y	N
4 ***Hilleary***	Y	Y	Y	N	Y	Y	N
5 Clement	N	Y	Y	Y	Y	Y	Y
6 Gordon	N	Y	Y	Y	N	Y	Y
7 ***Bryant***	Y	Y	Y	N	Y	Y	N
8 Tanner	N	Y	Y	Y	Y	Y	Y
9 Ford	N	Y	Y	Y	Y	Y	Y
TEXAS							
1 Sandlin	N	Y	Y	Y	N	Y	Y
2 Turner	Y	Y	Y	Y	Y	Y	Y
3 ***Johnson, Sam***	Y	Y	Y	N	Y	Y	N
4 Hall	Y	Y	Y	N	Y	Y	Y
5 ***Sessions***	Y	Y	Y	N	Y	Y	N
6 ***Barton***	Y	Y	Y	N	Y	Y	N
7 ***Archer***	Y	Y	Y	N	Y	Y	N
8 ***Brady***	Y	Y	Y	N	Y	Y	N
9 Lampson	Y	Y	Y	Y	Y	Y	Y
10 Doggett	N	Y	Y	Y	N	Y	Y
11 Edwards	N	Y	Y	Y	N	Y	Y
12 ***Granger***	Y	Y	Y	Y	Y	Y	N
13 ***Thornberry***	Y	Y	Y	N	Y	Y	N
14 ***Paul***	Y	Y	Y	N	N	Y	N
15 Hinojosa	N	Y	Y	Y	Y	+	Y
16 Reyes	N	Y	Y	Y	Y	P	Y
17 Stenholm	N	Y	Y	N	Y	N	Y
18 Jackson-Lee	N	Y	Y	Y	N	N	Y
19 ***Combest***	Y	Y	Y	N	Y	Y	N
20 Gonzalez	N	Y	Y	Y	N	Y	Y
21 ***Smith***	Y	Y	Y	N	Y	Y	N
22 ***DeLay***	Y	Y	Y	N	Y	Y	N
23 ***Bonilla***	Y	Y	Y	N	Y	Y	N
24 Frost	N	Y	Y	Y	N	Y	Y
25 Bentsen	N	Y	Y	Y	N	Y	Y
26 ***Armey***	Y	Y	Y	N	Y	Y	N
27 Ortiz	N	Y	Y	N	Y	Y	Y
28 Rodriguez	N	Y	Y	Y	Y	Y	Y
29 Green	N	Y	Y	Y	N	N	Y
30 Johnson, E.B.	N	Y	Y	Y	N	Y	Y
UTAH							
1 ***Hansen***	Y	Y	Y	N	Y	N	N
2 ***Cook***	Y	Y	Y	N	Y	Y	N
3 ***Cannon***	Y	Y	Y	N	Y	?	N
VERMONT							
AL *Sanders*	N	Y	Y	Y	N	Y	Y
VIRGINIA							
1 ***Bateman***	Y	Y	Y	N	Y	Y	N
2 Pickett	N	Y	Y	Y	Y	N	Y
3 Scott	N	Y	Y	Y	Y	N	Y
4 Sisisky	N	Y	Y	Y	Y	Y	Y
5 Goode	Y	Y	Y	N	Y	Y	N
6 ***Goodlatte***	Y	Y	Y	N	N	Y	N
7 ***Bliley***	Y	Y	Y	N	Y	Y	N
8 Moran	N	Y	Y	Y	Y	Y	Y
9 Boucher	?	Y	Y	Y	N	Y	Y
10 ***Wolf***	Y	Y	?	N	Y	Y	N
11 ***Davis***	Y	Y	Y	N	Y	Y	N
WASHINGTON							
1 ***White***	Y	Y	Y	N	Y	Y	N
2 ***Metcalf***	Y	Y	Y	N	Y	P	N
3 ***Smith, Linda***	Y	Y	Y	N	Y	Y	N
4 ***Hastings***	Y	Y	Y	N	Y	Y	N
5 ***Nethercutt***	Y	Y	Y	N	Y	Y	N
6 Dicks	N	Y	Y	Y	Y	Y	Y
7 McDermott	N	Y	Y	Y	N	Y	Y
8 ***Dunn***	Y	Y	Y	N	Y	Y	N
9 Smith, Adam	N	Y	Y	Y	N	?	Y
WEST VIRGINIA							
1 Mollohan	Y	Y	Y	N	Y	?	Y
2 Wise	N	Y	Y	Y	Y	Y	Y
3 Rahall	Y	Y	Y	N	Y	Y	Y
WISCONSIN							
1 ***Neumann***	Y	Y	Y	N	N	Y	N
2 ***Klug***	Y	Y	Y	Y	Y	Y	N
3 Kind	N	Y	Y	Y	N	Y	Y
4 Kleczka	N	Y	Y	Y	N	Y	Y
5 Barrett	N	Y	Y	Y	N	Y	Y
6 ***Petri***	Y	Y	Y	N	N	P	N
7 Obey	N	Y	Y	Y	N	?	Y
8 Johnson	N	Y	Y	Y	N	Y	Y
9 ***Sensenbrenner***	Y	Y	Y	N	N	Y	N
WYOMING							
AL ***Cubin***	Y	Y	Y	N	Y	Y	N

Southern states - Ala., Ark., Fla., Ga., Ky., La., Miss., N.C., Okla., S.C., Tenn., Texas, Va.

Key

Y	Voted for (yea).
#	Paired for.
+	Announced for.
N	Voted against (nay).
X	Paired against.
−	Announced against.
P	Voted "present."
C	Voted "present" to avoid possible conflict of interest.
?	Did not vote or otherwise make a position known.

Democrats · **Republicans** · *Independent*

498. H Res 581. Open Impeachment Inquiry/Adoption. Adoption of the resolution to authorize the Judiciary Committee to conduct an inquiry into whether sufficient grounds exist to impeach President Clinton. Adopted 258-176: R 227-0; D 31-175 (ND 17-134, SD 14-41); I 0-1. Oct. 8, 1998.

499. Procedural Motion/Adjourn. Obey, D-Wis., motion to adjourn. Motion rejected 58-349: R 0-209; D 58-139 (ND 48-96, SD 10-43); I 0-1. Oct. 8, 1998.

500. HR 4274. Fiscal 1999 Labor-HHS Appropriations/Previous Question. Dreier, R-Calif., motion to order the previous question (thus ending debate and the possibility of amendment) on adoption of the rule (H Res 584) to provide for House floor consideration of the bill to provide about $290 billion in fiscal 1999 funding for the Labor, Health and Human Services and Education departments and related agencies. Motion agreed to 224-201: R 220-0; D 4-200 (ND 4-145, SD 0-55); I 0-1. Oct. 8, 1998.

501. HR 4274. Fiscal 1999 Labor-HHS Appropriations/Procedural Motion. DeLay, R-Texas, motion to table (kill) the Furse, D-Ore., motion to reconsider the Dreier, R-Calif., motion to order the previous question. Motion agreed to 231-197: R 223-0; D 8-196 (ND 4-145, SD 4-51); I 0-1. Oct. 8, 1998.

502. HR 4274. Fiscal 1999 Labor-HHS Appropriations/Rule. Adoption of the rule (H Res 584) to provide for House floor consideration of the bill to provide about $290 billion in fiscal 1999 funding for the Labor, Health and Human Services and Education departments and related agencies. Adopted 214-209: R 201-22; D 13-186 (ND 8-136, SD 5-50); I 0-1. Oct. 8, 1998.

503. HR 4274. Fiscal 1999 Labor-HHS Appropriations/Procedural Motion. Dreier, R-Calif., motion to table (kill) the Obey, D-Wis., motion to reconsider the vote by which the House adopted the rule (H Res 584) to provide for House floor consideration of the bill to provide about $290 billion in fiscal 1999 funding for the Labor, Health and Human Services and Education departments and related agencies. Motion agreed to 230-192: R 221-0; D 9-191 (ND 5-140, SD 4-51); I 0-1. Oct. 8, 1998.

504. HR 4274. Fiscal 1999 Labor-HHS Appropriations/Parental Consent for Contraceptives Distribution. Istook, R-Okla., substitute amendment to the Greenwood, R-Pa., amendment to require parental consent or notification before minors can receive contraceptives from federally supported family planning clinics. The Greenwood amendment would have allowed clinics to dispense contraceptives to minors without parental consent or notification. Adopted 224-200: R 190-33; D 34-166 (ND 21-124, SD 13-42); I 0-1. Oct. 8, 1998. (Subsequently, the Greenwood amendment, as amended, was adopted by voice vote.)

	498	499	500	501	502	503	504
ALABAMA							
1 *Callahan*	Y	N	Y	Y	Y	Y	Y
2 *Everett*	Y	N	Y	Y	Y	Y	Y
3 *Riley*	Y	N	Y	Y	Y	Y	Y
4 *Aderholt*	Y	N	Y	Y	Y	Y	Y
5 Cramer	Y	N	N	N	N	N	Y
6 *Bachus*	Y	N	Y	Y	Y	Y	Y
7 Hilliard	N	N	N	N	N	N	N
ALASKA							
AL *Young*	Y	N	Y	Y	Y	Y	Y
ARIZONA							
1 *Salmon*	Y	N	Y	Y	Y	Y	Y
2 Pastor	N	Y	N	N	N	N	N
3 *Stump*	Y	N	Y	Y	Y	Y	Y
4 *Shadegg*	Y	N	Y	Y	Y	Y	Y
5 *Kolbe*	Y	N	Y	N	Y	N	Y
6 *Hayworth*	Y	N	Y	Y	Y	Y	Y
ARKANSAS							
1 Berry	N	N	N	N	N	N	N
2 Snyder	N	N	N	N	N	N	N
3 *Hutchinson*	Y	?	N	Y	Y	Y	Y
4 *Dickey*	Y	N	Y	Y	Y	Y	Y
CALIFORNIA							
1 *Riggs*	Y	N	Y	Y	Y	Y	Y
2 *Herger*	Y	N	Y	Y	Y	Y	Y
3 Fazio	N	Y	N	N	?	?	?
4 *Doolittle*	Y	N	Y	Y	Y	Y	Y
5 Matsui	N	Y	N	N	N	N	N
6 Woolsey	N	Y	N	N	N	N	N
7 Miller	N	Y	N	N	N	N	N
8 Pelosi	N	Y	N	N	N	N	N
9 Lee	N	Y	N	N	N	N	N
10 Tauscher	Y	N	N	N	N	N	N
11 *Pombo*	Y	N	Y	Y	Y	Y	Y
12 Lantos	N	N	N	N	?	N	N
13 Stark	N	Y	N	N	N	N	N
14 Eshoo	N	Y	N	N	N	N	N
15 *Campbell*	Y	N	Y	Y	Y	Y	Y
16 Lofgren	N	N	N	N	N	N	N
17 Farr	N	Y	N	N	N	N	N
18 Condit	Y	N	N	N	Y	N	N
19 *Radanovich*	Y	N	Y	Y	Y	Y	Y
20 Dooley	N	N	N	N	?	?	N
21 *Thomas*	Y	N	Y	Y	Y	Y	N
22 Capps, L.	N	N	N	N	N	N	N
23 *Gallegly*	Y	N	Y	Y	Y	Y	Y
24 Sherman	N	N	N	N	N	N	N
25 *McKeon*	Y	N	Y	Y	Y	Y	Y
26 Berman	N	N	N	N	N	N	N
27 *Rogan*	Y	N	Y	Y	Y	Y	Y
28 *Dreier*	Y	N	Y	Y	Y	Y	Y
29 Waxman	N	N	N	N	N	N	N
30 Becerra	N	Y	N	N	N	N	N
31 Martinez	N	Y	N	N	?	?	?
32 Dixon	N	N	N	N	N	N	N
33 Roybal-Allard	N	N	N	N	N	N	N
34 Torres	N	N	N	N	N	N	N
35 Waters	N	Y	N	N	N	N	N
36 Harman	N	Y	N	N	N	?	N
37 Millender-McD.	N	N	N	N	N	N	N
38 *Horn*	Y	N	?	Y	N	Y	N

	498	499	500	501	502	503	504
39 *Royce*	Y	N	Y	Y	Y	Y	Y
40 *Lewis*	Y	N	Y	Y	Y	Y	Y
41 *Kim*	Y	N	Y	Y	Y	Y	Y
42 Brown	N	Y	N	N	N	N	N
43 *Calvert*	Y	N	Y	Y	Y	Y	Y
44 *Bono, M.*	Y	N	Y	Y	Y	Y	Y
45 *Rohrabacher*	Y	N	Y	Y	Y	Y	Y
46 Sanchez	N	N	N	N	N	N	N
47 *Cox*	Y	N	Y	?	Y	Y	Y
48 *Packard*	Y	N	Y	Y	Y	Y	Y
49 *Bilbray*	Y	N	Y	N	Y	N	Y
50 Filner	N	Y	N	N	N	N	N
51 *Cunningham*	Y	?	Y	Y	Y	Y	Y
52 *Hunter*	Y	N	Y	Y	Y	Y	Y
COLORADO							
1 DeGette	N	N	N	N	N	N	N
2 Skaggs	N	N	N	N	N	N	N
3 *McInnis*	Y	N	Y	Y	Y	Y	Y
4 *Schaffer*	Y	N	Y	Y	Y	Y	Y
5 *Hefley*	Y	N	Y	Y	Y	Y	Y
6 *Schaefer*	Y	N	Y	Y	Y	Y	Y
CONNECTICUT							
1 Kennelly	N	?	?	?	?	?	?
2 Gejdenson	N	N	N	N	N	N	N
3 DeLauro	N	Y	N	N	N	N	N
4 *Shays*	Y	N	Y	N	N	N	N
5 Maloney	Y	N	N	N	N	N	N
6 *Johnson*	Y	N	Y	N	Y	N	Y
DELAWARE							
AL *Castle*	Y	N	Y	Y	N	Y	N
FLORIDA							
1 *Scarborough*	Y	N	?	Y	Y	Y	Y
2 Boyd	N	N	N	N	N	N	N
3 Brown	N	N	N	N	N	N	N
4 *Fowler*	Y	N	Y	Y	Y	Y	Y
5 Thurman	N	N	N	N	N	N	N
6 *Stearns*	Y	N	Y	Y	Y	Y	Y
7 *Mica*	Y	Y	Y	Y	Y	Y	Y
8 *McCollum*	Y	N	Y	Y	Y	Y	Y
9 *Bilirakis*	Y	N	Y	Y	Y	Y	Y
10 *Young*	Y	N	Y	Y	Y	Y	Y
11 Davis	N	N	N	N	N	N	N
12 *Canady*	Y	N	Y	Y	Y	Y	Y
13 *Miller*	Y	N	Y	N	Y	N	Y
14 *Goss*	Y	N	Y	Y	Y	Y	Y
15 *Weldon*	Y	N	Y	Y	Y	Y	Y
16 *Foley*	Y	N	Y	Y	Y	Y	N
17 Meek	N	Y	N	N	N	N	N
18 *Ros-Lehtinen*	Y	N	Y	N	Y	N	N
19 Wexler	N	N	N	N	N	N	N
20 Deutsch	N	N	N	N	N	N	N
21 *Diaz-Balart*	Y	N	Y	Y	Y	?	Y
22 *Shaw*	Y	N	Y	Y	Y	Y	Y
23 Hastings	N	N	N	N	N	N	N
GEORGIA							
1 *Kingston*	Y	N	Y	Y	Y	Y	Y
2 Bishop	N	N	N	N	N	N	N
3 *Collins*	Y	N	Y	Y	Y	Y	Y
4 McKinney	N	N	N	N	N	N	N
5 Lewis	N	Y	N	N	N	N	N
6 *Gingrich*	Y						Y
7 *Barr*	Y	?	Y	Y	Y	Y	Y
8 *Chambliss*	Y	N	Y	Y	Y	Y	Y
9 *Deal*	Y	N	Y	Y	Y	Y	Y
10 *Norwood*	Y	N	Y	Y	Y	Y	Y
11 *Linder*	Y	N	Y	Y	Y	Y	Y
HAWAII							
1 Abercrombie	N	−	N	N	N	N	N
2 Mink	N	Y	N	N	N	N	N
IDAHO							
1 *Chenoweth*	Y	N	Y	Y	Y	Y	Y
2 *Crapo*	Y	N	Y	Y	Y	Y	Y
ILLINOIS							
1 Rush	N	N	N	N	N	N	N
2 Jackson	N	N	N	N	N	N	N
3 Lipinski	Y	N	Y	N	N	N	Y
4 Gutierrez	N	N	N	N	N	N	N
5 Blagojevich	N	N	N	N	N	N	N
6 *Hyde*	Y	N	Y	Y	Y	Y	Y
7 Davis	N	N	N	N	N	N	N
8 *Crane*	Y	N	Y	Y	Y	Y	Y
9 Yates	N	Y	N	N	?	?	?
10 *Porter*	Y	N	Y	Y	Y	Y	Y
11 *Weller*	Y	N	Y	Y	Y	Y	Y
12 Costello	Y	N	Y	Y	Y	?	N
13 *Fawell*	Y	?	Y	Y	Y	?	N

ND Northern Democrats   SD Southern Democrats

	498	499	500	501	502	503	504
14 ***Hastert***	Y	N	Y	Y	Y	Y	Y
15 ***Ewing***	Y	N	Y	Y	Y	Y	Y
16 ***Manzullo***	Y	N	Y	Y	Y	Y	Y
17 Evans	Y	Y	N	N	N	N	N
18 ***LaHood***	Y	N	Y	Y	Y	Y	Y
19 Poshard	N	?	N	Y	N	N	?
20 ***Shimkus***	Y	N	Y	Y	Y	Y	Y
INDIANA							
1 Visclosky	N	N	N	N	N	N	Y
2 ***McIntosh***	Y	N	Y	Y	Y	Y	Y
3 Roemer	Y	N	N	N	N	N	Y
4 ***Souder***	Y	N	Y	Y	Y	Y	Y
5 ***Buyer***	Y	?	?	?	?	?	?
6 ***Burton***	Y	N	Y	Y	Y	Y	Y
7 ***Pease***	Y	N	Y	Y	Y	Y	Y
8 ***Hostettler***	Y	N	Y	Y	Y	Y	Y
9 Hamilton	Y	N	N	N	N	N	Y
10 Carson	N	N	N	N	N	N	N
IOWA							
1 ***Leach***	Y	N	Y	Y	N	Y	N
2 ***Nussle***	Y	N	Y	Y	Y	Y	Y
3 Boswell	Y	N	N	N	N	N	N
4 ***Ganske***	Y	N	Y	Y	N	Y	N
5 ***Latham***	Y	N	Y	Y	Y	Y	Y
KANSAS							
1 ***Moran***	Y	N	Y	Y	Y	Y	Y
2 ***Ryun***	Y	?	Y	Y	Y	Y	Y
3 ***Snowbarger***	Y	N	Y	Y	Y	Y	Y
4 ***Tiahrt***	Y	N	Y	Y	Y	Y	Y
KENTUCKY							
1 ***Whitfield***	Y	?	?	?	Y	Y	Y
2 ***Lewis***	Y	N	Y	Y	Y	Y	Y
3 ***Northup***	Y	N	Y	Y	Y	Y	Y
4 ***Bunning***	Y	N	Y	Y	Y	Y	Y
5 ***Rogers***	Y	N	Y	Y	Y	Y	Y
6 Baesler	N	?	N	N	N	N	N
LOUISIANA							
1 ***Livingston***	Y	N	Y	Y	Y	Y	Y
2 Jefferson	N	N	N	N	N	N	N
3 ***Tauzin***	Y	N	Y	Y	Y	Y	Y
4 ***McCrery***	Y	N	Y	Y	Y	Y	Y
5 ***Cooksey***	Y	N	Y	Y	Y	Y	Y
6 ***Baker***	Y	N	Y	Y	Y	Y	Y
7 John	Y	N	N	N	N	N	Y
MAINE							
1 Allen	N	Y	N	N	N	N	N
2 Baldacci	N	N	N	N	N	N	N
MARYLAND							
1 ***Gilchrest***	Y	N	Y	Y	N	Y	N
2 ***Ehrlich***	Y	N	Y	Y	N	Y	N
3 Cardin	N	N	N	N	N	N	N
4 Wynn	N	N	N	N	N	N	N
5 Hoyer	N	N	N	N	N	N	N
6 ***Bartlett***	Y	N	Y	Y	Y	Y	Y
7 Cummings	N	N	N	N	N	N	N
8 ***Morella***	Y	N	Y	Y	N	Y	N
MASSACHUSETTS							
1 Olver	N	Y	N	N	N	N	N
2 Neal	N	N	N	N	N	N	N
3 McGovern	N	Y	N	N	N	N	N
4 Frank	N	Y	N	N	N	N	N
5 Meehan	N	Y	N	N	N	N	N
6 Tierney	N	N	N	N	N	N	N
7 Markey	N	N	N	N	N	N	N
8 Kennedy	N	N	N	N	N	N	N
9 Moakley	N	Y	N	N	N	N	?
10 Delahunt	N	Y	N	N	N	N	N
MICHIGAN							
1 Stupak	N	N	N	N	N	N	Y
2 ***Hoekstra***	Y	N	Y	Y	Y	Y	Y
3 ***Ehlers***	Y	N	Y	Y	Y	Y	Y
4 ***Camp***	Y	N	Y	Y	Y	Y	Y
5 Barcia	N	N	N	Y	Y	Y	Y
6 ***Upton***	Y	N	Y	Y	N	Y	N
7 ***Smith***	Y	N	Y	Y	Y	Y	Y
8 Stabenow	N	N	N	N	N	N	N
9 Kildee	N	N	N	N	Y	Y	Y
10 Bonior	N	N	N	N	N	N	N
11 ***Knollenberg***	Y	N	Y	Y	Y	Y	Y
12 Levin	N	N	N	N	N	N	N
13 Rivers	N	N	N	N	N	N	N
14 Conyers	N	Y	N	N	N	N	N
15 Kilpatrick	N	Y	N	N	N	N	N
16 Dingell	N	N	N	N	N	N	N

	498	499	500	501	502	503	504
MINNESOTA							
1 ***Gutknecht***	Y	N	Y	Y	Y	Y	Y
2 Minge	Y	N	N	N	N	N	N
3 ***Ramstad***	Y	N	Y	Y	N	Y	N
4 Vento	N	N	N	N	N	N	N
5 Sabo	N	Y	N	N	N	N	N
6 Luther	N	N	N	N	N	N	N
7 Peterson	Y	N	N	N	Y	Y	Y
8 Oberstar	N	N	N	N	N	N	N
MISSISSIPPI							
1 ***Wicker***	Y	N	Y	Y	Y	Y	Y
2 Thompson	N	N	N	N	N	N	N
3 ***Pickering***	Y	?	?	Y	Y	Y	Y
4 ***Parker***	Y	N	Y	Y	Y	Y	Y
5 Taylor	Y	N	N	Y	Y	Y	Y
MISSOURI							
1 Clay	N	N	N	N	N	N	N
2 ***Talent***	Y	N	Y	Y	Y	Y	Y
3 Gephardt	N	Y	N	N	N	N	N
4 Skelton	Y	N	N	N	Y	N	Y
5 McCarthy	N	N	N	N	N	N	N
6 Danner	Y	N	N	N	N	N	Y
7 ***Blunt***	Y	N	Y	Y	Y	Y	Y
8 ***Emerson***	Y	N	Y	Y	Y	Y	Y
9 ***Hulshof***	Y	?	Y	Y	Y	Y	Y
MONTANA							
AL ***Hill***	Y	N	Y	Y	Y	Y	Y
NEBRASKA							
1 ***Bereuter***	Y	N	Y	Y	Y	Y	Y
2 ***Christensen***	Y	?	Y	Y	Y	Y	Y
3 ***Barrett***	Y	N	Y	Y	Y	Y	Y
NEVADA							
1 ***Ensign***	Y	?	Y	Y	Y	Y	Y
2 ***Gibbons***	Y	N	Y	Y	Y	Y	Y
NEW HAMPSHIRE							
1 ***Sununu***	Y	N	Y	Y	Y	Y	Y
2 ***Bass***	Y	N	Y	Y	N	Y	N
NEW JERSEY							
1 Andrews	N	Y	N	?	N	N	N
2 ***LoBiondo***	Y	N	Y	Y	Y	Y	Y
3 ***Saxton***	Y	N	Y	Y	Y	Y	Y
4 ***Smith***	Y	N	Y	Y	Y	Y	Y
5 ***Roukema***	Y	N	Y	Y	Y	Y	Y
6 Pallone	N	N	N	N	N	N	N
7 ***Franks***	Y	N	Y	Y	N	Y	N
8 Pascrell	N	N	N	N	N	N	N
9 Rothman	N	N	N	N	N	N	N
10 Payne	N	N	N	N	N	N	N
11 ***Frelinghuysen***	Y	N	Y	Y	Y	Y	N
12 ***Pappas***	Y	N	Y	Y	Y	Y	Y
13 Menendez	N	N	N	N	N	N	N
NEW MEXICO							
1 ***Wilson***	Y	N	Y	Y	Y	Y	Y
2 ***Skeen***	Y	N	Y	Y	Y	Y	Y
3 ***Redmond***	Y	N	Y	Y	Y	Y	Y
NEW YORK							
1 ***Forbes***	Y	N	Y	Y	Y	Y	Y
2 ***Lazio***	Y	N	Y	Y	N	Y	N
3 ***King***	Y	N	Y	Y	Y	Y	Y
4 McCarthy	Y	N	N	N	N	N	N
5 Ackerman	N	Y	N	N	N	N	N
6 Meeks	N	N	N	N	N	N	N
7 Manton	N	Y	N	N	N	N	N
8 Nadler	N	N	N	N	N	N	N
9 Schumer	N	N	N	N	N	N	N
10 Towns	N	Y	N	N	N	N	N
11 Owens	N	Y	N	N	N	N	N
12 Velázquez	N	N	N	N	N	N	N
13 ***Fossella***	Y	?	Y	Y	Y	Y	Y
14 Maloney	Y	N	Y	N	N	N	N
15 Rangel	N	N	N	N	N	N	N
16 Serrano	N	N	N	N	N	N	N
17 Engel	N	N	N	N	N	N	N
18 Lowey	N	Y	N	N	?	N	N
19 ***Kelly***	Y	N	Y	Y	Y	Y	N
20 ***Gilman***	Y	N	Y	Y	N	Y	N
21 McNulty	N	Y	N	N	N	N	N
22 ***Solomon***	Y	N	Y	Y	Y	Y	Y
23 ***Boehlert***	Y	N	Y	Y	N	Y	N
24 ***McHugh***	Y	N	Y	Y	N	Y	Y
25 ***Walsh***	Y	N	Y	Y	P	Y	Y
26 Hinchey	N	Y	N	N	N	N	N
27 ***Paxon***	Y	N	Y	Y	Y	Y	Y
28 Slaughter	N	Y	N	N	N	N	N
29 LaFalce	N	Y	N	N	N	N	Y
30 ***Quinn***	Y	N	Y	Y	Y	Y	Y

	498	499	500	501	502	503	504
31 ***Houghton***	Y	N	Y	Y	Y	Y	N
NORTH CAROLINA							
1 Clayton	N	Y	N	N	N	N	N
2 Etheridge	Y	N	N	N	N	N	N
3 ***Jones***	Y	N	Y	Y	Y	Y	Y
4 Price	N	N	N	N	N	N	N
5 ***Burr***	Y	N	Y	Y	Y	Y	Y
6 ***Coble***	Y	N	Y	Y	Y	Y	Y
7 McIntyre	Y	N	N	N	N	N	Y
8 Hefner	N	Y	N	N	N	N	N
9 ***Myrick***	Y	N	Y	Y	Y	Y	Y
10 ***Ballenger***	Y	N	Y	Y	Y	Y	Y
11 ***Taylor***	Y	N	Y	Y	Y	Y	Y
12 Watt	N	N	N	N	N	N	N
NORTH DAKOTA							
AL Pomeroy	N	N	N	N	N	N	N
OHIO							
1 ***Chabot***	Y	N	Y	Y	Y	Y	Y
2 ***Portman***	Y	N	Y	Y	Y	Y	Y
3 Hall	N	Y	N	N	Y	Y	Y
4 ***Oxley***	Y	?	Y	Y	Y	Y	Y
5 ***Gillmor***	Y	N	Y	Y	Y	Y	Y
6 Strickland	N	Y	N	N	N	N	N
7 ***Hobson***	Y	N	Y	Y	Y	Y	Y
8 ***Boehner***	Y	N	Y	Y	Y	Y	Y
9 Kaptur	N	N	N	N	N	N	N
10 Kucinich	Y	N	N	N	N	N	N
11 Stokes	N	N	N	N	N	N	N
12 ***Kasich***	Y	N	Y	Y	Y	Y	Y
13 Brown	N	N	N	N	N	N	N
14 Sawyer	N	N	N	N	N	N	N
15 ***Pryce***	+	–	+	+	+	+	–
16 ***Regula***	Y	N	Y	Y	Y	Y	Y
17 Traficant	N	N	N	N	N	N	Y
18 ***Ney***	Y	?	Y	Y	N	Y	Y
19 ***LaTourette***	Y	N	Y	Y	Y	Y	N
OKLAHOMA							
1 ***Largent***	Y	N	Y	Y	Y	Y	Y
2 ***Coburn***	Y	N	Y	Y	Y	Y	Y
3 ***Watkins***	Y	N	Y	Y	Y	Y	Y
4 ***Watts***	Y	N	Y	Y	Y	Y	Y
5 ***Istook***	Y	N	Y	Y	Y	Y	Y
6 ***Lucas***	Y	N	Y	Y	Y	Y	Y
OREGON							
1 Furse	N	Y	Y	N	N	N	N
2 ***Smith***	Y	N	Y	Y	Y	Y	Y
3 Blumenauer	N	N	N	N	N	N	N
4 DeFazio	N	Y	N	N	N	N	N
5 Hooley	N	N	N	N	N	N	N
PENNSYLVANIA							
1 Brady	N	N	N	N	N	N	N
2 Fattah	N	N	?	N	N	N	N
3 Borski	N	N	N	N	N	N	N
4 Klink	N	N	N	N	N	N	N
5 ***Peterson***	Y	N	Y	Y	Y	Y	?
6 Holden	N	N	N	N	N	N	Y
7 ***Weldon***	Y	N	Y	Y	Y	Y	Y
8 ***Greenwood***	Y	?	Y	Y	Y	Y	N
9 ***Shuster***	Y	N	Y	Y	Y	Y	Y
10 ***McDade***	Y	N	?	?	?	?	?
11 Kanjorski	N	N	N	N	N	N	Y
12 Murtha	N	N	N	N	Y	N	Y
13 ***Fox***	Y	N	Y	Y	Y	Y	Y
14 Coyne	N	N	N	N	N	N	N
15 McHale	Y	N	Y	N	N	N	N
16 ***Pitts***	Y	N	Y	Y	Y	Y	Y
17 ***Gekas***	Y	N	Y	Y	Y	Y	Y
18 Doyle	N	?	N	N	N	N	Y
19 ***Goodling***	Y	N	Y	Y	Y	Y	Y
20 Mascara	N	N	N	N	N	N	Y
21 ***English***	Y	N	Y	Y	Y	Y	Y
RHODE ISLAND							
1 Kennedy	N	?	N	N	N	N	N
2 Weygand	Y	N	N	N	N	N	N
SOUTH CAROLINA							
1 ***Sanford***	Y	N	Y	Y	Y	Y	Y
2 ***Spence***	Y	N	Y	Y	Y	Y	Y
3 ***Graham***	Y	N	Y	Y	Y	Y	Y
4 ***Inglis***	Y	N	Y	Y	Y	Y	Y
5 Spratt	Y	Y	N	N	N	N	N
6 Clyburn	N	N	N	N	N	N	N
SOUTH DAKOTA							
AL ***Thune***	Y	N	Y	Y	Y	Y	Y

	498	499	500	501	502	503	504
TENNESSEE							
1 ***Jenkins***	Y	N	Y	Y	Y	Y	Y
2 ***Duncan***	Y	N	Y	Y	Y	Y	Y
3 ***Wamp***	Y	?	Y	Y	Y	Y	Y
4 ***Hilleary***	Y	N	Y	Y	Y	Y	Y
5 Clement	N	N	N	N	N	N	N
6 Gordon	N	N	N	N	N	N	Y
7 ***Bryant***	Y	N	Y	Y	Y	Y	Y
8 Tanner	N	N	N	N	N	N	Y
9 Ford	N	N	N	N	N	N	N
TEXAS							
1 Sandlin	N	N	N	N	N	N	Y
2 Turner	Y	N	N	N	N	N	Y
3 ***Johnson, Sam***	Y	N	Y	Y	Y	?	Y
4 Hall	Y	N	N	Y	Y	Y	Y
5 ***Sessions***	Y	N	Y	Y	Y	Y	Y
6 ***Barton***	Y	N	Y	Y	Y	Y	Y
7 ***Archer***	Y	N	Y	Y	Y	Y	Y
8 ***Brady***	Y	N	Y	Y	Y	Y	Y
9 Lampson	Y	N	N	N	N	N	N
10 Doggett	N	N	N	N	N	N	N
11 Edwards	N	N	N	N	N	N	N
12 ***Granger***	Y	N	Y	Y	Y	Y	Y
13 ***Thornberry***	Y	N	Y	Y	Y	Y	Y
14 ***Paul***	Y	N	Y	Y	Y	Y	Y
15 Hinojosa	N	N	N	N	N	N	N
16 Reyes	N	N	N	N	N	N	N
17 Stenholm	Y	N	N	Y	Y	Y	Y
18 Jackson-Lee	N	Y	N	N	N	N	N
19 ***Combest***	Y	N	Y	Y	Y	Y	Y
20 Gonzalez	N	N	N	N	N	N	N
21 ***Smith***	Y	N	Y	Y	Y	Y	Y
22 ***DeLay***	Y	N	Y	Y	Y	Y	Y
23 ***Bonilla***	Y	N	Y	Y	Y	Y	Y
24 Frost	N	N	N	N	N	N	N
25 Bentsen	N	N	N	N	N	N	N
26 ***Armey***	Y	N	Y	Y	Y	Y	Y
27 Ortiz	N	N	N	N	Y	N	Y
28 Rodriguez	N	Y	N	N	N	N	N
29 Green	N	N	N	N	N	N	N
30 Johnson, E.B.	N	Y	N	N	N	N	N
UTAH							
1 ***Hansen***	Y	N	Y	Y	Y	Y	Y
2 ***Cook***	Y	N	Y	Y	Y	Y	N
3 ***Cannon***	Y	N	Y	Y	Y	Y	Y
VERMONT							
AL *Sanders*	N	N	N	N	N	N	N
VIRGINIA							
1 ***Bateman***	Y	N	Y	Y	Y	Y	Y
2 Pickett	Y	N	N	N	N	N	N
3 Scott	N	Y	N	N	N	N	N
4 Sisisky	Y	N	N	N	N	N	N
5 Goode	Y	N	N	Y	Y	Y	Y
6 ***Goodlatte***	Y	N	Y	Y	Y	Y	Y
7 ***Bliley***	Y	N	Y	Y	Y	Y	Y
8 Moran	Y	?	N	N	N	N	N
9 Boucher	N	N	N	N	N	N	N
10 ***Wolf***	Y	N	Y	Y	Y	Y	Y
11 ***Davis***	Y	N	Y	Y	Y	Y	N
WASHINGTON							
1 ***White***	Y	?	Y	Y	Y	Y	Y
2 ***Metcalf***	Y	N	Y	Y	Y	Y	Y
3 ***Smith, Linda***	Y	N	Y	Y	Y	Y	Y
4 ***Hastings***	Y	N	Y	Y	Y	Y	Y
5 ***Nethercutt***	Y	N	Y	Y	Y	Y	Y
6 Dicks	N	Y	N	N	N	N	N
7 McDermott	N	Y	N	N	N	N	N
8 ***Dunn***	Y	N	Y	Y	Y	Y	Y
9 Smith, Adam	N	N	N	N	N	N	N
WEST VIRGINIA							
1 Mollohan	N	N	Y	N	N	N	Y
2 Wise	N	?	N	N	N	N	N
3 Rahall	N	N	N	N	Y	N	Y
WISCONSIN							
1 ***Neumann***	Y	N	Y	Y	Y	Y	Y
2 ***Klug***	Y	N	Y	Y	N	Y	N
3 Kind	Y	N	N	N	N	N	N
4 Kleczka	N	N	N	N	N	N	N
5 Barrett	N	N	N	N	N	N	N
6 ***Petri***	Y	N	Y	Y	Y	Y	Y
7 Obey	N	Y	N	N	N	N	N
8 Johnson	N	Y	N	N	N	N	N
9 ***Sensenbrenner***	Y	N	Y	Y	Y	Y	Y
WYOMING							
AL ***Cubin***	Y	N	Y	Y	Y	Y	Y

Southern states - Ala., Ark., Fla., Ga., Ky., La., Miss., N.C., Okla., S.C., Tenn., Texas, Va.

505. HR 3150. Consumer Bankruptcy Revisions/Recommit. Nadler, D-N.Y., motion to recommit the bill to the conference committee with instructions to report it back with an amendment to retain the status quo on rules regarding the discharge of credit card debt and to stiffen penalties for companies that force bankrupt persons into reaffirmation agreements. Motion rejected 157-266: R 3-219; D 153-47 (ND 120-26, SD 33-21); I 1-0. Oct. 9, 1998.

506. HR 3150. Consumer Bankruptcy Revisions/Conference Report. Adoption of the conference report on the bill to revise the nation's bankruptcy laws by forcing most debtors to file for Chapter 13 relief, instead of Chapter 7, if they have an above-median income and the ability to pay off at least 25 percent of their debts over five years. Adopted (thus sent to the Senate) 300-125: R 224-1; D 76-123 (ND 49-96, SD 27-27); I 0-1. Oct. 9, 1998. A "nay" was a vote in support of the president's position.

507. H Res 565. Importance of Mammograms and Biopsies/Passage. Bliley, R-Va., motion to suspend the rules and pass the resolution to express the sense of the House that mammograms and biopsies are an important part of the fight against breast cancer. Motion agreed to 424-0: R 224-0; D 199-0 (ND 145-0, SD 54-0); I 1-0. Oct. 9, 1998. A two-thirds majority of those present and voting (283 in this case) is required for passage under suspension of the rules.

508. H Con Res 331. Sewage Facilities in Tijuana, Mexico/Passage. Gilman, R-N.Y., motion to suspend the rules and pass the bill to express the sense of Congress that the sewage and infrastructure facilities in Tijuana, Mexico, are inadequate. Motion rejected 250-174: R 222-2; D 28-171 (ND 16-129, SD 12-42); I 0-1. Oct. 9, 1998. A two-thirds majority of those present and voting (283 in this case) is required for passage under suspension of the rules.

509. H Res 557. Holocaust-Era Assets/Passage. Gilman, R-N.Y. motion to suspend the rules and pass the bill to express the sense of the House in support of U.S. government efforts to identify Holocaust-era assets. Motion agreed to 427-0: R 225-0; D 201-0 (ND 147-0, SD 54-0); I 1-0. Oct. 9, 1998. A two-thirds majority of those present and voting (285 in this case) is required for passage under suspension of the rules.

510. HR 3875. Nutrition Programs Reauthorization/Conference Report. Goodling, R-Pa., motion to suspend the rules and adopt the conference report on the bill to reauthorize through 2003 the Women, Infants and Children nutrition program and a national summer food program for children of low-income families. Motion agreed to 422-1: R 225-1; D 196-0 (ND 144-0, SD 52-0); I 1-0. Oct. 9, 1998. A two-thirds majority of those present and voting (282 in this case) is required for passage under suspension of the rules.

511. Fiscal 1999 Continuing Appropriations/Passage. Passage of the joint resolution to provide continuing appropriations through Oct. 12 for fiscal 1999 spending bills not yet enacted. The continuing resolution sets spending at fiscal 1998 levels. Passed 421-0: R 223-0; D 197-0 (ND 143-0, SD 54-0); I 1-0. Oct. 9, 1998.

Key

Y	Voted for (yea).
#	Paired for.
+	Announced for.
N	Voted against (nay).
X	Paired against.
–	Announced against.
P	Voted "present."
C	Voted "present" to avoid possible conflict of interest.
?	Did not vote or otherwise make a position known.

Democrats **Republicans** *Independent*

	505	506	507	508	509	510	511
ALABAMA							
1 *Callahan*	N	Y	Y	Y	Y	Y	Y
2 *Everett*	N	Y	Y	Y	Y	Y	Y
3 *Riley*	N	Y	Y	Y	Y	Y	Y
4 *Aderholt*	N	Y	Y	Y	Y	Y	Y
5 Cramer	N	Y	Y	Y	Y	Y	Y
6 *Bachus*	N	Y	Y	Y	Y	Y	Y
7 Hilliard	Y	N	Y	Y	Y	Y	Y
ALASKA							
AL *Young*	N	Y	Y	Y	Y	Y	Y
ARIZONA							
1 *Salmon*	N	Y	Y	Y	Y	Y	Y
2 Pastor	Y	Y	Y	N	Y	Y	Y
3 *Stump*	N	Y	Y	Y	Y	Y	Y
4 *Shadegg*	N	Y	Y	Y	Y	Y	Y
5 *Kolbe*	N	Y	Y	Y	Y	Y	Y
6 *Hayworth*	N	Y	Y	Y	Y	Y	Y
ARKANSAS							
1 Berry	N	Y	Y	Y	Y	Y	Y
2 Snyder	N	Y	Y	N	Y	Y	Y
3 *Hutchinson*	N	Y	Y	Y	Y	Y	Y
4 *Dickey*	N	Y	Y	Y	Y	Y	Y
CALIFORNIA							
1 *Riggs*	N	Y	Y	Y	Y	Y	Y
2 *Herger*	N	Y	Y	Y	Y	Y	Y
3 Fazio	N	Y	N	Y	Y	Y	Y
4 *Doolittle*	N	Y	Y	Y	Y	Y	Y
5 Matsui	Y	Y	Y	N	Y	Y	Y
6 Woolsey	Y	N	Y	N	Y	Y	Y
7 Miller	Y	N	Y	N	Y	Y	Y
8 Pelosi	Y	N	Y	N	Y	Y	Y
9 Lee	Y	N	Y	N	Y	Y	Y
10 Tauscher	N	Y	Y	N	Y	Y	Y
11 *Pombo*	N	Y	Y	Y	Y	Y	Y
12 Lantos	Y	N	Y	N	Y	Y	Y
13 Stark	Y	N	Y	N	Y	Y	Y
14 Eshoo	Y	N	Y	N	Y	Y	Y
15 *Campbell*	Y	Y	Y	Y	Y	Y	Y
16 Lofgren	Y	N	Y	N	Y	Y	Y
17 Farr	Y	N	Y	N	Y	Y	Y
18 Condit	N	Y	Y	Y	Y	Y	Y
19 *Radanovich*	N	Y	Y	Y	Y	Y	Y
20 Dooley	Y	N	Y	N	Y	Y	Y
21 *Thomas*	N	Y	Y	Y	Y	Y	Y
22 Capps, L.	Y	Y	Y	N	Y	Y	Y
23 *Gallegly*	N	Y	Y	Y	Y	Y	Y
24 Sherman	N	Y	Y	Y	Y	?	Y
25 *McKeon*	N	Y	Y	Y	Y	Y	Y
26 Berman	?	?	?	?	?	?	?
27 *Rogan*	N	Y	Y	Y	Y	Y	Y
28 *Dreier*	N	Y	Y	Y	Y	Y	Y
29 Waxman	Y	N	Y	N	Y	Y	Y
30 Becerra	Y	N	Y	N	Y	Y	Y
31 Martinez	Y	N	Y	N	Y	Y	Y
32 Dixon	Y	N	Y	N	Y	Y	Y
33 Roybal-Allard	Y	N	Y	N	Y	Y	Y
34 Torres	?	?	?	N	Y	Y	Y
35 Waters	Y	N	Y	N	Y	Y	Y
36 Harman	Y	N	Y	N	Y	Y	Y
37 Millender-McD.	Y	N	Y	Y	Y	Y	Y
38 *Horn*	N	Y	Y	Y	Y	Y	Y

	505	506	507	508	509	510	511
39 *Royce*	N	Y	Y	Y	Y	Y	Y
40 *Lewis*	N	Y	Y	Y	Y	Y	Y
41 *Kim*	N	Y	Y	Y	Y	Y	Y
42 Brown	Y	N	Y	N	Y	Y	Y
43 *Calvert*	N	Y	Y	Y	Y	Y	Y
44 *Bono, M.*	N	Y	Y	Y	Y	Y	Y
45 *Rohrabacher*	N	Y	Y	Y	Y	Y	Y
46 Sanchez	Y	N	Y	N	Y	Y	Y
47 *Cox*	N	Y	Y	Y	Y	Y	Y
48 *Packard*	N	Y	Y	Y	Y	Y	Y
49 *Bilbray*	N	Y	Y	Y	Y	Y	Y
50 Filner	Y	N	Y	N	Y	Y	Y
51 *Cunningham*	N	Y	Y	Y	Y	Y	Y
52 *Hunter*	N	Y	Y	Y	Y	Y	Y
COLORADO							
1 DeGette	Y	N	Y	N	Y	Y	Y
2 Skaggs	Y	N	Y	N	Y	Y	Y
3 *McInnis*	N	Y	Y	Y	Y	Y	Y
4 *Schaffer*	N	Y	Y	Y	Y	Y	Y
5 *Hefley*	N	Y	Y	Y	Y	Y	Y
6 *Schaefer*	N	Y	Y	Y	Y	Y	Y
CONNECTICUT							
1 Kennelly	?	?	?	?	?	?	?
2 Gejdenson	Y	N	Y	N	Y	Y	Y
3 DeLauro	Y	N	Y	N	Y	Y	Y
4 *Shays*	N	Y	Y	Y	Y	Y	Y
5 Maloney	N	Y	Y	Y	Y	Y	Y
6 *Johnson*	N	Y	Y	Y	Y	Y	Y
DELAWARE							
AL *Castle*	N	Y	Y	Y	Y	Y	Y
FLORIDA							
1 *Scarborough*	N	Y	Y	Y	Y	Y	Y
2 Boyd	N	Y	N	Y	Y	Y	Y
3 Brown	Y	N	Y	N	Y	Y	Y
4 *Fowler*	N	Y	+	+	+	Y	Y
5 Thurman	Y	N	Y	N	Y	Y	Y
6 *Stearns*	N	Y	Y	Y	Y	Y	Y
7 *Mica*	N	Y	Y	Y	Y	Y	Y
8 *McCollum*	N	Y	Y	Y	Y	Y	Y
9 *Bilirakis*	N	Y	Y	Y	Y	Y	Y
10 *Young*	N	Y	Y	Y	Y	Y	Y
11 Davis	N	Y	Y	N	Y	Y	Y
12 *Canady*	N	Y	Y	Y	Y	Y	Y
13 *Miller*	N	Y	Y	Y	Y	Y	Y
14 *Goss*	N	Y	Y	Y	Y	Y	Y
15 *Weldon*	N	Y	Y	Y	Y	Y	Y
16 *Foley*	N	Y	Y	Y	Y	Y	Y
17 Meek	Y	N	Y	N	Y	Y	Y
18 *Ros-Lehtinen*	N	Y	Y	Y	Y	Y	Y
19 Wexler	Y	N	Y	N	Y	Y	Y
20 Deutsch	N	Y	Y	N	Y	Y	Y
21 *Diaz-Balart*	N	Y	Y	Y	Y	Y	Y
22 *Shaw*	N	Y	Y	Y	Y	Y	Y
23 Hastings	Y	N	Y	N	Y	Y	Y
GEORGIA							
1 *Kingston*	N	Y	Y	Y	Y	Y	Y
2 Bishop	N	Y	Y	Y	Y	Y	Y
3 *Collins*	N	Y	Y	Y	Y	Y	Y
4 McKinney	Y	N	Y	N	Y	Y	Y
5 Lewis	Y	N	Y	N	Y	Y	Y
6 *Gingrich*							
7 *Barr*	N	Y	Y	Y	Y	Y	Y
8 *Chambliss*	N	Y	Y	Y	Y	Y	Y
9 *Deal*	N	Y	Y	Y	Y	Y	Y
10 *Norwood*	N	Y	Y	Y	Y	Y	Y
11 *Linder*	N	Y	Y	Y	Y	Y	Y
HAWAII							
1 Abercrombie	Y	N	Y	N	Y	Y	Y
2 Mink	Y	N	Y	N	Y	Y	Y
IDAHO							
1 *Chenoweth*	N	Y	Y	Y	Y	Y	Y
2 *Crapo*	N	Y	Y	Y	Y	Y	Y
ILLINOIS							
1 Rush	Y	N	Y	N	Y	Y	Y
2 Jackson	Y	N	Y	N	Y	Y	Y
3 Lipinski	Y	N	Y	N	Y	Y	Y
4 Gutierrez	Y	N	Y	N	Y	Y	Y
5 Blagojevich	Y	Y	Y	N	Y	Y	Y
6 *Hyde*	N	Y	Y	Y	Y	Y	Y
7 Davis	Y	N	Y	N	Y	Y	Y
8 *Crane*	N	Y	Y	Y	Y	Y	Y
9 Yates	N	Y	N	Y	Y	Y	?
10 *Porter*	N	Y	Y	Y	Y	Y	Y
11 *Weller*	N	Y	Y	Y	Y	Y	Y
12 Costello	N	Y	Y	Y	Y	Y	Y
13 *Fawell*	N	Y	Y	Y	Y	Y	Y

ND Northern Democrats **SD** Southern Democrats

	505	506	507	508	509	510	511
14 ***Hastert***	N	Y	Y	Y	Y	Y	Y
15 ***Ewing***	N	Y	Y	Y	Y	Y	Y
16 ***Manzullo***	N	Y	Y	Y	Y	Y	Y
17 Evans	Y	N	Y	N	Y	Y	Y
18 ***LaHood***	N	Y	Y	Y	Y	Y	Y
19 Poshard	?	?	?	?	?	?	?
20 ***Shimkus***	N	Y	Y	Y	Y	Y	Y
INDIANA							
1 Visclosky	Y	N	Y	N	Y	Y	Y
2 ***McIntosh***	N	Y	Y	Y	Y	Y	Y
3 Roemer	N	Y	Y	?	Y	Y	Y
4 ***Souder***	N	Y	Y	Y	Y	Y	Y
5 ***Buyer***	N	Y	Y	Y	Y	Y	Y
6 ***Burton***	?	Y	Y	Y	Y	Y	Y
7 ***Pease***	N	Y	Y	Y	Y	Y	Y
8 ***Hostettler***	N	Y	Y	Y	Y	Y	Y
9 Hamilton	N	Y	Y	N	Y	Y	Y
10 Carson	Y	N	Y	Y	Y	Y	Y
IOWA							
1 ***Leach***	N	Y	Y	Y	Y	Y	Y
2 ***Nussle***	N	Y	Y	Y	Y	Y	Y
3 Boswell	N	Y	Y	Y	Y	Y	Y
4 ***Ganske***	N	Y	Y	Y	Y	Y	Y
5 ***Latham***	N	Y	Y	Y	Y	Y	Y
KANSAS							
1 ***Moran***	N	Y	Y	Y	Y	Y	Y
2 ***Ryun***	N	Y	Y	Y	Y	Y	Y
3 ***Snowbarger***	N	Y	Y	Y	Y	Y	Y
4 ***Tiahrt***	N	Y	Y	Y	Y	Y	Y
KENTUCKY							
1 ***Whitfield***	N	Y	Y	Y	Y	Y	Y
2 ***Lewis***	N	Y	Y	Y	Y	Y	Y
3 ***Northup***	N	Y	Y	Y	Y	Y	Y
4 ***Bunning***	N	Y	Y	Y	Y	Y	Y
5 ***Rogers***	N	Y	Y	Y	Y	Y	Y
6 Baesler	N	Y	Y	Y	Y	Y	Y
LOUISIANA							
1 ***Livingston***	N	Y	Y	Y	Y	Y	Y
2 Jefferson	Y	N	Y	N	Y	Y	Y
3 ***Tauzin***	N	Y	Y	Y	Y	Y	Y
4 ***McCrery***	N	Y	Y	Y	Y	Y	Y
5 ***Cooksey***	N	Y	Y	Y	Y	Y	Y
6 ***Baker***	N	Y	Y	Y	Y	Y	Y
7 John	?	?	?	?	?	?	?
MAINE							
1 Allen	Y	N	Y	N	Y	Y	Y
2 Baldacci	Y	N	Y	N	Y	Y	Y
MARYLAND							
1 ***Gilchrest***	N	Y	Y	Y	Y	Y	Y
2 ***Ehrlich***	N	Y	Y	Y	Y	Y	Y
3 Cardin	N	Y	Y	N	Y	Y	Y
4 Wynn	Y	Y	Y	N	Y	Y	Y
5 Hoyer	N	Y	Y	N	Y	Y	Y
6 ***Bartlett***	N	Y	Y	Y	Y	Y	Y
7 Cummings	Y	N	Y	N	Y	Y	Y
8 ***Morella***	N	Y	Y	Y	Y	Y	Y
MASSACHUSETTS							
1 Olver	Y	N	Y	N	Y	Y	Y
2 Neal	Y	Y	Y	N	Y	Y	Y
3 McGovern	Y	N	Y	N	Y	Y	Y
4 Frank	N	Y	Y	N	Y	Y	?
5 Meehan	Y	N	Y	N	Y	Y	Y
6 Tierney	?	?	?	?	?	?	?
7 Markey	Y	N	Y	N	Y	Y	Y
8 Kennedy	Y	N	Y	N	Y	Y	Y
9 Moakley	Y	N	Y	N	Y	Y	Y
10 Delahunt	Y	N	?	N	Y	Y	Y
MICHIGAN							
1 Stupak	Y	N	Y	N	Y	Y	Y
2 ***Hoekstra***	N	Y	Y	Y	Y	Y	Y
3 ***Ehlers***	N	Y	Y	Y	Y	Y	Y
4 ***Camp***	N	Y	Y	Y	Y	Y	Y
5 Barcia	N	Y	Y	N	Y	Y	Y
6 ***Upton***	N	Y	Y	Y	Y	Y	Y
7 ***Smith***	N	Y	Y	Y	Y	Y	?
8 Stabenow	Y	N	Y	N	Y	Y	Y
9 Kildee	Y	N	Y	N	Y	Y	Y
10 Bonior	Y	N	Y	N	Y	Y	Y
11 ***Knollenberg***	N	Y	Y	Y	Y	Y	Y
12 Levin	Y	N	Y	N	Y	Y	Y
13 Rivers	Y	Y	Y	N	Y	Y	Y
14 Conyers	Y	N	Y	N	Y	Y	Y
15 Kilpatrick	Y	N	Y	N	Y	Y	Y
16 Dingell	Y	N	Y	N	Y	Y	Y

	505	506	507	508	509	510	511
MINNESOTA							
1 ***Gutknecht***	N	Y	Y	Y	Y	Y	Y
2 Minge	N	Y	Y	N	Y	Y	Y
3 ***Ramstad***	N	Y	Y	Y	Y	Y	Y
4 Vento	Y	N	Y	N	Y	Y	Y
5 Sabo	Y	N	Y	N	Y	Y	Y
6 Luther	Y	N	Y	N	Y	Y	Y
7 Peterson	N	Y	Y	Y	Y	Y	Y
8 Oberstar	Y	N	Y	N	Y	Y	Y
MISSISSIPPI							
1 ***Wicker***	N	Y	Y	Y	Y	Y	Y
2 Thompson	Y	N	Y	N	Y	Y	Y
3 ***Pickering***	N	Y	Y	Y	Y	Y	Y
4 ***Parker***	N	Y	Y	Y	Y	Y	Y
5 Taylor	N	Y	Y	Y	Y	Y	Y
MISSOURI							
1 Clay	Y	N	Y	N	Y	Y	Y
2 ***Talent***	N	Y	Y	Y	Y	Y	Y
3 Gephardt	Y	Y	Y	?	Y	Y	Y
4 Skelton	N	Y	Y	N	Y	Y	Y
5 McCarthy	Y	N	Y	N	Y	Y	Y
6 Danner	N	Y	Y	Y	Y	Y	Y
7 ***Blunt***	N	Y	Y	Y	Y	Y	Y
8 ***Emerson***	N	Y	Y	Y	Y	Y	Y
9 ***Hulshof***	N	Y	Y	Y	Y	Y	Y
MONTANA							
AL ***Hill***	N	Y	Y	Y	Y	Y	Y
NEBRASKA							
1 ***Bereuter***	N	Y	Y	Y	Y	Y	Y
2 ***Christensen***	N	Y	Y	Y	Y	Y	Y
3 ***Barrett***	N	Y	Y	Y	Y	Y	Y
NEVADA							
1 ***Ensign***	N	Y	Y	Y	Y	Y	Y
2 ***Gibbons***	N	Y	Y	Y	Y	Y	Y
NEW HAMPSHIRE							
1 ***Sununu***	N	Y	Y	Y	Y	Y	Y
2 ***Bass***	N	Y	Y	Y	Y	Y	Y
NEW JERSEY							
1 Andrews	Y	Y	Y	N	Y	Y	Y
2 ***LoBiondo***	N	Y	Y	Y	Y	Y	Y
3 ***Saxton***	N	Y	Y	Y	Y	Y	Y
4 ***Smith***	N	Y	Y	Y	Y	Y	Y
5 ***Roukema***	Y	N	Y	Y	Y	Y	Y
6 Pallone	Y	N	Y	N	Y	Y	Y
7 ***Franks***	N	Y	Y	Y	Y	Y	Y
8 Pascrell	Y	Y	Y	N	Y	Y	Y
9 Rothman	N	Y	Y	N	Y	Y	Y
10 Payne	Y	N	Y	N	Y	Y	Y
11 ***Frelinghuysen***	N	Y	Y	Y	Y	Y	Y
12 ***Pappas***	N	Y	Y	Y	Y	Y	Y
13 Menendez	Y	Y	Y	N	Y	Y	Y
NEW MEXICO							
1 ***Wilson***	N	Y	Y	Y	Y	Y	Y
2 ***Skeen***	N	Y	Y	Y	Y	Y	Y
3 ***Redmond***	N	Y	Y	Y	Y	Y	Y
NEW YORK							
1 ***Forbes***	N	Y	Y	Y	Y	Y	Y
2 ***Lazio***	N	Y	Y	Y	Y	Y	Y
3 ***King***	N	Y	Y	Y	Y	Y	Y
4 McCarthy	Y	Y	Y	N	Y	Y	Y
5 Ackerman	Y	N	Y	N	Y	Y	Y
6 Meeks	Y	N	Y	N	Y	Y	Y
7 Manton	Y	N	Y	N	Y	Y	?
8 Nadler	Y	N	Y	N	Y	Y	Y
9 Schumer	Y	N	Y	N	Y	Y	Y
10 Towns	Y	N	Y	N	Y	Y	Y
11 Owens	Y	N	Y	N	Y	Y	Y
12 Velázquez	Y	Y	Y	N	Y	Y	Y
13 ***Fossella***	N	Y	Y	Y	Y	Y	Y
14 Maloney	Y	Y	Y	N	Y	Y	Y
15 Rangel	Y	N	Y	N	Y	Y	Y
16 Serrano	Y	N	Y	N	Y	Y	Y
17 Engel	Y	N	Y	N	Y	Y	Y
18 Lowey	Y	N	Y	N	Y	Y	Y
19 ***Kelly***	N	Y	Y	Y	Y	Y	Y
20 ***Gilman***	N	Y	Y	Y	Y	Y	Y
21 McNulty	Y	N	Y	N	Y	Y	Y
22 ***Solomon***	N	Y	Y	Y	Y	Y	Y
23 ***Boehlert***	N	Y	Y	Y	Y	Y	Y
24 ***McHugh***	N	Y	Y	Y	Y	Y	Y
25 ***Walsh***	N	Y	Y	Y	Y	Y	Y
26 Hinchey	Y	N	Y	N	Y	Y	Y
27 ***Paxon***	N	Y	Y	Y	Y	Y	Y
28 Slaughter	Y	N	Y	N	Y	Y	Y
29 LaFalce	Y	N	Y	N	Y	Y	Y
30 ***Quinn***	N	Y	Y	Y	Y	Y	Y

	505	506	507	508	509	510	511
31 ***Houghton***	N	Y	Y	Y	Y	Y	Y
NORTH CAROLINA							
1 Clayton	Y	N	Y	N	Y	Y	Y
2 Etheridge	Y	Y	Y	N	Y	Y	Y
3 ***Jones***	N	Y	Y	Y	Y	Y	Y
4 Price	Y	Y	Y	N	Y	Y	Y
5 ***Burr***	N	Y	Y	Y	Y	Y	Y
6 ***Coble***	N	Y	Y	Y	Y	Y	Y
7 McIntyre	Y	Y	Y	Y	Y	Y	Y
8 Hefner	Y	N	Y	N	Y	Y	Y
9 ***Myrick***	N	Y	Y	Y	Y	Y	Y
10 ***Ballenger***	N	Y	Y	Y	Y	Y	Y
11 ***Taylor***	N	Y	Y	Y	Y	Y	Y
12 Watt	Y	N	Y	N	Y	Y	Y
NORTH DAKOTA							
AL Pomeroy	Y	Y	Y	N	Y	Y	Y
OHIO							
1 ***Chabot***	N	Y	Y	Y	Y	Y	Y
2 ***Portman***	N	Y	Y	Y	Y	Y	Y
3 Hall	Y	N	Y	Y	Y	Y	Y
4 ***Oxley***	N	Y	Y	Y	Y	Y	Y
5 ***Gillmor***	N	Y	Y	Y	Y	Y	Y
6 Strickland	Y	Y	Y	N	Y	Y	Y
7 ***Hobson***	N	Y	Y	Y	Y	Y	Y
8 ***Boehner***	N	Y	Y	Y	Y	Y	Y
9 Kaptur	Y	N	Y	N	Y	Y	Y
10 Kucinich	Y	N	Y	Y	Y	Y	Y
11 Stokes	Y	N	Y	N	Y	Y	Y
12 ***Kasich***	N	Y	Y	Y	Y	Y	Y
13 Brown	Y	N	Y	N	Y	Y	Y
14 Sawyer	Y	Y	Y	N	Y	Y	Y
15 ***Pryce***	–	+	+	+	+	+	+
16 ***Regula***	N	Y	Y	Y	Y	Y	Y
17 Traficant	Y	N	Y	Y	Y	Y	Y
18 ***Ney***	N	Y	Y	Y	Y	Y	Y
19 ***LaTourette***	N	Y	Y	Y	Y	Y	Y
OKLAHOMA							
1 ***Largent***	N	Y	Y	Y	Y	Y	Y
2 ***Coburn***	N	Y	Y	Y	Y	Y	Y
3 ***Watkins***	N	Y	Y	Y	Y	Y	Y
4 ***Watts***	N	Y	Y	Y	Y	Y	Y
5 ***Istook***	N	Y	Y	Y	Y	Y	Y
6 ***Lucas***	N	Y	Y	Y	Y	Y	Y
OREGON							
1 Furse	Y	N	Y	N	Y	Y	Y
2 ***Smith***	N	Y	Y	Y	Y	Y	Y
3 Blumenauer	Y	Y	Y	N	Y	Y	Y
4 DeFazio	Y	N	Y	N	Y	?	Y
5 Hooley	N	Y	Y	N	Y	Y	Y
PENNSYLVANIA							
1 Brady	Y	N	Y	N	Y	Y	Y
2 Fattah	Y	?	Y	N	Y	Y	Y
3 Borski	Y	N	Y	N	Y	Y	Y
4 Klink	Y	N	Y	N	Y	Y	Y
5 ***Peterson***	N	Y	Y	Y	Y	Y	Y
6 Holden	Y	Y	Y	N	Y	Y	Y
7 ***Weldon***	N	Y	Y	Y	Y	Y	Y
8 ***Greenwood***	N	Y	Y	Y	Y	Y	Y
9 ***Shuster***	N	Y	Y	Y	Y	Y	Y
10 ***McDade***	?	?	?	?	Y	Y	Y
11 Kanjorski	Y	N	Y	N	Y	Y	Y
12 Murtha	Y	N	Y	N	Y	Y	Y
13 ***Fox***	Y	Y	Y	Y	Y	Y	Y
14 Coyne	Y	N	Y	N	Y	Y	Y
15 McHale	Y	Y	Y	Y	Y	Y	Y
16 ***Pitts***	N	Y	Y	Y	Y	Y	Y
17 ***Gekas***	N	Y	Y	Y	Y	Y	Y
18 Doyle	Y	N	Y	N	Y	Y	Y
19 ***Goodling***	?	Y	Y	Y	Y	Y	Y
20 Mascara	Y	N	Y	N	Y	Y	Y
21 ***English***	N	Y	Y	Y	Y	Y	Y
RHODE ISLAND							
1 Kennedy	Y	Y	Y	N	Y	Y	Y
2 Weygand	N	Y	Y	N	Y	Y	Y
SOUTH CAROLINA							
1 ***Sanford***	N	Y	Y	Y	Y	Y	Y
2 ***Spence***	N	Y	Y	Y	Y	Y	Y
3 ***Graham***	N	Y	Y	Y	Y	Y	Y
4 ***Inglis***	N	Y	Y	Y	Y	Y	?
5 Spratt	Y	Y	Y	N	Y	Y	Y
6 Clyburn	Y	N	Y	N	Y	Y	Y
SOUTH DAKOTA							
AL ***Thune***	N	Y	Y	Y	Y	Y	Y

	505	506	507	508	509	510	511
TENNESSEE							
1 ***Jenkins***	N	Y	Y	Y	Y	Y	Y
2 ***Duncan***	N	Y	Y	Y	Y	Y	Y
3 ***Wamp***	N	Y	Y	Y	Y	Y	Y
4 ***Hilleary***	N	Y	Y	Y	Y	Y	Y
5 Clement	N	Y	Y	N	Y	Y	Y
6 Gordon	N	Y	Y	N	Y	Y	Y
7 ***Bryant***	N	Y	Y	Y	Y	Y	Y
8 Tanner	N	Y	Y	N	Y	Y	Y
9 Ford	Y	N	Y	N	Y	Y	Y
TEXAS							
1 Sandlin	Y	Y	Y	N	Y	Y	Y
2 Turner	Y	Y	Y	N	Y	Y	Y
3 ***Johnson, Sam***	N	Y	Y	Y	Y	Y	Y
4 Hall	N	Y	Y	Y	Y	Y	Y
5 ***Sessions***	N	Y	Y	Y	Y	Y	Y
6 ***Barton***	N	Y	Y	Y	Y	Y	Y
7 ***Archer***	N	Y	Y	Y	Y	Y	Y
8 ***Brady***	N	Y	Y	N	Y	Y	Y
9 Lampson	Y	N	Y	N	Y	?	Y
10 Doggett	Y	N	Y	N	Y	?	Y
11 Edwards	Y	N	Y	N	Y	Y	Y
12 ***Granger***	N	Y	Y	Y	Y	Y	Y
13 ***Thornberry***	N	Y	Y	Y	Y	Y	Y
14 ***Paul***	N	Y	Y	Y	Y	N	Y
15 Hinojosa	Y	N	Y	N	Y	Y	Y
16 Reyes	Y	N	Y	N	Y	Y	Y
17 Stenholm	N	Y	Y	Y	Y	Y	Y
18 Jackson-Lee	Y	N	Y	N	Y	Y	Y
19 ***Combest***	N	Y	Y	Y	Y	Y	Y
20 Gonzalez	Y	N	Y	N	Y	Y	Y
21 ***Smith***	N	Y	Y	Y	Y	Y	Y
22 ***DeLay***	N	Y	Y	Y	Y	Y	Y
23 ***Bonilla***	N	Y	Y	N	Y	Y	Y
24 Frost	N	Y	Y	N	Y	Y	Y
25 Bentsen	N	Y	Y	N	Y	Y	Y
26 ***Armey***	N	Y	Y	Y	Y	Y	Y
27 Ortiz	Y	N	Y	N	Y	Y	Y
28 Rodriguez	Y	N	Y	N	Y	Y	Y
29 Green	Y	N	Y	N	Y	Y	Y
30 Johnson, E.B.	Y	N	Y	N	Y	Y	Y
UTAH							
1 ***Hansen***	N	Y	Y	Y	Y	Y	Y
2 ***Cook***	?	Y	Y	Y	Y	Y	Y
3 ***Cannon***	N	Y	Y	Y	Y	Y	Y
VERMONT							
AL *Sanders*	Y	N	Y	N	Y	Y	Y
VIRGINIA							
1 ***Bateman***	N	Y	Y	Y	Y	Y	Y
2 Pickett	N	Y	Y	Y	Y	Y	Y
3 Scott	Y	N	Y	N	Y	Y	Y
4 Sisisky	N	Y	Y	Y	Y	Y	Y
5 Goode	N	Y	Y	Y	Y	Y	Y
6 ***Goodlatte***	N	Y	Y	Y	Y	Y	Y
7 ***Bliley***	N	Y	Y	Y	Y	Y	Y
8 Moran	N	Y	Y	Y	Y	Y	Y
9 Boucher	N	Y	Y	N	Y	Y	Y
10 ***Wolf***	N	Y	Y	Y	Y	Y	Y
11 ***Davis***	N	Y	Y	Y	Y	Y	Y
WASHINGTON							
1 ***White***	N	Y	Y	Y	Y	Y	Y
2 ***Metcalf***	N	Y	Y	Y	Y	Y	Y
3 ***Smith, Linda***	N	Y	Y	Y	Y	Y	Y
4 ***Hastings***	N	Y	Y	Y	Y	Y	Y
5 ***Nethercutt***	N	Y	Y	Y	Y	Y	+
6 Dicks	Y	Y	Y	N	Y	Y	Y
7 McDermott	Y	N	Y	N	Y	Y	Y
8 ***Dunn***	N	Y	Y	Y	Y	Y	Y
9 Smith, Adam	N	Y	Y	N	Y	Y	Y
WEST VIRGINIA							
1 Mollohan	N	Y	Y	N	Y	Y	?
2 Wise	N	Y	Y	Y	Y	Y	Y
3 Rahall	Y	N	Y	N	Y	Y	Y
WISCONSIN							
1 ***Neumann***	N	Y	Y	Y	Y	Y	Y
2 ***Klug***	N	Y	Y	Y	Y	Y	Y
3 Kind	Y	Y	Y	N	Y	Y	Y
4 Kleczka	N	Y	Y	N	Y	Y	Y
5 Barrett	Y	N	Y	N	Y	Y	Y
6 ***Petri***	N	Y	Y	Y	Y	Y	Y
7 Obey	Y	N	Y	N	Y	Y	Y
8 Johnson	N	Y	Y	N	Y	?	Y
9 ***Sensenbrenner***	N	Y	Y	Y	Y	Y	Y
WYOMING							
AL ***Cubin***	N	Y	Y	Y	Y	Y	Y

Southern states - Ala., Ark., Fla., Ga., Ky., La., Miss., N.C., Okla., S.C., Tenn., Texas, Va.

512. Steel Anti-Dumping Laws/Privileged Resolution. Davis, R-Va., motion to table (kill) the Thomas, R-Calif., motion to appeal the ruling of the chair that the Visclosky, D-Ind., privileged resolution regarding enhanced enforcement of steel anti-dumping laws did not constitute a question of the privileges of the House. Motion agreed to 219-204: R 218-4; D 1-199 (ND 1-146, SD 0-53); I 0-1. Oct. 10, 1998.

513. Expedited Consideration of Legislative Business/Previous Question. Dreier, R-Calif., motion to order the previous question (thus ending debate and the possibility of amendment) on the resolution to allow for expedited consideration of appropriations bills, appropriations conference reports and continuing resolutions for the remainder of the 105th Congress. The measure also allows the Speaker to schedule suspension bills on any day for the rest of the session. Motion agreed to 221-201: R 221-0; D 0-200 (ND 0-147, SD 0-53); I 0-1. Oct. 10, 1998. (Subsequently, the resolution was adopted by voice vote.)

514. European Union Compliance with World Trade Organization Rules/Rule. Adoption of the rule (H Res 588) to provide for House floor consideration of the bill to require the United States Trade Representative to respond to the European Union's non-compliance with rulings of the World Trade Organization concerning bananas and beef hormones. Adopted 243-179: R 218-4; D 25-174 (ND 10-136, SD 15-38); I 0-1. Oct. 10, 1998.

515. HR 4110. Veterans Benefits Changes/Adoption. Stump, R-Ariz., motion to suspend the rules and adopt the resolution (H Res 592) to concur in Senate amendments to the bill that makes several changes to education, housing and other benefits programs within the Department of Veterans Affairs. Motion agreed to (thus clearing the bill for the president) 423-0: R 222-0; D 200-0 (ND 147-0, SD 53-0); I 1-0. Oct. 10, 1998. A two-thirds majority of those present and voting (282 in this case) is required for passage under suspension of the rules.

516. HR 4567. Medicare Reimbursement Formula/Passage. Thomas, R-Calif., motion to suspend the rules and pass the bill to create a new interim Medicare reimbursement formula for home health care agencies until a prospective payment system is ready. Motion agreed to 412-2: R 214-1; D 197-1 (ND 144-1, SD 53-0); I 1-0. Oct. 10, 1998. A two-thirds majority of those present and voting (276 in this case) is required for passage under suspension of the rules.

517. H Con Res 334. Taiwan and the World Health Organization/Passage. Solomon, R-N.Y., motion to suspend the rules and pass the bill to express the sense of Congress that Taiwan should participate in the World Health Organization in an "appropriate and meaningful" manner. Motion agreed to 418-0: R 217-0; D 200-0 (ND 147-0, SD 53-0); I 1-0. Oct. 10, 1998. A two-thirds majority of those present and voting (279 in this case) is required for passage under suspension of the rules.

518. H Con Res 320. Condemning Nazi-Soviet Pact of Non-Aggression/Passage. Gilman, R-N.Y., motion to suspend the rules and pass the bill to condemn the 1939 Nazi-Soviet Pact of Non-Aggression, under which Nazi Germany and the former Soviet Union divided Eastern Europe into spheres of influence. Motion agreed to 417-0: R 216-0; D 200-0 (ND 147-0, SD 53-0); I 1-0. Oct. 10, 1998. A two-thirds majority of those present and voting (278 in this case) is required for passage under suspension of the rules.

Key

Y	Voted for (yea).
#	Paired for.
+	Announced for.
N	Voted against (nay).
X	Paired against.
−	Announced against.
P	Voted "present."
C	Voted "present" to avoid possible conflict of interest.
?	Did not vote or otherwise make a position known.

Democrats   **Republicans**
Independent

	512	513	514	515	516	517	518
ALABAMA							
1 *Callahan*	Y	Y	Y	Y	Y	Y	Y
2 *Everett*	Y	Y	Y	Y	Y	Y	Y
3 *Riley*	Y	Y	Y	Y	Y	Y	Y
4 *Aderholt*	Y	Y	Y	Y	Y	Y	Y
5 Cramer	N	N	N	Y	Y	Y	Y
6 *Bachus*	Y	Y	Y	Y	Y	Y	Y
7 Hilliard	N	N	N	Y	Y	Y	Y
ALASKA							
AL *Young*	Y	Y	Y	Y	Y	Y	Y
ARIZONA							
1 *Salmon*	Y	Y	Y	Y	Y	Y	Y
2 Pastor	N	N	Y	Y	Y	Y	Y
3 *Stump*	Y	Y	Y	Y	Y	Y	Y
4 *Shadegg*	Y	Y	Y	Y	Y	Y	Y
5 *Kolbe*	Y	Y	Y	Y	Y	Y	Y
6 *Hayworth*	Y	Y	Y	Y	Y	Y	Y
ARKANSAS							
1 Berry	N	N	Y	Y	Y	Y	Y
2 Snyder	N	N	N	Y	Y	Y	Y
3 *Hutchinson*	Y	Y	Y	Y	Y	Y	Y
4 *Dickey*	Y	Y	Y	Y	Y	Y	Y
CALIFORNIA							
1 *Riggs*	Y	Y	Y	Y	Y	Y	Y
2 *Herger*	Y	Y	Y	Y	Y	Y	Y
3 Fazio	N	N	N	Y	Y	Y	Y
4 *Doolittle*	Y	Y	Y	Y	Y	Y	Y
5 Matsul	N	N	N	Y	Y	Y	Y
6 Woolsey	N	N	N	Y	Y	Y	Y
7 Miller	N	N	N	Y	Y	Y	Y
8 Pelosi	N	N	N	Y	Y	Y	Y
9 Lee	N	N	N	Y	Y	Y	Y
10 Tauscher	N	N	N	Y	Y	Y	Y
11 *Pombo*	Y	Y	Y	Y	Y	Y	Y
12 Lantos	N	N	N	Y	Y	Y	Y
13 Stark	N	N	N	Y	Y	Y	Y
14 Eshoo	N	N	N	Y	Y	Y	Y
15 *Campbell*	Y	Y	Y	Y	Y	Y	Y
16 Lofgren	N	N	N	Y	Y	Y	Y
17 Farr	N	N	N	Y	Y	Y	Y
18 Condit	N	N	N	Y	Y	Y	Y
19 *Radanovich*	Y	Y	Y	Y	Y	Y	Y
20 Dooley	N	N	N	Y	Y	Y	Y
21 *Thomas*	Y	Y	Y	Y	Y	Y	Y
22 Capps, L.	N	N	N	Y	Y	Y	Y
23 *Gallegly*	Y	Y	Y	Y	Y	Y	Y
24 Sherman	N	N	N	Y	Y	Y	Y
25 *McKeon*	Y	Y	Y	Y	Y	Y	Y
26 Berman	?	?	?	?	?	?	?
27 *Rogan*	Y	Y	Y	Y	Y	Y	Y
28 *Dreier*	Y	Y	Y	Y	Y	Y	Y
29 Waxman	N	N	N	Y	Y	Y	Y
30 Becerra	N	N	N	Y	Y	Y	Y
31 Martinez	N	N	N	Y	Y	Y	Y
32 Dixon	N	N	N	Y	Y	Y	Y
33 Roybal-Allard	N	N	N	Y	Y	Y	Y
34 Torres	N	N	N	Y	?	Y	Y
35 Waters	N	N	N	Y	Y	Y	Y
36 Harman	N	N	?	Y	Y	Y	Y
37 Millender-McD.	N	N	N	Y	Y	Y	Y
38 *Horn*	N	Y	Y	Y	Y	Y	Y

	512	513	514	515	516	517	518
39 *Royce*	Y	Y	Y	Y	Y	Y	Y
40 *Lewis*	Y	Y	Y	Y	Y	Y	Y
41 *Kim*	Y	Y	Y	Y	Y	Y	Y
42 Brown	N	N	N	Y	Y	Y	Y
43 *Calvert*	Y	Y	Y	Y	Y	Y	Y
44 *Bono, M.*	Y	Y	Y	Y	Y	Y	Y
45 *Rohrabacher*	Y	Y	Y	Y	Y	Y	Y
46 Sanchez	N	N	N	Y	Y	Y	Y
47 *Cox*	Y	Y	Y	Y	Y	Y	Y
48 *Packard*	Y	Y	Y	Y	Y	Y	Y
49 *Bilbray*	Y	Y	Y	Y	Y	+	Y
50 Filner	N	N	N	Y	Y	Y	Y
51 *Cunningham*	Y	Y	Y	Y	Y	Y	Y
52 *Hunter*	Y	Y	N	Y	?	Y	Y
COLORADO							
1 DeGette	N	N	N	Y	Y	Y	Y
2 Skaggs	Y	N	N	Y	Y	Y	Y
3 *McInnis*	Y	Y	Y	Y	Y	Y	Y
4 *Schaffer*	Y	Y	Y	Y	Y	Y	Y
5 *Hefley*	Y	Y	Y	Y	Y	Y	Y
6 *Schaefer*	Y	Y	Y	Y	Y	Y	Y
CONNECTICUT							
1 Kennelly	?	?	?	?	?	?	?
2 Gejdenson	N	N	N	Y	Y	Y	Y
3 DeLauro	N	N	N	Y	Y	Y	Y
4 *Shays*	Y	Y	Y	Y	Y	Y	Y
5 Maloney	N	N	N	Y	Y	Y	Y
6 *Johnson*	Y	Y	Y	Y	Y	Y	Y
DELAWARE							
AL *Castle*	Y	Y	Y	Y	Y	Y	Y
FLORIDA							
1 *Scarborough*	Y	Y	Y	Y	Y	Y	Y
2 Boyd	N	N	Y	Y	Y	Y	Y
3 Brown	N	N	N	Y	Y	Y	Y
4 *Fowler*	Y	Y	Y	Y	Y	Y	Y
5 Thurman	N	N	N	Y	Y	Y	Y
6 *Stearns*	Y	Y	Y	Y	Y	Y	Y
7 *Mica*	Y	Y	Y	Y	Y	Y	Y
8 *McCollum*	Y	Y	Y	Y	Y	Y	Y
9 *Bilirakis*	Y	Y	Y	Y	Y	Y	Y
10 *Young*	Y	Y	Y	Y	Y	Y	Y
11 Davis	N	N	N	Y	Y	Y	Y
12 *Canady*	Y	Y	Y	Y	Y	Y	Y
13 *Miller*	Y	Y	Y	Y	Y	Y	Y
14 *Goss*	Y	Y	Y	Y	Y	Y	Y
15 *Weldon*	Y	Y	Y	Y	Y	Y	Y
16 *Foley*	Y	Y	Y	Y	Y	Y	Y
17 Meek	N	N	N	Y	Y	Y	Y
18 *Ros-Lehtinen*	Y	Y	Y	Y	Y	Y	Y
19 Wexler	N	N	N	Y	Y	Y	Y
20 Deutsch	N	N	N	Y	Y	Y	Y
21 *Diaz-Balart*	Y	Y	Y	Y	Y	Y	Y
22 *Shaw*	Y	Y	Y	Y	Y	Y	Y
23 Hastings	N	N	N	Y	Y	Y	Y
GEORGIA							
1 *Kingston*	Y	Y	Y	Y	Y	Y	Y
2 Bishop	N	N	Y	Y	Y	Y	Y
3 *Collins*	?	?	?	?	?	?	?
4 McKinney	N	N	N	Y	Y	Y	Y
5 Lewis	N	N	N	Y	Y	Y	Y
6 *Gingrich*							
7 *Barr*	Y	Y	Y	Y	Y	Y	Y
8 *Chambliss*	Y	Y	Y	Y	Y	Y	Y
9 *Deal*	Y	Y	Y	Y	Y	Y	Y
10 *Norwood*	Y	Y	Y	Y	Y	?	?
11 *Linder*	Y	Y	Y	Y	Y	Y	Y
HAWAII							
1 Abercrombie	N	N	Y	Y	Y	Y	Y
2 Mink	N	N	Y	Y	Y	Y	Y
IDAHO							
1 *Chenoweth*	Y	Y	Y	Y	Y	Y	Y
2 *Crapo*	Y	Y	Y	Y	Y	Y	Y
ILLINOIS							
1 Rush	N	N	N	Y	Y	Y	Y
2 Jackson	N	N	N	Y	Y	Y	Y
3 Lipinski	N	N	N	Y	Y	Y	Y
4 Gutierrez	N	N	N	Y	Y	Y	Y
5 Blagojevich	N	N	N	Y	Y	Y	Y
6 *Hyde*	Y	Y	Y	Y	Y	Y	Y
7 Davis	N	N	N	Y	Y	Y	Y
8 *Crane*	Y	Y	Y	Y	Y	Y	Y
9 Yates	N	N	N	Y	Y	Y	Y
10 *Porter*	Y	Y	Y	Y	Y	Y	Y
11 *Weller*	Y	Y	Y	Y	Y	Y	Y
12 Costello	N	N	N	Y	Y	Y	Y
13 *Fawell*	Y	Y	Y	Y	Y	Y	Y

	512	513	514	515	516	517	518
14 ***Hastert***	Y	Y	Y	Y	Y	Y	Y
15 ***Ewing***	Y	Y	Y	Y	Y	Y	Y
16 ***Manzullo***	Y	Y	Y	Y	Y	Y	Y
17 Evans	N	N	N	Y	Y	Y	Y
18 ***LaHood***	Y	Y	Y	Y	Y	Y	Y
19 Poshard	?	?	?	?	?	?	?
20 ***Shimkus***	Y	Y	Y	Y	Y	Y	Y
INDIANA							
1 Visclosky	N	N	N	Y	Y	Y	Y
2 ***McIntosh***	Y	Y	Y	Y	Y	Y	Y
3 Roemer	N	N	N	Y	Y	Y	Y
4 ***Souder***	Y	Y	Y	Y	Y	Y	Y
5 ***Buyer***	Y	Y	Y	Y	Y	Y	Y
6 ***Burton***	Y	Y	Y	Y	Y	Y	Y
7 ***Pease***	Y	Y	Y	Y	Y	Y	Y
8 ***Hostettler***	Y	Y	Y	Y	Y	Y	Y
9 Hamilton	N	N	N	Y	Y	Y	Y
10 Carson	N	N	N	Y	Y	Y	Y
IOWA							
1 ***Leach***	Y	Y	Y	Y	Y	Y	Y
2 ***Nussle***	Y	Y	Y	Y	Y	Y	Y
3 Boswell	N	N	Y	Y	Y	Y	Y
4 ***Ganske***	Y	Y	Y	Y	Y	Y	Y
5 ***Latham***	Y	Y	Y	Y	Y	Y	Y
KANSAS							
1 ***Moran***	Y	Y	Y	Y	Y	Y	Y
2 ***Ryun***	Y	Y	Y	Y	Y	Y	Y
3 ***Snowbarger***	Y	Y	Y	Y	Y	Y	Y
4 ***Tiahrt***	Y	Y	N	Y	Y	Y	Y
KENTUCKY							
1 ***Whitfield***	Y	Y	Y	Y	Y	Y	Y
2 ***Lewis***	Y	Y	Y	Y	Y	Y	Y
3 ***Northup***	Y	Y	Y	Y	Y	Y	Y
4 ***Bunning***	Y	Y	Y	Y	Y	Y	Y
5 ***Rogers***	Y	Y	Y	Y	Y	Y	Y
6 Baesler	N	N	Y	Y	Y	Y	Y
LOUISIANA							
1 ***Livingston***	Y	Y	Y	Y	Y	Y	Y
2 Jefferson	N	N	N	Y	Y	Y	Y
3 ***Tauzin***	Y	Y	Y	Y	Y	Y	Y
4 ***McCrery***	Y	Y	Y	Y	Y	Y	Y
5 ***Cooksey***	Y	Y	Y	Y	Y	Y	Y
6 ***Baker***	Y	Y	Y	Y	Y	Y	Y
7 John	N	N	Y	Y	Y	Y	Y
MAINE							
1 Allen	N	N	N	Y	Y	Y	Y
2 Baldacci	N	N	N	Y	Y	Y	Y
MARYLAND							
1 ***Gilchrest***	Y	Y	Y	Y	Y	Y	Y
2 ***Ehrlich***	Y	Y	Y	Y	Y	Y	Y
3 Cardin	N	N	N	Y	Y	Y	Y
4 Wynn	N	N	N	Y	Y	Y	Y
5 Hoyer	N	N	N	Y	?	Y	Y
6 ***Bartlett***	Y	Y	Y	Y	Y	Y	Y
7 Cummings	N	N	N	Y	Y	Y	Y
8 ***Morella***	Y	Y	Y	Y	Y	Y	Y
MASSACHUSETTS							
1 Olver	N	N	N	Y	Y	Y	Y
2 Neal	N	N	N	Y	Y	Y	Y
3 McGovern	N	N	N	Y	Y	Y	Y
4 Frank	N	N	N	Y	Y	Y	Y
5 Meehan	N	N	N	Y	Y	Y	Y
6 Tierney	N	N	N	Y	Y	Y	Y
7 Markey	N	N	N	Y	Y	Y	Y
8 Kennedy	N	N	N	Y	Y	Y	Y
9 Moakley	N	N	N	Y	Y	Y	Y
10 Delahunt	N	N	N	Y	Y	Y	Y
MICHIGAN							
1 Stupak	N	N	N	Y	Y	Y	Y
2 ***Hoekstra***	Y	Y	Y	Y	Y	Y	Y
3 ***Ehlers***	Y	Y	Y	Y	Y	Y	Y
4 ***Camp***	Y	Y	Y	Y	Y	Y	Y
5 Barcia	N	N	Y	Y	Y	Y	Y
6 ***Upton***	Y	Y	Y	Y	Y	Y	Y
7 ***Smith***	Y	Y	Y	Y	Y	Y	Y
8 Stabenow	N	N	Y	Y	Y	Y	Y
9 Kildee	N	N	N	Y	Y	Y	Y
10 Bonior	N	N	N	Y	Y	Y	Y
11 ***Knollenberg***	Y	Y	Y	Y	Y	Y	Y
12 Levin	N	N	N	Y	Y	Y	Y
13 Rivers	N	N	N	Y	Y	Y	Y
14 Conyers	N	N	N	Y	Y	Y	Y
15 Kilpatrick	N	N	N	Y	Y	Y	Y
16 Dingell	N	N	Y	Y	Y	Y	Y

	512	513	514	515	516	517	518
MINNESOTA							
1 ***Gutknecht***	Y	Y	Y	Y	Y	Y	Y
2 Minge	N	N	Y	Y	Y	Y	Y
3 ***Ramstad***	Y	Y	Y	Y	Y	Y	Y
4 Vento	N	N	N	Y	Y	Y	Y
5 Sabo	N	N	N	Y	N	Y	Y
6 Luther	N	N	N	Y	Y	Y	Y
7 Peterson	N	N	Y	Y	Y	Y	Y
8 Oberstar	N	N	N	Y	Y	Y	Y
MISSISSIPPI							
1 ***Wicker***	Y	Y	Y	Y	Y	Y	Y
2 Thompson	N	N	N	Y	Y	Y	Y
3 ***Pickering***	Y	Y	Y	Y	+	Y	Y
4 ***Parker***	?	?	?	?	?	?	?
5 Taylor	N	N	N	Y	Y	Y	Y
MISSOURI							
1 Clay	N	N	N	Y	Y	Y	Y
2 ***Talent***	Y	Y	Y	Y	Y	Y	Y
3 Gephardt	N	N	N	Y	Y	Y	Y
4 Skelton	N	N	N	Y	Y	Y	Y
5 McCarthy	N	N	N	Y	Y	Y	Y
6 Danner	N	N	N	Y	Y	Y	Y
7 ***Blunt***	Y	Y	Y	Y	Y	Y	Y
8 ***Emerson***	Y	Y	Y	Y	Y	Y	Y
9 ***Hulshof***	Y	Y	Y	Y	Y	Y	Y
MONTANA							
AL ***Hill***	Y	Y	Y	Y	Y	Y	Y
NEBRASKA							
1 ***Bereuter***	Y	Y	Y	Y	Y	Y	Y
2 ***Christensen***	Y	Y	Y	Y	Y	Y	Y
3 ***Barrett***	Y	Y	Y	Y	Y	Y	Y
NEVADA							
1 ***Ensign***	Y	Y	Y	Y	Y	?	?
2 ***Gibbons***	Y	Y	Y	Y	Y	Y	Y
NEW HAMPSHIRE							
1 ***Sununu***	Y	Y	Y	Y	Y	Y	Y
2 ***Bass***	Y	Y	Y	Y	Y	Y	Y
NEW JERSEY							
1 Andrews	N	N	N	Y	Y	Y	Y
2 ***LoBiondo***	Y	Y	Y	Y	Y	Y	Y
3 ***Saxton***	Y	Y	Y	Y	Y	Y	Y
4 ***Smith***	Y	Y	Y	Y	Y	Y	Y
5 ***Roukema***	Y	Y	Y	Y	Y	Y	Y
6 Pallone	N	N	N	Y	Y	Y	Y
7 ***Franks***	Y	Y	Y	Y	Y	Y	Y
8 Pascrell	N	N	N	Y	Y	Y	Y
9 Rothman	N	N	N	Y	Y	Y	Y
10 Payne	N	N	N	Y	Y	Y	Y
11 ***Frelinghuysen***	Y	Y	Y	Y	Y	Y	Y
12 ***Pappas***	Y	Y	Y	Y	Y	Y	Y
13 Menendez	N	N	N	Y	Y	Y	Y
NEW MEXICO							
1 ***Wilson***	Y	Y	Y	Y	Y	Y	Y
2 ***Skeen***	Y	Y	Y	Y	Y	Y	Y
3 ***Redmond***	Y	Y	Y	Y	Y	Y	Y
NEW YORK							
1 ***Forbes***	Y	Y	Y	Y	Y	Y	Y
2 ***Lazio***	?	?	?	Y	Y	Y	Y
3 ***King***	Y	Y	Y	Y	Y	Y	Y
4 McCarthy	N	N	N	Y	Y	Y	Y
5 Ackerman	N	N	N	Y	Y	Y	Y
6 Meeks	N	N	N	Y	Y	Y	Y
7 Manton	N	N	N	Y	Y	Y	Y
8 Nadler	N	N	N	Y	Y	Y	Y
9 Schumer	N	N	N	Y	Y	Y	Y
10 Towns	N	N	N	Y	Y	Y	Y
11 Owens	N	N	N	Y	Y	Y	Y
12 Velázquez	N	N	N	Y	Y	Y	Y
13 ***Fossella***	Y	Y	Y	Y	Y	Y	Y
14 Maloney	N	N	N	Y	Y	Y	Y
15 Rangel	?	?	?	?	?	?	?
16 Serrano	N	N	N	Y	Y	Y	Y
17 Engel	N	N	N	Y	Y	Y	Y
18 Lowey	N	N	N	Y	Y	Y	Y
19 ***Kelly***	Y	Y	Y	Y	Y	Y	Y
20 ***Gilman***	Y	Y	Y	Y	Y	Y	Y
21 McNulty	N	N	N	Y	Y	Y	Y
22 ***Solomon***	Y	Y	Y	Y	Y	Y	Y
23 ***Boehlert***	Y	Y	Y	Y	Y	Y	Y
24 ***McHugh***	Y	Y	Y	Y	Y	Y	Y
25 ***Walsh***	Y	Y	Y	Y	Y	?	?
26 Hinchey	N	N	N	Y	Y	Y	Y
27 ***Paxon***	Y	Y	Y	Y	Y	Y	Y
28 Slaughter	N	N	N	Y	Y	Y	Y
29 LaFalce	N	N	N	Y	Y	Y	Y
30 ***Quinn***	Y	Y	Y	Y	Y	?	?

	512	513	514	515	516	517	518
31 ***Houghton***	Y	Y	Y	Y	Y	Y	Y
NORTH CAROLINA							
1 Clayton	N	N	N	Y	Y	Y	Y
2 Etheridge	N	N	N	Y	Y	Y	Y
3 ***Jones***	Y	Y	Y	Y	Y	Y	Y
4 Price	N	N	N	Y	Y	Y	Y
5 ***Burr***	Y	Y	Y	Y	Y	Y	Y
6 ***Coble***	Y	Y	Y	Y	Y	Y	Y
7 McIntyre	N	N	N	Y	Y	Y	Y
8 Hefner	?	?	?	?	?	?	?
9 ***Myrick***	Y	Y	Y	Y	Y	Y	Y
10 ***Ballenger***	Y	Y	Y	Y	Y	Y	Y
11 ***Taylor***	Y	Y	Y	?	?	?	?
12 Watt	N	N	N	Y	Y	Y	Y
NORTH DAKOTA							
AL Pomeroy	N	N	N	Y	Y	Y	Y
OHIO							
1 ***Chabot***	Y	Y	Y	Y	Y	Y	Y
2 ***Portman***	Y	Y	Y	Y	+	Y	Y
3 Hall	N	N	N	Y	Y	Y	Y
4 ***Oxley***	Y	Y	Y	Y	Y	Y	Y
5 ***Gillmor***	Y	Y	Y	Y	Y	Y	Y
6 Strickland	N	N	N	Y	Y	Y	Y
7 ***Hobson***	Y	Y	Y	Y	Y	Y	?
8 ***Boehner***	Y	Y	Y	Y	Y	Y	Y
9 Kaptur	N	N	N	Y	Y	Y	Y
10 Kucinich	N	N	N	Y	Y	Y	Y
11 Stokes	N	N	N	Y	Y	Y	Y
12 ***Kasich***	Y	Y	Y	Y	Y	Y	Y
13 Brown	N	N	N	Y	Y	Y	Y
14 Sawyer	N	N	N	Y	Y	Y	Y
15 ***Pryce***	+	+	+	+	+	+	+
16 ***Regula***	Y	Y	Y	Y	Y	Y	Y
17 Traficant	N	N	N	Y	Y	Y	Y
18 ***Ney***	N	Y	N	Y	Y	Y	Y
19 ***LaTourette***	Y	Y	Y	Y	Y	Y	Y
OKLAHOMA							
1 ***Largent***	Y	Y	Y	Y	?	Y	Y
2 ***Coburn***	Y	Y	Y	Y	Y	Y	Y
3 ***Watkins***	Y	Y	Y	Y	Y	Y	Y
4 ***Watts***	Y	Y	Y	Y	Y	Y	Y
5 ***Istook***	Y	Y	Y	Y	Y	Y	Y
6 ***Lucas***	Y	Y	Y	Y	Y	Y	Y
OREGON							
1 Furse	N	N	N	Y	Y	Y	Y
2 ***Smith***	Y	Y	Y	Y	Y	Y	Y
3 Blumenauer	N	N	N	Y	Y	Y	Y
4 DeFazio	N	N	N	Y	Y	Y	Y
5 Hooley	N	N	N	Y	Y	Y	Y
PENNSYLVANIA							
1 Brady	N	N	N	Y	Y	Y	Y
2 Fattah	N	N	N	Y	Y	Y	Y
3 Borski	N	N	N	Y	Y	Y	Y
4 Klink	N	N	N	Y	Y	Y	Y
5 ***Peterson***	Y	Y	Y	Y	+	Y	Y
6 Holden	N	N	N	Y	Y	Y	Y
7 ***Weldon***	Y	Y	Y	Y	Y	Y	Y
8 ***Greenwood***	Y	Y	Y	Y	Y	Y	Y
9 ***Shuster***	Y	Y	Y	Y	Y	Y	Y
10 ***McDade***	Y	Y	Y	Y	Y	Y	Y
11 Kanjorski	N	N	N	Y	Y	Y	Y
12 Murtha	N	N	N	Y	Y	Y	Y
13 ***Fox***	Y	Y	Y	Y	Y	Y	Y
14 Coyne	N	N	N	Y	Y	Y	Y
15 McHale	N	N	N	Y	Y	Y	Y
16 ***Pitts***	Y	Y	Y	Y	Y	Y	Y
17 ***Gekas***	Y	Y	Y	Y	Y	Y	Y
18 Doyle	N	N	N	Y	Y	Y	Y
19 ***Goodling***	Y	Y	Y	Y	Y	Y	Y
20 Mascara	N	N	N	Y	Y	Y	Y
21 ***English***	Y	Y	Y	Y	?	Y	Y
RHODE ISLAND							
1 Kennedy	N	N	N	Y	Y	Y	Y
2 Weygand	N	N	N	Y	Y	Y	Y
SOUTH CAROLINA							
1 ***Sanford***	Y	Y	Y	Y	Y	Y	Y
2 ***Spence***	Y	Y	Y	Y	Y	Y	Y
3 ***Graham***	Y	Y	Y	Y	Y	Y	Y
4 ***Inglis***	Y	Y	Y	Y	Y	Y	Y
5 Spratt	N	N	N	Y	Y	Y	Y
6 Clyburn	N	N	N	Y	Y	Y	Y
SOUTH DAKOTA							
AL ***Thune***	Y	Y	Y	Y	Y	Y	Y

	512	513	514	515	516	517	518
TENNESSEE							
1 ***Jenkins***	Y	Y	Y	Y	Y	Y	Y
2 ***Duncan***	Y	Y	Y	Y	Y	Y	Y
3 ***Wamp***	Y	Y	Y	Y	Y	Y	Y
4 ***Hilleary***	Y	Y	Y	Y	Y	Y	Y
5 Clement	N	N	N	Y	Y	Y	Y
6 Gordon	N	N	Y	Y	Y	Y	Y
7 ***Bryant***	Y	Y	Y	Y	Y	Y	Y
8 Tanner	N	N	Y	Y	Y	Y	Y
9 Ford	N	N	N	Y	Y	Y	Y
TEXAS							
1 Sandlin	N	N	Y	Y	Y	Y	Y
2 Turner	N	N	Y	Y	Y	Y	Y
3 ***Johnson, Sam***	Y	Y	Y	Y	Y	Y	Y
4 Hall	N	N	Y	Y	Y	Y	Y
5 ***Sessions***	Y	Y	Y	Y	Y	Y	Y
6 ***Barton***	Y	Y	Y	Y	Y	Y	Y
7 ***Archer***	Y	Y	Y	Y	Y	Y	Y
8 ***Brady***	Y	Y	Y	Y	Y	Y	Y
9 Lampson	N	N	N	Y	Y	Y	Y
10 Doggett	N	N	N	Y	Y	Y	Y
11 Edwards	N	N	N	Y	Y	Y	Y
12 ***Granger***	Y	Y	Y	Y	Y	Y	Y
13 ***Thornberry***	Y	Y	Y	Y	Y	Y	Y
14 ***Paul***	Y	Y	Y	Y	N	Y	Y
15 Hinojosa	N	N	N	Y	Y	Y	Y
16 Reyes	N	N	N	Y	Y	Y	Y
17 Stenholm	N	N	Y	Y	Y	Y	Y
18 Jackson-Lee	N	N	N	Y	Y	Y	Y
19 ***Combest***	Y	Y	Y	Y	Y	Y	Y
20 Gonzalez	N	N	N	Y	Y	Y	Y
21 ***Smith***	Y	Y	Y	Y	Y	?	?
22 ***DeLay***	Y	Y	Y	Y	Y	Y	Y
23 ***Bonilla***	Y	Y	Y	Y	Y	Y	Y
24 Frost	N	N	N	Y	Y	Y	Y
25 Bentsen	N	N	N	Y	Y	Y	Y
26 ***Armey***	Y	Y	Y	Y	Y	Y	Y
27 Ortiz	N	N	Y	Y	Y	Y	Y
28 Rodriguez	N	N	Y	Y	Y	Y	Y
29 Green	N	N	N	Y	Y	Y	Y
30 Johnson, E.B.	N	N	N	Y	Y	Y	Y
UTAH							
1 ***Hansen***	Y	Y	Y	Y	Y	Y	Y
2 ***Cook***	Y	Y	Y	Y	Y	Y	Y
3 ***Cannon***	Y	Y	Y	Y	Y	Y	Y
VERMONT							
AL *Sanders*	N	N	N	Y	Y	Y	Y
VIRGINIA							
1 ***Bateman***	Y	Y	Y	Y	Y	Y	Y
2 Pickett	N	N	Y	Y	Y	Y	Y
3 Scott	N	N	N	Y	Y	Y	Y
4 Sisisky	N	N	N	Y	Y	Y	Y
5 Goode	N	N	N	Y	Y	Y	Y
6 ***Goodlatte***	Y	Y	Y	Y	Y	Y	Y
7 ***Bliley***	Y	Y	Y	Y	Y	Y	Y
8 Moran	N	N	N	Y	Y	Y	Y
9 Boucher	?	?	?	?	?	?	?
10 ***Wolf***	Y	Y	Y	Y	Y	Y	Y
11 ***Davis***	Y	Y	Y	Y	Y	Y	Y
WASHINGTON							
1 ***White***	Y	Y	Y	Y	Y	Y	Y
2 ***Metcalf***	N	?	Y	Y	Y	Y	Y
3 ***Smith, Linda***	Y	Y	Y	Y	Y	Y	Y
4 ***Hastings***	Y	Y	Y	Y	Y	Y	Y
5 ***Nethercutt***	+	+	+	+	+	+	+
6 Dicks	N	N	N	Y	Y	Y	Y
7 McDermott	N	N	N	Y	Y	Y	Y
8 ***Dunn***	Y	Y	Y	Y	Y	Y	Y
9 Smith, Adam	N	N	N	Y	Y	Y	Y
WEST VIRGINIA							
1 Mollohan	N	N	N	Y	Y	Y	Y
2 Wise	N	N	N	Y	Y	Y	Y
3 Rahall	N	N	N	Y	Y	Y	Y
WISCONSIN							
1 ***Neumann***	N	Y	N	Y	Y	Y	Y
2 ***Klug***	Y	Y	Y	Y	Y	Y	Y
3 Kind	N	N	N	Y	Y	Y	Y
4 Kleczka	N	N	N	Y	Y	Y	Y
5 Barrett	N	N	N	Y	Y	Y	Y
6 ***Petri***	Y	Y	Y	Y	Y	Y	Y
7 Obey	N	N	N	Y	Y	Y	Y
8 Johnson	N	N	N	Y	Y	Y	Y
9 ***Sensenbrenner***	Y	Y	Y	Y	Y	Y	Y
WYOMING							
AL ***Cubin***	Y	Y	Y	Y	Y	Y	Y

Southern states - Ala., Ark., Fla., Ga., Ky., La., Miss., N.C., Okla., S.C., Tenn., Texas, Va.

519. HR 2616. Charter Schools/Passage. Riggs, R-Calif., motion to suspend the rules and concur in Senate amendments to a bill to increase the authorization for the planning, design and startup of charter schools, with the goal of building up to 2,500 new schools by the year 2000. Motion agreed to (thus clearing the bill for the president) 369-50: R 208-10; D 160-40 (ND 121-26, SD 39-14); I 1-0. Oct. 10, 1998. A two-thirds majority of those present and voting (280 in this case) is required for passage under suspension of the rules.

520. S 852. National Standard for Salvaged Car Registration/Passage. Bliley, R-Va., motion to suspend the rules and pass the bill to establish national standards for the registration of salvaged and rebuilt cars. Motion agreed to 271-133: R 205-1; D 66-131 (ND 33-111, SD 33-20); I 0-1. Oct. 10, 1998. A two-thirds majority of those present and voting (270 in this case) is required for passage under suspension of the rules.

521. HR 3494. Sexual Predator Punishment/Senate Amendments. Hutchinson, R-Ark., motion to suspend the rules and agree with Senate amendments to provide "zero tolerance" for possession of child pornography. The bill would establish or increase penalties for Internet-based sex crimes against minors, as well as sentencing guidelines for crimes against children. Motion agreed to (thus clearing the bill for the president) 400-0: R 215-0; D 184-0 (ND 136-0, SD 48-0); I 1-0. Oct. 12, 1998. A two-thirds majority of those present and voting (267 in this case) is required for passage under suspension of the rules.

522. Steel Imports/Passage. Archer, R-Texas, motion to suspend the rules and adopt the concurrent resolution to express the sense of Congress that the president should take all necessary measures under existing law to respond to the significant increase of steel imports. Motion rejected 153-249: R 153-62; D 0-186 (ND 0-136, SD 0-50); I 0-1. Oct. 12, 1998. A two-thirds majority of those present and voting (268 in this case) is required for passage under suspension of the rules. A "nay" was a vote in support of the president's position.

523. S 2095. National Fish and Wildlife Foundation/Passage. Saxton, R-N.J., motion to suspend the rules and pass the bill to reauthorize through fiscal 2003 the National Fish and Wildlife Foundation, a nonprofit organization dedicated to the conservation and restoration of natural resources. Motion rejected 153-248: R 148-66; D 5-181 (ND 1-135, SD 4-46); I 0-1. Oct. 12, 1998. A two-thirds majority of those present and voting (268 in this case) is required for passage under suspension of the rules.

524. H Res 494. Commending Citizens of Guam/Adoption. Young, R-Alaska, motion to suspend the rules and adopt the resolution to express the sense of the House recognizing 100 years of Guam's loyalty and service to the United States and urging a reaffirmation of the commitment for increased self-government in Guam. Motion agreed to 410-0: R 217-0; D 192-0 (ND 143-0, SD 49-0); I 1-0. Oct. 13, 1998. A two-thirds majority of those present and voting (274 in this case) is required for passage under suspension of the rules.

525. S 1364. Federal Reports Elimination/Passage. Horn, R-Calif., motion to suspend the rules and pass the bill to eliminate, modify or phase out certain federal reports currently required by law. Motion agreed to (thus clearing the bill for the president) 390-19: R 216-0; D 173-19 (ND 131-12, SD 42-7); I 1-0. Oct. 13, 1998. A two-thirds majority of those present and voting (273 in this case) is required for passage under suspension of the rules.

Key

Y	Voted for (yea).
#	Paired for.
+	Announced for.
N	Voted against (nay).
X	Paired against.
–	Announced against.
P	Voted "present."
C	Voted "present" to avoid possible conflict of interest.
?	Did not vote or otherwise make a position known.

Democrats **Republicans**
Independent

		519	520	521	522	523	524	525
ALABAMA								
1	*Callahan*	Y	Y	Y	N	Y	Y	Y
2	*Everett*	Y	Y	Y	N	Y	Y	Y
3	*Riley*	Y	Y	Y	Y	Y	Y	Y
4	*Aderholt*	Y	Y	Y	Y	Y	Y	Y
5	Cramer	Y	Y	Y	N	N	Y	Y
6	*Bachus*	Y	Y	Y	N	N	Y	Y
7	Hilliard	N	N	Y	N	N	Y	N
ALASKA								
AL	*Young*	Y	Y	Y	Y	Y	Y	Y
ARIZONA								
1	*Salmon*	Y	Y	Y	N	Y	Y	Y
2	Pastor	Y	Y	Y	N	N	Y	Y
3	*Stump*	Y	Y	Y	Y	Y	Y	Y
4	*Shadegg*	Y	Y	Y	Y	Y	Y	Y
5	*Kolbe*	Y	Y	Y	N	Y	Y	Y
6	*Hayworth*	Y	Y	Y	Y	Y	Y	Y
ARKANSAS								
1	Berry	Y	Y	Y	N	N	Y	Y
2	Snyder	Y	Y	Y	N	N	Y	Y
3	*Hutchinson*	Y	Y	Y	N	Y	Y	Y
4	*Dickey*	Y	Y	Y	Y	Y	Y	Y
CALIFORNIA								
1	*Riggs*	Y	Y	Y	Y	Y	Y	Y
2	*Herger*	Y	Y	Y	Y	Y	Y	Y
3	Fazio	Y	N	Y	N	N	Y	Y
4	*Doolittle*	Y	Y	Y	Y	Y	Y	Y
5	Matsui	Y	N	Y	N	N	Y	Y
6	Woolsey	Y	N	Y	N	N	Y	Y
7	Miller	Y	N	Y	N	N	Y	Y
8	Pelosi	Y	N	Y	N	N	Y	Y
9	Lee	N	N	Y	N	N	Y	N
10	Tauscher	Y	P	Y	N	N	Y	Y
11	*Pombo*	Y	N	Y	N	Y	Y	Y
12	Lantos	Y	N	Y	N	N	Y	Y
13	Stark	N	N	Y	N	N	Y	Y
14	Eshoo	Y	N	Y	N	N	Y	Y
15	*Campbell*	Y	Y	Y	Y	Y	Y	Y
16	Lofgren	Y	N	P	N	N	Y	Y
17	Farr	Y	N	Y	N	N	Y	Y
18	Condit	Y	Y	Y	N	N	Y	Y
19	*Radanovich*	Y	Y	Y	Y	Y	Y	Y
20	Dooley	Y	Y	Y	N	N	Y	Y
21	*Thomas*	Y	Y	Y	N	Y	Y	Y
22	Capps, L.	Y	N	Y	N	N	Y	Y
23	*Gallegly*	Y	Y	Y	N	Y	Y	Y
24	Sherman	Y	Y	Y	N	N	Y	Y
25	*McKeon*	Y	Y	Y	N	Y	Y	Y
26	Berman	?	?	?	?	?	?	?
27	*Rogan*	Y	Y	Y	Y	Y	Y	Y
28	*Dreier*	Y	Y	Y	Y	Y	Y	Y
29	Waxman	Y	N	?	?	Y	Y	Y
30	Becerra	Y	N	Y	N	?	Y	Y
31	Martinez	Y	N	Y	N	N	Y	Y
32	Dixon	Y	N	Y	N	N	Y	Y
33	Roybal-Allard	Y	N	Y	N	N	Y	Y
34	Torres	Y	N	Y	N	N	Y	Y
35	Waters	N	N	Y	N	N	Y	N
36	Harman	Y	Y	Y	N	N	?	?
37	Millender-McD.	Y	N	Y	N	N	Y	Y
38	*Horn*	Y	Y	Y	N	Y	Y	Y

		519	520	521	522	523	524	525
39	*Royce*	Y	?	Y	N	Y	Y	Y
40	*Lewis*	Y	Y	Y	Y	Y	Y	Y
41	*Kim*	Y	Y	Y	Y	Y	Y	Y
42	Brown	Y	N	Y	N	N	Y	Y
43	*Calvert*	Y	Y	Y	Y	Y	Y	Y
44	*Bono, M.*	Y	Y	Y	Y	Y	Y	Y
45	*Rohrabacher*	Y	Y	Y	N	Y	Y	Y
46	Sanchez	Y	N	Y	N	N	Y	Y
47	*Cox*	Y	Y	Y	Y	Y	Y	Y
48	*Packard*	Y	Y	Y	Y	Y	Y	Y
49	*Bilbray*	Y	Y	Y	N	Y	Y	Y
50	Filner	N	N	Y	N	N	Y	Y
51	*Cunningham*	Y	Y	Y	N	Y	Y	Y
52	*Hunter*	Y	Y	Y	Y	Y	Y	Y
COLORADO								
1	DeGette	Y	N	Y	N	N	Y	Y
2	Skaggs	Y	N	+	–	–	Y	Y
3	*McInnis*	Y	?	Y	Y	Y	Y	Y
4	*Schaffer*	N	Y	Y	N	Y	Y	Y
5	*Hefley*	Y	Y	Y	Y	Y	Y	Y
6	*Schaefer*	Y	Y	Y	N	Y	Y	Y
CONNECTICUT								
1	Kennelly	?	?	?	?	?	?	?
2	Gejdenson	Y	N	Y	N	N	Y	Y
3	DeLauro	Y	N	Y	N	N	Y	Y
4	*Shays*	Y	Y	Y	N	N	Y	Y
5	Maloney	Y	Y	Y	N	N	Y	Y
6	*Johnson*	Y	Y	Y	Y	Y	Y	Y
DELAWARE								
AL	*Castle*	Y	Y	?	?	?	Y	Y
FLORIDA								
1	*Scarborough*	N	Y	?	?	?	?	?
2	Boyd	Y	N	Y	N	Y	Y	Y
3	Brown	N	N	Y	N	N	Y	Y
4	*Fowler*	Y	Y	Y	N	Y	Y	Y
5	Thurman	Y	N	Y	N	N	Y	Y
6	*Stearns*	Y	+	Y	N	Y	Y	Y
7	*Mica*	Y	Y	Y	Y	Y	Y	Y
8	*McCollum*	Y	?	?	?	?	?	?
9	*Bilirakis*	Y	Y	Y	N	Y	Y	Y
10	*Young*	Y	Y	Y	N	Y	Y	Y
11	Davis	Y	Y	Y	N	N	Y	Y
12	*Canady*	Y	Y	Y	Y	Y	Y	Y
13	*Miller*	Y	Y	Y	Y	Y	Y	Y
14	*Goss*	Y	Y	Y	Y	Y	Y	Y
15	*Weldon*	Y	Y	Y	N	Y	Y	Y
16	*Foley*	Y	Y	Y	N	Y	Y	Y
17	Meek	N	N	Y	N	N	Y	Y
18	*Ros-Lehtinen*	Y	Y	?	?	?	Y	Y
19	Wexler	Y	N	Y	N	N	?	?
20	Deutsch	Y	Y	+	–	–	+	+
21	*Diaz-Balart*	Y	Y	Y	N	Y	Y	Y
22	*Shaw*	Y	Y	Y	Y	Y	Y	Y
23	Hastings	N	N	Y	N	N	Y	N
GEORGIA								
1	*Kingston*	Y	Y	Y	Y	Y	Y	Y
2	Bishop	Y	N	Y	N	N	Y	Y
3	*Collins*	?	?	Y	Y	Y	Y	Y
4	McKinney	N	N	Y	N	N	Y	N
5	Lewis	Y	N	Y	N	N	Y	Y
6	*Gingrich*							
7	*Barr*	Y	Y	Y	Y	Y	Y	Y
8	*Chambliss*	Y	?	Y	N	Y	Y	Y
9	*Deal*	Y	P	Y	Y	Y	Y	Y
10	*Norwood*	?	?	?	?	?	Y	Y
11	*Linder*	Y	Y	Y	Y	Y	Y	Y
HAWAII								
1	Abercrombie	N	N	Y	N	N	Y	Y
2	Mink	N	N	Y	N	N	Y	N
IDAHO								
1	*Chenoweth*	N	Y	N	Y	Y	Y	Y
2	*Crapo*	N	Y	Y	Y	Y	Y	Y
ILLINOIS								
1	Rush	N	N	Y	N	N	Y	Y
2	Jackson	Y	N	Y	N	N	Y	Y
3	Lipinski	Y	N	Y	N	N	Y	Y
4	Gutierrez	Y	N	Y	N	N	Y	Y
5	Blagojevich	Y	N	Y	N	N	Y	Y
6	*Hyde*	Y	Y	Y	Y	Y	Y	Y
7	Davis	N	N	Y	N	N	Y	Y
8	*Crane*	Y	Y	Y	Y	Y	Y	Y
9	Yates	N	N	?	?	Y	Y	Y
10	*Porter*	Y	Y	Y	N	Y	Y	Y
11	*Weller*	Y	Y	Y	Y	Y	Y	Y
12	Costello	Y	N	Y	N	N	Y	Y
13	*Fawell*	Y	Y	Y	Y	Y	Y	Y

ND Northern Democrats   SD Southern Democrats

	519	520	521	522	523	524	525
14 ***Hastert***	Y	Y	Y	Y	Y	Y	Y
15 ***Ewing***	Y	Y	Y	N	N	Y	Y
16 ***Manzullo***	N	Y	Y	Y	Y	Y	Y
17 Evans	N	N	Y	N	N	Y	Y
18 ***LaHood***	Y	Y	Y	N	N	Y	Y
19 Poshard	?	?	?	?	?	?	?
20 ***Shimkus***	Y	Y	Y	N	N	Y	Y
INDIANA							
1 Visclosky	N	N	Y	N	N	?	?
2 ***McIntosh***	Y	?	Y	Y	N	Y	Y
3 Roemer	Y	N	Y	N	N	Y	Y
4 ***Souder***	Y	Y	Y	Y	N	?	?
5 ***Buyer***	Y	Y	Y	N	Y	Y	Y
6 ***Burton***	Y	Y	Y	N	Y	Y	?
7 ***Pease***	Y	Y	Y	N	N	Y	Y
8 ***Hostettler***	Y	Y	Y	N	N	Y	Y
9 Hamilton	Y	N	Y	N	N	Y	Y
10 Carson	Y	N	Y	N	N	Y	Y
IOWA							
1 ***Leach***	Y	Y	Y	Y	N	Y	Y
2 ***Nussle***	Y	Y	Y	Y	Y	Y	Y
3 Boswell	N	N	Y	N	N	Y	Y
4 ***Ganske***	Y	Y	Y	Y	N	Y	Y
5 ***Latham***	Y	Y	Y	Y	N	Y	Y
KANSAS							
1 ***Moran***	Y	Y	Y	Y	N	Y	Y
2 ***Ryun***	Y	Y	Y	Y	Y	Y	Y
3 ***Snowbarger***	Y	Y	Y	Y	Y	Y	Y
4 ***Tiahrt***	Y	Y	Y	Y	Y	Y	Y
KENTUCKY							
1 ***Whitfield***	Y	Y	Y	N	Y	Y	Y
2 ***Lewis***	Y	Y	Y	Y	Y	Y	Y
3 ***Northup***	Y	Y	Y	Y	Y	Y	Y
4 ***Bunning***	Y	Y	Y	N	Y	Y	Y
5 ***Rogers***	Y	Y	Y	Y	Y	Y	Y
6 Baesler	Y	Y	Y	N	N	Y	Y
LOUISIANA							
1 ***Livingston***	Y	Y	Y	Y	N	Y	Y
2 Jefferson	Y	N	Y	N	N	Y	Y
3 ***Tauzin***	Y	Y	Y	Y	Y	Y	Y
4 ***McCrery***	Y	Y	Y	Y	Y	?	?
5 ***Cooksey***	Y	Y	?	?	?	?	?
6 ***Baker***	Y	Y	Y	Y	Y	Y	Y
7 John	Y	Y	?	N	N	Y	Y
MAINE							
1 Allen	Y	N	Y	N	N	Y	Y
2 Baldacci	Y	Y	Y	N	N	Y	Y
MARYLAND							
1 ***Gilchrest***	Y	Y	Y	Y	N	Y	Y
2 ***Ehrlich***	Y	Y	Y	Y	N	Y	Y
3 Cardin	Y	N	Y	N	N	Y	Y
4 Wynn	Y	Y	Y	N	N	Y	N
5 Hoyer	Y	N	Y	N	N	Y	Y
6 ***Bartlett***	Y	Y	Y	Y	Y	Y	Y
7 Cummings	Y	Y	Y	N	N	Y	Y
8 ***Morella***	Y	Y	Y	Y	N	Y	Y
MASSACHUSETTS							
1 Olver	Y	N	Y	N	N	Y	Y
2 Neal	Y	N	Y	N	N	Y	Y
3 McGovern	Y	N	Y	N	N	Y	Y
4 Frank	Y	N	Y	N	N	Y	Y
5 Meehan	Y	?	Y	N	N	Y	Y
6 Tierney	Y	N	Y	N	N	Y	Y
7 Markey	Y	N	Y	N	N	Y	Y
8 Kennedy	Y	?	Y	N	N	Y	Y
9 Moakley	Y	N	Y	N	N	Y	Y
10 Delahunt	Y	N	Y	N	N	Y	Y
MICHIGAN							
1 Stupak	N	N	Y	N	N	Y	Y
2 ***Hoekstra***	Y	Y	Y	Y	Y	Y	Y
3 ***Ehlers***	Y	Y	?	?	?	Y	Y
4 ***Camp***	Y	Y	Y	Y	Y	Y	Y
5 Barcia	Y	N	Y	N	N	Y	Y
6 ***Upton***	Y	Y	Y	Y	N	Y	Y
7 ***Smith***	Y	Y	Y	N	Y	Y	Y
8 Stabenow	N	Y	Y	N	N	Y	Y
9 Kildee	Y	Y	Y	N	N	Y	Y
10 Bonior	N	N	Y	N	N	Y	Y
11 ***Knollenberg***	Y	Y	Y	Y	Y	Y	Y
12 Levin	Y	N	Y	N	N	Y	Y
13 Rivers	N	N	Y	N	N	Y	Y
14 Conyers	N	N	Y	N	N	Y	N
15 Kilpatrick	N	Y	+	–	–	+	+
16 Dingell	N	N	Y	N	N	Y	Y

	519	520	521	522	523	524	525
MINNESOTA							
1 ***Gutknecht***	Y	Y	Y	Y	N	Y	Y
2 Minge	Y	Y	Y	N	N	Y	Y
3 ***Ramstad***	Y	Y	Y	Y	N	Y	Y
4 Vento	Y	N	Y	N	N	Y	Y
5 Sabo	Y	N	Y	N	N	Y	Y
6 Luther	Y	N	Y	N	N	Y	Y
7 Peterson	Y	Y	Y	N	N	Y	Y
8 Oberstar	Y	N	Y	N	N	Y	Y
MISSISSIPPI							
1 ***Wicker***	Y	Y	Y	Y	Y	Y	Y
2 Thompson	N	N	Y	N	N	Y	N
3 ***Pickering***	Y	Y	Y	Y	Y	Y	Y
4 ***Parker***	?	?	Y	Y	Y	Y	Y
5 Taylor	N	Y	?	N	N	Y	Y
MISSOURI							
1 Clay	N	N	Y	N	N	Y	N
2 ***Talent***	Y	Y	Y	Y	Y	Y	Y
3 Gephardt	Y	Y	?	?	?	Y	Y
4 Skelton	Y	Y	Y	N	N	Y	Y
5 McCarthy	Y	N	+	–	–	Y	Y
6 Danner	Y	Y	Y	N	N	Y	Y
7 ***Blunt***	Y	?	Y	Y	Y	Y	Y
8 ***Emerson***	Y	Y	Y	N	Y	Y	Y
9 ***Hulshof***	Y	Y	Y	Y	N	Y	Y
MONTANA							
AL ***Hill***	Y	Y	Y	Y	Y	Y	Y
NEBRASKA							
1 ***Bereuter***	Y	Y	Y	Y	N	Y	Y
2 ***Christensen***	Y	Y	Y	Y	Y	Y	Y
3 ***Barrett***	Y	Y	Y	Y	Y	Y	Y
NEVADA							
1 ***Ensign***	?	?	Y	Y	N	Y	Y
2 ***Gibbons***	Y	Y	Y	Y	Y	Y	Y
NEW HAMPSHIRE							
1 ***Sununu***	Y	Y	Y	N	N	Y	Y
2 ***Bass***	Y	Y	Y	Y	N	Y	Y
NEW JERSEY							
1 Andrews	Y	Y	Y	N	N	Y	Y
2 ***LoBiondo***	Y	Y	Y	N	N	Y	Y
3 ***Saxton***	Y	Y	Y	N	Y	Y	Y
4 ***Smith***	Y	Y	Y	N	N	Y	Y
5 ***Roukema***	Y	Y	Y	Y	N	Y	Y
6 Pallone	Y	N	Y	N	N	Y	Y
7 ***Franks***	Y	Y	Y	Y	N	Y	Y
8 Pascrell	Y	Y	Y	N	N	Y	Y
9 Rothman	Y	N	Y	N	N	Y	Y
10 Payne	N	N	Y	N	N	Y	N
11 ***Frelinghuysen***	Y	Y	Y	Y	N	Y	Y
12 ***Pappas***	Y	Y	Y	N	N	Y	Y
13 Menendez	Y	N	Y	N	N	Y	Y
NEW MEXICO							
1 ***Wilson***	Y	Y	Y	N	Y	Y	Y
2 ***Skeen***	Y	Y	Y	N	Y	Y	Y
3 ***Redmond***	Y	Y	Y	N	Y	Y	Y
NEW YORK							
1 ***Forbes***	Y	?	Y	N	N	Y	Y
2 ***Lazio***	Y	Y	Y	Y	N	Y	Y
3 ***King***	Y	Y	Y	N	Y	Y	Y
4 McCarthy	Y	Y	Y	N	N	Y	Y
5 Ackerman	Y	N	Y	N	N	?	?
6 Meeks	Y	N	Y	N	N	Y	N
7 Manton	Y	N	Y	N	N	Y	Y
8 Nadler	Y	N	Y	?	?	Y	Y
9 Schumer	Y	N	Y	N	N	Y	Y
10 Towns	Y	N	Y	N	N	Y	N
11 Owens	Y	N	Y	N	N	Y	Y
12 Velázquez	Y	N	Y	N	N	Y	Y
13 ***Fossella***	Y	Y	Y	N	N	Y	Y
14 Maloney	Y	N	Y	N	N	Y	Y
15 Rangel	?	?	Y	N	N	Y	Y
16 Serrano	Y	N	Y	N	N	Y	Y
17 Engel	Y	N	Y	N	N	Y	Y
18 Lowey	Y	N	Y	N	N	Y	Y
19 ***Kelly***	Y	Y	Y	N	N	Y	Y
20 ***Gilman***	Y	Y	Y	Y	N	Y	Y
21 McNulty	Y	N	Y	N	N	Y	Y
22 ***Solomon***	Y	?	Y	Y	Y	Y	Y
23 ***Boehlert***	Y	Y	Y	N	N	Y	Y
24 ***McHugh***	Y	Y	Y	N	N	Y	Y
25 ***Walsh***	?	?	Y	N	N	Y	Y
26 Hinchey	Y	N	?	?	N	Y	Y
27 ***Paxon***	Y	Y	Y	Y	Y	Y	Y
28 Slaughter	Y	N	Y	N	N	Y	Y
29 LaFalce	Y	N	Y	N	N	Y	Y
30 ***Quinn***	?	?	Y	N	N	Y	Y

	519	520	521	522	523	524	525
31 ***Houghton***	Y	Y	Y	N	Y	Y	Y
NORTH CAROLINA							
1 Clayton	N	N	Y	N	N	Y	Y
2 Etheridge	Y	Y	Y	N	N	Y	Y
3 ***Jones***	N	Y	Y	Y	N	Y	Y
4 Price	Y	Y	Y	N	N	Y	Y
5 ***Burr***	Y	Y	Y	Y	Y	Y	Y
6 ***Coble***	Y	Y	Y	Y	Y	Y	Y
7 McIntyre	Y	Y	Y	N	N	Y	Y
8 Hefner	?	?	?	?	?	?	?
9 ***Myrick***	Y	Y	Y	Y	Y	Y	Y
10 ***Ballenger***	Y	Y	Y	Y	Y	Y	Y
11 ***Taylor***	?	?	Y	Y	Y	Y	Y
12 Watt	Y	N	Y	N	N	Y	Y
NORTH DAKOTA							
AL Pomeroy	Y	Y	Y	N	Y	Y	Y
OHIO							
1 ***Chabot***	Y	Y	Y	Y	N	Y	Y
2 ***Portman***	Y	Y	Y	Y	N	Y	Y
3 Hall	Y	N	Y	N	N	?	?
4 ***Oxley***	Y	Y	Y	Y	Y	Y	Y
5 ***Gillmor***	Y	Y	Y	Y	N	Y	Y
6 Strickland	Y	Y	Y	N	N	Y	Y
7 ***Hobson***	Y	Y	Y	Y	Y	Y	Y
8 ***Boehner***	Y	Y	Y	N	Y	Y	Y
9 Kaptur	Y	N	Y	N	N	Y	Y
10 Kucinich	N	N	Y	N	N	Y	Y
11 Stokes	N	N	Y	N	N	Y	Y
12 ***Kasich***	Y	Y	Y	Y	Y	Y	Y
13 Brown	Y	N	Y	N	N	Y	Y
14 Sawyer	Y	N	Y	N	N	Y	Y
15 ***Pryce***	+	+	+	+	+	+	+
16 ***Regula***	Y	Y	Y	Y	Y	Y	Y
17 Traficant	Y	Y	Y	N	N	Y	Y
18 ***Ney***	Y	Y	Y	N	Y	Y	Y
19 ***LaTourette***	Y	Y	Y	Y	N	Y	Y
OKLAHOMA							
1 ***Largent***	Y	Y	?	?	?	?	?
2 ***Coburn***	N	Y	Y	Y	N	Y	Y
3 ***Watkins***	Y	Y	Y	Y	Y	Y	Y
4 ***Watts***	Y	Y	Y	N	Y	Y	Y
5 ***Istook***	Y	Y	Y	Y	Y	Y	Y
6 ***Lucas***	Y	Y	Y	Y	Y	Y	Y
OREGON							
1 Furse	N	N	Y	N	N	Y	N
2 ***Smith***	Y	Y	Y	Y	N	Y	Y
3 Blumenauer	Y	N	Y	N	N	Y	Y
4 DeFazio	N	N	Y	N	N	Y	Y
5 Hooley	Y	Y	Y	N	N	Y	Y
PENNSYLVANIA							
1 Brady	Y	N	Y	N	N	Y	Y
2 Fattah	Y	N	Y	N	N	Y	Y
3 Borski	Y	N	?	?	?	Y	Y
4 Klink	Y	N	Y	N	N	Y	Y
5 ***Peterson***	Y	Y	Y	N	Y	Y	Y
6 Holden	Y	Y	Y	N	N	Y	Y
7 ***Weldon***	Y	Y	Y	N	N	Y	Y
8 ***Greenwood***	Y	Y	Y	Y	N	Y	Y
9 ***Shuster***	Y	Y	Y	Y	Y	Y	Y
10 ***McDade***	Y	Y	Y	?	?	?	?
11 Kanjorski	Y	N	Y	N	N	Y	Y
12 Murtha	Y	N	?	?	?	Y	Y
13 ***Fox***	Y	Y	Y	Y	N	Y	Y
14 Coyne	Y	N	Y	N	N	Y	Y
15 McHale	Y	N	Y	N	N	Y	Y
16 ***Pitts***	Y	Y	Y	Y	Y	Y	Y
17 ***Gekas***	Y	Y	Y	Y	Y	Y	Y
18 Doyle	Y	Y	Y	N	N	Y	Y
19 ***Goodling***	Y	Y	Y	N	Y	Y	Y
20 Mascara	Y	Y	Y	N	N	Y	Y
21 ***English***	Y	Y	Y	Y	N	Y	Y
RHODE ISLAND							
1 Kennedy	Y	N	Y	N	N	Y	Y
2 Weygand	Y	Y	Y	N	N	Y	Y
SOUTH CAROLINA							
1 ***Sanford***	Y	N	Y	N	N	Y	Y
2 ***Spence***	Y	Y	Y	N	Y	Y	Y
3 ***Graham***	Y	Y	?	?	?	?	?
4 ***Inglis***	Y	?	?	?	?	?	?
5 Spratt	Y	Y	?	?	?	?	?
6 Clyburn	N	N	Y	N	N	Y	N
SOUTH DAKOTA							
AL ***Thune***	Y	Y	Y	Y	Y	Y	Y

	519	520	521	522	523	524	525
TENNESSEE							
1 ***Jenkins***	Y	Y	Y	Y	Y	Y	Y
2 ***Duncan***	Y	Y	Y	N	Y	Y	Y
3 ***Wamp***	Y	Y	Y	Y	Y	Y	Y
4 ***Hilleary***	Y	Y	Y	Y	Y	Y	Y
5 Clement	Y	Y	Y	N	N	Y	Y
6 Gordon	Y	Y	Y	N	N	Y	Y
7 ***Bryant***	Y	Y	Y	Y	Y	Y	Y
8 Tanner	Y	Y	Y	N	N	Y	Y
9 Ford	Y	N	Y	N	N	Y	Y
TEXAS							
1 Sandlin	Y	Y	Y	N	N	Y	Y
2 Turner	Y	Y	Y	N	Y	Y	Y
3 ***Johnson, Sam***	Y	Y	Y	Y	Y	Y	Y
4 Hall	Y	Y	Y	N	Y	Y	Y
5 ***Sessions***	Y	Y	Y	Y	Y	Y	Y
6 ***Barton***	Y	Y	Y	Y	Y	Y	Y
7 ***Archer***	Y	Y	Y	Y	Y	Y	Y
8 ***Brady***	Y	Y	Y	Y	Y	Y	Y
9 Lampson	Y	Y	?	?	?	?	?
10 Doggett	Y	Y	Y	N	N	Y	Y
11 Edwards	Y	Y	Y	N	N	Y	Y
12 ***Granger***	Y	Y	Y	Y	Y	Y	Y
13 ***Thornberry***	Y	Y	Y	Y	Y	Y	Y
14 ***Paul***	N	?	P	N	N	Y	Y
15 Hinojosa	N	Y	Y	N	N	Y	Y
16 Reyes	Y	Y	Y	N	N	Y	Y
17 Stenholm	Y	Y	Y	N	Y	Y	Y
18 Jackson-Lee	Y	N	Y	N	N	Y	N
19 ***Combest***	Y	Y	Y	Y	Y	Y	Y
20 Gonzalez	Y	N	Y	N	N	Y	Y
21 ***Smith***	Y	Y	Y	Y	Y	Y	Y
22 ***DeLay***	Y	Y	Y	N	Y	Y	Y
23 ***Bonilla***	Y	Y	Y	Y	Y	Y	Y
24 Frost	Y	Y	Y	N	N	Y	Y
25 Bentsen	Y	Y	Y	N	N	Y	Y
26 ***Armey***	Y	Y	Y	Y	Y	Y	Y
27 Ortiz	Y	Y	Y	N	N	Y	Y
28 Rodriguez	Y	Y	Y	N	N	Y	Y
29 Green	Y	Y	Y	N	N	Y	Y
30 Johnson, E.B.	Y	N	Y	N	N	Y	N
UTAH							
1 ***Hansen***	Y	Y	Y	Y	Y	Y	Y
2 ***Cook***	Y	Y	Y	Y	N	Y	Y
3 ***Cannon***	N	Y	Y	Y	Y	Y	Y
VERMONT							
AL *Sanders*	Y	N	Y	N	N	Y	Y
VIRGINIA							
1 ***Bateman***	Y	Y	Y	Y	Y	Y	Y
2 Pickett	N	Y	Y	N	Y	Y	Y
3 Scott	N	N	Y	N	N	Y	Y
4 Sisisky	Y	Y	Y	N	N	Y	Y
5 Goode	N	Y	Y	N	N	Y	Y
6 ***Goodlatte***	Y	Y	Y	Y	N	Y	Y
7 ***Bliley***	Y	Y	Y	Y	Y	Y	Y
8 Moran	Y	Y	Y	N	N	Y	Y
9 Boucher	?	?	?	?	?	?	?
10 ***Wolf***	Y	Y	Y	Y	N	Y	Y
11 ***Davis***	Y	Y	Y	N	N	Y	Y
WASHINGTON							
1 ***White***	Y	Y	Y	Y	N	Y	Y
2 ***Metcalf***	Y	Y	Y	N	Y	Y	Y
3 ***Smith, Linda***	Y	Y	Y	Y	Y	Y	Y
4 ***Hastings***	Y	Y	Y	Y	Y	Y	Y
5 ***Nethercutt***	+	+	Y	Y	Y	Y	Y
6 Dicks	Y	N	Y	N	N	Y	Y
7 McDermott	N	N	Y	N	N	Y	Y
8 ***Dunn***	Y	Y	Y	Y	Y	Y	Y
9 Smith, Adam	Y	Y	Y	N	N	Y	Y
WEST VIRGINIA							
1 Mollohan	Y	Y	?	?	?	Y	Y
2 Wise	Y	Y	Y	N	N	Y	Y
3 Rahall	Y	Y	?	?	?	Y	Y
WISCONSIN							
1 ***Neumann***	Y	Y	Y	N	N	Y	Y
2 ***Klug***	Y	Y	Y	Y	?	Y	Y
3 Kind	Y	N	Y	N	N	Y	Y
4 Kleczka	Y	Y	Y	N	N	Y	Y
5 Barrett	Y	N	Y	N	N	Y	Y
6 ***Petri***	Y	Y	Y	N	N	Y	Y
7 Obey	Y	N	Y	N	N	Y	Y
8 Johnson	Y	Y	Y	N	N	Y	Y
9 ***Sensenbrenner***	N	Y	Y	N	N	Y	Y
WYOMING							
AL ***Cubin***	Y	Y	Y	N	Y	Y	Y

Southern states - Ala., Ark., Fla., Ga., Ky., La., Miss., N.C., Okla., S.C., Tenn., Texas, Va.

526. HR 4756. Year 2000 Computer Problem/Passage. Morella, R-Md., motion to suspend the rules and pass the bill to increase congressional oversight of the federal government's attempts to solve the so-called Year 2000 computer problem. The measure requires all federal agencies to submit a report to Congress outlining their progress on preparing their computers for the year 2000. Motion agreed to 407-3: R 214-3; D 192-0 (ND 143-0, SD 49-0); I 1-0. Oct. 13, 1998. A two-thirds majority of those present and voting (274 in this case) is required for passage under suspension of the rules.

527. S 1754. Public Health Program Consolidation/Passage. Bliley, R-Va., motion to suspend the rules and pass the bill to consolidate 37 Public Health Service grant programs and to require that priority be given to programs for minority health workers and professionals in underserved areas. Motion agreed to 303-102: R 115-101; D 187-1 (ND 140-0, SD 47-1); I 1-0. Oct. 13, 1998. A two-thirds majority of those present and voting (270 in this case) is required for passage under suspension of the rules.

528. S 1260. Class-Action Securities Litigation/Conference Report. Bliley, R-Va., motion to suspend the rules and adopt the conference report on the bill to require that all class-action securities lawsuits involving more than 50 parties be considered in federal court, where standards established in a 1995 securities law (PL 104-67) would apply. Motion agreed to (thus clearing the conference report for the president) 319-82: R 213-1; D 106-80 (ND 74-64, SD 32-16); I 0-1. Oct. 13, 1998. A two-thirds majority of those present and voting (268 in this case) is required for passage under suspension of the rules.

529. S 1722. Women's Health Research Programs/Passage. Bilirakis, R-Fla., motion to suspend the rules and pass the bill to authorize and coordinate medical research and related programs dealing with women's health. Motion agreed to (thus clearing the bill for the president) 401-1: R 212-1; D 188-0 (ND 140-0, SD 48-0); I 1-0. Oct. 13, 1998. A two-thirds majority of those present and voting (268 in this case) is required for passage under suspension of the rules.

530. HR 3963. Canyon Ferry Reservoir Cabin Sites/Passage. Hansen, R-Utah, motion to suspend the rules and pass the bill to direct the Interior Department to offer for sale 265 cabin sites near the Bureau of Reclamation's Canyon Ferry Reservoir in Montana. The bill requires the department to sell the lots to public owners at fair market value by sealed bid. Motion rejected 217-181: R 210-0; D 7-180 (ND 4-132, SD 3-48); I 0-1. Oct. 14, 1998. A two-thirds majority of those present and voting (266 in this case) is required for passage under suspension of the rules.

531. HR 559. Service-Connected Diseases/Passage. Stump, R-Ariz., motion to suspend the rules and pass the bill to add bronchiolo-alveolar carcinoma to the list of diseases presumed to be service-connected for certain veterans exposed to atomic radiation. The veterans or their surviving dependents would then be eligible for benefits. Motion agreed to 400-0: R 213-0; D 186-0 (ND 137-0, SD 49-0); I 1-0. Oct. 14, 1998. A two-thirds majority of those present and voting (267 in this case) is required for passage under suspension of the rules.

532. H Res 598. Enforcement of Steel Imports Laws/Adoption. English, R-Pa., motion to suspend the rules and adopt the resolution expressing the sense of the House that its integrity has been impugned because the anti-dumping provisions of the Trade and Tariff Act of 1930 have not been expeditiously enforced and calling for an import ban on steel from nations found to be violating international steel accords. Motion agreed to 345-44: R 159-44; D 185-0 (ND 136-0, SD 49-0); I 1-0. Oct. 15, 1998. A two-thirds majority of those present and voting (260 in this case) is required for passage under suspension of the rules.

Key

Y	Voted for (yea).	
#	Paired for.	
+	Announced for.	
N	Voted against (nay).	
X	Paired against.	
–	Announced against.	
P	Voted "present."	
C	Voted "present" to avoid possible conflict of interest.	
?	Did not vote or otherwise make a position known.	

Democrats **Republicans**
Independent

	526	527	528	529	530	531	532
ALABAMA							
1 *Callahan*	Y	N	Y	Y	Y	Y	?
2 *Everett*	Y	N	Y	Y	Y	Y	Y
3 *Riley*	Y	N	Y	Y	Y	Y	Y
4 *Aderholt*	Y	N	Y	Y	Y	Y	Y
5 Cramer	Y	Y	Y	Y	N	Y	Y
6 *Bachus*	Y	Y	Y	Y	Y	Y	Y
7 Hilliard	Y	Y	N	Y	N	Y	Y
ALASKA							
AL *Young*	Y	Y	Y	Y	Y	Y	Y
ARIZONA							
1 *Salmon*	Y	N	Y	Y	Y	Y	Y
2 Pastor	Y	Y	N	Y	N	Y	Y
3 *Stump*	Y	N	Y	Y	Y	Y	N
4 *Shadegg*	Y	N	Y	Y	Y	Y	Y
5 *Kolbe*	Y	N	Y	Y	?	?	N
6 *Hayworth*	Y	N	Y	Y	Y	Y	Y
ARKANSAS							
1 Berry	Y	Y	Y	Y	N	Y	Y
2 Snyder	Y	Y	Y	Y	N	Y	Y
3 *Hutchinson*	Y	Y	Y	Y	Y	Y	?
4 *Dickey*	Y	Y	Y	Y	Y	Y	Y
CALIFORNIA							
1 *Riggs*	Y	N	Y	Y	Y	Y	Y
2 *Herger*	Y	N	Y	Y	Y	Y	N
3 Fazio	Y	Y	Y	Y	N	Y	Y
4 *Doolittle*	Y	N	Y	Y	Y	Y	Y
5 Matsui	Y	Y	Y	Y	N	Y	Y
6 Woolsey	Y	Y	N	Y	N	Y	Y
7 Miller	Y	Y	Y	Y	N	Y	Y
8 Pelosi	Y	Y	Y	Y	N	Y	?
9 Lee	Y	Y	N	Y	N	Y	Y
10 Tauscher	Y	Y	Y	Y	N	Y	Y
11 *Pombo*	Y	N	Y	Y	Y	Y	Y
12 Lantos	Y	Y	Y	Y	N	Y	?
13 Stark	Y	Y	N	Y	N	Y	Y
14 Eshoo	Y	Y	Y	Y	N	Y	Y
15 *Campbell*	Y	N	Y	Y	N	Y	Y
16 Lofgren	Y	Y	Y	Y	N	Y	Y
17 Farr	Y	Y	Y	Y	N	Y	Y
18 Condit	Y	Y	Y	Y	N	Y	Y
19 *Radanovich*	Y	N	Y	Y	Y	Y	Y
20 Dooley	Y	Y	Y	Y	N	Y	Y
21 *Thomas*	Y	Y	Y	Y	Y	Y	N
22 Capps, L.	Y	Y	Y	Y	N	Y	Y
23 *Gallegly*	Y	Y	Y	Y	Y	Y	Y
24 Sherman	Y	Y	Y	Y	N	Y	Y
25 *McKeon*	Y	N	Y	Y	Y	Y	Y
26 Berman	?	?	?	?	?	?	?
27 *Rogan*	Y	N	Y	Y	Y	Y	N
28 *Dreier*	Y	N	Y	Y	Y	N	N
29 Waxman	Y	Y	N	Y	N	Y	Y
30 Becerra	Y	Y	N	Y	N	Y	Y
31 Martinez	Y	Y	Y	Y	N	Y	Y
32 Dixon	Y	Y	Y	Y	N	Y	Y
33 Roybal-Allard	Y	Y	N	Y	N	Y	Y
34 Torres	Y	Y	N	Y	?	?	?
35 Waters	Y	Y	N	Y	N	Y	Y
36 Harman	?	?	?	?	N	Y	Y
37 Millender-McD.	Y	Y	Y	Y	N	Y	Y
38 *Horn*	Y	Y	Y	Y	N	Y	Y

	526	527	528	529	530	531	532
39 *Royce*	Y	N	Y	Y	Y	Y	N
40 *Lewis*	Y	Y	Y	Y	Y	Y	Y
41 *Kim*	Y	Y	Y	Y	Y	Y	Y
42 Brown	Y	Y	N	Y	N	Y	Y
43 *Calvert*	Y	N	Y	Y	Y	Y	Y
44 *Bono, M.*	Y	N	Y	Y	Y	Y	Y
45 *Rohrabacher*	Y	N	Y	Y	Y	Y	Y
46 Sanchez	Y	Y	Y	Y	N	Y	Y
47 *Cox*	Y	N	Y	Y	Y	Y	Y
48 *Packard*	Y	Y	Y	Y	Y	Y	Y
49 *Bilbray*	Y	Y	Y	Y	Y	Y	Y
50 Filner	Y	Y	N	Y	N	Y	Y
51 *Cunningham*	Y	Y	Y	Y	Y	Y	Y
52 *Hunter*	Y	N	Y	Y	Y	Y	Y
COLORADO							
1 DeGette	Y	Y	N	Y	N	Y	Y
2 Skaggs	Y	Y	N	Y	N	Y	Y
3 *McInnis*	Y	N	Y	Y	Y	Y	Y
4 *Schaffer*	Y	N	Y	Y	Y	Y	Y
5 *Hefley*	Y	N	Y	Y	Y	Y	Y
6 *Schaefer*	Y	Y	Y	Y	?	?	Y
CONNECTICUT							
1 Kennelly	?	?	?	?	?	?	?
2 Gejdenson	Y	Y	Y	Y	N	Y	Y
3 DeLauro	Y	Y	Y	Y	N	Y	Y
4 *Shays*	Y	Y	Y	Y	Y	Y	Y
5 Maloney	Y	Y	Y	Y	N	Y	Y
6 *Johnson*	Y	Y	Y	Y	Y	Y	Y
DELAWARE							
AL *Castle*	Y	Y	Y	Y	Y	Y	Y
FLORIDA							
1 *Scarborough*	?	?	?	?	?	?	?
2 Boyd	Y	Y	Y	Y	N	Y	Y
3 Brown	Y	Y	N	Y	N	Y	Y
4 *Fowler*	Y	N	Y	Y	Y	Y	?
5 Thurman	Y	Y	N	Y	N	Y	Y
6 *Stearns*	Y	N	Y	Y	Y	Y	Y
7 *Mica*	Y	N	Y	Y	Y	Y	Y
8 *McCollum*	?	?	?	?	Y	Y	N
9 *Bilirakis*	Y	Y	Y	Y	Y	Y	Y
10 *Young*	Y	Y	Y	Y	Y	Y	Y
11 Davis	Y	Y	Y	Y	N	Y	Y
12 *Canady*	Y	N	Y	Y	Y	Y	Y
13 *Miller*	Y	N	Y	Y	Y	Y	N
14 *Goss*	Y	N	Y	Y	Y	Y	Y
15 *Weldon*	Y	Y	Y	Y	?	?	?
16 *Foley*	Y	N	Y	Y	Y	Y	Y
17 Meek	Y	Y	N	Y	N	Y	Y
18 *Ros-Lehtinen*	Y	Y	Y	Y	Y	Y	Y
19 Wexler	?	?	?	?	N	Y	Y
20 Deutsch	+	+	+	N	Y	Y	Y
21 *Diaz-Balart*	Y	Y	Y	Y	Y	Y	Y
22 *Shaw*	Y	N	Y	Y	Y	Y	Y
23 Hastings	Y	Y	N	Y	N	Y	Y
GEORGIA							
1 *Kingston*	Y	Y	Y	Y	Y	Y	Y
2 Bishop	Y	Y	Y	Y	N	Y	Y
3 *Collins*	Y	N	Y	Y	Y	Y	?
4 McKinney	Y	Y	N	Y	N	Y	Y
5 Lewis	Y	Y	N	Y	N	Y	Y
6 *Gingrich*							
7 *Barr*	Y	N	Y	Y	?	?	?
8 *Chambliss*	Y	N	Y	?	Y	Y	Y
9 *Deal*	Y	Y	Y	Y	Y	Y	?
10 *Norwood*	Y	N	Y	Y	Y	Y	Y
11 *Linder*	Y	N	Y	Y	Y	Y	Y
HAWAII							
1 Abercrombie	Y	Y	N	Y	N	Y	Y
2 Mink	Y	Y	N	Y	N	Y	Y
IDAHO							
1 *Chenoweth*	N	Y	Y	Y	Y	Y	Y
2 *Crapo*	Y	Y	Y	Y	Y	Y	Y
ILLINOIS							
1 Rush	Y	Y	Y	Y	N	Y	Y
2 Jackson	Y	Y	N	Y	N	Y	Y
3 Lipinski	Y	?	?	?	?	?	Y
4 Gutierrez	Y	Y	N	Y	N	Y	Y
5 Blagojevich	Y	Y	Y	Y	N	Y	Y
6 *Hyde*	Y	N	Y	Y	Y	Y	?
7 Davis	Y	+	–	+	–	+	Y
8 *Crane*	Y	N	Y	Y	Y	Y	N
9 Yates	Y	Y	N	Y	N	Y	Y
10 *Porter*	Y	Y	Y	Y	Y	Y	Y
11 *Weller*	Y	N	Y	Y	Y	Y	Y
12 Costello	Y	Y	Y	Y	N	Y	Y
13 *Fawell*	Y	Y	Y	Y	Y	Y	N

ND Northern Democrats   SD Southern Democrats

	526	527	528	529	530	531	532
14 ***Hastert***	Y	Y	Y	Y	Y	Y	Y
15 ***Ewing***	Y	Y	Y	Y	Y	Y	Y
16 ***Manzullo***	Y	N	Y	Y	Y	Y	N
17 Evans	Y	Y	N	Y	N	Y	Y
18 ***LaHood***	Y	N	Y	Y	Y	Y	Y
19 Poshard	?	?	?	?	?	?	?
20 ***Shimkus***	Y	Y	Y	Y	Y	Y	Y
INDIANA							
1 Visclosky	?	?	?	Y	?	?	Y
2 ***McIntosh***	Y	N	Y	Y	Y	Y	?
3 Roemer	Y	Y	Y	Y	N	Y	Y
4 ***Souder***	?	?	?	?	Y	Y	Y
5 ***Buyer***	Y	N	Y	Y	Y	Y	Y
6 ***Burton***	Y	N	Y	Y	Y	Y	Y
7 ***Pease***	Y	Y	Y	Y	Y	Y	Y
8 ***Hostettler***	Y	N	Y	Y	Y	Y	Y
9 Hamilton	Y	Y	Y	Y	N	Y	Y
10 Carson	Y	Y	N	Y	–	+	Y
IOWA							
1 ***Leach***	Y	Y	Y	Y	Y	Y	Y
2 ***Nussle***	Y	Y	Y	Y	Y	Y	Y
3 Boswell	Y	Y	Y	Y	N	Y	Y
4 ***Ganske***	Y	Y	Y	Y	Y	Y	Y
5 ***Latham***	Y	Y	Y	Y	Y	Y	Y
KANSAS							
1 ***Moran***	Y	Y	Y	Y	Y	Y	Y
2 ***Ryun***	Y	N	Y	Y	Y	Y	Y
3 ***Snowbarger***	Y	N	Y	Y	Y	Y	Y
4 ***Tiahrt***	Y	N	Y	?	Y	Y	Y
KENTUCKY							
1 ***Whitfield***	Y	N	Y	Y	Y	Y	Y
2 ***Lewis***	Y	N	Y	Y	Y	Y	Y
3 ***Northup***	Y	Y	Y	Y	Y	Y	N
4 ***Bunning***	Y	Y	Y	Y	Y	Y	Y
5 ***Rogers***	Y	Y	Y	Y	Y	Y	Y
6 Baesler	Y	Y	Y	Y	N	Y	Y
LOUISIANA							
1 ***Livingston***	Y	Y	?	Y	Y	Y	N
2 Jefferson	Y	Y	Y	Y	N	Y	Y
3 ***Tauzin***	Y	Y	Y	Y	?	Y	Y
4 ***McCrery***	?	?	?	?	Y	Y	Y
5 ***Cooksey***	?	?	?	?	Y	Y	?
6 ***Baker***	Y	N	Y	Y	Y	Y	Y
7 John	Y	Y	Y	Y	Y	Y	Y
MAINE							
1 Allen	Y	Y	Y	Y	N	Y	?
2 Baldacci	Y	Y	N	Y	N	Y	Y
MARYLAND							
1 ***Gilchrest***	Y	Y	Y	Y	Y	Y	Y
2 ***Ehrlich***	Y	N	Y	Y	Y	Y	Y
3 Cardin	Y	Y	Y	Y	N	Y	Y
4 Wynn	Y	Y	Y	Y	N	Y	Y
5 Hoyer	Y	Y	Y	Y	N	Y	Y
6 ***Bartlett***	Y	N	Y	Y	Y	Y	Y
7 Cummings	Y	Y	N	Y	N	Y	Y
8 ***Morella***	Y	Y	Y	Y	Y	Y	Y
MASSACHUSETTS							
1 Olver	Y	Y	N	Y	N	Y	Y
2 Neal	Y	Y	Y	Y	?	?	Y
3 McGovern	Y	Y	Y	Y	?	?	?
4 Frank	Y	Y	Y	Y	?	?	?
5 Meehan	Y	Y	Y	Y	N	Y	?
6 Tierney	Y	Y	N	Y	N	Y	Y
7 Markey	Y	Y	N	Y	N	Y	Y
8 Kennedy	Y	Y	Y	Y	Y	Y	Y
9 Moakley	Y	Y	Y	Y	N	Y	Y
10 Delahunt	Y	Y	N	Y	N	Y	Y
MICHIGAN							
1 Stupak	Y	Y	N	Y	N	Y	Y
2 ***Hoekstra***	Y	N	Y	Y	Y	Y	Y
3 ***Ehlers***	Y	Y	Y	Y	Y	Y	?
4 ***Camp***	Y	Y	Y	Y	Y	Y	N
5 Barcia	Y	Y	Y	Y	N	Y	Y
6 ***Upton***	Y	Y	Y	Y	Y	Y	Y
7 ***Smith***	Y	Y	Y	?	Y	Y	N
8 Stabenow	Y	Y	Y	Y	N	Y	Y
9 Kildee	Y	Y	N	Y	N	Y	Y
10 Bonior	Y	Y	N	Y	N	Y	Y
11 ***Knollenberg***	Y	Y	Y	Y	Y	Y	N
12 Levin	Y	Y	N	Y	N	Y	Y
13 Rivers	Y	Y	N	Y	N	Y	Y
14 Conyers	Y	Y	N	Y	?	?	Y
15 Kilpatrick	+	+	?	?	–	+	Y
16 Dingell	Y	Y	N	Y	N	Y	Y
MINNESOTA							
1 ***Gutknecht***	Y	Y	Y	Y	Y	Y	Y
2 Minge	Y	Y	Y	Y	N	Y	Y
3 ***Ramstad***	Y	Y	Y	Y	Y	Y	N
4 Vento	Y	Y	Y	Y	N	Y	Y
5 Sabo	Y	Y	Y	Y	N	Y	Y
6 Luther	Y	Y	Y	Y	N	Y	Y
7 Peterson	Y	Y	Y	Y	N	Y	Y
8 Oberstar	Y	Y	N	Y	N	Y	Y
MISSISSIPPI							
1 ***Wicker***	Y	N	Y	Y	Y	Y	Y
2 Thompson	Y	Y	N	Y	N	Y	?
3 ***Pickering***	Y	N	Y	Y	Y	Y	Y
4 ***Parker***	Y	N	Y	Y	Y	Y	Y
5 Taylor	Y	N	N	Y	N	Y	Y
MISSOURI							
1 Clay	Y	Y	N	Y	N	Y	Y
2 ***Talent***	Y	Y	Y	Y	Y	Y	Y
3 Gephardt	Y	Y	N	Y	N	Y	Y
4 Skelton	Y	Y	Y	Y	N	Y	Y
5 McCarthy	Y	Y	Y	Y	N	Y	Y
6 Danner	Y	Y	Y	Y	Y	Y	Y
7 ***Blunt***	Y	Y	Y	Y	Y	Y	?
8 ***Emerson***	Y	Y	Y	Y	Y	Y	Y
9 ***Hulshof***	Y	Y	Y	Y	Y	Y	N
MONTANA							
AL ***Hill***	Y	N	Y	Y	Y	Y	Y
NEBRASKA							
1 ***Bereuter***	Y	N	Y	Y	Y	Y	Y
2 ***Christensen***	Y	N	Y	Y	Y	Y	Y
3 ***Barrett***	Y	N	Y	Y	Y	Y	Y
NEVADA							
1 ***Ensign***	Y	Y	Y	Y	Y	Y	Y
2 ***Gibbons***	Y	N	Y	Y	Y	Y	Y
NEW HAMPSHIRE							
1 ***Sununu***	Y	N	Y	Y	Y	Y	N
2 ***Bass***	Y	N	Y	Y	Y	Y	Y
NEW JERSEY							
1 Andrews	Y	Y	Y	Y	N	Y	Y
2 ***LoBiondo***	Y	Y	Y	Y	Y	Y	Y
3 ***Saxton***	Y	Y	Y	Y	Y	Y	Y
4 ***Smith***	Y	Y	Y	Y	Y	Y	Y
5 ***Roukema***	Y	Y	Y	Y	Y	Y	Y
6 Pallone	Y	Y	Y	Y	N	Y	Y
7 ***Franks***	Y	Y	Y	Y	Y	Y	Y
8 Pascrell	Y	Y	Y	Y	N	Y	Y
9 Rothman	Y	Y	Y	Y	?	?	Y
10 Payne	Y	Y	N	Y	N	Y	Y
11 ***Frelinghuysen***	Y	Y	Y	Y	Y	Y	Y
12 ***Pappas***	Y	Y	Y	Y	Y	Y	Y
13 Menendez	Y	Y	N	Y	N	Y	Y
NEW MEXICO							
1 ***Wilson***	Y	Y	Y	Y	+	+	+
2 ***Skeen***	Y	Y	Y	Y	Y	Y	Y
3 ***Redmond***	Y	Y	Y	Y	Y	Y	Y
NEW YORK							
1 ***Forbes***	Y	Y	Y	Y	Y	Y	Y
2 ***Lazio***	Y	Y	Y	Y	Y	Y	Y
3 ***King***	Y	N	Y	Y	Y	Y	Y
4 McCarthy	Y	Y	Y	Y	N	Y	Y
5 Ackerman	?	?	?	?	N	Y	?
6 Meeks	Y	Y	N	Y	N	Y	Y
7 Manton	Y	Y	Y	Y	N	Y	Y
8 Nadler	Y	Y	N	Y	N	Y	Y
9 Schumer	Y	Y	N	Y	N	Y	Y
10 Towns	Y	Y	Y	Y	N	Y	Y
11 Owens	Y	Y	N	Y	N	Y	Y
12 Velázquez	Y	Y	Y	Y	N	Y	Y
13 ***Fossella***	Y	N	Y	Y	Y	Y	N
14 Maloney	Y	Y	Y	Y	N	Y	Y
15 Rangel	Y	Y	N	Y	N	Y	Y
16 Serrano	Y	Y	N	Y	N	Y	Y
17 Engel	Y	Y	N	Y	N	Y	Y
18 Lowey	Y	Y	P	Y	N	Y	Y
19 ***Kelly***	Y	Y	Y	Y	Y	Y	Y
20 ***Gilman***	Y	Y	Y	Y	Y	Y	Y
21 McNulty	Y	Y	Y	Y	N	Y	Y
22 ***Solomon***	Y	N	Y	Y	Y	Y	Y
23 ***Boehlert***	Y	Y	Y	Y	Y	Y	Y
24 ***McHugh***	Y	Y	Y	Y	?	?	Y
25 ***Walsh***	Y	Y	Y	Y	Y	Y	Y
26 Hinchey	Y	Y	N	Y	N	Y	Y
27 ***Paxon***	Y	Y	Y	Y	Y	Y	Y
28 Slaughter	Y	Y	Y	Y	N	Y	Y
29 LaFalce	Y	Y	Y	Y	N	Y	Y
30 ***Quinn***	Y	Y	Y	Y	Y	Y	Y
31 ***Houghton***	Y	Y	Y	Y	Y	Y	N
NORTH CAROLINA							
1 Clayton	Y	Y	N	Y	N	?	Y
2 Etheridge	Y	Y	Y	Y	N	Y	Y
3 ***Jones***	Y	N	Y	Y	Y	Y	Y
4 Price	Y	Y	Y	Y	N	Y	Y
5 ***Burr***	Y	N	Y	Y	Y	Y	N
6 ***Coble***	Y	N	Y	Y	Y	Y	N
7 McIntyre	Y	Y	Y	Y	N	Y	?
8 Hefner	?	?	?	?	?	?	?
9 ***Myrick***	Y	N	Y	Y	Y	Y	Y
10 ***Ballenger***	Y	N	Y	Y	Y	Y	N
11 ***Taylor***	Y	N	Y	Y	Y	Y	?
12 Watt	Y	Y	N	Y	?	?	Y
NORTH DAKOTA							
AL Pomeroy	Y	Y	Y	Y	Y	Y	Y
OHIO							
1 ***Chabot***	Y	N	Y	Y	Y	Y	Y
2 ***Portman***	Y	Y	Y	Y	Y	Y	Y
3 Hall	?	?	?	?	N	Y	Y
4 ***Oxley***	Y	N	Y	Y	Y	Y	Y
5 ***Gillmor***	Y	N	Y	Y	Y	Y	Y
6 Strickland	Y	Y	Y	Y	N	Y	Y
7 ***Hobson***	Y	Y	Y	Y	Y	Y	Y
8 ***Boehner***	Y	Y	Y	Y	Y	Y	Y
9 Kaptur	Y	Y	N	Y	N	Y	?
10 Kucinich	Y	Y	N	Y	N	Y	Y
11 Stokes	Y	Y	N	Y	N	Y	Y
12 ***Kasich***	Y	N	Y	Y	Y	Y	Y
13 Brown	Y	Y	Y	Y	N	Y	Y
14 Sawyer	Y	Y	Y	Y	N	Y	Y
15 ***Pryce***	+	+	+	+	+	+	+
16 ***Regula***	Y	Y	Y	Y	?	Y	Y
17 Traficant	Y	Y	Y	Y	Y	Y	Y
18 ***Ney***	Y	Y	Y	Y	Y	Y	Y
19 ***LaTourette***	Y	Y	Y	Y	Y	Y	Y
OKLAHOMA							
1 ***Largent***	?	?	?	?	?	?	?
2 ***Coburn***	Y	N	Y	Y	Y	Y	Y
3 ***Watkins***	Y	Y	Y	Y	Y	Y	Y
4 ***Watts***	Y	Y	Y	Y	Y	Y	Y
5 ***Istook***	Y	N	Y	Y	Y	Y	Y
6 ***Lucas***	Y	Y	Y	Y	Y	Y	Y
OREGON							
1 Furse	Y	Y	Y	Y	N	Y	?
2 ***Smith***	Y	?	?	?	?	?	Y
3 Blumenauer	Y	Y	Y	Y	N	Y	Y
4 DeFazio	Y	Y	N	Y	N	Y	Y
5 Hooley	Y	Y	Y	Y	N	Y	Y
PENNSYLVANIA							
1 Brady	Y	?	?	?	N	Y	Y
2 Fattah	Y	Y	N	Y	N	Y	Y
3 Borski	Y	Y	N	Y	N	Y	Y
4 Klink	Y	Y	N	Y	N	Y	Y
5 ***Peterson***	Y	Y	Y	Y	Y	Y	+
6 Holden	Y	Y	Y	Y	N	Y	Y
7 ***Weldon***	Y	Y	Y	Y	Y	Y	?
8 ***Greenwood***	Y	Y	Y	Y	?	?	?
9 ***Shuster***	Y	N	Y	Y	?	?	Y
10 ***McDade***	?	?	?	?	Y	Y	?
11 Kanjorski	Y	Y	N	Y	N	Y	Y
12 Murtha	Y	Y	?	?	N	Y	Y
13 ***Fox***	Y	Y	Y	Y	Y	Y	Y
14 Coyne	Y	Y	N	Y	N	Y	Y
15 McHale	Y	Y	Y	Y	N	Y	Y
16 ***Pitts***	Y	N	Y	Y	Y	Y	Y
17 ***Gekas***	Y	Y	Y	Y	Y	Y	Y
18 Doyle	Y	Y	Y	Y	N	Y	Y
19 ***Goodling***	Y	Y	Y	Y	Y	Y	Y
20 Mascara	Y	Y	Y	Y	N	Y	Y
21 ***English***	Y	Y	Y	Y	Y	Y	Y
RHODE ISLAND							
1 Kennedy	Y	Y	Y	Y	N	Y	Y
2 Weygand	Y	Y	Y	Y	N	Y	Y
SOUTH CAROLINA							
1 ***Sanford***	Y	N	Y	Y	Y	Y	N
2 ***Spence***	Y	N	Y	Y	Y	Y	Y
3 ***Graham***	?	?	?	?	?	?	?
4 ***Inglis***	?	?	?	?	?	?	?
5 Spratt	?	?	?	?	N	Y	Y
6 Clyburn	Y	Y	N	Y	N	Y	Y
SOUTH DAKOTA							
AL ***Thune***	Y	Y	Y	Y	Y	Y	Y
TENNESSEE							
1 ***Jenkins***	Y	Y	Y	Y	Y	Y	Y
2 ***Duncan***	Y	Y	Y	Y	Y	Y	Y
3 ***Wamp***	Y	Y	Y	Y	Y	Y	Y
4 ***Hilleary***	Y	Y	Y	Y	Y	Y	Y
5 Clement	Y	Y	Y	Y	N	Y	Y
6 Gordon	Y	Y	Y	Y	N	Y	Y
7 ***Bryant***	Y	Y	Y	Y	Y	Y	Y
8 Tanner	Y	Y	Y	Y	N	Y	Y
9 Ford	Y	Y	Y	Y	N	Y	Y
TEXAS							
1 Sandlin	Y	Y	Y	Y	N	Y	Y
2 Turner	Y	Y	Y	Y	N	Y	Y
3 ***Johnson, Sam***	Y	N	?	Y	Y	Y	Y
4 Hall	Y	Y	Y	Y	Y	Y	Y
5 ***Sessions***	Y	N	Y	Y	Y	Y	N
6 ***Barton***	Y	N	Y	Y	Y	Y	N
7 ***Archer***	Y	N	Y	Y	?	?	N
8 ***Brady***	Y	N	Y	Y	Y	Y	N
9 Lampson	?	?	?	?	N	Y	Y
10 Doggett	Y	Y	N	Y	N	Y	Y
11 Edwards	Y	Y	Y	Y	N	?	Y
12 ***Granger***	Y	Y	Y	Y	Y	Y	Y
13 ***Thornberry***	Y	Y	Y	Y	Y	Y	Y
14 ***Paul***	N	N	N	N	Y	Y	N
15 Hinojosa	Y	Y	Y	Y	N	Y	Y
16 Reyes	Y	Y	Y	Y	?	?	Y
17 Stenholm	Y	Y	Y	Y	N	Y	Y
18 Jackson-Lee	Y	Y	Y	Y	N	Y	Y
19 ***Combest***	Y	N	Y	Y	Y	Y	Y
20 Gonzalez	Y	Y	Y	Y	N	Y	Y
21 ***Smith***	Y	N	Y	Y	Y	Y	Y
22 ***DeLay***	Y	N	Y	Y	Y	Y	N
23 ***Bonilla***	Y	N	Y	Y	Y	Y	Y
24 Frost	Y	Y	N	Y	N	Y	?
25 Bentsen	Y	Y	Y	Y	N	Y	Y
26 ***Armey***	Y	Y	Y	Y	Y	Y	N
27 Ortiz	Y	Y	Y	Y	N	Y	Y
28 Rodriguez	Y	Y	Y	Y	N	Y	Y
29 Green	Y	Y	Y	Y	N	Y	+
30 Johnson, E.B.	Y	Y	N	Y	N	Y	+
UTAH							
1 ***Hansen***	Y	N	Y	Y	Y	Y	Y
2 ***Cook***	Y	Y	Y	Y	Y	Y	Y
3 ***Cannon***	N	N	Y	Y	Y	Y	Y
VERMONT							
AL *Sanders*	Y	Y	N	Y	N	Y	Y
VIRGINIA							
1 ***Bateman***	Y	Y	Y	Y	Y	Y	Y
2 Pickett	Y	Y	Y	Y	?	?	Y
3 Scott	Y	Y	N	Y	N	Y	Y
4 Sisisky	Y	Y	Y	Y	N	Y	Y
5 Goode	Y	?	?	?	Y	Y	Y
6 ***Goodlatte***	Y	Y	Y	Y	Y	Y	Y
7 ***Bliley***	Y	Y	Y	Y	Y	Y	N
8 Moran	Y	Y	Y	Y	N	Y	Y
9 Boucher	?	?	?	?	N	Y	Y
10 ***Wolf***	Y	Y	Y	Y	Y	Y	Y
11 ***Davis***	Y	Y	Y	Y	Y	Y	N
WASHINGTON							
1 ***White***	Y	Y	Y	Y	Y	Y	Y
2 ***Metcalf***	Y	Y	Y	Y	Y	Y	Y
3 ***Smith, Linda***	Y	N	Y	Y	Y	Y	Y
4 ***Hastings***	Y	N	Y	Y	Y	Y	?
5 ***Nethercutt***	Y	N	Y	Y	Y	Y	N
6 Dicks	Y	Y	Y	Y	N	Y	Y
7 McDermott	Y	Y	N	Y	N	Y	Y
8 ***Dunn***	Y	Y	Y	Y	Y	Y	N
9 Smith, Adam	Y	Y	Y	Y	N	Y	Y
WEST VIRGINIA							
1 Mollohan	Y	Y	N	Y	N	Y	Y
2 Wise	Y	Y	N	Y	?	Y	Y
3 Rahall	Y	Y	N	Y	N	Y	Y
WISCONSIN							
1 ***Neumann***	Y	N	Y	Y	Y	Y	Y
2 ***Klug***	Y	Y	Y	Y	Y	Y	Y
3 Kind	Y	Y	Y	Y	N	Y	Y
4 Kleczka	Y	Y	Y	Y	N	Y	Y
5 Barrett	Y	Y	Y	Y	N	Y	Y
6 ***Petri***	Y	N	Y	Y	Y	Y	Y
7 Obey	Y	Y	N	Y	N	Y	Y
8 Johnson	Y	Y	Y	Y	N	Y	Y
9 ***Sensenbrenner***	Y	N	Y	Y	Y	Y	Y
WYOMING							
AL ***Cubin***	Y	Y	Y	Y	Y	Y	Y

Southern states - Ala., Ark., Fla., Ga., Ky., La., Miss., N.C., Okla., S.C., Tenn., Texas, Va.

533. S 1733. Food Stamps Disbursement/Passage. Goodlatte, R-Va., motion to suspend the rules and pass the bill to direct the Social Security Administration to work with state agencies to ensure that food stamps are not issued to deceased individuals. Motion agreed to (thus clearing the bill for the president) 386-1: R 200-1; D 185-0 (ND 136-0, SD 49-0); I 1-0. Oct. 15, 1998. A two-thirds majority of those present and voting (258 in this case) is required for passage under suspension of the rules.

534. S 2133. Route 66 Designation/Passage. Hansen, R-Utah, motion to suspend the rules and pass the bill to designate Route 66 (approximately 2,200 miles of highway from Chicago to Santa Monica, Calif.) as "America's Main Street." Motion rejected 201-190: R 193-12; D 8-177 (ND 5-131, SD 3-46); I 0-1. Oct. 15, 1998. A two-thirds majority of those present and voting (261 in this case) is required for passage under suspension of the rules.

535. S 1132. Bandelier National Monument Expansion/Passage. Hansen, R-Utah, motion to suspend the rules and pass the bill to allow the National Park Service to extend the boundaries of Bandelier National Monument in New Mexico. Motion rejected 194-190: R 191-10; D 3-179 (ND 3-133, SD 0-46); I 0-1. Oct. 15, 1998. A two-thirds majority of those present and voting (256 in this case) is required for passage under suspension of the rules.

536. HR 4328. Fiscal 1999 Omnibus Appropriations/Rule. Adoption of the rule (H Res 605) to provide for House floor consideration of the conference report on the bill to provide almost $500 billion in new budget authority for those Cabinet departments and federal agencies whose fiscal 1999 appropriations bills were never enacted, and an additional $20.8 billion in "emergency" supplemental spending. Adopted 333-88: R 217-7; D 116-80 (ND 82-59, SD 34-21); I 0-1. Oct. 20, 1998.

537. H Res 604. Bandelier National Monument; S2133 Route 66 Designation/Rule. Adoption of the rule (H Res 604) to provide for House floor consideration of S1132 to allow the National Park Service to extend the boundaries of the Bandelier National Monument in New Mexico, and S2133 to designate Route 66 (approximately 2,200 miles of highway from Chicago to Santa Monica, Calif.) as "America's Main Street." Adopted 229-189: R 224-0; D 5-188 (ND 5-134, SD 0-54); I 0-1. Oct. 20, 1998.

538. HR 4328. Fiscal 1999 Omnibus Appropriations/Conference Report. Adoption of the conference report on the bill to provide almost $500 billion in new budget authority for those Cabinet departments and federal agencies whose fiscal 1999 appropriations bills were never enacted. The measure incorporates eight previously separate appropriations bills: Labor-HHS-Education, Interior, Treasury-Postal, Foreign Operations, Commerce-Justice-State, District of Columbia, Agriculture and Transportation. In addition, the bill provides $20.8 billion in "emergency" supplemental spending, including $6.8 billion for military spending ($1.9 billion of it for Bosnia operations), $5.9 billion for relief to farmers, $2.4 billion for anti-terrorism programs, $3.35 billion to address Year 2000 computer problems and $1.55 billion for disaster relief from Hurricane Georges. The measure also contains language to extend expiring tax provisions (at a cost of $9.7 billion over nine years), increase the number of H-1B visas for high-tech foreign workers, impose a three-year moratorium on new taxes on Internet access, implement the Chemical Weapons Convention and extend for six months Chapter 12 of the bankruptcy code, which is designed to help struggling farmers. Adopted 333-95: R 162-64; D 170-31 (ND 120-26, SD 50-5); I 1-0. Oct. 20, 1998. (HR 4328 was originally the fiscal 1999 Transportation Appropriations bill.) A "yea" vote was a vote in support of the president's position.

Key

Y	Voted for (yea).	
#	Paired for.	
+	Announced for.	
N	Voted against (nay).	
X	Paired against.	
−	Announced against.	
P	Voted "present."	
C	Voted "present" to avoid possible conflict of interest.	
?	Did not vote or otherwise make a position known.	

Democrats   **Republicans**
Independent

	533	534	535	536	537	538
ALABAMA						
1 *Callahan*	?	?	?	Y	Y	Y
2 *Everett*	Y	Y	Y	Y	Y	Y
3 *Riley*	Y	Y	Y	Y	Y	Y
4 *Aderholt*	Y	Y	Y	Y	Y	Y
5 Cramer	Y	N	N	Y	N	Y
6 *Bachus*	Y	Y	Y	Y	Y	N
7 Hilliard	Y	N	N	N	N	Y
ALASKA						
AL *Young*	Y	Y	Y	Y	Y	Y
ARIZONA						
1 *Salmon*	Y	Y	Y	N	Y	N
2 Pastor	Y	N	N	Y	N	Y
3 *Stump*	Y	Y	Y	Y	Y	Y
4 *Shadegg*	Y	Y	Y	Y	Y	Y
5 *Kolbe*	Y	Y	Y	Y	Y	Y
6 *Hayworth*	Y	Y	Y	Y	Y	Y
ARKANSAS						
1 Berry	Y	N	N	Y	N	Y
2 Snyder	Y	N	N	Y	N	Y
3 *Hutchinson*	?	?	?	Y	Y	Y
4 *Dickey*	Y	Y	Y	Y	Y	Y
CALIFORNIA						
1 *Riggs*	Y	Y	Y	Y	Y	N
2 *Herger*	Y	Y	Y	Y	Y	Y
3 Fazio	Y	N	N	?	?	?
4 *Doolittle*	Y	Y	Y	Y	Y	Y
5 Matsui	Y	N	N	Y	N	Y
6 Woolsey	Y	N	N	N	N	Y
7 Miller	Y	N	N	N	N	Y
8 Pelosi	?	?	?	Y	N	Y
9 Lee	Y	N	N	N	N	N
10 Tauscher	Y	N	N	?	?	Y
11 *Pombo*	Y	Y	Y	Y	Y	Y
12 Lantos	?	?	?	Y	Y	Y
13 Stark	Y	N	N	?	?	?
14 Eshoo	Y	N	N	Y	N	Y
15 *Campbell*	Y	N	Y	Y	N	Y
16 Lofgren	Y	N	N	N	N	Y
17 Farr	Y	N	N	N	N	Y
18 Condit	Y	N	N	N	N	Y
19 *Radanovich*	Y	Y	Y	Y	Y	Y
20 Dooley	Y	N	N	N	N	Y
21 *Thomas*	Y	Y	Y	Y	Y	Y
22 Capps, L.	Y	N	N	Y	N	Y
23 *Gallegly*	Y	Y	Y	Y	Y	Y
24 Sherman	Y	N	N	N	N	Y
25 *McKeon*	Y	Y	Y	Y	Y	Y
26 Berman	?	?	?	Y	Y	Y
27 *Rogan*	Y	Y	Y	Y	Y	Y
28 *Dreier*	Y	Y	Y	Y	Y	Y
29 Waxman	Y	N	N	Y	N	Y
30 Becerra	Y	N	N	?	?	Y
31 Martinez	Y	N	N	N	N	Y
32 Dixon	Y	N	N	N	N	Y
33 Roybal-Allard	Y	N	N	Y	N	Y
34 Torres	?	?	?	Y	N	Y
35 Waters	?	?	?	Y	N	Y
36 Harman	Y	N	N	Y	N	Y
37 Millender-McD.	Y	N	N	Y	N	Y
38 *Horn*	Y	Y	Y	Y	Y	Y

	533	534	535	536	537	538
39 *Royce*	Y	Y	Y	Y	Y	N
40 *Lewis*	?	Y	Y	Y	Y	Y
41 *Kim*	Y	Y	Y	Y	Y	Y
42 Brown	Y	N	N	N	N	Y
43 *Calvert*	Y	Y	Y	Y	Y	Y
44 *Bono, M.*	Y	Y	Y	Y	Y	Y
45 *Rohrabacher*	Y	Y	Y	Y	Y	Y
46 Sanchez	Y	N	N	N	N	Y
47 *Cox*	Y	Y	Y	Y	Y	Y
48 *Packard*	Y	Y	Y	Y	Y	Y
49 *Bilbray*	Y	Y	Y	Y	Y	N
50 Filner	Y	N	N	N	N	N
51 *Cunningham*	Y	Y	Y	Y	Y	Y
52 *Hunter*	Y	Y	Y	Y	Y	Y
COLORADO						
1 DeGette	Y	N	N	N	N	N
2 Skaggs	Y	N	N	N	N	N
3 *McInnis*	?	Y	Y	Y	Y	Y
4 *Schaffer*	Y	N	N	Y	N	N
5 *Hefley*	Y	Y	Y	Y	Y	N
6 *Schaefer*	Y	Y	Y	Y	Y	Y
CONNECTICUT						
1 Kennelly	?	?	?	Y	N	Y
2 Gejdenson	Y	N	N	Y	N	Y
3 DeLauro	Y	N	N	Y	N	Y
4 *Shays*	Y	N	Y	N	N	Y
5 Maloney	Y	N	N	Y	N	Y
6 *Johnson*	Y	Y	Y	Y	Y	Y
DELAWARE						
AL *Castle*	Y	Y	Y	Y	Y	N
FLORIDA						
1 *Scarborough*	?	?	?	N	Y	N
2 Boyd	Y	N	N	N	N	N
3 Brown	Y	N	?	Y	N	Y
4 *Fowler*	?	?	?	Y	Y	Y
5 Thurman	Y	N	N	N	N	N
6 *Stearns*	Y	Y	Y	Y	N	N
7 *Mica*	Y	Y	?	Y	Y	Y
8 *McCollum*	Y	Y	?	Y	Y	Y
9 *Bilirakis*	Y	Y	Y	Y	Y	Y
10 *Young*	Y	Y	Y	Y	Y	Y
11 Davis	Y	N	N	N	N	Y
12 *Canady*	Y	Y	Y	Y	Y	Y
13 *Miller*	Y	N	Y	Y	N	N
14 *Goss*	Y	Y	Y	Y	Y	Y
15 *Weldon*	?	?	?	Y	Y	N
16 *Foley*	Y	Y	Y	Y	Y	Y
17 Meek	Y	N	N	Y	N	Y
18 *Ros-Lehtinen*	Y	Y	Y	Y	Y	Y
19 Wexler	Y	N	N	N	N	Y
20 Deutsch	Y	N	N	N	N	Y
21 *Diaz-Balart*	Y	Y	Y	Y	Y	Y
22 *Shaw*	Y	Y	Y	Y	Y	Y
23 Hastings	Y	N	N	N	N	Y
GEORGIA						
1 *Kingston*	Y	Y	Y	Y	Y	Y
2 Bishop	Y	N	N	Y	N	Y
3 *Collins*	?	?	?	Y	Y	N
4 McKinney	Y	N	N	N	N	Y
5 Lewis	Y	N	N	Y	N	Y
6 *Gingrich*						Y
7 *Barr*	?	?	?	Y	Y	N
8 *Chambliss*	Y	Y	Y	Y	Y	Y
9 *Deal*	?	?	?	Y	Y	N
10 *Norwood*	Y	?	?	Y	Y	Y
11 *Linder*	Y	Y	Y	Y	Y	Y
HAWAII						
1 Abercrombie	Y	N	N	Y	N	Y
2 Mink	Y	N	N	Y	N	Y
IDAHO						
1 *Chenoweth*	Y	Y	Y	Y	Y	Y
2 *Crapo*	Y	Y	Y	Y	Y	Y
ILLINOIS						
1 Rush	Y	N	N	N	N	Y
2 Jackson	Y	N	N	N	N	Y
3 Lipinski	?	?	?	N	N	Y
4 Gutierrez	Y	N	N	N	N	Y
5 Blagojevich	Y	N	N	Y	N	Y
6 *Hyde*	?	?	?	Y	Y	Y
7 Davis	Y	N	N	N	N	Y
8 *Crane*	Y	Y	Y	Y	N	N
9 Yates	Y	N	N	N	N	N
10 *Porter*	Y	Y	Y	Y	Y	Y
11 *Weller*	Y	Y	Y	Y	Y	Y
12 Costello	Y	N	N	N	N	N
13 *Fawell*	?	?	Y	Y	N	Y

ND Northern Democrats   SD Southern Democrats

	533	534	535	536	537	538
14 ***Hastert***	Y	Y	Y	Y	Y	Y
15 ***Ewing***	Y	Y	Y	Y	Y	Y
16 ***Manzullo***	Y	Y	Y	Y	Y	N
17 Evans	Y	N	N	Y	N	Y
18 ***LaHood***	Y	Y	Y	Y	Y	N
19 Poshard	?	?	?	?	?	?
20 ***Shimkus***	Y	Y	Y	Y	Y	Y
INDIANA						
1 Visclosky	Y	N	N	Y	N	Y
2 ***McIntosh***	?	?	?	Y	Y	N
3 Roemer	Y	N	N	Y	N	Y
4 ***Souder***	Y	Y	Y	Y	Y	Y
5 ***Buyer***	Y	Y	Y	Y	Y	Y
6 ***Burton***	Y	Y	Y	Y	Y	Y
7 ***Pease***	Y	Y	Y	Y	Y	Y
8 ***Hostettler***	Y	Y	Y	Y	Y	N
9 Hamilton	Y	N	N	Y	N	Y
10 Carson	Y	N	N	N	N	Y
IOWA						
1 ***Leach***	Y	Y	Y	Y	Y	Y
2 ***Nussle***	Y	Y	Y	Y	Y	Y
3 Boswell	Y	Y	Y	Y	Y	Y
4 ***Ganske***	Y	N	Y	Y	Y	Y
5 ***Latham***	Y	Y	Y	Y	Y	Y
KANSAS						
1 ***Moran***	Y	Y	Y	Y	Y	Y
2 ***Ryun***	Y	Y	Y	Y	Y	Y
3 ***Snowbarger***	Y	Y	Y	Y	Y	Y
4 ***Tiahrt***	Y	Y	Y	N	Y	Y
KENTUCKY						
1 ***Whitfield***	Y	Y	Y	Y	Y	Y
2 ***Lewis***	Y	Y	Y	Y	Y	Y
3 ***Northup***	Y	Y	+	Y	?	Y
4 ***Bunning***	Y	Y	Y	Y	Y	Y
5 ***Rogers***	Y	Y	Y	Y	Y	Y
6 Baesler	Y	Y	N	Y	N	Y
LOUISIANA						
1 ***Livingston***	Y	Y	Y	Y	Y	Y
2 Jefferson	Y	N	N	Y	N	Y
3 ***Tauzin***	Y	Y	Y	Y	Y	Y
4 ***McCrery***	Y	Y	Y	Y	Y	Y
5 ***Cooksey***	?	?	?	Y	Y	Y
6 ***Baker***	Y	Y	Y	Y	Y	Y
7 John	Y	N	N	Y	N	Y
MAINE						
1 Allen	?	?	?	N	N	Y
2 Baldacci	Y	N	N	Y	N	Y
MARYLAND						
1 ***Gilchrest***	Y	Y	Y	Y	Y	Y
2 ***Ehrlich***	Y	Y	Y	Y	Y	Y
3 Cardin	Y	N	N	N	N	N
4 Wynn	Y	N	N	Y	N	Y
5 Hoyer	Y	N	N	N	N	Y
6 ***Bartlett***	Y	Y	Y	Y	Y	N
7 Cummings	Y	N	N	Y	N	Y
8 ***Morella***	Y	Y	Y	Y	Y	Y
MASSACHUSETTS						
1 Olver	Y	N	N	N	N	Y
2 Neal	Y	N	N	N	N	Y
3 McGovern	?	?	?	Y	N	Y
4 Frank	?	?	?	N	N	Y
5 Meehan	?	?	?	?	?	?
6 Tierney	Y	N	N	Y	N	Y
7 Markey	Y	N	N	Y	N	Y
8 Kennedy	Y	N	N	Y	N	Y
9 Moakley	Y	N	N	Y	N	Y
10 Delahunt	Y	N	N	Y	N	Y
MICHIGAN						
1 Stupak	Y	N	N	N	N	N
2 ***Hoekstra***	Y	Y	Y	Y	Y	N
3 ***Ehlers***	?	?	?	Y	Y	N
4 ***Camp***	Y	Y	Y	Y	Y	Y
5 Barcia	Y	N	Y	Y	Y	Y
6 ***Upton***	Y	Y	Y	Y	Y	N
7 ***Smith***	Y	Y	Y	Y	Y	N
8 Stabenow	Y	N	N	Y	N	Y
9 Kildee	Y	N	N	N	N	Y
10 Bonior	Y	N	N	N	N	Y
11 ***Knollenberg***	Y	Y	Y	Y	Y	Y
12 Levin	Y	N	N	Y	N	Y
13 Rivers	Y	N	N	N	N	N
14 Conyers	Y	N	N	N	N	Y
15 Kilpatrick	Y	N	N	Y	N	Y
16 Dingell	Y	N	N	Y	N	Y
MINNESOTA						
1 ***Gutknecht***	Y	Y	Y	Y	Y	Y
2 Minge	Y	N	N	N	N	N
3 ***Ramstad***	Y	Y	Y	Y	Y	Y
4 Vento	Y	N	N	N	N	Y
5 Sabo	Y	N	N	Y	N	Y
6 Luther	Y	N	N	N	N	N
7 Peterson	Y	N	N	N	N	N
8 Oberstar	Y	N	N	?	N	Y
MISSISSIPPI						
1 ***Wicker***	Y	Y	Y	Y	Y	Y
2 Thompson	?	?	?	N	N	Y
3 ***Pickering***	Y	Y	Y	Y	Y	Y
4 ***Parker***	Y	Y	Y	Y	Y	Y
5 Taylor	Y	N	N	N	N	N
MISSOURI						
1 Clay	Y	N	N	Y	N	Y
2 ***Talent***	Y	Y	Y	Y	Y	Y
3 Gephardt	Y	N	N	Y	N	Y
4 Skelton	Y	N	N	Y	Y	Y
5 McCarthy	Y	N	N	N	N	Y
6 Danner	Y	Y	N	Y	N	Y
7 ***Blunt***	?	?	?	Y	Y	Y
8 ***Emerson***	Y	Y	Y	Y	Y	Y
9 ***Hulshof***	Y	Y	Y	Y	Y	Y
MONTANA						
AL ***Hill***	Y	Y	Y	Y	Y	Y
NEBRASKA						
1 ***Bereuter***	Y	Y	Y	Y	Y	Y
2 ***Christensen***	Y	Y	Y	N	Y	N
3 ***Barrett***	Y	Y	Y	Y	Y	Y
NEVADA						
1 ***Ensign***	Y	Y	Y	N	Y	N
2 ***Gibbons***	Y	Y	Y	Y	Y	Y
NEW HAMPSHIRE						
1 ***Sununu***	Y	Y	Y	Y	Y	Y
2 ***Bass***	Y	Y	Y	Y	Y	Y
NEW JERSEY						
1 Andrews	Y	N	N	N	N	Y
2 ***LoBiondo***	Y	Y	Y	Y	Y	Y
3 ***Saxton***	Y	Y	Y	Y	Y	Y
4 ***Smith***	Y	Y	Y	?	Y	N
5 ***Roukema***	Y	Y	Y	Y	Y	N
6 Pallone	Y	N	N	Y	N	Y
7 ***Franks***	Y	N	Y	Y	Y	Y
8 Pascrell	Y	N	N	Y	N	Y
9 Rothman	Y	N	N	Y	N	Y
10 Payne	Y	N	N	N	N	Y
11 ***Frelinghuysen***	Y	N	Y	Y	Y	N
12 ***Pappas***	Y	Y	Y	Y	Y	N
13 Menendez	Y	N	N	N	N	Y
NEW MEXICO						
1 ***Wilson***	+	Y	Y	Y	Y	Y
2 ***Skeen***	Y	Y	Y	Y	Y	Y
3 ***Redmond***	Y	Y	Y	Y	Y	Y
NEW YORK						
1 ***Forbes***	Y	Y	Y	Y	Y	Y
2 ***Lazio***	Y	Y	Y	Y	Y	Y
3 ***King***	Y	Y	Y	Y	Y	N
4 McCarthy	Y	N	N	Y	N	Y
5 Ackerman	?	?	?	Y	N	Y
6 Meeks	Y	N	N	Y	N	Y
7 Manton	Y	N	N	Y	N	Y
8 Nadler	Y	N	N	N	N	Y
9 Schumer	Y	N	N	Y	N	Y
10 Towns	Y	N	N	N	N	Y
11 Owens	Y	N	N	N	N	Y
12 Velázquez	Y	N	N	Y	?	Y
13 ***Fossella***	Y	Y	Y	Y	Y	Y
14 Maloney	Y	N	N	Y	N	Y
15 Rangel	Y	N	N	Y	N	Y
16 Serrano	Y	N	N	Y	N	Y
17 Engel	Y	N	N	Y	N	Y
18 Lowey	Y	N	N	Y	N	Y
19 ***Kelly***	Y	Y	Y	Y	Y	Y
20 ***Gilman***	Y	Y	Y	Y	Y	Y
21 McNulty	Y	N	N	Y	N	Y
22 ***Solomon***	Y	Y	Y	Y	Y	Y
23 ***Boehlert***	Y	Y	Y	Y	Y	Y
24 ***McHugh***	Y	Y	Y	Y	Y	Y
25 ***Walsh***	Y	Y	Y	Y	Y	Y
26 Hinchey	Y	N	N	Y	N	Y
27 ***Paxon***	Y	Y	Y	Y	Y	Y
28 Slaughter	Y	N	N	Y	?	Y
29 LaFalce	Y	N	N	N	N	Y
30 ***Quinn***	Y	Y	Y	Y	Y	Y
31 ***Houghton***	Y	Y	Y	Y	Y	Y
NORTH CAROLINA						
1 Clayton	Y	N	N	N	?	Y
2 Etheridge	Y	N	N	N	N	Y
3 ***Jones***	Y	Y	N	Y	Y	N
4 Price	Y	N	N	Y	N	Y
5 ***Burr***	Y	Y	Y	Y	Y	N
6 ***Coble***	Y	Y	N	Y	Y	N
7 McIntyre	?	?	?	Y	N	Y
8 Hefner	?	?	?	Y	N	Y
9 ***Myrick***	Y	Y	N	Y	Y	Y
10 ***Ballenger***	Y	Y	Y	Y	Y	N
11 ***Taylor***	?	Y	Y	Y	Y	Y
12 Watt	Y	N	N	N	N	Y
NORTH DAKOTA						
AL Pomeroy	Y	N	N	Y	N	Y
OHIO						
1 ***Chabot***	Y	N	N	Y	Y	N
2 ***Portman***	Y	Y	Y	Y	Y	N
3 Hall	Y	N	N	Y	N	Y
4 ***Oxley***	Y	Y	Y	Y	Y	Y
5 ***Gillmor***	Y	Y	Y	Y	Y	Y
6 Strickland	Y	N	N	Y	N	Y
7 ***Hobson***	Y	Y	?	Y	Y	Y
8 ***Boehner***	Y	Y	Y	Y	Y	Y
9 Kaptur	?	?	?	Y	N	N
10 Kucinich	Y	N	N	Y	N	Y
11 Stokes	Y	N	N	Y	N	Y
12 ***Kasich***	Y	Y	Y	Y	Y	Y
13 Brown	Y	N	N	Y	?	Y
14 Sawyer	Y	N	N	Y	N	Y
15 ***Pryce***	+	+	+	+	+	+
16 ***Regula***	Y	Y	Y	Y	Y	Y
17 Traficant	Y	Y	Y	Y	Y	Y
18 ***Ney***	Y	Y	Y	Y	Y	Y
19 ***LaTourette***	Y	Y	Y	Y	Y	Y
OKLAHOMA						
1 ***Largent***	?	?	?	Y	Y	N
2 ***Coburn***	Y	Y	Y	Y	Y	N
3 ***Watkins***	Y	Y	Y	Y	Y	Y
4 ***Watts***	Y	Y	Y	Y	Y	Y
5 ***Istook***	Y	Y	Y	Y	Y	N
6 ***Lucas***	Y	Y	Y	Y	Y	Y
OREGON						
1 Furse	?	?	?	N	N	Y
2 ***Smith***	Y	Y	Y	Y	Y	Y
3 Blumenauer	Y	N	N	Y	N	N
4 DeFazio	Y	N	N	N	N	N
5 Hooley	Y	N	N	Y	N	Y
PENNSYLVANIA						
1 Brady	Y	N	N	Y	N	Y
2 Fattah	Y	N	N	Y	N	Y
3 Borski	Y	N	N	N	N	Y
4 Klink	Y	N	N	N	N	N
5 ***Peterson***	Y	Y	Y	Y	Y	Y
6 Holden	Y	N	N	N	N	N
7 ***Weldon***	?	?	?	N	Y	N
8 ***Greenwood***	?	?	?	Y	Y	Y
9 ***Shuster***	Y	Y	Y	Y	Y	Y
10 ***McDade***	?	?	Y	Y	Y	Y
11 Kanjorski	Y	N	N	N	N	N
12 Murtha	Y	N	N	Y	N	Y
13 ***Fox***	Y	Y	Y	Y	Y	Y
14 Coyne	Y	N	N	N	N	Y
15 McHale	Y	N	N	N	N	Y
16 ***Pitts***	Y	Y	Y	Y	Y	Y
17 ***Gekas***	Y	Y	Y	Y	Y	Y
18 Doyle	Y	N	N	Y	N	Y
19 ***Goodling***	Y	Y	Y	Y	Y	Y
20 Mascara	Y	N	N	Y	N	Y
21 ***English***	Y	Y	Y	Y	Y	Y
RHODE ISLAND						
1 Kennedy	Y	N	N	?	?	Y
2 Weygand	Y	N	N	?	?	Y
SOUTH CAROLINA						
1 ***Sanford***	Y	N	N	Y	Y	N
2 ***Spence***	Y	Y	Y	Y	Y	Y
3 ***Graham***	?	?	?	Y	Y	N
4 ***Inglis***	?	?	?	Y	Y	N
5 Spratt	Y	N	?	Y	N	Y
6 Clyburn	Y	N	N	N	N	Y
SOUTH DAKOTA						
AL ***Thune***	Y	Y	Y	Y	Y	Y
TENNESSEE						
1 ***Jenkins***	Y	Y	Y	Y	Y	Y
2 ***Duncan***	Y	Y	Y	Y	Y	N
3 ***Wamp***	Y	Y	Y	Y	Y	N
4 ***Hilleary***	Y	Y	Y	Y	Y	Y
5 Clement	Y	N	N	Y	N	Y
6 Gordon	Y	N	N	N	N	Y
7 ***Bryant***	Y	Y	Y	Y	Y	Y
8 Tanner	Y	N	N	Y	N	Y
9 Ford	Y	N	N	N	N	Y
TEXAS						
1 Sandlin	Y	N	N	Y	N	Y
2 Turner	Y	N	N	Y	N	Y
3 ***Johnson, Sam***	Y	Y	Y	Y	Y	N
4 Hall	Y	Y	N	Y	N	Y
5 ***Sessions***	Y	Y	Y	Y	Y	Y
6 ***Barton***	Y	Y	Y	Y	Y	N
7 ***Archer***	Y	Y	Y	Y	Y	Y
8 ***Brady***	Y	Y	Y	Y	Y	N
9 Lampson	Y	N	N	Y	N	Y
10 Doggett	Y	N	N	N	N	N
11 Edwards	Y	N	?	N	N	Y
12 ***Granger***	Y	Y	Y	Y	Y	Y
13 ***Thornberry***	Y	Y	Y	Y	Y	Y
14 ***Paul***	N	N	N	Y	Y	N
15 Hinojosa	Y	N	N	Y	N	Y
16 Reyes	Y	N	N	Y	N	Y
17 Stenholm	Y	N	N	Y	N	Y
18 Jackson-Lee	Y	Y	N	N	N	Y
19 ***Combest***	Y	Y	Y	Y	Y	Y
20 Gonzalez	Y	N	N	Y	N	Y
21 ***Smith***	Y	Y	Y	Y	Y	Y
22 ***DeLay***	Y	Y	Y	Y	Y	Y
23 ***Bonilla***	Y	Y	Y	Y	Y	Y
24 Frost	?	?	?	Y	N	Y
25 Bentsen	Y	N	N	N	N	Y
26 ***Armey***	Y	Y	Y	Y	Y	Y
27 Ortiz	Y	N	N	Y	N	Y
28 Rodriguez	Y	N	N	Y	N	Y
29 Green	+	–	–	N	N	Y
30 Johnson, E.B.	+	+	+	N	N	Y
UTAH						
1 ***Hansen***	Y	Y	Y	?	?	?
2 ***Cook***	Y	Y	Y	Y	Y	Y
3 ***Cannon***	Y	Y	Y	Y	Y	Y
VERMONT						
AL *Sanders*	Y	N	N	N	N	Y
VIRGINIA						
1 ***Bateman***	Y	Y	Y	Y	Y	Y
2 Pickett	Y	N	N	Y	N	Y
3 Scott	Y	N	N	Y	N	Y
4 Sisisky	Y	N	N	Y	N	Y
5 Goode	Y	N	N	Y	N	N
6 ***Goodlatte***	Y	Y	N	Y	Y	Y
7 ***Bliley***	Y	Y	Y	Y	Y	Y
8 Moran	Y	N	N	Y	N	Y
9 Boucher	Y	N	N	Y	N	Y
10 ***Wolf***	Y	Y	Y	Y	Y	N
11 ***Davis***	Y	Y	Y	Y	Y	Y
WASHINGTON						
1 ***White***	Y	Y	Y	Y	Y	N
2 ***Metcalf***	Y	Y	Y	Y	Y	Y
3 ***Smith, Linda***	Y	Y	Y	Y	Y	N
4 ***Hastings***	?	?	?	Y	Y	Y
5 ***Nethercutt***	Y	Y	Y	Y	Y	Y
6 Dicks	Y	N	N	Y	N	Y
7 McDermott	Y	N	N	N	N	N
8 ***Dunn***	Y	Y	Y	Y	Y	Y
9 Smith, Adam	Y	N	N	Y	N	N
WEST VIRGINIA						
1 Mollohan	Y	N	N	?	?	?
2 Wise	Y	N	N	Y	N	Y
3 Rahall	Y	N	N	N	N	Y
WISCONSIN						
1 ***Neumann***	Y	N	Y	Y	Y	N
2 ***Klug***	Y	Y	Y	Y	Y	N
3 Kind	Y	N	N	N	N	N
4 Kleczka	Y	N	N	N	N	N
5 Barrett	Y	N	N	N	N	N
6 ***Petri***	Y	Y	Y	Y	Y	N
7 Obey	Y	N	N	Y	N	Y
8 Johnson	Y	N	N	Y	N	N
9 ***Sensenbrenner***	Y	N	N	Y	Y	N
WYOMING						
AL ***Cubin***	Y	Y	Y	Y	Y	Y

Southern states - Ala., Ark., Fla., Ga., Ky., La., Miss., N.C., Okla., S.C., Tenn., Texas, Va.

Key

Y	Voted for (yea).
#	Paired for.
+	Announced for.
N	Voted against (nay).
X	Paired against.
−	Announced against.
P	Voted "present."
C	Voted "present" to avoid possible conflict of interest.
?	Did not vote or otherwise make a position known.

Democrats **Republicans**
Independent

539. Support U.S. Troops/Adoption. Adoption of the resolution to express congressional support for the troops in and around the Persian Gulf region and to reaffirm that it should be the policy of the United States to support efforts to remove Saddam Hussein's regime from power in Iraq and promote a democratic government to replace that regime. Adopted 417-5: R 221-2; D 195-3 (ND 142-2, SD 53-1); I 1-0. Dec. 17, 1998.

540. Procedural Motion/Adjourn. Bonior, D-Mich., motion to adjourn. Motion rejected 183-225: R 0-220; D 182-5 (ND 134-2, SD 48-3); I 1-0. Dec. 18, 1998.

541. Procedural Motion/Journal. Approval of the House Journal of Friday, Dec. 18, 1998. Approved 277-125: R 202-4; D 74-121 (ND 51-90, SD 23-31); I 1-0. Dec. 19, 1998.

542. H Res 611. Impeachment of President Clinton/Censure — Appeal Ruling of Chair. Armey, R-Texas, motion to table (kill) the Gephardt, D-Mo., appeal of the ruling of the chair that the Boucher, D-Va., motion to recommit with instructions was not germane. The Boucher motion would instruct the Judiciary Committee to report the resolution back to the House with an amendment to express the sense of the House that President Clinton "fully deserves" the "censure and condemnation" of the American people and the House because of his conduct. Motion agreed to 230-204: R 226-2; D 4-201 (ND 0-150, SD 4-51); I 0-1. Dec. 19, 1998. A "nay" was a vote in support of the president's position.

543. H Res 611. Impeachment of President Clinton/Article I — Grand Jury Perjury. Adoption of Article I of the resolution, which would impeach President Clinton for "perjurious, false and misleading testimony" during his Aug. 17, 1998, federal grand jury testimony about his relationship with former White House intern Monica Lewinsky, his prior testimony in the Paula Jones sexual harassment lawsuit and his attempts to influence others' testimony in both. Adopted 228-206: R 223-5; D 5-200 (ND 1-149, SD 4-51); I 0-1. Dec. 19, 1998. A "nay" was a vote in support of the president's position.

544. H Res 611. Impeachment of President Clinton/Article II — Civil Suit Perjury. Adoption of Article II of the resolution, which would impeach President Clinton for "perjurious, false and misleading testimony" in his Dec. 23, 1997, written answers and his Jan. 17, 1998, testimony in the Paula Jones federal sexual harassment civil lawsuit about his relationship with former White House intern Monica Lewinsky. Rejected 205-229: R 200-28; D 5-200 (ND 1-149, SD 4-51); I 0-1. Dec. 19, 1998. A "nay" was a vote in support of the president's position.

	539	540	541	542	543	544
ALABAMA						
1 *Callahan*	Y	N	Y	Y	Y	Y
2 *Everett*	Y	N	Y	Y	Y	Y
3 *Riley*	Y	N	Y	Y	Y	Y
4 *Aderholt*	Y	N	Y	Y	Y	Y
5 Cramer	Y	Y	N	N	N	N
6 *Bachus*	Y	N	Y	Y	Y	Y
7 Hilliard	Y	Y	N	N	N	N
ALASKA						
AL *Young*	Y	?	Y	Y	Y	Y
ARIZONA						
1 *Salmon*	Y	N	Y	Y	Y	Y
2 Pastor	Y	Y	?	N	N	N
3 *Stump*	Y	N	Y	Y	Y	Y
4 *Shadegg*	Y	N	Y	Y	Y	Y
5 *Kolbe*	Y	N	Y	Y	Y	Y
6 *Hayworth*	Y	N	Y	Y	Y	Y
ARKANSAS						
1 Berry	Y	Y	N	N	N	N
2 Snyder	Y	Y	N	N	N	N
3 *Hutchinson*	Y	N	Y	Y	Y	Y
4 *Dickey*	Y	N	N	Y	Y	N
CALIFORNIA						
1 *Riggs*	Y	N	?	Y	Y	Y
2 *Herger*	Y	N	Y	Y	Y	Y
3 Fazio	Y	Y	N	N	N	N
4 *Doolittle*	?	N	Y	Y	Y	Y
5 Matsul	Y	Y	N	N	N	N
6 Woolsey	Y	Y	N	N	N	N
7 Miller	?	?	?	?	?	?
8 Pelosi	Y	Y	?	N	N	N
9 Lee	N	Y	N	N	N	N
10 Tauscher	Y	Y	N	N	N	N
11 *Pombo*	Y	N	Y	Y	Y	Y
12 Lantos	Y	Y	N	N	N	N
13 Stark	Y	Y	N	N	N	N
14 Eshoo	Y	Y	N	N	N	N
15 *Campbell*	Y	N	Y	Y	Y	Y
16 Lofgren	Y	Y	N	N	N	N
17 Farr	Y	Y	N	N	N	N
18 Condit	Y	Y	N	N	N	N
19 *Radanovich*	Y	N	Y	Y	Y	Y
20 Dooley	Y	Y	N	N	N	N
21 *Thomas*	Y	N	Y	Y	Y	Y
22 Capps, L.	Y	Y	N	N	N	N
23 *Gallegly*	?	N	Y	Y	Y	Y
24 Sherman	Y	Y	N	N	N	N
25 *McKeon*	Y	N	Y	Y	Y	Y
26 Berman	Y	Y	N	N	N	N
27 *Rogan*	Y	N	Y	Y	Y	Y
28 *Dreier*	Y	N	Y	Y	Y	Y
29 Waxman	Y	Y	N	N	N	N
30 Becerra	Y	?	N	N	N	N
31 Martinez	Y	?	N	N	N	N
32 Dixon	Y	Y	N	N	N	N
33 Roybal-Allard	Y	?	N	N	N	N
34 Torres	Y	?	Y	N	N	N
35 Waters	Y	Y	?	N	N	N
36 Harman	Y	Y	N	N	N	N
37 Millender-McD.	Y	Y	N	N	N	N
38 *Horn*	Y	N	Y	Y	Y	Y

	539	540	541	542	543	544
39 *Royce*	Y	N	Y	Y	Y	Y
40 *Lewis*	Y	N	Y	Y	Y	Y
41 *Kim*	Y	N	Y	Y	Y	N
42 Brown	Y	Y	N	N	N	N
43 *Calvert*	Y	N	Y	Y	Y	Y
44 *Bono, M.*	Y	N	Y	Y	Y	Y
45 *Rohrabacher*	Y	N	Y	Y	Y	Y
46 Sanchez	+	Y	N	N	N	N
47 *Cox*	Y	N	Y	Y	Y	Y
48 *Packard*	Y	N	Y	Y	Y	Y
49 *Bilbray*	Y	N	Y	Y	Y	Y
50 Filner	Y	Y	N	N	N	N
51 *Cunningham*	Y	N	Y	Y	Y	Y
52 *Hunter*	Y	N	Y	Y	Y	Y
COLORADO						
1 DeGette	?	Y	N	N	N	N
2 Skaggs	Y	Y	N	N	N	N
3 *McInnis*	Y	N	Y	Y	Y	Y
4 *Schaffer*	Y	N	Y	Y	Y	Y
5 *Hefley*	Y	N	Y	Y	Y	Y
6 *Schaefer*	Y	?	Y	Y	Y	Y
CONNECTICUT						
1 Kennelly	Y	Y	N	N	N	N
2 Gejdenson	Y	Y	N	N	N	N
3 DeLauro	Y	Y	N	N	N	N
4 *Shays*	Y	N	Y	N	N	N
5 Maloney	Y	Y	Y	Y	N	N
6 *Johnson*	Y	N	Y	Y	Y	Y
DELAWARE						
AL *Castle*	Y	N	Y	Y	Y	N
FLORIDA						
1 *Scarborough*	?	N	Y	Y	Y	N
2 Boyd	Y	Y	N	N	N	N
3 Brown	Y	?	N	N	N	N
4 *Fowler*	Y	N	Y	Y	Y	Y
5 Thurman	Y	Y	N	N	N	N
6 *Stearns*	Y	N	Y	Y	Y	Y
7 *Mica*	Y	N	Y	Y	Y	Y
8 *McCollum*	Y	N	Y	Y	Y	Y
9 *Bilirakis*	Y	N	Y	Y	Y	Y
10 *Young*	Y	N	?	Y	Y	Y
11 Davis	Y	Y	N	N	N	N
12 *Canady*	Y	N	Y	Y	Y	Y
13 *Miller*	Y	N	Y	Y	Y	Y
14 *Goss*	Y	N	Y	Y	Y	Y
15 *Weldon*	Y	N	Y	Y	Y	Y
16 *Foley*	Y	N	Y	Y	Y	Y
17 Meek	Y	Y	N	N	N	N
18 *Ros-Lehtinen*	Y	N	Y	Y	Y	Y
19 Wexler	Y	Y	N	N	N	N
20 Deutsch	Y	Y	N	N	N	N
21 *Diaz-Balart*	Y	N	Y	Y	Y	Y
22 *Shaw*	Y	N	Y	Y	Y	Y
23 Hastings	Y	Y	N	N	N	N
GEORGIA						
1 *Kingston*	Y	N	Y	Y	Y	Y
2 Bishop	Y	Y	N	N	N	N
3 *Collins*	Y	N	Y	Y	Y	Y
4 McKinney	N	Y	N	N	N	N
5 Lewis	Y	Y	N	N	N	N
6 *Gingrich*	Y					
7 *Barr*	Y	N	Y	Y	Y	Y
8 *Chambliss*	Y	N	Y	Y	Y	Y
9 *Deal*	Y	N	Y	Y	Y	Y
10 *Norwood*	Y	N	Y	Y	Y	Y
11 *Linder*	Y	N	Y	Y	Y	Y
HAWAII						
1 Abercrombie	Y	Y	N	N	N	N
2 Mink	Y	Y	N	N	N	N
IDAHO						
1 *Chenoweth*	Y	N	?	Y	Y	Y
2 *Crapo*	Y	N	Y	Y	Y	Y
ILLINOIS						
1 Rush	?	Y	N	N	N	N
2 Jackson	Y	Y	Y	N	N	N
3 Lipinski	?	Y	N	N	N	N
4 Gutierrez	Y	Y	N	N	N	N
5 Blagojevich	Y	Y	N	N	N	N
6 *Hyde*	Y	N	Y	Y	Y	Y
7 Davis	Y	Y	N	N	N	N
8 *Crane*	Y	?	?	Y	Y	Y
9 Yates	Y	Y	N	N	N	N
10 *Porter*	Y	N	Y	Y	Y	Y
11 *Weller*	Y	N	Y	Y	Y	Y
12 Costello	Y	Y	N	N	N	N
13 *Fawell*	Y	N	Y	Y	Y	Y

ND Northern Democrats   SD Southern Democrats

	539	540	541	542	543	544
14 ***Hastert***	Y	N	Y	Y	Y	Y
15 ***Ewing***	Y	N	Y	Y	Y	Y
16 ***Manzullo***	Y	N	Y	Y	Y	Y
17 Evans	Y	Y	Y	N	N	N
18 ***LaHood***	Y	N	Y	Y	Y	Y
19 Poshard	Y	Y	N	N	N	N
20 ***Shimkus***	Y	N	Y	Y	Y	Y
INDIANA						
1 Visclosky	Y	Y	?	N	N	N
2 ***McIntosh***	Y	N	Y	Y	Y	Y
3 Roemer	Y	Y	Y	N	N	N
4 ***Souder***	Y	N	?	Y	N	N
5 ***Buyer***	Y	N	Y	Y	Y	Y
6 ***Burton***	Y	N	?	Y	Y	Y
7 ***Pease***	Y	N	Y	Y	Y	Y
8 ***Hostettler***	Y	N	Y	Y	Y	Y
9 Hamilton	Y	Y	Y	N	N	N
10 Carson	Y	Y	N	N	N	N
IOWA						
1 ***Leach***	Y	N	Y	Y	Y	Y
2 ***Nussle***	Y	N	Y	Y	Y	Y
3 Boswell	Y	Y	Y	N	N	N
4 ***Ganske***	Y	N	Y	Y	Y	Y
5 ***Latham***	Y	N	Y	Y	Y	Y
KANSAS						
1 ***Moran***	Y	N	Y	Y	Y	Y
2 ***Ryun***	Y	N	Y	Y	Y	Y
3 ***Snowbarger***	+	N	Y	Y	Y	Y
4 ***Tiahrt***	Y	N	Y	Y	Y	Y
KENTUCKY						
1 ***Whitfield***	Y	N	Y	Y	Y	Y
2 ***Lewis***	Y	N	Y	Y	Y	Y
3 ***Northup***	Y	N	Y	Y	Y	Y
4 ***Bunning***	Y	N	Y	Y	Y	Y
5 ***Rogers***	Y	N	Y	Y	Y	Y
6 Baesler	?	Y	N	N	N	N
LOUISIANA						
1 ***Livingston***	Y	N	Y	Y	Y	Y
2 Jefferson	Y	Y	N	N	N	N
3 ***Tauzin***	Y	N	Y	Y	Y	Y
4 ***McCrery***	Y	N	?	Y	Y	Y
5 ***Cooksey***	Y	N	Y	Y	Y	Y
6 ***Baker***	Y	N	Y	Y	Y	Y
7 John	Y	Y	Y	N	N	N
MAINE						
1 Allen	Y	?	N	N	N	N
2 Baldacci	Y	Y	N	N	N	N
MARYLAND						
1 ***Gilchrest***	Y	N	Y	Y	Y	Y
2 ***Ehrlich***	Y	N	Y	Y	Y	Y
3 Cardin	Y	Y	Y	N	N	N
4 Wynn	Y	Y	N	N	N	N
5 Hoyer	Y	Y	Y	N	N	N
6 ***Bartlett***	Y	N	Y	Y	Y	Y
7 Cummings	Y	Y	Y	N	N	N
8 ***Morella***	Y	N	Y	N	N	N
MASSACHUSETTS						
1 Olver	Y	Y	N	N	N	N
2 Neal	Y	Y	N	N	N	N
3 McGovern	Y	Y	N	N	N	N
4 Frank	Y	Y	?	N	N	N
5 Meehan	Y	Y	N	N	N	N
6 Tierney	Y	Y	N	N	N	N
7 Markey	Y	Y	N	N	N	N
8 Kennedy	Y	?	?	N	N	N
9 Moakley	Y	Y	Y	N	N	N
10 Delahunt	Y	Y	N	N	N	N
MICHIGAN						
1 Stupak	Y	Y	N	N	N	N
2 ***Hoekstra***	Y	N	Y	Y	Y	Y
3 ***Ehlers***	Y	N	Y	Y	Y	Y
4 ***Camp***	Y	N	Y	Y	Y	Y
5 Barcia	Y	Y	Y	N	N	N
6 ***Upton***	Y	N	Y	Y	Y	Y
7 ***Smith***	Y	N	Y	Y	Y	Y
8 Stabenow	Y	Y	Y	N	N	N
9 Kildee	Y	Y	Y	N	N	N
10 Bonior	Y	Y	N	N	N	N
11 ***Knollenberg***	Y	N	?	Y	Y	Y
12 Levin	Y	Y	N	N	N	N
13 Rivers	Y	Y	Y	N	N	N
14 Conyers	N	Y	Y	N	N	N
15 Kilpatrick	Y	Y	N	N	N	N
16 Dingell	Y	Y	Y	N	N	N

	539	540	541	542	543	544
MINNESOTA						
1 ***Gutknecht***	Y	N	Y	Y	Y	Y
2 Minge	Y	Y	Y	Y	N	N
3 ***Ramstad***	Y	N	Y	Y	Y	N
4 Vento	Y	Y	N	N	N	N
5 Sabo	Y	Y	N	N	N	N
6 Luther	Y	Y	N	N	N	N
7 Peterson	Y	Y	N	N	N	N
8 Oberstar	Y	?	N	N	N	N
MISSISSIPPI						
1 ***Wicker***	Y	N	Y	Y	Y	Y
2 Thompson	Y	Y	N	N	N	N
3 ***Pickering***	Y	N	?	Y	Y	Y
4 ***Parker***	Y	N	Y	Y	Y	Y
5 Taylor	Y	N	N	Y	Y	Y
MISSOURI						
1 Clay	Y	Y	N	N	N	N
2 ***Talent***	Y	N	Y	Y	Y	Y
3 Gephardt	Y	Y	N	N	N	N
4 Skelton	Y	Y	N	N	N	N
5 McCarthy	Y	Y	Y	N	N	N
6 Danner	Y	Y	Y	N	N	N
7 ***Blunt***	Y	N	Y	Y	Y	Y
8 ***Emerson***	Y	?	Y	Y	Y	Y
9 ***Hulshof***	Y	N	Y	Y	Y	Y
MONTANA						
AL ***Hill***	Y	N	Y	Y	Y	Y
NEBRASKA						
1 ***Bereuter***	Y	N	Y	Y	Y	Y
2 ***Christensen***	Y	N	Y	Y	Y	Y
3 ***Barrett***	Y	N	Y	Y	Y	Y
NEVADA						
1 ***Ensign***	Y	N	N	Y	Y	N
2 ***Gibbons***	Y	N	Y	Y	Y	N
NEW HAMPSHIRE						
1 ***Sununu***	Y	N	Y	Y	Y	Y
2 ***Bass***	Y	N	Y	Y	Y	Y
NEW JERSEY						
1 Andrews	Y	Y	Y	N	N	N
2 ***LoBiondo***	Y	N	Y	Y	Y	Y
3 ***Saxton***	Y	N	Y	Y	Y	Y
4 ***Smith***	Y	N	?	Y	Y	Y
5 ***Roukema***	Y	N	Y	Y	Y	Y
6 Pallone	Y	Y	N	N	N	N
7 ***Franks***	Y	N	Y	Y	Y	Y
8 Pascrell	Y	Y	N	N	N	N
9 Rothman	Y	Y	Y	N	N	N
10 Payne	Y	Y	N	N	N	N
11 ***Frelinghuysen***	Y	N	Y	Y	Y	Y
12 ***Pappas***	Y	N	Y	Y	Y	Y
13 Menendez	Y	Y	N	N	N	N
NEW MEXICO						
1 ***Wilson***	Y	N	Y	Y	Y	Y
2 ***Skeen***	Y	N	Y	Y	Y	Y
3 ***Redmond***	Y	N	Y	Y	Y	Y
NEW YORK						
1 ***Forbes***	Y	N	Y	Y	Y	Y
2 ***Lazio***	Y	N	Y	Y	Y	N
3 ***King***	Y	N	Y	Y	N	N
4 McCarthy	Y	Y	N	N	N	N
5 Ackerman	Y	Y	N	N	N	N
6 Meeks	Y	Y	N	N	N	N
7 Manton	?	?	N	N	N	N
8 Nadler	Y	Y	Y	N	N	N
9 Schumer	Y	Y	Y	N	N	N
10 Towns	Y	?	?	N	N	N
11 Owens	Y	?	N	N	N	N
12 Velázquez	Y	Y	N	N	N	N
13 ***Fossella***	Y	N	?	Y	Y	Y
14 Maloney	Y	Y	?	N	N	N
15 Rangel	Y	Y	?	N	N	N
16 Serrano	Y	Y	N	N	N	N
17 Engel	Y	Y	N	N	N	N
18 Lowey	Y	Y	Y	N	N	N
19 ***Kelly***	Y	N	Y	Y	Y	N
20 ***Gilman***	Y	N	Y	Y	Y	N
21 McNulty	Y	Y	N	N	N	N
22 ***Solomon***	Y	N	Y	Y	Y	Y
23 ***Boehlert***	Y	N	Y	Y	Y	Y
24 ***McHugh***	Y	N	Y	Y	Y	Y
25 ***Walsh***	Y	N	Y	Y	Y	Y
26 Hinchey	Y	?	N	N	N	N
27 ***Paxon***	Y	N	Y	Y	Y	Y
28 Slaughter	Y	Y	?	N	N	N
29 LaFalce	Y	Y	N	N	N	N
30 ***Quinn***	Y	N	Y	Y	Y	Y

	539	540	541	542	543	544
31 ***Houghton***	Y	N	Y	Y	N	N
NORTH CAROLINA						
1 Clayton	Y	Y	N	N	N	N
2 Etheridge	Y	Y	N	N	N	N
3 ***Jones***	Y	N	Y	Y	Y	Y
4 Price	Y	Y	N	N	N	N
5 ***Burr***	Y	N	Y	Y	Y	Y
6 ***Coble***	Y	N	Y	Y	Y	Y
7 McIntyre	Y	Y	Y	N	N	N
8 Hefner	Y	?	N	N	N	N
9 ***Myrick***	Y	N	Y	Y	Y	Y
10 ***Ballenger***	Y	N	Y	Y	Y	Y
11 ***Taylor***	?	?	Y	Y	Y	Y
12 Watt	Y	Y	Y	N	N	N
NORTH DAKOTA						
AL Pomeroy	Y	Y	N	N	N	N
OHIO						
1 ***Chabot***	Y	N	Y	Y	Y	Y
2 ***Portman***	Y	N	Y	Y	Y	Y
3 Hall	Y	Y	N	N	N	N
4 ***Oxley***	Y	N	Y	Y	Y	Y
5 ***Gillmor***	Y	N	Y	Y	Y	Y
6 Strickland	Y	Y	N	N	N	N
7 ***Hobson***	Y	N	Y	Y	Y	N
8 ***Boehner***	Y	N	Y	Y	Y	Y
9 Kaptur	Y	?	Y	N	N	N
10 Kucinich	Y	Y	N	N	N	N
11 Stokes	Y	Y	Y	N	N	N
12 ***Kasich***	Y	N	Y	Y	Y	Y
13 Brown	Y	Y	N	N	N	N
14 Sawyer	Y	Y	N	N	N	N
15 ***Pryce***	Y	–	+	Y	Y	N
16 ***Regula***	Y	N	Y	Y	Y	Y
17 Traficant	Y	Y	Y	N	N	N
18 ***Ney***	Y	N	Y	Y	Y	N
19 ***LaTourette***	Y	N	Y	Y	Y	Y
OKLAHOMA						
1 ***Largent***	Y	N	?	Y	Y	Y
2 ***Coburn***	Y	N	Y	Y	Y	Y
3 ***Watkins***	Y	N	Y	Y	Y	Y
4 ***Watts***	Y	N	Y	Y	Y	Y
5 ***Istook***	Y	N	Y	Y	Y	Y
6 ***Lucas***	Y	N	Y	Y	Y	Y
OREGON						
1 Furse	P	Y	N	N	N	N
2 ***Smith***	Y	N	Y	Y	Y	Y
3 Blumenauer	Y	Y	Y	N	N	N
4 DeFazio	Y	Y	N	N	N	N
5 Hooley	Y	Y	N	N	N	N
PENNSYLVANIA						
1 Brady	Y	Y	N	N	N	N
2 Fattah	Y	Y	N	N	N	N
3 Borski	Y	Y	N	N	N	N
4 Klink	Y	Y	N	N	N	N
5 ***Peterson***	Y	N	Y	Y	Y	Y
6 Holden	Y	Y	N	N	N	N
7 ***Weldon***	Y	N	Y	Y	Y	Y
8 ***Greenwood***	Y	N	Y	Y	Y	N
9 ***Shuster***	Y	N	Y	Y	Y	Y
10 ***McDade***	Y	?	?	Y	Y	Y
11 Kanjorski	Y	Y	N	N	N	N
12 Murtha	?	Y	Y	N	N	N
13 ***Fox***	Y	N	Y	Y	Y	Y
14 Coyne	Y	Y	N	N	N	N
15 McHale	Y	N	Y	N	Y	Y
16 ***Pitts***	Y	N	Y	Y	Y	Y
17 ***Gekas***	Y	N	Y	Y	Y	Y
18 Doyle	Y	Y	N	N	N	N
19 ***Goodling***	Y	N	Y	Y	Y	Y
20 Mascara	Y	Y	N	N	N	N
21 ***English***	Y	N	N	Y	Y	N
RHODE ISLAND						
1 Kennedy	Y	Y	N	N	N	N
2 Weygand	Y	Y	Y	N	N	N
SOUTH CAROLINA						
1 ***Sanford***	N	N	Y	Y	Y	N
2 ***Spence***	Y	N	Y	Y	Y	Y
3 ***Graham***	Y	N	Y	Y	Y	N
4 ***Inglis***	Y	N	Y	Y	Y	Y
5 Spratt	Y	Y	Y	N	N	N
6 Clyburn	Y	Y	N	N	N	N
SOUTH DAKOTA						
AL ***Thune***	Y	N	Y	Y	Y	Y

	539	540	541	542	543	544
TENNESSEE						
1 ***Jenkins***	Y	N	Y	Y	Y	Y
2 ***Duncan***	Y	N	Y	Y	Y	Y
3 ***Wamp***	Y	N	Y	Y	Y	Y
4 ***Hilleary***	Y	N	Y	Y	Y	Y
5 Clement	Y	Y	Y	N	N	N
6 Gordon	Y	?	Y	N	N	N
7 ***Bryant***	Y	N	Y	Y	Y	Y
8 Tanner	Y	Y	Y	N	N	N
9 Ford	Y	Y	N	N	N	N
TEXAS						
1 Sandlin	Y	Y	Y	N	N	N
2 Turner	Y	Y	N	N	N	N
3 ***Johnson, Sam***	Y	N	?	Y	Y	Y
4 Hall	Y	N	Y	Y	Y	Y
5 ***Sessions***	Y	N	?	Y	Y	Y
6 ***Barton***	Y	N	?	Y	Y	Y
7 ***Archer***	Y	N	Y	Y	Y	Y
8 ***Brady***	Y	N	Y	Y	Y	Y
9 Lampson	Y	Y	Y	N	N	N
10 Doggett	Y	Y	Y	N	N	N
11 Edwards	Y	Y	Y	N	N	N
12 ***Granger***	Y	N	Y	Y	Y	Y
13 ***Thornberry***	Y	N	Y	Y	Y	Y
14 ***Paul***	N	N	?	Y	Y	Y
15 Hinojosa	Y	Y	N	N	N	N
16 Reyes	Y	Y	N	N	N	N
17 Stenholm	Y	Y	Y	Y	Y	Y
18 Jackson-Lee	Y	Y	N	N	N	N
19 ***Combest***	Y	N	Y	Y	Y	Y
20 Gonzalez	Y	?	?	N	N	N
21 ***Smith***	Y	N	Y	Y	Y	Y
22 ***DeLay***	Y	N	Y	Y	Y	Y
23 ***Bonilla***	Y	N	Y	Y	Y	Y
24 Frost	Y	Y	N	N	N	N
25 Bentsen	Y	Y	Y	N	N	N
26 ***Armey***	Y	N	Y	Y	Y	Y
27 Ortiz	Y	Y	N	N	N	N
28 Rodriguez	Y	Y	N	N	N	N
29 Green	Y	Y	N	N	N	N
30 Johnson, E.B.	Y	Y	N	N	N	N
UTAH						
1 ***Hansen***	Y	N	Y	Y	Y	Y
2 ***Cook***	Y	N	Y	Y	Y	Y
3 ***Cannon***	Y	N	Y	Y	Y	Y
VERMONT						
AL *Sanders*	Y	Y	Y	N	N	N
VIRGINIA						
1 ***Bateman***	Y	N	Y	Y	Y	Y
2 Pickett	Y	Y	N	N	N	N
3 Scott	Y	Y	Y	N	N	N
4 Sisisky	Y	Y	Y	N	N	N
5 Goode	Y	N	Y	Y	Y	Y
6 ***Goodlatte***	Y	N	Y	Y	Y	Y
7 ***Bliley***	Y	N	Y	Y	Y	Y
8 Moran	Y	Y	Y	N	N	N
9 Boucher	Y	Y	Y	N	N	N
10 ***Wolf***	Y	N	Y	Y	Y	Y
11 ***Davis***	Y	N	?	Y	Y	Y
WASHINGTON						
1 ***White***	Y	N	Y	Y	Y	Y
2 ***Metcalf***	Y	N	Y	Y	Y	Y
3 ***Smith, Linda***	Y	N	?	Y	Y	Y
4 ***Hastings***	Y	N	Y	Y	Y	Y
5 ***Nethercutt***	Y	N	Y	Y	Y	Y
6 Dicks	Y	Y	N	N	N	N
7 McDermott	Y	Y	N	N	N	N
8 ***Dunn***	Y	N	Y	Y	Y	Y
9 Smith, Adam	Y	Y	Y	N	N	N
WEST VIRGINIA						
1 Mollohan	Y	Y	Y	N	N	N
2 Wise	Y	?	Y	N	N	N
3 Rahall	Y	Y	Y	N	N	N
WISCONSIN						
1 ***Neumann***	Y	N	Y	Y	Y	Y
2 ***Klug***	Y	N	?	Y	Y	N
3 Kind	Y	Y	Y	N	N	N
4 Kleczka	Y	Y	Y	N	N	N
5 Barrett	Y	N	Y	N	N	N
6 ***Petri***	Y	N	Y	Y	Y	Y
7 Obey	Y	Y	Y	N	N	N
8 Johnson	Y	?	Y	N	N	N
9 ***Sensenbrenner***	Y	N	Y	Y	Y	Y
WYOMING						
AL ***Cubin***	Y	N	Y	Y	Y	Y

Southern states - Ala., Ark., Fla., Ga., Ky., La., Miss., N.C., Okla., S.C., Tenn., Texas, Va.

Key

Y	Voted for (yea).
#	Paired for.
+	Announced for.
N	Voted against (nay).
X	Paired against.
–	Announced against.
P	Voted "present."
C	Voted "present" to avoid possible conflict of interest.
?	Did not vote or otherwise make a position known.

Democrats **Republicans**
Independent

---

545. H Res 611. Impeachment of President Clinton/Article III — Obstruction of Justice. Adoption of Article III of the resolution, which would impeach President Clinton for obstruction of justice, concealing evidence and delaying proceedings in the Paula Jones federal sexual harassment civil lawsuit. Adopted 221-212: R 216-12; D 5-199 (ND 1-148, SD 4-51); I 0-1. Dec. 19, 1998. A "nay" was a vote in support of the president's position.

546. H Res 611. Impeachment of President Clinton/Article IV — Abuse of Power. Adoption of Article IV of the resolution, which would impeach President Clinton for abuse of office for refusing to respond or lying in response to 81 written questions submitted to him by the House Judiciary Committee. Rejected 148-285: R 147-81; D 1-203 (ND 0-149, SD 1-54); I 0-1. Dec. 19, 1998. A "nay" was a vote in support of the president's position.

547. Impeachment of President Clinton/Appointment of Managers. Adoption of the resolution to appoint and authorize managers, drawn from the Republican membership of the House Judiciary Committee, to conduct the impeachment trial against President Clinton in the Senate. Adopted 228-190: R 223-2; D 5-187 (ND 1-137, SD 4-50); I 0-1. Dec. 19, 1998.

	545	546	547
ALABAMA			
1 *Callahan*	Y	Y	Y
2 *Everett*	Y	Y	Y
3 *Riley*	Y	Y	Y
4 *Aderholt*	Y	Y	Y
5 Cramer	N	N	N
6 *Bachus*	Y	Y	Y
7 Hilliard	N	N	N
ALASKA			
AL *Young*	Y	Y	Y
ARIZONA			
1 *Salmon*	Y	Y	Y
2 Pastor	N	N	N
3 *Stump*	Y	Y	Y
4 *Shadegg*	Y	N	Y
5 *Kolbe*	N	N	Y
6 *Hayworth*	Y	Y	Y
ARKANSAS			
1 Berry	N	N	N
2 Snyder	N	N	N
3 *Hutchinson*	Y	Y	Y
4 *Dickey*	Y	N	Y
CALIFORNIA			
1 *Riggs*	Y	N	Y
2 *Herger*	Y	Y	Y
3 Fazio	N	N	N
4 *Doolittle*	Y	Y	Y
5 Matsui	N	N	N
6 Woolsey	N	N	N
7 Miller	?	?	?
8 Pelosi	N	N	N
9 Lee	N	N	N
10 Tauscher	N	N	N
11 *Pombo*	Y	Y	Y
12 Lantos	N	N	N
13 Stark	N	N	N
14 Eshoo	N	N	N
15 *Campbell*	Y	N	Y
16 Lofgren	N	N	N
17 Farr	N	N	N
18 Condit	N	N	N
19 *Radanovich*	Y	Y	Y
20 Dooley	N	N	N
21 *Thomas*	Y	Y	Y
22 Capps, L.	N	N	N
23 *Gallegly*	Y	Y	Y
24 Sherman	N	N	N
25 *McKeon*	Y	Y	Y
26 Berman	N	N	N
27 *Rogan*	Y	Y	Y
28 *Dreier*	Y	Y	Y
29 Waxman	N	N	N
30 Becerra	N	N	N
31 Martinez	N	N	N
32 Dixon	N	N	N
33 Roybal-Allard	N	N	N
34 Torres	N	N	N
35 Waters	N	N	N
36 Harman	N	N	N
37 Millender-McD.	N	N	N
38 *Horn*	Y	N	Y

	545	546	547
39 *Royce*	Y	Y	Y
40 *Lewis*	Y	Y	Y
41 *Kim*	N	N	Y
42 Brown	N	N	N
43 *Calvert*	Y	Y	Y
44 *Bono, M.*	Y	Y	Y
45 *Rohrabacher*	Y	Y	Y
46 Sanchez	N	N	N
47 *Cox*	Y	Y	Y
48 *Packard*	Y	Y	Y
49 *Bilbray*	Y	N	Y
50 Filner	N	N	N
51 *Cunningham*	Y	Y	Y
52 *Hunter*	Y	Y	Y
COLORADO			
1 DeGette	N	N	?
2 Skaggs	N	N	N
3 *McInnis*	Y	N	Y
4 *Schaffer*	Y	Y	Y
5 *Hefley*	Y	N	Y
6 *Schaefer*	Y	Y	Y
CONNECTICUT			
1 Kennelly	N	N	?
2 Gejdenson	N	N	N
3 DeLauro	N	N	N
4 *Shays*	N	N	N
5 Maloney	N	N	N
6 *Johnson*	N	N	Y
DELAWARE			
AL *Castle*	N	N	Y
FLORIDA			
1 *Scarborough*	Y	N	Y
2 Boyd	N	N	N
3 Brown	N	N	N
4 *Fowler*	Y	Y	Y
5 Thurman	N	N	N
6 *Stearns*	Y	Y	Y
7 *Mica*	Y	Y	Y
8 *McCollum*	Y	Y	Y
9 *Bilirakis*	Y	Y	Y
10 *Young*	Y	Y	Y
11 Davis	N	N	N
12 *Canady*	Y	Y	Y
13 *Miller*	Y	Y	Y
14 *Goss*	Y	N	Y
15 *Weldon*	Y	Y	Y
16 *Foley*	Y	N	Y
17 Meek	N	N	N
18 *Ros-Lehtinen*	Y	N	Y
19 Wexler	N	N	N
20 Deutsch	N	N	N
21 *Diaz-Balart*	Y	Y	Y
22 *Shaw*	Y	N	Y
23 Hastings	N	N	N
GEORGIA			
1 *Kingston*	Y	Y	Y
2 Bishop	N	N	N
3 *Collins*	Y	Y	Y
4 McKinney	N	N	N
5 Lewis	N	N	N
6 *Gingrich*	Y	Y	Y
7 *Barr*	Y	Y	Y
8 *Chambliss*	Y	Y	Y
9 *Deal*	Y	Y	Y
10 *Norwood*	Y	Y	Y
11 *Linder*	Y	Y	Y
HAWAII			
1 Abercrombie	N	N	N
2 Mink	N	N	N
IDAHO			
1 *Chenoweth*	Y	Y	Y
2 *Crapo*	Y	Y	Y
ILLINOIS			
1 Rush	N	N	N
2 Jackson	N	N	N
3 Lipinski	N	N	?
4 Gutierrez	N	N	N
5 Blagojevich	N	N	N
6 *Hyde*	Y	Y	Y
7 Davis	N	N	N
8 *Crane*	Y	Y	Y
9 Yates	N	N	N
10 *Porter*	Y	N	Y
11 *Weller*	Y	N	Y
12 Costello	N	N	?
13 *Fawell*	Y	N	Y

ND Northern Democrats   SD Southern Democrats

	545	546	547
14 *Hastert*	Y	Y	Y
15 *Ewing*	Y	Y	Y
16 *Manzullo*	Y	Y	Y
17 Evans	N	N	N
18 *LaHood*	Y	Y	Y
19 Poshard	N	N	?
20 *Shimkus*	Y	N	Y

INDIANA

	545	546	547
1 Visclosky	N	N	N
2 *McIntosh*	Y	N	Y
3 Roemer	N	N	N
4 *Souder*	Y	N	Y
5 *Buyer*	Y	Y	?
6 *Burton*	Y	Y	Y
7 *Pease*	Y	Y	Y
8 *Hostettler*	Y	Y	Y
9 Hamilton	N	N	N
10 Carson	N	N	N

IOWA

	545	546	547
1 *Leach*	N	N	Y
2 *Nussle*	Y	Y	Y
3 Boswell	N	N	N
4 *Ganske*	Y	N	Y
5 *Latham*	Y	N	Y

KANSAS

	545	546	547
1 *Moran*	Y	N	Y
2 *Ryun*	Y	Y	?
3 *Snowbarger*	Y	Y	Y
4 *Tiahrt*	Y	Y	Y

KENTUCKY

	545	546	547
1 *Whitfield*	Y	N	Y
2 *Lewis*	Y	Y	Y
3 *Northup*	Y	N	Y
4 *Bunning*	Y	Y	Y
5 *Rogers*	Y	N	Y
6 Baesler	N	N	N

LOUISIANA

	545	546	547
1 *Livingston*	Y	Y	Y
2 Jefferson	N	N	N
3 *Tauzin*	Y	N	Y
4 *McCrery*	Y	N	Y
5 *Cooksey*	Y	Y	Y
6 *Baker*	Y	Y	Y
7 John	N	N	N

MAINE

	545	546	547
1 Allen	?	?	?
2 Baldacci	N	N	N

MARYLAND

	545	546	547
1 *Gilchrest*	Y	N	Y
2 *Ehrlich*	Y	N	Y
3 Cardin	N	N	N
4 Wynn	N	N	N
5 Hoyer	N	N	N
6 *Bartlett*	Y	Y	Y
7 Cummings	N	N	N
8 *Morella*	N	N	N

MASSACHUSETTS

	545	546	547
1 Olver	N	N	N
2 Neal	N	N	?
3 McGovern	N	N	N
4 Frank	N	N	N
5 Meehan	N	N	N
6 Tierney	N	N	N
7 Markey	N	N	N
8 Kennedy	N	N	N
9 Moakley	N	N	N
10 Delahunt	N	N	N

MICHIGAN

	545	546	547
1 Stupak	N	N	N
2 *Hoekstra*	Y	Y	Y
3 *Ehlers*	Y	Y	Y
4 *Camp*	Y	Y	Y
5 Barcia	N	N	N
6 *Upton*	Y	N	Y
7 *Smith*	Y	Y	Y
8 Stabenow	N	N	N
9 Kildee	N	N	N
10 Bonior	N	N	N
11 *Knollenberg*	Y	Y	Y
12 Levin	N	N	N
13 Rivers	N	N	N
14 Conyers	N	N	?
15 Kilpatrick	N	N	N
16 Dingell	N	N	N

MINNESOTA

	545	546	547
1 *Gutknecht*	Y	Y	Y
2 Minge	N	N	N
3 *Ramstad*	Y	N	Y
4 Vento	N	N	N
5 Sabo	N	N	N
6 Luther	N	N	N
7 Peterson	N	N	N
8 Oberstar	N	N	N

MISSISSIPPI

	545	546	547
1 *Wicker*	Y	Y	Y
2 Thompson	N	N	N
3 *Pickering*	Y	Y	Y
4 *Parker*	Y	N	Y
5 Taylor	Y	Y	Y

MISSOURI

	545	546	547
1 Clay	N	N	N
2 *Talent*	Y	Y	Y
3 Gephardt	N	N	N
4 Skelton	N	N	N
5 McCarthy	N	N	–
6 Danner	N	N	?
7 *Blunt*	Y	Y	Y
8 *Emerson*	Y	N	Y
9 *Hulshof*	Y	N	Y

MONTANA

	545	546	547
AL *Hill*	Y	N	Y

NEBRASKA

	545	546	547
1 *Bereuter*	Y	N	Y
2 *Christensen*	Y	Y	Y
3 *Barrett*	Y	Y	Y

NEVADA

	545	546	547
1 *Ensign*	Y	N	Y
2 *Gibbons*	Y	Y	Y

NEW HAMPSHIRE

	545	546	547
1 *Sununu*	Y	Y	Y
2 *Bass*	Y	N	Y

NEW JERSEY

	545	546	547
1 Andrews	N	N	N
2 *LoBiondo*	Y	N	Y
3 *Saxton*	Y	N	Y
4 *Smith*	Y	Y	Y
5 *Roukema*	Y	Y	Y
6 Pallone	N	N	N
7 *Franks*	Y	N	Y
8 Pascrell	N	N	N
9 Rothman	N	N	N
10 Payne	N	N	N
11 *Frelinghuysen*	Y	N	Y
12 *Pappas*	Y	Y	Y
13 Menendez	N	N	N

NEW MEXICO

	545	546	547
1 *Wilson*	Y	Y	Y
2 *Skeen*	Y	Y	Y
3 *Redmond*	Y	Y	Y

NEW YORK

	545	546	547
1 *Forbes*	Y	Y	Y
2 *Lazio*	Y	N	Y
3 *King*	N	N	Y
4 McCarthy	N	N	N
5 Ackerman	N	N	N
6 Meeks	N	N	N
7 Manton	N	N	N
8 Nadler	N	N	N
9 Schumer	N	N	N
10 Towns	N	N	N
11 Owens	N	N	N
12 Velázquez	N	N	N
13 *Fossella*	Y	N	Y
14 Maloney	N	N	N
15 Rangel	N	N	N
16 Serrano	N	N	N
17 Engel	N	N	N
18 Lowey	N	N	N
19 *Kelly*	Y	N	Y
20 *Gilman*	Y	N	Y
21 McNulty	N	N	N
22 *Solomon*	Y	Y	Y
23 *Boehlert*	N	N	N
24 *McHugh*	Y	N	Y
25 *Walsh*	Y	N	Y
26 Hinchey	N	N	N
27 *Paxon*	Y	Y	Y
28 Slaughter	N	N	N
29 LaFalce	N	N	N
30 *Quinn*	Y	N	Y

	545	546	547
31 *Houghton*	N	N	N

NORTH CAROLINA

	545	546	547
1 Clayton	N	N	?
2 Etheridge	N	N	N
3 *Jones*	Y	Y	Y
4 Price	N	N	N
5 *Burr*	Y	N	Y
6 *Coble*	Y	Y	Y
7 McIntyre	N	N	N
8 Hefner	N	N	N
9 *Myrick*	Y	Y	Y
10 *Ballenger*	Y	Y	Y
11 *Taylor*	Y	Y	Y
12 Watt	N	N	N

NORTH DAKOTA

	545	546	547
AL Pomeroy	N	N	N

OHIO

	545	546	547
1 *Chabot*	Y	Y	Y
2 *Portman*	Y	N	Y
3 Hall	N	N	N
4 *Oxley*	Y	Y	Y
5 *Gillmor*	Y	N	Y
6 Strickland	N	N	N
7 *Hobson*	Y	N	Y
8 *Boehner*	Y	Y	Y
9 Kaptur	N	N	N
10 Kucinich	N	N	N
11 Stokes	N	N	N
12 *Kasich*	Y	N	Y
13 Brown	N	N	N
14 Sawyer	N	N	N
15 *Pryce*	Y	N	Y
16 *Regula*	N	N	Y
17 Traficant	N	N	N
18 *Ney*	Y	N	Y
19 *LaTourette*	Y	N	Y

OKLAHOMA

	545	546	547
1 *Largent*	Y	N	Y
2 *Coburn*	Y	Y	Y
3 *Watkins*	Y	Y	Y
4 *Watts*	Y	Y	Y
5 *Istook*	Y	Y	Y
6 *Lucas*	Y	Y	Y

OREGON

	545	546	547
1 Furse	N	N	?
2 *Smith*	Y	Y	?
3 Blumenauer	N	N	N
4 DeFazio	N	N	N
5 Hooley	N	N	N

PENNSYLVANIA

	545	546	547
1 Brady	N	N	N
2 Fattah	N	N	N
3 Borski	N	N	N
4 Klink	N	N	N
5 *Peterson*	Y	Y	Y
6 Holden	N	N	N
7 *Weldon*	Y	N	Y
8 *Greenwood*	Y	N	Y
9 *Shuster*	Y	N	Y
10 *McDade*	Y	Y	Y
11 Kanjorski	N	N	N
12 Murtha	N	N	?
13 *Fox*	Y	Y	Y
14 Coyne	N	N	N
15 McHale	Y	N	Y
16 *Pitts*	Y	Y	Y
17 *Gekas*	Y	Y	Y
18 Doyle	N	N	N
19 *Goodling*	Y	Y	Y
20 Mascara	N	N	N
21 *English*	N	N	Y

RHODE ISLAND

	545	546	547
1 Kennedy	N	N	N
2 Weygand	N	N	N

SOUTH CAROLINA

	545	546	547
1 *Sanford*	Y	Y	Y
2 *Spence*	Y	Y	Y
3 *Graham*	Y	Y	Y
4 *Inglis*	Y	Y	Y
5 Spratt	N	N	N
6 Clyburn	N	N	N

SOUTH DAKOTA

	545	546	547
AL *Thune*	Y	N	Y

TENNESSEE

	545	546	547
1 *Jenkins*	Y	N	Y
2 *Duncan*	Y	Y	Y
3 *Wamp*	Y	Y	Y
4 *Hilleary*	Y	Y	Y
5 Clement	N	N	N
6 Gordon	N	N	N
7 *Bryant*	Y	Y	Y
8 Tanner	N	N	N
9 Ford	N	N	N

TEXAS

	545	546	547
1 Sandlin	N	N	N
2 Turner	N	N	N
3 *Johnson, Sam*	Y	Y	Y
4 Hall	Y	N	Y
5 *Sessions*	Y	Y	Y
6 *Barton*	Y	Y	Y
7 *Archer*	Y	Y	Y
8 *Brady*	Y	Y	Y
9 Lampson	N	N	N
10 Doggett	N	N	N
11 Edwards	N	N	N
12 *Granger*	Y	N	Y
13 *Thornberry*	Y	N	Y
14 *Paul*	Y	Y	Y
15 Hinojosa	N	N	N
16 Reyes	N	N	N
17 Stenholm	N	N	N
18 Jackson-Lee	N	N	N
19 *Combest*	Y	N	Y
20 Gonzalez	N	N	N
21 *Smith*	Y	Y	Y
22 *DeLay*	Y	Y	Y
23 *Bonilla*	Y	N	Y
24 Frost	N	N	N
25 Bentsen	N	N	N
26 *Armey*	Y	Y	Y
27 Ortiz	N	N	N
28 Rodriguez	N	N	N
29 Green	N	N	N
30 Johnson, E.B.	N	N	N

UTAH

	545	546	547
1 *Hansen*	Y	Y	Y
2 *Cook*	Y	Y	Y
3 *Cannon*	Y	Y	Y

VERMONT

	545	546	547
AL *Sanders*	N	N	N

VIRGINIA

	545	546	547
1 *Bateman*	Y	Y	Y
2 Pickett	N	N	N
3 Scott	N	N	N
4 Sisisky	N	N	N
5 Goode	Y	N	Y
6 *Goodlatte*	Y	Y	Y
7 *Bliley*	Y	Y	Y
8 Moran	N	N	N
9 Boucher	N	N	N
10 *Wolf*	Y	Y	Y
11 *Davis*	Y	N	Y

WASHINGTON

	545	546	547
1 *White*	Y	N	Y
2 *Metcalf*	Y	Y	Y
3 *Smith, Linda*	Y	Y	Y
4 *Hastings*	Y	Y	Y
5 *Nethercutt*	Y	N	Y
6 Dicks	N	N	N
7 McDermott	N	N	N
8 *Dunn*	Y	Y	Y
9 Smith, Adam	N	N	N

WEST VIRGINIA

	545	546	547
1 Mollohan	N	N	N
2 Wise	N	N	N
3 Rahall	N	N	N

WISCONSIN

	545	546	547
1 *Neumann*	Y	Y	Y
2 *Klug*	Y	N	Y
3 Kind	N	N	N
4 Kleczka	N	N	N
5 Barrett	N	N	N
6 *Petri*	Y	N	Y
7 Obey	N	N	N
8 Johnson	N	N	N
9 *Sensenbrenner*	Y	Y	Y

WYOMING

	545	546	547
AL *Cubin*	Y	Y	Y

Southern states - Ala., Ark., Fla., Ga., Ky., La., Miss., N.C., Okla., S.C., Tenn., Texas, Va.

House Roll Call Votes By Subject

271 P2 FM 122
08/18/99 33700   SELB
INFORMATION CONSERVATION, INC.